Don Wright's Guide To
FREE
CAMPGROUNDS

First printing 2007
Printed in the United States of America

Don Wright's Guide to FREE Campgrounds

    Rev. ed. of VanMeer's Guide to Free Campgrounds, 1984
I.   Campsites, facilities, etc. -- United States -- Directories
II.   Free Campgrounds, U.S.A.
III.   Title: Guide to FREE Campgrounds
IV.   Don Wright's Guide to FREE Campgrounds, 1986
V.   Don Wright's Guide to FREE Campgrounds, 1988
VI.   Don Wright's Guide to FREE Campgrounds, 1990
VII.   Don Wright's Guide to FREE Campgrounds, 1993
VIII. Don Wright's Guide to FREE Campgrounds, 1995
IX.   Don Wright's Guide to FREE Campgrounds, 1997
X.   Don Wright's Guide to FREE Campgrounds, 1999
XI.   Don Wright's Guide to FREE Campgrounds, 2002
XII.   Don Wright's Guide to FREE Campgrounds, 2005

ISBN 0-937877-49-2

Cottage Publications, Inc.
P.O. Box 2832
Elkhart, IN 46515-2832
1-800-272-5518

Visit our website at: www.cottagepub.com
e-mail us at: info@cottagepub.com

CO TE TS & ABBREVIATIO S

Abbreviations

approx	•	approximately
ave	•	avenue
bldg	•	building
blk	•	block
BLM	•	Bureau of Land Mgmt.
cfga	•	campfire - grill area
co	•	county
d	•	dock
drkg wtr	•	drinking water
E	•	east
elec	•	electric
elev	•	elevation
FH or FR	•	forest road
Hwy	•	highway
hrs	•	hours
jct	•	junction
L	•	Launch (boat)
LD	•	Labor Day
MD	•	Memorial Day
mi	•	miles
N	•	north
Prim	•	primitive
r	•	rental
S	•	south
st	•	street
tbls	•	tables
W	•	west
wtr	•	water

INTRODUCTION

This is not just another ordinary campground guide. This is the only guide that lists thousands of campgrounds across the USA where you can stay absolutely **FREE.** In addition, to make your travels easier, we have added thousands more campgrounds with overnight fees of **$12 or less.**

For the first time since Guide to Free Campgrounds appeared in 1980, we are offering two editions of it -- an Eastern Edition and a Western Edition. By adding thousands of $12-and-under campsites to the additional thousands of FREE campgrounds, we created an enormous collection of camping places that could not be published or updated efficiently in one edition -- nearly 1,000 pages of free and low-cost campgrounds without any advertising!

Our two-edition directories of low-cost campgrounds, Camping on a Shoestring, are now blended into this book, and they have been discontinued. The result is two books instead of three and a packaging that will enable you to find campgrounds more easily. By including campgrounds with fees of $12 or less, we have been able to add hundreds of small campgrounds not available in any other campground directory -- those invaluable city and county parks, national forest and Bureau of Land Management campgrounds, public campgrounds operated by utility firms and lumber companies, overnight stops created by Lions and Kiwanis clubs, state-operated fishing camps, low-cost off-season campgrounds, fairground camping areas and especially the mom-and-pop private campgrounds where we all enjoy stopping for a few days.

We've expanded our coverage in middle America where sometimes it seems that every small town provides free or low-cost campsites for visitors. Travelers through the Midwestern states of Iowa, South Dakota, Nebraska, Missouri, Kansas and North Dakota will particularly note the addition of more locally owned public campgrounds as well as small privately operated ones.

Our listings of state-operated fishing lakes, hunting areas and wildlife management areas where primitive camping is allowed continues to increase. Experienced users of Guide to Free Campgrounds will notice new entries that include boondock camps, dispersed national forest camps, fairgrounds, wildlife area camps, coyote camps and even a few private campgrounds where no fees are charged.

Each campground in this book is carefully researched, and the information is updated at least bi-annually. We make every effort to keep this continually changing information as accurate as possible by means of field researchers, government sources, reader feedback and, in many cases, personal site visits.

Popular campgrounds that were previously deleted from this book because small fees were charged are now back. They include low-cost National Forest, Bureau of Land Management, National Park and Corps of Engineers sites.

Public campgrounds remain the heart of this book, whether they are free or have fees that must be paid. Those parks offer incred-ible savings to budget-conscious travelers, but they also have other advantages. They are generally found in peaceful and scenic settings. They are commonly located by a lake, river or ocean and offer numerous recreational opportunities, such as boating, fishing, swimming or waterskiing. Public campgrounds often have hiking trails, and almost all have easy access to nature.

Significantly, most campers today spend the majority of their nights in campgrounds where overnight fees are charged, where they have access to a wide variety of facilities (such as electricity and water hookups) or services (swimming pools, rec halls, etc.). Now, we're providing information about the least expensive of those campgrounds along with the free ones.

Guide to Free Campgrounds and its companion books (including our extremely popular Camping With the Corps of Engineers) are available nation-wide in bookstores, at RV dealerships, camping supply stores, some discount department stores and all Camping World outlets. They also can be purchased by mail directly from us, from Camping World, Camper's Choice or from various other sources. They distributed to the bookstore trade by BookWorld Services of Sarasota, Florida; they are distributed to RV dealerships and camping supply outlets by Stag-Parkway Distribution, Arrow Distributing and Northwest Trailer Parts.

The campgrounds in this book are listed alphabetically by state and by towns within each state. All towns are listed and indexed on the maps found at the beginning of each state section, but individual campgrounds are not. On each map you'll also find an index of the towns in the state. Use this as you would a table of contents to find the town you are looking for.

At the beginning of each state section, we've listed sources for general tourist information and additional camping data. You'll find many valuable suggestions for locating additional campgrounds from these sources. In this section, we've also listed campgrounds in parks and wilderness areas that aren't near towns.

As a service to our readers, we have begun adding special travel tips and detailed fishing tips to our listings. Most of the states in the first half of the book include these tips; more will be added to future editions.

Fishing tips are based upon a combination of our own knowledge about the lakes and streams identified and upon contributions from field researchers who are active campers and fishermen. Travel tips represent our best suggestions as a result of our own travels and our research for this guide's companion book, Guide to Free Attractions (now being updated for its Sixth Edition).

MAPS

Maps have been provided with each state, answering complaints about our Tenth Edition from readers who disliked the maps we used and our grid system of map coordinates.

Although we've listed thousands of free campgrounds in this

guide, we've by no means exhausted all the possibilities. Here are a few suggestions for places to check if there isn't a free campground listed in the area you want to stay.

NATIONAL FORESTS AND BUREAU OF LAND MANAGEMENT

You can legally camp anywhere on national forest land, and most places on BLM property. The only problem is that much of the forest area is so dense that campground areas (even if all the "official" sites are taken) might be your best bet. Find a spot at the edge of the campground.

Most state and national forests and BLM lands have so-called "dispersed" sites that may be utilized free. Thousands of those dispersed locations are available throughout the west and in the national forests of Maine, Minnesota and Michigan. Dispersed sites are basically locations where boondock camping has occurred often enough that the sites almost appear to be semi-developed camping locations. Frequently, the government agencies responsible for developing campsites begin to add facilities such as pit toilets, picnic tables and campfire grill areas to the dispersed areas, and formal development of official sites begins to take shape.

Some of the best dispersed sites that are popular among traveling campers are in Arizona around the rim of the Grand Canyon. Others are on the shores of lakes throughout the Upper Peninsula of Michigan and off the dirt roads in northern Minnesota. Our plans for future editions of this guide are to add even more dispersed locations.

CITY PARKS

We have listed numerous city parks in this guide that allow camping, but there are still many to be discovered. Stop at a service station, the local Chamber of Commerce or the police station and ask if there is a park or other free or low-cost place to spend the night.

FACILITIES AT LOW-COST CAMPGROUNDS

You'll be surprised at how many facilities low-cost campgrounds offer -- from drinking water to hot showers and full hookups. Our readers frequently tell us low-cost sites are valuable for them because they like to search out inexpensive places where they can either just park for the night or spend a few days while they economize.

A WORD ABOUT "RV SIZE LIMITS"

Throughout this book, you will see references to RV size limits at campgrounds. Please do not interpret this to mean those sites are not open to larger RVs. The "limits" are really general recommendations on the length of RVs that either fit easily on the sites or can maneuver on the grounds without scraping trees. No one is going to ask you to leave a campground because you have a 30-foot motorhome and the "size limit" is 16 feet.

LONG-TERM VISITOR AREAS (LTVAs)

The Bureau of Land Management (BLM) established nine LTVAs in 1983 in the California desert and along the lower Colorado River where visitors may camp for the entire winter. Winter visitors who wish to stay in an LTVA may do so by purchasing a long-term visitor permit for $100 and selecting a location in one of the designated Long-Term Visitor Areas. The permit covers the long-term season from October 1 to May 31. Permit holders may move from one LTVA to another without incurring additional user fees. Guests are allowed to stay with permit holders for short stays during the season at no charge.

STATE PARKS

Most state part systems include campgrounds that offer sites for $12 or less. However, many of those states also charge daily entry fees which sometimes cause overall fees to be higher than our $12 guidelines. In cases when the overnight fees are under $12 when the entry fees are disregarded, we have elected to include those state park facilities in this book. If you intend to camp several times in a particular state's parks, we suggest you invest in the annual entry permits which most states offer.

CORPS OF ENGINEERS

Users of our best-selling *GUIDE TO FREE CAMPGROUNDS* probably already are aware that the U.S. Army Corps of Engineers eliminated many of its cost-free camping facilities during 1994. Low fees are now charged at most of those sites, and so they are included in this book.

NATIONAL FORESTS

Campgrounds at national forests have become favorite overnight spots of campers who want to reduce their travel costs. As a consequence, many national forest sites are experiencing heavy daily usage, and forest administrators are hard pressed to maintain those sites and keep them both attractive and rustic. Almost across the board, campsite fees at national forest areas have been increased dramatically during the past three years; in some cases, fees have more than doubled. In addition, the forest service is tending toward hiring professional concessionaires to operate the campgrounds, and that tendency also has resulted in higher camping fees.

UPDATED FEES

At various points within the text of this book, you will find references to "fee status uncertain" or "at last report." In these cases, the campgrounds have been listed in this edition even though we were uncertain, at presstime, of exact fee amounts. In each case, we verified that the campground offered low-fee sites, but exact fees either were unavailable to us or had not yet been set for the upcoming camping season.

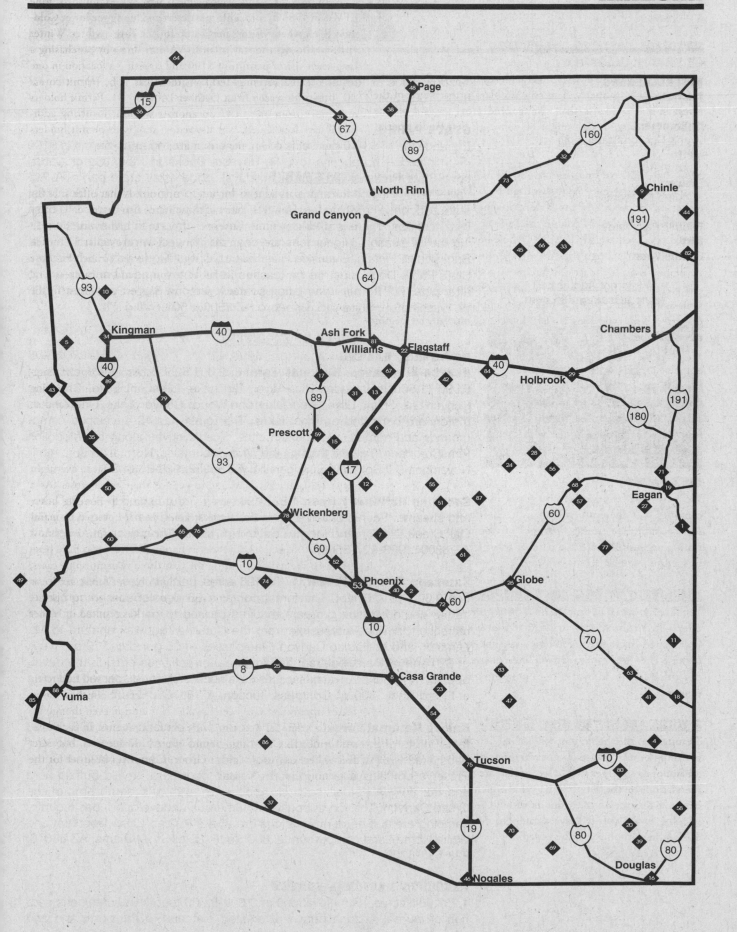

ARIZONA

Capital:
Phoenix
Nickname:
Grand Canyon State
Motto:
"God Enriches"
Flower:
Saguaro Blossom
Tree:
Foothill Palo Verde
Bird:
Cactus Wren

Internet Address:
www.arizonaguide.com

Arizona Office of Tourism, 1110 West Washington, Suite 155, Phoenix, AZ 85007; 602/364-3700. Internet: www.arizonaguide.com.

STATE PARKS

Entrance fee of $3-10 per vehicle. An annual unlimited entry permit is $100 ($45 limited -- no access to Lake Havasu, Buckskin Mountain or Cattail cove State Parks on Fri-Sun or holidays), good at all state parks. A $15 Valley Verde Regional Pass is available for visitors to six state parks. Most state park base camping fees are $12 per night without hookups, $19 base with hookups. There is a 15-day limit. Lower 7-day rates are available during the off-season. Higher fees are charged on weekends and holidays at Buckskin Mountain, Buckskin River Island, Cattail Cove and Hake Havasu State Parks Dogs must be on leashes at all times, and owners clean up after pets. For further information contact: Arizona State Park Board, 800 W. Washington, Suite 415, Phoenix, AZ 85007; 602-542-4174.

NATIONAL FORESTS

Apache-Sitgreaves National Forest. 2,003,525 acres in elevations of 5,000-11,500 ft. Includes Blue River, Big Lake, Crescent Lake, Chevelon Canyon Lake, Luna Lake, Greer lakes and Woods Canyon Lake. Only electric motors are permitted on most lakes. The forest has 48 developed campgrounds and numerous dispersed sites. Scenic drives along the Mogollon Rim, Coronado Trail and through the White Mountains. Normal season: April-November. PO Box 640, Springerville, AZ 85938; 928-333-4301.

Coconino National Forest. 1,821,496 acres. Trout fishing in several lakes and streams. Scenic drives around the Peaks, Lake Mary-Long Valley Rd, Oak Creek Canyon and Mogollon Rim Rd. 182 S. Thompson St., Flagstaff, AZ 86001. 928-527-3600.

Coronado National Forest. 1,780,196 acres, partly in New Mexico. Elevation 3,000-10,720 feet. The forest contains 39 developed campgrounds; its fee demonstration program requires passes to park vehicles at most recreation facilities accessible from the Catalina Highway enroute to Mt. Lemmon and at Sabino Canyon. Day passes of $5 per day, $10 per week or $20 annually are required in many area for activities outside the developed campgrounds. The passes also are necessary for dispersed camping at Lizard Rock. 300 W. Congress, Tucson, AZ 85701; 520/388-8300.

Kaibab National Forest. 1,557,274 acres, with elevations of 3,000-10,418 feet. Points of interest include Cataract, White Horse, Dogtown and Kaibab Lakes -- all with low-fee campgrounds. Grand Canyon National Game Preserve contains a famous North Kaibab deer herd, a wild buffalo herd and the unique Kaibab squirrel. Access to north and south rims of the Grand Canyon. The forest boasts of numerous undeveloped, backcountry camping areas. Fee dump stations are at the Kaibab Lake, Dogtown and White Horse Lake campgrounds. 800 South Sixth St., Williams, AZ 86046; 928-635-8200.

PRESCOTT NATIONAL FOREST

1,237,061 acres, with elevations of 3,000-8,000 feet. In mountainous section of central Arizona between forested plateaus to the north and arid desert to the south. The forest has 14 developed campgrounds, 7 picnic areas, 4 group reservation campgrounds and 2 group reservation picnic areas. Some roads are quite primitive. The forest has joined the federal Recreational Fee Demonstration Project and is testing fees, discounts and incentives at 29 recreation sites near Prescott and on Mingus Mountain near Jerome. Included are campgrounds, day-use areas and trailheads at Lynx Lake, Groom Creek, Wolf Creek, Indian Creek, White Spar, Thumb Butte and Granite Basin. Annual and four-month seasonal passes are available for $40 and $20, respectively. Holders of the passes get 25% discounts on camping fees at Groom Creek Horse Camp, Indian Creek, Lower Wolf Creek, White Spar and Yavapai Campgrounds on Monday through Thursday nights. A new 4-for-3 camping discount is in effect at the same campgrounds: Campers staying four nights pay for three. 344 S. Cortez St., Prescott, AZ 86303; 928-443-8000.

TONTO NATIONAL FOREST

Four wilderness areas totaling 360,000 acres are part of this national forest: Pine Mountain Wilderness (which stretches into Prescott National Forest), Superstition Wilderness, Mazatzal Wilderness and Sierra Ancha Wilderness. The forest also has several dispersed, undeveloped campsites which formerly were free, but daily vehicle fees have been implemented for those near Apache and Roosevelt Lakes. Visitors to those area now must pay $6 daily vehicle fees. In addition, boating fees of $4 are now charged in the same areas, so boat-in campers must pay $10 -- $6 for a vehicle pass and $4 for a boating pass. Campgrounds where fees are charged are not free off season because the campgrounds are closed when fees are not collected. Activities include horseback riding and hiking. Free wilderness permits are required. For maps of Tonto National Forest, Superstition Wilderness and Cave Creek-Mazatzal Mountains Area (at a nominal cost), and for further information contact: Superintendent, Tonto National Forest, 2324 East McDowell Rd., Phoenix, AZ 85006; 602-225-5200.

Canyon de Chelly National Monument's free Cottonwood campsite is one mile east of Chinle. It is open all year, but water is available only from April to October. Fees are charged at Spider Rock Campground, a private, primitive facility. PO Box 588, Chinle, AZ 86503.

Chiricahua National Monument has 30 campsites and 17 miles of trails. A $5 per person entry fee is now charged for adults; America the Beautiful passes honored. 13063 East Bonita Canyon Rd, Willcox, AZ 85643. 530-824-3560.

Glen Canyon National Recreation Area has 178 campsites and good hiking, but no developed hiking trails. Vehicle pass for 1-7 days is $15; annual pass $30; America the Beautiful passes honored. Boating fees, $8 for 1-7 days; $30 annual vessel permit. PO Box 1507, Page, AZ 86040. 928-608-6200.

GRAND CANYON NATIONAL PARK

Backcountry camping is allowed all year throughout much of the park. A backcountry permit is now $10 per person plus $5 per person per day "impact" fee in addition to a vehicle admission fee ($25 for seven days). America the Beautiful passes are accepted. Reservations are required and can be made beginning Oct. 1 for the upcoming year; write Backcountry Reservations Office in care of the park. 16 backcountry camping areas are available. Reservations also can be made in person at reservations office on the North Rim from Nov-May or on the South Rim all year.

Permits are required for any hiking or camping below the rim. Camping below the rim is limited to 7 nights per hike, with a limit of 2 nights per campground. To make reservations contact: Back-country Reservation Office, Box 129, Grand Canyon, AZ 86023; 928-638-7888. This office does not make reservations for group or individual campground space on the rim, river trips, lodging or trips into the Havasupai Indian Reservation.

RV camping is available at Mather and Desert View Campgrounds on the South Rim, North Rim Campground on the North Rim (reservatons required at 877-4446777) and Tuweep Campground on the remote Northwest Rim.

Lake Mead National Recreation Area, 32 miles west of Kingman on SR 68, has both developed and primitive campsites. Entrance fees are $5 per vehicle for 1-5 days or $20 annually; America the Beautiful passes are honored. Numerous areas can be reached by boat, vehicle or backpack. Primitive camping, accessible by boat along the shoreline, is permitted anywhere outside developed areas or areas marked with no-camping signs, with a 15-day or 30-day limit. Vehicle camping is allowed only in designated areas of the backcountry. Campground fees are $10 per site; maximum stay is 90 days; after 15 days backcountry, campers must change sites. Sites with full hookups are available at concessioner-operated locations. 601 Nevada Highway, Boulder City, NV 89005. 702-293-8906.

Navajo National Monument is southwest of Keyenta. It offers 30 free primitive campsites and features preserved ruins of three villages left behind by prehistoric Pueblo Indians. HC 71, Box 3, Tonalea, AZ 86044.

Organ Pipe Cactus National Monument, south of Ajo, has 208 campsites, but backcountry camping is now closed for hiking and camping due to an increase in illegal border activity. Box 100, Ajo, AZ 85321.

Petrified Forest National Park permits wilderness backpacking & camping, but there are no developed campsites. Backpacking permits are free, but a 7-day $10 park entry fee is charged ($20 annually); federal America the Beautiful passes are accepted. PO Box 2217, Petrified Forest National Park, AZ 86028.

Saquaro National Monument has no developed campgrounds. Old Spanish Trail, Rte 8, Box 695, Tucson, AZ 85730.

Bureau of Land Management's Lake Havasu Field Office is participating in the national Fee Demonstration Program and has implemented fees for facilities and services which had been free. Lake Havasu shoreline campsites are now $10 for day use and $10 per site. At Empire Landing Campground, a $3 per vehicle day use fee is charged in addition to the $10 per night campground fee. At formerly free Crossroads Campground, $4 is charged for each site. A $3 per boat trailer fee is charged at Take-Off Point boat ramp, and day use of the Bullfrog area is now $3 per vehicle. Annual passes are being considered. Funds from the program are earmarked for new signs; repair and replacing picnic tables, grills and restrooms; stabilizing eroding lakeshores, and improving trail systems and connecting paths at shoreline campsites. 2610 Sweetwater Ave., Lake Havasu City, AZ 86406; 928-505-1200.

Bureau of Land Management, Safford field office, 711 Fourteenth Ave, Safford AZ 85546; 928-348-4400.

This district manages the Aravaipa Canyon Wilderness, which is open to tent camping and backpacking by reservation and permit. An entry fee of $5 per person (up from $1.50) is charged. Reservations must be confirmed 15-30 days in advance of the visit, and permits are issued at that time. Fees are collected at the wilderness parking areas through self-service registration boxes. Aravaipa Canyon is a deep wilderness gorge of outstanding natural beauty, rich in history and Western lore. Prehistoric ruins are scattered throughout the area, and activities include sightseeing, plant or bird study, horseback riding and exploring features such as hidden waterfalls, canyon pools, and wildlife-viewing (deer, javelina, coyotes, mountain lions, bighorn sheep, bats and coati-mundi).

Bureau of Land Management, Yuma Field Office, 2555 East Gila Ridge Rd, Yuma, AZ 85365; 928-317-3200.

NOTE: Probably the ultimate in low-cost camping is available from the Yuma office of the Bureau of Land Management at its LaPosa and Imperial Dam Long Term Visitor Area sites. Although actually located in California, they are in close proximity to Yuma and Quartzite, Arizona, respectively. To meet the long-term needs of winter visitors while, at the same time, protecting the desert environment, in 1983 the BLM established eight LTVAs where visitors may camp the entire winter. Currently, a winter-long visit (Sept. 15-April 15) to any of the LTVAs is available to holders of a special $140 permit. Short-term 14-day permits are $30. From April 16 to Sept. 14, fees are $5 per day or $50 for the season. Permit holders may move from one LTVA to another at no cost. Golden Eagle, Golden Age and Golden Access Passports as well as American the Beautiful discounts do not apply to LTVA fees. Campers who wish to stay on the desert outside of an LTVA may camp free in one location on undeveloped public land for up to 14 days in any 28-day period. Short-term camping in the Quartzsite area is limited, but there are two designated camping areas at milemarkers 99 and 112 adjoining Highway 95. Annual permits are available only at the bureau's Yuma office. An LTVA permit also allows the holder access to day use facilities at Senator Wash and Squaw Lake recreation areas. For locations of the LaPosa and Imperial Dam LTVAs, see entries under Yuma and Quartzite.

White Mountain Apache Tribe Reservation. Several campgrounds have plenty of sites except during the major holiday weekends. Campgrounds are open all year, but services are provided only between May 15 and September 15. Camping permits of $8 per day are required, and camping is permitted only at designated sites, all of which have some combination of fire ring, picnic table, trash barrel, toilet and drinking water. However, primitive camping is permitted at some of the most remote places on the reservation, and campers are required to pack out their trash. Most designated campsites are at fishing lakes and streams, and anglers must purchase daily fishing permits. Wildlife & Outdoor Recreation Division, PO box 220, Whiteriver, AZ 85941. 928-338-4385.

ALPINE (1)

Alpine Divide   **$10**
Apache-Sitgreaves National Forest
4 mi N of Alpine on US 191. $10 May-Sept; free approx 10/1-11/15 and 4/15-5/15; 14-day limit. 11 sites (tents & very small RVs). Tbls, toilets, cfga, drkg wtr (no wtr, toilets or trash services after 10/15). Picnicking, nearby fishing. Elev 8550 ft; 5 acres, adjacent to highway at foot of Escdilla Mtn.

Aspen Campground   **$10**
Apache-Sitgreaves National Forest
2 mi N of Alpine on US 191; 5 mi W on FR 249; 6 mi S on FR 276; at bend in Black River canyon. $6. 5/1-11/1; 14-day limit. 6 sites. Tbls, toilets, cfga, drkg wtr. Elev 7780 ft. Fishing, hiking.

Blue Crossing   **FREE**
Apache-Sitgreaves National Forest
On FR 281/Apache CR 2104 to Blue River unbridged crossing; just south of Upper Blue Campground. Free. May-Oct; 14-day limit. 4 sites (RVs under 22 ft; no tents). Tbls, toilets, cfga, firewood, no drkg wtr. Hiking, picnicking, fishing. Elev 6200 ft. 1 acre. Scenic. River. Adjacent to Blue Range Primitive Area. Pack out trash.

Blue River   **FREE**
Apache-Sitgreaves National Forest
3 mi E of Alpine on US 191; S on FR 281 (Blue River Rd) along Blue River. Free. Undesignated primitive sites. No facilities, no drkg wtr, no trash service. Camp 100 ft from river. Hiking, horseback riding, fishing.

Buckalou   **FREE**
Apache-Sitgreaves National Forest
9 mi S of Alpine on US 191 & Buckalou Rd. Free. All year; 14-day limit. Primitive undesignated sites; no facilities, no drkg wtr.

Buffalo Crossing   **$10**
Apache-Sitgreaves National Forest
1.9 mi NW of Alpine on US 191; 5 mi W on FR 249; 6 mi SW on FR 276. $10 during 5/1-10/30; free rest of year; 14-day limit. 16 sites (lots of RV space). Tbls, toilets, cfga, drkg wtr. Picnicking, fishing. Elev 7540 ft. Stream. Scenic. On East Fork of Black River.
Fishing tip: Fishing is best in the spring after high runoff. River is stocked weekly with rainbow trout, and it also contains native brown and brookies. Live bait fish prohibited.

Butterfly Cienega   **FREE**
and Ackre Lake
Apache-Sitgreaves National Forest
22 mi S of Alpine on US 191 to Hannagan Meadow; 2 mi S on FR 24. Free. All year; 14-day limit. Tbls, toilets, cfga, no drkg wtr. Fishing, boating.
Fishing tip: Catch-and-rellease only at Ackre Lake; artificial lures only. Best fishing for Apache trout and grayling is in the late fall.

Deer Creek   **$10**
Apache-Sitgreaves National Forest
1.9 mi N of Alpine on US 191; 5 mi W on gravel FR 249; 6 mi S on FR 276. $10 during 5/1-10/30; free rest of year; 14-day limit. 6 sites. Tbls, toilets, cfga, drkg wtr. Hiking, fishing. On E Fork of Black River.

Diamond Rock   **$10**
Apache-Sitgreaves National Forest
1.9 mi NW of Alpine on US 191; 5 mi W on FR 249; 5.9 mi SW on FR 276. $10 during 5/1-10/30; free rest of year; 14-day limit. 12 sites (RVs under 22 ft). Tbls, toilets, cfga, piped drkg wtr. Picnicking, fishing. Elev 7900 ft. 6 acres. Stream. Scenic. On East Fork of Black River. Camp features CCC-era Adirondack shelters.

Double Cienega   **FREE**
Apache-Sitgreaves National Forest
About 27 mi S of Alpine on US 191; 3 mi W on FR 25; right for qtr mi in FR 25B; right on short loop rd (very poor rds, impassable when wet). Free. 5/15-11/15; 14-day limit. Primitive undesignated sites. No facilities, no drkg wtr, no trash service. Hiking, hunting.

54 Road   **FREE**
Apache-Sitgreaves National Forest
23 mi SW of Alpine on US 191 to Hannagan Meadow; 5 mi S of Hannagan Meadow. Free. All year; 14-day limit. Primitive undesignated sites. No facilities, no drkg wtr.

Hannagan   **Donations**
Apache-Sitgreaves National Forest
23 mi SW of Alpine on US 191. 5/1-9/15; 14-day limit. 8 sites (RVs under 17 ft). Free, but donations accepted. Tbls, toilets, cfga, drkg wtr. Picnicking, hiking, fishing (4 mi). Elev 9100 ft. 3 acres. Scenic. Jump off point to Blue Range Primitive Area. Pack out trash.

Horse Spring   **$10**
Apache-Sitgreaves National Forest
2 mi N of Alpine on US 191; 5 mi W on gravel FR 249; 6 mi S on FR 276. $10. 5/1-10/30; 14-day limit. 27 sites. Tbls, toilets, cfga, drkg wtr, group ramada, picnic area. Free off-season, but no wtr, toilets or trash service after 10/15. Trout fishing in East Fork of Black River.

K.P. Cienega   **FREE**
Apache-Sitgreaves National Forest
28 mi SW of Alpine on AZ 191; 1.3 mi SE on FR 155. 5/1-9/15; 14-day limit. Free, but donations accepted. 5 sites (RVs under 17 ft). Tbls, toilets, cfga, piped drkg wtr, horse corrals. Picnicking, hiking, fishing (2 mi). Elev 9000 ft. 2 acres. Scenic. Access point to Blue Range Primitive Area. Pack out trash. Popular among horsemen on trail rides.

Luna Lake   **$10**
Apache-Sitgreaves National Forest
5 mi SE of Alpine on US 180; 1 mi N on FR 570. $10. 5/15-9/15; 14-day limit. 51 sites (32-ft RV limit). Tbls, toilets, cfga, drkg wtr. Group sites available by reservation. 2 handicap-accessible toilets at group area; 2 at lake. Boating(rl), fishing (trout), nearby mountain biking trails, hiking, tackle shop. Elev 8000 ft; 8 acres.
*Fishing tip*s: Good population of rainbow, brook and cutthroat trout, most pansize from annual stockings; some larger from previous stockings. 120-acre lake.

Lost Cienega   **FREE**
Apache-Sitgreaves National Forest
21 mi S of Alpine on US 191; 1 mi N of Hannagan Meadow. Free. All year; 14-day limit. Primitive undesignated sites; no facilities, no drkg wtr.

Racoon Campground   **$10**
Apache-Sitgreaves National Forest
2 mi N of Alpine on US 191; 5 mi W on FR 249; 6 mi S on FR 276 to East Fork camping area. Racoon is a new area developed to replace campsites too close to the creek. $10. May-Oct; 14-day limit. 10 sites. Tbls, toilets, cfga, drkg wtr. Fishing, hiking

Round Cienega   **FREE**
Apache-Sitgreaves National Forest
1.9 mi NW of Alpine on US 180; W on FR 249 toward Big Lake; 3 mi E of Big Lake. Free. All year; 14-day limit. Primitive undesignated sites; no facilities, no drkg wtr. Hiking.

Terry Flat   **FREE**
Apache-Sitgreaves National Forest
5 mi N of Alpine on US 191, then FR 56 to Terry Flat Loop Rd. Free. All year; 14-day limit. Camp along loop rd at pullout areas. No facilities; no trash service. Hunting, hiking, picnicking. Elev 9600 ft.

Upper Blue   **FREE**
Apache-Sitgreaves National Forest
4.5 mi SE of Alpine on US 180, then 20 mi S on Apache CR 2104. Free. 4/1-12/1; 14-day limit. 3 sites (RVs under 16 ft); 2 acres. Toilets, piped drkg wtr, cfga, tbls, 2 camp shelters. Picnicking, hiking, fishing. Pack out trash. Elev 6,200 ft.

West Fork   **FREE**
Apache-Sitgreaves National Forest
6 mi W & N of Buffalo Crossing (see that entry) on West Fork of the Black River. Free. May-Oct; 14-day limit. 70 undesignated sites along river for RVs or tents; some tbls & toilets, cfga; no drkg wtr. Biking, hiking.
Fishing tip: Stream stocked each week with rainbow trout during spring & summer; also native brown trout present.

Wildcat Point   **FREE**
Apache-Sitgreaves National Forest
About 27 mi S of Alpine on US 191; 3 mi W on FR 25; camp where FR 25 crosses the Black River. Free. All year; 14-day limit. Primitive undesignated sites; no facilities, no drkg wtr. Fishing.
Fishing tip: Black River is stocked weekly with rainbow trout and also contains native browns and brookies. Live bait fish prohibited.

APACHE JUNCTION (2)

Lost Dutchman State Park **$12**
5 mi NE of Apache Junction on SR 88. $12 base. All year; 15-day limit. 35 sites and group camping for 20 RVs. Tbls, flush toilets, showers, cfga, drkg wtr, no hookups, dump, visitor center. Desert interpretive trails, rockhounding, campfire programs. At base of Superstition Mountains; hiking access via Siphon Draw Trail. Excellent views. 292 acres.

The Point **$10**
Tonto National Forest
15.7 mi NE of Apache Junction on AZ 88; 2.7 mi NE, BY BOAT. $6 daily use fee plus $4 daily boat fee. All year; 14-day limit. 3 tent sites. Tbls, toilets, cfga, no drkg wtr. Boating(l 2 mi; r 4 mi); swimming, waterskiing, picnicking, fishing. Elev 1700 ft. 1 acre. Canyon Lake.

Tortilla Campground **$6**
Tonto National Forest
18 mi Ne of Apache Junction on SR 88. $6 Tonto Pass required. 10/1-4/30; 14-day limit. 77 sites (22-ft RV limit). Tbls, flush toilets, cfga, drkg wtr hookups, dump, store, wtr hookups. Nearby fishing, boating. Elev 1800 ft; 25 acres.

ARIVACA (3)

Arivaca Lake **FREE**
Coronado National Forest
1 mi S of Arivaca on FR 216; 5 mi E on FR 39; E to 90-acre lake. Free. All year; 14-day limit. Primitive undesignated sites. Tbls, toilet, cfga, no drkg wtr, no trash service. Boating(l - elec mtrs), fishing, birdwatching. Summer temperatures around 100.
Fishing tip: 90-acre Arivaca Lake has good fishing for largemouth bass, catfish or bluegills.

BOWIE (4)

Indian Bread Rocks **FREE**
Picnic Area and Camping
Bureau of Land Management
S of Bowie on Apache Pass Rd, then W on dirt rd to Happy Camp Canyon. Free. Primitive, undeveloped sites. 5 tbls, 1 toilet, cfga, no drkg wtr. Hiking, picnicking, hunting.

Joy Valley **FREE**
Rockhound Area
Bureau of Land Management
16 mi NE of Bowie. From Texaco service station in Bowie, N half mi; right at graded dirt rd; approx 8.5 mi; E (right) again; follow directional signs after crossing the San Simon River (rds may be impassable in July, Aug or Sept due to thunderstorms and flash floods). Free. All year; 14-day limit. No designated sites. Tbls, cfga. Hiking, hunting, picnicking, rockhounding. Elev 3650 ft.
Travel tip: Visit nearby Fort Bowie National Historic Site (11 mi S of town on I-10 & Apache Pass Rd; exhibits on fort's history of 1862-94.

BULLHEAD CITY (5)

Colorado River Nature Center
FREE
Bureau of Land Management
From Hwy 95 just S of the S connection with Bullhead City Bypass, go W on Richardo Rd, which becomes the dirt access rd to the river beach area. Free, Undeveloped sandy beach with undesignated tent sites (no vehicles allowed). The 500-acre CRNC is managed by the BLM, Bullhead City & Arizona Game & Fish Dept. OHV access, boating, swimming, hiking.

Davis Campground **$12**
Mohave County Park
1 mi N of Bullhead City on SR 95; W on paved rd below dam on Colorado River. $12 base. All year; 14-day limit. 171 sites (40-ft RV limit). Base fee for beach area site without hookups or facilities; hookups $17-20. Tbls, flush toilets, cfga, drkg wtr, showers, dump, visitor center, coin laundry. Swimming, boating(ld), fishing. 365 acres.

Katherine Landing **$10**
Lake Mead National Recreation Area
3 mi N of Bullhead City on SR 95; 1 mi W on SR 68; 3.4 mi NW on access rd. $10. All year; 30-day limit. 173 sites. Tbls, toilets, flush toilets, cfga, drkg wtr, dump, coin laundry. Boating(l), waterskiing, fishing, swimming, Hoover Dam tours & visitor center. On SE shore of Lake Mojave.

CAMP VERDE (6)

Beaver Creek **$7.50**
Coconino National Forest
12 mi N of Camp Verde on I-17; 2 mi E on FR 618; at Wet beaver Creek. $7.50 with federal Senior Pass; others pay $15. All year; 7-day limit. 13 sites (22-ft RV limit). Tbls, toilets, cfga, drkg wtr. Fishing, hiking (trails into Beaver Creek Wilderness), swimming. Free picnic area across FR 618. Elev 3900 ft; 3 acres.
Fishing tip: Wet Beaver Creek contains planted trout, generally stocked in April, May, August & Sept.

Bullpen Campground **FREE**
Coconino National Forest
6.5 mi SE of Camp Verde on Alt SR 260; E on FR 626. Free. All year; 14-day limit. Tbls, toilets, cfga, no drkg wtr. Hiking, fishing. Elev 3200 ft.

Clear Creek **$7.50**
Coconino National Forest
6.5 mi SE of Camp Verde on Alt SR 260; 1 mi E on FR 626. $7.50 with federal Senior Pass; others pay $15. All year; 7 day limit. Free during 12/15-3/15. 18 sites & 1 group site for up to 80 persons (32-ft RV limit). Tbls, toilets, cfga, drkg wtr. Swimming, fishing, hiking. Elev 3200 ft; 6 acres.

West Clear Creek **FREE**
Coconino National Forest
6.5 mi SE of Camp Verde on Alt SR 260; 1 mi E on FR 626 to West Clear Creek. Free. All year; 14-day limit. Tbls, toilets, cfga, no drkg wtr. Hiking, fishing. Elev 3200 ft.

CAREFREE (7)

Bartlett Flat **$6**
Tonto National Forest
7 mi E of Carefree on FR 24; 6 mi on FR 205; 7 mi on FR 19; 3.5 mi on FR 459. $6 Tonto Pass vehicle fee. All year; 14-day limit. Primitive undesignated sites; RVs under 16 ft. Fishing, boating on Bartlett Lake. Minimum-development site; not recommended for trailers.

CCC Campground **$6**
Tonto National Forest
20.5 mi NE of Carefree on FR 24 (Bloody Basin Rd); gravel portion narrow with blind curves. $6. All year; 14-day limit. 10 sites (16-ft RV limit). Tbls, toilets, cfga, no drkg wtr. Picnicking, hiking. Elev 3300 ft. 3 acres. Serves as trailhead for Cave Creek Trail #4. Minimum development facility. On former site of Civilian Conservation Corps camp.

Fisherman's Point **$6**
Tonto National Forest
7 mi E of Carefree on FR 24; 17 mi on FR 205. $6 Tonto Pass required. All year; 14-day limit. Primitive undesignated sites (no trailers). Toilets, cfga, no drkg wtr. Minimum-development site. Fishing, boating; access point to Verde River.

Horseshoe **$6**
Tonto National Forest
6.5 mi E of Carefree on FR 24 (Bloody Basin Rd.); 15.5 mi NE on FR 205; half mi NE on FR 205A. $6 Tonto Pass required. All year; 14-day limit. 12 sites (RVs under 16 ft). Tbls, toilets, cfga, drkg wtr. Picnicking, fishing, boating. Elev 1900 ft. 4 acres. Access to Verde River; just downstream from Horseshoe Dam. Steep grades and/or sharp turns; space too tight for large RVs.

Jojoba Boating Camp **$6**
Tonto National Forest
7 mi E of Carefree on FR 24; 6 mi on FR 205; 7 mi on FR 19. $6 Tonto Pass required. All year; 14-day limit. Undesignated primitive sites (RVs under 16 ft). Toilets, cfga, no drkg wtr. Paved boat launch to Bartlett Lake. Fishing, boating. Elev 1800 ft.

Mesquite Campground **$6**
Tonto National Forest
6.6 mi E on FR 22; 15.2 mi NE on FR 205. $6 Tonto Pass required. All year; 14-day limit. About 12 undesignated primitive sites. Toilets, cfga, no drkg wtr. Fishing, boating, picnicking, hiking. Access to Verde River. Minimum-development site. Elev 1900 ft.

Needle Rock $6
Tonto National Forest
2.3 mi SE of Carefree on FR 25; 2.4 mi N on FR 20. $6 Tonto Pass required. All year; 14-day limit. 10 sites (16-ft RV limit). Toilets, tbls, cfga, no drkg wtr. Fishing, picnicking, boating, hiking. Access to Verde River. Minimum-development area.

Ocotillo Boating Camp $10
Tonto National Forest
7 mi E of Carefree on FR 24; 17 mi on FR 205; .4 mi on FR 2100. On Horseshoe Reservoir. $6 Tonto Pass plus $4 boat pass. All year; 14-day limit. Undesignated primitive (RVs under 16 ft). Toilets, cfga, no drkg wtr. Fishing, boating (paved ramp). Elev 1950 ft.

Rattlesnake $6
Tonto National Forest
6.6 mi E of Carefree on CR 21; 6.3 mi E on FR 205; 7 mi E on FR 19; 1 mi on FR 459. $6 Tonto Pass required. All year; 14-day limit. Undesignated primitive sites; RVs under 16 ft. Toilets, cfga, no drkg wtr. Fishing, picnicking, boating, hiking. Minimum-development site. On Bartlett Lake.

Riverside $6
Tonto National Forest
6.5 mi E of Carefree on FR 24; 6 mi E on FR 205; 9 mi SE on FR 19; 1 mi SW on FR 162. $6 Tonto Pass required. All year; 14-day limit. 12 sites (RVs not recommended). Toilets, tbls, cfga, no drkg wtr, no trash service. Fishing, boating/waterskiing (3 mi); picnicking. Elev 1600 ft. 1 acre. Access to Verde River for canoeing, rafting, tubins. Steep grades and/or sharp turns.

Seven Springs $6
Tonto National Forest
20 mi NE of Carefree on FR 24 (Bloody Basin Rd) in chapparal desert. $6 Tonto Pass required. All year; 14-day limit. 23 sites. Tbls, toilets, cfga, no drkg wtr. Picnicking, nature trail. Elev 3400 ft. 3 acres above smal stream. Access rds have steep grades or sharp turns and aren't recommended for RVs longer than 16 feet. Closed temporarily in 2007 due to 2006 wildfire.

Sheep Bridge FREE
Tonto National Forest
6.6 mi E of Carefree on CR 51; 30 mi N on FR 24; 11.7 mi SE on FR 269. Free. All year; 14-day limit. Undesignated site. Cfga, no drkg wtr, no toilets, no trash service. Picnicking, fishing, hiking. Minimum-development site.

South Bend Cove $6
Tonto National Forest
6.6 mi E of Carefree on CR 17; 6.3 mi E on FR 205; 7.2 mi E on FR 19; .1 mi E on FR 185. $6 Tonto Pass required. All year; 14-day limit. Undesignated sites. Toilets, cfga, no drkg wtr. Picnicking, fishing, hiking.

CASA GRANDE (8)

Jim Korsten FREE
West Pinal County Park
Stanfield exit 151 from I-8, N on SR 84 1.2 mi (12 mi W of Stanfield). All year; 3-day limit. Undesignated sites. Trash cans, no drkg wtr. Up to 40-ft RVs.

Pinal County Fairgrounds $12
On SR 287 at 11-Mile Corner -- 11 mi E of Casa Grande, 11 mi S of Coolidge & 11 mi N of Eloy. $12 if space is available. All year. 50 sites. Tbls, flush toilets, cfga, drkg wtr, showers, elec/wtr. Pond, waterfall, fiishing.

CHINLE (9)

Cottonwood FREE
Canyon de Chelly
National Monument
1 mi SE of Chinle on AZ 7, half mi S of visitor center. Free. All year; 5-day limit. 95 sites (RVs under 35 ft). Tbls, flush toilets, cfga, spigot drkg wtr, laundry, dump. Store, ice, food nearby. Campfire programs during summer. Hiking, picnicking, boating, fishing (Navajo Tribal Fishing Permit required) nearby. Motorbikes prohibited. No pets in canyon floor areas or on self-guiding White House Trail; otherwise on leash. 3 group sites available by reservation. Reader says "a super free camp."
Travel tip: Try the self-guided trail from White House Overlook to the White House Ruins. Attend ranger campfire programs at campground on summer evenings.

CHLORIDE (10)

Chloride Municipal Park FREE
21 mi N of Kingman via US 93, then 4 mi E on paved rd. Go into town, turn right at Union 76 station, go one block & turn left. Go about a block to ballfield. Free. All year. Overnight parking while in town. No facilities. Sightseeing. Old 1800s mining town. Murals on rocks 1.3 mi from town.

Chloride VFW Post 2190 FREE
In Chloride at 4953 Tennessee St. Free. All year. No facilities.

CLIFTON (11)

Blackjack FREE
Apache-Sitgreaves National Forest
15 mi S of Clifton on US 191; 19 mi E on SR 78. Free. All year; 14-day limit. About 10 primitive sites; 16-ft RV limit Few facilities. Tbls, 1 toilet, cfga, no drkg wtr. No trash service. Hinting, hiking.

Cherry Lodge FREE
Apache-Sitgreaves National Forest
16 mi N of Clifton on US 191. Free. All year; 1-day limit. Primitive undesignated sites; 32-ft RV limit. 4 picnic sites. Drkg wtr, tbls, toilets, cfga. Elev 6500 ft.
Travel tip: US 191 is part of the route followed by Francisco de Coronado as he looked for the legendary Seven Cities of Cibola in 1540; route very scenic, especially well known for fall foliage.

Coal Creek FREE
Apache-Sitgreaves National Forest
15 mi S of Clifton on US 191; 15 mi S on SR 78. Free. All year; 14-day limit. 5 primitive sites; 16-ft RV limit. Tbls, toilets, cfga, no drkg wtr, no trash service. Hunting, picnicking, hiking. Popular among Hwy 78 travelers.

FR 217 Dispersed Sites FREE
Apache-Sitgreaves National Forest
26 mi N of Clifton on US 191; NW on FR 217 (very narrow after 20 mi); numerous pull-out sites on FR 217 & US 191. Free. All year; 14-day limit. No facilities, no drkg wtr. Fishing, hiking.

FR 475 Dispersed Sites FREE
Apache-Sitgreaves National Forest
25.5 mi N of Clifton on US 191; E on FR 475; numerous pull-out sites on FR 475 & US 191 offer free primitive camping; no facilities, no drkg wtr. Fishing, hiking.

Granville FREE
Apache-Sitgreaves National Forest
16 mi N of Clifton on US 191. Free. All year; 14-day limit. 11 sites; 16-ft RV limit. Tbls, cfga, piped drkg wtr (available only Apr-Nov). 5 acres. Horse corrals. Picnicking, horseback riding. Trash service only in summer.

Honeymoon FREE
Apache-Sitgreaves National Forest
26 mi N of Clifton on US 191; 24 mi NW on FR 217 (very narrow last 5 mi); at Eagle Creek. Under the rim on Eagle Creek. Free. All year; 14-day limit. 4 sites (RVs under 16 ft). Tbls, cfga, toilets. No wtr. Picnicking, fishing, horseback riding, hiking. Elev 5600 ft. 5 acres. Self-clean up area; pack out trash.

Lower Juan Miller FREE
Apache-Sitgreaves National Forest
25.5 mi N of Clifton on US 191; 1.5 mi E on FR 475. Free. All year; 14-day limit. 4 sites (RVs under 16 ft). Tbls, toilets, cfga, no drkg wtr, trash service only in summer. Hiking. 2 acres.

Strayhorse FREE
Apache-Sitgreaves National Forest
54 mi N of Clifton on AZ 191. Free. 5/15-9/30; 14-day limit. 7 sites (RVs under 17 ft). Tbls, toilets, cfga, piped drkg wtr. Picnicking, horseback riding, hunting. Elev 8200 ft. 2 acres. Horse corrals. Trash service only in summer.

Upper Juan Miller FREE
Apache-Sitgreaves National Forest
25.5 mi N of Clifton on US 191; 1 mi E on FR 475; narrow access rd, unsuitable for RVs &

often closed by snow in winter. Free. All year; 14-day limit. 4 sites. Tbls, toilets, cfga, no drkg wtr, trash service only in summer. Hiking. 2 acres; elev 6100 ft.

CORDES JUNCTION (12)

Salt Ground Trailhead   **FREE**
Prescott National Forest
34 mi SW of Cordes Junction on US 17. Free. All year; 14-day limit. Primitive undesignated area; RVs under 17 ft. No facilities. Hiking. Elev 5300 ft.

Travel tip: Ghost towns & deserted mining camps are plentiful in the nearby Bradshaw Mountains. Good gold prospecting & rockhounding. Roads unpaved, rough.

COTTONWOOD (13)

Dead Horse Ranch   **$12**
State Park
1.8 mi NW on Main St from US 89A milepost 353 in Cottonwood; half mo N on North 10th St. $12 base. All year; 15-day limit. Base fee for no hookups; $19 base with hookups; lower 7-day rate during off-season. 45 sites and group area. Tbls, flush toilets, showers, cfga, drkg wtr, wtr hookups($), elec($), dump. 26 picnic sites with grills, wtr, flush toilets. Hiking trails along Verde River, fishing, horse trails, visitor center, stocked pond. Elev 3300 ft.

Fishing tip: The upper Verde River is stocked with trout every other week between Nov & March.

Verde Valley Fairgrounds   **$12**
From northbound SR 89A (S Main St), W on SR 89 (Cottonwood St); right (N) on 12th St to fairground entrance on E side at Cherry St. $12. All year. 40-60 RV sites with elec/wtr. Flush toilets, no showers, dump.

CROWN KING (14)

Coal Camp Trailhead   **FREE**
Prescott National Forest
7 mi SE of Crown King. Free. All year; 14-day limit. 1 site; no facilities. Hiking, picnicking. Elev 6500 ft.

Hazlett Hollow Patch   **$6**
Prescott National Forest
Half mi S of Crown King on FR 259; 7 mi SE on FR 52 (unimproved dirt road). $6. 5/1-9/30; 14-day limit. 15 sites (32-ft RV limit). Tbls, toilets, cfga, drkg wtr, shelters. Fishing, hiking trails. Elev 6000 ft; 5 acres. Most walls & walkways were built by the Civilian Conservation Corps in the 1930s.

Kentuck Springs   **FREE**
Horsethief Basin Recreation Area
Prescott National Forest
Half mi S of Crown King on FR 259; 6.8 mi SE on FR 52. Free. 5/1-11/30; 14-day limit. 27 sites; 7 acres (RVs under 32 ft). Tbls, toilets, cfga, firewood, no drkg wtr. Pack out trash. Picnicking, hiking, fishing (2 mi). Elev 6000 ft.

DEWEY (15)

Powell Springs   **$6**
Prescott National Forest
d8.3 mi NE of Dewey on AZ 169; 5 m N on FR 372 (Cherry Rd); far off the beaten path. $6. All year; 14-day limit. 10 sites (22-ft RV limit). Tbls, toilets, cfga, no drkg wtr. Picnicking. Elev 5300 ft. 3 acres. No trash service.

DOUGLAS (16)

Bathtub   **$10**
Coronado National Forest
N of Douglas on Leslie Canyon Rd; N on FR 74 and FR 74E. $10. All year; 14-day limit. 11 walk-in tent sites. Tbls, toilets, cfga, drkg wtr (no wtr Nov-Mar). Fishing, hiking nearby. Elev 6300 ft; 50 acres.

Camp Rucker   **$5**
Coronado National Forest
N of Douglas on Leslie Canyon Rd; N on FR 74 & FR 74E (27 mi E of Elfrida). $5. All year; 14-day limit. 9 sites (16-ft RV limit). Available to individuals if not being used by groups. Free 12/1-4/1, but no wtr. Tbls, toilets, cfga, drkg wtr. Excellent trout fishing, hiking. Elev 6100 ft; 50 acres.

Cypress Park   **$10**
Coronado National Forest
N of Douglas on Leslie Canyon Rd; N on FR 74 and FR 74E. $10. 4/1-11/31; 14-day limit. Free during off-season, but no drkg wtr. 16-ft RV limit; 7 sites. Tbls, toilets, cfga, drkg wtr. Fishing, hiking nearby. Elev 6200 ft; 30 acres.

Rucker Forest Camp   **$10**
Coronado National Forest
N of Douglas on Leslie Canyon Rd; N on FR 74 and FR 74E. $10. All year; 14-day limit; free 12/1-4/1, but no wtr. 14 sites (16-ft RV limit). Tbls, toilets, cfga, drkg wtr. Fishing, picnicking, hiking. Elev 6500 ft; 50 acres.

Rucker Lake   **$10**
Coronado National Forest
N of Douglas on Leslie Canyon Rd; N on FR 74, following signs to lake. $10. All year; 14-day limit. 8 sites; 16-ft RV limit. Tbls, toilets, cfga, drkg wtr (Apr-Nov). Biking, hiking, horseback riding.

DRAKE (17)

Bear Siding   **FREE**
Prescott National Forest
SW of Drake at the end of FR 492A (on the Verde River); rough/rocky access rd; impassable during wet/winter weather. Free. All year (weather permitting); 14-day limit. Undesignated sites, primitive camping. No drkg wtr or other facilities. Fishing (AZ fishing license required; bass, catfish, carp); hiking. 10 acres. Quiet, beautiful spot; very popular on weekends. Patrolled regularly by Forest Service personnel and Yavapai County Sheriff's Dept. No shooting allowed.

DUNCAN (18)

Round Mountain   **FREE**
Rockhound Area
Bureau of Land Management
Approx 10 mi S of Duncan; US 70 S of Duncan into New Mexico; W (right) about 4.5 mi from state line; approx 7 mi on graded dirt rd to BLM sign that gives further directions. Rds may be impassable during summer rainy season. Free. All year. 4 sites. Tbls, toilets, cfga. No drkg wtr. Elev 4100 ft. Hunting, hiking, rockhounding, picnicking.

EAGAR (19)

Water Canyon   **FREE**
Apache-Sitgreaves National Forest
2 mi S of Eagar on FR 285 (Water Canyon Rd). Free. All year; 14-day limit. Dispersed primitive camping at numerous pullouts along rd. No facilities; no trash service. Hiking, fishing, picnicking, hunting.

ELFRIDA (20)

Sycamore   **$10**
Coronado National Forest
14.7 mi N of Elfrida on US 191; 12 mi E on AZ 181; 10.5 mi W on FR 41. $10; free 12/1-4/1, but no wtr; 14-day limit. 5 sites (16-ft RV limit). Tbls, toilets, cfga, no drkg wtr. Picnicking. Elev 6200 ft. 35 acres. Stream. Scenic. Hiking.

West Turkey Creek   **$10**
Coronado National Forest
14.7 mi N of Elfrida on US 191; 12 mi E on AZ 181; 8.5 mi W on FR 41. $10 during 4/1-11/31; 14-day limit. 7 tent sites (no RVs). Tbls, toilets, cfga, no drkg wtr. Picnicking. Elev 5900 ft. 20 acres. Stream. Scenic.

FLAGSTAFF (22)

Ashurst Lake   **$7**
Coconino National Forest
17.3 mi SE of Flagstaff on FR 3 (Lake Mary Rd); 4 mi E on FR 82E. $7 with federal Senior Pass during about 5/1-10/15; others pay $14. Free rest of yr, but no wtr & only 1 toilet at boat launch. 14-day limit. 50 sites (22-ft RV limit). Tbls, toilets, cfga, drkg wtr. Boating(I--8 hp limit), fishing, windsurfing. Elev 7000 ft; 20 acres. Concessionaire operated. Day use $7.

Bonito Campground   **$8**
Coconino National Forest
12 mi NE of Flagstaff on US 89; 2 mi E on FR 545. $8 with federal Senior Pass; others pay $16. 4/15-10/15; 14-day limit. 44 sites; 42-ft RV limit. Tbls, flush toilets, cfga, drkg wtr. Nature programs, interpretive programs, lava flows, hiking.

Dairy Springs $7
Coconino National Forest
20 mi S of Flagstaff on FR 3 (Lake Mary Rd); 3.5 mi W on FR 90. $7 with federal Senior Pass; others pay $12 during 5/1-10/15; free rest of yr, but no wtr or toilets; 14-day limit. 30 sites (35-ft RV limit). Tbls, toilets, cfga, drkg wtr, store, coin laundry. Boating, fishing, hiking, nature trail, windsurfing, horseback riding. Elev 7000 ft; 17 acres. Concessionaire-operated. Day use $7.

Double Springs $7
Coconino National Forest
13.5 mi SE of Flagstaff on FR 3 (Lake Mary Rd); 5 mi SW on FR 90. $7 with federal Senior Pass; others pay $14 during 5/1-10/15; free rest of yr, but no wtr or toilets. 14-day limit. 15 sites (35-ft RV limit). Tbls, toilets, cfga, drkg wtr, store, coin laundry. Boating, fishing, hiking, windsurfing, campfire program. Elev 7000 ft; 9 acres. Concessionaire-operated. Day use $7.

Canyon Vista $7
Coconino National Forest
6 mi SE of Flagstaff on FR 3 (Lake Mary Rd); near Walnut Canyon and Lower Lake Mary. $7 with federal Senior Pass; others pay $14 during 4/20-10/15; free rest of yr, but no wtr or toilets. 14-day limit. 11 sites; 22-ft RV limit. Tbls, toilets, cfga, drkg wtr. Hiking, rock climbing, horseback riding. Day use $7.

Cinder Hills OHV Area FREE
Coconino National Forest
7 mi NE of Flagstaff on US 89; E on FR 776; camp at posted areas along rd. Free. No facilities. Hiking, picnicking, OHV activities. 13,500 acres. No glass containers.

Forked Pine $7
Coconino National Forest
17.3 mi SE of Flagstaff on FR 3 (Lake Mary Rd); 4 mi E on FR 82E. $7 with federal Senior Pass; others pay $14 during 5/1-10/15; free rest of yr, but no wtr & no toilets except 1 at boat launch. 14-day limit. 25 sites (16-ft RV limit). Tbls, toilets, cfga, drkg wtr. Boating(l), fishing, hiking, windsurfing. Ashurst Lake. Elev 7100 ft; 20 acres. Concessionaire-operated. Day use $7.

Fort Tuthill $9
Coconino County Park
4 mi S of Flagstaff on I-17; exit 337 on W side of interstate; cross US 89A, then half mi into park. $9 base; 14-day limit. Base fee for no hookups; $13 for water hookup; (elec not available). 100 sites (no elec). Tbls, flush toilets, cfga, drkg wtr, playground. Picnicking, sightseeing. Elev 7000 ft; 355 acres. Group camping $6 each.

Lakeview $7
Coconino National Forest
13.2 mi SE of Flagstaff on FR 3 (Lake Mary Rd). $7 with federal Senior Pass; others pay $14. Open about 4/1-10/15; 14-day limit. 30 sites; 28-ft RV limit. Campground reno-

vated in 2002. Tbls, toilets, cfga, drkg wtr. Boating(l), fishing, waterskiing, windsurfing. Elev 6900 ft; 15 acres. Concessionaire operated. Day use $7.

Little Elden Springs Horse Camp $8
Coconino National Forest
5 mi N of Flagstaff on US 89; 2 mi W on FR 556; N on FR 556A. $8 with federal Senior Pass; others pay $16. About 5/1-10/15; 14-day limit. 15 pull-through sites; 35-ft RV limit. Designed for horsemen. Tbls, toilets, cfga, drkg wtr. Bridle trails, hiking. Elev 7200 ft.

Lockett Meadow $10
Coconino National Forest
12.5 mi NE of Flagstaff on US 89 to FR 420 (directly across from Sunset Crater turnoff); 1 mi W on FR 420; right on FR 552 at Lockett Meadow sign; dirt rd closed early spring & late fall due to snow. $10. MD-10/15; 14-day limit. Free off-season when rd is open, but no drkg wtr & maybe no toilets. 17 sites; RVs larger than 20 ft discouraged. Tbls, toilets, cfga, no drkg wtr. Hiking, mountain biking. Trail to an ancient volcono. Elev 8600 ft. New fire rings & tbls installed 2004.

Pinegrove Campground $8
Coconino National Forest
19 mi S of Flagstaff on Hwy 3 (Lake Mary Rd). $8 with federal Senior Pass; others pay $16. 4/20-10/15; 14-day limit. 46 sites; 33-ft RV limit. Tbls, flush toilets, cfga, drkg wtr, coin showers, dump ($5 for non-campers). Fishing, boating(l), biking, hiking. $8 day use fee.

Rest Area #2 FREE
Unmarked; about 5 mi S of Flagstaff on Alt US 89 on east side of hwy. Free. Open area near small stream. All year; 1 night limit. Piped sprg wtr. Picnicking.

FLORENCE (23)

Boondock Area FREE
From jct of US 89 and US 60, past rest areas on north, past tree on south, across railroad tracks to gate on south. Turn south thru gate and go 1 mi. Free. All year. Undesignated sites. No facilities. Wtr in Florence.
Travel tip: Cochran Ghost town is 16 mi E of Florence on Kelvin Hwy, then N on dirt rd to Gila River. A few original buildings still stand. Or see The Riderless Horse 7 mi S of Florence on SR 80/89; a statue of Tom Mix's favorite horse stands where the cowboy died in a car wreck.

FOREST LAKES (24)

Al Fulton/Mosquito Lake FREE
Apache-Sitgreaves National Forest
4 mi W of Forest Lakes on SR 260, along FRs 181, 171, 79. Free. All year; 14-day limit. 57 primitive dispersed sites on FR 171 & numerous undesignated spaces along other

rds such as FR 195, FR 9350, FR 509V, FR 84 and FR 9354. No facilities; no trash service. Fishing, boating at Woods Canyon Lake & Willow Springs Lake. Hiking, hunting, picnicking.

Baca Meadow FREE
Apache-Sitgreaves National Forest
5 mi E of Forest Lakes on SR 260; 2 mi on FR 300, then 4 mi On FR 86. Free. All year; 14-day limit. Primitive dispersed camping area; no facilities; no trash service. Hiking, picnicking. Black Canyon & Willow Springs Lakes nearby.
Fishing tip:At Black Canyon Lake (1 mi), use worms or powerbait from shore; boaters try cowbells, black or brown wooly worms. Elec motors only. At Willow Springs, fish from shore with salmon eggs, powerbaits or worms; boaters troll small lures or bottom fish with worms.

Rim Lakes Recreation Area FREE
Apache-Sitgreaves National Forest
4 mi W of Forest Lakes on SR 260; camp at numbered sites along FRs 180, 181, 9512E and 79. Free. 75 primitive sites. No facilities, cfga, no drkg wtr. Fire restrictions may apply. Popular sites for OHV use.

GILA BEND (25)

Painted Rock/Petroglyph $8
Bureau of Land Management
20 mi W of Gila Bend on I-8 to exit 102; 11 mi N on Painted Rocks Rd; half mi on Painted Rock Point Rd. $8 (day use $2). All year; 14-day limit. 30 sites. Tbls, toilets, cfa, sun shelters, no drkg wtr. Many examples of Indian petroglyphs. Rockhounding, hiking. No public access to Painted Rocks dam. Host Oct-Apr.

GLOBE (26)

Cholla Campgrund $6
Tonto National Forest
N of Globe on Hwy 88 to Roosevelt Lake, then N on Hwy 188; E at campgrond sign. $6 Tonto Pass required. All year; 14-day limit during Apr-Sept, 6-month limit Oct-Mar. America's largest solar-powered campground. 206 sites; 32-ft RV limit. Tbls, toilets, cfga, drkg wtr, showers, free dump. Boating(l), fishing, waterskiing, hiking, playgrounds, visitor center.

Grapevine Bay $6
Tonto National Forest
21 mi N of Globe on Hwy 88; 2 mi E on FR 84. $6 Tonto Pass required. All year; 16-day limit. Primitive undesignated sites; 24-ft RV limit. Toilets, cfga, no drkg wtr. Fishing, hiking.

Icehouse CCC Camp FREE
Tonto National Forest
6 mi S of Globe on FR 112. Free. All year; 14-day limit. Undesignated primitive sites; RVs under 16 ft; 30 acres. Tbls, toilets, cfga,

no drkg wtr. Picnicking, hiking. Minimum-development site.

Travel tip: Globe's annual historic home & building tour is held 3rd weekend of Feb. See McMillan Ghost Town near US 60, 10 mi NE of Globe.

Indian Point $6
Tonto National Forest

30.2 mi N of Globe on SR 88; 11.2 mi N on SR 188; right at A+ Crossing sign (milepost 255) for 2.4 mi to campground sign, then follow sign 1.3 mi (includes ford over Tonto Creek). At N end of Roosevelt Lake. New campground. $6 Tonto Pass. All year; 14-day limit. 54 sites. Tbls, toilets, cfga, drkg wtr, fish cleaning stations. Boating(l), fishing, sailing, waterskiing. 19,200-acre lake.

Jones Water   FREE
Tonto National Forest

17.2 mi NE of Globe on US 60. Free. All year; 14-day limit. 12 sites; 7 acres (RVs under 16 ft) & space for self-contained RVs. Tbls, toilets, cfga, piped drkg wtr. Picnicking. Elev 4500 ft.

Travel tips: Attend Globe's "Apache Day" all-Indian celebration on 3rd weekend of Oct; Indian food booths, crafts, paintings, quilts, entertainment, fashion show. 40 mi NE of Globe (E of Seneca Lake) US 60 crosses Salt River Canyon -- scenic area similar to Grand Canyon; stop at roadside park.

Pinal   FREE
Tonto National Forest

2.5 mi SW of Globe on FR 112; 2.5 mi SW on FR 55; 9.5 mi SW on FR 651; large RVs might have problems on the narrow, winding rd. Free. 4/15-10/31; 14-day limit. 14 sites; 6 acres (RVs under 16 ft). Tbls, toilets, cfga, piped drkg wtr. Wtr off during winter. Elev 7500 ft.

Travel tip: Visit Clara T. Woody Museum 1 mi S of Globe on Jesse Hayes Rd; archaeological exhibits from nearby Besh-ba-Gowah ruins, a town inhabited by Salado Indians 1225-1400.

Pioneer Pass   FREE
Tonto National Forest

8.6 mi S of Globe on FR 112. Free. 4/1-12/31; 14-day limit. 33 sites (RVs under 16 ft). Tbls, toilets, cfga, piped drkg wtr. Wtr off during winter. Elev 6000 ft. 18 acres. Steep grades and/or sharp turns.

Sulphide Del Rey   FREE
Tonto National Forest

2.5 mi SW on FR 112; 2.5 mi SW on FR 55, then 5 mi SW on FR 651. Free. 4/1-12/31; 14-day limit. 10 primitive sites (RVs under 16 ft). Tbls, toilets, no drkg wtr. Picnicking. Developed by Boy Scouts. Minimum-development site.

Timber Camp   FREE
Tonto National Forest

27 mi NE of Globe on US 60. Free. All year; 14-day limit. Primitive undesignated sites for equestrians only when not reserved for group use; 32-ft RV limit. Toilet, no other facilities; no trash service. Hiking, picnicking, hunting.

Windy Hill $6
Tonto National Forest

23 mi N of Globe on Hwy 88; right for 2 mi on FR 82. $6 Tonto Pass required. All year; 14-day limit Apr-Sep, 6-month limit Oct-Apr. 346 sites; 32-ft RV limit. Tbls, flush toilets, cfga, drkg wtr, showers, playgrounds, amphitheater, dump. Fishing, boating(l), hiking. Visitor center.

Note: Just 20 miles east of Globe on US70 is the SAN CARLOS APACHE RESERVATION, 1.8 million acres of pristine desert, mountains and lakes. Once the home of Geronimo, the Apache warrior who terrorized settlers, miners and cattlemen in the 1870s and 1880s, the Reservation is now a prime attraction for hunters, fishermen, hikers, and nature lovers. There are plenty of dry camping areas that only require a modest daily fee of $10 for families. Boating and fishing on San Carlos Lake, the largest body of water in southeastern Arizona, costs $7 per person per day. At the lake headquarters are 12 RV sites with full hookups; in the near future, the tribe plans to expand its services to RVers. For now, there are boat ramps, a marina, a store for groceries and fishing supplies. Trout fishing may be found in a number of ponds, or "tanks" scattered throughout the Reservation.

GREER (27)

Benny Creek Campground $8
Apache-Sitgreaves National Forest

2 mi N of Greer on SR 373; on N shore of Bunch Reservoir. $8. 5/15-10/15; free rest of year when gate is unlocked; 14-day limit. 24 sites (24-ft RV limit; no tents). Tbls, toilets, cfga, drkg wtr. Fishing, hiking, boating(l), swimming. Elev 8300 ft; 4 acres.

Fishing tip: Lake contains rainbow and brown trout. Early spring fishing after ice thaws is best time.

Bunch Boat Launch   FREE
Apache-Sitgreaves National Forest

2 mi N of Greer on AZ 373. Free. Open May-Nov. Primitive undesignated area; 22-ft RV limit. No facilities. Fishing, boating, Elev 8300 ft.

Ditch Camp & North Fork $8
White Mountain Apache Reservation

W of Greer on SR 260; S on SR 473 (Hawley Lake Rd) past Cyclone Lake (closed to the public). $8. Apr-Nov; 10-day limit. 15 sites. Tbls, toilets, cfga, drkg wtr. Fishing.

Fishing tip: This section of the White River's North Fork is catch-and-release only, and no bait is permitted. River contains numerous browns up to 13 inches as well as some 3-5 pounds and 1-pound Apache trout. Some stream structures have been built to provide fish cover.

Drift Fence Lake Campground $8
White Mountain Apache Reservation

W of Greer on SR 260; S on SR 273 (Sunrise Lake Turnoff); 3 mi S of Reservation Lake to Drift Fence Lake. $8. Apr-Nov; 10-day limit. 3 sites. Tbls, toilets, cfga, drkg wtr. Fishing, boating. 16-acre lake. Elev 9000 ft.

Fishing tip: If possible, use small boat or tube rig to fish for Apache & brown trout with flies, corn or worms; fish coves wtih flies or gang spinners. Lake also contains bass, catfish. Lake is heavily stocked with trout in summer and gets larger fish around the holidays.

Gabaldon   FREE
Apache-Sitgreaves National Forest

2 mi N of Greer on AZ 373; 6 mi SE on FR 87; 4 mi SE on AZ 273. Free. 6/1-9/10; 14-day limit. 5 sites (RVs under 16 ft). Tbls, toilets, cfga, no drkg wtr. Mountain climbing, picnicking, fishing, boating. Elev 8500 ft. 3 acres. Botanical. Stream. Campground only for horse users of the Mt. Baldy Wilderness Area; limited corral facilities. Self-cleanup area; no wtr for horses at site.

Government Springs   FREE
Apache-Sitgreaves National Forest

1 mi S of Greer on AZ 373. May-Nov. Free. Primitive undesignated area; 16-ft RV limit. No facilities. Fishing, boating. Pack out trash. 3 picnic sites. Elev 8500 ft.

Horseshoe Cienega $8
White Mountain Apache Reservation

W of Greer on SR 260; S on access rd to Horseshoe Cienega Lake. $8. Apr-Nov; 10-day limit. Numerous sites. Tbls, toilets, cfga, drkg wtr, store. Fishing, boating(rl). At 121 acres, it is the reservation's 4th largest lake.

Fishing tip: State's second-best brown trout, 16 lbs 7 oz, and brook trout, 4 lbs 15 oz, were caught here. Excellent brown & brook trout fishing off the dam after October; use Rapalas for browns. Lake also contains Apache trout & grayling. Try for rainbows in late summer at W arm on powerbaits or cowbells; use flies for brookies. Fish deep for brown in summer. Catch-and-release for browns & rainbows using artificials only.

McCoy's Bridge Campground $8
White Mountain Apache Reservation

W of Greer on SR 260; S on SR 473 (Hawley Lake Turnoff); at North Fork of White River. $8. Apr-Nov; 10-day limit. 10 sites. Tbls, toilets, cfga, drkg wtr. Fishing.

Fishing tip: This area gets a weekly stocking of Apache trout in summer. Drift flies and worms with the current or cast spinners.

Pacheta Lake Campground $8
White Mountain Apache Reservation

W of Greer on SR 260; S on SR 273 (Sunrise Turnoff) & Rd Y-20 to Pacheta Lake. $8. Apr-Nov; 10-day limit. 15 sites. Tbls, toilets, cfga, drkg wtr. Fishing, boating.

Fishing tip: Use wooly buggers and mosquito-type flies for troup; catch-and-release; artificial lures only.

Reservation Lake   **$8**
White Mountain Apache Reservation
W of Greer on SR 260; S on SR 273 (Sunrise Turnoff) to Reservation Lake. $8. Apr-Nov; 10-day limit. 60 sites. Tbls, toilets, cfga, drkg wtr, store. Fishing, boating(lr). 280-acre lake, elev 9000 ft.

Fishing tip: Lake contains numerous rainbow, brook & brown trout. State record brown (22.9 poounds) was caught here in 1999 on a four-inch Rapala. Shore fishing is good, but trolling and fly fishing from boat produces more catches. Use gang spinners or cast flies or lures in the coves. Trolling produces best early and late in the day; use Rapalas and Z-rays.

River Boat Launch
                        FREE
Apache-Sitgreaves National Forest
2 mi N of Greer on AZ 373. Free. May-Nov. Primitive undesignated area; no facilities; 22-ft RV limit. Fishing, boating. Elev 8300 ft.

Rolfe C. Hoyer   **$8**
Apache-Sitgreaves National Forest
2 mi N of Greer on AZ 373, across from Greer Lakes. $8 with federal Senior Pass; others pay $16. 5/15-9/30; 14-day limit. 100 sites; 32-ft RV limit. Tbls, flush toilets, cfga, drkg wtr, dump. Fishing, hiking, nature walks, interpretive programs. Elev 8300 ft.

SU Knolls   **FREE**
Apache-Sitgreaves National Forest
SW of Greer on SR 273; 1.5 mi N of Crescent Lake. Free primitive undesignated camping; no facilities, no drkg wtr. Hiking, fishing.

Tonto Lake Campground   **$8**
White Mountain Apache Reservation
33 mi SE of Fort Apache via reservation rds Y-70 and Y-40 near Pacheta Lake Campground. $8. Apr-Nov; 10-day limit. Tent sites, cfga, tbls. Fishing for rainbow & Apache trout.

Tunnel Boat Launch   **FREE**
Apache-Sitgreaves National Forest
2 mi N of Greer on AZ 373. Free. May-Nov; 14-day limit. Primitive undesignated area; 22-ft RV limit. No facilities. Fishing, boating. Elev 8300 ft.

Fishing tip: Clear shoreline makes casting easy. Fly fishing best in late fall. Lake is well known for its large brown troup; it also contains rainbows.

Winn   **$7**
Apache-Sitgreaves National Forest
2 mi N of Greer on SR 373; 6 mi SW on FR 87; 3 mi S on SR 273; 1 mi NE on FR 554. $7 with federal Senior Pass; others pay $14 Fees charged 5/15-10/15; free rest of year; 14-day limit. 63 sites; 45-ft RV limit. Tbls, toilets, cfga, drkg wtr. Fishing, hiking nearby. Elev 9300 ft; 25 acres. Concessionaire-operated.

HEBER (28)

Bear Canyon Lake   **FREE**
Apache-Sitgreaves National Forest
38 mi SW of Heber on AZ 260, FR 300 & FR 89 (2.6-mi primitive dirt rd). Free. May-Oct; 14-day limit. Primitive undesignated sites around lake. Toilets, cfga, no drkg wtr. Artificial lure fishing, boating. Elev 7800 ft.

Fishing tip: Lake is stocked with catchable size rainbow trout in spring & summer. Also contains grayling.

Bear Canyon Lake   **FREE**
Dispersed Site
Apache-Sitgreaves National Forest
Follow SR 260 SW of Heber to FR 300; W on FR 300, then 3 mi N on FR 89 to lake entry. Hike 1 mi S from parking lot toward lake. Free. Primitive undesignated tent sites. All year; 14-day limit. Toilets, cfga, no drkg wtr, no trash service.

Black Canyon Dispersed   **FREE**
Apache-Sitgreaves National Forest
18 mi SW of Heber on SR 260 and FR 86 to lake; half mi S of lake to dispersed area. Free. Primitive undesignated sites. No facilities, no drkg wtr. Fishing, boating.

Black Canyon Rim   **$12**
Apache-Sitgreaves National Forest
22 mi SW of Heber on SR 260; 3 mi S on FR 300; N on FR 86. $12. 5/15 10/15; free rest of year; 14-day limit. 21 sites; 16-ft RV limit. Tbls, toilets, cfga, drkg wtr (no wtr, toilets or trash service during free period). Hiking; nearby fishing & boating. Elev 7600 ft; 20 acres. Pack out trash; self-service area.

Brookbank/Nelson Lake   **FREE**
Apache-Sitgreaves National Forest
13 mi W of Heber on SR 260; half mi S on FR 300; W of Black Canyon Lake. Free. May-Oct; 14-day limit. Primitive undesignated sites along rd. No facilities; no drkg wtr. Hiking, horseback riding, fishing, boating(l - elec mtrs only).

Fishing tip: Long, narrow 100-acre Nelson Lake contains rainbow, cutthroat, brown & brook trout. Spring & fall best time for browns; summers yield good rainbows. Recent improvements include 2 covered fishing stations. Trout fishing good from shore; boaters troll small spinners. Limit of 6 trout during 5/1-9/1.

Chevelon Canyon Lake   **FREE**
Apache-Sitgreaves National Forest
38 mi SW of Heber on AZ 260; FR 300 to FR 169; FR 169 to FR 169B. Free. Apr-Oct; 14-day limit. Primitive designated campsites. Toilet. Trophy fishing; artificial lures & special size rules (check state fish regs). Elev 6500 ft. No trash service.

Fishing tip: Try Rapalas, Kastmaster, Z-ray or cowbells at Chevelon Canyon Lake for trout. Artificial lures only; 10-14 inchers may not be kept. Float tube recommended or fish from shore; boat access hard. Very remote lake.

Chevelon Canyon   **FREE**
Backpacker Sites
Apache-Sitgreaves National Forest
38 mi SW of Heber on AZ 260; FR 300 to FR 169; FR 169 to FR 169B; backpack upstream & downstream from Chevelon Canyon Lake. Free dispersed tent camping; no facilities. Fishing, hiking.

Chevelon Crossing   **FREE**
Apache-Sitgreaves National Forest
1.5 mi W of Heber on AZ 260; 16.5 mi NW on FR 504. Free. All year; 14-day limit. 7 sites; RVs under 16 ft; 6 acres. Toilet, tbls, cfga, no drkg wtr, no trash service. Picnicking, fishing, rockhounding. Elev 6300 ft. 5 acres. Stream. Geological. 34 mi S of Winslow, AZ. Self clean-up area. On Chevlon Creek.

Crook Campground   **$12**
Apache-Sitgreaves National Forest
22 mi SW of Heber on SR 260; 3.5 mi NW on FR 300; qtr mi on FR 105. $12 during 5/15-10/30; free rest of yr but no wtr; 14-day limit. 26 sites; 32-ft RV limit. Tbls, toilets, cfga, drkg wtr, dump($). Fishing, boating(l), summer ranger programs. Elev 7500 ft; 15 acres.

Durfee Crossing   **FREE**
Apache-Sitgreaves National Forest
1.5 mi W of Heber on AZ 260; 16.5 mi NW on FR 504 to Chevelon Crossing campground; Durfee is just S of Chevelon. Free. Primitive undesignated sites; no facilities. Fishing, hiking.

FR 169 Dispersed Sites   **FREE**
Apache-Sitgreaves National Forest
38 mi SW of Heber on AZ 260; FR 300 to FR 169. Camp within 50 feet of marked posts along FR 159; road signs indicate if camping is allowed within 300 ft of the road or at a numbered post. Free. All year; 14-day limit. No facilities. Hiking, fishing.

Gentry   **$10**
Apache-Sitgreaves National Forest
2.5 mi E of Heber on SR 260; nearly 4 mi SE on FR 300. Formerly free, now $10 during 5/15-10/15; free rest of year. 14-day limit. 6 sites (RVs under 16 ft). Toilets, cfga, tbls, no drkg wtr. Picnicking, hiking. Pack out trash. Elev 7,725 ft.

Horseshoe Lake   **FREE**
Apache-Sitgreaves National Forest
22 mi SW of Heber on SR 260; NW on FR 300 to FR 76; about 2 mi N of the Promontory Butte area of Mogollon Rim. Free. All year; 14-day limit. Primitive undesignated sites; no facilities. Fishing, hiking.

Mogollon   **$12**
Apache-Sitgreaves National Forest
22 mi SW of Heber on SR 260; 4.5 mi NW on FR 300. $12. 5/1-10/30; free rest of yr, weather permitting; 14-day limit. 26 sites (32-ft RV limit). Tbls, toilets, cfga, drkg wtr. Fishing, boating(l), hiking. Elev 7500 ft; 15 acres.

Rim **$12**
Apache-Sitgreaves National Forest
6 mi W of Heber on SR 260; qtr mi NW on FR 300. $12. 5/15-9/15; 14-day limit. 26 sites (32-ft RV limit). Tbls, toilets, cfga, drkg wtr. Hiking, picnicking; nearby boating & fishing. Elev 7600 ft; 15 acres. Near visitor center

Sinkhole **$12**
Apache-Sitgreaves National Forest
27 mi W of Heber on SR 260; half mi N on FR 149 toward Willow Springs Lake. $12. 5/1-9/15; free rest of year, weather permitting; 14-day limit. 26 sites (32-ft RV limit). Toilets, cfga, drkg wtr, no tbls. Hiking, fishing, boating (8 hp limit), mountain biking. Elev 7600 ft; 15 acres.

Twin Springs **FREE**
Apache-Sitgreaves National Forest
12 mi S of Heber on SR 260, then N on FRs 99, 122, 210. Free. All year; 14-day limit. Primitive dispersed RV sites throughout area. No facilities, no trash service. Boating & fishing at Black Canyon Lake; hiking, picnicking, hunting.

Willow Springs Lake **FREE**
Recreation Area
Apache-Sitgreaves National Forest
1.5 mi E of Heber on AZ 260. 5/15-10/15; 14-day limit. Free. Undesignated sites. Toilets, cfga, tbls, no drkg wtr. RVs under 22 ft. Fishing, boating, picnicking. Motors 8 hp or less. Boat launch.
Fishing tip: Good-size rainbow trout can be caught from Willow Springs Lake.

HOLBROOK (29)

Backcountry Camps **$10**
Petrified Forest
National Park
25 mi E of Holbrook on I-40 to exit 311. Camp free, but $10 weekly entry fee. Hike into Painted Desert or into assigned areas. No facilities; no trash service. Also camp free at Crystal Forest museum and at gift shop across the rd; picnic tbls, no other facilities.

Cholla Lake **$10**
Navajo County Park
8 mi W of Holbrook on I-40; S on exit 277 (Joseph City business loop), then E on park access rd 1.7 mi; on N shore of Cholla Lake. $10 base. All year. Base fee for no hookups; $14 for wtr/elec (50% discount for seniors; lower rates for multiple nights). 20 sites. Tbls, flush toilets, cfga, drkg wtr, dump, showers. Fishing, boating, swimming.

JACOB LAKE (30)

Buck Farm Overlook **FREE**
Backcountry Camping Area
Kaibab National Forest
20 mi E of North Kaibab Visitor Center at Jacob Lake on US 89A to FR 445 (Buffalo Ranch Headquarters turnoff); then 23.5 mi

S to FR 445's fork; 2 mi on left fork to FR 445H, then 3 mi to end of rd. Free. All year; 14-day limit. Undesignated primitive sites; no facilities. Suggested use: early fall to early summer to avoid summer heat.
Travel tips: Sightseeing, wildlife viewing. 100-yd hike to edge of Marble Canyon. Scenic drive off the E rim of plateau into House Rock Valley & past the Buffalo Ranch. Spectacular view into Marble Canyon, with Vermilion Cliffs to the north and Navajo Mountoun on E horizon. Elev 5500 ft.

Crazy Jug Point **FREE**
Backcountry Camping Area
Kaibab National Forest
From North Kaibab Visitor Center at Jacob Lake, S one-qtr mi on AZ 67 to FR 461; then 9 mi W on FR 461 & FR 462 to FR 422; then 11.5 mi S (5 miles beyond Big Springs) to FR 425; turn right on FR 425 for 10 mi to Big Saddle Point; turn S onto FR 292; 1.5 mi on FR 292 & FR 292B to end of rd. 32 mi of good gravel rd. Free. All year; 14-day limit. Undesignated primitive sites; no facilities. Sightseeing, hiking, picnicking. Wildlife viewing. Elev 7450 ft.
Travel tips: Panoramic view of Grand Canyon National Park looking into Tapeats Amphitheater. Spectacular canyonlands view; Fishtail Mesa to the W, Steamboat Mountain & Powell Plateau to the S. Opportunity to view fox, deer, hawks, eagles, squirrels.

Demotte **$12**
Kaibab National Forest
24 mi S of Jacob Lake on SR 67; qtr mi W on US 616. $12. Free 11/1-5/14; fee rest of year; 14-day limit. 22 sites (32-ft RV limit). Tbls, flush toilets, cfga, drkg wtr, store. No wtr, trash pickup during free period. Elev 8700 ft; 14 acres. Closed in 2006 for reconstruction.
Travel tip: Drive 7 mi N of park entrance to North Rim of the Grand Canyon. Horseback riding at nearby concession. Guided hikes available from concession at North Rim Country Store.

East Rim Viewpoint **FREE**
Backcountry Camping Area
Kaibab National Forest
26.5 mi S of Jacob Lake on AZ 67 (.7 mi beyond DeMotte camp entrance); turn left (E) onto FR 611; about 1.4 mi E of AZ 67, FR 611 intersects FR 610; continue E on FR 611 3 more mi. Last 4.5 mi gravel rd, okay for RVs in dry weather. Free. All year; 14-day limit. Late spring to late fall best period. Undesignated sites. Toilets, cfga. No tbls or drkg wtr. Hiking, picnicking, wildlife viewing, bird-watching.
Travel tips: Panoramic view of House Rock Valley, Vermilion Cliffs, Marble Canyon, North Canyon. Cool summer camping. Access to trailhead for East Rim Trail #7 into Saddle Mountain Wilderness. Elev 8800 ft. Access to trailhead for East Rim Trail #7 leading into Saddle Mountain Wilderness.

Indian Hollow **FREE**
Kaibab National Forest
25.9 mi S of Jacob Lake on AZ 67; 17.8 mi NW on FR 422; 7.8 mi SW on FR 425; 4.7 mi W on FR 232. Rough rds last 4.5 mi. Free. 5/1-11/15; 14-day limit. 3 sites (RVs under 32 ft). Tbls, toilets, cfga, no drkg wtr. Picnicking, rockhounding, hiking. Elev 6000 ft. 2 acres. Scenic. Trailhead for Thunder River Trail into Grand Canyon. Snow blocks access in winter. Rare bighorn sheep seen regularly.

Jacob Lake **$7**
Kaibab National Forest
1 mi N of Jacob Lake on US 89A; qtr mi E on US 89A. $7 with federal Senior Pass; others pay $14. 5/15-11/1; 14-day limit. 53 sites (32-ft RV limit); 2 handicap sites; 2 small group sites. Tbls, flush toilets, cfga, drkg wtr, store, dump nearby ($10 to dump, 50 cents per gallon wtr). Hiking (nature trails), visitor center, picnicking, boating (8-hp limit), horseback riding, chuckwagon rides, guided forest tours, nature programs, nature trails. 44 mi N of N rim of Grand Canyon. 27 acres; elev 7900 ft.

Jumpup Point **FREE**
Backcountry Camping Area
Kaibab National Forest
W off AZ 67 on FR 461 one-third mi S of Visitor Center in Jacob Lake; 9 mi on FRs 461 & 462 to FR 422; 2 mi S to FR 423; 5 mi W to FR 427; 2.3 mi S to FR 236; 7 mi W to FR 201; 10.3 mi S (left) on FR 201 to end of rd. First 25 mi good gravel rds; last 11 mi rough, not suitable for cars or RVs. Protruding rocks in road bed over last few mi. Free. All year; 14-day limit. Undesignated primitive sites; no facilities. Wildlife viewing, sightseeing. Elev 5650 ft.
Travel tip: Spectacular canyonland panoramic view; Kamab Creek Canyon just to the W, Jumpup Canyon to the E & S. Grand Canyon in the distance.

Marble Viewpoint **FREE**
Backcountry Camping Area
Kaibab National Forest
26.5 mi S on AZ 67 from Jacob Lake (.7 mi beyond DeMotte camp entrance); turn left (E) onto FR 611 for 1.4 mi, then S on FR 610 for 6 mi to FR 219; N on FR 219 for 4 mi to road's end. Last 11.5 mi on gravel rd suitable for RVs in dry weather. Free. All year; 14-day limit. Spring-fall best period. Primitive open camping; no facilities. Hiking, picnicking, bird-watching, wildlife viewing. Nights cool & windy.
Travel tip: Spectacular panoramic view of House Rock Valley, Vermilion Cliffs, Marble Canyon, North Canyon, Saddle Mountain Wilderness.

Parissawampitts Point **FREE**
Backcountry Camping Area
Kaibab National Forest
From quarter mi S of visitor center on AZ 67, take FRs 461 & 462 W 9 mi to FR 422, then S 19 mi (12.3 mi beyond Big Springs) to FR

206; then S 3.5 mi and W on FR 214 8 mi to end of road. Good gravel roads. Free. All year; 14-day limit. Be prepared for summer thunderstorms. Undesignated primitive sites; no facilities. Hiking, sightseeing, picnicking. Elev 7570 ft. Panoramic view of Grand Canyon.

Quaking Aspen Spring FREE
Backcountry Camping Area
Kaibab National Forest
S on AZ 67 from North Kaibab Visitor at Jacob Lake (.7 mi past Demotte camp entrance) to FR 422; 2 mi W to FR 270; 1 mi S to FR 222; 5 mi W to FR 206; 4 mi S. Last 12 mi good gravel & dirt rds. Free. All year; 14-day limit. Sightseeing, wildlife viewing, hiking. Elem 7800 ft. Scenic, cool meadow along bottom of Quaking Aspen Canyon makes camping attractive in fringes of aspen/spruce trees. Fall colors spectacular.

Sowats Point FREE
Backcountry Camping Area
Kaibab National Forest
W on FR 461 off AZ 67 just S of forest visitor center in Jacob Lake; 9 mi W on FRs 461 7 462 to FR 422; 11.5 mi S (5 mi beyond Big Springs) to FR 425; 8 mi S to FR 233; 9.5 mi W to end of rd. Mostly good gravel rds, but last 2-3 mi are rough; high-clearance vehicles recommended. See Crazy Jug Point entry for alternate RV or auto route. Free. All year; 14-day limit. Undesignated primitive sites; no facilities. Sightseeing, wildlife viewing, hiking.

Travel tip: Canyonland panoramic view; Mount Trumbull on western horizon; Powell Plateau & Grand Canyon Nat'l. Park on the S.

Timp Point FREE
Backcountry Camping Area
Kaibab National Forest
26.5 mi S of Jacob Lake on AZ 67 (.7 mi beyond DeMotte camp entrance), then W 2 mi on FR 422 to FR 270; S 1 mi, then W 5 mi on FR 222; W one-qtr mi to FR 271; follow FR 271 8 mi to its end. Last 16.5 mi on good gravel rds. Free. All year; 14-day limit. Undesignated prim camping; no facilities. Hiking, sightseeing, picnicking. Elev 7600 ft. Wildlife viewing.

Travel tip: Point has panoramic view of Grand Canyon and tributary canyons. Only known, easily accessible point on the Kaibab Plateau where it is possible (with binoculars) to see Thunder River emerge from N wall of Tapeats Canyon.

JEROME (31)

Mingus Mountain $6
Prescott National Forest
6.6 mi SW of Jerome on US 89A; 2.5 mi SE on FR 104. Located on top of Mingus Mtn. Tough rd for RVs. $6 ($15 will be charged at 19 elec sites beginning in 2008). 5/1-12/12; 14-day limit. 25 sites (RVs under 40 ft). Tbls, toilets, cfga, no drkg wtr. Horseback riding, hiking, picnicking, hunting. 10 acres. Pack

out trash. Panoramic view of Verde Valley. Acces to North Mingus Trail. Elev 7500 ft. Camp upgraded with new toilets, more sites & wtr system being rebuilt.

Potato Patch $10
Prescott National Forest
6.5 mi SW of Jerome on US 89A (on Mingus Mtn). $10 without hookups. 5/1-11/1; 14-day limit. 42 sites (including 12 new RV sites with elec, $15); 40-ft RV limit. Tbls, toilets, cfga, drkg wtr. Hiking, picnicking. 4 acres. Access to Woodchute·Trail 102 & Woodchute Wilderness. Elev 7000 ft.

KAYENTA (32)

Betatakin FREE
Main Campground
Navajo National Monument
22 mi SW of Kayenta on US 160; 9 mi N/NW on AZ 564 to the monument headquarters; campground is just beyond visitor center. Free. May-Oct.; 7-day limit. 30 sites (RVs under 28 ft). Tbls, flush toilets, cfga, dump, wtr in restrooms. Picnicking, hiking. In the summer, campfire programs are given on the archeology, history, and natural history of the monument. Elev 7300 ft. No wood fires allowed; only charcoal or propane. Sites quite close. No entry fee to park. In summer, overflow space available at a more primitive campground 1 mi N.

Travel tip: A Navajo Tribal Guild concession in visitor center sells objects made by the Indians; visitor center offers displays & films on the Anasazi culture and 20-min video about the Betatakin cliff dwelling.

Keet Seel FREE
Backcountry Campground
Navajo National Monument
20 mi SW of Kayenta on US 160; 9 mi N/NW on AZ 564 to the monument headquarters; 9 mi N of visitor center, on rough trail. Hike in or horseback ride in. Free. MD-LD; 1 night limit. Undesignated tent sites. Hiking, horseback riding. Elev 7300 ft. 60 acres. No wood fires allowed; only charcoal/propane. Backcountry permit required. Ranger-guided tours of Keet Seel ruins.

Mitten View Campground $10
Monument Valley Navajo Reservaton
24 mi N of Kayenta on US 163; 4 mi E; near visitor center of Navajo National Monument. $10 during early April to 10/15; $5 rest of year for self-contained RVs. All year; 14-day limit. Tbls, toilets, cfga, drkg wtr, coin laundry, showers($), dump. 99 sites (32-ft RV limit). Picnicking, hiking, sightseeing.

KEAMS CANYON (33)

Hopitu Trailer Park FREE
Hopi Indian Reservation
Near Keams Canyon, on Hwy 264, 5 mi W of Hwy 87. Free. All year; 7-day limit. 33 sites; 40 acres. Pay showers, tbls. Store, ice, laundry nearby. Picnicking.

Keams Canyon FREE
Hopi Indian Reservation
On Hwy 264 opposite trading post. Free. All year; 2-day limit. About 12 unspecified sites (RVs under 24 ft). Toilets, showers, cfga, tbls. Elev 5500 ft.

Travel tip: In summer, kachina dance ceremonies are held at nearby Hopi villages.

KINGMAN (34)

Bonelli Landing $5
Lake Mead National Recreation Area
75 mi NW of Kingman on US 93 & Bonelli Landing access. Camp free, but $5 entry fee ($20 annually). All year; 15-day limit. Undesignated sites. Tbls, toilets, cfga, no drkg wtr. Fishing, swimming, picnicking, boating(l). Elev 1230 ft.

Gregg's Hideout $5
Lake Mead National Recreation Area
70 mi N of Kingman; on SE shore, E of Temple Bar. Camp free, but $5 entry fee ($20 annually). All year; 15-day limit. Undesignated sites. Undeveloped.

Hualapai Mountain $12
Mohave County Park
From I-40 exit 51 at Kingman, 1.9 mi S on Stockton Hill Rd; 11 mi on Hualapai Mountain Rd. $12 base. All year; 14-day limit (RV sites closed during winter). Base fee for no hookups; $20 for full hookups. 96 sites. Tbls, flush toilets, cfga, drkg wtr, playground, sports fields. Hiking, picnicking. 2300 acres. Weekly & monthly rates available.

Monkey Cove $5
Lake Mead National Recreation Area
70 mi N of Kingman. Camp free, but $5 entry fee ($20 annually). All year; 15-day limit. Undesignated sites. Undeveloped.

Travel tip: Stop at White Hills Ghost Town, 50 mi N of Kingman off Rt 93; now mostly old diggings, it was rowdiest silver mine between Globe & Virginia City.

Packsaddle Recreation Site
FREE
Bureau of Land Management
15 mi NW of Kingman on US 93, then 6 mi NE on Chloride-Big Wash Rd. Free. 5/1-11/1; 14-day limit. 7 sites. Tbls, toilets, cfga, no drkg wtr. Hiking, picnicking, rockhounding. Elev 6200 ft.

Travel tip: Goldenroad & Oatman ghost towns are SW of Kingman. Little remains of Goldenroad; Oatman has many empty buildings, picturesque ruins. Area honeycombed with abandoned mine shafts, dilapidated buildings.

Pierce Ferry FREE
Lake Mead National Recreation Area
77 mi N of Kingman off US 93. Free. All year; 15-day limit. Elev 1300 ft. Primitive sites. Fishing, boating.

Temple Bar   **$10**
Lake Mead National Recreation Area
80 mi N of Kingman on US 93. $10. All year; 30-day limit. 153 sites. Tbls, flush toilets, cfga, drkg wtr, coin laundry, dump. Fishing, hiking, boating(l), swimming, waterskiing.

Wild Cow Springs Recreation Site   **$5**
Bureau of Land Management
Approx 12 mi SE of Kingman on Hualapai Mtn Rd to Hualapai Mt Co Pk; approx 5 mi S on winding dirt rd through co pk, to campground. $5. 5/1-11/1; 14-day limit. 24 sites. Toilets, cfga, no tbls, no drkg wtr. Hunting, hiking. Elev 7200 ft. 10 acres. High-clearance vehicles recommended; large RVs discouraged.

Windy Point Recreation Site   **$4**
Bureau of Land Management
21 mi N of Kingman on US 93; right on dirt rd located 2 mi N of AZ 62 (Chloride Rd) for approx 10.2 mi to campground. $4. 5/1-11/1; 21-day limit. 7 primitive sites (RVs under 20 ft). 13 acres. Tbls, flush toilets, cfga, no drkg wtr. Dump at nearby rest area. Hunting, hiking, picnicking, rockhounding. Elev 6100 ft.

LAKE HAVASU CITY (35)

Havasu National   **FREE**
Wildlife Refuge
N of Lake Havasu City and S of Topock on Arizona shoreline of Lake Havasu for 2 mi S of Topock Gorge. Free. All year. Undesignated camping area; no facilities. Hiking, fishing, boating, wildlife watching. Refuge is home of the Harris hawk, one of America's rarest birds of prey.
   Travel tip: If camped here in January, consider attending the annual Dixieland Jazz Festival at Lake Havasu City the third weekend. Community's annual Snowbird Jamboree is held for winter visitors the 4th Sat of Feb. On last Fri-Sun in April, the Topock-Seligman area holds fund-raiser to preserve last remaining portion of Route 66; classic car show big attraction.
   Fishing tip: Lake Havasu has good fishing for bass, crappie and catfish.

Lake Havasu   **$10**
Shoreline Boat-in Campsites
Bureau of Land Management
From Lake Havasu City S to Parker Dam on Arizona side of the lake. $10 with federal Senior Pass; others pay $20 ($10 overnight plus $10 day use). All year; 14-day limit. 105 lakeshore sites, most with tbl, cfga, toilet, trash can, shade ramada. Accessible only by boat from launches at Take-off Point, Havasu Spring near the dam on Hwy 95, Cattail Cove and Windsor Beach State Park or from the island in Lake Havasu City.

LITTLEFIELD (36)

Virgin River Canyon   **$8**
Bureau of Land Management
Arizona Strip District
16 mi N of Littlefield on I-15 at Little Pockets

interchange. Adjacent to the Virgin River and Cedar Pockets Rest Area. $8. All year; no time limit. 75 sites. Tbls, flush toilets, cfga, drkg wtr, dump. Scenic overlook, interpretive trail, 2 river access trails. Fishing, hiking, picnicking. Elev 2250 ft.

LUKEVILLE (37)

Alamo Canyon Backcountry Camp   **$8**
Organ Pipe Cactus
National Monument
2 mi N of Lukeville on SR 85 to visitor center. $8 camping fee plus $8 entry fee for 7 days. $16 (holders of federal Senior Pass camp for half price). All year; 7-day limit. 4 tent sites in desert at mouth of canyon. Toilets, cfga, no drkg wtr, no trash service. Backcountry sites temporarily closed in 2007 due to illegal border activity.

Twin Peaks Campground
Organ Pipe Cactus   **$12**
National Monument
5 mi N of Lukeville on Hwy 85. $10. All year; 14-day limit. $8 entry fee also charged. Holders of federal Senior Pass camp at half price. 208 sites (35-ft RV limit). Tbls, flush toilets, cfga, drkg wtr, dump, visitor center. Hiking, picnicking, sightseeing. 330,000 acres.

MARBLE CANYON (38)

Lees Ferry   **$10**
Glen Canyon
National Recreation Area
5 mi N of Marble Canyon on US 89A. $10. All year; 14-day limit. $15 per vehicle entry fee and $8 per boat also charged (good for 1-7 days). 54 sites. Tbls, flush toilets, cfga, drkg wtr, store. Boating(l), fishing, swimming. Elev 3100 ft; 15 acres.

MCNEAL (39)

Double Adobe RV Park   **$12**
At 5057 W. Double Adoble Rd W of Lowell. $12 base for primitive or tent sites; $17 full hookups (extra for elec heat or A/C); discounts for AARP, ATA, AAA, Good Sam. Tbls, flush toilets, showers, cfga, drkg wtr. Trap shooting range, horse boarding.

MESA (40)

Bagley Flat   **FREE**
Tonto National Forest
27 mi N of Mesa on AZ 87; 4 mi SE on FR 204; 1 mi E on FR 206, 5 mi E, BY BOAT ON SAGUARO LAKE. Free All year; 14-day limit. 38 tent sites. Tbls, toilets, cfga, no drkg wtr. Swimming beach, waterskiing, picnicking, fishing, boating(lr 5 mi). Elev 1500 ft. 5 acres.
   Travel tip: On first Fri-Sun of Nov, Mesa holds huge "Fine Folk Festival" featuring ethnic food booths, 250 artisans, national & local entertainmers, kids' activities.

Fishing tip: Lake loaded with yellow bass, has good population of largemouth and channel catfish. Try small jig-and-spinners for yellows; plastic worms, black jigs & chartreuse spinnerbaits for largemouth.

Coon Bluff Recreation Area   **$6**
Tonto National Forest
7 mi from Mesa on US 60/70; 12 mi N on FR 204 (Power Rd/Bush Hwy); left for 1 mi on FR 204E. $6. Winter camping only, 11/1-3/31; 1-day limit. About 4 primitive sites. Tbls, toilets, cfga, no drkg wtr. Swimming, fishing, rafting, tubing.

Goldfield Campground   **$6**
Tonto National Forest
7 mi from Mesa on US 60/70; 11 mi on FR 204; 1 mi on FR 204E. $6. Camp only during 11/1-3/31; 1-day limit. Undesignated primitive sites; no facilities, no drkg wtr. Fishing, boating.

Phon D. Sutton   **$6**
Tonto National Forest
7 mi NE of Mesa on US 60 (Superstition Hwy); 11 mi N on FR 204 (Power Rd/Bush Hwy); left on FR 169 (Phon D. Sutton Rd) for 1 mi. $6. Camp only during 11/1-3/31; 1-day limit. 2 large, level paved areas, each the size of a football field, for about 15 sites. Tbls, cfga, toilets, no drkg wtr. Fishing, hiking, tubing, rafting, swimming. River access point.
   Travel tip: Mesa Chamber of Commerce offers "tag-a-long" tours of scenic & historical destinations between Nov & Apr; each participant drives own vehicle.

Water Users Campground   **$6**
Tonto National Forest
7 mi NE of Mesa on US 60/70; 15 mi N on FR 204. $6 Tonto Pass required. Camp only during 11/1-3/31; 1-day limit. Primitive undesignated sites; no facilities, no drkg wtr. Fishing, boating.

MORENCI (41)

Safford-Morenci Trail/East   **FREE**
Bureau of Land Management
6 mi W of Morenci off US 191 on Lower Eagle Creek Rd (5 mi gravel). Free. All year; 14-day limit. Undesignated primitive tent sites; no facilities. Backcountry hiking trail. Picnicking.

MORMON LAKE (42)

Kinnikinick   **$7**
Coconino National Forest
2 mi S of Mormon Lake on FR 90; 2.1 mi SE on CR FH3; 4.8 mi E on FR 125; 4.6 mi SE on FR 82. Free 10/1-5/18; rest of year, $7 with federal Senior Pass; others pay $14. 14-day limit. 18 sites; 22-ft RV limit. Tbls, toilets, cfga, no drkg wtr. Fishing, boating(l). Day use $7.
   Fishing tip: Kinnikinick Lake is stocked with trout. Mormon Lake (state's largest natural lake) has low, marshy waters

more suitable to duck hunting than fishing -- it began to dry up in 1924.

Travel tip: Excellent area for horseback riding, berry-picking in fall; no horses in the campground.

NEEDLES, (CA.) (43)

Ft. Mohave Indian Reservation
Along river N of Needles, off AZ 95. Fee status uncertain, but low fee charged. 200 primitive sites; no facilities. Wtr available along hwy. Boating, fishing. Contact law enforcement officer for permits.

Beale Slough   **FREE**
Bureau of Land Management
From I-40 S of Needles, take the Five-Mile Rd exit E toward Colorado River; follow dirt rd under the railroad bridge; turn right (S) for 1 mi to interpretive sign. Free. Primitive undesignated sites at slough created during channelization of river. Also follow dirt rd N or S along river to unmarked turnouts available for camping. No facilities. No vehicles on beach. Fishing, boating, hiking, OHV use.

NEW ORAIBI (45)

Oraibi Wash Campground   **FREE**
Hopi Indian Reservation
1 mi E of New Oraibi on AZ 264; on sandy beach. Free. All year; 7-day limit. 7 sites (RVs under 24 ft). 1 acre. Tbls, toilets, cfga, no drkg wtr. Store, ice, food, laundry nearby. Reservations accepted. Picnicking.

Pumpkin Seed Point   **FREE**
Hopi Indian Reservation
E of Oraibi on rocky promontory. Free. All year; no time limit. 3 sites. Tbls, cfga, no drkg wtr, no toilets.

NOGALES (46)

Patagonia Lake State Park   **$12**
12 mi NE of Nogales on SR 82. $12 base. All year; 15-day limit. 105 RV sites; 14 boat-in tent sites. Base fee for tent sites & RV sites without hookups; $19 base for hookups. Lower 7-day rate during off-season. Somesites accessible only by boat. Tbls, flush toilets, showers, cfga, drkg wtr, store, dump, marina. Fishing, boating(ld), hiking, swimming. Half mi trail to Sonoita Creek Elev 4000 ft; 640 acres.

White Rock   **$10**
Coronado National Forest
7 mi N of Nogales on I-19; 9 mi W on Hwy 289 (Ruby Rd). $10. All year; 14-day limit. 15 sites; RVs under 23 ft. Tbls, flush toilets, cfga, drkg wtr. Handicapped facilities. Boating(l--elec mtrs only), fishing, hiking. Elev 4000 ft; 28 acres. No firewood.

Fishing tip: 49-acre Pena Blanca Lake contains largemouth bass, crappie and catfish, and in cooler months, stocked trout can be caught.

ORACLE (47)

Peppersauce   **$10**
Coronado National Forest
15 mi SE of Oracle on FR 382; qtr mi W on FR 29. $10. All year; 14-day limit. 19 small sites (RVs under 22 ft; sites quite small). Tbls, toilets, cfga, firewood, piped drkg wtr. Rockhounding, picnicking. Elev 4700 ft. 10 acres. Scenic. Many large sycamore. Only campground on N side of Mt. Lemmon. Reader says entry rd very poor. Base for 4WD use.

PAGE (48)

Lone Rock   **$8**
Glen Canyon National Recreation Area
13 mi N of Page on US 89. $8 plus $15 vehicle entry fee for 1-7 days. All year; 14-day limit. Undesignated primitive sites (RVs under 20 ft). 25 acres. Tbls, toilets, cfga, outdoor cold shower, dump. Swimming, fishing, picnicking.

Fishing tip: Fish the Colorado River below Glen Canyon Dam for trophy rainbow trout (8-10 pounds) and small brook & cutthroats. Float from Lee's Ferry. Use spinners, plastic jigs or fly-fish a shrimp or black woolly worm pattern in the deep holes.

Travel tips: Huge "Festival of Lights Boat Parade" held first Sat of Dec; decorated & lighted boats parade on Lake Powell; cookie contest; entertainment. Also, John W. Powell Museum in town, with geological displays, Indian artifacts.

PALO VERDE (CA) (49)

Oxbow Campground   **$5**
Bureau of Land Management
Lake Havasu District
3 mi S of Palo Verde on SR 78; 1 mi E on gravel rd from sign marked "Colorado River." Camp is at old river channel oxbow in both Arizona & California. $5 (or $50 annually). All year; 14-day limit. Undesignated, unmarked primitive sites. No facilities. Boating(l), fishing, hiking, swimming, picnicking. Near popular OHV trails & Cibola National Wildlife Refuge. Free use permit required. No open fires; use charcoal grills or propane stoves.

PARKER(50)

Crossroads   **$4**
Bureau of Land Management
Yuma District
8 mi NW of Parker (in California) on Parker Dam Rd. All year. $4 (or $50 annual). All year; 14-day limit. 12 undeveloped sites. Tbls, toilets, cfga, no drkg wtr. Along Colorado River. Boat trailer fees expected to be levied.

Empire Landing   **$10**
Bureau of Land Management
9 mi N of Parker on Parker Dam Rd, on California side of the Colorado River in the Parker Dam Recreation Area (7 mi N of Earp).

$10 (or $50 annual). All year; 14-day limit. 50 RV sites & 28 walk-in tent sites. Tbls, flush toilets, cfga, drkg wtr, cold showers, dump. Fishing, boating, rockhounding, swimming beach. 20 acres. $3 day use fee charged. Closed for renovation until October 2007.

La Paz County Park   **$11**
8 mi N of Parker on Hwy 95; on Colorado River. $11 base. All year; 4-month limit. Base fee for dry camping; $13 at 35 waterfront shade ramada sites with wtr hookups; RV sites with wtr/elec/CATV, $16; weekly & monthly rates available. 600 sites. Tbls, flush toilets, showers, beach, playground, dump ($7 non-campers). Golf($), fishing, waterskiing, boating(l), horseshoes, volleyball, tennis, softball, jet skiing. 160 acres.

PAYSON (51)

Aspen Campground   **$8**
Apache-Sitgreaves National Forest
N of Payson on SR 260 toward Heber; 5 mi W on FR 300; right at Woods Canyon Lake Rd for 0.75 mi; near Rim Visitor Center. $8 with federal Senior Pass; others pay $16 ($6 at overflow area). 5/1-10/31; 14-day limit. 136 sites; 45-ft RV limit. Tbls, toilets, cfga, drkg wtr, dump nearby, picnic area. Boating(l), fishing, interpretive trail.

Blue Ridge   **$8**
Coconino National Forest
51 mi N of Payson on SR 87; 1 mi on FR 138; on Blue Ridge Reservoir. $8. MD-9/18; 14-day limit. 10 sites (22-ft RV limit). Tbls, toilets, cfga, drkg wtr. Fishing, hiking, picnicking, boating. Elev 7300 ft; 5 acres.

Camp Bonito   **FREE**
Apache-Sitgreaves National Forest
E of Payson on SR 260; NW on FR 300; 1 mi E on FR 115; 2 mi on FR 91; 1.5 mi E of Ohaco Lookout on FR 40. All year; 14-day limit. Undesignated primitive sites; no facilities; no trash pickup. Picnicking, hiking, horseback riding.

Canyon Point   **$10**
Apache-Sitgreaves National Forest
NW of Payson on SR 260; at milepost 287. $10 base with federal Senior Pass; others pay $20 (elec hookups, $4). 5/15-10/15; 14-day limit. 88 sites (32 with elec). Tbls, flush toilets, cfga, drkg wtr, showers ($3), dump ($5 non-campers), public phone. Hiking trails, interpretive programs, fishing.

Christopher Creek   **$6.50**
Tonto National Forest
21 mi NE of Payson on SR 260; S at milepost 271. $6.50 with federal Senior Pass; others pay $13. 4/1-10/31; 14-day limit. 43 sites; 22-ft RV limit. Tbls, toilets, cfga, drkg wtr. Campfire program, fishing, hiking, horseback riding. Elev 5100 ft. Firewood $5.

Deer Lake   **FREE**
Apache-Sitgreaves National Forest
E of Payson on SR 260; 7 mi NW on FR 300; 2.3 mi N on FR 169; qtr mi E on access rd. Free. All year; 14-day limit. Undesignated primitive sites; camp anywhere except on lakeshore. No facilities except cfga; no trash service. Fishing, hiking, picnicking.

Double Cabin   **FREE**
Apache-Sitgreaves National Forest
E of Payson on SR 260; 16 mi NW on FR 300; 4 mi N on FR 115; 1 mi E of Ohaco Lookout on FR 40. Free. All year; 14-day limit. Undesignated primitive sites; no facilities except cfga; no trash service. Hiking, picnicking. Ruins of old cabin nearby.

First Crossing   **FREE**
Tonto National Forest
2 mi N of Payson on SR 87; 7 mi on FR 199; on East Verde River. Free. All year; 14-day limit. Undeveloped primitive sites on 10 acres (16-ft RV limit). Tbls; no toilets, cfga, no drkg wtr. Trout fishing, boating, hiking.

Flowing Spring   **FREE**
Tonto National Forest
3.5 mi N of Payson via AZ 87; & FR 272. Free. All year; 14-day limit. Undesignated camping area on 20 acres; 16-ft RV limit. Toilets, no drkg wtr, no trash service. Trout fishing. East Verde River access. Elev 4600 ft.

FR 34 Dispersed Sites   **FREE**
Apache-Sitgreaves National Forest
E of Payson on SR 260; 16 mi NW on FR 300; 4 mi N on FR 115 to Ohaco Lookout; pick up FR 56, follow it to FR 225; follow FR 225 to FR 34. Free primitive camping within 300 feet of FR 34. No facilities. Hiking, fishing.

Houston Mesa Camp   **$7.50**
Tonto National Forest
Half mi N of Payson on US 87; right at campground sign for qtr mi; left into campground. $7.50 with federal Senior Pass; others pay $12. 2/1-11/30; 14-day limit. 75 sites; 30-ft RV limit. Tbls, toilets, cfga, drkg wtr, dump, showers. Hiking, horseback riding, interpretive trail. 30 equestrian sites $12. Firewood $5.

Knoll Lake   **$12**
Coconino National Forest
29 mi NE of Payson on SR 260; 19 mi NW on FR 300; 4 mi E on FR 295E. $12. MD-9/30; 14-day limit. 33 sites (32-ft RV limit). Tbls, toilets, cfga, drkg wtr. Boating(l), hiking, fishing. Elev 7400 ft; 20 acres. Campground was closed in 2006 for renovation.

Lower Tonto Creek   **$12**
Tonto National Forest
17 mi NE of Payson on SR 260; qtr mi N on FR 289. $12. 4/1-10/30; 14-day limit. Free LD-MD, but no wtr or trash service. 17 sites (22-ft RV limit). Tbls, toilets, cfga, drkg wtr. Dump($5) at Ponderosa Campground on SR 260. Fishing, hiking trails. Tours of nearby trout hatchery. Elev 5600 ft; 14 acres.

Ponderosa Campground   **$6.50**
Tonto National Forest
15 mi NE of Payson on SR 260; S to site. $6.50 with Senior Pass; others pay $13. All year; 14-day limit. 61 sites; 45-ft RV limit. Tbls, toilets, cfga, drkg wtr, dump ($3 for campers; $5 for others). Self-guided Albert Nature Trail, campfire programs.

Second Crossing   **FREE**
Tonto National Forest
2 mi N of Payson on AZ 87; 8.5 mi on FR 199. Free. May-Sep; 14-day limit. Undeveloped primitive sites on 2 acres (RVs under 16 ft). No toilets, cfga, no drkg wtr. Fishing, swimming. East Verde River access point. Minimum-development site. Elev 5100 ft.

Spillway   **$9**
Apache-Sitgreaves National Forest
N of Payson on SR 260 toward Heber; 5 mi W on FR 300; right at Woods Canyon Lake Rd for 0.75 mi; across from Rim Visitor Center. $0 with federal Senior Pass; others pay $18 ($6 at overflow). 5/15-9/15; 14-day limit. 26 sites; 16-ft RV limit. Tbls, toilets, cfga, drkg wtr, picnic area, dump nearby. Boating(l), fishing, interpretive nature trail. Elev 7500 ft.

Third Crossing   **FREE**
Tonto National Forest
2 mi N of Payson on AZ 87; 9.5 mi on FR 199. Free. May-Sep; 14-day limit. Undeveloped primitive sites on 5 acres (RVs under 17 ft). No toilets, cfga, no drkg wtr. Fishing. East Verde River access point. Minimum-development site.

Upper Tonto Creek   **$12**
Tonto National Forest
17 mi NE of Payson on SR 260; 1 mi N on CR 289. $12. 4/1-10/30; free rest of year, but no drkg wtr during free period; 14-day limit. 9 sites (RVs under 17 ft). Tbls, toilets, cfga, drkg wtr, dump nearby($), nature trails. Hiking, fishing, swimming. Elev 5600 ft; 7 acres.

Verde Glen   **FREE**
Tonto National Forest
2 mi N of Payson on AZ 87; 10.5 mi on FR 199; half mi E on FR 64. Free. Apr-Nov; 14-day limit. Undeveloped primitive sites on 20 acres (RVs under 17 ft). Toilets, cfga, no drkg wtr, no trash service. Fishing, hiking. River access point. Minimum-development site.

Water Wheel   **FREE**
Tonto National Forest
2 mi N of Payson on AZ 87; 8 mi on FR 199. Free. Apr-Nov; 14-day limit. Undeveloped primitive sites (RVs under 16 ft). Toilets, cfga, no drkg wtr. Fishing. River access point. Minimum-development site. Elev 5000 ft.

PEORIA (52)

Desert Tortois Campground   **$5**
Lake Pleasant Regional Park
Maricopa County Park
N of SR 74 off Castle Springs Rd at Lake Pleasant. $5 base. All year; 14 day limit. Base fee for primitive shoreline camping; $10 for semi-developed sites; $18 for developed sites. 76 sites. Tbls, toilets, cfga, drkg wtr, site remadas, elec, showers. Boating(l), fishing, hiking. Part of 23,662-acre park.

Main Entrance Camping   **$5**
Lake Pleasant Regional Park
Maricopa County Park
N of SR 74 off Castle Hot Springs Rd at Lake Pleasant; primitive camping along shoreline near park's main entrance. $5. All year; 14-day limit. Several sites (no RV size limit). Tbls, toilets, cfga, no drkg wtr. Boating(l), fishing, hiking. 23,662-acre park.

North Entrance Camping   **$5**
Lake Pleasant Regional Park
Maricopa County Park
N of SR 74 off Castle Hot Springs Rd past the main entrance; primitive shoreline camping on Lake Pleasant near entrance. $5. All year; 14-day limit. Several sites. Tbls, toilets, cfga, no drkg wtr. Boating(l), fishing, hiking. 23,662-acre park.

Roadrunner Campground   **$5**
Lake Pleasant Regional Park
Maricopa County Park
N of SR 74 off Castle Springs Rd at Lake Pleaant. $5 base. All year; 14-day limit. Base fee for primitive sites; $10 for semi-developed sites; $18 for developed sites. 72 sites. Tbls, toilets, cfga, drkg wtr, site remadas. All RV sites have wtr/elec hookups; tent sites in picnic area. Boatin(l), fishing, picnicking, hiking.

White Tanks Regional Park   **$10**
Maricopa County Park
15 mi W of Peoria via Olive/Dunlap Ave. $10 plus park entry fee. All year; 14-day limit. 40 sites and group camping area. Tbls, flush toilets, cfga, showers, picnic sites, (wtr may not be available). Hiking, horseback riding, waterfall(1 mi), Indian petroglyphs. Elev 1400 ft; 26,337 acres.

✪ PHOENIX (53)

Ben Avery Shooting Range   **$10**
Arizona Game & Fish Dept.
25 mi N of Phoenix on I-17. $10 base. All year; 14-day limit. Base fee without hookups; $25 with wtr/elec. 100 sites. Tbls, flush toilets, cfga, drkg wtr, showers, playground. Shooting range, archery range, hiking trails. Camping only for registered shooters.

Black Canyon Trailhead   **$5**
Maricopa County Park
25 mi N of Phoenix on I-17; on Carefree Hwy (SR 74). $5. All year; 14-day limit. 100

sites (36-ft RV limit). Tbls, toilets, cfga, drkg wtr, elec/wtr. Camping by reservation only. Shooting ranges, archery range; 5 mi of trails & practice area.

PICACHO (54)

Picacho Peak State Park $12
8 mi E of Picacho on I-10. $12 base. All year; 15-day limit. Base fee for sites without hookups; hookups $19 base. Lower 7-day rate during off-season. 95 sites; tents only in group use area. Tbls, flush toilets, cfga, drkg wtr, showers, no dump, horse facilities. Horseback riding, hiking trails (trail to Picacho Peak summit). 3400 acres.

PINE (55)

Clints Well FREE
Coconino National Forest
21.9 mi N of Pine on AZ 87; quarter mi N on FR FH3. Free. 4/15-11/15; 14-day limit. 7 sites (RVs under 23 ft), plus space in trees for several self-contained RVs. Tbls, toilets, cfga, firewood, no drkg wtr. Picnicking. Elev 7000 ft. 3 acres.
Fishing tip: Blue Ridge Reservoir (9 mi) has good trout fishing.

Kehl Springs FREE
Coconino National Forest
13 mi N of Pine on AZ 87; 7.1 mi E on FR 300. Free. All year; 14-day limit. 8 sites (RVs under 23 ft). Tbls, toilets, cfga, firewood, no drkg wtr. Picnicking, mountain biking, fishing, boating. Elev 7500 ft. 6 acres.
Travel tip: Short hike to edge of the Mogollon Rim for spectacular view of the Pine-Payson country.
Fishing tip: Knoll Lake (21 mi) regularly produces some excellent trout. Nearby meadow colored by wildflowers in spring.

Rock Crossing $8
Coconino National Forest
3 mi SW of Blue Ridge Ranger Station; 25 mi on FR 751. $8. 5/15-10/1; 14-day limit. 35 sites (32-ft RV limit). Toilets, tbls, cfga, drkg wtr. Boating(l), fishing. Elev 7500 ft; 25 acres.

PINEDALE (56)

Hub Point FREE
Apache-Sitgreaves National Forest
S of Pinedale on FR 130, past Lons Canyon turnoff; E on FR 219; right on FR 139 for qtr mi, then take Hub Point turnoff on FR 919 for qtr mi. Free. All year; 14-day limit. Primitive undesignated camping area. Hiking, picnicking, hunting.

Lons Canyon FREE
and Lons Spring
Apache-Sitgreaves National Forest
S of Pinedale on FR 130 (off SR 260) to Lons Canyon cutoff, follow signs. Free. All year; 14-day limit. Primitive undesignated camping

areas scattered throughout the canyon. No facilities; no trash service. Picnicking, hiking, horseback riding.

PINETOP-LAKESIDE (57)

A-1 Lake Campground $8
White Mountain Apache Reservation
22 mi E of Pinetop on SR 260. $8. 5/15-9/15; 10-day limit. 4 sites. Tbls, toilets, cfga, drk wtr. Site can be muddy in snow or rain. Fishing, boating(l), hiking. Lake named for an Apache chief who was called A-1 by soldiers who thought his name was too hard to pronounce. 24-acre lake; elec 8900 ft.
Fishing tip: Most anglers fish for trout using waders, tubes, rafts or canoes. Shoreline usually clear for casting. Try glitter powerbait & worms near the parking area in early morning. Lake has native rainbows, brookies and Apaches, with fish stocked twice monthly in summer.

Alchesay Springs Campground $8
White Mountain Apache Reservation
S of Pinetop-Lakeside on Hwy 73. $8. Apr-Nov; 10-day limit. 10 RV sites. Tbls, toilets, cfga, drkg wtr. Fishing. Alchesay Fish Hatchery nearby.
Fishing tip: North Fork of White River below the fish hatchery is stocked twice monthly in the summer with 8-inch and 12-inch Apache trout; put-and-take fishing.

Bog Creek Campground $8
White Mountain Apache Reservation
E of Pinetop via SR 260 (just E of McNary) on reservation rd. $8. Apr-Nov; 10-day limit. 5 sites. Tbls, toilets, cfga, drkg wtr. Fishing. Elev 7500 ft.

Bog Tank Campground $8
White Mountain Apache Reservation
E of Pinetop via SR 260; right on reservation rd past Bog Creek & Shush-B-Zazhe camps to Bog Tank Lake; across Hwy 260 from Horseshoe Cienega Lake. $8. All year; 10-day limit. 10 sites. Tbls, toilets, cfga, drkg wtr. Fishing, boating. 12-acre lake.
Fishing tip: Catch pan-size rainbow trout shore fishing from the dam, the E shore or NW corner in late afternoon. Large 15-inch Apache trout are stocked the first week of June. Use flies, worms, corn and z-rays. Live bait fish prohibited.

Brown Spring FREE
Dispersed Area
Apache-Sitgreaves National Forest
From Pinetop-Lakeside, follow SR 260 to McNary, then NE on FR 224 toward Vernon, following signs to Lake Mountain fire lookout; then 1.5 mi N of lookout. Free primitive undesignated sites. No facilities.

Cooley Lake Campground $8
White Mountain Apache Reservation
S of Pinetop-Lakeside via SR 260; 1 mi S of Hon-Dah just off SR 73. $8. Apr-Nov; 10-day

limit. 10 sites. Tbls, toilets, cfga, drkg wtr. Fishing, boating.
Fishing tip: 11-acre lake contains trout, bass, sunfish, channel catfish. Use worm & corn for trout; best at night.

East Fork Campground $8
White Mountain Apache Reservation
S of Pinetop-Lakeside on SR 73; NE on R-25; at East Fork of White River. $8. Apr-Nov; 10-day limit. 15 sites. Tbls, toilets, cfga, drkg wtr. Fishing, birdwatching.
Fishing tip: Since this area gets little use, it is stocked twice monthly during the summer with 8-inch and 12-inch Apache trout. Some big browns can be caught too.

Los Burros FREE
Apache-Sitgreaves National Forest
E of Pinetop-Lakeside to McNary; 8 mi NE of McNary on FR 224. Free. 5/15-10/15; 14-day limit. 10 sites (RVs under 22 ft). 12 acres. Tbls, 1 toilet, cfga, firewood, no drkg wtr. Picnicking, hiking. Elev 7900 ft. No trash service.

Lower Log Road Campsites $8
White Mountain Apache Reservation
E of Pinetop-Lakeside via SR 260; about 100 primitive sites scattered along Lower Log Rd. $8. Apr-Nov; 10-day limit. Tbls, toilets, cfga, drkg wtr. Fishing. Sites get heavy use.
Fishing tip: Smallmouth bass are present in this section of the White River's North Fork, but the most popular fishing is for summertime Apache trout. Apaches of 8 and 12 inches are stocked weekly, and not all are caught, so fishing remains good until October. Most effective are worms and flies drifted with the current and spinners retrieved across-stream. Farther from campsites, wild browns and rainbow can be caught.

Pierce Spring FREE
Apache-Sitgreaves National Forest
E of Pinetop-Lakeside on SR 260 to McNary; about 10 mi NE of McNary on FR 224; right on FR 96 for 1 mi; right on unmarked access rd. Free. All year; 14-day limit. Primitive dispersed camping area; no facilities; no trash service. Horseback riding, picnicking.

Porter Spring/Lons Canyon FREE
Apache-Sitgreaves National Forest
E of Pinetop-Lakeside on SR 260 to McNary; 13 mi NE of McNary on FR 224. Free. All year; 14-day limit. Primitive undesignated sites; no facilities, no drkg wtr. Fishing, hiking.

Reservation Flat FREE
Apache-Sitgreaves National Forest
E of Pinetop-Lakeside on SR 260 to McNary; 6 mi N of McNary on FR 224; 1.5 mi on FR 9. All year; 14-day limit. Free primitive dispersed camping area; no facilities; no trash service. Picnicking, hiking.

Ryan Ranch Campground $8
White Mountain Apache Reservation
E of Pinetop-Lakeside on SR 260, then S

past Horseshoe Cienega Lake; at North Fork of the White River. $8. Apr-Nov; 10-day limit. 5 sites. Tbls, toilets, cfga, drkg wtr. Fishing, hiking.

Fishing tip: North Fork of White River is stocked twice monthly in the summer with 8-inch and 12-inch Apache trou; very little fishing pressure.

Scott Reservoir **FREE**
Apache-Sitgreaves National Forest
S of Pinetop-Lakeside on SR 260; 1.5 mi E on FR 45 (Porter Mountain Rd), following signs to lake. Free. All year; 14-day limit. 12 primitive designated sites. Toilets, cfga, tbls, no drkg wtr. Fishing, picnicking, hiking.

Fishing tip: Scott Reservoir contains rainbow trout, brown trout, channel catfish, sunfish, largemouth bass.

Shush-Be-Tou Lake Camp **$8**
White Mountain Apache Reservation
15 mi SE of Pinetop via SR 260; right on reservation rd past Bog Creek & Shush-Be Zazhe Campgrounds. $8. May-Nov; 10-day limit. 10 sites. Tbls, toilets, cfga, drkg wtr. Fishing, boating. Elev 7600 ft.

Fishing tip: Troll for Apache, rainbow & brown trout in early spring. Lake also contains lots of bluegills.

Shush-Be Zazhe Campground **$8**
White Mountain Apache Reservation
E of Pinetop via SR 260; right on reservation rd past Bog Creek Campground. $8. May-Oct; 10-day limit. 6 sites. Tbls, toilets, cfga, drkg wtr. Fishing, boating.

PORTAL (58)

Herb Martyr **$10**
Coronado National Forest
4 mi SW of Portal on FR 42; 3 mi SW on FR 42A. $10. All year; 14-day limit. 7 tent sites; no RVs. Tbls, toilets, cfga, no drkg wtr, no trash service. Hiking trails, picnicking. Elev 5800 ft; 60 acres.

Idlewilde **$10**
Coronado National Forest
2 mi W of Portal on FR 42 (or access from Rodeo, NM); must ford stram, which is impassable in wet weather. $10. About 4/15-10/31; free rest of year when open, but usually closed Nov-Mar; 14 day limit. 10 sites; 16-ft RV limit. Tbls, toilets, cfga, drkg wtr (no wtr during free period). Hiking, picnicking. Nature trails. Cave Creek Canyon Visitor Center nearby. Elev 5000 ft; 50 acres.

John Hands **FREE**
Coronado National Forest
4 mi SW of Portal on FR 42. Free. All year; 14-day limit. 6 tent sites; no RVs. Tbls, toilets, cfga, no drkg wtr, no trash service. Elev 5600 ft; 40 acres. Hiking, picnicking.

Pinery Canyon/Cave Creek **FREE**
Coronado National Forest
2 mi W of Portal on CR 42; 16 mi W on FR

42. Free. 4/1-11/30; 14-day limit. 4 sites (16-ft RV limit). Tbls, toilets, cfga, no drkg wtr, no trash service. Picnicking, hiking trails. Elev 7000 ft. 30 acres.

Travel tip: Stop at Paradise ghost town 6 mi NW of Portal; briefly active mining town in early 1900s; a few residents, old jail & ruins of various businesses.

Rustler Park **$10**
Coronado National Forest
13 mi W of Portal on FR 42 to Onion Saddle; 3 mi SW on FR 42D (or access from Rodeo, NM). $10. Open 4/1-11/30; 14-day limit. 25 sites (22-ft RV limit). Tbls, toilets, cfga, no drkg wtr. Pack out trash; no service. Hiking trails, picnicking. Elev 8300 ft; 200 acres.

Stewart **$10**
Coronado National Forest
2.3 mi W of Portal on FR 42. $10. All year; free 12/1-4/15; 14-day limit. 6 sites (22-ft RV limit). Tbls, toilets, cfga, drkg wtr (no wtr during free period; wtr purification recommended). Hiking, picnicking. Elev 5100 ft.

Sunny Flat **$10**
Coronado National Forest
3 mi SW of Portal on FR 42. $10 during 4/1-10/31; free rest of year, but no wtr. All year; 14-day limit. 14 sites (28-ft RV limit). Tbls, toilets, cfga, drkg wtr (wtr purification recommended). Picnicking, hiking. Elev 5200 ft; 70 acres.

PRESCOTT (59)

Groom Creek Horse Camp **$10**
Prescott National Forest
6.5 mi S of Prescott on Mt. Vernon Ave (FR 52) to Groom Creek, then three-fourths mi S. $10. 5/1-10/31; 14-day limit. 37 sites for equestrian campers. Redeveloped campground a joint venture with Desert Saddlebag Club of Phoenix; sites can handle large RVs & horse trailers. Tbls, toilets, cfga, drkg wtr, horse tethers. Horseback riding, hiking trails.

Hilltop **$10**
Prescott National Forest
4.9 mi E on Hwy 69 from Prescott to 1.8 mi past Bradshaw Ranger District office; 3.5 mi on Walker Rd, then left at campground sign about half mi. $10. 4/15-10/31; 7-day limit. 38 sites (40-ft RV limit). Tbls, toilets, cfga, drkg wtr. Boating (elec motors only), fishing, hiking, gold panning, no swimming. Short walk to 55-acre Lynx Lake. Elev 5500 ft.

Indian Creek **$6**
Prescott National Forest
4 mi SW of Prescott on US 89; half mi S on FR 63. Nestled along Indian Creek between the White Spar Hwy & the Groom Creek cutoff #97. $6. 5/1-9/30; 14-day limit. 27 sites (32-ft RV limit). Tbls, toilets, cfga, no drkg wtr. Hunting, hiking. Scenic. Elev 5800 ft; 10 acres.

Lower Wolf Creek **$6**
Prescott National Forest
7.6 mi S of Prescott on CR 52; 0.9 mi W on FR 97. $6. 5/1-10/31; 14-day limit. 20 sites (40-ft RV limit). Tbls, toilets, cfga, no drkg wtr. Hiking, hunting. 7 acres.

Lynx Lake **$10**
Prescott National Forest
4.9 mi E on Hwy 69; left for 3 mi on Walker Rd (FR 197) to campground sign; left on access rd; on W shore of 55-acre Lynx Lake. $10. 4/1-10/31; 7-day limit. 36 sites (40-ft RV limit). Tbls, flush toilets, cfga, drkg wtr. Boating (elec motors only), fishing, hiking, gold panning, no swimming. Elev 5500 ft.

Fishing tip: Lynx Lake contains trout, bluegills and channel catfish.

Thumb Butte **$2**
Prescott National Forest
4 mi W of Prescott via Gurley St. $2. All year; 1-day limit. Primitive undesignated area, about 20 sites; 32-ft RV limit. 21 picnic sites. No facilities. Elev 5700 ft. Primarily a group day-use area.

Travel tips: Annual "Territorial Days" festival held in Prescott 2nd Sat & Sun of June; sports tournaments, arts & crafts, historic home tour. Also, 4 mi N of Prescott on US 89 is Granite Dells, with 2 mi of beautiful granite formations along hwy.

White Spar **$10**
Prescott National Forest
2.5 mi S of Prescott on US 89; CG is just off FR 62. $10. 5/1-10/31 (11 sites open all year); 14-day limit. 60 sites (40-ft RV limit). Tbls, toilets, cfga, drkg wtr. Hiking, picnicking. Reservations available. Elev 5700 ft; 20 acres.

Travel tip: World's oldest rodeo, "Frontier Days," is held during 4th of July week at Prescott; started in 1888.

Yavapai Campground **$10**
Prescott National Forest
In Prescott, follow Grove Ave N from Gurley St to 4th traffic light, bearing left through the light, then 3.2 mi on Iron Springs Rd to Granite Basin Lake; left on FR 374 about 4 mi. $10. All year; 14-day limit. 25 sites; 40-ft RV limit. Tbls, toilets, cfga, drkg wtr. Boating (no mtrs), fishing, no swimming, hiking.

QUARTZSITE (60)

Kofa National **FREE**
Wildlife Refuge
15 mi S of Quartzite off SR 95. Free. All year. Undesignated sites; no facilities; no drkg wtr. Hiking, picnicking, sightseeing. Excellent backpacking. Primitive terrain. Scenic, rugged. Camping not for first-timers.

Travel tip: During Jan & Feb, join 250,000 other campers at Quartzite's annual Pow Wow, a gigantic gem & mineral show and flea market, held the first Wed-Sun in Feb. Also, see Kofa Ghost Town 28 mi S of Quartzite on US 60/70, then 24 mi

ARIZONA

ARIZONA

on SR 95; site of the rich King of Arizona gold mine 1896-1910; mostly ruins.

LaPosa $140
Long-Term Visitor Area
Bureau of Land Management
1 mi S on SR 95 from I-10 exit 6 mi S of Quartzsite. $140. All year. Fee is for whole winter season of 9/15-4/15. $5 daily or $50 seasonally during 4/16-9/14 or $30 for 14 days. 2,000 sites on 11,400 acres. Drkg wtr (8 faucets), trash pickup, dump, cfga, 10 toilets, dance floor, ramada. Rockhounding, picnicking, hiking, sightseeing.

ROOSEVELT (61)

Bachelors Cove $6
Tonto National Forest
1.6 mi NW of Roosevelt on AZ 88; 7.3 mi NW on AZ 188. $6. All year; 14-day limit. Approx 10 sites; 16-ft RV limit. Toilets, no tbls, no drkg wtr. Swimming, boating ($4 boat fee), fishing, waterskiing, picnicking. Elev 2100 ft. 5 acres. Roosevelt Lake, paved launch area.

Bermuda Flat $6
Tonto National Forest
1.6 mi NW of Roosevelt on AZ 88; 8.9 mi NW on AZ 188. $6. 2/6 11/14; 14-day limit. About 25 primitive sites for tents & self-contained RVs; 32-ft RV limit. Toilets, no tbls, no drkg wtr. Swimming, boating(rl - $4 boat fee), fishing, waterskiing. Elev 2100 ft; 18 acres. Roosevelt Lake. Minimum development site. Formerly named Horse Pasture.

Burnt Corral Recreation Site $6
Tonto National Forest
17 mi W of Roosevelt on SR 188; qtr mi W on FR 183; on Apache Lake. $6. All year; 14-day limit. 79 sites. Tbls, toilets, cfga, drkg wtr. Swimming, boating(l - $4 boat fee), fishing, waterskiing, campfire programs, interpretive programs. 38 acres.

Cholla Bay $6
Tonto National Forest
1.6 mi NW of Roosevelt on AZ 88; 8.1 mi NW on AZ 188. $6. All year; 4-day limit. 206 tent sites (RVs under 17 ft okay). Toilets, cfga, tbls, no drkg wtr. Swimming, boating ($4 boat fee), fishing, waterskiing, picnicking. Elev 2100 ft. 3 acres. Roosevelt Lake.

Schoolhouse Point $6
Tonto National Forest
7.3 mi SE of Roosevelt on AZ 88; 3.5 mi NE on FR 447. $6. All year; 14-day limit. 211 sites; 32-ft RV limit. Toilets, tbls, drkg wtr, amphitheater, fish cleaning stations. Dump 6 mi. Swimming, boating(l), fishing, picnicking, waterskiing. Elev 2100 ft. 35 acres. Stream. Access to Salt River. Roosevelt Lake. Small boats can be launched.

SAFFORD (63)

Arcadia $10
Coronado National Forest
7.5 mi S of Safford on US 191; 11 mi SW on SR 366; long RVs have difficulty negotiating SR 366 switchbacks. $10. All year, but closed when snow closs SR 366; 14-day limit. 19 sites (22-ft RV limit). Tbls, toilets, cfga, no drkg wtr. Hiking trails, picnicking. Elev 6700 ft; 10 acres.

Aravaipa Canyon $5
Primitive Area East
Bureau of Land Management
15 mi W of Safford on US 70 to Aravaipa-Klondyke Rd, then follow gravel rd 45 mi. $5. All year; 5-day limit. Fee $5 per person, and permit is needed to enter the wilderness (contact Safford District office, 602/428 4040). Limited to 20 visitors per day. Primitive, undesignated tent camping area. Toilets, cfga, no drkg wtr. Golden Age or Golden Access passes may not be applied to the wilderness permit.

Black Hills FREE
Rockhound Area
Bureau of Land Management
17 mi NE of Safford, just off US 191; access rd from AZ 666; approx 1 mi to parking area. Free. All year. No designated sites. Tbls, toilets, cfga, drkg wtr. Trash pickup. Hunting, hiking, picnicking, fishing.
Travel tip: Check rockhound areas administered by BLM for agates & other semi-precious stones.

Bonita Creek FREE
Bureau of Land Management
From 8th Ave near Safford airport, follow signs NE on Sanchez Rd to Bonita Creek. Free. All year; 14-day limit. Primitive undesignated sites along the creek. No facilities, no wtr or trash service. Hiking, bird-watching.

Clark Corrals FREE
Coronado National Forest
7.5 mi S of Safford on US 191; 28 mi SW on SR 366; 7 mi on FR 803. Free. May-Oct; 14-day limit. 2 sites (26-ft RV limit). Tbls, toilets, cfga, no drkg wtr. Horse corrals. Horseback riding, hiking, picnicking. Elev 9000 ft.

Columbine Corrals $10
Coronado National Forest
7.5 mi S of Safford on US 191; 28 mi SW on SR 366; across from visitor information station. $10. 5/15-11/15; 14-day limit. 6 sites (16-ft RV limit). Tbls, toilets, cfga, drkg wtr; corrals & wtr for horses. Horseback riding, hiking & riding trails, picnicking. Elev 9500 ft. Visitor center open 4/15-9/15.

Cunningham Camp $10
Coronado National Forest
8 mi S of Safford on US 191; 26 mi SW on Hwy 366; switchbacks too tight for large RVs. $10. 4/15-11/15; 14-day limit. 10 sites (22-ft RV limit due to rd switchbacks). Tbls,

toilets, cfga, no drkg wtr. Horse feed & wtr no longer furnished. 2 vehicles per site. Pipe corral, bridle trails. Horseback riding, mountain biking, hiking.

Fourmile Canyon $5
Bureau of Land Management
15 mi NW of Safford on Hwy 70 to Aravaipa-Klondyke Rd; 30 mi W on graded gravel rd to Klondyke; 1 mi W on Fourmile Canyon Rd. $5. All year. 10 dirt pull-through sites (30 ft RV limit). Toilets, drkg wtr, cfga. Elev 3500 ft. Picnicking, hiking. Permit needed to travel in Aravaipa Canyon.

Hospital Flat $10
Coronado National Forest
7.5 mi S of Safford on US 191; 23 mi SW on SR 366; large vehicles have difficulty negotiating SR 366 switchbacks. $10 during 5/15-10/1; free rest of year; 14-day limit. 11 tent sites. Tbls, toilets, cfga, drkg wtr. Hiking, picnicking, nature trails, fishing. Site of old Fort Grant Tent Hospital. Elev 9000 ft; 20 acres.
Fishing tip: Big Creek contains native trout but is not stocked. A half-mile to mile hike is needed to reach good fishing areas.

Hot Well Dunes Recreation Area $3
Bureau of Land Management
7 mi E of Safford on Hwy 70; 25 mi S on Haekel Rd. $3 (or $30 annually). All year; 14-day limit. 10 sites. Tbls, toilets, cfga, no drkg wtr. 2 natural artesian hot tubs with wtr at 106 degrees. Fishing, hiking. Heavily used weekends.

Owl Creek Campgruond $5
Bureau of Land Management
Gila Box Riparian
National Conservation Area
10 mi E of Safford on US 70; N on US 191 to milepost 160 (4 mi S of Clifton); left on Black Hills Back Country Byway to campground, about 10 mi S of Clifton. $5. All year; 14-day limit. 7 sites. Tbls, cfga, shad ramadas, toilets, drkg wtr. Boating, fishing, hiking, hunting.

Riggs Flat $10
Coronado National Forest
7.5 mi S of Safford on US 191; 27.5 mi SW on SR 366; 4 mi W on FR 803; 1 mi S on FR 287; on Riggs Flat Lake. Large vehicles have difficulty negotiating SR 366 switchbacks. $10 during MD-LD; free earlier & later, but no wtr; 14-day limit. 31 sites (22-ft RV limit). Tbls, toilets, cfga, drkg wtr. Boating (l--elec motors only), fishing, hiking trails. Elev 8600 ft; 50 acres.

Riverview Campground $5
Bureau of Land Management
Gila Box Riparian
National Conservation Area
Safford District
5 mi E of Safford on US 70 to town of Solomon; left on Sanchez Rd; after crossing Gila River bride, continue 7 mi to Bonita Creek

and Gila Box RNCA sign; turn left for 2.5 mi on dirt rd to Gila Box Riparian National Conservation Area. $5. All year; 14-day limit. 13 sites. Tbls, toilets, cfga, drkg wtr, shade ramadas, volleyball court. Fishing, boating, hiking, river floating, hunting.

Roper Lake State Park $10-12
6 mi S of Safford on US 191; 21 mi SW on SR 366; half miN on FR 137; long RVs have difficulty negotiating SR 366 switchbacks. $10-12 base. All year; 15-day limit. Base fee for no hookups; sites with hookups, $16 base. 71 sites; 1 group site ($10 plus $20 reservation fee); lower 7-day rate during off-season. Tbls, flush toilets, cfga, drkg wtr, showers, dump, shade ramadas. Fishing, boating (dl--elec motors only), swimming beach, windsurfing, natural hot spring, hiking trails. Elev 3130 ft; 320 acres.

Round the Mountain Trailhead   FREE
Coronado National Forest
7.5 mi S of Safford on US 191; 7 mi SW on SR 366. Free. All year; 14-day limit. 3 sites (26-ft RV limit). Tbls, toilets, cfga, no drkg wtr, corral. Wtr for horses only. Corrals, Horseback riding, hiking, picnicking.

Safford-Morenci Trail   FREE
Bureau of Land Management
The West Ranch trailhead is approx 12 mi NE of Safford on San Juan Mine Rd (W end). Free. All year. Primitive tent sites. Hunting, hiking. Informative signs. Back-country hiking trail. Elev 4700 ft.

Shannon $10
Coronado National Forest
7.5 mi S of Safford on US 191; 21.5 mi SW on SR 366; half mi N on FR 137; large RVs have difficulty negotiating SR 366 switchbacks. $10. 4/15-11/14; 14-day limit. 11 sites (RVs under 17 ft). Tbls, toilets, cfga, no drkg wtr. Hiking, nature trails (including to top of 10,000-ft Heliograph Peak. Elev 9100 ft; 10 acres.

Soldier Creek $10
Coronado National Forest
7.5 mi S of Safford on US 191; 29.2 mi SW on SR 366; half mi W on FR 34; qtr mi E on FR 656. $10 during MD-LD; free earlier & later, weather permitting; 14-day limit. 12 sites (RVs under 23 ft). Tbls, flush toilets, cfga, no drkg wtr. Hiking, nature trails. Elev 9300 ft; 7 acres.

Spring Canyon Picnic Area   FREE
Bureau of Land Management
From 8th Ave near Safford airport, follow signs to Bonita Creek NE on Sanchez Rd; area is about 3 mi past first sign along River. Free. All year; 14-day limit. Primitive sites with 2 tbls, cfga, no other facilities, no wtr, no trash service. Hiking, canoeing, fishing.

Fishing tip: Work the river's deep pools with live bait for catfish.

Stockton Pass Picnic Area   FREE
Coronado National Forest
16.5 mi S of Safford on US 191; 12 mi W on AZ 266; half mi NE on FR 198. Free. All year; 1-day limit. 7 sites; RVs under 16 ft. 11 picnic sites; 10 acres. Tbls, toilets, cfga, firewood, no drkg wtr. Picnicking, horseback riding (1 mi). Elev 5600 ft.

Fishing tip: Try Roper Lake, which is stocked with bass, bluegill and catfish; only electric motors allowed on boats.

Turkey Creek   FREE
Bureau of Land Management
13 mi W of Safford on US 70; 32 mi SW on dirt Aravaipa-Klondyke Rd; at Klondyke, follow signs 10 mi to Aravaipa Canyon Wilderness; Turkey Creek at E end of wilderness. Free. Primitive undesignated sites. No facilities except cfga, but toilets at wilderness parking lot. No drkg wtr. Free permit needed to use wilderness. Primarily a hiker camp for those going into the canyon. Nearby Aravaipa Canyon camp is $5 per person.

ST. GEORGE, (UT.) (64)

Arizona Strip   FREE
Bureau of Land Management
E from Bloomington exit of I-15, then S on River Rd to Arizona state line; follow signs on dirt rd; start at Black Rock Mountain. Primitive, undeveloped campsites on 3.2 million acres N of Grand Canyon & S of Utah line; includes 8 wilderness areas. Free. All year; 14-day limit. Undeveloped, few amenities. Rvs not recommended off-highway (Vermilion Cliffs highway suggested). Wildlife viewing (antelope, deer, bigho`, coyotes, mountain lions); hiking, backpacking, mountain biking, rockhounding, boating. Interagency visitor information center in St. George. Attractions include Dominguez-Escalante Interpretive Site on US 89A, 21 mi E of Jacob Lake; Virgin River Canyon's towering multi-colored cliffs, 20 mi SW of St. George; historic one-room Mount Trumbull Schoolhouse; Nampaweap Petroglyph Site; Sawmill Historic Site/Uinkaret Pueblo; Little Black Mountain Petroglyph Site.

SALOME (65)

Centennial Park $5
La Paz County Park
Just E of Salome off Hwy 60 on Centennial Park Rd. $5. All year. 26 primitives sites. Tbls, toilets, cfga, drkg wtr, playground, dump ($5 campers, $7 non-campers), showers ($1, $7 for non-campers). Picnicking, hiking, tennis, horseshoes, basketball, volleyball, rockhounding. Weekly rate $30; monthly $75. Greasewood Desert Golf Course at N nd of park.

SECOND MESA (66)

Second Mesa Campground   FREE
and Trailer Park
Hopi Indian Reservation
Jct Hwys 264 & 87, 5 mi NW on Hwy 264; on top of Second Mesa next to Cultural Center. Free. All year; 2-day limit. 6 sites; 10 acres. Tbls, flush toilets, pay showers, laundry. Picnicking. Elev 6000 ft.

Travel tip: Hopi Arts and Crafts Guild nearby; offers pottery, jewelry, basket weavings.

SEDONA (67)

Bootlegger Campground $9
Coconino National Forest
9 mi N of Sedona (18 mi S of Flagstaff) on US 89A in Oak Creek Canyon. $9 with federal Senior Pass; others pay $18. 4/15-10/31; 7-day limit. 10 paved tent sites (no RVs except pickup campers, vans). Tbls, toilets, cfga, no drkg wtr. Fishing, hiking.

Cave Springs Campground $10
Coconino National Forest
13 mi N of Sedona (14 mi S of Flagstaff) on US 89A in Oak Creek Canyon. $10 with federal Senior Pass; others pay $20. 4/15-10/15; 7-day limit. 82 sites; 35-ft RV limit. Tbls, toilets, cfga, drkg wtr, coin showers. Fishing, swimming, hiking. Crowded on weekends.

Manzanita Campground $9
Coconino National Forest
6 mi N of Sedona (21 mi S of Flagstaff) on US 89A in Oak Creek Canyon. $9 with federal Senior Pass; others pay $18. All year; 7-day limit. 18 sites for tents & small sleep-in vehicles; no trailers. Tbls, toilets, cfga, drkg wtr. Fishing, swimming, hiking.

Pine Flat Campground $10
Coconino National Forest
12 mi N of Sedona (14 mi S of Flagstaff) on US 89A in Oak Creek Canyon. $10 with federal Senior Pass; others pay $20. 3/3-11/15; 7-day limit. 56 sites; 30-ft RV limit. Tbls, toilets, cfga, drkg wtr, coin showers. Fishing, swimming, hiking.

SHOW LOW (68)

Cibeque Creek Campground $8
White Mountain Apache Reservation
About 25 mi S of Show Low on US 60; NW on access rd to town of Cibeque, then N of Cibeque on service rds 12 and O-20; at Cibeque Creek. $8. All year; 14-day limit. 10 sites. Tbls, toilets, cfga, drkg wtr. Fishing. Elev 6000 ft. Closed due to fire.

Fishing tip: Creek is stocked with Apache trout N of town toward the Rim, and the creek produces some of the state's big-gest brown trout

Fence Tank   **FREE**
Apache-Sitgreaves National Forest
3 mi S of Show Low on SR 260; left on FR 136 at sign marked Joe Tank Rd; after 1.8 mi, left on FR 140 for 2.2 mi; accessible only to high-clearance vehicles. Free. May-Oct; 14-day limit. Primitive undesignated sites. No facilities, no drkg wtr, no trash service. Hiking, wildlife viewing.

Fool Hollow Lake   **$6**
State Recreation Area
Apache-Sitgreaves National Forest
W through Show Low from US 60 on Hwy 260; right on Old Linden Rd and West Adams; right on 16th Ave (Fool Hollow Rd); in Apache-Sitgreaves National Forest. $6-7.50 base without hookups with federal Senior Pass; others pay $12-15 base; elec hookups $7-10. All year; 15-day limit. 123 sites; 45-ft RV limit. Tbls, flush toilets, cfga, drkg wtr, dump, showers, fish cleaning stations. Fishing, boating(l--8 hp limit), hiking. Elev 6500 ft; 700 acres. Operated by the state on forest service land in cooperation with city of Show Low. More campsites to be added.

   Fishing tip: Anglers catch trout, catfish, bass, bluetill, walleyes and crappie. Live bait fish prohibited. From shore, use worms, marsh-mallows, salmon eggs or powerbait. Boaters use spinners or flies. Lake stocked with pan-size trout. Bass anglers try scented plastic worms or crankbaits near rocky shorelines or weed areas early or late in the day. Catch crappies and sunfish off piers with worms.

Hawley Lake Campground   **$8**
White Mountain Apache Reservation
SE of Show Low on SR 260 past McNary; right on Hwy 473. $8. All year. 100 shoreline sites. Tbls, flush toilets, cfga, drkg wtr. Fishing, boating (l - elect mtrs). Elev 8000 ft.

   Fishing tip: This lake contains rain-bow, cutthroat, brown and brook trout, and shoreline fishing is quite good. Use worms, grasshoppers and yellow power-bait lures W of the boat dock; troll with z-rays & spinners. Ice fishing popular; large browns caught most often in the fall.

Lakeside   **$12**
Apache-Sitgreaves National Forest
10 mi SE of Show Low on SR 260; just acros highway from ranger station. $12 base; $14 for premium site. 5/1-9/30; 14-day limit. 82 sites (32-ft RV limit). Tbls, toilets, cfga, drkg wtr, visitor center, store, coin laundry. Dump ($6). Handicap-designated campsites at either side of toilet; paved sidewalks to sites. Summer interpretive programs, fish-ing, boating(l), hiking. Elev 7000 ft; 13 acres. Concessionaire-operated.

Salt River Canyon Campground   **$10**
White Mountain Apache Reservation
SW of Show Low (past Carrizo) on US 60 at Salt River. $10 per person. All year; 10-day limit. 8 sites. Tbls, toilets, cfga, drkg wtr. Fishing, whitewater rafting, boating, kayak-ing.

   Fishing tip: Salt River contains good popu-lation of smallmouth bass. Use small spinners, crawfish along rock walls and gravel bars.

Show Low Lake   **$12**
Navajo County Park
4 mi SE of Show Low on SR 260; 1 mi N on Show Low Lake Rd. $12-14 without hookups; $18 with elec (50% discount for seniors). May-Sept. 71 sites. Tbls, flush toilets, cfga, drkg wtr, showers ($3), dump, store. Fishing, boating (rl--limit 8 hp), pic-nicking ($2). Elev 7000 ft.

Sunrise Lake Campground   **$8**
White Mountain Apache Reservation
SE of Show Low on SR 260 past McNary, then right on Hwy 273; at entrance to Sunrise Park Resort. $8. All year. 200 primitive sites. Tbls, portable toilets, cfga, drkg wtr; showers at the lodge. Fishing, boating (elect mtrs). Elev 8700 ft.

   Fishing tip: This is one of the best trout lakes on the reservation, but a slot limit requires that fish 12-16 inches be released. Still, many rainbows are 16-20 inches, and the lake also contains grayling. Both shore fishing and trolling are excellent. Lake can get rather rough in high winds.

Sunrise RV Park   **$8**
White Mountain Apache Reservation
SE of Show Low on SR 260 past McNary, then right on Hwy 273; at Sunrise Park Resort. $8. All year; 10-day limit. 20 RV sites with elec. Tbls, cfga. Flush toilets, show-ers, coin laundry at the resort; no wtr, but available at nearby general store. Fishing, boating (elec mtrs).

SIERRA VISTA (69)

Ramsey Vista   **$10**
Coronado National Forest
8 mi S of Sierra Vista on SR 92; 7 mi W on Carr Canyon Rd (FR 368); sharp switchbacks cannot be negotiated by trailers & motor-homes. $10. All year; 14-day limit. 8 sites for tents, vans, pickup campers or trailers under 20 ft. Tbls, toilets, cfga, no drkg wtr. Handi-cap-accessible toilet; handicap accessible campsite with accessible picnic table, ped-estal grill, hard tent pad. Hiking, sightseeing, picnicking, horseback trails & corrals.

   Travel tip: Visit Fort Huachuca Trading Post just W of town; still in excellent condi-tion, it dates to mid-1800s, built in response to Indian Wars of 1870s and 1880s; only post still active in state from that peri-od; museum has large weapons display.

Reef Townsite   **$10**
Coronado National Forest
8 mi S of Sierra Vista on SR 92; 5 mi W on Carr Canyon Rd (FR 368); sharp switchbacks can-not be negotiated by trailers & motorhomes. $10 during 5/15-10/30; free 11/1-5/14 but no wtr; 14-day limit. 14 sites for tents, vans, pick-up campers, trailers under 20 ft. Tbls, toilets,

cfga, drkg wtr, food prep areas. 2 handicap-accessible campsites with trails to toilets; both with pedestal grill, wheelchair-designed tbl, hard tent pad. Hiking, sightseeing, picnicking, horseback trails. Elev 7200 ft; 20 acres. Group camping area has 16 sites on 10 acres. Built on site for old mining town.

San Pedro   **$2**
Riparian National Conservation Area
Bureau of Land Management
E of Sierra Vista in vast 58,000-acre area of Cochise County between St. David and the Mexican border. $2 per person. Primitive camping permitted in backcountry areas, but not in parking areas. Permit required, avail-able from self-service pay stations at all visitor parking areas. 7-day limit each location. No facilities. Bird watching, hiking, picnicking, horseback riding.

SONOITA (70)

Lakeview   **$10**
Coronado National Forest
30 mi SE of Sonoita on SR 83. $10. All year; 14-day limit. 65 sites (32-ft RV limit). Tbls, toilets, cfga, drkg wtr, store, dump, fishing pier. 3 handicap-accessible toilets with paved entry ramps; 3 tbls accessible by paved trail; 2 tbls accessible by compacted soil trail. Hiking, fishing, boating(rl--8 hp limit). Parker Canyon Lake. Concessionaire-operated. Elev 5400 ft; 50 acres; $5 day-use fee.

SPRINGERVILLE (71)

Brookchar   **$10**
Big Lake Recreation Area
Apache-Sitgreaves National Forest
4 mi SW of Springerville on SR 260; 23 mi S on SR 261; left at stop sign near Crescent Lake; 2.5 mi to Big Lake Recreation Area. Brookchar is in the RA past the visitor's cen-ter. $10. 5/15-9/30; free rest of year; 14-day limit. 13 walk-in tent sites. Tbls, flush toilets, cfga, drkg wtr, visitor center, store, showers. Dump 1 mi. Boating(lr), fishing, hiking & bik-ing trails, nature trail, horseback riding. Elev 9100 ft; 9 acres. 400-acre lake.

   Fishing tip: Big Lake contains rainbow, cutthroat and brook trout. A very popu-lar lake, it is stocked each spring and fall with more than 30,000 trout. Live bait fish prohibited. From shore, use worms, salmon eggs or Rainbow powerbait off rocky points; boaters troll slowly and deep with small Cowbells, Flatfish or Rapalas.

Burro Mountain   **FREE**
Apache-Sitgreaves National Forest
4 mi SW of Springerville on SR 260; 23 mi S on SR 261; 4 mi W of Crescent Lake. Free. All year; 14-day limit. Primitive undesignated sites; no facilities, no drkg wtr.

Carnero Lake   **FREE**
Apache-Sitgreaves National Forest
About 11 mi W of Springerville on SR 260; 5

mi N to Carnero Lake. Free. All year; 14-day limit. Primitive undesignated sites; no facilities, no drkg wtr. Fishing, hiking.

Burr Case Malpais Campground   **$10**
1.5 mi NW of Springerville on US 60/180/191. $10 base. All year. Base fee for primitive sites without hookups (3-night limit); full hookups $15.90. 58 sites. Tbls, flush toilets, cfga, drkg wtr, hookups($), dump, showers, coin laundry. Fishing, hunting. Weekly, monthly rates available.

CC Cabin   **FREE**
Apache-Sitgreaves Natinal Forest
About 11 mi W of Springerville on SR 260; 6 mi N. Free. All year; 14-day limit. Primitive undesignated sites; no facilities, no drkg wtr.

Cutthroat   **$12**
Big Lake Recreation Area
Apache-Sitgreaves National Forest
4 mi SW of Springerville on SR 260; 23 mi S on SR 261; left at stop sign near Crescent Lake; 2.5 mi to Big Lake Recreation Area. Cutthroat is the last CG in the RA past the visitor's center; hike to sites. $12 during 5/15-9/30; no free off-season camping; 14-day limit. 18 tent sites. Tbls, toilets, cfga, drkg wtr, showers, store, dump, visitor center. Fishing, boating(lr), hiking & biking trails, horseback riding, nature trail. Elev 9100 ft; 10 acres.

Grayling   **$7**
Big Lake Recreation Area
Apache-Sitgreaves National Forest
4 mi SW of Springerville on SR 260; 23 mi S on SR 261; left at stop sign near Crescent Lake; 2.5 mi to Big Lake Recreation Area. Grayling is in the RA past the visitor's center and Rainbow CG. $7 with federal Senior Pass; others pay $14. 5/15-9/30; free rest of year; 14-day limit. 23 sites (22-ft RV limit). Tbls, flush toilets, cfga, drkg wtr, tackle shop, visitor center, store, dump, showers. Fishing, Boating(lr), hiking & biking trails, horseback riding(r), mountain biking. Elev 9200 ft; 15 acres.

Lyman Lake State Park   **$12**
14 mi N of Springerville on US 180/61; 1.6 mi E on SR 81 from US 180/61 jct to N end of Lyman Lake. $12 base. All year; 15-day limit. Base fee for no hookups; $19 base for hookups; lower 7-day rate during off-season. 67 sites (45-ft RV limit). Tbls, flush toilets, cfga, drkg wtr, dump, general store, boat concession. Swimming, boating(l), fishing, waterskiing, hiking, petroglyph tours. Buffalo herd. Elev 6000 ft; 1180 acres.

Mexican Hay Lake   **FREE**
Apache-Sitgreaves National Forest
About 3 mi SW of Springerville on SR 260; 3 mi S on SR 261. Free. All year; 14-day limit. Primitive undesignated sites; no facilities, no drkg wtr. Fishing.

Fishing tip: 69-acre lake is choked with weeds, and heavy shoreline brush makes it necessary to use a small boat or tube for fishing.

Mineral Creek   **FREE**
Apache-Sitgreaves National Forest
W of Springerville on SR 260 (about 5 mi SE of Vernon), then just S. Free. All year; 14-day limit. Primitive undesignated sites; no facilities, no drkg wtr. Fishing, hiking.

Rainbow   **$7-8**
Big Lake Recreation Area
Apache-Sitgreaves National Forest
4 mi SW of Springerville on SR 260; 23 mi S on SR 261; left at stop sign near Crescent Lake; 2.5 mi to Big Lake Recreation Area. Rainbow is in the RA past the visitor's center. $7 base with federal Senior Pass ($8 for pull-through); others pay $14 & $16. 5/15-9/30; 14-day limit. 152 sites (32 ft RV limit). Tbls, flush toilets, cfga, drkg wtr, visitor center, store, dump, showers. Boating(lr), fishing, hiking & biking trails, nature trail, horseback riding(r). Elev 9200 ft; 46 acres.

South Fork Camp   **$10**
Apache-Sitgreaves National Forest
5 mi W of Springerville via AZ 260 and AZ 560 at end of FR 4124 south of AZ 260. $10 during 5/15-9/15; free rest of year, but no wtr or trash service. 14-day limit. 8 sites; RVs under 33 ft. Toilets, cfga, tbls, drkg wtr. Fishing, picnicking, hiking trail.

SUPERIOR (72)

Devils Canyon   **FREE**
Tonto National Forest
6 mi E of Superior on US 60-70. Free. All year; 1-day limit. 5 sites (no RV size limit, but trailers not recommended). Tbls, toilets, cfga, no drkg wtr. Hiking, rock climbing. Elev 4000 ft.

Oak Flat   **FREE**
Tonto National Forest
4 mi NE of Superior on US 60. Free. All year; 14-day limit. 16 sites (RVs under 22 ft). Tbls, toilets, cfga, no drkg wtr. Rockhounding, picnicking. Elev 4200 ft. 20 acres. Steep grades and/or sharp curves.

Travel tips: Nearby is Apache Leap, the cliff where 75 Indian braves leaped to their death to avoid capture by soldiers.

TONALEA (73)

Elephant Feet Indian   **FREE**
1 mi E of US 160. Free. All year. 3 sites. Tbls, toilets, cfga, no drkg wtr. Picnicking. Elev 5000 ft.

TUCSON (75)

Bog Springs   **$10**
Coronado National Forest
S of Tucson on I-19 to Continental; follow Madera Canyon signs 7 mi SE on FR 62 and 6 mi S on FR 70. $10. All year; 14-day limit. 13 sites (22-ft RV limit). Tbls, toilets, cfga, drkg wtr. Hiking, picnicking. Elev 5600 ft; 15 acres. Excellent birdwatching.

Catalina State Park   **$12**
9 mi N of Tucson on SR 77. $12. Open Fri before MD-Tues after LD; 15-day limit. Base fee for no hookups; sites with hookups $19 base. 48 sites (no RV size limit). Tbls, flush toilets, showers, cfga, drkg wtr, dump, visitor center, equestrian center. No hookups. Hiking, nature trails, horse facilities, horseback riding, birdwatching. Elev 2650 ft; 5,500 acres.

East Unit, Backcountry Camp   **$6**
Saguaro National Park
3 mi E on Old Spanish Trail Rd. Hike or ride horseback to camping area. $6. All year. Sites free by permit, but $6 entry fee. 7 sites. No facilities; no wtr. Obtain free permit at visitor center.

Gilbert Ray   **$10**
Pima County Campground
Tucson Mountain Park
12 mi W of Tucson on SR 86; 8 mi N on Kinney Rd. $10 for tents or non-hookup RV sites; $20 with elec. All year. 130 RV sites. Tbls, flush toilets, drkg wtr, elec($), dump, no grill areas. Hiking trails, archery, firing ranges, horseback riding. Saguaro National Monument, Arizona-Sonora Desert Museum, Old Tucson nearby. Elev 3000 ft. 20,000 acre park.

General Hitchcock   **$10**
Coronado National Forest
27 mi NE of Tucson via Hitchcock Hwy (milepost 12). $5 fee plus $5 daily permit, $10 weekly permit or $20 annual permit. All year; 14-day limit. 11 tent sites. Toilets, tbls, cfga, no drkg wtr. Picnicking, hiking. Elev 6000 ft.

Gordon Hirabayashi Camp   **$10**
Coronado National Forest
From jct with Tanque Verde Rd in Tucson, 4.2 mi on Catalina Hwy to forest, then 7 mi to campground (on the right on mtn route). $10. All year; 14-day limit. 12 sites. Tbls, toilets, cfga, no drkg wtr. Corral. Hiking, horseback riding.

Molino Basin   **$10**
Coronado National Forest
21.3 mi NE on FR 33; .1 mi NW on FR 5. 10/15-4/30; 14-day limit. $10. 37 sites (RVs under 23 ft). Tbls, toilets, cfga, no drkg wtr. Picnicking, hiking. Elev 4400 ft. 65 acres. Mountains. Grassy terrain.

Prison Camp   **$5**
Coronado National Forest
19 mi NE of Tucson on Catalina Hwy, at milepost 7. $5 daily, $10 weekly or $20 annual forest pass required. All year; 14-day limit. 8 sites; 22-ft RV limit. Tbls, cfga; no other facilities. Climbing, hiking, horseback riding. Temporarily closed at presstime in 2007.

Rose Canyon   **$8.50**
Coronado National Forest
NE of Tucson on Catalina Hwy between mileposts 17 & 18; at Rose Canyon Lake.

$8.50 with federal Senior Pass; others pay $17. Apr-Nov; 14-day limit. 74 sites; 22-ft RV limit. Tbls, toilets, cfga, drkg wtr. Fishing, hiking. Elev 7000 ft.

Spencer Canyon $8
Coronado National Forest
21From Tanque Verde rd in Tucson, 25.7 mi N on Hitchcock Hwy (milepost 22). $8 with federal Senior Pass; others pay $16. 4/15-10/15; 14-day limit. 60 sites; 22-ft RV limit. Tbls, toilets, cfga, drkg wtr. Hiking, sightseeing. Elev 8000 ft; 65 acres.

WENDEN (76)

Alamo Lake State Park $10
38 mi N of Wenden on Alamo Access Rd. $10-12 base. All year; 15-day limit. Base fee for no hookups; hookup sites $19 base. About 250 sites (no RV size limit). Tbls, flush toilets, cfga, drkg wtr, dump, elec($), store. Swimming, boating(lr), fishing. 8,400 acres. On Williams River; river access to Lake Havasu by boat.

WHITERIVER (77)

Lower Big Bonito Creek $8
White Mountain Apache Reservation
S & E of Whiteriver (and Fort Apache) on SR 73; S on Reservation Rd Y-70. $8. Apr-Nov; 10-day limit. 2 sites. Tbls, toilets, cfga, drkg wtr. Fishing.

Fishing tip: Hike along the creek to find cool, clear pools holding brown & rainbow trout. Use flies and worms.

Rock Creek Campground $8
White Mountain Apache Reservation
SE of Whiteriver on SR 73, E of East Fork crossing. $8. Apr-Nov; 10-day limit. 2 sites. Tbls, toilets, cfga, drkg wtr. Fishing.

Upper Big Bonita Creek $8
White Mountain Apache Reservation
SE of Whiteriver on SR 73; S on reservation rd Y-70 to Big Bonita Creek. $8. Apr-Nov; 10-day limit. 6 sites. Tbls, toilets, cfga, drkg wtr. Fishing.

Fishing tip: Clear, cold pools hold rainbow and brown trout. Ask locally for tips on lures.

WHY (86)

Coyote Howls East $8
City Park
Several primitive sites are located along US 85 (north of Organ Pipe Cactus National Monument). $8 daily; $35 weekly; $70 monthly. Groups up to 15 sites, $7 each; larger groups, $6. 600 sites Tbls, flush toilets, cfga, showers, drkg wtr, library, card room, community building, dump. No hookups. 200 acres.

WICKENBURG (78)

Constellation City Park $5
1 mi N of US 60 on El Recreo St. $5. All year; 7-day limit. 35 sites; no RV size limit. No facilities. Sightseeing, picnicking.

WIKIEUP (79)

Burro Creek Recreation Site $10
Bureau of Land Management
14 mi SE of Wikieup on US 93; half mi W on Burro Creek Rd. $10. All year; 21-day limit. 30 sites. Tbls, flush toilets, cfga, drkg wtr, dump ($10 non-campers), picnic area, desert garden. Rockhounding, hiking, fishing.

WILLCOX (80)

Bonita Canyon $12
Chiricahua National Monument
31 mi SE on SR 186; 3.1 mi E on Hwy 181E. $12. All year; 14-day limit. $5 per adult entry fee also charged. 22 sites (29-ft RV limit); group camping area. Tbls, flush toilets, cfga, drkg wtr, visitor center, museum, grey wtr dump. Hiking trails, campfire programs, sightseeing. Elev 5400 ft; 12,000 acres.

Cochise Stronghold $10
Coronado National Forest
SW of Willcox on I-10 to US 191; 18 mi S on US 191; 9.5 mi W on Ironwood Rd/FR 84. $10. All year; 14-day limit. 10 sites (22-ft RV limit), plus 8 walk-in tent sites. Tbls, toilets, cfga, drkg wtr; some handicap sites & facilities. Hiking, picnicking. Cochise Trail and Stronghold Nature Trail. Elev 5000 ft; 30 acres.

WILLIAMS (81)

Cataract Lake $10
Kaibab National Forest
One-third mi W of Williams on I-40; qtr mi W on CR 749. $10. 5/1-10/1; 14-day limit. 18 sites (22-ft RV limit). Tbls, toilets, cfga, drkg wtr, dump ($3 dump, $5 dump & fill wtr). Boating(l--8 hp limit), fishing, hiking. Concessionaire-operated. Elev 6800 ft; 9 acres.

Cataract Lake $6
Coconino County Park
2 mi NW of Williams just off I-40 at Country Club Rd exit. $6. 5/1-10/31; 14-day limit. 30 sites. Tbls, toilets, cfga, drkg wtr, central kitchen ramadas. Boating (6 hp limit), fishing. Elev 6800 ft; 15 acres. Group sites $4 per unit.

Dogtown Lake $12
Kaibab National Forest
3 mi SE of Williams on SR 173; 2 mi E on FR 140; 1 mi N on FR 132. $12 during 5/15-10/1; free or reduced fees rest of year, but no wtr or services. 51 sites; 35-ft RV limit. Tbls, toilets, cfga, drkg wtr, group ramada by reservation, dump ($7 for campers, $12 visitors), firewood ($6). Boating (l--elec mtrs), fishing, hiking, nature trails. Elev 7000 ft; 60 acres.

Fishing tip: Dogtown Lake is well known for its trout, crappies & channel catfish.

Kaibab Lake Campground $7.50
Kaibab National Forest
2 mi E of Williams on I-40; 2 mi N on SR 64; half mi NW on FR 747. $7.50 with federal Senior Pass; others pay $15 during 5/15-10/1; free rest of year, but no wtr or trash service. 14-day limit. 63 sites (35-ft RV limit). Tbls, toilets, cfga, drkg wtr. Dump fee $7 for campers, $12 for visitors. Handicap-accessible toilet with paved path to 2 paved sites. Boating(l--8 hp limit), fishing, hiking, interpretive programs, no swimming. Concessionaire-operated. Elev 6800 ft; 36 acres. Day use $5.

Fishing tip: Good rainbow, brown & brook trout fishing at nearby Kaibab Lake. Channel catfish also stocked.

Ten-X $10
Kaibab National Forest
47 mi N of Williams on SR 64/US 180. $10. 5/1-9/30; 14-day limit. 70 sites (40-ft RV limit). Group sites available. Tbls, toilets, cfga, drkg wtr. Nature trails, campfire programs, picnicking. Camp is 8 mi from Grand Canyon NP. Elev 6600 ft; 46 acres.

White Horse Lake $7.50
Kaibab National Forest
8 mi S of Williams on FR 173; 9 mi E on FR 110; 3 mi E on FR 109. $7.50 with federal Senior Pass; others pay $15. 5/1-10/1; free rest of year; 14-day limit. 94 sites; 38-ft RV limit. Tbls, toilets, cfga, drkg wtr, store. Dump fee $7 for campers, $12 for visitors; firewood $6. Boating(rl--elec motors only), fishing, hiking.Elev 7000 ft; 44 acres. Concessionaire-operated.

WINKLEMAN (83)

Aravaipa Canyon $5
Primitive Area West
Bureau of Land Management
10 mi S of Winkleman on AZ 77 to Aravaipa Rd; 13 mi E (gravel for 8 mi). $5 per person, and permit is needed to enter the wilderness (contact Safford District office, 602/428-4040). Primitive, undeveloped tent camping area. Limited to 30 visitors per day. Backpacking area. 3-day limit. Toilets, cfga, no drkg wtr.

WINSLOW (84)

Homolovi Ruins State Park $10-12
4 mi E on I-40 to exit 257; 1.2 miN on Hwy 87; 1.2 mi W on paved access rd. $10-12 base. All year; 15-day limit. Base fee for no hookups; hookups $14 base. 52 sites. Tbls, flush toilets, cfga, drkg wtr, visitor center, dump. Interpretive programs, interpretive trails through Anasazi ruins, picnicking; handicap-accessible trail. Elev 4900 ft; 4,5ƒ00 acres.

Travel tip: Be sure to see Meteor Crater, W of town off I-40, and the display at the Museum of Astrology, including a 1,406-pound meteorite. Just NE of town on SR 87 is Little Painted Desert County Park featuring numerous religious scenes.

WINTERHAVEN (CA.) (85)

Senator Wash Boat-In $5
Bureau of Land Management
From Winterhaven exit of I-8, go N 20 mi on CR S-24; left on Gerguson Lake Rd for 4 mi to Senator Wash boat ramp near Imperial Dam. Travel by boat to camping areas on N & S shores: $5 (or $50 annually). All year; 14-day limit. 1 toilet, outdoor showers, pay phone at boat ramp. Boating(l), fishing, swimming area, waterskiing, hiking. Permit required; open fires prohibited about MD-LD.

Senator Wash North Shore $5
Bureau of Land Management
From Winterhaven exit of I-8, go N 22 mi on CR 2-24; follow Senator Wash Rd 2 mi to South Mesa Campground; proceed through campground & follow signs to North Shore. $5 (or $50 annually). Holders of Long-Term Visitor Area permits also may use the day-use facilities. All year; 14-day limit. Primitive undesignated sites on about 60 acres. Tbls, toilets, cfga, no drkg wtr; dump at South Mesa (fee charged 9/15-4/15). Boating(l), fishing, swimming, hiking, waterskiing. Free permit required. No trash service. Fires restricted about MD-LD; cook on charcoal grills or propane stoves. Formerly free.

Senator Wash South Shore $5
Bureau of Land Management
From I-8 exit at Winterhaven, follow CR S-24 about 22 mi N; follow Senator Wash Rd 2 mi to South Mesa Campground, then left about 200 yds; turn right on reservoir access rd. $5 (or $50 annually). Holders of Long-Term Visitor Area permits also may use the day-use facilities. All year; 14-day limit. Primitive undesignated sites on 50 acres. Tbls, flush toilets, outdoor showers, drkg wtr, gravel beach; dump at South Mesa (fee 9/15-4/15); no trash service. Boating(l), fishing, swimming, hiking.

YOUNG (87)

Airplane Flat FREE
Tonto National Forest
23 mi NE of Young on unpaved SR 288/FR 512; rigt on FR 33 for 5 mi. Free. Apr-Nov; 14-day limit. Undeveloped tent/RV sites (RVs under 16 ft). Toilets, cfga, tbls, no drkg wtr. Fishing, picnicking. Elev 6600 ft. Pack out trash. Stream for artificial lure & fly fishing only (1 mi). FR 12 & SR 288 unpaved. Near Canyon Creek. Handicapped facilities.
  Fishing tip: Fishing in Canyon Creek is limited to artificial lures.

Alderwood FREE
Tonto National Forest
11 mi N of Young on SR 288; right on FR 200 for 7 mi; left on FR 200A for half mi. Free. Apr-

Nov; 14-day limit. Undesignated, undeveloped sites. Tbls, toilets, cfga, no drkg wtr. Fishing, picnicking. Elev 5200 ft. Pack out trash. To reach Lower Haigler Creek, turn left at second 4-way intersection on FR 249 (unpaved SR 288). Minimum-development site.

Colcord Ridge FREE
Tonto National Forest
23 mi NE of Young on FR 12 & FR 33. Free. Apr-Nov; 14-day limit. Undeveloped tent & RV sites (RVs under 32 ft). Toilets, cfga, tbls, no drkg wtr. Picnicking, hiking. Elev 7600 ft. Pack out trash. Artificial fly & lure fishing only (5 mi). SR 288 & FR 12 unpaved. Minimum-development site.

Haigler Canyon FREE
Tonto National Forest
3 mi NW of Young on AZ 288; 9 mi on FR 200. Free. Apr-Nov; 14-day limit. Sites (RVs under 16 ft). No drkg wtr. Picnicking, fishing. Wtr cold for swimming; rocky. Elev 5300 ft. Minimum-development site.

Lower Canyon Creek FREE
Tonto National Forest
22 mi NE of Young on FR 12 & FR 188. Free. May-Nov. 1-day limit. Facilities: Undeveloped. RVs under 16 ft. Toilets, cfga, no drkg wtr. Fly & lure fishing only. Picnicking. Elev 6400 ft. SR 288 & FR 12 unpaved.

Rose Creek FREE
Tonto National Forest
23.4 mi S of Young on AZ 288. Free. 4/1-11/15; 14-day limit. 5 sites (16-ft RV limit). Tbls, toilets, cfga, piped drkg wtr, no trash service. Picnicking, fly & lure fishing only. Stream within 1 mi of SR 228 and FS 12. Elev 5400 ft. 5 acres.

Upper Canyon Creek FREE
Tonto National Forest
31 mi NE of Young. Free. Apr-Oct; 14-day limit. Undeveloped sites (RVs under 16 ft). Tbls, toilets, no drkg wtr. Fly fishing, picnicking. Elev 6700 ft. Near Canyon Creek. Minimum-development site.

Valentine Ridge FREE
Tonto National Forest
3 mi NE on AZ SR 288; 17 mi NE on FR FH12; 3 mi NE on FR FH188. Free. 5/15-11/15; 14-day limit. 9 sites (RVs under 16 ft). Tbls, toilets, cfga, firewood, no drkg wtr. Picnicking, hiking, fly & lure fishing only. Stream within 1 mi of SR 228 and FS 12. Elev 6900 ft. 5 acres. Mountains. Near Canyon Creek.

Workman Creek FREE
Tonto National Forest2
22 mi N of SR 88 on SR 288, then along Workman Creek on FR 487, past Workman Creek Falls. High-clearance vehicles advised; RVs discouraged. Free. Apr-Nov; 14-day limit. 3 sites at Cascade and Falls Recreation Sites. Tbls, cfga, toilets, no drkg wtr. Fishing, hiking, no trash service. Elev 5400-7748 ft.

YUMA (88)

Imperial Dam $140
Long-Term Visitor Area
Bureau of Land Management
From I-8 Winterhaven exit, 24 mi N of Yuma on CR S-24 in California; follow Senator Wash Rd 2 mi. $140. All year. Fee is for whole winter season of 9/15-4/15. $5 daily or $50 seasonally during 4/16-9/14 or $30 for 14 days. About 2,000 sites on 3,500 acres. Toilets, cfga, drkg wtr, grey & black wtr dumps, outdoor showers, ramadas; limited facilities in winter. Rockhounding, hiking, fishing, boating, swimming.

Mittry Lake FREE
Bureau of Land Management
7 mi E of Yuma on SR 95; 9.5 mi N on Avenue 7E to 600-acre Mittry Lake. Free. All year; 10-day limit. Numerous undesignated sites.. Toilet, cfga, no drkg wtr. Fishing jetty. Boating(l), hiking, fishing, swimming, duck hunting. About 2,400 acres of marshland managed jointly by BLM, BOR & state game & fish department. Free permit required. Large fishing jetties.

Rest Area FREE
21 mi N of Yuma on W side of US 95 at big brick gate & sign to US Army Proving Grounds. Free. All year; 1 night limit. Spaces for self-contained RVs (no tent camping). Tbls, toilets, cfga. Picnicking.

Squaw Lake $5
Bureau of Land Management
24 mi NE of Yuma on CR S-24 in California (or exit CR S-24 from I-8 at Winterhaven; go N 20 mi; left on Ferguson Lake Rd, then follow signs 4 mi). $5 daily use fee or $50 annually. All year; 14-day limit. 125 RV sites (30-ft RV limit) & numerous dispersed tent sites. Tbls, flush toilets, cold outdoor showers, cfga, drkg wtr, gray water dump (dump station at nearby South Mesa), beach. Boating(l), fishing, swimming, hiking. 15 acres. No open fires MD-LD.

YUCCA (89)

Havasu Backcountry North FREE
Bureau of Land Management
Access N side of Mohave Mountains off I-40 at Franconia Wash. Or try the El Paso Natural Gas Pipeline area from I-40's Gem Acres exit. For the eastern portion of the Havasu backcountry north, drive S on Alamo Rd from I-40 in Yucca; rd continues to Rawhide Mountains & N shore of Alamo Lake. Free. All year; 14-day limit. Primitive dispersed camping; no facilities. Get access guide from BLM office in Havasu City. Favorite areas for dune buggies, OHV, motorcycles, mountain biking, rockhounding.

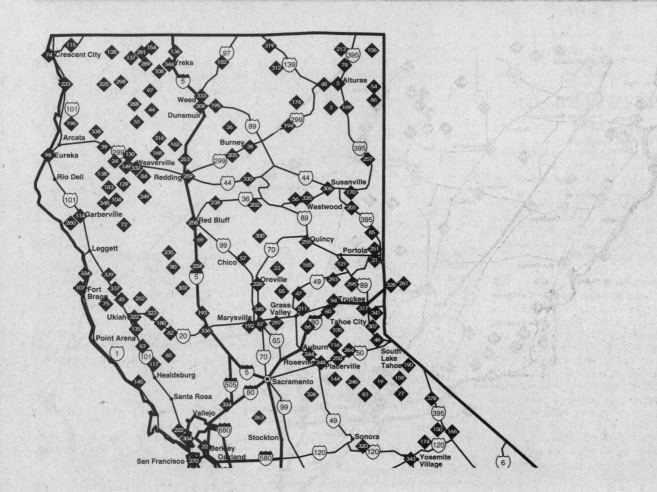

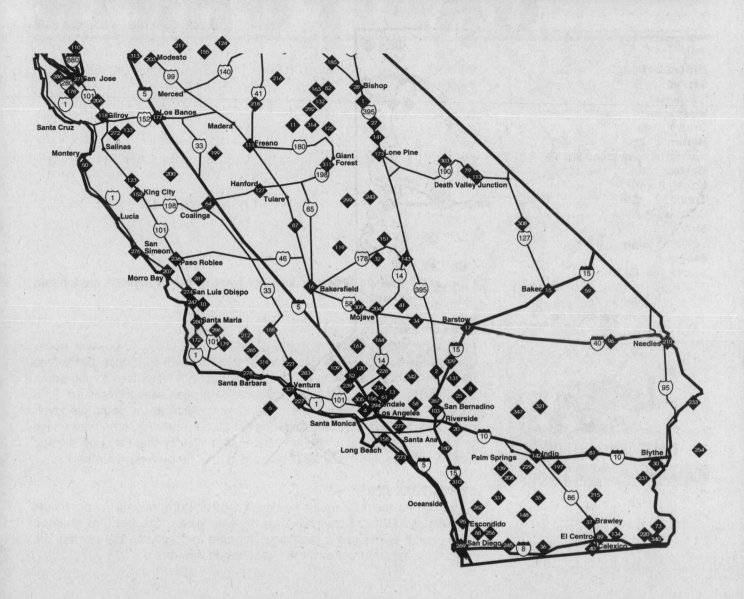

CALIFORNIA

MISCELLANEOUS
Capital:
Sacramento
Nickname:
Golden State
Motto:
"Eureka" (I have found it)
Flower:
Golden Poppy
Tree:
California Redwood
Bird:
California Valley Quail
Song:
"I Love you, California"

Internet Address:
www.gocalif.com

California Division of Tourism, PO Box 1499, Sacramento, CA 95812-1499. 1 800-462-2543.

Dept of Parks and Recreation; P.O. Box 942896, Sacramento, CA 94296-0001. 916/653-6995.

Dept of Fish and Game, 1416 Ninth St., Sacramento, CA 95814. 916/445-0411.

Department of Forestry, 1416 9th ST., Sacramento, CA 95814. 916/653-5123.

REST AREAS
Overnight stops are not permitted. RV sanitary dump stations are located at several rest areas.

STATE PARKS
Fees at developed sites are now $12-18 per night without hookups; hookups are $9 added to the base fee; showers are 25-50 cents. Entry fees vary from park to park, and non-campers must pay entry fees to use dump stations. Premium sites are an additional $10; peak season rates are $3-5 higher. Pets are allowed; there is no longer a charge for dogs. Undeveloped sites are $9-15. Trail campsites are $3 per person. Some parks have "environmental" sites, which are walk-in tent sites in relatively undisturbed natural settings; fees vary. Reservations are $7.50 by Reserve America.

STATE FORESTS
Camping facilities are quite rustic. Most campgrounds have pit toilets or none at all, and some have no drinking water. No fees are charged for camping at the rustic facilities. Campfire and special use permits are required, available free from the forest headquarters.

DEATH VALLEY NATIONAL PARK
Free camping is available at backcountry sites and at the Emigrant campground, but entry fees of $20 per vehicle are charged, good for seven days. Fees of $12-18 are charged at other camping areas. Holders of the new America the Beautiful Senior Passes and Golden Age Passports camp at half price. All sites are on a first-come, first-served basis. Camping is recommended from May through October. Camping is limited to 30 days. From June through September, daytime temperatures are commonly in the 100s; the rest of the year, highs range from the 60s to the 90s. Fires are permitted only in grills or camp stoves. Firewood gathering is prohibited. Death Valley National Monument, PO Box 579 Death Valley, CA 92328; 760-786-3200.

JOSHUA TREE NATIONAL PARK
Two deserts merge in the park--the Mohave and the Colorado--and camping areas are located in both. Fees are charged at the Black Rock and Cottonwood campgrounds and at the group campsites. A park entry fee of $15 for 7 days ($30 annual pass) is charged. Among the free campgrounds, Hidden Valley is open all year, the others from about October through May.

Horses permitted at Ryan campground. Length of stay, 14-day limit (30 days at Hidden Valley June 1-Oct. 1). RVs up to 32 feet long permitted. Backcountry camping permitted in much of the park, but no water is available. Drinking water available only at Cottonwood and Black Rock Canyon campgrounds, visitor center, Oasis visitor center and Indian Cove ranger station. Evening ranger programs at Cottonwood. Summer temperatures commonly exceed 100 degrees.

REDWOOD NATIONAL PARK

There are no camping fees for Redwood National Park hike-in sites. (State park hike-in sites are $3 per person.) Campers must park in the parking lot and walk 1/4 to 1/2 mile to campsites. All have sites with fire rings and toilets. Use metal food caches where available. Redwood, Prairie Creek, Crescent City, Jedediah Smith, and Hiouchi Information Centers provide information for Redwood National and State Parks. Over 200 miles of trails are available. Regularly scheduled ranger-guided programs are available during the summer. Environmental education programs are offered during the spring and fall at two outdoor schools.

Bureau of Land Management, 95825 Federal Building, Room W1834, 2800 Cottage Way, Sacramento, CA 95825. The BLM manages 15.2 million acres of public land -- nearly 15% of the state's land area.

LONG-TERM VISITOR AREAS. To meet long-term needs of winter visitors and protect fragile desert resources elsewhere, the BLM established eight Long-Term Visitor Areas (LTVAs) in the California desert and along the lower Colorado River where visitors may camp for the entire winter. Winter visitors who wish to stay in an LTVA may do so by purchasing a long-term visitor permit for $140 and selecting a location in one of the designated LTVAs. The permit covers the long-term use season from Sept. 15 to April 15. Permit holders may move from one LTVA to another without incurring additional user fees. Short-term fees are $5 daily or $50 seasonally during 4/16-9/14 or $30 for 14 days in the winter. Within the Mule Mountain LTVA, long-term visitor permits are not required of campers who stay for less than 14 days. LTVAs were chosen because of their popularity with winter visitors in the past and encompass locations where access roads have been developed and facilities are available nearby. In most cases, drinking water, showers and bathrooms are not available onsite. Garbage and sewage must be transported to the nearest dumpsite. Obtain permits at LTVA host and entrance stations, visitor information centers, from uniformed BLM employees in the field or by contacting BLM offices in Arizona in southern California. Permits are not available through the mail.

DESERT CAMPING. Campers who wish to stay on the desert outside of an LTVA may camp on undeveloped public lands for up to 14 days in any 28-day period in one location at no charge unless otherwise posted. After 14-days, short-term campers must move to a new site outside a 25-mile radius of their original campsite. Visitors must arrive in a self-contained camping unit wit a permanently affixed waste water holding tank of at least 10 gallons capacity. Units not self-contained are allowed only at Mule Mountain, Imperial and LaPosa LTVAs. Short-term camping in the Quartz-site area is limited, but there are two designated camping areas, at Mile Marker 99 and Mile Marker 112 adjoining Highway 95.

CORPS OF ENGINEERS

Many formerly free areas were converted to charge sites a few years ago, and camping fees are now $10 or more per night. Corps of Engineers, 1325 J St, Sacramento, CA 95814. 916-557-5100.

Mid-Pacific Region, U.S. Bureau of Reclamation, 2800 Cottage Way, Sacramento, CA 95814.

Mountain Home Demonstration State Forest. Reached via SR 190 to Springville, then the Balch Park Road and Bear Creek Road northeast of town. Twenty miles of maintained trails in the forest provide a superior opportunity to experience giant sequoias at close range. A wilderness permit is required for backpacking into the Golden Trout Wilderness area. For information: P.O. Box 517, Springville, CA 93265. Phone 209/539-2321 (summer) or 539-2855.

Jackson Demonstration State Forest, P.O. Box 1185, Fort Bragg, CA 95437. 707/964-5674.

NATIONAL FORESTS

Free, required wilderness permits provide entry to wilderness and primitive areas and authorize the building of campfires. A group needs only one permit. Permits are valid in contiguous national forests and areas managed by the National Park Service and are issued at ranger station and Forest Service field offices near points of entry. Campers may also write to individual national forests for permits. Unless otherwise posted, camping outside developed campgrounds is permitted on National Forest lands. For the foreseeable future, significant changes are being felt in the fee structures of national forests. Eighty-three forest service projects were included in a Recreation Fee Demonstration Program aimed at raising funds for forest maintenance and improvement and testing whether fees can be applied to services that were otherwise free. Generally speaking, most test fees are $5 per day or $30 annually. Those charges usually are applied either per-person or per-vehicle. Several national forest service projects are affected by the program; each is outlined under the applicable national forest on the following pages; holders of federal Senior Passes such as America the Beautiful and Golden Age passes pay half rates for the charges levied. In southern California, four national forests now require visitors to purchase $5 daily or $30 annual "Adventure Passes." Those forests are Angeles, Cleveland, Los Padres and San Bernardino. The forest service and the U.S. Army Corps of Engineers started a joint campground reservation service; its toll-free number is 877-444-6777.

Angeles National Forest. 701 N. Santa Anita Ave., Arcadia, CA 91006; 626-574-1613. Free off-season camping is permitted at several campgrounds. During the off-season, water supplies are shut off and trash service is halted. Some roads into the campgrounds are closed during snow periods, however. This forest now charges daily/annual Adventure Pass fees for vehicles of $5 daily or $30 annually. Campfire permits are required all year for any type of campfire (open wod fire, charcoal fire or liquid or gas fuel portable stoves) at all trail cmps and at any area outside developed forest service recreation sites.

Cleveland National Forest. 10845 Rancho Bernardo Rd, Suite 200, San Diego, CA 92127; 858-673-6180. As part of the Recreation Fee Demonstration Program, this forest now charges $5 daily and $30 annual Adventure Pass fees for vehicles. The forest has 460,000 acres. Besides camping, it offers opportunities for fishing, hunting, mountain biking, OHV activities, hiking. Federal Senior Passes such as the Golden Age Passport and the America the Beautiful pass.

Eldorado National Forest. Offers free off-season camping at some of its fee sites. However, snow often prevents access during the free periods because most forest roads are not plowed. The forest does not charge fees when all services such as water are not available. Wilderness permits are $5 per person. Fees are charged at some campgrounds for pets. Short parking spurs are 25 feet long; long spurs are generally 50 feet.California campfire permits are required when camping outside maintained campgrounds. 100 Forni Rd., Placerville, CA 95667; 530-622-5061.

Inyo National Forest. Unlike some other forests in California, it does not permit free off-season camping in parks where seasonal fees are charged. Inyo's campgrounds are closed during off-season periods. Campground fees are typically $11-$17. 351 Pacu Lane, Suite 200, Bishop, CA 93514. 760-873-2400.

Klamath National Forest. The forest straddles the California/Oregon border and both sides of I-5. Several of the campgrounds where overnight fees are charged are open all year, but services are provided and fees collected only between May or June and the end of October. 1312 Fairlane Rd, Yreka, CA 96097; 530-842-6131.

Lake Tahoe Basin Management Unit. Operates 11 public campgrounds in the area just north of Lake Tahoe along Hwy 89 near Camp Richardson. Wilderness permits are $5 per person. 35 College Dr., South Lake Tahoe, CA 96150; 530-543-2600.

Lassen National Forest. 2550 Riverside Drive, Susanville, CA 96130; 530-257-2151. The forest surrounds Lassen Volcanic National Park and is famous both for its volcanic exploration and its outstanding fly-fishing for trout at Hat Creek. Some campgrounds are free during the winter, but no water or services are provided; virtually all campgrounds are open until Nov 1, even if services are ended earlier by concessionaires. Transient occupancy taxes are charged at fee-campgrounds in Plumas County. Catch-and-release policies are in effect at some of the forest's best trout and salmon stream; only artificial lures with barbless hooks may be used.

Los Padres National Forest. The forest's recreational settings include ocean beaches, sub-alpine forest, chaparral, desert badlands and riparian areas. As part of the Recreation Fee Demonstration Program, this forest now charges $5 daily and $30 annual fees for vehicles. 6755 Hollister Ave, Suite 150, Goleta, CA 93117; 805 968-6640.

Mendocino National Forest. This forest has a substantial number of developed free campgrounds as well as several dispersed sites where no fees are charged. Campfire permits are required for areas other than developed campgrounds. Boating, fishing and swimming opportunities are provided at various lakes and streams. Rockhounds can find agate and jasper along Big Stoney Creek from Red Bridge to Mine Camp; jadeite and nephrite along the Eel River; serpentine in the Fouts Spring area, the eastern edge of the forest and at McCloud Ridge and Blue Banks; quartz crystals at the Big Butts-Shinbone area; chrome at the Red Mountain area west of the town by that name, and fossils in the Rice Valley area. At press-time, this forest was not a participant in the Recreation Fee Demonstration Program. 825 North Humboldt Ave, Willows, CA 95988; 530-934-3316.

Modoc National Forest. Campsites for which fees are charged are available for free camping (without water available) before Memorial Day and after Labor Day, weather permitting. The forest has numerous primitive, undeveloped sites for which no fees are ever charged as well as 20 developed campground. It is the most remote of California's national forests and offers secluded, uncrowded camping and recreational opportunities. 800 W. 12th St., Alturas, CA 96101; 530-233-5811.

Plumas National Forest. Generally, fee campgrounds are open from April through October; those at higher elevations are open in mid to late May. Fees are charged at campgrounds having a water system, maintained restrooms and trash collection. Self-serve campground charge no fees and depend upon users to pack out their trash, use their own toilet paper and keep toilets clean. Five lakes in the forest have recreational areas with camping, picnicking, swimming, boating, fishing and hiking. The Feather Falls Recreation Area boasts of the sixth largest waterfall in America. 159 Lawrence St., Quincy, CA 95971; 530-283-2050.

San Bernardino National Forest. Numerous primitive, undeveloped sites are available for camping, by permit., but campers must purchase either daily or annual Adventure Passes in order to park and use the forest's recreational facilities. That vehicle pass is $5 or $30 annually. Free off-season camping is not permitted at campgrounds where fees are charged; forest campgrounds are closed 10/16-4/14, and no camping is permitted during the closed period. Developed campgrounds generally open in May and close in October. Camping is allowed in designated dispersed areas and at Yellow Post sites; no fees are charged, but no services are provided, and campers must have Adventure Passes. Free Post sites are within remote areas on backroads or trails where campfires are allowed all year; a free visitor permit is required. Wilderness campsites are accessible only by foot or horseback and require a wilderness permit which can be reserved up to three months in advance from the local ranger station. 602 S. Tippecanoe Ave., San Bernardino, CA 92408; 909-382-2600.

Sequoia National Forest. Offers free camping at its numerous primitive, dispersed areas, with camping outside of its 50 developed campgrounds anywhere on forest land with a campfire permit. To protect the Kern River, no camping is allowed from the Live Oak day-use area up-canyon 6 miles (milepost 24) within 100 feet of the water. Forest features more than 30 groves of giant sequoia trees with diameters of up to 30 ft; largest is the Boole Tree, standing 269 ft high with a 90-ft circumference. Trout are found in nearly every stream & lake, and the unique golden trout are found in high country streams of the Golden Trout Wilderness. 1839 South Newcomb St., Porterville, CA 93257; 599-784-1500.

Shasta-Trinity National Forest. 3644 Avtech Parkway, Redding, CA 96002; 530-226-2500. Generally, dispersed camping is allowed outside of developed sites; exceptions are within the Trinity National Recreation Area, at Claire Engle (Trinity) Lake, and at Lewiston Lake, where camping is prohibited within a quarter mile of the high-water mark. An access fee also was implemented for boat ramp access. Some formerly free dispersed sites now have camping fees, but more free dispersed sites have been added to this book. As part of the Recreation Fee Demonstration program, Shasta Trinity charges daily parking fees at various sites; $5 passes are required at North Gate, Brewer Creek and Clear Creek trailheads; a $15-per-person pass is required at the Mt. Shasta Summit; camping fees are charged at McBride Springs, Fowlers Cattle Camp; a daily vehicle is charged at the McCloud Reservoir boat ramp, and an annual forest pass for $25 includes recreational parking for one vehicle, participation in the Summit program by one person and parking at the McCloud Reservoir. Free campfire permits are required outside designated campsites from May 1 through October. Most campgrounds are open 5/15-9/15, although some sites are open off-season, as weather permits, with reduced services and no water.

Sierra National Forest. This forest's 1.3 million acres are in central California, on the western slope of the Sierra Nevada mountains, south of the Merced River and north of Kings River. The forest has several cost-free campgrounds, but most camps are now $13-20. 1800 Tollhouse Rd., Clovis, CA 93611; 559-297-0706.

Six Rivers National Forest. Located in the northwest corner of the state, this scenic area is best known for its rugged coastline, roaring rivers and majestic redwood groves. Developed campgrounds are equipped with vault or flush toilets, fire rings or stoves, tables, parking for two vehicles and drinking water (unless otherwise noted). Dispersed camping is free except in Aikens Creek West and is limited to 30 days per year. A campfire permit is required for all use of fires, gas lanterns, barbecues and campstoves outside developed campgrounds. The forest has several cost-free campgrounds. 1330 Bayshore Way, Eureka, CA 95501; 707-442-1721.

Stanislaus National Forest. Has more than 40 developed campgrounds. Ideal camping time is May-Oct. Most campgrounds fill quickly on holiday weekends. Some camps can accommodate all size RVs. Campfire permits are required for building fires or using campstoves outside an RV away from a developed campground. Dispersed camping is not allowed within the boundaries of the forest's recreation areas -- Brightman, Clark Fork, Lake Alpine, Pinecrest or Tuolumne-Lumsden. 19777 Greenley Rd., Sonora, CA 95370; 209-532-3671.

Tahoe National Forest. Pacific Gas & Electric Co. is now managing developed campgrounds north of Lake Spaulding and south of Jackson Meadow Rd. Fees are charged at those sites. 631 Coyote St., Nevada City, CA 95959; 530-265-4531.

Toiyabe National Forest. Most of this forest is in Nevada, but about 1 million acres overlap into California just east of Lake Tahoe and north of Yosemite National Park. Most of the California campgrounds in this forest have camping fees higher than $12, but seniors with either the Golden Age Passport or the new America the Beautiful Senior Pass can camp at those facilities for half price. HCR 1, Box 1000, Bridgeport, CA 93517; 916-932-7070.

ABERDEEN (1) S

Goodale Creek $5
Bureau of Land Management
2 mi W of Aberdeen off US 395 on Aberdeen Cutoff Rd. $5; formerly free. About 4/15-11/1. Special Long-Term Visitor Area (LTVA) permits can now be used at Crowley, Tuttle Creek and Goodale Creek Campgrounds. These LTVA permits are $300 for the period between the first Saturday in March through 11/1. 62 sites; pit toilets, tbls, cfga, no drkg wtr. Fishing, mountain biking, hiking, hunting. 40 acres; elev 4,100 ft. Pack out trash. Donations accepted. Beware of snakes.

ADELANTO (2) S

City Park FREE
US 395 W of I-15 and Victorville, visible from hwy. Free. All year; 24-hour limit. 10 undesignated sites, large parking area. Toilets, drkg wtr, no size limit.

ADIN (3) N

Ash Creek FREE
Modoc National Forest
1/10 mi S of Adin on CA 299, 8.3 mi SE on CR 527; half mi N on FR 38N47 (off Adin-Madeline Rd). Free. 5/1-10/15. 14-day limit. 7 sites, RVs under 22 ft. Tbls, toilets, cfga, no drkg wtr. Rockhounding, picnicking, fishing. Elev 4,800 ft; 7 acres.
Fishing tip: Scenic Ash Creek offers excellent trout fishing most of the year.

Howard's Gulch $6
Modoc National Forest
25 mi E of Adin on SR 299; 6 mi NW on Hwy 139. $6. 5/1-10/30; 14 day limit. 11 sites; 22-ft RV limit. Tbls, toilets, cfga, drkg wtr. Fishing, hiking. Elev 4700 ft.
Fishing tip: Catch bass and catfish from the nearby South Fork of Pit River or try for bass and bluegill from nearby Beeler Reservoir (7 miles).

Lower Rush Creek $6
Modoc National Forest
7.5 mi NE of Adin on CA 299; half mi NE on FR 40N39; rd not recommended for trailers. $6 MD-LD; free rest of year; 14-day limit. 10 sites (RVs under 22 ft). Tbls, toilets, cfga, piped drkg wtr. No wtr during free period. Picnicking, fishing. Elev 4400 ft; 5 acres. Mountains. Lower Rush Creek.

Upper Rush Creek $6
Modoc National Forest
7.5 mi NE of Adin on CA 299; 2.3 mi NE on FR 40N39; rd not recommended for trailers. $6 May-Oct; free rest of year; 14-day limit. 13 sites (RVs under 22 ft). Tbls, toilets, cfga, piped drkg wtr. No wtr during free period. Picnicking, fishing. Elev 5200 ft; 4 acres.

Willow Creek $6
Modoc National Forest
1 mi S of Adin on CA 299; 14.5 mi SE on CA 139. $6 fee MD-LD; free rest of year; 14-day limit. 8 sites (RVs under 32 ft). Used heavily by travelers to Reno. 5 acres, flat terrain. Tbls, toilets, cfga, piped drkg wtr. No wtr during free period. Picnicking, trout fishing. Elev 5200 ft.

ALTADENA (4) S

Idlehour Trail Camp $5
Angeles National Forest
2.9 mi NE of Altadena on Trail 2N453; .2 mi NE on Trail 2N452; 1.5 mi N on Trail 12W16. $5 daily or $30 annually. All year; 14-day limit. 4 tent sites. Tbls, no toilets, no drkg wtr. Campfire permit required. Elev 2,500 ft; 2 acres. Stream. Closed during high fire danger, call local ranger station for details. Hiking access only.

Millard $5
Angeles National Forest
1.1 mi N of Altadena on Lake Ave; 1.1 mi W on Loma Alta Dr; 1.7 mi N on CR 2N65 to Cheney Trail in Millard Canyon. $5 daily or $30 annually. All year; 14-day limit. 5 tent sites. Tbls, toilets, cfga, no drkg wtr. Hiking, picnicking. Elev 1,900 ft; 1 acre. Stream wtr. 200-yard walk from parking area to first site. Millard Falls 1 mi.

Mount Lowe Trail Camp $5
Angeles National Forest
4 mi N of Altadena on Trail 12W14; one-fifth mi N on FR 2N50 (primitive rds); from locked gate, hike 3.5 mi along old railroad bed. $5 daily or $30 annually. All year; 14-day limit. 4 tent sites. Tbls, toilets, no drkg wtr. Hiking, picnicking, horseback riding, fishing 4 mi. Elev 4,500 ft; 2 acres. Nature trails. Hiking and equestrian access only. Hitching rail. Fire closure restrictions in summer. Campfire permit required.

ALTURAS (5) N

Ballard Reservoir FREE
Modoc National Forest
17 mi W of Alturas on Hwy 299 to Canby; 1.5 mi S on CR 54; keep to left as road narrows, following signs to lake. Free. Undesignated primitive sites; no facilities. Hiking, trout fishing.

Big Sage Reservoir FREE
Modoc National Forest
3 mi W of Alturas on Hwy 299; 6 mi N on Crowder Flat Rd #3; right on CR 180 for 3 mi. Free. 5/30-10/15; 14-day limit. 6 primitive sites (22-ft RV limit). Tbls, toilets, cfga, no drkg wtr. Pack out trash. Fishing, hiking, boating(l). On Big Sage Reservoir. Elev 5100 ft.
Fishing tip: Big Sage is an excellent bass lake; cast shorelines & dropoffs in early spring, using jigs, spinnerbaits, crankbaits;

try deep-runners & plastic worms in summer. The lake also contains good populations of crappie and catfish.
Travel tip: Modoc County Museum in Alturas has extensive firearms collection dating from 15th to 20th Century; regional Indian artifacts; outdoor displays; native-plant display. Donations accepted.

Jane's Reservoir FREE
Modoc National Forest
3 mi W of Alturas on Hwy 299; about 26 mi N on Crowder Flat Rd, past Big Sage Reservoir; W for qtr mi on Jane's Reservoir turn-off. Free. May-Oct; 14-day limit. Primitive undesignated sites. Tbls, toilets, cfga, no drkg wtr. Fishing, boating(l). Devil's Garden wild horse herd nearby.

Pepperdine FREE
Modoc National Forest
13 mi SE of Alturas on CR 56; 6 mi E on FR 41N31 (Parker Creek Rd); 1 mi S on Pepperdine Rd. Free. 6/1-10/15. 5 sites (RVs under 17 ft). Tbls, toilets, cfga, piped drkg wtr. Picnicking, fishing (4 mi), hiking, horseback riding. Elev 6800 ft. Trailhead to South Warner Wilderness. Corrals & parking available.

Reservoir C FREE
Modoc National Forest
1 mi W of Alturas on Hwy 299; 9.5 mi N on CR 73 (Crowder Flat Rd); left 7 mi on Triangle Ranch Rd. Free. 6 primitive sites; 22-ft RV limit. Tbls, toilet, cfga, no drkg wtr. Fishing, hiking, 4-wheeling, boating(l).

ANACAPA ISLAND (6) S

Anacapa Island CG $7.50
Channel Islands National Park
14 mi S of Ventura; boat access only; hike half mi from dock. $7.50 with federal Senior Pass; others pay $15. All year; 14-day limit. 7 primitive sites. No supplies, fuel, wtr. Pack out trash. Tbls. Island limit, 30 persons. Hiking, picnicking, fishing, scuba diving, snorkeling. Reservations required (included in $15 fee). 154-step stairway to camping areas. No shade. Pack in wood or fuel. Sea lions, sea birds. 699 acres. Visitor center. 877-444-6777.
Fishing tip: Fishing pressure is heavy around the island, but good catches of kelp bass, black sea bass and canary rockfish are made; occasionally barracuda and yellowtail in summer; in fall, area south of island is noted for broadbill swordfish & striped marlin.

ANGELUS OAKS (8) S

Thomas Hunting Ground $5
San Bernardino National Forest
4 mi W of Angelus Oaks on FR 1N12. $5 daily or $30 annually. 5/15 11/30. 10-day limit. 6 sites; RVs under 22 ft. 15 acres. Tbls, toilets, cfga. No drkg wtr. Hiking, picnicking. Elev 6800 ft. Elev, 6,800 ft. 15 acres.

ARROYO GRANDE (10) S

Agua Escondido $5
Los Padres National Forest
27.5 mi E on CR 32 (Arroyo Grand-Huasna Rd.); 1.5 mi N on FR 30S07; 2 mi N on FR 30S02. $5 daily or $30 annually. Deer season only; 14-day limit. 3 tent sites; 1 acre. Tbls, toilets, cfga, no drkg wtr. Deer hunting, hiking, picnicking; horseback riding. Horse troughs. Elev 2200 ft.

Balm of Gilead Trail Camp $5
Los Padres National Forest
Garcia Mountain Wilderness
19 mi NE on Pozo-Arroyo Grande CR; 6 mi E on Forest Trail 15E06. $5 daily or $30 annually. Tent sites. Hiking.

Buckeye Trail Camp $5
Los Padres National Forest
Garcia Mountain Wilderness
19 mi NE on Pozo-Arroyo Grande CR; 3.5 mi E on forest Trail 15E06. $5 daily or $30 annually. 1 tent site. Tbl, toilet, cfga. Hiking, picnicking.

Hi Mountain $5
Los Padres National Forest
10 mi NE of Arroyo Grande forest service station off Pozo-Hi Mountain Rd. $5 daily or $30 annually. All year; 14-day limit. 11 primitive undesignated sites; 16-ft RV limit. Tbls, toilet, cfga, no drkg wtr.

Oceano Dunes $6
State Vehicular Recreation Area
Just SW of Arroyo Grande, off Hwy 1. $6 plus $4 entry fee. All year; by reservation 5/15-9/15 & on holidays. Primitive camping on 1,500 acres. Tbls, toilets, cfga, drkg wtr. Beach, sand dunes, off-road vehicle activities.

Stony Creek $5
Los Padres National Forest
Garcia Mountain Wilderness
20 mi E on CR 32 (Arroyo Grande-Huasna Rd.); 1.7 mi N on FR 30S02; then 2 mi NW on FR 31S09. $5 daily or $30 annually. Road impassable in wet weather. All year; 14-day limit. 6 tent sites; 3 acres. Tbls, toilets, cfga, piped spring drkg wtr shut off 10/1 5/1). Deer hunting, hiking, picnicking. Horseback riding 1 mi. Elev 2000 ft.

AUBERRY (11) S

Squaw Leap FREE
Management Area
Bureau of Land Management
5 mi NW on San Joaquin River off Hwy 145; in San Joaquin River Gorge. Free. All year; 14-day limit. 7 walk-in family tent sites & 2 group tent sites. Toilets, cfga, tbls, no drkg wtr. Horse hitching post. Diverse plants, animals of interest to naturalists. Fishing on San Joaquin River, hiking, horseback riding, mountain biking, hunting, picnic area.

Smalley Cove $10
Pacific Gas & Electric
20 mi N of Clovis on Hwy 168; 2.8 mi N on Auberry Rd; 8.5 mi NE on Powerhouse Rd to Kerckhoff Reservoir. $10. All year; 14-day limit. 5 sites. Tbls, toilets, cfga, drkg wtr. Fishing, boating.

AZUSA (13) S

Coldbrook $12
Angeles National Forest
18 mi N on SR 39 (San Gabriel Canyon Rd) from I-210 (Azusa Canyon exit) at Azusa. $12 without Adventure Pass; $10 with pass. All year; 14-day limit. 22 sites (22-ft RV limit). Tbls, toilets, cfga, drkg wtr. Fishing, hiking. On North Fork of San Gabriel River. Elev 3350 ft. Closed during 2007 due to mud slides from wildfires.

Fishing tip: West, east & north forks of San Gabriel River are well stocked with trout.

Crystal Lake Recreation Area $12
Angeles National Forest
From I-210 at Azusa, 26 mi N on SR 39 (San Gabriel Canyon Rd). $12. All year; 14-day limit. (Fee is $10 for those with Adventure Pass.) 52 sites. Tbls, flush & portable toilets, cfga, drkg wtr. Hiking, fishing. Elev 5800 ft. Closed in 2007 due to mud slides from wild fires.

BAKER (15) S

East Mojave FREE
National Scenic Area
Bureau of Land Management
Primitive camping permitted on disturbed areas adjacent to roads within the 1.5-million-acre scenic area. Area accessible from either I-15 on the north or I-40 on the south. Free. Backpackers may camp at any previously disturbed site. Petroglyphs are scattered throughout the area, protected by law. Designated as America's first national scenic area in 1980. Includes volcanic cinder cones, desert tortoises, cattle operations, sand dunes, historic & modern mines, rock formations, Joshua trees, wildflowers in April & May. Best period for visiting, Oct-May. Stores in Goffs, Cima, Nipton.

Travel tip: Devil's Playground is 18 mi SE of Baker; westerly winds drive sand to an area where winds from the north, south & east converge.

Little Dunes Camping FREE
Dumont Dunes OHV Area
Bureau of Land Management
About 31 mi N of Baker on Hwy 127 to OHV area E of hwy & S of Amargosa River; camping area is directly off Hwy 127 1 mi S of Dumont Rd. Free, but $60 seasonal use permit required. Primitive camping anyywhere within the riding area; 14-day limit. No facilities. ATV use, motorcycling, 4WD touring, hiking, rockhounding.

BAKERSFIELD (16) S

Auxiliary Dam $5
Isabella Lake
Sequoia National Forest
50 mi NE on Hwy 178; 1 mi E of Lake Isabella. $5 daily or $35 annual permit required for lakeshore camping. All year; 14-day limit. Undesignated open sites. Tbls, toilets, cfga, flush toilets, hot showers. Fishing, swimming, picnicking; boating (l). Elev 3000 ft; 200 acres. Kern River (1.5 mi).

Fishing tip: Try early spring for largemouth bass & trout; cast the shoreline and dropoffs for bass, using jig-and-pig, crank-baits & spinnerbaits. Lake has an excellent population of huge bass.

Travel tip: Visit Ballarat ghost town, located about 23 mi N of Trona on SR 178, then 4 mi E on gravel rd. A few buildings left from 1890s gold camp. Nearby Panamint City (11 mi NE of Ballarat on rough dirt rd) ghost town has some shacks, large silver smelter chimneys from 1870s.

Chimne Peak Campground FREE
Bureau of Land Management
50 mi E of Bakersfield on SR 178, then continue NE on SR 178; N on Canebrake Rd to Chimney Creek. Free. Mar-Nov; 14-day limit. 32 sites. Tbls, toilets, cfga, no drkg wtr, no trash service. Hiking, biking. Elev 5700 ft.

Evans Flat FREE
Sequoia National Forest
45 mi NE of Bakersfield via Rancheria Rd. (Road 25S15 -- dirt rd). Free. 5/1-10/31; 14-day limit. 20 sites. Toilets, tbls, cfga, drkg wtr. 20-ft RV limit. Large-group camping. No trash pickup. Elev 6,200 ft. Suitable for horse camping; fenced pasture adjacent to cpgrnd.

Stine Cove Rec Area FREE
Sequoia National Forest
On E side of Lake Isabella off Sierra Way. Free. All year; 14-day limit. Open camping; no RV length limit. Chemical toilets, tbls, cfga, no drkg wtr. Fishing, boating.

Fishing tip: Lake Isabella is stocked with chinook salmon in addition to containing largemouth bass, bluegill, crappie and rainbow trout.

Walker Pass Trailhead FREE
Bureau of Land Management
14 mi E of Onyx on Hwy 178 or 15 mi W of Hwy 14 on Hwy 178. Free. All year, but may be inaccessible in winter; 14-day limit. 11 primitive sites. Tbls, toilets, cfga, drkg wtr Apr-Oct. Horse corral. Hiking, horseback riding, hunting. On Pacific Crest National Scenic Trail. Elev 5000 ft. Donations accepted.

BARSTOW (17) S

Afton Canyon Campground $6
Bureau of Land Management
From I-5 exit, S 3 mi following signs on Afton

Canyon Rd; 38 mi E of Barstow. $6. All year; 14-day limit. 22 sites. Tbls, toilets, cold showers, drkg wtr (limited). Scenic cliffs, wildlife area. Mojave River. East Mojave National Preserve. Equestrian camp by permit.

Owl Canyon Campground   **$6**
Rainbow Basin Natural Area
Bureau of Land Management
8 mi N of Barstow via Camp Irwin Rd; 2 mi W on Fossil Beds Rd. (Exit I-15 or I-40 at E Main; W to Yucca St railroad bridge on Ft Irwin Rd to Fossil Bed Rd; right on Rainbow Basin Rd. $6. All year; 14-day limit. 31 sites. Tbls, toilets, cold showers, drkg wtr (limited), cfga. Rockhounding, gold panning, hiking, horseback riding. Scenic cliffs. Adjacent to Rainbow Basin Natural Landmark. Elev 3000 ft; 40 acres.

BEAR VALLEY (19) N

Bloomfield   **$8**
Stanislaus National Forest
15.8 mi NE on CA 4; .8 mi SE on FR 8N01 (Highland Lakes Rd); .1 mi S on FR 8N29 (rds narrow, unpaved). $8. 6/15-10/31; 14-day limit. Unimproved; About 20 primitive dispersed sites (RVs under 16 ft); not recommended for trailers. Tbls, toilets, drkg wtr. Stream. 5 acres. Fishing, picnicking, boating (3 mi). Elev 8000 ft. RV dump station at Calaveras Big Trees State Park on Hwy 4 NE of Arnold; use fee. Campfire permit required.

Hermit Valley   **FREE**
Stanislaus National Forest
12.1 mi NE of Bear Valley on CA 4; qtr mi S on FR 8N22. Free. 6/15-10/1; 14-day limit. Dispersed sites in lower valley & NE upper valley at Grouse Flat. 50 acres, about 25 spaces for large RVs. Tbls, toilets, cfga, no drkg wtr. River. Swimming, picnicking, fishing, deer hunting. Campfire permit required. Elev 7500 ft. RV dump station at Calaveras Big Trees State Park on Hwy 4 NE of Arnold; use fee.

Highland Lakes   **$8**
Stanislaus National Forest
16 mi NE of Bear Valley on SR 4; 4.5 mi SE on FR 8N01; half mi SW on FR 8N33. $8. 6/15-10/31; 14-day limit; route not recommended for trailers. 35 sites. Tbls, toilets, cfga, drkg wtr. Hiking, swimming, fishing, hunting. No trash service. Elev 8600 ft; 5 acres.

Lake Alpine   **FREE**
Backpack Camp
Stanislaus National Forest
4 mi NE of Bear Valley on Hwy 4, at E end of Lake Alpine near Silver Valley trailhead. Free. 6 tent sites (no vehicles). Wtr & toilets across rd at Chickaree Picnic Area. Parking at Silver Valley trailhead or picnic area. One-night limit.

Lake Alpine Campground   **$9**
Stanislaus National Forest
4 mi NE of Bear Valley on Hwy 4, at E end of Lake Alpine. $9 with federal Senior Pass; others pay $18. 6/15-9/30; 14-day limit. 25 sites; 27-ft RV limit. Tbls, flush toilets, cfga, drkg wtr. Boating(l), fishing, hiking, biking, summer interpretive programs. Dump at nearby Calaveras Big Tree State Park ($2).

Pacific Valley   **FREE**
Stanislaus National Forest
10 mi NE of Bear Valley on SR 4; 1 mi S on FR 8N12 (6 mi W of Ebbetts Pass). along Pacific Creek. Free. 6/15-10/1; 14-day limit. 15 dispersed sites (RVs under 16 ft); not recommended for trailers. Tbls, toilets, cfga, no drkg wtr. Fishing, picnicking. Elev 7600 ft. Good early season deer camp. Campfire permit required. Equestrians camp at S end of site.

BEAUMONT (20) S

Bogart   **$12**
Riverside County Park
From I-10 at Beaumont, 4.5 mi N on Beaumont Ave; at N end of Cherry Valley Ave. $12. All year. 40 sites. Tbls, flush toilets, cfga, drkg wtr, playground. Hiking, horseback riding, fishing. 414 acres.

BECKWOURTH (21) N

Crocker   **FREE**
Plumas National Forest
7 mi N on CR 111 (Beckworth-Genessee Rd.); qtr mi W on FR 24N36. Free. 5/15-10/15;; 14-day limit. 10 sites (RVs under 32 ft). Tbls, toilets, no drkg wtr. Hunting, picnicking, boating (d--rent, 5 mi); swimming (4 mi); fishing (1 mi). Elev 5800 ft; 1 acre; Crock Creek/Lake Davis (4 mi). Dump station ($2) at Grizzly Campground, 8 mi N of Portola just off CR 126.

Fishing tip: Try Lake Davis for brown & lake trout.

BERKELEY (22) N

Tilden Regional Park   **FREE**
East Bay Regional Park District
Off Wildcat Canyon Rd and Grizzly Park Blvd in Berkeley, just N of Hwy 24 (take Fish Ranch Rd exit E of the Calidecott Tunnel, drive uphill & turn right at Grizzly Peak Blvd. Free. All year; 10-day limit. Equestrian camping; primitive tent sites. Tbls, toilets, cfga, no wtr except for horses. Visitor center, carousel, nature area. Hiking, biking, horseback riding.

BERRY CREEK (23) N

Little North Fork   **FREE**
Plumas National Forest
14 mi N on CR 27562 (Oroville-Bucks Lake Rd); 5 mi NE on FR 23N60; half mi N on FR 23N15. Free. 5/15-10/15; 14-day limit. 27 sites (RVs under 16 ft); tbls, toilets, cfga, no drkg wtr. Hunting, picnicking, fishing, hiking.

Elev 4000 ft; 3 acres. Off Oroville-Bucks Lake Rd. on Little North Fork of Feather River.

Fishing tip: River has excellent seasonal runs of striped bass, shad & steelhead. Try trout in late May when water clears.

Milsap Bar   **FREE**
Plumas National Forest
9 mi NE of Berry Creek on CR 27562; half mi S on CR 44603; 7 mi E on FR 22NG2. Free. 5/1-11/1; 14-day limit. 20 sites (RVs under 17 ft). Toilets, cfga, no drkg wtr, tbls. Elev 1600 ft.

Rogers Cow Camp   **FREE**
Plumas National Forest
15 mi NE on CR 27562; half mi W on FR 23N15; off Oroville-Bucks Lake Rd. Half mi W of Merrimac. Free. 5/15-11/30; 14-day limit. 8 RV/tent sites. Elev 4100 ft; 1 acre. Tbls, toilets, cfga, no drkg wtr. Stream. Berry picking, picnicking.

BIG BAR (24) N

Big Bar   **FREE**
Shasta-Trinity National Forest
1 mi SE of Big Bar on CA 299 across bridge from Big Bar Ranger Station. Free. 6/1-10/1; no service Oct-May; 14-day limit. 3 sites (RVs under 16 ft). Tbls, toilets, cfga, no drkg wtr. Swimming, picnicking, fishing. Elev 1200 ft.

Big Flat   **$8**
Shasta-Trinity National Forest
3.7 mi E of Big Bar on Hwy 299. $8 during 5/1-11/1; $6 rest of year; 14-day limit; 10 sites (22-ft RV limit). Tbls, toilets, cfga, drkg wtr. Hiking, fishing, swimming.

Hayden Flat   **$10**
Shasta-Trinity National Forest
6.2 mi NW of Big Bar on SR 299; 1 mi SW of Denny on CR 402 (winding rd). $10 during 7/1-11/1; $6 rest of year. 14-day limit. 36 sites (RVs under 26 ft). Tbls, toilets, cfga, drkg wtr, beach. Swimming, fishing. 8 acres. No trash service.

BIG BEAR CITY (25) S

Coldbrook   **FREE**
San Bernardino National Forest
W of Big Bear city on Hwy 18; on S end of Big Bear Lake just off Metcalf Bay. Free. All year; 14-day limit. 36 sites; 25-ft RV limit. Toilets, tbls, cfga, drkg wtr. Fishing, hiking.

Siberia Creek Group Camp   **$5**
San Bernardino National Forest
10 mi W on SR 18, then W qtr mi, 3.5 mi hike SE down steep trail. $5 daily or $30 annually. 6/1-9/15; 14-day limit. 10 sites. Tbls, toilets, cfga, no drkg wtr. Fishing, picnicking.

Travel tip: Take Gold Fever Trail Tour, beginning at Big Bear Ranger Station, 8 mi E of Fawnskin, near Big Bear Lake on SR 38. 3-hour car tour of trail, including many interesting sights & sites from gold rush days.

BIG BEND (26) N

Hawkins Landing $12
Pacific Gas & Electric
Shasta-Trinity National Forest
2.1 mi N of Big Bend on Hwy 299; 3.3 mi W on FR 38N11 to Iron Canyon Reservoir spillway; right 1 mi. $12. All year; 14-day limit. 10 sites (30-ft RV limit). Tbls, toilets, cfga, drkg wtr. Fishing. Site operated by PG&E in cooperation with the national forest.
Fishing tip: Try the trout in Iron Canyon Reservoir; spring best time for the lunker rainbow and browns, but small trout can be caught all season.

BIG PINES (27) S

Baker Creek $10
Inyo County Campground
Half mi N of Big Pines on US 395; 1 mi W on Baker Creek Rd. $10. All year; 15-day limit. 70 sites. Tbls, toilets, cfga, drkg wtr. Fishing. Elev 4000 ft; 10 acres.
Fishing tip: Good trout fishing on Baker Creek and the whole Big Pine Creek drainage; use salmon eggs & Panther Martin spinners. Also try nymphs with a split shot near bottom.

First Falls FREE
Inyo National Forest
10.5 mi SW on Glacier Lodge Rd. Walk-in sites only. Free. 5/1-10/15; 14-day limit. 5 tent sites. Tbls, cfga, toilets, no drkg wtr. Picnicking, fishing, swimming, horseback riding, hunting. Elev 8300 ft. On trail to John Muir Wilderness.

Glacier View (Triangle) $10
Inyo County Park
Half mi N of Big Pines on US 395; at Hwy 168. $10. 4/15-10/15; 15 day limit. 40 sites. Tbls, flush toilets, cfga, drkg wtr.

Grandview FREE
Inyo National Forest
Half mi N on US 395; 13 mi NE on CA 168; 5.5 mi N on CR 4S01 (White Mountain Rd); primitive rds. Free (donations accepted). 5/1-10/31; 14-day limit. 26 sites (RVs under 45 ft). Tbls, toilets, cfga, firewood, no drkg wtr. Picnicking, hiking. Elev 8600 ft; 2 acres. Botanical. Serves Ancient Bristlecone Pine Forest. Nature trails 5 mi.
Travel tip: Visit Ancient Bristlecone Pine Forest, about 17 mi from Big Pines via SR 168, then a paved unmarked rd to Schulman Memorial Grove. Some of the gnarled pine trees are more than 4,500 years old. Naturalist on duty at visitor center in grove.

Table Mountain Camp $6.50
Angeles National Forest
1 mi from Big Pines on Table Mountain Rd. $6.50 with federal Senior Pass; others pay $13. May-Nov; 14-day limit. 115 sites; 32-ft RV limit. Tbls, toilets, cfga, drkg wtr. Visitor center. OHV activities.

Taboose Creek $10
Inyo County Park
12.5 mi S of Big Pines on US 395; 2.5 mi W on Taboose Creek Rd. $10. All year; 14-day limit. 55 sites. Tbls, pit toilets, cfga, drkg wtr. Fishing, hiking, picnicking. John Muir Trail nearby. Elev 3900 ft.
Fishing tip: Best luck for rainbow and brown trout in Taboose Creek is the section between Independence and Big Pine; the state plants catchable size trout there.

BISHOP (28) S

Horton Creek Campground $5
Bureau of Land Management
8.5 mi NW of Bishop on US 395; W on Sawmill Rd; 3 mi W on Round Valley Rd. $5 (formerly free). About 5/15-11/1; 14-day limit. Day use only rest of year. 53 primitive sites. Tbls, pit toilets, cfga, no drkg wtr. Fishing, hiking. Near Tungsten Hills for mountain biking, horseback riding, OHV use. Be watchful for mountain lions. Elev 4975 ft.
Fishing tip: Horton Creek is stocked regularly with rainbows, brook and brown trout.

Mosquito Flat Trailhead FREE
Inyo National Forest
30 mi W of Bishop on US 395 to Tom's Place, then 7 mi on FR 12 (Rock Creek Rd). Free. About 6/1-LD; 1-day limit. Tbls, toilets, cfga, no drkg wtr, beach. Hiking, swimming. Elev 10,100 ft.

Pleasant Valley $10
Inyo County Park
5.5 mi N of Bishop on US 395; NE on access rd. $10. All year; 14 day limit. 200 sites. Tbls, toilets, cfga, drkg wtr. Fishing, picnicking. Pleasant Valley Reservoir. Elev 4300 ft; 42 acres.
Fishing tip: For trout, fish caddis flies in the river leading into the lake.

BLYTHE (30) S

Coon Hollow $5
Bureau of Land Management
Long-Term Visitor Area
14 mi W of Blythe on I-10 to Wiley Well Rd; 13 mi S of I-10 via graded dirt Wiley Well Rd. $140 permit for season 9/15-4/15 or $30 for 14 days in winter; $5 per day or $50 for period of 4/16-9/14. 25 primitive sites. Tbls, toilets, cfga, no wtr. Dump at Wiley Well rest area on I-10 at Wiley Well Rd. Excellent geode-hunting at nearby geode beds. Pick up map at rock shop in Blythe. Federal Senior Pass discounts do not apply to LTVA fees.
Travel tip: Excellent geode-hunting at nearby geode beds. Pick up map at rock shop in Blythe.

Mayflower $12
Riverside County Park
6 mi NE of Blythe, just N of 6th Ave & Colorado River Rd. $12 base. All year. Base fee

for no hookups; $18 with elec & wtr. About 180 sites. Tbls, flush toilets, cfga, showers, dkrg wtr, dump, pool. Swimming, boating(l), fishing. 24 acres.

Midland $5
Bureau of Land Management
Long Term Visitor Area
From I-10 at Lovekin Blvd exit, N 6 blocks, then NW 4 mi on Midland Rd. $5 daily or $50 for season during 4/16-9/14; $140 seasonal permit for season 9/14-4/15 or $30 for 14 days. 14-day limit. Undesignated sites. Sanitary dump. No toilets, no drkg wtr. Geode hunting nearby. Pick up map at rock shop in Blythe. Federal Senior Pass discounts do not apply to LTVA fees.

Miller Park FREE
Riverside County Park
12 mi SW of Blythe at Hwy 78 & 38th Ave; on Colorado River. Free. Primitive undesignated sites on 5 undeveloped acres. No facilities, no wtr. Boating, fishing

Mule Mountain $5
Bureau of Land Management
Long-Term Visitor Area
From I-10 at Wiley's Well Rd exit, S 9 mi; or, from Hwy 78, N 25 mi on Milpitas Wash Rd. Camping area on both sides of rd from Wiley's Well Camp to Coon Hollow Camp. $5 daily during 4/16-9/14 or $50 for season; $140 permit for season 9/15-4/15 or $30 for 14 day; 14-day limit at each site. Undesignated sites. Toilets, trash pickup at Wiley's Well and Coon Hollow Camps; dump, drkg wtr, toilets and trash pickup at Wiley's Well Rest Stop on I-10. Federal Senior Pass discounts do not apply to LTVA fees.

Wiley Well $5
Bureau of Land Management
Long-Term Visitor Area
14 mi W of Blythe on I-10 to Wiley Well Rd; 9 mi S of I-10. Free 14 days. $5 daily or $50 for season during 4/16-9/14; $140 permit for season 9/15-4/15 or $30 for 14 days. 21 primitive sites. Tbls, cfga, toilets, no drkg wtr. Dump at Wiley Well rest area on I-10 at Wiley Well Rd. Excellent geode-hunting at nearby geode beds. Pick up map at rock shop in Blythe. Golden Eagle, Golden Age & Golden Access Passport discounts do not apply to LTVA fees.
Travel tip: Excellent geode-hunting at nearby geode beds. Pick up map at rock shop in Blythe. Find "thunder eggs" in hillside ash areas; also check nearby Hidden Saddle & Potato Patch Geode Beds for fireagates, chalcedony roses, other gemstones.

BODFISH (32) S

Breckenridge FREE
Sequoia National Forest
9 mi S of Bodfish on CR P483Y; 7 mi W on FR 28S06; 1.6 mi SW on FR 28S07; paved and dirt rd. Free. 5/1-10/31; 14-day limit. 8

sites (20-ft RV limit). Tbls, toilets, cfga, no drkg wtr. Pack out trash. Fishing, hiking, picnicking. Elev 7100 ft; 3 acres. Nondrinkable spring wtr. Mill Creek.

BORON (34) S

Boondock Area   FREE
SR 58 W of 4-Corners near Mojave and Edwards AFB. Free. All year. Many dry washes accessible from the road 100-500 yds for self-contained RVs. In case of Columbia landings or major air events, plan on arriving a day early.

BORREGO SPRINGS (35) S

Arroyo Salado $6
Primitive Campground
Anza-Borrego Desert State Park
16 mi E of Borrego Springs on CR 522. $6. All year; 15-day limit. Primitive open camping. Tbls, toilets, cfga, no drkg wtr. No open fires. Fishing, rockhounding, hiking.

Backcountry Camping $5
Anza-Borrego Desert State Park
From Borrego Springs, follow Palm Canyon Dr & Montezuma Valley Rd. $6 daily pass ($30 annually). Camp throughout the park, boondocking without facilities. Fishing, hiking, rockhounding. 600,000 acres of open area.

Culp Valley Primitive Area $5
Anza-Borrego Desert State Park
10 mi SW of Borrego Springs on CR S22, just inside W park entrance. $5. All year; 15-day limit Primitive open camping. Tbls, toilets, cfga, no drkg wtr. No open fires. Rockhounding, hiking.

Ocotillo Wells   FREE
State Vehicle Recreation Area
About 12 mi E of Borrego Springs (near town of Ocotillo Wells) on Borrego Springs Rd & SR 78. Free. All year. Primitive sites with tbls, cfga, shade ramadas, toilets, no drkg wtr, dump. Primarily an OHV use area for all-terrain vehicles, 4WD and motorcycles.

Sheep Canyon $5
Anza-Borrego Desert State Park
NW of Borrego Palm Canyon Campground. $5. All year; 15-day limit. Small number of primitive undesignated sites. Tbls, toilets, cfga, no drkg wtr. Hiking, rockhounding.

Yaqui Pass Primitive Area $5
Anza Borrego Desert State Park
5 mi S of Borrego Springs on CR 53; right on Yaqui Pass Rd for 4 mi. $5. All year; 15-day limit. Tbls, toilets, cfga, no drkg wtr. No open fires. Rockhounding, hiking.

Yaqui Well $5
Primitive Campground
Anza-Borrego Desert State Park
5 mi S of Borrego Springs on CR 53; right for

6 mi on CR 53 (Yaqui Pass Rd). $5. All year; 15-day limit. 10 numbered primitive sites & numerous undesignated sites. Tbls, toilets, cfga, no drkg wtr. No open fires. Hiking, rockhounding.

BOULEVARD (36) S

Cottonwood $6
McCain Valley Recreation Area
Bureau of Land Management
2 mi E of Boulevard on co rd; 7 mi NW on McCain Valley Rd. $6. All year; 14-day limit. 30 sites. Tbls, toilets, cfga, no drkg wtr. On W edge of McCain Valley national Cooperative Land and Wildlife Management Area. Picnicking, hiking, biking, horseback riding. No OHV. Elev 3000-4500 ft.

Lark Canyon $6
Off-Highway Vehicle Area
McCain Valley Recreation Area
Bureau of Land Management
2 mi E of Boulevard on co rd; 7 mi NW on McCain Valley Rd. $6. 15 sites. All year; 14-day limit. Tbls, toilets, cfga, no drkg wtr. Popular OHV area. Within the McCain Valley National Cooperative Land and Wildlife Management Area. Picnicking, biking, mountain biking. Elev 4000 ft.

BRAWLEY (37) S

Gecko/Grays Well $25
Imperial Sand Dunes Recreation Area
Bureau of Land Management
27 mi E of Brawley on SR 78, 3 mi S on BLM's paved Gecko Rd; sites along Gecko Rd & along Grays Well Rd S of I-8. $25 weekly for 1-7 days; $90 annually. All year. 19 hardened RV sites. Toilets, cfga, no drkg wtr. Hiking, horseback riding, interpretive programs. 250 acres. Largest sand dunes recreation area in America; 40 mi long, 5 mi wide. Popular ORV area. Visitor center.

Osborne Overlook $5
Bureau of Land Management
24 mi E of Brawley on CA 78; 2 mi E of Gecko Rd. $5. All year, 3-day limit. 75 sites. Tbls, toilets, cfga, no drkg wtr. Hunting (dove, pheasant, duck); dune buggying, motorbike trail-riding; picnicking. Elev 500 ft; 15 acres. Motorbike trails. Imperial Sand Dunes.

Roadrunner Campground $25
Imperial Sand Dunes Recreation Area
Bureau of Land Management
27 mi E of Brawley on SR 78; S to end of BLM's paved Gecko Rd. $25 weekly for 1-7 days; $00 annually. All year. Tbls, toilets, cfga, no drkg wtr. Hiking, horseback riding, interpretive programs. 250 acres. Largest sand dunes recreation area in America; 40 mi long, 5 mi wide. Popular ORV area. Visitor center.

Wiest Lake $7
Imperial County Park
5 mi N of Brawley on Hwy 111; 2 mi E on

Rutherford Rd; on S shore of Wiest lake. $7 base. All year; 14-day limit. Base fee for non-hookup sites; $12 with hookups. 44 sites. Tbls, flush toilets, cfga, showers, drkg wtr, hookups($), dump. Fishing, boating(l). Monthly rate available.

BRIDGEPORT (37B) N

Desert Creek   FREE
Toiyabe National Forest
From SR 338 in Nevada, pick up FR 027; follow it S, watching for campground signs. Free. About 5/1-11/1; 14-day limit. 13 sites. Tbls, toilets, cfga, no drkg wtr. Fishing. Elev 6300 ft.

Green Creek $6.50
Toiyabe National Forest
6 mi S of Bridgeport on US 395; 7 mi W on Green Creek Rd. $6.50 with federal Senior Pass; others pay $13. About 5/15-10/1; 14-day limit. 11 sites (22-ft RV limit). Tbls, toilets, cfga, drkg wtr. Hiking, fishing. Elev 7500 ft.

Green Creek   FREE
State Wildlife Area
6 mi S of Brideport on US 395; 7 mi W on Green Lake Rd. Free. All year; 14-day limit. Primitive camping on 720 acres along 3 mi of Green Creek. Fishing (brown, brook & rainbow trout), hunting.

Obsidian $8
Toiyabe National Forest
12 mi N of Bridgeport on US 395; 4 mi W on rough, dirt FR 66. $8. About 6/15-10/15; 14-day limit. 14 sites (30-ft RV limit). Tbls, toilets, cfga, no drkg wtr, no trash service. Hiking, fishing. Elev 7800 ft. Poorly maintained at last report.

Walker River   FREE
State Wildlife Area
14 mi NW of Bridgeport on US 395 to Sonora Junction; continue about 10 mi N to town of Walker; wildlife area just N of Walker in East Walker River Canyon. Free. All year; 14-day limit. Primitive camping on 1,367 acres; no facilities. Hunting, fishing.

BURNEY (38) N

Big Pine $12
Lassen National Forest
5 mi NE of Burney on SR 299; 28 mi S on SR 89 (4 mi S of Old Station). $12. 4/15-10/31; 14-day limit. 19 sites (22-ft RV limit). Tbls, toilets, cfga, drkg wtr. Fishing at Hat Creek. Lassen Volcanic National Park nearby. Hiking Pacific Crest Trail. Elev 4600 ft; 3 acres.
Fishing tip: The upper section of Hat Creek has a put-and-take fishery, supported by annual stockings, while the lower section is a specially regulated wild trout area with several public accesses on private land.

Butte Creek FREE
Lassen National Forest
5 mi E of Burney on Hwy 299; 23 mi SE on CA 89; 10 mi E on CA 44; 2.5 mi S on FR 32N21 (off CA 44, 2 mi S on rd to Butte Lane and NE part of Lassen Volcanic National Park). Free. 5/15-10/1; 14-day limit. 20 sites (RVs under 22 ft). 2 acres. Tbls, toilets, cfga, no drkg wtr. Dump near the Merrill Campground at Eagle Lake. Fishing, picnicking. Elev 5600 ft.
Travel tip: Visit nearby Lassen Volcanic National Park, with its lava flows, hot springs, mud pools and a now-dormant volcano which erupted for several years earlier this century.
Fishing tip: Try Butte Creek's rainbow trout & chinook salmon. Drift worms or salmoon eggs or match a current hatch with flies.

Dusty Campground $6
Pacific Gas & Electric
Lassen National Forest
5 mi E of Burney on SR 299; 7 mi N on Hwy 89; 7.5 mi W on Clark Creek Rd; 1 mi E on access rd; on N shore of Lake Britton. $6-12. 6/1-10/15; 14 day limit. 7 primitive sites; 20-ft RV limit. Tbls, toilets, cfga, no drkg wtr. Fishing, boating.
Fishing tip: Lake Britton offers good angling opportunity and contains brown & rainbow trout, largemouth & smallmouth bass, crappie, channel catfish and bluegills. Spinners, spoons and minnow-like lures work best. Live or dead bait fish prohibited.

Honn $11
Lassen National Forest
5 mi NE of Burney on Hat Creek; 14 mi S on Hwy 89. $11. All year; 14-day limit. 6 sites. Tbls, toilets, cfga, no drkg wtr. Dump across from Hat Creek Camp on Hwy 89. Hiking. Elev 3400 ft. Limited turn-around space for RVs.

McArthur-Burney Falls $9
Memorial State Park
Just outside Burney on SR 89; at Lake Britton. $9 for 6 hike-in environmental campsites; $15 base off-season, $20 peak season at 129 developed sites; 32-ft RV limit. All year; 15-day limit. Tbls, flush toilets, showers($), cfga, drkg wtr, dump, visitor center, store. Hiking, nature trails, swimming. 910 acres; 5 mi of streamside & lake shoreline. Park's main attraction is 129-ft waterfall

BURNT RANCH (39) N

Burnt Ranch $8
Shasta-Trinity National Forest
Half mi W of Burnt Ranch on Hwy 299; N to camp; just above Trinity River. $8. 5/15-10/31; 14-day limit. 16 sites (25-ft RV limit). Tbls, toilets, cfga, drkg wtr. Small waterfall, fishing. Elev 1000 ft.

Denny FREE
Shasta-Trinity National Forest
7 mi W on Hwy 299; 19 mi NE on FR 7N01 (Denny Rd.). Free. All year; 14-day limit. 16 sites (RVs under 25 ft). Tbls, toilets, cfga, no drkg wtr. Camp is self-service 7/1-10/30. Rockhounding, picnicking. Fishing & swimming 1 mi. Elev 1400 ft; 5 acres. Difficult access for RVs. Requires careful driving. On New River.

CALEXICO (40) S

Tamarisk LTVA $140
Bureau of Land Management
22.5 mi E of Calexico on SR 98; access via a gravel rd from hwy. All year. By $140 seasonal fee or $30 for 14 days during 9/15-4/15; during 4/16-9/14, $5 per day or $50 for season. Undesignated sites. No tbls, toilets, drkg wtr. Dump at Holtville City Dump Station on Holt Rd (S-32), 2 blocks S of Evan Hewes Hwy (S-80); no charge. Hiking, rockhounding. Golden Eagle, Golden Age & Golden Access Passport discounts do not apply to LTVA fees.

CALIFORNIA CITY (41) S

Airport RV Park $10
At 22636 Airport Way near California City. $10. All year. 13 sites. Tbls, flush toilets, cfga, drkg wtr, showers, modem hookups, dump.

CALLAHAN (44) N

East Fork FREE
Klamath National Forest
27 mi SW of Callahan on FH 93. Formerly fee site; now free all year. 14-day limit. 9 sites (50-ft RV limit). Tbls, toilets, cfga, drkg wtr. Scenic. Fishing, hiking, picnicking, swimming. Elev 2600 ft.
Fishing tip: Good steelhead & salmon fishing on the adjoining Salmon River. Upstream on South Fork are deep holes excellent for salmon or steelhead.
Travel tip: Explore old mining areas upstream from camp on the South Fork. 2 mi downstream is historic town of Cecilville.

Kangaroo Lake $10
Klamath National Forest
2 mi E of Callahan on SR F1089; 9.5 mi NE on SR F1219; 6.7 mi S on FR 41N08; E on FR 41N08. Free 10/16-5/15; $10 rest of yr. 18 sites (32-ft RV limit). Tbls, toilets, cfga, drkg wtr. Swimming, boating (no motors), fishing, hiking trails. Elev 6000 ft; 3 acres. Sites for handicapped & elderly. Elev 6500 ft. 25-acre lake.
Fishing tip: This lake is one of the few high mountain lakes accessible by vehicle, with only a 5-minute walk. It features 2 fishing piers, native brook and brown trout and stocked rainbow of up to 25 inches.
Travel tip: See Callahan Ranch Hotel in town; built as a stagecoach stop in 1854; still serves travelers.

Trail Creek $10
Klamath National Forest
16.6 mi SW of Callahan on CR FH93; .3 mi S on FR 39N08. $10. MD-10/15; free rest of year. 14-day limit. 12 sites (22-ft RV limit). Tbls, cfga, toilets, drkg wtr; no wtr during free period. Swimming, creek fishing, nature trails. Elev 4700 ft; 4 shaded acres. Hike to several lakes in Trinity Alps Wilderness.
Travel tip: Numerous old buildings, old mining dumps can be seen 30 mi S of Callahan on SR 3 along the Trinity River & its branches; some gold panning done today.

CALPELLA (45) N

Miti Park $8
Lake Mendocino
Corps of Engineers
Off US 101 2 mi S of Calpella; E side of dam; boat access only. $8. 4/1-9/30; 14-day limit. 10 sites. Toilets, cfga, no drkg wtr. Swimming, boating, fishing.
Fishing tip: This lake is well known for its excellent striped bass and huge catfish. It also contains smallmouth bass and crappie.

CAMP RICHARDSON (46) N

Bayview $11
Lake Tahoe Basin Management
5.3 mi NW on Hwy 89. $10. About 5/1-10/15; 1-day limit. 12 sites (20-ft RV limit); 4 acres. Toilets, cfga, tbls, drkg wtr. Dump 5 mi. Hiking trails. Elev 6800 ft.
Travel tip: Visit the Lake Tahoe Forest Service Visitor Center, 3 mi N of South Lake Tahoe on Hwy 89; watch trout & kokanee salmon in Taylor Creek through underground viewing chamber.
Fishing tip: Beautiful Lake Tahoe has excellent fishing for lake trout, rainbow trout & kokanee salmon.

CAMPTONVILLE (47) N

Lower Carlton Flat FREE
Tahoe National Forest
12 mi NE on Hwy 49. Free. 4/1-11/15; 14-day limit. Undeveloped sites on 12 acres (16-ft RV limit). Tbls, toilets, cfga, drkg wtr. Swimming, fishing.

Ramshorn Camp $6.50
Tahoe National Forest
15 mi NE of Camptonville on Hwy 49 just past Convict Flat picnic area. Formerly free, now $6.50 with federal Senior Pass; others pay $13. 5/15-9/30; 14-day limit. 16 sites. Tbls, toilets, cfga, no drkg wtr. Fishing, hiking. Elev 2200 ft.

CANBY (48) N

Cottonwood Flat FREE
Modoc National Forest
4 mi SE of Canby on CA 299; 4.1 mi W on CR 84; 3.5 mi W on FR 41N44; half mi NW on FR 42N10. Free. MD-10/15; 14-day limit.

10 sites (RVs under 22 ft). Tbls, toilets, cfga, drkg wtr. Rockhounding, picnicking; primarily a hunter camp. Elev 4700 ft; 6 acres. Historic. Hulbert Creek and Pit River 4 mi.

Lassen Creek Campground FREE
Modoc National Forest
5 mi N of Canby on Hwy 139. Free. May-Oct; 21-day limit. Primitive undesignated sites. Tbls, toilets, cfga, no drkg wtr. Hiking, no fishing in Lassen Creek. Rockhounding nearby. Elev 4700 ft.

Reservoir F FREE
Modoc National Forest
6 mi N of Canby on Hwy 139; 4 mi N on Mowitz Rd 46 to Reservoir F jct, then E on FR 43N36 for 6 mi. Free. May-Oct; 14-day limit. 6 primitive sites; 22-ft RV limit. Tbls, toilets, cfga, no drkg wtr. Fishing, boating, hiking.

CARMEL (50) S

Andrew Molera State Park $10
21 mi S of Carmel on Hwy 1; backpack access to camp., about one-third mi. $10. All year. 24 walk-in tent sites. Toilets, cfga, drkg wtr. Swimming, fishing, hiking, biking, horseback riding. Beach.

Bottchers Gap $12
Los Padres National Forest
8 mi S of Carmel on Hwy 1; 9 mi E on Palo Colorado Rd (CR 5012). $12. All year; 14-day limit. 11 walk-in tent sites. Tbls, toilets, cfga, no drkg wtr. Hiking.

China Camp FREE
Los Padres National Forest
22 mi SE of Carmel on Carmel Valley Rd; 10 mi S on Tassajara Rd (FR 18S02). Free. All year; 14-day limit 6 tent sites; 20-ft RV limit. Tbls, toilets, cfga, no drkg wtr. Hiking. Elev 4300 ft.

White Oaks FREE
Los Padres National Forest
22 mi SE of Carmel on Carmel Valley Rd; 8 mi S on Tassajara Rd. Free. 7 sites; 20-ft RV limit. All year; 14-day limit. Tbls, toilets, cfga, no drkg wtr. Hiking, fishing at Anastasia Creek. Elev 4200 ft.

CASTAIC (52) S

Bouquet $5
Angeles National Forest
6 mi S of Castaic on I-5; E on Magic Mountain Parkway to Valencia Blvd; left 2 mi to Bouquet Canyon Rd, then N 12 mi. $5 daily or $30 annually. All year; 14-day limit. 4 tent sites. Tbls, toilets, cfga, no drkg wtr. Bouquet Canyon Creek offers good trout fishing.
Fishing tip: Bouquet Canyon Creek offers good trout fishing. Also try nearby Castaic Lake for Florida-strain largemouth bass as well as trout and catfish.

Frenchman's Flat $5
Angeles National Forest
10 mi N of Castaic on I-5, then N on Pyramid Lake Rd. $5 daily or $30 annually. All year; 14-day limit. Primitive undesignated sites; 32-ft RV limit. Tbls, toilets, cfga, no drkg wtr. Closed in early 2007 due to forest fire.
Fishing tip: Catch trout, catfish, bluegill, crappie, striped bass, largemouth & smallmouth bass at nearby Pyramid Lake. Western creek arms regarded as best fishing spots; try submerged points & dropoffs.

Oak Flat $5
Angeles National Forest
10 mi N of Castaic on I-5; 3 mi NW on Templin Hwy; qtr mi N on FR 6N46. $5 daily or $30 annually. All year; 14-day limit. 27 sites (18-ft RV limit). Tbls, toilets, cfga, drkg wtr. Fishing, hiking trails, biking. 7 acres; elev 2800 ft.

CECILVILLE (53) N

Matthews Creek $6
Klamath National Forest
8.5 mi NW of Cecilville on CR FH93. $6. 6/1-10/31; free rest of year; 14-day limit. 12 sites (RVs under 47 ft). Tbls, toilets, cfga, drkg wtr; no wtr or trash service during free period. Swimming, fishing. 11 acres on South Fork Salmon River.

Shadow Creek FREE
Klamath National Forest
7.2 mi NE of Cecilville on Callahan-Cecilville Rd. Free. 5/1-10/15; free rest of yr, but no trash service; 14-day limit. 5 sites (RVs under 50 ft). Tbls, toilets, cfga, no drkg wtr. Swimming, fishing, hiking. On Shadow Creek (no fishing) and E Fork Salmon River. Elev 2900 ft.

CEDARVILLE (54) N

Cedar Pass FREE
Modoc National Forest
8 mi W of Cedarville on CA 299. Free. 5/30-10/15; 14-day limit. 17 sites (RVs under 23 ft). Tbls, toilets, cfga, no drkg wtr. Picnicking, fishing. Elev 5900 ft; 10 acres. Mountains. Dense forest. Stream. Pack out trash.

Stough Reservoir FREE
Modoc National Forest
5.1 mi W of Cedarville on CA 299; half mi N on FR 45N39. Free. 5/30-10/15. 14 sites (22-ft RV limit). Tbls, toilets, cfga, drkg wtr. Rockhounding, picnicking. Elev 6300 ft; 3 acres.

CHALLENGE (55) N

Strawberry $9
Sly Creek Recreation Area
Plumas National Forest
17 mi N of Challenge, off LaPorte Rd. $9 with federal Senior Pass; others pay $18. MD-LD; 14-day limit. 10 sites. Tbls, toilets, cfga, drkg wtr. Fishing, boating(l),swimming, waterskiing. Elev 4000 ft; 2 acres. At Sly Creek Reservoir.

CHESTER (56) N

Hamilton Beach Dispersed FREE
Pacific Gas & Electric
Lassen National Forest
About 30 mi SW of Chester near Hamilton Beach fishing access sites on Lake Almanor. Free. All year; 14-day limit. Toilets, cfga, tbls, no drkg wtr. Primarily a site for hunters & fishermen. Fishing, hunting, hiking, boating(l).
Fishing tip: Good fishing from shore as well as boats for German brown trout, rainbows and landlocked salmon as well as both smallmouth & largemouth bass and catfish. Best spots for browns in summer are W shoreline near West Shore Cove and the forest service boat launch. Also try the dam and the shoreline near the camping area. For browns, use broken-back Rebels and Rapalas, Z-Rays, Needlefish. Crawdad, shad and rainbow patterns are best.

Horseshoe Lake $10
Backcountry Campsites
Lassen Volcanic National Park
15 mi NW of Chester on Juniper Lake Rd; 1.5 mi W by foot on trail. $10 entry fee for 7 days; camp free with permit. All year; 14-day limit 12 tent sites. Toilets. Fishing, boating (no motor boats). Elev 6540 ft. Snag Lake. Small pets on leash. Hang food from trees to avoid attracting black bears. Horseshoe Lake contains brook & rainbow trout but is not a great fishing lake.

Juniper Lake $10
Lassen Volcanic National Park
13 mi NW of Chester on Juniper Lake Rd. at E shore of Juniper Lake (1 mi from ranger station); rd not suitable for RVs. $10. 6/29-9/16 (depends on snow); 14-day limit. 18 sites, 1 group site; equestrian sites $10 plus $4 per horse. RVs not recommended. Tbls, toilets, cfga, no drkg wtr. Elev 6792 ft. $25 annual entry fee or $10 for 7 days.

Soda Springs FREE
Lassen National Forest
11.5 mi W of Chester on CA 36; 20 mi SW on CA 32; half mi NE on FR 26N19 (Soda Springs Rd.). Free. 5/25-10/15; 14-day limit. 10 sites (RVs under 22 ft). Tbls, toilets, cfga, well drkg wtr. Fishing, picnicking. Elev 3600 ft; 4 acres. Big Chico Creek.
Fishing tip: Try Deer Creek for rainbow trout; Dept of Fish & Game stocks it each May & June. Some steelhead also in Alder. And don't forget the bass, trout, kokanee & king salmon of Lake Almanor!

Soldier Creek $11
Lassen National Forest
S of Chester on Hwy 89 to Humboldt Rd; 1 mi right on Humboldt Rd, then bear right at fork; right at Fanani Meadows jct. $11. 5/15-11/1; 14-day limit. Primitive undesignated

sites (about 15). Tbls, toilets, cfga, no drkg wtr. Fishing, hunting.

Warner Valley $10
Lassen Volcanic National Park
Off Hwy 36, 16 mi NW on oil and dirt rd; 1 mi W of Warner ranger station. $10 from early Oct until snowfall; $14 rest of year ($7 with federal Senior Pass); 14-day limit. Also $10 entry fee to park for 7 days. 18 tent/RV sites. Tbls, drkg wtr, toilets, cfga. Hiking trail to lakes & Devil's Kitchen Geothermal Area. Elev 5600 ft.

CHICO (57) N

Butte Creek Campground $5
Bureau of Land Management
20 mi NE of Chico on SR 32 to Forest Ranch, then 3.5 mi SE on graded dirt Doe Mill Rd. $5. All year; 14-day limit. Primitive area with 23 gold mining or dredging sites; no facilities, no drkg wtr. Gold panning, rockhounding, fishing, hiking, rafting. Dredging permitted during 4th Sat in May until 10/15. Area is quite cool.
Travel tip: Visit the Chico Museum in town; art & regional history exhibits, Chinese temple from late 1800s that was shipped to site & reassembled; donations accepted. Also see Honey Run Covered Bridge off Hwy 99, 5 mi up Humbug/Honey Run Rd; one of the few covered bridges left in California; 3 levels, built 1894 of native pine; picnic grounds.

CHINO (58) S

Prado Regional Park $10
San Bernardino County Park
In Chino on Hwy 83, S of Hwy 60 & N of Hwy 91. $10 base. All year; 1-month limit. Base fee for no hookups & overflow; $22 with hookups ($132 weekly). 75 RV sites. Tbls, flush toilets, cfga, showers, drkg wtr, dump, store, playground. Fishing, horseback riding, golf, dog training, boating(r), soccer, horseshoes, shooting ranges, air gun range. Entry fee charged.

CHOWCHILLA

Hidden View Campground $7
Hensley Lake
Corps of Engineers
From jct with Hwy 99 at Chowchilla, follow signs on Avenue 26. $7 with federal Senior Pass; others pay $14 at basic sites. Premium sites with wtr/elec, $20 ($10 with federal Senior Pass). All year; 14-day limit. 55 sites (14 with hookups); 65-ft RV limit. Tbls, flush toilets, cfga, drkg wtr, dump, showers, beach, playground, fish cleaning station. Fishing, hiking, swimming, waterskiing, boating (l), biking, evening shows Fri & Sat. 3-day minum stay on holiday weekends.

CIMA (59) S

Camp Rock Springs FREE
Providence Mountains
Bureau of Land Management
35 mi NW of Essex off I-40 via Essex & Black Canyon Rd, then N through outcroppings to Cedar Canyon, E on Cedar Canyon Rd, 5 mi past Black Canyon Rd., right onto dirt track to Camp Rock Springs. Free. Undesignated sites. Drkg wtr from spring to the W. Hiking, rockhounding. Petroglyphs in rocks above campsite.
Travel tip: Providence ghost town is 25 mi N of Essex on dirt rd, W of Needles; rock buildings left as reminders of silver mining town of 1880s.

CISCO GROVE (60) N

Woodchuck FREE
Tahoe National Forest
3 mi NE of I-80 at Cisco Grove on Rattlesnake Rd; steep, winding rd; RVs not recommended. Free. 6/15-10/15; 14-day limit. 8 sites (RVs under 16 ft). Tbls, toilets, cfga, no drkg wtr. Picnicking. Fishing & swimming 3 mi. Elev 6300 ft; 5 acres. On Rattlesnake Creek; Sterling Lake 3 mi.

CLAREMONT (61) S

Manker Flat $12
Angeles National Forest
From Foothill Blvd in Claremont, take Mills Ave (Mt. Baldy Rd) 9 mi N (reach Foothill via Mountain Ave N from I-10). $12 (discount of $2 for those with Adventure Pass). May-Oct; 14-day limit. 21 sites; 16-ft RV limit. Tbls, flush toilets, cfga, drkg wtr. Hiking to San Antonio Falls.

CLEARLAKE OAKS (62) N

Blue Oaks FREE
Indian Valley Recreation Area
Bureau of Land Management
Ukiah District
E of Clearlake Oaks 15.5 mi on SR 20; N on Walker Ridge Rd (narrow, dirt) to Reservoir Access Rd., left 2.4 mi to camp, 1.5 mi farther to lake. Free. All year; 14-day limit. 6 sites. Toilets, cfga, drkg wtr. Fishing, boating, hunting, off-road vehicles, hiking, swimming, horseback riding, biking. Marina & store at dam.

Kowalski Camp FREE
Indian Valley Recreation Area
Bureau of Land Management
14 mi E of Clearlake Oaks on Hwy 20; N on Walker Ridge Rd to Indian Valley Reservoir; check in at store; boat-in access to W shore of lake (1 mi by boat, hike-in on Indian land prohibited). Free. All year; 14-day limit 3 primitive tent sites. Tbls, cfga, no toilets, no drkg wtr. Hiking, boating, fishing. Day use parking fee charged by Yolo County.

Lower Hunting Creek FREE
Knoxville Recreation Area
Bureau of Land Management
From Hwy 29 at Lower Lake (near Clear Lake), 15 mi SE on Morgan Valley Rd. (Berryessa-Knoxville Rd); 2 mi S on Devilhead Rd. Free. 5 sites. All year; 14-day limit. 5 sites. Tbls, toilets, cfga, drkg wtr. Hunting.
Fishing tip: Try the Putah Creek section of the lake for bass in early spring; troll deep for trout during summer; fish the mouths of Putah & Pope Creeks in fall, using minnows. Nighttime bass fishing is best along the S shore.
Travel tip: Knoxville ghost town is 20 mi E of Lower Lake toward Lake Berryessa; once a mining town, now popular with rockhounds. Also stop at Sturmer Winery, 1 mi S of Lower Lake on SR 29; tours & wine-tastings free.

Walker Ridge FREE
Indian Valley Reservoir
Bureau of Land Management
Ukiah District
E of Clearlake Oaks, off SR 20; N on Walker Ridge Rd to reservoir (steep, winding narrow dirt rds; large RVs not recommended; some rds impassable during wet weather). Free. All year; 14-day limit (Sept-May best time). Undesignated offroad sites; 17,000 acres; 4,000-acre lake. No facilities except at Blue Oak and Wintun locations. Fishing, 10 mph boating, hunting, off-road vehicles, hiking, swimming. Marina & store near dam. Cross dam to access 2.5-mi Kowalski hiking trail.
Fishing tip: Indian Valley Lake offers quite good rainbow trout & largemouth bass fishing, along with catfish, crappies & sunfish. Cache Creek below dam is stocked with brown trout.

CLOVERDALE (63) N

Navarro Beach Campground $10
Navarro River Redwoods State Park
49 mi N of Cloverdale on US 101; within state park at mouth of Navarrow River on the ocean. $10 during 9/16-5/14; $15 peak season. All year; 15-day limit. 10 primitive sites; 30-ft RV limit. Tbls, toilets, cfga, no drkg wtr. Hiking, fishing.

Paul M. Dimmick $10
Wayside State Campground
Navarro River Redwoods State Park
49 mi N of Cloverdale on US 101; within state park at milemarker 8 on Hwy 128. $10 during 9/16-5/14; $15 peak season. All year; 15-day limi. 23 sites; 30-ft RV limit, but suggested only for small rigs. Tbls, toilets, cfga, drkg wtr (except in winter). Catch-and-release fishing in Navarro River with barbless hooks.

COALINGA (64) S

Coalinga Mineral Springs $11
Fresno County Parks
Bureau of Land Management
14 mi W of Coalinga on Hwy 198; right on Coalinga Mineral Springs Rd for 5 mi. $11 ($5

for seniors). All year; 14-day limit. 20 sites. Tbls, flush toilets, cfga, no drkg wtr. Horseback riding, hunting, birdwatching, hiking. Operated by Fresno County.

Los Gatos Creek Park   **$11**
Fresno County Parks
18 mi W of Coalinga on Los Gatos Creek Rd. $11 ($5 for seniors). All year; 14-day limit. 44 sites plus 17 overflow sites. Tbls, flush toilets, cfga, no drkg wtr.

COBB (65) N

Boggs Mountain   **FREE**
Demonstration State Forest
1 mi N of Cobb on Hwy 175; turn at sign for fire station. All year; 14-day limit. 15 primitive sites at Calso Ridge Camp; 2 sites at Ridge Camp; no toilets, cfga, no drkg wtr except at Houghton Springs and Big Springs camping areas. Picnicking, hiking, horseback riding. Camp in designated areas only. Campfire & camping permit required; acquire from ranger station. 3,453 acres.

COLFAX (66) N

Bear River Campground   **$10**
Inland Fishing Access
Placer County Park
2 mi N of Colfax off I-80 on Weimar rd; 3 mi E on Placer Hills Rd; 1 mi N on Plum Tree Rd on Milk Ranch Rd. $10. All year; 14-day limit. 25 primitive sites. Tbls, toilets, cfga, drkg wtr. Swimming, hiking, canoeing, fishing, horseback riding, gold panning.

COLUSA (67) N

Colusa-Sacramento River   **$12**
State Recreation Area
In Colusa, from Hwy 20 (Market St), turn right on 10th St to the levee. $12 off-season; $15 in-season. MD-12/31; 15-day limit. 14 sites; 27-ft RV limit. Tbls, flush toilets, cfga, drkg wtr, showers, dump, coin laundry, store. Boating(l), fishing, hiking.
Fishing tip: At the park is one of the best stretches of the Sacramento River for catching king salmon, steelhead, rainbow trout and striped bass.

CORNING (69) N

Woodson Bridge   **$11**
State Recreation Area
At Corning, 6 mi E on South Ave from I-5; on both sides of Sacramento River. $11 base off-season; $14 in-season. All year; 15-day limit. 41 sites plus boat-in camp on W bank. 31-ft RV limit. Tbls, flush toilets, showers, cfga, drkg wtr, coin laundry, dump. Fishing, swimming, horseshoes, birdwatching, nature trails. 328 acres.
Fishing tip: This area of the river offers excellent fishing for king salmon, steelhead, striped bass, catfish and bluegill.

COVELO (72) N

Atchison Dispersed Camp   **FREE**
Mendocino National Forest
E of Covelo on FR 7. Free. All year; 14-day limit. 3 sites; 22-ft RV limit. Tbls, toilet, cfga, no drkg wtr, no trash service. Elev 4300 ft.

Boardman Dispersed Camp
FREE
Mendocino National Forest
NE of Covelo on RD M1 (Indian Dick Rd). Free. All year; 14-day limit. 3 sites. Tbls, toilets, cfga, no drkg wtr, no trash service.

Eel River   **$8**
Mendocino National Forest
1.5 mi N of Covelo on CR 162; 11.1 mi E on CR 338; .2 mi S on FR 1N02 (next to Eel River Work Center). $8. 4/1-12/1; 14-day limit. 16 sites on 6 acres (22-ft RV limit). Tbls, toilets, cfga, drkg wtr. Swimming, fishing, picnicking, boating. Elev 1500 ft.
Fishing tip: The Eel River is well known for its steelhead, chinook & coho.

Georges Valley   **FREE**
Dispersed Camp
Mendocino National Forest
E of Covelo at NE terminus of Indian Dick Rd (RD M-1). Free. All year; 14-day limit. Primitive undesignated sites; no facilities, no drkg wtr. Hiking. Trailhead.

Green Springs   **FREE**
Dispersed Camp
Mendocino National Forest
E of Covello at Yolla-Bolly Middle Eel Wilderness. Free. All year; 14-day limit. 4 primitive sites. Tbls, toilets, cfga, spring wtr, no trash service. Popular trailhead & mountain biking camp.

Hammerhorn Lake   **$6**
Mendocino National Forest
2.6 mi N of Covelo on Hwy 162; 11.1 mi E on CR 338; 22.4 mi N on FR 1N02; half mi E on FR 23N01 (18 mi N of Eel River Work Center via Rd 1, Indian Dick Rd. Free. 6/1-10/1; 14-day limit. 9 sites (22-ft RV limit). Tbls, toilets, cfga, drkg wtr, fishing piers, no trash service. 1 disability site with adjoining toilet. Hiking, fishing, boating(l).
Fishing tip: This small lake has a surprisingly large population of big rainbow trout.

Howard Meadows   **FREE**
Howard Lake Basin Recreation Area
Mendocino National Forest
2.6 mi E of Covelo on CA 162; 11.1 mi E on CR 38; 17.5 mi N on FR 1N02 (12 mi N of Eel River Work Center via Rd M1, Indian Dick Rd; take rd to the left of the Little Doe Campground for 4 mi; bear left at three-point jct; at 12-acre Howard Lake. Free. All year; 14-day limit. 9 primitive sites. Toilet, cfga, no tbls, no drkg wtr, no trash service. High-clearance vehicles suggested. Fishing, boating(l).

Little Doe   **FREE**
Mendocino National Forest
2.6 mi E of Covelo on CA 162; 11.1 mi E on CR 38; 17.5 mi N on FR 1N02 (12 mi N of Eel River Work Center via Rd M1, Indian Dick Rd. Free. 6/15-9/30; 14-day limit. 13 sites (RVs under 22 ft). Tbls, toilets, cfga, no wtr. Picnicking, hiking. Elev 3600 ft; 8 acres. No trash pickup; pack out trash. Mountains.
Fishing tip: Camp is on N side of Howard Lake, stocked with good size rainbow trout.

Rattlesnake Creek   **FREE**
Mendocino National Forest
From Hammerhorn Junction, N on Rd M1 (Indian Dick Rd), cross the cement bridge at Rattlesnake Creek; turn left. Free. All year; 14-day limit. 2 sites. No toilets, cfga, no tbls, no drkg wtr, no trash service. Swimming hole upstream.

Rock Cabin   **FREE**
Dispersed Camp
Mendocino National Forest
About 30 mi NE of Eel River Station at N end of Indian Dick Rd. Free. All year; 14-day limit. 3 primitive sites; no facilities, no drkg wtr, no trash service. Trailhead for Yolla-Bolly Middle Eel Wilderness. Elev 6250 ft.

Soldier Ridge   **FREE**
Dispersed Camp
Mendocino National Forest
E of Covelo at NE terminus of Indian Dick Rd (RD M-1). Free. All year; 14-day limit. Primitive undesignated sites; no facilities, no drkg wtr.

Surveyor Dispersed Camp   **FREE**
Mendocino National Forest
E of Covelo off FR 7, about 7 mi E of Eel River Station. Free. All year; 14-day limit. 3 primitive sites. Toilet, cfga, tbl, no drkg wtr, no trash service.

Wells Cabin   **FREE**
Mendocino National Forest
2.5 mi E of Covelo on SR 162; 11 mi E on CR 338; 12 mi NE on FH 7; 4 mi N on CR 23N69. Free. 7/1-10/31; 21-day limit. 25 sites (RVs under 22 ft). Tbls, drkg wtr, toilets, cfga. Wtr only during high-use season; no trash service. Picnicking, hiking. Elev 6300 ft; 8 acres. Day hike to Anthony Peak Lookout (1 mi). Not a good site for RVs.

Y Campground   **FREE**
Mendocino National Forest
From Covelo, follow directions to Atchison Camp & continue 2.4 mi; sign at turnoff says to Keller Place -- campground is half mi on the right. Free. All year; 14-day limit. Primitive undesignated sites; no facilities, no drkg wtr, no trash service. Scenic.

COYOTE RIDGE (73) S

Boondock Area   **FREE**
Bureau of Land Management
On Colorado River between Imperial and Laguna Dams. W on old Senator Wash Rd

from SR 524. Free. All year. Dry camp in rugged landscape; level spaces for all size rigs. No desert septic tanks allowed. Drkg water, dump nearby. CB Channel 23 monitored.

CRESCENT CITY (74) N

Environment Camp   **$9**
Tolowa Dunes State Park
5 mi NW of US 101 in Crescent City on Northcrest Dr/Lake Earl Dr; left on Lower Lake Rd for 2.5 mi; left on Kellogg Rd for 1 mi; walk-in access qtr mi. $9. All yr; 14-day limit. 6 environmental tent sites. Tbls, toilets, cfga, no drkg wtr. Biking, hiking, horseback riding, fishing, boating(l). 10,000 acres.

DeMartin Walk-In Camp   **FREE**
Redwood National Park
S of Crescent City in the park; park at mile-marker 14.4 on E side of US 101; hike in half mi; or park at N end of Wilson Creek bridge & hike 3 ml; or at the Hostel & hike 3 mi. Free. All year; 14-day limit. 10 tent sites. Drkg wtr, tbls, cfga, trash cans, toilets. On Pacific Coast Trail; Wilson Creek.
    Fishing tip: Fall & winter, use salmon eggs & crankbaits to catch steelhead & salmon from the Smith River nearby. During summer, catch rainbow trout from the Smith on flies.
    Travel tip: Miller Redwood Company, 4 mi S of town on US 101, offers free guided tours weekdays.

Flint Ridge Walk-In Camp   **FREE**
Redwood National Park
S of Crescent City in the park; park on Coastal Dr as it crests at ocean-view ridge; or on W side (trailhead across rd & qtr mi in), or at trailhead on N end of Coastal Dr at Douglas Bridge parking lot (then hike 4.2 mi in on Flint Ridge Trail. Free. All year; 14-day limit. 10 tent sites. Drkg wtr, tbls, cfga, toilets, trash cans.
    Travel tip: Watch migrating whales from trail near camp.
    Fishing tip: Fall & winter, use salmon eggs & crankbaits to catch steelhead & salmon from the Smith River nearby. During summer, catch rainbow trout from the Smith on flies.

Little Bald Hills   **FREE**
Horse/Backpack Camp
Redwood National Park
Park at trailhead off the E end of Howland Hill Rd. Hike or ride horseback 4.5 mi to camp. Free. All year; 14-day limit. Undesignated sites. Toilets, cfga, drkg wtr, tbls, horse bar, trash cans.

Nickel Creek Walk-In Camp
FREE
Redwood National Park
4 mi S of Crescent City in the park; park at end of Enderts Beach Rd. Free. All year; 14-day limit. 5 tent sites. No drkg wtr, tbls, cfga, toilets, trash cans. In brushy creek canyon above beach. Scenic.
    Travel tip: Rellim Demonstration Forest,

4 mi S of town on Hamilton Rd, just off US 101, offers diorama of early logging & lumber industry; logging tools, photos, forest trails. Free.

Redwood Creek Hike-In   **FREE**
Redwood National Park
S of Crescent City in the park on gravel bar of Redwood Creek past the first footbridge to qtr mi on either side of Tall Trees Grove. Free. All year, but June through Sept recommended. Undesignated tent sites.
    Travel tip: Brother Jonathan Cemetery on 9th St & Taylor Rd has graves of victims of the Brother Jonathan shipwreck in 1865.

CROWLEY (75) N

Crowley Lake Campground   **$5**
Bureau of Land Management
From Crowley and US 395, 5.5 mi N and W of Tom's Place overlooking Crowley Lake & Long Valley on Crowley Lake Dr. $5; previously free. About 5/15-11/1; 14-day limit. Special Long-Term Visitor Area (LTVA) permits can now be used at Crowley, Tuttle Creek and Goodale Creek Campgrounds. These LTVA permits are $300 for the period between the first Saturday in March through 11/1. 47 sites. Tbls, toilets, cfga, no drkg wtr, dump, group camping. Fishing (3 mi to lake), boating(lr), OHV use. Elev 7000 ft.
    Fishing tip: Try the lake for trout and Sacramento perch, both near the dam & at upper end of lake near Long Valley River.

DARDANELLE (77) N

Beardsley   **FREE**
Stanislaus National Forest
From SR 108 near Dardanelle, 7 mi on Beardsley Rd. Free. May-Oct; 14-day limit. 26 sites (including 10 at day-use area); 22-ft RV limit. Toilets, cfga, no drkg wtr, no tbls. Fishing, hiking, boating(l), swimming. Elev 3400 ft.
    Fishing tip: Beardsley Lake contains rainbow trout, eastern brook trout and German browns. The browns are making a nice comeback, and plenty in the 12-14 inch range can be caught. Use Goldeneye lures or nightcrawlers. The lake is stocked annually with 20,000 catchable-size browns and 10,000 pounds of rainbows. Middle Fork Stanislaus River also contains rainbow, eastern brook and German brown trout.

Brightman Flat   **$12**
Stanislaus National Forest
Brightman Recreation Area
1.2 mi NW of Dardanelle on SR 108. $12. 5/15-10/15; 14-day limit. 33 sites (RVs under 23 ft). Tbls, toilets, cfga, drkg wtr. Mountain climbing, hiking, picnicking, fishing. Elev 5600 ft; 5 acres. Middle fork of Stanislaus River. Nature trails 3 mi. Columns of the Giants 2.5 mi. Geological.
    Fishing tip: The upper section of Middle Fork Stanislaus River is easily accessible

from SR 108. The river is stocked each summer with rainbow trout and also contains eastern brook and German brown trout.

Clark Fork   **$12**
Stanislaus National Forest
Clark Fork Recreation Area
3 mi W of Dardanelle on SR 108; 6 mi NE on Clark Fork Rd; qtr mi SE on FR 7N40Y. $12 (B loop, $13). May-Oct; 14-day limit. 88 sites; 50-ft RV limit. Tbls, toilets, cfga, drkg wtr, dump. Fishing, hiking, boating(l).
    Fishing tip: Clark Fork River is within easy walking distance of Clark Fork Rd. It is regarded as a good rainbow trout stream.

Clark Fork Horse Camp   **$7**
Stanislaus National Forest
Clark Fork Recreation Area
3 mi W of Dardanelle on SR 108; 6 mi NE on Clark Fork Rd; qtr mi SE on FR 7N40Y; near Clark Fork Campground. $7. 5/1-10/31; 14-day limit. 14 sites; 22-ft RV limit. Tbls, toilets, cfga, no drkg wtr. Fishing, horseback riding. Elev 6200 ft. Dump station at Clark Fork Campground.

Fence Creek   **$6**
Stanislaus National Forest
Clark Fork Recreation Area
21 mi E of Pinecrest on Fence Creek Rd, just off Clark Fork Rd. $6. 5/1-10/31; 14-day limit. 38 sites; 22-ft RV limit. Tbls, toilets, cfga, no drkg wtr. Elev 6100 ft.
    Fishing tip: Try Clark Fork River for rainbow trout May-Nov.

Herring Creek   **FREE**
Stanislaus National Forest
1.1 mi N of Strawberry on SR 108; 7.5 mi NE on FR 5N11. 5/15-10/15; 14-day limit. 7 sites (RVs under 22 ft). Tbls, toilets, cfga, no drkg wtr. Hiking, picnicking, fishing. Elev 7300 ft.

Herring Reservoir   **FREE**
Stanislaus National Forest
From SR 108 near Strawberry, 7 mi NE on Herring Creek Rd (FR 5N11). Free. May-Oct; 14-day limit. 42 sites; 22-ft RV limit. Toilets, cfga, no drkg wtr, no tbls. Fishing, hiking. Elev 7350 ft.

Niagara Creek   **$6**
Stanislaus National Forest
7.5 mi SW of Dardanelle on SR 108; qtr mi NE on FR 5N011; half mi NE on FR 6N24. $6. 5/1-10/31; 14-day limit. 10 sites (RVs under 23 ft). Tbls, toilets, cfga, no drkg wtr. Mountain climbing (elev 6600 ft). Nature trails. Trail of Ancient Dwarfs, half mi. Fishing.

Niagara ORV Trailhead   **$6**
Stanislaus National Forest
7.5 mi SW on CA 108; 2 mi SE on FR 5N011. $6. 5/1-10/31; 14-day limit. 10 sites (RVs under 23 ft). Tbls, toilets, cfga, no drkg wtr. Picnicking, fishing (1 mi). Elev 7000 ft; 5 acres. Niagara Creek. 2.5 mi to Niagara Ridge ORV route. Free RV dump stations at Clark Fork Campground, Dardanelle Resort

and near Pinecrest on Hwy 108, half mi W of Summit Ranger District office.

Pigeon Flat   **$10**
Stanislaus National Forest
Brightman Recreation Area
1.4 mi E on SR 108; .1 mi E on FR 6N43Y; .1 mi E on Trail 0. Walk in campground. $10. 5/15-10/16; 14-day limit. 7 tent sites. Tbls, toilets, cfga, no drkg wtr. Picnicking, hiking, fishing (small trout in Stanislaus River), mountain climbing. Elev 6000 ft; 2 acres. Middle fork of Stanislaus River. Column of the Giants, one fifth mi. Nature trails 1 mi.

Sand Flat   **$9**
Stanislaus National Forest
Clark Fork Recreation Area
2.7 mi NW of Dardanelle on SR 108; 7 mi NE on FR 7N83. $9. 5/15-10/15; 14-day limit. 68 sites; 40-ft RV length limit. Tbls, toilets, cfga, drkg wtr. Fishing. Elev 300 ft.
Fishing tip: The lower section of Middle Stanislaus River contains good populations of rainbow, eastern brook and German brown trout. Access also from Beardsley Campground.

DAVIS CREEK (78) N

Plum Valley   **FREE**
Modoc National Forest
2.4 mi SE of Davis Creek on FR 45N04; 1 mi SE on FR 45N35. Free. 5/1-10/15. 7 sites (RVs under 16 ft). Tbls, toilets, cfga, no drkg wtr. Picnicking, rockhounding, fishing, boating. Elev 5600 ft; 4 acres. Lake. South fork of Davis Creek.
Travel tip: This campground is within the historic Highgrade Mining District, and numerous abandoned mines are nearby; stay out of the mines, but explore close by obsidian rockhounding areas. Obtain permit for personal collecting from the Davis Creek store.

DEATH VALLEY (79) S

Emigrant Junction   **FREE**
Death Valley National Park
Jct of CA 190 and Emigrant Canyon Rd. Apr-Oct; 30-day limit. Camp free, but $10 entry fee ($10 with federal Senior Pass). 10 sites (RVs under 30 ft). Tbls, flush toilets, cfga, drkg wtr. Picnicking. Elev 2000 ft.

Furnace Creek   **$12**
Death Valley National Park
N of Wildrose ranger station near Furnace Creek visitor center. $12 during 4/15-10/15; $18 rest of year ($9 with federal Senior Pass). 14-day limit. 136 sites. Tbls, flush toilets, cfga, drkg wtr, dump.

Wildrose   **FREE**
Death Valley National Park
Half mi W of Wildrose ranger station in Wildrose Canyon; 4WD suggested. All year; 30-day limit. Camp free, but $20 entry fee

($10 with federal Senior Pass). 23 primitive backcountry sites. Toilets, cfga, tbls, drkg wtr (except in winter).

Saline Valley Marsh   **FREE**
Bureau of Land Management
Death Valley National Park
N of Death Valley, then gravel rds from US 395 and SR 190; oasis in middle of barren Saline Valley, now part of the national park. Free. All year; 30-day limit. Primitive, undeveloped camping; no facilities, no drkg wtr. Hiking, rockhounding.
Travel tip: Area contains remains of the Saline Valley Salt Works and tram, listed on National Register of Historic Places. There, exceptionally pure salt deposits were once mined; the tram is the most scenic, historic and best preserved of its kind in America.

DESERT CENTER (81) S

Corn Springs   **$6**
Bureau of Land Management
8 mi E of Desert Center via I-10 & US 60. Half mi SE on Chuckwalla Rd; 6 mi W on Corn Springs Rd. $6. All year; 14-day limit. 14 sites next to palm tree oasis. Tbls, toilets, cfga, drkg wtr, cold showers. 50 acres.

DINKEY CREEK (82) S

Gigantea   **$6.50**
Sierra National Forest
1.6 mi S on CR PN44 (Dinkey Creek Rd); 6 mi SE on McKinley Grove Rd. 6/1-10/31; 14-day limit. Formerly free, now $6.50 with federal Senior Pass; others pay $13. 10 sites (RVs under 36 ft). Tbls, toilets, cfga, no drkg wtr. Picnicking, hiking. Elev 6500 ft. Botanical. Half mi from McKinley Grove of giant sequoias.

Sawmill Flat   **FREE**
Sierra National Forest
12.9 mi SE of Dinkey Creek on FR 11S40; 3.3 mi S on FR 11S12. Free. 6/1-10/31; 14-day limit. 15 sites (22-ft RV limit). Tbls, toilets, no drkg wtr. Picnicking, fishing, swimming, hiking. Elev 6700 ft. Wishon Reservoir, 6 mi.

Voyager Rock   **FREE**
Sierra National Forest
14 mi E on FR 11S40; 8 mi N on FR 40S16; 3 mi N on Trail 28E34 (Courtright Rd); on E side of Courtright Reservoir (last 3 mi on trail recommended for short wheelbase 4x4 vehicles); also accessible by boat. Free. 6/1-10/31; 14-day limit. 14 tent or pickup camper sites. Tbls, toilets, cfga, no drkg wtr. Mountain climbing, swimming, picnicking, fishing, hiking. Elev 8200 ft; 3 acres. Lake.

DORRINGTON (83) N

Boards Crossing   **FREE**
Stanislaus National Forest
From CA 4 S of Dorrington, qtr mi SE on FR 5N02 (Boards Crossing Rd); 4 mi SE on CR

5N75; tenth mi W on FR 5N60. Free. June-Oct; 14-day limit. 5 dispersed tent sites; not recommended for trailers. Tbls, toilets, drkg wtr, cfga. Picnicking, swimming, fishing, deer hunting. Calaveras Memorial 4 mi S. Campfire permit required. Elev 3800 ft.
Fishing tip: Try the North Fork of Stanislaus River (adjacent to camp), where rainbow trout are stocked each summer.

DOUGLAS CITY (84) N

Douglas City Campground   **$10**
Bureau of Land Management
Half mi W of Douglas City on SR 299 & Steiner Flat Rd. Free 11/1-5/1; rest of year, $10; 14-day per year limit. 18 sites. Tbls, flush & pit toilets, cfga, drkg wtr (no wtr during free period), beach. Fishing, boating, hiking, swimming, rockhounding, gold panning. Elev 1500 ft. Along Trinity River. Scenic.

Steelbridge   **$5**
Trinity River Recreation Area
Bureau of Land Management
41 mi W of Redding on US 299 to Steelbridge Rd, just 3 mi E of Douglas City; 2 mi to campground at Trinity River. $5. All year; 14-day limit. 9 sites (30 ft RV limit). Toilets, no drkg wtr (wtr at Junction City sites 1.5 mi W of Junction City). Fishing, hunting, rafting, canoeing. 3,500 acres of recreation area along 40 miles of Trinity River. High winds through steep, forested mountains from Lewiston to Helena. Rds easily accessible. Elev 1500-3500 ft.
Fishing tip: Great salmon fishing in Trinity River here during Sept & early Oct; then steelhead fishing from mid-Oct through Nov.

Steiner Flat   **FREE**
Bureau of Land Management
W of Douglas City on SR 299 & Steiner Flat Rd, just beyond Douglas City Campground. Free. All year; 14-day limit. Primitive undesignated sites. Tbls, toilets, cfga, no drkg wtr. Hiking, fishing, boating, swimming. Elev 1500 ft.

DOYLE (85) N

Fort Sage OHV Area   **FREE**
Bureau of Land Management
2 mi N of Doyle on US 395 to Laver Crossing, then follow signs. Free. All year; 14-day limit. 5 primitive sites; cfga, toilets, no drkg wtr, OHV staging facilities, no trash service. Trail system for motorcyclists of all abilities. Nearby horseback riding, mountain biking, hiking, wild horse viewing.

Meadow View   **FREE**
Plumas National Forest
6.6 mi W of Doyle on CR 331 (Doyle Grade Rd); .9 mi NW on CR 101. Free. 4/25-10/15; 14-day limit. 6 sites (RVs under 22 ft). Tbls, toilets, cfga, no drkg wtr. Picnicking. Fishing, 3 mi. Hunting, big & small game, 1 mi. Elev 6100 ft; 2 acres. Dump nearby. Last Chance Creek.

Fishing tip: Excellent fishing for both largemouth bass (spring) and rainbow trout (spring & early summer).

EAGLEVILLE (86) N

Emerson   **FREE**
Modoc National Forest
1.1 mi S on CR 1; 3 mi SW on FR 40N43; access very steep for RVs; poor roads. Free. 7/1-10/15; 14-day limit. 4 sites (16-ft RV limit). Tbls, toilets, cfga, no drkg wtr. Picnicking, fishing, hiking. Elev 6000 ft; 2 acres. Mountains. Dense forest area. Trailhead to South Warner Wilderness. Very good fishing (also swimming) at nearby Emerson Lake (3.5 mi).

Patterson   **FREE**
Modoc National Forest
3.3 mi S of Eagleville on CR 1 (Surprise Valley Rd); 5.1 mi SW on FR 39N01; 4.8 mi W on FR 39N01; .3 mi E on FR 39N28 (near South Warner Wilderness); access steep for RVs -- consider coming from Likely. 7/1-10/15; 14-day limit. 5 sites (RVs under 17 ft). Tbls, toilets, cfga, piped drkg wtr. Hiking, picnicking. Elev 7200 ft; 6 acres. Nature trails. Fishing in East Creek. Corrals available. Site is a major equestrian trailhead to South Warner Wilderness.

EARLIMART (87) S

Colonel Allensworth   **$10**
State Historic Park
7 mi W of Earlimart on CR J22. $10. All year; 15-day limit. 15 sites; 35-ft RV limit. Tbls, flush toilets, cfga, drkg wtr, showers, visitor center, dump. Historic park memoralizes the only California town founded, financed and governed by black Americans.

EL CAJON (88) S

Boulder Oaks   **$10**
Cleveland National Forest
About 30 mi E of El Cajon on I-8; exit S at Kitchen Creek-Cameron Station jct; right on southern frontage rd for 1 mi. $10-12. All year; 14-day limit. 30 sites; 27-ft RV limit. Tbls, toilets, cfga, drkg wtr. Nearby hiking, fishing. Elev 3500 ft. Fires may be forbidden. Closed Mar-May during arroyo toad breeding season.

Cibbets Flat   **$10**
Cleveland National Forest
About 35 mi E of El Cajon on I-8; 4.5 mi N on Kitchen Creek Rd. $10. All year; 14-day limit. 25 sites; 27-ft RV limit. Tbls, toilets, cfga, drkg wtr. Fishing. Camp host in summer.

EL CENTRO (89) S

Hot Springs   **$140**
Bureau of Land Management
Long-Term Visitor Area
From I-8, E of El Centro 12.5 mi, take Hwy 114 N. east on Old Hwy 80 (front-age rd) for 1 mi to site. $140 seasonal fee or $30 for 14 days during 9/15-4/15; during 4/16-9/14, $5 per day or $50 for season. 14-day limit. No toilets, no drkg wtr. Dump at Holtville City Dump Station on Holt Rd (S-32), 2 blocks S of Evan Hewes Hwy (S-80); no charge. Federal Senior Pass discounts do not apply to LTVA fees.
Travel tip: Community of Calipatria, N of El Centro on SR 115, is the lowest-elevation town in the Western Hemisphere; American flag flies at sea-level atop 180-ft flagpole.

Plaster City Open Area   **FREE**
Bureau of Land Management
17 mi W of El Centro. Exit I-8 on Dunnaway Rd. Free. All year; 14-day limit. Primitive undesignated camping in 41,000-acre open desert area. No facilities, no drkg wtr. OHV activities, photography.

Superstition Mtn Open Area   **FREE**
Bureau of Land Management
From Hwy S-80 to Huff Rd to Wheeler Rd. Follow Wheeler to one of several popular primitive camping areas or to the base of Superstition Mountains. Free. All year; 14-day limit. Primitive undesignated camping; no facilities, no drkg wtr. OHV activities.

ELK CREEK (90) N

Plaskett Meadow   **$8**
Mendocino National Forest
4.5 mi N on CR 306; 30 mi NW on Alder Springs Rd. $8. 6/15-10/15; 14-day limit. 34 sites (RVs under 17 ft). Tbls, toilets, cfga, drkg wtr. Swimming, boating, fishing, hiking. Nature trails. No boat motors. Elev 6000 ft. 2 small trout fishing lakes.

Plaskett Meadows Picnic   **FREE**
Mendocino National Forest
36 mi NW of Elk Creek on Forest Hwy, across lake from Plaskett Campground. Free. 7/15-10/15; 14-day limit. Primitive undesignated sites. Tbls, toilet, cfga, no drkg wtr. Parking area. Fishing, picnicking, boating.

Stony Gorge   **FREE**
Mendocino National Forest
Half mi N of Elk Creek, then half mi E on SR 162, then half mi S. Free. Elev 5000 ft. 2/1-7/31; 14-day limit. 125 sites. Tbls, toilets, cfga, drkg wtr. Picnicking, fishing, swimming, boating.

Telephone Camp   **FREE**
Mendocino National Forest
4.5 mi N of Elk Creek on CR 306; 36 mi NW on CR 307. Free. 6/15-10/15; 14-day limit. 13 sites (RVs under 22 ft). Tbls, toilets, cfga, piped drkg wtr. Picnicking, swimming, boating, fishing (3 mi). Elev 6600 ft; 6 acres. Scenic. Located on edge of Dry Meadow in red fir timber area. Gravity wtr system. Pinto Creek.

EMIGRANT GAP (94) N

Carr Lake   **FREE**
Tahoe National Forest
Pacific Gas & Electric
4.8 mi E of Emigrant Gap on I-80; 4.6 mi W on CA 20; 8.4 mi N on FR 18N18; 2.1 mi E on FR 18N16. Free. 6/15-9/30; 14-day limit. 20 tent sites. Tbls, toilets, cfga, no drkg wtr. Swimming, picnicking, fishing, boating (l). Elev 6700 ft; 2 acres. Lake. Hand-off boat launching site. PG&E expected to levy fees at this camp in 2007.

Grouse Ridge   **FREE**
Tahoe National Forest
4.8 mi E of Emigrant Gap on I-80; 4.6 mi W on CA 20; 6.4 mi N on FR 18N18; 4.6 mi NE on FR 18N14 (Grouse Ridge Rd); near Grouse Ridge Lookout. Free. 6/15-9/30; 14-day limit; closed in winter. 9 sites (RVs under 16 ft). Tbls, toilets, cfga, piped drkg wtr. Picnicking; fishing & swimming 1 mi. Elev 7400 ft; 3 acres. Many small lakes nearby in the Grouse Lakes area. Milk Lake and Sanford Lake, quarter mi.

Sterling Lake   **FREE**
Tahoe National Forest
8.3 mi E of Emigrant Gap on I-80; 6.1 mi NE on FR 17N16 (Fordyce Lake Rd). Free. 6/15-9/30; 14-day limit. 6 sites on 2 acres. Tbls, toilets, cfga, no drkg wtr. Swimming, picnicking, fishing, boating (l; hand-off boat launching). Elev 7000 ft.

ESSEX (96) S

Hole-in-the-Wall   **$12**
National Park Service
Mojave National Preserve
16 mi NW of Essex on Essex Rd; 12 mi N on Black Canyon Rd. $12. All year; 14-day limit. 35 RV/tent sites & 2 walk-in sites. Tbls, toilets, cfga, drkg wtr, dump. Scenic volcanic rock walls & formations. Iron rings set in rock for climb down to Wildhorse Canyon. Ramadas. Group camping area. New campground designed particularly for motor-homes. Free primitive camping allowed on disturbed areas adjacent to roads; backpackers may camp at any previously disturbed site. Elev 4400 ft.

Mid Hills Campground   **$12**
Mojave National Preserve
16 mi NW of Essex on Essex Rd; 19 mi N on Black Canyon Rd; 2 mi on unpaved Wild Horse Canyon Rd. $12. All year; 14-day limit. 26 sites. Tbls, toilets, cfga, drkg wtr. Hiking, sightseeing. Motorhomes longer than 26 ft might have trouble maneuvering. Free primitive camping allowed on disturbed areas adjacent to roads; backpackers may camp at any previously disturbed site. Elev 5600 ft.

Primitive Camping   **FREE**
Bureau of Land Management
Mojave National Preserve
16 mi NW of Essex on Essex Rd; 12 mi N

on Black Canyon Rd. Free primitive camping allowed on disturbed areas adjacent to roads; backpackers may camp at any previously disturbed sites. No facilities. Elev 4200 ft. Here are the primary roadside camping areas:

Kelso Dunes -- near the gate and end of the access road to the dunes (2-3 sites).

Rainy Day Mine Site -- 15.2 mi S of Baker on Kelbaker Rd; go qtr mi N of Kelbaker Rd on the road leading to the mine; 4x4 vehicles only; no RVs (3-4 sites).

Black Canyon Rd -- 5.2 mi S of Hole-in-the-Wall visitor center on E side of Black Canyon Rd (3-4 sites).

Powerline Site -- 11.8 mi N of Kelso on Kelbaker Rd, where powerlines cross the rd (2-3 sites).

Caruthers Canyon -- 5.5 mi W of Ivanpah Rd on New York's Mountains Rd; 1.5-2.7 mi N of New York's Mtns Rd to sites; no RVs (3-4 sites).

Sunrise Rock -- 10.4 mi S of I-15 on E side of Cima Rd; trailhead for Teutina Peak is nearby on opposite side of Cima Rd.

Providence Mountain   FREE
Bureau of Land Management
N 16 mi from I-40 interchange at Essex to Providence Mountains. Free. All year; 14-day limit. Dry camping permitted throughout area. Park no farther than 300 ft from rd. Limestone caves nearby ($), tours daily mid-Sept to mid-June. Nature trails, canyons, petroglyphs.

Travel tip: Providence ghost town is about 25 mi N of Essex on dirt rd, W of Needles; rock buildings left as reminders of silver mining town of 1880s.

Providence Mountain $12
State Recreation Area
17 mi NW of I-40 near Essex on Essex Rd (60 mi W of Needles). $12. All year; 15-day limit. 6 primitive sites; 32-ft RV limit. Tbls, cfga, toilets, no drkg wtr. Hiking, nature trail. Site of Mitchell Caverns, the only limestone cave in the state park system. 5,250 acres.

ETNA (97) N

Hotelling Campground   FREE
Klamath National Forest
43 mi W of Etna between FR 93 & South Fork of Salmon River. Free. All year; 14-day limit. 5 rustic sites with toilet, cfga, no drkg wtr. Trash service May-Oct. Good access to river. Elev 1760 ft.

Travel tip: City is gateway to the Salmon River country to the west and an entrance to the Marble Mountains Primitive Area.

Red Bank Campground   FREE
Klamath National Forest
33 mi W of Etna on Etna/Somes Bar Rd. Free. All year; 14-day limit. 5 rustic sites. Toilets, cfga, no drkg wtr. Trash service May-Oct. Near North Fork of Salmon River. 1760 elevation.

EUREKA (98) N

Baxter Environmental Camp $10
Humboldt Redwoods State Park
4 mi N of Burlington Campground on Avenue of the Giants; left on Mattole Rd for 6 mi, following signs for Honeydew; camp's gate on left side of Mattole Rd, marked with small sign; use lock combination provided at registration at Burlington. Park at 2nd lock gate, hike to campsites. $10 during 9/15-5/14; $12 peak season. 2 tent sites. Tbls, drkg wtr (must be treated), pit toilet, cfga, food locker. Showers at Albee Creek and Cuneo Creek Campgrounds (both within 1 mi). Hiking.

Hamilton Barn $10
Environmental Camp
Humboldt Redwoods State Park
Register at Burlington Campground. From Burlington, 4 mi N on Avenue of the Giants; left on Mattole Rd for 6 mi, following signs for Honeydew; camp's gate on right side of rd; open gate lock with combination provided at registration; drive 1 mi to parking area, walk 50-200 yds to sites. $10 during 9/16-5/14; $12 peak season. 3 tent sites. Toilets, cfga, drkg wtr (must be purified), cfga, food locker; showers at Albee Creek and Cuneo Creek Campgrounds (both within 1 mi). Hiking, poor fishing. Interpretive program at Albee Creek.

Trail Camps $3
Humboldt Redwoods State Park
S of Eureka on US 101. $3 per person. All year; 3-day limit. Johnson Trail Camp, 2.5 mi from Big Tree area; no drkg wtr, no open fires, no horses or dogs. Whiskey Flat Trail Camp, 4.5 mi from Big Tree area; 5 sites, toilet, no drkg wtr, no open fires, no dogs or horses. Hanson Ridge Trail Camp, 6.5 mi from Big Tree area; 5 sites, toilet, no drkg wtr, no open fires, no dogs or horses. Grasshopper Trail Camp, half mi from fire lookout; 5 sites, untreated drkg wtr at lookout July-Oct. Bull Creek Trail Camp, along Bull Creek, 14 mi from Grasshopper Rd; 5 sites, toilet, no drkg wtr, no open fires, no dogs or horses.

FALL RIVER MILLS (100) N

Cinder Cone   FREE
Wilderness Study Area
Bureau of Land Management
Plateau 6 mi SE of Fall River Mills off US 299. Free. May-October. 13 sites. Tbls, cfga, no drkg wtr. Hunting. Elev 3500 ft. Boil wtr before using. Very scenic area. Mountain biking, hiking, birdwatching, fishing.

Travel tip: Fort Crook Museum in Fall River Mills has extensive collection of Indian artifacts; pioneer history & genealogy files; picnic, barbecue facilities. Free.

Pit River Campground $8
Bureau of Land Management
5 mi W on US 299, then follow Campground Rd. On Pit River. Free. 5/1-12/1; 14-day limit.

10 sites. Tbls, bbq, toilets, cfga, no drkg wtr. Fishing, swimming, birdwatching, hiking, mountain biking. 40 mi N of Lassen Volcanic National Park. Elev 3000 ft; 10 acres. Please clean site before leaving. This campground is being updated and will become a fee site in 2007; 10 sites planned with elec, new tbls, cfga.

Fishing tip: The Pit River offers great trout fishing, with lots of rainbows available in the 20-inch range. Try silver-and-green or orange Hum Dingers.

Popcorn Cave Campground   FREE
Cinder Cone Wilderness Study Area
4 mi S of Fall River Mills on Cassel Rd; left for 7 mi on Cinder Cone Rd; no sign for campground. Free. All year; 14-day limit. Undeveloped primitive site is access to the wilderness study area, with its extensive lava flows and numerous caves. No facilities, no drkg wtr, no trash service. Campround gets few visitors. Hiking, cave exploring, hunting, birdwatching.

FONTANA (103) S

Applewhite $10
San Bernardino National Forest
N of Fontana on Sierra Ave to I-5; 9 mi N on Lytle Creek Rd. $10 (double site $15). All year; 14-day limit. 44 sites (30 ft RV limit). Tbls, flush toilets, cfga, drkg wtr. Fishing. Elev 3300 ft.

FOREST GLEN (104) N

Fern Camp   FREE
Shasta-Trinity National Forest
About 3 mi W of Forest Glen on SR 36; S on dirt FR 1S23 about 5 mi, past Pickett Peak Camp. Free. 6/1-11/1; 14-day limit. 2 tent sites. Toilet, cfga, no drkg wtr.

Forest Glen $6
Shasta-Trinity National Forest
Qtr mi W of Forest Glen on SR 36. $6. 5/20-11/1; 14-day limit. 15 sites (RVs under 16 ft); 2 picnic sites. Tbls, toilets, cfga, no drkg wtr. Fishing, swimming, hiking. Groceries. Near S fork of Trinity River. Elev 2300 ft.

Hells Gate $6
Shasta-Trinity National Forest
1 mi E of Forest Glen on FR 29N58. $6; free if wtr is shut off. 5/20-11/1; 14-day limit. 15 sites (RVs under 16 ft). Tbls, toilets, cfga, drkg wtr. Fishing, swimming, hiking, birdwatching. Groceries. 10 more sites for tents & RVs half mi beyond camp on dirt rd. South Ford National Recreation Trail. Elev 2300 ft; 4 acres. On S fork of Trinity River.

Pickett Peak Camp   FREE
Shasta-Trinity National Forest
About 3 mi W of Forest Glen on SR 36; S on dirt FR 1S23 about 3 mi. Free. 6/1-11/1; 14-day limit. 2 primitive tent sites. Toilet, cfga, no drkg wtr.

Scotts Flat   **FREE**
Shasta-Trinity National Forest
3 mi S of Forest Glen on FR 29N58. Free. MD-11/1; 14-day limit. 7 sites (20-ft RV limit). Tbls, toilets, cfga, no drkg wtr. Swimming, fishing, hiking. South Fork Trinity River National Recreation Trail.

FORESTHILL (105) N

Ahart   **$7**
Tahoe National Forest
36 mi E of Foresthill on Mosquito Ridge Rd, just past French Meadows Reservoir. $7 with federal Senior Pass; others pay $14. MD-LD; free rest of year when accessible; 14-day limit. 12 sites (22-ft RV limit). Tbls, toilets, cfga, no drkg wtr. On Middle Fork of American River. Fishing.

Parker Flat   **FREE**
Tahoe National Forest
15 mi NE of Foresthill on Sugar Pine Rd past Sugar Pines Campground, then left on dirt rd; at Sugar Pine Reservoir. Free. All year; 14-day limit. 7 sites primarily for OHV users, but okay for small RVs & tenters. Tbls, toilets, cfga, drkg wtr in summer. Fishing, hiking, boating.

Poppy   **FREE**
Tahoe National Forest
41.5 mi E of Foresthill on FR 96; half mi NW BY BOAT, then 1 mi NW by trail. Also trail access from McGuire Beach Parking Lot, 3.5 mi NE of Foresthill on FR 17N12; 1 mi SW by foot; on NW shore of French Meadows Reservoir. Free. MD-10/31; 14-day limit. 12 tent sites. Tbls, toilets, cfga, no drkg wtr. Swimming, picnicking, fishing, waterskiing. Elev 5300 ft; 4 acres.
Fishing tip: Try French Meadows Lake for rainbow trout, using live minnows or small spinners.

Robinson Flat   **FREE**
Tahoe National Forest
33 mi NE of Foresthill on CR K3125 (Mosquito Ridge Rd); narrow, winding mountain rd; not recommended for RVs. Free. MD-10/31; 14-day limit. 14 sites; 30-ft RV limit. Tbls, toilets, cfga, no drkg wtr (only nondrinkable spring wtr). Horseback riding, hiking, picnicking. Fishing, 2 mi. Elev 6800 ft; 5 acres. Nature trails. Little Duncan Creek 2 mi. Equestrian trails.

Secret House   **FREE**
Tahoe National Forest
18.7 mi NE of Foresthill on CR K3125 (Foresthill Divide Rd); narrow, winding mountain rd; not recommended for RVs. Free. MD-LD; 14-day limit. 2 tent sites; 1 acre. Tbls, toilets, cfga, piped drkg wtr. Nature trails. Elev 5400 ft. Hiking, picnicking, fishing (2 mi).

Sugar Pine   **FREE**
OHV Staging Area
Tahoe National Forest
8 mi N of Foresthill on Foresthill Rd; about 8 mi W on Sugar Pine Rd. Free. All year; 14-day limit. Open undesignated sites for RVs only; no tents. Tbls, toilets, cfga, drkg wtr. Staging area for off-highway vehicles. Boating(l), swimming, fishing, hiking. Dump nearby. Sugar Pine Trail open for both foot and bike traffic; a pleasnt 3.5-mil trail around lake, accessed from campground or boat ramp.

Talbot   **FREE**
Tahoe National Forest
28.5 mi E of Foresthill on FR 15N10 (Mosquito Ridge Rd); 1 0 mi NE on FR 15N08; 8.3 mi NE on FR 17N12; rough, narrow rd, not recommended for RVs. Free. 6/15-9/15; 14-day limit. 5 sites. Tbls, toilets, cfga, no drkg wtr. Horseback riding, swimming, picnicking, fishing, waterskiing, hiking, boating (d--3 mi). Elev 5600 ft; 6 acres. Nature trails, 1 mi. Stalls for parking horse trailers; hitching rails at trailhead. On middle fork of American River, 5 mi above French Meadows Reservoir.
Fishing tip: Try the American River for steelhead, chinook salmon & striped bass.

Upper Hell Hole   **FREE**
Eldorado National Forest
20 mi E of Foresthill on FR 96; 8.8 mi NE on FR 10; 8.8 mi E on FR 8; 13.5 mi SE on FR 2; 3 mi BY BOAT at E end of Hell Hole Reservoir. Also by trail. Free. 6/15-9/15. 15 tent sites. Tbls, toilets, no drkg wtr. Swimming, picnicking, fishing, boating (l--3 mi), sailing, waterskiing. Elev 4600 ft; 8 acres. Campfire permit required.
Fishing tip: Good brown trout fishing, particularly in early summer.

FORT BIDWELL (106) N

Fee Reservoir   **FREE**
Bureau of Land Management
Susanville District
7 mi E of Fort Bidwell. 5/1-11/1; 14-day limit. 10 sites. Tbls, toilets, cfga, no drkg wtr. Boating, fishing. Water service due for repair.

FORT BRAGG (107) N

Jackson   **FREE**
Demonstration State Forest
SR 20 between Willits and Fort Bragg. Free. All year. Rustic-type camping only; 20 scattered campgrounds ranging from one campsite to several. Tbls, pit toilets, cfga, trash pickup, no drkg wtr. Picnicking, hiking, horseback riding. Coastal fishing and recreation within 20 mi of most campsites. Sandy beach, tidal pools. Permit required. Magnificent view of ocean. Best weather, Sept-Oct. 50,200 acres.
Travel tip: Tour Georgia-Pacific Logging Museum and mill in Fort Bragg; museum contains historical exhibits on logging. Also see Mendocino Coast Botanical Gardens 2 mi S on SR 1; encompasses 17 acres of woods, meadows & gardens; paths lead from a nursery through the gardens, "Fern Canyon" and native forest to scenic ocean bluffs.

FORT JONES (108) N

Bridge Flat   **FREE**
Klamath National Forest
21.2 mi W of Fort Jones on CR 7F01. Free. May-Oct; 14-day limit. 4 sites (32-ft RV limit). Tbls, toilets, cfga, no drkg wtr or trash service. Swimming, boating, fishing, hiking, whitewater rafting. Primarily a backpacker camp for nearby Marble Mountain Wilderness. Scott River, Kelsey Trail. Elev 2000 ft.
Travel tip: Fort Jones Museum, in town, contains Indian & pioneer artifacts.

Hidden Horse   **$10**
Klamath National Forest
25 S of Fort Jones on Hwy 3; 11 mi on Callahan-Cecilville Rd turnoff. $10 during May-Oct; free rest of year, but no wtr or trash service. 6 sites. Tbls, toilets, cfga, drkg wtr, 4 corral stalls, horse mounting ramp. Horseback riding, hiking.

Indian Scotty   **$10**
Klamath National Forest
17.7 mi W of Fort Jones on CR 7F01; qtr mi SW on FR 44N45; on Scott River. Free 10/15-5/15; $10 rest of year; 14-day limit. 28 sites (RVs under 30 ft). Tbls, toilets, cfga, no drkg wtr during free period. Swimming, fishing, horseshoes. Elev 2400 ft; 18 acres. Popular.
Travel tip: Scott Bar ghost town is 26 mi NW of Fort Jones on gravel rd; many old buildings, some of which are still used by gold prospectors.

Mt. Ashland Campground   **FREE**
Klamath National Forest
Atop Mt. Ashland 1 mi W of Mt. Ashland Ski Resort, 10.5 mi off I-5. Free. May-Oct; 14-day limit. 9 sites. Tbls, toilets, cfga, no drkg wtr, no trash service.

Scott Mountain   **FREE**
Klamath National Forest
33 mi S of Fort Jones on Hwy 3. Free. All year; 14-day limit. 5 sites. Tbls, toilet, cfga, no drkg wtr, no trash service. Hiking. Pacific Crest Trail passes nearby, making this camp a nice resting place for hikers. Elev 3500 ft.

FRAZIER PARK (109) S

Chuchupate   **$5**
Los Padres National Forest
3 mi from the Chuchupate ranger station off Frazier Mountain Rd (FR 8N04). $5 daily or $30 annually. May-Oct; 14-day limit. 30 sites; 24-ft RV limit. Tbls, toilets, cfga, no drkg wtr. Hiking, hunting. Elev 6000 ft.

Chula Vista   **FREE**
Los Padres National Forest
17 mi W on CR FH95 to parking lot on Mt. Pinos; walk 500 ft. Free. All year; 14-day limit. 12 walk-in sites plus self-contained RVs in parking lot; 4 acres. Tbls, toilets, cfga, drkg wtr. Picnicking. Elev 8300 ft. No campfires in parking lot. Lots of star-gazing at this campground.

Dome Springs   **FREE**
Los Padres National Forest
3.4 mi W of Frazier Park on CR FG95; 18 mi SW of Frazier Park on CR N03 (Lockwood Valley Rd); 3 mi N on dirt FR 8N04 (which is 7 mi E of SR 33). Sandy access rd; 4WD may be needed. Free. All year; 14-day limit. 4 sites. Tbls, toilet, cfga, no drkg wtr. Hiking. Badland terrain.

Fishbowls Trail Camp   **$5**
Los Padres National Forest
SW of Frazier Park via Lake of the Woods, Lockwood Valley Rd (CR 9N03), Thorn Meadows Spur Rd (7N03C), Cedar Creek Rd to its end, then 1 mi up a ridge on Trail 22W10 and 2 mi on Fishbowls Trail (21W05). Easier hike is by Fishbowls Trail from Grade Valley paralleling Piru Creek. $5 daily or $30 annually. No facilities except 2 stoves, cfga, 2 tbls. Hiking, fishing. Elev 5200 ft.

Halfmoon   **$5**
Los Padres National Forest
3.4 mi W of Frazier Park on CR FG95; 20.4 mi SW on CR 9N03 (Lockwood Valley Rd); 8.8 mi SE on FR 7N03 (Grade Valley Mutau Rd) to its end. $5 daily or $30 annually. 5/1-11/30; 14-day limit. 10 sites on 10 acres (RVs under 22 ft). Tbls, cfga, firewood, no drkg wtr. Picnicking. Elev 4700 ft. Usually accessible by 2WD; not accessible in wet weather. Along Little Piru Creek.

McDonald Cabin Trail Camp   **$5**
Los Padres National Forest
S of Frazier Park via Lake of the Woods, FR 9N03 and FR 7N03, then E of Mutau Flat on the Little Mutau & Alder Creek (20W11) trails. $5 daily or $30 annually. Undesignated tent sites. All year; 14-day limit. 1 stove, cfga, no drkg wtr, no toilet. Fishing, hiking. Ruins of stone cabin.

McGill   **$12**
Los Padres National Forest
W of Frazier Park on Frazier Mountain & Cutty Valley Rd; left for 6 mi on Mt Pinos Rd. $12. 4/15-11/15; 14-day limit. 78 sites (30-ft RV limit). Tbls, toilets, cfga, no drkg wtr. Hiking, interpretive trail. Elev 7400 ft; 25 acres.

Mount Pinos   **$10**
Los Padres National Forest
W of Frazier Park on Frazier Mountain & Cutty Valley Rd; left for 6 mi on Mt. Pinos Rd. $10. 5/15-10/1; 14-day limit. 19 sites (26 ft RV limit). Tbls, toilets, cfga, drkg wtr. Elev 7800 ft. 12 acres. Adventure pass charged outside campground. Concession.

Pine Springs   **$5**
Los Padres National Forest
3.4 mi W of Frazier Park on CR FH95 (Frazier Mountain Park Rd); 10.4 mi SW on CR 9N03 (Lockwood Valley Rd); 2.8 mi S on FR 7N03 (Grade Valley Rd); 1 mi W on FR 7N03A; a limited area for RVs because of narrow dirt rd; not accessible during wet weather. $5 daily or $30 annually. 5/15-11/1; 14-day

limit. 12 sites on 10 acres (RVs under 22 ft). Tbls, toilets, cfga, no drkg wtr. Picnicking. Elev 5800 ft.

Pleito Creek   **FREE**
Los Padres National Forest
About 12 mi NW of Frazier Park via Frazier Rd, Lake of the Woods, FR 9N05, FR 9N22 and Pleito Canyon Rd (FR 21W01); access only by 4WD, foot, horse or motorcycle. Free. All year; 14-day limit. 3 sites. Tbls, toilets, cfga, no drkg wtr. Fishing, horseback riding. Elev 5000 ft.

Salt Creek   **FREE**
Los Padres National Forest
SW of Frazier Park via Lake of the Woods, Mt. Pinos Hwy, unimproved FR 9N22 and then hike or ride horse or motorcycle or 4WD on Salt Creek Trail 20W03. Free. May-Oct; 14-day limit. 2 tent sites. Toilet, tbl, cfga, no drkg wtr, 1 stove. Fishing, hiking. Elev 3000 ft. On designated 4WD trail.

Stone House Trail Camp   **$5**
Los Padres National Forest
3.4 mi W of Frazier Park on CR FG95; 20.4 mi SW on CR 9N03 (Lockwood Valley Rd); 8.8 mi SE on FR 7N03 (Grade Valley Mutau Rd) to Halfmoon Campground; about 2 mi NE on FR 7N13, then hike 1 mi by Trail 20W07 & half mi S on Trail 24W03. Or, hike in from N on Trail 20W07 from FR 8N12 just S of Lockwood Flat. $5 daily or $30 annually. 2 tent sites. No facilities, no drkg wtr except that purified from Mutau Creek. Hiking, fishing. Elev 4450 ft.

Thorn Meadows   **FREE**
Los Padres National Forest
From Frazier Park exit of I-5, W on Lockwood Valley Rd to Lake of the Woods, then 12 mi SW; left on FR 7N03 for 7 mi, to its end (4WD recommended; on Piru Creek. Free. 5/1 10/15; 14-day limit. 5 sites (16-ft RV limit). Tbls, toilets, cfga, no drkg wtr, corral. Fishing, hiking, horseback riding. Elev 5000 ft.

FREMONT (110) S

Sunol Regional Wilderness   **$12**
East Bay Regional Park District
From Fremont area, N on I-60 to Calaveras Rd exit; right on Calaveras Rd to Geary Rd, then to park. All year; 10-day limit. $12 (includes parking fee). 4 primitive tent sites. Tbls, toilets, cfga, drkg wtr. Hiking, horseback riding, nature programs. Make reservations in advance: 510-862-636-1684.

FRESNO (111) S

Camp 4   **FREE**
Sequoia National Forest
65 mi E of Fresno along Kings River via SR 180, Piedra Rd, Trimmer Springs RD (FR 11S12), and Davis Rd (FR 12S01); paved and dirt rd, not suitable for RVs. Free. 4/15-7/15; 14-day limit. 5 sites on 1 acre (RVs under 16

ft). Tbls, toilets, cfga, no drkg wtr. Swimming; picnicking; river fishing.

Fishing tip: Kings River is a wild trout fishery upstream from Pine Flat Reservoir to the confluence of its middle & south forks. Its primary fish is rainbow trout, although browns are also present, and trout size is among the best in California. Smallmouth and spotted bass also are present below Garnet Dam.

Camp 4 1/2   **FREE**
Sequoia National Forest
64 mi E of Fresno on Kings River via SR 180, Piedra Rd., Trimmer Springs Rd (FR 11S12), and Davis Rd (FR 12S01); paved and dirt rds. Free. 4/15-7/15; 14-day limit. 5 primitive sites (RVs under 16 ft). Tbls, toilets, cfga, no drkg wtr. Swimming, picnicking, fishing. Elev 1000 ft; 3 acres. Kings River. Wtr available at Camp 4 1/2 Guard Station.

Choinumni Park   **$11**
Fresno County Parks
On Piedra Rd near Pine Flat Lake dam. $11 ($5 for seniors). All year; 14-day limit. 75 sites. Tbls, flush toilets, cfga, drkg wtr, dump, playground. Fishing, boating.

Colonel Allensworth   **$10**
State Historic Park
About 60 mi S of Fresno on Hwy 99; at Earlimart, 8 mi W on Avenue 56; 2 mi S on Hwy 43. $10. All year; 15-day limit. 15 sites (30-ft RV limit) and 51-site overflow. Tbls, flush toilets, cfga, drkg wtr, showers, visitor center. Restored historic town.

Lost Lake Recreation Area   **$11**
Fresno County Park
19 mi N of Fresno below Friant Dam. $11 ($5 for seniors). All year; 14-day limit. 42 sites. Tbls, toilets, cfga, drkg wtr. Fishing, hiking, birdwatching, nature study, softball field, playground, beach ball facility. 70-Acre primitive nature study area; 38-acre lake.

Mill Flat   **FREE**
Sequoia National Forest
66 mi E of Fresno along Kings River via SR 180, Piedra Rd, Trimmer Springs Rd (FR 11S12), and Davis Rd (FR 12S01); paved and dirt rds. Free. 4/15-7/15; 14-day limit 5 tent sites. Tbls, toilets, cfga, no drkg wtr. Swimming, picnicking, fishing. Elev 1100 ft; 2 acres. Kings River.

Fishing tip: Very good bass & trout fishing in spring when water of Pine Flat Lake is high; cast 67-mi shoreline with jigs, crank baits & spinnerbaits for bass; use minnows & small spinners for trout.

Pine Flat Recreation Area   **$11**
Fresno County Park
37 mi E of Fresno on Belmont Ave/Trimmer Springs Rd; right on Pine Flat Rd for 3 mi. $11 ($5 for seniors). 55 sites (and 60 overflow sites). Tbls, flush toilets, cfga, drkg wtr, dump, showers, playground. Fishing, boating(rl), waterskiing. 1,120 acres.

FURNACE CREEK (113) S

Mesquite Spring $12
Death Valley National Park
NW of Furnace Creek on SR 190 to 5 mi S of Scotty's Castle. on Grapevine Rd. $12. All year; 30-day limit. 30 sites. Tbls, flush toilets, cfga, drkg wtr, dump.

Sunset $12
Death Valley National Park
In town near visitor center. $12. 10/1-4/1; 30-day limit. 1,000 sites (no RV size limit). Tbls, flush toilets, cfga, drkg wtr, dump. Nature programs, hiking. Visitor center nearby.

Texas Spring $7
Death Valley National Park
1.5 mi S of Furnace Creek visitor center. $7 with federal Senior Pass; others pay $14. 10/1-4/1; 30-day limit. 92 sites Tbls, toilets, cfga, drkg wtr, dump. Nature programs, hiking, exploring.

GARBERVILLE (114) N

Watts Lake Primitive Area FREE
Six Rivers National Forest
9.5 mi E of Garberville on CR 229 toward Zenia Guard Station, then 17.3 me E on CR 516 and 4 mi N on FR 2S08. Free. June-Oct; 30-day limit. Undesignated primitive camping area. Space for 2 tents, 3 small RVs. Toilet, no other facilities. Fishing, picnicking.

Travel tip: Take "Avenue of the Giants" tour; scenic bypass of US 101 splits off between Garberville & Phillipsville, follows Eel River. Redwood groves to visit include Rockefeller Forest & Children's Forest in Humboldt Redwoods State Park.

GASQUET (115) N

Baker Flat Primitive Area FREE
Six Rivers National Forest
6 mi N of US 199 on CR 316 and FR 18N17. Free. All year; 30-day limit Undesignated primitive camping area. No facilities. Hunting, hiking.

Big Flat $8
Six Rivers National Forest
Smith River National Recreation Area
8.2 mi SW of Gasquet on US 199; 17.2 mi SE on CR 427; qtr mi N on CR 405. (11 mi NE of Crescent City.) $8. MD-LD; 14 day limit. 28 sites on 8 acres (RVs under 23 ft). Tbls, toilets, cfga, firewood, no drkg wtr or trash service. Swimming, hunting, picnicking, fishing.

Grassy Flat $10
Six Rivers National Forest
Smith River National Recreation Area
4.5 mi E of Gasquet on US 199. $10. About MD-LD; 14-day limit. 19 sites; 30-ft RV limit. Tbls, toilets, cfga, drkg wtr. Fishing (Smith River), kayaking. 3 acres.

Mud Springs Primitive Area FREE
Six Rivers National Forest
1.5 mi S of Pigeon Roost on forest's Low Standard Rd. Free. All year; 30-day limit.FL Undesignated primitive camping area. No facilities. Hunting, hiking.

Muslatt Lake Primitive Area FREE
Six Rivers National Forest
3 air mi E of Big Flat Station on FR 15N36. Free. All year; 30-day limit. Undesignated primitive camping area. No facilities. Fishing, hunting, hiking.

Rattlesnake Lake Primitive FREE
Six Rivers National Forest
2.5 mi NE of Pigeon Roost on FR 18N07. Free. All year; 30-day limit. Undesignated primitive camping area. No facilities. Fishing, hunting, hiking.

Sanger Lake Primitive Area FREE
Six Rivers National Forest
E of US 199, between Sanger and Young's Peaks on FR 18N07. Free. All year; 30-day limit. Undesignated primitive camping area. No facilities. Fishing, hunting, hiking.

Soldiers Well Primitive Area FREE
Six Rivers National Forest
1.5 mi N of Pigeon Roost on forest's Low Standard Rd along Little Rattlesnake Mountain. Free. All year; 30-day limit. Undesignated prim camping area. No facilities. Hunting, hiking.

GEORGETOWN (116) N

Big Meadows $10
Eldorado National Forest
22 mi E of Georgetown on Wentworth Springs Rd; 27 mi NE on FR 2; camp is 1.5 mi NW of Hell Hole Reservoir. $10. 5/15-10/31; 14-day limit. 54 sites. Tbls, flush & pit toilets, cfga, drkg wtr. One handicap site. Fishing, swimming, boating, hiking, 4WD. Elev 5300 ft.

Dru Barner Park $8
Eldorado National Forest
22 mi E of Georgetown on Wentworth Springs Rd; left on gravel Bypass Rd for 1.5 mi. $8. All year; 14-day limit. 8 sites. Flush toilets, cfga, drkg wtr tbls. Primarily an equestrian camp. Bridle trail nearby. Biking. No motorcycles. Elev 3000 ft.

Hell Hole $10
Eldorado National Forest
22 mi E of Georgetown on Wentworth Springs Rd; 29 mi NE on FR 2; 1 mi NW of Hell Hole Reservoir. $10. All year; 14-day limit. 10 walk in tent sites. Tbls, toilets, cfga, drkg wtr. Fishing, hiking, swimming, boating. Elev 5200 ft.

Ponderosa Cove Overflow $8
Eldorado National Forest
18 mi E on CR 12N29. $8. 4/15-11/1; 14-day limit. 12 sites on 6 acres (RVs under 16 ft). Tbls, toilets, cfga, firewood, drkg wtr. Swimming, fishing, boating, picnicking. Elev 5000 ft. Overflow for Stumpy Meadows Camp.

Stumpy Meadows $8.50
Eldorado National Forest
17 mi E of Georgetown on Wentworth Springs Rd; at Stumpy Meadows Lake. $8.50 with federal Senior Pass; others pay $17. 4/15-11/1; 14-day limit. 40 sites. Tbls, toilets, cfga, drkg wtr. Boating(l), fishing, swimming. Elev 4400 ft. Dump near Ponderosa Cove Overflow camp.

GEYSERVILLE (117) N

Boat-in/Hike-in Camping $10
Lake Sonoma
Corps of Engineers
3 mi S of Geyserville off US 101, 13 mi NW of Healdsburg. $10 during 10/1-3/31; $14 rest of year ($7 with federal Senior Pass). All year; 14-day limit. Primitive shoreline camping at 15 campgrounds with 115 sites, plus 2 group sites. Access by boat or foot. Toilets, cfga, no tbls or drkg wtr. Campers must register at visitor center. Boating, fishing, waterskiing on 2,700-acre lake. State fish hatchery nearby. Boat launch fee.

GILROY (118) S

Coyote Lake $10
Santa Clara County Park
From Hwy 101 at Gilroy, 1.75 mi E on Leavesley Rd; 6 mi N on New Ave; right on Roop Rd, which becomes Gilroy Hot Springs Rd, for 3 mi, then left on Coyote Reservoir Rd. $10 for seniors (60 or older) Mon-Thurs at tent or car-camping sites; $9 car camping during 11/1-2/28; $18 all other car camping sites; $25 at RV sites. All year; 14-day limit. 74 sites. Tbls, flush toilets, cfga, drkg wtr, showers. Fishing, boating($), hiking. 635-acre lake.

Mt. Madonna $10
Santa Clara County Park
10 mi W of Gilroy on Hwy 152 (Hecker Pass Hwy). $10 for seniors Mon-Thurs at tent or car-camping sites; $9 car camping during 11/1-2/28; $18 all other car camping sites; $25 at RV sites. All year; 14-day limit. 100 sites at 4 campgrounds. Tbls, flush toilets, showers, cfga, drkg wtr. Hiking, horseback riding, fishing, archery, nature trails, visitor center. 3,219 acres.

GLENNVILLE (119) S

Alder Creek FREE
Sequoia National Forest
8 mi E of Glennville on SR 155; 3 mi S on FR 25S04 (Alder Creek Rd); paved and dirt rds. Free. 5/1-10/31; 14-day limit. 13 sites (20-ft

RV limit). Tbls, toilets, cfga, no drkg wtr. Fishing, picnicking. Elev 3900 ft; 5 acres. Alder Creek and Cedar Creek. No trash collection.

Cedar Creek   **FREE**
Sequoia National Forest
10 mi E of Glennville on SR 155 (paved rd); unsuitable for trailers. Free. All year; 14-day limit. 11 sites on 2 acres; unsuitable for trailers. Tbls, toilets, cfga, piped spring drkg wtr May-Oct. No trash pickup. Fishing, picnicking. Elev 4800 ft.

Frog Meadow   **FREE**
Sequoia National Forest
26 mi NE of Glennville via SR 155 and FR FH 90 (paved but narrow road). Free. 6/16-10/15; 14-day limit. 10 sites (RVs under 17 ft). Tbls, toilets, cfga, no drkg wtr. Picnicking; fishing (1 mi). Elev 7500 ft; 4 acres. Tobias Creek (1 mi). Used mostly as fall hunt camp.

Panorama   **$7.50**
Sequoia National Forest
21 mi NE of Glennville via SR 155 and FRs 23S16 and 23S15 (paved, narrow rd; not advisable for RVs). Within the Giant Sequoia National Monument. $7.50 with federal Senior Pass; others pay $15 (formerly free). All year; 14-day limit. 10 primitive tent sites. Tbls, toilets, cfga, no drkg wtr. Picnicking; fishing (4 mi). Elev 6800; 4 acres. Deep Creek and Capinero Creek (4 mi).

GORMAN (120) S

Buck Creek Camp   **$5**
Los Padres National Forest
.9 mi S on FR 8N01; 4.5 mi SE on FR 7N08; 1.8 mi SW on Trail 18W01. Located on Buck Creek Trail; 8 mi from Alamo Mountain, BY FOOT or HORSEBACK. $5 daily or $30 annually. 5/15-10/31; 14-day limit. 1 tent site. Tbls, cfga, no toilets/drkg wtr. Hiking, horseback riding, picnicking, fishing. Elev 4200 ft; 1 acre. Scenic. Stream. Popular. Rugged backcountry. Steep canyons, dense stands of Bigcone Douglas fir and rugged peaks viewed along trail.

Cottonwood OHV Campground   **$5**
Los Padres National Forest
About 25 mi SE of Gorman on FR 8N01; about 2 mi N on dirt FR 8N12 (Lockwood Creek Rd) to Sunset Camp; 3 mi N on rocky Lockwood OHV Trail (with challenging steep pitches); NW on Cottonwood Camp OHV spur. $5 daily or $30 annually. All year; 14-day limit. 1 streamside site. No facilities except cfga; no drinking wtr. Hiking, 4WD use, fishing.

Dutchman   **$5**
Los Padres National Forest
23 mi S from I-5 on Hungry Valley Rd & Alamo Rd (FR 7N01--rough dirt rd). $5 daily or $30 annually. 5/1-10/15; 14-day limit. 8 sites (16-ft RV limit). Tbls, toilets, cfga, no drkg wtr. Pack out trash. Elev 4800 ft.

Gold Hill   **$5**
Los Padres National Forest
10 mi Se of Gorman (about 6 mi from Hungry Valley SVRA) on FR 8N01 (Gold Hill Rd); next to Piru Creek. $5 daily or $30 annually. All year; 14-day limit. About 17 sites. Dispersed cfga, sometimes portable toilets, no other facilities, no tbls, no drkg wtr. Primarily used by motorcyclists. Elev 4000 ft. W of Hungry Valley State Vehicular Recreation Area.

Hardluck   **$5**
Los Padres National Forest
9 mi S of Gorman; 7 mi SE on SR 180; 6.5 mi SE on FH78; 4.5 mi NE on FR 14S11; along Piru Creek. $5 daily or $30 annually. All year; 14-day limit. 26 sites (32-ft RV limit). Tbls, toilets, cfga, no drkg wtr. Swimming, fishing. Hungry Valley State Vehicular Recreation Area nearby. Elev 2750 ft.

Hungry Valley   **$6**
State Vehicular Recreation Area
1 mi N of Gorman on Peace Valley Rd. $6 base plus $4 entry fee. All year; 15-day limit. 150 primitive sites on 2,000 acres. Tbls, toilets, cfga, no drkg wtr, shade ramadas. Off road vehicle area. Hiking. 19,000 acres.

Kings Camp   **$5**
Los Padres National Forest
8 mi SE of Gorman on FR 8N01; qtr mi S on FR 8N01A. $5 daily or $30 annually. 5/1-11/15; 14-day limit. 7 RV sites; 3 tent sites. Tbls, toilets, cfga, no drkg wtr. Swimming. Hungry Valley State Vehicular Recreation Area (4WD area) nearby. Elev 4200 ft.

Little Mutau Creek Trail Camp   **$5**
Los Padres National Forest
Follow directions to Twin Pines Campground below, then continue SE on Alamo Loop Rd & FR 8N01; hike SW on Trail 20W10 to E shore of Little Mutau Creek, then NW along creek on Trail 20W10 to camp. Or, drive from Frazier Park to Mutau Flat; hike 4 mi E on Trail 20W10 & Trail 20W01. $5 daily or $30 annually. All year; 14-day limit. 1 site. No facilities except cfga, 1 stove; purify wtr from seasonal creek.

Lockwood Flat 4WD Camp   **$5**
Los Padres National Forest
About 25 mi SE of Gorman on FR 8N01; about 2 mi N on 4WD dirt FR 8N12 (Lockwood Creek Rd) to Sunset Camp; 3 mi N on rocky Lockwood 4WD Trail (with challenging steep pitches) past Cottonwood Camp spur. $5 daily or $30 annually. All year; 14-day limit. 5 primitive sites in canyon-type camp. Dispersed cfga, no other facilities, no drkg wtr. Hiking, fishing, 4WD trails.

Los Alamos   **$12**
Angeles National Forest
8 mi S of Gorman on I-5; W at Smokey Bear Rd exit, follow signs. $12. All year; 14-day limit. 93 sites; some group sites; 26-ft RV limit. Tbls, flush toilets, cfga, drkg wtr, dump. Boating(l), fishing. Launch at Emigrant Landing. Elev 3600 ft.

Sunset 4WD Camp   **FREE**
Los Padres National Forest
About 25 mi SE of Gorman on FR 8N01; about 2 mi N on 4WD dirt FR 8N12 (Lockwood Creek Rd) to Sunset Camp. Free. All year; 14-day limit. 2 sites in canyon-type setting. Hiking, fishing, 4WD use. Elev 4300 ft.

Twin Pines   **$5**
Los Padres National Forest
13 mi SE of Gorman on FR 7N01 (Alamo Loop Rd) to Alamo Mtn. $5 daily or $30 annually. 5/1-11/15; 14-day limit. 5 tent sites. Tbls, toilets, cfga, no drkg wtr. Swimming. Elev 6600 ft.

GRAEAGLE (121) N

Lakes BasinCampground   **$7**
Lakes Basin Recreation Area
Plumas National Forest
8 mi S of Graegle on Gold Lake Rd off Hwy 89. $7 with federal Senior Pass; others pay $14. All year; 14-day limit. 23 sites. Tbls, toilets, cfga, drkg wtr. Fishing, boating, hunting, hiking, swimming. Elev 6300 ft. Closed in early 2007 due to road damage; June opening expected.

GRANT GROVE (122) S

Big Meadow   **FREE**
Sequoia National Forest
1.4 mi S of Grant Grove on SR 180; 6.5 mi SE on US FH78 (General's Hwy); 4.4 mi NE on FR 14S11 (Horse Corral Rd). Paved access rds. Free. 5/15-10/1; 14-day limit. 25 sites (RVs under 22 ft). Tbls, toilets, cfga, no drkg wtr. Wtr available at Big Meadow Guard Station, 1.5 mi W of campground. Fishing, picnicking; horseback riding/rental (4 mi). Elev 7600 ft; 15 acres. Big Meadow Creek. Public phone three-fourths mi.

Buck Rock   **FREE**
Sequoia National Forest
1.4 mi S of Grant Grove on SR 180; 6.5 mi SE on US FH78 (General's Hwy); 3.2 mi NE on FR 14S01 (Horse Corral Rd); .2 mi N on FR 13S04 (Buck Rock Rd). Paved and dirt rds. Free. 5/15-10/1; 14-day limit. 5 sites on 2 acres (RVs under 16 ft). Tbls, toilets, cfga, no drkg wtr. Wtr available, public phone at Big Meadow Guard Station, 1 mi E of campground. Picnicking, fishing. Elev 7600 ft.

Landslide   **$7.50**
Sequoia National Forest
6 mi NE of Grant Grove on SR 180; 7 mi S on Hume Rd (FR 13S09) past Hume Lake, then up Tenmile Rd, 1.5 mi past Tenmile Campground. $7.50 with federal Senior Pass; others pay $15. 5/15-10/1; 14-day limit. 9 sites (RVs under 16 ft). Tbls, toilets, cfga, nondrinkable spring wtr. Fishing, boating (lr-- 4 mi). Elev 5800 ft; 2 acres. Landslide Creek and Hume Lake (3 mi).
Fishing tip: Try nearby Hume Lake, where the state stocks catchable-size rainbow trout

each summer. The lake also contains brown trout and smallmouth bass.

Tenmile $7.50
Sequoia National Forest
Giant Sequoia National Monument
6 mi NE of Grant Grove on SR 180; 7 mi S on Hume Rd (FR 13S09), around Hume Lake and up Tenmile Rd. $7.50 with federal Senior Pass; others pay $15 (formerly free). May-Oct; 14-day limit. 13 sites (RVs under 22 ft). Tbls, toilets, cfga, drkg wtr. Picnicking; fishing; boating (rl--5 mi), hiking & biking in 2 sequoia groves. Elev 5800 ft; 5 acres. Scenic. Tenmile Creek and Hume Lake (4 mi).

Fishing tip: Rainbow trout are self-sustaining in lower parts of Tenmile Creek; upper portions contain both rainbow and eastern brook trout. The stream is primary pools and riffles.

Upper Stony Creek $7.50
Sequoia National Forest
Giant Sequoia National Monument
13 mi SE of Grant Grove on General's Hwy. $7.50 with federal Senior Pass; others pay $15. MD-LD; 14-day limit. 19 sites; 22-ft RV limit. Tbls, flush toilets, cfga, drkg wtr. Hiking, horseback riding, biking in Jennie Lakes Wilderness. Public phone half mi.

GREENFIELD (123) S

Escondido FREE
Los Padres National Forest
19 mi from US 101 in Greenfield ; 7 mi S on Indians Rd (winding, dirt). Free. 5/1-11/1; 14-day limit. 9 tent sites. Tbls, toilets, cfga, drkg wtr. Hiking, backpacking.

GROVELAND (124) S

Lost Claim $12
Stanislaus National Forest
12 mi E of Groveland on SR 120. $12. 5/15-9/15; 14-day limit. 10 sites (22-ft RV limit). Tbls, toilets, cfga, drkg wtr, cold showers. Elev 3100 ft; 5 acres. Trailers not recommended.

Lumsden FREE
Stanislaus National Forest
7.5 mi E of Groveland on SR 120; .9 mi N on CR 6210 (CR A36210, Ferretti Rd); 4.3 mi E on FR 1N10. Free. All year; 14-day limit. 10 sites; 22-ft RV limit. Tbls, toilets, cfga, no drkg wtr. Swimming, plcnicking, fishing, hiking. Elev 1500 ft; 4 acres. 5 mi of dirt rd (one lane); very steep, not advised for trailers or large motorhomes; use extreme caution. 12 mi from Groveland Ranger Station. On Tuolumne River.

Lumsden Bridge FREE
Stanislaus National Forest
7.5 mi E of Groveland on SR 120; .9 mi N on CR 6210 (CR A3610, Ferretti Rd); 5.5 mi E on FR 1N10. Free. 4/15-11/1; 14-day limit. 9 sites; 22-ft RV limit. Tbls, toilets, cfga,

no drkg wtr. Swimming, hiking, picnicking, fishing. Elev 1500 ft; 2 acres. 16 mi from Groveland Ranger station. 5 mi of one-lane dirt rd, very steep, not advisable for trailers or large motorhomes; use extreme caution. Tuolumne River. RV dump station at Naco West, S of Hwy 120, 19 mi E of Groveland; $5 use fee.

Moore Creek Group FREE
Stanislaus National Forest
10.5 mi E of Groveland on SR 120; 2 mi S on FR 2505. Free. All year; 14-day limit. 1 group site (RVs under 22 ft). Tbls, toilets, cfga. Picnicking, hiking; fishing/swimming (5 mi). Elev 2800 ft; 1 acre. Flat terrain. Moore Creek. One group site, 2S05, is on Moore Creek Rd S of Buck Meadows, capacity for 40 people. Reservations accepted through Groveland ranger office.

South Fork FREE
Stanislaus National Forest
7.5 mi E of Groveland on SR 120; .9 mi N on CR 6210 (CR A36210, Ferretti Rd); 4.6 mi E on FR 1N10. Free. 4/15-11/1; 14-day limit. 8 sites; 22-ft RV limit. Tbls, toilets, cfga, no drkg wtr. Hiking, swimming, picnicking, fishing. Elev 1500 ft; 2 acres. River; rafting. Lumsden Rd not suitable for large RVs.

The Pines $12
Stanislaus National Forest
9 mi E of Groveland on SR 120. $12. All year; 14-day limit. 12 sites for tents, small RVs; 22-ft RV limit. Tbls, toilets, cfga, drkg wtr. Elev 3200 ft.

HANFORD (127) S

Kings County Fairgrounds $12
From jct of Hwy 198 & 10th Ave at Hanford, half mi S on 10th Ave. $12 base. All year. Base fee for dry camping; $15 full hookups. 250 sites. Tbls, flush toilets, drkg wtr, showers, dump. About 2 mi from fair site.

HAPPY CAMP (128) N

Curly Jack $10
Klamath National Forest
On Curly Jack Rd at Happy Camp. $10 during 5/1-11/1; free rest of year; 14-day limit. 17 sites (30-ft RV limit). Tbls, toilets, cfga, drkg wtr (no wtr or trash service during free period). Fishing, swimming. Access to Klamath River.

Norcross Campground FREE
Klamath National Forest
16 mi S of Happy Camp on Elk Creek Rd. Free. All year; 14-day limit. 6 sites. Tbls, toilets, cfga, no drkg wtr (except for horses), no trash service. Hiking, horseback riding. Camp is staging area for various trails into Marble Mountain Wilderness. Elev 2400 ft.

Sulphur Springs FREE
Klamath National Forest
13.9 mi S on CR 7C001 (Elk Creek Rd); hike 50 yds. Free. 5/1-10/31; 14-day limit. 7 walk-in tent sites. Tbls, toilets, cfga, no drkg wtr. Swimming, picnicking, fishing, horseback riding. Elev 2400 ft; 4 acres. Elk Creek trailhead. Warm springs (75 degrees) along Elk Creek.

Fishing tip: Fall & winter, use salmon eggs & crankbaits to catch steelhead & salmon from the Klamath River nearby. During summer, catch rainbow trout from the Smith on flies.

West Branch $8
Klamath National Forest
7.7 mi N of Happy Camp on CR 7C01; 5.2 mi NW on CR 8C002; .3 mi NW on FR 40S07; 1.2 mi NW on FR 18N31. $8 during 5/1-10/31; free rest of year; 14-day limit. 15 sites on 15 acres (RVs under 22 ft). Tbls, toilets, no drkg wtr. Picnicking; swimming/fishing (1 mi). Near Indian Creek. Elev 2200 ft. No trash service. Quiet, secluded.

HAYFORK (129) N

Cold Springs Camp FREE
Shasta-Trinity National Forest
8 mi S of Hayfork on SR 3; About 2 mi W on CR 353. Free. MD-11/1; 14-day limit. 2 primitive tent sites, cfga; no facilities, no drkg wtr.

Philpot FREE
Shasta-Trinity National Forest
8 mi S of Hayfork on SR 3; half mi W on CR 353; .3 mi N on FR rd. Also, 1 mi W of Peanut off SR 3. Free. 5/20-10/15; 14-day limit. 6 tent sites on 2 acres. Tbls, toilets, cfga, firewood, piped drkg wtr. Picnicking, stream fishing, hiking (interpretive trail).

Shiell Gulch FREE
Shasta-Trinity National Forest
3 mi E of Hayfork on SR 3; 7 mi S on CR 302. Free. 7/1-10/15; 14-day limit. 5 tent sites Tbls, toilets, cfga, no drkg wtr. Fishing, hiking.

HEALDSBURG

Liberty Glen Campground $8
Lake Sonoma
Corps of Engineers
From US 101 near Healdsburg, W on Dry Creek Rd 15 mi, following signs. $8 with federal Senior Pass; others pay $16. All year; 14-day limit. 97 sites; 46-ft RV limit. Tbls, toilets, cfga. Wtr system being repaired, so no drkg wtr, showers, dump until completed. Biking, hiking, ranger programs, horseback riding, playground. No lake shoreline at camp.

HELENA (130) N

Hobo Gulch   **FREE**
Shasta-Trinity National Forest
20 mi N of Helena on CR 421 and FR 34N07 (Hobo Gulch Rd). Free. All year; 14-day limit. 10 sites; 16-ft RV limit. Tbls, toilets, cfga, no drkg wtr. Swimming, picnicking, fishing, hiking, horseback riding (corral). Elev 2900 ft; 5 acres. Not advisable for RVs. Adjoins primitive area. Trinity River. Self-service facility.
Fishing tip: Fish the North Fork of the Trinity River in fall and early winter for steelhead, coho & chinook.
Travel tip: Silverado Museum in Helena contains memorabilia of author Robert Louis Stevenson, including first editions, original manuscripts & photos. Free.

HIGH SIERRA (132) S

Ward Lake   **$6.50**
Sierra National Forest
1.5 mi SW of High Sierra on FR 5S80; 2.1 mi SE on FR 7S01 (5 mi S of Mono Hot Springs). $6.50 with federal Senior Pass; others pay $13. 6/1-10/31; 14-day limit. 17 sites; 40-ft RV limit. Tbls, toilets, cfga, no drkg wtr. Swimming, fishing. Elev 7400 ft; 3 acres. Scenic. Large RVs should not use Kaiser Pass Rd.

HOLLISTER (133) S

Bolado Park   **$5**
San Benito County Fairgrounds
From Hwy 1, S of Morgan Hill & N of Salinas, take Hwy 25 E about 10 mi to Hollister, then S on Hwy 25 about 8 mi. $5 tents; $15 RVs. All year. Tbls, toilets, cfga, drkg wtr.

Clear Creek   **FREE**
Management Area
Bureau of Land Management
35 mi S of Hollister on Hwy 25, past Pinnacles National Monument; left onto Coalinga-Los Gatos Creek CR to mgt area turnoff. Free. All year; 14-day limit. Free dispersed camping everywhere except San Benito Mtn Natural Area. Six staging areas have pit toilets and trash dumpsters. Beware of natural asbestos in soil and water. Hiking, biking, rockhounding, goldpanning, OHV activity. Area contains about 150 semi-precious minerals and gemstones, including serpentine, jadite, cinnabar, tremolite, topazite and benitoite.

Hollister Hills   **$6**
State Vehicular Recreation Area
6 mi S of Hollister on Cienega Rd. $6 plus $4 entry fee. All year; 14-day limit. 125 primitive sites. Tbls, flush toilets, cfga, drkg wtr. Off-road vehicle area; motorcycle & 4WD trails. 6,627 acres.

Oak Flat Campground   **FREE**
Clear Creek Management Area
Bureau of Land Management
From Hwy 25 S of Hollister, 14 mi E on Coal-inga-Los Gatos Creek CR; left across San Benito River to camp. Free. All year; 14-day limit. 100 primitive sites. Toilets, cfgq, no tbls, no drkg wtr. Hiking, biking, rockhounding. Beware of natural asbestos in soil and wtr.

HOLTVILLE (134) S

Heber Dunes   **FREE**
State Vehicular Recreation Area
I-8, S on Orchard Rd, W on King Rd, half mi E on Heber Rd. Free. All year; 3-day limit. 75 sites; 340 acres. Drkg wtr, flush toilets, cfga, tbls. Fishing.

Walker Park   **FREE**
Imperial County park
W edge of Holtville on SR 115 off I-80. Free. All year; 3-day limit. 50 sites on 5 acres; pull-through spaces. Tbls, toilets, cfga, drkg wtr. Picnicking, fishing. Golf nearby.

HOPLAND (135) N

Sheldon Creek   **FREE**
Cow Mountain Recreation Area
Bureau of Land Management
Off US 101, 12 mi E of Hopland on Highland Springs Rd. Free. All year; 14-day limit. 6 tent sites. Tbls, toilets, cfga, drkg wtr. Hunting, hiking, picnicking, horseback riding, hunting. Elev 2500 ft. Mountainous terrain. Trails. Small pets.
Travel tip: Take a day off for touring local wineries & tasting samples. Tours offered at Bel Arbes Winery, Fetzer Vineyards, McDowell Valley Vineyards & Milano Winery.

HORNBROOK (136) N

Juniper Point Camp   **FREE**
Pacific Gas & Electric Company
11 mi E of Hornbrook on co rd (Hornbrook is 12 mi N of Yreka on I-5). Free. May-Oct. 9 sites. Toilets. Swimming. Klamath River. Half mi from Mirror Cove Camp.
Fishing tip: Fall & winter, use salmon eggs & crankbaits to catch steelhead & salmon from the Klamath River. During summer, catch rainbow trout from the Smith on flies.
Travel tip: Visit the Siskiyou County Museum in Yreka. Also, the courthouse there contains a highly valued gold display from local diggings.

Mirror Cove Camp   **FREE**
Pacific Gas & Electric Company
11 mi E of Hornbrook on co rd (Hornbrook is 12 mi N of Yreka on I-5). Free. May-Oct. 10 sites. Toilets. Swimming; boating (l). Half mi from Juniper Point.
Fishing tip: Fall & winter, use salmon eggs & crankbaits to catch steelhead & salmon from the Klamath River. During summer, catch rainbow trout from the Smith on flies.

HORSE CREEK (137) N

Sarah Totten   **$10**
Klamath National Forest
6 mi SW of Horse Creek on SR 96 (qtr mi E of Hamburg). $10. All year; 14-day limit; free during 11/15-6/1. 8 sites (22-ft RV limit). Tbls, toilets, cfga, drkg wtr (no wtr or trash service during free period). Group site by reservation. On Klamath River. Fishing, picnicking. 5 acres.

HYAMPOM (138) N

Big Slide   **FREE**
Shasta-Trinity National Forest
5 mi N of Hyampom on CR 311 (Lower South Fork Rd). Free. MD-10/15; 14-day limit. 8 sites; 16-ft RV limit. Tbls, toilets, cfga, no drkg wtr. Swimming, fishing, hiking. On South Fork of Trinity River. Elev 1200 ft.
Fishing tip: Great salmon fishing in Trinity River here during Sept & early Oct; then steelhead from mid-Oct through Nov.

Slide Creek   **FREE**
Shasta-Trinity National Forest
About 6 mi N of Hyampon on CR 311 (Lowre South Ford Rd), past Big Slide Campground. Free. All year; 14-day limit. 5 primitive sites. Toilets, cfga, no drkg wtr. Fishing, hiking.

Underwood Camp   **FREE**
Primitive Area
Six Rivers National Forest
Remote camping & fishing area adjacent to Underwood Creek & its confluence with the South Fork of Trinity River. Access over single-lane rd from Underwood co rd near Hyampom. Free. All year; 30-day limit. Undesignated primitive camping area. No facilities. Fishing, hunting.
Fishing tip: Try fall fishing for steelhead, chinook & coho on the Trinity River.

IDYLLWILD (139) S

Boulder Basin   **$10**
San Bernardino National Forest
9 mi N of Idyllwild on Hwy 243; 6 mi E on FR 4S01 (Black Mountain Rd). $10. 5/15-11/15; 14-day limit. 34 sites (22-ft RV limit). Tbls, toilets, cfga, drkg wtr. Hiking trails. Elev 7300 ft.

Dark Canyon   **$12**
San Bernardino National Forest
8 mi N of Idyllwild on Hwy 243; 3 mi on FR 4S02 (Stone Creek Campground Rd). $12. 4/15-10/15; 14-day limit. 17 sites (22-ft RV limit). Tbls, toilets, cfga, drkg wtr. Hiking trails, fishing (San Jacinto River and Dark Canyon Creek).

Fern Basin   **$10**
San Bernardino National Forest
8 mi N of Idyllwild on Hwy 243; 1 mi on FR 4S02 past Stone Creek Campground. $10. 5/15-10/15; 14-day limit. 22 sites (15-ft RV

limit). Tbls, toilets, cfga, drkg wtr. Hiking trails. Elev 5300 ft. Minimum 3-day stay on holiday weekends.

Marion Mountain $10
San Bernardino National Forest
8 mi N of Idyllwild on Hwy 243; 2 mi on FR 4S02 past Stone Creek Campground & Fern Basin Camp. $10. 5/15-10/15; 14-day limit. 24 sites (15-ft RV limit). Tbls, toilets, cfga, drkg wtr. Hiking trails. Elev 6600 ft.

Stone Creek Campground $11
Mount San Jacinto State Park
6 mi N of Idyllwild on Hwy 243. $11 during 9/16-5/14; $15 rest of year. All year; 15-day limit. 50 primitive sites (24-ft RV limit). Tbls, toilets, cfga, rkg wtr. Fishing, nature trails, hiking.

INDEPENDENCE (141) S

Independence Creek $10
Inyo County Campground
Half mi W on Market St in Independence, via US 395. $10. All year; 14-day limit. 25 sites (no RV size limit). Tbls, pit toilets, cfga, drkg wtr. Wheelchair access. Fishing. Elev 3900 ft; 10 acres.
Fishing tip: Independence Creek is stocked with rainbow and brown trout. They are planted from the campground to above Seven Pines Village.

Lower Gray's Meadow $6.50
Inyo National Forest
5 mi W of Independence on CR 13S02 (Onion Valley Rd). $6.50 with federal Senior Pass; others pay $13. About 3/15-10/15; 14-day limit. 52 sites; 32-ft RV limit. Tbls, flush toilets, cfga, drkg wtr. Fishing, swimming. Elev 6000 ft. 15 acres.
Fishing tip: Indepence Creek is regularly stocked with trout.

Oak Creek FREE
Inyo National Forest
1.5 mi NW of Independence on US 395; 2.5 mi W on CR 13S04 (North Oak Creek Dr). Free. All year; 14-day limit. 22 sites; 36-ft RV limit. Tbls, flush toilets, cfga, no drkg wtr. Hiking, fishing (poor fishing). Elev 5000 ft. 10 acres. Upper campsites secluded; rd not passable by RVs.

Onion Valley $6.50
Inyo National Forest
13 mi W of Independence on CR 13S02 (Onion Valley Rd). $6.50 with federal Senior Pass; others pay $13. About 6/5-10/1; 14-day limit. 29 sites; 28-ft RV limit. Tbls, flush toilets, cfga, drkg wtr. Fishing, hiking. Elev 9200 ft. 8 acres.

Symmes Creek FREE
Bureau of Land Management
5 mi W via Onion Valley Rd, 1.5 mi S on Foothill Rd. Free. 5/1-11/1; 14-day limit. 55 sites on 40 acres. Tbls, cfga, toilets, no drkg wtr.

Picnicking, fishing. Elev 5185 ft.
Fishing tip: Symmes Creek is well stocked with trout. Campground has very good access.
Travel tips: Eastern California Museum in town; large collection of western Ameri-cana & Indian artifacts. Or, tour Mount Whitney State Fish Hatchery, 4 mi W of Independence on US 395; considered state's most beautiful hatchery.

Tinnemaha $10
Inyo County Campground
19.5 mi N of Independence on US 395; half mi W on Fish Spring Rd; 2 mi N on Tinnemaha Rd. $10. All year; 14-day limit. 47 sites (no RV size limit). Tbls, toilets, cfga, no drkg wtr. Elev 4400 ft; 10 acres.
Fishing tip: Rainbow and brown trout are planted regularly in Tinnemaha Creek near the campground.

INDIO (142) S

Pinyon Flat $8
San Bernardino National Forest
About 10 mi W of Indio on SR 111 to Palm Desert; 14 mi SW of Palm Desert on SR 74, crossing Santa Rosa Indian Reservation. $8. All year; 14-day limit. 18 sites (15-ft RV limit). Tbls, toilets, cfga, drkg wtr. Wheelchair access. Hiking. Nearby Santa Rosa Wilderness contains bighorn sheep.

INYOKERN (143) S

Chimney Creek FREE
Bureau of Land Management
15 mi N of Inyokern on US 395; 13 mi W on CR 152 (Nine Mile Canyon-Kennedy Meadow Rd). Free; donations accepted. All year; 14-day limit; may be inaccessible in winter. 36 sites on 40 acres (25-ft RV limit). Tbls, no drkg wtr, cfga; limited facilities in winter. Elev 5700 ft. Pack out trash. Pacific Crest Trail 2 mi. Horses & pets welcome. Host Apr-Sept.

Fish Creek $7
Sequoia National Forest
15 mi N of Inyokern on US 395; 23.6 mi NW on CR 152; 8.6 mi NW on FR 21S02 (paved and dirt rd sometimes steep). $7. Open June-Nov; 14-day limit. 40 sites (12 for RVs up to 27 ft). Tbls, toilets, cfga, firewood, piped spring drkg wtr, no trash service. Horseback riding; picnicking; fishing (in season with barbless flies only). Elev 7400 ft; 2 acres. Fish Creek. Supplies at Kennedy Meadows and Troy Meadows.

Fossil Falls Campground $6
Bureau of Land Management
About 50 mi N of Inyokern on E side of US 395; use Cinder Rd exit; in Mojave Desert at foot of eastern Sierra Nevada. $6. All year; 14-day limit. 12 sites. Tbls, toilets, cfga, no drkg wtr, no trash service. Hiking, exhibits, rockhounding. Hike to 40-ft waterfall, best viewed late fall, winter, early spring.

Kennedy Meadows $10
Sequoia National Forest
15 mi N of Inyokern on US 395; 23.6 mi NW on CR 152; 2.2 mi N on CR 152; .4 mi N on FR 22S11 (paved and dirt rd sometimes steep). $10. All year; 14-day limit. 38 sites (RVs under 31 ft). Tbls, toilets, cfga, firewood, piped spring drkg wtr available 5/15-9/30. Swimming, picnicking, fishing. Elev 6100 ft; 15 acres. S fork Kern River. No trash pickup.
Fishing tip: Native California golden trout have been reestablished in this area of the river. Brown trout are stocked each summer, and hybrid rainbow-golden trou are also found. Fishing is allowed within the Golden Trout Wilderness between the last Saturday in April and Nov. 15, using only artificial lures with barbless hooks.

Long Valley FREE
Bureau of Land Management
15 mi N of Inyokern on US 395; 26 mi NW on CR 152 (Nine Mile Canyon Rd). Free; donations accepted. All year; 14-day limit; may be inaccessible in winter. 13 sites on 15 acres. Toilets, tbls, cfga, no drkg wtr. Limited facilities in winter. Fishing, hiking, horseback riding/rental. Elev 9000 ft. Nature trails. Long Valley Creek. Located in Lamont Meadows-Long Valley Recreation Area. Small pets. Pack out trash.Trailhead for 3-mile trail down South Fork of Kern River. Elev 5200 ft.

Short Canyon FREE
Bureau of Land Management
NW of Inyokern on US 395 to Leliter Rd exit (1 mi past SR 14 jct); on W side of hwy, follow Short Canyon signs, taking graded dirt rd W to Powerline Rd, then half mi S to jct with BLM Route SE138; follow that graded rd to Short Canyon parking lot & trailhead. Free dispersed primitive camping; no facilities, no drkg wtr, no trash service. Hiking, horseback riding, birdwatching, photography. Spectacular wildflower displays in spring -- bright yellow coreopsis, orange California poppies, white buckwheats, purple gilias, blue phacelias.

Spangler Hills FREE
Off-Highway Use Area
Bureau of Land Management
E of Inyokern on SR 178 into Ridgecrest, then S on College Heights Blvd to OHV's N boundary. Free. All year; 14-day limit. Primitive undesignated sites on 57,000-acre public area designated for OHV activities. No facilities; no drkg wtr. Hiking, horseback riding. Area is home to protected desert tortoise. Most popular OHV staging area is E of Trona-Red Mountain Rd on BLM Rt RM143; large camping area available there.

Troy Meadow $10
Sequoia National Forest
15 mi N on Inyokern on US 395; 23.6 mi NW on CR 152; 9.9 mi NW on FR 21S02 (paved and dirt rd sometimes steep). $10. 6/1-11/15; 14-day limit. 73 sites (60-ft RV limit). Tbls, toi-

lets, cfga, firewood, piped drkg wtr available 5/15-9/30. Picnicking; fishing (in season with barbless flies only); horseback riding (1 mi). Elev 7800 ft; 15 acres. Stream. Fish Creek (2 mi). No trash pickup. Closed during 2006 for reconstruction; sites upgraded for RVs up to 60 ft; to open in summer of 2007.

JACKSON (144) N

Middle Fork Consumnes   **FREE**
Eldorado National Forest
28 mi E of Jackson on Hwy 88; 10 mi N on Cat Creek Rd. Free. 5/1-11/15; 14-day limit. 11 primitive sites. Toilets, cfga, no drkg wtr. Swimming, fishing. Elev 5600 ft.

Pardoes Point   **$9.50**
Eldorado National Forest
40 mi E of Jackson on Hwy 88; right on Bear River Reservoir Rd for 5 mi; on SE shore of Lower Bear River Reservoir. $9.50 with federal Senior Pass; others pay $19. 6/1-10/30; 14-day limit. 10 sites. Tbls, toilets, cfga, drkg wtr. Fishing, boating(l), picnicking 4WD.

Sugar Pine Point   **$10**
Eldorado National Forest
40 mi E of Jackson on Hwy 88; right on Bear River Reservoir Rd for 2.5 mi to Y, then left 3 mi on unpaved access rd; on N shore of Lower Bear River Reservoir. $10. All year; 14-day limit. 10 sites; 50-ft RV limit. Tbls, toilets, cfga, no drkg wtr. Fishing, boating, picnicking, swimming, 4WD. Elev 6000 ft.

JULIAN (148) S

Bow Willow   **$7**
Anza-Borrego Desert State Park
12 mi E of Julian on SR 78; 31 mi S on CR S2. $7 during 9/16-5/14; $9 peak season. All year; 15-day limit. 16 primitive sites. Tbls, toilets, cfga, limited drkg wtr, shade ramadas. Hiking to Bow Willow & Rockhouse Canyons. Carrizo Badlands nearby.

Mountain Spring Canyon   **$5**
Anzo-Borrego Desert State Park
12 mi E of Julian on SR 78; about 28 mi S on CR S2, just N of Bow Willow. $5. All year; 15-day limit. Primitive undesignated sites with tbls, toilets, cfga, no drkg wtr. Hiking, rockhounding.

JUNCTION CITY (149) N

Junction City   **$10**
Bureau of Land Management
Shasta-Trinity National Forest
1.5 mi W of Junction City on Hwy 299; on Trinity River. $10 during 5/1-11/1; $4 rest of yr, but no wtr; 14-day limit. 21 sites (22-ft RV limit). Tbls, toilets, cfga, drkg wtr. Fishing. Elev 1500 ft. May be free in 2007.

Ripstein   **FREE**
Shasta-Trinity National Forest
14.8 mi N of Junction City on CR P401 (Canyon Creek Rd). Free. 7/1-10/1; 14-day limit.

10 sites; 22-ft RV limit. Tbls, toilets, cfga, no drkg wtr. Hiking, picnicking, fishing. Elev 3000 ft; 5 acres. Canyon Creek. Trailhead of Salmon-Trinity Alps Primitive Area (2 mi). Self-service facility.
Fishing tip: Try the trout in Canyon Creek, but keep in mind they're small.

JUNE LAKE (150) N

Aerie Crag   **$8**
Inyo National Forest
5.9 mi W of June Lake on SR 158; right at RV Campground sign; on ridge above Rush Creek; RV camping only. $8. About 4/15-10/31; 3-day limit. 10 RV sites. Tbls, flush toilets, cfga, no drkg wtr. Dump stations at Mobile station in June Lake ($5) and nearby Fern Creek Lodge (free).

Big Springs   **FREE**
Inyo National Forest
11.5 mi SE of June Lake off US 395; 7 mi S on SR 158 (June Lake Loop Rd); 1.5 mi NE on Owens River Rd; bear left at fork for qtr mi. Free. 5/1-11/1; 21-day limit. 26 sites (RVs under 45 ft). Tbls, toilets, cfga, firewood, no drkg wtr. Picnicking, hiking. Elev 7300 ft; 4 acres. Deadman Creek.

Deadman   **FREE**
Inyo National Forest
2.4 mi NE of June Lake on SR 158; 6.5 mi SE on SR 395; 3 mi SW on FR 2S05. Free. 6/1-10/15; 14-day limit. 30 RV sites (RVs under 45 ft). Tbls, toilets, cfga, no drkg wtr. Picnicking, fishing. Elev 7800 ft; 8 acres. Stream.
Fishing tip: Rainbow and brown trout are planted in Deadman Creek at the campground.

Glass Creek   **FREE**
Inyo National Forest
2.4 mi NE of June Lake on SR 158 (June Lake Loop Rd); 6 mi SE on US 395; .2 mi W on FR 2S24. Free. 5/15-11/1; 21-day limit. 50 sites (RVs under 40 ft). Tbls, toilets, cfga, no drkg wtr. Hiking, picnicking, fishing. Elev 7600 ft; 15 acres. Glass Creek. Store available.
Fishing tip: The state plants brown and rainbow trout in Glass Creek at the campground.

Hartley Springs   **FREE**
Inyo National Forest
2 mi NE of June Lake on SR 158; 2 mi SE on US 395; 1.5 mi S on FR 2S78. Free. 6/1-9/30; 14-day limit. 20 sites on 18 acres (RVs under 40 ft). Tbls, toilets, cfga, no drkg wtr. Picnicking. Elev 8400 ft. Store.

KERNVILLE (151) S

Brush Creek   **FREE**
Sequoia National Forest
20 mi N of Kernville on CR PM99 (Sierra Hwy--along Kern River). Paved rd. Free. All year; 1-day limit. Undeveloped sites (RVs under 22 ft). Toilets, cfga, firewood, no tbls, no drkg wtr. Fishing (in Brush Creek using

only barbless flies). Elev 3800 ft; 3 acres. Brush Creek. Campfire permit required. Well suited for self-contained RVs. Supplies at Roads End and Fairview. Commercial rafting May-Oct. Firewood from local businesses.
Fishing tip: Try Brush Creek's steelhead & salmon in the winter.

Camp 9   **$10**
Sequoia National Forest
5 mi S of Kernville on Sierra Way Rd (SR 99); on E shore of Lake Isabella. $10. All year; 14-day limit. 109 primitive sites; no RV size limit. Tbls, flush toilets, cfga, drkg wtr, dump ($7). Fish cleaning area. Boating(l), fishing.
Fishing tip: For bass, try jigs & plastic lures and nightcrawlers near points and structure. Crawdads are always good if you can get them. Best areas are Orrick, Boulder Gulch, Brown's Cove, Tammy's Landing area and the flats of North Fork.

Corral Creek   **FREE**
Sequoia National Forest
8.9 mi N of Kernville on CR PM99; along the Kern River. Free. All year; 14-day limit. Undeveloped sites (RVs under 22 ft); suited for self-contained RVs. Tbls, toilets, cfga, firewood, no drkg wtr. Picnicking, swimming, fishing. Elev 3000 ft; 5 acres. Raft rental on Kern River, May-Oct. Firewood available from local businesses. Campfire permit required.
Travel tip: Kern Valley Museum in town displays local native Indian artifacts, history of gold mining, lumbering, ranching in valley.
Fishing tip: The Kern River is stocked with rainbow trout near the campgrounds every week during the summer. Use Power Bait, salmon eggs, worms. Spin fishermen, try Panter Martin, Super Duper, Blue Fox, Mepps and Rooster Tails. Hottest spots seem to be at Road's End, Fairview, Johnsondale bridge, Riverside Park.

Horse Meadow   **$10**
Sequoia National Forest
20 mi N of Kernville on Sierra Way; right on Sherman Pass Rd for 6.5 mi; right for 4 mi at sign for Horse Meadow; follow signs 3 mi on dirt rd. $10. 6/1-11/1; 14-day limit. 41 sites (22-ft RV limit). Tbls, toilets, cfga, drkg wtr, no trash service. Horseback riding, hiking, fishing.
Fishing tip: Try nearby Salmon Creek, which is not heavily fished due to its poor access. It contains California golden trout, which were introduced there nearly 100 years ago and are now self-sustaining. Brown trout also are present. Access from FR 22S15 to the Salmon Creek Trail (33E36)

Limestone   **$7.50**
Sequoia National Forest
19 mi NW of Kernville on Sierra Way Rd. $7.50 with federal Senior Pass; others pay $15. 4/1-11/30; 14-day limit. 22 sites (30-ft RV limit). Tbls, toilets, cfga, no drkg wtr. Fishing, hiking. Along the Kern River. Elev 3800 ft.

Fishing tip: This section of the Kern River has a good population of stocked brown and rainbow trout as well as native rainbows. Nearby Brush Creek contains self-sustaining rainbows, accessible via a dirt road off Sherman Pass Rd (FR 22S05).

KING CITY (152) S

Memorial Campground   FREE
Los Padres National Forest
From US 101 in King City, 18 mi S on CR G14; 6 mi N on Mission Rd; left for 16 mi on CR 4050 (Del Venturi-Milpitas Rd). Free. All year; 14-day limit. 8 tent sites. Tbls, toilets, cfga, no drkg wtr. Hiking.

KLAMATH RIVER (154) N

Beaver Creek   FREE
Klamath National Forest
Half mi E of Klamath River on SR 96; 5 mi N on FR 48N01 (Beaver Creek Rd). Free. May-Oct; 14-day limit. 8 sites; 24-ft RV limit. Tbls, toilets, cfga, no drkg wtr. Fishing, hiking, hunting. Elev 2400 ft.
Fishing tip: There is good trout fishing at Beaver Creek.

KNIGHTS FERRY (155) N

Horseshoe Road Campground $8
Stanislaus River Parks
Corps of Engineers
W on Sonora & Orange Blossom Rds to Horseshoe Bend; boat-in, hike-in or bike-in access only. $8. All year; 14-day limit. 18 sites. Tbls, toilets, cfga, no drkg wtr. Fishing, canoeing, boating, hiking. Information center has salmon exhibits; nearby covered bridge.

LA CANADA-FLINTRIDGE (156) S

Bear Canyon Trail Camp $5
Angeles National Forest
10 mi NE of La Canada on SR 2 (Angeles Crest Hwy); half mi S on FR 2N57; 1.5 mi SW on Trail 11W14; 3 mi SW on Trail 12W08. Hiking access only. $5 daily or $30 annually. 4/1-11/30; 14-day limit. 3 tent sites on 2 acres. Tbls, cfga, no toilets, tank drkg wtr. Boating, fishing, hiking.

Buckhorn $12
Angeles National Forest
From I-210 at La Canada, 35 mi N from Angeles Crest Hwy exit (Hwy 2). $12. 4/1-11/15; 14-day limit. 38 sites; 16-ft RV limit. Tbls, toilets, cfga, drkg wtr. High Desert National Recreation Trail to backcountry; Cooper Canyon 1.5-mi hike. Elev 6300 ft.

Chilao Recreation Area $12
Angeles National Forest
From I-210 at La Canada, 26 mi N from Angeles Crest Hwy exit (Hwy 2). $12. 4/1-11/15; 14-day limit. 111 sites; 28-ft RV limit,

but 1 site for 36 ft. Tbls, toilets, cfga, limited drkg wtr. Elev 5300 ft. Visitor center 1 mi being restored 2007 & 2008.

Commodore Switzer Trail Camp $5
Angeles National Forest
.8 mi NW on La Canada on SR 118; 10 mi NE on SR 2; half mi S on FR 2N57 (Switzer Rd); 1 mi SW on Trail 11W14. $5 daily or $30 annually. All year. 1 tent site; 2 acres. Cfga, no toilets/tbls/drkg wtr. Hiking; stream fishing (1 mi).

DeVore Trail Camp $5
Angeles National Forest
.8 mi NW on La Canada on SR 118; 14.6 mi NE on SR 2 (Angeles Crest Hwy); 5.6 mi SE on FR 2N24; 1.2 mi E on Trail 11W12. $5 daily or $30 annually. All year; 14-day limit. 6 tent sites for hikers, bikers, equestrians. Tbls, no toilets, no drkg wtr. Picnicking, hiking, horseback riding. Elev 2900 ft; 2 acres. Stream. Campfire permit required. Hiking and equestrian access only. On Gabrielino NRT.
Travel tip: Visit Mount Wilson Observatory (10 mi NE of town on SR 2, then 5 mi SE on Mount Wilson Rd); museum with planetary models & photos; visitors can see telescopes. Free.

Gould Mesa $5
Angeles National Forest
NE of La Canada on FS hiking trails. $5 daily or $30 annually. All year; 14-day limit. 3 tent sites. Tbls, cfga, no drkg wtr. Hiking, fishing, picnicking. Hiking or equestrian access only. Gabrielino NRT.

Horse Flats $12
Angeles National Forest
From I-210 at La Canada, 29 mi N from Angeles Crest Hwy exit (Hwy 2); left at Santa Clara Divide Rd at Three Points for 3 mi. $12. Apr-Nov; 14-day limit. 25 sites (22-ft RV limit). Tbls, toilets, cfga, no drkg wtr. Elev 5700 ft.

Messenger Flat $8
Angeles National Forest
From I-210 at La Canada, 9 mi N from Angeles Crest Hwy exit (Hwy 2); left on CR N3 (Angeles Forest Highway for 12 mi; left for 11 mi on Santa Clara Divide Rd. $8. Apr-Nov; free rest of year; 14-day limit. 10 tent sites. Horse facilities, tbls, toilets, cfga, no drkg wtr. Pacific Crest Trail. Elev 5900 ft. Road may close with heavy snow.

Monte Cristo $8
Angeles National Forest
From I-210 at La Canada, 9 mi N from Angeles Crest Hwy exit (Hwy 2); left on CR N3 (Angeles Forest Highway) for 9 mi. $8 during May-Nov; free rest of year; 14-day limit. 19 sites (30-ft RV limit). Tbls, toilets, cfga, drkg wtr. Elev 3600 ft.

Oakwilde Trail Camp $5
Angeles National Forest
2.5 mi E of La Canada on SR 118; 41.5 mi N

on Trail 11W14. Access by foot or by horse (Gabrielino NRT) only. $5 daily or $30 annually. All year; 14-day limit. 7 tent sites. Tbls, toilets, cfga, no drkg wtr. Campfire permit required. Boating; picnicking; hiking; fishing (1 mi). Elev 1800 ft; 1 acre. Dark Canyon Creek. Closed during high fire danger.

Valley Forge Walk-In Camp $5
Angeles National Forest
.8 mi NW of La Canada on Hwy 118; 14.3 mi NE on Hwy 2 to Red Box Ranger Station; park in lot there, walk 4.5 mi to campground. $5 daily or $30 annually. All year; 14-day limit. 12 tent sites. Tbls, toilets, cfga, no drkg wtr. Fishing, hiking. Campfire permit required.
Travel tip: Descanso Gardens in La Canada Flintridge displays more than 100,000 camellias; also roses, berried plants, azaleas, orchids, Japanese teahouse & garden. Free only on third Tues of each month.

West Fork Walk-In Camp $5
Angeles National Forest
.8 mi NW of La Canada on Hwy 1.18; 14.3 mi NE on Hwy 2 to Red Box Ranger Station; park in lot there, walk, bike or horseback 3 mi to campground. $5 daily or $30 annually. All year; 14-day limit. 7 tent sites. Tbls, toilets, cfga, drkg wtr. Fishing, hiking. Campfire permit required.

LAGUNA BEACH (158) S

Crystal Cove State Park $11
Off Pacific Coast Hwy between Laguna Beach and Corona del Mar; park in El Moro lot, hike inland 3 mi, mostly uphill on strenuous trail. $11 during 9/16-5/14; $15 rest of year. All year; 15-day limit. Primitive undesignated tent sites; no facilities except toilets & tables; no drkg wtr, no trash service; fires restricted to backpack stoves. Horseback riding, hiking, surfing, scuba diving, swimming, mountain biking, tidepool exploration.

LAKE ALPINE (159) N

Lodgepole Overflow   FREE
Stanislaus National Forest
2 mi W of Lake Alpine on Hwy 4. Free. June-Oct; 48-hour limit. Open only when other Alpine Basin camps are full. 20 primitive undesignated sites. Chemical toilets, cfga, tbls, drkg wtr. Reservations & fees for groups. Elev 7290 ft.

Mosquito Lake $5
Stanislaus National Forest
6.6 mi NE of Lake Alpine on SR 4. $5. 6/1-11/1; 14-day limit. 11 sites; 40-ft RV limit. Toilets, tbls, cfga, no drkg wtr. Fishing, boating. Elev 8260 ft. Campfire permit required. Primarily day-use area, but limited camping.

Sand Flat   FREE
Stanislaus National Forest
9 mi S of Lake Alpine on Hwy 4 to Big Mead-

ows Group Camp; 2 mi S on steep 4WD rd. No RVs recommended. (Note: Do not confuse this free camp with Sand Bar Flat fee campground west of Dardanelle.) Free. 6/1-9/30; 14-day limit. 6 tent sites. Tbls, toilets, cfga, no drkg wtr. Primarily 4WD camp along North Fork of Stanislaus River. Primitive; campfire permit required. Elev 5800 ft.

Stanislaus River   **$8**
Stanislaus National Forest
7 mi S of Lake Alpine on Hwy 4, pass Tamarack; 4 mi S on Spicer Reservoir Rd. $8. 6/1-10/31; 14-day limit. 25 sites (35-ft RV limit). Tbls, toilets, cfga, drkg wtr. Fishing, boating; on North Fork of Stanislaus River.

LAKE ELSINORE (160) S

Blue Jay Campground   **$7.50**
Cleveland National Forest
5.7 SW of Lake Elsinore on SR 74, then about 5 mi NW on North Main Divide Rd following signs. $7.50 with federal Senior Pass; others pay $15. All year; 14-day limit. 50 sites; 20-ft RV limit. Tbls, toilets, cfga, drkg wtr. Biking, hiking. Elev 3400 ft.

El Cariso North   **$7.50**
Cleveland National Forest
5.9 mi SW of Lake Elsinore on SR 74. $7.50 with federal Senior Pass; others pay $15. May-Oct; 14-day limit. 24 sites; 22-ft RV limit. Tbls, toilets, cfga, drkg wtr. Hiking.

Upper San Juan Camp   **$7.50**
Cleveland National Forest
About 10 mi SW of Lake Elsinore on SR 74. $7.50 with federal Senior Pass; others pay $15. May-Nov; 14-day limit. 18 sites; 32-ft RV limit. Tbls, toilets, cfga, drkg wtr. Biking, hikng, horseback riding.

Wildomar Campground   **$10**
Cleveland National Forest
5.7 mi SW of Lake Elsinore on SR 74; 10 mi E on Killen Trail Rd. (narrow last half mi). $10. All year; 14-day limit. 11 sites; 22-ft RV limit. Tbls, toilets, cfga, well drkg wtr. Hiking, OHV trails. Elev 2400 ft.

LAKE HUGHES (161) S

Lower Shake   **$5**
Angeles National Forest
5.2 mi W of Lake Hughes on CR N2 (Elizabeth Lake-Pine Canyon Rd); 5.2 mi W on FR 7N03; .3 mi S on FR 7N34. $5 daily or $30 annually. Elev 4300 ft. 5/1-12/15; 14-day limit. About 5 tent sites. No facilities, cfga, no drkg wtr. Hiking, picnicking. No longer operated as a developed campground.

Sawmill Meadows   **$5**
Angeles National Forest
5.4 mi W of Lake Hughes on CR N2 (Elizabeth Lake-Pine Canyon Rd); 4.6 mi W on FR 7N23. $5 daily or $30 annually. All year; 14-day limit. 8 sites (RVs under 16 ft). Tbls,

toilets, cfga, firewood, no drkg wtr, no trash service. Picnicking. Elev 5200 ft; 4 acres.

Upper Shake   **$5**
Angeles National Forest
5.8 mi W of Lake Hughes on CR N2; 1.8 mi w on FR 7N23; .8 mi SE on FR 7N230. $5 daily or $30 annually. 5/1-11/30; 14-day limit. 18 sites (22-ft RV limit). Tbls, toilets, cfga, no drkg wtr. Picnicking, hiking. Elev 4300 ft; 4 acres.

LAKEHEAD (162) N

Beehive Point   **$6**
Shasta-Trinity National Forest
4 mi SE of Lakehead on I-5; 3.7 mi E on gravel rd; on Shasta Lake shoreline. $6 during 5/15-9/15; free rest of year but no trash service Portable toilets, cfga, no drkg wtr. Undesignated primitive sites; 30-ft RV limit. Picnicking, swimming, fishing, boating.

Fishing tip: In summer, catch big trout and salmon from Shasta Lake by fishing 80-125 eet deep. Try white Cripplure or a tandem single-blade spinner at the mouth of Dry Creek or Toupee Island.

Gooseneck Cove   **FREE**
Shasta-Trinity National Forest
1 mi S of Lakehead on I-5; 3 mi SW BY BOAT (9 mi NW of Pitrina Bridge on I-5). Free. All year; 14-day limit. 8 tent sites. Tbls, toilets, cfga, no drkg wtr. Swimming, picnicking, waterskiing, fishing; boating (d; rl--3 mi). Elev 1100 ft; 4 acres. On Sacramento River Arm. Unit of Whiskeytown-Shasta-Trinity National Recreation Area. Nearest boat ramps at Sugarloaf, Antlers or Salt Creek.

Fishing tip: Sacramento River offers an unusual treat in June -- shad fishing; or try the salmon during the September run. River produced state's record 88-pound chinook salmon, and it has excellent fishing for striped bass and largemouth.

Gregory Beach   **$6**
Shasta-Trinity National Forest
4.5 mi S of Lakehead on I-5; 2.5 mi SW on CR 7H01 (Salt Creek Rd). On Shasta Lake shore next to Gregory Creek Campground ($14 fee). $6 during 4/1-9/15; free rest of year (open periods depend upon bald eagle habitat protection). Portable toilets, cfga, no drkg wtr. All year; 14-day limit. Undesignated primitive sites; 30-ft RV limit. Fishing, swimming, boating. Elev 1067 ft.

Fishing tip: Veteran rainbow trout fishermen look for big concentrations of plankton when searching for Lake Shasta fish. The phosphorescent clouds of phyto and zooplankton provide natural food for trout and salmon and attract large schools that can be caught on Cripplures and Hum Dingers using downriggers.

Lower Salt Creek   **$6**
Shasta-Trinity National Forest
4.5 mi S of Lakehead on I-5; 2 mi SW on CR 7H01 (Salt Creek Rd); on Shasta Lake. $6 during 4/1-9/15; free rest of year but no trash

service; 14-day limit. Primitive undesignated sites; 30-ft RV limit. Portable toilets, cfga, no drkg wtr. Fishing, swimming, boating. Elev 1885 ft.

Nelson Point   **$9**
Shasta-Trinity National Forest
3 mi S of Lakehead on I-5; 1 mi E from Salt Creek exit. $9. 4/1-9/15; 14-day limit. 8 sites (16-ft limit). Tbls, toilets, cfga, no drkg wtr. Fishing, boating, swimming.

LAKESHORE (163) S

Badger Flat   **FREE**
Sierra National Forest
7 mi E of Lakeshore on Kaiser Pass Rd. Free. 6/15-10/15; 14-day limit. 15 sites (22-ft RV limit). Tbls, toilets, cfga, no drkg wtr, horse facilities. Fishing, hiking, horseback riding. Elev 8200 ft; 5 acres. Scenic. Along Rancheria Creek. Huntington Lake. Note for all Sierra NF sites: Half of Kaiser Pass Rd is rough, narrow, with blind curves; large RVs not recommended.

Bolsillo   **FREE**
Sierra National Forest
16 mi E of Lakeshore on CR M2710; 17 mi NE on FR 4S01. Free. 6/1-10/31; 14-day limit. 3 tent sites; 1 acre. Tbls, toilets, cfga, piped drkg wtr. Visitor center across from campground. Stream. Fishing, picnicking, hiking, horseback riding (1 mi). Elev 7400 ft.

Portal Forebay   **$6.50**
Sierra National Forest
13.5 mi NE of Lakeshore on Kaiser Pass Rd; on Forebay Lake. $6.50 with federal Senior Pass; others pay $13 5/15-10/1; 14-day limit. 11 sites (16-ft RV limit). Tbls, toilets, cfga, no drkg wtr. Hiking, fishing.

Sample Meadows   **FREE**
Sierra National Forest
14 mi E of Lakeshore on CR M2710; 9.8 mi NE on FR 5S80; 3 mi NW on FR 7S05 (Low Standard access rd). Free. 5/15-10/1; 14-day limit. 16 sites (RVs under 16 ft). Tbls, toilets, cfga, no drkg wtr. Fishing, picnicking. Elev 7800 ft; 7 acres. Scenic. Kaiser Creek.

West Kaiser   **FREE**
Sierra National Forest
Follow directions to Sample Meadows Camp; beyond Sample Meadows, rd becomes a maintained, graded dird rd for 10 mi; West Kaiser is at turnoff for Kaiser Diggings. Free. 6/1-9/15; 14-day limit. 8 sites; 26-ft RV limit. Tbls, toilets, cfga, no drkg wtr. Fishing, hiking. Some sites on West Kaiser Creek.

LANCASTER (164) S

Saddleback Butte State Park   **$12**
17 mi E of Lancaster on Ave J East; on W edge of Mojave Desert. $12. All year; 14-day limit. 50 sites (30-ft RV limit). Tbls, flush toilets, cfga, drkg wtr, dump. Hiking trails,

birdwatching, 4.5-mile bridle trail, no hunting or OHV. Elev 6500 ft; 2,955 acres.

LA PORTE (165) N

Cleghorn Bar FREE
Plumas National Forest
13 mi N of LaPorte. Go N on LaPorte Rd, then just N of Onion Valley, turn W for 10 mi. following signs; 4WD necessary for access. Free. All year; 14-day limit. 26 sites. Tbls, toilet, cfga, no drkg wtr, no trash service. Fishing, 4WD activity. On Middle Fork Feather River.

LEE VINING (166) N

Aspen Grove $8
Mono County Park
7 mi W of Lee Vining on SR 120. $8. 5/15-10/1. 56 sites (RVs under 20 ft). Tbls, toilets, cfga, no drkg wtr. Fishing. Elev 8000 ft. Lee Vining Creek.

Cattleguard $7
Inyo National Forest
Just S of Lee Vining on US 395; 3 mi W on SR 120. $7 with federal Senior Pass; others pay $14. 5/1-10/15. 16 sites; 30-ft RV limit. Tbls, portable toilets, cfga, no drkg wtr. Elev 7500 ft.

Junction $12
Inyo National Forest
10 mi W of Lee Vining on SR 120; .1 N on FR 1N04. $12. 6/1-10/15; 14-day limit. 13 sites (RVs under 30 ft). Tbls, toilets, cfga, no drkg wtr. Mountain climbing, picnicking, fishing, hiking, boating (ld--1 mi). Elev 9600 ft; 5 acres. Stream. Scenic. Tioga Lake. 1 mi E of Yosemite National Park. Nature Trails (1 mi).

Lower Lee Vining Creek $7
Inyo National Forest
5 mi W of Lee Vining on SR 120. $7 with federal Senior Pass; others pay $14. 5/1-10/15; 14-day limit. 54 sites (RVs under 25 ft). Tbls, toilets, cfga, drkg wtr. Fishing, hiking. Elev 7000 ft. Large pine & aspen shade trees.

Lundy Canyon $7
Mono County Park
Inyo National Forest
5 mi N of Lee Vining on US 395 to access rd. $7 with federal Senior Pass; others pay $14. 5/15-10/1; 14-day limit. 51 sites 924-ft RV limit). Tbls, toilets, cfga, no drkg wtr. Mono Lake nearby. Elev 8000 ft.

Sawmill - Tioga Pass Area $12
Inyo National Forest
10 mi SW of Lee Vining on SR 120; 1.5 mi NW on CR 1N04; walk to campground. $12. 6/1-10/15; 14-day limit. 12 tent sites. Tbls, toilets, no drkg wtr. Mountain climbing, hiking, picnicking, fishing; boating (rl-1 mi). Elev 9800 ft; 2 acres. Saddlebag Lake.

Upper Lee Vining Creek $7
Inyo National Forest
5 mi W of Lee Vining on SR 120. $7 with federal Senior Pass; others pay $14. 5/1-10/1; 14-day limit. 55 sites. Tbls, toilets, cfga, no drkg wtr. Fishing, hiking. Elev 7500 ft.

LEMONCOVE

Horse Creek Campground $8
Kaweah Lake
Corps of Engineers
From dame just NE of Lemoncove, 3 mi E on SR 198, following signs. $8 with federal Senior Pass; others pay $16. All year; 14-day limit. 80 sites; 35-ft RV limit. Tbls, flush toilets, cfga, drkg wtr, showers, dump ($ for non-campers), fish cleaning stations, playground. Hiking, fishing, boating(l), waterskiing, summer campfire programs.

LEWISTON (168) N

Ackerman $12
Shasta-Trinity National Forest
8 mi N of Lewiston on CR 105 at NW shore of Lewiston Lake. $12 during 4/1-10/31; $6 rest of year; 14-day limit. 66 sites (40-ft RV limit). Tbls, toilets, flush toilets, cfga, drkg wtr, dump. Fishing, hiking, canoeing, boating (ramps nearby). 20 acres.
Travel tip: Stop at the fish hatchery below Lewiston Dam; admission free.
Fishing tip: Lewiston Lake is known for its big trout and also contains bass, catfish and bluegills.

Cooper Gulch $12
Shasta-Trinity National Forest
4.2 mi N of Lewiston on CR 105 on S side of Lewiston Lake. $12. 4/1-10/31 (free 11/1-11/15 but no wtr); 14-day limit. 5 sites (16-ft RV limit). Tbls, toilets, cfga, drkg wtr. Swimming, boatng(l), fishing, canoeing, hiking. 6 acres.
Fishing tip: Lake has rather good trout fishing, but you'll have to search out the good spots. There's variety, though, with rainbows, browns, brooks & kokanee salmon. Launch boat 1 mi N at Pinecove ramp or at Pinecove Marina.

Mary Smith $11
Shasta-Trinity National Forest
2 mi N of Lewiston on CR 105; qtr mi N on FR 33N79, at S end of Lewiston Lake. $11. 5/1-9/15; 14-day limit. 18 tent sites. Tbls, flush toilets, cfga, drkg wtr. Fishing., hiking, canoeing 8 acres.

Tunnel Rock $6
Shasta-Trinity National Forest
7.2 mi N on CR 105; on NW side of Lewiston Lake. $6. All year; 14 day limit. 6 sites (2 for small RVs such as fold-out or truck camper). Tbls, toilets, cfga, no drkg wtr. Picnicking, fishing, boating. Boat launch 1 mi Elev 1900 ft; 2 acres. Foothills.
Fishing tip: Located near some of the best fishing on Lewiston Lake.

LIKELY (169) N

Blue Lake $7
Modoc National Forest
8.5 mi E of Likely on CR 64; 7 mi SE on FR 39N01; 1.2 mi S on FR 38N30. Free LD-MD, weather permitting; $7 rest of year; 14-day limit. 48 sites on 24 acres (32-ft RV limit). Tbls, toilets, cfga, drkg wtr. No wtr during free period. Swimming, fishing, boating(l), hiking & nature trails. Elev 6000 ft. Site sometimes closed due to nesting bald eagles.
Fishing tip: Launch small boat from camp, try rainbow trout and brown trout. Lake also populated with catfish, largemouth bass, bluegills.

Mill Creek Falls $6
Modoc National Forest
8.6 mi E of Likely on CR 64; 2.4 mi N on CR 64; 6 mi E on CR 64; 1.2 mi N on FR 40N46. $6. Free LD-MD, weather permitting; 14-day limit. 19 sites (22-ft RV limit). Tbls, toilets, cfga, drkg wtr (no wtr during free period). Picnicking, hiking, fishing, swimming. Elev 5700 ft; 6 acres. Mountains. Dense forest. Trailhead to Mill Creek Falls, Clear Lake and South Warner Wilderness.
Fishing tip: Rainbow trout are planted each summer at South Fork Pit River near the campground. Other good nearby trout waters are Mill Creek, Poison Creek and South Fork Fitzhugh Creek.

Soup Springs Campground $6
Modoc National Forest
8.6 mi E of Likely on CR 64; 2.4 mi N on CR 64; 1 mi N on FR 42N0S; 6.4 mi E on FR 40N24. $6. 7/1-10/15. 14 sites on 2 acres (RVs under 22 ft). Tbls, toilets, cfga, piped drkg wtr. Picnicking, horseback riding; fishing (2 mi). Elev 6800 ft. Stream. Near trailheads to South Warner Wilderness. Corrals available.

LITCHFIELD (170) N

Belfast Petroglyph Site FREE
Bureau of Land Management
W of Litchfield on Hwy 395, then 4 mi W on Center Rd; 4.5 mi N on Belfast Rd; no camping within qtr mi of archaeological sites. Free. All year; 14-day limit. Undesignated sites; no facilities, no drkg wtr. Fishing, hiking, hunting, petroglyph viewing.

LONE PINE (173) S

Cottonwood Lakes $6
Backpacker Camp
Inyo National Forest
Hiker staging area for Cottonwood Lakes Trail. $6 for walk-in sites; 4 per tent. 5/26-10/30; 1-night limit. 12 undesignated sites. Toilet, cfga, drkg wtr. Picnicking, hiking. Elev 10,000 ft.

Diaz Lake Recreation Area   **$10**
Inyo County Park
2 mi S of Lone Pine on US 395; on N edge of Mojave Desert. $10. All year; 15-day limit. 200 sites. Tbls, flush toilets, solar showers, cfga, drkg wtr, playground, beaches. Boating(l$), fishing, waterskiing, swimming. Elev 3700 ft. Lake was formed in 1872 by an earthquake.

Fishing tip: Diaz Lake contains bass, catfish and bluegills as well as rainbow and alpers trout planted during trout season.

Golden Trout   **$6**
Backpacker Camp
Inyo National Forest
3 mi W of Lone Pine on CR 15S02 (Whitney Portal Rd); 15 mi S on SR 190. $6. MD-11/1; 1-day limit. 18 tent sites. Tbls, toilets, cfga, drkg wtr. Hiking, fishing.

Horseshoe Meadows   **$12**
Equestiran Campground
Inyo National Forest
5 mi W of Lone Pine on Whitney Portal Rd; 15 mi SW on Horseshoe Meadows Rd. $12. MD-10/30; 1-day limit. 10 equestrian sites, several hike-in tent sites. Tbls, toilets, cfga, drkg wtr, pack station, horse facilities. Bridle trails, hiking, fishing. Elev 10,000 ft.

Lone Pine   **$7**
Inyo National Forest
6 mi W of Lone Pine on CR 15S02 (Whitney Portal Rd). $7 with federal Senior Pass; others pay $14. About 4/15-10/15; 14-day limit. 43 sites (32-ft RV limit). Tbls, toilets, cfga, drkg wtr. Hiking, fishing, swimming. Elev 6000 ft.

Fishing tip: Lone Pine Creek is stocked with rainbow and brown trout. Find best spots along Whitley Portal Rd.

Portagee Joe   **$10**
Inyo County Park
13 mi W of Lone Pine on CR 15S02 (Whitney Portal Rd). $10. All year; 14-day limit. 15 sites. Tbls, toilets, cfga, drkg wtr. Hiking, fishing. Elev 3700 ft. 260 acres.

Tuttle Creek   **$5**
Bureau of Land Management
3 mi W of Lone Pine on Whitney Portal Rd; 1.5 mi S on Horseshoe Meadow Rd; W on winding dirt rd. $5 (formerly free). About 3/10-11/1; 14 day limit. Special Long-Term Visitor Area (LTVA) permits can now be used at Crowley, Tuttle Creek and Goodale Creek Campgrounds. These LTVA permits are $300 for the period between the first Saturday in March through 11/1. 85 sites on 50 acres. Tbls, toilets, cfga, no drkg wtr. Fishing, picnicking, horseback riding. Fee was charged; may be again. Elev 5120 ft. Interagency visitor center at S end of Lone Pine.

Fishing tip: Tuttle Creek is stocked with rainbow and brown trout; access from Horseshoe Meadow Rd.

Whitney Trailhead   **$6**
Inyo National Forest
13 mi W of Lone Pine on CR 15S02 (Whitney Portal Rd). $6. About MD-10/15; 1-day limit. 10 walk-in tent sites. Tbls, toilets, cfga, drkg wtr. Hiking. Elev 8300 ft.

LONG BARN (174) N

Crandall   **FREE**
Motorcycle Staging Area
Stanislaus National Forest
7 mi N of Long Barn on SR 108, then N on FR 4N01 to Spring Gap. Free. May-Oct; 14-day limit. Primitive dispersed sites; 40-ft RV limit. No facilities. Limited to motorcyclist and ATV campers. 60 mi of cycle trails; good riding. Elev 5000 ft.

Fraser Flat   **$7.50**
Stanislaus National Forest
6 mi NE of Long Barn on SR 108; from Spring Gap turnoff, 3 mi N on FR 4N14 (Fraser Flat Rd), a steep, winding rd for 20-30 mph travel. $7.50 with federal Senior Pass; others pay $15. May-Oct; 14-day limit. 38 sites (22-ft RV limit). Tbls, toilets, cfga, drkg wtr, accessible fishing pier. Fishing, hunting. Elev 4800; 13 acres. On South Fork of Sanislaus River.

Hull Creek   **$5**
Stanislaus National Forest
12 mi SE of Long Barn on FR 3N01. $5 fee 6/1-10/1, but free winter camping permitted; 14-day limit. 18 sites; 22-ft RV limit. Tbls, toilets, cfga, drkg wtr. Ranger station (11 mi). Hiking, picnicking, trout fishing. Secluded meadow with small stream. Elev 5600 ft; 5 acres. Hull Creek (dry in summer).

Fishing tip: Try trout fishing on Hull Creek.

Sand Bar Flat   **$7**
Stanislaus National Forest
6 mi NE of Long Barn on SR 108; 6 mi N on FR 4N01; 3 mi NE on FR 4N88; 3 mi N on FR 4N85; on Middle Fork (Lower) Stanislaus River. Rd not recommended for large RVs. $7. 5/15-11/15; 14-day limit. 10 sites (22-ft RV limit). Tbls, toilets, cfga, drkg wtr. Swimming, fishing. Elev 5400 ft; 6 acres.

Trout Creek Camp   **FREE**
Stanislaus National Forest
15 mi E of Long Barn on Rd 3N01. Free. All year; 14-day limit. Primitive dispersed sites; 40-ft RV limit. Some tbls, cfga, toilets seasonally. Okay to camp overnight with horses. Campfire permit required.

LOOKOUT (176) N

Lava Camp   **FREE**
Modoc National Forest
15 mi N of Lookout on CR 91; 9.2 mi NW on FR 42N03. 6/1-10/30. 12 sites (RVs under 32 ft). Free. Tbls, toilets, cfga, no drkg wtr. Rockhounding, picnicking. Elev 4400 ft; 9 acres. Scenic.

LOS BANOS (177) S

Cottonwood Creek   **FREE**
State Wildlife Area
About 20 mi W of Los Banos on SR 152, past N shore of San Luis Lake; wildlife area at county line, accessible via Dinosaur Point Rd. Free. All year; 14-day limit. Free primitive camping only in parking lot of Upper Cottonwood Creek unit. No facilities. Hunting, hiking.

Fishing tip: This lake is best known for its striped bass; fish river channels during sumer; watch for stripers chasing bait fish along the surface in early spring and fall.

Los Banos   **FREE**
State Wildlife Area
About 2 mi N of Los Banos on SR 165; half mi E on Henry Miller Ave. Free. All year; 14-day limit. Primitive camping on 6,217 acres. Drkg wtr, cfga, toilets. Hike or drive along levees. Hunting, fishing, hiking, boating.

Los Banos Creek Reservoir   **$10**
San Luis Resevior
State Recreation Area
5 mi W of Los Banos on SR 152; 1 mi S on Volta Rd; 1 mi E on Pioneer Rd; 5 mi S on Canyon Rd. $10. All year; 15-day limit. 20 sites (30-ft RV limit). Tbls, toilets, cfga, drkg wtr. Boating(l), fishing, canoeing, sailboarding, horseback riding, swimming. Equestrian sites.

Madeiros Campground   **$10**
San Luis Reservoir
State Recreation Area
12 mi W of Los Banos on SR 152; N on SR 33; on San Luis Reservoir. $10. All year; 15-day limit. 350 primitive sites; 30-ft RV limit. Tbls, toilets, cfga, drkg wtr. Boating(l), fishing, horseback riding, boating(l), sailing.

North Grasslands   **FREE**
State Wildlife Area
About 5 mi N of Los Banos on Hwy 168; NE on Wolfsen Rd to Salt Slough Unit; for China Island Unit, continue N on Hwy 168 about 10 mi, then W on Hwy 140. Free. Primitive camping on 7,069 acres of restored & created wetlands. No facilities. Hunting, fishing, boating.

O'Neill Forebay   **FREE**
State Wildlife Area
12 mi W of Los Banos on SR 152; N on SR 33 to O'Neill Forebay Lake, Free. All year; 14-day limit. Primitive camping on 700 acres. Fishing, hunting, hiking.

Panoche Hills   **FREE**
Bureau of Land Management
Between Lost Banos & Coalinga on I-5, take Little Panoche Rd exit, then 14 mi W; Panoche Access Point is nearly across from Mercy Hot Springs spa. Free. All year, but area closed to vehicles 4/15-10/15 to reduce fire hazards; 14-day limit. Park within 15 ft of roadways; no motorcycles or ATVs. Primitive

undesignated camping; no facilities, no drkg wtr. Hiking, biking, horseback riding. 26,000 acres.

San Luis Reservoir　　FREE
State Wildlife Area
About 15 mi W of Los Banos on SR 152 to San Luis Lake. Access to W side of area from Dinosaur Point Rd. Free. All year; 14-day limit. Primitive camping on 902 acres at San Luis and O'Neill Forebay Lakes. Drkg wtr, toilets. Fishing, boating, hiking, hunting.

Tumey Hills　　FREE
Bureau of Land Management
Between Los Banos & Coalinga on I-5, take Panoche Rd exit W about 1.5 mi to graded dirt access; a second access point 5 mi farther on S side of rd. Free. All year; 14-day limit. Primitive undesignated camping on 36,000 acres of public land in San Benito & Fresno Counties. No facilities, no drkg wtr. Camp within 15 feet of existing roads. Biking, hiking, horseback riding, hunting.

Volta State Wildlife Area　　FREE
About 9 mi W of Los Banos on SR 152; 2 mi N on Volta Rd; hal mi NW on Ingomar Grade Rd. Free primitive camping alowed only at check station during waterfowl season. No facilities. 2,891 acres

LOS GATOS (178) S

Castle Rock State Park　　$11
2.5 mi SE of Saratoga Gap on SR 35; main parking lot 2 mi S of Hwy 9 on Skyline Blvd. $11. All year; 15-day limit. 25 primitive walk-in tent sites. Tbls, toilets, cfga, drkg wtr. Hiking, rock climbing.

LOS OLIVOS (179) S

Ballard Camp　　$5
Figueroa Mountain Recreation Area
Los Padres National Forest
13 mi W of Los Banos on Figueroa Mountain Rd to area of Figueroa Campground; hike or ride by horseback N along trail to camp. $5 daily or $30 annually. 2 primitive tent sites. No facilities; wtr available from nearby spring.

Davy Brown Campground　　$5
Figueroa Mountain Recreation Area
Los Padres National Forest
20.6 mi NE of Los Olivos on Figueroa Mountain Rd; 3.8 mi N on Sunset Valley Rd to campground sign (on left). $5 daily or $30 annually. All year; 14-day limit 13 sites; 25-ft RV limit. Tbls, toilets, cfga, drkg wtr (shut off in winter). Hiking, horseback riding, mountain biking, trout fishing.

Figueroa　　$5
Figueroa Mountain Recreaton Area
Los Padres National Forest
13 mi NE of Los Olivos on Fugueroa Mountain Rd. $5 daily or $30 annually. All year; 14-day limit. 33 sites (25-ft RV limit). Tbls,

toilets, cfga, drkg wtr. Hiking trails; scenic; wheelchair access.

LUCERNE (180) N

Lakeview　　FREE
Mendocino National Forest
2 mi NW of Lucerne on SR 20; 5 mi NE on FR 8; 3 mi SE on FR 15N09. Free. 5/1-10/15; 14-day limit. 9 sites (RVs under 16 ft). Tbls, toilets, no drkg wtr, cfga, no trash service. Picnicking. Elev 3400 ft; 3 acres. Scenic. Check Upper Lake Ranger Station about Rice Fork crossing. Good view of Clear Lake.

Fishing tip: California's largest natural lake, Clear Lake, offers excellent spring fishing for largemouth bass, big crappie & bluegills. During summer, try night fishing for catfish.

MACDOEL (182) N

Juanita Lake　　$10
Klamath National Forest
Qtr mi SW of Macdoel on US 97; 6.5 mi W on Meiss Lake-Sam's Neck Rd; 1.2 mi S on FR 46N04 (Butte Valley Rd). Free 11/1-5/15; $10 rest of yr; 14-day limit. 23 sites (32-ft RV limit). Tbls, toilets, cfga, drkg wtr; no wtr or trash service during free period. Swimming, boating (l--no motors), fishing, hiking. Elev 5100 ft; 20 acres; Group site ($30) by reservation. Trail, piers for handicapped. Winter access mainly by snowmobile.

Fishing tip: 55-acre Juanita Lake offers good bass fishing early in spring and through mid-summer. Try jigs & spinnerbaits early; switch to crankbaits & plastic worms as water warms. Concentrate on points & dropoffs. The lake also is stocked with rainbow & brown trout.

Travel tip: Several miles W of town is the Meiss Lake State Wildlife Refuge. After climbing Mt. Hebron summit, the road drops down to Grass Lake; a vista point is located 1 mi S of Grass Lake and provides a panoramic view to the south of Mt. Shasta.

Martins Dairy　　$8
Klamath National Forest
12 mi S of MacDoel on SR 97; 11 mi NW on FR 46N10; 2 mi NW on FR 46N12; .2 mi NE on FR 46N09. $8 during MD-10/31; free rest of year. 14-day limit. 8 sites (RVs under 26 ft). Tbls, toilets, cfga, piped drkg wtr. No wtr or trash service during free period. Hunting, birdwatching mountain biking, fishing. At headwaters of Little Shasta River. Elev 6000 ft; 8 acres. Little Shasta Spring.

Fishing tip: Rainbow and brown trout are stocked regularly in the Little Shasta River; catch perrywinkles from under rocks for bait.

Shafter　　$6
Klamath National Forest
3.7 mi SW of Macdoel on US 97; 2.2 mi E on CR ZK03l; 5.3 mi S on CR 8Q01. $6 during May-Oct; free rest of year; 14-day limit. 10

sites (RVs under 33 ft). Tbls, toilets, cfga, drkg wtr. Swimming, boating, fishing. Elev 4400 ft; 11 acres. No wtr or trash service during free period. Popular during hunting season.

Fishing tip: Butte Creek is stocked with rainbow & brown troup; good fishing early in season.

MAD RIVER (183) N

Bailey Canyon　　$12
Six Rivers National Forest
13 mi SE of Mad River on Lower Mad River Rd; at Ruth Lake. $12. MD-9/15; 14-day limit. 25 sites (22-ft RV limit). Tbls, toilets, cfga, drkg wtr. Boating, fishing, hiking, waterskiing.

Fishing tip: Besides rainbow trout, bass and catfish, anglers at Rush Lake catch an occasional kokanee salmon.

Brown's Canyon　　FREE
Primitive Area
Six Rivers National Forest
From just W of Mad River, travel 4 mi S of SR 36 on paved Van Duzen Rd, on bank of Van Duzen River. Free. Apr-Nov; 30-day limit. Undesignated primitive camping area; space for 2 RVs & 2 tents. No facilities. Boil creek water before using. Fishing, hunting, picnicking.

Fishing tip: Van Duzen River offers excellent steelhead, chinook & coho fishing.

Fir Cove　　$12
Six Rivers National Forest
12 mi SE of Mad River on Lower Mad River Rd; at Ruth Lake. $12. Holidays & weekends only, May-Oct; reserved group camping otherwise. 19 sites (22-ft RV limit). Tbls, toilets, cfga, drkg wtr. Boating(l), fishing, hiking, waterskiing.

Mad River Campground　　$12
Six Rivers National Forest
5 mi SE of Mad River on SR 36; 3 mi N of dam. $12. All year; 14 day limit. 40 sites (30-ft RV limit). Tbls, toilets, cfga, drkg wtr. NHunting, hiking, fishing, picnicking, swimming. Elev 2500 ft. Closed in 2007 due to road construction.

MAMMOTH LAKES (185) S

Big Springs　　FREE
Inyo National Forest
1 mi E of Mammoth Lakes on SR 203; bear left (N) on US 395 to Lee Vining, then 7.3 mi and right for 2.1 mi on Owens River Rd. Free. About 4/15-11/15; 21-day limit. 26 sites. Tbls, toilets, cfga, no drkg wtr. Trout fishing. Elev 7300 ft.

Deadman Campground　　FREE
Inyo National Forest
1 mi E of Mammoth Lakes on SR 203; 8.1 mi N on US 395; left at Deadman Creek Rd for 1.2 mi; bear left at "Y," for 1.6 mi to lower

section and 1.8 mi to upper section; on both sides of creek. 30 sites for tents, fold-outs, truck campers. Free. 6/1-10/15; 14-day limit. Tbls, toilets, cfga, no drkg wtr. Hiking, fishing, OHV activities.

Hartley Springs   **FREE**
Inyo National Forest
1 mi E of Mammoth Lakes on SR 203; bear left (north) on US 395 to Lee Vining, then 11.3 mi; left at Hartley Springs sign, then bear right at "Y" onto FR 2548 for nearly 1 mi; final leg of rd is rough. Free. 6/1-10/1; 14-day limit. 20 sites. Tbls, toilets, cfga, no drkg wtr.

MARICOPA (188) S

Caballo   **FREE**
Los Padres National Forest
9 mi S of Maricopa on SR 166; 27 mi SE on CR FH95; half mi N on FR 9N27 (3 mi W of town of Pine Mountain Club). $5 daily or $30 annually. 5/1-11/15; 14-day limit. 5 sites. Free. Tbls, toilets, cfga, no drkg wtr. Swimming. Elev 5800. Rd has ruts; 4WD may be needed.

Campo Alto   **$5**
Los Padres National Forest
9 mi S of Maricopa on SR 166; 27 mi SE on FR9N07 (Cerro Noroeste Rd) to its end. $5 daily or $30 annually. 5/15-11/15; 14-day limit. Open for winter sports when rd is plowed. About 19 sites (RVs under 32 ft). Tbls, toilets, cfga, no drkg wtr. Hiking, picnicking, mountain climbing. Elev 8200 ft; 10 acres. At summit of Cerro Noroeste Mountain, Mount Abel. Operated by Kern County. Supplies in Lake-of-the-Woods (15 mi).

Marian   **FREE**
Los Padres National Forest
9 mi S of Maricopa on SR 166; 15 mi SE on CR/FH 95; 1 mi N on FR 9N27 (3 mi W of town of Pine Mountain Club). Free. 5/1-11/15; 14-day limit. 5 sites (16-ft RV limit). Tbls, toilets, cfga, no drkg wtr. 4WD may be needed.

Sheep Camp   **$5**
Los Padres National Forest
9 mi S of Maricopa on SR 166; 26.5 mi SE on CR FH95; 2.5 mi SE on Trail 21W03. Hiking from Mount Pinos: 2 mi on Trail 21W03 from Condor Observation Point. Hiking from Mount Abel: 3 mi on Trail 21W03. Hiking from Lockwood Valley: 7 mi on trail past Three Falls Boy Scout Camp. $5 daily or $30 annually. 5/15-11/15; 14-day limit. 4 tent sites. Cfga, no drkg wtr, no tbls, no toilets. Wtr in spring qtr mi above camp, but purify it. Hiking, horseback riding. Elev 8400 ft; 1 acres. Scenic; site under a stand of Jeffrey pines. Elev and steep pitches in trail make hiking a challenge.

Toad Springs   **FREE**
Los Padres National Forest
9 mi S of Maricopa on SR 166; 15 mi SE on CR FH95 (Mill Potrero Hwy); half mi SW on FR 9N09 (Quatal Canyon Rd). Free. 5/1-11/15; 14-day limit. 5 sites on 2 acres (RVs under 16 ft). Tbls, toilets, cfga, firewood, no drkg wtr. Picnicking. Elev 5700 ft.

Valle Vista   **$5**
Los Padres National Forest
9 mi S of Maricopa on SR 166; 12 mi S on CR FH95 (Mt. Abel Rd). Suitable for small RVs. $5 daily or $30 annually. All year; 14-day limit. 7 sites on 4 acres (RVs under 32 ft). Tbls, toilets, cfga, no drkg wtr. Picnicking. Elev 4800 ft. Operated by Kern County.

MARIPOSA (190) S

Jerseydale   **FREE**
Sierra National Forest
5 mi NE of Mariposa on Hwy 140; 6 mi E on Triangle Rd; 3 mi N on Jerseydale Rd. Free. 5/1-11/30; 14-day limit. 8 sites; 24-ft RV limit. Tbls, toilets, cfga, drkg wtr. Fishing nearby.

McCabe Flat   **$10**
Merced River Recreation Area
Bureau of Land Management
Hwy 140 to Briceville, turn left & follow dirt river rd 2.5 mi W; RVs over 18 ft not recommended on bridge. $10 and free. All year; 14-day limit. 11 walk-in tent sites; 3 RV sites. Tbls, toilets, cfga, no drkg wtr. Whitewater rafting, trout fishing, rockhounding, prospecting, horseback riding, swimming, gold panning.

Railroad Flat   **$10**
Merced River Recreaton Area
Bureau of Land Management
Hwy 140 to Briceville, turn left & follow dirt river rd 4.8 mi W; RVs over 18 ft not recommended on bridge. $10 and free. All year; 14-day limit. 3 walk-in tent sites; 6 RV sites. Tbls, toilets, cfga, no drkg wtr. Whitewater rafting, trout fishing, rockhounding, prospecting, horseback riding, swimming, gold panning.

Summit Camp   **FREE**
Sierra National Forest
12.6 mi E of Mariposa on CR 49; 6.8 mi NE on CR 5S092; high-clearance vehicles suggested. Free. All year, weather permitting; 14-day limit. 14 sites on 2 acres (RVs under 22 ft). Tbls, toilets, cfga, piped drkg wtr. Picnicking. Elev 5800 ft.
   Travel tip: California State Mining & Mineral Museum, 2 mi S of Mariposa at the fairgrounds, has one of the world's largest gem & mineral collections; also an assay office, stamp mill, full-scale replica of a mine.

Willow Placer   **$10**
Merced River Recreaton Area
Bureau of Land Management
Hwy 140 to Briceville, turn left & follow dirt

river rd 3.8 mi W; RVs over 18 ft not recommended on bridge. $10 and free. All year; 14-day limit. 7 walk-in tent sites; 1 RV site. Tbls, toilets, cfga, no drkg wtr. Whitewater rafting, trout fishing, rockhounding, prospecting, horseback riding, swimming.

MARKLEEVILLE (191) N

Centerville Flat   **FREE**
Toiyabe National Forest
2 mi E of Markleeville on SR 4; E on Hwy 89, then N on forest service rd. Free. Open June-Sept; 14-day limit. Undeveloped primitive area; about 10 undesignated sites. Tbls, toilets, cfga, no drkg wtr. Hiking, picnicking. Elev 6000 ft.

Wolf Creek Meadows   **FREE**
Toiyabe National Forest
7 mi E of Markleeville on SR 4; E on Wolf Creek Rd. Free. Open June-Sept; 14-day limit. Undeveloped primitive area; about 10 undesignated sites. Tbls, toilets, cfga, no drkg wtr. Hiking, fishing, picnicking. Elev 6400 ft.

MARYSVILLE (192) N

Boat-in Campsites   **$10**
Englebright Lake
Corps of Engineers
21 mi E of Marysville on SR 20. Boat-in sites only around 815-acre lake. $10 during May-Oct; free rest of year; 14-day limit. 100 primitive sites. Toilets, cfga, no drkg wtr. Boating, fishing, hiking. 916/639-2343.

Spencerville   **FREE**
State Wildlife Area
E of Spencerville on Erle Rd, then NE on Spencerville Rd. Free. All year; 14-day limit. Primitive camping on 11,448 acres. Hunting, fishing.

MAXWELL (193) N

East Park Reservoir   **FREE**
Bureau of Reclamation
20 mi W of Maxwell on access rds. Near Mendocino National Forest. Free. Primitive sites. Drkg wtr, toilets, tbls. Fishing, boating(l), swimming, hiking trails, waterskiing.

MCARTHUR (194) N

Ahjumawi Lava Spring State Park   **$9**
3.5 mi N of McArthur on dirt road, then by boat from Big Lake unimproved PG&E ramp; no vehicle access. $9. All year; 30-day limit. 9 primitive environmental sites (3 at Crystal Springs, 3 on shore of Horr Pond, 3 just W of Ja-She Creek). Toilets, cfga, camp stoves, no drkg wtr. Boating, fishing, hiking. 6,000 acres.

MCCLOUD (195) N

A.H. Hogue $7
Modoc National Forest
17 mi E of McCloud on Hwy 89 to Bartle, then 31 mi N on FR 46 (Powder Hill Rd); follow Medicine Lake Rd to site. $7. MD-LD; free rest of yr, but no wtr; 14-day limit. 24 sites; 30-ft RV limit. Tbls, toilets, cfga, drkg wtr, beach. Fishing, swimming, boating. Elev 6700 ft. On Medicine Lake.

Fishing tip: Once the center of a volcano, 640-acre Medicine Lake is quite deep and holds a good population of rainbow and brook trout.

Ah-Di-Na $8
Shasta-Trinity National Forest
16 mi S of McCloud on FR 16 to McCloud Lake; 4 mi S on unpaved rd from S side of lake (very winding rd). $8. 5/1-11/15; 14-day limit. 16 tent sites. Tbls, flush toilets, cfga, drkg wtr. Fishing, swimming. 30 acres. Fruit orchard in season. Elev 2300 ft.

Algoma FREE
Shasta-Trinity National Forest
13 mi E on SR 89; half mi S on FR 39N06. Free. 5/1-11/1; 14-day limit. 8 sites (RVs under 32 ft). Tbls, toilets, cfga, no drkg wtr. Picnicking, fishing. Elev 3900 ft; 5 acres. Flat terrain.

Bullseye Lake FREE
Modoc National Forest
17 mi E of McCloud on Hwy 89 to Bartle; NE 31 mi on Power Hill Rd (FR 46), then pass Medicine Lake on Medicine Lake Rd to Bullseye Lake. Free. July-Oct; 14-day limit. Undesignated primitive sites; tbls, cfga, toilets, no drkg wtr. 22-ft RV limit. Fishing, swimming, hiking, ice caves.

Cattle Camp $12
Shasta-Trinity National Forest
9.5 mi E of McCloud on SR 89; half mi S on FR 40N44. $12. 5/1-11/1; 14-day limit. 25 sites (RVs under 32 ft). Well drkg wtr, firewood, tbls, flush toilets, cfga. Picnicking; fishing; swimming (1 mi). Elev 3700 ft; 7 acres. River. Flat terrain. Renovated campground has new handicap facilities, restrooms, added sites.

Fishing tip: Try trout fishing on the nearby Lower McCloud River; barbless hooks and catch-and-release required on some sections. Also big brown trout & smallmouth bass on McCloud section of Shasta Lake; summer best time.

Travel tip: Also nearby are the Falls of the McCloud River; three waterfalls tumble through a sheer walled gorge.

Fowlers Camp $12
Shasta-Trinity National Forest
6 mi E of McCloud on SR 89; at McCloud River. $12. 5/1-11/1; 14-day limit. 39 sites; 30-ft RV limit. Tbls, toilets, cfga, drkg wtr. Fishing (poor), hiking, swimming. Easy hike to 2 waterfalls. Elev 3600 ft.

Harris Spring FREE
Shasta-Trinity National Forest
16 mi E of McCloud on SR 89; 17 mi N on FR 43N15. 8/15-11/1. 15 sites (RVs under 26 ft). Tbls, toilets, cfga, firewood, piped drkg wtr. Picnicking, hiking. Elev 4800 ft; 7 acres. McCloud River. 10 mi S of proposed Medicine Lake Highlands Rec. Area. E of Mt. Shasta. Elev 4800 ft.

Trout Creek FREE
Shasta-Trinity National Forest
17 mi N of SR 89 on Pilgrim Creek Rd. Free. June-Oct; 14-day limit. About 10 undesignated sites; 30-ft RV limit. Tbls, toilets, cfga, no drkg wtr, no trash service. Fishing, swimming.

MCKINLEYVILLE (196) N

Clam Beach $10
Humboldt County Park
2 mi W of US 101 at McKinleyville, following signs; next to Little River State Beach. $10. All year; 3-day limit. 50 sites. Tbls, toilets, cfga, drkg wtr. Fishing, clamming, beachcombing.

MECCA (197) S

Corvina Beach $12
Salton Sea State Recreation Area
14 mi SE of Mecca on SR 111; on shore of Salton Sea. $12. All year; 30-limit. 500 primitive sites. Tbls, toilets, cfga, drkg wtr. Boating(l), fishing. Showers($) at the headquarters area. 228 ft below sea level.

Fishing tip: Salton Sea contains corvina of up to 37 pounds and tilapia of about 3 pounds as well as gulf croaker and sargo.

Headquarters $12
Salton Sea State Recreation Area
10 mi SE of Mecca on SR 111; next to Varner Harbor and park's visitor center. $12 without hookups off-season; $17 in-season (35-ft limit); $18 base off-season with hookups (40-ft limit). All year; 30-day limit. 25 sites. Tbls, flush toilets, cfga, drkg wtr, showers($), dump. Wheelchair access. Boating, fishing.

Mecca Beach $12
Salton Sea State Recreation Area
12 mi SE of Mecca on SR 111. $12. All year; 30-day limit. 110 sites (30-ft RV limit). Tbls, flush toilets, cfga, drkg wtr, showers($), beach. Fishing, boating, swimming.

New Camp $12
Salton Sea State Recreation Area
At park's headquarters area. $12. All year; 30-day limit. Tbls, flush toilets, cfga, drkg wtr, showers($). Boating, fishing, swimming.

Salt Creek Beach $12
Salton Sea State Recreation Area
17 mi SE of Mecca on SR 111; strip beach on the Salton Sea. $12. All year; 30-day limit. 150 primitive sites. Tbls, toilets, cfa, no drkg wtr. Fishing, boating. Excellent birdwatch-ing at mouth of creek. Tbls, toilets, cfga, no drkg wtr.

MENDOTA (199) S

Mendota State Wildlife Area FREE
Half mi S of Mendota on SR 180; 1 mi E on Panoche Rd. Free. All year; 14-day limit. Primitive camping on 11,882 acres at Fresno Slough; no facilities. Hunting, fishing, hiking.

MERCY HOT SPRINGS(200) S

Little Panoche Reservoir FREE
State Wildlife Area
Access from various roads N, W & S of Mercy Hot Springs; four units of wildlife area; lake accessible via Hwy J1 (Little Panoche Rd) NE of town. Free. All year; 14-day limit. Primitive camping on 828 acres; undeveloped. Fishing, hunting.

MILFORD (201) N

Conklin Park FREE
Plumas National Forest
5.5 mi SE of Milford on CR 336; 6 mi S on FR 26N70; .2 mi NE on FR 26N91, on Willow Creek. Free. 5/1-10/15; 14-day limit. 9 sites on 2 acres (RVs under 22 ft). Tbls, toilets, cfga, no drkg wtr. Picnicking, hiking. Fishing/big game hunting (1 mi). Elev 5900 ft.

Laufman FREE
Plumas National Forest
From US 395 at Milford, 3 mi SE on Milford Grade Rd. Free. 5/1-10/15; 14-day limit. 6 sites (22-ft RV limit). Tbls, toilets, cfga, no drkg wtr. Hiking, picnicking. Elev 5100 ft.

MINERAL (202) N

Backcountry Sites $10
Lassen Volcanic National Park
NE of Mineral on SR 89 to Manzanita Lake entrance. $10 entry fee for 7 days; camping free with written permit. All year; first come, first-served basis; 14-day limit. Undesignated tent sites. No facilities, but hot showers, coin laundry, food service, store at Manzanita Lake campground. Fishing, picnicking, hiking, boating, sightseeing. Dormant volcanos, cinder cones, lava flows, thermal springs. Hang food high from trees to avoid attracting bears.

Fishing tip: Although not stocked with trout, this lake holds trophy rainbows. Fishing is especially good just after the spring thaw. No motorized boats are allowed, and it is an excellent float tube lake. Barbless hooks and artificial lures are required for this strictly catch-and-release fishing.

Crags Camp $12
Lassen Volcanic National Park
Manzanita Lake entrance station, 4.5 mi NE on Lassen Park Rd. $12. MD-9/17; 14-day limit. Primarily an overflow area for Manzani-

ta Lake campground. 45 sites (35-ft RV limit). Tbls, toilets, cfga, drkg wtr. Fishing, hiking. $10 entry fee for 7 days. Elev 5700 ft.

Southwest Walk-In Camp   **$7**
Lassen Volcanic National Park
NE of Mineral on SR 89 (Lassen Park Rd) just beyond S entrance station. $7 with federal Senior Pass during 5/15-10/15 (others pay $14); free in late Sept until snowfall. 14-day limit. 21 walk-in tent sites. Tbls, toilets, drkg wtr, cfga, store. Boating, hiking, sightseeing. Dormant volcanos, cinder cones, lava flows, thermal springs. Elev 7000 ft. $10 entry fee for 7 days.

MODESTO (203) S

McHenry Avenue Campground   **$8**
Stanislaus River Park
Corps of Engineers
6 mi N of Modesto on McHenry Ave, across Stanislaus River; W on river rd; boat-in access only. $8. All year; 14-day limit. 19 sites. Tbls, toilets, cfga, drkg wtr. Boating, fishing, canoeing, rafting, hiking.

MOJAVE (204) S

Red Rock Canyon State Park   **$12**
25 mi NE of Mojave on SR 14. $12. All year; 14-day limit. 50 sites (30-ft RV limit). Tbls, toilets, cfga, drkg wtr, dump. 2 handicap sites. Hiking, rockhounding. 10,384 acres. Nature hikes, campfire programs.

MONTGOMERY CREEK (205)N

Madrone   **FREE**
Shasta-Trinity National Forest
2 mi SW of Montgomery City on US 299; 2.5 mi W on CR 6L005 (Fender Ferry Rd; 17 mi NW on FR N8G01. Free. 4/15-11/15; 21-day limit. 13 sites (RVs under 16 ft). Tbls, toilets, cfga, no drkg wtr. Fishing; picnicking. Elev 1200 ft; 6 acres. On Squaw Creek. Unit of Whiskeytown-Shasta-Trinity National Recreation area; mainly a backpacker camp.

MORGAN HILL (206) S

Henry W. Coe State Park   **$12**
From US 101 in Morgan Hill, follow East Dunne Ave across Anderson Lake bridge, then 13 mi; narrow, winding rd, not advised for RVs over 22 ft). $12. All year; 15-day limit. 20 primitive sites; some trail campsites for $3 per person. Tbls, toilets, cfga, drkg wtr, same shade ramadas. Hiking, biking, birdwatching, horseback riding. Visitor center.

MORRO BAY (207) S

Montana De Oro State Park   **$11**
2 mi S of Morro Bay on Hwy 1; 4 mi on South Bay Blvd to Los Osos, then 5 mi W on Pecho Valley Rd. $11 for primitive sites off-season; $15 in-season. All year; 7-day limit. 50 primitive sites along S side of creek; 27-ft RV limit. Tbls, toilets, cfga, wood stoves, no drkg wtr. Equestrian sites have pipe corrals. Fishing, horseback riding, biking. Visitor center.

MOUNTAIN CENTER (208) S

Thomas Mountain   **$5**
San Bernardino National Forest
SE on SR 74 past Lake Hemet to FR 6S13; W 4 mi; left for 3 mi on FR 5S13. $5 daily or $30 annually. All year; 14-day limit. 6 tent sites. Tbls, toilets, cfga, no drkg wtr. Fishing at Lake Hemet.

Tool Box Springs   **$5**
San Bernardino National Forest
SE on SR 74 past Lake Hemet to FR 6S13; W 4 mi; left for 4.5 mi on FR 5S13. $5 daily or $30 annually. All year; 14-day limit. 6 tent sites. Tbls, toilets, cfga, no drkg wtr. Elev 6500 ft.

MOUNT SHASTA (209) N

Castle Lake   **FREE**
Shasta-Trinity National Forest
11.6 mi SW on CR 2M002; half mi below lake. Free. 6/1-10/15; 7-day limit. 6 sites (16-ft RV limit). Tbls, toilets, cfga, no drkg wtr. Picnicking, hiking. Elev 5400 ft; 5 acres. Mountains. Stream. Castle Lake is half mi from campsite; fishing not very good.

Gumboot   **FREE**
Shasta-Trinity National Forest
3.5 mi SE of Mount Shasta on CR 2M002; 11.1 mi SW on FR 40N30; half mi S on FR 40N37. Free. 6/1-10/30; 7-day limit. 4 sites (RVs under 16 ft). Tbls, toilets, no drkg wtr. Swimming, picnicking, fishing. Elev 6200 ft; 10 acres. Lake. Campfire permit required.
Fishing tip: Plenty of trout in lake, but they're generally small.

McBride Spring   **$12**
Shasta-Trinity National Forest
4.5 mi NE of Mount Shasta on CR FH98. $12. All year; 7-day limit. Free off-season, 10/1-MD. 10 sites on 2 acres (RVs under 16 ft). Tbls, toilets, cfga, drkg wtr. No wtr off-season. Winter camping. Elev 5000 ft.
Travel tip: Mount Shasta Fish Hatchery and Sisson Hatchery Museum are half mi W of I-5; rears up to 10 million trout per year; museum on geology of area.

Panther Meadow   **FREE**
Shasta-Trinity National Forest
13.4 mi NE of Mount Shasta on CR FH98. Free. 6/15-9/30; 7-day limit. 10 walk-in sites. Tbls, toilets, cfga, no drkg wtr. Mountain climbing, picnicking, hiking. Elev 7400 ft; 5 acres. Scenic. Stream. Mt Shasta Ski Bowl (2 mi). Primarily a hiker camp.

Toad Lake   **FREE**
Shasta-Trinity National Forest
3.5 mi SE on CR 2M002; .2 mi N on FR 41N53; 12.6 W on 4WD rd FR 40N64; qtr mi hike to camp. Free. 6/1-10/1; 14-day limit. 6 tent sites. Tbls, toilets, cfga, firewood, no drkg wtr, no trash service. Picnicking, boating, swimming, fishing. Elev 7000 ft; 10 acres. Mountains. Toad Lake.

Toad Lake Cabin   **FREE**
Shasta-Trinity National Forest
3.5 mi SE of Mount Shasta on CR 2M002; qtr mi N on FR 41N53; 12 mi W on FR 40N64. Next to Toad Lake Campground. Free. Undesignated sites. Tbls, toilets, cfga, no drkg wtr.

NEEDLES (210) S

Beale Slough   **FREE**
Bureau of Land Management
From I-40 S of Needles, take the Five-Mile Rd exit E toward Colorado River; follow dirt rd under the railroad bridge; turn right (S) for 1 mi to interpretive sign. Free. Primitive undesignated sites at slough created during channelization of river. Also follow dirt rd N or S along river to unmarked turnouts available for camping. No facilities. No vehicles on beach. Fishing, boating, hiking, OHV use.

Bigelow Cholla Garden   **FREE**
Bureau of Land Management
From I-40 W of Needles, exit US 95 & follow dirt rd S about 200 ft; right to access the Four Corners Pipeline, then W along area's S boundary. Free primitive undesignated sites; no facilities; no drkg wtr. All year, but very high temperatures in summer; 14-day limit. This area contains the state's largest concentration of Bigelow cholla catus.

Chemehuevi Wash   **FREE**
Recreation Area
Bureau of Land Management
20 mi S of Needles on US 95; E of Havasu Lake Rd to Havasu Landing; 17 mi to the recreation area via 3 routes. Free. All year; 14-day limit. Summer temperatures very hot. Dispersed primitive camping; no facilities, no drkg wtr. Rockhounding, gold panning, fishing, hiking, horseback riding, OHV use.

Ft. Mohave Indian Reservation   **N/A**
Along river N of Needles, off AZ 95, in Arizona. Low fee. All year. 200 primitive sites; no facilities. Wtr available along hwy. Boating, fishing. Ask law enforcement officer for permits.

NEVADA CITY (211) N

Bowman Lake   **FREE**
Tahoe National Forest
23.2 mi E of Nevada City on SR 20; 16.2 mi N on FR 18. RV access from Graniteville Rd recommended. Free. 6/15-9/30; 14-day limit. 7 sites (RVs under 22 ft). Tbls, toilets,

cfga, no drkg wtr. Swimming, boating (d), waterskiing, picnicking, fishing. Elev 5600 ft; 3 acres.

Fishing tip: Good-size trout can be caught from Bowman Lake.

Travel tip: Visit American Victorian Museum in Nevada City; structures from 19th Century contain art, crafts exhibits, Victorian artifacts; donations.

Canyon Creek   **FREE**
Tahoe National Forest
23.2 mi E of Nevada City on SR 20; 13.2 mi N on FR 18; 2.3 mi SE on FR 18N13. RV access from Graniteville Rd recommended. Free. 6/15-9/30; 14-day limit. 20 sites (RVs under 22 ft). Tbls, toilets, cfga, no drkg wtr. Picnicking, fishing, boating (l), swimming (1 mi). Elev 6000 ft; 5 acres. On Canyon Creek 1 mi below Faucherie Reservoir.

Travel tip: Nevada City Winery offers free tours & samples daily.

Jackson Creek   **FREE**
Tahoe National Forest
23.2 mi E of Nevada City on SR 20; 13.2 mi N on FR 18; 4 mi E on CR 843. 6/15-9/30; 14-day limit. RV access from Graniteville Rd recommended. Free. 14 sites (RVs under 22 ft). Tbls, toilets, cfga, no drkg wtr. Picnicking. Swimming, waterskiing, boating (d), fishing (1 mi). Elev 5600 ft; 7 acres. On Jackson Creek, 1 mi above Bowman Lake.

South Yuba River Campground   **$5**
Bureau of Land Management
10 mi N of Nevada City on North Bloomfield Rd; 1.5 mi on dirt/gravel rd from bridge at Edwards Crossing. $5. 4/1-10/15; 14 day limit. 16 sites (30-ft RV limit). Toilets, drkg wtr, tbls, cfga. Hiking, hunting, fishing, horseback riding, gold panning. Elev 2500 ft. 12 mi hiking/riding & bridle trail, swimming, mountain biking, trout fishing, rockhounding. South Yuba River. Malakoff Diggins State Historical Park nearby.

NEW CUYAMA (212) S

Aliso   **$5**
Los Padres National Forest
3 mi W of New Cuyama on SR 166; 4 mi S on CR AL1S0 (Aliso Canyon Rd); 1 mi S on FR 11N02. $5 daily or $30 annually. All year; 14 day limit. 10 sites (RVs under 28 ft). Tbls, toilets, cfga, no drkg wtr. Boil well wtr before drkg. Horseback riding, hiking. Elev 3200 ft; 3 acres. Elev 3200 ft. Popular camp during deer season.

Ballinger   **$5**
Los Padres National Forest
10 mi E of New Cuyama on SR 166; 4 mi S on SR 33; 3 mi E to end of FR 9N10 (Ballinger Canyon Rd); at Ballinger Canyon OHV Area. $5 daily or $30 annually. All year; 14-day limit. 20 sites (RVs under 32 ft). Tbls, toilets, cfga, no drkg wtr. Elev 3000 ft; 8 acres. Mainly used by motorcycles & 4WD, but RVs

okay. Hungry Valley Recreation Area nearby for ORV enthusiasts.

Bates Canyon   **$5**
Los Padres National Forest
10 mi W of New Cuyama on SR 166; 8 mi S on FR 11N01. $5 daily or $30 annually. All year; 14-day limit. 6 sites (RVs under 16 ft). Tbls, toilets, cfga, no drkg wtr. Elev 2900 ft; 1 acre. Entrance into San Rafael Wilderness.

Hog Pen Springs   **$5**
Los Padres National Forest
3 mi W of New Cuyama on SR 166; 4 mi S on CR AL1S0 (Aliso Canyon Rd); 1 mi S on FR 11N02; 2 mi S on Trail 27W01, BY FOOT OR 4WD. $5 daily or $30 annually. 5/1-11/30; 14-day limit. 7 tent sites; 1 acre. Tbls, toilets, cfga, piped drkg wtr. Hiking, picnicking, horseback riding (1 mi). Elev 3600 ft.

Nettle Spring   **$5**
Los Padres National Forest
10 mi E of New Cuyama on SR 166; 16 mi S on SR 33; 8 mi NE on FR 8N06; 8 mi on dirt rd in Apache Canyon. $5 daily or $30 annually. All year; 14-day limit. 9 sites (RVs under 22 ft). Tbls, toilets, cfga, no drkg wtr. Picnicking, hiking. Elev 4400 ft; 4 acres. Not recommended for RVs. Popular area for 4WD.

Ozena   **$5**
Los Padres National Forest
10 mi E on SR 166; 20 mi S on SR 33; 1.5 mi E on CR 9N03 (Lockwood Valley Rd). $5 daily or $30 annually. All year; 14-day limit. 12 sites on 15 acres (RVs under 32 ft). Tbls, toilets, cfga, drkg wtr. Elev 3600 ft.

Painted Rock   **$5**
Los Padres National Forest
4 mi S of New Cuyamon CR 11N02; 1 mi S on Trail 26W01; 5 mi SW on Trail 27W04. $5 daily or $30 annually. 5/1-11/1; 14-day limit. 3 tent sites; 1 acre. Tbls, toilets, cfga, no drkg wtr (wtr at Montgomery Spring, but must be purified). Hiking, horseback riding, picnicking.

Rancho Nuevo   **FREE**
Los Padres National Forest
10 mi E of New Cuyama on SR 166; 19 mi on SR 33; 1 mi W on FR 704; 1 mi SW on FR 7N04A (sandy river crossing; 4WD recommended). Free. 4/1-11/30; 14-day limit. 2 sites. Tbls, toilets, cfga, no drkg wtr. Picnicking, horseback riding (1 mi). Elev 3600 ft; 1 acre. Stream. Heavily mineralized spring, not recommended for human consumption by state board of health because of high salt content. The spring is famous for its therapeutic qualities.

Salisbury Potrero   **$5**
Los Padres National Forest
4 mi S of New Cuyama on CR 11N02; 6 mi SE on Trail 26W01. $5 daily or $30 annually. 5/1-10/30; 14-day limit. 2 tent sites; 1 acre. Tbls, cfga, no toilets, no drkg wtr. Hiking, picnicking, horseback riding. Elev 4500 ft.

Tinta   **FREE**
Los Padres National Forest
10 mi E of New Cuyama on SR 166; 19 mi on SR 33; 1 mi W on FR 7N04 (Tinta Rd); 2 mi NW on FR 7N04J (not recommended for RVs). Free. 4/1-11/30; 14-day limit. 3 primitive undeveloped sites. Tbls, toilets, cfga, no drkg wtr. Picnicking. Elev 3600 ft; 1 acre. Stream. At head of Tinta Canyon motorcycle trail. Only OHVs may be operated on roads & designated trails around this camp.

Upper Rancho Nuevo   **$5**
Los Padres National Forest
10 mi E of New Cuyama on SR 166; 16.7 mi S on SR 33; 1.5 mi W on FR 7N04A; 5 mi W on Trail 24W03. $5 daily or $30 annually. 5/1-11/30; 14-day limit. 4 tent sites. Cfga, no tbls, no toilets, no drkg wtr. Hiking, horseback riding. Elev 4500 ft; 1 acre. Camp surrounded by pinion pines, chaparral and yucca in a beautiful secluded canyon. Stream.

Yellowjacket   **$5**
Los Padres National Forest
10 mi E of New Cuyama on SR 166; 13.6 mi S on SR 33; 5.5 mi NE on FR 8N06; 4 mi S on Trail 23W44. $5 daily or $30 annually. All year; 14-day limit. 1 tent site; 1 acre. Tbl, cfga, undrinkable wtr, no toilets. Hiking, horseback riding, picnicking.

NEW PINE CREEK (213) N

Cave Lake   **FREE**
Modoc National Forest
6.2 mi SE of New Pine Creek on FR 48N01 (dirt rd quite steep for large RVs). Free. 7/1-10/15; 14-day limit. 6 tent sites. Tbls, toilets, cfga, piped drkg wtr, firewood. Picnicking, boating, swimming, trout fishing, hiking, canoeing. Trail. Elev 6600 ft; 8 acres. No motor boats. 1 mi from Highgrade National Recreation Area.

Fishing tip: Near Cave Lake Camp can be found some excellent stream fishing: Try Twelve Mile Creek, Dismal Creek and Bidwell Creek for trout.

Lily Lake   **FREE**
Modoc National Forest
6.4 mi SE of New Pine Creek on FR 48N01. Free. 7/1-10/15; 14-day limit. 6 sites (15-ft RV limit). Tbls, toilets, cfga, no drkg wtr. Swimming, fishing, picnicking, boating, rockhounding, hunting, canoeing. Elev 6600 ft; 4 acres. Lily Lake. No motor boats. 1 mi from Highgrade National Recreation Area.

NILAND (215) S

Bombay Beach   **$12**
Salton Sea State Recreation Area
18 mi NW of Niland on SR 111; farthest S of the park's campgrounds. $12. All year; 30-day limit. 200 primitive sites; 35-ft RV limit. Tbls, toilets, cfga, drkg wtr. Fishing, boating.

Fishing tip: Near good fishing for giant corvina; most are 5-8 pounds, with occasional 30-pounder caught. Lake record is 37 pounds.

Hazard Unit   **FREE**
Imperial State Wildlife Area
About 2 mi NW of Niland on SR 111; W on McDonald Rd to smallest section of wildlife area. Free. All year; 14-day limit. Toilets, cfga, drkg wtr. Hunting, fishing, boating.

Ramer Unit   **FREE**
Imperial State Wildlife Area
About 8 mi S of Niland on SR 111, S of Calipatria at Ramer Lake. Free. All year; 14-day limit. Primitive camping. Toilets, cfga, drkg wtr. Hunting, fishing, boating.

Red Hill Marina   **$7**
Imperial County Park
5 mi S of Niland on Hwy 111; right on Sinclair Rd, then right on Garst Rd for about 1.5 mi; left on Red Hill Rd. $7 base. All yaer; 14-day limit. 115 sites. Tbls, flush toilets, showers, cfga, drkg wtr, hookups($). Boating(l), fishing. Fee not verified for 2007.

Slab City   **FREE**
Boondock Camp
4 mi E of Niland on Beal Rd. Free desert camping at former Marine Corps training camp where concrete slab foundations are all that's left. Register at Christian Center in mobile bldg on main street. Free. No facilities; pack out trash, haul in wtr from Niland; dump in Niland. Swap meets on weekends. Large population of Loners on Wheels members during winter.
Fishing tip: Salton Sea contains saltwater corvina, sargo, gulf croaker, tilapia.

Wister Unit   **FREE**
Imperial State Wildlife Area
About 3 mi NW of Niland on SR 111; on E shore of Salton Sea. Free. All year; 14-day limit. Primitive camping. Toilets, cfga, drkg wtr. Hunting, fishing, boating.

NORTH FORK (216) S

China Bar   **FREE**
Sierra National Forest
4.6 mi SE of North Fork on CR 225; 33.2 mi NE on FR 4S81; 1.5 mi S on FR 6S25; 3.5 mi NE, BY BOAT or trail. Free. 6/15-9/15; 14-day limit. 6 tent sites. Tbls, toilets, cfga, no drkg wtr. Boating, fishing Elev 3400 ft; 3 acres. Boat camp on San Joaquin River inlet or Jackass Creek inlet to Mammoth Pool Reservoir.
Fishing tip: Trout fishing quite good in spring on Mammoth Pool Reservoir.

Clover Meadow   **FREE**
Sierra National Forest
4.6 mi S of North Fork on CR 225; 38 mi NE on FR 4S81 (Minarets Rd); 1.4 mi N on FR 5S30. Free. 6/15-10/15; 14 day limit. 7 sites (20-ft RV limit). Tbls, toilets, cfga, drkg wtr. Hiking, backpacking. Trailhead parking for Ansel Adams Wilderness. Elev 7000 ft.

Fish Creek   **$7**
Sierra National Forest
4.6 mi S of North Fork on CR 225; 18 mi NE on FR 4S81. During 4/15-11/15, $7 with federal Senior Pass; others pay $14 (free walk-in camping after LD); 14-day limit. 7 sites (20-ft RV limit). Tbls, toilets, cfga, no drkg wtr. Fishing, picnicking. Elev 4600 ft.
Travel tip: Sierra Mono Indian Museum at jct of CRs 225, 228 & 274 displays artifacts unique to the Mono Indians; also wildlife exhibits, tools, jewelry, basket collection.

Granite Creek   **FREE**
Sierra National Forest
4.6 mi SE of North Fork on CR 225; 50.6 mi NE on FR 4S81; 1.4 mi N on FR 5S30; 3.4 mi NE on FR 5S071. Free. 6/1-10/31; 14-day limit. 20 sites on 5 acres; 20-ft RV limit. Tbls, toilets, cfga, no drkg wtr. Hiking, fishing. Elev 6900 ft. Upper loop has horse corrals; no horses in lower loop.

Little Jackass   **FREE**
Sierra National Forest
4.6 mi SE on CR 225; 35 mi NE on FR 4S81; 1.5 mi SE on FR 6S22. Free. 5/1-10/15; 14-day limit. 5 sites (RVs under 21 ft). Tbls, toilets, cfga, firewood. Picnicking, fishing, swimming, hiking. Elev 4800 ft; 3 acres. Mountains.

Redinger Lake   **FREE**
Sierra National Forest
From post office in North Fork, 4.3 mi E on Hwy 41; right on Italian Bar Rd (FR 225) for 3.8 mi; ring on FR 235 for 2.1 mi to paved parking area at spillway. Free. All year; 14-day limit. Undeveloped pavement camping; 25-ft RV limit. No tbls, cfga, trash service or drkg wtr; pit toilets. Fishing, hiking, boating (l), waterskiing. No campfires; use charcoal or hibachis. No camping on beaches or either side of lake.

Upper Chiquito   **FREE**
Sierra National Forest
Half mi E of North Fork on CR 225; 9 mi NE on CR 274; 23 mi NE on FR 5S07. Free. 6/1-10/31; 14-day limit. 20 sites (RVs under 22 ft). Toilets, cfga, no drkg wtr. Fishing, picnicking. Elev 6800 ft; 6 acres. Chiquito Creek. Near Chiquito TrailHead accessing Ansel Adams Wilderness & Yosemite.

Whiskey Falls   **FREE**
Sierra National Forest
1.5 mi E on CR 225; 7 mi NE on FR 8S09; 1.5 mi E on FR 8S70. Free. 6/1-11/15; 14-day limit. 14 sites (RVs under 22 ft). Tbls, toilets, cfga, no drkg wtr. Picnicking, fishing, swimming.

OAKDALE (217) S

Valley Oak   **$8**
Stanislaus River Park
Corps of Engineers
1.5 mi N of Oakdale on SR 120; 3 mi E on Rodden Rd; boat-in access only. $8. All year;

14-day limit. 10 sites. Tbls, toilets, cfga, drkg wtr. Canoeing, fishing, boating, hiking.

OAKHURST (218) S

Bowler Group Camp   **FREE**
Sierra National Forest
While driving N from Oakhurst on Hwy 41, turn right on FR 222 for 5.5 mi, then left on Beasore Rd (FR 7) for about 20 mi. Free. July-Oct; 14-day limit. 12 group sites (20-ft RV limit). Tbls, toilets, cfga, no drkg wtr. Horses allowed.

Jerseydale Campground   **FREE**
Sierra National Forest
From northbound SR 41 in Oakhurst, left on Hwy 49 for 15 mi; right on Triangle Rd for 2.5 mi; bear left on Triangle at jct with Westfall Rd; after 2.1. right on Jerseydale Rd for 2.2 mi, then turn at FR 4S82 just past the fire station. Camp also reachable from Mariposa. Free. May-Nov; 14-day limit. 8 sites (on slopes); 24-ft RV limit. Tbls, toilets, cfga, drkg wtr (must be boiled), no trash service.

Kelty Meadow   **$7**
Sierra National Forest
5 mi N of Oakhurst on SR 41; 10 mi NE on CR 632 (Sky Ranch Rd); on Willow Creek. $7 with federal Senior Pass; others pay $14. (formerly free). MD-10/1; 14-day limit. 11 sites . Tbls, toilets, cfga, no drkg wtr, horse facilities. Horseback riding, hiking, fishing. Campground is in the area 7 mi N of Bass Lake known as Kelty Meadow. Elev 5800 ft.

Nelder Grove   **FREE**
Sierra National Forest
.2 mi N of Oakhurst on CR 426; 4 mi N on SR 41; 8.1 mi NE on FR 6S10; 10.3 mi NW on FR 4S04 (steep, narrow entrance rd). Free. 5/21-9/30; 14-day limit. 7 sites (RVs under 22 ft). Tbls, toilets, cfga, no drkg wtr. Hiking, picnicking, fishing. Elev 5300 ft; 3 acres. Scenic. Nature trails. California Creek. Located within Nelder Grove of giant sequoias. Interpretive display.
Travel tip: Fresno State Historical Park, NE of town via SR 41 & CR 426 to School Rd., has a collection of historic buildings typical of those found in a local late-19th Century community.

Summit Campground   **FREE**
Sierra National Forest
From Yosemite-Sierra Visitor Bureau in Oakhurst, go 13.5 mi to Yosemite NP entrance, then make left for 4.5 mi to Wawona; left at Wawona Hotel, through golf course and E for 4.5 mi; left on FR 5S09A. Free. June-Oct; 14-day limit. 6 sites (RVs not recommended) Tbls, toilets, cfga, no drkg wtr, no trash service. High-clearance vehicles recommended.

OGILBY (220) S

Dunes Vista　　　　　**$125**
Long-Term Visitor Area
Bureau of Land Management
From I-8 exit, qtr mi N on Ogilby Rd. Long-Term Visitor Area on W side of rd. $125 annual permit or $5 daily. Free camping in desert outside LTVA for up to 14 days. No facilities, but facilities at Yuma; dump at RV Dump A Tank, Ave 3E exit off I-8. Golden Eagle, Golden Age & Golden Access Passport discounts do not apply to LTVA fees.

OJAI (221) S

Cherry Creek　　　　　**FREE**
Los Padres National Forest
1 mi W on SR 150; 23.5 mi NW on SR 33; 2.8 mi S on W. Tecuya Rd 9N19, then Cherry Creek OHV Route 113; access only by OHV. Free. 11/1-6/30; 14-day limit. 2 tent sites. Cfga, no tbls, no toilets, no drkg wtr. Swimming, fishing. Elev 4500 ft; 2 acres. Stream. Closed during fire season, 7/1-10/31.

Howard Creek　　　　　**$5**
Los Padres National Forest
1 mi W of Ojai on SR 150; 14.8 mi NW on SR 33; 2.2 mi E on FR 7N03 (Sespe River Rd); 1.2 mi NE on FR 5N03. $5 daily or $30 annually. All year; 14-day limit. 6 sites (no trailers). Toilets, cfga, no tbls, no drkg wtr. Hiking, picnicking, fishing. Elev 3200 ft; 2 acres. Geological interest. Howard/Sespe Creeks.

Lions Canyon　　　　　**$5**
Los Padres National Forest
1 mi W of Ojai on SR 150; 14.7 mi NW on SR 33; 5.5 mi E on FR 7N03 (Sespe River Rd). $5 daily or $30 annually. 4/1-1/1; 14-day limit. 22 sites (16-ft RV limit). Tbls, toilets, cfga, drkg wtr. Swimming, fishing, hiking. On Sespe Creek.

Matilija　　　　　**$5**
Los Padres National Forest
1 mi W of Ojai on SR 150; 5 mi NW on SR 33; 7.3 mi NW on FR 5N13; 1.2 mi N on Trail 23W07. $5 daily or $30 annually. 1/1-7/1; 14-day limit. 5 tent sites. Toilets, cfga, no tbls, no drkg wtr. Hiking, swimming, picnicking, fishing. Elev 2000 ft; 2 acres. Located along trail, 3 mi from the end of a 5-mi spur (Matilija Reservoir Rd). On upper N fork of Matilija Reservoir.

Middle Lion　　　　　**$5**
Los Padres National Forest
Rose Valley Recreation Area
1 mi W of Ojai on SR 150; 14.8 mi NW on SR 33; 5.4 mi E on FR 7N03 (Sespe River Rd); 1 mi S on FR 22W06. $5 daily or $30 anually. All year; 14-day limit. 8 sites (RVs under 31 ft). Tbls, toilets, cfga, no drkg wtr. Hiking, picnicking, fishing, mountain biking, horseback riding. Elev 3300 ft; 5 acres. Scenic. Lion Creek.

Murietta Trail Camp　　　　　**$5**
Los Padres National Forest
Located along trail 1.5 mi from the end of a 5-mi spur (Matilija Reservoir Rd); 7 mi N of Ojai on SR 33. $5 daily or $30 annually. 11/15-6/30; 14-day limit. 5 tent sites. Toilets, cfga, no tbls, no drkg wtr (boil creek wtr). Hiking.

Oak Flat Trail Camp　　　　　**$5**
Los Padres National Forest
1 mi W of Ojai on SR 150; 14.5 mi NW on SR 33; 11.5 mi E on FR 7N04; 1 blk SE on trail. $5 daily or $30 annually. 4/1-11/31; 14 day limit. 3 tent sites. Tbls, cfga, no toilets, no drkg wtr. Hiking, swimming, picnicking, fishing, horseback riding. Scenic.

Pine Mountain　　　　　**$5**
Los Padres National Forest
1 mi W of Ojai on SR 150; 29.2 mi NW on SR 33; 5 mi E on FR 6N06. $5 daily or $30 annually. 4/1-12/31; 14-day limit. 6 tent sites. Tbls, toilets, cfga, no drkg wtr. Hiking, fishing, horseback riding. Elev 6700 ft; 5 acres. Located in large timber. Dry camp; wtr available quarter mi down trail at Raspberry Spring.

The Pines Trail Camp　　　　　**$5**
Los Padres National Forest
5 mi E of Ojai on SR 150; 1 mi NE on co hwy; 1.8 mi NE on Trail 22W08. $5 daily or $30 annually. All year; 14-day limit. 3 tent sites. Cfga, no tbls, no toilets, no drkg wtr. Hiking.

Potrero Seco Trail Camp　　　　　**$5**
Los Padres National Forest
1 mi W of Ojai on SR 150; 30 mi NW on SR 33; 3 mi W on Trail 6N03. $5 daily or $30 annually. Elev 4900 ft. 4/1-12/1; 14-day limit. 2 tent sites. Cfga, wtr, no tbls. Hiking.

Reyes Creek　　　　　**$5**
Los Padres National Forest
36 mi N of Ojai on SR 33; 3 mi E on CR 9N03; 2 mi S on FR 7N11. $5 daily or $30 annually. All year; 14-day limit. 30 sites (22-ft RV limit). Tbls, toilets, cfga, drkg wtr. Fishing, hiking.

Reyes Peak　　　　　**$5**
Los Padres National Forest
1 mi W of Ojai on SR 150; 29.2 mi NW on SR 33; 6 mi E on FR 6N06. $5 daily or $30 annually. May-Nov; 14-day limit. 6 sites on 15 acres; 16-ft RV limit. Tbls, cfga, no toilets, no drkg wtr. Horseback riding, hiking. Scenic.

Rose Valley Falls　　　　　**$5**
Los Padres National Forest
Rose Valley Recreation Area
15 mi N of Ojai on Hwy 33; 5.5 mi E on Sespe River Rd. $5 daily or $30 annually. All year; 14-day limit. 9 sites (30-ft RV limit). Tbls, toilets, cfga, no drkg wtr. Swimming, fishing. Elev 3400 ft.

Sespe Hot Springs Trail Camp　　　　　**$5**
Los Padres National Forest
1 mi W of Ojai on SR 150; 14.8 mi NW on SR 33; 21 mi E on FR 7N03 (Sespe River Rd); 1 mi N on Trail 20W12. Access by foot or 4-wheel drive. $5 daily or $30 annually. 4/1-12/31; 14-day limit. 5 tent sites. Tbls, toilets, cfga, no drkg wtr. Hiking, swimming, picnicking, fishing, horseback riding. Elev 3200 ft; 2 acres. Scenic. Sespe Creek stocked annually with rainbow trout.

OLEMA (222) N

Coast Camp　　　　　**$7.50**
Point Reyes National Seashore
Half mi NW of Olema on Bear Valley Rd. to park headquarters. 8 mi from trailhead on nearly level trails, or 6 mi via Inverness Ridge on steeper trails. $7.50 with federal Senior Pass; others pay $15. All year; 4-day limit. Total stay in backcountry limited to 4 days. 14 tent sites. Groups (8 or more) limited to certain sites, with maximum of 25 per group and only one group per night. Tbls, toilets, cfga, drkg wtr. Only gas stoves, charcoal in grills provided or canned heat may be used for cooking. Wood fires prohibited except for driftwood fires on the beach. Hitchrail for horses. No motorbikes or pets. Camping permit required, available at park headquarters. Reservations recommended. Nature trails. On an open, grassy bluff about 200 yds above beach. No trees.

Glen Camp　　　　　**$7.50**
Point Reyes National Seashore
Half mi NW of Olema on Bear Valley Rd. to park headquarters. 4.6 mi from trailhead on nearly level trails. $7.50 with federal Senior Pass; others pay $15. All year; 4-day limit. Total stay in backcountry limited to 4 days. 12 tent sites. No parties more than 8 persons. Tbls, toilets, cfga, drkg wtr. Hiking, horseback riding, swimming (in ocean), picnicking, fishing. Only gas stoves, charcoal in grills provided or canned heat may be used for cooking. Wood fires prohibited except for driftwood fires on the beach. Hitchrail for horses. No motorbikes or pets. Camping permit required, available at park headquarters. Reservations recommended. Nature trails. In a small, wooded valley 2 mi from ocean.

Sky Camp　　　　　**$7.50**
Point Reyes National Seashore
Half mi NW of Olema on Bear Valley Rd to park headquarters. 2.8 mi from trailhead on W side of Mt Wittenberg. $7.50 with federal Senior Pass; others pay $15. All year; 4-day limit. Total stay in backcountry limited to 4 days. 12 primitive walk-in tent sites. Groups limited to certain sites, with maximum of 25 per group and only one group (of more than 8 persons) per night. Tbls, toilets, cfga, drkg wtr. Hiking, horseback riding, swimming (in ocean), picnicking, fishing. Only gas stoves, charcoal in grills provided or canned heat may be used for cooking. Wood fires prohibited except for driftwood fires on the beach. Hitchrail for horses. No motorbikes or pets. Camping permit required, available at park

headquarters. Reservations recommended. Nature trails. Elev 1025 ft. Good view of Drakes Bay and surrounding hills.

Wildcat Camp $7.50
Point Reyes National Seashore

Half mi NW of Olema on Bear Valley Rd. to park headquarters. 7 mi by foot to campground from trailhead. $7.50 with federal Senior Pass; others pay $15. All year; 4-day limit. Total stay in backcountry limited to 4 days. 7 tent sites, each for 9-25 persons on Saturday; other times, both groups and small camping parties may use sites. Tbls, toilets, cfga, drkg wtr. Hiking, horseback riding, swimming (in ocean), picnicking, fishing. Only gas stoves, charcoal in grills provided or canned heat may be used for cooking. Wood fires prohibited except for driftwood fires on the beach. Organized juvenile groups must have one adult supervisor for each eight juveniles. Camp is in a grassy meadow near a small stream that flows into the sea. No trees; easy beach access. Hitchrail for horses. No motorbikes. Camping permit required; available at park headquarters. Reservations recommended. Nature trails. No pets.

ORICK (223) N

Dry Lagoon Walk-In Camp $10
Humboldt Lagoons State Park

About 11 mi S of Orick on US 101 (13 mi N of Trinidad) at milemarker 114.5; obtain combination to a locked gate & register at Patrick's Point SP, 10 mi S on Hwy 101. $10 during 9/16-5/14; $12 peak season. All year; 15-day limit. 6 primitive walk-in environmental tent sites. Tbls, toilets, cfga, no drkg wtr. Visitor center. Fishing, hiking, boating, canoeing, beachcombing, birdwatching, whalewatching, agate hunting.

Gold Bluffs Beach Campground $11
Prairie Creek Redwoods State Park

5 mi N of Orick on US 101; 4 mi W on Davison Rd; register at park visitor center or beach station for directions & lock combination to campground; short hike from parking for 3 environmental tent sites. $11 for environmental sites; $15 base for 25 developed sites (27-ft RV limit). All year, weather permitting. Tbls, toilets, cfga, food lockers, no drkg wtr, no trash service for environmental camps; developed sites have tbls, flush toilets, solar showers, drkg wtr, food lockers. Two backpacker camp areas also available in the park. Nature study, beachcombing, hiking trails (70 mi), birdwatching, biking trails, nature trail, visitor center.

Stone Lagoon Boat-In Camp $10
Humbolt Lagoons State Park

About 1.5 mi S of the Redwood Information Center S of Orick at N end of Stone Lagoon. $10 during 9/16-5/14; $12 peak season. All year; 15-day limit. 6 dispersed sites in cove across lagoon from visitor center, accessible by boat or foot. Toilets, cfga, tbls, food lockers, no drkg wtr. Fishing, hiking, boat-

ing, canoeing, beachcombing, birdwatching, whalewatching, agate hunting. Self-register near boat ramp at visitor center.

ORLAND (224) N

Buckhorn $10
Black Butte Lake
Corps of Engineers

14 mi W of I-5 at Orland on CR 200 (Newville Rd) past dam; half mi SW of jct with Black Butte Rd. $10 during Oct-March; $15 rest of year. All year; 14-day limit. 65 sites. Tbls, flush toilets, cfga, drkg wtr, showers, playground, beach, amphitheater, dump. Boating(l), fishing, hiking, swimming.

Orland Buttes Campground $7.50
Black Butte Lake
Corps of Engineers

From I-5 at Orland, 6 mi W on CR 200; 3.3 mi SW on CR 206; half mi W. $7.50 with federal Senior Pass; others pay $15. 4/1-9/15; 14-day limit. 35 sites (18 pull-through); 35-ft RV limit. Tbls, flush toilets, cfga, drkg wtr, dump, beach, fish cleaning station. Horseback riding, swimming, waterskiing, fishing.

ORLEANS (225) N

Aikens Creek West $8
Six Rivers National Forest

10.5 mi SW of Orleans on SR 96 (5 mi E of Weitchpec); on Klamath River. $8. 6/1-11/1; 14-day limit. 29 sites (35-ft RV limit). Tbls, flush toilets, cfga, drkg wtr, dump. Wheelchair access. Fishing, swimming. Multi-family sites available.

Beans Camp Campground
FREE
Klamath National Forest

From Hwy 96 at S end of Orleans, follow FR 15N01 (Eyesee Rd) 17 mi; right on FR 12N22 for half mi for first two sites; four other sites down the hill. Free. All year; 14-day limit. 6 sites. Tbls, toilets, cfga, no drkg wtr, no trash service. Secluded at 4000-ft elev. Administered by Six Rivers NF.

E-Ne-Nuck $10
Six Rivers National Forest

10.2 mi SW of Orleans on SR 96; next to Bluff Creek camp at Klamath River. $10. 7/1-11/5; 14-day limit. 11 sites (30-ft RV limit). Tbls, toilets, cfga, drkg wtr. Swimming, boating, fishing. Formerly named Bluff Creek.

Fish Lake Campground $10
Six Rivers National Forest

10.7 mi SW of Orleans on SR 96; 7.7 mi NW on FR 16N01. $10. May-Sept; 14-day limit. 24 sites; 12 acres; 20-ft RV limit. Toilets, tbls, drkg wtr. Dump at nearby Aikens Creek Campground. Hiking, fishing, picnicking, swimming. Multi-family sites available.

Frog Pond Campground FREE
Klamath National Forest

24 mi N of Orleans on SR 96; just past bridge over Klamath River & qtr mi before Dillon Creek Campground, turn on FR 14N69; at 3-way jct, veer left onto FR 14N21 for several miles, then onto dirt rd FR 13N13 to camp. Free. May-Oct; 14-day limit. 3 sites. Tbls, toilet, cfga, no drkg wtr, no trash service. Fishing in Frog Pond, also named Lake Oogarmomtok. Administered by Six Rivers NF.

Nordheimer $8
Klamath National Forest

About 7 mi N of Orleans on SR 96; 14 mi E on Hwy 93; on Salmon River. $8 during 5/1-10/31; free rest of year; 14-day limit. 8 sites. Toilets, cfga, drkg wtr. No wtr or trash service during free period. Boating(l), fishing, whitewater rafting. Secluded. Remnants of historic mining operations are nearby; some fruit trees remain from homesteading activities. Administered by Six Rivers NF.

Travel tip: Remnants of historic mining operations are nearby; some fruit trees remain from homesteading activities.

Pearch Creek Campground $10
Six Rivers National Forest

1 mi NE of Orleans on SR 96. $10. MD-11/1; 14-day limit. 10 sites (22-ft RV limit) Toilets, tbls, cfga, drkg wtr, dump. Hiking, fishing, picnicking, swimming.

OROVILLE (226) N

Feather Falls FREE
Plumas National Forest

Follow Oro Dam Blvd NE of Oroville; right on Olive Hwy for 8 mi; right on Forbestown Rd for 7 mi; left on Lumpkin Rd for 10 mi to trailhead turnoff; left for 1.5 mi; at Feather Falls trailhead. Free. All year; 14-day limit. 20 sites. Tbls, toilets, cfga, piped drkg wtr. Hiking, fishing. Elev 2500 ft.

Oroville State Wildlife Area FREE

Just SW of Oroville off SR 70 & S of SR 162. Free. All year; 14-day limit. Primitive camping on 11,870 acres bordered by 12 mi of river channels. Fishing, hunting, hiking, canoeing.

Fishing tip: The 15,500-acre Lake Oroville is quite heavily fished, but its variety of fish is attractive: coho and king salmon, trout, bass and crappie. 19-pound salmon & 3-pound crappie have been caught. "Bassmaster Magazine" ranks lake as having the state's best bass fishing.

OXNARD (227) S

Thornhill Broome Campground $11
Point Mugu State Park

15 mi S of Oxnard on SR 1. $11 off-season; $15 in-season. 7-day limit. 88 primitive sites (31-ft RV limit). Tbls, toilets, cfga, drkg wtr, no showers, no shade. Fishing, surfing, beachcombing.

PALMDALE (228) S

Big Buck Trail Camp $5
Angeles National Forest
5.4 mi S of Palmdale on SR 14; 9.5 mi S on CR N3 (Angeles Forest Hwy); 5.2 mi W on FR 3N17; 1 mi S on FR 4W24; hike in only. $5 daily or $30 annually. 3/1-10/30; 14-day limit. 3 undesignated tent sites. Tbls, cfga, no toilets, no drkg wtr. Hiking, picnicking. Trail camp for Pacific Crest Trail. Elev 5500 ft.

Mount Pacifico $5
Angeles National Forest
5.4 mi S of Palmdale on SR 14; 9.5 mi S on CR N3 (Angeles Forest Hwy); 6.5 mi E on FR 3N17. $5 daily or $30 annually. 5/15-11/15; 14-day limit. 7 sites (suitable primarily for pickup campers). Tbls, toilets, cfga, firewood, no drkg wtr. Picnicking, horseback riding. Elev 7100 ft; 1 acre. Good weather may lengthen season. Closed in early 2007 due to road damage; reopening expected late July.

South Fork $5
Angeles National Forest
From Palmdale, follow 156th St (Valyermo Rd) to Big Rock Creek Rd, then 2 mi. $5 daily or $30 annually. May-Nov (or weather permitting); 14-day limit. 21 sites; 16-ft RV limit. Tbls, toilets, cfga, no drkg wtr. Picnicking, hiking trails. Stocked trout in Big Rock Creek. Elev 4500 ft.

PALM DESERT (229) S

Santa Rosa FREE
State Wildlife Area
SE and SW of Palm Desert, access from SR 74. Free. All year; 14-day limit. Primitive camping on 103,862 acres; no facilities. Hiking, hunting. Area contains nation's largest herd of penninsular bighorn sheep.

PALO VERDE (231) S

Mule Mountain $140
Long-Term Visitor Area
Bureau of Land Management
N on SR 78 to Bradshaw Rd; left on Bradshaw Trail (dirt rd) to Wiley's Well Camp. LTVA on both sides of Wiley's Well Rd 9 mi S to Coon Hollow Camp. $140 seasonal permit or $30 for 14 days during 9/15-4/15; $5 per day or $50 seasonal during 4/16-9/14. 14-day limit. Undesignated sites. Toilets at Wiley's Well and Coon Hollow Camps; toilets, drkg wtr, dump at Wiley's Well rest area on I-10. Hiking, hunting, picnicking. Camping in desert outside LTVA free for 14 days within 28-day period. LTVA permits not required for stays of less than 14 days. Federal Senior Pass discounts do not apply to LTVA fees.

Oxbow Campground $5
Bureau of Land Management
Lake Havasu District
3 mi S of Palo Verde on SR 78; 1 mi E on gravel rd from sign marked "Colorado River."

Camp is at old river channel oxbow in both Arizona & California. $5 (or $50 annually). All year; 14-day limit. Undesignated, unmarked primitive sites. No facilities. Boating(l), fishing, hiking, swimming, picnicking. Near popular OHV trails & Cibola National Wildlife Refuge. Free use permit required. No open fires; use charcoal grills or propane stoves.

Palo Verdes County Park FREE
Imperial County
3 mi S of Palo Verde on SR 78; at oxbow of Colorado River. Free. All year; 3-day limit. About 30 undesignated sites. Tbls, flush toilets, cfga, drkg wtr. Swimming, picnicking, fishing (catfish, bass), hunting (pheasant, dove, duck), boating (no motor boats). Elev 100 ft; 10 acres. Oxbow Lagoon/Colorado River (3 mi). Cibola National Wildlife Refuge nearby.
Travel tip: Rockhound at Lunada Bay on Palo Verdes Peninsula, reached by short, steep walk from roadside turnoff on Paseo del Mar; excellent selection of rocks, shells.

PARKER (ARIZONA) (233) S

Crossroads $4
Bureau of Land Management
8 mi NW of Parker (in California) on Parker Dam Rd. $4 or $50 annual. All year; 14-day limit. 12 undeveloped sites. Tbls, toilets, cfga, no drkg wtr. Along Colorado River. Boat trailer fees expected to be levied.

Empire Landing $10
Bureau of Land Management
9 mi N of Parker on Parker Dam Rd, on California side of the Colorado River in the Parker Dam Recreation Area (7 mi N of Earp). $10. all year; 14-day limit. 50 drive-to sites & 28 walk-to tent sites along the river. Tbls, flush toilets, cfga, drkg wtr, cold showers, dump. Fishing, hiking, rockhounding, boating. 20 acres. $3 for day use.

PASADENA (234) S

Fall Creek Trail $5
Angeles National Forest
From I-210 N of Pasadena, 9 mi N on Hwy 2 (Angeles Crest Highway); left on Angeles Forest Hwy (CR N3) for 4 mi; W on Mt. Gleason Ave, then N on FR 3N27 for 1 mi; at Big Tujunga Creek. $5 daily or $30 annually. All year; 14-day limit. 10 hike-in sites. Tbls, toilets, cfga, no drkg wtr. Fishing, hiking, mountain biking. Campfire permit required. Elev 3500 ft.

PASKENTA (235) N

Dead Mule FREE
Mendocino National Forest
28 mi W of Paskenta. S on RD 23N02, right on RD 23N50; left on Rd 23N54 to campground. Free. 6/1-11/1. 2 RV/tent sites. Tbls, toilets, cfga, no trash service. Wtr W of camp. Elev 5000 ft.

Del Harleson FREE
Mendocino National Forest
21 mi SW of Paskenta. S on RD 23N02; left on RD 23N69; left on RD 23N03; left on RD 23N74 to campground. Free. 5/15-11/15. 4 sites. Tbls, toilets, cfga, no drkg wtr. Elev 4200 ft.

Kingsley Glade FREE
Mendocino National Forest
22 mi W of Paskenta on RD 23N01; left on RD 24N01 to campground. Free. 6/1-11/1. 4 sites, edge of meadow. Toilets, cfga, tbls, drkg wtr, hitching posts, corral. Riding trails. Swimming, fishing 5 mi at Thomas Creek, horseback riding. Elev 4500 ft.

Mud Flat FREE
Mendocino National Forest
10 mi SW of Paskenta. S on RD 23N02; right on RD 23N69 to campground. Free. 4/1-11/1. Sites. Tbls, toilets, cfga. Gravity wtr system. Hiking, picnicking. Elev 2200 ft.

Sugar Springs FREE
Mendocino National Forest
35 mi W of Paskenta. S on RD 23N02; right on Rd 23N69; right on Rd 23N41 to campground. Free. 6/1-11/1. 2 sites. Tbls, toilets, cfga, no trash service. Wtr W of camp. Hiking, picnicking. Elev 5400 ft.

Sugarfoot Glade FREE
Mendocino National Forest
24 mi W of Paskenta on FR 24N01. Free. Open 5/15-11/15; 14-day limit. 6 primitive sites. Tbls, cfga, toilets, no wtr (creek dry in summer), no trash service.

Three Prong FREE
Mendocino National Forest
25. mi W of Paskenta on RD 23N01; left on Rd 24N13 to campground. Dirt rds. Free. 6/1-11/1. 6 sites. Tbls, toilets, cfga, no trash service. Wtr piped to campground. Hiking, picnicking. Elev 4800 ft.

Whitlock FREE
Mendocino National Forest
15 mi NW of Paskenta on CR 23N01; .7 mi NW on CR 23N41. Dirt rds. 6/1-10/31; 14-day limit. 3 sites (RVs under 22 ft). Tbls, toilets, cfga. Gravity wtr system. Wtr only during heavy use season. Hiking, picnicking. 2 acres; elev 4300 ft. Fall hunting camp.

PAYNES CREEK (238) N

Black Rock FREE
Lassen National Forest
8.5 mi SE of Paynes Creek on CR 202; 22 mi SE on CR 28N29. Free (formerly $10). All year; 14-day limit. 4 sites; 1 acre. Tbls, toilets, cfga, no drkg wtr. Stream. Hiking, picnicking, fishing. Elev 2100 ft.

Paynes Creek FREE
Bureau of Land Management
Redding Field Office
Near Paynes Creek, follow Jelly Ferry Rd 3

mi N of I-5 to Bend, then 2 mi NE on Bend Ferry Rd. Free. All year; 14-day limit. Primitive undesignated sites. Tbls, toilets, cfga, no drkg wtr. Parking for horse trailers. No camping near mouth of Inks Creek. Fishing, horseback riding, hiking. Mouth of Inks Creek & areas near it are closed to camping.

PEARBLOSSOM (239) S

Sycamore Flat $5
Angeles National Forest
S of Pearblossom on Longview Rd; left on Valyermo Rd, pass ranger station; right on Big Rock Rd for 2 mi. $5 daily or $30 annually Adventure Pass. All year; 14-day limit. 11 sites (18-ft RV limit). Tbls, toilets, cfga, drkg wtr.

PIEDRA

Island Campground $8
Pine Flat Lake
Corps of Engineers
9.5 mi NE of Piedra on Trimmer Springs Rd, then S following signs. $8 with federal Senior Pass; others pay $16. All year; 14-day limit. 97 sites (including 60 overflow); 65-ft RV limit. Tbls, flush toilets, coin showers, cfga, drkg wtr, fishing pier, fish cleaning station. Fishing, boating (l), hiking.

PIERPOINT (243) S

Peppermint FREE
Sequoia National Forest
Giant Sequoia National Monument
26.5 mi E of Pierpoint on SR 190; 3 mi S on FR 90; half mi E on FR 21S07. Free. 5/17-9/30; 14-day limit. About 19 dispersed sites on 10 acres; 22-ft RV limit. Tbls, toilets, cfga, no drkg wtr. Picnicking, swimming, stream fishing, horseback riding & rental (2 mi). Elev 7100 ft.

PILOT POINT (244) N

Avery Pond $11
Folsom Lake State Recreation Area
S of Pilot Hill on Rattlesnake Bar Rd; park at Rattlesnake Bar, hike 1.1 mi by trail. $11. 2 hike-in environmental tent sites. Tbls, toilet, cfga, no drkg wtr or trash service. Fishing, hiking.
Fishing tip: The South Fork of American River is a topnotch trout fishery, with plenty of wild rainbow and brown trout both above and below the Class III rapids. The pools are accessible only by rafts from the Chili Bar Park upstream. Try Countdown Rapalas or black-and-gold Panther Martin spinners.

PINE VALLEY (245) S

Agua Dulce $5
Cleveland National Forest
E of Pine Valley off Sunrise Hwy. $5 (or $30 annual Adventure Pass). 5/30-LD; 14-day

limit. 5 individual walk-in tent sites (in addition to group camping areas). Tbls, toilets, cfga, drkg wtr. Hiking. Elev 5,900 ft.

Bobcat Meadows $5
Cleveland National Forest
6.3 mi E of Pine Valley on I-8; follow Buckman Springs Rd 3.3 mi; right on Corral Canyon Rd (FR17S04) at ORV sign for 5.9 mi (rd quite narrow in places); bear left at "Y" onto Skye Valley Rd for .2 mi; next to ORV area. $5. All year; 14-day limit. $5 daily pass fee or $30 annually. 20 sites; 27-ft RV limit. Tbls, toilets, cfga, no drkg wtr, no trash service. Hiking, ORV use.

Burnt Rancheria $7.50
Cleveland National Forest
E of Pine Valley on I-8, then 9.4 mi N on Sunrise Hwy (Hwy S1). $7.50 with federal Senior Pass; others pay $15. 5/15-10/31; 14-day limit. 111 sites; 40-ft RV limit. Tbls, flush toilets, cfga, drkg wtr. Hiking, fishing, biking, horseback riding. 2-night minimum stay on weekends; 3-night holiday weekends.

Corral Canyon $5
Cleveland National Forest
6.3 mi E of Pine Valley on I-8; follow Buckman Springs Rd 3.3 mi; right on Corral Canyon Rd (FR 17S04) at ORV sign for 5.9 mi (rd quite narrow in places); bear right at "Y" for 1.4 mi. Next to ORV area. $5. All year; 14-day limit. $5 daily pass fee or $30 annually. 20 sites; 27-ft RV limit. Tbls, toilets, cfga, no drkg wtr. Hiking, ORV use. Elev 3500 ft.

Laguna Campground $7.50
Cleveland National Forest
E of Pine Valley on I-8, then 13 mi N on Sunrise Hwy (Hwy S1) to just past 26-mile marker. $7.50 with federal Senior Pass; others pay $15. All year; 14-day limit. 104 sites; 45-ft RV limit. Tbls, flush toilets, cfga, drkg wtr, coin showers. Interpretive programs, biking, fishing, hiking.

PIONEER (246) N

Caples Lake $8
Eldorado National Forest
42 mi E of Pioneer on SR 88. $8 with federal Senior Pass; others pay $16. MD-9/15; 14-day limit. 34 sites; 35-ft RV limit. Tbls, toilets, cfga, drkg wtr. Boating, fishing, hiking. Elev 7800 ft.

Kirkwood Lake $9.50
Eldorado National Forest
40 mi E of Pioneer on SR 88 to half mi W of town of Kirkwood; left at sign for Kirkwood Ski Resort for half mi. $9.50 with federal Senior Pass; others pay $19. 6/15-10/15; 14-day limit. 12 sites with short parking spurs. Tbls, toilets, cfga, drkg wtr, bear lockers. Boating, fishing, hiking (rainbow trout). Elev 7600 ft.

Lumberyard FREE
Eldorado National Forest
19.9 mi NE of Pioneer on SR 88; .1 mi SW on Ellis Rd. Free. 6/1 11/1; 14-day limit. 5 sites (RVs under 16 ft). Tbls, cfga, no drkg wtr, toilets. Boating (rl), picnicking; swimming, fishing. Elev 6200 ft; 2 acres.

Mokelumne FREE
Eldorado National Forest
19.9 mi NE of Pioneer on SR 88; 12 mi S on Ellis Rd. Free. 5/1 11/16; 14-day limit. 8 sites. Toilets, cfga, no drkg wtr, no tbls. Swimming; picnicking; fishing; boating. Elev 3200 ft; 2 acres. On Mokelumne River. Salt Springs Reservoir 4 mi. Reservoir boating potentially dangerous due to steep, narrow canyon.
Fishing tip: Try for chinook salmon in the Mokelumne.

Moore Creek FREE
Eldorado National Forest
19 mi NE of Pioneer on SR 88; 12 mi S on Ellis Rd. Free. 5/1-11/15. 8 sites (RVs under 16 ft). Toilets, cfga, no drkg wtr, no tbls. Swimming, fishing, picnicking, boating(l-4 mi). Swimming holes nearby. Elev 3200 ft; 5 acres. On Mokelumne River.
Fishing tip: Boating on Salt SPS Reservoir often hazardous because of steep, narrow canyon. Some trout fishing on the Mokelumne River, but most fish caught are quite small.

Pipi Campground $9.50
Eldorado National Forest
11 mi E of Pioneer on SR 88; 0.8 mi NW on Omo Ranch Rd; 5.9 mi N on North/South Rd. $9.50 with federal Senior Pass; others pay $19. 4/15-11/30; 14-day limit. 51 sites; 35-ft RV limit. Tbls, toilets, cfga, drkg wtr, fishing piers. Fishing, OHV use.

Silver Lake $10
Eldorado National Forest
36 mi E of Pioneer on SR 88. $10 with federal Senior Pass; others pay $20. About 5/1-10/31; 14-day limit. 62 sites; 35-ft RV limit. Tbls, toilets, cfga, drkg wtr. Fishing, hiking, boating. Elev 7200 ft.

South Shore $9.50
Eldorado National Forest
19.9 mi NE of Pioneer on SR 88; 3.5 mi N on Bear River Rd. $9.50 with federal Senior Pass; others pay $19. About 6/15-10/15; 14-day limit. 22 sites; 35-ft RV limit. Tbls, toilets, cfga, drkg wtr. Fishing, hiking.
Fishing tip: Check out the rainbow, mackinaw & brown trout fishing at nearby 700-Bear River Lake.

White Azalea FREE
Eldorado National Forest
19.9 mi NE of Pioneer on SR 88; 12 mi S on Ellis Rd; narrow rd not recommended for RVs. Free. 5/1-11/15; 14-day limit. 6 RV/tent sites (RV limit, 16 ft). Toilets, cfga, no drkg wtr, no tbls. Swimming; picnicking; fishing;

boating (ld--3 mi). Elev 3500 ft; 2 acres. On Mokelumne River. Salt Springs Reservoir 3 mi. Reservoir boating potentially dangerous due to steep, narrow canyon.

Woods Lake **$8**
Eldorado National Forest
45 mi NE of Pioneer on SR 88; S at sign for Woods Lake Recreation Area for 1.5 mi. Rd unsuitable for large RVs. $8 with federal Senior Pass; others pay $16. 6/15-10/15; 14-day limit. 25 small sites. Boating, fishing, hiking. Elev 8200 ft.

PISMO BEACH (247) S

Oceano Dunes **$8**
State Vehicle Recreation Area
At nearby Arroyo Grande, exit US 101 at Grand Ave; 4 mi W on Grand Ave to camping area. $8. All year. About 1,000 primitive sites for off-road vehicles. Tbls, toilets, cfga, no drkg wtr. ORV activities.

Pismo Dunes OHV **$6**
State Recreation Area
3 mi S of Pismo Beach on SR 3. $6. All year; 14-day limit. 500 primitive sites. Tbls, toilets, cfga, no drkg wtr. Area for use of off-road vehicles, horseback riding, fishing, hiking. 2,500 acres of sand dunes. Pack out trash.

PLACERVILLE (248) N

Capps Crossing **$8**
Eldorado National Forest
12 mi E of Placerville on US 50; 6 mi S on Sly Park Rd; 13 mi E on Mormon Emigrant Trail; 6 mi S on Capps Crossing Rd. $8 with federal Senior Pass; others pay $16. 5/15-9/15; 14-day limit. 11 sites. Tbls, toilets, cfga, drkg wtr. Fishing at North Fork of Consumnes River. Hiking, swimming. Elev 5200 ft.

China Flat **$8**
Eldorado National Forest
29 mi E of Placerville on US 50; at Kyburz, 3 mi S on Silver Fork Rd. $8 with federal Senior Pass; others pay $16. MD-9/30; 14-day limit. 18 sites (22-ft RV limit). Tbls, toilets, cfga, drkg wtr. Swimming, fishing, motorcycling, biking, 4WD, hiking. On Silver Fork of American River. Elev 4800 ft.

Gerle Creek **$10**
Eldorado National Forest
21 mi E of Placerville on US 50; 27 mi N on Ice House Rd (FR 3); follow Gerle Creek signs at fork. $10 with federal Senior Pass; others pay $20. MD-9/30; 14-day limit. 50 sites; 30-ft RV limit. Tbls, toilets, cfga, drkg wtr, fishing pier. Biking, boating, fishing (brown trout), horseback riding, interpretive trail. Elev 5300 ft.

Ice House **$10**
Eldorado National Forest
21 mi E of Placerville on US 50; 11 mi N on Ice House Rd (FR 3). $10 with federal Senior

Pass; others pay $20. 5/15-10/15; 14-day limit. 83 sites (including RV-only section near boat ramp); 35-ft RV limit. Tbls, toilets, cfga, drkg wtr, dump ($5). Hiking/biking trail, fishing, boating(l), swimming, waterskiing.
Fishing tip: 700-acre Ice House Lake contains mackinaw, brown & rainbow trout.

Loon Lake **$10**
Eldorado National Forest
21 mi E of Placerville on US 50; 28 mi N on Ice House Rd (FR 3) to fork; follow right fork for 5 mi. $10 with federal Senior Pass; others pay $20. 6/15-10/15; 14-day limit (2-night minimum stay on weekends). 53 sites; 45-ft RV limit. Tbls, toilets, cfga, drkg wtr. Boating(l), fishing, hiking. No horses allowed in main campground; group camping available at equestrian area. Elev 6378 ft.
Fishing tip: 900-acre Loon Lake contains brown & rainbow trout.

Sand Flat **$8**
Eldorado National Forest
28 mi E of Placerville on US 50 at South Fork of American River. $8 with federal Senior Pass; others pay $16. MD-LD; 14-day limit. 29 sites. Tbls, toilets, cfga, drkg wtr. Fishing, swimming, hiking.

Silver Fork **$8**
Eldorado National Forest
29 mi E of Placerville on US 50; at Kyburz, 8 mi S on Silver Fork Rd. $8 with federal Senior Pass; others pay $16. MD-9/30; 14-day limit. 35 sites. Tbls, toilets, cfga, drkg wtr. Fishing, swimming, hiking. Elev 5600 ft.

Sunset Campground **$9**
Eldorado National Forest
21 mi E of Placerville on US 50; 16 mi N on Ice House Rd; at Union Valley Reservoir. $9 with federal Senior Pass; others pay $18. MD-9/30; 14-day limit. 131 sites; 35-ft RV limit. Tbls, toilets, cfga, drkg wtr, beach, coin showers at nearb Fashoda tent camp parking lot, dump ($5). Boating(l), fishing, hiking, swimming, trail biking.
Fishing tip: The huge, 25,000-acre lake features kokanee salmon as well as brown, rainbow & mackinaw trout.

Wench Creek **$9**
Eldorado National Forest
21 mi E of Placerville on US 50; 19 mi N on Ice House Rd; on E shore of Union Valley Reservoir. $9 with federal Senior Pass; others pay $18. MD-LD; 14-day limit. 100 sites; 35-ft RV limit. Tbls, flush toilets, cfga, drkg wtr, coin showers at Fashoda tent camp parking lot. Fishing, boating, biking trail.

Wolf Creek **$9**
Eldorado National Forest
21 mi E of Placerville on US 50; 21 mi N on Ice House Rd (FR 3); 1.75 mi on FR 31; left on Wolf Creek turnoff for half mi; on N shore of Union Valley Reservoir. $9 with federal Senior Pass; others pay $18. MD-LD; 14-day limit. 42 sites; 35-ft RV limit. Tbls, toi-

lets, cfga, drkg wtr, coin showers at nearby Fashoda camp. Boating, fishing, hiking. Elev 4900 ft.

Wrights Lake **$9**
Eldorado National Forest
21 mi E of Placerville on US 50; 11 mi N on Ice House Rd (FR 3); right on Wrights Lake Tie Rd for 9 mi; left for 2 mi on Wrights Lake Rd. $9 with federal Senior Pass; others pay $18. About 7/1-10/1; 14-day limit. 82 sites (including 15 for equestrians); 35-ft RV limit. Tbls, toilets, cfga, drkg wtr. Boating (no mtrs), fishing, hiking, horseback riding, biking. Elev 7000 ft.

Yellowjacket Campground **$10**
Eldorado National Forest
21 mi E of Placerville on US 50; 21 mi N on Ice House Rd (FR 3) to Yellowjacket turnoff, then half mi; on N shore of Union Valley Reservoir. $10 with federal Senior Pass; others pay $20. 5/15-9/30; 14-day limit. 40 sites; 35-ft RV limit. Tbls, flush toilets, cfga, drkg wtr, dump ($5). Boating(l), hiking, fishing, waterskiing. Elev 4900 ft.

PLATINA (249) N

Basin Gulch **$6**
Shasta-Trinity National Forest
5 mi W of Platina on SR 36; 1.2 mi S on FR 29N13. $6. 5/15-10/31; 14-day limit. 13 sites (20-ft RV limit). Tbls, toilets, cfga, no drkg wtr. Fishing. 9 acres on Middle Fork of Cottonwood Creek.

Beegum Gorge **FREE**
Shasta-Trinity National Forest
Qtr mi E of Platina on SR 36; 1.9 mi S on CR 1C001; 4.2 mi SW on FR 28N06; rd from SR 36 unsafe for RVs. Free. 5/1-10/31; 14-day limit. 2 sites (RVs not recommended). Tbls, toilets, cfga, no drkg wtr. Swimming, hiking trail, picnicking, fishing. Elev 2100 ft; 1 acre. Beegum Creek.

Deerlick Springs **FREE**
Shasta-Trinity National Forest
5 mi W of Platina on SR 36; 5.2 mi N on CR B005; qtr mi N on FR 30N44; 5.2 mi N on FR 31N01. Free. 5/20-10/31; 14-day limit. 13 sites (22-ft RV limit). Tbls, toilets, cfga, no drkg wtr. Swimming, fishing, hiking trails. 6 acres. Elev 3100 ft.

White Rock **FREE**
Shasta-Trinity National Forest
5 mi W of Platina on SR 36; 14.4 mi S on FR 29N13; 5.6 mi S on FR 29N19. Free. 5/15-10/31; 14-day limit. 3 tent sites. Tbls, toilets, cfga, firewood, no drkg wtr. Picnicking. Elev 4800 ft; 1 acre. Stream. Adjacent to White Oak Guard Station.

POLLOCK PINES (250) N

Pleasant **FREE**
Eldorado National Forest
8.5 mi E of Pollock Pines on US 50; 34 mi N

on Ice House Rd (Soda Springs-Riverton Rd) & Loon Lake Rd; 2.5 mi NE on Trail 15E03, by foot and by boat along NE side of Loon Lake (by boat from lake's boat ramp). Free. 6/15-10/1; 14-day limit. 10 tent sites. Toilets, cfga, firewood, no drkg wtr. Boating, swimming, hiking, picnicking, fishing, waterskiing, sailing. Elev 6500 ft; 4 acres.

Fishing tip: Good rainbow trout fishing in Loon Lake during late spring & summer.

Strawberry Point   **$8**
Eldorado National Forest
8.5 mi E of Pollock Pines on US 50; 10.5 mi N on CR 17N12; 1.5 mi E on FR 11N37. On N shore of Ice House Reservoir. $8 during MD-10/15; free rest of year; 14-day limit. 10 sites. Tbls, toilets, cfga, no drkg wtr, dump. Swimming, boating(l), fishing.

Fishing tip: Try Ice House Reservoir for trout during summer; it is restocked each June.

Wentworth Springs   **FREE**
Eldorado National Forest
8.5 mi E of Pollock Pines on US 50; 24.5 mi N on CR 17N12; 3.5 mi N on FR 17N12 (Ice House Rd); 3 mi E on FR 14N02. Access for 4WD & motorcycles only. FREE. 6/15-10/1; 14-day limit. 8 sites. Tbls, toilets, cfga, no drkg wtr. Hiking, swimming, picnicking, fishing, hunting. Elev 6200 ft. Stream. Gerle Creek and Loon Lake (1 mi). Point of departure for NW end of Desolation Wilderness Area.

Fishing tip: Try Loon Lake in early spring for rainbow trout.

PORTERVILLE

Tule Recreation Area   **$8**
Success Lake
Corps of Engineers
From dam near Porterville, 2 mi E on SR 190, then N following signs. $8 for basic site & $10.50 with elec/wtr for holders of federal Senior Pass; others pay $16 & $21. All year; 14-day limit. 103 sites (9 with elec); 65-ft RV limit. Tbls, flush toilets, showers, fish cleaning station, dump, playground. Boating(l), fishing, hiking, golf, Saturday campfire programs MD-LD. 3-day minimum stay on holiday weekends.

PORTOLA (251) N

Lightning Tree   **$9**
Plumas National Forest
Lake Davis Recreation Area
2.5 mi E of Portola on SR 70; 9.9 mi NW on CR 112 (Grizzly Rd); on Davis Lake. 5/1-11/15; 7-day limit. $9 for 17 family sites (RVs under 32 ft); $16 for 21-site multiple-family area; no drkg wtr. Picnicking, swimming, fishing, boating. Elev 5900 ft; 12 acres. For self-contained RVs only. Dump station ($2) at Grizzly Campground, 8 mi N of Portola just off CR 126.

Fishing tip: Excellent trout and large-

mouth bass fishing available from Davis Lake in spring & early summer. Western & northern shorelines offer best access for float tubes.

Travel tip: Portola Railroad Museum, 1 mi S of SR 70 on CR A15, features 70 pieces of railroad rolling stock, housed in old 16,000 sq ft Western Pacific diesel service shop.

POTTER VALLEY (252) N

Oak Flat   **FREE**
Mendocino National Forest
18.1 mi NE of Potter Valley on CR 240; 3 mi NE on FR 20N01. Free. 5/15-9/30; 14-day limit. 12 sites (RVs under 22 ft). Tbls, toilets, cfga, no drkg wtr. Store, ice, gas, laundry, showers (1 mi). Swimming, picnicking, fishing, sailing, boating (rld), hiking, waterskiing. Elev 1800 ft; 4 acres. Lake. Plenty of overflow space; primarily a motorcycle camp & weekend overflow site on heavy weekends.

Fishing tip: There are trout in Lake Pillsbury, but they are hard to catch; some lunkers are occasionally hooked, though.

Travel tip: Free tour & samples at Braren Pauli Winery on Hawn Creek Rd near Potter Valley.

PROJECT CITY (253) N

Arbuckle Flat Boat Camp   **FREE**
Shasta-Trinity National Forest
5.5 mi N of Project City on I-5; 15 mi E by boat. (15 mi E of Pit River Bridge, located on I-5.) Free. All year; 14-day limit. 11 tent sites. Tbls, toilets, cfga, no drkg wtr. Swimming, picnicking, fishing, waterskiing, boating (d). Elev 1100 ft; 4 acres. On shore of Shasta Lake; boat access only. Unit of the Whiskeytown-Shasta-Trinity National Recreation Area.

Fishing tip: Shasta Lake has excellent population of largemouth bass in addition to largemouth, catfish & crappies.

Greens Creek Boat Camp   **FREE**
Shasta-Trinity National Forest
5.5 mi N of Project City on I-5; 5 mi E by boat. (5 mi from Pit River Bridge, located on I-5.) Free. 4/1-9/30; 14-day limit. 9 tent sites. Tbls, toilets, cfga, no drkg wtr. Store, food, ice, gas (2 mi). Swimming, picnicking, fishing, waterskiing. Boating (d, rl--2 mi). Elev 1000 ft; 6 acres. Geological interest. On McCloud River Arm of Shasta Lake. Unit of the Whiskeytown-Shasta-Trinity National Recreation Area.

Ski Island   **FREE**
Shasta-Trinity National Forest
4 mi N of Project City on I-5; 12 mi NE on CR 4Gf100; .1 mi NW by boat. (3 mi E of Pit River Bridge, located on I-5.) Free. All year; 14-day limit. 23 tent sites. Tbls, toilets, cfga, no drkg wtr. Store, ice, gas, food, dump (1 mi). Swimming, waterskiing, picnicking, fishing. Boating (ld; r--1 mi). Elev 1100 ft; 9 acres. Amphitheater. On Pit arm shore of Shasta Lake. Unit of the Whiskeytown-Shasta-Trinity National Recreation Area.

QUARTZSITE (ARIZONA) (254) S

La Posa LTVA   **$140**
Bureau of Land Management
From I-10 at Quartzsite, take US 95 S 1 mi; site on four graded roads on both sides of US 95. $140 permit for season or $30 for 14 days during 9/15-4/15; $5 per day or $50 seasonal during 4/16-9/14. Undesignated sites. Sanitary dump 2 mi N of Quartzite. Toilets, drkg wtr, telephone, trash disposal. Federal Senior Pass discounts do not apply to LTVA fees.

Short-Term Boondock Area   **FREE**
Bureau of Land Management
Near Quartzite at Milepost 99 and Milepost 112 adjoining Hwy 95. Free. Undesignated primitive camping areas; no facilities. 14-day limit. Self-contained RVs of any length may be parked in these areas but must move to new sites outside of a 25-mile radius after the 14-day period. RVers use these sites primarily while taking part in events and activities in Quartzite.

QUINCY (255) N

Brady's Camp   **FREE**
Plumas National Forest
6.5 mi E of Quincy on SR 70; take Squirrel Creek turnoff, then 8 mi toward Argentine Lookout. Free. 5/15-10/31; 14-day limit. 4 primitive tent sites. Tbls, toilets, cfga, no drkg wtr. Picnicking, fishing. Elev 7200 ft; 4 acres. Scenic. Stream. Argentine Lookout.

Deanes Valley   **FREE**
Plumas National Forest
5.4 mi W of Quincy on CR 414 (Quincy Spanish Ranch Rd); 4 mi S on FR 24N29; 1 mi S on FR 24N28. Free. 4/1-10/31; 14-day limit. 7 sites (RVs under 22 ft). Tbls, toilets, cfga, no drkg wtr. Swimming, picnicking, fishing, horseback riding, hiking. Elev 4400 ft; 7 acres. Nature trails. S fork of Rock Creek.

Travel tip: Plumas County Museum in Quincy displays historical documents, photos, period rooms of the late 1800s, mining & logging exhibits, woven baskets & artifacts from local Indians.

Lower Bucks   **$7**
Plumas National Forest
18 mi SW of Quincy on CR PL414; 4 mi NW on FR 24N33; 2 mi w on FR 24N24. $7 with federal Senior Pass; others pay $14. 5/1-10/30; 14-day limit. 6 RV sites (RVs under 22 ft). Tbls, toilets, cfga, firewood, drkg wtr. Dump. Picnicking; boating (rld--5 mi); swimming, fishing, hiking. Elev 5200 ft; 6 acres. Mountains. Self-contained RVs only on Lower Bucks Lake.

Silver Lake   **FREE**
Plumas National Forest
5.7 mi W of Quincy on CR 414 (Quincy Spanish Ranch Rd); 8.4 mi W on FR 24N30. Free.

5/1-10/31; 14-day limit. 8 sites (RVs under 22 ft). Tbls, toilets, cfga, no drkg wtr. Horse-back riding, picnicking, fishing, boating (ld), hiking. Elev 5800 ft; 5 acres. Lake trailhead. Entrance to Bucks Lake Wilderness.

Fishing tip: Silver Lake well known for its rainbow trout.

Snake Lake　　　　　　　　　**FREE**
Plumas National Forest
5 mi W of Quincy on Bucks Lake Rd; 5 mi N. Free. 4/1-10/30; 14-day limit. 7 tent sites. Tbls, toilets, cfga, no drkg wtr. Fishing. Elev 4200 ft. Popular in winter for snowmobiling & cross-country skiing.

Fishing tip: Try Snake Lake in summer for rainbow trout; troll or drift with live minnows.

Taylor Lake　　　　　　　　　**FREE**
Plumas National Forest
18 mi N of Quincy on Hwy 89; 5 mi E on CR 214 to Taylorsville; 2 mi N on CR 214; 10 mi E on FR 27N10; 1 mi on FR 27N57. Free. Undesignated primitive sites; no facilities, no drkg wtr. Hiking, trout fishing.

RAMONA (256) S

Arroyo Salado　　　　　　　　**$5**
Primitive Camp Area
Anza-Borrego Desert State Park
16 mi E on CR S22 from Borrego Springs. $5 daily permit or $30 annually. All year. Open camping; no facilities, no drkg wtr. Open fires prohibited. Thimble Trail trailhead 3 mi W. Elev 800 ft.

Travel tip: Woodward Museum in town filled with antiques; outside are bunkhouse, blacksmith shop, freight & stage wagons, town jail built of sheet iron in 1880.

Blair Valley　　　　　　　　　**$5**
Environmental Camps
Anza-Borrego Desert State Park
12 mi E of Julian on Hwy 78; 5 mi S on CR S2. $5 daily permit or $30 annually. Walk-in tent sites. All year. Tbls, cfga, no drkg wtr. Reservations requested (619/767-5311). Hik-ing trails nearby.

Culp Valley Primitive Camp　　　**$12**
Anza Borrego Desert State Park
From Ramona, E on Hwy 78 to Santa Isabel; left on Hwy 79; right on S2 ten mi; left on 522 (Montezuma Grade). $12. All year. Open camping; no facilities. Good pullouts near the California Riding & Hiking Trail. Hiking. Pets on 6-ft leash; rabies certification of veri-fication required; not allowed on hiking trails. Park says, "Leave dogs home." Very hot in summer (100-110 degrees plus) and yet cooler than the desert floor by 10 degrees. No ground fires. Barbecues and camp stoves okay.

Fish Creek　　　　　　　　　　**$5**
Anza-Borrego Desert State Park
12 mi S of Hwy 78 in Ocotillo Wells on Split Mountain Rd. $5 daily permit or $30 annually.

All year. 15 sites. Tbls, toilets, cfga, no drkg wtr. Scenic "Erosion Road" drive is on dirt & paved roads, directed by markers at 1-mi intervals. Sites include Font's Point Wash, Palo Verde Wash and Borrego Badlands.

Travel tip: Scenic "Erosion Road" drive is on dirt & paved roads, directed by markers at 1-mi intervals. Sites include Font's Point Wash, Palo Verde Wash and Borrego Bad-lands.

Mountain Palm Springs　　　　**$5**
Primitive Camp Area
Anza-Borrego Desert State Park
15 mi N on CR S2 from I-8 at Ocotillo. $5 daily permit or $30 annually. All year. Open RV or tent camping; no designated sites. Toilets, no drkg wtr, no cfga. Hiking trails nearby.

Yaqui Pass　　　　　　　　　　**$5**
Primitive Camp Area
Anza-Borrego Desert State Park
5 mi S on CR S3 from Borrego Springs; 4 mi W on Yaqui Pass Rd (CR S3). $5 daily permit or $30 annually. Primitive open RV or tent camping; no facilities, no drkg wtr. Hiking trails nearby.

Yaqui Well　　　　　　　　　　**$5**
Primitive Camp Area
Anza-Borrego Desert State Park
5 mi S on CR S3 from Borrego Springs; 6 mi on CR S3 (Yaqui Pass Rd). $5 daily permit or $30 annually. Primitive open RV or tent camping; toilets, no drkg wtr. Open fires pro-hibited. Mainly used for overflow from Tama-risk Grove campground. Trails nearby.

RAVENDALE (257) N

Dodge Reservoir　　　　　　　**FREE**
Bureau of Land Management
25 mi E of Ravendale on dirt rd; follow signs from US 395. Rough rd; not recommended for RVs. (54 mi N of Susanville). Free. All year (but not accessible in winter); 14-day limit. 12 tent sites. Tbls, cfga, toilets. No drkg wtr. Hunting, fishing, hiking, swimming, picnick-ing. No boat launch available; cartop boats may be used. Elev 5700 ft.

Fishing tip: 400-acre Dodge Reservoir is stocked with Eagle Lake rainbow trout.

RED BLUFF (258) N

Alder Creek　　　　　　　　　　**$11**
Lassen National Forest
44 mi E of Red Bluff on SR 36, then E on SR 36/89; 8 mi S on Hey 32; at Deer Creek. $11 during 4/1-11/1; free rest of year. 6 sites (trailers discouraged). Tbls, toilets, cfga, no drkg wtr. Trout fishing.

Fishing tip: Upper Susan River supports rainbow, brown & brook trout. Match a cur-rent hatch with flies or drift live bait (live or dead fish prohibited as bait). At beaver ponds, try small spinners.

Sycamore Campground　　　　　**$12**
Red Bluff Recreational Area
Mendocino National Forest
From I-5 at Red Bluff, 100 yds E on SR 36; half mi S on Sale Lane; on Sacramento River. $12. Apr-Nov; 14-day limit. 30 sites; no RV size limit; 8 picnic sites. Tbls, flush toilets, cfga, drkg wtr. Boating(l), swimming, water-skiing. No wtr during winter. 488 acres.

Tehama　　　　　　　　　　　　**FREE**
State Wildlife Area
E of Red Bluff on SR 99, then NE on Hogs-back Rd into refuge; or, about 15 mi NE of Red Bluff on Hwy 36, then S on Plum Creek Rd. Free. All year; 14-day limit. Primitive camping, no facilities. 46,862 acres. Hiking, hunting (turkey, deer, wild pigs).

Tomhead Saddle　　　　　　　**FREE**
Shasta-Trinity National Forest
13 mi W of Red Bluff on SR 36; 5 mi SW on CR 181 (Cannon Rd); 19 mi W on CR 146; 4.8 mi SW on FR 27N04. Free. 5/15-10/31. 5 sites. Tbls, toilets, cfga, no drkg wtr. Hiking, picnicking, horseback riding. Elev 5700 ft; 5 acres. Horse corral. Adjacent to Yolla Bolly Wilderness.

Travel tip: Stop at Red Bluff Salmon Lad-der, 2 mi S of Red Bluff on Williams Ave; watch thousands of salmon ascend the lad-der at the Public Television Salmon Viewing Plaza on Sale Lane, where underwater TV cameras monitor the fish in order to count them; most activity, Sept-April.

Toomes Camp　　　　　　　　**FREE**
Mendocino National Forest
65 mi W of Red Bluff; near Yolla Bolly Wil-derness. Free. 6/1-10/31; 14-day limit. 2 sites. Tbls, toilet, cfga, no drkg wtr, no trash service.

Willow Lake　　　　　　　　　　**FREE**
Lassen National Forest
55 mi E of Red Bluff on Hwy 36; left on Wilson Lake Rd (FR 29N19). Free. Late May-11/1; 14-day limit. Undesignated sites; no facilities. Fishing, hiking.

REDDING (259) N

Brandy Creek　　　　　　　　　**$7**
Whiskeytown National Recreation Area
11 mi NW of Redding on SR 299; 5 mi W on S Shore Rd (JFK Dr). $7 in winter; $14 in summer ($7 with federal Senior Pass). All year; 14-day limit. Fee depends upon avail-ability of wtr. 46 sites for self-contained RVs under 30 ft. Tbls, cfga, drkg wtr, dump, ice. Swimming, picnicking, fishing, deer hunting, boating (rld), horseback riding, waterskiing. Ranger program. Elev 1210 ft; 20 acres. On Whiskeytown Lake.

Fishing tip: Rainbow trout are often caught from the river near the picnic area and at jct of Soda Creek. Use flies & lures with barbless hooks; catch-and-release required within the park.

Jones Valley Inlet $6
Shasta-Trinity National Forest
7.5 mi E of Redding on Hwy 299; 9 mi N on Dry Creek Rd from Bella Vista. $6 during 3/1-10/15; free rest of year; 14-day limit. Portable toilets, cfga, drkg wtr. Undesignated primitive sites (30-ft RV limit). Boating, swimming, fishing on Shasta Lake.

Fishing tip: Shasta Lake has excellent population of largemouth bass in addition to smallmouth, catfish & crappies.

Travel tips: Redding Museum of Art and History at Caldwell Park in Redding contains regional Indian & art exhibits; free. Also, guided tours of Shasta Dam, 8 mi N of Redding on I-5, then 6 mi W; world's highest overflow dam, with drop 3 times as steep as Niagara Falls; 20-minute film in visitor center; free.

Mariners Point $9
Shasta-Trinity National Forest
7.5 mi E of Redding on Hwy 299; at Dry Creek Rd, pick up CR 5J050 for 4 mi. $9. South area open 8/1-10/15; North area open 7/1-10/15. Both sections likely to be closed rest of the year due to bald eagle nest protection. 7 sites; 16-ft RV limit. Tbls, toilets, cfga, no drkg wtr.

Fishing tip: Shasta Lake's best shoreline fishing for trout is at McCloud Bridge. Rainbow are stocked heavily in the summer, and in fall, brown trout move upstream to spawn.

Oak Bottom $7
Whiskeytown National Recreation Area
From I-5's Whiskeytown-Eureka exit, 15 mi W on Hwy 299 (8 mi W of Redding). $7 with federal Senior Pass at RV section; others pay $14 ($16-18 during season at tent area). Tbls, flush toilets, cfga, drkg wtr, showers (no wtr in winter), dump, interpretive center, beaches. Boating, fishing, hiking, swimming.

Old Cow Creek FREE
Latour Demonstration State Forest
50 mi E of Redding. Free. June-Oct, depending on snow. 2 sites (RVs under 16 ft). Tbls, cfga, no drkg wtr. Picnicking, fishing, swimming, hiking, horseback riding (corral avail). Elev 5600 ft.

Old Station FREE
Latour Demonstration State Forest
50 mi E of Redding. Free. June-Oct, depending on snow. 1 site (RV under 16 ft). Picnicking, fishing, swimming, hiking, horseback riding. Thousand Lakes Wilderness Area.

Shasta OHV Area $10
Shasta-Trinity National Forest
Bureau of Land Management
7 mi N of Redding on I-5; 4 mi W on Shasta Dam Blvd; 2 mi N on Lake Blvd to Shasta Dam. $10. All year; 14-day limit. 22 sites (30-ft RV limit); 4 picnic sites. Tbls, toilets, cfga, drkg wtr. Biking, horseback riding, fishing. Next to Chappe-Shasta off-highway vehicle staging area. Permit needed for access across Shasta Dam; acquire 72 hrs in advance.

Sims Flat $12
Shasta-Trinity National Forest
40 mi N of Redding on I-5; 1 mi S on Sims Rd; on Sacramento River. $12. 4/15-11/27; 14-day limit. 20 sites (24-ft RV limit). Tbls, flush toilets, cfga, drkg wtr. Trout fishing, boating, hiking.

South Cow Creek FREE
Latour Demonstration State Forest
50 mi E of Redding. Free. June-Oct, depending on snow. 2 sites. Tbls, drkg wtr, cfga. Picnicking, fishing, swimming, hiking, horseback riding. Thousand Lakes Wilderness Area.

REDWAY (260) N

Honeydew Creek $8
King Range National Conservation Area
Bureau of Land Management
From US 101 at South Fork/Honeydew exit, follow signs to Honeydew, then follow Wilder Ridge Rd 2 mi toward Ettersburg. $8. All year; 14-day limit. 5 sites. Tbls, toilets, cfga, no drkg wtr. Hunting, fishing, hiking. Creek is an important salmon spawning stream; do not use soap in it.

Horse Mountain $8
King Range National Conservation Area
Bureau of Land Management
17.5 mi W of Redway on Shelter Cove Rd; 6 mi N on Kings Peak Rd. $8. All year; 14-day limit. 9 sites (20-ft RV limit). Tbls, toilets, cfga, no drkg wtr. Hiking, 4WD, mountain biking, fishing, surfing, horseback riding, swimming, boating. Water-based service available at Shelter Cove, about 30 minutes away at ocean.

Mattole Beach $8
King Range National Conservation Area
Bureau of Land Management
US 101 to Redway from Garberville; W about 30 mi; through Honeydew for 15 mi, then left to end of Lighthouse Rd. $8. Large RVs not recommended. All year; 14-day limit. 14 sites. Portable toilets, no drkg wtr, cfga, beach. Hunting, fishing, hiking, swimming. Steep, winding dirt rds; some impassable during wet weather. Crowded & noisy in summer.

Nadelos $8
King Range National Conservation Area
Bureau of Land Management
17 mi W of Redway on Shelter Cove Rd; 2 mi S on Chemise Mtn Rd. $8. All year; 14-day limit. 8 tent sites. Tbls, toilets, cfga, drkg wtr. Hiking, biking, surfing, fishing, boating, exhibits. Elev 1840 ft. 15 minutes from Shelter Cove for boating, fishing, surfing.

Sinkyone $9
Wilderness State Park
17 mi W of Redway on Briceland Rd, following signs to Whitehorn; 6 mi farther to 4-corner fork; take middle fork, then 4 mi to Usal Beach; last 10 mi unpaved. $9 during 9/16-5/14; $12 peak season. All year; 14-day limit. 22 hike-in tent sites & 15 primitive drive-to sites at Usal Beach (large RVs not recommended). Also $3 per person trail camps along 15-mi Lost Coast Trail. Tbls, toilets, cfga, no drkg wtr. Hiking, backpacking trails.

Tolkan Campground $8
King Range National Conservation Area
Bureau of Land Management
17.5 mi W of Redway on Shelter Cove Rd; 3.5 mi N on Kings Peak Rd. $8. All year; 14-day limit. 9 sites (20-ft RV limit). Tbls, toilets, cfga, drkg wtr, cold showers. Wheelchair access. Fishing. No pets. Elev 1800 ft; 50 acres.

Wailaki $8
King Range National Conservation Area
Bureau of Land Management
17 mi W of Redway on Shelter Cove Rd; 2 mi S on Chemise Mtn Rd. $8. All year; 14-day limit. 13 sites (20-ft RV limit). Tbls, toilets, cfga, drkg wtr. Hiking, 4WD trails, biking, hiking, birdwatching, exhibits.

RENO (NEVADA) (261) N

Lookout $6
Toiyabe National Forest
NW of Reno on I-80 to Verdi exit; 11 mi on Old Dog Valley Rd. $6. 6/1-9/30; 14-day limit. 22 sites (22-ft RV limit). Tbls, toilets, cfga, no drkg wtr. Rockhounding, hiking. Elev 6700 ft.

RINCON (262) S

Fry Creek $12
Cleveland National Forest
From Rincon (20 mi E of I-15 on SR 76), 8.5 mi N on CR S6; across rd from Observatory camp. $12. 5/1-11/30. 15 sites (16-ft RV limit; no trailers). Tbls, toilets, cfga, drkg wtr. Near Palomar Observatory. Elev 4800 ft.

Observatory $12
Cleveland National Forest
From Rincon (20 mi E of I-15 on SR 76), 8.5 mi N on CR S6. $12. May-Nov; 14-day limit. 42 sites (22 & 27-ft RV limit). Tbls, flush toilets, cfga, drkg wtr. Near Palomar Observatory. Elev 4800 ft.

RIVERTON (264) N

Airport Flat FREE
Eldorado National Forest
27 mi N of Riverton on Ice House-Loon Lake Rd; where rd forks for Gerle Creek Campground or Loon Lake, take Gerle Creek branch for 3 mi. FREE. All year; 14-day limit. 16 sites. Tbls, toilets, cfga, no drkg wtr. Fishing, swimming, motorcyclingm ATV, 4WD. Elev 5300 ft.

Fishing tip: Try Ice House Reservoir for trout during summer; it is restocked each June. Or, pop over to Union Valley for a chance at its rainbows.

Azalea Cove FREE
Eldorado National Forest
14 mi from Hwy 50 on Ice House-Loon Lake Rd, then access by bike, trail or boat from Sunset boat ramp; along the Union Valley bike trail on E shore of Union Valley Lake. Free. Tent sites. Toilets, tbls, cfga, no drkg wtr, no trash service. Biking, swimming, boating. Elev 4900 ft.

Camino Cove FREE
Eldorado National Forest
7 mi N of Hwy 50 on Ice House-Loon Lake Rd; 3 mi W on Peavine Ridge Rd; 5 mi N on Bryant Springs Rd past West Point boat ramp, then 1.5 mi E to campground turnoff on the right; on NW shore of Union Valley Lake. Free. 32 sites. Toilets, cfga, no tbls, no drkg wtr. Fishing, boating, hiking. Elev 4875.

Jones Fork $8
Eldorado National Forest
From US 50 at Riverton, 12 mi N on Ice House Rd at Union Valley Reservoir in the Crystal Basin. $8. All year; 14-day limit. 10 sites. Tbls, toilets, cfga, no drkg wtr. Fishing, hiking, boating, swimming, biking. Elev 4900 ft.

North Shore RV Camp $8
Eldorado National Forest
About 29 mi N of Hwy 50 at Riverton on Ice House and Loon Lake Rds in the Crystal Basin; on NW shore of Loon Lake. $8. 6/15-10/15; 14 day limit. 15 sites for self-contained RVs and tents. Tbls, toilets, cfga, no drkg wtr. Fishing, boating, swimming, hiking, biking. Elev 6378 ft.

Northwind $8
Eldorado National Forest
11 mi N of Riverton on Soda Springs-Riverton Rd; right on Ice House Rd; on N shore of Ice House Reservoir. $8. 3/1-12/31; 14-day limit. 9 sites for self-contained RVs & tents. Tbls, toilets, cfga, no drkg wtr. Fishing, boating, swimming, biking, hiking. Elev 5500 ft.

West Point FREE
Eldorado National Forest
7 mi N of Hwy 50 on Ice House Rd; 3 mi E on Peavine Ridge Rd; 5 mi N on Bryant Springs Rd to just past the boat ramp on NW shore of Union Valley Lake. Free. Apr-Nov; 14-day limit. 8 sites. Toilets, cfga, no tbls, no drkg wtr. Boating(l), fishing, hiking. Elev 4875 ft.

SAN BERNARDINO (267) S

Holcomb Valley $12
San Bernardino National Forest
Follow Hwy 30 from San Bernardino to Hwy 330, then 35 mi on Hwy 330 to Big Bear Lake dam; at fork, bear left on Hwy 38 for 10 mi; left on FR 3N09 (Van Dusen Canyon Rd) for 3 mi; left on FR 3N16. $12. All year; 14-day limit; may be inaccessible in winter. 19 sites; 25-ft RV limit. Tbls, toilets, cfga, no drkg wtr. Elev 7400 ft.

Fishing tip: Try Big Bear Lake for spring trout; rainbows are planted each year in Holcomb Creek. Big Bear is populated with rainbow & brown trout, coho salmon, bass, bluegill, catfish & crappies.

SAN DIEGO (269) S

Arroyo Seco & Granite Springs $3
Cuyamaca Rancho State Park
40 mi E of San Diego on I-8; 5 mi N on Hwy 79. $3 per person. All year; 7-day limit. 3 primitive trail campsites at each area. Pit toilets, no cfga (use backpack stoves), drkg wtr seasonally, but wtr tastes bad at Granite Springs. Horse corrals at each camp, but pack in feed because grazing prohibited. Sites in remote, unlighted area; register at park headquarters, Paso Picacho kiosk or Green Valley kiosk.

✪ SAN FRANCISCO (270) N

Bicentennial FREE
Golden Gate National Recreation Area
N on US 101. ext Alexander, 3 mi W on Bunker Rd to Visitor Center. Free. May-Nov, depending on weather; 3-day limit. Reservations required (415-331-1540). 3 primitive tent sites. Cfga, toilets, tbls, no drkg wtr. Fires only in grills, designated fire rings or campstoves. Winters wet; fog common in summer; cliffs prone to landslides & covered with poison oak.

Hawk Camp FREE
Golden Gate National Recreation Area
N on US 101, ext Alexander, 3 mi W on Bunker Rd to visitor center. Backpack only to campground up steep 3.5-mi Bobcat Trail. Free. May-Nov, depending on weather; 3-day limit. Reservations required. 3 primitive tent sites. Toilets, tbls, no drkg wtr. No fires permitted. Winters wet; fog common in summer; cliffs prone to landslides & covered with poison oak. Most primitive of park's camping areas. In Gerbode Valley.

Haypress Camp FREE
Golden Gate National Recreation Area
N on US 101, ext Alexander, 3 mi W on Bunker Rd to visitor center. Backpack only to campground, 3/4 mi from Tennessee Valley parking lot. Free. 7/1-10/30; 3-day limit. Reservations required. 5 primitive sites. Cfga, tbls, toilets, no drkg wtr. Fires only in grills, designated fire rings or campstoves.

Kirby Cove FREE
Group Campground
Golden Gate NRA
N of San Francisco just W of US 101. On the beach. Free. May-Nov, depending on weather & road conditions. 3-day limit. Reservations required. Number & type of vehicle restricted. 4 tent sites accommodating 12-65 campers. Tbls, cfga, toilets, drkg wtr. Fires only in grills, designated fire rings or campstoves. Four cars per sites permitted in parking lot.

SAN JOSE (271) S

Joseph D. Grant $10
Santa Clara County Park
From Hwy 101 at San Jose, follow Alum Rock Ave. E to Mt. Hamilton Rd, then right for 8 mi. $10 for seniors Mon-Thurs at tent or car-camping sites; $9 car camping during 11/1-2/28; $18 all other car camping sites; $25 at RV sites. All year; 14-day limit. 22 sites. Tbls, flush toilets, showers, cfga, drkg wtr. Hiking, mountain biking, fishing, horseback riding. 9,522 acres.

Uvas Canyon $10
Santa Clara County Park
From Hwy 101 at San Jose, W on Bernal Ave; S on McKean Rd (turning into Uvas Rd); right on Croy Rd for 4.5 mi. $10 for seniors Mon-Thurs at tent or car-camping sites; $9 car camping during 11/1-2/28; $18 all other car camping sites; $25 at RV sites. All year; 14-day limit. 25 sites. Toilets, tbls, cfga, drkg wtr. Hiking, waterfalls.

Westridge Trail Camp $3
The Forest of Nisene Marks State Park
From Hwy 1 at Aptos, follow State Park Rd N to Soquel Rd; then E, under railroad bridge to Aptos Creek Rd on left; follow signs. $3 per person during 9/16-5/14; $11 rest of year. Tent camping. Tbls, toilets, drkg wtr; no fires (only backpack stoves). Hiking, biking.

SAN JUAN BAUTISTA (272) S

Fremont Peak State Park $11
11 mi S of SR 156 in San Juan Bautista on San Juan Canyon Rd. $11 off-season; $15 in-season. All year; 30-day limit. 28 primitive sites; 26-ft motorhome limit, 18-ft trailer limit. Tbls, toilets, cfga, drkg wtr. Hiking. Park features an astronomical observatory with a 30-inch telescope which is open for public programs on selected evenings.

SAN LUIS OBISPO (274) S

Sulphur Pot Trail Camp $5
Los Padres National Forest
18 mi N of San Luis Obispo on SR 101; 11 mi E on Pozo-Arroyo Grande co rd; 8.5 mi N on Lopez Canyon Rd; 2.5 mi on Trail 13E03. $5 daily or $30 annually. 1 tent site. Tbls, cfga. Hiking, picnicking.

Upper Lopez Trail Camp $5
Los Padres National Forest
18 mi N of San Luis Obispo on SR 101; 11 mi E on Pozo-Arroyo Grande Co Rd; 8.5 mi N on Lopez Canyon Rd; 2.5 mi on Trail 13E03. $5 daily or $30 annually. 1 tent site. Tbls, cfga, drkg wtr.

SAN SIMEON (276) S

Alder Creek FREE
Los Padres National Forest
24.5 mi N of San Simeon on SR 1; 8 mi E on

CALIFORNIA

FR 23S01 (Willow Creek Rd -- unsurfaced). Free. All year; 14-day limit. 2 tent sites. Tbls, toilets, cfga, no drkg wtr. Hiking, picnicking, fishing. Elev 2300 ft; 3 acres. Alder Creek.

Nacimiento $10
Los Padres National Forest
35 mi N of San Simeon on SR 1; 8 mi E on Nacimiento-Ferguson Rd. $10. All year; 14-day limit. 8 sites; 25-ft RV limit. Tbls, toilets, cfga, no drkg wtr. Fishing, hiking, hunting.

Washburn Campground
San Simeon State Park $11
On Hwy 1 midway between Los Angeles & San Francisco. $11 base. MD-12/31; 15-day limit. 268 sites. Base fee for primitive sites at Washburn loop off-season; $15 in-season; 31-ft RV limit, no access to flush toilets or showers, but dump. $20-25 for developed sites at Sam Simeon Creek loop; 35-ft RV limit with flush toilets, cfga, showers($), drkg wtr. Hiking, nature trails, fishing.

SANTA BARBARA (278) S

Blue Canyon $5
Los Padres National Forest
8 mi N of Santa Barbara on SR 154; 22 mi E on FR 5N12, .7 mi E on FR 5N15; 1.4 mi N on Trail 26W14. $5 daily or $30 annually. All year; 14-day limit. 1 tent site. Tbls, cfga, firewood, no toilets, no drkg wtr. Horseback riding, hiking, boating (no motors). 1 acre. Stream.

Bluff Camp $5
Los Padres National Forest
13.5 mi NW on SR 154; 6.5 mi NE on FR 5N18; 1.5 mi E on FR 5N15 by foot or horse; 17.2 mi N on FR 9N11. $5 daily or $30 annually. 11/15-6/30; 14-day limit. 3 tent sites. Tbls, toilets, cfga, firewood. Picnicking, fishing, hiking, horseback riding. Elev 4500 ft; 2 acres. Mountains. Brushy terrain. Stream.

Fremont Campground $7.50
Los Padres National Forest
10 mi NW of Santa Barbara on SR 154; 2.5 mi E on Paradise Rd. $7.50 with federal Senior Pass; others pay $15. 4/1-10/1; 14-day limit. 15 sites; 25-ft RV limit. Tbls, flush toilets, cfga, drkg wtr. Swimming, fishing, mountain biking, hiking. 2-day minimum stay on weekends; 3-day holiday weekends.

Happy Hollow $5
Los Padres National Forest
10 mi NW on SR 154; 5.6 mi NW on FR 5N18; 3 mi E on FR 5N15 BY FOOT, HORSE OR MOTORCYCLE; 7.1 mi N on Trail 9N11 BY FOOT, HORSE OR MOTORCYCLE. $5 daily or $30 annually. All year; 14-day limit. Closed during fire season. 3 tent sites. Tbls, toilets, firewood. Picnicking, hiking, horseback riding. Elev 4300 ft; 3 acres. Mountains. Brush terrain.

Hidden Potrero $5
Los Padres National Forest
13.5 mi N of Santa Barbara on SR 154; 2 mi E on FR 5N13; 4.9 mi NE on Trail 5N15 BY FOOT, HORSE OR MOTORCYCLE. $5 daily or $30 annually. 11/15-6/30; 14-day limit. 1 tent site. Tbls, cfga, firewood, no drkg wtr, no toilet. Hiking, picnicking, horseback riding (rental--4 mi). Elev 2700 ft; 1 acre. Closed during fire season.

Indian Creek Trail Camp $5
Los Padres National Forest
10 mi N of Santa Barbara on SR 154; 6.5 mi E on FR 5N18; 14.5 mi NE on FR 9411; 6 mi SE on Trail 26W08. $5 daily or $30 annually. End of fire season to June 30. Undesignated sites, undrinkable stream wtr. Hiking. Elev 2300 ft.

Little Pine Spring $5
Los Padres National Forest
10 mi NW of Santa Barbara on SR 154; 6.7 mi E on Paradise Rd; along the Santa Cruz Trail on N side of Little Pine Mtn, 6 mi from Upper Oso. $5 daily or $30 annually. All year; 14-day limit. Primitive undesignated tent sites. Tbls, ice can stove, horse trough, no drkg wtr except for horses. Horseback riding, hiking, mountain biking.

Lower Caliente $5
Upper Santa Ynez Recreation Area
Los Padres National Forest
8 mi NW of Santa Barbara on SR 154; 25 mi E on East Camino Cielo to the old Pendola Station; right on Big Caliente Rd for 2 mi. $5 daily or $30 annually. All year; 14-day limit. 2 sites. Toilet, cfga, no drkg wtr, no trash service. Swimming, hiking, biking, horseback riding. Campground usually full on weekends during deer season.

Los Prietos Campground $7.50
Los Padres National Forest
10 mi NW of Santa Barbara on SR 154; 3.7 mi E on Paradise Rd. $7.50 with federal Senior Pass; others pay $15. 4/1-10/1; 14-day limit. 8 sites; 30-ft RV limit. Tbls, flush toilets, cfga, drkg wtr. Hiking, fishing, swimming, nature trails. Santa Ynez River.

Lower Camuesa $5
Los Padres National Forest
10 mi NW of Santa Barbara on SR 154; 6.7 mi E on Paradise Rd; 1.5 mi N on Camuesa Dr to Upper Oso Campground; follow the Camuesa/Buckhorn OHV route to camp. $5 daily or $30 annually. All year; 14-day limit. 3 hike-in or OHV-in tent sites. Tbls, toilet, cfga, no drkg wtr. Hiking, mountain biking, horseback riding, OHV.

Matias Potrero $5
Lower Santa Ynez Recreation Area
Los Padres National Forest
10 mi NW of Santa Barbara on SR 154; 11 mi E on Paradise Rd; hike or horseback 1.5 mi S on Matais Potrero connector trailhead from S side of Paradise Rd (qtr mi before Live Oak day use area). $5 daily or $30 annually. All

year; 14-day limit. 1 tent site. Tbl, cfga, horse corral, water trough, no drkg wtr except for horses, no trash service.

Middle Camuesa $5
Los Padres National Forest
10 mi NW of Santa Barbara on SR 154; 6.7 mi E on Paradise Rd; follow trail to Upper Oso Camp, then take Camuesa/Romero OHV route to site. $5 daily or $30 annually. All year; 14-day limit. 1 tent site. Tbl, cfga, no toilet, no drkg wtr, no trash service.

Middle Santa Ynez $5
Upper Santa Ynez Recreation Area
Los Padres National Forest
8 mi N of Santa Barbara on SR 154; 22 mi E on FR 5Nl12; 8.8 mi N on FR 5N15. $5 daily or $30 annually. All year; 14-day limit. 9 sites. Tbls, toilets, cfga, no drkg wtr. Hiking, picnicking, mountain biking, swimming, fishing, horseback riding. Elev 1800 ft; 3 acres. quarter mi W of Pendola Guard Station. Travel via San Marcos Pass Rd. Rd not advisable in wet weather or for travel trailers; okay for motorhomes. Stream. Site usually full on weekends during deer season mid-Aug to late Sept.

Mono $5
Upper Santa Ynez Recreation Area
Los Padres National Forest
8 mi N of Santa Barbara on SR 154; 22 mi E on FR 5N12 (E Camino Cielo Rd); 13.1 mi E on FR 5Nl15. $5 daily or $30 annually. All year; 14-day limit. 3 walk-in sites (no trailers). Toilets, firewood, no drkg wtr. Hiking, picnicking, fishing, bridle trails, biking, swimming. Elev 1400 ft; 4 acres. Closed during fire season. 5 mi W of Pendola Guard Station. Narrow mountain dirt rds; not advisable in wet weather or for trailers; okay for motorhomes. Mono Creek. Camp usually full on weekends during deer season.

Nineteen Oaks $5
Los Padres National Forest
10 mi NW of Santa Barbara on SR 154; 6.7 mi E on Paradise Rd; hike or horseback 2 mi N on Santa Cruz Trail. $5 daily or $30 annually. All year; 14-day limit. 2 tent sites. Tbls, cfga, no toilets, no drkg wtr. Horseback riding, hiking, mountain biking.

P-Bar Flat $5
Upper Santa Ynez Recreation Area
Los Padres National Forest
8 mi N of Santa Barbara on SR 154; 22 mi E on FR 5N12; 9.7 mi N on FR 5N15. $5 daily or $30 annually. All year; 14-day limit. 4 sites (no trailers). Toilets, cfga, tbls, no drkg wtr, no trash service. Hiking, picnicking, fishing, swimming. Elev 1500 ft; 1 acre. 1 mi W of Pendola Guard Station. Travel via San Marcos Pass Rd. Narrow mountain dirt rds; not advisable in wet weather or for trailers. Stream. Nature trails (2 mi). Campground is usually full on weekends during deer season.

Santa Cruz Trail Camp $5
Los Padres National Forest
10 mi NW of Santa Barbara on SR 154; 5.6 mi E on FR 5N18 (Paradise Rd); 1.5 mi N on FR 5N15; 10 mi N on Trail 27N09. BY FOOT OR HORSE. $5 daily or $30 annually. 11/15 (end of fire season) to 6/30; 14-day limit. 7 tent sites. Tbls, toilets, cfga, no drkg wtr. Hiking, picnicking, fishing, swimming, horseback riding, biking.

Santa Ynez $8
Santa Ynez Recreation Area
Los Padres National Forest
10 mi N of Santa Barbara on SR 154; 8 mi E on Paradise Rd. $8. 4/1-11/1; 14-day limit. 34 sites (22-ft RV limit). Tbls, toilets, cfga, drkg wtr. Fishing, horseback riding, swimming, hiking.

Upper Oso $7.50
Los Padres National Forest
10 mi N of Santa Barbara on SR 154; 1.5 mi N on FR 5N15 (Camuesa Dr). $7.50 with federal Senior Pass; others pay $15 ($10 & $20 per day with horse corral). 25 sites (13 with corrals & long spurs); 22-ft RV limit. Flush toilets, tbls, cfga, drkg wtr. Swimming, hiking, horseback riding, nature trails, OHV, ATV. Elev 1200 ft.

White Oaks $5
Los Padres National Forest
12.1 mi NW of Santa Barbara on Hwy 154; 6.2 mi E on FR 5N18; 2.1 mi SE on FR 5N20. $5 daily or $30 annually. All year; 14-day limit. 8 sites (RVs under 16 ft). Tbls, toilets, cfga, drkg wtr. Fishing. Elev 4200 ft. Near Anastasia Creek.

SANTA MARIA (280) S

Baja Campground FREE
Los Padres National Forest
25 mi E of Santa Maria on Hwy 166; 3 mi N on Branch Creek Rd. Free. All year; 14-day limit. 1 site. Tbl, toilet, cfga, no drkg wtr. Hunting, mountain biking, OHV activitites.

Barrel Springs $5
Los Padres National Forest
3 mi N of Santa Maria on US 101; 15 mi E on SR 166; 8 mi S on co rd; 8 mi SE on FR 11N04. $5 daily or $30 annually. All year; 14 day limit. 6 sites (no RVs). Tbls, toilets, cfga, piped drkg wtr. Hiking, picnicking. Elev 1000 ft; 2 acres. Stream. Scenic 4x4 drive. Road impassable in wet weather.

Brookshire Springs $5
Los Padres National Forest
3 mi N of Santa Maria on US 101; 15 mi E on SR 166; 6 mi E on FR 11N04. $5 daily or $30 annually. All year; 14-day limit. 2 sites (RVs under 16 ft). Tbls, toilets, cfga, piped drkg wtr. Hiking, picnicking.

Buck Spring $5
Los Padres National Forest
E of Santa Maria on SR 166; 2 mi on FR 30S022. $5 daily or $30 annually. All year; 14-day limit. 1 site. Tbl, toilet, cfga, no drkg wtr. OHV activities, hunting. Elev 1500 ft.

Colson Canyon $5
Los Padres National Forest
3 mi N of Santa Maria on US 101; 15 mi E on SR 166; 8.5 mi S on Buckhorn Canyon Rd; 4 mi E on FR 11N64. All year; 14-day limit. $5 daily or $30 annually. 5 sites (limited RV space). Tbls, toilets, cfga, spring wtr. Scenic drive. Hiking, picnicking. Elev 2000 ft; narrow, steep dirt rd; trailers not recommended. Rd impassable in wet weather.

Horseshoe $5
Los Padres National Forest
7 mi E of Santa Maria on Betteravia Rd; 4.5 mi E on Mesa Rd; 4.5 mi N on Tepusquet Canyon Rd; 17.5 mi NE on Colson Canyon Rd. $5 daily or $30 annually. 3 sites. May-Oct; 14-day limit. Tbls, toilet, cfga, no drkg wtr. Hiking, OHV activities. Elev 1600 ft.

Lazy Campground FREE
Los Padres National Forest
3 mi N of Santa Maria on US 101; 15 mi E on SR 166; 8.5 mi S on CR 554; 11.5 mi NE on FR 11N04; high-clearance vehicle needed. Free. 11/15-7/1; 14-day limit. 2 sites (no trailers). Tbls, toilets, cfga, no drkg wtr. Hiking, picnicking, OHV use, mountain biking, horseback riding.

Miranda Pine Springs FREE
Los Padres National Forest
3 mi N of Santa Maria on US 101; 15 mi E on SR 166; 8 mi E on FR 11N04; 10 mi E on FR 11N03. Free. All year; 14-day limit. 3 primitive sites. Tbls, toilet, cfga, no drkg wtr. Hiking, picnicking. Elev 4000 ft.

Wagon Flat $5
Los Padres National Forest
3 mi N on US 101; 15 mi E on SR 166; 8.5 mi S on CR 554; 10.5 mi NE on FR 11N04. $5 daily or $30 annually. All year; 14-day limit. 3 sites (RVs under 16 ft). Tbls, toilets, cfga. Picnicking, hiking. Elev 1400 ft; 1 acre. Mountains. On North Fork of La Brea Creek. Scenic drive; rd impassable in wet weather.

SANTA MARGARITA (281) S

American Canyon $5
Los Padres National Forest
1.1 mi E of Santa Margarita on SR 58; 17.2 mi E on CR 21 (Pozo Rd); 7 mi SE on FR 30S02; 2.1 mi NE on FR 30S04. $5 daily or $30 annually. All year; 14-day limit. 14 sites; limited RV space (16 ft RV limit). Tbls, toilets, cfga, piped spring drkg wtr. Deer hunting, horseback riding, hiking. Elev 1700 ft. Trail access only during deer season.

KCL Campground FREE
Carrizo Plain National Monument
From Hwy 58 E of Santa Margarita & W of McKittrick, 13 mi S on Soda Lake Rd; right on Selby Rd for qtr mi. Free. All year; 14-day limit. 8 sites. Tbls, cfga, portable toilets, no drkg wtr, no trash service. Archaeological exploring, birdwatching, hiking, horseback riding, hunting, wild horse viewing. Camp was formerly owned by Kern County Land Company. Very remote location.

Friis $5
Los Padres National Forest
22.5 mi E of Santa Margarita on Pozo-Santa Margarita Rd (#21); 4 mi NE on FR 29S02; 1 mi N on undesignated FS rd. $5 daily or $30 annually. All year; 14-day limit. 3 sites. Toilets, cfga, spring wtr. Hiking.

La Panza $5
Los Padres National Forest
1.1 mi E of San Margarita on Hwy 58; 19 mi E on CR 21; 10 mi NE on FR 29S01. All year; 14-day limit. $5 daily or $30 annually. 15 sites (RVs under 16 ft). Tbls, toilets, cfga, drkg wtr; limited facilities in winter. Elev 2400 ft.

Navajo $5
Los Padres National Forest
21 mi SE on Pozo-Santa Margarita Rd (#21); 4 mi E on FR 29S02. $5 daily or $30 annually. All year; 14-day limit. 2 sites (no RVs). Tbls, toilets, cfga, spring wtr. Hiking, picnicking, OHV activities.

Selby Campground FREE
Carrizo Plain National Monument
Bureau of Land Management
From Hwy 58 E of Santa Margarita & W of McKittrick, 13 mi S on Soda Lake Rd; right on Selby Rd for two mi. Free. All year; 14-day limit. 5 primitive sites. Tbls, toilets, cfga, no drkg wtr, no trash service. Archaeological study, hiking, horseback riding, birdwatching.

SANTA PAULA (283) S

Big Cone Trail Camp $5
Los Padres National Forest
On Santa Paula Creek, approx 6 mi by SR 150 and 4 mi BY TRAIL from Santa Paula. $5 daily or $30 annually. 11/1-6/30; 14-day limit. 6 tent sites. Tbls, toilets, cfga, stream wtr. Hiking, picnicking.
   Travel tip: Visit the Unocal Oil Museum in Santa Paula; historical material depicting the story of oil; model of an oil field; free.

SANTA YNEZ (285) S

Cachuma $5
Figueroa Mountain Recreation Area
Los Padres National Forest
2 mi E of Santa Ynez on SR 246; 2 mi SE on SR 154; 12 mi NE on FR 7N07 (Happy Canyon Rd; narrow mountain road, not recommended for trailers). $5 daily or $30 annually. All year; 14-day limit. 6 sites (RVs under 22 ft). Tbls, toilets, cfga, firewood, no drkg wtr. Picnicking, horseback riding, swimming, hiking, biking. Elev 2100 ft; 2 acres. Stream. 8 mi E of Figueroa Mountain (wtr available

there). Camp usually full weekends mid-Aug to late Sept during deer season.

Fishing tip: Nearby Lake Cachuma provides excellent fishing for huge largemouth bass; best time is early spring, using jigs & spinnerbaits; in summer, try plastic worms and deep-running crankbaits. Also fish there for trout, catfish, bluegill, crappie & smallmouth bass.

Travel tip: Tour a couple of local wineries; Gainey Vineyard offers tour of crushing, laboratory, barrel, bottle aging areas & has space for picnicking; Santa Ynez Winery has free tours & tastings daily by reservation. Both near SR 246.

Manzana Schoolhouse Trail Camp $5
Los Padres National Forest
13 mi NE of Santa Ynez on FR 7N07 (Happy Canyon Rd, not recommended for trailers); 5 mi NW on CR 10N08; 2 mi N on Trail 30W07; 2.5 mi N on Trail 30W13. $5 daily or $30 annually. All year; 14-day limit. 8 tent sites. Tbls, toilets, cfga, no drkg wtr. Hiking, picnicking, fishing. Sisquoc River.

Nira $5
Figueroa Mountain Recreation Area
Los Padres National Forest
10 mi NE of Santa Ynez on CR 3350; 6 mi N on FR 7N07 (Happy Canyon Rd, not recommended for trailers); 5 mi N on FR 8N09 (Figueroa Mountain Rd). $5 daily or $30 annually. All year; 14-day limit. 12 sites (RVs under 22 ft). Tbls, toilets, cfga, drkg wtr (must be obtained at Davy Brown Campground. Hiking, picnicking, fishing. Elev 2000 ft; 3 acres. Manzana River. Entrance into San Rafael Wilderness. Horses allowed in separate areas of site.

SARATOGA (286) S

Sanborn County Park $10
Santa Clara County
2 mi W of Saratoga on Hwy 9; left on Sanbord Rd for 1 mi. $10 base. MD-LD, 14-day limit; 30-day limit reat of year. Base fee for walk-in tent sites. $10 for seniors Mon-Thurs at tent or car-camping sites; $9 car camping during 11/1-2/28; $18 all other car camping sites; $25 at RV sites. Walk-in sites open about 3/15-10/15. 58 sites (30-ft RV limit). Tbls, flush toilets, cfga, drkg wtr, dump, hookups($). Hiking, nature trail, picnicking, nature display. 3,600 acres.

SAWYERS BAR (288) N

Bacon Rind   FREE
Klamath National Forest
10 mi S of Sawyer Bar on FR 39N23. Free. All year; 14-day limit. Dispersed overnight site, rustic. No facilities, no trash service. Near Eddy Gulch & Blue Ridge Lookouts. Elev 5000 ft.

Big Flat Campground   FREE
Klamath National Forest
20 mi W of Coffee Creek Guard Station. Free. June-Oct; 14-day limit. 9 rustic sites. No drkg wtr or trash service; toilets, cfga. Starting point for Preachers Peak to Caribou Mountains ridge lines & lakes. Access delayed until late in summer. Within Shasta-Trinity National Forest, but administered by Klamath NF.

Idlewild $10
Klamath National Forest
6.2 mi NE of Sawyers Bar on CR 2E01 (narrow, but with turnouts); along North Fork of Salmon River. Free. All year; 14-day limit. 18 sites (48-ft RV limit). Tbls, toilets, cfga, drkg wtr. Trailhead camp for backpackers. Fishing. Elev 2600 ft; 11 acres.

Mulebridge Campground   FREE
Klamath National Forest
2 mi upstream from Idlewild campground (see directions above). Free. All year; 14-day limit. 5 small rustic sites with tbls, cfga, toilet, no drkg wtr (except for horses. Trash service in summer. Stock corral with area for group camping. Trailhead for North Fork Trail into Marble Mountain Wilderness.

SCOTT BAR (289) N

Lovers Camp   FREE
Klamath National Forest
13.6 mi SW of Scott Bar on CR 7F01; 5.4 mi SW on FR 44N4S; 1.7 mi SW on FR 43N45. Free. 5/28-10/15. 8 walk-in tent sites. Tbls, toilets, cfga, firewood, no drkg wtr (except for horses), no trash service. Picnicking, fishing, stock unloading area, corral. Elev 4300 ft; 5 acres. Canyon Creek (1 mi). Trailhead to Sky High Lakes, Deep Lake & Marble Valley in Marble Mountain Wilderness Area.

SEIAD VALLEY (291) N

Fort Goff   FREE
Klamath National Forest
4.7 mi NW of Seiad Valley on SR 96. Free. All year; 14-day limit. 5 walk-in tent sites. Tbls, toilets, cfga, no drkg wtr, no trash service. Fishing, picnicking. Elev 1400 ft; 4 acres. On banks of scenic Klamath River. Pack out trash.

Fishing tip: Good angling for steelhead and salmon in Klamath River during fall & winter run.

Grider Creek   FREE
Klamath National Forest
1.5 mi E of Seiad Valley on Hwy 96; right on Walker Creek Rd, then right on Grider Creek Rd for 6 mi. Along Grider Creek. Free. 10 sites (32-ft RV limit). Tbls, toilets, cfga, no drkg wtr, no trash service. All year; 14-day limit. Elev 1400 ft. Corral, loading ramp. Trailhead for Pacific Crest Trail into Marble Mountain Wilderness.

Fishing tip: Excellent fishing in Grider Creek.

O'Neil Creek $8
Klamath National Forest
5.1 mi SE of Seiad Valley on SR 96. $8 during 6/1-11/15; free rest of yr; 14-day limit. 11 sites (RVs under 22 ft). Tbls, toilets, no drkg wtr. Picnicking, mountain climbing. Elev 1500 ft; 9 acres. Scenic. Stream.

Fishing tip: Close to Klamath River steelhead trout & salmon fishing.

SHAVER LAKE (292) S

Kirch Flat   FREE
Sierra National Forest
19 mi SE of Shaver Lake on FR 40; then follow FR 11S12 south past Teakettle Experimental Area & Black Rock Lake; camp is E of Pine Reservoir on N side of Kings River. Free. All year; 14-day limit. 17 sites; 35-ft RV limit. Tbls, toilets, cfga, no drkg wtr. Fishing, rafting, hiking. Elev 1100 ft.

SIERRA CITY (293) N

Berger Creek $10
Tahoe National Forest
5 mi NE of Sierra City on SR 49; 1.3 mi NW on CR F424 (Gold Lake Rd); 2.4 mi NW on CR 20N16. $10. 6/15-10/15; 14-day limit. 9 sites (RVs under 22 ft). Tbls, toilets, cfga, no drkg wtr. Fishing, picnicking, boating (dr--2 mi), swimming (3 mi). Elev 5900 ft; 5 acres. Packer Lake.

Fishing tip: Good trout fishing at Packer, Tamarack Lakes & others nearby; Tamarack particularly well known for its golden trout.

Travel tip: Kentucky Mine & Museum, 1 mi NE of town via SR 49 in Sierra County Historical Park, is on site of a hard-rock gold mine; tools, photos, documents & mineral samples displayed to depict mining camp life during California's gold rush era.

Diablo $10
Tahoe National Forest
5 mi NE on SR 49; 1.3 mi NW on CR F424; 2.9 mi NW on FR 20N16. $8. 6/1-10/1; 14-day limit. 18 undeveloped sites; tents & self-contained RVs. Tbls, cfga, toilets, no drkg wtr. Fishing & swimming at Packer Lake (2 mi).

Sierra $10
Tahoe National Forest
7 mi NE of Sierra City on SR 49. $10 during 6/15-10/15; free rest of year, but no services. 14-day limit. 16 sites (RVs under 22 ft). Tbls, toilets, cfga, no drkg wtr. Swimming, picnicking, fishing, boating (rld--5 mi). Elev 5600 ft; 5 acres. On N Yuba River. Sardine Lakes (5 mi).

Snag Lake Tree   FREE
Tahoe National Forest
5 mi NE of Sierra City on SR 49; 5.3 mi N on CR FH24 (Gold Lake Rd). Free. 6/1-10/1; 14-day limit. 12 sites (RVs under 22 ft). Tbls, toilets, cfga, no drkg wtr. Lake water. Swimming, picnicking, fishing, waterskiing, boat-

ing (rld--2 mi at Gold Lake); no motor boats). Elev 6600 ft; 5 acres.

Fishing tip: Adjacent to Snag Lake, which has fair fishing. Gold Lake (2 mi) offers good brown trout angling.

SIERRA MADRE (294) S

Hoegees $5
Angeles National Forest
1.2 mi E of Sierra Madre on CR SMDR; 4.2 mi N on CR 2N41; 3 mi W on Trail 11W15; 3 mi NW on Trail 11W15. $5 daily or $30 annually. All year; 14-day limit. 15 tent sites. Tbls, toilets, no drkg wtr. Hiking, picnicking, horseback riding. Elev 2600 ft; 3 acres. Stream. Closed during high fire danger; see local ranger station. Campfire permit required.

Spruce Grove Trail Camp $5
Angeles National Forest
1.2 mi E of Sierra Madre on CR SMDR; 4.2 mi N on CR 2N41; 4 mi NW on Trail 11W14. $5 daily or $30 annually. All year; 14-day limit. 7 tent sties. Tbls, toilets, cfga, no drkg wtr. Picnicking, horseback riding, hiking. Elev 3000 ft; 1 acre. Stream. Closed during high fire danger; see local ranger station for details; campfire permit required. Hiking or horse access by Gabrielino NRT.

SIERRAVILLE (295) N

Antelope Valley FREE
State Wildlife Area
About 10 mi NE of Sierraville on SR 49 (Loyalton Rd) to Loyalton, then S on Antelope Valley Rd into refuge. Free. All year; 14-day limit. Primitive camping in 5,616-acre refuge. No facilities. Hunting, hiking. Refuge surrounded by Tahoe National Forest.

Bear Valley FREE
Tahoe National Forest
Quarter mi E of Sierraville on SR 49; 7.3 mi E on FR 20N04 (Lemon Canyon Rd); Rd not recommended for trailers. Free. 5/15-10/15; 14-day limit. 10 sites (RVs under 16 ft). Tbls, toilets, cfga, piped drkg wtr. Fishing, picnicking. Elev 6700 ft; 1 acre. At the head of Bear Valley Creek.

Gold Lake 4x4 Camp FREE
Lakes Basin Recreation Area
Plumas National Forest
10 mi S of Hwy 89 off Gold Lake Hwy 4; 4-wheel drive required. Free. All year; 14-day limit. 16 sites. Tbls, toilets, cfga, no drkg wtr. Fishing, boating(l), waterskiing Elev 6250 ft.

Haven Lake FREE
Lakes Basin Recreation Area
Plumas National Forest
20 mi W of Sierraville on SR 49; 5 mi N on Gold Lake Rd. Free. Undesignated primitive sites; no facilities, no drkg wtr. Hiking, fishing.

Fishing tip: Try another lake unless you like to catch small brook trout.

SISQUOC (296) S

Alejandro Trail Camp $5
Los Padres National Forest
4.5 mi NE of Sisquoc on Colson Canyon Rd; 4 mi NE on FR 11N04; 1 mi S by trail. $5 daily or $30 annually. 1 tent site. Tbls, cfga, no drkg wtr.

SMARTVILLE (297) N

Boat-in Camping $10
Corps of Engineers
Engelbright Lake
Hwy 20 near Smartville, 3 mi on Mooney Flat Rd; boat-in to about 100 sites. Free 10/1-5/1; $10 rest of year; 14-day limit. Undesignated sites. No facilities except cfga. Fishing, boating, hiking. Contact park manager for details, 916/639-2343.

Fishing tip: Cast shorelines in early spring for largemouth bass, using spinnerbaits & jigs; use plastic worms & nightcrawlers in summer. Lake also has good numbers of rainbow & brook trout.

Travel tip: In Marysville, visit Mary Aaron Museum; historic memorabilia from 1850-1900; restored kitchen, country store museum, mining equipment. Donations.

SOMESBAR (298) N

Dillon Creek $10
Klamath National Forest
15 mi N of Somesbar on SR 96. $10. All year; 14-day limit (free during winter, depending on weather). 21 sites (RVs under 23 ft). Tbls, toilets, cfga, drkg wtr. No wtr or trash service during free period. Biking, swimming, boating(l), hiking, good bank fishing. Nature trails. Administered by Six Rivers NF.

George Geary's FREE
Klamath National Forest
Half mi N of Somes Bar on SR 93; 1.5 mi E. Free. 11/1-5/1; 14-day limit. Rustic dispersed sites. No facilities, no trash service. Boating (l), fishing, hunting. Administered by Six Rivers NF.

Green Riffle FREE
Klamath National Forest
2 mi N of Somes Bar on SR 96; along Klamath River. Free. All year; 14-day limit. Rustic dispersed sites. Toilets, cfga, no drkg wtr, no trash service. Fishing, boating(l). Administered by Six Rivers NF.

Oak Bottom $10
Klamath National Forest
12 mi E of Somesbar on SR 96; 2.5 mi E on FR 93. $10. All year; 14 day limit. Free during winter when wtr shut off. 26 sites (RVs under 31 ft). Tbls, toilets, cfga, drkg wtr. Boating, fishing, biking, swimming, whitewater rafting. Near Salmon River. Administered by Six Rivers NF.

Persido Bar FREE
Klamath National Forest
10 mi N of Somes Bar on SR 96; along Klamath River. Free. All year; 14-day limit. Rustic dispersed sites. Tbls, toilets, cfga, no drkg wtr, no trash service. Boating(l), fishing. Administered by Six Rivers NF.

Roger's Creek FREE
Klamath National Forest
2.5 mi N of Somes Bar on SR 96; along Klamath River. Free. All year; 14-day limit. Rustic dispersed sites. Toilets, cfga, no drkg wtr, no trash service. Fishing, boating(l). Administered by Six Rivers NF.

Ti-Bar Flat FREE
Klamath National Forest
7 mi N of Somes Bar on SR 96. Free. All year; 14-day limit. 5 rustic sites. Toilet, cfga, no trash service; drkg wtr at Ti-Bar fire station E of campground. Boating(l), fishing, drifting, rafting. Large, flat dispersed area. Administered by Six Rivers NF.

Travel tip: Remnants of historic mining operations are nearby; some fruit trees remain from homesteading activities.

SPRINGVILLE (299) S

Balch County Park $8
Mountain Home State Forest
Sequoia National Forest
Tulare County Park
21 mi NE of Springville on Balch Park Rd & Bear Creek Rd. $8 for seniors; $16 all others. 5/1-11/1; 14-day limit. 71 sites (30-ft RV size limit). Tbls, toilets, cfga, drkg wtr. Fishing. Elev 6500 ft. Managed by Tulare County.

Frasier Mill FREE
Mountain Home State Forest
23 mi NE of Springville via Bear Creek Rd. Difficult access for RVs. Free. 6/1-10/31; 14-day limit. 46 sites (RVs under 20 ft). Tbls, drkg wtr, firewood, cfga, toilets. Horseback riding, picnicking, fishing, hiking, hunting.

Hedrick Pond FREE
Mountain Home State Forest
19 mi NE of Springville via Bear Creek Rd. Free. 6/1-10/31; 14-day limit. 15 sites (RVs under 20 ft). Tbls, drkg wtr, cfga, toilets. Picnicking, fishing, hunting, hiking, horseback riding (pack station) and backcountry trails. Elev 6300 ft.

Fishing tip: Hedrick Pond has a good population of stocked rainbow trout.

Hidden Falls FREE
Mountain Home State Forest
20 mi NE of Springville via Bear Creek Rd, Summit Rd and River Rd. Free. 6/1-10/31; 14-day limit. 5 tent sites. Tbls, drkg wtr, cfga, toilets. Picnicking, fishing, hiking, hunting, horseback riding (pack station). Elev 5900 ft.

Jack Flat FREE
Sequoia National Forest
.8 mi E of Springville on SR 190; 12.3 mi N on

CR 239; 2 mi NE on FR 19S09. (Paved and rocky rd, not recommended for cars.) Free. 5/1-10/31; 14-day limit. 2 sites (no trailers). Tbls, toilets, piped spring drkg wtr. Swimming, picnicking, fishing (fly fishing only), hiking. Elev 4300 ft; 1 acre. River. Campfire permit required.

Methuselah Group Camp   **FREE**
Mountain Home State Forest
3 mi N on Balch Park Rd from just E of Springville; 15 mi E on Bear Creek Rd. Free. RVs not Recommended. 5/1-10/1; 14-day limit. Group sites for 20-100 persons. Tbls, toilets, cfga, no drkg wtr. Elev 5900 ft.

Moses Gulch   **FREE**
Mountain Home State Forest
3 mi N of Springville on SR 190; 22 mi E on Bear Creek Rd, Summit Rd and River Rd. Free. 6/1-10/31; 14-day limit. 6 sites (RVs under 16 ft). 20 acres. Tbls, toilets, firewood, drkg wtr. Hiking, picnicking.

Shake Camp Campground   **FREE**
Mountain Home State Forest
18 mi NE of Springville via Bear Creek, Summit and River Rds. Free. 6/1-10/31, weather permitting; 14-day limit. 11 sites (RVs under 16 ft). Tbls, drkg wtr, cfga, toilets. Picnicking, fishing nearby, hiking, horseback riding (rentals & corrals nearby), hunting. Trailhead to Golden Trout Wilderness nearby. Pack station nearby.
   Travel tip: Make sure to see the Adam Tree, on 3 mi Loop Trail starting at Shake Camp corral area; 31 ft in diameter, 247 ft tall.

Sunset Point Campground   **FREE**
Mountain Home State Forest
22 mi NE of Springville via Bear Creek Rd. Free. 6/1-10/31, weather permitting; 14-day limit. 4 sites (RVs under 20 ft). Tbls, drkg wtr, cfga, toilets. Picnicking, fishing nearby, hiking, horseback riding (corrals nearby), hunting. Trailhead to Golden Trout Wilderness nearby.

STIRLING CITY (300) N

Philbrook   **FREE**
Lassen National Forest
11 mi N of Stirling City on CR 91513; 4 mi E on CR 92523. Free. 6/1-10/1; 14-day limit. 10 sites (RVs under 23 ft). Tbls, toilets, cfga, no drkg wtr. Swimming, boating, fishing.

STONYFORD (302) N

Cedar Camp   **FREE**
Mendocino National Forest
6.5 mi W of Stonyford on CR 18N01 (Fouts Spring Rd); 10.7 mi S on FR 18N07 (John Smith Rd); 2 mi SW on FR 17N02. Access up Trough Ridge or Little Stony Rd is poor for RVs. Free. 6/15-10/15; 14-day limit. 5 sites. Tbls, toilets, cfga, no drkg wtr, no trash service. Picnicking. Fishing, swimming, boat-

ing (5 mi). Elev 4300 ft; 2 acres. Power boats prohibited on lake. Little Stony Creek (5 mi). Located in timer area, mature stand of mixed fir and pines.

Davis Flat   **FREE**
Mendocino National Forest
9.5 mi W of Stonyford on FR 18N03. Free. All year; 14-day limit. 70 dispersed sites. 12 Tbls, toilets, cfga, drkg wtr. In designated ORV area. Hiking, motorcycling.

Digger Pine Flat   **FREE**
Mendocino National Forest
6.1 mi S of Stonyford on CR 32 (Lodoga Stonyford Rd); 3.8 mi SW on CR 42 (Goat Mountain Rd). Free. All year. 7 sites (RVs under 16 ft). Tbls, toilets, cfga, no drkg wtr, no trash service. Swimming, picnicking, fishing. Elev 1500 ft; 2 acres. Botanical area (5 mi). Located in Little Stoney Creek drainage. Site very popular in winter when stream is in full flow. ORV trail access; recommended ORV camping.

Diversion Dam   **FREE**
Mendocino National Forest
3 mi W of Stonyford on CR 18N01 (Fouts Spring Rd). Free. All year. 7 sites. Tbls, toilets, cfga, no drkg wtr. Hiking, picnicking. Elev 1300 ft. In open grove of oaks. Very dry site in the summer.

Dixie Glade   **FREE**
Mendocino National Forest
13 mi W of Stonyford on Rd M10. All year; 14-day limit. 8 sites. Tbls, toilet, cfga, sometimes drkg wtr, no trash service. Fishing, hiking. Elev 3700 ft.
   Fishing tip: Excellent native trout fishing is within 1 mi at South Fork of Stony Creek.

Fouts Campground   **FREE**
Mendocino National Forest
8.8 mi W of Stonyford on CR 18N01 (Fouts Spring Rd); .3 mi N on CR 18N03. Free. All year; 14-day limit. 11 sites (RVs under 17 ft). Tbls, toilets, cfga, drkg wtr gravity piped. Swimming, picnicking, fishing, rockhounding. Elev 1600 ft; 7 acres. Stony Creek. Snow Mountain Jasper (5 mi). Digger pine trees in N end of camp. Heavy ORV use 10/1-6/1.

Letts Lake Complex   **$10**
Mendocino National Forest
8 mi W of Stonyford on Fouts Springs Rd; 6 mi SW on FR 18N01; 3 mi SE on FR 17N02. $10. 4/15-11/1; 14-day limit. 44-site complex consists of three camps -- Main Letts, Saddle, Stirrup and Spillway. 20-ft RV limit. Tbls, toilets, cfga, drkg wtr. Fishing, boating(elec mtrs), canoeing on 30-acre lake. Historic landmark. Elev 4500 ft.

Mill Creek   **FREE**
Mendocino National Forest
8.7 mi W of Stonyford at Mill Creek on CR 18N01 (Fouts Spring Rd). Free. All year; 14-day limit. 6 sites (RVs under 22 ft). Tbls, toilets, cfga, no drkg wtr. Rockhounding,

swimming, picnicking, fishing. Elev 1600 ft; 2 acres. Small roadside campground. In winter and early spring stream flow is up. Snow Mountain Jasper is at the site. Heavy ORV use 10/1-6/1

Mill Valley   **$8**
Mendocino National Forest
9 mi W of Stonyford on Fouts Springs Rd; 6 mi SW on FR 18N01; 1.5 mi S on FR 17N02. $8. 4/15-11/1; 14-day limit. 15 sites (RVs under 16 ft). Tbls, toilets, cfga, drkg wtr. Lily Pond lake. Hiking, fishing. Letts Lake 1 mi. Elev 4200 ft; 5 acres.

North Fork   **FREE**
Mendocino National Forest
9 mi W of Stonyford on CR 18N01 (Fouts Spring Rd); 2.3 mi N on CR 18N03. All year; 14-day limit. 6 sites (RVs under 16 ft). Tbls, toilets, cfga, no drkg wtr, no trash service. Swimming, picnicking, fishing, rockhounding. Elev 1700 ft; 3 acres. Adjacent to year-long stream (Stony Creek). Camp is located in open grove of oak trees. Snow Mountain Jasper is at the site. High OHV use between Oct & June.

Old Mill   **FREE**
Mendocino National Forest
6.5 mi W of Stonyford on CR 18N01 (Fouts Spring RD); 7.1 mi S on FR 18N07 (John Smith Rd). Free. 5/1-11/1; 14-day limit. 10 sites (RVs under 16 ft). Tbls, toilets, cfga, gravity piped drkg wtr, no trash service. Rockhounding, picnicking. Fishing (5 mi). Elev 3600 ft; 3 acres. Located in mature stand of mixed pine and fir. Small RVs can use the site, but main access rd up Trough Ridge is narrow.

South Fork   **FREE**
Mendocino National Forest
9.5 mi W of Stonyford on FR 18N03. Free. All year; 14-day limit. 5 sites. Tbls, toilet, cfga, no drkg wtr. Fishing, hiking. On South Fork of Stony Creek.

STOVEPIPE WELLS (303) S

Mahogany Flat   **FREE**
Death Valley National Park
9 mi SW of Stove Pipe Wells on SR 190; 29 mi SE on Wildrose Canyon Rd. Difficult rd access. All year; recommended May-Oct; 30-day limit. Camp free, but $20 park entry fee ($10 with federal Senior Pass). 10 hike-in or 4WD sites. Tbls, toilets, cfga, no drkg wtr. Hiking, picnicking. Elev 8200 ft; 9 me SE of Wildrose Ranger Station. Fires only in grills or campstoves.

Pinyon Mesa   **FREE**
Death Valley National Park
Check location at Emigrant Ranger Station, just SW of Stovepipe Wells on SR 190. All year; recommended May-Oct; 30-day limit. Camp free, but $20 park entry fee ($10 with federal Senior Pass). 2 4WD or hike-in sites.

Tbls, toilets, cfga, no drkg wtr. Hiking, picnicking. Fires only in grills or campstoves.

Stovepipe Wells   **$12**
Death Valley National Park
In Stovepipe Wells on CR 190. $12 plus entry fee. 10/1-4/31; 30 day limit. 200 sites (30-ft RV limit). Tbls, flush toilets, cfga, drkg wtr.

Thorndike Camp   **FREE**
Death Valley National Park
9 mi SW of Stovepipe Wells on SR 190; 29 me SE on Wildrose Canyon Rd. All year; recommended May-Oct; 30-day limit. Camp free, but $20 park entry fee ($10 with federal Senior Pass). 8 4WD or hike-in sites (no RVs). Tbls, toilets, cfga, no drkg wtr. Hiking, picnicking. 8 mi SE of Wildrose Ranger Station. Fires only in grills or campstoves.

Wildrose Campground   **FREE**
Death Valley National Park
9 mi SW of Stovepipe Wells on SR 190; 21 mi S on Wildrose Canyon Rd at ranger station. All year; recommended May-Oct; 30-day limit. 20 4WD or hike-in sites (no RVs). Tbls, toilets, cfga, no drkg wtr. Hiking, picnicking. Elev 4000 ft. Camp free, but $20 park entry fee ($10 with federal Senior Pass).

STRAWBERRY (304) N

Cascade Creek   **$6**
Stanislaus National Forest
9.1 mi NE of Strawberry on SR 108; quarter mi NE on FR 5N28. $6. 5/1-10/15; 14-day limit. 14 sites (RVs under 22 ft). 12 sites. Tbls, toilets, cfga, no drkg wtr. Hiking, mountain climbing, picnicking. Elev 6000 ft; 3 acres. Cascade Creek. Trail of the Ancient Dwarfs (4.6 mi).

Mill Creek   **$6**
Stanislaus National Forest
11.2 mi NE on SR 108; half mi NE on FR 5N21; half mi N on FR 5N26. $6. 5/1-10/15; 14-day limit. 17 sites (RVs under 23 ft). Tbls, toilets, cfga, firewood, no drkg wtr. Hiking, mountain climbing, picnicking, fishing. Elev 6200 ft; 3 acres. Donnell Vista (3.6 mi). Rock Garden Nature Trail (2.8 mi). Trail of the Ancient Dwarfs (2.8 mi).

SUNLAND (305) S

Tom Lucas Trail Camp   **$5**
Angeles National Forest
6 mi NE of Sunland on CR 2N78 (Big Tujunga Rd); 3.5 mi NE on Trail 13W03. $5 daily or $30 annually. All year; 14-day limit. 2 tent sites. Tbls, toilets, cfga, no drkg wtr. Hike-in trail camp. Horseback riding, hiking, picnicking. Elev 2900 ft; 1 acre. Scenic. Stream. Obtain free required fire permit at Big Tujunga Station.

SUSANVILLE (306) N

Biscar Reservoir   **FREE**
Bureau of Land Management
34 mi N of Susanville on Hwy 395; 6 mi W on Karlo Rd to Lower Biscar Reservoir. Free. About 4/15-11/15; 14-day limit. Primitive undesignated sites; no facilities, no drkg wtr. Fishing, hunting, birdwatching. Pack out trash.

Fredonyer Peak   **FREE**
Bureau of Land Management
21 mi N of Susanville on Hwy 139; camp along dirt rd used by bikers cycling to Fredonyer Peak (a 4-8 hr bike trip). Free primitive camping; no facilities, no drkg wtr. Hiking, biking, photography. Scenic.

North Eagle Lake   **$8**
Bureau of Land Management
29 mi N of Susanville on SR 139; 1 mi W on CR A1. $8. 5/15-12/1; 14-day limit. 20 sites. Tbls, toilets, cfga, drkg wtr, dump. Biking, boating, fishing, hiking Elev 5200 ft; 3 acres.

Fishing tip: Eagle Lake is home of the Eagle Lake trout, a sub-species of rainbow that grows quickly, reaching three pounds by the third year and up to 9 pounds. Use spoons or minnow-type lures, worms and flies. Bait fish prohibited. Near camp, rocks & reed patches make up the shoreline.

Ramhorn Springs   **FREE**
Bureau of Land Management
45 mi N of Susanville on US 395; 3 mi E on Post Camp Rd. Free. All year, but not always accessible. 12 sites (28-ft RV limit). Tbls, toilets, cfga, no drkg wtr. Popular hunting camp. Picnicking, hiking. Elev 5000 ft.

Roxie Peconom   **FREE**
Lassen National Forest
W of Susanville off SR 36. Free. May-Oct; 14-day limit. 10 walk-in tent sites sites. Tbls, toilets, cfga, drkg wtr. Dump station 7 mi. Elev 4800 ft.

Willow Creek Canyon   **FREE**
Bureau of Land Management
11 mi E of Susanville on Hwy A27; just before Willow Creek, turn N on Belfast Rd for 3-5 mi. Free. All year; 14-day limit. Primitive undesignated camping in remote canyon area. No facilities; no drkg wtr. Hiking, fishing, archaeological exploring. Petroglyph area nearby.

TAHOE CITY (307) N

Emerald Bay State Park   **$11**
22 mi S of Tahoe City on Hwy 89, adjacent to D.L. Blisss SP. $11 base. 5/15-10/1; 15-day limit. Base fee off-seaon for 20 boat-in tent sites with chemical toilets, cfga, tbls, drkg wtr; $15 in-season. $20 off-season for 100 developed sites; 18-ft RV limit; tbls, flush toilets, cfga, drkg wtr, showers($). Fishing, boating, swimming, hiking, tours of castle-like mansion. Sites are usually full on week-

ends, but not weekdays. Very scenic lake, often photographed.

TECOPA (308) S

Tecopa Hot Springs   **$10**
Inyo County Park
3 mi NW of Tecopa on county rd. $10. All year; 9-month limit. 365 sites. Tbls, toilets, cfga, drkg wtr, elec($). Wheelchair access. Free mineral baths (108 degrees). Exercise classes, dance classes, lectures, movies, horshoes, outdoor dances, nearby rockhounding for opals, amethysts, petrified wood. Near Death Valley National Park.

TEMECULA (310) S

Dripping Springs   **$12**
Cleveland National Forest
11 mi E of Temecula on SR 79. $12. All year; 14-day limit. 33 sites (22-ft RV limit). Tbls, toilets, cfga, drkg wtr. Agua Tibia Wilderness nearby. Hiking (Dripping Springs Trail). This is primarily an equestrian campground.

Fishermans Camp   **$5**
Cleveland National Forest
2 mi N on US 395; 2 mi NW on SR 71; 12 mi W on CR 7S01; 4 mi NW on FR 6S082; 2 mi W on FR 7S07. $5. All year; 14-day limit. $5 daily pass fee or $30 annually. 5 sites (no trailers). Tbls, toilets, cfga, no drkg wtr. Hiking, picnicking, horseback riding. Elev 1200 ft; 12 acres. Stream.

Oak Grove Campground   **$7.50**
Cleveland National Forest
About 25 mi SE of Temecula on SR 79. $7.50 with federal Senior Pass; others pay $15. All year; 14-day limit. 81 sites; 27-ft RV limit. Tbls, flush toilets, cfga, drkg wtr. Hiking trails, inerpretive programs.

THREE RIVERS (311) S

Atwill Mill   **$12**
Sequoia National Park
24 mi SE of Three Rivers on SR 198. Rd to campground is steep, narrow and winding; rd closed in winter because of snow conditions. $12. Free in winter (Nov-May). 14-day limit 6/14-9/14; 30-day limit rest of year. 21 tent sites. Tbls, toilets, cfga, piped drkg wtr. Store, gas, pay showers 3 mi at Silver City. Picnicking, fishing nearby. Elev 6645 ft. Food must be kept in provided storage lockers. Single-trip entry fee $20 per vehicle for 7 days; annual permit $30.

Fishing tip: Excellent trout fishing here from the Middle Fork of the Kaweah River with size 12-18 Adams and Yellow Humpy dry flies or size 10-16 Western Coachmen wet flies.

Travel tip: Don't miss seeing the park's General Grant Tree, second in size to the General Sherman Tree, reputed to be the largest and one of the oldest living things, which is in the Giant Forest in adjoining Sequoia National Park.

Backcountry Camping   **Free**
Kings Canyon National Park
N of Three Rivers on SR 198 to Grant Grove Village; E on SR 180. All year; June-Nov recommended. Free undesignated sites throughout the park, but $15 per trip for wilderness permit. Hike in or ride in by horseback. Picnicking, fishing, hiking. Free backcountry permit required. Reservations for permit must be made at least 7 days in advance by mail. Some permits at park on first-come basis in summer. Hang food high from trees. Single-trip entry fee per vehicle for 7 days; annual fee available.

Fishing tip: Trout fishing is fairly good at most of the lakes and streams in the national park. The best are the South Fork of the San Joaquin River and the Middle and South Forks of Kings River; other good streams are Granite, Bubbs and Lewis Creeks, and good catches of golden trout are made near the headwaters of the Kern River.

Backcountry Camping   **Free**
Sequoia National Park
E of Three Rivers off SR 198. Free camping, but $15 per trip wilderness permit required. All year. June-Nov recommended. Undesignated sites throughout the park. Hike in or ride in by horseback. Picnicking, fishing, hiking. Free backcountry permit required. Reservations for permit must be made at least 7 days in advance by mail. Some permits at park on first-come basis in summer. Fires only in designated fire rings or campstoves. Hang food on wires or poles provided, or high in trees. Single-trip entry fee per vehicle for 7 days; annual fee available.

Cold Springs   **$12**
Sequoia National Park
24 mi up Mineral King Rd from SR 198. Access rd too narrow and steep for RVs. $12. Free in winter (Nov-MD). 14-day limit 6/14-9/14; 30-day limit rest of year. 32 tent sites. Tbls, toilets, cfga, piped drkg wtr, trash cans. Store, gas, food, pay showers at Silver City (2 mi). Picnicking, fishing nearby. $10 single-trip entry fee per vehicle for 7 days; annual fee available. Food must be kept in provided storage lockers. Elev 7500 ft.

South Fork   **$12**
Sequoia National Park
15 mi SE of Three Rivers on S Fork Rd. Steep, narrow access rd with limited turn-around in campground, so RVs discouraged. Free in winter (11/1-5/15); $12 rest of year. 14-day limit 6/14-9/14; 30-day limit rest of year. Peak-season reservations required. 13 sites. Tbls, drkg wtr, cfga, toilets, trash cans. Picnicking, skiing. Wtr available only Apr-Nov, not during free period. Elev 3600 ft. Park entry fee charged.

Fishing tip: Excellent trout fishing during spring & fall in South Fork of Kaweah River.

TIONESTA (312) N

Blanche Lake   **FREE**
Modoc National Forest
From Hwy 139 near Tionesta, 18.5 mi W on CR 97; 1 mi N on FR 44N75; half mi on FR 44N38. Free. Jul-Oct; 14-day limit. Primitive undesignated sites; tbls, cfga, toilets, no drkg wtr. Near Modoc Volcanic Scenic Byway and Lava Beds National Monument. Elev 6500 ft.

Payne Springs   **FREE**
Modoc National Forest
From Hwy 139 near Tionesta, 15.5 mi W on CR 97; left oon FR 43N42 1.8 mi, then qtr mi on FR 43N17. Free. July-Oct; 14-day limit. Primitive sites; 20-ft limit. Tbls, toilets, cfga, no drkg wtr. In Medicine Lake Highlands. Near Lava Beds National Monument

TRACY (313) S

Carnegie   **$6**
State Vehicular Recreation Area
6 mi W of I-580, between Tracy & Livermore at 18600 Corral Hollow Rd. $6. All year; 14-day limit. 50 sites. Tbls, flush toilets, cfga, drkg wtr. Off-road vehicle activities. Daily or annual entry fee also charged. 1,500 acres.

TRIMMER (314) S

Black Rock   **$10**
Sierra National Forest
Pacific Gas & Electric Company
20 mi E of Trimmer on Trimmer Springs Rd (FR 40); 10 mi NW on Black Rock Rd (FR 11S12). $10. All year; 14-day limit. Free in winter, but limited facilities. 10 sites. Tbls, toilets, cfga, drkg wtr. Fishing, hiking, kayaking, rafting.

Bretz Mill   **FREE**
Sierra National Forest
9 mi E of Trimmer on Trimmer Springs Rd; 15 mi N on Big Creek Rd. Free. All year; 14-day limit. 10 sites (24-ft RV limit). Tbls, toilets, cfga, no drkg wtr. Fishing, swimming, hiking. Elev 3300 ft.

TRINITY CENTER (316) N

Captain's Point   **FREE**
Boat-In Camp
Shasta-Trinity National Forest
1 mi S on FR 36N28; 8 mi S BY BOAT; on W shore of main arm of Trinity Lake, the northernmost boat-access campground. Free. All year; 14-day limit. 3 tent sites. Tbls, toilets, cfga, no drkg wtr. Picnicking; fishing; boating (rld--4 mi); swimming; waterskiing; hiking. Elev 2400 ft; 1 acre. Mountains. Launch boats from Clark Springs & Alpine View campgrounds.

Fishing tip: Trinity Lake has some of the state's best smallmouth bass fishing.

Clear Creek   **FREE**
Shasta-Trinity National Forest
5 mi N on SR 3; 11.2 mi SE on CR 106; 2 mi SE on FR 36N65. Free. 6/15-9/10; 14-day limit. 22 sites (RVs under 23 ft). Tbls, toilets, cfga, no drkg wtr. Picnicking, fishing, hiking. Elev 3500 ft; 7 acres. Foothills. Dense forest. Clear Creek. Open all year; snows in winter. Hunter camp in fall.

Eagle Creek   **$9**
Shasta-Trinity National Forest
12.2 mi N of Trinity Center on SR 3; 3.7 mi NE on CR 1089. $9. All year; free but no wtr 11/1-4/30; 14-day limit. 17 sites (40-ft RV limit). Tbls, toilets, cfga, drkg wtr. On Trinity River. Swimming, fishing. Elev 2800 ft; 10 acres.

Goldfield   **FREE**
Shasta-Trinity National Forest
7 mi N on SR 3; 4 mi W on CR 104. Free. 5/16-9/10; 14-day limit. Open all year. 6 sites on 4 acres; 16-ft RV limit. Tbls, toilets, cfga, no drkg wtr. Picnicking, fishing, swimming, hiking. Boulder Creek trailhead. Elev 3000 ft.

Horse Flat   **FREE**
Shasta-Trinity National Forest
12.2 mi N of Trinity Center on SR 3; 1.5 mi N on CR 1089; 2.8 mi NW on FR 38N27. Free. 5/26-9/10; 14-day limit. Open until 10/31 with no services. 16 sites; 16-ft RV limit. Tbls, toilets, cfga, no drkg wtr. Hiking, picnicking, fishing, berry-picking, horseback riding; corral. Elev 3000 ft; 12 acres. On Eagle Creek. Trailhead to Sal-mon Trinity Alps Primitive Area. 7 mi N of Coffee Creek Ranger Station.

Fishing tip: Not much fishing on Eagle Creek, but plenty of small trout in the upper Trinity River.

Travel tip: Scott Museum of Trinity Center, on airport rd half mi E of town, off SR 3, displays Indian artifacts, historical items; barbed wire collection; stagecoach; free guided tours. Donations.

Jackass Springs   **FREE**
Shasta-Trinity National Forest
5.8 mi N on SR 3; 19.9 mi SE on CR 106; 4.5 mi W on CR 119. Free. All year; 14-day limit. 21 sites (RVs under 32 ft). Tbls, toilets, cfga, no drkg wtr. Picnicking, hiking, boating, swimming, fishing, waterskiing. Elev 2400 ft; 7 acres. Mountains. Open all year; snow in winter. Unpaved access rd.

Preacher Meadow   **$11**
Shasta-Trinity National Forest
1.5 mi SW of Trinity Center on SR 3; qtr mi SW on FR 36N98; along Swift Creek. $11. 5/1-10/31; 14-day limit. 63 sites (40-ft RV limit). Tbls, toilets, cfga, drkg wtr. Hiking, fishing. Elev 2900 ft; 6 acres.

Travel tip: The campground contains three large ponderosa pines with scars believed to have been made about 100 years ago by local Wintu Indians who regarded the inner cambium layer of the trees as a food source

Scott Mountain FREE
Shasta-Trinity National Forest
16 mi N of Coffee Creek on Hwy 3. Free. All year; 14-day limit. 7 sites; 15-ft RV limit. Tbls, toilets cfga, no drkg wtr. Hiking trail camp (pacific Crest Trail) leading into Trinity Alp Wilderness. Elev 5,400 ft.

Trinity River $9
Shasta-Trinity National Forest
9.5 mi N of Trinity Center on SR 3; on the Trinity River. $9 during 5/15-10/31; $5 rest of year but no wtr; 14-day limit. 7 sites (40-ft RV limit). Tbls, toilets, cfga, drkg wtr. Fishing, gold panning. Elev 2500 ft.

TRUCKEE (317) N

Alpine Meadows $12
Martis Creek Lake
Corps of Engineers
On N side of dam, 4 mi NE of SR 267. $12. May to mid-Nov; 14-day limit. 25 sites (30-ft RV limit). Tbls, toilets, cfga, drkg wtr. Fishing.

Boyington Mill $6.50
Tahoe National Forest
7 mi E of Truckee on I-80; 3.1 mi N on CR 21N03. $6.50 with federal Senior Pass; others pay $13. 5/15-10/1; 14-day limit. 12 sites on 3 acres (RVs under 32 ft). Tbls, toilets, cfga, firewood, drkg wtr. Picnicking, swimming, river fishing, waterskiing, boating (l--4 mi). Elev 5700 ft.

Davies Creek FREE
Tahoe National Forest
7 mi E of Truckee on US 80; 9 mi N on CR 21N03 (Stampede Dam Rd); 2 mi W on CR 19N03 (Henness Pass Rd). Free. 5/1-10/31; 14-day limit. 7 sites (RVs under 22 ft). Tbls, toilets, cfga, firewood, no drkg wtr. Horse ok, fishing, picnicking, boating (ld), swimming, waterskiing. Elev 6000 ft; 4 acres. Davies Creek and Stampede Reservoir (1 mi). Historic immigrant trail.
Fishing tip: Try rainbow & brown trout and kokanee salmon fishing at Stampede Reservoir. The lake frequently serves up trophy sizes. Stockings in 2001 included 12,000 pounds of catchable rainbows, 50,000 mackinaw fingerlings and 3,000 pounds of catchable browns along with 30,000 kokanee.

Sagehen Creek FREE
Tahoe National Forest
9 mi N of Truckee on SR 89; 1.5 mi SW on FR 18N11 (Sagehen Summit Rd). Free. All year, weather permitting. 14-day limit. 10 undeveloped sites on 10 acres (22-ft RV limit). Tbls, toilets, cfga, no drkg wtr. Fishing, picnicking. Elev 6500 ft.

TUCUYA RIDGE (318) S

Cherry Creek FREE
Los Padres National Forest
2 mi from Tecuya Ridge BY 4-WHEEL DRIVE, MOTORBIKE, HORSE OR FOOT. Free. May-Oct. 2 tent sites. Toilets. Spring wtr in trough should be purified before drinking. Hiking, horseback riding. Elev 5200 ft.

TULELAKE (319) N

Headquarters $7
Modoc National Forest
4 mi S of Tulelake on Hwy 139; 4.8 mi W on CR 111; 20 mi SW on CR 48N04; 14 mi S on FR 47N75. $7; free LD-MD, weather permitting; 14-day limit. 9 sites (16-ft RV limit). Tbls, toilets, cfga, drkg wtr, beach. No wtr during free period. Boating, fishing, picnicking, swimming. On Medicine Lake.
Travel tip: Visit the nearby Klamath Basin National Wildlife Refuges -- Tule Lake, Lower Klamath & Clear Lake. Primary attractions are the migrating waterfowl and, in fall, nearly one million birds; in winter, bald eagles nest there.

Hemlock $7
Modoc National Forest
4 mi S of Tulelake on SR 139; 4.7 mi W on CR 111; 20 mi SW on CR 48N04; 14 mi S on FR 47N75. $7. Free LD-MD, weather permitting; 14-day limit. 19 sites on 10 acres (RVs under 23 ft). Tbls, toilets, cfga, drkg wtr, beach. No wtr during free period. Swimming, boating(l), fishing, water skiing. On Medicine Lake.
Fishing tip: Hemlock and Headquarters Campgrounds are good spots from which to catch trout from Medicine Lake.

Indian Well $10
Lava Beds National Monument
30 mi S of Tulelake off SR 139; three-fourth mi from park headquarters. $10 ($6 in winter); wtr available at headquarters in winter. Also $10 entry fee for 7 days. Winter temperatures 20-40 degrees. 43 sites for tents & small RVs. Tbls, toilets, cfga, drkg wtr. Elev 4770 ft; 80 acres.
Travel tip: Nature program, visitor center, nearly 200 lava tube caves -- 21 open, pictographs, wildlife photography are highlights. Klamath National Wildlife Refuge nearby is winter nesting area for bald eagles.

Medicine Lake $7
Modoc National Forest
4 mi S of Tulelake on SR 139; 4.7 mi W on CR 111; 20 mi SW on CR 48N04; 14 mi S on FR 47N75. $7. Free LD-MD, weather permitting; 14-day limit. 22 sites on 21 acres (22-ft RV limit). Tbls, toilets, cfga, drkg wtr, beach. No wtr during free period. Swimming, boating(l), fishing, waterskiing.
Fishing tip: Try rainbow & brook trout from Medicine Lake in summer; lake formed naturally in crater of old volcano. Arctic grayling also can be caught near this campground.
Travel tip: Visit nearby Lava Beds National Monument (15 mi).

TWENTYNINE PALMS (321)S

Backcountry Camps FREE
Joshua Tree National Park
Throughout most of park. Hike in. All year. Recommended times, fall, winter or spring. Camp free, but 7-day $15 entry fee charged (free with federal Senior Pass). Undesignated camping areas. No drkg wtr, no facilities. Drkg wtr at Cottonwood campground, Cottonwood Visitor Center, Oasis Visitor Center, Indian Cove Ranger Station. Hiking, picnicking. Summer temperatures exceed 100 degrees.
Travel tip: Visit Twentynine Palms Museum on Adobe Rd; exhibits of area settlement by Indians, pioneers, miners.

Belle Campground $10
Joshua Tree National Park
Half mi E of Twentynine Palms on SR 62; 9 mi S on Utah Trail. $10. All year; 14-day limit 10/1-6/1; rest of year, 30-day limit. 7-day entry fee also charged (free with federal Senior Pass). 18 sites, among rock formations (32 ft RV limit). Tbls, toilets, cfga, no drkg wtr. Hiking, picnicking. Elev 3800 ft.

Black Rock Canyon $7.50
Joshua Tree National Park
12 mi W of Twentynine Palms on SR 62; 5 mi S of Yucca Valley on Joshua Lane. $7.50 with federal Senior Pass; others pay $15 plus entry fee. 10/1-5/31; 14-day limit. 100 sites (32-ft RV limit). Tbls, flush toilets, cfga, drkg wtr, dump. Wheelchair access. Hiking, ranger talks, wayside exhibits, horseback riding, mountain biking. Horse owners must provide wtr. Elev 4000 ft.

Cottonwood Campground $7.50
Joshua Tree National Park
At south entrance to park. $7.50 with federal Senior Pass; others pay $15 plus entry fee. All year; 14-day limit 10/1-6/1; rest of year, 30-day limit. 62 sites. Tbls, flush toilets, cfga, drkg wtr, dump.

Hidden Valley Campground $10
Joshua Tree National Park
12 me SE of Joshua Tree. $10. All year; 14-day limit 10/1-6/1; 30 days rest of year. 7-day entry fee also charged (free with federal Senior Pass). 39 sites (RVs under 33 ft). Tbls, toilets, cfga, no drkg wtr. Hiking, picnicking; nature program (Nov-May). Elev 4200 ft. Magnificent rock formations in the Wonderland of Rocks. Drkg wtr at Cottonwood Campground & Visitor Center, Oasis Visitor Center, Indian Cove Ranger Station. Summer temperatures above 100 degrees.

Indian Cove $7.50
Joshua Tree National Park
4.8 mi W of Twentynine Palms on Twentynine Palms Hwy (SR 62); 2.5 mi S on Indian Cove Rd. $7.50 with federal Senior Pass; others pay $15 plus entry fee. All year; 14-day limit (30-day limit during 6/1-10/1). 101 sites. Tbls, toilets, cfga, no drkg wtr (wtr at Indian Cove ranger station).

Jumbo Rocks $10
Joshua Tree National Park
1 mi E of Twentynine Palms on SR 62; 11 mi S on Utah Trail. $10. All year; 14-day limit 10/1-6/1; rest of year, 30-day limit. 7-day entry fee also charged (free with federal Senior Pass). 124 sites (32-foot RV limit). Tbls, toilets, cfga, no drkg wtr. Hiking trails, picnicking, nature program May-Nov. Elev 4400 ft.

Ryan Campground $10
Joshua Tree National Park
16 mi SE of Joshua Tree on Park Blvd-Quail Springs Rd. $10. All year; 14-day limit 10/1-6/1; 30 days limit rest of year. 7-day entry fee also charged (free with federal Senior Pass). 31 sites (RVs under 33 ft). Tbls, toilets, cfga, no drkg wtr. Hiking, picnicking, horseback riding. Elev 4300 ft. Only monument campground allowing horses. Trails. Drkg wtr at Cottonwood Campground & Visitor Center, Oasis Visitor Center, Indian Cove Ranger Station. Summer temperatures above 100 degrees. Beautiful campground, but toilets often odoriforous. No fee for horses.

White Tank $10
Joshua Tree National Park
Half mi E of Twentynine Palms on SR 62; 10 mi S on Utah Trail. $10. All year; 14-day limit 10/1-6/1; rest of year, 30-day limit. 7-day entry fee also charged (free with federal Senior Pass). 15 very small sites sites (small RVs only). Tbls, toilets, cfga, no drkg wtr. Hiking trails, picnicking. Elev 3800 ft. Sites among rock formations.

UKIAH (322) N

Buckhorn   FREE
Cow Mountain Recreation Area
Bureau of Land Management
US 101 to Talmage Rd in Ukiah, E 1.5 mi to Eastside Rd; .3 mi S to Mil Creek Rd, then E 16 mi. Only ORV or 4WD vehicles can negotiate last 2 miles; very rough rd. Free. All year; 14-day limit. 4 tent sites. Toilets, no drkg wtr. ORV use, hiking, hunting, rifle range, horseback riding.
Travel tip: Visit Grace Hudson Museum and Sun House in Ukiah; displays work of Indian painter Grace Carpenter Hudson; Pomo Indian basketry, photos, historical exhibits.

Bu-Shay Campground $10
Lake Mendocino
Corps of Engineers
5 mi N of Ukiah on US 101; 2.7 mi E on SR 20; after crossing Russian River bridge, turn left 1 mi. $10 with federal Senior Pass; others pay $20. 4/15-9/30; 14-day limit. 164 sites; 40-ft RV limit. Tbls, flush toilets, cfga, drkg wtr, coin showers, dump, playground. Hiking, fishing, biking, waterskiing, evening programs on weekends.

Che-Ka-Ka Campground $8
Lake Mendocino
Corps of Engineers
2 mi N of Ukiah on US 101 on N. State St; E

(right) to Lake Mendocino Dr. to top of hill, following signs. $8 with federal Senior Pass; others pay $16. 4/15-9/30; 14-day limit. 23 sites; 43-ft RV limit. Tbls, flush toilets, cfga, drkg wtr, playground, beach. Boating(l), fishing, hiking, swimming, waterskiing, golf, biking.

Cow Mountain   FREE
Recreation Area
Bureau of Land Management
1.5 mi E on Talmage Rd, one-third mi S on Eastside Rd; 3 mi E on Mill Creek Rd (becomes one lane through county park 1-2 mi after Talmage, then one-lane narrow dirt rd with infrequent turnouts, steep; 7 mi N on Mendo Rock Rd (goes off at 45-degree angle, difficult for large RVs to negotiate & no turn-around for 5 mi, also steep one-lane gravel with hairpin turns. Free. All year. 10 tent sites (no RVs). Toilets, drkg wtr, tbls, cfga. Hunting, hiking, fishing, mountain biking, horseback riding. Elev 2500 ft. At McClure Creek. Mountainous terrain. Russian River. Closes during poor weather. 60,000 acres.
Travel tip: Held Poage Memorial Home & Research Library in Ukiah open by appt; 1903 house with collections of Indian artifacts, children's toys, kitchen antiques, Mendocino memorabilia. Free.

Fuller Grove $6.50
Pacific Gas & Electric
Mendocino National Forest
6 mi N of Ukiah on US 101; 5 mi E on SR 20; 26 mi NW on CR 240 (Potter Valley-Lake Pillsbury Rd); on NW shore of 2280-acre Lake Pillsbury next to Pogie Point camp. $6.50 with federal Senior Pass; others pay $13. All year; 14-day limit. 30 sites (22-ft RV limit). Tbls, toilets, cfga, drkg wtr. Boating(l), fishing. Elev 1900 ft. Fee for pets. Camp operated by PG&E.
Fishing tip: Lake Pillsbury contains a large population of rainbow and brown trout as well as some salmon. Rental boats, bait and tackle are available.

Goat Rocks Primitive Camp   FREE
Cow Mountain Recreation Area
Bureau of Land Management
From US 101 in Ukiah, 1.5 mi E on Talmage Rd; right on Eastside Rd for one-third mi; left on Mill Creek Rd for 3 mi; park at Mendo Rock Rd & hike or ride horse on Glen Eden Trail E about 4 mi. Free. 2 tent sites. Tbls, no toilet, cfga, wtr for animals. Hiking, horseback riding, mountain biking.

Ky-En Campground $10
Lake Mendocino
Corps of Engineers
5 mi N of Ukiah on US101; 1 mi E on Hwy 20; 0.8 mi E on Marina Dr. $10 for basic sites & $11 premium sites with federal Senior Pass; others pay $20 & $22. All year; 14-day limit. 103 sites (2 pull-through); 35-ft RV limit. Tbls, flush toilets, cfga, drkg wtr, coin showers, dump, elec, playground, beach. 2-day minimum stay on weekends; 3-day minimum holiday weekends.

Mayacmus Campground   FREE
North Cow Mountain Recreation Area
Bureau of Land Management
From US 101, 1.5 mi E on Talmage Rd; one-third mi right on Eastside Rd; 3 mi left on Mill Creek Rd; 7 mi left on Mendo Rock Rd. Free. All year; 14-day limit. 9 tent sites; no RVs. Tbls, toilets, cfga, no drkg wtr. Hiking, horseback riding, hunting.
Travel tip: Free tours of local wineries -- Baccala Vineyards, Cresta Blanca Vineyards, Parducci Winery, Parsons Creek Winery, Tijsseling Vineyards, Whaler Vineyard.

Navy Camp $6.50
Pacific Gas & Electric
Mendocino National Forest
6 mi N of Ukiah on US 101; 5 mi E on SR 20; 26 mi NW on CR 240 (Potter Valley-Lake Pillsbury Rd; next to Gravelly Valley air strip. $6.50 with federal Senior Pass; others pay $13. All yaar;; 14-day limit. 20 sites. Tbls, toilets, cfga, drkg wtr (except Oct-May). Fee for pets. Operated by PG&E.

Pogie Point $6.50
Pacific Gas & Electric
Mendocino National Forest
6 mi N of Ukiah on US 101; 5 mi E on SR 20; 26 mi NW on CR 240 (Potter Valley-Lake Pillsbury Rd); on NW shore of 2280-acre Lake Pillsbury. $6.50 with federal Senior Pass; others pay $13. All year; 14-day limit. 45 sites, tbls, toilets, cfga, drkg wtr (except in winter). Fishing, buating. Elev 1900 ft. Fee for pets. Camp now operated by PG&E.

Red Mountain Campground   FREE
Cow Mountain Recreation Area
Bureau of Land Management
Exit US 101S at Talmage Rd in Ukiah; 1.5 mi E on Talmage Rd; right on Eastside Rd for qtr mi; left on Mill Creek Rd for 8 mi; veer right where rd forks (following sign), then nearly q mi to camp. Steep uphill one-lane dirt rd with infrequent turnouts; large RVs not recommended. All year. 14-day limit; subject to closure during wet winter weather. 7 tent sites, 3 RV sites and group area. Cfga, tbls, drkg wtr, toilets. Picnicking, hunting, fishing, hiking. Elev 2500 ft. Mountainous terrain. Popular among off-road motorcyclists; horseback riding; motorcycle trails.

South Red Mountain   FREE
Cow Mountain Recreation Area
Bureau of Land Management
1.5 mi S of Ukiah on US 101; 1.6 mi E on Talmage Rd; 2 mi E on Mill Creek Rd; 6 mi E on New Cow Mountain Rd. Free. May-Oct; 14-day limit. 12 sites (no RVs). Toilets, no drkg wtr. Boil wtr before use. Fishing, hunting, hiking. Elev 2500 ft. Mendocino Lake and Russian River (2 mi). Mountainous terrain.

Sunset Point $6.50
Pacific Gas & Electric
Mendocino National Forest
6 mi N of Ukiah on US 101; 5 mi E on SR 20; 26 mi NW on CR 240 (Potter Valley-Lake

Pillsbury Rd); on E shore of 2280-acre Lake Pillsbury. $6.50 with federal Senior Pass; others pay $13. May-Sept; 14-day limit. 54 sites. Tbls, toilets, cfga, drkg wtr (except in winter). Nature trail, fishing, boating(l). Fee for pets. Camp now operated by PG&E.

Trout Creek $12
Pacific Gas & Electric
5 mi E on SR 20 from jct with US 101 near Ukiah; 2 m from Eel River Bridge (E of Van Arsdale Reservoir). $12. May-Oct; 14-day limit. 15 sites. Tbls; toilets, cfga, drkg wtr. Fishing. Status not verified for 2007.

UPPER LAKE (323) N

Bear Creek FREE
Mendocino National Forest
17 mi N of Upper Lake on CR 301 (FR 1N02); 6 mi E on CR 18N01; 1.5 mi E on FR 17N33. Free. 5/1-10/15; 14-day limit. 16 sites (RVs under 16 ft). Tbls, toilets, cfga, no drkg wtr. Swimming, picnicking, fishing. Elev 2300 ft; 6 acres. Creek. Check at Upper Lake Ranger Station for info on Rice Fork crossing.

Deer Valley FREE
Mendocino National Forest
12 mi N of Upper Lake on CR 301 (FR 1N02); 4.5 mi E on FR 16N01. Free. 4/1-11/1; 14-day limit. 13 sites on 4 acres. Tbls, toilets, cfga, no drkg wtr, no trash service. Picnicking. Elev 3700 ft. Primarily a deer hunting camp.

Lower Nye Trailhead FREE
Mendocino National Forest
17 mi N of Upper Lake on CR 301 (FR 1N02); 6 mi E on CR 18N01 (Rice Creek Rd); 14 mi N on FR 18N04. Free. 5/1-9/15; 14-day limit. 6 sites. Tbls, toilets, cfga, no drkg wtr. Picnicking, hiking. On Skeleton Creek. Elev 3300 ft; 2 acres. Check at Upper Lake Ranger Station for info on creek crossing.

Middle Creek $6
Mendocino National Forest
8 mi N of Upper Lake on CR 301 (FR 1N02). $6. All year; 21-day limit. 26 sites. Tbls, toilets, cfga, drkg wtr. Nature trails; motorcycle trails nearby. Elev 2000 ft. Adjoining picnic area absorbed into campground.

VACAVILLE (324) N

Lake Solano $8
Solano County Park
Bureau of Reclamation
11 mi N of Vacaville on I-505; 5 mi W on Hwy 128; left on Pleasant Valley Rd. $8 for seniors at non-hookup sites; others pay $15 ($21-23 for hookups; seniors pay $14). All year; 14-day limit. 90 sites (40 with hookups); 35-ft RV limit. Tbls, flush toilets, cfga, drkg wtr, dump, showers, hookups ($). Boating (lr), fishing. Administered by county.
Fishing tip: Lake Solano is among the best fly fishing waters in the Sacramento Valley. It contains both brown and rainbow trout.

VALLEY SPRINGS (326) N

Acorn East $10
New Hogan Lake
Corps of Engineers
Half mi S of Valley Springs on SR 26; 1 mi S on Hogan Dam Rd; three-fourths mi E on Hogan Pkwy. $10 during 10/1-3/31 ($12 rest of year). All year; 14-day limit. 70 sites; 65-ft RV limit. Tbls, flush toilets, cfga, drkg wtr, showers (50 cents for 5 minutes), dump. Boating(l), fishing, hiking.

Acorn West $12
New Hogan Lake
Corps of Engineers
Half mi S of Valley Springs on SR 26; 1 mi S on Hogan Dam Rd; three-fourths mi E on Hogan Pkwy. $12 Sun-Thurs during 4/1-9/30 ($16 Fri-Sat); $12 all week 10/1-3/31. All year; 14-day limit. 58 sites; 65-ft RV limit. Tbls, flush toilets, cfga, drkg wtr, showers (50 cents for 5 minutes), dump, hookups($), amphitheater, fish cleaning station. Fishing, boating, hiking. Requires 2-day minimum stay on weekends, 3-day stay holiday weekends.

Deer Flat $10
New Hogan Lake
Corps of Engineers
Half mi S of Valley Springs on SR 26; 1 m S on Hogan Dam Rd; 0.7 mi E to Acorn West Campground (to register); boat access to campsites on E side of dam. $10. 5/1-9/30; 14-day limit. Primitive boat-in tent sites. Tbls, toilets, cfga, no drkg wtr. Fishing, boating, swimming.

Oak Knoll $10
New Hogan Lake
Corps of Engineers
Half mi from Valley Springs on SR 26; 1.8 mi E on Lime Rd; 1.4 mi S on Petersburg Rd. $10. 4/1-9/30; 14-day limit. 50 primitive sites (8 pull-through); 65-ft RV limit. Tbls, toilets, cfga, drkg wtr, dump. Fishing. Requires 2-day minimum stay on weekends & 3-day stay holiday weekends.

VENTURA (327) S

San Miguel Island $7.50
Channel Islands National Park
55 nautical mi (4 hrs) from Ventura Harbor by commercial ferry; it is the farthest W of the Channel Islands. Campground is 1 mi hike uphill from beach landing. $7.50 with federal Senior Pass; others pay $15. 9 tent sites. Toilets, tbls, windbreaks, food cabinets; bring cookstove; no open fires. Visits limited to 200 persons annually, by reservation only (877-444-6777). Very foggy & windy. Ranger-led hikes, beach exploring, birdwatching, scuba diving, snorkeling, kayaking, fishing. Western beach, Point Bennett, is only place in the world where up to six different species of seals & sea lions can be viewed (in winter, as many as 50,000 breed there)

Santa Barbara $7.50
Island Campground
Channel Islands National Park
45 nautical mi S by commercial ferry. Camping area one-third mi from boat landings; hike half mi up steep switchback trail. $7.50 with federal Senior Pass; others pay $15. All year; 14-day limit. 8 tent sites. No supplies; pack in food, water, fuel. Tent capable of being securely anchored recommended due to wind. No shade. Pack out trash. Fires only in campstoves in summer. Sea lions, sea birds, cormorants, gray whales. Scuba diving, snorkeling, hiking, birdwatching. Ferry runs once a week in summer. Reservations required; call 877-444-6777; cost included in camping fee. 639 acres.
Travel tip: In Ventura, take free tour of Donald C. Tillman Water Reclamation Plant and Japanese Garden; huge gardens feature beautiful lawns, paths, banzai trees; teahouse, zigzag bridges.
Fishing tip: Thick kelp beds on N side of island provide cover for fish; most popular are rockfish, kelp bass, sheepshead.

Santa Cruz Island $7.50
Channel Islands National Park
17-29 mi from Ventura Harbor by commercial ferry (2 hrs). $7.50 with federal Senior Pass; others pay $15. All year; 14-day limit. Two campgrounds: one in Scorpion Valley with 40 tent sites and a new backcountry campground at Del Norte on N side of island. To reach the new camping area, follow ranch road trail from Prisoner Landing for 3.5 mi; 4 sites withtoilet but no wtr; fires prohibited.

VERDI (NEVADA) (328) N

Hunting Camp #1 FREE
Toiyabe National Forest
3 mi NW on FR 027. Free. All year; 14-day limit. Undesignated primitive area, undeveloped. Toilet, cfga, no drkg wtr. Horses permitted. Primarily a hunter's camp.

Hunting Camp #2 FREE
Toiyabe National Forest
3.5 mi NW on FR 027. Free. 4/1-11/1; 14-day limit. Undesignated primitive area, undeveloped. Toilet, cfga, no drkg wtr. Horses permitted. Primarily a hunter's camp.

Hunting Camp #4 FREE
Toiyabe National Forest
NW of Verdi on FR 027. Free. 4/1-11/1; 14-day limit. Undesignated primitive area, undeveloped. Toilet, cfga, no drkg wtr. Primarily a hunter's camp.

VIOLA (330) N

North Battle Creek Reservoir $10
Pacific Gas & Electric
3.5 mi E of Viola on SR 44; 5 mi N on CR 32N17; 4 mi E on CR 32N31; half mi on CR 32N18. $10. All year; 14-day limit. 10 sites & 5 walk-in sites. Tbls, toilets, cfga, drkg wtr.

Canoeing, fishing, boating (elec mtrs), hiking. Elev 5600 ft. Status not verified for 2007.

WARNER SPRINGS (331) S

Indian Flats   **$5**
Cleveland National Forest
2 mi NW of Warner Springs on SR 79; 6 mi N on FR 9S05. $5. June-Feb; 14-day limit. 17 sites; 16-ft RV limit. Tbls, toilets, cfga, no drkg wtr. Hiking. Elev 3600 ft.

WEAVERVILLE (332) N

Bridge Camp   **$11**
Shasta-Trinity National Forest
10 mi N of Weaverville, then 13.5 mi NE on SR 3; 1.5 mi NW on CR 112; 2 mi NW on FR 35N33. $11 during 4/1-10/31; $6 rest of year, but no wtr; 14-day limit. 10 sites (12-ft RV limit). Tbls, toilets, cfga, drkg wtr. Nature trails. Swimming, fishing, hiking, horseback riding (corrals). Bait, restaurant, 2 mi. On Stuart Fork arm of Whiskeytown-Shasta-Trinity National Recreation Area.

Clark Springs   **$11**
Shasta-Trinity National Forest
18 mi N of Weaverville on SR 3; at Mule Creek Station. $11. 3/1-9/15; free 3/1-5/15 but no wtr. 21 tent sites (small RVs okay); 34 picnic sites. Tbls, flush toilets, cfga, drkg wtr, beach. Swimming, boating(dl), fishing. On Stuart Fork arm in Whiskeytown-Shasta-Trinity National Recreation Area.

East Weaver   **$10**
Shasta-Trinity National Forest
2 mi NE of Weaverville on SR 3; 1.5 mi N on CR 228 (East Weaver Rd); along East Weaver Creek. $10 during 4/1-10/31; $6 rest of year but no wtr; 14-day limit. 15 sites (16-ft RV limit). Tbls, toilets, cfga, drkg wtr. Hiking, fishing. Elev 2800 ft; 5 acres.

Mariners Roost   **FREE**
Boat-In Camp
Shasta-Trinity National Forest
13.3 mi NE of Weaverville on SR 3; 5.2 mi E, BY BOAT on Clair Engle Lake. Free. All year; 14-day limit. 7 tent sites. Tbls, toilets, cfga, firewood, no drkg wtr. Swimming, fishing, picnicking, boating(d; lr--2 mi). Elev 2400 ft; 3 acres. A lakeshore camp on E Fort Stuart fork arm of Clair Engle Lake, E shore, located just E of the Ridgeville Boat-In Camp. Boat ramps at Clark Springs, Alpine View campgrounds. Trinity unit of Whiskeytown-Shasta-Trinity National Recreation Area.

Minersville   **$7.50**
Shasta-Trinity National Forest
17 mi NE of Weaverville on SR 3; 1 mi SE on FR 33N28. During peak season, $7.50 with federal Senior Pass; others pay $15; during 11/1-5/1, $7.50 for all, but no drkg wtr. All year; 14-day limit. 21 sites (35-ft RV limit). Tbls, flush toilets, cfga, drkg wtr. Boating(l), fishing, swimming, waterskiing. Near Clair

Engle Lake on Stuart Fork arm in Whiskeytown-Shasta-Trinity National Recreation Area. 11 acres.

Fishing tip: Bass fishing best in early spring; use jigs & spinnerbaits along dropoffs, points and underwater structure. Trout fishing best in early spring too. In summer, drift minnows for trout; use deep-running crankbaits & plastic worms for bass.

Travel tip: In Weaverville, visit J.J. (Jake) Jackson Museum; features displays on history from days of the Indian through the gold rush; Indian relics, Chinese weapons, bottle collection, old jail cells; audio visual program. Donations.

Pigeon Point   **$12**
Shasta-Trinity National Forest
15 mi W of Weaverville on Hwy 299. $12 ($8 at 2 walk-in tent sites). May-Oct; 14-day limit. 10 sites (25-ft RV limit). Tbls, toilets, cfga, drkg wtr. Swimming beach, fishing. Trinity River.

Ridgeville Boat-In Camp   **FREE**
Shasta-Trinity National Forest
13.3 mi NE of Weaverville on SR 3; 5 mi E, BY BOAT, on Clair Engle Lake to the Stuart Fork arm; camp on western shore at end of peninsula at arm's entrance just W of the Mariners Roost Boat-In Camp. Free. All year; 14-day limit. 21 tent sites. Tbls, toilets, cfga, no drkg wtr. Boat ramps at Clark Springs, Alpine View campgrounds. Boating, fishing.

Fishing tip: Keep in mind, Clair Engle also has good population of brown trout & kokanee salmon.

Ridgeville Island   **FREE**
Shasta-Trinity National Forest
13.6 mi NE of Weaverville on SR 3; 3.6 mi E, BY BOAT, on Clair Engle Lake. Free. All year. 3 tent sites. Tbls, toilets, cfga, firewood, no drkg wtr. Waterskiing, swimming, picnicking, fishing, boating (d; rl--1 mi). Elev 2400 ft; 6 acres. An island lakeshore camp on Fort Stuart fork arm of Clair Engle Lake, N shore. Trinity unit of Whiskeytown-Shasta-Trinity National Recreation Area.

Rush Creek   **$6**
Shasta-Trinity National Forest
8 mi N of Weaverville on SR 3; left at camp sign for qtr mi. $6. 5/1-9/1; 14-day limit. 10 primitive RV & tent sites; 16-ft RV limit. Tbls, toilets, cfga, no drkg wtr, no trash service. Primarily an overflow camp. Hiking, fishing, swimming, gold panning.

Stoney Point   **$12**
Shasta-Trinity National Forest
14 mi NE of Weaverville on SR 3. On Clair Engle Lake. $12 during 5/1-10/31; $6 rest of year but no wtr; 14-day limit. 21 tent sites. Tbls, flush toilets, cfga, drkg wtr, beach. Swimming, fishing, boating, waterskiing. 11 acres. At Stuart Fork arm of the Whiskeytown-Shasta-Trinity National Recreation Area.

Fishing tip: Excellent fishing for bass, catfish and trout from Trinity Lake as well as for trout in the Stuart's Fork of the Trinity River.

WEED (333) N

Lake Shastina   **FREE**
Shasta Cascade
Wonderland Association
2.5 mi NE of Weed on Hwy 97; 1 mi W on Ordway Rd, then N on Edgewood-Big Springs Rd to westbound lake turnoff. Free. Undesignated primitive camping area; portable toilets, cfga, drkg wtr. Fishing, boating(l).

Fishing tip: Try camping here in late spring for the excellent crappie fishing; use small jigs & minnows. Catch trout and bass.

WESTPORT (334) N

Westport-Union Landing   **$10**
State Beach
3 mi N of Westport (16 mi N of Fort Bragg) on SR 1. $10 off-season; $15 peak season. All year; 15-day limit. 130 primitive sites (35-ft RV limit). Tbls, pit toilets, cfga, drkg wtr. Scenic. Fishing, beachcombing, diving.

WESTWOOD (335) N

Echo Lake   **FREE**
Lassen National Forest
On Rd 10 near Silver Lake. Free. May-Nov; 14-day limit. Undesignated sites, no tbls, no cfga, no drkg wtr. Fishing, hiking.

Fishing tip: Rainbow & brook trout from Silver Lake typically are 7-15 inches. Fish by boat, tube or shore with surface flies mornings and evenings; use worms or salmon eggs during the day.

WILLIAMS (336) N

Cache Creek   **FREE**
State Wildlife Area
About 18 mi SW of Williams on Hwy 20; at main & N fork of Cache Creek. Public access S of Hwy 20 on Hwy 16. Free. All year; 14-day limit. Primitive camping on 2,632 acres. Hunting, hiking, fishing.

Indian Valley   **FREE**
State Wildlife Area
About 17 mi SW of Williams on Hwy 20; 8 mi N on Bear Valley Rd; W on Bartlett Springs Rd to N shore of Indian Valley Lake; follow signs. Free. All year; 14-day limit. Primitive camping on 4,990 acres surrounding the lake. Hunting, fishing, boating, canoeing.

Fishing tip: Indian Valley Lake holds a wide variety of fish, including trout, catfish, steelhead and largemouth & smallmouth bass.

WILLOW CREEK (338) N

Andy's Camp   **FREE**
Primitive Area
Six Rivers National Forest
Near Willow Creek at jct of Grogan Trail 6E16 and FR 8N10. Free. All year; 30-day limit. Undeveloped primitive camping area. No

facilities except small stock corral. Horseback riding, hunting, hiking, picnicking. Used by hunters and backpackers. Also trailhead of Grogan Trail 6E16.

Boise Creek Campground   **$8**
Six Rivers National Forest
1 mi W of Willow Creek on Hwy 299. $8. All year; 14-day limit. 17 sites (35-ft RV limit). Toilets, tbls, no drkg wtr, cfga. Hiking, fishing, picnicking.

Box Camp Primitive Area   **FREE**
Six Rivers National Forest
1 mi E of Hoopa Valley Indian Reservation, just S of FR 8N01; adjacent to small tributary of Tish Tang Creek. Free. Fall use by hunters; 30-day limit. Undeveloped primitive camping area. No facilities. Hunting, picnicking, hiking.

Clark Camp Primitive Area   **FREE**
Six Rivers National Forest
1 mi NW of Groves Prairie, just S of FR 7N10. Camp alongside small creek. Free. All year; 30-day limit. Undeveloped primitive camping area. No facilities. Hunting, picnicking, hiking, fishing.

Clear Lake   **FREE**
White Rock Springs
Primitive Camping Area
Six Rivers National Forest
Adjacent to FR 6N01, 7 mi SE of SR 299 area of Berry Summit. Free. All year; 30-day limit. Fall primary use period. Numerous hunter camps in area. No facilities. Hunting, picnicking, hiking.

Cold Springs Primitive Area   **FREE**
Six Rivers National Forest
4 mi S of Horse Mountain on FR 6N01. Free. All year, depending on weather; 30-day limit. Fall primary use period. Undeveloped primitive camping area. No facilities except spring wtr. Hunting, hiking. Small ridgetop camp & spring was historically used in conjunction with Humboldt Trail. Elev 5000 ft.

Cow Chip Springs   **FREE**
Primitive Area
Six Rivers National Forest
On a small flat of Last Chance Ridge adjacent to FR 6N01. Free. All year; 30-day limit. Undeveloped primitive camping area. No facilities. Hunting, hiking.

East Fork Willow Creek   **$8**
Six Rivers National Forest
6 mi W of Willow Creek on SR 299. $8. Forest entry information site. All year; limit 7 days in calendar yr; free off-season. 13 primitive sites; 20-ft RV limit. Information display, 3 vault toilets, tbls, no drkg wtr. Hunting, hiking, picnicking. Pack out trash.

Gray's Falls   **$10**
Six Rivers National Forest
12 mi E of Willow Creek on Hwy 299. $10. 5/1-9/15; 14-day limit. 33 sites (35-ft RV limit). 1 handicap site. Tbls, flush toilets, cfga, drkg wtr. Fishing, tubing, hiking.

Grizzly Camp   **FREE**
Primitive Area
Six Rivers National Forest
From Hawkins Bar over CR 402 and FRs 7N26 and 7N53. Free. All year; 30-day limit. Undeveloped prim camping area. No facilities. Hunting, backpacking. Trailhead for SE end of Horse Trail Ridge Nat'l Recreation Trail 6E08.

Groves Prairie   **FREE**
Primitive Area
Six Rivers National Forest
Large meadow divided by Prairie Creek, 6.5 air mi NE of Hawkins Bar on FR 7N04. Free. All year; 30-day limit. Undeveloped primitive camping area. No facilities. Hiking, fishing.

Happy Camp Primitive Area   **FREE**
Six Rivers National Forest
4 air mi NE of Hawkins Bar by FRs 7N04 and 6N10. Free. All year; 7-day limit in calendar yr. Remote, undeveloped primitive camping area. Toilets, tbls, block fireplaces. Hunting, hiking.

Horse Linto Primitive Area   **FREE**
Six Rivers National Forest
7 mi NE of Willow Creek on FR 10N02. Free. All year; limit 7 days in calendar yr. 3 undeveloped primitive sites; 20-ft RV limit. Fire pits, toilets, tbls, trash cans, no drkg wtr. Fishing, swimming.

Robinson Camp   **FREE**
Primitive Area
Six Rivers National Forest
1.5 mi SE of Grouse Mountain on the Humboldt Trail. Free. All year; 30-day limit. Undeveloped primitive camping area. Rustic user-built improvements, spring flowing into trough. Bear and deer hunting.

Rooster Rock   **FREE**
Primitive Area
Six Rivers National Forest
10 mi S of SR 299 at Berry Summit area, adjacent to Snow Camp Rd. Free. All year; 30-day limit. Undeveloped primitive camping area. No facilities.

Surprise Beach   **FREE**
Primitive Area
Six Rivers National Forest
On South Fork of Trinity River, 12 mi S of SR 299. Accessible from South Fork Rd over short section of FS Low Standard Rd starting about 3 mi SE of Willow Creek. Near Surprise Creek. Free. All year; 30-day limit. Undesignated primitive camping area. No facilities. Swimming, fishing, hiking.

   Fishing tip: Try fall fishing for steelhead, chinook & coho on the Trinity River.

Trail Head-6E08   **FREE**
Primitive Area
Six Rivers National Forest
Near jct of Trail 6E08 and FR 10N02. Free. All year; 30-day limit. Undeveloped primitive camping area. No facilities. Hunting, hiking,

backpacking. Site is trailhead for W end of Horse Trail Ridge National Recreation Trail 6E08.

WILLOWS (339) N

Stony Gorge Reservoir   **FREE**
Bureau of Reclamation
21 mi W of Willows on SR 162. Near Mendocino National Forest. Free. Primitive sites. Tbls, toilets, cfga, drkg wtr. Picnic sites. Swimming, boating(l), fishing. Lake level low after Aug.

WINTERHAVEN (340) S

Imperial Dam   **$140**
Long-Term Visitor Area
Bureau of Land Management
From I-8 at Winterhaven, NE 20 mi on Imperial County Hwy (S-24), then W on Senator Wash Rd. Free 4/14-9/14; $140 for winter season or $30 for 14 days during 9/15-4/15; during 4/16-9/14, $5 per day or $60 for season. No facilities. Gray water dump at Quail Hill. Dump at Kripple Kreek. Drkg wtr, dump, toilets at South Mesa. Gray water dump at Coyote Ridge. Federal Senior Pass discounts do not apply to LTVA fees.

Pilot Knob   **$140**
Long-Term Visitor Area
Bureau of Land Management
From I-8 at Winterhaven's Sidewinder Rd exit, qtr mi S on Sidewinder Rd. Site on gravel terrace on both sides of rd. $140 for season or $30 for 14 days during 9/15-4/15; during 4/16-9/14, $5 daily or $50 for season. Undesignated sites. No facilities. Dump ($) and water fills($) at Tank and Mobile Wash, I-8 at Ave 3E in Yuma. Federal Senior Pass discounts do not apply to LTVA fees.

Senator Wash North Shore   **$5**
Bureau of Land Management
19.7 mi N of Winterhaven on CR S24; 3 mi W on Senator Wash Rd to South Mesa Campground, then left following signs. $5 daily or $50 annually. All year; 14-day limit. Undesignated sites on 60 acres. Tbls, flush toilets, cfga, drkg wtr; dump at South Mesa (fee 9/15-4/15). Boating(l), fishing, OHV activities, hiking, swimming.

Senator Wash South Shore   **$5**
Bureau of Land Management
19.7 mi N of Winterhaven on CR S24; 3 mi W on Senator Wash Rd to South Mesa Campground, then 200 yds to reservoir access rd. All year; 14-day limit. $5 daily or $50 annually. Undesignated sites on 50 acres. Tbls, flush toilets, dump, drkg wtr, no trash service. Swimming, waterskiing, boating (l), fishing (catfish, bass). Elev 180 ft. Senator Wash Reservoir.

Squaw Lake   **$5**
Bureau of Land Management
From I-8 near Winterhaven, 20 mi N on CR S-

24 to sign for Senator Wash & Squaw Lake. $5 daily use fee or $50 annually. All year; 14-day limit. 125 sites (30-ft RV limit) & numerous dispersed tent sites. Tbls, flush toilets, cfga, cold outdoor showers, drkg wtr, gray water dump (dump station at nearby South Mesa). Boating(l), fishing, swimming, hiking.

WOODFORDS (341) N

Crystal Springs   **$12**
Toiyabe National Forest
1 mi W of Woodfords on SR 88. $12. About 4/15-9/30; 14-day limit. 22 sites (22-ft RV limit). Tbls, toilets, cfga, drkg wtr. Fishing, hiking. West Fork of Carson River. Elev 6000 ft.

Fishing tip: The West Fork of Carson River is heavily stocked with catchable size rainbow and cutthroat trout. For handicapped fishermen, the best access are two fishing platforms built at the Hope Valley Wildlife Area near Hwys 88 & 89. Try pitching crickets anchored with tiny split shot.

Hope Valley   **$12**
Toiyabe National Forest
About 10 mi W of Woodfords on SR 88; 1.5 mi S on Blue Lakes Rd. $12. About 6/15-9/30; 14-day limit. 20 sites (22-ft RV limit). Tbls, toilets, cfga, drkg wtr. Fishing, hiking. Elev 7300 ft.

Indian Creek Reservoir   **$11**
Bureau of Land Management
Near Woodfords, 3 mi S on Hwy 89 to Airport Blvd; right on access rd. $11 for 10 walk-in sites; $15 for RVs. 5/1-9/30; 14-day limit. Base fee for 10 tent sites; 19 RV sites (24-ft RV limit); group camping by reservation. Tbls, flush toilets, cfga, showers, drkg wtr, dump. Fishing. Elev 6000 ft.

Kit Carson   **$12**
Toiyabe National Forest
5 mi W of Woodfords on SR 88. $12. About 5/15-9/15; 14-day limit. 12 sites (22-ft RV limit). Tbls, toilets, cfga, drkg wtr. West Fork of Carson River. Fishing, hiking. Elev 6900 ft.

Markleeville   **$10**
Toiyabe National Forest
About 10.5 mi S of Woodfords on Hwy 89 (half mi S of Markleeville). $10. 4/15-10/15; 14-day limit. 10 sites (20-ft RV limit). Tbls, toilets, cfga, drkg wtr. Fishing at Markleeville Creek. Elev 5500 ft.

Red Lake   **FREE**
State Wildlife Area
About 10 mi SW of Woodfords on SR 88; at Red Lake. Free. All year; 14-day limit. Primitive camping on 860 acres. Hunting, fishing, canoeing, boating, hiking.

Silver Creek   **$6.50**
Toiyabe National Forest
About 10 mi S of Woodfords on Hwy 89 to Markleeville; 16 mi S on SR 4. $6.50 with federal Senior Pass; others pay $13. MD-LD; 14-day limit. 22 sites (22-ft RV limit). Tbls, toilets, cfga, drkg wtr. Fishing. Elev 6800 ft.

Snowshoe Springs   **$12**
Toiyabe National Forest
4 mi W of Woodfords on SR 88. $12. About 5/15-9/15; 14-day limit. 13 tent sites. Tbls, toilets, cfga, drkg wtr. Fishing. West Fork of Carson River. Elev 6600 ft.

Turtle Rock   **$10**
Alpine County Park
3.5 mi S of Woodfords on SR 89. $10 ($8 for seniors). 5/1-10/15 (depending upon weather). 25 sites (30-ft RV limit). Tbls, toilets, cfga, drkg wtr. Elev 6000 ft.

WRIGHTWOOD (342) S

Apple Tree   **$5**
Angeles National Forest
3 mi from Wrightwood on Angeles Crest Hwy to Big Pines; bear right on Big Pines Hwy (CR N4) for 2 mi. $5 daily or $30 annually. All year; 14-day limit. 8 tent sites, 1 group site. Tbls, toilets, cfga, drkg wtr in summer. Elev 6200 ft.

Blue Ridge   **$5**
Angeles National Forest
5.6 mi W of Wrightwood on SR 2 (Angeles Crest Hwy); 3.8 mi SE on FR 3N06. $5 daily or $30 annually. 5/1-10/31; 14-day limit. 8 sites (RVs under 21 ft). Tbls, toilets, cfga, no drkg wtr. Hiking, picnicking. Elev 7900 ft; 3 acres. Snow closes access rd Dec April. Nature trails (on Pacific Crest Trail).

Cabin Flat   **$5**
Angeles National Forest
5.6 mi W of Wrightwood on SR 2 (Angeles Crest Hwy); 14.9 mi SE on FR 3N06. 4WD necessary; walk-in sites. $5 daily or $30 annually. 5/15-10/31; 14 day limit. 12 sites (RVs under 16 ft). Tbls, toilets, cfga, firewood, no drkg wtr. Picnicking, fishing. Elev 5400 ft; 2 acres. Snow closes access rd Dec-April. Prairie Ford of San Gabriel River. Pacific Crest Trail connection. Note: Closed in 2007 for RV use to protect endangered mountain yellow legged frog.

Cooper Canyon Trail Camp   **$5**
Angeles National Forest
26.7 mi W of Wrightwood on SR 2 (Angeles Crest Hwy); 1.5 mi NE on FR 3N02. $5 daily or $30 annually. 5/15-10/31; 14-day limit. 8 sites (no trailers). Tbls, toilets, cfga, no drkg wtr. Fishing, picnicking. Elev 6300 ft; 2 acres. Stream. Hiking access only on Pacific Crest Trail.

Fish Fork   **$5**
Angeles National Forest
5.6 mi SW of Wrightwood on SR 2; 14.9 mi SE on FR 3N06; 5.6 mi SW on Trail 8W091. $5 daily or $30 annually. 5/15-10/15; 14-day

limit. (Snow Dec-Apr; access rd closed.) 1 site (no RVs). Toilets, cfga, no drkg wtr. Fishing, picnicking. Elev 3400 ft; 1 acre. Stream.

Guffy   **$5**
Angeles National Forest
5.6 mi W of Wrightwood on SR 2 (Angeles Crest Hwy); 7.2 mi SE on FR 3N06; 4WD necessary to reach site. $5 daily or $30 annually. 5/15-10/31; 14-day limit. 6 sites (RVs under 16 ft). Tbls, toilets, cfga, no drkg wtr. Hunting, hiking, picnicking. Elev 8300 ft; 2 acres. Snow closes access rd Dec-Apr. Trail connects to Pacific Crest Trail.

Lake Campground   **$12**
Angeles National Forest
3 mi from Wrightwood on Angeles Crest Hwy to Big Pines; bear right on Big Pines Hwy (CR N4) for 2.5 mi. $12. May-Dec; free rest of yr, but no wtr; 14-day limit. 8 sites (18-ft RV limit). Tbls, toilets, cfga, drkg wtr. Fishing. On Jackson Lake. Elev 6100 ft.

Little Fish Fork   **$5**
Angeles National Forest
5.6 mi W of Wrightwood on SR 2; 12 mi SE on FR 3N06; 2.8 mi W on Trail 3N08; 2.3 mi SW on Trail 8W30. $5 daily or $30 annually. 5/15-10/15; 14-day limit. (Snow Dec-Apr; access rd closed.) 2 tent sites. Cfga, no tbls, no toilets, no drkg wtr. Hiking, picnicking, fishing. Elev 6000 ft; 2 acres.

Little Jimmy Trail Camp   **$5**
Angeles National Forest
19.8 mi W of Wrightwood on SR 2 (Angeles Crest Hwy); 2.7 mi SE on Trail 9W03. Hiking access only. $5 daily or $30 annually. 5/15 10/15; 14-day limit. 16 tent sites. Tbls, toilets, no drkg wtr. Hiking, picnicking. Elev 7400 ft; 6 acres. Free fire permit required. Hiking access only on Pacific Crest Trail.

Lupine   **$5**
Angeles National Forest
5.6 mi W of Wrightwood on SR 2 (Angeles Crest Hwy); 12 mi SE on FR 3N06. $5 daily or $30 annually. 6/15-10/31; 14-day limit. 11 walk-in tent sites. Tbls, toilets, cfga, firewood, no drkg wtr except from spring. Hunting, picnicking, fishing. Elev 6600 ft; 3 acres. Snow closes access rd Dec-Apr. Prairie Fork of San Gabriel River.

Mine Gulch   **$5**
Angeles National Forest
5.6 mi NW of Wrightwood on SR 2 (Angeles Crest Hwy); 14.9 mi SE on FR 3N06; 2.1 mi W on Trail 8W091. $5 daily or $30 annually. 5/15 10/15; 14-day limit. 5 tent sites. Toilets, cfga, no tbls, no drkg wtr. Hiking, picnicking, fishing. Elev 4500 ft; 1 acre. Snow closes access rd Dec-Apr.

Mountain Oak   **$12**
Angeles National Forest
3 mi from Wrightwood on Angeles Crest Hwy to Big Pines; bear right on Big Pines Hwy (CR N4) for 3 mi. $12. All year; free when wtr is

shut off; 14-day limit. 17 sites (18-ft RV limit). Tbls, toilets, cfga, drkg wtr. Elev 6200 ft.

Peavine $5
Angeles National Forest
3 mi from Wrightwood on Angeles Crest Hwy to Big Pines; bear right on Big Pines Hwy (CR N4) for 2.5 mi. $5 daily or $30 annually. All year; 14-day limit. 4 tent sites. Tbls, toilets, cfga, drkg wtr.

Upper Fish Fork $5
Angeles National Forest
6 mi NW of Wrightwood on SR 2; 9 mi SE on FR 3N06; 3 mi S on Trail 8W10. $5 daily or $30 annually. 5/15-10/15; 14-day limit. 1 tent site. Cfga, no tbls, no toilets, no drkg wtr. Hiking, fishing.

YOSEMITE VILLAGE (343) N

Bridalveil Creek $7
Yosemite National Park
About 8 mi E of Wawona Rd (Hwy 41) on Glacier Point Rd (S of Yosemite Village). $7 with federal Senior Pass; others pay $14. 7/1-9/15; 14-day limit. 110 sites; 35-ft motorhome limit, 24-ft trailer limit. Tbls, cfga, drkg wtr, flush toilets, food lockers.

Crane Flat $10
Yosemite National Park
On Big Oak Flat Rd (Hwy 120) at Craine Flat, NW of Yosemite Village. $10 with federal Senior Pass; others pay $20. 7/1-9/30; 14-day limit. 166 sites; 35-ft motorhome limit, 27-ft trailer limit. Tbls, flush toilets, cfga, drkg wtr, food locker.

Hodgen Meadows $7
Yosemite National Park
N of Yosemite Valley on Big Oak Flat Rd (SR 120). Holders of federal Senior Pass pay $7 during 10/15-4/15 (others pay $14) and $10 rest of year (others pay $20); 14-day limit. 105 sites; 27-ft trailer limit, 35-foot motorhme limit. Tbls, flush toilets, cfga, drkg wtr, food locker. Dump at Upper Pines Camp. Fishing.

Lower Pines $10
Yosemite National Park
In Yosemity Valley near Curry Village. $10 with federal Senior Pass; others pay $20. Mar-Oct; 14-day limit. 60 sites; 40-ft motorhome limit, 35-ft trailer limit. Tbls, flush toilets, drkg wtr, cfga, food locker, dump.

North Pines $10
Yosemite National Park
In Yosemite Valley near Curry Village. $10 with federal Senior Pass; others pay $20. Apr-Sept; 14-day limit. 81 sites; 40-ft motorhome limit, 35-ft trailer limit. Tbls, cfga, flush toilets, drkg wtr, food lockers.

Porcupine Flat $10
Yosemite National Park
30 mi NE of Yosemite Village on Old Big Oak Flat Rd. Just N of Tioga Rd. $10 plus entry

fee. About 7/1-10/15; 14-day limit. 52 sites; 24-ft trailer limit, 35-ft motorhome limit. Tbls, toilets, cfga, no drkg wtr. Fishing. Trails to Yosemite Creek & Snow Creek. Elev 8100 ft.

Tamarack Flat $10
Yosemite National Park
23 mi NE of Yosemite Village on Old Big Oak Flat Rd; 4 mi E of Gin Flat. $10 plus entry fee. 6/10-10/15; 14-day limit. 52 sites; RVs not recommended. Tbls, toilets, cfga, no drkg wtr. Fishing.

Tuolumne Meadows $10
Yosemite National Park
On Tioga Rd at Tolumne Meadows N of Yosemite Village. $10 with federal Senior Pass; others pay $20. 7/1-9/30; 14-day limit. 304 sites; 35-ft RV limit. Tbls, flush toilets, cfga, drkg wtr, dump, food locker.

Upper Pines Campground $10
Yosemite National Park
In Yosemite Valley near Curry Village. $10 with federal Senior Pass; others pay $20. All year; 14-day limit. 238 sites; 35-ft motorhome limit, 24-ft trailer limit. Tbls, flush toilets, cfga, drkg wtr, dump, food locker.

Wawona Campground $7
Yosemite National Park
1 mi N of Wawano on Wawano Rd (SR 41) and S of Yosemite Valley. Holders of federal Senior Pass pay $7 during Oct-Apr (others pay $14) and $10 rest of year (others pay $20). 14-day limit. 93 sites; 35-ft RV limit. Tbls, flush toilets, cfga, drkg wtr, dump. Fishing.

White Wolf $7
Yosemite National Park
20 mi E of Yosemite Buck Meadows on Big Oak Flat Rd (SR 120), 1 mi Off Tioga Rd. $7 with federal Senior Pass; others pay $14. 6/1-9/15; 14-day limit. 74 sites (27-ft RV limit). Tbls, flush toilets, cfga, drkg wtr. Fishing, ranger programs, hiking. Elev 8000 ft; 18 acres.

Yosemite Creek $10
Yosemite National Park
35 mi from Yosemite Village on Old Tioga Rd; 4 mi S of New Tioga Rd. $10 plus entry fee. 6/1-10/15; 14-day limit. 40 tent sites. Tbls, toilets, cfga, no drkg wtr. Fishing. Pets only at W end of camp. Elev 7600 ft; 5 acres.

YREKA (344) N

Copco Reservoir FREE
Bureau of Land Management
33 mi NE on Yreka on US 99 (N Central Valley). Free. May-Nov. Undesignated sites. Wtr. Water sports, boating (l), hunting, fishing. Elev 2500 ft. On Klamath River. Cooperative area; Bureau of Land Management & Pacific Power & Light Co.
Fishing tip: Fall & winter, use salmon eggs & crankbaits to catch steelhead & salmon

from the Klamath River. During summer, catch rainbow trout from the Smith on flies.
Travel tip: Greenhorn Park at Greenhorn Reservoir displays restored miner's cabin, has outdoor activities; free.

Tree of Heaven $10
Klamath National Forest
8 mi N of Yreka on SR 263; 4 mi W on SR 96. $10. All year; free during 11/15-5/15; 14-day limit. 20 sites (22-ft RV limit). Tbls, toilets, cfga, drkg wtr (no wtr in winter). Swimming, fishing, boating(l), hikng, horseshoes, volleyball. On Klamath River. Elev 2100 ft; 6 acres. Paved birding nature trail with interpretive signs.

YUBA CITY (345) N

Live Oak Municipal Park $10
1 mi W on Pennington Rd from Live Oak (8.5 mi N of Yuba City on Hwy 99 to Live Oak). $10 (California seniors, $8; disabled, $5). All year; 14-day limit. 12 sites (30-ft RV limit). Tbls, toilets, cfga, drkg wtr.
Travel tip: 15 mi NW of Yuba City on Hwy 99 is Gray Lodge Refuge; waterfowl nestings, pheasant, hawk, other species viewed along auto route; admission charged except to those with current California fishing or hunting licenses or California Wildlife Pass.

YUCCA VALLEY (347) S

Morongo Valley Park FREE
5 mi W of Yucca Valley on Hwy 62. Free. All year. 6 sites. Tbls, toilets, cfga, no drkg wtr. Near Joshua Tree National Park.

ZENIA (348) N

Bear Springs FREE
Primitive Area
Six Rivers National Forest
2 mi N of Zenia Guard Station on FR 2S08. Free. All year; 30-day limit. Used June-Oct. Undeveloped prim camping area; space for 1 RV, 1 tent. No facilities. Hunting, hiking, picnicking.

Bear Wallow Springs FREE
Six Rivers National Forest
3.5 mi N of Zenia Guard Station on oiled logging rd, FR 2S08. Jan-Oct. Used June-Oct. 3 undeveloped primitive sites. Toilet; no other facilities. Fall deer hunting. Elev 4900 ft. Pleasant summer climate. Good scenery. Toilet located below middle unit.

Black Lassic Primitive Area FREE
Six Rivers National Forest
5 mi from jct of CR 511 and FR 1S07, on FR 1S07. Free. All year; 30-day limit. Used June-Oct. 1 undeveloped primitive site. Spring water trough (boil before using). Hunting, hiking. Unique geologic & botanical area. Elev 5000 ft.

Grizzly Primitive Area   **FREE**
Six Rivers National Forest
FR 2S08 to FR 2S17 a short distance, then turn right for .9 mi up 4WD rd to Grizzly Mtn. Free. All year; 30-day limit. Camp hot, dry during summer. Undeveloped primitive camping area; no facilities. Hunting, hiking.

Red Lassic Primitive Area   **FREE**
Six Rivers National Forest
On FR 1S07 about 5 mi from jct with CR 511. Free. June-Oct; 30-day limit. Undeveloped primitive camping area. No facilities. Hunting, hiking. Unique geologic and botanical area.

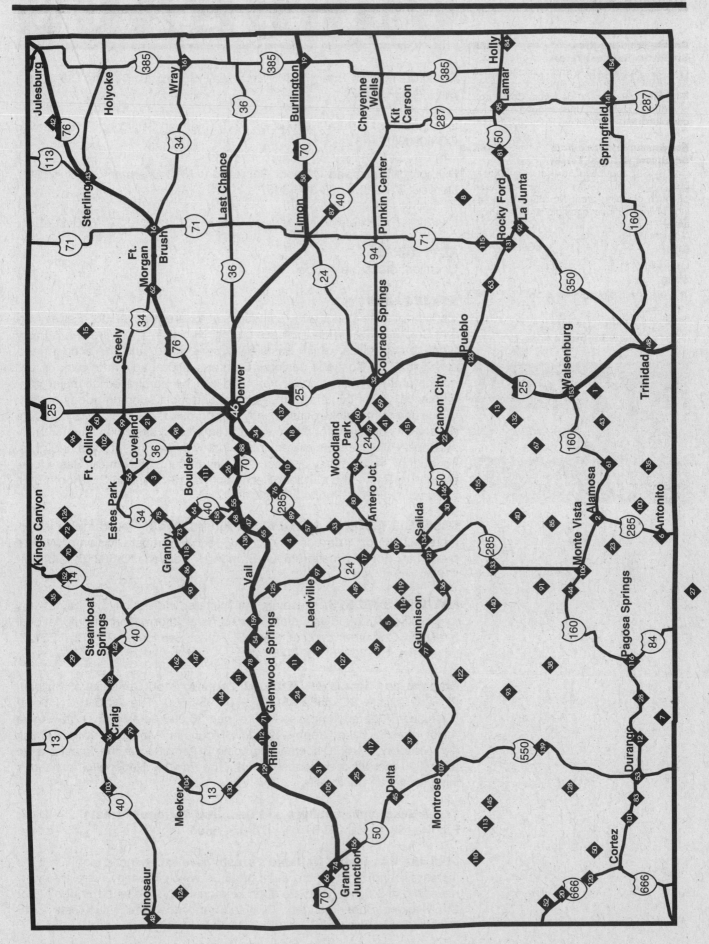

COLORADO

MISCELLANEOUS
Capital:
Denver
Nickname:
Centennial State
Motto:
Nil Sine Numine (Nothing Without Providence)
Flower:
Rocky Mountain Columbine
Tree:
Colorado Blue Spruce
Bird:
Lark Bunting
Song:
"Where the Columbines Grow"

Internet Address:
www.colorado.com

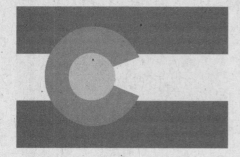

Colorado Tourism Board, 1675 Broadway, Suite 320, Denver, CO 80202; 800/COLORADO.

Department of Natural Resources, 1313 Sherman St., Room 718, Denver, CO 80203; 866-3311.

Division of Parks and Outdoor Recreation, 1313 Sherman St., Suite 618, Denver CO 80203. 303-866-3437.

Division of Wildlife, 6060 Broadway, Denver, CO 80216; 303/825-1192.

REST AREAS
Overnight stops are not permitted.

STATE PARKS
Visitors to state parks and recreation areas are required to display current Colorado State Parks passes on their vehicles. There are two primary types: a daily pass, which costs $4-7 per vehicle, and the annual pass, at $55 ($27 for Colorado seniors). Both are valid at any state park or recreation area for the calendar year and can be purchased at major park entrances, visitor centers, campgrounds and most sporting goods outlets. In addition to the parks pass, nightly campground fees are now $12 or $14 ($8 at a few parks) for primitive sites, $14 for basic sites plus fees for utility hookups. Primitive sites are equipped just with fire rings, tables and grills. For further information, contact the Department of Natural Resources, Division of Parks and Outdoor Recreation, 1313 Sherman St., Room 618, Denver, CO 80203. Phone 303/866-3437.

COLORADO DIVISION OF WILDLIFE PROPERTIES. Free camping is permitted for up to 14 days in any 45-day period on most Division of Wildlife properties. For information, 6060 Broadway, Denver, CO 80216; 303/297-1192.

NATIONAL FORESTS. These are administered individually by the national forest offices around the state. For general information about national forests in Colorado, contact the U.S. Forest Service at P.O. Box 25127, Lakewood, CO 80225; 303-275-5350.

Arapaho and Roosevelt National Forests, 2150 Centre Ave, Building E, Fort Collins, CO 80526-8119; 970-295-6600. The Arapaho National Recreation Area encompasses more than 36,000 acres and contains five major lakes -- Lake Granby, Shadow Mountain, Monarch, Willow Creek and Meadow Creek. Dispersed camping is permitted in the forests; drive up to 300 feet off open roads to park. The Pawnee National Grassland is included within the forests.

Grand Mesa, Uncompahgre and Gunnison National Forests, 2250 U.S. Highway 50, Delta, CO 81416. 970-874-6600.

Pike and San Isabel National Forests have experienced significant fee increases, and most of the campgrounds which formerly were free now have fees of $11-14. Most are open Memorial Day weekend through Labor Day weekend Superintendent, Pike and San Isabel National Forests, 2840 Kachina Drive, Pueblo, CO 81008. 719-553-1400.

Rio Grande National Forest consists of 1.86 million acres in southwestern Colorado. 1803 W. Highway 160, Monte Vista, CO 81144.

Routt National Forest, 2468 Jackson St, Laramie, WY 82070. Numerous developed sites are available, but camping is not permitted at picnic grounds, trailheads, within 100 feet of lakes, streams & trails or where otherwise posted. Fees are now charged at all campgrounds, and camping is no longer free part of the year when water service is off.

San Juan National Forest, 15 Burnett Court, Durango, CO 81301. This forest consists of more than 2 million acres in southwestern Colorado. Not many of its campgrounds are free, but most are low-fee and can be found in this guidebook. At Pagosa areas campgrounds, RVers are charged higher rates than tenters.

White River National Forest, 900 Grand Ave., Box 948, Glenwood Springs, CO 81602. 970-945-2421. Approximately 70 campgrounds, picnic areas, boat rams and observation sites are scattered throughout the forest's 2.1 million areas. Nearly three dozen campgrounds with fees of $12 or less are included in this guidebook.

BLACK CANYON OF THE GUNNISON NATIONAL PARK

Free camping is no longer available at 12 hike-in sites in the backcountry. A vehicle entry fee (or annual pass) is charged, and there is a $12 overnight charge for camping at the North Rim and South Rim campgrounds ($18 at Loop B, South Rim). Campgrounds are open mid-April through October, but exact dates at the North Rim depend upon road and snow conditions, and South Rim fees are $12 in the off-season at Loop A. Water is provided from mid-or late-May through September; it should be used sparingly because it has to be hauled in. Camping areas are 8200 feet elevation near the rim of the 1800-foot deep Black Canyon. RVs are permitted at the North Rim and South Rim locations, but not in the backcountry. Limit of stay is 14 days; 7 in the backcountry. Large RVs may have difficulty traveling the dirt access road to North Rim in wet weather; call the park for up to date road conditions. Evening ranger programs are scheduled at the South Rim sites. Fires permitted only in grills provided or campstoves. Firewood gathering is prohibited. For information, 102 Elk Creek, Gunnison, CO 81230. 970-641-2337.

COLORADO NATIONAL MONUMENT

Free camping is no longer available at Saddlehorn campground in the off-seasons; fees are charged all year, but entry fees are charged only from April through September. The campground is open all year on a first-come, first-served basis. Flush toilets available only in warmer months; vault toilets are provided the rest of the year. Backcountry camping is allowed all year throughout much of the park, but backcountry campers are requested to register before hiking or horseback riding to the various locations. The monument is rugged territory where fossils of dinosaurs have been unearthed. Wildlife include mule deer, coyotes, mountain lions and desert bighorn sheep. A vehicle entry fee (or annual fee) is charged. Evening ranger programs and a visitor center are available at Saddlehorn campground. Facilities there include drinking water and flush toilets; 14-day limited stay. Open fires prohibited; cook on charcoal grills provided or on campstoves. Waste water sinks are situated in each campground comfort station; sanitary dumping stations are in the neighboring communities of Fruita and Grand Junction. Backcountry camping is permitted anywhere except within 50 yards of a trail or one quarter mile of the road. For information, Colorado National Monument, Fruita, CO 81521.

CURECANTI NATIONAL RECREATION AREA

Fees are charged at all campgrounds in the recreation area except the boat-in backcountry campsites. Most campgrounds are open from May to October, with exact dates depending upon snow and road conditions. No camping fees are collected at developed campgrounds from Oct 1 to mid May. See Gunnison entries in Guide to Free Campgrounds. Drinking water during off-season periods can be obtained at the Elk Creek picnic area and at Cimarron. Campgrounds remain open until closed by snow or freezing temperatures. Generally, sites are accessible at Elk Creek year-round and at Lake Fork and Cimarron from mid-April through mid-November. Campfire programs and nature walks are scheduled throughout the summer. Backcountry camping is allowed from April through October along the lakeshore on a first-come, first-served basis. See listings under Gunnison. Several sites are located on Blue Mesa, Morrow Point and Crystal Lakes. For information, Curecanti National Recreation Area, 102 Elk Creek, Gunnison, CO 81230.

DINOSAUR NATIONAL MONUMENT

Free camping is permitted at all back-country locations, but entry fees of $10 per vehicle for 7 days are charged ($20 annually). Camping is $8-12 per night at the monument's campgrounds (free at Rainbow Park). For information, Dinosaur National Monument, 4545 E. Hwy 40, Dinosaur, CO 81610. 970-374-3000.

Bureau of Land Management

Although camping outside improved campsites is not prohibited, it is not encouraged except in designated primitive areas because of sanitary, fire, litter and surface damage problems. Except where specifically prohibited, camping is allowed outside of developed areas. Fees are charged for camping in some of BLM's developed sites in Colorado. Fees vary widely. Bureau of Land Management, 2850 Youngfield St., Lakewood, CO 80215 7076. 303-239-3600.

U.S. Bureau of Reclamation, Building 67, Denver Federal Center, Denver, CO 80225; 236-8098.

Bureau of Outdoor Recreation, PO Box 2587, Denver Federal Center, Building 41, Denver, CO 80255.

AGUILAR (1)

Spanish Peaks   **FREE**
State Wildlife Area
18 mi SW of Aguilar on co rd. Free. All year;
14-day limit during 45-day period. Primitive
campsites. Toilets, drkg wtr, cfga, tbls. Big
game, small game & turnkey hunting. Hiking,
picnicking. Elev 6500 ft; 5500 acres. Camping, fires only in designated areas.

ALAMOSA (2)

Backcountry Camps   **$3**
Great Sand Dunes
National Park
15 mi E from Alamosa on US 160; 16 mi N
on CR 150. $3 per person entry fee (or $15
annual for family); backcountry camping is
free but permit required from visitor center.
Trailheads lead into the Sangre de Cristo
Mountains, and two sites along the Medano
Pass Jeep Road are reserved for backpackers who hike 4 miles along 4x4 trail. Fires
prohibited; wtr usually available but must
be purified; firewood gathering prohibited;
make fires only in grills provided or in campstoves.
   Travel tip: Nearby is the Alamosa Wildlife
Refuge (3 mi S of town), bordering the Rio
Grande River; habitat for Canadian geese &
the near-extinct whooping crane; best times
spring & fall; special tours, programs, handicap facilities. Free.

Pinyon Flats   **$7**
Great Sand Dunes
National Park
15 mi E of Alamosa on US 160; 16 mi N on
CR 150. $7 with federal Senior Pass; others
pay $14. All year; 14-day limit. 88 sites; 32-ft
RV limit. Tbls, flush toilets, cfga, drkg wtr,
dump (no wtr during winter). Sightseeing,
hiking, backpacking. $3 per person entry fee
(or $15 annual) also charged.

ALLENSPARK (3)

Twin Sisters   **FREE**
State Wildlife Area
4 mi N of Allenspark on Hwy 7 to Meeker
Park; 2.5 mi N on FR 119; 1 mi W on FR
325. Free. All year; 14-day limit in 45-day
period. Primitive camping; no facilities. Hiking, hunting.

ALMA (4)

Alma   **FREE**
State Wildlife Area
1.5 mi N of Alma on Hwy 9; qtr mi NW on CR
4. Free. All year; 14-day limit during a 45-day
period. Primitive campsites. Tbls, toilets,
cfga. Fishing, picnicking. Elev 10,000 ft; 240
acres. 7 mi of stream.
   Fishing tip: Catch rainbow, brown & brook
trout in middle fork of the South Platte River.

Kite Lake   **$7**
Pike National Forest
6 mi NW of Alma on CR 8. Road of Ten is
rough, too steep for trailers. Free 10/2-4/30;
$7 rest of year; 14-day limit. 7 tent sites.
Tbls, toilets, no drkg wtr or trash service.
Mountain climbing, picnicking, fishing. Elev
12,000 ft; 3 acres. Lake. Historic mining area.
3 peaks over 14,000 ft (2 mi). Not recommended for trailers.

ALMONT (5)

Almont   **$10**
Gunnison National Forest
1 mi SW of Almont on SR 135. $10. 5/15-
10/15; 16-day limit.t). 10 sites; 28-ft RV limit
Tbls toilets, cfga, drkg wtr. Fishing.

Cold Spring   **$8**
Gunnison National Forest
16.1 mi NE of Almont on FR 742. MD-10/30;
14-day limit. $8. 5/15-9/30; 16-day limit. 6
sites (RVs under 16 ft). 2 acres. Tbls, toilets,
cfga, no drkg wtr. Fishing, picnicking. Elev
9000 ft.

Dinner Station   **$12**
Gunnison National Forest
32.5 mi NE of Almont on FR 742. $12during
5/15-10/15; free 10/15-12/1. 16-day limit. 22
sites (35-ft RV limit). Tbls, toilets, cfga, drkg
wtr. Fishing (Taylor River). Taylor Park Reservoir nearby. Elev 9600 ft; 12 acres.

Dorchester   **$12**
Gunnison National Forest
39.5 mi NE of Almont on FR 742. $12 during
MD-10/15; free 10/15-12/1. 16-day limit. 10
sites (28-ft RV limit). Tbls, toilets, cfga, drkg
wtr. Hiking, ranger station, fishing.

Lodgepole   **$12**
Gunnison National Forest
14.6 mi NE of Almont on FR 742. $12. 5/15-
9/30; 16-day limit. 17 sites (35-ft RV limit).
Tbls, toilets, cfga, drkg wtr. Hiking, fishing
(Taylor River). Elev 8800 ft; 4 acres.

Lottis Creek   **$9**
Gunnison National Forest
17.5 mi NE of Almont on FR 742. $9 with
federal Senior Pass; others pay $18 during
5/15-9/30; center loop free about 10/1-12/1.
16-day limit. 28 sites (35-ft RV limit). Tbls,
toilets, cfga. drkg wtr. Wheelchair access.
Fishing (Taylor River & Lottis Creek), hiking.

Mirror Lake   **$10**
Gunnison National Forest
26.6 mi NE of Almont on FR 742; 7.6 mi SE
on FR 765; 3.1 mi E on FR 211. $10. 6/15-
9/30; 16-day limit. 10 sites (RVs under 17
ft). Tbls, toilets, cfga, no drkg wtr. Fishing,
boating (no motors), hiking trails, picnicking.
Elev 11,000 ft; 4 acres. Stream. Geological.
On shore of Mirror Lake (36 surface acres).
Historic Tincup townsite (2 mi E).

Mosca   **$12**
Gunnison National Forest
7.2 mi NE of Almont on FR 742; 12 mi N
on FR 744; on SE shore of Spring Creek
Reservoir. $12 during 6/1-10/15; free about
10/15-12/1. 16-day limit. 16 sites (35-ft RV
limit). Tbls, toilets, cfga, drkg wtr. Boating(ld),
fishing, hiking.

North Bank   **$12**
Gunnison National Forest
7.7 mi NE of Almont on FR 742. $12 during
5/15-10/15; free about 10/15-12/1. 16-day
limit. 17 sites (35-ft RV limit). Tbls, toilets,
cfga, drkg wtr. Fishing (Taylor River). Elev
8800 ft; 6 acres.

Rivers End   **$12**
Gunnison National Forest
28.3 mi NE of Almont on FR 742; on NE
shore of Taylor Park Reservoir. $12 during
about 5/15-10/15; free 10/15-12/1. 16-day
limit. 18 sites (35-ft RV limit). Tbls, toilets,
cfga, drkg wtr. Fishing, boating(ld).

Rosy Lane   **$12**
Gunnison National Forest
10 mi NE of Almont on FR 742. $12 without
hookups ($6 with federal Senior Pass); $18
with elec ($12 with federal Senior Pass).
5/15-9/15; 16-day limit. 20 sites (35-ft RV
limit). Tbls, toilets, cfga, drkg wtr. Fishing.

Spring Creek   **$10**
Gunnison National Forest
7.2 mi NE of Almont on FR 742; 2 mi N on FR
744. $10. 5/15-10/15; 14-day limit. 12 sites
(35-ft RV limit). Tbls, toilets, cfga, drkg wtr.
Fishing (Spring Creek). Elev 8600 ft; 4 acres.

ANTONITO (6)

Conejos   **$12**
Rio Grande National Forest
23 mi W of Antonito on SR 17; 7 mi NW on
FR 250. $12. MD-LD; 14-day limit. 16 sites;
25-ft RV limit. Tbls, toilets, cfga, drkg wtr.
Fishing, hiking. Elev 8700 ft; 10 acres. This
campground alternateswith Spectacle Lake
Camp staying open until 11/15 for big game
hunting and fall color visitors.
   Fishing tip: The Conejos River highly
regarded as a wild trout stream and has more
public access fishing than any other major
river in Colorado.

Cumbres Pass Dispersed   **FREE**
Rio Grande National Forest
At the top of Cumbres Pass just off SR 17;
behind old Cumbres & Toltec Scenic Railroad
station. Free. MD-LD; 14-day limit. Primitive undesignated sites; cfga, toilet nearby,
no drkg wtr, no trash service. Hiking. Elev
10,000 ft.

La Manga Creek   **FREE**
Dispersed Camping Area
Rio Grande National Forest
24 mi W of Antonito on SR 17; 1 mi N on FR
114; at La Manga Creek. Free. MD-LD; 14-

day limit. No facilities, no drkg wtr, no trash service. Hiking, fishing. Elev 10,300 ft.

Lake Fork $12
Rio Grande National Forest
23 mi W of Antonito on SR 17; 7.5 mi NW on scenic FR 250 to access rd. $12. MD-LD; 14-day limit. 18 sites (25-ft RV limit). Tbls, toilets, cfga, drkg wtr. Fishing, coin laundry, hiking. Elev 10,100 ft; 10 acres. Reduced services after Labor Day for big game hunting & fall color.

Mix Lake $12
Rio Grande National Forest
23 mi W of Antonito on SR 17; 21.5 mi NW on scenic FR 250; .7 mi W on FR 2506B. $12. MD-LD; 14-day limit. 22 sites; 25-ft RV limit. Tbls, toilets, cfga, drkg wtr. Hiking, fishing. Elev 10,100 ft; 10 acres.

Old La Manga FREE
Dispersed Camping Area
Rio Grande National Forest
24 mi W of Antonito on SR 17; half mi W on FR 250 to Elk Creek Campground, then half mi SW on FR 128. Free. MD-LD; 14-day limit. Primitive undesignated sites, no facilities, no drkg wtr, no trash service. Hiking, fishing. Elev 8800 ft.

South Fork FREE
Dispersed Camping Area
Rio Grande National Forest
3 mi N of Rocky Mountain Lodge, W of FR 250 between the road and the Conejos River at the South Fork trailhead. Free. MD-LD; 14-day limit. Primitive undesignated sites. 1 pit toilet, parking for horse trailers; no drkg wtr, no trash service. Hiking, horseback riding, fishing at Conejos River. Elev 9100 ft.

Spectacle Lake $12
Rio Grande National Forest
24 mi W of Antonito on SR 17; 6 mi NW on FR 250. $12. MD-LD; 14-day limit. 24 sites; 25-ft RV limit. Tbls, toilets, cfga, drkg wtr. Fishing, hiking, no boating. Elev 8700 ft; 17 acres. This camp alternates with Conejos Camp is staying open with reduced services until 11/15 for big game hunting & fall color viewing.

Trail Creek FREE
Dispersed Camping Area
Rio Grande National Forest
23 mi W of Antonito on SR 17; 10 mi NW on scenic FR 250, past access rd to Lake Fork Camp. Free. MD-LD; 14-day limit. Designated undeveloped camping area. No facilities, no drkg wtr, no trash service. Fishing, hiking.

Trujillo Meadows $7
Rio Grande National Forest
34 mi W of Antonito on SR 17; SW to FR 118; 3 mi NW to Trujillo Meadows Rd 7 FR 118.1B. $7 with federal Senior Pass; others pay $14. MD-LD; 14-day limit. 50 sites (25-ft RV limit). Tbls, toilets, cfga, drkg wtr. Fishing,

boating(l). 60 acres. Portions of campground remain open in fall for hunters.

ARLINGTON (8)

Adobe Creek Reservoir FREE
(Blue Lake)
State Wildlife Area
10 mi E, then 3 mi S on co rds; on CR 10. Free. All year; 14-day limit in 45-day period. Campsites, tbls, toilets, cfga. Waterfowl hunting, fishing, picnicking, hunting, boating(l), waterskiing, sailboarding. 5,147 acres of water; boat ramp. Elev 4128 ft. Public access prohibited 11/1 through waterfowl hunting season.

Fishing tip: Lake populated with largemouth bass, walleye, crappies, channel catfish, northern pike, wiper, tiger muskies & white bass.

ASPEN (9)

Lincoln Creek FREE
Dispersed Sites
White River National Forest
11 mi SE of Aspen on SR 82 (no RVs over 35 ft on Hwy 82). Rd not maintained for passenger cars. Free. 6/14-11/14; 14-day limit. 24 tent sites. No facilities. Fishing.

Travel tip: If you're in this area during late June, be sure to attend the Snowmass Balloon Festival -- a series of races and maneuvers with hot-air balloons.

Fishing tip: This camping area is just a short distance from Roaring Fork River, one of the state's best rainbow trout streams. Between April & October, only artificial lures may be used, and the daily limit is two fish.

Lincoln Gulch $6.50
White River National Forest
10.5 mi SE of Aspen on SR 82 (no RVs over 35 ft on Hwy 82); half mi SW on FR 106 (rough gravel); qtr mi W on access rd. $6.50 with federal Senior Pass; others pay $13. 5/20-LD; 5-day limit. 7 sites (30 ft RV limit). Tbls, toilets, cfga, drkg wtr. Fishing, hiking, biking, 4WD. At Lincoln Creek & Roaring Fork River. Secluded. Elev 9700 ft.

Lostman $6.50
White River National Forest
14.2 mi SE of Aspen on SR 82 (no RVs over 35 ft on Hwy 82). $6.50 with federal Senior Pass; others pay $13. MD-LD; 5-day limit. 10 sites (30-ft RV limit). Tbls, toilets, cfga, drkg wtr. Fishing, hiking, picnicking. At Lostman Creek & Roaring Fork River. Elev 10,700 ft.

Portal $11
White River National Forest
11.9 mi SE of Aspen on SR 82 (no RVs over 35 ft on Hwy 82); 7 mi on Lincoln Creek Rd. At Grizzly Reservoir. $11 during 6/19-9/7; 5-day limit; free rest of year. 7 sites (RVs under 21 ft). Tbls, toilets, cfga, firewood, no drkg wtr or trash service; pack it out. Hiking, picnicking, boating (d), fishing. Elev 10,700 ft; 3 acres. Near Lostman Reservoir.

Travel tip: While in the area, visit the historic ghost town of Ashcroft -- once a booming city with two main streets and three hotels; it was the town to where silver miner Horace Tabor brought his famous bride, Baby Doe. Now only 9 buildings remain. It's 12 mi S off Hwy 82 just N of Aspen on Castle Creek Rd (FR 102).

Fishing tip: Roaring Fork River offers good fishing for rainbow & brown trout; also whitefish.

Weller Lake $6.50
White River National Forest
11.4 mi SE of Aspen on SR 82; .1 mi S on FR 104. 6/15-9/15; 5-day limit. $6.50 with federal Senior Pass; others pay $13. 11 sites (RVs under 40 ft). Tbls, toilets, cfga, firewood, drkg wtr. Hiking, picnicking, fishing. Elev 9400 ft; 3 acres. Scenic. Nature trails, fishing, picnicking. Adjacent to Roaring Fork River.

BAILEY (10)

Deer Creek $6.50
Pike National Forest
2.5 mi N on US 285; 8 mi NW on FR 100. $6.50 with federal Senior Pass; others pay $13. 5/1-9/15; 14-day limit. 13 sites (30-ft RV limit). Tbls, toilets, cfga, no drkg wtr. Fishing, hiking. Elev 9000 ft; 5 acres.

Meridian $6.50
Pike National Forest
2.3 mi N of Bailey on US 285; 6.5 mi NW on FR 100; 1 mi N on FR 102. $6.50 with federal Senior Pass; others pay $13. On Elk Creek. 5/1-9/15; 14-day limit. 18 sites (RVs under 30 ft). Drkg wtr, toilets, cfga, tbls. Trailhead; wilderness access. Fishing, hiking.

BASALT (11)

Basalt FREE
State Wildlife Area
3.2 mi E of Basalt on FR 105 (Frying Pan Rd) to signs; N to site. For Christine Unit, half mi W of Basalt on Hwy 82; dirt access rd N to site. Watson Divide Unit, 6 mi S of Basalt on Hwy 82; N on dirt access rd. Free. Camp only during big-game hunting season, 3 days before & 3 days after. Primitive campsites. Toilets, cfga, drkg wtr. Hunting, picnicking, fishing, shooting range. No boating. No camping within qtr mi of Fryingpan River. Elev 5800 ft; 4170 acres; 3 acres of water.

Travel tip: Small group tours are provided on Tues & Fri afternoons at the Rocky Mountain Institute SE of Basalt in Snowmass; it's a research center operating with a wide variety of energy-efficient techniques.

Fishing Tip: Don't neglect the brown trout fishing in Fryingpan River; it's famous for its big browns, and also for large rainbows as well as containing brookies and cutthroat. The whole stretch of water between Basalt & Reudi Reservoir is excellent. Only flies & lures are permitted; daily limit, 2 fish over 16 in.

Chapman　　FREE
White River National Forest
24.5 mi E of Basalt on CR 105 (Frying Pan Rd). Free before & after fee season, but no services or wtr; $15 during 5/20-11/11 ($7.50 with federal Senior Pass); 14-day limit. 83 sites, including 13 walk-in sites; 50-ft RV limit. Tbls, toilets, cfga, drkg wtr. Hiking, fishing, canoeing, swimming, horseshoes; boating at Chapman Reservoir; ball field; interpretive trail. At Frying Pan River. Elev 8800 ft; 13 acres. 2-night minimum stay on weekends during fee period.

Coke Oven State　　FREE
State Wildlife Area
33 mi E of Basalt on FR 105 (Fryingpan River Rd). Free. All year; 14-day limit. Primitive undesignated sites; no facilities, no drkg wtr. About 300 acres for hunting, hiking, fishing.

Dearhamer　　FREE
White River National Forest
23.5 mi E of Basalt on CR 105. Free before & after fee season, but no wtr or services; $15 during MD-11/15 ($7.50 with federal Senior Pass); 14-day limit. 13 sites (35-ft RV limit). Tbls, toilets, cfga, drkg wtr. Swimming, boating(l), fishing, waterskiing, mountain biking. Ruedi Reservoir.

Dinkle Lake　　FREE
Dispersed Sites
White River National Forest
From SR 82 at Emma, 1 mi S on CR 7; 5 mi SW on CR 6; 2 mi S on CR 6A (dirt rd) to lake. Free. Several undesignated primitive camping areas around perimeter of lake. No facilities, no drkg wtr. Picnicking, fishing. Area also can be reached from just S of Carbondale, off SR 133.
Fishing tip: Good rainbow and brook trout opportunities at Dinkle and also from nearby Thomas Lakes, reached via a 3.5-mi trail.

Elk Wallow　　$7
White River National Forest
23 mi E of Basalt on CR 105; 3.3 mi E on FR 15501. $7. MD-11/15; 14-day limit. 7 sites (RVs under 30 ft). Tbls, toilets, cfga, no drkg wtr, no trash service. Fishing, picnicking. Horseback riding (3 mi, r--4 mi). Elev 9000 ft; 2 acres. North Fork of Fryingpan River. Ruedi Dam (12.7 mj).
Fishing tip: From here, fish the Fryingpan for trout but remember, within four miles of the dam, catch-and-release must be practiced, and artificial lures are required.

BAYFIELD (12)

Graham Creek　　$10
San Juan National Forest
N on CR 501/FR 600 from US 160 at Bayfield for 15 mi to Vallecito Dam; 3.5 mi NW on FR 603; on Vallecito Reservoir about 2 mi N of Old Timers Camp. $10. MD-LD; 14-day limit. 25 sites; 35-ft RV limit. Tbls, toilets, cfga, drkg wtr. Boating(l), fishing, horseback riding.

Fishing tip: Vallecito is a very popular fishing lake, containing German brown, rainbow and cutthroat trout as well as kokanee salmon and northern pike.

Middle Mountain　　$12
San Juan National Forest
N on CR 501/FR 600 from US 160 at Bayfield for 15 mi to Vallecito Dam; qtr mi W on FR 602; on Vallecito Reservoir. $12 during MD-LD ($14 lakefront sites); free rest of yr, but no wtr or services. 24 sites; 35-ft RV limit. Tbls, toilets, cfga, drkg wtr. Boating(l), fishing.

North Canyon　　$12
San Juan National Forest
N on CR 501/FR 600 from US 160 at Bayfield for 15 mi to Vallecito Dam; 4 mi NW on FR 603; on Vallecito Reservoir. $12. MD-LD; 14-day limit. 21 sites; 35-ft RV limit. Tbls, toilets, cfga, drkg wtr. Boating(l), fishing.

Old Timers　　$10
San Juan National Forest
N on CR 501/FR 600 from US 160 at Bayfield for 15 mi to Vallecito Dam; 2 mi NW on FR 603; on SE shore of Vallecito Reservoir. $10. MD-LD; 14-day limit. 10 sites; 25-ft RV limit. Tbls, toilets, cfga, drkg wtr. Fishing, boating(l).

Pine Point　　$12
San Juan National Forest
N on CR 501/FR 600 from US 160 at Bayfield for 15 mi to Vallecito Dam; 4.5 mi NW on FR 603; on Vallecito Reservoir. $12 (lakefront sites $14). MD-LD; 14-day limit. 30 sites; 35-ft RV limit. Tbls, toilets, cfga, drkg wtr. Fishing, boating(l).

Pine River　　$10
San Juan National Forest
N on CR 501/FR 600 from US 160 at Bayfield for 15 mi to Vallecito Dam; 4.5 mi NW on FR 603; mi E on FR 602. $10 during MD-LD; free rest of yr, but no trash service. 6 sites; 20-ft RV limit. Tbls, toilets, cfga, no drkg wtr. Hiking, backpacking, horseback riding. Horse corrals.

Riverside RV Park　　$12
On Hwy 160 at Bayfield, 41743 Hwy 160. $12 base; $18.69 full hookups. 4/1-10/31. 84 sites; 45-ft RVs. Drkg wtr, tbls, flush toilets, showers, cfga, coin laundry, dump, hookups($), CATV($). Fishing, horseshoes.

BEULAH (13)

Ophir Creek　　$6.50
San Isabel National Forest
11.7 mi SW of Beulah on SR 76; 3 mi NW on SR 165. $6.50 with federal Senior Pass; others pay $13. MD-LD (free through Oct with reduced services); 10-day limit. 31 sites (30-ft RV limit). Tbls, toilets, cfga, drkg wtr. Hiking, fishing. Elev 8900 ft; 14-acres.

BRIGGSDALE (15)

Crow Valley　　$10
Pawnee National Grassland
Roosevelt National Forest
Half mi W of Briggsdale on SR 14; half mi N on CR 77. $10 (double site, $14); half price during winter, but no wtr. 5/1-10/1 with wtr; 14-day limit. 10 sites (35-ft RV limit). Tbls, toilets, cfga, drkg wtr. Handicap trail, farm equipment museum. Elev 4800 ft.

BRUSH (16)

Memorial Park　　$10
Municipal V.F.W. Park
In Brush, 2 blocks S of traffic light on Clayton St. 4/1-10/31; 7-day limit. 66 sites; 24 for RVs. Tbls, flush toilets, cfga, drkg wtr, dump, showers, elect, shelter, playground. First night free; $10 per night thereafter. Swimming, picnicking. Golf & tennis nearby. Elev 4300 ft; Register at police station; $10 deposit.

Prewitt Reservoir Camp　　$3
State Wildlife Area
15 mi NE of Brush on US 6; 1 mi E on access rd. $3 permits. All year; 14-day limit. $3 daily permits for those without Colorado hunting or fishing licenses; $5 annually for those with licenses. Undesignated primitive sites. Tbls, toilets, cfga, no drkg wtr. Fishing, hunting, boating(l). 2400-acre lake.

BUENA VISTA (17)

Arkansas Valley　　$8
Adventures Rafting
13 mi S of Buena Vista on US 24, milepost 197; on Arkansas River. $8 per person. 5/1-11/15. 10 rustic tent sites. Whitewater rafting, fishing, hiking, biking, horseshoes, volleyball.

Bootleg　　$7
San Isabel National Forest
2 mi S of Buena Vista, at jct of US 24 & US 285, travel 5 mi S on US 285; 6 mi W on CR 162 from Northrop; on the Colorado Trail (no vehicle access). $7. 6 tent sites. Tbls, toilets, cfga, no drkg wtr, no trash service. Fishing, hiking, rafting.

Collegiate Peaks　　$6.50
San Isabel National Forest
10.5 mi W of Buena Vista on SR 306; on Cottonwood Creek. $6.50 with federal Senior Pass; others pay $13. MD-10/1; 14-day limit. 56 sites (50-ft RV limit). Tbls, flush toilets, cfga, drkg wtr. Fishing, hiking trails, OHV trail. Elev 9800 ft; 11 acres.

Cottonwood Lake　　$6.50
San Isabel National Forest
7 mi SW of Buena Vista on SR 306; 3.5 mi SW on FR 210. $6.50 with federal Senior Pass; others pay $13. MD-10/15; 7-day limit. 28 RV sites (40-ft RV limit). Tbls, toilets, cfga,

drkg wtr, new solar water heating system. Fishing. No tenting. Elev 9600 ft. Open in 2007 after being closed for 2 years for reconstruction.

Railroad Bridge $7
Bureau of Land Management
Arkansas Headwaters
State Recreation Area
From US 24 in Buena Vista, turn E at traffic light for 2 blks, past railroad tracks; left on N. Colorado Ave, which becomes CR 371 (dirt & narrow in places) for 6.2 mi. $7 with federal Senior Pass; others pay $14. All year; 14-day limit. 14 sites. Tbls, toilets, cfga, no drkg wtr, no trashservice. Fishing, rock hunting.

Ruby Mountain $7
Bureau of Land Management
Arkansas Headwaters
State Recreation Area
7 mi S of Buena Vista on US 285; follow signs from Fisherman's Bridge. $7 with federal Senior Pass; others pay $14. All year; 14-day limit. 22 sites (30-ft RV limit). Tbls, toilets, cfga, no drkg wtr. Fishing, boating, canoeing, rafting, hiking, rock hunting. No trash service. Elev 7500 ft.

BUFFALO CREEK (18)

Buffalo $7
Pike National Forest
Half mi SE of Buffalo Creek on CR 126; 5.6 mi SW on FR 543; qtr mi E on FR 550. $7 with federal Senior Pass; others pay $14. 5/15-9/15; 14-day limit. 41 sites (30-ft RV limit). Tbls, toilets, cfga, drkg wtr. Fishing, hiking, mountain biking. Elev 7400 ft.

Green Mountain $6.50
Pike National Forest
Half mi SE of Buffalo Creek on CR 125; 7.7 mi SW on FR 543. $6.50 with federal Senior Pass; others pay $13. 5/1-9/15; 14-day limit. 6 tent sites. Tbls, toilets, cfga, drkg wtr. Picnicking, hiking, fishing. Near Wellington Lake & Buffalo Creek. Elev 7500 ft.

Platte River $12
Pike National Forest
16.6 mi SE of Buffalo Creek on CR 126; 4 mi N on CR 67. $12. All year; 14-day limit. 10 tent sites. Tbls, toilets, cfga, drkg wtr. Fishing, rafting. Elev 6300 ft.

CAHONE (20)

Bradfield Recreation Area $8
Bureau of Land Management
5 mi E of Cahone to Dolores River, then follow signs (qtr mi downstream from Bradfield bridge). $8. 4/1-10/31; 14-day limit. 22 sites (30-ft RV limit). Tbls, toilets, cfga, drkg wtr. Boating, fishing. No trash service.

CAMPION (21)

Lon Hagler $3
State Wildlife Area
3.5 mi W of Campion on CR 14W; 1.5 mi Non CR 21S. $3. All year; 5-day limit in 15-day period. Primitive undesignated sites. Toilets, cfga, tbls. 181 acres. Hiking, hunting, fishing, boating, archery range.

CANON CITY (22)

Five Points $7
Bureau of Land Management
Arkansas Headwaters
State Recreation Area
16 mi W of Canon City on US 50. $7 with federal Senior Pass; others pay $14. All year; 14-day limit. 20 sites (30-ft RV limit). Tbls, toilets, cfga, no drkg wtr, no trash service. Fishing, rafting, picnicking. Elev 6000 ft.

Floyd's RV Park $12
On Hwy 50 milepost 293, 3 mi E of Hwy 115 (17 mi E of Canon City). $12 base. All year. Base fee for tent sites; $20 full hookups. 47 sites; 45-ft RV limit. Tbls, flush toilets, cfga, drkg wtr, showers, dump, coin laundry.

Oak Creek FREE
San Isabel National Forest
Direction: 12.3 mi SW of Canon City on CR 143. Free. All year; 10-day limit. 15 sites; 9 acres. 25-ft RV limit. Tbls, toilets, cfga, drkg wtr at well within qtr mi, no trash service. Picnicking, hiking. Elev 7600 ft.
Travel tip: See the Rudd Stone House and Cabin at the Canon City municipal building; built 1860, furnished with articles of that era, Indian artifacts, big-game trophies. African artifacts, guns, Indian items, circus performer memorabilia, spoon collection, Army memorabilia, 19th Century carriage, school bells, doll collection, gemstone exhibit, cattle brands.
Fishing tip: Try Texas Creek and the small streams & lakes near it along Hwy 69 W of town; good brown trout fishing. Or, fish the Arkansas River below Salida for browns.

CAPULIN (23)

La Jara Reservoir FREE
State Wildlife Area
15 mi W of Capulin on co rd. Free. 5/1-11/31; 14-day limit during 45-day period. 50 primitive sites; 100 acres. Primitive. Tbls, toilets, cfga, drkg wtr, no trash service. Boating(l), hunting, picnicking, fishing. Camp within 300 ft of reservoir & W of dam, as posted. 1,241-acre lake. Elev 9700 ft.
Fishing tip: Fish from boat for pan-size brook trout in good numbers; not many big fish caught here, though.

CARBONDALE (24)

Avalanche $7
White River National Forest
13.5 mi S of Carbondale on SR 133; 2.6 mi E on FR 310. $7 with federal Senior Pass during MD-11/15; others pay $14; free rest of season, but no wtr or services; 14-day limit. 13 sites (25-ft RV limit). Tbls, toilets, cfga, drkg wtr. Fishing, hiking. Along Avalanche Creek. Elev 7400 ft; 3 acres.

Bogan Flats $7.50
White River National Forest
22.5 mi S of Carbondale on SR 133; 1.5 mi E on CR 314. $7.50 with federal Senior Pass; others pay $15. Free after regular season ends, but no wtr or services. MD-11/15; 14-day limit. 37 sites (spaces for 40-ft RVs). Tbls, toilets, cfga, drkg wtr. Fishing, hiking. Crystal River. Yule Creek marble quarry nearby. Elev 7600 ft.

CEDAREDGE (25)

Cobbett Creek (Carp Lake) $12
Grand Mesa National Forest
16 mi N of Cedaredge on SR 65. $12. 6/15-10/1; 16-day limit. 20 sites (30-ft RV limit). Tbls, toilets, cfga, drkg wtr. Fishing, hiking, boating. Elev 10,300 ft.

Crag Rest $10
Grand Mesa National Forest
16 mi N of Cedaredge on SR 65; 3.5 mi E on FR 121; on Eggleston Lake. $10. 6/15-LD; 16-day limit. 11 sites (27-ft RV limit). Hiking, fishing. Elev 10,300 ft; 4 acres.

Fish Hawk FREE
Grand Mesa National Forest
16 mi N of Cedaredge on SR 65; 6 mi E on FR 121. Free. 6/20-9/30; 14-day limit. 5 sites (RVs under 16 ft). Tbls, toilets, cfga, piped drkg wtr. Picnicking, fishing, boating (1 mi; r--2 mi), horseback riding. Elev 10,200 ft; 1 acre.

Kiser Creek $10
Grand Mesa National Forest
15 mi N of Cedaredge on SR 65; 3 mi E on FR 121; S on FR 123. $10. 6/15-9/15; 30-day limit. 12 sites (16-ft RV limit). Tbls, toilets, cfga, no drkg wtr. Fishing, boating(r), hiking trails. Groceries. Elev 10,100 ft; 4 acres.

Island Lake $12
Grand Mesa National Forest
16.2 mi N of Cedaredge on SR 65; 1 mi W on FR 116. $12 during about 6/15-LD; free MD-11/15. 16-day limit. 41 sites (45-ft RV limit). Tbls, toilets, cfga, drkg wtr. Fishing, boating (l), hiking.

Little Bear $12
Grand Mesa National Forest
16.2 mi N of Cedaredge on SR 65; half mi W on FR 116. $12. 5/15-10/1; 16-day limit. 36 sites (22-ft RV limit). Tbls, flush toilets, cfga,

drkg wtr. Boating(lr), fishing, hiking. Elev 10,200 ft; 30 acres. Visitor center.

Ward Lake $12
Grand Mesa National Forest
16 mi N of Cedaredge on SR 65; 1 mi E on FR 121. $12 during about 6/15-LD; free MD-12/1. 16-day limit. 40 sites (20-ft RV limit). Tbls, toilets, cfga, drkg wtr. Fishing, boating(dr), hiking. Elev 10,200 ft; 30 acres.

Weir & Johnson $10
Grand Mesa National Forest
16 mi N of Cedaredge on SR 65; 10 mi E on FR 121; 3 mi E on FR 126. $10. 6/15-9/15; 16-day limit. 12 sites (22 ft. RV limit). Tbls, toilets, cfga, no drkg wtr. Boating, fishing, hiking. Between Weir Lake & Johnson Lake. Elev 10,500 ft.

CENTRAL CITY (26)

Cold Springs $6.50
Arapaho National Forest
5 mi N of Central City-Blackhawk on Hwy 119. $6.50 with federal Senior Pass; others pay $13. Late May to fall hunting season; 14-day limit. 38 sites; 55-ft RV limit. Tbls, toilets, cfga, drkg wtr. Hiking, fishing, mountain biking, gold panning. Elev 9200 ft.

Columbine $12
Arapaho National Forest
2 mi NW of Central City on CR 279. $12. 5/26 to fall hunting season; 14-day limit. 47 sites (55-ft RV limit). Tbls, toilets, cfga, drkg wtr. Hiking, fishing, mountain biking. Elev 9200 ft; 4 acres.

CHIMNEY ROCK (28)

First Fork Hunter Camp FREE
San Juan National Forest
Half mi E of Chimney Rock on US 160; 10.5 mi N on FR 622. Free. 5/15-11/25; 14-day limit. 10 sites (RVs under 22 ft). Toilets, cfga, no drkg wtr. Rockhounding, hunting, picnicking, fishing. Elev 7100 ft; 2 acres. Piedra River.

Fishing tip: Most streams that flow into the Piedra are stocked with cutthroat trout; only artificial lures may be used on Piedra just N of Hwy 160 (try gray & brown nymphs).

Lower Piedra $10
San Juan National Forest
19 mi N of Chimney Rock on FR 621; on W bank of Piedra River. $10 for tents, $12 for RVs. 5/15-LD; 14-day limit. 17 sites (RVs under 35 ft). Tbls, toilets, cfga, no drkg wtr. Horseback riding, picnicking, fishing, hiking. Elev 6000 ft; 6 acres.

Ute $10
San Juan National Forest
5.5 mi SE of Chimney Rock on US 160. $10 for tents, $12 RVs. MD-LD; 14-day limit. 26 sites (RVs under 36 ft). Tbls, toilets, cfga,

firewood, piped drkg wtr. Picnicking, fishing, hunting. Elev 6900 ft; 60 acres. Chimney rock (13 mi).

CLARK (29)

Hahns Peak Lake $10
Routt National Forest
10.6 mi N of Clark on CR 129; 2.5 mi W on FR 486. $10. 6/15-10/31; 14-day limit. 25 sites (RVs under 40 ft). Tbls, toilets, cfga. Boating(l), fishing. Electric motors only. Elev 8500 ft; 11 acres.

Fishing tip: On the way from Clark, you'll pass the turnofff for Steamboat Lake (just W of CR 129); it's stocked annually with hundreds of thousands of rainbow fingerlings. Lots of one-foot rainbows are caught, but some larger too; also browns & Snake River cutthroat. Another possibility is Pearl Lake, 3 mi E of CR 129; only artificial lures may be used.

Hinman $12
Routt National Forest
1 mi N of Clark on CR 129; 6 mi NE on FR 400. $12. 6/10-10/15; 14-day limit. 13 sites (RVs under 23 ft). Tbls, toilets, cfga. Fishing. Elev 7600 ft; 6 acres.

Fishing tip: Elk River is highly regarded for its excellent brook and rainbow trout fishing, and the section of water between Hinman and Seed House Campgrounds provides the best catches; favorite time of locals is late summer when pools are at low levels.

Seed House $12
Routt National Forest
1 mi N of Clark on CR 129; 9.5 mi NE on FR 400. $12. 6/15-10/31; 14-day limit. 24 sites (RVs under 22 ft). Tbls, toilets, cfga. Fishing. Elev 8000 ft; 10 acres.

Fishing tip: See Hinman entry. If you've got a 4WD, also try N of the campground on FR 431 along the North Fork of Elk River; that section has lots of small brooks and rainbows. Late summer is best time.

COALDALE (30)

Coaldale $9
San Isabel National Forest
4.1 mi SW of Coaldale on FR 249. At Hayden Creek. $9. 5/18-10/15; 14-day limit. 11 sites (RVs under 26 ft). Tbls, toilets, cfga, no drkg wtr. Hiking, picnicking, fishing. Elev 7800 ft; 4 acres. Formerly named Hayden Creek #2.

Hayden Creek $11
San Isabel National Forest
5.2 mi SW of Coaldale on CR 6. $11. 5/18-10/15; 14-day limit. 11 sites (RVs under 36 ft). Tbls, toilets, cfga, well drkg wtr. Hiking, picnicking, fishing. Elev 8000 ft; 4 acres. Hayden Creek. Hiking trail. Open to motorcycles.

COLLBRAN (31)

Aspen Grove Campground $12
Vega State Park
12 mi E of Collbran on Hwy 330. $12. May-Sept. 27 basic sites; 30-ft RV limit. Tbls, pit toilets, cfga, drkg wtr, dump at Oak Point Camp. Interpretive programs, boating(l), waterskiing, sailboarding, fishing, hiking trails, mountain biking trails, bridle trails, hunting, winter sports (excellent snowmobile system). Elev 8000 ft; 898 acres. Entry fee.

Fishing tip: Best bet at Vega Reservoir is for rainbow trout, although some cutthroat are also caught.

Big Creek $10
Grand Mesa National Forest
14 mi S of Collbran on FR 121. $10 during 7/1-9/15; free rest of year. 16-day limit. 26 sites (30-ft RV limit). Tbls, toilets, cfga, no drkg wtr. Trout fishing, boating(l).

Cottonwood Lake $10
Grand Mesa National Forest
12 mi S of Collbran on FR 121; 4 mi W on FR 257. $10 during 6/15-9/15; free rest of year. 16-day limit. 36 sites; 32-ft RV limit. Tbls, toilets, cfga, drkg wtr. Fishing, boating(l), hunting, hiking. Elev 10,100 ft; 27 acres.

Pioneer Campground $12
Vega State Park
12 mi E of Collbran on Hwy 330. $12. May-Sept. 10 primitive walk-in tent sites. Tbls, pit toilets, cfga, drkg wtr. Interpretive programs, boating(l), waterskiing, sailboarding, fishing, hiking trails, mountain biking trails, bridle trails, hunting, winter sports (excellent snowmobile system). Elev 8000 ft; 898 acres. Entry fee.

Plateau Creek FREE
State Wildlife Area
3.5 mi W of Collbran on Hwy 330; quarter mi N on Sunnyside Rd. Free. Camping during big-game season only. Vehicles prohibited 12/1-5/1; 14-day limit during 45-day period. 1,347 acres. Primitive campsites. No facilities, no campfires. Picnicking, hiking. Elev 6200 ft; 1,350 acres.

COMO (33)

Selkirk $7
Pike National Forest
3.5 mi NW on CR 33; half mi NW on CR 50; 1.7 mi NW on FR 406. $7 during 5/1-10/1; free rest of year; 14-day limit. 15 sites (25-ft RV limit). Tbls, toilets, cfga, no drkg wtr or trash service. Fishing (Tarryall Creek).

CONIFER (34)

Osprey $11
Pike National Forest
1 mi S of Conifer on US 285; 17 mi SE on FR 97; at South Platte River. $11 during 5/1-10/15; $7 rest of year; 14-day limit. 10

tent sites, portable toilets, cfga, no drkg wtr. Fishing, canoeing.

Fishing tip: The South Platte River contains rainbow and brown trout.

Ouzel   **$11**
Pike National Forest
1 mi S of Conifer on US 285; 20 mi SE on FR 97; at South Platte River. $11 during 5/1-10/15; $7 rest of year; 14-day limit. 13 small tent sites. Portable toilets, cfga, no drkg wtr. Fishing, canoeing, rafting. Elev 6000 ft.

COWDREY (35)

Big Creek Lakes   **$10**
Routt National Forest
18.2 mi NW of Cowdrey on CR 6; 5.7 mi SW on FR 600. $10. 6/15-LD; 14-day limit. 54 sites; 45-ft RV limit. Tbls, toilets, cfga. Swimming, boating(l), fishing, waterskiing, hiking trails. Elev 9000 ft; 17 acres.

CRAIG (36)

Duffy Mountain Access   **$8**
State Parks River Acces Site
Bureau of Land Management
19 mi W of Craig on US 40; 6.5 mi S on CR 17 to Government Bridge at Yampa River, then N to river on BLM Rd 1593 just before cattle guard (stay left at all intersections). $8. All year; 14-day limit. 5 primitive sites. Toilet, cfga, no drkg wtr. Boating(l), fishing.

Freeman   **$12**
Routt National Forest
13.2 mi NE of Craig on SR 13; 9 mi NE on FR 112. $12. 6/15-10/31; 14-day limit. 17 sites; RVs under 22 ft. Tbls, toilets, cfga, drkg wtr; some handicap facilities. Fishing, hiking. Elev 8800 ft; 9 acres. At Freeman Reservoir.

Travel tip: Be sure to see Brown's Park National Wildlife Refuge 80 mi W of Craig on SR 318; hawks, eagles, antelope, waterfowl; free primitive camping (see entry); roaming wild horse herd and rockhounding at Sand Wash Basin. Fremont Indian rock art in Irish Canyon and Vermillion Cliffs.

Juniper Canyon   **$8**
State Parks River Access Site
Bureau of Land Management
About 20 mi W of Craig on US 40; 3.5 mi S on CR 53; left on CR 74 for 8 mi to Yampa River. $8 All year; 14-day limit. 12 primitive sites. Toilet, cfga, no drkg wtr. Boating(l), fishing, rafting.

Little Yampa Canyon   **FREE**
Special Recreation
Management Area
Bureau of Land Management
SW of Craig along the Yampa River by boat. 53 river mi from Craig Golf Course to bridge at Juniper Hot Springs. 40 mi from Hwy 13 bridge to Government Bridge on Moffat CR 17. 4x4 travel in Duffy Mountain/Little Yampa Canyon area. By road: US 40 from craig to

Lay; CR 17 S to Duffy Mountain access rd; follow signs, then 4x4 track. Longer boat trip: N from near Yampa to Steamboat, then W past Craig and Maybell into Dinosaur National Monument, linking with the Green River. Free. May-Sept best time. Many good, primitive campsites along river. Some cfga, toilets. Fishing, hunting, rafting, kayaking. Several trail developments underway. Flatwater floating. Juniper Canyon has a large rapids not suitable for canoes; short run for rafters and kayakers. 17,000 acres. Raptor & cliff swallow nests; golden & bald eagles, turkey vultures, osprey, ducks, beaver, elk, deer.

Loudy Simpson Park   **FREE**
Moffat County Park
S of Craig off SR 394 at the developed ball field complex at Yampa River. Free. All year. No facilities. Camping by permission only. Boating(l), fishing.

Sawmill Creek   **$10**
Routt National Forest
13 mi N of Craig on SR 13; 12.6 mi NE on FR 110. $10. 7/1-10/31; 14-day limit. 6 sites (RVs under 22 ft). Tbls, toilets, cfga, no drkg wtr or trash service. Mountain climbing, picnicking, fishing. Elev 9000 ft; 4 acres. Closed in 2006; 2007 status unclear.

South Beach   **$8**
Yampa Project Pump Station
State Parks River Access Site
Bureau of Land Management
About 3 mi S of Craig on SR 13 at Yampa River bridge; large graveled pull-off area; park on W side of pump station near toilet. $8. 2-night limit. Primitive undesignated camping. Toilet, cfga, no drkg wtr. Fishing but no boat or canoe launching at water intake channel.

CRAWFORD (37)

North Rim   **$12**
Black Canyon of
Gunnison National Monument
From Crawford on Hwy 92, follow signs to North Rim Rd (closed in winter). $12. 4/15-10/15; 14-day limit. 13 sites. Tbls, toilets, cfga, drkg wtr. Hiking, sightseeing, fishing, rafting. No entry fee to North Rim.

Smith Fork   **FREE**
Dispersed Sites
Gunnison National Forest
6.5 mi E of Crawford on FR 712. Free. 5/15-11/15; 14-day limit. 5 sites. Tbls, toilets, cfga, piped drkg wtr. Picnicking, fishing, hiking. Elev 7500 ft; 2 acres. Foothills. Stream. Crawford Reservoir (7 mi). Black Canyon National Monument (25 mi).

CREEDE (38)

Bristol Head   **$11**
Rio Grande National Forest
22 mi SW of Creede on SR 149; qtr mi on FR 510; at South Clear Creek. $11. MD-LD;

14-day limit. 16 sites (32-ft RV limit). Tbls, toilets, cfga, drkg wtr. Fishing, hiking. Scenic qtr-mi trail to waterfall overlook. Elev 9600 ft; 15 acres.

Fishing tip: Four fishing access points to North Clear Creek are by primitive dirt roads marked with white arrows leading off FR 513 (Continental Reservoir/Rito Hondo Rd).

Crooked Creek   **FREE**
Rio Grande National Forest
20.1 mi S of Creede on Sr 149; 1.8 mi W on FR 520 (Rio Grande Reservoir Rd). Free. 5/1-10/31; 14-day limit. 3 primitive sites; no facilities; toilet across the road. Elev 9200 ft.

Hanson's Mill Dispersed   **FREE**
Rio Grande National Forest
7.3 mi SE of Creede on SR 149; 9.5 mi NW on FR 600 (Pool Table Rd). Free. MD-Oct; 14-day limit. Primitive undesignated sites. No wtr, no trash service; 1 pit toilet. Hiking & 4WD trails; fishing at East Bellows Creek. Elev 10,800 ft.

Ivy Creek   **FREE**
Rio Grande National Forest
6.5 mi SW of Creede on SR 149; 4 mi SW on FR 523; 2.7 mi SW on FR 528; 2 mi SW on FR 526 (rough rd). Free. MD-11/15; 14-day limit. 4 sites (1 developed with tbl & cfga). Most suitable for tents, pickups, foldouts. Toilet, no drkg wtr, no trash collection. Rockhounding, picnicking, fishing, hiking. Elev 9200 ft; 9 acres. Stream. Trailhead to Weminuche Wilderness Area via Ivy Creek Trail at camp.

Travel tip: At Old Creede Cemetery (at Creede Museum) is original gravesite of Bob Ford, who killed Jesse James.

Lost Trail Campground   **FREE**
Rio Grande National Forest
20.5 mi SW of Creede on SR 149; 18.1 mi SW on FR 520 (Rio Grande Reservoir Rd). Free; donations accepted. MD-LD; 14-day limit. 7 sites (RVs under 32 ft). Tbls, toilets, cfga, well drkg wtr, no trash service. Hiking, picnicking, fishing, horseback riding/rental. Elev 9500 ft; 3 acres. Scenic. Stream. Limited space for RV maneuvering. Camp ususually full mid-June through Aug.

Love Lake   **FREE**
Rio Grande National Forest
6 mi SW of Creede on SR 149; 4 mi S on FR 523 (Middle Creek Rd); stay right at the Y, following FR 523 anoher 3.5 mi, then bear left on Karper Ranch Rd for 3.5 mi; at Love Lake. Free undeveloped sites suitable for group; no facilities, no drkg wtr, no trash service. Hiking, fishing, boating (no mtrs). 5-acre lake; also fish North Clear Creek below waterfall.

Marshall Park   **$12**
Rio Grande National Forest
7 mi SW of Creede on SR 149; qtr mi on FR 523.1A. $12 during MD-LD; free rest of year, but no wtr or trash service; 14-day limit. 18 sites (30-ft RV limit). Tbls, toilets, cfga, drkg wtr. Fishing. 12 acres. Elev 8800 ft.

North Clear Creek $11
Rio Grande National Forest
23 mi SW of Creede on SR 149; 2 mi N on FR 510. $11. MD-LD; free rest of season, but no wtr or trash service; 14-day limit. 27 sites; 30-ft RV limit. Tbls, toilets, cfga, drkg wtr. Fishing. Elev 9600 ft; 15 acres.

North Lime Creek Trailhead FREE
Rio Grande National Forest
6.5 mi SW of Creede on SR 149; 4 mi SW on FR 523; 8 mi SW on FR 528. Free. 6/15-9/15; 30-day limit. 2 primitive sites. Tbl, toilet, cfga, no drkg wtr. Rockhounding, hiking, picnicking, fishing. Elev 10,000 ft; 12 acres. Trailhead to Weninuche Wilderness Area.

Travel tip: In Creede, visit the Creede Museum in the old railroad depot built in 1981; hand-drawn fire wagon, horse-drawn hearse; replica of a shafthouse.

Rio Grande Dispersed Area FREE
Rio Grande National Forest
10 mi SW of Creede on SR 149; sign says "Rio Grande Fisherman's Area"; through gated fence, 1 mi S on FR 529. On Rio Grande River. Free. MD-LD; 14-day limit. 4 sites (RVs under 32 ft). 8 acres. Tbls, toilet, cfga, firewood, well drkg wtr. Fishing, picnicking. Elev 8900 ft.

Fishing tip: Good spot for brown trout & some rainbows using dry flies & small spinners.

Rito Hondo Reservoir FREE
Dispersed Camping Area
Rio Grande National Forest
27.3 mi W of Creede on SR 149; 3.3 mi NW on FR 513. Free. MD-LD; 14-day limit. 35 primitive sites; no facilities except 1 toilet; no drkg wtr, no trash service. Boating(l), fishing, hiking. Elev 10,200 ft.

Rito Hondo Reservoir FREE
State Wildlife Area
27.3 mi W of Creede on Hwy 149; 2 mi NW on FR 513 (Rito Hondo Rd) to fork; take right fork 200 yds to lake. Free. All year; 14-day limit during 45-day period. Primitive camp area. Toilets, cfga, no drkg wtr. Fishing (41-acre Rito Hondo Lake) for wild brook trout & stocked rainbows.

River Hill $12
Rio Grande National Forest
18 mi SW of Creede on SR 149; 9 mi W on FR 520 (Rio Grande Reservoir Rd) to FR 520.2D (River Hill Rd). $12. MD-LD; 14-day limit. 23 sites (32-ft RV limit). Tbls, toilets, cfga, drkg wtr, gray water dump. Fishing. 15 acres. Elev 9300 ft. Camp usually full mid-June through Aug.

Road Canyon FREE
Rio Grande National Forest
20.5 mi SW of Creede on SR 149; 6 mi SW on FR 520; at Road Canyon Reservoir. Free. 6/1-9/15. 6 sites (RVs under 32 ft). 14-day limit. Tbls, toilets, cfga, no drkg wtr. No trash collection. Horseback riding, boat-

ing (ld), picnicking, fishing. Elev 9300 ft; 9 acres. Undeveloped overflow camping area is across the road.

Fishing tip: Reservoir has several parking areas for fishermen.

Silver Thread $11
Rio Grande National Forest
24.5 mi SW of Creede on SR 149. $11 during MD-LD; free rest of season, but no wtr or trash service; 14-day limit. 13 sites (30-ft RV limit). Tbls, toilets, cfga, drkg wtr. Fishing, hiking. Elev 9700 ft; 18 acres.

Thirty Mile $12
Rio Grande National Forest
18 mi SW of Creede on SR 149; 12 mi on FR 520 to FR 520.2C. $12. MD-LD; 14-day limit. 39 sites (30-ft RV limit). Tbls, toilets, cfga, drkg wtr, gray water dump. Fishing, hiking. 30 acres. Elev 9300 ft. Full mid-June through Aug.

CRESTED BUTTE (39)

Avery Peak FREE
Gunnison National Forest
7.3 mi N of Crested Butte on SR 3; 1.5 mi N on FR 317. Free. 6/4-10/29; 14-day limit. 10 sites (RVs under 16 ft). Tbls, toilets, cfga, no drkg wtr. Picnicking, fishing. Elev 9600 ft; 4 acres. Scenic. Stream. Rocky Mountain Biological Lab/historic Gothic townsite (2 mi S).

Travel Tip: At Crested Butte's Center for the Arts Building is the Mountain Bike Hall of Fame; displays on mountain biking; town calls itself the mountain-biking capital of the world.

Cement Creek $12
Gunnison National Forest
7.5 mi SE of Crested Butte on SR 135; 4 mi NE on FR 740. $12. 5/15-10/15; 16-day limit. 13 sites (28-ft RV limit). Tbls, toilets, cfga, drkg wtr. Fishing (Cement Creek), hot springs nearby, hiking.

Gothic $8
Gunnison National Forest
11.4 mi N of Crested Butte on FR 317. $8. 6/15-9/15; 16-day limit. 4 sites for tents or short RVs. Tbls, toilets, cfga, firewood, no drkg wtr. Picnicking, fishing, hiking. Elev 9600 ft; 3 acres. Mountains; dense forest; stream. 2 mi NW of Rocky Mountain Biological Laboratory and Gothic townsite. 1 mi SE of Gothic Natural Area.

Lake Irwin $7
Gunnison National Forest
7 mi W of Crested Butte on Hwy 2; N on FR 826 from Lake Irwin turnoff. $7 with federall Senior Pass; others pay $14. 6/15-9/15; 16-day limit. 32 sites; 35-ft RV limit. Tbls, toilets, cfga, drkg wtr. Fishing, hiking, picnicking, boating(l).

Lost Lake $12
Gunnison National Forest
15 mi W of Crested Butte on SR 135; 3 mi S on FR 706. $10 during about 6/15-9/30; free 10/1-11/15. 16-day limit. 11 sites (RVs under 22 ft). Tbls, toilets, cfga, no drkg wtr. Boating (d), picnicking, fishing, hiking. Elev 9600 ft; 3 acres. Lake. West Elk Wilderness (3.5 mi).

Fishing tip: Try the small ponds near the Roaring Judy fish hatchery; huge trout are caught there, including a 30-pound brown in 1988; good fishing for small rainbows.

CRESTONE (40)

North Crestone Creek $9
Rio Grande National Forest
1.2 mi N of Crestone on FR 950. $9 during MD-LD; free LD-11/30 or until snow closes access (no wtr or trash service); 14-day limit. 13 sites; 25-ft RV limit. Tbls, toilets, cfga, drkg wtr. Horse loading facilities. Horseback riding, hiking, fishing. Elev 8300 ft; 8 acres.

CRIPPLE CREEK (41)

Cripple Creek Gold $12
Campground & Horse Company
6 mi N of Cripple Creek on Hwy 67, milepost 58 (12 mi S of Divide). $12-$15. All year. 25 sites; 45-ft RV limit. Tbls, flush toilets, cfga, drkg wtr, showers, elec($), coin laundry, playground, dump. Mountain biking, horseback riding, hiking.

Sand Gulch Campground $4
Shelf Road Recreation Site
Bureau of Land Management
From Cripple Creek, qtr mi S on Second St; angle right onto CR 88. From N side of Canon City, follow Fields Ave north; it becomes Shelf Rd (CR 9). Off old toll rd behind red BLM gate. $4. All year. Primitive undesignated sites. Toilets, tbls, no drkg wtr, cfga. Hiking, rock climbing.

The Banks Campground $4
Shelf Road Recreation Site
Bureau of Land Management
From Cripple Creek, qtr mi S on Second St; angle right onto CR 88. From N side of Canon City, follow Fields Ave north; it becomes Shelf Rd (CR 9). Off old toll rd; continue down Shelf rd from Sand Gulch Camp. $4. All year. Primitive undesignated sites. Toilets, tbls, no drkg wtr, cfga. Hiking, rock climbing.

CROOK (42)

Jumbo Reservoir $3
State Wildlife Area
NE of Crook on US 138 to Red Lion Station; 2 mi N on CR 95. $3. All year. Undesignated sites near Jumbo Lake. Toilets, cfga, no drkg wtr. Fishing, boating, hiking, waterskiing, hunting, boating(l).

CUCHARA (43)

Bear Lake $6.50
San Isabel National Forest
3.5 mi S of Cuchara on SR 12; 4.2 mi W on FR 422 (good rd). $6.50 with federal Senior Pass; others pay $13. MD-10/15; 14-day limit. 14 sites (40-ft RV limit). Tbls, toilets, cfga, drkg wtr. Fishing, hiking. Elev 10,700 ft; 5 acres.
Fishing tip: Bear Lake offers fair fishing for cutthroat and brook trout.

Blue Lake $6.50
San Isabel National Forest
3.5 mi S of Cuchara on SR 12; 3.5 mi W on FR 422. $6.50 with federal Senior Pass; others pay $13. MD-10/15; 14-day limit. 15 sites (40-ft RV limit). Tbls, toilets, cfga, drkg wtr. Hiking, fishing. Elev 10,500 ft; 8 acres.

DEL NORTE (44)

Cathedral FREE
Rio Grande National Forest
8.8 mi W of Del Norte on US 160; 1.6 mi N on CR 18; 3.1 mi N on FR 650; 7 mi NW on FR 640. Free. MD-LD; 14-day limit. 33 sites (RVs under 35 ft). Tbls, toilets, cfga, firewood, well drkg wtr. Picnicking, fishing, hiking. Elev 9500 ft; 16 acres. Mountain, dense forest, stream.
Travel Tip: Attractions in and around Del Norte include the Barlow-Sanderson Stage Station, a renovated express station; Rio Grande County Museum with historical displays & demonstrations; La Ventana Arch, one of nature's most spectacular wonders.

Schrader Creek Dispersed FREE
Rio Grande National Forest
7.5 mi from Del Norte on Pinos Creek Rd 330 (CR 14A); N on FR 333 (Schrader Creek Rd) via 4WD vehicle. Free. MD-LD; 14-day limit. Numerous primitive undesignated tent sites; no facilities; no drkg wtr. Fishing, 4WD use.

DELTA (45)

Columbine FREE
Uncompahgre Mesa National Forest
30 mi SW of Delta on CR 2214; 2.5 mi S on FR 402. Free. 6/10-9/30. 6 sites; 32-ft RV limit. Toilets, tbls, cfga, no drkg wtr. Hiking. Secluded.

Escalante FREE
State Wildlife Area
4 mi W of Delta on 5th St. Other tracts 12 mi W of Delta from Hwy 50 (8 separate units). Free. 8/1-3/14 on 2 tracts; all year on others; 14-day limit during 45-day period. Primitive campsites. Hunting, some fishing. Elev 7800 ft; 7598 acres; 5 acres of water; 5 mi of streams.
Travel tip: Tour the nearby Hotchkiss National Fish Hatchery; main supplier of rainbow trout for reservoirs in western Colorado and New Mexico. Free.

Gunnison Gorge $10
National Conservation Area
Bureau of Land Management
About 10 mi E of Delta on SR 92 near Austin; follow signs to Peach Valley Rd. $10. All year. $5 per day combination day use/camping fee, so overnight equals 2 days; $15 for 2 nights. Tbls, toilets, cfga, no drkg wtr. Fishing, hiking, rock climbing. Area established by Congress in 1999. 57,700 acres.

Paonia State Park $7
E of Delta on Hwy 92 to Hotchkiss, then N on Hwy 133 through Paonia and 16 mi to park; Spruce Campground (8 sites) is on upper end of the lake along SR 133; Hawsapple Campground (7 sites) is across Muddy Creek, then right on CR 2 for half mi. $7. Primitive sites. Tbls, toilets, cfga, no drkg wtr. Fishing, boating (l), waterskiing, horseback riding.
Fishing tip: Paoni is known for its northern pike, with most caught from late June until late August. Fish below the dam for trout, using Grizzly Shrimp or wooley brown bear.
Travel tip: When in Delta, stop off at Confluence Park, a 265-acre city park in the developmental stages; foot & bike paths, stocked fishing lakes, picnic areas.

⊛ DENVER (46)

Backcountry Camps $15
Rocky Mountain National Park
65 mi NW of Denver on US 36. $15 per visit backcountry fee during 6/1-9/30; also $15 for 7 days or $30 annual entry fee. 14-day limit. 269 designated backcountry & cross-country sites; some for horseback riders. Get permit at backcountry office of park headquarters. Open fires prohibited; no facilities, no drkg wtr, no trash service.

DILLON (47)

Davis Springs $5
White River National Forest
19.2 mi NW of Dillon on SR 9; 3 mi NW on FR 30. $5. 5/15-11/1; 14-day limit. 7 sites (RVs under 16 ft). Tbls, toilets, cfga, no trash service. Picnicking, fishing, boating(ld-3 mi, r-5 mi); swimming, waterskiing. Elev 8200 ft; 12 acres. Mountains, hardwood forest. Next to Green Mountain Reservoir. Note: Closed in 2007 until further notice.
Fishing tip: Green Mountain Reservoir is well known for its kokanee salmon, which are among the biggest in Colorado. Lake also contains plenty of trout.

Elliot Creek $10
White River National Forest
30.2 mi NW of Dillon on SR 9; 3 mi SW on CR 30. $10 or special season pass for $65. MD-LD; 14-day limit. 24 sites (RVs under 22 ft). Tbls, flush & pit toilets, cfga, firewood, no drkg wtr. Picnicking, fishing, boating (rld--2 mi); swimming, waterskiing. Elev 8300 ft; 13 acres. Mountains, grassy terrain. Elliott Creek. Adjacent to Green Mountain Lake.

McDonalds Flats $10
White River National Forest
19 mi NW of Dillon on SR 9; 5 mi NW on CR 30 on W side of Green Mountain Reservoir. $10 or special season pass for $65. About 5/15-10/15; 14-day limit; free when wtr is shut off in fall. 13 sites (32-ft RV limit). Tbls, toilets, cfga, drkg wtr. Swimming, boating(l), fishing, hiking. Elev 8200 ft; 24 acres.

Prairie Point $10
White River National Forest
22 mi NW of Dillon on SR 9. $10 or special $65 seasonal pass. MD-LD (open only during high-use periods); 14-day limit. 31 sites; 20-ft RV limit). Tbls, toilets, cfga, drkg wtr. Boating(d), fishing, waterskiing, swimming. Near upper end of Green Mountain Reservoir. Elev 9100 ft; 25 acres.

Prospector $6.50
White River National Forest
3.5 mi SE of Dillon on US 6; 3 mi W on CR 1. $6.50 with federal Senior Pass; others pay $13. About 5/15-9/15; 14-day limit. Services & fees may be reduced in fall. 106 sites (32-ft RV limit). Tbls, toilets, cfga, drkg wtr. Boating(dl), fishing, hiking. Elev 9100 ft; 25 acres.

Sugar Loaf $12
Arapaho National Forest
9 mi N of Dillon on Hwy 9; 5 mi SE on CR 30; 1 mi on FR 138. Free 11/1-MD; $12 rest of year; 14-day limit. 11 sites (23-ft RV limit). Tbls, toilets, cfga, drkg wtr. Fishing, hiking, mountain biking & OHV trails. Elev 9000 ft; 8 acres. Closed 2006 & early 2007 due to hazardous trees from beetle infestation.

Willows $10
White River National Forest
30.2 mi NW of Dillon on SR 9; 1 mi SW on CR 30. $10 or special $65 seasonal pass. About 5/15-9/15; 14-day limit. 35 sites (RVs under 32 ft). Tbls, toilets, no drkg wtr. Picnicking, fishing, boating, waterskiing. Elev 8200 ft; 18 acres. Mountains, grassy terrain. Adjacent to Green Mountain Reservoir.

DINOSAUR (48)

Echo Backcountry Camp $8
Dinosaur National Monument
2 mi E of Dinosaur on US 40; 25 mi N on Scenic Drive; 13 mi NE on unpaved Echo Park Rd (13 mi of steep terrain; no oversize vehicles or RVs recommended. Extremely scenic, however. Worth the effort). Unpaved rds impassable when wet, closed in winter. $8 daily plus $10 entry fee. 5/1-10/31; 15-day limit. Free rest of year. 17 renovated tent sites & 4 walk-in sites. Wtr faucets (no wtr from early fall to late spring due to potential damage to pipes from freezing). Boating (earth boat launch; special permit required for boating), whitewater running craft only; fishing; no swimming. 5 acres. Ranger station. Elev 5100 ft; 5 acres. Attendant. At jct of Yampa & Green Rivers. Free backcountry permit required.

Green River Campground   **$12**
Dinosaur National Monument
5 mi E of Dinosaur Quarry. $12. 4/1-10/1; 14-day limit. 88 sites. Tbls, flush toilets, cfga, drkg wtr. Fishing, hiking, ranger talks.

Rainbow Park   **FREE**
Dinosaur National Monument
Located N of Dinosaur on a series of unmarked gravel co rds; inquire directly from a park ranger. From Jensen, 3 mi N on SR 149; 5 mi NW on Brush Creek Rd; 4 mi N on gravel rd along Brush Creek; 12 mi E on Island Park Rd (rough, impassable when wet); RVs discouraged due to sharp turns. Free daily but $10 entry fee. Open about 7/1-11/1; 15-day limit. About 4 undesignated primitive sites. Tbls, toilets, cfga, no drkg wtr. Whitewater rafting (special permit required); no swimming (unexpected currents). Stop at headquarters, 2 mi E of Dinosaur; free audio-visual program & exhibits about the park; get backcountry permits there.

DIVIDE (49)

The Crags   **$11**
Pike National Forest
4.5 mi S of Divide on SR 67; 3.5 mi E on FR 383; narrow, steep access rd. $11. 5/15-10/1; 14-day limit. 17 sites (RVs under 22 ft). Toilets, cfga, tbls, drkg wtr. Fishing, hiking, picnicking. Elev 10,100 ft; 7 acres. Nature trails. Camp has problems with bears.

DOLORES (50)

Bradfield   **$8**
San Juan National Forest
2 mi W of Dolores on Hwy 145; right on Hwy 184 for 8 mi; right on US 666 for 13 mi, then right for 1 mi on FR 505. $8. MD-LD (free off-season); 14-day limit. 22 sites; 45-ft RV limit. Tbls, toilets, cfga, drkg wtr. Boating(l), fishing.

Burro Bridge   **$12**
San Juan National Forest
12.5 mi NE of Dolores on Hwy 145; 23 mi NE on FR 535; on West Dolores River. $12. MD-11/15 (if demand indicates); 14-day limit. 15 sites (35-ft RV limit). Tbls, toilets, cfga, drkg wtr. Fishing, picnicking, hiking, horseback riding (corrals). Elev 9000 ft. Corrals($).

Cabin Canyon   **$10**
San Juan National Forest
7 mi NW of US 666 on FR 505; 34 mi E on FR 504; on Dolores River at Lone Dome. $10. 5/15-LD; 30-day limit. 13 sites (45-ft RV limit). Tbls, toilets, cfga, drkg wtr, dump nearby. Fishing, picnicking, concrete barrier-free trail along river. 4WD & mountain biking nearby on FR 475. Elev 6300 ft; 5 acres.

Ferris Canyon   **$10**
San Juan National Forest
10 mi from US 666 on FR 504. $10 ($5 off-season). 5/15-11/15; 14-day limit. 7 sites;

45-ft RV limit. Tbls, toilets, cfga, drkg wtr, dump. Fishing, picnicking. Elev 6300 ft.

Groundhog Reservoir   **FREE**
State Wildlife Area
26 mi W of Dolores on FR 526 (11th St in town); 5 mi E on FR 533. Free. All year; 14-day limit in 45-day period. 13 sites. Tbls, toilets, cfga, drkg wtr, store. Boating(l), fishing, hiking, hunting.

House Creek   **$12**
San Juan National Forest
From 11th St in Dolores, 6 mi N on Dolores-Norwood Rd (FR 526); 5.4 mi SE on House Creek Rd (FR 528); at McPhee Reservoir. $12 (may be $5 off-season). 5/15-9/15; 14-day limit. 45 sites; 50-ft RV limit. Tbls, toilets, cfga, drkg wtr, dump. Hiking, fishing, boating(l). Elev 7000 acres.

Mavreeso   **$12**
San Juan National Forest
13 mi NE of Dolores on SR 145; 6 mi NE on FR 535. $12. 5/15-9/15; 30-day limit. 14 sites (35-ft RV limit). Tbls, toilets, cfga, drkg wtr, dump. Fishing. Elev 7600 ft; 9 acres.

McPhee Campground   **$12**
San Juan National Forest
7 mi S of Dolores on Hwy 145 & W on Hwy 184; N on CR 25, then on FR 271. $12 base ($7 off-season); $15 with elec. MD until closed by weather; 14-day limit. $6 may be charged off-season. 76 sites (12 walk-in); 50-ft RV limit. Tbls, flush toilets, drkg wtr, showers, dump, elec($3), full hookups($5). Boating(l), hiking, fishing.

Sage Hen Area   **FREE**
McPhee Reservoir
San Juan National Forest
4.2 mi W on Hwy 184 from jct with Hwy 145; N at entrance sign. Free overnight camping on beach. Toilet, trash pickup.
Travel tip: Tour the Escalante Ruins overlooking McPhee Reservoir; excavated ruins were once inhabited by the Anasazi.
Fishing tip: Try the Dolores River downstream from the dam for large rainbow, cutthroat & brown trout up to 20 inches. Also, excellent smallmouth & largemouth bass fishing at the lake, which also produces lots of small rainbow trout.

West Dolores   **$12**
San Juan National Forest
13 mi NE of Dolores on SR 145; 7.5 mi NE on FR 535. $12. 5/15-10/25; 30-day limit. 18 sites (35-ft RV limit). Tbls, toilets, cfga, drkg wtr, dump. Fishing. Elev 7800 ft; 10 acres.

DOTSERO (51)

Bull Gulch   **FREE**
Wilderness Study Area
Bureau of Land Management
N of Dotsero on Colorado River, near Burns. Public access by raft from river. Free. May-Sept; 14-day limit. Unrestricted camping.

No facilities. Hiking, wildlife viewing. 15,000 acres. Bald eagle & prairie falcon nests. High canyons. Elev 6400 ft.

Hack Lake   **FREE**
Bureau of Land Management
From I-70 at Dotsero, 6.5 mi N on CR 301 (Colorado River Rd); NW on Sweetwater Rd to Sweetwater Lake (site of fores service campground). Hike into backcountry on Hack Lake-Ute Trail. Free. Primitive undesignated camping; no facilities except at Sweetwater Lake. Access only by hiking & horseback. Hunting, horseback riding, fishing at secluded lakes.

DOVE CREEK (52)

Mountain Sheep Point   **FREE**
Recreation Site
Bureau of Land Management
From E end of town, follow Dolores River access rd 5 mi to river; follow signs to site. Free. 4/1-10/31; 14-day limit. 3 sites (30-ft RV limit). Tbls, toilets, cfga, no drkg wtr. Fishing, boating(l), hiking, hunting, mountain biking. Elev 6100 ft; 7 acres.
Fishing tip: Try Dolores River for brown, rainbow & cutthroat trout up to 20 inches.

DURANGO (53)

Florida   **$12**
San Juan National Forest
15 mi E of Durango on CR 240 (Florida Rd); 7 mi N on FR 596; on Florida River. $12 during MD-LD; full fee required off-season unless wtr is off, then $6. 20 sites; 35-ft RV limit. Tbls, toilets, cfga, drkg wtr. Fishing, hiking.

Haviland Lake   **$7**
San Juan National Forest
18 mi N of Durango on US 550; 1 mi on FR 671 across dam. $7 with federal Senior Pass; others pay $14 (lakeside sites $11 & $18, respectively). 11 sites with elec, $3-4 extra. 6/15-9/15; 14-day limit. 43 sites; 65-ft RV limit. Tbls, toilets, cfga, drkg wtr. Fishing, boating (no mtrs), hiking. Picnic area, $7.

Junction Creek   **$12**
San Juan National Forest
5 mi NW of Durango on FRs 171 & 573; on Junction Creek Rd. $12. MD-10/15; 14-day limit. 34 sites; 50-ft RV limit. Tbls, toilets, cfga, drkg wtr. Fishing, hiking. Colorado Trail. Elev 7300 ft; 38 acres. Sites may be half price off-season.

Miller Creek   **$10**
San Juan National Forest
15 mi E of Durango on CR 240 (Florida Rd); 3 mi N on FR 596 (2 mi N of dam). $10. MD-LD; 14-day limit. When wtr is off after LD, fee is half price. 12 sites; 35-ft RV limit. Tbls, flush toilets, cfga, drkg wtr. Fishing, boating(l).

Snowslide Campground   **$12**
San Juan National Forest
11 mi W of Durango on US 160; 5 mi N on CR 124 (LaPlata Canyon Rd). $12 during MD-LD; free rest of season. 13 sites; 30-ft RV limit. Tbls, cfga, no drkg wtr, no toilets, no trash service. Drkg wtr available at nearby Kroeger Campground, toilets at Miners Cabin & Madden dispersed camping areas. Fishing at La Plata River.

Transfer Park   **$12**
San Juan National Forest
15 mi E of Durango on CR 240 (Florida Rd); 8 mi N on CR 243. $12. MD-LD; 14-day limit. 25 sites; 35-ft RV limit. Hiking, backpacking, fishing, horseback riding; horse unloading area. Site was once used for transferring ore and supples between pack mules and wagons.

EAGLE (54)

Fulford Cave   **$8**
White River National Forest
12.1 mi S on CR 307; 6 mi E on FR 415; at East Brush Creek. $8. About 5/15-10/31; 14-day limit. 7 sites (25-ft RV limit). Tbls, 1 toilet, cfga, drkg wtr. Hiking, fishing. Visitors can explore cave or visit historic mining town of Fulford.

Fishing tip: Adjacent East Brush Creek contains brook and rainbow trout.

Yeoman Park   **$8**
White River National Forest
12.1 mi S of Eagle on CR 307; 6 mi SE on FR 154; .1 mi S on FR 15416; near Brush Creek. $8. About 5/15-10/31; 14-day limit. 23 sites (RVs under 30 ft). Tbls, toilets, cfga, firewood, spring drkg wtr. Hiking, picnicking, fishing, mountain climbing, horseback riding. Elev 9000 ft; 20 acres. Stream. Geological. Nature trails. Extensive beaver colony nearby.

Fishing tip: Brush Creek contains brook & rainbow trout. Also, much of Eagle River between Wolcott & Gypsum is designated public water heavily populated with rainbow & brown trout 10-14 inches long. Try 12-16 elk hair caddis imitation flies.

EMPIRE (55)

Mizpah   **$11**
Arapaho National Forest
6 mi W of Empire on US 40. $10. 5/26-9/10; 14-day limit. 10 sites (35-ft RV limit). Tbls, toilets, cfga, drkg wtr. Hiking, fishing. Elev 9200 ft; 5 acres.

ESTES PARK (56)

Backcountry Camps   **$15**
Rocky Mountain National Park
Hike in or horseback to designated backcountry sites from park headquarters or the Kawuneeche Visitor Center at Grand Lake. $15 per trip backcountry permit fee plus $15

for 7-day or $30 annual entry fee. 7-day limit June-Sept; 15 days longer rest of year. 269 designated tent sites. Cfga, toilets.

Meeker Park Overflow   **$8**
Roosevelt National Forest
13 mi S of Estes Park on SR 7 at milemarker 11. $8 during mid-May to 1st weekend after LD; free off-season. 29 sites; 30-ft RV limit. Portable toilets, cfga, no drkg wtr, no tbls. Tends to be full due to proximity to Rocky Mountain NP. Elev 8600 ft.

FAIRPLAY (57)

Buffalo Springs   **$10**
Pike National Forest
14.5 mi S of Fairplay on US 285; half mi W on FR 431. $10. 5/1-9/30; 14-day limit. 18 sites (RVs under 31 ft). 9 acres. Tbls, toilets, cfga, well drkg wtr. Rockhounding, picnicking, hiking trails, biking. Elev 9000 ft.

Fourmile   **$10**
Pike National Forest
1.3 mi S of Fairplay on US 285; W on CR 18. $10. MD-10/15; 14-day limit. 14 sites (22-ft RV limit). Tbls, toilets, cfga, drkg wtr. Hiking, fishing (Fourmile Creek). Near 1,000-year-old trees. Elev 10,762 ft.

Horseshoe   **$10**
Pike National Forest
1.3 mi S of Fairplay on US 285; 5.5 mi W on CR 18. $10. 5/1-10/1; 14-day limit. 19 sites (25-ft RV limit). Tbls, toilets, cfga, drkg wtr. Hiking, fishing. Elev 10,800 ft; 8 acres.

Weston Pass   **$10**
Pike National Forest
5 mi S of Fairplay on US 285; 7 mi SW on CR 5; 4.1 mi SW on CR 22. $10. 5/25-9/10; 14-day limit. 14 sites (RVs under 26 ft). Tbls, toilets, cfga, no drkg wtr. Picnicking, fishing. Elev 10,200 ft; 6 acres. Stream. Nearby Weston Pass Rd was former historic toll rd.

FLAGLER (58)

Flagler Reservoir   **FREE**
State Wildlife Area
E on Rd 4 at Flagler City Park (1 block off I-70), 3 mi to lake. Free. All year; 14-day limit during 45-day period. 5 separate, multiple sites. Some with tbls. Pit toilets, drkg wtr. Fishing, small-game hunting, boating(l), picnicking. Elev 5000 ft; 568 acres; 160 acres of water.

Fishing tip: Flagler Reservoir contains yellow perch, crappie, largemouth bass, channel catfish, northern pike, tiger muskies.

FORT COLLINS (60)

Bliss State Wildlife Area   **FREE**
60 mi W of Fort Collins on Hwy 14. Free. All year; 14-day limit. Undesignated primitive sites. Toilet, cfga, no tbls, no drkg wtr. Fishing, hunting No boating.

Dixon Lake   **FREE**
State Wildlife Area
From I-25 at Prospect St exit in Fort Collins, 7.1 mi W to Overland Trail; three-fourths mi S to Rd 42C; W one mi. Free. All year; 14-day limit in 45-day period. Primitive camping; no facilities. Picnicking, photography, boating(no motors), fishing.

Travel tip: Tour Anheuser Busch Brewery, opened in 1988, followed by visit to the Clydesdale horse hamlet.

Dutch George Flats   **$7**
Roosevelt National Forest
11 mi N of Fort Collins on Hwy 287; 17 mi W on Hwy 14 (Poudre Canyon Hwy). $7 during off-season when water is off; $14 rest of year except $7 with federal Senior Pass. 20 sites; 33-ft RV limit. Tbls, toilets, cfga, drkg wtr. Hiking, fishing. Elev 6500 ft.

Horsetooth Campground   **$12**
Larimer County Park
5 mi S of town on Taft Hill Rd; 2 mi W on CR 38E. $12 base; $17 with elec plus $6 daily ($75 annual, $35 senior) park use fee. All year; 14-day limit. 100 tent sites & 115 drive-through sites (no RV size limit). Tbls, showers, flush toilets, cfga, drkg wtr, dump, store. Boating, swimming, fishing, duck hunting. Horsetooth Reservoir. Reduced facilities in winter.

Jack's Gulch   **$7.50**
Roosevelt National Forest
11 mi N of Fort Collins on Hwy 287; 22 mi W on Hwy 14 (Poudre Canyon Hwy). $7.50 base during off-season when wtr turned off; $15 rest of year except $7.50 with federal Senior Pass; equestrian sites $25; $5 surcharge for 20 elec hookups. 14-day limit. 70 sites (including 6 horse camping sites with small corrals); 50-ft RV limit. Tbls, toilets, cfga, drkg wtr, elec($). Hiking, fishing, horseback riding, mountain biking. Elev 8100 ft.

Kelly Flats   **$7.50**
Roosevelt National Forest
11 mi N of Fort Collins on Hwy 287; 22 mi W on Hwy 14 (Poudre Canyon Hwy). $7.50 during off-season when wtr turned off; $15 rest of year except $7.50 with federal Senior Pass. 14-day limit. 29 sites; 40-ft RV limit. Tbls, toilets, cfga, drkg wtr. Hiking, fishing, mountain biking. Elev 6600 ft.

Lower Unit   **FREE**
Cherokee Park State Wildlife Area
22 mi N from Fort Collins on US 287; W on Cherokee Park Rd 6 mi. Free. All year; 14-day limit during 45-day period. Primitive campsites. Toilets, tbls, cfga. Hunting, fishing, picnicking, hiking. Elev 6,500-8,000 ft. Camp only in designated areas. Fires only in designated areas. Vehicles prohibited except in parking areas.

Middle Unit   **FREE**
Cherokee Park State Wildlife Area
22 mi N from Fort Collins on US 287; W 8

mi on Cherokee Park Rd. Vehicles prohibited from day after Labor Day through day before Memorial Day. Free. All year; 14-day limit during 45-day period. Primitive campsites. Toilets, tbls, cfga. Hunting, fishing, picnicking, hiking. Elev 6,500-8,000 ft. Camp only in designated areas. Fires only in designated areas.

Mountain Park $7.50
Roosevelt National Forest
11 mi N of Fort Collins on Hwy 287; 19 mi W on Hwy 14 (Poudre Canyon Hwy). $7.50 during off-season when wtr not available; $15 rest of year except $7.50 with federal Senior Pass; $30 double or large sites ($15 off-season & for seniors; $5 surcharge for elec. 55 sites; 50-ft RV limit. Tbls, toilets, cfga, drkg wtr, coin showers, elec($). Hiking, fishing, mountain biking, 4WD. Elev 6500 ft.

Narrows $7
Roosevelt National Forest
11 mi N of Fort Collins on Hwy 287; 16 mi W on Hwy 14 (Poudre Canyon Hwy). $7 during off-season when wtr not available; $14 rest of year except $7 with federal Senior Pass. 15 sites; 30-ft RV limit. Tbls, toilets, cfga, drkg wtr. Tents only in lower section. Hiking, fishing, rafting, 4WD. Elev 6400 ft.

Stove Prairie $7
Roosevelt National Forest
11 mi N of Fort Collins on Hwy 287; 25 mi W on Hwy 14 (Poudre Canyon Hwy). $7 during off-season when wtr not available; $14 rest of year except $7 with federal Senior Pass. 9 sites; 30-ft RV limit. Tbls, toilets, cfga, drkg wtr. Hiking, fishing, mountain biking, rafting, 4WD. Elev 6000 ft.

Upper Unit FREE
Cherokee Park State Wildlife Area
22 mi N from Fort Collins on US 287; 22 mi W on Cherokee Park Rd 80C. Vehicles prohibited from day after Labor Day through day before Memorial Day. Free. All year; 14-day limit during 45-day period. Primitive sites. Toilets, tbls, cfga. Hunting, fishing, picnicking, hiking. Camp & fires only in designated areas.

Watson Lake FREE
State Wildlife Area
NW of Fort Collins and LaPorte on US 287; 1 mi W on Rist Canyon Rd across Poudre River; turn N. Sites. No RV size limit; 14-day limit. Camp only in established areas. Toilets, cfga, tbls. Dump & wtr at Phillips service station on US 287 N in Fort Collins with purchase of fuel or propane. Fishing at lake or river. No boating, ice fishing, hunting. No parking on the S dam.
Fishing tip: Watson Lake is regularly stocked with trout, and N end is open only to fly or lure fishing; lake is heavily fished.
Travel tip: Visit Fort Collins Museum, 200 Mathews St; turn-of-century Carnegie Library displays artifacts from Pre-Columbian and Plains Indians; relics from old Fort Collins military post; rare Folsom arrow and spear points; log cabins, historic school house.

FORT GARLAND (61)

Mountain Home Reservoir FREE
State Wildlife Area
2.5 mi E of Fort Garland on Hwy 160 to Trinchera Rd; 2 mi to Icehouse Rd; 1 mi W. Free. Primitive camping. Toilets, no other facilities, no trash service. All year; 14-day limit in 45-day period. Fishing, boating(l), toilets, cfga. Elev 8145 ft; 1,120 acres.

Ute Creek Campground $10
From Hwy 160 at Fort Garland, 1 block N on Narcisso, then W on 5th St; at Ute Creek. $10 tents; $15 RVs. All year. 30 sites; 45-ft RV limit. Tbls, toilets, cfga, drkg wtr, hookups($), showers, coin laundry. Fishing.

FORT MORGAN (62)

Riverside City Park FREE
Canfield Recreation Area
From I-76 exit 80 at Fort Morgan, drive to 1600 N. Man St at the South Platte River. Free. 16 sites at 240-acre park. Tbls, toilets, cfga, drkg wtr, elec($), pool. Playgrounds, swimming, horseshoes, fitness trails, fishing, volleyball, tennis.

FOWLER (63)

Fowler RV Park (Private) $10
4 blocks E of Main in Fowler on Hwy 96. $10. 4/1-11/1. Base fee for tent sites; $20 full RV hookups. 41 sites; 45-ft RV limit. Tbls, flush toilets, cfga, drkg wtr, showers, dump, hookups($), CATV.

FRASER (64)

Byers Creek $12
Arapaho National Forest
6.5 mi SW of Fraser on FR 160. $12. MD-LD; 14-day limit. 6 sites (32-ft RV limit). Tbls, toilets, cfga, drkg wtr. Fishing, hiking, biking. At St. Louis & Byers Creeks in Fraser Experimental Forest. Elev 9360 ft.

St. Louis Creek $12
Arapaho National Forest
3 mi SW of Fraser on CR 73 (St. Louis Creek Rd). $12. MD-LD; 14-day limit. 16 sites (25-ft RV limit). Tbls, toilets, cfga, drkg wtr. Fishing, hiking, snowmobiling, mountain biking. Elev 8900 ft; 6 acres. In Fraser Experimental Forest.

FRISCO (65)

Pine Cove $12
Peninsula Recreation Area
White River National Forest
2.3 mi SE of Frisco on SR 9. $12. About 5/15-9/15; 10-day limit. 55 sites (50-ft RV limit). Tbls, toilets, cfga, drkg wtr. Boating(l), fishing, swimming, hiking. On Dillon Reservoir. Elev 9000 ft; 5 acres.

FRUITA (66)

Saddlehorn Campground $10
Colorado National Monument
3.5 mi S of Fruita on SR 340. $10. All year; 14-day limit. 80 sites; 26-ft RV limit. Flush toilets, drkg wtr (except in winter), charcoal grills, tbls. Dump station in Fruita. Picnicking, hiking. Wood fires prohibited. Visitor center 4 mi from Fruita entrance open all year. Pets on leash, not permitted on trails or in backcountry. Daily entry fee charged Apr-Sept.

GARDNER (67)

Huerfano FREE
State Wildlife Area
13 mi SW of Gardner on CR 580. Area both sides of Huerfano River NW of Walsenburg. Free. All year; 14-day limit during 45-day period. Primitive campsites. Toilets, cfga, tbls. No drkg wtr. Hiking, boating(l), fishing, hunting, picnicking, backpacking. Elev 7600 ft; 544 acres. 343 water acres.
Fishing tip: Excellent trout fishing in Huerfano River; or hike to nearby Huerfano Gorge where high-altitude Upper and Lower Lily Lakes & Lost Lake contain large native trout-rainbows, brookies, browns, cutthroat.

Mt. Evans FREE
State Wildlife Area
W on I-70 from to El Rancho Rd. exit; S to Hwy 74 to Evergreen Lake; 6.4 mi W on Upper Bear Creek Rd; 3 mi W on CR 480. Free. 5-day limit during 45-day period except during big-game season in designated campgrounds. Vehicles prohibited day after Labor Day through June 14 except during regular rifle deer and elk seasons. Public access prohibited 1/1-6/14. 15 primitive sites. Tbls, cfga, toilets, no drkg wtr. Big game, small game hunting, swimming, fishing. 4,846 acres. Small streams contain trout.

GEORGETOWN (68)

Clear Lake $11
Arapaho National Forest
4 mi S of Georgetown on CR 118 (Guanella Pass Rd). $11. 5/16-9/10; 14-day limit. 8 sites (25-ft RV limit). Tbls, toilets, cfga, drkg wtr. Picnicking, fishing, hiking. Elev 10,000 ft. South Clear Creek.

Guanella Pass $11
Arapaho National Forest
5 mi S of Georgetown on CR 118 (Guanella Pass Rd). $11. 6/1-9/15; 14-day limit. 18 sites; 45-ft RV limit. Tbls, toilets, cfga, drkg wtr. Fishing, hiking, mountain biking. Elev 10,900 ft.

GILLETTE (69)

Pikes Peak (Bison)   **FREE**
State Wildlife Area
2 mi S of Gillette on dirt rd; 1.5 mi E to Bison Reservoir, then NE of reservoir. Free. 7/15-3/31; 14-day limit in 45-day period. Primitive camping; no facilities. Bighorn sheep hunting, photography.

GLENDEVEY (70)

Hohnholz Lakes   **FREE**
State Wildlife Area
5 mi N from Glendevey on Laramie River Rd; W at sign. Scenic drive. Free. All year; 14-day limit during 45-day period. Primitive camping only at Laramie River camping area. Toilets, cfga, tbls. Fishing, hiking, picnicking. Hunting. 111 acres of water among 3 lakes. Access to Forrester Creek, Grace Creek.
Fishing tip: Laramie River, Forrester Creek & Grace Creek, all adjoining the area, offer excellent fishing for brook, native rainbow and brown trout. Lakes contain primarily rainbow. Use artificial lures only.

GLENWOOD SPRINGS (71)

Bison Lake   **FREE**
White River National Forest
16.9 mi E of Glenwood Springs on US 6/24; 2 mi N on CR 301; 25.5 mi NW on FR 600; W on FR 601 past former Klines Folly Camp, then take left fork for 8 mi; right on FR 640 for 2 mi; at Bison Lake. Free. July-Sept; 14-day limit Undesignated primitive sites. No toilet, no other facilities, no drkg wtr, no trash service. No fishing at Bison Lake; brook trout at nearby Heart Lake. Toilet removed in 2006.

Coffee Pot Springs   **$6**
White River National Forest
18 mi E of Glenwood Springs on US 6/24; 2 mi N on CR 301; 20.6 mi NW on FR 600; at French Creek. Free before & after regular season of 6/1-11/1, when $6 fee is charged. 14-day limit. 10 sites (RVs under 21 ft). 20 acres. Tbls, toilets, cfga, firewood, piped drkg wtr. Picnicking, horseback riding; fishing (5 mi). Elev 10,100 ft.
Travel tip: Just before heading NW on FR 600 toward the campground, the 20-mi section of Colorado River through Glenwood Canyon (just below the Shoshone power plant) offers popular and exciting rafting opportunities.

Deep Lake   **$6**
White River National Forest
16.9 mi E of Glenwood Springs on US 6/24; 2 mi N on CR 301; 26.5 mi NW on FR 600; on E side of Deep Lake. $6 during 7/1-10/31; free rest of year, but no services; 14-day limit. 37 sites (RVs under 36 ft). Tbls, toilets, cfga, firewood, no drkg wtr. Boating (ld); picnicking, fishing. Elev 10,500 ft; 8 acres.
Fishing tip: Deep Lake is stocked regularly with rainbow trout and also contains lakers.

Travel tip: A 1-mi trail from the Glenwood Canyon section along the Colorado River leads to spectacular scenery and a series of waterfalls below Hanging Lake; 200 yards above the lake, the creek spouts out of a cliff called Spouting Rock; hike from a parking area on the N side of I-10.

Supply Basin   **$6**
White River National Forest
16.9 mi E of Glenwood Springs on I-70; 2 mi N on CR 301; 25.5 mi NW on FR 600; left on FR 640, half mi past Klines Folly camp, on Heart Lake. $6 during 7/1-10/1; free rest of year; 14-day limit. 6 sites (25-ft RV limit). Tbls, toilets, cfga, no drkg wtr. Boating (d), picnicking, fishing. Elev 10,700 ft; 2 acres.
Fishing tip: Nearby 480-acre Heart Lake contains stocked brook trout, but fishing is difficult due to shallow shoreline; boat fishing is good, but gas-powered motors prohibited.

Sweetwater Lake   **$8**
White River National Forest
18 mi E of Glenwood Springs on I-70; 7 mi N of Dotsero on CR 37; 10 mi NW on CR 17; S on FR 607. $8. 6/1-11/1; 14-day limit. 9 sites (30-ft RV limit). Tbls, toilets, cfga, no drkg wtr (but at resort nearby). On S end of Sweetwater Lake. Fishing, hiking, horseback riding, canoeing. Elev 7700 ft. No trash service after mid-Sept.
Fishing tip: Sweetwater Lake contains rainbow, brown & brook trout and also kokanee salmon. Good fishing from shore or by boat (no motors).

Thompson Creek   **FREE**
Recreation Site
Bureau of Land Management
Grand Junction District
S of Glenwood Springs on Freeman Creek Rd and co rds to Thompson Creek in Pitkin County. Free. 4/1-8/31, 8-day limit; 9/1-3/32, 14-day limit. Primitive undesignated campsites. Toilets (May-Sept), no drkg wtr. Hiking, biking, fishing, horseback riding. Very scenic. Enviromental education opportunities. Dinosaur footprints reported here.
Travel tip: Experience the natural hot springs baths of Glenwood Springs while you're in this area. The Glenwood Hot Springs Pool is known best, but the Yampah Hot Springs Vapor Caves are an interesting diversion; soothing 115-degree steam baths available in three natural caves.

White Owl   **$6**
White River National Forest
16.9 mi E of Glenwood Springs on US 6/24; 2 mi N on CR 301; 24 mi NW on FR 15600; .8 mi W on FR 6002D; on 21-acre White Owl Lake. $6. 7/1-10/30; 14-day limit. Free off-season, but no trash service. 11 sites (RVs under 30 ft). Tbls, toilets, cfga, firewood, no drkg wtr, no trash service. Picnicking, fishing, boating. Elev 10,600 ft; 1 acre. Scenic.
Fishing tip: The 21-acre lake is stocked with brook, brown & rainbow trout, but popu-

lation depleted by winter kill. It is not heavily fished. Better fishing for trout at nearby Heart Lake and Deep Lake.

GOULD (72)

Aspen   **$10**
Routt National Forest
1 mi SW of Gould on FR 740; qtr mi W on FR 741. $10. MD-LD; 14-day limit. 7 sites (RVs under 23 ft). Tbls, toilets, cfga, drkg wtr. Fishing. Elev 8900 ft. Near Colorado State Forest.

Pines   **$10**
Routt National Forest
3.5 mi SE of Gould on FR 740. $10. MD-LD; 14-day limit. 11 sites (RVs under 20 ft). Tbls, toilets, cfga, drkg wtr. Fishing. Elev 9200 ft; 5 acres.

GRANBY (73)

Denver Creek   **$12**
Arapaho National Forest
3 mi NW of Granby on US 40; 12 mi NW on SR 125. $12. MD-LD (free later in fall, but no wtr); 14-day limit. 22 sites (25-ft RV limit). Tbls, toilets, cfga, drkg wtr. Fishing, OHV trails. Elev 8800 ft; 9 acres.

Sawmill Gulch   **$10**
Arapaho National Forest
3 mi NW of Granby on US 40; 10 mi NW on SR 125. $10. MD-LD; 14-day limit. 6 sites (32-ft RV limit). Tbls, toilets, cfga, drkg wtr. Fishing, OHV trails. Elev 8780 ft.

GRAND JUNCTION (74)

Big Dominguez   **FREE**
Recreation Site
Bureau of Land Management
SE on US 50 from Grand Junction; right (W) on SR 141 at Whitewater; SW 14 mi; left on Divide Rd at Uncompahgre National Forest sign for 5 mi; left at BLM sign to sign for site; 4 mi. Watch for rock slides last 2 mi; RVs not recommended. Free. 5/15-10/15; 14-day limit. 9 sites. Tbls, cfga, toilets, no drkg wtr. Fishing, hiking, picnicking, horseback riding. Pack out trash. Also, primitive camping permitted along Dominguez Creek rd. Elev 7500 ft.

Black Ridge Canyons   **FREE**
Colorado Canyons
National Conservation Area
Bureau of Land Management
10 mi W of Grand Junction. Acess by one of two roads that parallel the southern boundary. Upper Road open 4/15-8/15; Lower Road open 8/15-2/15; high-clearance 4x4 required last 1.5 mi; roads hazardous when wet. Free primitive camping May-Oct; no facilities, no drinking wtr. Float campers required to have portable toilets and fire pans for cooking; backbackers shuld carry stoves. No camping in and around the arches.

COLORADO

Hay Press   **FREE**
Grand Mesa National Forest
10 mi SW of Grand Junction on SR 340; 20 mi S on CR 400. At Little Fruita Reservoir No. 3. Free. MD-11/15; 16-day limit. 11 sites (RVs under 16 ft). Tbls, toilets, cfga, no drkg wtr. Picnicking. Elev 9300 ft; 2 acres. Colorado National Monument (14 mi N). Hay Press Creek.

Travel tip: While here, you can take part in an actual dinosaur dig at Rabbit Valley Dinosaur Quarry, 24 mi W of Grand Junction; tours organized by the Museum of Western Colorado. The free museum also has exhibits on western Colorado from prehistoric times.

Miracle Rock   **FREE**
Recreation Site
Bureau of Land Management
1 mi E from Grand Junction on SR 340; left to Colorado National Monument for 7.5 mi past monument's east entrance; left at Glade Park store sign for 5 mi; S on 16.5 Rd for 6.6 mi; W 8 mi, then S on 9.8 Rd for 1.1 mi. Free. 5/1-11/1; 14-day limit. 4 sites (30-ft RV limit). Tbls, toilets, cfga, no drkg wtr. Hiking, picnicking. Elev 6600 ft; 6 acres. Scenic. Primarily for tents; RVs not recommended.

Mud Springs   **$5**
Recreation Site
Bureau of Land Management
1 mi from Grand Junction on SR 340; left to Colorado National Monument for 7.5 mi past monument's east entrance; left at Glade Park store sign for 5 mi; S on 16.5 Rd for 6.6 mi. Free only 10/1-10/15; $5 during 5/15-10/1; 14-day limit. 14 sites (RVs under 30 ft). 8 acres. Toilets, cfga, firewood, tbls, drkg wtr. Hiking, rockhounding, picnicking. Elev 8100 ft.

Rabbit Valley   **FREE**
Colorado Canyons
National Conservation Area
Bureau of Land Management
W of Grand Junction on I-70 to Rabbit Valley exit; turn left, crossing I-70 going S, to area (26 mi total, near Utah border). Free. 3/1-12/15; 7-day limit. 3 sites. Tbls, toilets, cfga, no drkg wtr. 24 sq mi of high desert. Hiking, biking, OHV, hunting, horseback riding. No vehicle access to Colorado River. Very hot in summer. Backcountry camping allowed. Road to Castle Rock and Knowles Canyon overlook too rough, narrow for RVs. Wood scarce.

GRAND LAKE (75)

Grand Lake City Park   **FREE**
From US 34, follow signs E to Grand Lake, then 2 blocks past 4-way stop; left on Hancock St 1 block to parking lot designated for self-contained RVs. Free. 48-hour limit. No facilities.

GRANT (76)

Burning Bear   **$6.50**
Pike National Forest
5.2 mi NW of Grant on FR 118. $6.50 with federal Senior Pass; others pay $13. 5/1-9/15; 14-day limit. 14 sites (RVs under 21 ft). Tbls, toilets, cfga, well drkg wtr. River, stream, fishing, trailhead, wilderness area, hiking. Elev 9500 ft; 6 acres. At jct of Bear Creek & Scott Gomer Creek.

Geneva Park   **$6.50**
Pike National Forest
7 mi NW of Grant on FR 118; qtr mi NW on FR 119. $6.50 with federal Senior Pass; others pay $13. 5/1-9/15; 14-day limit. 26 sites (RVs under 21 ft). Tbls, toilets, cfga, no drkg wtr. Fishing, stream, hiking, trailhead. Scenic drive. Elev 9800 ft. On Geneva Creek.

Hall Valley   **$6.50**
Pike National Forest
3.1 mi W of Grant on US 285; 4.7 mi NW on FR 120. $6.50 with federal Senior Pass; others pay $13. 5/1-9/15; 14-day limit. 9 sites (RVs under 21 ft). Tbls, toilets, cfga, no drkg wtr. Fishing, picnicking. Elev 9900 ft; 4 acres. Stream.

Handcart   **$6.50**
Pike National Forest
3.1 mi W of Grant on US 285; 4.9 mi NW on FR 120. $6.50 with federal Senior Pass; others pay $13. 5/1-10/15; 14-day limit. 11 tent sites. Tbls, toilets, cfga, well drkg wtr. Picnicking, fishing, hiking. Elev 9800 ft; 5 acres. Mountains, dense forest, stream. Near North Fork of South Platte River.

GUNNISON (77)

Backcountry Camps   **FREE**
Curecanti National Recreation Area
W of Gunnison along lakeshore. Free. April-Oct, depending upon ice conditions. Undesignated tent sites on Blue Mesa, Morrow Point, Crystal Lake. 14-day limit. No facilities. Picnicking, fishing, hiking, boating. Boating fees are charged at Blue Mesa Lake: $4 for 2 days; $10 for 2 weeks; $30 annually.

Fishing tip: Excellent fishing at all three lakes, with Blue Mesa providing the best action from rainbow, brown, mackinaw & brook trout; also large quantities of kokanee salmon.

Travel tip: Tour Aberdeen Quarry 6 mi SW of town on South Beaver Creek; open during summer for self-guided tours; famed granite quarry (1889-92) supplied stone for state capitol in Denver.

Cebolla Boat-In Camp   **FREE**
Curecanti National Recreation Area
Between Elk Creek marina (16 mi W of Gunnison on US 50) and Lake Fork Marina (27 mi W of Gunnison on US 50) on S side of lake. Boat access only. Free. Apr-Oct; 14-day

limit. 2 sites. Toilets, tbls, cfga. Picnicking, fishing, boating, hiking. Burn driftwood only. Wildflowers in spring. Wooded. Birds of prey nest in tree snags and rocky cliffs.

Cochetopa Canyon   **FREE**
Special Recreation Management Area
Bureau of Land Management
SE of Gunnison on SR 114 along Cochetopa River. Access by co rds. Free. Apr-Nov; 14-day limit. 14 primitive sites at 6 roadside pull-offs along Cochetopa Creek. 3 have toilets, no tbls or drkg wtr. Pack out trash. Limited scattered facilities. Swimming, fishing, hunting, hiking, backpacking. Small, rugged canyon. Accessible roadside camping. Scenic.

Commissary   **FREE**
Gunnison National Forest
26.1 mi W of Gunnison on US 50; half mi NW on SR 92; 9.2 mi N on FR 721. At Soap Creek. 5/27-10/23; 16-day limit. 7 sites (RVs under 16 ft). Tbls, toilets, cfga, no drkg wtr. Fishing, picnicking. Elev 7900 ft; 2 acres. Stream. Curecanti National Recreation Area (approx 10 mi S).

Dry Gulch   **$12**
Curecanti National Recreation Area
Just N of US 50, 17 mi W of Gunnison; on Blue Mesa Lake. $12. All year; 14-day limit. 9 sites. Tbls, cfga, toilets, drkg wtr. Burn driftwood only. Drkg wtr during winter available at Elk Creek picnic area. Area may be closed by snow or freezing temperatures. Blue Mesa Lake boat fees $4 for 2 days; $10, two weeks; $30 annual. Boating, fishing.

Elk Creek   **$12**
Curecanti National Recreation Area
16 mi W of Gunnison on US 50; on Blue Mesa Lake. $12 ($18 with elec -- $12 with federal Senior Pass). All year, depending on weather (heavy snowfalls generally close the campground from Dec to March); 14-day limit. 160 sites (no RV size limit). Flush toilets, drkg wtr, dump, cfga, hot showers, dump. No wtr or flush toilets in winter. Boating (rld), picnicking, swimming, fishing. In winter, snowmobiling. Elev 7480 ft. Evening ranger programs. Sites usually accessible all year. During winter, wtr available at picnic area.

Gateview Campground   **FREE**
Curecanti National Recreation Area
7 mi W of Powderhorn on SR 149, then 6 mi N on improved gravel rd. Free. 5/15-11/15; 14-day limit. 6 sites; 22-ft RV limit. Tbls, cfga, toilets, drkg wtr. Boating, picnicking, fishing, hiking. Campground may be closed in winter by snow or freezing temperatures. Obtain drkg wtr in winter at Elk Creek picnic area.

Lake Fork Campground   **$6**
Curecanti National Recreation Area
27 mi W of Gunnison on US 50; near Blue Mesa Dam. Ordinarily $12, but wtr system shut down in 2007 for repairs, so fee is $6. 4/15-9/30; 14-day limit. 90 sites (limited number of sites available for tents); no RV

size limit. Tbls, cfga, flush toilets, dump, fish cleaning station, drkg wtr. Boating (l); picnicking; fishing. Elev 7580 ft. During cold weather wtr available at Elk Creek picnic area. Evening ranger program.

Lake Fork Canyon   **FREE**
Boat-In Camp
Curecanti National Recreation Area
27 mi W of Gunnison on US 50; S to camp from marina. Boat access only Free.. Apr-Nov; 14-day limit. 2 tent sites. Tbls, toilets, cfga. Fishing, boating, picnicking, hiking. Short distance from secluded cove among blue spruce, firs. Small stream runs through area in spring; boil water before drinking.

Ponderosa   **$12**
Curecanti National Recreation Area
Half mi W of Blue Mesa Dam via the Soap Creek Rd off US 50. RVs can make that 6-mi drive, but rd can be very muddy and hazardous when wet. $12. About 4/15-9/30; 14-day limit. 28 sites. Tbls, toilets, cfga, drkg wtr. Boating(l), picnicking, fishing, hiking. Sites among pine trees at shoreline of Soap Creek arm of Blue Mesa Lake. 22-ft RV limit. Elev 8000 ft; 1,000 acres.

Red Bridge Campground   **$5**
Curecanti National Recreation Area
7 mi W of Powderhorn on SR 149; watch for sign on the right that says "Red Bridge and Gateview"; exit on good travel rd for 2 mi. $5. 5/15-11/15; 14-day limit. Primitive sites. Tbls, toilets, cfga, no drkg wtr. Boating, fishing.

Red Creek   **$12**
Curecanti National Recreation Area
19 mi W of Gunnison on US 50. $12. 5/15-11/15; 14-day limit. Boating, picnicking, fishing, hiking. 2 sites; 22-ft RV limit. Tbls, cfga, toilets, drkg wtr. Burn driftwood only. Obtain drkg wtr in winter at Elk Creek picnic area.

Red Creek Dispersed Sites   **FREE**
Curecanti National Recreation Area
19 mi W of Gunnison on US 50. All year; 14-day limit. Primitive dispersed sites along dirt rd around Red Creek Campground, where fee is charged. Free. Obtain drkg wtr in winter at Elk Creek picnic area and Cimarron campground.

Soap Creek   **$12**
Gunnison National Forest
26.1 mi W of Gunnison on US 50; half mi NW on SR 92; 7.2 mi N on FR 721; half mi NE on FR 824. $12. 6/14-9/30; 16-day limit. 21 sites (RVs under 35 ft). Tbls, toilets, cfga, piped drkg wtr. Fishing, picnicking. Elev 7700 ft; 8 acres. Curecanti National Recreation Area approx 9 mi S. On-site horse corral & unloading ramp.

Stevens Creek   **$12**
Curecanti National Recreation Area
12 mi W of Gunnison on US 50. $12. 5/1-11/1; 14-day limit. Boating(l), picnicking, fishing, hiking. 53 sites (no RV size limit).

Tbls, toilets, cfga, camp store, drkg wtr. Evening ranger programs on summer weekends. Launch for small boats. Elev 7540 ft.

The Bridge Campground   **$5**
Curecanti National Recreation Area
On Hwy 149 between Lake City & Gunnison, upstream from Red Bridge Camp. $5. 5/1-11/1; 14-day limit. Primitive sites. Tbls, toilets, cfga, no drkg wtr. Fishing, bating(l).

Turtle Rock   **FREE**
Boat-In Camp
Curecanti National Recreation Area
16 mi W of Gunnison on US 50 to Elk Creek marina; half mi S of Elk Creek on S side of lake. BOAT ACCESS ONLY. Free. Apr-Oct; 14-day limit. 3 tent sites. Toilets, tbls, cfga. Fishing, boating, hiking, picnicking. Popular with canoeists. Burn driftwood only.

West Elk   **FREE**
Boat-In Camp
Curecanti National Recreation Area
Between Lake Fork marina (27 mi W of Gunnison) and Elk Creek marina (16 mi W of Gunnison) on N shore of lake. Boat access only from either marina; 1 hr by hand-powered craft. Next to inlet of West Elk Creek. Free. Apr-Oct; 14-day limit. 2 tent sites. Toilets, tbls, cfga. Fishing, boating, hiking, picnicking. Burn driftwood only. Two log cabins stand at side of creek. Moor boats on W shore just before bottleneck near the creek mouth to avoid submerged timber. Developed trail leads to campsites.

GYPSUM (78)

Community Recreation Site   **FREE**
Eagle River Recreation Area
Bureau of Land Management
2 mi W of Gypsum on US 6 & 24 to Gypsum Recreation Site, then W; on Eagle River Free. All year; 7-day limit (14 days off-season). Primitive undesignated sites; no facilities. Fishing, river-running, hiking. Elev 6200 ft.

Deep Creek   **FREE**
Bureau of Land Management
Grand Junction District
About 6 mi W of Gypsum on US 6/24; 1 mi N on CR 301 (Colorado River Rd) along Colorado River; 2 mi W on Coffee Pot Rd. Free. 5/1-10/1; 14-day limit. Primitive camping area; roadside & walk-in camping. Toilets (May-Sept), cfga. No drkg wtr. Very scenic, good fishing, wildlife viewing, rafting, hiking, horseback riding, OHVs, hunting, spelunking. Visitor information.

Fishing tip: Much of Eagle River between Wolcott & Gypsum is designated public water heavily populated with rainbow & brown trout 10-14 inches long. Try 12-16 elk hair caddis imitation flies. Deep Creek contains brown, rainbow, brook & cutthroat trout.

Gypsum Campground   **$10**
Upper Colorado Recreation Area
Bureau of Land Management
From I-70 exit 140 at Gypsum, follow frontage rd on S side of interchange westward along Eagle River about 2 mi; camp between the road & river. $10. 7-day limit during 4/1-8/31; 14 days 9/1-3/31. Primitive undesignated sites. Tbls, toilets, cfga, no drkg wtr. Fishing, boating(l), hiking, picnicking.

Fishing tip: Eagle River between Gore Creek & the Colorado River at Dottier has a 2-trout limit. Fly fishing is quite popular and productive. State leases fishing rights between Wolcott and Eagle.

Lava Flow Recreation Site   **FREE**
Eagle River Recreation Area
Bureau of Land Management
W of Gypsum on US 6 & 24, past Gypsum, Community and Horse Pasture sites. Free. All year; 7-day limit (14 days off-season). Primitive undesignated sites; no facilities, no drkg wtr. Fishing, river-running, hiking.

Lede Reservoir   **FREE**
White River National Forest
17.1 mi SE of Gypsum on FR 412 (last mile narrow & rough). Free. 6/1-10/1; 14-day limit. About 3 undesignated sites (RVs under 22 ft). Toilet, cfga, no drkg wtr, no trash service. Boating(l), canoeing, picnicking, fishing. Elev 9500 ft; 3 acres. 27-acre Lede Reservoir.

Fishing tip: Catchable-size rainbow trout are stocked in Lede Reservoir regularly. Lake 32 ft deep. Dirt ramp for launching small boats.

HAMILTON (ROUTT CTY) (79)

Indian Run   **FREE**
State Wildlife Area
12 mi E of Hamilton on Hwy 317; 6 mi S of Pagoda on CR 67. Free. All year; 14-day limit during a 45-day period. Primitive undeveloped campsites. Toilets, tbls, no drkg wtr, cfga. Hunting on 2,039 acres. Horse corral. Elev 6700 ft.

Fishing tips: Excellent fishing for native trout in four streams, including South Fork of the Williams Fork River.

HARTSEL (80)

Antero Reservoir   **FREE**
State Wildlife Area
5 mi SW of Hartsel on Hwy 24. Free. All year; 14-day limit during a 45-day period. About 60 primitive campsites; 1,000 acres. Tbls, toilets, drkg wtr; fires prohibited. Fishing (4,000-acre lake), boating(l), picnicking. Elev 9000 ft.

Fishing tip: Antero Reservoir and South Fork of South Platte River contain rainbow, brown and cutthroat trout.

HASTY (81)

John Martin Reservoir   **FREE**
State Wildlife Area
4 mi N of Hasty on CR 40. Free. All year except during waterfowl season; 14-day limit during 45-day period. Primitive camping. Toilets, cfga, no drkg wtr. Boating(l), fishing, hiking, hunting. Elev 3700 ft.

Fishing Tip: John Martin Reservoir provides an excellent variety of fishing opportunities because it is stocked with largemouth & smallmouth bass, walleye, crappie, sunfish, white bass, hybrid bass and channel catfish in addition to trout. Try the mouth of the Arkansas River and the shorelines of Rule Creek.

HAYDEN (82)

Elkhead Reservoir Area   **$8**
Yampa River State Park
About 10 mi W of Hayden on US 40, then NE on 29 Rd to reservoir. $8 for dispersed camping at the East Beach area; $8 for 25 primitive sites at Elks Campground. All year. Toilets, tbls, cfga, no drkg wtr. Fishing, boating(l).

HESPERUS (83)

Kroeger   **$10**
San Juan National Forest
11 mi N of Hesperus on US 160; 7 mi N on FR 571. $10. MD-LD; 14-day limit. 11 sites; 35-ft RV limit at 1 site. Tbls, toilets, cfga, drkg wtr, no trash service. Fishing. Elev 9000 ft; 2 acres.

HOLLY (84)

Arkansas River/Holly   **FREE**
State Wildlife Areas
1 mi N of Holly on CR 34 to Holly; 4 mi E on Hwy 50, then 1 mi S on CR 39 to Arkansas River. Free. All year; 14-day limit in 45-day period. Primitive camping; no facilities. Hunting, photography, hiking. Fishing at Arkansas River. Holly 55 acres; Arkansas River 98 acres.

HOOPER (85)

UFO Watchtower Camground   **$10**
2.5 mi N of Hooper on Hwy 17; at gift shop devoted to alien themes. $10. All year. 24 sites; 45-ft RVs. Tbls, toilets, cfga, drkg wtr.

HOT SULPHUR SPRINGS (86)

Hot Sulphur Springs   **FREE**
State Wildlife Area
3 mi W of Hot Sulphur Springs on US 40, then along Colorado River through Byers Canyon; short dirt rd leads to primitive camping area beside river. Four individual sections allow camping. Free. All year; 14-day limit. 50 sites. Tbls, toilets, cfga, drkg wtr. Along river are pullouts for overnight parking & fishing. Fishing, picnicking, big-game hunting. Elev 7600 ft; 5 acres. Part of 1,173-acre area.

Fishing tip: This section of the Colorado River is quite popular for trout fishing, partly because it is one of the few places where there is public access; through Byers Canyon is a 2-mile section where wading produces large rainbows & browns.

Travel tip: Grand County Historical Museum on E end of town is housed in a 1924 school; exhibits on skiing, Indian artifacts, pioneer women, development of area.

HUGO (87)

Hugo   **FREE**
State Wildlife Area
Kinny Lake tract: 12 mi S of Hugo on CR 109;; 2.5 mi E on CR 2G; 1 mi E on CR 2. Clingingsmith tract: 14 mi S on CR 102; 2.2 mi E on CR 2G. Free. All year; 14-day limit during 45-day period. Primitive campsites. Toilets, cfga, tbls. Hunting, fishing, picnicking, hiking. Elev 4800 ft; 3600 acres. 26 water acres. Boating on Kinney Lake (no motors); no boating in Clingingsmith area.

Travel tip: Visit Lincoln County Museum in town; open by appt (719-743-2209); restored old family home containing authentic antique pieces; costume room with clothing dating to 1800s.

IDAHO SPRINGS (88)

Echo Lake   **$12**
Arapaho National Forest
14 mi SW of Idaho Springs on SR 103. $12. 5/26-9/15; 14-day limit. 18 sites (55-ft RV limit). Tbls, toilets, cfga, drkg wtr. Fishing, hiking. Elev 10,600 ft; 4 acres.

West Chicago Creek   **$11**
Arapaho National Forest
6 mi SW of Idaho Springs on SR 103; 4 mi SW on FR 188. $11. 5/26-9/15; 14-day limit. 16 sites (45-ft RV limit). Tbls, toilets, cfga, drkg wtr. Fishing, hiking. Elev 9600 ft; 3 acres.

JEFFERSON (89)

Aspen   **$10**
Pike National Forest
2 mi W of Jefferson on CR 35; 1 mi N on CR 37; 1.7 mi NW on FR 401. $10. 5/1-9/22; 14-day limit. 12 sites (25-ft RV limit). Tbls, toilets, cfga, drkg wtr. Boating(l), fishing, hiking. Elev 9900 ft; 5 acres.

Jefferson Creek   **$10**
Pike National Forest
2 mi NW of Jefferson on CR 35; 1 mi N on CR 37; 3 mi NW on FR 401. $10. 5/1-9/22; 14-day limit. 17 sites (25-ft RV limit). Tbls, toilets, cfga, drkg wtr. Fishing, hiking. Elev 10,000 ft; 28 acres.

Fishing tip: Jefferson Creek contains brook trout and stocked rainbows. A daily fee is charged to enter the area.

Kenosha Pass   **$7**
Pike National Forest
4 mi NE of Jefferson on US 285. $7 with federal Senior Pass; others pay $14. 5/1-9/15; 14-day limit. 25 sites (24-ft RV limit). Tbls, toilets, cfga, drkg wtr. Hiking. Elev 10,000 ft; 11 acres.

Lodgepole   **$10**
Pike National Forest
2 mi NW of Jefferson on CR 35; 1 mi N on CR 37; 1.2 mi NW on FR 401. $10. 5/1-9/1; 14-day limit. 35 sites (25-ft RV limit). Tbls, toilets, cfga, drkg wtr. Hiking, fishing. Elev 9900 ft; 15 acres.

Lost Park Camp   **$7**
Pike National Forest
1.2 mi NE of Jefferson on US 285; 19.7 mi E on FR 127; 4 mi E on FR 134. $7. Elev 10,000 ft. 5/25-9/30; 14-day limit. 12 sites on 4 acres (RVs under 23 ft). Tbls, toilets, cfga, firewood, no drkg wtr, no trash service. Fishing, picnicking. Elev 10,000 ft.

Michigan Creek   **$7**
Pike National Forest
3 mi NW of Jefferson on CR 35; 2 mi NW on CR 54; 1 mi NW on FR 400. $7 during 5/1-10/1; free rest of year; 14-day limit. 13 sites (25-ft RV limit). Tbls, toilets, cfga, no drkg wtr, no trash service. Fishing, hiking. Fourmile Creek. Elev 10,000 ft; 6 acres. Campground renovated in 2001.

Tarryall Reservoir   **FREE**
State Wildlife Area
15 mi SE of Jefferson on CR 77 to reservoir. Free. All year; 14-day limit during a 45-day period. Primitive campsites. Toilets, cfga, no drkg wtr, fishing jettys. Hunting, fishing, picnicking. Elev 9000 ft; 886 acres. Water 175 acres. Boat ramp.

Fishing tip: Try the creek below the lake for brook & rainbow trout; large ones are caught there.

Karval Reservoir   **FREE**
State Wildlife Area
From Hwys 94/109 jct, S 10 mi on Hwy 109. Free. All year; 14-day limit during 45-day period. Primitive campsites. Toilets (except in winter), cfga, drkg wtr, tbls, shelters. Hunting, fishing, hiking, picnicking, boating (no motors). Elev 5100 ft; 235 acres. 22-acre lake.

Fishing tip: Karval Lake contains channel catfish, largemouth bass, wiper, hybrid bluegills, grass carp and rainbow trout.

KREMMLING (90)

Cataract Creek   **$10**
White River National Forest
Quarter mi E of Kremmling on US 40; 12.3 mi SE on SR 9; 4.7 mi SE on CR 30 (at Green Mountain Lake); 2.1 mi SW on CR 1725 near Lower Cataract Lake. Access rd not recommended for low-clearance vehicles. $10

or special $65 seasonal permit. 5/1-10/1; 14-day limit. 4 primitive undeveloped sites; 21-ft RV limit. Tbls, toilets, cfga, drkg wtr. Hiking, picnicking, fishing, boating (rld--3 mi). Elev 8600 ft; 4 acres. Stream. Nature trails. Trailhead to Gore Range Eagles Nest Primitive Area.

Cow Creek North $10
White River National Forest
Qtr mi E of Kremmling on US 40; about 14.5 mi SE on SR 9; SW on access rd to NE shore of Green Mountain Lake. $10 or special $65 seasonal pass. 5/15-11/1; 14-day limit. 32 primitive undeveloped sites. Tbls, toilets, cfga, no drkg wtr. Fishing, boating, swimming, canoeing. Part of Arapaho National Forest.

Cow Creek South $10
White River National Forest
Qtr mi E of Kremmling on US 40; about 14.5 mi SE on SR 9; SW on access rd to NE shore of Green Mountain Lake. $10 or special $65 seasonal pass. 5/15-11/1; 14-day limit. Free during early spring & late fall. 10 primitive undeveloped sites. Toilets, cfga, no drkg wtr. Fishing, boating, swimming, canoeing. Part of Arapaho National Forest.

Elliott Creek $10
White River National Forest
Qtr mi E of Kremmling on US 40; 12 mi SE on SR 9; 3 mi SW on CR 30. At Elliott Creek near NW shore of Green Mountain Lake. $10 or special $65 seasonal pass. MD-LD; 14-day limit. About 24 primitive undeveloped sites (RVs under 22 ft). Tbls, pit toilets, cfga, no drkg wtr. Picnicking, fishing, boating (rld--2 mi); swimming, waterskiing. Elev 8000 ft; 13 acres. Part of Araphao National Forest.

Gore Canyon FREE
Bureau of Land Management
Downstream from Kremmling on Colorado River, through Gore Canyon by floatboat. Access from SW only by hiking trail from the BLM Pumphouse Recreation Site 11.1 mi downstream from Kremmling. Free. May-Sept. Primitive camping on riverbank. Hiking, sightseeing, whitewater rafting. Only for expert kayakers; risky Class V rapids and Class VI waterfalls.

Pumphouse Recreation Site $10
Upper Colorado Recreation Area
Bureau of Land Management
On Upper Colorado River S of Kremmling 1 mi on SR 9; W on CR 1 (Trough Rd) 14 mi; pass Inspiration Point; right on access rd; 2 mi to site. $10. 4/15-10/1; 14-day limit. 12 sites; limited RV space (30-ft limit). Toilets, tbls, cfga, drkg wtr (from about 6/1-LD). Whitewater float trips, fishing, hiking, sightseeing. Raft launching. Primary raft launch area. Float trip map, $1 from BLM, Kremmling Resource Area Office, P.O. Box 68, Kremmling 80459. Elev 7000 ft.

Radium $6
Upper Colorado Recreation Area
Bureau of Land Management
1 mi S of Kremmling on SR 9; 14 mi W on CR 1 (Trough Rd); then 25 mi, past Inspiration Point & Pumphouse site. $6. 4/1-10/30; 14-day limit. 6 sites (30-ft RV limit). Tbls, toilets, cfga, no drkg wtr. River rafting, fishing, mountain biking.

Radium FREE
State Wildlife Area
2.5 mi S of Kremmling on Hwy 9 to CR 1; SW 12 mi along Colorado River on Trough Rd to State Bridge. Area surrounds town of Radium on both sides of river. Free. All year; 14-day limit during 45-day period. Primitive scattered sites plus developed campground E of Radium near confluence of Colorado River & Sheephorn Creek. Tbls, toilets, cfga, no drkg wtr. Fishing, boating, picnicking, hiking, hunting. Motor travel limited to established rds. 11,483 acres; quarter mile of Blacktail Creek; 1.5 mi of Colorado River.
Fishing tip: The Colorado at this point provides very good brook trout fishing as well as angling for rainbow, brown and cutthroat trout.

Rock Creek FREE
State Wildlife Area
6 mi NW of Kremmling on US 40; left for 12 mi on Hwy 134; left on Fr 206 for 2.5 mi. Free. All year; 14-day limit. Primitive undesignated camping. Toilets, cfga, no tbls, no drkg wtr. Fishing, birdwatching.

State Bridge FREE
Bureau of Land Management
S of Kremmling on Hwy 131 to bridge. Or hiking trail from BLM Pumphouse Recreation Site, 11.1 mi downstream from Kremmling (see Pumphouse entry), downstream from Radium Camp. Float Colorado River to half mi below SR 131 bridge. Free. May-Sept. Rafting, kayaking, canoeing. Relatively easy stretch of whitewater. Class II or III rapids.

LA GARITA (91)

Poso Campground $5
Rio Grande National Forest
6.3 mi NW of La Garita on CR 41G; 1.5 mi W on FR 690; 1.1 mi SW on FR 675. $5 during MD-LD; free rest of year, but no wtr or trash service; 14-day limit. 4 acres. 11 sites (RVs under 25 ft). Tbls, toilets, cfga, firewood, well drkg wtr, trash collection. Rockhounding, picnicking, stream fishing. Elev 9000 ft. On South Fork of Carnero Creek; near Cave Creek.

Stormking Campground $7
Rio Grande National Forest
10 mi NW of La Garita on CR G; 4.5 mi N on CR 41G (after 3.5 mi, becomes dirt & narrows to 1 lane). $7 during MD-LD; free LD-11/15, but no wtr or trash service; 14-day limit. 3 tent sites, 8 RV sites (RVs under 26 ft). Tbls,

toilets, cfga, firewood, well drkg wtr, trash collection. Picnicking, rockhounding, 4WD nearby on FR 786. Elev 9200 ft; 4 acres. Middle Fork of Carnero Creek.

LA JUNTA (92)

Carrizo Canyon Picnic Area FREE
Comanche National Grassland
58 mi S of LaJunta on Hwy 109; 18 mi E on Hwy 160; 7 mi S on CR 3; 3 mi E on CR P; 2 mi S on CR 6; 1.5 mi W on CR M; 1.9 mi S on FR 539. Free. All year; 14-day limit. Dispersed camping. Tbls, toilets, cfga, no drkg wtr. Fishing, hiking, rock art exploration

Vogel Canyon Picnic Area FREE
Comanche National Grassland
13 mi S of LaJunta on Hwy 109; 1 mi W on CR 802 to sign for Vogel Canyon; 2 mi S. Free. All year; 14-day limit. Dispersed camping allowed at parking area, not on hiking trails. Tbls, toilet, cfga, no drkg wtr. Hiking, horseback riding (2 hitching rails & bridle trails), birdwatching. Ancient rock art nearby.

LAKE CITY (93)

Big Blue $8
Gunnison National Forest
10 mi N of Lake City on SR 149; 9 mi NW on FR 868 (rd slippery when wet; trailers not recommended; steep rd). $8. 6/1-LD; 16-day limit. 8 tent, 3 short RV sites. Tbls, toilets, cfga, no drkg wtr. Picnicking, hiking, fishing. Big Blue Creek.
Fishing tip: Try for trout nearby below the riffles of Lake Fork of the Gunnison; use dry flies & small spinners. Closer to Lake City, larger fish are quite often caught on nymphs, spinners & flies.

Cebolla $8
Gunnison National Forest
9 mi SE of Lake City on SR 149; 8 mi NE on FR 788. $8. 5/15-9/15; 16-day limit. 5 sites (16-ft RV limit). Tbls, toilets, cfga, drkg wtr. Fishing (Cebolla Creek).

Deer Lakes $12
Gunnison National Forest
9 mi SE of Lake City on SR 149; 3 mi NE on FR 788. $12. 7/1-9/15; 16-day limit. 12 sites (30-ft RV limit). Tbls, toilets, cfga, drkg wtr. Fishing. Elev 10,900 ft; 5 acres.

Hidden Valley $8
Gunnison National Forest
9 mi S of Lake City on SR 149; 7 mi NE on FR 788. $8. About 6/1-9/15; 16-day limit. 4 tent sites. Tbls, toilets, cfga, drkg wtr. Hiking, fishing.

Mill Creek $7
Bureau of Land Management
2.5 mi S of Lake City on SR 149; 10 mi W on rd to Lake San Cristobal. $7. 6/1-10/30; free off-season, but no drkg wtr. 22 sites (35-ft

RV limit). Tbls, toilets, cfga, drkg wtr. Fishing, mountain biking, hiking, rockhounding, off-roading. Nearby ghost towns. Elev 9,500 ft.

Slumgullion   **$10**
Gunnison National Forest
9 mi SE of Lake City on SR 149; NE on FR 788. $10 during about 5/15-10/15; free 10/15-12/1. 16-day limit. 19 sites (30-ft RV limit). Tbls, toilets, cfga, drkg wtr. Hiking. Elev 11,500 ft; 7 acres.

Spruce   **$8**
Gunnison National Forest
9 mi SE of Lake City on SR 149; 8 mi NE on FR 788. $8. 6/1-9/15; 16-day limit. 9 sites (22-ft RV limit). Tbls, toilets, cfga, drkg wtr. Fishing (Cebolla Creek), hiking.

Williams Creek   **$12**
Gunnison National Forest
2 mi S of Lake City on SR 149; 6 mi SW on FR 907. $12. 5/15-10/15; 16-day limit. 23 sites; 20-ft RV limit. Tbls, toilets, cfga, drkg wtr. Fishing. Elev 9200 ft; 10 acres.

LAKE GEORGE (94)

Blue Mountain   **$10**
Pike National Forest
1.3 mi SW of Lake George on FR 245; half mi S on FR 240. $10. 4/27-9/22; 14-day limit. 21 sites (35-ft RV limit). Tbls, toilets, cfga, drkg wtr. Fishing, hiking. Elev 8200 ft.

Cove   **$10**
Pike National Forest
1 mi SW of Lake George on CR 61; 8.3 mi SW on FR 96. $10. 5/1-9/30; 14-day limit. 4 sites (16-ft RV limit). Tbls, toilets, cfga, no drkg wtr. Secluded. Elev 8400 ft.

Happy Meadows   **$10**
Pike National Forest
1.2 mi NW of Lake George on US 24; 1.2 mi N on CR 77; .7 mi NE on CR 112. $10 during 5/1-10/1; free rest of year but no wtr or trash service; 14-day limit. 10 sites (22-ft RV limit). Tbls, toilets, cfga, drkg wtr. Fishing (South Platte River). Elev 7900 ft.

Riverside   **$10**
Pike National Forest
2.5 mi SW of Lake George on FR 245. $10 during 5/1-10/1; free rest of year; 14-day limit. 19 sites (30-ft RV limit). Tbls, toilets, cfga, no drkg wtr. Fishing. Elev 8000 ft; 6 acres.

Round Mountain   **$10**
Pike National Forest
5.2 mi NW of Lake George on US 24. $10. 4/27-9/22; 14-day limit. 16 sites (35-ft RV limit). Tbls, toilets, cfga, drkg wtr. Near Elevenmile Reservoir. Elev 8500 ft.

Spillway   **$10**
Pike National Forest
9.5 mi SW of Lake George on FR 246. $10.

4/27-9/22; 14-day limit. 23 sites (25-ft RV limit). Tbls, toilets, cfga, drkg wtr. Hiking, fishing. Elev 8500 ft.

Springer Gulch   **$10**
Pike National Forest
6.5 mi S of Lake George on FR 245. $10. 5/1-10/1; 14-day limit. 15 sites (25-ft RV limit). Tbls, toilets, cfga, drkg wtr. Fishing, hiking trails, rock climbing.

Spruce Grove   **$10**
Pike National Forest
1.2 mi NW of Lake George on US 24; 12.2 mi SW on CR 77. $10. 4/10-10/30; 14-day limit. 27 sites (35-ft RV limit). Tbls, toilets, cfga, drkg wtr. Fishing (Tarryall Creek), hiking. Elev 8600 ft.

Twin Eagles Trailhead   **$7**
Pike National Forest
1.2 mi NW of Lake George on US 24; 11.2 mi SW on CR 77. $7 during 5/1-10/1; free rest of year 14-day limit. 9 sites; 22-ft RV limit. Tbls, toilets, cfga, no drkg wtr. Fishing, hiking (Twin Eagles Trail). Elev 8600 ft.

LAMAR (95)

Mike Higbee   **FREE**
State Wildlife Area
4 mi E of Lamar on Hwy 50. Free. All year; 14-day limit in 45-day period. Primitive camping; no facilities. Hunting, pond fishing, archery & rifle ranges.

Travel tip: See the Madonna of the Trail Monument in town; one of 12 such monuments sponsored by the Daughters of the American Revolution to mark the National Old Trails; unveiled in 1928; each of the 12 is in a different state; U.S. Hwy 50 through Lamar is one of the National Old Trails.

Queens   **FREE**
State Wildlife Area
5 mi W of Lamar on US 50; 16 mi n on Hwy 287; 1 mi E on co rd. Follow signs. Free. All year except 12/1 through waterfowl season on Lower (south) Queens and Nee Noshe Lakes; 11/1 through waterfowl season on Upper (north) Queen (including the channel), Nee Grande and Sweetwater (Nee So Pah) Lakes. Primitive campsites with toilets, picnic tables, cfga. 1900 acres. Waterfowl hunting, fishing for northern pike, walleye, bass, catfish. Boating(l). Waterskiing on Upper Queens and Nee Noshe Reservoirs. Elev 3800 ft.

Thurston Reservoir   **FREE**
State Wildlife Area
9 mi N of US 50 at Lamar on Hwy 196; 1 mi W on CR TT; right on CR 7 to lake. All year; 14-day limit during 45-day period. Primitive undesignated sites. Toilets, cfga, no drkg wtr. Boating(l), fishing.

LAPORTE (96)

Aspen Glen   **$11**
Roosevelt National Forest
4 mi N of Laporte on US 287; 51 mi W on Hwy 14. $11 during 5/1-9/30; $5.50 if no water available. 14-day limit. 8 sites (30-ft RV limit). Tbls, toilets, cfga, drkg wtr. Boating, fishing, hiking trails, biking. On Joe Wright Creek; 3 lakes within 2 mi -- Chambers, Lost & Barnes Meadow. Elev 8660 ft.

Big Bend   **$12**
Roosevelt National Forest
4 mi N of Laporte on US 287; 41 mi W on SR 14. $12 ($6 in winter, but no wtr). All year; 14-day limit. 6 sites (20-ft RV limit). Tbls, toilets, cfga, drkg wtr. Hiking, fishing. On Cache La Poudre River. Elev 7700 ft.

Big South   **$12**
Roosevelt National Forest
4 mi N of Laporte on US 287; 51 mi W on SR 14. $12. 5/1-9/30; 14-day limit. 4 sites (RVs under 26 ft). Tbls, toilets, cfga, no drkg wtr. Picnicking, fishing, swimming, boating (l--4 mi). Elev 8400 ft; 1 acre. Lake. Scenic. Confluence of Big South Poudre River and Joe Wright Creek.

Browns Park   **$11**
Roosevelt National Forest
4 mi N of Laporte on US 287; 55 mi W on SR 14; 21 mi N on CR 103. $11. 6/1-11/15; 14-day limit. 28 sites (RVs under 31 ft). Tbls, toilets, cfga, no drkg wtr. Hiking, picnicking, fishing. Elev 8400 ft; 10 acres. Stream. Trailhead to Rawah Wilderness. McIntyre and Link Trailhead. Beside Jinks Creek. Scenic.

Grandview   **$11**
Roosevelt National Forest
4 mi N of LaPorte on US 287; 61 mi W on SR 14; 14 mi SE on FR 156 (Long Draw Rd). $11. 6/1-9/30; 1-day limit. 9 tent sites. Tbls, toilets, cfga, drkg wtr. Picnicking, boating, fishing. Elev 10,000 ft; 4 acres. Scenic. At inlet of Long Draw Reservoir.

Fishing tip: This is one of the best places for catching trout on the Cache la Poudre River.

Long Draw   **$11**
Roosevelt National Forest
4 mi N of Laporte on US 287; 61 mi W on SR 14; 9 mi SE on FR 156 (Long Draw Rd). $11 ($5.50 in winter, but no wtr). 6/15-11/30; 14-day limit. 25 sites (RVs under 31 ft). Tbls, toilets, cfga, drkg wtr. Picnicking, hiking, fishing. Elev 10,000 ft; 6 acres. Mountains, dense forest. Half mi N of Long Draw Reservoir.

Lory State Park   **$8**
N on US 287 from Laporte; left at Bellvue exit (CR 52E); 1 mi W on CR 52E; 1 mi S on CR 23N, then S on CR 25G. $8. All year; 14-day limit. 6 backcountry tent sites on 2,000 acres. Tbls, toilets, cfga, drkg wtr at picnic areas. Interpretive programs by appt; 17 pic-

nic sites; 25 mi of hiking trails; 15 mi of biking & mountain biking trails; 20 mi of horseback trails; hunting; boating, fishing, waterskiing at Horsetooth Reservoir. Elev 7015 ft; 2479 acres. Entry fee.

Fishing tip: Horsetooth Reservoir is operated by Larimer County Parks Department; access on W side by foot only. Five covers offer bass, trout, walleye fishing.

Skyline   **FREE**
Roosevelt National Forest
4 mi N of Laporte on US 287; 55 mi W on SR 14; 4 mi N on FR 190. Free. All year; 14-day limit. Flat, dispersed camping in area of former 8-site campground; 2 acres. No facilities except cfga; no drkg wtr. Fishing. Elev 8600.

Sleeping Elephant   **$12**
Roosevelt National Forest
4 mi N of Laporte on US 287; 46 mi W on SR 14. $12 during 5/15-10/1; $6 when wtr not available; 14-day limit. 15 sites (20-ft RV limit). Tbls, toilets, cfga, drkg wtr. Fishing, hiking, mountain biking. Elev 7800 ft; 6 acres.

Tom Bennett   **$10**
Roosevelt National Forest
4 mi N of Laporte on US 287; 27 mi W on SR 14; 11 mi S on CR 131; 5 mi W on FR 145. $10. 5/15-10/31; 14-day limit. 12 sites (RVs under 21 ft). Tbls, toilets, cfga, no drkg wtr. Fishing, picnicking, hiking, mountain biking. Elev 9000 ft; 3 acres. Poudre River. Near Pin Gree Park.

Tunnel   **$6.50**
Roosevelt National Forest
4 mi N of Laporte on US 287; 59 mi W on SR 14; 21 mi N on CR 103. $6.50 in winter when wtr not available; $13 during 5/1-9/30, but $6.50 with federal Senior Pass; 14-day limit. 49 sites (40-ft RV limit). Tbls, toilets, cfga, drkg wtr. Fishing, hiking, biking. Elev 8600 ft; 18 acres.

LEADVILLE (97)

Elbert Creek   **$11**
San Isabel National Forest
3.6 mi SW of Leadville on US 24; .7 mi W on SR 300; 6.5 mi SW on CR 11. $11. 6/1-9/30; 14-day limit. 17 sites (16 ft RV limit). Tbls, toilets, cfga, drkg wtr. Fishing, hiking. Elev 10,000 ft; 12 acres. At Elbert Creek & Halfmoon Creek.

Fishing tip: Halfmoon Creek contains brook and brown trout, with rainbows stocked below the trailhead.

Camp Hale Memorial   **$12**
White River National Forest
17 mi N of Leadville on US 24; qtr mi E on FR 729; 1 mi S on FR 716. $11 during MD-LD. 10-day limit. 21 sites (60-ft RV limit). Tbls, toilets,cfga, drkg wtr. On East Fork of Eagle River. Fishing, mountain biking, hiking, rock climbing.

Halfmoon   **$11**
San Isabel National Forest
3.6 mi SW of Leadville on US 24; .7 mi W on SR 300; 5.5 mi SW on FR 11; near Elbert Creek. $11. 5/15-9/30; 14 day limit. 22 sites (16-ft RV limit). Tbls, toilets, cfga, drkg wtr. Fishing, hiking. Elev 9800 ft; 14 acres.

Half Moon   **FREE**
Dispersed Campsite
White River National Forest
5 mi S of Leadville on US 24; right on FR 707 (Tigiwon Rd) for 8.5 mi. Free. 6/1-9/15; 14-day limit. 7 primitive undesignated sites; no facilities, no drkg wtr. Picnicking, hiking, fishing. Two trailheads for Holy Cross Wilderness Area.

Fishing tip: Halfmoon Creek along FR 110 provides excellent brook trout fishing; use spinners, worms, flies.

Travel tip: In Leadville, take self-guided tour of Heritage Museum & Gallery on E 9th St; mining & cultural artifacts from Victorian Leadville; dioramas of mining history.

Tabor   **$12**
San Isabel National Forest
2 mi W of Leadville on CR 37; 2.5 mi W on CR 4; 3 mi W on CR 9C. $12. 5/15-9/15; 14-day limit. 44 RV sites (no tents); 37-ft RV limit. Tbls, flush toilets, cfga, drkg wtr, dump. Hiking, fishing.

Tigiwon   **$10**
White River National Forest
5 mi S of Leadville on US 24; right on FR 707 (Tigiwon Rd) 6 mi (rough rd, high-clearance vehicles needed). $10 during LD-MD; free rest of year; 10-day limit. 9 sites; 30-ft RV limit, but RV use discouraged. Also old stone lodge available to groups of up to 150 by free reservations. Tbls, toilets, cfga, no drkg wtr. Picnicking, hiking, no fishing. Elev 9900 ft.

Fishing tip: No creeks nearby, but just W of Leadville on 6th St, then NW on Turquoise Lake Rd is Turquoise Lake, where good fishing opportunities await for brown, rainbow & cutthroat trout & kokanee salmon.

Travel tip: Visit Leadville National Fish Hatchery 4 mi W of Leadville on Hwy 24, then 2 mi S on Hwy 300; tours of the hatchery, built 1889; cutthroat & rainbow trout are reared. Free.

LOVELAND (99)

Boyd Lake State Park   **$9**
1 mi E of Loveland; SR 34 W of I-25; N on Madison Ave. $9 for seniors with state park Aspen Leaf pass on Sun-Thurs (full price on Fri-Sat; others pay full price of $18. All year. 148 basic sites; 32-ft RV limit. 90 picnic sites. Tbls, toilets, cfga, drkg wtr, dump, showers. Swimming, snack bar, boating(ldr), waterskiing, sailboarding(r), fishing, hiking trail, biking trails, hunting, winter sports. 197 acres. Entry fee.

Fishing tip: Try underwater ridges and inlets for bass, crappie, walleye and rainbow trout.

Carter Lake   **$12**
Larimer County Campground
5 mi W of Loveland on US 34; 2 mi S on CR 29; qtr mi W on CR 18E. $12 base; $17 with elec, plus $6 daily ($75 annual) park use fee. All year; 14-day limit. 190 sites; 35-ft RV limit. Tbls, flush toilets, cfga, drkg wtr, dump, beach. Swimming, boating (drl), fishing.

Flatiron Reservoir   **$12**
Larimer County Campground
5 mi W of Loveland on US 34; 2 mi S on CR 29; W on CR 18E. $12 plus $6 daily ($75 annual) park use fee. All year; 14-day limit. 50 sites; 30-ft RV limit. Tbls, toilets, cfga, drkg wtr. Hiking, fishing, picnicking. Elev 5,500 ft.

Pinewood Lake   **$12**
Larimer County Campground
5 mi W of Loveland on US 34; 2 mi S on CR 29; W on CR 18E. $12 plus $6 daily ($75 annual) park use fee. All year; 14-day limit. 25 sites; 30-ft RV limit. Tbls, toilets, cfga, drkg wtr. Swimming, boating(l), fishing, hiking, picnicking. Elev 6200 ft. Reduced facilities in winter.

MANASSA (100)

Sego Springs   **FREE**
State Wildlife Area
3 mi E of Manassa on Hwy 142; half mi N on access rd. Free. 7/15-2/15; 14-day limit in 45-day period. Primitive camping. No facilities. Fishing. No fires.

Travel tip: If you're in this area during late July, consider attending the Mormon Pioneer Days Celebration (held the weekend closest to July 24), featuring rodeos, parades, carnival.

MANCOS (101)

Mancos State Park   **$12**
Qtr mi N of Mancos on Hwy 184; 4 mi E on CR 42 (FR 561), then N to park. $12. All year. 34 basic sites; 45-ft RV limit. Tbls, toilets, cfga, drkg wtr, dump. Interpretive programs, boating(l), sailboarding, fishing, hiking trails, biking trails, bridle trails, winter sports. Elev 7800 ft; 334 acres. Entry fee.

Target Tree   **$12**
San Juan National Forest
7 mi E of Mancos on US 160. $12. MD-9/30; 14-day limit. 25 sites (45-ft RV limit). Tbls, toilets, cfga, drkg wtr. Fishing, picnicking, interpretive trail. Elev 7800 ft. Indians once used the site's trees for for target practice, and many are still scarred from arrows and bullets.

MASONVILLE (102)

Buckhorn Canyon   **FREE**
Roosevelt National Forest
4 mi N of Masonville on US 287; 15 mi W on SR 14; 10 mi S on CR 27. Free. 5/1-10/31; 14-day limit. 17 acres. 10 sites (RVs under

32 ft). Individual sites along rd. Tbls, toilets, cfga, no drkg wtr. Fishing, picnicking. Elev 8300 ft.

MAYBELL (103)

Browns Park   FREE
State Wildlife Area
Quarter mi W of Maybell on US 40 from Maybell; NW on CR 318 to CR 10; W to Beaver Creek Unit. To reach Cold Spring Mountain Unit, continue on CR 318 to CR 110; W to access rd; S to property. Free. All year; 14-day limit during 45-day period. Primitive campsites. No facilities. Big-game hunting, fishing, picnicking. Elev 8700 ft. 2 mi of Beaver Creek.

Bull Canyon, Willow Creek,   FREE
Skull Creek Wilderness Study Areas
Bureau of Land Management
W of Maybell on US 40; N on co rds. Areas N of highway, S of Dinosaur National Monument. Free. All year; 14-day limit. Accessible earlier and later in spring & fall than higher-elevation areas. Primitive backcountry camping; no facilities. Scenic viewing, hiking, backpacking, viewing wildlife, photography, horseback riding. 39,000 acres in the three areas. Colorful canyons, sandstone cliffs, rock outcrops. Archaeological sites (protected by law). Bull Canyon WSA can be viewed from Dinosaur Monument's Plug Hat picnic area.

Calloway Recreation Site   FREE
Bureau of Land Management
NW on SR 318 for 45 mi to CR 10N; right for about 15 mi; left (W) on CR 72. Follow signs to site. Free. All year; 14-day limit. 3 primitive RV sites. Toilet, cfga, no drkg wtr, no tbls. Hiking, hunting, sightseeing, picnicking.

Cold Spring Mountain Area   FREE
State Wildlife Area
NW of Maybell in NW corner of state, off SR 318 to CR 10N and CR 72. Lower portion of mountain accessible in Browns Park. Follow signs to camping areas. Free. All year; 14-day limit. Primitive camping at 5 camp areas. Pit toilets; 3 areas have fire rings; no drkg wtr. Hunting, hiking, backpacking, photography, fishing in Beaver Creek. Top of mountain wet until mid-June, restricting vehicle use.

Crook Campground   FREE
Browns Park
National Wildlife Refuge
50 mi NW of Maybell on SR 318, past access rd to Lodore Hall Nat'll Historic Site, left on gravel tour rd 1 mi. Free. All yr; 14-day limit during 45-day period. 20 sites for tents of self-contained RVs. No facilities or drkg wtr. Wtr nearby at Subheadquarters and refuge headqtrs. Hiking, hunting, fishing, sightseeing. Swing bridge across Green River. Bridge under capacity for RVs; OK for cars & light trucks.

Cross Mountain   FREE
Wilderness Study Area
Bureau of Land Management
W of Maybell on US 40, through Elk Springs, then NW on Deerlodge Park Rd to parking area at Yampa River at SE end of Dinosaur National Monument. Hike in to canyon rim or backcountry. Free. All year; 14-day limit. Primitive hike-in backcountry camping. No facilities. Hiking, backpacking, photography, hunting, fishing, scenic viewing. Numerous side canyons allow for exploration and boulder scrambling. Yampa River kayaking for experts. Spectacular view of canyon from 1000-ft height at rim. Big horn sheep, mountain lion, deer, elk, golden eagle, bald eagle. S end of mountain excellent for day hikes; N end good for backpacking & camping.

Travel tip: Take a comparatively easy rafting trip on the Yampa River from Deerlodge Park at E end of Dinosaur National Monument; raft through the Yampa River Canyon with its 1,000-foot walls.

Deerlodge Campground $8
Dinosaur National Monument
18 mi SW of Maybell on US 40; 14 mi W to campground. $8 plus $10 entry fee; free in winter, but no wtr. All year; 14-day limit. Exact dates depend on snow conditions. 8 primitive tent sites. Tbls, toilets, cfga, no drkg wtr. Boating (earth launch-- whitewater running craft only; rafting permit required); fishing, picnicking, no swimming (ice-cold water and unexpected currents). Elev 5000 ft; 2 acres. Ranger station. Launching area for Yampa River trips. Popular put-in spot for raft trips down the Yampa River, through the scenic Yampa River Canyon.

Diamond Breaks   FREE
Wilderness Study Area
Bureau of Land Management
NW of Maybell on SR 318 and W of Browns Park National Wildlife Refuge. Free. All year; 14-day limit. Primitive camping; no facilities. Photography, nature study, viewing wildlife, day hikes, backpacking. Scenic mountainous area. Solitude. Adjacent to north end of Dinosaur National Monument. Spectacular views into Canyon of Lodore. 36,000 acres.

Douglas Mountain   FREE
Bureau of Land Management
NW of Maybell on SR 318 to CR 12 and CR 10 (through Greystone) and CR 116 (Douglas Mountain Blvd dirt, poorly maintained). Free. All year; 14-day limit. Primitive camping. No facilities. Deer & elk hunting, sightseeing, hiking, backpacking, horseback riding. Good views to north from Douglas Mountain Blvd. High-clearance vehicles recommended. Scenic: pine forests, red sandstone outcrops.

East Cross Mountain $8
State Parks River Access Site
Bureau of Land Management
13.6 mi W of Maybell on US 40; 2.4 mi N on CR 85; turn on BLM Rd 1551 for about 1.5 mi to fork, then bear left to Yampa River. $8.

All year; 14-day limit. 4 primitive sites. Toilets, tbls, cfga, no drkg wtr. Boating(l), fishing.

Gates of Lodore $8
Dinosaur National Monument
41 mi NW of Maybell on SR 318; 4 mi SW on unpaved rds. $8 per site plus $10 entry fee. 5/15-10/15; 15-day limit. Free camping in winter, but no wtr. 17 sites (30-ft RV limit). Tbls, toilets, cfga, wtr faucets. Boating (concrete launch -- whitewater running craft only; special rafting permit required); fishing; picnicking; no swimming (cold water & dangerous currents). Elev 5600 ft; 6 acres. River. N portal to Lodore Canyon. Pets on leash. Spectacular scenery where the Green River created the 2,300-foot-deep Lodore Canyon. River runs wild.

Irish Canyon   FREE
Bureau of Land Management
About 40 mi NW of Maybell on SR 318, then 4 mi N through Irish Canyon on Moffat County Rd 10N (gravel rd) for 8 mi. 4/15-11/30; 14-day limit. 6 sites (30-ft RV limit). Tbls, cfga, toilet. No drkg wtr, no trash service. Picnicking, wildlife viewing, hunting, hiking, sightseeing. 14,400 acres.

Travel tip: Interpretive exhibit, Indian petroglyphs near canyon entrance via short trail. Ponds, wild horse herd at Sand Wash Basin. Vermillion Badlands. Very scenic route with steep, colorful canyon walls.

Little Snake   FREE
State Wildlife Area
20 mi N of Maybell on CR 19. Free. Camping period from 3 days before big game hunting seasons until 3 days after in self-contained RVs. Primitive camping, undesignated sites. No facilities, no drkg wtr. Big-game hunting camp on 4860 acres.

Maybell Bridge $8
State Parks River Access Site
Bureau of Land Management
3 mi E of Maybell on US 40; just E of Yampa River. $8. All year; 14-day limit. 6 primitive sites. Toilets, cfga, no drkg wtr. Boating(l), fishing.

Rocky Reservoir   FREE
Recreation Site
Bureau of Land Management
NW of Maybell on SR 318 about 45 mi; right on SR 10N for about 15 mi; left (W) on CR 72; follow signs. Free. All year; 14-day limit. 3 primitive RV sites. Toilet, tbl, fire rings, no drkg wtr, no trash service. Hunting, hiking, sightseeing, picnicking.

Sand Wash Basin   FREE
Bureau of Land Management
NW of Maybell, accessible from SR 318. Dirt rds hazardous when wet. Free. All year; 14-day limit. Prim. camping, undesignated sites. No facilities. Hunting, rockhounding, trail bike riding.

Travel tip: Fossils and petrified wood can

be collected (fossil permit to dig for fossils; 25-pound daily limit of petrified wood). Wild horses can be viewed.

Swinging Bridge Camp   FREE
Browns Park
National Wildlife Refuge
58 mi NW of Maybell on SR 318, past access to Lodore Hall National Historic Site and past access rd to Crook campground, then left on gravel tour 2 mi. Free. All year. 15 sites for tents or self-contained RVs. Cfga, shade trees; no drkg wtr or other facilities. Wtr nearby at Subheadquarters and refuge headquarters. Hiking, hunting, fishing, sightseeing. Next to swinging bridge across Green River. Bridge under capacity for RVs, okay for cars and trucks. Boating on Butch Cassidy pond (no motors) & Green River.

West Cold Spring   FREE
Wilderness Study Area
Bureau of Land Management
NW of Maybell on SR 318 to N side of Browns Park. Free. All year; 14-day limit. Primitive undesignated camping. No facilities. Hunting, backpacking, scenic viewing, fishing, trail hiking. Beaver Creek Canyon. 17,000 acres.

MEEKER (104)

Bel Aire Unit   FREE
Oak Ridge
State Wildlife Area
2 mi E of Meeker on Hwy 13; 18 mi E on CR 8; 1.5 mi S on CR 17 (S of Buford), then W on dirt rd. Free. 7/15-10/30; 14-day limit during 45-day period. Primitive undesignated sites. Tbls, toilets, cfga, drkg wtr. Hunting, fishing, picnicking.

Fishing tip: Excellent fishing for trout & whitefish in the South Fork of the White River; many deep pools with large rainbows & cutthroat; 6 mi of river restricted to artificial lures. Also, very good trout fishing (rainbow & some cutthroat) all year at Avery Lake.

Travel tip: Visit Spring Cave, Hwy 13 E two mi; right on CR 8 for 18 mi; right on South Fork Rd to South Fork Campground in White River National Forest; hike half mi to cave; second largest cave in Colorado; many passages unexplored; one section, called Thunder Road, has one of the largest underground streams in America.

East Marvine $6.50
White River National Forest
2 mi E of Meeker on SR 13; 29 mi E on CR 8; 6.5 mi SE on FR 12 (Marvine Creek Rd). $6.50 with federal Senior Pass; others pay $13. MD-11/15; 14-day limit (fees may be reduced if opening is extended and services reduced; horse sites $15. 7 sites; 50-ft RV limit. Tbls, toilets, cfga, drkg wtr, corrals ($5). Fishing, hiking, horseback riding. Elev 8200 ft. Overflow camping on left side of rd.

Hill Creek   FREE
White River National Forest
2 mi E of Meeker on SR 13; 18 mi E on CR 8; 8 mi SE on CR 10 (South Fork Rd); half mi NE on FR 2328 (access rd steep, so 4WD recommended). Free. MD-11/1; 14-day limit. 10 undeveloped sites. Toilets, cfga, hitching posts, no drkg wtr. Hiking, picnicking, fishing, horseback riding. Elev 8000 ft; 3 acres. Stream. Scenic. Next to Flattops Wilderness. Elev 8000 ft.

Himes Peak $6.50
White River National Forest
2 mi E of Meeker on SR 13; 41 mi E on CR 8; 5 mi SE on FR 205 (Trappers Lake Rd). $6.50 with federal Senior Pass; others pay $13. Fees may be less if services are reduced, and in early 2007, water system was not operating. MD-11/15; 14-day limit. 11 sites (36-ft RV limit). Tbls, toilets, cfga, drkg wtr. Hiking, fishing, horseback riding, hiking. Elev 9500 ft.

Fishing tip: Fishing access to North Fork of White River, Big Fish Creek, Big Fish Lake, Boulder Lake, Doris Lake, Robinson Lake, Gwendylin Lake, McBride Lake.

Jensen   FREE
State Wildlife Area
9 mi NE of Meeker on Hwy 13; access via CR 30 at top of Nine-mile Gap. Free. 7/15-12/1; 14-day limit during 45-day period. Primitive camping, only in 3 designated undeveloped areas; no facilities, no drkg wtr. Big-game hunting on 5955 acres.

Fishing tip: See entry for Bel Aire Unit of Oak Ridge SWA.

Travel tip: Hike half mi from nearby South Fork Campground to Spring Cave, the state's second largest cave; underground stream thought to be one of the largest of its kind in the U.S. For experienced spelunkers only!

Marvine $6.50
White River National Forest
2 mi E of Meeker on SR 13; 29 mi E on CR 8; 4.5 mi SE on FR 12 (Marvine Creek Rd). $6/50 with federal Senior Pass; others pay $13. MD-11/15; 14-day limit. 24 sites (60-ft RV limit); horse camping okay at 3 sites, $15 with corrals. Tbls, toilets, cfga, drkg wtr. Fishing, hiking, horseback riding. Marvine Creek & Marvine Lakes; trailhead to lakes. Elev 8100 ft; 5 acres.

Oak Ridge   FREE
State Wildlife Area
2 mi N of Meeker on Hwy 13 to CR 8; E 25 mi. Camping at Lake Avery and at area's north and south access points. On White River at 260-acre Lake Avery. Also sites at end of a short access rd from SR 132 about 2 mi E of the lake and from CR 6 on the N side. Free. 7/16-10/30; 14-day limit during 45-day period. 50 primitive lakeside campsites (camp only in designated areas). Toilets, tbls, cfga, drkg wtr. Hunting, hiking, picnicking, lake trout fishing, horseback riding. Elev 6200 ft; 11,765 acres. Lake Avery Wildlife

Area. White River. Eagles, rattlesnakes, marmots, porcupine. Boat ramp at Lake Avery. Horse corrals & loading ramps.

Fishing tip: Try whitefish & trout in Lake Avery during early spring or summer.

South Fork $6.50
White River National Forest
2 mi E of Meeker on SR 13; 23 mi E on CR 8; 9.5 mi S on CR 10; half mi SE on FR 200. $6.50 with federal Senior Pass; others pay $13. About 5/15-11/15; 14-day limit. 18 sites (36-ft RV limit). Tbls, toilets, cfga, drkg wtr. Fishing, swimming, hiking, picnicking. Elev 8000 ft; 6 acres. Season may be extended with reduced services.

MESA (105)

Jumbo $10
Grand Mesa National Forest
13 mi S of Mesa on SR 64; S on FR 252. $10 with federal Senior Pass; others pay $20. MD-LD; 14-day limit. 26 sites (45-ft RV limit). Tbls, toilets, cfga, drkg wtr. Boating(l), fishing, hiking, bike trails. Mesa Lakes nearby. Elev 9800 ft; 10 acres.

Spruce Grove $10
Grand Mesa National Forest
15 mi S of Mesa on SR 65. $10. 6/15-10/1; free rest of year, but no drkg wtr; 30-day limit; 16 sites (22-ft RV limit). Tbls, toilets, cfga, drkg wtr. Hiking, picnicking, fishing. Elev 10,000 ft.

MONTE VISTA (106)

Alamosa   FREE
Rio Grande National Forest
12 mi S of Monte Vista on SR 15; 17.4 mi W on FR 250 (Alamosa-Conejos River Rd). Free. MD-LD; 14-day limit. 10 sites (RVs under 26 ft). 3 acres. Tbls, toilets, cfga, firewood, drkg wtr, no trash collection. Picnicking, horseback riding, no fishing in the Alamosa River. Elev 8600 ft.

Comstock   FREE
Rio Grande National Forest
2 mi S of Monte Vista on SR 15; 16.5 mi SW on FR 265 (Rock Creek Rd); very rough road. Free. MD-LD; 14-day limit. 8 sites (RVs under 31 ft). 3 acres. Tbls, toilets, cfga, firewood, no drkg wtr, no trash collection. Stream fishing, picnicking, horseback riding. Elev 9600 ft.

Hot Creek   FREE
State Wildlife Area
20 mi S of Monte Vista on Hwy 15; where highway turns E, turn right on gravel rd marked for Hot Creek and La Jara Reservoir; 3 mi to wildlife area. Free. 4/30-12/1; 14-day limit in 45-day period. No snowmobiles. Primitive unrestricted camping. Toilets at La Jara Reservoir. Hunting, no fishing. 3,494 acres; elev 9000 ft. Solitude. Desert bighorn sheep.

Rio Grande   **FREE**
State Wildlife Area
3 mi E of Monte Vista on Sherman Ave. Free. 7/15-2/15; 14-day limit. Primitive camping only in areas with toilets. No fires. Hiking, fishing, hunting.

Fishing tip: Four miles of Rio Grande River, including numerous oxbows, winds through the wildlife preserve, and the oxbows are excellent places to catch largemouth bass, channel catfish and northern pike.

Rock Creek   **FREE**
Rio Grande National Forest
2 mi S of Monte Vista on SR 15; 13.5 mi SW on FR 265 (Rock Creek Rd; gravel to within 1 mi of campground). Free. MD-LD; 14-day limit. 13 sites (RVs under 31 ft). 6 acres on Rock Creek. Tbls, toilets, cfga, drkg wtr, no trash collection. Fishing, picnicking, horseback riding. Elev 9400 ft.

Stunner Campground   **FREE**
Rio Grande National Forest
12 mi S of Monte Vista on SR 15; 33.7 mi W on FR 250; quarter mi SW on FR 380. (Approx 14 mi W of Alamosa Campground). On Alamosa River. Free. MD-LD; 14-day limit. 10 sites (RVs under 26 ft). 3 acres. Tbls, toilets, cfga, firewood, drkg wtr, no trash collection. Picnicking, horseback riding, stream fishing. Elev 9800 ft.

Terrace Reservoir   **FREE**
State Wildlife Area
12 mi S of Monte Vista on Hwy 15; 9 mi W on FR 250. Free. All year; 14-day limit during 45-day period. Primitive camping; no facilities. Fishing. Elev 8525 acres.

MONTROSE (107)

Big Cimarrona   **$8**
Uncompahgre National Forest
20 mi E of Montrose on US 50; 20 mi S on CR 69. At Cimarron River. $8 during MD-LD; free LD-11/15. 16-day limit. 10 sites (RVs under 20 ft). 2 acres. Tbls, toilets, cfga, no drkg wtr. Fishing, picnicking. Elev 8600 ft. Closed in 2006; status uncertain for 2007.

Travel tip: Montrose County Historical Museum, in old railroad depot, has exhibits on area's settlement; homesteader cabin & country store.

Beaver Lake   **$10**
Uncompahgre National Forest
20 mi E of Montrose on US 50; 20.5 mi S on FR 858 (Big Cimarron Rd). $10. MD-10/1; 14-day limit. 11 sites; 20-ft RV limit. Tbls, toilets, cfga, drkg wtr (no wtr after 9/15). Fishing, hiking.

Billy Creek   **FREE**
State Wildlife Area
16 mi SE from Montrose on Hwy 550 to Billy Creek, then half mi E on CR 2. Three other tracts with different entrances. Free. All year; 14-day limit during 45-day period. Primitive camping. No facilities. Big-game hunting, picnicking, river fishing. Elev 6000-8000 ft; 5591 acres.

Travel tip: On the way from Montrose, stop at the Ute Indian Museum, just off Hwy 550; exhibits about the state's Ute Indians, especially Chief Ouray; artifacts. Fee.

Cimarron Creek   **$12**
Curecanti National Recreation Area
20 mi E of Montrose on US 50. $12. Apr-Dec; 14-day limit. 21 sites (no RV size limit). Individual sites indicated by tbls & firepits. Drkg wtr, dump, flush toilets, store. Intermittent evening campfire programs.

East Portal   **$12**
Curecanti National Recreation Area
8 mi E of Montrose on US 50; 7 mi on SR 347; 6 mi on East Portal access rd. (Buses, trailers and motorhomes larger than 22 feet are prohibited on the last 6 mi. This portion is steep, narrow, hazardous descent into the Black Canyon of the Gunnison.) $12. 4/15-11/15; 14-day limit. Campground may be closed by snow or freezing temperatures. 15 shaded sites. Toilets, cfga, tbls, drkg wtr. During cold weather, drkg wtr available at Elk Creek picnic area. Near historic Gunnison River Diversion Tunnel.

Iron Spring   **FREE**
Uncompahgre National Forest
24 mi SW of Montrose on SR 90. MD-11/15;16-day limit. Free. 10 sites (RVs under 22 ft). 4 acres. Tbls, toilets, cfga, no drkg wtr. Picnicking. Elev 9500 ft. Picnicking, hiking.

Silver Jack   **$7**
Uncompahgre National Forest
10 mi E of Montrose on US 50; 20 mi S on FR 858 (Big Cimarron Rd). $7 with federal Senior Pass; others pay $14. MD-LD; 16-day limit. 60 sites; 30-ft RV limit. Tbls, toilets, cfga, drkg wtr. Fishing, boating (no mtrs), hiking.

South Rim   **$10**
Black Canyon of
Gunnison National Monument
6 mi E of Montrose on US 50; 5 mi N on Hwy 37. $10 ($15 with elec). 4/15-10/15; 14-day limit. 88 sites; 22-ft RV limit. Tbls, toilets, cfga, drkg wtr, visitor center. Hiking, sightseeing, rafting, fishing.

Travel tip: Cimarron Visitor Center nearby for Curecanti National Recreation Area; railroad exhibits including narrow-gauge engine, freight car, caboose, coal tender; livestock corrals and loading pens, stock cars with historical significance; picnicking.

NATHROP (109)

Cascade   **$6.50**
San Isabel National Forest
Half mi S of Nathrop on US 285; 5.5 mi W on CR 162; 3.2 mi W on FR 212; along Chalk Creek near Chalk Cliffs. $6.50 with federal Senior Pass; others pay $13. MD-9/1; 7-day limit. 21 sites (35-ft RV limit). Tbls, flush & pit toilets, cfga, drkg wtr. Fishing, hiking trails, swimming, horseback riding. Elev 9700 ft; 8 acres.

Fishing tip: Chalk Creek contains brook, brown and stocked rainbow trout. Good pool fishing in this cobble-bottom stream.

Chalk Lake   **$6.50**
San Isabel National Forest
Half mi S of Nathrop on US 285; 5.5 mi W on CR 162; 3 mi SW on FR 212; along Chalk Creek. $6.50 with federal Senior Pass; others pay $13. MD-9/1; lower fees charged during 5/17-5/23 & 9/2-10/28; 7-day limit. 20 sites (50-ft RV limit). Tbls, toilets, cfga, drkg wtr. Fishing, hiking, swimming, horseback riding. Elev 8700 ft; 4 acres. 2-day minimum stay on weekends; 3-day minimum on holiday weekends.

Iron City   **$10.50**
San Isabel National Forest
Half mi S of Nathrop on US 285; 15 mi W on CR 162; half mi NE on FR 212. $10.50 with federal Senior Pass; others pay $21. 6/1-9/15; 7-day limit. 15 sites (25-ft RV limit). Tbls, toilets, cfga, drkg wtr. Fishing, hiking. Elev 9900 ft; 21 acres.

Mt. Princeton   **$6.50**
San Isabel National Forest
Half mi S of Nathrop on US 285; 5.5 mi W on CR 162; 2.5 mi W on FR 212; at Chalk Creek. $6.50 with federal Senior Pass; others pay $13. MD-9/1; 7-day limit. 19 sites (45-ft RV limit). Tbls, toilets, cfga, drkg wtr. Hiking, fishing, horseback riding, swimming. Elev 8900 ft.

NATURITA (110)

Dry Creek Basin   **FREE**
State Wildlife Area
17 mi SE of Naturita on Hwy 141. Free. All year; 14-day limit during 45-day period. Restricted primitive camping. No facilities; 7,833 acres plus 17,000 BLM property & 1,280 acres of leased state land. Hunting, picnicking, fishing in 11 stocked ponds. Elev 7000-8000 ft.

NEDERLAND (111)

Backcountry Campsites   **$8**
Golden Gate Canyon State Park
S of Nederland on SR 119, then E on Gap Rd; hike into backcountry $8 for 4 3-sided shelters or 19 hike-in tent sites (no facilities, no fires). All year; 14-day limit. Obtain permits at visitor center. Entry fee.

Rainbow Lakes   **$8**
Roosevelt National Forest
6.5 mi N of Nederland on SR 72; 5 mi W on CR 116. Extremely rough rd leading to site. $8 during 6/15-10/15; 7-day limit; free rest of year. 16 sites (20-ft RV limit). Toilets, tbls, cfga, no drkg wtr, no trash service. Fishing, picnicking, hiking, cross-country skiing. Elev 10,000 ft; 10 acres.

NEW CASTLE (112)

Garfield Creek   **FREE**
State Wildlife Area

2 mi SW of New Castle on CR 312; S along Garfield Creek. Free. Camping only during elk and deer seasons, 3 days before season & 3 days after. Primitive designated campsites. Toilets, cfga. 4,804 acres. Hunting.

Fishing tip: Nearby Elk Creek (just NW of New Castle) offers excellent fishing for small rainbow trout; the numbers make up for their size; easy river access on FR 603.

Travel tip: Try a whitewater rafting trip on the South Canyon section of the Colorado River between New Castle & Glenwood Springs.

Meadow Lake   **$6.50**
White River National Forest

9 mi NW of New Castle on CR 245; 20.5 mi N on FR 244; 3.5 mi E on FR 601; 3 mi S on FR 823. $6.50 with federal Senior Pass. 7/1-10/24; 14-day limit. 10 sites (16-ft RV limit). Tbls, toilets, cfga, drkg wtr, fishing pier. Fishing, hiking, mountain biking, boating(l), fishing pier. Elev 9600 ft. Operated by Rocky Mountain Recreation.

NORWOOD (113)

Miramonte Reservoir   **FREE**
State Wildlife Area

1 mi E on Hwy 145 (Lone Cone Rd), then 17 mi S on FR 610 (Dolores-Norwood Rd); at NW base of Lone Coune Mountain. Access limited to snowmobiles after Dec. 1. Free. All year; 14-day limit within 45-day period. 50 RV sites; 510 acres. Camp only in designated areas. Tbls, cfga, toilets, dump, drkg wtr, shelter. Fishing, hiking, picnicking, firewood, waterfowl hunting, boating (l).

Fishing tip: Miramonte at times produces quite good catches of rainbow trout. Avoid the nearby San Miguel River below Norwood; fishing is poor.

OHIO CITY (114)

Comanche Campground   **FREE**
Gunnison National Forest

From northbound SR 76 at Ohio City, left on FR 771.1 (Gold Creek Rd) for 2.5 mi. Free. 5/15-9/15; 16-day limit. 4 small sites. Tbls, toilets, cfga, no drkg wtr, no services. Hiking, fishing.

Gold Creek   **FREE**
Gunnison National Forest

8 mi NE of Ohio City on FR 771. Free. 5/15-9/15; 16-day limit. 6 small sites. Tbls, toilets, cfga, no drkg wtr, no services. Mountain climbing, picnicking, hiking, fishing. Elev 10,000 ft; 2 acres. Scenic. Trails to high country lakes begin across access rd.

ORDWAY (115)

Lake Henry   **FREE**
State Wildlife Area

1 mi N of Ordway on CR 20. Free. All year; 14-day limit in 45-day period. Scattered shoreline sites. No facilities, no drkg wtr. Fishing, boating(l), hunting.

Meredith Reservoir   **FREE**
State Wildlife Area

3 mi E of Ordway on CR G; 1 mi S on CR 21. Free. All year except 11/1 through migratory waterfowl season; 14-day limit during 45-day period. Primitive campsites. Toilets, tbls, cfga. Fishing, hiking, picnicking, waterfowl hunting. Elev 4254 ft; 3220 acres of water. Boat ramp.

Fishing tip: Reservoir contains walleye, channel catfish, wipers, tiger muskies.

Olney Springs   **FREE**
State Wildlife Area

5 mi W of Ordway on Hwy 96; 1 mi N of Olney Springs on CR 7. All year; 14-day limit during 45-day period. Primitive undesignated sites; no facilities, no drkg wtr. Fishing, canoeing, hiking.

Ordway Reservoir   **FREE**
State Wildlife Area

2 mi N of Ordway; W side of Hwy 71. Free. All year; 14-day limit during 45-day period. Primitive campsites. Toilets, tbls, cfga. Fishing, hiking, picnicking. Elev 4300 ft; 12-acre lake.

Fishing tip: Reservoir contains rainbow trout, catfish, bass, perch.

Travel tip: Stop at Korinek Trout Farm, 3 mi W of town on Hwy 96, then 5 mi S on Lane 15; Private, but visitors welcome daily 8-5; see trout being reared. Free.

PAGOSA SPRINGS (116)

Blanco River   **$12**
San Juan National Forest

13.1 mi SE of Pagosa Springs on US 84; 1.8 mi E on FR 656. $12 for RVs, $10 tents. MD-LD; 14-day limit. 6 sites (RVs under 35 ft). Tbls, toilets, cfga, drkg wtr. Community picnic areas with ball diamond, horseshoe pits and volleyball court. Softball, volleyball, horseshoes, picnicking, fishing, hiking. Elev 7200 ft; 8 acres.

Fishing tip: Blanco River is heavily populated with trout but is only lightly fished.

Bridge   **$12**
San Juan National Forest

2.5 mi W of Pagosa Springs on US 160; 17 mi N on FR 631 (Piedra Rd); at Williams Creek. $12 for RVs, $10 tents. 5/15-10/31; 30-day limit. 19 sites; 50-ft RV limit. Tbls, toilets, cfga, drkg wtr. Fishing.

Cimarrona   **$12**
San Juan National Forest

2.5 mi W of Pagosa Springs on US 160; 20 mi N on FR 631 (Piedra Rd); 3 mi N on FR 640; at Cimarrona Creek. $12 for RVs, $10 tents. MD-LD; 30-day limit. 21 sites; 35-ft RV limit. Tbls, toilets, cfga, drkg wtr. Fishing, hiking, horseback riding. 1 mi to pack animal ramp & corral.

East Fork   **$12**
San Juan National Forest

10 mi E of Pagosa Springs on US 160; left for 0.7 mi on FR 667 (East Fork Rd); on East Fork of San Juan River. $12 for RVs, $10 tents. MD-9/30; 30-day limit. 26 sites; 35-ft RV limit. Tbls, toilets, cfga, drkg wtr. Fishing, hiking; OHV use nearby. Elev 7600 ft; 20 acres.

Middle Fork Hunter Camp   **FREE**
San Juan National Forest

2 mi W of Pagosa Springs on US 160; 15.5 mi NW on CR 631; 5 mi NE on FR 636. Free. 5/15-11/25; 14-day limit. 10 tent sites. Tbls, toilets, cfga, no drkg wtr. Hunting, hiking, picnicking. 5 acres.

Fishing tip: Detour westward on US 160 to jct of Hwy 151, fish Lake Capote for rainbow & cutthroat; average size 12-14 inches; get tribal fishing permit.

Travel tip: Visit the Chimney Rock Archeological Area S of Hwy 160 between Durango and Pagosa Springs; tours daily at 9 mid-may through mid-Sept; unique rock spires mark the northernmost area of the Chacoan Empire.

Navajo State Park   **$7**

17 mi W of Pagosa Springs on US 160; 18 mi SW on CR 151; 2 mi S on CR 982; at Navajo Lake. $7 base. All year. Base fee at primitive sites with cfga & tbls ($3 off-season at Windsurf Beach & Arbles Point); $12 at non-elec sites ($7 off-season at Tiffany & Rosa); $16 with elec ($12 off-season at Carracas); $20 full hookups ($16 off-season at Rosa). 110 sites. Tbls, toilets, cfga, drkg wtr, hookups($), showers, dump. Visitor center, interpretive programs, snack bar, boating(ldr), waterskiing, sailboarding, fishing, hiking trails, hunting, mountain biking trails, winter sports. Elev 6100 ft; 2,672 acres. Entry fee.

Fishing tip: Navajo Lake contains kokanee salmon, smallmouth bass, northern pike, crappie and several types of trout.

Teal   **$12**
San Juan National Forest

2.5 mi W of Pagosa Springs on US 160; 20 mi N on FR 631 (Piedra Rd); 1.5 mi N on FR 640; on Williams Creek Reservoir. $12 for RVs, $10 tents. MD-LD; 14-day limit. 16 sites; 35-ft RV limit. Tbls, toilets, cfga, drkg wtr. Fishing, boating (l). 10 acres; elev 8300 ft.

West Fork   **$12**
San Juan National Forest

14 mi E of Pagosa Springs on US 160; left for 1.5 mi on FR 648 (West Fork Rd); on West Fork of San Juan River. $12 for RVs, $10 tents. MD-9/30; 30-day limit. 28 sites; 35-ft

RV limit. Tbls, toilets, cfga, drkg wtr. Fishing, hiking. Elev 8000 ft; 10 acres.

Williams Creek $12
San Juan National Forest
2/5 mi W of Pagosa Springs on US 160; 20 mi N on FR 631 (Piedra Rd); half mi N on FR 640; near Williams Creek Reservoir (4 mi N of Bridge Campground). $12 for RVs, $10 tents. MD-LD; 14-day limit. 67 sites; 45-ft RV limit. Tbls, toilets, cfga, drkg wtr, free dump nearby at Piedra & Williams Creek Rds. Fishing. Elev 8300 ft; 12 acres.

Wolf Creek $12
San Juan National Forest
14 mi E of Pagosa Springs on US 160; left for half mi on FR 648 (West Fork Rd). $12 for RVs, $10 tents. MD-LD; 30-day limit. 26 sites; 35-ft RV limit. Tbls, toilets, cfga, drkg wtr. Fishing. Elev 8000 ft; 6 acres.

PAONIA (117)

Erikson Springs $10
Gunnison National Forest
About 18 mi NE of Paonia on SR 133; 7 mi E on CR 12. $10 during about 6/1-9/30; free 10/1-11/15. 16-day limit. 18 sites (35-ft RV limit). Tbls, toilets, cfga, drkg wtr. Fishing (Anthracite Creek), hiking. Paonia State Recreation Area nearby. Elev 6800 ft.

PARSHALL (118)

Horseshoe $10
Routt National Forest
16.8 mi SE of Parshall on CR 3. $10. 6/1-11/15; 14-day limit. 7 sites (RVs under 26 ft). Tbls, toilets, cfga. Fishing, mountain biking, hiking & OHV trails. Elev 10,000 ft.

Fishing tip: Nearby Williams Fork Reservoir has a wide variety of excellent fishing opportunities -- rainbow & brown trout, northern pike, kokanee salmon.

Hot Sulphur Springs   FREE
State Wildlife Area
2 mi E of Parshall on US 40. Free. All year; 14-day limit. Camp only at Lone Buck Campground, Pioneer Park or Beaver Creek area. 50 sites (RVs under 16 ft). Tbls, toilets, cfga, no drkg wtr except at E end of Pioneer Park bridge. Fishing, picnicking, big-game hunting, shooting range, birdwatching. Elev 7600 ft.

South Fork $11
Roosevelt National Forest
25 mi S of Parshal on US 40, in Williams Fork Valley, off CR 3 on FR 138. $11. MD-9/15. 11 sites; 23-ft RV limit. Tbls, toilets, cfga, drkg wtr, corral, accessible boardwalk. Hiking, horseback riding, OHV trails. Elev 8970 ft. This campground was closed in 2006 due to hazardous trees; status uncertain in 2007.

Williams Fork Reservoir   FREE
State Wildlife Areas
Just E of Parshall at Williams Fork Reservoir

and several state access areas on the Colorado River, including Kemp and Breeze units. Free primitive camping. Some toilets, but mostly dry camping. Boating(l), fishing.

Fishing tip: The best fishing is below the reservoir off US 40 near Parshall. Use dry flies for browns and rainbows.

PITKIN (119)

Middle Quartz $8
Gunnison National Forest
1.5 mi NE of Pitkin on FR 765; 5.5 mi NE on FR 767. $8. About 6/1-LD; 16-day limit. 5 sites (RVs under 16 ft). Tbls, toilets, cfga, no drkg wtr. Mountain climbing, picnicking, fishing. Elev 10,200 ft; 3 acres. Stream. Historic.

Pitkin $7
Gunnison National Forest
1 mi E of Pitkin on FR 765. $7 with federal Senior Pass; others pay $14. 5/15-9/30; 16-day limit. 23 sites (35-ft RV limit). Tbls, toilets, cfga, drkg wtr. Fishing (Quartz Creek), 4WD trails. Ranger station nearby. Elev 9400 ft; 8 acres.

Quartz $10
Gunnison National Forest
4 mi N of Pitkin on FR 765. $10. About 6/1-LD; 16-day limit. 10 sites (16-ft RV limit). Tbls, toilets, cfga, drkg wtr. Fishing (North Quartz Creek), rockhounding.

PLEASANT VIEW (120)

Big Water Spring   FREE
Hunter Camp
San Juan National Forest
1 mi NW on US 666; 5 mi N on CR 505; 20 mi N on FR 504. Free. 9/1-11/15; 14-day limit. 1 site (RV under 32 ft). Tbls, toilets, well drkg wtr. Picnicking, hiking. Elev 8200 ft; 10 acres. Mountains.

Travel tip: See nearby Lowry Pueblo Ruins, 9 mi W of US 160 at Pleasant View; ruins of a civilization that mysteriously disappeared 1,000 years ago; a National Historic Landmark.

PONCHA SPRINGS (121)

Monarch Park $10
San Isabel National Forest
14.5 mi W of Poncha Springs on US 50; .7 mi E on FR 231; at South Fork of Arkansas River. $10. 6/11-9/1; 14-day limit. 36 sites (45-ft RV limit). Tbls, toilets, cfga, drkg wtr, fishing dock. Hiking & mountain biking trails, fishing, 4x4 activities. 2-day minimum stay on weekends. Elev 10,500 ft; 17 acres.

North Fork Reservoir $6
San Isabel National Forest
6 mi W of Poncha Springs on US 50; 10.2 mi N on CR 240. $6. 6/18-9/20; 14-day limit. 8 sites (RVs under 26 ft). Tbls, toilets, cfga, dump, no drkg wtr, no trash service.

Boating, picnicking, fishing (no motors). Elev 11,000 ft.

Fishing tip: North Fork Reservoir has some of the area's best trout fishing.

O'Haver Lake $10
San Isabel National Forest
4.5 mi S of Poncha Springs on US 285; 2.3 mi SW on CR 200; 1.5 mi W on CR 202; rd has several sharp curves. $10. 5/17-9/1; 14-day limit. 29 sites (45-ft RV limit). Tbls, toilets, cfga, drkg wtr. Fishing, hiking & biking trails, fishing pier, weekend interpretive programs. 2-day minimum stay on weekends. Elev 9200 ft. 15-acre lake. $4 day use fee for access to lake.

POWDERHORN (122)

Cebolla Creek   FREE
Recreation Site
Bureau of Land Management
S from SR 149 at Powderhorn turnoff; S on CR 27 along Cebolla Creek for 8 mi; right to area marked "Cebolla Campground." Free. 6/1-10/15; 14-day limit. 3 sites (30 ft RV limit). Tbls, toilet, cfga, no drkg wtr. Pack out trash. Fishing, swimming, picnicking. Elev 9500 ft.

Cebolla Creek $8
State Wildlife Area
14.7 mi SW of Powderhorn on CR 27 along Cebolla Creek. $8. All year. 5 sites (RVs under 22 ft). No facilities. Swimming, picnicking, fishing, hunting. 1,427 acres straddling creek. Elev 8,800-10,000 ft.

Powderhorn Primitive Area   FREE
Special Recreation Management Area
Bureau of Land Management
SW of Powderhorn, NE of Lake City on both sides of Lake Fork of Gunnison River off CR 58 (Indian Creek Rd). Hike-in or horseback ride-in. Free. Apr-Nov; 14-day limit. Primitive camping. No facilities. Hiking, fishing, hunting, hiking. Powderhorn Lakes. 43,000-acre wilderness study area. Elk breeding ground. Bighorn sheep. Three trailheads provide good non-motorized access. Park at Powderhorn Lakes Trailhead. Low-impact camping all along the trail; use existing sites & fire rings. Good trout fishing at upper and lowr Powderhorn Lakes.

PUEBLO (123)

Davenport $6.50
San Isabel National Forest
35 mi SW of Pueblo on Hwy 78; 2 mi N on Hwy 165; 2 mi E on FR 382. $6.50 with federal Senior Pass. MD-LD; 14-day limit. 12 tent sites. Tbls, toilets, cfga, drkg wtr. Hiking, ORV activities, fishing.

RANGELY (124)

Rangely Camper Park   **$12**
Western Rio Blanco
Metropolitan Recreation & Park District
At 940 E. Rangely Ave on NE side of town; at the White River. $12 without hookups; $14 with elec. 23 sites for RVs under 30 ft. Tbls, toilets, cfga, drkg wtr, showers, dump. Volleyball, horseshoes, fishing ponds

RED CLIFF (125)

Blodgett   **$12**
White River National Forest
3 mi S of Red Cliff on US 24; half mi SW on FR 703 (Homestake Rd). $12. MD-LD; 10-day limit. 6 sites (30-ft RV limit). Tbls, toilets, cfga, drkg wtr. Fishing, hiking. At Eagle River & Homestake Creek.

Gold Park   **$12**
White River National Forest
3 mi S of Red Cliff on US 24; 9 no SW on FR 703. $12. MD-LD; 10-day limit. 11 sites (40-ft RV limit). Tbls, toilets, cfga, drkg wtr. Fishing, hiking. Elev 9300 ft; 4 acres. Homestake Creek nearby.

Homestake Road   **FREE**
Dispersed Camping Area
White River National Forest
3 mi S of Red Cliff on US 24; SW on FR 703 (Homestake Rd) between Blodgett and Gold Park Campgrounds. Free. Primitive undesignated sites along the road near Homestake Creek. No facilities, not drkg wtr.

Hornsilver   **$12**
White River National Forest
2.5 mi S of Red Cliff on US 24; at Homestake Creek. $12 during MD-9/15; 10-day limit; free rest of year if accessible, but no wtr or trash service. 12 sites (30-ft RV limit). Tbls, toilets, cfga, drkg wtr. Fishing, hiking. Eagle River. Elev 8800 ft; 5 acres.

RED FEATHER LAKES (126)

Dowdy Lake   **$10**
Roosevelt National Forest
1 mi E of Red Feather Lakes on CR 74E; half mi N on FR 218 (gravel). $10 with federal Senior Pass at RV sites & off-season when wtr not available ($7.50 at tent sites); $20 & $15 for non-seniors and in-season when wtr is available. All year; 10-day limit. 62 sites (40-ft RV limit). Tbls, toilets, cfga, drkg wtr. Picnicking, boating(l), fishing, hiking, biking. Elev 8100 ft. Campground was reconstructed in 2006, and sites were enlarged.
Fishing tip: Good trout fishing at nearby Parvin Lake, but fishing is restricted to artificial lures.

North Fork Poudre   **$10**
Roosevelt National Forest
1 mi S of Red Feather Lakes on CR 4; 7 mi W on FR 162. $10. 6/15-10/1; 14-day limit.
9 sites (RVs under 31 ft). Tbls, toilets, cfga, no drkg wtr. Fishing, picnicking, horseback riding. Elev 9200 ft; 3 acres. Stream. Beside north fork of Poudre River.

REDSTONE (127)

McClure   **$10**
Gunnison National Forest
9 mi SW of Redstone on US 133. $10 during MD-10/1; free 10/1-11/15. 16-day limit. 17 sites (35-ft RV limit). Tbls, toilets, cfga, drkg wtr. Hiking, fishing (Lee Creek). McClure Pass nearby. Elev 8000 ft; 5 acres.

RICO (128)

Cayton   **$12**
San Juan National Forest
6 mi NE of Rico on SR 145; half mi E on FR 578. $12 ($6 when wtr not available). 6/15 through hunting season; 30-day limit. 27 sites; 35-ft RV limit. Tbls, toilets, cfga, drkg wtr, dump ($5). Fishing, hiking. Elev 9400 ft; 11 acres. Popular in summer.

RIFLE (129)

Little Box Canyon   **FREE**
White River National Forest
3 mi N of Rifle on SR 13; 11.2 mi NE on SR 355; 2.2 mi N on CR C217; 25 mi N on FR 825. Free. 5/1-10/31; 14-day limit. 4 sites. Tbls, toilets, cfga, no drkg wtr. Fishing, picnicking. Elev 7600 ft; 1 acre.
Fishing tip: Rifle Gap Reservoir offers excellent scenery and clear waters along with a wide variety of fishing opportunities. Most fishermen try for brown & rainbow trout, but Rifle Gap also has good fishing for largemouth and smallmouth bass and walleye.
Travel tip: Watch for a herd of buffalo at the NW end of Rifle Falls State Park, and visit the ice caves N of the 50-ft falls; while there, explore limestone caves.

Rifle Mountain Park   **$7**
Hwy 13 N out of rifle; right on SR 325 past Rifle Gap SP; stay right over the dam & pass Rifle Falls SP. $7 (plus $5 day use fee or $40 annually). Primitive sites. Tbls, toilets, cfga, drkg wtr. Hiking, fishing, spelunking, rock climbing. Free camping is available just outside the park on NFS and BLM land. 50-ft waterfall.
Fishing tip: Lake contains rainbow & German brown trout, walleye, channel catfish, smallmouth & largemouth bass.

West Rifle Creek   **FREE**
State Wildlife Area
4 mi NE of Rifle on Hwy 13; 6 mi on Hwy 325; 1 mi NW on CR 252. Free. Camping LD-12/31 (deer & elk seasons); 14-day limit during 45-day period. 6 primitive campsites. Toilets, cfga, tbls, drkg wtr. Hiking, hunting, fishing. Elev 7700 ft; 320 acres; 2 mi of water.

RIO BLANCO (130)

Piceance   **FREE**
State Wildlife Area
20 mi N of Rio Blanco on Hwy 13; then follow signs on CR 5 (4 different entrances). Free. All year; 14-day limit during 45-day period. Primitive campsites. Toilets, cfga, tbls, drkg wtr. Fishing, hunting on 29,000 acres; elev 6200 ft. Campfires only in designated areas.
Fishing tip: Two ponds at Little Hills Experimental Station stocked with rainbow & brook trout. Smallmouth, largemouth bass, northern pike & crappie are available at Rio Blanco Lake.

ROCKY FORD (131)

Rocky Ford West   **FREE**
State Wildlife Area
3 mi N of Rocky Ford on Hwy 17; 1 mi E on CR 805. Free. Primitive campsites; no facilities. Fishing in Arkansas River, hiking, hunting.
Travel tip: Rocky Ford claims to be the "melon capital of the world," and produce stands dot the Arkansas Valley from August until first frost, offering exceptional produce.

Timpas Creek   **FREE**
State Wildlife Area
4 mi S of Rocky Ford on Hwy 71; 2 mi NE on Hwy 266, across river bridge; 1 mi S on CR 21; 1 mi W on CR Z. Free. All year; 14-day limit during 45-day period. Primitive camping. No facilities. Hunting, fishing. Lots of water potholes; 141 acres; elev 4000 ft. Fires prohibited.

RYE (132)

Lake Isabel La Vista   **$12**
San Isabel National Forest
8 mi NW of Rye on SR 165. Holders of federal Senior Pass pay $12 at 19 RV sites with elec & $7 at 10 walk-in tent sites; others pay $19 & $14. 4/20-10/15; 14-day limit. 50-ft RV limit. Tbls, toilets, cfga, drkg wtr. Fishing, hiking, boating(no mtrs), swimming. Elev 8400 ft; 25 acres. 2-day minimum stay on weekends.
Fishing tip: This lake is quite good for children learning to fish because of open shore areas. The lake contains lake trout (mackinaw), brown, cutthroat and rainbow trout.

Lake Isabel St. Charles   **$7**
San Isabel National Forest
10 mi NW of Rye on SR 165; 1 mi W on FR 308. $7 with federal Senior Pass; others pay $14. MD-LD; 14-day limit. 15 sites (35-ft RV limit). Tbls, cfga, drkg wtr, flush toilets. Hiking, fishing, boating(l). Elev 8400 ft; 10 acres. 2-day minimum stay on weekends.

Lake Isabel South Side   **$7**
San Isabel National Forest
10 mi NW of Rye on SR 165; half mi W on

FR 308. $7 with federal Senior Pass; others pay $14. MD-LD; 14-day limit. 8 RV sites (40-ft RV limit). Tbls, toilets, cfga, drkg wtr. Boating(ld), fishing, hiking. Elev 8400 ft. 2-day minimum stay on weekends.

SAGUACHE (133)

Buffalo Pass $5
Rio Grande National Forest
27.6 mi NW of Saguache on SR 114; 1.7 mi S on FR 775. $5 during MD-LD; free 10/10-11/30 for hunters but no wtr or trash service; 14-day limit. 26 sites (RVs under 25 ft). Tbls, toilets, cfga, firewood, drkg wtr, trash collection. Picnicking. Elev 9100 ft; 37 acres. Located at old Indian camp site and on old stage route.

Horse Canyon Road Area FREE
Rio Grande National Forest
33 mi NW of Saguache on SR 114; 4 mi S on county rd, then 1.5 mi E on county rd to Saguache Park Rd 787; 8 mi S on Rd 787 to N end of Saguache Park, at jct with Middle Fork Saguache Rd (FR 744) about 1.5 mi W of Stone Cellar Campground. Find several good primitive sites along the roads in this area, including North Ford Rd 766, FR 745 and FR 744. Free. All year; 14-day limit. No facilities; no drkg wtr. Hiking, fishing.

Luders Creek $5
Rio Grande National Forest
22 mi NW of Saguache on SR 114; 11 mi NW on FR 750 (CR NN 14). $5. MD through hunting season; 14-day limit. 6 sites (RVs under 26 ft). Tbls, toilets, cfga, firewood, no drkg wtr, no trash service. Picnicking. Elev 9200 ft; 2 acres. Near old Cochetopa Pass on Ute Trail. FR 750 was one of the famous toll roads leading west built by Otto Mears in 1876. 4WD rds 2 mi E.

Stone Cellar $7
Rio Grande National Forest
22 mi NW of Saguache on SR 114; 18.7 mi NW on FR 750; 16.4 mi S on FR 787. $7. MD until snow closes access; 14-day limit. 4 sites (RVs under 26 ft). Tbls, toilets, cfga, firewood, well drkg water, no trash service. Picnicking, fishing. Elev 9500 ft; 3 acres. Rolling hills, grassy terrain. Stream. Near Indian and Soldier Battleground. Pets on leash. On middle fork of Saguache Creek. 4WD activities nearby on FRs 774 & 776.

Trickle Mountain FREE
Wildlife Habitat Area
Bureau of Land Management
From Saguache on US 285, W 15 mi on SR 114. Area is N of highway. Free. All year; 14-day limit. No established campsites; undesignated camping. 52,565 acres. One of few places where bighorn sheep, elk, mule deer, pronghorn use same area; large pronghorn herd.
Travel tip: Visit the Russell Lakes Waterfowl Management Area, 4 mi S, 1 mi E of U.S. 285; beautiful refuge for white-faced ibis, some swans, a variety of sandpipers and the snowy egret. Free.

SALIDA (134)

Angel of Shavano $6.50
San Isabel National Forest
10 mi W of Salida on US 50; 4 mi N on CR 240; 1 mi on gravel rd; access rd rough, so high-clearance vehicles recommended; near North Fork of South Arkansas River. $6.50 with federal Senior Pass; others pay $13. 5/15-10/15; 14-day limit. 20 sites; 30-ft RV limit. Tbls, toilets, cfga, drkg wtr. Hiking, fishing. Elev 9200 ft; 10 acres.

Hecla Junction Recreation Site $7
Bureau of Land Management
Arkansas Headwaters
State Recreation Area
N of Salida on SR 291 to jct with US 285; N half mi, then NE on CR 129; 2.5 mi to site. $7 with federal Senior Pass; others pay $14. All year; 14-day limit. 22 sites (30-ft RV limit). Tbls, toilets, cfga, no drkg wtr, no trash service. Fishing, swimming, boating, rafting, hiking. Elev 7300 ft.

Rincon $7
Bureau of Land Management
Arkansas Headwaters
Recreation Area
9 mi SE of Salida on US 50; on Arkansas River. $7 with federal Senior Pass; others pay $14. All year; 14-day limit. 8 sites. Tbls, toilets, cfga, no drkg wtr, no trash service. Swimming, fishing, biking, hiking, boating(l). Elev 6750 ft.

Salida East FREE
Bureau of Land Management
Just E of Salida on N side of US 50. Free. Primitive undesignated camping; no facilities.

SAN LUIS (135)

Rito Seco FREE
Municipal Park
7 mi NE of San Luis on Hwy 150; right on CR 1690. Primitive undesignated camping on land donated to town by Forbes Trinchera Ranch. Toilets, tbls, drkg wtr. Fishing, hiking, picnicking.
Fishing tip: Try Sanchez Reservoir, 5 mi S of town. Excellent fishing for huge northern pike, some up to 30 or 40 pounds; also walleyes & yellow perch, some small trout. 28 free primitive campsites open all year around the lake.

SARGENTS (136)

Snowblind $10
Gunnison National Forest
1.1 mi NE of Sargents on US 50; 6.9 mi N on FR 888. $10. 5/15-9/15; 16-day limit. 22 sites (RVs under 22 ft). Tbls, toilets, cfga, no drkg wtr. Mountain climbing, picnicking, fishing. Elev 9800 ft; 10 acres. Stream. Scenic. Old mining town of Whitepine is 2 mi N. Canyon Creek Trailhead 1 mi SW.

SEDALIA (137)

Devils Head $7
Pike National Forest
10 mi W of Sedalia on SR 67; 9 mi SE on FR 300; half mi SE on FR 3008C. $7 with federal Senior Pass; others pay $14. MD-9/15; 14-day limit. 21 sites (22-ft RV limit). Tbls, toilets, cfga, drkg wtr. Hiking, dirt biking. Elev 8800 ft; 10 acres. Fire lookout tire open to visitors.

Flat Rocks $7
Pike National Forest
10 mi SW of Sedalia on SR 67; 4.7 mi S on FR 300. $7 with federal Senior Pass; others pay $14. 5/15-10/15; 14-day limit. 19 sites (20-ft RV limit). Tbls, toilets, cfga, drkg wtr. Elev 8200 ft; 8 acres. Primarily an OHV campground.

Indian Creek $7
Pike National Forest
10 mi SW of Sedalia on SR 67; .3 mi W on CR 67. $7 with federal Senior Pass; others pay $14. 5/1-9/15; 14-day limit. 11 sites (20-ft RV limit). Tbls, toilets, cfga, drkg wtr. Mountain biking, hiking, fishing. Elev 7500 ft. Horseman sites $16 ($8 for seniors).

Jackson Creek $6.50
Pike National Forest
10 mi W of Sedalia on Hwy 67; 13.9 mi S on FR 300; 1.5 mi NE on FR 502. $6.50 with federal Senior Pass. 5/1-9/15; 14-day limit. 9 sites (20-ft RV limit). Tbls, toilets, cfga, no drkg wtr. Hiking, trailhead. Scenic drive.

SILVERTHORNE (138)

Blue River $12
White River National Forest
From I-70 exit 205 at Silverthorne, 6 mi N on Hwy 9. $12. MD-LD; 10-day limit (services & fees reduced after LD). 24 sites; 25-ft RV limit. Tbls, toilets, cfga, drkg wtr. Fishing, biking. Camp is closed periodically due to bear problems. Traffic noises.
Fishing tip: Above this area, Blue River is closed to fishing Oct-Jan; best times for trout between here and Breckenridge are early spring for rainbows and early fall for browns & brooks.

Lowry $6.50
White River National Forest
About 4 mi E of Silverthorne on Hwy 6; right on Swan Mountain Rd. $6.50 with federal Senior Pass at sites without elec ($11.50 with elec); others pay $13 & $18. MD-LD; 14-day limit. Fee & services may be reduced in fall. 24 sites; 50-ft RV limit. Tbls, toilets, cfga, drkg wtr, elec($), dump. Fishing, boating, hiking. Elev 9300 ft.

SILVERTON (139)

Alpine Triangle   **FREE**
Special Recreation Management Area
Bureau of Land Management
Primitive loop rd connecting Silverton, Lake City and Ouray over Engineer & Cinnamon Passes. Free. All year; 14-day limit. Hike-in, backcountry, 4x4, rural and roadway camping areas. Primitive; scattered facilities. Skiing, rockhounding, kayaking, rafting, sightseeing, fishing, trailbiking. Scenic, picturesque mining remnants. Off-road 4/4 activities. 5 hiking trails. Access to 14,000-ft peaks. 64,000 acres.

Travel tips: Blair Street, once the wide-open street of the Silverton mining camp of 1880s, now has buildings with false facades that serve as movie set backdrop each day at 5 p.m., Blair & 12th Sts become scene of reenacted gunfights. The ghost towns of Eureka and Animas Forks are NE of Silverton on SR 110, a dirt road that is too rough for RVs; four-wheel drive vehicles recommended; ruins of Sunnyside Mine also nearby.

Purgatory   **$12**
San Juan National Forest
22 mi SW of Silverton on US 550. $12. 5/15-9/15; 14-day limit. 14 sites; 30-ft RV limit. Tbls, toilets, cfga, drkg wtr. Hiking. Elev 8800 ft; 6 acres.

Sig Creek   **$10**
San Juan National Forest
21 mi SW of Silverton on US 550; 6 mi W on FR 578 (Hermosa Park Rd). $10 during MD-LD (free off-season, but no wtr or services); 14-day limit. 9 sites (30-ft RV limit). Tbls, toilets, cfga, drkg wtr. Fishing, hiking. 4 acres.

South Mineral   **$7**
San Juan National Forest
4 mi NW of Silverton on US 550; 5 mi W on FR 585. $7 with federal Senior Pass; others pay $14. MD-9/15; 14-day limit. 26 sites; 26-ft RV limit. Tbls, toilets, cfga, drkg wtr. Fishing, hiking. Elev 9800 ft; 12 acres.

South Mineral   **FREE**
Dispersed Camping Area
San Juan National Forest
4 mi NW of Silverton on US 550; 1-5 mi W on FR 585. Free. All year; 14-day limit. Primitive, designated open sites along FR 585 on way to South Mineral Campground, where fee is charged. No facilities. Fishing, hiking. Elev 9800 ft.

SOUTH FORK (140)

Cross Creek   **$11**
Rio Grande National Forest
2 mi SW of South Fork on US 160; from jct of FR 360 (Beaver Creek Rd), E to campground. $11 during MD-LD; free LD-11/15, but no wtr or trash service; 14-day limit. 12 sites; 25-ft RV limit. Tbls, toilets, cfga, drkg wtr. Boating(l), fishing. Beaver Reservoir qtr mi N. Elev 8840 ft.

Fishing tip: Beaver Reservoir contains all sizes of rainbow, brook and native cutthroat trout as well as koakaee salmon; paved boat ramp at S end. Also fish the stream at S end of lake.

Highway Springs Camp   **$7**
Rio Grande National Forest
5.2 mi SW of South Fork on US 160. On South Fork of Rio Grande. $7 during MD-LD; 14-day limit. Camp alternates staying open until 11/15 for hunters and fall color viewing. 11 sites (RVs under 36 ft); also 5 sites without tbls. 4 acres. Tbls, toilets, cfga, firewood, no drkg wtr. Store, food, ice, gas, showers, dump (2 mi). Fishing, picnicking. Elev 8400 ft.

Fishing tip: Along several sections of US 160, the South Fork provides good fishing for rainbows, cutthroat & brown trout.

Lower Beaver Creek Camp   **$12**
Rio Grande National Forest
2.4 mi SW of South Fork on US 160; 3 mi S on FR 360. $12 fee MD-LD. Camp alternates staying open (free) until 11/15 for hunters & fall color viewing; 14-day limit. 23 sites (RVs under 36 ft). Firewood, drkg wtr (during free season, no trash collection or drkg wtr). 7 acres. Boating (d), horseback riding.

Palisade   **$12**
Rio Grande National Forest
9.5 mi N of South Fork on Hwy 149. $12 during MD-LD; free rest of season, but no wtr or trash service; 14 -ft limit. 12 sites (30-ft RV limit). Tbls, toilets, cfga, drkg wtr. Fishing. This is the only campground between South Fork & Creede; it is usually full mid-June through Aug.

Park Creek   **$12**
Rio Grande National Forest
9 mi SW of South Fork on US 160. $12. MD-LD; alternates staying open until 11/15 for hungers & fall color viewing (reduced services, no wtr); 14-day limit. 20 sites; 35-ft RV limit. Tbls, toilets, cfga, drkg wtr. Fishing. Elev 8500 ft.

Tucker Ponds Camp   **$10**
Rio Grande National Forest
Approx 11 mi W of South Fork on US 160; 3 mi S on FR 390. $10 fee 6/15-9/15; 14-day limit. Alternates being open free until 11/15 for hunters & fall color viewing. 19 sites (RVs under 35 ft). 16 acres. Tbls, toilets, cfga, firewood, drkg wtr. During free period, no wtr, no trash collection. Berry picking, picnicking, lake fishing. Elev 9700 ft.

Upper Beaver Camp   **$12**
Rio Grande National Forest
2.4 mi SW of South Fork on US 160; 4 mi S on FR 360. (1 mi farther S of FR 360 past Beaver Creek campground.) $12 fee MD-LD; free alternate years until 11/15 for hunters & fall color viewing. 14-day limit. 16 sites (RVs under 36 ft). 5 acres. Firewood, drkg wtr. During free period, no trash collection or

drkg wtr. Boating(d), horseback riding, fishing. Elev 8400 ft.

SPRINGFIELD (141)

Two Buttes Reservoir   **FREE**
State Wildlife Area
18 mi N of Springfield on US 385/287; 3 mi E on CR B5. Free. 5/1-10/31. 75 sites. Tbls, toilets, cfga, drkg wtr, dump. Store (1 mi). Boating (rl); picnicking, swimming, fishing; waterfowl, small game hunting. Pets on leash. 4,995 land acres; 1,798 water acres. Water level varies. Elev 4400 ft.

Fishing tip: Two Buttes Reservoir dries up periodically, but the area's Black Hole ponds contain largemouth bass, catfish, wipers and grass carp.

Travel tip: Consider taking an overnight chuckwagon trip. The Kirkwell Cattle Company specializes in overnight tours into the remote areas of southwest Baca County and historical "cedar break" area.

STEAMBOAT SPRINGS (142)

Dry Lake   **$10**
Routt National Forest
4 mi N of Steamboat Springs on CR 36 (Strawberry Park Rd); 3 mi E on FR 60 (Buffalo Pass Rd). $10 ($5 when water unavailable). 6/10-11/15; 14-day limit. 8 sites (RVs under 17 ft). Tbls, toilets, cfga, no drkg wtr. Picnicking, fishing (nearby). Elev 8000 ft.

Travel tip: If you're camping here between the middle of June and mid-Aug, try attending the nation's largest weekly professional rodeo every Fri & Sat night at the local rodeo grounds.

Dumont Lake   **$12**
Routt National Forest
22.3 mi SE of Steamboat Springs on US 40; 1.5 mi NE on FR 311; half mi N on FR 312. $12 ($6 when water is unavailable). 6/15-10/1; 14-day limit. 22 sites (RVs under 41 ft). Tbls, toilets, cfga, drkg wtr. Boating(l), fishing. Elev 9500 ft; 5 acres.

Fishing tip: This well-stocked lake offers good rainbow fishing with small spinners or live bait. Excellent fly fishing in nearby streams.

Granite Campground   **$8**
Routt National Forest
4 mi S of Buffalo Pass on FR 310; high-clearance vehicles suggested. $8. 6/15-10/1; 14-day limit. 8 sites (4 walk-in); 22-ft RV limit. Tbls, toilets, cfga, no drkg wtr or trash service. Fishing, boating (no mtrs). On shore of recently enlarged Fish Creek Reservoir.

Meadows   **$10**
Routt National Forest
15 mi SE of Steamboat Springs on US 40. $10. 7/1-9/15; 14-day limit. 30 sites (RVs under 41 ft). Tbls, toilets, cfga, drkg wtr. Fishing. Elev 9300 ft; 7 acres.

Fishing tip: Nearby Pearl Lake contains

cutthroat trout and grayling; best time is mid to late May. Fishing is restricted to flies and artificial lures.

Travel tip: Visit Fish Creek Falls 3 mi E of town on Fish Creek Falls Rd; it has a drop of 283 feet. Hiking trail leads to the Continental Divide. Picnic area, historic bridge, handicap trail. Best flow is late spring, early summer. Overlook trail above falls leads to a second set of falls.

Service Creek   FREE
State Wildlife Area
4.5 mi S of Steamboat Springs on Hwy 131; 7 mi SE on CR 18. Free. Open to camping only during elk & deer seasons, 3 days before & 3 days after. Primitive campsites; 309 acres. Tbls, toilets, cfga. Hunting, fishing, picnicking.

Fishing tip: Try fishing the eddies & pools of the Yampa River, especially in late summer; good rainbows, browns, whitefish and even some northern pike.

Stagecoach State Park $8
4 mi E of Steamboat Springs on US 40; 5 mi S on SR 131; 7 mi S on CR 14; in Yampa Valley. $8 base. All year. 92 sites. Base fee for 9 primitive sites at McKinley Campground; $14 for 18 basic sites at Harding Spur Camp; $12 for basic sites at Pinnacle Camp ($18 with elec); $18 for elec sites at Junction City Camp. Tbls, toilets, cfga, drkg wtr, dump, showers, elec($). Interpretive programs, swimming, snack bar, boating(ldr), waterskiing, sailboarding(r), fishing, hiking trails, biking trails, winter sports. Elev 7250 ft; 866 acres. Entry fee.

Fishing tip: Lake is well known for its fast-growing rainbows of 10-16 inches; some brown, brook and Snake River cutthroat. Also large northern pike of up to 20 pounds. In spring, try small gold or gold-and-orange lures near shore for trout. Summer & early fall, troll 15-18 feet with small spoons. For pike, use large, bright lures during spring and early summer, fished near shorelines; try deep points in late summer.

Summit Lake $10
Routt National Forest
4 mi N of Steamboat Springs on CR 36; 11.6 mi E on FR 60. $10. 7/10-9/30; 14-day limit. 16 sites (22-ft RV limit). Tbls, toilets, cfga, drkg wtr (no wtr after LD). Fishing, picnicking. Elev 10,300 ft. 1 mi S of Mt Zirkel Wilderness.

Walton Creek $12
Routt National Forest
17 mi SE of Steamboat Springs on US 40. Easy access. $12. 6/15-9/15; 14-day limit. 14 sites (RVs under 23 ft). Tbls, toilets, drkg wtr, cfga. Fishing.

SWEETWATER (144)

Sweetwater Lake Resort $10
From I-70 exit 133, drive 7 mi to Anderson's Camp, then 10 mi W along Sweetwater Creek to 3406 Sweetwater Rd. $10 base. 5/15-11/15. 20 primitive RV or tent sites; 45-ft RV limit (1 site with elec/wtr, $15). Tbls, toilets, cfga, drkg wtr, laundry. Trout fishing, hiking, boating(r), volleyball, horseshoes, mountain biking, horseback riding.

TELLURIDE (145)

Alta Lakes   FREE
Dispersed Sites
Uncompahgre National Forest
S on SR 145 from Telluride to Boomerang Rd (FR 632), the 3 mi E to lakes. Free. Undesignated primitive camping for tents or self-contained RVs; about 7 sites. Toilet, cfga, no drkg wtr. Fishing, picnicking, hiking.

Travel tip: See Bridal Veil Falls, 2.5 mi SE of town off SR 145; falls with a drop of more than 365 feet; Colorado's highest; listed in National Register of Historic Places. Free.

Illium Valley   FREE
Dispersed Sites
Uncompahgre National Forest
5 mi W of Telluride on SR 145; S on FR 625 (Illium Valley Rd). Free. Undesignated primitive sites along road next to South Fork of San Miguel River. Picnicking, hiking, fishing.

Travel tip: Tulluride's historic Victorian buildings are worth seeing; whole town is designated as a national historic landmark; its past includes visits by famous people such as Sarah Bernhardt, Lillian Gish, William Jennings Bryan and Butch Cassidy.

Matterhorn $8
Uncompahgre National Forest
12 mi SW of Telluride on Hwy 145. $8 base with federal Senior Pass without hookups ($12 with hookups); others pay $16 & $24. 6/1-9/30; 7-day limit. 26 sites; 35-ft RV limit. Tbls, flush toilets, cfga, drkg wtr, showers, hookups($). Fishing, hiking.

Priest Lake   FREE
Dispersed Sites
Uncompahgre National Forest
14 mi S of Telluride on SR 145. All year; 14-day limit. Primitive undesignated sites. No facilities except toilet, cfga. Fishing, hiking.

TEXAS CREEK (146)

Maytag   FREE
Bureau of Land Management
2 mi E of Texas Creek on US 50; at Arkansas River. Free. Primitive undesignated sites; about 8 spaces. Lower rd close to river has turnaround space. Fishing, hunting.

TOPONAS (147)

Blacktail Creek $10
Routt National Forest
Half mi S of Toponas on Hwy 131; 13 mi E on Hwy 134. $10. 6/1-11/15; 14-day limit. 8 RV sites (RVs under 23 ft); 2 tent sites. Tbls, toilets, cfga, drkg wtr. Elev 9100 ft.

Lynx Pass $10
Routt National Forest
Half mi S of Toponas on SR 131; 9 mi E on SR 134; 2.5 mi N on FR 270. $10. 6/15-9/30; 14-day limit. 11 sites (RVs under 19 ft). Tbls, toilets, cfga, drkg wtr, nature trails. Fishing, hiking, biking. Elev 9000 ft; 8 acres.

TRINIDAD (148)

James M. John   FREE
and Lake Dorothey
State Wildlife Area
S on I-25 17 mi from Trinidad to Folsom exit at Raton, NM; then NM Hwys 526 and 72 up Sugarite Canyon 12 mi; area begins at state line. Access limited to foot or horseback from parking areas. Free. All year; 14-day limit during 45-day period. Primitive tent camping. Toilets, cfga, tbls. Camping prohibited within 200 yards of lake or 100 feet of stream except in designated areas. Fishing; small game, deer, turkey hunting; picnicking. 4800 acres. 4-acre lake.

Travel tip: In Trinidad, visit A.R. Mitchell Memorial Museum of Western Art; art by famous painters; folk art; Indian artifacts; features work by A.R. Mitchell; early Hispanic religious folk art; housed in a 1906 department store. Donations.

TWIN LAKES (149)

Dexter $11
San Isabel National Forest
4 mi E of Twin Lakes on SR 82; half mi SW on FR 170. $11. 5/1-10/14; 14-day limit. 24 sites (37-ft RV limit). Tbls, toilets, cfga, drkg wtr. Hiking, fishing. Elev 9300 ft; 5 acres.

Parry Peak $12
San Isabel National Forest
2.6 mi SW of Twin Lakes on SR 82. $12. 5/15-9/15; 14-day limit. 26 sites (32-foot RV limit). Tbls, toilets, cfga, drkg wtr. Hiking, fishing. Elev 9500 ft; 10 acres.

Fishing tip: Twin Lakes stocked with rainbow trout; also contains brook, brown & cutthroat trout, some kokanee salmon.

Twin Peaks $12
San Isabel National Forest
3 mi W of Twin Lakes on SR 82. $12. 5/15-9/15; 14-day limit. 39 sites (32-ft RV limit). Tbls, toilets, cfga, drkg wtr. Hiking, fishing.

VICTOR (151)

Skagway Reservoir   FREE
and Beaver Creek
State Wildlife Area
Half mi E of Victor on CR 67; 6.5 mi S on CR 441. Free. All year; 14-day limit during 45-day period. Primitive camping for self-contained RVs; 90 acres. Toilets, cfga. Boating(l), fishing, picnicking. Elev 9000 ft.

Fishing tip: Skagway Reservoir contains rainbow & brook trout and northern pike. Beaver Creek contains rainbows and some browns & brookies.

Travel tip: At Victor, visit the Lowell Thomas Museum; mining memorabilia & the Lowell Thomas family collection. Fee.

WALDEN (152)

Colorado State Forest   **$12**
21 mi E of Walden on SR 14. $12. All year. 158 basic sites plus backcountry areas. Tbls, toilets, cfga, drkg wtr, dump (at Ranger Lakes parking lot). Boating(l), fishing, hiking trails, biking trails, bridle trails, horse facilities, winter sports. Elev 10,000 ft; 70,000 acres (50,000 in backcountry). Entry fee. The following are campground and camping areas within Colorado State Forest:

Ranger Lakes. Accessible directly from Hwy 14, about 6 mi W of Cameron Pass.; camp within short walk of lakes. 32 sites, some newly renovated. Tbls, toilets, cfga, drkg wtr, dump. Fishing, nature trail, summer interpretive programs weekend evenings. No boats.

The Crags. Access steep, narrow & winding; not recommended for large RVs. 26 sites. Tbls, toilets, cfga, drkg wtr. Access rd steep, narrow, winding; not recommended for RVs.

North Michigan Reservoir. 48 sites around the lake. Drkg wtr, cfga, toilets, tbls. Fishing, but no swimming; no-wake boating. 2 boat ramps. Sites on S side newly renovated.

Bochman. 1 mi N of North Michigan Reservoir. Toilets, cfga, drkg wtr 52 sites, most undesignated.

Ruby Jewel Lake. Access via Ruby Jewel Rd. Backcountry camping. Artificial lures only for lake's cutthroat trout.

Kelly Lake. Backcountry camping. Access via Ruby Jewel trailhead through Hidden Valley -- a 4-mile hike; also via Kelly Lake Trail. Artificial lures only for lake's golden & cutthroat trout & some grayling.

Clear Lake. Backcountry camping. Access from Clear Lake Trailhead at end of CR 41 -- an 8-mile hike with 1,200-ft elevation gain. Good backpacking & bridle trail. Cutthroat trout; artificial lures only.

American Lakes. Backcountry camping. Access by American Lakes trailhead or Michigan Ditch Rd; 5-mile hike. Cutthroat & rainbow trout; artificial lures only.

Delaney Butte Lakes   **FREE**
State Wildlife Area
Half mi W of Walden on SR 14 to CR 18; 4.5 mi W to CR 5; 1 mi N. Follow signs. Free. All year; 14-day limit during 45-day period. 150 primitive sites. Tbls, toilets, cfga, drkg wtr, shelters. Boating (rl), waterskiing, picnicking, fishing, small-game hunting. Elev 8100 ft; 300 acres. Pets. 150 water acres. Bleak terrain, few trees. Gusty winds.

Fishing tip: State Div of Wildlife manages 6 lakes in area with good fishing; camping (with toilet facilities) available at East & South Delaney Butte Lakes (rainbow, brook trout); North Lake (brown trout); Lake John (rainbow, cutthroat, brown trout); Cowdrey Lake (rainbow); Seymour Lake (rainbow). Summer weeds can be problem at North Delaney Butte; early spring, late fall best times.

Hidden Lakes   **$10**
Routt National Forest
13 mi SW of Walden on SR 14; 10.5 mi N on CR 234; 1.2 mi W on FR 60. $10. 6/15-LD; 14-day limit. 9 sites (RVs under 20 ft). Tbls, toilets, cfga, drkg wtr. Fishing, boating. Elev 8900 ft.

Murphy   **FREE**
State Wildlife Area
1 mi E of Walden on CR 12. Free. All year; 14-day limit in 45-day period. Primitive camping; no facilities. Fishing, photography. No hunting.

Fishing tip: Try the nearby North Platte River; its deep pools contain large brown trout as well as plenty of small ones; use spinners & live bait early in spring; in late summer, wade the shallow edges and use flies.

Owl Mountain   **FREE**
State Wildlife Area
13 mi E of Walden on Hwy 14; 6 mi S on CR 25. Free. All year; 14-day limit. Primitive undesignated camping at 920-acre wildlife area. Hunting, hiking.

Seymour Lake   **FREE**
State Wildlife Area
From jct of SR 14 & SR 125, 16.2 mi W on SR 14 to CR 28; 1 mi on CR 28; 1 mi on CR 28 to CR 11; 4 mi on CR 11. Free. All year; 14-day limit during 45-day period. Undesignated primitive campsites. Toilets, cfga, tbls, no drkg wtr. Picnicking, boating(l).

Fishing tip: Try this 11-acre lake for rainbow trout; they aren't as big as those in Lake John and the Delaney Buttes, but they are plentiful.

Teal Lake   **$10**
Routt National Forest
13 mi SW of Walden on SR 14; 10.5 mi W on CR 24; 1 mi E on FR 60. $10. 6/1-LD; 14-day limit. 17 sites; 22-ft RV limit. Tbls, toilets, cfga, drkg wtr. Fishing, hiking.

Walden Reservoir   **FREE**
State Wildlife Area
Half mi W of Walden on Hwy 15; half mi W on CR 12. Free. All year; 14-day limit in 45-day period. Primitive camping; no facilities. Hunting.

WALSENBURG (153)

Apishapa   **FREE**
State Wildlife Area
18.5 mi NE of Walsenburg on Hwy 10; SE 20 mi past Mica Butte. Follow signs. Free. All year; 14-day limit during 45-day period. Primitive camping. No facilities. Hunting, hiking. Scenic. 8,000 acres. Canyons, cedar plains. Apishapa River. Solitude.

WALSH (154)

Burchfield   **FREE**
State Wildlife Area
11 mi E of Walsh on CR DD. Free. All year. 14-day limit in 45-day period. Camping space near dry lake; 117 acres. No facilities. Small-game hunting. Elev 4000 ft.

WESTCLIFFE (155)

Alvarado   **$6.50**
San Isabel National Forest
3.5 mi S of Westcliffe on SR 69; 5.2 mi W on CR 302; 1.3 mi SW on FR 302. $6.50 with federal Senior Pass; others pay $13. 5/15-9/1; 14-day limit. 50 sites (29-ft RV limit). Tbls, toilets, cfga, drkg wtr. Hiking, fishing. Secluded. Equestrian sites $16 ($8 for seniors).

DeWeese Reservoir   **FREE**
State Wildlife Area
5 mi NW of Westcliffe on Hwy 69; 1.5 mi N on Copper Gulch Rd, then follow signs. Free. All year; 14-day limit in 45-day period. Primitive undesignated sites. Tbls, toilets, cfga, no drkg wtr. Boating(l), fishing, hunting.

Lake Creek   **$12**
San Isabel National Forest
About 12 mi NW of Westcliffe on SR 69 to Hillside; 3 mi W on FR 300. $12. MD-10/15; 14-day limit. 11 sites (tents or small RVs). Tbls, toilets, cfga, drkg wtr. Fishing, hiking. Secluded.

Fishing tip: Lake Creek is stocked with rainbow trout from Jct 82 to Lackawanna Gulch.

Middle Taylor Creek   **FREE**
State Wildlife Area
8 mi W of Westcliff on Hermit Lakes Rd. Free. All year; 14-day limit during 45-day period. Primitive campsites. Toilets, cfga, tbls. Hunting, fishing. Elev 11,000 ft; 486 acres. Small stream. National forest access.

Fishing tip: Try De Weese Reservoir, NW of Westcliffe on Hwy 69, then N on CR 241 about 4 mi. Stocked regularly with pan-size rainbow trout; also consider Grape Creek just below the lake; it runs through public land and offers good fishing for rainbows & browns.

Travel tip: Visit the unique Bishop Castle, 24 mi W of I-25 on Hwy 165 near Rye; castle built by hand by one man, Jim Bishop; now 3 stories high; eventually will have a moat and drawbridge; project started in 1969; topped by a dragon designed to belch real fire; 58-foot tower (meant to be even taller) with spiral staircase; supported by visitor donations.

WHITEWATER (156)

Divide Fork   **FREE**
Uncompahgre National Forest
13 mi SW of Whitewater on SR 141; 15 mi SW on FR 402. Free. 5/20-11/1. 11 sites (RVs

under 23 ft). Tbls, toilets, cfga, no drkg wtr. Picnicking. Elev 9200 ft; 4 acres.

WINTER PARK (158)

Idlewild $12
Arapaho National Forest
1 mi S of Winter Park on US 40. $12. MD-LD; 14-day limit. 24 sites (32-ft RV limit). Tbls, toilets, cfga, drkg wtr. Fishing, mountain biking, hiking. Elev 9000 ft; 10 acres.

Robbers Roost $12
Arapaho National Forest
5 mi S of Winter Park on US 40 at base of Berthoud Pass. $12. MD-LD; 14-day limit. 11 sites (25-ft RV limit). Tbls, toilets, cfga, drkg wtr. Fishing, mountain biking, hiking. Elev 9826 ft.

WOLCOTT (159)

Castle Peak FREE
Wilderness Study Area
Bureau of Land Management
N on SR 131 from Wolcott several mi, left on dirt rd labeled "Milk Creek." Follow signs to Horse Mountain. Free. All year; 14-day limit. Undesignated sites. No facilities. Fishing, hunting, hiking, backpacking, horse trails. Elev from 8000 ft. Streams, lakes.

Wolcott Campground $10
Upper Colorado Recreation Area
Bureau of Land Management
From I-70 exit 157 at Wolcott, 1.7 mi W on Hwy 6; at Eagle River. $10. All year; 7-day limit during 4/1-8/31; 14 days 9/1-3/31. Undeveloped primitive camping area. Toilets, cfga, tbls, no drkg wtr. Boating(l), fishing, rock climbing, picnicking.

WOODLAND PARK (160)

Big Turkey $7
Pike National Forest
11.6 mi NW of Woodland Park on SR 67; .8 mi SW on FR 200; 3.9 mi SW on FR 360. $7 with federal Senior Pass; others pay $14. 5/1-9/15; 14-day limit. 10 sites (RVs under 16 ft). 4 acres. Tbls, toilets, cfga, no drkg wtr. Stream fishing, picnicking. Elev 8000 ft. On Turkey Creek. Still closed in 2007 after fire damage in 2002.

Goose Creek $7
Pike National Forest
24 mi NW of Woodland Park on SR 67; 2.9 mi SW on CR 126; 12 mi SW on FR 211. $7 with federal Senior Pass; others pay $14. 5/1-9/15; 14-day limit. 10 sites (RVs under 21 ft). Tbls, toilets, cfga, well drkg wtr. Fishing, picnicking. Elev 8100 ft; 4 acres. Scenic. Nature trail. Lost Creek Scenic Area (1 mi). Near access to Lost Creek Wilderness Area. Re-opened in 2006 after major fire damage in 2002.

Springdale $11
Pike National Forest
4 mi E on FR 22 from US 24 to Woodland Park; 1.7 mi E on FR 300 (Rampart Range Rd). $11. 5/15-9/30; 14-day limit. 13 sites; 16-ft RV limit. Tbls, toilets, cfga, no drkg wtr. Rampart Range Lake nearby. Elev 9100 ft.
Fishing tip: 50-acre Rampart Range Lake contains brown, cutthroat, rainbow and lake (mackinaw) trout.

WRAY (161)

Beecher Island FREE
Municipal Park
5 mi S of Wray on US 385; 13 mi SE on CR 61. Free. All year. 30 sites. Tbls, flush toilets, cfga, firewood, drkg wtr, showers, playground.
Travel tip: In Wray, visit the Wray Museum on Hwy 34 across from courthouse; Indian artifacts, Beecher Island relics, photos and nature collections, replicas from Smithsonian-sponsored digs in the area.

Wray City Park FREE
At US 385 & US 34 in town. Free. 1-night limit. Adjoining rest area in city park which permits overnight parking. Enter from center of town.

YAMPA (162)

Bear Lake $10
Routt National Forest
13 mi SW of Yampa on CR 7. $10. 6/1-10/1; 14-day limit. 43 sites (30-ft RV limit). Tbls, toilets, cfga, drkg wtr. Boating(l), fishing, picnicking, hiking trails. Elev 9700 ft; 20 acres.

Bear River Dispersed Site $3
Routt National Forest
10-20 mi SW of Yampa on FR 900; along Bear River. $3. All year; 14-day limit. 32 dispersed undesignated sites; 30-ft RV limit. Tbls, fire grates. Toilets & trash deposit at Yamcolo Reservoir boat ramp nearby. Fishing, hiking, mountain biking. Elev 9300 ft-10,200 ft.

Chapman Reservoir $10
Routt National Forest
5 mi W/NW of Yampa on CR 17; left on CR 132 (FR 16) for 7 mi; 1 mi S on FR 940. $10. 6/15-9/30; 14-day limit. 12 sites; 35-ft RV limit. Tbls, toilets, cfga, no drkg wtr. Fishing, boating, hiking, canoeing, swimming.

Cold Springs $10
Routt National Forest
7 mi SW of Yampa on CR 7; 8.6 mi SW on FR 900. At Stillwater Reservoir. $10. 6/1-10/1; 14-day limit. 5 sites (RVs under 23 ft). Tbls, drkg wtr, toilets, cfga. Boating, fishing. Elev 10,500 ft.

Crosho Lake Recreation Area $5
Routt National Forest
4 mi N/NW of Yampa on CR 17; 6 mi W on CR 15; at S end of Crosho Lake. 5. 6/15-11/15; 14-day limit. 10 dispersed primitive

sites; 25-ft RV limit. Toilets, cfga, no drkg wtr, no trash service, no tbls. Fishing, hiking, mountain biking.

Gardner Park Reservoir FREE
Recreation Area
Routt National Forest
About 7 mi S/SW of Yampa on CR 7; 3 mi on FR 900; left on FR 910 for 2 mi; at Gardner Park Reservoir. Free. About 6/15-11/15; 14-day limit Primitive dispersed sites. Toilets, cfga, no drkg wtr, no tbls or trash service. Interpretive trail, boating, hiking, fishing.

Lagunita Lake FREE
Recreation Area
Routt National Forest
20 mi SW of Yampa on SR 134; 3 mi N on FR 270; just before Lynx Pass Campground. Free. Primitive dispersed sites. Toilets, cfga, no drkg wtr. Fishing, hiking, biking. Elev 8900 ft.

Red Dirt Reservoir FREE
Recreation Area
Routt National Forest
11 mi S of Yampa on Hwy 131; 20 mi E on FR 134; 8 mi N on FR 100; 2 mi N on FR 101. Free. About 6/15-11/15; 14-day limit. Primitive dispersed sites around lake. Toilet, cfga, no drkg wtr, no trash service. Fishing, mountain biking, hiking.

Sheriff Reservoir $10
Routt National Forest
W of Yampa on CR 16, then S on FR 959. $10. 6/15-11/15; 14-day limit. 6 sites (20-ft RV limit). Tbls, toilets, cfga, no drkg wtr. Boating(l), fishing, hiking trails, horseback riding. Elev 9800 ft.

Trout Creek FREE
Recreation Area
Routt National Forest
About 5 mi N/NW of Yampa on CR 17; left on CR 132 for about 4 mi; 5 mi N/NW on FR 925; at Trout Creek. Free. June-Nov; 14-day limit. Primitive undesignated sites. Toilet, cfga, no drkg wtr, no trash service. Fishing.

Vaughn Lake $10
Routt National Forest
5 mi N of Yampa on SR 131; 18.2 mi W on FR 16. $10. 6/15-11/15; 14-day limit. 6 sites (22-ft RV limit). Tbls, toilets, cfga, no drkg wtr. Boating(ld - elec mtrs), picnicking, fishing, hunting. Elev 9500 ft; Trailhead nearby to Flat Tops Wilderness.

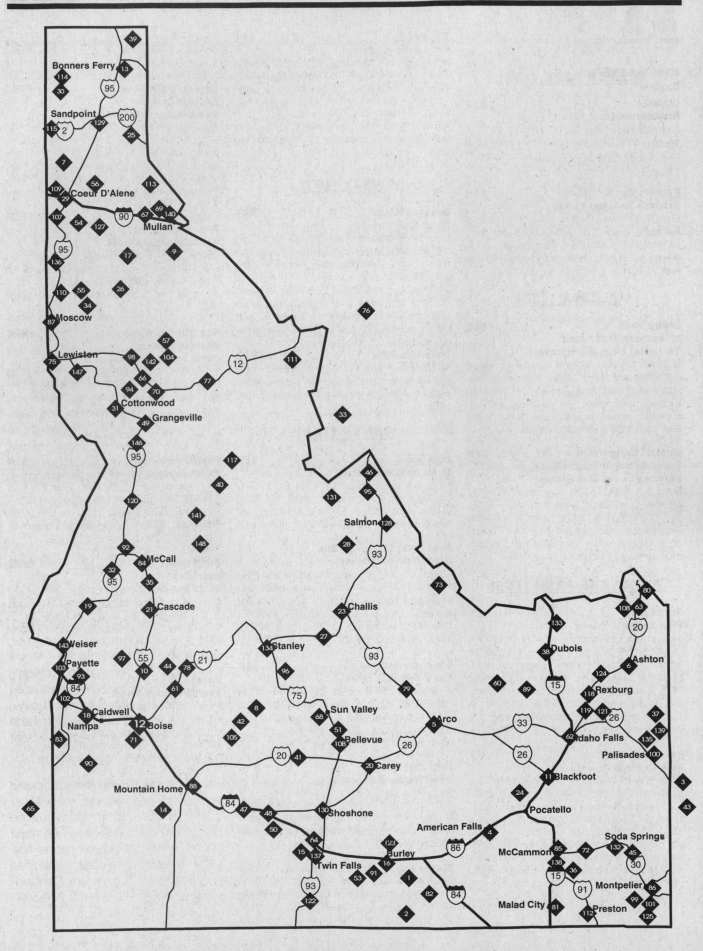

IDAHO

MISCELLANEOUS
Capital:
Boise
Nickname:
Gem State
Motto:
Esto Perpetua (It Is Forever)
Flower:
Syringa (Mock Orange)
Tree:
Western White Pine
Bird:
Mountain Bluebird
Song:
"Here We Have Idaho"

Internet Address:
www.visitid.org

Idaho Division of Tourism Development, 700 West State St, PO Box 83720, Boise, ID 83720-0093; 208-334-0093; 800/VISIT-ID.

Dept of Fish and Game, 600 S. Walnut St., Boise, ID 83707. 208/334-3700.

Idaho Parks and Recreation, Statehouse Mall, PO Box 83720, Boise, ID 83720; 208/334-4199.

REST AREAS
Overnight stops at most state rest areas are not permitted.

STATE PARKS
Campsites $9 to $22 per night, depending upon amenities. Primitive sites without amenities are $9; standard sites (table, grill, campspur, vault toilet, no water) are $12; "serviced" sites (with water OR electric hookups) are $16; serviced sites with water and electric are $20 or $22; full hookups, $24. Maximum length of stay, 15 days in any 30-day period. Seniors (62 or older) may camp for half price at nine parks during Monday and Thursday. Day-use fees of $4 are no loner charged in addition to camping fees. Monthly rates for campsites are available. Pets on leashes are permitted in campgrounds. RV size restrictions range from 22 feet to 35 feet. Handicapped camping sites area available in each campground. For more information, write Idaho Department of Parks and Recreation, PO Box 83720, Boise, ID 83720-0065; 208/334-4199.

NATIONAL FORESTS
U.S. Forest Service, 1249 S. Vinell Way, Boise, ID 83709. 208-373-4100.

Bitterroot National Forest. No fees are charged for camping at the forest's five recreation sites in Idaho. 316 N. 3rd St., Hamilton, MT 59840. 406/363-7161.

Boise National Forest. At 2.6 million acres, it is one of the nation's largest. Located in south-central Idaho, it is characterized by forested mountains, high rolling meadows, deep canyons and water, timber, forage, mineral and wildlife resources. There are 70 developed campgrounds and nearly 800 miles of trails. Boise National Forest, 1249 S. Vinnell Way, Boise, ID 83709. 208/373-4100.

Caribou National Forest and Curlew National Grasslands. Located in the southeast corner of the state. There are no specified backcountry or wilderness camping areas. Camping in any unimproved site is regulated only by a 16-day limit. All refuse must be packed out, and campfires must be attended at all times. In excess of 1,000 miles of trails are open to hiking, horseback riding and trail biking. The forest has several developed campgrounds. For further information, contact Forest Supervisor, Caribou-Targhee National Forest, 1405 Hollipark Dr, Idaho Falls, ID 83401; 208-524-7500.

Challis National Forest. This 2.5-million-acre forest is located in the central part of the state. The Middle Fork of the Salmon Wild and Scenic River flows 106 miles through the Idaho Primitive Area. There are free campsites along the river, and a primitive trail parallels it. Nearly 1,600 miles of trails and 35 developed camp and picnic sites are found in the forest. For a free guide and map that pinpoint river campsites and campgrounds accessible by vehicle, contact Forest Service, Intermountain Region, 324-25th St., Ogden, UT 84401. Information about the forest from Salmon-Challis National Forest, 1206 S. Challis St., Salmon, ID 83467. 208/756-5100.

Clearwater National Forest. This forest includes 1.8 million acres ranging in elevation from 1,600 feet to almost 9,000. Much of it is snowbound December through May. All campgrounds are located near streams or rivers. Facilities which are not closed by accessibility may be used without charge during the off-season. Camping elsewhere in the forest is permitted unless otherwise posted. Numerous attractive roadside campsites are available. Of special interest to readers of this book: The forest's two main rivers, the North Fork of the Clearwater and the Lochsa, are paralleled by road -- Forest Roads 247 and 250 on the North Fork and Highway 12 along the Lochsa. There are numerous no-cost "dispersed" campsites along both roads. An RV sewage dump station is available for use at Wilderness Gateway Campground, NE of Kooskia on US 12. 12730 Highway 12, Orofino, ID 83544; 208/476-4541.

Nez Perce National Forest. Located entirely within Idaho County in north-central Idaho. It offers primitive recreational opportunities for hikers, backpackers, horseback riders and river floaters. It has 29 campgrounds, 4 picnic areas and a private hot springs resort. Nez Perce National Forest, 1005 Highway 13, Grangeville, ID 83530. 208/983-1950.

Payette National Forest. This 2-million-acre area is in west-central Idaho. It has 25 developed camp and picnic grounds and more than 2,400 miles of trails. 800 W. Lakeside Avel, PO Box 1026, McCall, ID 83638. 208/634-0700.

St. Joe, Kaniksu and Coeur D'Alene National Forests. Grouped together in north Idaho, they feature moderately steep to rugged mountains with the large and beautiful lakes of Priest, Pend Oreille and Coeur D'Alene. Fishing, swimming, berry-picking, horseback riding and dispersed camping. Primitive, designated campsites are provided near Gospel Hill and Meadow Creek. The forests do not have free off-season periods; fees are charged the entire time the campgrounds are open. Contact Idaho Panhandle National Forests, 3815 Schreiber Way, Coeur d'Alene, ID 83815. 208/765-7223.

Salmon National Forest. In east-central Idaho bordering Montana, it is extremely mountainous with numerous lakes, rivers and streams. There are 21 developed camp and picnic grounds and 1,100 miles of trails in the forest. All sites for which fees are charged are free during the off-season. Weather may prevent access, however. 1206 S. Challis St., Salmon, ID 83467. 208/756-5100.

Bighorn Crags Area--Idaho Primitive Area. Camping and hiking in this remote section of the primitive area requires detailed planning or a guide. Primitive campsites with toilet facilities are Crags Camp (main trailhead), Big Clear Lake, Birdbill Lake, Heart Lake, Terrace Lake and Welcome Lake.

Sawtooth National Forest. More than 2 million acres in south-central Idaho and some of northern Utah. There are 87 developed camp and picnic grounds and more than 1,500 miles of trails. Many of the campgrounds for which fees are charged are available without charge before and after the "managed" season. Fees are charged only if all standardly available services, such as drinking water and toilets, are still offered. Water supplies are shut off during the free period. Contact the nearest district ranger office for specific site availability. Sawtooth National Forest, 2647 Kimberly Road East, Twin Falls, ID 83301. 208/737-3200.

Targhee National Forest. Located in southeast Idaho, bordering Montana on the north and including a bit of Wyoming on the east. This 1.8 million-acre area has 31 developed camp and picnic sites as well as 1,500 miles of trails. The forest has numerous undeveloped, dispersed camping areas that are open to camping without charge. Inquire at the appropriate district ranger offices for further information on dispersed sites. Generally, developed campgrounds are open either from Memorial Day weekend or in mid-June until after Labor Day. Some campgrounds are open to free dry camping until access is blocked by snow; water and trash service are not provided during free periods. Targhee National Forest, 1405 Hollipark Dr, Idaho Falls, ID 83401; 208-524-7500.

CRATERS OF THE MOON NATIONAL MONUMENT
There are no backcountry campsites, but camping is permitted anywhere in the 68-square-mile wilderness so long as it is one mile within the wilderness boundary. Entrance fees are not collected when the park road is closed because of snow (usually mid-October to late April). Camping fees of $6 are collected at Lava Flow Campground when the water supply is turned off (usually mid-October to late April). Otherwise camping fees at the 52-site facility are $10; no hookups are available. No wood fires; dump stations and showers are not available. A wilderness permit is required for camping in the wilderness.

Corps of Engineers, Albeni Falls Dam, 2576 East Hwy 2, Oldtown, ID 83822.

U.S. Bureau of Reclamation, 1150 N. Curtis Rd, Boise, ID 83706. 208/378-5312.

ALBION (1)

Bennett Springs   **FREE**
Sawtooth National Forest
5.5 mi SE of Albion on SR 77; 4.9 mi SW on FR 549. 5/30-101; 14-day limit. 6 sites. Tbls, toilets, cfga, firewood. Picnicking, hiking, fishing (2 mi). Elev 8000 ft; 5 acres. Mountains. Streams.

Lake Cleveland   **$8**
Sawtooth National Forest
5.5 mi SE of Albion on SR 77; 10 mi W on FR 549 (very rough). $8. 7/10-10/15; 14-day limit. 29 sites. Tbls, toilets, cfga, drkg wtr. Fishing.

ALMO (2)

City of Rocks   **$12**
National Reserve
3 mi SW of Almo on Elba Almo Rd. $12. 4/1-11/1; 15-day limit. Managed jointly by National Park Service and Idaho Department of Parks & Recreation. 90 primitive sites. Tbls, toilets, cfga, no drkg wtr. Mountain biking, rock climbing, horseback riding. 14,300-acre scenic geologic area.

ALPINE (WYOMING) (3)

Alpine   **$8**
Targhee National Forest
3 mi NW of Alpine on US 26; at E edge of Palisades Reservoir. $8 during MD-LD; free LD-closure, but no wtr; 14-day limit. 15 sites (32-ft RV limit). Tbls, toilets, cfga, drkg wtr. Fishing, hiking, horseback riding. Snake River; Yellowstone and Grant Teton National Parks.

McCoy Creek   **$8**
Targhee National Forest
5 mi S of Alpine on US 89; 6 mi NW on FR 087; at S end of Palisades Reservoir. $8 during MD-LD; free LD-10/31, but no wtr; 14-day limit. 19 sites (32-ft RV size limit). Tbls, flush toilets, cfga, drkg wtr. Boating(l), canoeing, swimming, fishing, waterskiing. Elev 5800 ft; 4 acres.

AMERICAN FALLS (4)

Great Rift Backcountry   **FREE**
Bureau of Land Management
From I-86 exit 40 N of American Falls, NE on SR 39 past American Falls dam, then left on Center Pleasant Valley Rd (Rd 2600-S) for 7 mi; 6 mi N on Lava Bed Rd; 6 mi on dirt Crystal Cave Rd to vicinity called "The Frying Pan." Free. 4/1-11/31; 14-day limit. Primitive undesignated camping; no facilities. The 635-square-mile Great Rift is the largest, deepest and most recent volcnic rift system in continental U.S. Explore lava caves, spatter caves, ice tubes, cinder cones.

Indian Springs   **$12**
Swimming & RV Park
1.5 mi S of I-86 on Hwy 37 at exit 36 near American Falls. $12 base for primitive camping; 125 sites with elec/wtr; 36 full hookups ($18). Tbls, flush toilets, cfga, showers, drkg wtr, dump, pool, coin laundry, snack bar. Volleyball, horseshoes, driving range, game room

Massacre Rocks State Park   **$10**
10 mi SW of American Falls on I-86, exit 28. $10 for seniors at sites with elec/wtr (others pay $20. All year; 15-day limit. 40 sites (55-ft RV limit). Tbls, toilets, cfga, drkg wtr, dump, showers. Limited facilities in winter. Boating(l), fishing, hiking trails, nature program, mountain biking, horseshoes, visitor center. Elev 4400 ft; 990 acres. Register Rock from Oregon Trail pioneers.

Pipeline Recreation Site   **FREE**
Bureau of Land Management
Pocatello Field Office
1 mi W on N Frontage Rd; N toward river. Free. 4/15-10/31; 14-day limit. 5 sites (25-ft RV limit). Toilets, cfga, tbls. Boating, fishing, picnicking.

Fishing tip: American Falls Reservoir is one of the best rainbow trout lakes in the region, especially along Sportsman Bay near Aberdeen or by the dam.

Travel tip: Visit the American Falls Fish Hatchery 1.5 mi NW of town on SR 39; 1 mi S on country rd; see how fish are reared. 226-2015.

Willow Bay   **$11**
City Recreation Area
From I-86 exit 40 at American Falls, NW 1.5 mi on Hwy 39; 2 mi NE on Fort Hall Rd & follow signs to marina at American Falls Reservoir. $11 base. 4/1-10/1. 35 developed sites plus about 60 undeveloped sites. Tbls, flush toilets, cfga, drkg wtr, hookups($), showers, dump, coin laundry, playground. Boating(ld), horseshoes, fishing, volleyball, waterskiing, windsurfing, biking, swimming.

ARCO (5)

Lava Flow   **$10**
Craters of the Moon National Monument
18 mi S of Arco on US 20. $10 plus entry fee; $6 off-season but no wtr. All year; 14-day limit. 52 sites (35-ft RV limit). Tbls, toilets, cfga, drkg wtr. Hiking, winter sports, visitor center, interpretive programs.

ASHTON (6)

Cave Falls   **$10**
Targhee National Forest
5 mi N of Ashton on SR 47; 7 mi E on CR 36; half mi S of Yellowstone National Park. IN WYOMING. $10. MD-9/15; 16-day limit. 23 sites (22-ft RV limit). Tbls, toilets, cfga, drkg wtr. Swimming, fishing, hiking trails. Elev 6200 ft; 16 acres.

Grandview   **$**
Targhee National Forest
15 mi E of Ashton on SR 47 (Mesa Falls Scenic Byway). Fees unavailable. 6/1-9/30. 14-day limit. 5 sites on 6 acres (RVs under 22 ft). Tbls, toilets, cfga, firewood, no drkg wtr. Horseback riding, picnicking, fishing nearby. Elev 6200 ft. 47 mi to West Yellowstone.

Fishing tip: Nearby Henrys Fork River has excellent rainbow trout fishing; or, drive N to Henry Lake for big rainbows, cutthroat and hybrid bass.

Travel tip: Here can be found the Lower and Upper Mesa Falls, two of the last undisturbed waterfalls on consequence in the West; Lower Mesa can easily be seen at the Grandview campground; for Upper Mesa Falls, follow the highway N of the campground about half mi to a gravel rd on the left side; this falls plunges 114 feet.

Pole Bridge   **FREE**
Targhee National Forest
12 mi NE of Ashton on US 47; 3.5 mi N on CR 294; 2.5 mi E on FR 156; 4.5 mi N on FR 150; at Warm River. Free. 6/1-10/31. 14-day limit. 20 sites (RVs under 23 ft). Tbls, toilets, cfga, firewood, well drkg wtr. Fishing, picnicking.

Riverside   **$12**
Targhee National Forest
16.5 mi N of Ashton on US 20; 1 mi SE on FR 304; at Henry's Fork River. $12. 5/10-10/1; 16-day limit. 55 sites (35-ft RV limit). Tbls, toilets, cfga, drkg wtr. Fishing, boating. Elev 6200 ft; 24 acres.

Warm River   **$12**
Targhee National Forest
10 mi NE of Ashton on SR 47; near confluence of Warm River & Henrys Fork. $12 during 5/15-10/15; free 9/24-10/15, but no wtr; full hookups $23. 16-day limit. 29 sites (22-ft RV limit). Flush toilets, cfga, drkg wtr, Fishing, hiking, floating, biking, horseback riding. Handicap access. Elev 5200 ft; 7 acres.

West End   **$**
Targhee National Forest
18 mi N of Ashton on US 20; 15 mi NW on FR 167; on Island Park Reservoir. Fees unavailable. Elev 6200 ft. MD-10/15; 16-day limit. 19 sites (RVs under 23 ft) Tbls, toilets, cfga. Swimming, boating (ld), picnicking, fishing, waterskiing, berry picking, horseback riding. Elev 6200 ft; 15 acres.

ATHOL (7)

Farragut State Park   **$12**
4 mi E of Athol on SR 54; off US 95. $12 at standard sites without hookups. All year; 15-day limit. 184 sites (60-ft RV limit); hookup sites $20 & $22. Tbls, flush toilets, cfga, drkg wtr, dump, elec($), showers, fish cleaning station. Limited facilities in winter. Swimming, boating(l), fishing, ski trails, snowmobiling, hiking trails, horseback riding, mountain biking, playground, horseshoes,

volleyball, nature walks, waterskiing, interpretive programs, visitor center, shooting range, volleyball, disc golf. 3,923 acres. Lake Pend Oreille.

Fishing tip: The world record kamloops (37 pounds) was caught in Lake Pend Oreille. The lake also contains rainbow & lake trout, crappie, bass and whitefish.

ATLANTA (8)

Neinmeyer　　　　　　　　　　**FREE**
Boise National Forest
27 mi W of Atlanta on FR 268. Free. 6/1-10/31; 14-day limit. 8 sites (RVs under 22 ft). Tbls, toilets, cfga, firewood. Picnicking, fishing, horseback riding. Elev 3800 ft; 2 acres. Adjacent to middle fork of Boise River. Minimum-maintenance site.

Fishing tip: Good spot to fish for rainbow and brown trout.

Power Plant　　　　　　　　　**FREE**
Boise National Forest
2.5 mi NE of Atlanta on FR 268; near headwaters of Middle Fork of Boise River. Free. Elev 5800 ft. 6/1-10/1; 14-day limit. 24 sites on 18 acres (RVs under 22 ft). Tbls, toilets, cfga, drkg wtr. Horseback riding, hiking, picnicking, fishing. Gateway to Sawtooth Wilderness Area.

Queens River　　　　　　　　　**FREE**
Boise National Forest
6 mi W of Atlanta on FR 268; at Middle Fork Boise River. Free. 6/1-9/30; 14-day limit. 4 tent sites. Tbls, toilets, cfga, firewood, no drkg wtr. Fishing, picnicking, horseback riding, biking. Elev 5000 ft; 2 acres. Minimum maintenance.

AVERY (9)

Beaver Creek　　　　　　　　　**FREE**
St. Joe National Forest
29 mi E of Avery on FR 50 (St. Joe River Rd); 8 mi S on FR 218. Free. 6/1-10/31; 14-day limit. 3 sites. Tbls, toilet, cfga, no drkg wtr, no trash service. Hiking, fishing (cutthroat trout).

Conrad Crossing　　　　　　　**FREE**
St. Joe National Forest
29 mi E of Avery on FR 50 (St. Joe River Rd). Free. 6/1-10/30; 14-day limit. 8 sites (3 on river, 5 above hwy); RVs under 16 ft. Tbls, toilets, cfga, well drkg wtr June-Oct. Fishing (cutthroat trout), picnicking, swimming. Elev 3600 ft; 5 acres. Historic Montana trail. On St. Joe Wild & Scenic River, trout waters.

Fly Flat　　　　　　　　　　　**FREE**
St. Joe National Forest
29 mi E of Avery on FR 50 (St. Joe River Rd); 4 mi S on FR 218. Camp free, but donations accepted. About 6/1-10/31; 14-day limit. 14 sites (RVs under 32 ft). Tbls, toilets, cfga, firewood, drkg wtr June-Oct. Picnicking, fishing, hiking, swimming. Elev 3500 ft; 6 acres. 5 mi

N of Red Ives Ranger Station. On St. Joe River, wild trout waters.

Heller Creek　　　　　　　　　**FREE**
St. Joe National Forest
29 mi E of Avery on FR 50; 10 mi S on FR 218; 13.7 mi E on FR 320. Free. Elev 4700 ft. 6/15-10/31; 14-day limit. 4 sites on 4 acres (RVs under 22 ft). Tbls, toilets, cfga, no drkg wtr. Memorial. Rd 320 is very rough. Alternative route from Superior, MT, better for low-clearance vehicles. Heller grave site.

Line Creek Stock Camp　　　　**FREE**
St. Joe National Forest
29 mi E of Avery on St. Joe River Rd (FR 50); 10 mi S on Red Ives Rd (FR 218). Free. All year; 14-day limit. 9 pull-through sites for stock trailers. Tbls, toilets, cfga, no drkg wtr. Feed bunks, hitching posts, trailhead parking. Hiking, horseback riding.

Fishing tip: Fish for wild trout at the start of the wild portion of St. Joe River.

Mammoth Springs　　　　　　　**FREE**
St. Joe National Forest
22 mi E of Avery on FR 50; 14 mi S on FR 509; 2.5 mi S on FR 201. Free. 6/15-10/15; 14-day limit. 8 sites (RVs under 23 ft). Tbls, toilets, cfga, drkg wtr Jul-Oct. Picnicking, berry picking. 1 mi to Dismal Lake. Elev 5700 ft.

Packsaddle　　　　　　　　　　**FREE**
St. Joe National Forest
5 mi E of Avery on FR 50; at St. Joe River. Free. 6/1-10/31; 14-day limit. 2 sites. Tbls, toilet, cfga, no drkg wtr, no trash service. Fishing, hiking, horseback riding. Trailead for Packsaddle Nelson Ridge National Recreation Trail.

Spruce Tree　　　　　　　　　**FREE**
St. Joe National Forest
29 mi E of Avery on FR 50 (St. Joe River Rd); 12 mi S on FR 218 (Red Ives Rd). Free. 6/1-10/31; 14-day limit. 9 sites (35-ft RV limit). Tbls, toilets, cfga, drkg wtr June-Oct, no trash service. Swimming, fishing, hiking to virgin backcountry.

Squaw Creek　　　　　　　　　**FREE**
St. Joe National Forest
4.8 mi N of Avery on CR 456; 1 mi S on Old Moon Pass Rd. MD-11/1. 5 undesignated tent sites. Tbls, toilets, cfga, firewood, no drkg wtr. Picnicking, fishing. Elev 2600 ft; 2 acres. North Fork St. Joe River. Sites not suitable for RVs.

Tin Can Flat　　　　　　　　　**$6**
St. Joe National Forest
11 mi E of Avery on FR 50 (St. Joe River Rd); at St. Joe River. $6. About 5/15-10/31; 14-day limit. 11 sites (32-ft RV limit). Tbls, toilets, drkg wtr, cfga, no trash service. Hiking, fishing.

Turner Flat　　　　　　　　　**$6**
St. Joe National Forest
8 me E of Avery on FR 50; at St. Joe River. $6. About 5/15-10/31; 14-day limit. 11 sites (32-ft RV limit). Tbls, toilets, drkg wtr, cfga, no trash service. Hiking, fishing.

BANKS (10)

Big Eddy　　　　　　　　　　　**$10**
Boise National Forest
15 mi N of Banks on SR 55; on North Fork of Payette River. $10. 5/1-10/1; 14-day limit. 5 sites (32-ft RV limit). Tbls, toilets, cfga, no drkg wtr. Picnicking, fishing, swimming, boating. Elev 3600 ft.

Fishing tip: Try the excellent trout fishing near camp.

Canyon　　　　　　　　　　　　**$10**
Boise National Forest
8.2 mi N of Banks on SR 55; in narrow canyon formed by North Fork of Payette River. $10. 5/15-10/1; 14-day limit. 7 sites (30-ft RV limit) Tbls, toilets, cfga, drkg wtr. Trout fishing, whitewater rafting. Elev 3600 ft. Closed during 2007.

Cold Springs　　　　　　　　　**$10**
Boise National Forest
9.5 mi N on SR 55; at North Fork of Payette River. $10. 4/15-10/20; 14-day limit. 6 sites (25-ft RV limit). Tbls, toilets, cfga, drkg wtr. Trout fishing, whitewater rafting. Elev 3600 ft. Closed during 2007.

Swinging Bridge　　　　　　　**$10**
Boise National Forest
3.2 mi N of Banks on SR 55. $10. 4/20-10/20; 14-day limit. 11 sites (25-ft RV limit). Tbls, toilets, cfga, drkg wtr. Fishing. Elev 4000; 6 acres.

BELLEVUE (10B)

Copper Creek　　　　　　　　　**FREE**
Sawtooth National Forest
25 mi E & N of Bellevue on Muldoon Canyon Rd 25, then N & E on FR 134. Free. 5/15-10/15. 5 sites (RVs under 22 ft). Tbls, toilets, cfga, firewood, no drkg wtr. Horseback riding, picnicking, fishing, rockhounding. Agates 2 mi W of campground. Elev 6400 ft.

BLACKFOOT (11)

Cutthroat Trout　　　　　　　**FREE**
Bureau of Land Management
Pocatello Field Office
7 mi N of Blackfoot on Hwy 91; 10 mi E on Wolverine rd; right on Cedar Creek Rd for 13 mi; right on Trail Creek Bridge Rd for 6 mi; road turns into Lincoln Creek Rd; 1 mi to camp. Free. 5/1-10/31; 14-day limit. 3 primitive sites (15-ft RV limit). Tbls, toilets, cfga, no drkg wtr. Fishing.

Graves Creek   **FREE**
Bureau of Land Management
Pocatello Field Office
7 mi N of Blackfoot on Hwy 91; 10 mi E on Wolverine Rd; right on Cedar Creek Rd for 13 mi; right on Trail Creek Bridge Rd for 6 mi; road turns into Lincoln Creek Rd; 1 mi to camp. Free. 5/1-10/31; 14-day limit. 5 sites (15-ft RV limit). Tbls, toilets, cfga, no drkg wtr. Fishing.

McTucker Ponds   **FREE**
Bingham County Park
13 mi W of Blackfoot on Hwy 39; left for 3 mi at sign for McTucker Ponds; near upper end of American Falls Reservoir. Free. All year. Primitive undesignated sites near 8 small gravel pits. No facilities except cfga; no drkg wtr. Fishing, hiking, birdwatching.
Fishing tip: The ponds contain channel catfish, largemouth bass and bluegill and are stocked annually with rainbow trout.

Sage Hen Flats   **FREE**
Bureau of Land Management
7 mi N of Blackfoot on Hwy 91; 10 mi E on Wolverine Rd; right on Cedar Creek Rd for 13 mi; right on Trail Creek Bridge Rd for 6 mi; rd turns into Lincoln Creek Rd; 6 mi to camp. Free. 5/1-10/31; 14-day limit. 5 sites (15-ft RV limit). Tbls, toilets, cfga, no drkg wtr. Fishing.

✪ BOISE (12)

Badger Creek   **FREE**
Boise National Forest
16 mi E of Boise on SR 21; at Lucky Peak Nursery, go 21 mi E on FR 268. Free. Elev 3400 ft. 4/15-10/15; 14-day limit. 5 sites; 1 acre. Tbls, toilets, cfga, firewood, no drkg wtr. Picnicking, fishing, horseback riding. On Middle Fork of Boise River.

Cottonwood   **FREE**
Boise National Forest
16 mi E of Boise on SR 21; 15 mi E on FR 268 & FR 377; at Cottonwood Creek. Free. 4/15-10/31; 14-day limit. 3 tent sites (no trailers). Tbls, toilets, cfga, firewood. Boating, waterskiing, horseback riding, picnicking, fishing. Elev 3300 ft; 2 acres. Within 1 mi of the Cottonwood Ranger Station. Minimum maintenance camp. Secluded.

Cove Recreation Site   **FREE**
Snake River Birds of Prey
National Conservation Area
Bureau of Land Management
35 mi S of Boise. From I-84 exit 44, follow SR 69 S 8 mi; e mi S on Swan Falls Rd to boundary of conservation area. Free. All year; 14-day limit. Developed sites at campground & free dispersed camping throughout the area. Toilets, tbls, cfga, drkg wtr. Educational programs, interpretive displays, fishing, hiking, horseback riding, biking, boating(l). Area contains largest concentration of nesting birds in North America; about 800 pairs of falcons, eagles, hawks & owls.

Riverside Campground   **FREE**
Boise National Forest
16 mi N of Boise on SR 21; from Lucky Peak Nursery, go 62 mi E on FR 268; on Middle Fork of Boise River. Free. 6/1-9/30; 14-day limit. 11 sites. Tbls, toilets, cfga, no drkg wtr. Hiking (trailhead from Power Plant Camp 1 mi E), fishing, horseback riding. Elev 5600 ft.

Shafer Butte   **$8**
Boise National Forest
16 mi NE of Boise on Bogus Basin Rd; 3 mi N on FR 374; 1.5 mi E on Shafer Butte Rd. $8. MD-LD; 14-day limit. 7 sites (22-ft RV limit). Tbls, toilets, cfga, drkg wtr. Hiking.

Troutdale   **FREE**
Boise National Forest
16 mi E of Boise on SR 68; 28 mi NE on FR 268. Free. Elev 3600 ft. 4/15-10/31; 14-day limit. 5 sites on 2 acres (RVs under 22 ft). Tbls, toilets, cfga, firewood, no drkg wtr. Picnicking, fishing, horseback riding. On middle fork of Boise River. Minimum maintenance.

BONNERS FERRY (13)

Blue Lake RV Park   **$10**
8 mi S of Bonners Ferry on US 95. $10 for primitive & tent sites; $17-20 with hookups. 4/1-10/31. 45 sites. Tbls, flush toilets, showers, cfga, drkg wtr, coin laundry, dump. Swimming, hiking, fishing.
Travel tip: While in the area, drive over Moyie Bridge on US 2; bridge hovers between canyon walls suspended 450 feet above the river; just S of bridge is rd to Moyie Falls, a spectacular sight.

Meadow Creek   **$6**
Kaniksu National Forest
From US 2, N of Bonners Ferry, 11 mi N on Meadow Creek Rd (CR 34); at Moyi River. $6. MD-LD; 14-day limit. 22 sites. Tbls, toilets, cfga, drkg wtr. Fishing (brook & cutthroat trout), berry-picking, boating.

Smith Lake Campground   **FREE**
Kaniksu National Forest
5 mi N of Bonners Ferry on US 95; 2 mi N CR 35. Free. 5/15-9/15; 14-day limit. 7 sites. Tbls, toilets, cfga, drkg wtr. Hiking, fishing, boating(l), swimming. On an isolated patch of forest, so get permission from landowner for access.

BRUNEAU (14)

Bruneu River   **FREE**
Recreation Area
Bureau of Land Management
If traveling west, from Hwy 51, take the Grasmere-Rowland Rd; if east (preferred), access via the Bruneau-Three Creek Rd. Both rds are rough, 4WD required. Free. Primitive undesignated tent camping; no facilities. Fishing, whitewater rafting, hunting.

Cottonwood Campground   **$8**
Idaho Power Company
State Fish & Game Department
5.7 mi W of Bruneau on SR 78; N to Bruneau Arm of C.J. Strike Reservoir. $8. All year; 14-day limit. 40 sites. Tbls, toilets, cfga, drkg wtr. Fishing, boating(l), hiking.
Fishing tip: The lake area near the campground is an excellent place to fish by float tube. Cast back toward the overhanging brush or rocky shoreline for smallmouth bass and crappies. Or, fish from shore near camp for bluegill, perch, crappie, trout and bass.

BUHL (15)

Miracle Hot Springs   **$10**
10 mi W of Buhl on Hwy 30. $10 base for primitive sites; $20 with elec. 35 sites. Tbls, flush toilets, cfga, drkg wtr, hookups($), spa, pool. Fishing, swimming, volleyball.

BURLEY (16)

4 Families RV Park   **$10**
In Burley at 900 N. Overland Ave; exit 208 from I-84. $10 base. 16 sites. Tbls, toilets, cfga, drkg wtr, hookups. No other information available.

Milner Recreation Area   **$5**
Bureau of Land Management
7 mi W of Burley on US 30; 1 mi N at the Milner Historic/Recreation Area sign; 3 mi W on gravel rd. $5 (Sept-March sportsman pass, $15; annual pass $25). 5/1-10/31; 14-day limit. Tbls, toilets, cfga. Boating(l), fishing, hiking.

CALDER (17)

Big Creek   **FREE**
St. Joe National Forest
6 mi E on CR 347; 3 mi NW on FR 537. Free. 6/1-10/31; 14-day limit. 9 sites; 30-ft RV limit. Toilets, cfga, drkg wtr, tbls. Hiking, fishing, horseback riding. Site of former CCC camp.

Donkey Creek   **FREE**
St. Joe National Forest
11 mi E of Calder on FR 50; 8 mi S on FR 321; at Marble Creek. Elev 2800 ft. 2 sites on 2 acres (RVs under 22 ft). Tbls, toilets, cfga, firewood. Berry picking, fishing. Historic site.
Travel tip: The nearby Marble Creek Historical Site exhibits early 1900s equipment & techniques, including a replica logging flume. Several other artifacts, including cabins, are scattered throughout the area and can be explored.

CALDWELL (18)

Sandhollow RV Park   **$10**
From I-84's Caldwell exit 17, 1 mi S on Old Hwy 30 from Sandhollow Store; 1 mi E on Hollow Rd. $10 ($50 weekly; $200 monthly). 10 sites; 35-ft RV limit. Drkg wtr, dump, hookups.

CAMBRIDGE (19)

Brownlee   **$8**
Payette National Forest
16.5 mi NW of Cambridge on SR 71; 1 mi E on FR 044; at Brownlee Creek. $8 during 5/15-10/31; $5 during 4/15-5/30 & 9/10-10/31; 16-day limit. 11 sites on 4 acres (RVs under 17 ft). Tbls, toilets, cfga, drkg wtr. Horseback riding, picnicking, fishing. Elev 4200 ft. Closest forest campground to Brownlee Reservoir, perhaps the best fishing lake in Idaho.

Copperfield Park   **$8**
Idaho Power Company
Hwy 71 from Cambridge to Oxbow, Oregon; right on OR 86. $8 for RVs ($5 tents) during Nov-March; sites $16 & $10 in-season. All year; 14-day limit. 62 sites (50-ft RV limit). Tbls, flush toilets, cfga, drkg wtr, dump, elec($), showers. Hiking, fishing.

Hells Canyon Park   **$8**
Idaho Power Company
Hwy 71 from Cambridge toward Brownlee Dam; right just before crossing Snake River Bridge; half mi N. $8 for RVs ($5 tents) during Nov-March; sites $16 & $10 in-season. All year; 14-day limit. 24 sites (40-ft RV limit). Tbls, flush toilets, showers, drkg wtr, dump, elec($). Handicap access. Fishing, hiking, boating(ld), hunting.

McCormick Park   **$8**
Idaho Power Company
28 mi N of Cambridge on Hwy 71 to Snake River; follow signs (on Idaho side of Oxbow Reservoir). $8 for RVs ($5 tents) during Nov-March; $16 & $10 in-season. All year; 14-day limit. 34 sites (30-ft RV limit). Tbls, flush toilets, showers, drkg wtr, cfga, elec/wtr, dump. Fishing, swimming, boating (ld). 12 acres.

Woodhead Park   **$8**
Idaho Power Company
Hwy 71 from Cambridge toward Brownlee Dam; half mi before reaching dam. $8 for RVs ($5 tents) during Nov-March; sites $16 & $10 in-season. All year; 14-day limit. 124 sites; 40-ft RV limit. Tbls, flush toilets, drkg wtr, elec, showers, cfga, dump. Handicap access. Hiking, fishing, boating. 65 acres.

CAREY (20)

Fish Creek Reservoir   **FREE**
Bureau of Land Management
Shoshone Field Office
Turn N on Hwy 93 about 6 mi E of Carey; proceed about 5 mi; signed. May be difficult access in winter. Free. 5/1-10/31; 14-day limit. Designated primitive sites (RVs under 30 ft) on N shore; dispersed sites around the lake. Toilets, cfga, no drkg wtr. Trout fishing, boating (ld), picnicking, sightseeing.

High-Five Campground   **$7**
Bureau of Reclamation
15 mi NW of Carey on co rd. $7 5/15-9/30; 14-day limit. 4 sites (60-ft RV limit). Tbls, toilets, cfga, drkg wtr. Fishing, picnicking, boating(l).

Little Wood Lake   **$7**
Bureau of Reclamation
10 mi N of Carey on Durfee Lane, Dry Creek Rd & Hunt Lane; at Little Wood River Reservoir. $7. 5/15-9/30; 14-day limit. 21 sites (30-ft RV limit). 206 acres. Tbls, drkg wtr, toilets, cfga. Swimming, picnicking, fishing, boating (l).
   Fishing tip: This lake contains rainbow, cutthroat and brook trout and kokanee salmon.

Silver Creek   **FREE**
Bureau of Land Management
Shoshone Field Office
7 mi S on Hwys 20/26/93, then follow signs 2 mi N. May be difficult access in winter. Free. 4/15-11/30; 14-day limit. Undesignated sites. Toilets, tbls, cfga, no drkg wtr. Fishing, picnicking, bird hunting.
   Fishing tip: Excellent rainbow and brown trout fishing on Silver Creek; use small spinners & flies.

CASCADE (21)

Big Sage Campground   **$9**
Bureau of Reclamation
Lake Cascade State Park
2.2 mi S of Cascade on Cascade Reservoir. $9 at primitive sites; seniors pay half price weekdays. 5/1-10/31; 15-day limit. 100 undeveloped, undefined primitive sites in open area (or at plowed parking lot in winter, but no wtr). Tbls, toilets, cfga, drkg wtr. Boating, fishing, hiking, swimming.

Blue Heron Campground   **$12**
Bureau of Reclamation
Lake Cascade State Park
S of Cascade on Cascade Reservoir. $12 at 12 standard sites during 5/1-10/31 ($9 for primitive camping at parking lot off-season, but no wtr); seniors pay half price weekdays. 15-day limit. Toilets, cfga, drkg wtr. Fishing, boating, swimming, hiking.

Buck Mountain   **FREE**
Boise National Forest
35 mi E of Cascade on Warm Lake Rd; 2 mi N on Johnson Creek Rd. Free. 6/15-10/30; 14-day limit. 4 sites (RVs under 16 ft). Tbls, toilets, cfga, firewood. Picnicking, fishing. Elev 6500 ft; 1 acre. Johnson Creek.

Buttercup Campground   **$12**
Bureau of Reclamation
Lake Cascade State Park
22.4 mi N of Cascade on W side of Cascade Reservoir. $12; seniors pay half price weekdays. 5/1-10/31; 15-day limit. 30 standard sites (32-ft RV limit). Tbls, toilets, cfga, drkg wtr, dump. Fishing, boating(l), swimming, hiking.
   Fishing tip: Cascade Lake contains coho salmon, rainbow trout, smallmouth bass and perch.

Crown Point   **$12**
Bureau of Reclamation
Lake Cascade State Park
W of Hwy 55 on Old State Highway, following signs; on Cascade Reservoir. $12; seniors pay half price weekdays. 5/1-10/31; 15-day limit. 38 standard sites without hookups (32-ft RV limit). Tbls, toilets, cfga, drkg wtr, dump. Fishing, boating(l), swimming, hiking.

Curlew   **$9**
Bureau of Reclamation
Lake Cascade State Park
S on Lakeshore Dr from Cascade; right on West Side Rd for 20 mi; on N side of Cascade Lake. $9; seniors pay half price weekdays. 5/1-10/31; 14-day limit. 25 primitive tent sites. Tbls, portable toilets, cfga, drkg wtr. Swimming, fishing, boating, hiking.

French Creek   **$10**
McCall Recreation Area
Boise National Forest
4 mi S of Cascade on CR 10422; 1 mi W on CR 10922; 4 mi N on FR 10922. $10. 5/15-9/15; 14-day limit. 21 sites (RVs under 30 ft). Tbls, toilets, cfga, drkg wtr. Boating(l), fishing, swim-ming, waterskiing. On Cascade Reservoir. Elev 4000 ft; 49 acres.

Golden Gate   **FREE**
Boise National Forest
35 mi E of Cascade on Warm Lake Rd; 23 mi N on Johnson Creek Rd; at South Fork of Salmon River. Free. 6/1-10/30; 14-day limit. 9 sites (RVs under 22 ft). Tbls, toilets, cfga, drkg wtr. Fishing, swimming, hiking, ATV activities, horseback riding, mountain biking.

Huckleberry Campground   **$12**
Bureau of Reclamation
Lake Cascade State Park
21 mi N of Cascade, on W side of Cascade Reservoir. $12. 5/1-10/31; 15-day limit. 33 standard sites without hookups (32-ft RV limit). Tbls, toilets, cfga, drkg wtr, dump. Hiking, boating(l), fishing, swimming. Formerly was named West Mountain North.

Ice Hole   **FREE**
Boise National Forest
35 mi E of Cascade on Warm Lake Rd; 19 mi N on Johnson Creek Rd; at South Fork of Salmon River. Free. 6/15-10/31; 14-day limit. 10 sites (RVs under 16 ft). Tbls, cfga, toilets, no drkg wtr. Fishing, swimming, hiking, ATV activities, horseback riding, mountain biking. Elev 5200 ft; 6 acres. Adjacent to Johnson Creek.

Pen Basin   **FREE**
Boise National Forest
1 mi N of Cascade on SR 55; 35 mi NE on FR 22 (Warm Lake Rd); 2.5 mi SE on FR 579; near Johnson Creek. Free. Elev 6700 ft. 6/15-

10/30; 14-day limit. 6 sites on 9 acres (RVs under 22 ft). Tbls, toilets, cfga, firewood. Picnicking, horseback riding, fishing, hiking.

Penny Springs   **FREE**
Boise National Forest
1 mi N of Cascade on SR 55; 23.5 mi NE on FR 22 (Warm Lake Rd); 4.5 mi N on FR 401 (South Fork Rd); near South Fork of Salmon River. Free. 5/1-11/30; 14-day limit. 4 tent sites. Tbls, toilets, cfga, no drkg wtr. Picnicking. Fishing 2 mi. Elev 5200 ft; 4 acres.

Picnic Point   **$6**
Boise National Forest
25 mi NE of Cascade on Warm Lake Rd; at Warm Lake. $6. 5/15-11/15; 14-day limit. 8 walk-in tent sites. Tbls, toilets, cfga, drkg wtr. Fishing, hiking, boating.

Poison Creek   **$12**
Bureau of Reclamation
Lake Cascade State Park
23.5 mi N of Cascade on W side of Cascade Reservoir. $12; seniors pay half price weekdays. All year; wtr only 5/15-10/15; 15-day limit. 20 standard sites (32-ft RV limit). Tbls, toilets, cfga, drkg wtr, dump. Hiking, boating(l), fishing, swimming.

Shoreline   **$10**
Boise National Forest
1 mi N of Cascade on SR 55; 24 mi NE on FR 22; 1 mi SW on FR 489. $10. 5/15-MD; 14-day limit. Parking fee of $2 at overflow sites. 31 sites (40-ft RV limit). Tbls, toilets, cfga, drkg wtr. Boating(l), fishing, swimming, waterskiing. Elev 5300 ft; 20 acres. Groceries.

Smith's Ferry   **FREE**
Boise Cascade Corp.
18 mi S of Cascade on SR 15. Free. 5/1-10/31; 14-day limit. 10 sites. Tbls, toilets, cfga, firewood, wtr hookup. Picnicking. Swimming & fishing nearby. River nearby. Mountainous.

South Fork Salmon River   **$10**
Boise National Forest
1 mi N of Cascade on SR 55; 23 mi NE on FR 22 (Warm Lake Rd). $10. 5/15-11/1; 14-day limit (camp may be closed during spawning season, 7/1-9/15, to protect salmon). 14 sites (RVs under 23 ft). Tbls, toilets, cfga, drkg wtr. Fishing, swimming. 10 acres. Chinook travel 700 miles from Pacific Ocean to spawn here. Elev 5100 ft.

Sugarloaf Campground   **$12**
Bureau of Reclamation
Lake Cascade State Park
8.8 mi N of Cascade. $12; seniors pay half price weekdays. 5/1-10/15; 14-day limit. 72 sites (32-ft RV limit). Tbls, toilets, cfga, drkg wtr. Boating(l), fishing, hiking, swimming.

Summit Lake   **FREE**
Boise National Forest
1 mi N of Cascade on SR 15; 32 mi NE on FR 22 (Warm Lake Rd); 7 mi SE on FR 579. Free. Elev 7200 ft. 6/15-10/30; 14-day

limit. 3 sites (RVs under 16 ft). Tbls, toilets, cfga, firewood, no drkg wtr. Picnicking, fishing boating(l), hiking, waterskiing. Between Warm Lake Creek and Summit Lake.

Trout Creek   **FREE**
Boise National Forest
35 mi E of Cascade on Warm Lake Rd; 8 mi N on Johnson Creek Rd; at Trout Creek. Free. 6/15-10/30; 14-day limit. 5 sites (RVs under 16 ft). Tbls, toilets, cfga, firewood, no drkg wtr. Horseback riding, hiking, picnicking, fishing. Elev 6200 ft; 2 acres.

Van Wyck Campground   **$12**
Bureau of Reclamation
Lake Cascade State Park
From jct of SR 55 & Old State Hwy, 2 mi W on Old State Hwy. $12 during 5/1-10/15, $9 at boat launch parking lot off-season, but no wtr (seniors pay half price weekdays); 15-day limit. 22 sites (32-ft RV limit). Tbls, flush toilets, cfga, drkg wtr, dump. Boating(l), fishing, hiking, swimming.

Warm Lake   **$10**
Boise National Forest
1 mi N of Cascade on SR 55; 26 mi NE on FR 22; qtr mi SE on FR 579RA. $10. 5/15-LD; 14-day limit. 12 sites (30-ft RV limit). Tbls, toilets, cfga, drkg wtr. Boating, fishing, swimming.

West Mountain   **$12**
Bureau of Reclamation
Lake Cascade State Park
23 mi N of Cascade, on W side of Cascade Reservoir. $12; senior pay half price weekdays. 5/15-10/15; 15-day limit. 18 sites (32-ft RV limit). Tbls, flush toilets, cfga, drkg wtr, dump. Hiking, boating(l), fishing, swimming.

Yellow Pine   **FREE**
Boise National Forest
35 mi E of Cascade on Warm Lake Rd; 25 mi N on Johnson Creek Rd; at South Fork of Salmon River. Free. 6/1-10/15; 14-day limit. 14 sites (RVs under 25 ft). Tbls, toilets, cfga, drkg wtr. Fishing, hiking. Elev 4800 ft; 12 acres. Groceries. Adjacent to Johnson Creek. Historic pioneer cemetery nearby.

CHALLIS (23)

Bayhorse Lake   **FREE**
Challis National Forest
10 mi S of Challis on US 93; 7.5 mi N on FR 051; between Bayhorse & Little Bayhorse Lakes. Free. 7/1-9/10. 7 sites on 12 acres (RVs under 21 ft). Tbls, toilets, cfga, firewood, no drkg wtr. Horseback riding, picnicking, fishing, rockhounding, OHV activity, biking, hiking. Trailers not advised; steep, narrow rds. Elev 8600 ft. Historic brickyard at Little Bayhorse Lake.

Bayhorse Recreation Site   **$10**
Bureau of Land Management
Challis Field Office
5 mi W of Challis on SR 75. $10. All year; 14-

day limit. 11 sites (28-ft RV limit). Tbls, toilets, drkg wtr. Hiking, boating, fishing, picnicking. Elev 5200 ft; 4 acres.

Travel tip: At Challis, stop at visitor center of the new state park, Land of the Yankee Fork; directions to the ghost towns of Bonanza and Custer; both were big mining towns of 1880s, now deserted; all that's left of Custer are a gold dredge, a few homes and schoolhouse containing a museum.

Big Creek   **FREE**
Challis National Forest
17 mi N of Challis on US 93 to Ellis; 28 mi S on Farm-to-Market Rd; about 4 mi E on FR 097; at confluence of North & South Forks of Big Creek. Free. 6/1-9/30; 14-day limit. 3 sites. Tbls, toilets, cfga, no drkg wtr. Fishing, hiking, horseback riding, OHV use, biking.

Boulder White Clouds   **FREE**
Trailhead Campground
Sawtooth National Recreation Area
18 mi SW of Challis on US 93/SR 75; 18 mi S on East Fork Rd (FR 120); on East Fork of Salmon River. Free. May-Oct; 14-day limit. Fishing, hiking in the White Cloud Peaks area.

Cottonwood Recreation Site   **$10**
Bureau of Land Management
Challis Field Office
15 mi N of Challis on Hwy 93. $10. All year; 16-day limit. 13 sites; 30-ft RV limit. Tbls, toilets, cfga, drkg wtr, dump. Hiking, picnicking, fishing, boating(l). Elev 5000 ft.

Deadman Hole   **FREE**
Recreation Site
Bureau of Land Management
Challis Field Office
2 mi S of Challis on Hwy 93; 12 mi W on Hwy 75; on river side of hwy. Free. All year; 14-day limit. Undesignated sites. Toilets, cfga, drkg wtr, no trash service. Access & interior rds are rough dirt.

Land of the Yankee Fork   **$7**
State Historic Area
At US 93 & SR 75 between Challis and Sunbeam. $7 base. All year; 15-day limit. Base fee for primitive sites; $9 for basic sites. Tbls, flush toilets, cfga, drkg wtr. Hiking, biking, horseback riding, guided walks, gold dredge tours, ghost town tours, gold panning.

Little Bayhorse Lake   **FREE**
Challis National Forest
10 mi S of Challis on US 75; 7 mi W on FR 051; on Little Bayhorse Lake. Free. 7/1-9/15; 16-day limit. 3 dispersed sites. Tbls, toilets, cfga, firewood, no drkg wtr. Picnicking, fishing, boating. Elev 8400 ft; 7 acres. Little Bayhorse Lake. Trailers not advised; steep, narrow rd.

Little Boulder Recreation Site   **$6**
Bureau of Land Management
Challis Field Office
2 mi S of Challis on Hwy 93; right on Hwy

75 for 17 mi; left on East Fork Salmon River Rd for about 20 mi. $6. All year; 14-day limit. 3 sites. Toilet, cfga, drkg wtr. Hiking, horseback riding. Site used as staging area for horsemen.

Mahoney Creek   **FREE**
Challis National Forest
26 mi from Challis on FR 086. Free. 7/1-9/30; 14-day limit. 2 sites. Tbls, toilet, cfga, no drkg wtr. Hiking, fishing, horseback riding. Elev 9100 ft.

Mill Creek   **$5**
Challis National Forest
4.5 mi W of Challis on CR 70; 11 mi W on FR 70 (narrow rd); on Yankee Fork of Salmon River. $5. 6/15-9/30; 1-day limit. 15 sites (RVs under 35 ft). Tbls, toilets, cfga, firewood, piped drkg wtr. Rockhounding, picnicking, fishing, horseback riding. Elev 7500 ft; 3 acres. Narrow rd; trailers over 22 ft not advised. Historic Custer Adventure Motorway.

Morgan Creek   **FREE**
Recreation Site
Bureau of Land Management
Challis Field Office
10 mi NW of Challis on US 93. Free. All year. 4 sites. Tbls, toilets, cfga, no drkg wtr. Rockhounding, fishing, hiking. No trash service.

Morse Creek Campground   **FREE**
Challis National Forest
17 mi N of Challis on US 93 to Ellis; 10 mi SE on Farm-to-Market Rd; 6 mi E on FR 094. Free. 6/15-9/15; 14-day limit. 3 sites. Tbls, toilet, cfga, no dkrg wtr. Trout fishing, hiking, horseback riding, nature trail, biking. Elev 6500 ft.

Mosquito Flat   **FREE**
Challis National Forest
13 mi W of Challis on FR 070; 4 mi N on FR 080; on shore of Mosquito Flat Reservoir. Free. 6/15-9/15; 14-day limit. 9 sites; 32-ft RV limit. Tbls, toilet, cfga, no drkg wtr. Fishing, hiking, biking, horseback riding, boating(l).

Sleeping Deer   **FREE**
Transfer Camp
Challis National Forest
6 mi NW of Challis on CR 80; 5 mi NW on FR 80; 34 mi NW on FR 86 (no RVs permitted). Free. Elev 9400 ft. 7/1-10/1; 15-day limit. 4 sites. Firewood. Picnicking, fishing, horseback riding. Trailhead at edge of Frank Church River of No Return Wilderness.

Little West Fork   **FREE**
Challis National Forest
8 mi N of Challis on US 93; 6 mi NW on FR 055; 4 mi W on FR 057; at West Fork of Morgan Creek. Free. 6/1-9/30; 14-day limit. 1 site. Toilet, tbl, cfga, no drkg wtr. Fishing, hiking, biking, horseback riding. Elev 6600 ft.

CLARK FORK (25)

Porcupine Lake   **FREE**
Kaniksu National Forest
9 mi N of Clark Fork on FR 419 (Lightning Creek Rd); 6 mi SW on FR 632 (Porcupine Creek Rd). Free. Elev 4800 ft. 6/15-9/15; 14-day limit. 5 sites on 2 acres (RVs under 22 ft). Tbls, toilets, cfga, no drkg wtr. Fishing, hiking, biking, boating(l).
Fishing tip: Try the nearby Lake Pend Oreille for some excellent fishing; see Whiskey Rock Bay entry.
Travel tip: At Cabinet Gorge Dam, 8 mi E of town on SR 200, is scenic overlook from which to view this horseshoe-shaped dam located on the Clark Fork River.

Whiskey Rock Bay   **FREE**
Kaniksu National Forest
30 mi SW on FR 278; or 10 mi S by boat from Garfield Bay. On Lake Pend Oreille N shore. Free. 5/1-11/30; 14-day limit. 9 sites (15-ft RV limit). Toilets, tbls, cfga, drkg wtr. Swimming, boating(d), fishing, picnicking.
Fishing tip: Lake Pend Orielle has a well-deserved reputation as a fisherman's paradise. Fourteen species of game fish are there, including kokanee, largemouth bass & bluegill. World's record kamloops trout and a 32-pound dollar varden were caught in the lake.
Travel tip: While exploring the southern end of the lake, stop at the museum of Farragut State Park; natural history & old Navy photo exhibits

CLARKIA (26)

Cedar Creek   **FREE**
St. Joe National Forest
3.5 mi N of Clarkia on SR 3; at the St. Maries River. Free. 6/1-10/31; 14-day limit. 3 tent sites. Tbls, toilets, cfga, firewood, no drkg wtr. Swimming, picnicking, cutthroat fishing.
Travel tip: Stop at nearby Emerald Creek, where the National Forest Service administers summer treasure digs for star garnets; the blue or black stones are found only in Idaho and India; surfaces reflect stars of four to six points; permits issued on-site; guides demonstrate techniques; shovel, bucket, wash screen needed (can be rented there).

Crater Lake   **FREE**
Backcountry Camp
Bureau of Land Management
Coeur d'Alene Field Office
24 mi E of Clarkia on FR 301; on S side of Grandmother Mountain WSA. Free. Crater Lake nearby; no trail. 7/1-9/30; 14-day limit. Primitive campsites along rd. Tbl, cfga, toilet, no drkg wtr, no trash service.

Crater Peak   **FREE**
Backcountry Camp
Bureau of Land Management
Coeur d'Alene Field Office
23 i E of Clarkia on FR 301; on S side of Grandmother Mountain WSA. Free. 7/1-9/30;

14-day limit. Primitive campsites along rd. Tbl, cfga, toilet, no drkg wtr, no trash service.

Emerald Creek   **$6**
St. Joe National Forest
5.3 mi NW of Clarkia on SR 3; 5.5 mi S on FR 447. $6. About 5/15-10/1; 14-day limit. 18 sites (RVs under 23 ft). Tbls, toilets, cfga, drkg wtr. Fishing, rockhounding (garnets). 10 acres.

Orphan Point Saddle Camp   **FREE**
Bureau of Land Management
Coeur d'Alene Field Office
From Hwy 3 at Clarkia, 26 mi E on FR 301. Roadside sites on S side of Grandmother Mountain WSA. Free. 7/1-9/30; 14-day limit. Tbl, toilet, cfga, no drkg wtr, no trash service. Trailhead for Lookout Mountain & Delaney Creek trails.

CLAYTON (27)

East Fork Recreation Site   **$10**
Bureau of Land Management
Challis Field Office
4 mi E of Clayton on US 93; at confluence of East Fork & Salmon Rivers. $10. Free 10/1-4/30; 14-day limit. 9 sites (25-ft RV limit). Some pull-through spaces. Tbls, toilets, cfga, piped drkg wtr. No wtr during free period. Hiking, trailbiking, picnicking, fishing, hunting, horseback riding. Elev 5500 ft; 5 acres.

Herd Lake Recreation Site   **FREE**
Bureau of Land Management
Challis Field Office
5 mi E of Clayton on SR 75; S on East Fork Rd to Herd Lake Rd; 10 mi SE on Herd Lake Rd. Free. All year. Undesignated sites. Toilets, tbls, cfga, no drkg wtr. Fishing, canoeing.

Holman Creek   **$11**
Sawtooth National Forest
Sawtooth National Recreation Area
7 mi W of Clayton on SR 75; near Salmon River. $11 during MD-10/15; free rest of season, but no wtr or services; 10-day limit. 10 sites (22-ft RV limit; no RV turnaround at sites 7-10). Tbls, toilets, drkg wtr, cfga. Fishing, hiking, boating.
Fishng tip: Excellent fishing in the Salmon River for trout & steelhead, but only hatchery steelhead with clipped adipose fin may be kept.

Zeigler Hole   **FREE**
Recreation Site
Bureau of Land Management
Challis Field Office
5 mi S of Clayton. Free. All year. Undesignated sites. Toilets, tbls, cfga, no drkg wtr.

COBALT (28)

Crags   **$5**
Salmon National Forest
9 mi SW of Cobalt on FR 055; 7 mi NW on

FR 112; 13 mi N on FR 113; 2 mi N on FR 114 (rough rds not recommended for RVs). $5. Free 10/1-6/30; 14-day limit. 24 sites. Tbls, toilets, cfga, drkg wtr. Elev 8400 ft; 27 acres. Entrance to Bighorn Crags & Idaho Panhandle Primitive Area. Hiking, fishing.

Deep Creek   FREE
Salmon National Forest
3.5 mi N of Cobalt on FR 055 (Panther Creek Rd). Free. 5/15-11/15. 3 sites on 2 acres (RVs under 16 ft). Tbls, toilets, cfga, firewood, drkg wtr. Picnicking, fishing, horseback riding. Panther Creek polluted by mine waste, but trout in Deep Creek. Elev 4900 ft.

McDonald Flat   FREE
Salmon National Forest
5 mi SW of Cobalt on FR 055 (Panther Creek Rd). Free. 5/15-11/15. 6 sites (RVs under 21 ft). Tbls, toilets, cfga, no drkg wtr. Picnicking, fishing, horseback riding. Elev 5400 ft; 6 acres.

Middle Fork Peak   FREE
Salmon National Forest
13 mi S of Cobalt on FR 055 (Panther Creek Rd); 27 mi W on FR 112; semi-developed camping area. Free. 7/1-10/1; 14-day limit. 3 sites on 2 acres (RVs not recommended). Tbls, toilets, cfga, firewood, horse facilities, no drkg wtr; pack out trash. Picnicking, horseback riding. Trail entrance to Frank Church-River of No Return Wilderness. Elev 9000 ft.

Yellowjacket Lake   FREE
Salmon National Forest
13 mi S of Cobalt on FR 055 (Panther Creek Rd); 7 mi W on FR 112; veer to right at FR 113 for 16 mi. Free. 7/1-10/1; 14-day limit. 7 sites (RVs not recommended). Tbls, toilets, cfga, firewood, piped drkg wtr; pack out trash. Picnicking, fishing, boating (no mtrs). Horseback riding 1 mi. Elev 8000 ft; 5 acres. Adjacent to small coldwater lake.

COEUR D'ALENE (29)

Bell Bay $10
Coeur d'Alene National Forest
12 mi NE of Coeur d'Alene on FR 268; 11 mi E on FR 612 (6 mi NW of Harrison). $10 base. MD-9/14; 14-day limit. Base fee for Upper Loop, 15 sites; Lower Loop, $12, 12 sites (22-ft RV limit). Toilets, tbls, cfga, drkg wtr. Boating(lr), fishing, swimming, waterskiing, recreational program. Overlooks Canada Lake on E side of Coeur D'Alene Lake.

Beauty Creek $7
Coeur d'Alene National Forest
7 mi E of Coeur d'Alene on I-90; exit 22, then 3 mi W on SR 97; 1 mi SE on FR 438. $7 with federal Senior Pass; others pay $14. 5/1-9/15; 14-day limit. 20 sites (32-ft RV limit). Tbls, toilets, cfga, drkg wtr. Boating(l), fishing, waterskiing, hiking.

Honeysuckle $12
Coeur d'Alene National Forest
11 mi NE of Coeur d'Alene on FR 268 (Fernan Lake Rd); 11 mi E on FR 612; at Little North Fork of Coeur d'Alene River. $12. MD-9/14; 14-day limit. 7 sites (16-ft RV limit). Tbls, toilets, cfga, drkg wtr. Handicap access. Fishing, hunting, hiking, rafting, OHV activity, mountain biking.

Killarney Lake Boat Launch $8
Bureau of Land Management
Coeur d'Alene Field Office
I-90 at Coeur D'Alene to Rose Lake Exit; 4 mi S on Hwy 3; 3.5 mi W on Killarney Lake Rd. $8. All year; 14-day limit. 11 sites (22-ft RV limit). Tbls, toilets, cfga, drkg wtr. Hiking, boating (ld), fishing, picnicking. 500-acre Lake Killarney.

Killarney Lake Picnic Site   FREE
Bureau of Land Management
Coeur d'Alene Field Office
I-90 at Coeur D'Alene to Rose Lake Exit; 4 mi S on Hwy 3; 4 mi W on Killarney Lake Rd; access by foot or boat. Free. 5/1-9/30; 14-day limit. 2 tent sites, 1 picnic site. Tbl, toilet, cfga, no drkg wtr, no trash service. Boating(d), fishing, hiking.

Mica Bay Boater Park $8
Lake Coeur D'Alene Recreation Area
Bureau of Land Management
Coeur d'Alene Field Office
6 mi S of Coeur D'Alene on Hwy 95; left on Putnam for 2 mi; right on Tall Pines, then right on Loff's Bay Rd; boat access to Mica Bay. $8. 5/1-9/30; 14-day limit. 16 tent sites, 4 mooring docks. Tbls, toilets, cfga, drkg wtr, playground, no trash service. Boating, fishing.

Popcorn Island   FREE
Bureau of Land Management
Coeur d'Alene Field Office
19 mi E of Coeur D'Alene on I-90 to Rose Lake/St. Maries exit; 4 mi S on Hwy 3, then right on Killarney Lake Rd for 3.5 mi; access by boat to 1-acre Popcorn Island on N end of Killarney Lake. Free. 5/1-9/30; 14-day limit. 1 site with toilet, tbl, cfga, boat dock, no drkg wtr, no trash service. Boating, fishing.

Sheep Springs   FREE
Recreation Site
Bureau of Land Management
Coeur d'Alene Field Office
21 mi S of Coeur d'Alene via Latour Creek and Rochat Divide Rds or from St. Maries 11 mi E on St. Joe River Rd & 12 mi N on Rochat Divide Rd. Rough rds & mountainous terrain. Free. 5/1-10/31; 14-day limit. 3 primitive sites (21-ft RV limit). Tbl, toilets, cfga, drkg wtr. Hiking, fishing, picnicking. Primarily for hunters, fishermen. Trail leads to Crystal Lake, where primitive tent camping is permitted.

Tingley Springs   FREE
Bureau of Land Management
Coeur d'Alene Field Office
25 mi E of Coeur d'Alene on I-90 to Cataldo exit 40; 30 mi S on Latour Creek-Rochat Divide Rd; 1 mi W on Phillips Draw Rd. Free. 6/1-9/30; 14-day limit. 6 primitive sites. Tbls, toilet, cfga, drkg wtr, no trash service.

Windy Bay Boater Park $8
Lake Coeur D'Alene Recreation Area
Bureau of Land Management
Coeur d'Alene Field Office
16 mi S of Coeur D'Alene on W side of Lake Coeur D'Alene; boat access to Windy Bay. $8. 5/1-9/30; 14-day limit. 14 tent sites. Tbls, toilets, cfga, no drkg wtr. 7 mooring docks. Fishing, boating, swimming.

COOLIN (30)

Geisinger Campground   FREE
Kaniksu National Forest
11 mi N of Coolin to E shore of Priest Lake; access by boat or trail to Upper Priest Lake from Lions Head Campground in Priest Lake State Park. Free. 5/15-9/15; 14-day limit. 2 sites. Toilet, cfga, no drkg wtr, no trash service. Fishing, boating, hiking.

Navigation Campground   FREE
Kaniksu National Forest
9 mi N of Priest River on SR 57; 12 mi NE on FRs 1339 & 2512; from Beaver Creek Campground, travel by canoe to Upper Priest Lake sites. Free. 6/1-9/30; 14-day limit. 5 boat-in tent sites. Boating, canoeing, fishing.

Fishing tip: Catch huge mackinaw trout in Priest Lake or hook cutthroat and brook trout in Priest River.

Priest Lake State Park $12
11 mi N of Coolin on E shore of Priest Lake. $12 base. All year; 15-day limit. Limited facilities in winter. Base fee for standard sites without hookups ($9 off-season, but no wtr); sites with hookups, $20 & $22. 151 sites (50-ft RV limit). Tbls, flush toilets, cfga, drkg wtr, dump, elec($), showers. Beach, swimming, boating (ld), fishing, tobogganing, snowmobiling, hiking trails, nature program, horseshoes, volleyball, rafting, canoeing. 463 acres.

Trapper Creek   FREE
Kaniksu National Forest
11 mi N of Coolin on E shore of Priest Lake; access by boat or trail to Upper Priest Lake from either Lions Head Campground in Pries Lake State Park or from Beaver Creek Campground. Free. 5/15-9/15; 14-day limit. 4 tent sites. Tbls, toilet, cfga, no drkg wtr, no trash service. Fishing, hiking, boating.

COTTONWOOD (31)

Pine Bar Recreation Site $6
Bureau of Land Management
Cottonwood Field Office
11 mi S of Cottonwood on Graves Creek Rd; 4 mi E on Salmon River Rd; at Lower Salmon

River. $6. All year; 14-day limit. 7 sites. 30 acres. Tbls, cfga, toilets, drkg wtr, trash collection, beaches. Boating(l), swimming, picnicking, fishing, hunting. Put-in spot for floaters.

Travel tip: Visit Weis Rockshelter, 8 mi S of town in Grave Creek Canyon; archaeo-logical site of extensive excavations which confirmed human habitation in this area thousands of years ago.

COUNCIL (32)

Big Flat $8
Payette National Forest
12 mi S of Council on US 95; 14 mi SE & E on FR 206. $8 during MD-10/15; $5 off-season, but no wtr; 16-day limit. 13 single sites, 3 double sites (RVs under 45 ft). Tbls, toilets, cfga, no drkg wtr. Picnicking, horseback riding, fishing, berry-picking. Elev 4050 ft; 3 acres. Adjacent to Little Weiser River.

Black Lake FREE
Hells Canyon Nat. Recreation Area
Wallowa-Whitman National Forest
34 mi N of Council on CR 002; 7 mi N on FR 105; 16 mi N on FR 112; .1 mi E on FR 114. Rds steep, not recommended for RVs. Free. Elev 7200 ft. 6/30-9/30. 4 sites on 25 acres (RVs under 22 ft). Tbls, toilets, cfga, firewood, piped drkg wtr. Boating, swimming, picnicking, fishing, rockhound-ing, hiking, nature trails, horseback riding. In Hills Canyon National Recreation Area (non-wilderness).

Fishing tip: Best bet for great fishing is to try nearby Cascade Lake for its variety of game fish, including rainbow, cutthroat and brown trout, coho salmon & perch. Good lake for casting from shore if you don't have a boat.

Travel tip: Tour Council Lumber Mill, off Hwy 95 on Galena St. near Council; by appt (208-253-4225); a Boise Cascade mill; uses the only outdoor electrical overhead crane in Idaho to haul logs to the mill, where they are cut into rough lumber and loaded into rail cars.

Cabin Creek $8
Payette National Forest
4 mi S of Council on US 95; 10 mi E on FR 186, along Middle Fork of Weiser River. $8 during MD-10/15; free off-season, but no wtr. 16-day limit. 12 sites on 5 acres (RVs under 23 ft). Tbls, toilets, cfga, piped drkg wtr. Picnicking, horseback riding, fishing. Elev 4150 ft.

Evergreen $8
Payette National Forest
14 mi N of Council on US 95; on Weiser River. $8. 6/1-9/10; 16-day limit. 12 sites (RVs under 22 ft). Tbls, toilets, cfga, drkg wtr, store. Fishing. Elev 3650 ft; 4 acres. Site was closed in 2006 for reconstruction; due to reopen in 2007.

Huckleberry $8
Payette National Forest
30 mi NW of Council on FR 002; 5 mi NE on FR 105; 1 mi E on FR 110; at Bear Creek. $8 during 6/10-9/10; free off-season, but no wtr. 16-day limit. 8 single sites, 1 double site (RVs under 45 ft). Tbls, toilets, cfga, drkg wtr. Horseback riding, picnicking, fishing. Elev 4950 ft; 4 acres. Near Hells Canyon/Seven Devils Scenic Area. Stream.

Lafferty Camp $8
Payette National Forest
24 mi NW of Council on FR 002. $8. All year; 16-day limit. Free off-season if wtr is shut off. 16-day limit. 8 sites (16-ft RV limit). Tbls, new toilets, cfga, drkg wtr. Horseback riding, picnicking, hiking, fishing for Crooked River rainbow trout. Elev 4300 ft.

DARBY (MONTANA) (33)

Indian Creek FREE
Bitterroot National Forest
4 mi S of Darby on US 93; 14 mi W on CR 473; 37 mi W on FR 468; 5 mi N on FR 6223; at Selway River. Free. 6/15-9/15; 10-day limit. 6 sites (includes 4 hunter camps); 25-ft RV limit. Tbls, toilets, cfga, no drkg wtr. Hiking, hunting, fishing, biking.

Indian Trees $10
Bitterroot National Forest
4 mi S on US 93; 14 mi SW on CR 473; 37 mi W on FR 468; 5 mi N on FR 6223. $10. 5/20-9/30; 14-day limit. 16 sites (50-ft RV limit). Tbls, toilets, cfga, drkg wtr. Hiking.

Magruder Crossing FREE
Bitterroot National Forest
4 mi S of Darby on US 93; 14 mi SW on CR 423; 37 mi W on FR 468; at Selway River. Free. 6/15-11/1; 10-day limit. 4 sites; 30-ft RV limit. Toilet, tbls, cfga, no drkg wtr. Fishing, hiking, horseback riding, biking.

Paradise FREE
Bitterroot National Forest
4 mi S of Darby on US 93; 14 mi W on CR 473; 37 mi W on FR 468; 11 mi N on FR 6223; at Selway River. Free. 6/15-11/26; 10-day limit. 11 sites (RVs under 16 ft). Toilets, cfga, no drkg wtr. Fishing, hiking, horseback riding, boating(l).

Raven Creek FREE
Bitterroot National Forest
4 mi S of Darby on US 93; 14 mi W on CR 473; 37 mi W on FR 468; 2 mi N on FR 6223; at Selway River. Free. 6/1-9/15; 14-day limit. 2 sites; 25-ft RV limit. Toilet, cfga, no drkg wtr. Fishing, hiking.

Slate Creek FREE
Nez Perce National Forest
4 mi S of Darby on US 93; 22 mi S on CR 473; 2 mi S on CR 96. Free. 6/1-9/15; 14-day limit. 4 sites (RVs under 23 ft). Toilets, cfga, tbls, drkg wtr. Fishing, boating.

DEARY (34)

Little Boulder Creek $8
Clearwater National Forest
4 mi E of Deary on ID 8; 3 mi SE on CR 1963; at Potlatch River. $8. MD-LD; 14-day limit. 17 sites (35-ft RV limit). Toilets, tbls, drkg wtr, cfga. Fishing. Near Palouse River, hiking, biking.

DONNELLY (35)

Amanita $10
Boise National Forest
4.8 mi SW of Donnelly on CR 422. $10. 5/15-9/15; 14-day limit. 10 sites (RVs under 23 ft). Tbls, toilets, cfga, drkg wtr. Fishing, swimming, boating(l), waterskiing. Cascade Reservoir. Elev 5000 ft; 4 acres.

Kennally Creek $8
Payette National Forest
3 mi W of Donnelly on SR 55; 10 mi E on FR 388. $8. All year; 16-day limit. Free off-season if wtr is shut off. 10 sites (26-ft RV limit). Tbls, toilets, cfga, drkg wtr. Fishing, hiking, picnicking, horseback riding. Horse unloading ramp, hitching rails. Elev 6000 ft. Pack out trash.

Lakeside City Park FREE
Half mi SW of Donnelly. Free. All year. 5 sites (RVs under 20 ft). Tbls, toilets, cfga, firewood, sanitary station, playground. Store nearby. Swimming, picnicking, fishing, boat-ing (rd).

Fishing tip: This is a good location from which to explore Cascade Reservoir. Its large variety of game fish includes rainbow, cutthroat and brown trout, coho salmon & perch. Good lake for casting from shore if you don't have a boat.

Travel tip: Swing past the Roseberry Ghost Town; Farm-to-Market Rd branches off Hwy 55 just N of Donnelly; 19th Century church, jailhouse, city hall, old Finnish church & cemetery.

Rainbow Point $10
Boise National Forest
4.7 mi SW of Donnelly on CR 422. $10. 5/15-9/15; 14-day limit. 12 sites (RVs under 24 ft). Tbls, toilets, cfga, drkg wtr. Boating(l), fish-ing, swimming, waterskiing. Cascade Reser-voir. Elev 5000 ft; 11 acres.

Southwestern Idaho $6
Senior Citizens Recreation Assoc.
E of Donnelly on Siscra Rd; near Cascade Reservoir (watch for signs on SR 55 S of town). $6 base. 175 sites. Tbls, flush toilets, showers, cfga, drkg wtr, hookups($), dump. 60-acre park leased from Bureau of Recla-mation; designed for seniors, but open to all.

DOWNEY (36)

Cherry Creek   **FREE**
Caribou National Forest
4 mi SW of Downey on CR 80 N; 6 mi S on FR 20047. Free. 5/15-9/30. 4 tent sites (no trailers). Tbls, toilets, cfga, firewood, piped drkg wtr. Picnicking, fishing, horseback riding. Elev 6000 ft; 5 acres. Pack out garbage.

Summit   **$8**
Caribou National Forest
10 mi SW of Downey on CR 80N; 1.5 mi W on co rd; 1 mi W on FR 41. $8. MD-9/30; 16-day limit. 12 sites (32-ft RV limit). Tbls, toilets, cfga, drkg wtr. Fishing, hiking, horseback riding, biking. Elev 6200 ft.

DRIGGS (37)

Mike Harris   **$10**
Targhee National Forest
13 mi SE of Driggs on SR 33; half mi S on FR 80330; at Harris Creek & Trail Creek jct. $10. 5/20-9/15; 14-day limit. 12 sites (22-ft RV limit). Tbls, toilets, cfga, drkg wtr. Fishing, hiking trailhead. Elev 6200 ft; 5 acres.

Teton Canyon   **$10**
Targhee National Forest
6 mi E of Driggs on CR 09; 4.5 mi S on FR 09; in Wyoming. $10. 5/15-9/15; 16-day limit. 19 sites (30-ft RV limit). Tbls, toilets, cfga, drkg wtr. Beginning of Teton Crest Trail into Jedediah Smith Wilderness. Fishing, hiking. Elev 7270 ft; 4 acres.

DUBOIS (38)

Lamont E. Hodges   **FREE**
Dubois Memorial City Park
Center of Dubois off SR 15-91 (gravel access rds); at Beaver Creek. Free. All year. 4 undesignated RV sites (no tents). Flush toilets, drkg wtr, tbls, cfga. About 2-3 acres.

Stoddard   **$10**
Wagon Wheel Court
At 330 W. 4th, at Thomas St. in Dubois. $10. 3 sites. Tbls, toilets, cfga, drkg wtr. No other information.

Waring City Park   **FREE**
In Dubois behind city-county building & courthouse. Free. Tbls, toilet, cfga, drkg wtr, dump nearby, playground.

Webber Creek   **FREE**
Targhee National Forest
25 mi NW of Dubois on CR A3; 2.3 mi W on FR 196. Free. Elev 7000 ft. 6/15-9/15. 4 sites on 5 acres (RVs under 16 ft). Tbls, toilets, cfga, firewood, no drkg wtr. Picnicking, fishing, horseback riding.

EASTPORT (39)

Copper Creek   **$6**
Kaniksu National Forest
S of Eastport 2 mi to the Three Mile Jct (US 95 & US 2); N on US 95 to the Mount Hall Jct (US 95 & SR 1); right on US 95 for 13.5 mi; E on Copper Falls Rd (FR 2517) for half mi; at Moyie River. $6. Elev 2500 ft. MD-LD; 14-day limit. 16 sites (RVs under 32 ft). Tbls, toilets, cfga, firewood, well drkg wtr. Picnicking, fishing, berry picking, horseback riding. Copper Falls 1 mi. 8 acres.

Robinson Lake   **$8**
Kaniksu National Forest
7 mi S of Eastport on US 95; 1 mi N on FR 448. $8. MD-LD; 14-day limit. 10 sites; 32-ft RV limit. Toilets, tbls, cfga, drkg wtr. Boating(l), fishing, swimming, hiking. 60-acre lake. Handicap access to 3 sites. Elev 2800 ft.

ELK CITY (40)

Bear Creek   **FREE**
Nez Perce National Forest
12 mi W of Elk City on SR 14; 3 mi N on FR 1858; at Newsome Creek. Free. May-Sept; 14-day limit. 4 undeveloped sites. Toilet, cfga, no drkg wtr.

Bridge Creek   **FREE**
Nez Perce National Forest
3 mi SW of Elk City on SR 14; 14 mi SE on FR 222; 12 mi NE of Red River Ranger Station on FR 234. Free. Elev 4800 ft. 6/1-10/31; 14-day limit. 5 sites on 3 acres (RVs under 16 ft). Tbls, toilets, cfga, firewood, no drkg wtr. Picnicking, fishing, swimming, horseback riding. 1 mi from Red River Hot Springs.

Crooked River #3   **FRE**
Nez Perce National Forest
6 mi W of Elk City on SR 14; 3 mi S on FR 233. Free. May-Sept; 14-day limit. 5 undeveloped sites straddling Crooked River; 12 parking spaces. Toilet, cfga, no drkg wtr. N of campgrounds are historic dredgings from the gold rush days.
   Fishing tip: Crooked River contains brook & rainbow trout.

Ditch Creek   **FREE**
Nez Perce National Forest
3 mi SW of Elk City on SR 14; 14 mi SE on FR 222; 4 mi NE on FR 234; at Red River. Free. Elev 4500 ft. 6/1-10/31; 14-day limit. 4 sites on 3 acres (RVs under 16 ft). Tbls, toilets, cfga, no drkg wtr. Berry picking, picnicking, fishing, horseback riding. Stock-handling facilities. Red River Hot Springs at end of the road.

Fivemile Campground   **FREE**
Nez Perce National Forest
7 mi W of Elk City on SR 14; 11 mi S on FR 233; at Crooked River & Five Mile Creek. Free. 4 undeveloped sites. Toilet, cfga, no drkg wtr. Nice swimming area, fish pond. Historic spots date from gold rush period.

French Gulch   **FREE**
Nez Perce National Forest
6 mi S of Elk City on CR 1818; at Red River.

Free. June-Oct; 14-day limit. 3 sites. Tbls, toilets, cfga, no drkg wtr. Fishing, hiking, ATV activity.

Granite Springs   **FREE**
Nez Perce National Forest
3 mi SW of Elk City on SR 14; 15 mi SE on FR 222; 17 mi E on FR 468. Free. 7/15-10/15; 14-day limit. 4 sites (RVs under 16 ft). Piped drkg wtr, toilets, no tbls. Horseback riding, biking, hiking trails. 6700 ft; 4 acres. Primarily a developed hunters' camp. Stock-handling facilities. The Nez Perce used a trail through the camp for their migrations to reduce chances of meeting their enemies, the Blackfeet.

Halfway House   **FREE**
Nez Perce National Forest
32 mi W of Elk City on SR 14; 5 mi SW on FR 233; 1.5 mi S on FR 311; at Crooked Creek. Free. 6/15-10/30; 14-day limit. 4 sites (RVs under 16 ft). Tbls, toilets, cfga, no drkg wtr. Picnicking, fishing, horseback riding. Elev 5000 ft; 4 acres. Dixie Guard Station and Airfield. Trailhead into Gospel-Hump Wilderness. Stock handling facilities available.

Legget Creek   **FREE**
Nez Perce National Forest
14 mi W of Elk City on SR 14; across the road from the Clearwater River. Free. June-Oct; 14-day limit. 6 undeveloped sites. Toilets, cfga, no drkg wtr. Cutthroat & rainbow trout fishing.

Limber Luke   **FREE**
Nez Perce National Forest
10 mi N of Elk City on CR 1854 and FR 443; at Limber Luke Creek. Free. May-Sept; 14-day limit. 1 tent site. Toilet, cfga, no drkg wtr. Hiking, horseback riding, OHV activity, biking.

MacKay Bar   **FREE**
Nez Perce National Forest
32 mi W of Elk City on SR 14; S on FR 233; 1.5 mi S on FR 222 (steep, winding dirt rds last 6 mi). Free. 16/15-10/31; 14-day limit. 3 sites (for tents & small campers). Tbls, toilets, cfga, no drkg wtr. Picnicking, hiking, boating, swimming, fishing (white sturgeon & steelhead), floating, horseback riding, OHV activity. Elev 2300 ft; 5 acres. Mountains. Grassy terrain. Trailhead into River of No Return Wilderness. Permit needed to float river 6/20-9/10.

Magruder Corridor   **FREE**
Backcountry Byway Dispersed Sites
Nez Perce National Forest
S of Elk City to Red River Ranger Station, then E on FR 468; primitive road follows Nez Perce trail between Frank Church and Selway-Bitterroot Wilderness areas. May-Oct; 14-day limit. Primitive dispersed sites along the byway. No facilities except some toilets. Historical markers, ranger stations. Fishing, mountain biking, hiking.

Newsome Campground   **FREE**
Nez Perce National Forest
About 12 mi W of Elk City on SR 14; 5.5 mi N on FR 1858; at Newsome Creek. May-Sept. 6 sites for tents, pickup campers. Tbls, toilet, cfga, no drkg wtr. Fishing, hiking trails. Nearby are remains of historic Newsome townsite from gold rush era. Group camping free in the field across the road.

Orogrande Campground   **FREE**
Nez Perce National Forest
6 mi W of Elk City on SR 14; 12 mi S on FR 233. Free. June-Oct; 14-day limit. 11 undeveloped sites. Toilets, cfga, no drkg wtr. Near the Orogrande townsite, trading center for the Buffalo Hump mining town. Site's name means "course gold" from the ore found there.

Orogrande Summit   **FREE**
Nez Perce National Forest
W of Elk City on SR 14, then S on FR 233 (23 mi total). Free. 7/1-9/30; 14-day limit. 5 sites. Tbls, toilets, cfga, no drkg wtr. Hiking, horseback riding.

Oxbow Campground   **FREE**
Nez Perce National Forest
12 mi W of Elk City on SR 14; 2 mi N on FR 1858; at Newsome Creek. Free. 6/1-9/30; 14-day limit. 1 site. Toilet, cfga, no drkg wtr. Fishing, hiking, mountain biking.

Poet Creek   **FREE**
Nez Perce National Forest
3 mi SW of Elk City on SR 14; 15 mi SE on FR 222; 25 mi E on FR 468. Free. 7/15-10/15; 14-day limit. 4 sites (RVs under 16 ft). Tbls, toilets, cfga, firewood, no drkg wtr. Picnicking, fishing, horseback riding. Elev 5100 ft; 5 acres. Trailhead into Salmon River & River of No Return Wilderness. Breaks Primitive Area. Stock-handling facilities.

Red Horse Mine Camp   **FREE**
Nez Perce National Forest
12 mi W of Elk City on SR 14; 4 mi N on FR 1858. Free. May-Oct; 14-day limit. Undeveloped area for tents, campers. Toilets, cfga, no drkg wtr.

Red River   **FREE**
Nez Perce National Forest
3 mi SW of Elk City on SR 14; 14 mi SE on FR 222; 6 mi NE of Red River Ranger Station on FR 234. Free. MD-9/15; 14-day limit. 40 sites (16-ft RV limit). Tbls, toilets, cfga, firewood, piped drkg wtr. Berry picking, picnicking, fishing, horseback riding, hiking, biking. Elev 4600 ft; 25 acres.
Fishing tip: Red River contains rainbow & brook trout, mountain whitefish.

Sam's Creek   **FREE**
Nez Perce National Forest
32 mi W of Elk City on SR 14; 3 mi SW on Mackay Bar Rd (FR 233); 1 mi on FR 311. Free; at Crooked Creek & Sams Creek. Free. Elev 5200 ft. 6/15-10/31; 16-day limit. 3 sites on 2 acres (RVs under 16 ft). Tbls, toilets, cfga, no drkg wtr. Picnicking, hiking, fishing. No horses.

Sing Lee Campground   **FREE**
Nez Perce National Forest
13 mi W of Elk City on SR 14; 4.5 mi N on FR 1858; at Newsome Creek. Free. 6/1-10/31; 14-day limit. Fishing, hiking.

Six Mile Campground   **FREE**
Nez Perce National Forest
16 mi W of Elk City on SR 14; 10 mi SW on FR 492. Free. Sept-Oct; 14-day limit. 2 tent sites. Toilet, cfga, no drkg wtr. Area closed to motor vehicles; trails in Gospel Hump Wilderness closed to bikes. Hiking, horseback riding.

Table Meadows   **FREE**
Nez Perce National Forest
3 mi N of Elk City via CR 1854; 7 mi N FR 283 (Ericson Ridge Rd); 5.1 mi NW on FR 420. 6/1-10/30. 6 sites (RVs under 16 ft). Toilets, cfga, no drkg wtr. Berry picking, horseback riding. Elev 4500 ft; 7 acres. West fork American River adjacent to site.

Wildhorse Lake   **FREE**
Nez Perce National Forest
10 mi W of Elk City on SR 14; 16 mi SW on FR 233; 2 mi NW on FR 2331. Steep, narrow, winding rds. Free. Elev 7500 ft. 7/1-9/30; 14-day limit. 6 sites on 10 acres (RVs under 16 ft). Tbls, toilets, cfga, firewood, no drkg wtr. Picnicking, fishing, swimming, boating. Trailhead into Gospel-Hump Wilderness. No horses.

FAIRFIELD (41)

Abbot   **$2**
Sawtooth National Forest
18 mi N of Fairfield on FR 094; 27 mi W on FR 337; at South Fork of Boise River. $2. Elev 4000 ft. 5/15-9/30; 14-day limit. 7 sites on 5 acres (RVs under 16 ft). Tbls, toilets, cfga, firewood, no drkg wtr. Picnicking, fishing, horseback riding.

Bird Creek   **$2**
Sawtooth National Forest
18 mi N of Fairfield on FR 094; 24 mi W on FR 337; at South Fork of Boise River. $2. Elev 5000 ft. 5/15-10/31; 14-day limit. 5 sites (RVs under 22 ft). Tbls, toilets, cfga, firewood, no drkg wtr. Picnicking, fishing, horseback riding.

Bounds   **$6**
Sawtooth National Forest
18 mi N of Fairfield on FR 094; 1 mi W on FR 337; at South Fork of Boise River. $6. 6/1-9/30; 14-day limit. 12 sites. Tbls, toilets, cfga, drkg wtr. Hiking, fishing.

Canyon Transfer Camp   **$4**
Sawtooth National Forest
26 mi N of Fairfield on FR 094 and FR 227, past Big Smokey Guard Station. $4. 6/1-9/30; 14-day limit. 6 sites. Tbls, toilets, cfga, drkg wtr. Fishing, hiking.

Chaparral   **$2**
Sawtooth National Forest
18 mi N of Fairfield on FR 094; 26 mi W on FR 337; at South Fork of Boise River. $2. Elev 4600 ft. 5/15-9/30; 14-day limit. 7 sites (RVs under 22 ft). Tbls, toilets, cfga, firewood, no drkg wtr. Picnicking, fishing.

Five Points   **FREE**
Sawtooth National Forest
5.9 mi N of FR 093; 11.4 mi N on FR 094. Free. Elev 5500 ft. 6/1-9/30; 14-day limit. 5 sites (RVs under 16 ft). Tbls, toilets, cfga, firewood, no drkg wtr. Picnicking, fishing, horseback riding.

Skeleton Creek   **FREE**
Sawtooth National Forest
18 mi N of Fairfield on FR 094; 16 mi W on FR 337; on South Fork of Boise River. Free. Elev 5300 ft. 6/1-9/30; 14-day limit. 5 undeveloped sites; no facilities. 4 acres. Picnicking, fishing, horseback riding, hiking trails.

South Boise   **FREE**
Sawtooth National Forest
18 mi N of Fairfield on FR 094; 10 mi N on FR 012; near headwaters of South Fork of Boise River. Free. 6/1-9/30; 14-day limit. 2 undesignated sites. Toilets, cfga, no other facilities. Picnicking, fishing, horseback riding, hiking.

Willow Creek   **$2**
Sawtooth National Forest
18 mi N of Fairfield on FR 094; 23 mi W on FR 337; at South Fork of Boise River. $2. Elev 5100 ft. 5/15-9/30; 14-day limit. 5 sites on 5 acres (RVs under 16 ft). Tbls, cfga, firewood, no drkg wtr. Picnicking, fishing, swimming, horseback riding.

FEATHERVILLE (42)

Baumgartner   **$10**
Sawtooth National Forest
12 mi E of Featherville on FR 227. $10; at South Fork of Boise River. MD-9/14; 14-day limit. 39 sites. Tbls, flush toilets, cfga, drkg wtr. Hiking, fishing, 111-degree hot springs, nature trail.

FREEDOM (WYOMING) (43)

Pinebar   **FREE**
Caribou National Forest
1 mi N of Freedom on CR 34; 9.5 mi W on SR 34; on Tin Cup Creek. Free. 5/1-11/1; 14-day limit. 5 sites (30-ft RV limit). Tbls, toilets, cfga, drkg wtr, firewood. Horseback riding, picnicking, fishing. Extensive hiking trail system.

Tin Cup   **FREE**
Caribou National Forest
1 mi N of Freedom, Wyoming, on CR 111; 2.6

mi W on SR 34; at Tin Cup Creek. Free. 5/1-10/31; 14-day limit. 5 sites (16-ft RV limit). Toilets, drkg wtr, cfga, tbls. Fishing, picnicking, extensive hiking trails, biking.

GARDEN VALLEY (44)

Boiling Springs   **$8**
Boise National Forest
2.5 mi W of Garden Valley on SR 17; 22 mi N on FR 698. $8. Elev 4000 ft. 4/20-10/20; 14-day limit. 9 sites on 3 acres (RVs under 30 ft). Tbls, toilets, cfga, firewood, no drkg wtr. Picnicking, fishing, horseback riding. Adjacent to middle fork of Payette River.

Hardscrabble   **$8**
Boise National Forest
2.5 mi W of Garden Valley on SR 17; 14 mi N on FR 698. $8. Elev 3400 ft. 5/15-9/30. 6 sites on 2 acres (RVs under 24 ft). Tbls, toilets, firewood, cfga, no drkg wtr. Picnicking, fishing, horseback riding. Adjacent to middle fork of Payette River.

Hot Springs   **$10**
Boise National Forest
2 mi E of Garden Valley on SR 17. $10 during 4/1-9/20; free off-season; 14-day limit. 10 sites (35-ft RV limit). Tbls, toilets, cfga, drkg wtr. Fishing.

Riverpond Campground   **$10**
Near Garden Valley at 5683 Bogart; at Middle Fork of Payette River. $10 for primitive & tent sites; $15 with hookups. All year. 15 sites. Tbls, toilets, cfga, drkg wtr, hookups($).

Rattlesnake   **$10**
Boise National Forest
2.5 mi W of Garden Valley on SR 17; 18 mi N on FR 698. $10. Elev 3800 ft. 4/20-10/20; 14-day limit. 11 sites on 7 acres (RVs under 36 ft). Tbls, toilets, cfga, firewood, no drkg wtr. Picnicking, fishing, horseback riding. Adjacent to Middle Fork of Payette River.

Silver Creek   **$10**
Boise National Forest
2.5 mi W of Garden Valley on SR 17; 19 mi N on FR 698; 7 mi NE on FR 671. $10. 4/20-10/20; 14-day limit. 5 sites (RVs under 31 ft). Tbls, toilets, cfga, firewood, drkg wtr. Picnicking, fishing, horseback riding, hiking.

South Fork Payette   **FREE**
Recreation Site
Bureau of Land Management
3 mi E of Garden Valley, off Alder Creek Rd, S side of river. Free. 5/1-10/31; 14-day limit. Primitive undesignated sites; no facilities. Fishing.

Tie Creek   **$10**
Boise National Forest
2.5 mi W of Garden Valley on SR 17; 11 mi N on FR 698. $10. Elev 3200 ft. 4/20-10/20; 14-day limit. 8 sites on 4 acres (RVs under 36 ft). Tbls, toilets, cfga, firewood, well drkg wtr. Picnicking, fishing, horseback riding. Adjacent to middle fork of Payette River.

Trail Creek   **$8**
Boise National Forest
2.5 mi W of Garden Valley on SR 17; 19 mi N on FR 698. $8. Elev 3800 ft. 4/20-10/20; 14-day limit. 11 sites on 5 acres (RVs under 36 ft). Tbls, toilets, cfga, firewood, piped drkg wtr. Picnicking, fishing, horseback riding. Adjacent to Middle Fork of Payette River.

GEORGETOWN (45)

Summit View   **$8**
Caribou National Forest
2.4 mi E on CR 102; 6 mi N on FR 95 (Georgetown Canyon Rd). $8. 5/15-10/15 (no wtr after LD); 14-day limit. 17 sites (32-ft RV limit). Tbls, toilets, cfga, drkg wtr. Hiking, biking, fishing, horseback riding, OHV activity.

GIBBONSVILLE (46)

Twin Creek   **$5**
Salmon National Forest
5 mi NW of Gibbonsville on SR 93; half mi NW on FR 449. $5. Free 9/15-MD; 14-day limit. 40 sites on 21 acres (32-ft RV limit). Tbls, toilets, cfga, drkg wtr. No drkg wtr during free period. Nature trails, fishing, horse ramp.

GLENNS FERRY (47)

Three Island Crossing   **$10**
State Park
On W. Madison St, off I-84 at Glenns Ferry. $10 for seniors weekdays; others pay $20 for sites with elec/wtr. No RV size limit. Tbls, flush toilets, cfga, drkg wtr, showers, dump. Swimming, fishing, hiking, guided walks, interpretive center, historical programs. Site of a key river crossing on the Oregon Trail. 513 acres; elev 2484 ft.

GOODING (48)

Little City of Rocks   **FREE**
Bureau of Land Management
Shoshone Field Office
W from SR 46 about 12.5 mi N of Gooding; dirt rd 1 mi. RV parking S of rock wall recommended. Free. All year; 14-day limit. Undeveloped primitive area; limited camping opportunities. No facilities, no wtr. Pack out trash. Picnicking, hiking, sightseeing.
   Travel tip: Excellent rock formations of diatomite (similar to England's White Cliffs of Dover); see outcrops 8 mi W of the camping area. Rds to nearby Gooding City of Rocks should not be attempted without 4WD.

Thorn Creek Reservoir   **FREE**
Bureau of Land Management
Shoshone Field Office
18 mi N on Hwy 46; 4 mi E on dirt rd to reservoir. Difficult access in winter and after rain. Free. 5/1-10/31; 14-day limit. 10 tent sites. Toilets, tbls, cfga. Boating (small boats), fishing (shrimp-fed trout), hiking, birdwatching, picnicking.

GRANGEVILLE (49)

Castle Creek   **$8**
Nez Perce National Forest
1 mi E of Grangeville on SR 13; 10 mi SE on CR 17; 6 mi SE on SR 14. $8 (Canadian, $13). 6/1-10/1; 14-day limit. 8 sites (RVs under 22 ft). Toilets, cfga, tbls, drkg wtr. Dump at South Fork Campground. Hiking, swimming, fishing, picnicking. Camp free when wtr shut off.

Fish Creek Meadows   **$8**
Nez Perce National Forest
1 mi E of Grangeville on SR 13; 1 mi S on CR 17; 6.8 mi SE on FR 221. $8 ($Canadian, $10). 5/15-9/30; 24-day limit. 8 sites on 3 acres (RVs under 24 ft). Tbls, toilets, cfga, firewood, no drkg wtr. Picnicking, berry picking, fishing, horseback riding, hiking trails. Camp free when wtr shut off.

Meadow Creek   **FREE**
Nez Perce National Forest
1 mi E of Grangeville on SR 13; 10 mi SE on CR 17; 9 mi SE on SR 14; between Meadow Creek & South Fork of Clearwater River. Free. 6/1-10/1; 10-day limit. 3 sites for tents or pickup campers (no trailers). Tbls, toilets, cfga, firewood, no drkg wtr. Picnicking, hiking, fishing. Elev 2300 ft; 3 acres. Mountains.

Mountain View MH & RV Park   **$10**
From Main St in Grangeville, half mi N on Hall St. $10-12 base; $17-19 hookups. All year. 32 sites; 70-ft RV limit. Tbls, flush toilets, cfga, drkg wtr, hookups($), coin laundry, CATV, dump.

Sourdough Saddle Camp   **FREE**
Nez Perce National Forest
25 mi E of Grangeville on SR 14; 5 mi S on FR 212/1894; 15 mi W on FR 492. Sept-Oct; 14-day limit. Undeveloped area for 5 camping units. Toilets, tbls, cfga, no drkg wtr. Pack out trash. Hiking, horseback riding.

South Fork   **$8**
Nez Perce National Forest
1 mi E of Grangeville on Hwy 13; 9.9 mi SE on CR 17; 6 mi SE on SR 14. $8 (Canadian, $10). 6/1-10/1; 14-day limit. 8 sites (RVs under 22 ft); 1 multi-family picnic site. Toilets, tbls, cfga, drkg wtr, dump. Fishing, swimming. Camp free when wtr shut off.

HAILEY (51)

Bridge Camp   **FREE**
Sawtooth National Forest
2.6 mi N of Hailey on SR 75; 9 mi W on FR 097; at Deer Creek. Free. 5/15-10/15. 3 dispersed sites (no trailers). Tbls, toilets, cfga, no drkg wtr. Picnicking, fishing, horseback riding. Elev 5600 ft; 2 acres. Douglas fir seed production area.

Federal Gulch   **FREE**
Sawtooth National Forest
6.1 mi N of Hailey on SR 75; 11.5 mi E on FR 118; at East Fork of Wood River. Free. Elev 5700 ft. 5/15-10/15; 14-day limit. 9 sites on 2 acres (RVs under 22 ft). Tbls, toilets, cfga, firewood, piped drkg wtr. Hiking, picnicking, fishing, horseback riding. 17 mi SE of Sun Valley. Trailhead to Pioneer Mountains.

Sawmill   **FREE**
Sawtooth National Forest
6.1 mi N of Hailey on SR 75; 10.9 mi E on FR 118; at East Fork of Wood River. Free. 5/15-10/15. 5 tent sites (no trailers). Tbls, toilets, cfga, firewood, no drkg wtr. Picnicking, fishing, horseback riding. Elev 5600 ft; 2 acres. 16 mi SE of Sun Valley.

Wolftone Camp   **FREE**
Sawtooth National Forest
2.6 mi N of Hailey on SR 75; 8.1 mi W on FR 097; at Deer Creek. Free. Elev 5500 ft. 5/15-10/15. 3 dispersed sites. Tbls, toilets, cfga, firewood, no drkg wtr. Picnicking, fishing, horseback riding. 103-degree Clarendon Hot Springs nearby.

HANSEN (53)

Bear Gulch   **$5**
Sawtooth National Forest
35.8 mi S of Hansen on CR G3 (FR 515). $5. Elev 4900 ft. 6/1-9/30; 14-day limit. 8 sites on 3 acres (RVs under 16 ft). Tbls, toilets, cfga, firewood, piped drkg wtr. Picnicking, horseback riding, fishing. Near Shoshone Wildlife Pond.

Diamondfield Jack   **FREE**
Sawtooth National Forest
26 mi S of Hansen on CR G3 (FR 515). Free. All year; 14-day limit. 8 sites (RVs under 32 ft). Toilets, tbls, cfga, no drkg wtr. Fishing, picnicking. Winter sports activities. Elev 7000 ft.

Lower Penstemon   **$5**
Sawtooth National Forest
24 mi S of Hansen on CR G3 (Rock Creek Rd). $5. All year; 14-day limit. 5 sites (16-ft RV limit). Tbls, toilets, cfga, drkg wtr. Group camping available. Popular winter sports.

Pettit Lake   **$8**
Sawtooth National Forest
28 mi S of Hansen on CR G3. MD-LD; 14-day limit. $8. 12 sites (RVs under 22 ft). Toilets, cfga, tbls, drkg wtr. Fishing, picnicking.

Schipper   **$5**
Sawtooth National Forest
15.2 mi S on CR G3; at Birch Creek. $5. 4/1-10/15; 14-day limit. 6 tent sites. Tbls, toilets, drkg wtr, cfga. Fishing, picnicking. Elev 4600 ft.

Upper Penstemon   **$5**
Sawtooth National Forest
24 mi S of Hansen on CR G3 (Rock Creek

Rd); near base of Magic Mountain. $5. All year; 14-day limit. 8 sties. Tbls, toilets, cfga, drkg wtr. Fishing, hiking, winter sports.

HARRISON (54)

Harrison City Campground   **$9**
On Hwy 97 in Harrison. $9 base; $17 full hookups. 5/1-11/30. 28 sites. Tbls, flush toilets, cfga, drkg wtr, dump, showers, hookups($), coin laundry.

HARVARD (55)

Giant White Pine   **$8**
Clearwater National Forest
8.5 mi N of Harvard on SR 6. $8. MD-LD; 14-day limit. 14 sites (RVs under 30 ft). Tbls, toilets, cfga, drkg wtr. Hiking trails, observation site. Camp may be open free until 11/1 after wtr is off.

Laird Park Recreation Area   **$8**
Clearwater National Forest
3 mi NE of Harvard on SR 6; 1 mi SE on FR 447; at Palouse River. $8. MD-LD; 14-day limit. 31 sites (35-ft RV limit). Tbls, toilets, cfga, drkg wtr, 7 picnic sites. Fishing, nature trails, swimming beach, playground. Large group picnic area may be reserved for $25 per day.
    Fishing tip: Brook trout can be caught above and below the campground.

Pines RV Park (Priv)   **$12**
2 mi from Harvard on SR 6. $12. All year. 16 sites with full hookups. Tbls, flush toilets, showers, cfga, drkg wtr, elec, dump. Weekly/monthly rates available.

HAYDEN LAKE (56)

Mokins Bay   **$12**
Coeur d'Alene National Forest
12 mi E of Hayden Lake on FR 3090; E at "Public Camp" sign. $12. MD-LD; 14-day limit. 16 sites (RVs under 22 ft). Tbls, toilets, cfga, firewood, piped drkg wtr. Picnicking, fishing, boating, waterskiing. Nearest public boat launch 5 mi by rd at N end of lake.

HEADQUARTERS (57)

Aquarius   **$8**
Clearwater National Forest
42 mi NE of Headquarters on Hwy 11; 25 mi NE on FR 247; at North Fork of Clearwater River. $8. MD-LD; 14-day limit. 9 sites (RVs under 32 ft). Tbls, toilets, cfga, drkg wtr. Fishing, boating, hiking, horseback riding Elev 1700 ft. May be open free without water until about 10/15.

E.C. Rettig Area   **FREE**
Potlatch Corporation
2 mi S of Headquarters on SR 11. Free. 6/1-11/15; 14-day limit. 9 sites (RVs under 20 ft). 4 tbls above SR 11 used for camping; 5 tbls below SR 11 for picnicking. Spring

& creek drkg wtr must be purified. Hiking, picnicking, fishing. Elev 3250 ft; 4 acres. No motorbikes.

Grandad   **FREE**
Corps of Engineers
Dworshak Project
NE of Headquarters on Silver Creek-Big Island Rd at Grandad Bridge, Mile 40 on Dworshak Reservoir. Free. 10 sites in undeveloped parking area, restrooms, seasonal launch ramp. Overnight camping spaces. No drkg wtr. Fishing, boating.

HOWE (60)

Summit Creek   **FREE**
Recreation Site
Bureau of Land Management
Challis Field Office
41 mi NW on co rd; 9.5 mi NE on Summit Rd. (30 mi S of Patterson.) Free. Elev 7000 ft. All year; 16-day limit. 7 sites on 1 acre (30-ft RV limit). Tbls, toilets, cfga, no drkg wtr. Hiking, fishing. On Little Lost River.

IDAHO CITY (61)

Bad Bear   **$10**
Boise National Forest
9.5 mi NE of Idaho City on SR 21. $10. 6/1-10/15; 14-day limit. 5 sites (RVs under 23 ft). Tbls, toilets, cfga, drkg wtr. Fishing, hiking.

Bald Mountain Camp   **FREE**
Boise National Forest
1 mi N of Idaho City on SR 21; 6 mi SE on FR 304; 1 mi SE on FR 203. Free. 7/1-9/30; 14-day limit. 4 sites. Tbls, toilets, cfga, no drkg wtr. Hiking, mountain biking, horseback riding, OHV activities. Trail leads to Middle Fork of Boise River.

Black Rock   **$8**
Boise National Forest
3 mi NE of Idaho City on SR 21; 18 mi E on FR 327. $8 base; $10 for larger sites. About 6/1-10/15; 14-day limit. 11 sites. Tbls, toilets, cfga, drkg wtr. Fishing, horseback riding, hiking. Adjacent to N fork of Boise River.

Bonneville   **$10**
Boise National Forest
18 mi NE of Idaho City on SR 21; half mi N on FR 25. $10. 5/1-9/30; 14-day limit. 23 sites (RVs under 30 ft). Tbls, toilets, cfga, firewood, drkg wtr. Picnicking, fishing, hiking, boating. Elev 4700 ft; 2 acres. Mountains. Stream. Natural hot springs quarter mi upstream from camp. Boating suitable for whitewater craft only on S fork of the Payette River.

Grayback Gulch   **$10**
Boise National Forest
2.6 mi SW of Idaho City on SR 21. $10. MD-LD; 14-day limit. 18 sites (RVs under 23 ft). Tbls, toilets, cfga, drkg wtr. Fishing, swimming.

Ten Mile   **$10**
Boise National Forest
9.3 mi NE of Idaho City on SR 21. $10. 6/1-10/15; 14-day limit. 14 sites (RVs under 23 ft). Tbls, toilets, cfga, drkg wtr. Fishing.

IDAHO FALLS (62)

Kelly's Island   **$5**
Bureau of Land Management
23 mi NE of Idaho Falls on US 26. $5. 5/1-11/15; 14-day limit. 14 sites (RVs under 23 ft). Tbls, toilets, cfga, drkg wtr. Boating, fishing, hiking.

North Tourist Park   **FREE**
Municipal Campground
NE on US 26-91 to Lincoln St. and N Yellowstone Hwy (US 26); paved access rds. Free. All year; 1-day limit. About 20 undesignated sites in pull-through areas. Toilets, near city golf course and large shopping center. Site of a Peter "Wolf" Toth Indian sculpture, carved from huge log.
Fishing tip: Gem Lake, at town's S city limits, offers trophy-size trout making their way downstream on the Snake River.
Travel tip: N of town on I-15, at Spencer, is the Spencer Opal Mine; open pit mine is only place in North America where opals are plentiful enough to mine commercially; get digging permit at the Opal Shop; produces high quality star opals.

South Tourist Park   **FREE**
Municipal Campground
US 26-91 exit off I-15; 2.5 mi to Southside rest area at S Yellowstone. Free. All year; 1-day limit. 4 back-in sites. Tbls, toilets, cfga, drkg wtr, playground. Picnicking, fishing, boating (l). Snake River.
Fishing tip: This section of the river produces trophy-size cutthroat trout up to two feet long; also, good brown trout.
Travel tip: See The Lavas, 10 mi S on U.S. 91 to Shelley; 4 mi W on county rd; caves created by lava; good place for finding Indian arrowheads, other artifacts; although an extension of Craters of the Moon (for which there is a charge), this area is free and filled with rock flows and lava tubes.

Shady Rest Campground   **$12**
On US 91 in Idaho Falls; at 2200 N. Yellowstone Hwy. $12 base; $20 full hookups. 55 sites. Tbls, flush toilets, cfga, drkg wtr.

Tex Creek   **FREE**
Wildlife Management Area
14 mi NE of Idaho Falls on US 26; just after milepost 350, turn right at Ririe Dam/Recreation Area sign; follow Meadow Creek Rd SE past the dam. Free. All year; 10-day limit. Primitive camping in designated areas; no facilities. Hunting, hiking, horseback riding.

ISLAND PARK (63)

Henry's Lake State Park   **$12**
15 mi W of Yellowstone NP's W gate at 3917 E. 5100 N. $12 without hookups, $20 with elec/wtr. All year; 15-day limit. 44 sites; 60-ft RV limit. Tbls, flush toilets, cfga, drkg wtr, showers, dump, fish cleaning station. Boating(ld), fishing, hiking, biking, guided walks, interpretive hiking trail. 585 acres; elev 6470 ft.
Fishing tip: Henry's Lake contains cutthroat trout averaging 3-5 pounds, cutthroat-rainbow hybrids up to 12 pounds; brook trout up to 3 pounds. Excellent stream fishing nearby at Henry's Ford, Madison and Gallatin Rivers.

Valley View   **$10**
RV Campground & Laundromat
On Hwy 20 across from Henry's Lake. $10 base for tents; $16 for RVs without hookups; $21 full hookups. 5/1-11/30. 53 sites; 75-ft RV limit. Tbls, flush toilets, cfga, drkg wtr, showers, hookups ($), coin laundry.

West End   **FREE**
Dispersed Camping Area
Targhee National Forest
On FR 167 at Island Park Reservoir; open area by a bend of the lake. Free. MD-9/15; 14-day limit. Primitive undesignated sites. Toilet, cfga, tbls, drkg wtr (half mi). Boating(l), fishing.

JEROME (64)

Big Tree RV Park   **$12**
At 300 First Ave W, Jerome. $12 base; $15 with hookups. 25 sites. Tbls, flush toilets, cfga, drkg wtr.

JORDAN VALLEY (OR.) (65)

North Fork Recreation Site   **FREE**
Bureau of Land Management
Owyhee Field Office
27 mi SE of Jordan Valley, Oregon, on Owyhee Uplands Backcountry Byway; at North Fork of Owyhee River. Free. 5/1-10/31; 7-day limit. Primitive sites. Toilets, cfga, no drkg wtr, no trash service. Biking, fishing, hiking, horseback ridking.

Owyhee Uplands   **FREE**
National Backcountry Byway
Bureau of Land Management
Owyhee Field Office
Starting 5 mi SE of Jordan Valley, Oregon, or 3 mi from Grand View, ID, on Owyhee Byway along the Owyhee River. Free. Secluded primitive sites all along the road at riverside. Some are like the small, tree-shaded picnic area at Poison Creek near E end of byway. No facilities. Fishing, boating, hiking, horseback riding.

KAMIAH (66)

Riverfront City Park   **FREE**
At E end of town on US 12 by Clearwater River. $5 with elec; free without hookups. All year; 2-day limit. 6 sites. Tbls, flush toilets, cfga, drkg wtr, elec($), beach, covered barbecue bldg. Boating(l), fishing, swimming, waterskiing, nature trail, playground, badminton, horseshoes.
Travel tip: Nearby are Nez Perce Indian graves (behind First Presbyterian Church, N of town on No Kid Lane. Also Heart of the Monster in Nez Perce National Historic Park; large rock formation prominent in Indian legends, said to be all that is left of the monster Koos-Koos-Ki, from which various Indian nations said to have begun.
Fishing tip: Try the Clearwater River & its tributaries for trout, bass, steelhead & whitefish.

KELLOGG (67)

Chrystal Gold Mine RV Park   **$10**
I-90 exit 54 to Miner's Memorial on N side of freeway; 2 mi W on Silver Valley Rd. No charge for camping; $10 for mine tour (not required to camp). All year. 21 sites; 40-ft RV limit. Tbls, toilets, cfga, drkg wtr, dump, wtr hookups.

KETCHUM (68)

Baker Creek   **FREE**
Sawtooth National Forest
Sawtooth National Recreation Area
15 mi N of Ketchum on SR 75. Free. All year; 14-day limit. Primitive undeveloped sites (RVs under 32 ft). Tbls, toilets, firewood, no drkg wtr. Picnicking, fishing, swimming, snowmobile area.
Travel tip: Tour the Sawtooth Nat'l Recreation Area; visitor center off SR 75 at Redfish Lake (8 mi N of town); immense, picturesque area includes hundreds of mountain lakes; nature trails, hiking, fishing, free park programs (slide shows, tours, lectures); visitor center has exhibits on plants, animals, geology.

Boulderview   **$10**
Sawtooth National Forest
Sawtooth National Recreation Area
11.5 mi N of Ketchum on SR 75; turn S at signs for Easley & Boulderview Camps; 1 mi on FR 040. $10. About MD-LD; 16-day limit. 10 sites (40-ft RV limit). Tbls, toilets, cfga, drkg wtr. Fishing, hiking. Elev 6800 ft. Closed by flood damage early in 2007; check with ranger district for status.

Boundary Campground   **FREE**
Sawtooth National Forest
From Ketchum, go NE through Sun Valley about 4 mi on FR 408; at Trail Creek. Free. 5/15-10/15; 14-day limit. 6 sites. Tbls, toilets, cfga, no drkg wtr, laundry facilities. Hiking, horseback riding, fishing.

Travel tip: NE of camp on FR 137 is trailhead for the Pioneer Cabin Trail (7.6 mi round trip), leading to a rustic cabin built in 1937 by Union Pacific Railroad as a ski shelter; cabin is a popular destination for day hikers, who typically picnic on the front steps.

Caribou $8
Sawtooth National Forest
Sawtooth National Recreation Area
7 mi N of Ketchum on SR 75; 3 mi E on FR 146; near NRA visitor center. $8 during about MD-9/15; free before & after fee season, but no services or wtr; 16-day limit. 7 sites on 60 acres (RVs under 22 ft). Tbls, toilets, cfga, drkg wtr. Picnicking, fishing, hiking trails. Difficult navigation for trailers. Visitor center, interpretive programs, drkg wtr, dump at the NRA headquarters. Elev 6100 ft.
Travel tip: Nearby on SR 75 is the Sawtooth National Fish Hatchery, where more than 3 million chinook salmon are reared each year; tours three times daily in summer.

Cottonwood FREE
Sawtooth National Forest
6 mi W of Ketchum on FR 227; at Warm Springs Creek. Free. 5/15-10/15; 14-day limit. 1 site; no facilities, no drkg wtr, no trash service. Fishing. 124-degree Warfield Hot Springs 2 mi W.

Cougar FREE
Sawtooth National Forest
Sawtooth National Recreation Area
7 mi N on SR 75; 3 mi N on FR 146. Free. 6/15-10/1; 16-day limit. 10 sites; 5 acres. Toilets, cfga, tbls, no drkg wtr. Hiking, picnicking, fishing. Elev 6450 ft.

Easley $10
Sawtooth National Forest
Sawtooth National Recreation Area
14.5 mi N of Ketchum on SR 75; turn S at sign; at Big Wood River. $10. MD-LD; 16-day limit. 10 sites (40-ft RV limit). Tbls, toilets, cfga, drkg wtr. Swimming, fishing, hiking. Elev 6800 ft. Closed in early 2007 by flood damage; check status with ranger district.

East Fork Baker Creek FREE
Sawtooth National Forest
15 mi N of Ketchum on SR 75; 3 mi S on FR 162. Free. 6/1-11/15; 14-day limit. 2 sites. Tbls, toilet, cfga, no drkg wtr. Fishing, hiking.

Murdock $11
Sawtooth National Forest
Sawtooth National Recreation Area
7 mi N of Ketchum on SR 75; 1 mi E on FR 146. $11 during bout MD-9/30; free before & after season, but no wtr or services; 16-day limit. 12 sites on 60 acres (RVs under 22 ft). Tbls, toilets, no cfga, drkg wtr. Picnicking, fishing, hiking trails. Visitor center with exhibits, interpretive programs, dump 2 mi down canyon at headquarters. Elev 6200 ft.

North Fork $11
Sawtooth National Forest
Sawtooth National Recreation Area
8.1 mi N of Ketchum on SR 75; at Big Wood River. $11-$13 during about MD-9/30; 9 sites free before & after season, but no wtr or services; 16-day limit. 29 sites (RVs under 23 ft). Tbls, toilets, cfga, drkg wtr. Fishing, hiking, biking. Visit center, exhibits, interpretive programs, dump are across SR 75 at recreation area headquarters. Elev 5900 ft; 40 acres.

Park Creek $5
Challis National Forest
12 mi NE of Ketchum on SR 75; 26 mi NE on Sun Valley Rd, becoming Trail Creek Rd. $5. 6/15-10/15; 14-day limit. 12 sites (32-ft RV limit). Tbls, toilets, cfga, drkg wtr. Hiking trails, fishing, horseback riding (corral just W on FR 141). Elev 7700 ft; 10 acres.

Phi Kappa $5
Challis National Forest
15 mi NE of Ketchum on SR 75; 23 mi NE on Sun Valley Rd, becoming Trail Creek Rd. $5. 6/15-10/15; 14-day limit. 21 sites (32-ft RV limit). Tbls, toilets, cfga, drkg wtr (naturally rusty color). Hiking trails, fishing. Elev 7600 ft; 8 acres.

Prairie Creek FREE
Sawtooth National Forest
Sawtooth National Recreation Area
18 mi N of Ketchum on SR 75. Free. All year; 16-day limit. Primitive undeveloped sites (RVs under 32 ft). Tbls, toilets, cfga, no drkg wtr. Picnicking, swimming, fishing, cross-country skiing. 60 acres.

Starhope $5
Challis National Forest
20 mi NE of Ketchum on SR 75; 23.1 mi E on FR 135 (Sun Valley Rd/Trail Creek Rd); 13 mi SW on Copper Basin Rd; 9 mi on Copper Basin Loop Rd 138. $5. 6/30-10/15; 14-day limit. 21 sites (32-ft RV limit). Tbls, toilets, cfga, drkg wtr, hitching post. Fishing, hiking trails, horseback riding. Elev 8000 ft; 9 acres.

Wildhorse $5
Challis National Forest
20 mi NE of Ketchum on SR 75; 3 mi on FR 135; 6 mi S on FR 136. $5. 6/1-10/15; 14-day limit. 12 sites (22-ft RV limit). Tbls, toilets, cfga, drkg wtr. Hiking trails, fishing. Elev 7400 ft; 30 acres.

Wood River $11
Sawtooth National Forest
Sawtooth National Recreation Area
10 mi NW of Ketchum on SR 75; second camp on S side of hwy after passing NRA headquarters; at Big Wood River. $11 during about MD-LD; 10-day limit; 8 sites free off-season, but no wtr or services. 30 sites (22-ft RV limit). Tbls, flush toilets, cfga, drkg wtr. Hiking, fishing, swimming. Elev 6300 ft; 41 acres.

KINGSTON (69)

Bumblebee $12
Coeur d'Alene National Forest
7 mi NE of Kingston on FR 9; 3 mi NW on FR 209; on North Fork of Coeur d'Alene River. $12. MD-LD; 14-day limit. 25 sites (16-ft RV limit). Tbls, toilets, cfga, drkg wtr. Fishing, hiking, kayaking. 10 acres. Elev 2200 ft.

KOOSKIA (70)

CCC Camp FREE
Nez Perce National Forest
23.5 mi E of Kooskia on US 12; 7 me SE on FR 223; at Selway River. Free. 6/1-11/15; 14-day limit. 6 undesignated sites. Tbls, toilets, cfga, no drkg wtr. Swimming, fishing, horseback riding, picnicking.
Fishing tip: Fenn Pond across the rd is stocked with rainbow trout; fishing in the river is catch & release.

Johnson Bar FREE
Nez Perce National Forest
23.5 mi E of Kooskia on US 12; 4 mi SE on FR 223; on Selway River. Free. MD-11/1; 14-day limit. 7 undesignated sites (RVs under 22 ft); groups okay. Tbls, toilets, cfga, firewood, no drkg wtr, beach. Swimming, picnicking, fishing, boating, rafting in spring. Elev 1600 ft; 5 acres. Visitor center (1 mi). Scenic. River.

Knife Edge River Portal FREE
Dispersed Campground
Clearwater National Forest
1 mi N of Kooskia on Hwy 13; 33.5 mi E on US 12; at Lochsa River. Free. MD-LD; 14-day limit. Primitive undesignated sites; no longer a formal campground; recently rebuilt for river access but still used for camping, as are about a dozen other sites on the river. No facilities; no drkg wtr. Fishing, biking, boating, hiking. Undeveloped boat ramp. May be closed to camping in May & June for river running season.

Race Creek FREE
Nez Perce National Forest
23.5 mi E of Kooskia on US 12; 20.5 mi SE on FR 223 (gravel rd for 13 mi); at upper Selway River. Free. MD-11/1; 14-day limit. 3 sites (RVs under 22 ft). Tbls, toilets, cfga, firewood, piped drkg wtr. Handicapped facilities. Hiking, picnicking, fishing (Meadow Creek), boating, horseback riding, horse feedrack, hitching rails, horse loading ramp. Elev 1800 ft; 4 acres. At Bitterroot Wilderness Trailhead. End-of-rd facilities for Bitterroot Wilderness Portal.

River Junction RV Park $10
Near Kooskia at milepost 74 on US 12. $10 base; $20 full hookups. Apr-Nov. 35 sites; 45-ft RV limit. Tbls, dump, cfga, flush toilets, drkg wtr, hookups ($), coin laundry. Swimming, fishing, boating.

Slims   **FREE**
Nez Perce National Forest
23.5 mi E of Kooskia on US 12; 21 mi SE on FR 223; 2 mi S on FR 290; at Meadow Creek. Free. MD-11/1; 14-day limit. 2 sites (RVs under 16 ft). Tbls, toilet, cfga, firewood, no drkg wtr. Stock loading ramps, hitching rails, fed rack. Picnicking, fishing, hiking, horseback riding. Elev 1800 ft; 4 acres. Scenic. End of rd facilities for Meadow Creek Country. Trailhead for Meadow Creek Recreation Trail.

Twentymile Bar   **FREE**
Nez Perce National Forest
23.5 mi E of Kooskia on US 12; 10.5 mi SE on FR 223; at Selway River. Free. MD-11/1; 14-day limit. 2 unimproved sites (RVs under 22 ft). Tbls, toilets, cfga, firewood, no drkg wtr. Boating, swimming from sandy bar, picnicking, fishing. Carry-down boat access.

Twentythreemile Bar   **FREE**
Nez Perce National Forest
23.5 mi E of Kooskia on US 12; 12 mi SE on FR 223; at Selway River. Free. MD-11/1; 14-day limit. 1 site. Toilet, cfga, no drkg wtr. Very steep access to river. Fishing, swimming, boating.

KUNA (71)

Celebration Park   **FREE**
Snake River Birds of Prey
National Conservation Area
Bureau of Land Management
Bruneau Field Office
SW of Kuna on CanAda Rd, leading into Victory Lane; at end of rd. Free. All year; 14-day limit. Primitive undesignated sites within state's only archaeological park. Toilets, cfga, drkg wtr. Boating(l), interpretive displays, educational programs, hiking. Petroglyphs.

LAVA HOT SPRINGS (72)

Big Springs   **$8**
Caribou National Forest
10 mi N of Lava Hot Springs on Bancroft Hwy; 8 mi W on FR 036. $8. MD-9/30; 14-day limit. 29 sites (16-ft RV limit). Tbls, toilets, cfga, drkg wtr. Fishing, hiking, biking, horseback riding, OHV activity. 3 equestrian sites; corrals. Newly renovated.

Chesterfield Reservoir   **FREE**
Caribou County Park
E of Hot Springs on Hwy 30, then 10 mi N on Old Route 30; left on Kelly-Toponce Rd for 10 mi, then turn on Nipper Rd at sign for Chesterfield Reservoir. Free. May-Sep; 14-day limit. 3 primitive sites. Tbls, toilet, cfga, no drkg wtr. Boating, fishing.
Fishing tip: Chesterfield Lake produces trophy trout, and 20-inch rainbows are routine. Launch a float tube above the dam. Use a black leech trailed by a scud pattern or Zugbug. Early mornings, focus on shallow water close to shore.

Rivers Edge RV Park   **$10**
At 101 W. Portneuf (Hwy 30), Lava Hot Springs. $10 base. All year. 87 sites. Tbls, flush toilets, showers, drkg wtr, hookups($), cfga.

LEADORE (73)

Big Eightmile   **FREE**
Salmon National Forest
6.7 mi W of Leadore on Lee Creek Rd; at second jct, bear left at Big Eightmile Creek on FR 097 for 7 mi. Free. 6/15-10/15. 10 sites (RVs under 25 ft). Tbls, toilets, cfga, firewood, drkg wtr; no trash service. Picnicking, fishing, horseback riding. Elev 6500 ft.

Lema's Store & RV Park   **$10**
On SR 28 at Leadore. $10. Apr-Nov. 10 sites. Tbls, flush toilets, cfga, drkg wtr, hookups, dump, store. Fishing.

Meadow Lake   **$5**
Salmon National Forest
16.8 mi SE of Leadore on SR 28; 6 mi W on FR 002. $5. 7/1-9/15; free rest of year; 14-day limit. 18 sites (24-ft RV limit). Tbls, toilets, cfga, drkg wtr. Fishing, swimming, boating, hiking. Scenic. No wtr during free period. Elev 9160 ft.
Fishing tip: Fish for trout in either the lake or in Meadow Creek.

McFarland Recreation Site   **$5**
Bureau of Land Management
Salmon Field Office
10 mi NW on Hwy 28. Free 11/1-4/30; rest of year, $5. 14-day limit. 10 sites (RV limit 28 ft). Some pull-through. Toilets, tbls, cfga, drkg wtr. Hiking, fishing, picnicking. Elev 5370 ft; 6 acres.
Travel tip: Visit the Lemhi Ghost Town 29 mi SE of town on SR 28; 1858 Mormon settlement failed because of Indian attacks; ruins of Fort Lemhi walls still stand; town and county named for Lemhi, a figure in the Book of Mormon.

Smokey's Cubs   **FREE**
Recreation Site
Bureau of Land Management
Salmon Field Office
4 mi E of Leadore off Hwy 28 South, on Railroad Canyon Rd. Free. All year; 14-day limit. 10 sites (28-ft RV limit). Tbls, toilets, cfga. Hiking, fishing, picnicking.

LEWISTON (75)

Black Pine Cabin Area   **FREE**
Potlatch Corporation
25 mi SE of Lewiston on CR P2 near Soldiers Meadow Reservoir (gravel access rds). Free. 6/1-11/15; 14-day limit. 10 sites (RVs under 20 ft). Tbls, toilets, cfga. Stream & spring drkg wtr must be boiled. Picnicking. Fishing & hiking nearby. Elev 4800 ft; 1 acre. No motorbikes.
Travel tip: Stop at the Nez Perce National

Historic Park Visitor Center 12 mi E of town on US 95; mementos from Lewis & Clark expedition, Indian cultural relics, historical displays. Audiovisual program on Nez Perce culture; park includes 24 different sites in north-central Idaho; interesting rock formations; battlefields; fur company post. Free.

Hells Gate State Park   **$12**
4 mi S of Lewiston; on Snake River. W on US 12; turn on Snake River Ave, just prior to Snake River bridge. $12 base; $20 with elec. All year; 15-day limit. 93 developed sites; 60-ft RV limit. Showers, tbls, flush toilets, cfga, drkg wtr, dump, store, playground. Volleyball, horseshoes, fishing, swimming, boating(ldr), hiking, biking, horseback riding, guided walks, education center, summer campfire programs. 960 acres.
Fishing tip: Most anglers are attracted to the park by the fall and winter steelhead runs on the Snake, Salmon and Clearwater Rivers. Also available: salmon, smallmouth bass, trout, catfish, sturgeon.
Travel tip: The Nez Perce National Historic Park is nearby, with its fascinating displays of artifacts on the traditional life of the Nez Perce people.

Lake Waha   **FREE**
Bureau of Reclamation
State Dept. of Wildlife & Parks
5 mi S of Lewiston on Tammany Creek Rd; 10 mi S on Waha Rd. Free. All year; 7-day limit. Primitive undesignated sites; limited facilities. Boating(l), fishing, swimming. 180-acre lake developed by Bureau of Reclamation, patrolled by Lewiston Orchards Irrigation District, managed by state.
Fishing tip: This 180-acre lake contains smallmouth bass and rainbow trout.

Soldiers Meadow Reservoir   **FREE**
Bureau of Reclamation
State Dept of Wildlife & Park
5 mi S of Lewiston Orchards on Tammany Creek Rd, then 14 mi S on Waha Rd, past the lake, then E on Soldiers Meadow Rd. All year; 7-day limit. Primitive camping. Tbls, toilets, cfga, no drkg wtr. Boating(l), fishing, swimming, hiking. 124-acre lake built by Bureau of Reclamation; patrolled by Lewiston Orchards Irrigation District, managed by state.
Fishing tip: The lake contaiins trout, kokanee salmon and crappie. Boat motors may be used, but only at trolling speed. Several nearby streams are stocked with rainbow and brook trout.

Sweetwater Creek   **FREE**
Recreation Area
Potlatch Corporation
21 mi SE of Lewiston on CR P2; 1.3 mi E of Lake Waha on rd to Webb Ridge; take left branch 1.3 mi E of Waha Store. Free. 6/1-10/1; 14-day limit. 13 sites (RVs under 20 ft). Tbls, toilets, cfga. Drkg wtr must be boiled. Picnicking, fishing nearby in Waha Lake. Elev 3385; 2 acres. In Orchards Tree Farm.

LOLO HOT SPRINGS (MT.) (76)

Hoodoo Lake   **FREE**
Clearwater National Forest
11 mi SW of Lolo on US 12; 17 mi S on FR 111 & FR 360; in Idaho. Free. 6/15-9/15 or until inaccessible; 14-day limit. 2 sites. Tbl, toilet, cfga, no drkg wtr. Hiking, horseback riding. Elev 5756 ft.

Jerry Johnson   **$8**
Clearwater National Forest
30 mi SW of Lolo Hot Springs on US 12, in Idaho at Lochsa River. $8. MD-9/30; 14-day limit. 15 sites (22-ft RV limit). Tbls, toilets, cfga, drkg wtr. Fishing, hiking. Elev 3100 ft; 6 acres. Trail to Jerry Johnson Hot Springs, which averages 118 degrees.
   Fishing tip: Local waters contain chinook salmon, steelhead, cutthroat & bull trout, mountain whitefish. Some species are catch-and-release.
   Travel tip: Lolo Pass Visitors Center offers excellent displays of the Lolo Trail, the Lewis & Clark expedition and the River of No Return Area.

Powell   **$8**
Clearwater National Forest
18 mi W of Lolo Hot Springs on US 12, in Idaho at Lochsa River. $8 base; $15 with elec. MD-10/15; 14-day limit. 39 sites (32-ft RV limit). Tbls, flush toilets, cfga, drkg wtr. Fishing, hiking. Lewis & Clark passed through here on their way to the Pacific. Camp may be open free without wtr until about 11/1.

Wendover   **$8**
Clearwater National Forest
22 mi W of Lolo Hot Springs on US 12, in Idaho at Lochsa River. $8. MD-9/30; 14-day limit. 27 sites (32-ft RV limit). Tbls, toilets, cfga, drkg wtr. Fishing, hiking & bridle trails. Elev 3280 ft.

White Sands   **$8**
Clearwater National Forest
22 mi W of Lolo Hot Springs on US 12; 1 mi S on Elks Summit Rd; in Idaho at Lochsa River. $8. 6/1-9/15 or until inaccessible; 14-day limit. 6 sites (32-ft RV limit). Tbls, toilets, cfga, drkg wtr. Swimming, fishing, hiking.

Whitehouse   **$8**
Clearwater National Forest
22 mi W of Lolo Hot Springs on US 12 in Idaho at Lochsa River and Whitehouse Pond. $8. MD-9/30; 14-day limit. 13 sites (32-ft RV limit). Tbls, toilets, cfga, drkg wtr. Fishing, hiking, horseback riding. Whitehouse Pond named for a member of the Lewis & Clark expedition; it was noted in his journal.

LOWELL (77)

Apgar   **$8**
Clearwater National Forest
7 mi E of Lowell on US 12; at Lochsa River.

$8. MD-10/10; 14-day limit. 7 sites (22-ft RV limit). Tbls, toilets, cfga, drkg wtr. Fishing, hiking, rafting.

Boyd Creek   **FREE**
Nez Perce National Forest
12 mi E of Lowell on Selway Rd 223; on Selway River. Free. 6/1-11/1; 14-day limit. 5 sites. Tbls, toilets, cfga, no drkg wtr. Horse loading ramp & feed rack. Trailhead for East Boyd National Recreation Trail. Terrain very steep. Swimming, boating, fishing.

Colgate   **FREE**
Clearwater National Forest
60 mi E of Lowell on US 12; at milepost 147. Free. Undesignated camping area. About 7 sites. Tbls, toilets, cfga, no drkg wtr. Fishing.

Gedney Creek   **FREE**
Nez Perce National Forest
19 mi E of Lowell on Selway River Rd 223; at Selway River, below Selway Falls. Free. 5/15-11/15; 14-day limit. Undeveloped tent sites. Toilet, no drkg wtr. Hiking, fishing, rafting, horseback riding. Limited parking space.

Glover Creek   **FREE**
Nez Perce National Forest
16 mi E of Lowell on Selway River Rd 223. Free. 5/15-10/31; 14-day limit. 7 sites (16-ft RV limit). Tbls, toilets, cfga, drkg wtr, handicapped facilities. Hitching rail, horse loading ramp. Trailhead for Glover National Recreation Trail. Terrain is very steep; limited maneuvering space for trailers.

O'Hara Bar   **$10**
Nez Perce National Forest
At Lowell, 12.7 mi SE on CR 223; 1 mi S on FR 651; at Selway River. $10. 5/15-10/1; 14-day limit. 34 sites (20-ft RV limit). Tbls, cfga, drkg wtr, toilets. Swimming, boating, fishing. Permit (by lottery) needed to float river from Selway Falls to Lowell during 5/15-7/31.
   Fishing tip: Fish the river for rainbow and cutthroat trout, but practice catch & release unles fishing in Fenn Pond across from the ranger station. Boat carry-down access at river.

Selway Falls   **FREE**
Nez Perce National Forest
21 mi E of Lowell on Selway River Rd 223; 1 mi S on FR 290; at Meadow Creek. Free. 6/1-10/31; 14-day limit. 7 sites. Tbls, toilets, cfga, no drkg wtr, handicapped facilities. Limited maneuvering space for trailers. Swimming, boating, fishing. Permit (by lottery) needed to float river from Selway Falls to Lowell during 5/15-7/31.

Slide Creek   **FREE**
Nez Perce National Forest
11 mi E of Lowell on Selway Rd 223; at Selway River. Free. May-Oct. Unimproved camping area. Toilet, cfga, no drkg wtr. Sandy beach. Hiking, fishing, swimming, kayaking.

Twentyfivemile Bar   **FREE**
Nez Perce National Forest
15 mi E of Lowell on Selway River Rd 223; at Selway River. 5/15-10/1; 14-day limit. Undeveloped sites at river bar. Toilet, cfga, no drkg wtr. Swimming, fishing. Carry-down boat access.

Wild Goose   **$8**
Clearwater National Forest
2 mi W of Lowell on US 12; at Lochsa River. $8. MD-10/10; 14-day limit. 6 sites (22-ft RV limit). Tbls, toilets, cfga, drkg wtr. Hiking, fishing.

Wilderness Gateway   **$8**
Clearwater National Forest
27 mi E of Lowell on US 12; at Lochsa River. $8. 4/15-11/1; 14-day limit. 89 sites (35-ft RV limit). Tbls, flush toilets, cfga, drkg wtr, dump. Fishing, hiking, swimming, rafting, horseback riding. Handicap access.

LOWMAN (78)

Barney's   **$8**
Boise National Forest
36 mi NE of Lowman on SR 21; 28 mi W on FR 579; 7.5 mi S on FR 555. $8. All year; 14-day limit. 6 sites (22-ft RV limit). Tbls, toilets, cfga, drkg wtr. Fishing, boating(l), hiking.

Bear Valley   **FREE**
Boise National Forest
36 mi NE of Lowman on SR 21; 1s mi N on FR 579 (Landmark-Stanley Rd); at Bear Valley Creek. Free. Elev 6400 ft. 7/1-9/30; 14-day limit. 10 sites; 20 acres (22-ft RV limit). Tbls, toilets, cfga, no drkg wtr. Picnicking, fishing, horseback riding, hiking.

Bull Trout Lake   **$10**
Boise National Forest
34 mi NE of Lowman on SR 21; 2 mi W on FR 250. $10 during 7/1-9/30; free off-season; 14-day limit. 36 sites on 15 acres (69 ft RV limit). Toilets, drkg wtr. Boating (no motors), boat ramp, fishing, nature trails. Several other lakes nearby. Elev 6900 ft.

Boundary Creek   **$5**
Challis National Forest
34.8 mi NE of Lowman on FR 668 (Boundary Creek Rd); on Middle Fork of Salmon River. $5. 6/15-9/15; 14-day limit. 14 sites (22-ft RV limit). Tbls, toilets, cfga, drkg wtr. Fishing, hiking, picnicking, floating on Marsh Creek. Elev 5800 ft; 6 acres.

Cozy Cove   **$8**
Boise National Forest
36 mi NE of Lowman on SR 21; 28 mi W on FR 579; 11 mi S on FR 555. $8. 7/1-9/30; 14-day limit. 9 sites (RVs under 16 ft). Tbls, toilets, cfga, firewood, drkg wtr. Boating(d), picnicking, fishing, waterskiing, horseback riding. Elev 5200 ft; 15 acres. Adjacent to Deadwood Reservoir.

Daggar Falls #1   **$5**
Challis National Forest

32 mi NE of Lowman on FR 082; N on FR 668 Boundary Creek Rd). $5 during 6/15-9/30; free rest of season; 14-day limit. 10 sites. Tbls, toilets, cfga, drkg wtr (RVs under 22 ft). Picnicking, fishing, hiking, horseback riding. Near the West and Middle Forks of Salmon River. Elev 5800 ft.

Fishing tip: Excellent fishing for wild cutthroat salmon (catch & release) and hatchery salmon, identified by clipped adipose fins.

Daggar Falls #2   **FREE**
Challis National Forest

32 mi NE of Lowman on FR 082; 13 mi N on FR 668. Elev 5800 ft. 6/15-9/10. 10 sites on 6 acres (RVs under 22 ft). Tbls, toilets, cfga, firewood, piped drkg wtr. Picnicking, fishing, horseback riding.

Deer Flat Campground   **FREE**
Boise National Forest

36 mi NE of Lowman on SR 21; 22 mi E on Cape Horn Turnoff (Landmark-Stanley Rd/FR 579); at confluence of Deer Creek, North Fork & South Fork. Elev 6400 ft. Free. 7/1-9/30; 14-day limit. 7 sites on 3 acres (RVs under 32 ft). Tbls, toilets, cfga, firewood, no drkg wtr. Picnicking, fishing, horseback riding.

Edna Creek   **$10**
Boise National Forest

18 mi N of Lowman on SR 21. $10. 6/1-10/15; 14-day limit. 9 sites (RVs under 17 ft). Tbls, toilets, cfga, drkg wtr. Fishing.

Fir Creek   **FREE**
Boise National Forest

33 mi NE of Lowman on FR 082; 1 mi NE on FR 470. Free. 7/1-9/30; 14-day limit. 5 sites (RVs under 16 ft). Tbls, toilets, cfga, drkg wtr, firewood. Picnicking, fishing, horseback riding, kayaking, rafting. Elev 6300 ft; 2 acres. Stream. Fishing restricted. Wilderness canoeing, kayaking, rafting on Bear Valley Creek. Elev 6400 ft.

Graham Bridge Camp   **FREE**
Boise National Forest

11 mi S of Lowman on SR 21; 3 mi E of FR 384; 33.5 mi SE on FR 522 (poor rd last 14 mi; RVs not recommended). Free. 8/1-10/15; 14-day limit. 4 sites (no trailers). Tbls, toilets, cfga, firewood, no drkg wtr. Picnicking, fishing, horseback riding. Elev 5600 ft; 2 acres. Stream.

Grandjean   **$10**
Sawtooth National Forest
Sawtooth National Recreation Area

21 mi NE of Lowman on SR 21; 6 mi E on FR 524; left on FR 824 at Sawtooth Lodge. $10 during 6/15-9/15; free rest of year, but no wtr or services; 10-day limit. 31 sites (22-ft RV limit). Tbls, toilets, cfga, drkg wtr. Swimming, fishing, hiking. 10 sites allow horses, have hitchlines. Trailhead to Sawtooth Wilderness. On South Fork of Payette River. Natural hot springs 1.5 mi. Elev 5400 ft.

Helende View   **$8**
Boise National Forest

11 mi E of Lowman on SR 21. $8. MD-LD; 14-day limit. Free when wtr shut off. 10 sites (RVs under 32 ft). Tbls, toilets, cfga, firewood, no drkg wtr. Picnicking, fishing, horseback riding. Elev 4000 ft; 3 acres. River. Boating suitable for whitewater craft only on south fork of Payette River.

Hower's Campground   **$8**
Boise National Forest

36 mi NE of Lowman on SR 21 to milepost 109.2; 28 mi W on FR 579; 7.5 mi S on FR 555; on Deadwood Reservoir. $8. 7/1-9/30; 14-day limit. 10 sites (22-ft RV limit). Tbls, toilets, cfga, drkg wtr. Fishing, boating(l), hiking.

Johnson Creek   **FREE**
Boise National Forest

11 mi S of Lowman on SR 21; 3 mi E on FR 384; 27 mi E on FR 312; on North Fork of Boise River. Free. 8/1-10/15; 14-day limit. 3 sites. Tbls, toilets, cfga, firewood, no drkg wtr. Picnicking, fishing, hiking, horseback riding. Elev 5600 ft; 2 acres.

Kirkham Hot Springs   **$10**
Boise National Forest

5 mi E of Lowman on SR 21. $10. MD-LD; 14-day limit. 17 sites (RV limit 32 ft). Parking fee of $2 at overflow sites. Drkg wtr, pit toilets, cfga, laundry, dump, tbls. Boating, fishing, swimming, picnicking. Natural hot springs on site. Boating suitable for whitewater craft only on south fork of Payette River.

Mountain View   **$10**
Boise National Forest

Half mi E of Lowman on SR 21. $10. MD-9/30; 14-day limit. Parking fee of $2 at overflow sites. 14 sites (RVs under 33 ft). Tbls, toilets, cfga, drkg wtr. Fishing.

Park Creek   **$8**
Boise National Forest

3 mi N of Lowman on FR 582. $8. MD-9/30; 14-day limit. 26 sites. Tbls, toilets, cfga, drkg wtr. Fishing, hiking.

Pine Flats   **$10**
Boise National Forest

5 mi W of Lowman on SR 17. $10. 4/20-10/20; 14-day limit. Parking fee of $2 at overflow sites. 24 sites (32-ft RV limit) and walk-in sites. Tbls, toilets, cfga, drkg wtr. Fishing. South Fork Payette River. Elev 4400 ft; 22 acres.

Riverside   **$8**
Boise National Forest

36 mi NE of Lowman on SR 21 to milepost 104.2; 28 mi W on FR 579; 7 mi S on FR 555. $8. 7/1-9/30; 14-day limit. 8 sites (RVs under 22 ft). Tbls, toilets, well drkg wtr, cfga, firewood. Picnicking, fishing, boating, hiking, horseback riding, biking. Elev 5200 ft; 3 acres. Adjacent to Deadwood Reservoir. Due to water level changes, boats may have to be launched at other lakes later in season.

Willow Creek   **FREE**
Boise National Forest

11 mi S of Lowman on SR 21; 23 mi E on FR 268. Free. 6/1-10/31; 14-day limit. 4 sites (16-ft RV limit). Tbls, toilets, cfga, firewood, drkg wtr. Picnicking, fishing, horseback riding. At Arrowhead Lake's Boise River inlet.

MACKAY (79)

Borah Peak Trailhead   **FREE**
Challis National Forest

20 mi N of Mackay on US 93; 3 mi on Borah Peak access rd. Free. 5/1-11/31; 14-day limit. 5 primitive sites. Toilet, cfga, no drkg wtr. Hiking. Elev 7200 ft.

Broad Canyon Trailhead   **FREE**
Challis National Forest

16 mi N of Mackay on US 93; left on Trail Creek Rd for 18 mi; left on Copper Basin Rd for 13 mi; right on Copper Basin Loop Rd for 7.5 mi; right on Broad Canyon Rd for half mi. Free. 6/15-10/15; 14-day limit. 8 primitive sites. Toilet, cfga, no drkg wtr. Hiking.

Deep Creek Recreation Site   **FREE**
Bureau of Land Management
Challis Field Office

15 mi NW of MacKay on US 93; 19 mi SW on Trail Creek Rd. Free. All year; 14-day limit. Undesignated sites. Toilet, tbls, cfga, no drkg wtr. Hiking, picnicking, fishing. No trash service.

Fall Creek Trailhead   **FREE**
Dispersed Camping Area
Challis National Forest

16 mi N of Mackay on US 93; left on Trail Creek Rd for 18 mi; left on Copper Basin Rd; keep to the right for 3.5 mi on Wildhorse Creek Rd; left on Fall Creek Rd for 1.5 mi. Free. 6/15-10/15; 14-day limit. Primitive undesignated sites. Toilet, cfga, no drkg wtr. Elev 7200 ft.

Garden Creek   **FREE**
Recreation Site
Bureau of Land Management
Challis Field Office

35 mi NW of Mackay on US 93. Free. All year; 14-day limit. 3 sites. Tbls, toilet, no drkg wtr. Picnicking, hiking. No trash service.

Iron Bog   **$5**
Challis National Forest

14 mi SE of Mackay on US 93; 10 mi SW on Antelope Creek Rd; 7.2 mi SW on FR 137. $5. 6/1-10/1; 14-day limit. 21 sites (24 ft RV limit). Tbls, toilets, cfga, drkg wtr. Fishing, hiking trails. Elev 7200 ft; 30 acres.

Joseph T. Fallini Campground   **$6**
Mackay Reservoir Recreation Site
Bureau of Land Management
Challis Field Office

5 mi NW of Mackay on US 93. $6 at 4 tent sites, $10 at 18 RV sites with hookups. 14-day limit. 59 sites (28-ft RV limit). Tbls, toilets,

cfga, drkg wtr, dump. Boating(l), fishing, hiking, picnicking, swimming. No drkg wtr during free period. Elev 6000 ft; 80 acres.

Lake Creek Trailhead **FREE**
Challis National Forest
16 mi N of Mackay on US 93; left on Trail Creek Rd for 18 mi; left on Copper Basin Rd for 18 mi to second turnoff to Copper Basin Loop Rd at Copper Basin guard station; right for 4 mi on Copper Basin Loop Rd. Free. 6/15-10/15; 14-day limit. 4 primitive sites. Toilet, cfga, no drkg wtr, hitching rails, horse loading ramp. Hiking, horseback riding.

Mill Creek Trailhead **FREE**
Challis National Forest
7 mi S of Mackay on US 93; left on Pass Creek Rd for 28 mi; left on Little Lost/Pahsimeroi Rd for qtr mi; right on Sawmill Canyon Rd; right on Mill Creek Rd. Free. 6/1-10/31; 14-day limit. 4 primitive sites. Toilet, cfga, no drkg wtr. Fishing, hiking.

Timber Creek **$5**
Challis National Forest
7 mi S of Mackay on US 93; 28 mi NE on Pass Creek Rd (FR 122); 13 mi N on Sawmill Canyon Rd (FR 101); at Little Lost River. $5. 6/15-10/15; 14-day limit. 12 sites (32-ft RV limit). Tbls, toilets, cfga, drkg wtr. Hiking, fishing, horseback riding (horse loadking ramp). Elev 7430 ft.

MACKS INN (80)

Big Springs **$12**
Targhee National Forest
14.5 mi SE of Macks Inn on SR 84. $12 during MD-9/15; free but no wtr after 9/15. 16-day limit. 15 sites (32-ft RV limit). Tbls, toilets, cfga, drkg wtr, hiking. Elev 6400 ft; 8 acres. Headwaters of Henrys Fork River. Big Springs Water Trail is 2-3 hour float or canoe trip to above Island Park Reservoir. Watch trout feed in springs.

Flatrock **$12**
Targhee National Forest
W of US 20 at Macks Inn; on shore of Henry's Fork. $12; $17 with elec. About 5/15-10/1; 16-day limit. 45 sites (32-ft RV limit). Tbls, toilets, cfga, drkg wtr. Swimming, fishing, canoeing, hiking.

Macks Inn Resort **$10**
1 block S of Macks Inn on US 20. $10 for tents; $18 for RV sites. 5/15-10/1. 79 sites. Tbls, flush toilets, cfa, drkg wtr, hookups($), store, dump, coin laundr, playground. Hiking, fishing, boating (r), canoeing (r), swimming, horseshoes, badminton, volleyball.

Upper Coffee Pot **$12**
Targhee National Forest
Qtr mi S of Macks Inn on US 20; 2 mi SW on FR 130. $12 base; $17 with elec. MD-10/15; free but no wtr 9/15-10/15. 14-day limit. 14 sites (16-ft RV limit). Tbls, toilets, cfga, drkg

wtr (no wtr after LD). Swimming, fishing, hiking. On shore of Henry's Fork River.

Fishing tip: Fishing is quite good at the campground for trout and kokanee salmon.

MALAD CITY (81)

Curlew National Grasslands **$10**
16 mi W of Malad. $10. All year; 14-day limit. Primitive sites. Tbls, toilets, cfga, drkg wtr. Hiking, birdwatching, fishing, swimming.

Dry Canyon Campground **FREE**
Caribou National Forest
3.5 mi N of Malad City on I-15; 17 mi E on Westin Hwy; 6 mi W on FR 53. Free. MD-9/30; 14-day limit. 3 sites. Tbls, toilets, cfga, no drkg wtr. Hiking, biking, horseback riding. Elev 6400 ft.

MALTA (82)

Lake Fork **FREE**
Sawtooth National Forest
18.6 mi E on FR 568; on N end of Sublett Reservoir. Free. Elev 5500 ft. 6/1-11/5; 14-day limit. Undesignated sites; no facilities, no drkg wtr. Picnicking, hiking, boating, swimming, fishing, waterskiing.

McClendon Spring **FREE**
Recreation Site
Bureau of Land Management
Burley Field Office
1.5 mi W of Malta on Hwy 77; N 3 mi to campground. Free. 4/15-10/31; 14-day limit. 2 sites (25-ft RV limit). Toilets, cfga, tbls, no drkg wtr. Hiking, picnicking.

Sublett **FREE**
Sawtooth National Forest
20.8 mi E of Malta on FR 568; around N end of Sublett Reservoir at Sublett Creek. Free. Elev 5500 ft. 6/1-10/30; 14-day limit. 9 sites on 10 acres (RVs under 22 ft). Tbls, toilets, cfga, firewood, drkg wtr. Picnicking, horseback riding, Fishing, swimming, boating(l).

MARSING (83)

River Haven RV Park **$10**
2.5 mi upriver from Marsing on Old Bruneau Hwy. $10 base; $18 RV hookups. 55 sites. Tbls, flush toilets, cfga, showers, drkg wtr, coin laundry, store, dump, hookups($). Fishing.

MCCALL (84)

Black Lee **FREE**
Payette National Forest
15 mi E of McCall on Lick Creek Rd. Free. All year; 16-day limit. Primitive undesignated sites, good for large groups & large RVs. Tbls, toilets, cfga, no drkg wtr, no trash service. Hiking.

Travel tip: While in McCall, tour McCall Fish Hatchery, 300 Mather Rd, by lake out-

let at W end of town; self-guided tours; guided group tours by appt (208-634-2690); hatchery raises a million chinook salmon, half million rainbow trout, 300,000 cutthroat trout annually; egg incubation, early rearing, outdoor rearing ponds shown.

Buckhorn Bar **$8**
Payette National Forest
39 mi NE of McCall on FR 48; 7.5 mi S on FR 674. $8 during MD-9/30; $5 off-season, but no wtr; 16-day limit. 10 single sites (4 walk-in tent sites) & 2 double walk-in tent sites. 30 & 45-ft RV limit. Tbls, toilets, cfga, firewood, piped drkg wtr. Horseback riding, picnicking, fishing, hiking trails. Elev 3800 ft; 5 acres. Stream. Adjacent to S fork of Salmon River.

Camp Creek **$8**
Payette National Forest
39 mi NE of McCall on FR 48; 11.5 mi S on FR 674. $8 during MD-9/30; $5 off-season, but no wtr; 16-day limit. 4 sites. Tbls, toilet, cfga, no drkg wtr. Pack out trash. Fishing, hiking, horseback riding. Elev 4000 ft.

Chinook **$5**
Payette National Forest
39 mi NE of McCall on FR 48 (Warren Wagon Rd). 8 mi NE of Warren on FR 21. Adjacent to Secesh River-Loon Lake trailhead. $5 during MD-9/30; free rest of year. 9 sites. Tbls, toilets, cfga, no drkg wtr. Horse trailer parking, horse unloading ramp, hitching rails. Loon Lake Trail access. Elev 5700 ft; 10 acres.

Four Mile Creek **$8**
Payette National Forest
39 mi NE of McCall on FR 48, then S on FR 674; along South Fork of Salmon River Rd. $8 during MD-9/30; $5 off-season when wtr is shut off; 16-day limit. 4 sites. Tbls, cfga, toilet, drkg wtr. Pack out trash. Fishing, hiking trails.

Lake Fork **$8**
Payette National Forest
9.5 mi E of McCall on FR 48 (Lick Creek Rd). $8. MD-9/30; $5 rest of season, but no drkg wtr; 16-day limit. 9 sites (22-ft RV limit). Tbls, toilets, cfga, drkg wtr. Hiking, fishing. Pack out trash. Elev 5600 ft.

Lakeview Village RV Park **$12**
Half mi E on Pine St from Hwy 55; 1 mi N on Davis St. $12 base; $16 full hookups. 5/15-9/15. 84 sites. Tbls, flush toilets, cfga, drkg wtr, showers, coin laundry.

Ponderosa **$8**
Payette National Forest
31 mi NE of McCall on FR 48 (Lick Creek Rd). $8 during MD-9/30; $5 off-season, but no wtr; 16-day limit. 14 sites (RVs under 23 ft). Tbls, toilets, cfga, drkg wtr. Hiking, fishing, picnicking. Lick Creek. Pack out trash. Elev 4050 ft.

Ponderosa State Park **$12**
2 mi NE of McCall, off SR 55 on East Lake Dr;

at Payette Lake. $12 without hookups, $20 with elec/wtr. 6/15-10/31; 15-day limit. 80-ft sites. Flush & pit toilets, cfga, drkg wtr, showers, education center, dump. Boating(l), boat camping, fishing, swimming, horseshoes, volleyball, hiking, biking, guided walks. 1,470 acres; elec 5050 ft.

Poverty Flat $8
Payette National Forest
NE of McCall along Salmon River Rd. $8 during MD-9/30; free rest of year if wtr is shut off. 16-day limit. 8 sites (including 4 walk-in tent sites). Tbls, toilet, cfga, drkg wtr. Pack out trash. Hitch rails. Fishing, hiking, horseback riding.

Rapid Creek FREE
Payette National Forest
16 mi S of Mccall on Hwy 55; E of FR 388. Free. All year; 16-day limit. Primitive undesignated sites; 22-ft RV limit. Tbls, toilets, cfga, no drkg wtr, no trash service.

Secash River Horse Camp $8
Payette National Forest
31 mi NE of McCall on Lick Creek Rd. $8 during MD-9/30; $5 rest of year if wtr is shut off; 16-day limit. 5 sites. Tbls, toilet, cfga. Drkg wtr across rd at Ponderosa Campground. Pack out trash. Fishing, hiking, horseback riding. Hitch rails.

Slick Rock Mountain FREE
Recreation Area
Payette National Forest
11 mi E of McCall on FR 48. Free. June-Sept; 14-day limit. Dispersed camping at 5400 ft elevation. No facilities. Rock climbing, hiking.

Upper Payette Lake $8
Payette National Forest
18.5 mi N of McCall on FR 21 (Warren Wagon Rd); 1 mi N on FR 495. $8 (double sites $10); walk-in camping $5 off-season if wtr is shut off. All year; 14-day limit. 10 sites (22-ft RV limit). Tbls, toilets, drkg wtr, cfga. Fishing, swimming, boating(l). Pack out trash.

MCCAMMON (85)

Goodenough Creek FREE
Bureau of Land Management
Pocatello Field Office
From McCammon, cross over I-15 & travel about 1 mi W to fork; take left fork S for qtr mi, then right on Goodenough Creek access rd for 2 mi; at foot of Bannock Range. Free. 6/1-10/31; 14-day limit. 13 primitive sites. Tbls, toilets, cfga, no drkg wtr. Hiking trail, biking.

MONTPELIER (86)

Montpelier Canyon $4
Caribou National Forest
3.3 mi E of Montpelier on US 89. $4. 5/15-10/15; 14-day limit. 14 sites (32-ft RV limit).

Tbls, toilets, cfga, drkg wtr. Fishing. Elev 6100 ft; 6 acres.

MOSCOW (87)

McCroskey State Park $9
30 mi N of Moscow on US 95 & Skyline Dr (an 18-mi gravel rd that traverses the park). $9 at primitive sites; standard sites without hookups $12. All year; 15-day limit. 3 primitive roadside camping areas; 25-ft RV limit. Tbls, pit toilets, cfga, drkg wtr, no trash service. Horseback riding, mountain biking, hiking. Drkg wtr at milepost 8.25 on Skyline Dr.

Robinson Lake $10
Latah County Parks & Recreation
5 mi E of Moscow on Robinson Park Rd. $8 12 RV sites, numerous tent spaces. Tbls, toilets, cfga, drkg wtr. Volleyball, horseshoes, ballfields.

MOUNTAIN HOME (88)

Big Roaring River Lake $7
Boise National Forest
30 mi NE of Mountain Home on SR 20; 29 mi NE on FR 61; 1.5 mi NE on FR 172; 3 mi S on FR 129. $7. 7/15-9/30; 14 day limit. 12 sites (RVs under 22 ft). Tbls, toilets, cfga, firewood, drkg wtr. Boating (no motors), picnicking, fishing, hiking trails, horseback riding. Elev 8200 ft; 7 acres. Lake. Four high alpine lakes nearby. Pack out trash.

Big Trinity Lake $7
Boise National Forest
35 mi NE of Mountain Home on SR 20 to Pine/Featherville exit; 29 mi N on SR 61; 15 mi NW on FR 172; 3 mi S on FR 129 to Guard Station Junction. $7. 7/15-10/1; 14 day limit. 17 sites (RVs under 22 ft). Tbls, toilets, cfga, firewood, piped drkg wtr. Boating (no motors), picnicking, fishing, horseback riding, hiking. Elev 7900 ft; 7 acres. Four high alpine lakes nearby. Pack out trash.

Bruneau Dunes State Park $12
Off I-84 near Mountain Home; westbound exit 112 or eastbound exit 90; Hwy 78 off SR 51. $12 base. All year; 15-day limit. Base fee for standard sites ($20 with elec); seniors pay half price weekdays. 35-ft RV limit. Tbls, flush toilets, cfga, drkg wtr, showers, dump, observatory, store. Hiking, horseback riding, boating(l), fishing, swimming, volleyball. 4,800 acres; elev 2470 ft.

C.J. Strike Parks $6
Idaho Power Company
Bureau of Land Management
Hwy 67 to Grandview from Mountain Home; SE on Hwy 78, turn left at high school, N to C.J. Strike Dam. $6. Three parks. All year. 50 sites (40-ft RV limit). Tbls, toilets, cfga, drkg wtr, handicap sites, pull-through sites. Fishing, hiking, boating(l), horseback riding.
Fishing tip: Try the Snake River just S of town; drive NE to Anderson Ranch Reservoir,

with its excellent kokanee salmon fishing, or fly fish for trout below the dam in the south fork of the Boise River.

Castle Creek FREE
Boise National Forest
24 mi NE of Mountain Home on SR 20; 5 mi NE on FR 134; 14 mi N on FR 113; at Anderson Ranch Reservoir. Free. 5/1-10/31; 14-day limit. 2 sites (RVs under 16 ft okay). Tbls, toilets, cfga, no drkg wtr. Picnicking, fishing, boating, waterskiing. Elev 4300 ft; 2 acres. Mountains.
Fishing tip: Lake has excellent fishing for bass and salmon. Boat ramp at Fall Creek Campground.

Curlew Creek $4
Boise National Forest
35 mi NE of Mountain Home on SR 20; abou 14 mi N on SR 61; In vicinity of Dog Creek camp. $4. 7/1-9/30; 14-day limit. 12 RV sites. Tbls, toilets, cfga, no drkg wtr. Fishing, hiking, boating(l), waterskiing.
Fishing tip: Lake offers excellent fishing for smallmouth bass and kokanee salmon. Catch fat rainbows below the dam.

Dog Creek $8
Boise National Forest
29 mi NE of Mountain Home on SR 20; 13 mi NE on FR 163; 14 mi N on FR 156. $8; some double sites at $12. 13 sites (RVs under 23 ft). 5/15-10/1; 14-day limit. Tbls, toilets, cfga, drkg wtr. Fishing, hiking. Elev 4400 ft; 6 acres.

Elk Flat Campground $8
Boise National Forest
29 mi NE of Mountain Home on SR 20; 22 mi NE on FR 61; on East Fork Boise River. $8 (double sites $12). 5/1-9/30; 14-day limit. 36 sites. Tbls, toilets, cfga, drkg wtr. Fishing, hiking, boating(l), OHV activities, horseback riding, biking.

Evans Creek FREE
Boise National Forest
24 mi NE of Mountain Home on SR 20; 5 mi NE on FR 134; 9 mi on FR 113. Free. 6/1-10/1; 14-day limit. 10 sites. Tbls, toilets, cfga. Picnicking, fishing, boating, waterskiing. Boat ramp at Fall Creek Campground.

Ice Springs FREE
Boise National Forest
24 mi NE of Mountain Home on SR 20; 5 mi NE on FR 134; 9 mi NE on FR 113; 5 mi N on FR 125; at Fall Creek. Free. Elev 5000 ft. 6/1-10/31; 14-day limit. 4 sites (RVs under 16 ft). Tbls, toilets, cfga, firewood, well drkg wtr. Store, food, gas 5 mi. Picnicking, horseback riding. Fishing, horseback riding, biking, hiking.

Jack's Creek FREE
Sportsman's Access Area
Idaho Power Company
State Wildlife Management Area
Hwy 67 to Grandview from Mountain Home;

SE on Hwy 78; turn left at high school; N to C.J. Strike Dam. Free. 8/1-2/1; 10-day limit. 50 primitive sites in designated area. Toilet, cfga, no drkg wtr. Boating(l), fishing.

Little Roaring River Lake   **FREE**
Boise National Forest
29 mi NE of Mountain Home on SR 20; 29 mi N on FR 61; 15 mi NE on FR 172; 3 mi S on FR 129; between Upper Roaring River & Little Roaring River Lake. Free. 6/1-9/30; 14-day limit. 17 sites. Tbls, toilets, cfga, firewood, no drkg wtr. Picnicking, fishing, horseback riding. Elev 7900 ft; 2 acres. No motor boats. 4 high alpine lakes nearby.

Little Wilson Creek   **FREE**
Boise National Forest
About 24 mi NE of Mountain Home on SR 20, then 7 mi N to Anderson Ranch Reservoir on FRs 134 & 113. Free. 5/15-10/15; 14-day limit. 2 tent sites. Tbls, toilets, cfga, no drkg wtr. Picnicking, fishing, boating, waterskiing. Elev 4200 ft; 1 acre. Mountains.

Pine RV Campground   **$6**
Boise National Forest
35 mi NE of Mountain Home on US 20; about 20 mi N around Anderson Ranch Reservoir on SR 61 & FR 128. $6. 5/1-10/31; 14-day limit. 7 RV sites. Tbls, toilets, cfga, no drkg wtr. Fishing, boating(l), hiking.

Spillway Campground   **FREE**
Boise National Forest
24 mi N of Mountain Home on US 20; 5 mi N on FRs 134 & 113; at Anderson Ranch Reservoir. Free. 5/1-10/31; 14-day limit. 4 sites. Tbls, toilets, cfga, no drkg wtr. Fishing, boating(l).

MUD LAKE (89)

Birch Creek   **FREE**
Bureau of Land Management
25 mi NW of Mud Lake on Hwy 28; no sign on SR 28, but access rd between mileposts 40 & 41. Free. 5/1-9/30; 14-day limit. 12 sites (25-ft RV limit). Tbls, toilets, cfga, no drkg wtr. Fishing. Quiet.

Haven Motel & Trailer Park   **$12**
On Hwy 33 in Mud Lake (1079 East 1500 N). $12. 13 sites. Tbls, toilets, cfga, drkg wtr, hookups, dump.

MURPHY (90)

Silver City Ghost Town   **FREE**
Bureau of Land Management
Owyhee Field Office
From Hwy 78 near Murphy, turn off at Silver City sign; unpaved access rds. Primitive undesignated camping areas near the town. Free. 6/1-11/30; 14-day limit. 6 sites, no facilities. Biking, fishing, hiking, horseback riding.

MURTAUGH (91)

Cauldron Rim   **FREE**
Bureau of Land Management
Exit 188 from I-84, S 3 mi, then E 1.5 mi, S 2 mi, then E on gravel rd and S to canyon rim. Watch signs last 2 mi. Last half mi into canyon difficult access; not recommended for RVs. Free. All year; 14-day limit. Undesignated camping spaces. No facilities. Limited camping opportunities. Picnicking, hiking. Beautiful waterfall, historic site.
Fishing tip: Nearby Murtaugh Lake provides fishing wharfs and an opportunity to catch some big catfish.

NEW MEADOWS (92)

Cold Springs   **$8**
Payette National Forest
8 mi SW of New Meadows on US 95; 4 mi W on FR 089; 1 mi W on FR 091; on Lost Valley Reservoir. $8 during 5/15-10/15; $5 off-season if wtr is off. 14-day limit. 32 single sites, 5 double sites ($10). 30 & 50-ft RV limit. Tbls, toilets, cfga, drkg wtr, dump. Boating(l), fishing, waterskiing, berry picking. Elev 4820 ft; 21 acres.

Grouse   **$8**
Payette National Forest
6 mi E of New Meadows on SR 55; 10.5 mi N on FR 257; half mi W on FR 273; .1 mi N on FR 278; at Goose Lake. $8; double sites $10. About 7/1-LD; 14-day limit. 22 sites (RVs under 16 ft). Tbls, toilets, cfga, drkg wtr. Swimming, boating(no mtrs), fishing. Elev 6350 ft. Pack out trash.

Hazard Lake   **$8**
Payette National Forest
6 mi E of New Meadows on SR 55; 22 mi N on FR 257 (Goose Lake Mountain Rd); .1 mi E on FR 259. $8 during 7/1-10/15; free off-season if wtr is off; 14-day limit. 12 sites (22-ft RV limit). Tbls, toilets, cfga, drkg wtr. Picnicking, fishing, boating (no mtrs), horseback riding. Elev 7100 ft; 5 acres. Scenic.

Last Chance Campground   **$8**
Payette National Forest
SE of New Meadows (7 mi W of McCall) on SR 55; 2 mi N on FR 453. $8 (double site $10). 5/15-10/15; free off-season if wtr is off; 16-day limit. 19 single sites, 3 double sites (45-ft RV limit). Tbls, toilets, cfga, drkg wtr. Hiking, picnicking. Elev 4650 ft.

Meadows RV Park   **$12**
2.5 mi E of New Meadows on Hwy 55. $12 base; $22 full hookups. 4/15-10/31. 37 sites. Tbls, flush toilets, cfga, drkg wtr, showers, coin laundry, dump, hookups($). Fishing, horseshoes, volleyball.

Pinehurst Resort   **$8**
At 5604 Hwy 95 near New Meadows (13 mi S of Riggins). $8 for primitive sites, $15 full hookups. 8 sites. Tbls, toilets, cfga, drkg wtr,

store. Volleyball, horseshoes, fishing, swimming, kayaking, rafting.

Zim's Hot Springs (Private)   **$10**
4 mi N of New Meadows on Hwy 95. $10 base; $16 full hookups. 12 sites; 35-ft RV limit. Tbls, flush toilets, cfga, drkg wtr, showers, dump, hookups($). Fishing, pool($), game room, hiking.

NEW PLYMOUTH (93)

Payette River   **FREE**
Wildlife Management Area
From SR 30 in New Plymouth, half miES on Idaho St; 1.5 mi N on Holly Ave; 0.7 mi E on NW Second Ave. Free. Primitive designated camping area; no facilities; 10-day limit. Bird-watching, fishing, hunting.
Fishing tip: The WMA's ponds contain bass, and rainbow trout are plentiful in the Payette River.

NEZPERCE (94)

Nezperce RV Park   **$10**
In Nezperce at 404 Oak St. $10. 6 sites. Tbls, toilets, cfga, drkg wtr. No other information.

NORTH FORK (95)

Spring Creek   **FREE**
Salmon National Forest
16.9 mi W of North Fork on Salmon River Rd (FR 30). Free.. 3/15-11/1; 14-day limit. 5 sites & several undeveloped sites; 32-ft RV limit. Tbls, toilets, cfga, drkg wtr. Fishing, boating, swimming, floating.
Fishing tip: Fishing is excellent here for cutthroat and rainbow trout, steelhead and whitefish.

OBSIDIAN (96)

Smokey Bear   **$10**
Sawtooth National Forest
Sawtooth National Recreation Area
9.8 mi S of Obsidian on SR 75; 3.4 mi SW on FR 205; at Alturas Lake. $10 during MD-LD; free rest of year, but no wtr or services; 14-day limit. 12 sites (16-ft RV limit). Tbls, toilets, cfga, drkg wtr. Boating(l), fishing, hiking, swimming. Pack out trash. Perkins Lake nearby.

OLA (97)

Antelope   **$10**
Boise National Forest
10 mi NE of Ola on FR 618; 6.7 mi NE on FR 626; 2.3 mi NE on FR 614. $10. 4/20-10/10; 14-day limit. 20 sites (30-ft RV limit). Tbls, toilets, cfga, drkg wtr. Boating(l), fishing, swimming. Sagehen Reservoir. 12 acres.

Hollywood Point   **$10**
Boise National Forest
10 mi NE of Ola on FR 618; 6.7 mi NE on FR

626; 4.5 mi E on FR 614; on Sagehen Reservoir. $10. 4/20-10/20; 14-day limit. 6 sites (22-ft RV limit). Tbls, toilets, cfga, drkg wtr. Fishing, swimming, boating, hiking.

Sagehen Creek   **$10**
Boise National Forest
10 mi NE of Ola on FR 618; 6.7 mi NE on FR 626; 3.5 mi NE on FR 614. $10. 4/20-10/20; 14-day limit. 15 sites (RVs under 32 ft). Tbls, toilets, cfga, drkg wtr. Fishing, swimming, boating(l). 11 acres.

OROFINO (98)

Canyon Creek   **FREE**
Corps of Engineers
Dworshak Project
11 mi N on Orofino/Elk River Rd on Dworshak Lake. Steep, winding gravel rd. Free. Open unless closed by snow; 14-day limit. 17 gravel sites (RVs under 22 ft). Toilets, tbls, cfga, no drkg wtr. Fishing, hiking, boating(l), swimming, waterskiing, hunting. Elev 1600-1650 ft.

Travel tip: Just off SR 7 near Orofino is the Dworshak National Fish Hatchery, the world's largest producer of steelhead; free self-guided tours illustrate the life cycle of these sea-going trout.

Fishing tip: Dworshak Reservoir has excellent fish populations, including top-notch fishing for kokanee salmon and rainbow trout.

Cold Springs Group Camp   **FREE**
Corps of Engineers
Dworshak Project
20 mi from Orofino on Orofino-Elk River Rd to Dent Acres boat launching ramp, or 17 mi to trailhead at Dent Bridge. Access BY BOAT OR FOOT. 14 river mi or 4-mi trail, moderate difficulty. Free. 6/1-9/30; 14-day limit. Primitive camp, 6-8 sites. Tent pads, tbls, cfga, toilets, no drkg wtr. Boating, fishing, waterskiing, picnicking, hiking. Groups only. Reservations required. P.O. Box 48, Ahsahka, ID 83520; 208/ 476-3294.

Dworshak State Park   **$12**
24 mi NE of Orofino, off US 12 on county rd (last 2 mi twisting, narrow 10% downgrade). $12 base ($20 with elec); seniors pay half price weekdays. 105 sites; 50-ft RV limit. Tbls, flush toilets, cfga, drkg wtr, showers, dump, beach, playground, fish cleaning station. Boating(ld), horseshoes, volleyball, swimming, fishing, hiking. 850 acres; elev 1600 ft.

Mini-Camps   **FREE**
Corps of Engineers
Dworshak Project
From Orofino, go to any of the 6 boat launching sites on Dworshak Lake. Mini-camps are accessible by boat or foot. Free. 6/1-9/30; 14-day limit. 121 tent sites around 184 mi of shoreline (1-4 tents per camp). Tent pads, tbls, cfga, toilets (toilets closed during win-

ter). Picnicking, boating, fishing, waterskiing, hunting. Lake level fluctuates.

Orofino City Park   **FREE**
N end of River Bridge on SR 7 and US 12. Free. All year; 1-day limit. 25 sites. Tbls, toilets. Picnicking, fishing.

Travel tip: Stop at the Lewis & Clark Canoe Camp 5 mi W of town on US 12; it's where Lewis & Clark camped in 1805 and built dugout canoes for part of their trek.

Pink House Recreation Site   **$10**
Clearwater River Recreation Area
Bureau of Land Management
3 mi W of Orofino between US 12 & Clearwater River. $10 base at 3 tent sites; $18 with hookups at 15 RV sites. All year; 14-day limit. Large developed camping area. Tbls, toilets, cfga, drkg wtr. Fishing, hiking, boating(l).

Fishing tip: This site is renowned for its steelhead fishing and has been a popular day-use area.

OVID (99)

Emigration   **$10**
Caribou National Forest
10.5 mi W of Ovid on SR 36. $10. 6/15-LD; 14-day limit. 25 sites (RVs under 23 ft). Tbls, flush toilets, cfga, drkg wtr. Hiking & biking trails, picnicking, horseback riding, OHV activity. Elev 7100 ft; 17 acres.

PALISADES (100)

Bear Creek   **FREE**
Targhee National Forest
2.6 mi SE of Palisades on US 26; 1.5 mi S on FR 076; 4.5 mi on FR 058. Free. Elev 5800 ft. 6/1-10/31; 14-day limit. 6 sites (RVs under 22 ft). No facilities. Picnicking, fishing, boating, swimming, horseback riding.

Calamity   **$12**
Targhee National Forest
2.6 mi S of Palisades on US 26; 1.1 mi SW on FR 058; on Palisades Reservoir. $12 during MD-LD; free LD-9/30, but no wtr; 14-day limit. 41 sites (26-ft RV size limit). Tbls, toilets, cfga, drkg wtr. Boating(l), fishing, swimming, waterskiing. Elev 5700 ft; 21 acres.

Palisades Creek   **$10**
Targhee National Forest
2 mi E of Palisades on FR 255. $10. 6/25-LD; 14-day limit. 8 sites (22-ft RV limit). Tbls, toilets, cfga, drkg wtr, handicapped facilities. Hiking trailhead, fishing, horseback riding (stock loading ramp). Elev 5600 ft; 10 acres.

PARIS (101)

Paris Springs   **$8**
Caribou National Forest
Qtr mi S of Paris on US 89; 3.8 mi W on FR 421; 1 mi W on FR 427. $8 during 6/1-LD; $4 after LD. 14-day limit. 9 sites (RVs under 23

ft). Tbls, toilets, cfga, drkg wtr. Hiking trails, fishing, biking, horseback riding, OHV activity. Nearby ice cave filled with ice all year.

PARMA (102)

Fort Boise   **FREE**
Wildlife Management Area
From SR 20/26 about 3 mi from Parma, follow Old Fort Boise Rd 2 mi W. Free. All year; 5-day limit. Primitive camping in designated areas, and pack-in tent camping. No facilities. Fishing, boating(l), hunting, hiking.

Old Fort Boise RV Park   **$7**
Parma City Park
On S side of Parma, E side of Hwy 95 between E. Stockton Rd & N. Parma Rd. $7 for tents; $13 with hookups ($10 seniors). 5/1-10/15. 10 back-in sites. Tbls, flush toilets, cfga, drkg wtr, showers, 20-amp elec, dump.

PAYETTE (103)

Lazy River RV Park   **$10**
4 mi N of Payette on Hwy 95; 11575 N. River Rd. $10 base. 12 sites. Tbls, toilets, cfga, drkg wtr, showers, dump, coin laundry, hookups ($).

PIERCE (104)

Campbell's Pond Area   **FREE**
Potlatch Corporation
6 mi N of Pierce on SR 11 to Hollywood Jct; 2.5 mi W on Hollywood Grangement Rd; left at Campbell's Pond turnoff; half mi S on co rd (gravel access rds). Free. 6/1-11/15; 14-day limit. 10 sites (RVs under 20 ft). Tbls, toilets, cfga, drkg wtr (must be boiled). Hiking, picnicking, fishing (stocked pond). Elev 3330 ft; 4 acres. No motor bikes.

Cedars   **FREE**
Clearwater National Forest
Half mi S of Pierce on SR 11; NE on FR 250. Free. Elev 3800 ft. 5/31-11/30 (or until inaccessible); 14-day limit. 5 sites on 5 acres (RVs under 16 ft). Tbls, toilets, cfga, firewood, no drkg wtr. Swimming, picnicking, fishing, hiking, horseback riding, OHV activity. On upper North Fork of Clearwater River & Long Creek. Scenic.

Fishing tip: This camp is well situated to take advantage of the excellent cutthroat, brook, dolly varden and rainbow trout fishing in the North Fork.

Hidden Creek   **$7**
Clearwater National Forest
Half mi S of Pierce on SR 11; 58 mi NE on FR 250. $7. MD-LD; 14-day limit. 13 sites (RVs under 23 ft). Tbls, toilets, cfga, drkg wtr, no trash service. Fishing (cutthroat trout). Elev 3500 ft; 5 acres. On North Fork Clearwater River. Camp free when wtr shut off.

Hollywood Campground   **FREE**
Potlatch Corporation
6.5 mi N of Pierce on SR 11. Free. 6/1-11/15; 14-day limit. 12 sites (RVs under 20 ft). Tbls, toilets, cfga, drkg wtr (must be boiled). Picnicking. Fishing & hiking nearby.

Kelly Forks   **$7**
Clearwater National Forest
Half mi S of Pierce on SR 11; 49 mi NE on FR 250; at confluence of Kelly Creek & North Fork of Clearwater River. $7. MD-LD; 14-day limit. 14 sites (RVs under 33 ft). Tbls, toilets, cfga, drkg wtr, no trash service. Boating, fishing (catch & release cutthroat). Elev 2700 ft; 5 acres. Camp free when wtr shut off.

Noe Creek   **$7**
Clearwater National Forest
Half Mi S of Pierce on Hwy 11; 49 mi NE on FR 250; at North Fork of Clearwater River. $5. MD-10/31; 14-day limit. 6 sites (RVs under 23 ft). Tbls, toilets, cfga, drkg wtr. Fishing; hiking trails nearby.

Washington Creek   **$7**
Clearwater National Forest
29 mi NE of Pierce on FR 250; 6 mi NW on FR 249. $7. MD-LD; 14-day limit. 23 sites (RVs under 23 ft). Tbls, toilets, cfga, drkg wtr. Fishing, hiking trails. On north fork of Clearwater River. 8 acres. Elev 2100 ft. Camp may be free during LD-10/15, but no wtr.

Weitas   **FREE**
Clearwater National Forest
34 mi NE of Pierce on FR 250. Free. 5/31-9/30 or until inaccessible; 14-day limit. 6 sites. Tbls, toilets, cfga, firewood, no drkg wtr. Picnicking, fishing, berry picking, boating(d). Elev 2500 ft; 4 acres. Scenic. On N fork of Clearwater River.
   Fishing tip: This camp is well situated to take advantage of the excellent cutthroat, brook, dolly varden and rainbow trout fishing in the North Fork.

PINE (105)

Nester's Riverside Campground **$10**
At Anderson Ranch Recreation Area. $10 base. All year. 15 sites. Tbls, toilets, cfga, drkg wtr, store. Fishing, boating, swimming.

Pine Resort (Private)   **$10**
At headwaters of Anderson Ranch Reservoir. $10 base. All year. 16 sites. Tbls, toilets, cfga, drkg wtr, dump, restaurant, coin laundry, hookups($). Fishing, boating, swimming.

PLUMMER (107)

Heyburn State Park   **$12**
Between Plummer & St. Maries on SR 5, off US 95; at S tip of Coeur d'Alene Lake. $12 base, $20 with elec/wtr (seniors pay half price weekdays). 5/1-10/31; 15-day limit. 132 sites in 3 campgrounds; 55-ft RV limit. Tbls, drkg wtr, flush & pit toilets, cfga,

showers, dump, playground, beach. Fishing, boating(ldr), swimming, volleyball, horseback riding, biking, hiking, guided walks, bird-watching, waterskiing. 7,838 acres.

POCATELLO (106)

Scout Mountain   **$8**
Caribou National Forest
10 mi S of Pocatello on CR 231; 3.8 mi SE on FR 1. $8. MD-9/30; 14-day limit. 25 sites. Tbls, toilets, cfga, drkg wtr. Hiking trails, biking, horseback riding, OHV activity. Crestline Cycle Trail starts just N of camp. Elev 6500 ft; 26 acres.

PONDS LODGE (108)

Box Canyon   **$12**
Targhee National Forest
2.2 mi S of Ponds Lodge on US 20; 8 mi SW on CR 134; 9 mi NW on FR 284; at Henrys Fork River. $12. MD-10/5; 14-day limit. 17 sites (22 ft RV limit). Tbls, toilets, cfga, drkg wtr. Hiking, fishing, boating. Elev 6200 ft; 9 acres.

Buffalo   **$12**
Targhee National Forest
Half mi N of Ponds Lodge on US 20; qtr mi E on FR 138. $12 base; $17 with elec. MD-9/15; free 9/15-10/15 but no wtr. 14-day limit. 105 sites (32-ft RV limit). Tbls, flush toilets, cfga, drkg wtr (no wtr LD-10/15). Fishing, hiking, canoeing, swimming. Elev 6200 ft; 90 acres. Adjacent to Buffalo River.

Buttermilk   **$12**
Targhee National Forest
2 mi N of Ponds Canyon on US 20; 2 mi NW on FR 30; 3.5 mi SW on FR 126. $12 base; $17 with elec. MD-LD; 16-day limit. 52 sites (32-ft RV limit). Tbls, toilets, cfga, drkg wtr. Swimming, boating(l), fishing, waterskiing. E arm of Island Park Reservoir. Group camping available by reservation.

McCrea Bridge   **$12**
Targhee National Forest
2 mi N of Ponds Lodge on US 20; 2.2 mi NW on FR 30. $12. 5/15-9/15; 16-day limit. 25 sites (32-ft RV limit). Tbls, toilets, cfga, drkg wtr. Swimming, fishing, boating(l), waterskiing. On Henrys Fork River at Island Park Reservoir. Elev 6200 ft.

POST FALLS (109)

Westside Resort (Private)   **$12**
7 mi NW of Post Falls off Hwy 53 on W. Hauser Lake Rd; near Hauser. $12 base. 10 sites. Tbls, toilets, showers, drkg wtr, hookups, coin laundry, store. Fishing, swimming.

POWELL (111)

Elk Summit   **FREE**
Clearwater National Forest
17 mi S of Powell on FR 360. Free. 7/1-10/31;

14-day limit. 15 sites (many suitable for horse & stock use with hitching rails & wtr). Tbls, toilets, cfga, no drkg wtr, no trash service. Horseback riding, hiking. Trailhead to Selway Bitterroot Wilderness. Elev 5756 ft.

PRESTON (112)

Albert Moser   **$10**
Caribou National Forest
4 mi SE of Preston on SR 91; 10 mi NE on Cub River Rd; on Cub River. $10 during MD-LD; $5 during LD-10/30 but no wtr; 14-day limit. 9 sites (RVs under 17 ft). Tbls, toilets, cfga, drkg wtr. Fishing, hiking trails, horseback riding, biking, OHV activity.

Willow Flat   **$12**
Caribou National Forest
4 mi SE of Preston on SR 91; 10 mi NE on Cub River Rd & FR 406; along North Fork of St. Charles Creek. $12 during MD-LD; $6 after LD, but no wtr; 14-day limit. 51 sites (RVs under 23 ft). Tbls, toilets, cfga, drkg wtr. Hiking trails, fishing, horseback riding, OHV activity. Elev 6000 ft; 30 acres.

PRICHARD (113)

Berlin Flats   **$12**
Coeur d'Alene National Forest
14 mi N of Prichard; right along Shoshone Falls Creek for 7 mi on FR 412. $12. MD-LD; 14-day limit. 9 sites (RVs under 22 ft). Tbls, toilets, cfga, firewood, piped drkg wtr. Picnicking, fishing, berry picking. Elev 2600 ft.

Big Hank   **$12**
Coeur d'Alene National Forest
20 mi NW of Prichard on FR 208; 1 mi NE on FR 306; at Coeur d'Alene River. $12. MD-LD; 14-day limit. 30 sites (22-ft RV limit). Tbls, toilets, cfga, drkg wtr. Hiking, fishing, kayaking, boating(l), rafting. 10 acres.

Devil's Elbow   **$12**
Coeur d'Alene National Forest
14 mi NW of Prichard on FR 208. $12. MD-LD; 14-day limit. 20 sites (22-ft RV limit). Tbls, portable toilets, cfga, drkg wtr. Boating(l), fishing, hiking. On Coeur d'Alene River.

Kit Price   **$12**
Coeur d'Alene National Forest
11 mi NW of Prichard on FR 208. $12. 5/1-9/30; 14-day limit. 52 sites (22-ft RV limit). Tbls, toilets, cfga, drkg wtr. Fishing, kayaking, rafting. On Coeur d'Alene River. Nearby Shoshone rest stop has dump.

PRIEST LAKE (114)

Navigation   **FREE**
Kaniksu National Forest
35 mi N of Priest River on SR 57; 3 mi E on FR 1339; eighth mi N on FR 237; 5 mi N on Trail 291 or by boat (on NW side of upper Priest Lake). Free. 6/15-9/15. 5 tent sites. Tbls, toilets, cfga, firewood, no drkg wtr, no

trash service. Berry picking, picnicking, fishing, boating(d). Elev 2400 ft; 6 acres. Lake. Scenic. Sandy beach.

Fishing tip: Priest Lake offers world-class mackinaw trout & kokanee salmon as well as trophy rainbows & cutthroats. In summer, there are plenty of fishing charters ready to help you land a few big ones.

Travel tip: On W side of Priest Lake is the Roosevelt Grove of Ancient Cedars -- a virgin forest with trees up to 12 feet across and 150 feet tall; near the grove is a short trail to beautiful Granite Falls.

PRIEST RIVER (115)

Boat-in Camps   **$8**
Bartoo Island
Kaniksu National Forest
Fees of $8 are charged at several boat-in tent camping areas at Bartoo Island on Priest Lake. Unless indicated, portable toilets are needed. Fees are collected at the Kallispell Bay boat ramp. They include:
Sunshine -- 7 sites; E side; pit toilet
Solo 1 -- 1 site; S end
Solo 2 -- 1 site; W side
North Bartoo -- 4 sites; N end
South Bartoo -- 5 sites; S end
South Bartoo Group -- 4 sites
West Sunshine -- 3 sites; E side
Sunrise Group -- 4 sites; NE side
Cedars Group -- 1 site; N end

Boat-in Camps   **$8**
Kalispell Island
Kaniksu National Forest
Fees of $8 are charged at several free boat-in tent camping areas at Kalispell Island on Priest Lake. Portable toilets are needed at most locations. Pack out trash. Fees collected at Kalispell Bay ramp. The areas include:
Shady -- 1 site, N end of island
Silver -- 10 sites; S end
Silver Cover -- 3 sites; S end; pit toilet
Selkirk Family Camp -- 2 sites; SE side
Kalispell Vista -- 2 sites; W side, pit toilet
North Cove -- 6 sites, NE end; pit toilet
West Shores -- 2 sites; W side
Peninsula -- 3 sites; SW side
Rocky Point -- 8 sites, NE end, pit toilet
Schneider -- 7 sites; SE end, pit toilet
Three Pines -- 8 sites, SE side, pit toilet
Cottonwood -- 4 sites, E side

Osprey   **$11**
Kaniksu National Forest
25 mi N of Priest River on SR 57; 2 mi NE on FR 237 at S end of Priest Lake; 1 mi past Outlet Camp. $11. MD-LD; 14-day limit. 16 sites (20-ft RV limit). Tbls, toilets, cfga, drkg wtr. Swimming, hiking, fishing, boating(lr), beach, waterskiing. On W shore of Priest Lake. Carry-down boat access or launch at Kalispell Bay ramp.

Outlet   **$11**
Kaniksu National Forest
25 mi N of Priest River on SR 57; 1 mi NE on FR 237. $11. 5/15-9/15 14-day limit. 31 sites

(22-ft RV limit). Tbls, flush toilets, cfga, drkg wtr, beach. Fishing, boating(l), hiking, swimming. On W shore of Priest Lake. Carry-down boat access or launch at Kalispell Bay ramp.

Plowboy   **FREE**
Kaniksu National Forest
In Upper Priest Lake Scenic Area on shore of lake; accessible by boat or trail. Free. 6/15-9/15; 10-day limit. 4 tent sites. Tbls, toilets, cfga, no drkg wtr. Picnicking, fishing, boating, swimming, hiking. Elev 2400 ft; 6 acres. Rolling hills, dense forest. Sandy beach. No dock. Pets on leash.

Stagger Inn   **FREE**
Kaniksu National Forest
35 mi N of Priest River on SR 57; 14 mi NW on FR 302. Free. 6/1-8/31. 4 tent sites. Tbls, toilets, cfga, no drkg wtr, no trash service. Picnicking, fishing, hiking, berry picking, hiking. Elev 3200 ft; 1 acre. Scenic. Roosevelt grove of ancient cedars (half mi NW). Pets on leash. Spectacular Granite Falls.

RED RIVER (117)

Deep Creek Campground   **FREE**
Bitterroot National Forest
55 mi E of Red River on FR 468. Free. 6/1-10/31; 14-day limit. 6 sites; 30-ft RV limit. Tbls, toilet, cfga, no drkg wtr. Fishing, hunting, hiking. Access point to Selway-Bitterroot and River of No Return Wilderness.

REXBURG (118)

Beaver Dick Park   **FREE**
Madison County Park
6 mi W of Rexburg on SR 33; at Henry's Fork of Snake River. Free. All year; 5-day limit. 20 RV sites, numerous tent sites. Tbls, toilets, cfga, drkg wtr. Boating, fishing, swimming.

Twin Bridges Park   **FREE**
Madison County Park
15 mi SW of Rexburg on Archer Hwy; at South Fork of Snake River. Free. All year; 5-day limit. 25 RV sites, numerous tent sites. Tbls, toilets, cfga, drkg wtr. Boating(d), fishing, swimming.

RIGBY (119)

Jefferson County Lake   **$5**
Jefferson County Park
On US 20 near Rigby. $5 base. 4/1-10/1. Primitive camping areas with tbls, flush toilets, cfga, drkg wtr, showers. Fishing, hiking, swimming.

RIGGINS (120)

Allison Creek   **FREE**
Picnic Campground
Nez Perce National Forest
From US 95 at Riggins, 9 mi up Salmon River Rd 1614. March-Nov; 14-day limit.

Undeveloped camping area adjacent to picnic grounds. Tbls, cfga, toilets, no drkg wtr. Fishing, picnicking, hiking.

Papoose   **FREE**
Nez Perce National Forest
1 mi S of Riggins on US 95; 5.4 mi on Papoose Creek Rd (FR 517) from mouth of Squaw Creek; rd not recommended for trailers or motorhomes. July-Oct; 14-day limit. 2 undeveloped spaces for small RVs. Tbls, toilet, cfga, no drkg wtr. Pack out trash. Cool, shady picnic area, Papoose Cave. Hiking, picnicking, fishing. Near Hells Canyon National Recreation Area.

Travel tip: Riggins is the area's whitewater capital for float trips; water excursions to abandoned mines, old Indian fishing camps, burial grounds, ancient Indian drawings. Also jet boat access of half day or longer.

Seven Devils   **FREE**
Hells Canyon National Recreation Area
Wallowa-Whitman National Forest
1.2 mi S of Riggins on US 95; 16.5 mi SW on FR 517 (Squaw Creek Rd); last 15 mi gravel & steep. Free. 6/30-10/1; 14-day limit. 10 sites for small RVs or tents. Tbls, toilets, cfga, no drkg wtr. Hiking, picnicking, fishing. Elev 72 ft; 9 aces. Not recommended for large RVs because of parking space & steep, narrow access. Seven Devils Lake. Within Hells Canyon-Seven Devils Scenic Area. End of rd facility.

Travel tip: Stop at the Rapid River Fish Hatchery near Riggins; one of the Northwest's most successful chinook salmon hatcheries; see adult chinook around May through Sept.

Shorts Bar/Island Bar   **FREE**
Bureau of Land Management
Cottonwood Field Office
2 mi E of Riggins on Big Salmon Rd; along Lower Salmon River. Free. Unveveloped primitive camping; no facilities, no trash service. Fire plans required for camp & cooking fires. Fishing, boating, rafting, kayaking, swimming. Put-in spot for floating river.

Spring Bar   **$8**
Nez Perce National Forest
1.5 mi S of Riggins on US 95; 11 mi E on FR 1614 (Salmon River Rd). $8 (Canadians $13). 4/1-10/31. 15 sites (accommodates most RVs). Tbls, toilets, cfga, firewood, piped drkg wtr. Rockhounding, picnicking, fishing, boating(ld). Elev 2000 ft; 4 acres. Scenic. River of No Return. Popular take-out point for float trips. Gold prospecting. Fall & spring steelhead fishing.

Windy Saddle   **FREE**
Nez Perce National Forest
15-20 mi SW of Riggins on FR 517 off Hwy 95. Free. May-Oct; 14-day limit. 4 sites. Tbls, toilets, cfga, no drkg wtr. Fishing, horseback riding (horse ramps), hiking. Wilderness trailheads. In Seven Devils Mountains 2 mi from Heaven's Gate Vista Point.

RIRIE (121)

Ririe Reservoir   **$6**
Bureau of Reclamation
Bonneville County Park
1 mi E of Ririe off Hwy 26, S on county rd to headquarters. $6. 5/15-10/15; 14-day limit. 49 sites (35-ft RV limit). Tbls, flush toilets, cfga, drkg wtr, showers, dump. Fishing, hiking, swimming, boating(l).
Fishing tip: This 1,560-acre lake contains rainbow & cutthroat trout, kokanee salmon, largemouth & smallmouth bass.

ROGERSON (122)

Backwaters   **FREE**
Bureau of Land Management
8 mi W of Rogerson on Three Creek Rd to dam at Salmon Falls Creek Reservoir; or W of Hwy 93 following signs; on E shore of lake about 13 mi S of dam. Free. Primitive undesignated sites. Toilet, tbls, cfga, no drkg wtr. Boating, fishing. Canoe on Salmon Falls Creek in spring.

Big Sandy Bay   **FREE**
Bureau of Land Management
8 mi W of Rogerson on Three Creek Rd to dam at Salmon Falls Creek Reservoir; or W of Hwy 93 following signs; on E shore of lake about 6.5 mi S of dam. Free. Primitive undesignated sites. Toilet, tbls, cfga, no drkg wtr. Boating, fishing. Canoe on Salmon Falls Creek in spring; take out at Backwaters in spring.

Greys Landing   **FREE**
Bureau of Land Management
8 mi W of Rogerson on Three Creek Rd to dam at Salmon Falls Creek Reservoir; or W of Hwy 93 following signs; on E shore of lake about 6 mi S of dam. Free. Primitive undesignated sites. Toilet, tbls, cfga, no drkg wtr. Boating(l), fishing. Canoe on Salmon Falls Creek in spring; take out at Backwaters site.

Jarbridge River   **FREE**
Recreation Area
Bureau of Land Management
Follow Jarbridge Rd (Three Creek Rd) to Murphy Hot Springs. Free. All year; 14-day limit. Primitive undesignated camping; no facilities. Fishing, hunting, whitewater rafting.

Lud Drexler Park   **$5**
Bureau of Land Management
Burley Field Office
8 mi W of Rogerson on Jarbridge (Three Creek Rd); next to Salmon Falls Dam. $5 and free. All year; 14-day limit. 20 sites (fees); about 60 free RV spaces near high-water mark. Tbls, toilets, cfga, drkg wtr, dump. Boating(l), fishing, swimming, hiking, waterskiing. Elev 5000 ft.
Fishing tip: Salmon Falls Creek Lake contains brown trout, chinook & kokanee salmon, crappie, smallmouth bass and walleye. Trophy walleyes are common.

Norton Bay   **FREE**
Bureau of Land Management
Burley Field Office
8 mi W of Rogerson on Three Creek Rd to dam at Salmon Falls Creek Reservoir; or W of Hwy 93 following signs; on E shore of lake about 7 mi S of dam. Free. Primitive undesignated sites. Toilet, tbls, cfga, no drkg wtr. Boating, fishing. Canoe on Salmon Falls Creek in spring; take out at Backwaters site.

RUPERT (123)

Lake Walcott State Park   **$12**
11 mi NE of Rupert on SR 24 at Minidoka Dam; at NW end of Lake Walcott. $12 base, $20 with elec/wtr. All year; 15-day limit. 60-ft sites. Tbls, flush toilets, cfga, drkg wtr, showers. Fishing, boating(l), horseshoes, disc golf. 65 acres; 20,700-acre lake.

Walcott Park & Campground   **$6**
Bureau of Reclamation
7 mi E of Rupert on Hwy 24; 6 mi E on CR 400N; at Minidoka Dam. $6. All year; 14-day limit. 22 sites (60-ft RV limit). Tbls, flush toilets, cfga, drkg wtr, dump. Fishing, hiking, playground. Minidoka National Wildlife Refuge

ST. ANTHONY (124)

Sand Creek   **FREE**
Wildlife Management Area
From St. Anthony, follow SR 20 (Business) E 1.5 mi; N at sportsman's access sign for 16 mi to Sand Creek ponds. Free. All year; 10-day limit. Primitive designated camping areas; no facilities. Fishing, hunting, hiking, horseback riding.

ST. CHARLES (125)

Bear Lake State Park   **$12**
5 mi E of St. Charles off Hwy 89 to T, then S 5 mi. $12 base; $20 with elec/wtr; seniors pay have rate weekdays. 4/1-11/30; 15-day limit. 47 sites (RVs under 60 ft). Tbls, toilets, cfga, drkg wtr, dump, elec($). Swimming, boating(rl), fishing, waterskiing, volleyball, winter sports. 20-mile lake on Utah border; 2-mile beach on N; half-mi beach on E. Wildlife refuge.

Beaver Creek   **FREE**
Caribou National Forest
About 11 mi W of St. Charles on FR 11. Free 5/15-9/15; 14-day limit. 5 sites. Tbls, toilets, cfga, drkg wtr. Fishing, hiking. Access to High Line National Recreation Trail.

Cloverleaf   **$10**
Caribou National Forest
1.2 mi N of St. Charles on US 89; 7 mi W on FR 412. $10. MD-9/30; no wtr after LD; 14-day limit. 18 sites (22-ft RV limit). Tbls, flush toilets, cfga, drkg wtr. Hiking, fishing, picnicking, mountain biking, horseback riding. Elev 6900 ft; 7 acres. Nearby Minnetonka Cave open for tours June-LD.

Porcupine   **$10**
Caribou National Forest
1.2 mi N of St. Charles on US 89; 2.5 mi W on CR 312; 5 mi W on FR 412; at St. Charles Creek. $10. MD-9/30; no wtr after LD; 14-day limit. 15 sites (22-ft RV limit). Tbls, flush toilets, cfga, drkg wtr. Hiking, biking, fishing, picnicking, horseback riding, OHV activity. Elev 6800 ft; 4 acres.

ST. MARIES (127)

Al Vanderpoel Area   **FREE**
Potlatch Corporation
15 mi SW of St. Maries at jct of US 95 and SR 30. Free. 5/1-11/15; 14-day limit. 4 sites (RVs under 20 ft). Tbls, toilets, cfga, drkg wtr (must be boiled). Picnicking, fishing, hunting, bike trails, hiking. Elev 2700 ft; 6 acres. Santa Creek wtr safe if boiled. Small pets on leash.

Camp 3   **FREE**
St. Joe National Forest
35 mi E of St. Maries on FR 50 to Marble Creek Historical Site; 15 mi S on FR 321 (Marble Creek Rd). Free. 4 sites. Tbls, toilets, cfga, no drkg wtr; horse loading ramp, no trash service. Fishing. Elev 3200 ft.

Ed's R&R Shady River   **$9.45**
RV Park (Private)
In St. Maries at 1211 Lincoln. $9.45 base. 14 sites. Tbls, toilets, cfga, drkg wtr, dump, elec($), store. Fishing.

Huckleberry   **$12**
Bureau of Land Management
Coeur D'Alene Field Office
29 mi E of St. Maries on St. Joe River Rd. $12 without hookups; $15 with elec & wtr. 6/1-10/31; free rest of year; 14-day limit. 33 sites (26-ft RV limit). Tbls, toilets, cfga, drkg wtr (no wtr during free period), dump. Fishing, swimming, hiking, boating, canoeing, rafting.
Travel tip: Stop at the St. Joe Ghost Town, 12 mi E on St. Joe River Rd; town had reputation of being tougher than Dodge City or the Alaskan gold camps; now little remains.

Marble Creek   **FREE**
St. Joe National Forest
35 mi E of St. Maries on FR 50 to Marble Creek Historical Site; 6 mi S on FR 321 (Marble Creek Rd). Free. 6/15-9/15; 14-day limit. 2 sites. Hiking, fishing (cutthroat trout).
Travel tip: Marble Creek Historical Site has exhibits of early 1900s logging, including photos, artifacts and a replica logging flume.

Misty Meadows   **$9**
RV Park & Camping
3 mi from St. Maries on Calder Avery Rd. $9 base; $19 full hookups 4/30-9/15. 30 sites; 40-ft RV limit. Tbls, flush toilets, cfga, drkg wtr, hookups($). Fishing, boating, swimming.

Shadowy St. Joe $6
St. Joe National Forest
1 mi E of St. Maries on US 3; 10 mi E on FR 50; at St. Joe River. $6. 5/15-9/30; 14-day limit. 14 sites (22-ft RV limit). Tbls, toilets, cfga, drkg wtr. Fishing, swimming, boating(l), swimming.

SALMON (128)

Agency Creek   FREE
Recreation Site
Bureau of Land Management
Salmon Field Office
22 mi SE of Salmon on SR 28 to Tendoy; 10 mi E on co rd. Free. 6/1-9/30; 14-day limit. 3 sites. Tbls, toilets, cfga, no drkg wtr. Hiking, picnicking.

Cougar Point $4
Salmon National Forest
5 mi S of Salmon on US 93; 12 mi W on FR 021. $4. 5/15-9/30; 14-day limit. About 12 undesignated sites (20 ft RV limit). Tbls, toilets, cfga, no drkg wtr. Elev 6600 ft; 15 acres. Hiking.

Iron Lake $5
Salmon National Forest
5 mi S of Salmon on US 93; 20 mi W on FR 021; 21 mi S on FR 020 (Salmon River Mountain Rd). $5. Free 9/21-7/1; 14-day limit. About 6 undesignated primitive sites (20-ft RV limit). Tbls, toilets, cfga, drkg wtr, stock facilities. No wtr during free period. Boating, fishing, horseback riding.
Travel tip: Stop at Lemhi County Historical Museum, 210 Main St in town; Indian artifacts, household items, tools from pioneer era; Asian antiques. Free.

Morgan Bar $5
Bureau of Land Management
Salmon Field Office
3.2 mi N of Salmon on US 93; left on Diamond Creek Rd (at the Lemhi County Fairgrounds) for 1.5 mi; on Salmon River. $5. 5/1-9/31; 14-day limit 8 sites; 28-ft RV limit. Tbls, toilets, cfga, drkg wtr. Boating(l), fishing, swimming.

Shoup Bridge $5
Bureau of Land Management
Salmon Field Office
5 mi S of Salmon on US 93; right just past Shoup bridge. $5. 4/1-10/31; 14-day limit. 5 sites; 28-ft RV limit. Tbls, toilets, cfga, drkg wtr. Fishing, hiking, boating(l). Primary river access.

Tower Rock Recreation Site $5
Bureau of Land Management
10 mi N of Salmon on US 93. $5 ($3 with federal Senior Pass). 3/15-11/30; 14-day limit. 6 sites (some pull-through); 28-ft RV limit. Toilets, tbls, cfga, drkg wtr. Picnicking, hiking, boating(l), fishing. Primary river access site.

Wallace Lake $4
Salmon National Forest
3.2 mi N of Salmon on US 93; 14 mi NW on FR 023; 4 mi S on FR 020 (rough, unpaved). $4. Free 9/21-6/14; 14-day limit. About 12 undesignated primitive sites; 20-ft RV limit. Tbls, toilets, cfga, drkg wtr. Fishing, boating (carry-down acess). Elev 8200 ft; 11 acres.

Williams Lake   FREE
Salmon National Forest
5 mi S of Salmon on US 93; 3 mi S on CR 021 (Williams Creek Rd) to "Y"; take left "Y" for 9 mi SW on FR 028, staying to the right to trailhead; access to camp by boat or trail; boaters put in at Williams Lake boat ramp. Free. All year; 14-day limit. 2 sites. Tbls, toilets, cfga, firewood, no drkg wtr. Picnicking, fishing, boating, swimming, hiking. Elev 5300 ft; 2 acres.

Williams Lake Recreation Site $5
Bureau of Land Management
Salmon Field Office
4 mi SW on US 93, cross Shoup Bridge; 7 mi on forest rds, following signs. $5 during 5/1-10/31; free rest of year; 14-day limit. 11 sites (28-ft RV limit). Toilets, tbls, cfga, no drkg wtr. Hiking, boating, fishing, swimming. Access to forest service boat ramp.

SANDPOINT (129)

Green Bay   FREE
Kaniksu National Forest
16 mi SE of Sandpoint on US 10A; also accessible by boat; at Lake Pend Oreille. Free. 5/1-11/1; 14-day limit. 3 tent sites. Toilets, cfga, tbls, no drkg wtr. Fishing, boating, swimming beach, fishing.
Fishing tip: Lake Pend Orielle has a well-deserved reputation as a fisherman's paradise. Fourteen species of game fish are there, including kokanee, largemouth bass & bluegill. World's record kamloops trout and a 32-pound dolly varden were caught in the lake.
Travel tip: For an unusual shopping experience, stop at the Cedar Bridge Public Market, downtown Sandpoint; old bridge now a solar-heated shopping mall with two-story plaza of shops & restaurants; nation's first marketplace on a bridge; excellent views of Lake Pend Oreille and mountains.

Round Lake State Park $12
10 mi S of Sandpoint off US 95, W on Dufort Rd. $12. All year; 15-day limit. 51 sites; 24-ft RV limit. Drkg wtr, tbls, cfga, flush toilets, showers, dump, education center, beach. Horseshoes, swimming, fishing, boating(l), hiking, guided walks. 142 acres; elev 2122 ft.
Fishing tip: This shallow 58-acre lake contains brook trout, rainbow trout, largemouth bass, sunfish and crappie.

SHOSHONE (130)

Burren West $10
RV & Trailer Resort
18 mi N of Shoshone on Hwy 75; turn at West Magic Reservoir sign for 10 mi. $10 base; $20 full hookups. 45 sites. Tbls, toilets, cfga, drkg wtr, hookups($), coin laundry, store.

Hot Springs Landing   FREE
Magic Reservoir Recreation Area
Bureau of Land Management
Shoshone Field Office
18 mi N of Shoshone, then follow signs .8 mi S of US 20 on dirt rd. Free. All year; 14-day limit. Undesignated sites near reservoir. Tbls, cfga, toilets, no drkg wtr. Pack out trash. Dump at Westshore Lodge. Fishing (trout, perch), boating(ld), hiking, picnicking.
Fishing tip: Magic Reservoir contains a large population of rainbow trout as well as brown trout 10-12 pound that are caught frequently.

Lava Recreation Sites   FREE
Magic Reservoir Recreation Area
Bureau of Land Management
Shoshone Field Office
18 mi N of Shoshone on Hwy 75; 10 mi NW from SR 75 at Big Wood River, then follow co rd and signs E. Access difficult in winter or after rain. Free. 4/1-10/31; 10-day limit. 30 pull-through sites (RVs under 30 ft) and undesignated sites at lakeshore. Toilets, cfga, tbls, no drkg wtr. Pack out trash. Dump at Westshore Lodge. Boating (primitive launch, docks at Lava Point), fishing (trout, perch), picnicking.
Fishing tip: For a change from lake fishing, try for rainbow trout at Big Wood River.

Magic City Boat Ramp   FREE
Magic Reservoir Recreation Area
Bureau of Land Management
Shoshone Field Office
18 mi N of Shoshone, then follow signs 5 mi W from SR 75. Free. All year; 14-day limit. Undesignated sites. No facilities, no drkg wtr. Dump at Westshore Lodge. Boating(ld), fishing (trout & perch), hiking.

Magic Dam   FREE
Magic Reservoir Recreation Area
Bureau of Land Management
Shoshone Field Office
18 mi N of Shoshone, then follow signs about 5 mi W from SR 75. Free. 4/1-10/31; 10-day limit. Undesignated sites. Tbls, toilets, no drkg wtr. Pack out trash. Dump at Westshore Lodge. Fishing (trout, perch), boating (primitive access), hiking. Also stream fishing below dam.

Moonstone Recreation Site   FREE
Magic Reservoir Recreation Area
Bureau of Land Management
Shoshone Field Office
18 mi N of Shoshone, then follow signs half mi S of US 20 on dirt rd. Low level of use; plenty of solitude. Free. 4/1-10/31; 10-day limit. 5

sites & undesignated sites near reservoir (RVs under 30 ft). Tbls, cfga, toilets, no drkg wtr. Pack out trash. Dump at Westshore Lodge. Boating(l), fishing (trout, perch), hiking.

Myrtle Point Recreation Site   **FREE**
Magic Reservoir Recreation Area
Bureau of Land Management
Shoshone Field Office
18 mi N of Shoshone on Hwy 75; 9 mi NW on co rd; follow signs 2 mi E. Free. 4/1-10/31; 10-day limit. 30 pull-through sites (RVs under 30 ft) and undesignated sites at lakeshore. Toilets, cfga, no drkg wtr. Pack out trash. Dump at Westshore Lodge. Boating, fishing (trout, perch), picnicking.

Richfield Diversion   **FREE**
Magic Reservoir Recreation Area
Bureau of Land Management
Shoshone Field Office
18 mi N of Shoshone on SR 75, then 2.5 mi W following signs. Last 1.5 mi rough, not suitable for RVs or passenger cars; area little used because of rough access. Free. All year; 14-day limit. Undesignated campsites. Primitive. Toilet, no drkg wtr. Dump at Westshore Lodge. Fishing (trout, perch), hiking, boating.

Seagull Point   **FREE**
Magic Reservoir Recreation Area
Bureau of Land Management
Shoshone Field Office
18 mi N of Shoshone on SR 75, then NW 6 mi at Big Wood River and E 1.5 mi. Watch signs. Last 1.5 mi rough, not recommended for RVs; may be closed in spring to protect nesting waterfowl. Free. All year; 14-day limit. Parking area for self-contained RVs. No facilities, no trash service. Dump at Westshore Lodge. Fishing (trout, perch), boating, bird watching.

Silver Creek South   **FREE**
Bureau of Land Management
Shoshone Field Office
33 mi NE of Shoshone on US 26/93; 2 mi W on Pacabo Cutoff Rd; BLM sign indicates a turn left off the highway; sites is about 1 mi. Free. All year; 14-day limit. Primitive camping near the riparian zone along Silver Creek. Hiking, fishing. Silver Creek Preserve, a nearby fly-fishing hot spot, is operated by the Nature Conservancy.

SHOUP (131)

Corn Creek   **$5**
Salmon National Forest
28.8 mi W of Shoup on FR 030 (Salmon River Rd). $5. 6/1-10/31; free rest of year; 14-day limit. 16 sites (22-ft RV limit). Tbls, toilets, cfga, drkg wtr. Boating(l), fishing, swimming, hiking, horse ramp. No wtr during free period. Pack out trash. Access to Salmon River, Frank Church-River of No Return Wilderness.

Horse Creek Hot Springs   **FREE**
Salmon National Forest
1.5 mi NE of Shoup on FR 030 (Salmon River Rd); 18 mi NW on FR 038 (Spring Creek Rd); 5 mi NW on FR 044. Free. 6/15-10/15. 9 sites on 11 acres (RVs under 23 ft). Tbls, toilets, cfga, no drkg wtr. Horseback riding, picnicking, fishing. Access to Frank Church-River of No Return Wilderness. Elev 6200 ft.

SODA SPRINGS (132)

Caribou County Park   **FREE**
Blackfoot Reservoir
12 mi N of Soda Springs on Hwy 34; at Blackfoot Reservoir (ask further directions locally). May-Sept; 14-day limit. About 100 scattered sites. Toilets, cfga, no drkg wtr. Fishing, boating.

Cold Springs   **FREE**
Caribou National Forest
9.1 mi S of Soda Springs on CR 425; 2 mi S on FR 425. Free. Elev 6100 ft. 5/25-10/30; 14-day limit. 3 sites (RVs under 22 ft). Tbls, toilets, cfga, firewood, piped drkg wtr. Picnicking, fishing, hiking.
Travel tip: See Captive Geyser in Soda Springs business district; erupts hourly, Apr-Oct; featured in Ripley's "Believe It or Not"; it is prevented from erupting if wind conditions indicate it will spray all over business area; carbon dioxide tober.

Diamond Creek   **FREE**
Caribou National Forest
10.1 mi N of Soda Springs on SR 34; 14 mi E on CR 30C (Blackfoot River Rd); 11 mi SE on FR 102. Free. 6/1-10/31; 14-day limit. 12 rustic sites. Toilets, cfga, no tbls, drkg wtr. Hiking, fishing, picnicking.
Travel tip: Stop at Beer Spring 1 mi N of town; Hooper Spring got its nickname from pioneers, who said its natural soda water tasted like beer; visitors can sample it.

Blackfoot Reservoir   **FREE**
Bureau of Land Management
Pocatello Field Office
11 mi N of Soda Springs on Hwy 34 at SW end of Blackfoot Reservoir. Free. 5/1-10/31; 14-day limit. 16 developed sites, 20 dispersed sites. Toilets, cfga, drkg wtr, tbls. Hiking, boating(l), fishing, picnicking. Fees planned in 2007.
Fishing tip: Fishing success at Blackfoot Lake depends on water conditions, but unless hit by drought, the lake produces good catches of big cutthroat & rainbow trout.

Eightmile Canyon   **$5**
Caribou National Forest
9.2 mi S of Soda Springs on Bailey Creek-Eightmile Rd; 4 mi S on FR 425. $5. Elev 7200 ft. 6/1-9/30; 14-day limit. 7 sites on 5 acres (RVs under 16 ft). Tbls, toilets, cfga, firewood, no drkg wtr. Picnicking, fishing, hiking, horseback riding, OHV activity. Part of Cache NF, administered by Caribou NF.

Maple Grove Campground   **$5**
Bureau of Land Management
S of Soda Springs on SR 34 to about 6 mi N of Preston; left for 3 mi on SR 36; left at sign that says "Oneida Narrows," and go N along Bear River to Redpoint & Maple Grove camps; at Oneida Narrows Reservoir. $5. 5/1-10/31; 14-day limit. 13 sites. Tbls, toilets, cfga. Fishing, boating(l), swimming.

Mill Canyon   **FREE**
Caribou National Forest
10.1 mi N of Soda Springs on SR 34; 11.4 mi E on Blackfoot River Rd; 7 mi on FR 99; at Blackfoot Narrows of Blackfoot River. Free. 6/1-10/15; 14-day limit. 10 sites (32-ft RV limit). Pull-through sites. Tbls, toilets, cfga, drkg wtr. Hiking, fishing.
Fishing tip: Besides Yellowstone cutthroat trout, the Blackfoot River contains rainbows and brookies. The river is open to fishing upstream from the reservoir between July 1 and Nov. 30. Access the river by driving 12 mi N of Soda Springs on SR 34. Please release the Yellowstones if you catch them.

Morgans Bridge   **FREE**
Bureau of Land Management
Pocatello Field Office
11 mi N of Soda Springs on SR 34; 4 mi W on China Cap Rd; 14 mi NW on Government Dam Rd; 14 mi N on Corral Creek Rd & Trail Creek Rd; on Blackfoot River. Free. 5/1-10/31; 14-day limit. 5 primitive sites. Toilets, tbls, cfga. Floating, tubing, fishing.

Redpoint Campground   **FREE**
Bureau of Land Management
Pocatello Field Office
S of Soda Springs on SR 34 to about 6 mi N of Preston; left for 3 mi on SR 36; left at sign that says "Oneida Narrows," and go N along Bear River to Redpoint & Maple Grove camps; at Bear River below Oneida Narrows Reservoir dam. Free. 5/1-10/31. About 8 primitive sites. Tbls, toilets, cfga. Tubing, rafting, fishing, caving.

Sucker Trap Campsite   **FREE**
Caribou County Park
12 mi N of Soda Springs on SR 34; half mi E on Blackfoot River Rd; at Blackfoot River. Free. May-Sep; 14-day limit. 20 sites. Toilets, cfga, no drkg wtr, dump. Fishing, boating.

Trail Creek Bridge Camp   **FREE**
Bureau of Land Management
Pocatello Field Office
11 mi N of Soda Springs on SR 34; 4 mi W on China Cap Rd; 14 mi NW on Government Dam Rd; 20 mi N on Corral Creek Rd, Lincoln Creek Rd & Trail Creek Rd; at Blackfoot River. Free. 5/1-10/31; 14-day limit. 6 primtive sites. Tbls, toilets, cfga, no drkg wtr. Fishing, boating, hiking.

SPENCER (133)

Spencer Stag Station   **$12**
At Spencer, just W of I-15 exit. $12 for RVs;

tents free. All year. 14 RV sites. Tbls, toilets, cfga, drkg wtr, hookups.

Stoddard Creek $6
Targhee National Forest
3.5 mi N of Spencer on US 15; 1 mi NW on FR 02. $6 (double site, $12). MD-9/15; 16-day limit. 22 sites (22-ft RV limit). Tbls, toilets, cfga, drkg wtr. Hiking, fishing, biking, horseback riding. 6 acres.

STANLEY (134)

Banner Creek FREE
Challis National Forest
22 mi W of Stanley on SR 21. Free. 7/1-9/15. 3 sites (RVs under 22 ft). Tbls, toilets, cfga, firewood, drkg wtr. Horseback riding, picnicking, fishing in nearby streams. Elev 6500 ft.

Basin Creek $11
Sawtooth National Forest
Sawtooth National Recreation Area
8.9 mi E of Stanley on SR 75; near Salmon River. $11 about MD-9/30; free rest of year, but no wtr or services; 10-day limit. 15 sites (22-ft RV limit). Tbls, toilets, cfga, drkg wtr. Fishing. Elev 6100 ft; 5 acres.

Beaver Creek $5
Challis National Forest
17 mi NW of Stanley on SR 21; 3 mi N on Beaver Creek Rd (FR 008). $5. 7/1-9/30; 14-day limit. 8 sites (32-ft RV limit. Tbls, toilets, cfga, drkg wtr. Handicap access. Fishing, hiking, horseback riding. Elev 6400 ft.

Bench Creek FREE
Challis National Forest
24 mi W of Stanley on SR 21. 6/15-9/15; 14-day limit. 5 sites (RVs under 16 ft). Toilets, tbls, cfga, drkg wtr. Fishing, picnicking, horseback riding, hiking. Elev 6500 ft.
   Fishing tip: Fish for trout at Bench Creek and nearby Bull Trout Lake (bull trou may not be harvested).

Blind Creek $5
Challis National Forest
14.9 mi NE of Stanley on SR 75; 1 mi N on Yankee Fork Rd; in canyon of Yankee Fork of Salmon River. $5. 6/15-9/10; 14-day limit. 5 sites (32-ft RV limit). Tbls, toilets, cfga, drkg wtr. Fishing, hiking. Interpretive & historical tours nearby.

Bonanza CCC Campground FREE
Challis National Forest
15 mi E of Stanley on SR 75; 7 mi N on FR 013; near ghost town of Bonanza. Free family camping off-season; group camping by reservation rest of year. 10 sites. Tbls, toilets, cfga, drkg wtr (no wtr during tree period of 9/2-5/31). Hiking, fishing, horseback riding.
   Travel tip: Explore the ghost town and cemetery shared by towns of Custer & Bonanza; tour nearby Yankee Drredge.

Custer 1 FREE
Challis National Forest
14.9 mi NE of Stanley on US 75; 8 mi N on FR 13; 4 mi NE on FR 070; near ghost town of Custer. 7/1-9/30; 14-day limit. 6 sites (RVs under 32 ft). Tbls, cfga, toilets, no drkg wtr. Fishing at Fivemile Creek, hiking, picnicking. Closed during 2007.
   Travel tip: Visit the Ghost Towns of Bonanza and Custer, found 12 mi E of town on SR 75, then 8 mi N on gravel rd; both were big mining towns of 1880s, now deserted; all that's left of Custer are a gold dredge, a few homes and schoolhouse containing a museum.

Deadwood Reservoir $6
Boise National Forest
21 mi W of Stanley on SR 21; 21 mi W on FR 579; 7 mi S on FR 555; at Deadwood Lake. $6. 29 sites. Tbls, toilets, cfga, drkg wtr. Fishing, boating. (3 free camps on E side of lake: Riverside, Hower's, Cozy Cove.)

Dutchman Flat FREE
Sawtooth National Recreation Area
Sawtooth National Forest
15.8 mi NE of Stanley on SR 75. Free. Elev 5800 ft. About 5/20-9/30; 10-day limit. 5 sites on 3 acres (RVs under 16 ft). Tbls, toilets, cfga, firewood, well drkg wtr. Store, food, gas, ice (1 mi). Rockhounding, hiking, picnicking, fishing, horseback riding.

Eightmile FREE
Challis National Forest
14.9 mi NE of Stanley on US 75; 3 mi N on FR 13; 6.5 mi NE on FR 70; at Eightmile Creek. Free. 6/15-9/10; 14-day limit. 2 sites on 2 acres (RVs under 16 ft). Tbls, toilets, cfga, firewood, no drkg wtr. Picnicking, fishing. Elev 7000 ft.

Elk Creek $10
Sawtooth National Recreation Area
Sawtooth National Forest
8 mi NW of Stanley on SR 21; at Valley Creek. $10 about 6/15-9/15; free rest of season, but no wtr or services; 14-day limit. 3 walk-to tent sites. Tbls, toilets, cfga, drkg wtr, no trash service. Fishing (trout), hiking, horseback riding. Elev 6541 ft.

Flatrock $5
Challis National Forest
14.9 mi NE of Stanley on SR 75; 2 mi N on FR 013; at Yankee Fork of Salmon River. $5. 6/1-9/30; 14-day limit. 9 sites (32-ft RV limit). Tbls, toilets, cfga, drkg wtr. Fishing.

Iron Creek $11
Sawtooth National Forest
Sawtooth National Recreation Area
2 mi W of Stanley on SR 21; 4 mi S on FR 619. $11 about MD-9/15; free rest of year, but no wtr or services; 14-day limit. 9 sites (22-ft RV limit). Tbls, toilets, cfga, drkg wtr. Hiking, fishing for wild cutthroat. Elev 6600 ft; 35 acres.

Jerry's Creek FREE
Challis National Forest
15 mi E of Stanley on US 93; 5 mi N on FR 013. Free. 7/1-9/15; 16-day limit. 3 sites (RVs under 22 ft). Tbls, toilets, cfga, firewood, no drkg wtr. Picnicking, fishing.

Josephus Lake FREE
Challis National Forest
17 mi N of Stanley on SR 21; 12 mi N on FR 008. Free. 7/1-9/30; 14-day limit. 3 sites. Tbls, toilets, cfga, no drkg wtr. Fishing, hiking. Elev 7200 ft.

Lakeview $10
Sawtooth National Forest
Sawtooth National Recreation Area
5 mi N of Stanley on SR 21; 3.5 mi W on FR 455; at Stanley Lake. $10. About MD-9/15; 14-day limit. 6 sites (22-ft RV limit). Tbls, toilets, cfga, drkg wtr. Fishing, hiking, boating (ramp at Stanley Lak Inlet).

Lola Creek $5
Challis National Forest
17 mi NW of Stanley on SR 21; 2 mi NW on FR 083. $5. 6/1-9/15; 16-day limit. 21 sites (RVs under 17 ft). Tbls, toilets, cfga, drkg wtr. Fishing, hiking, horseback riding. Access to River of No Return Wilderness Area. Horse stalls & loading ramps.

Lower O'Brien $11
Sawtooth National Forest
Sawtooth National Recreation Area
16.9 mi E of Stanley on SR 75; 4 mi S on FR 454 (Robinson Bar Rd); at Stanley River. $11. About 6/15-8/15; 10-day limit. 10 sites (22-ft RV limit). Tbls, toilets, cfga, drkg wtr. Fishing, boating, hiking. Road narrow & crosses a narrow bridge. Elev 5800 ft; 4 acres.

Mormon Bend $11
Sawtooth National Forest
Sawtooth National Recreation Area
7 mi E of Stanley on SR 75; at Salmon River. $11 about MD-10/31; free rest of year, but no wtr or services; 10-day limit. 15 sites (22-ft RV limit). Tbls, toilets, cfga, drkg wtr. Fishing, boating. Designated river put-in site. Elev 6100 ft; 15 acres.

Pole Flat $5
Challis National Forest
14.9 mi NE of Stanley on SR 75; 3 mi N on FR 013; in canyon of Yankee Fork of Salmon River. $5. 6/15-9/30; 16-day limit. 12 sites (32-ft RV limit). Tbls, toilets, drkg wtr, cfga. Fishing, horseback riding. Elev 6200 ft; 8 acres.

Redfish Inlet $10
Transfer Camp
Sawtooth National Recreation Area
Sawtooth National Forest
5 mi S of Stanley on SR 75; 1.7 mi SW on FR 70214; 4.3 mi SW on Trail 7101. Access by boat, foot or horse only. $10. 6/15-9/15; 10-day limit. 6 tent sites. Tbls, toilets, cfga, firewood, no drkg wtr. Swimming, picnick-

ing, fishing, hiking, mountain climbing. Elev 6500 ft; 5 acres. Stream. Scenic. Trailhead to Sawtooth Wilderness.

Riverside $11
Sawtooth National Forest
Sawtooth National Recreation Area
6.8 mi E of Stanley on SR 75; on Salmon River. $11. About MD-9/15; 10-day limit. 17 sites (25-ft RV limit). Tbls, toilets, cfga, drkg wtr. Fishing, hiking, boating.
Fishing tip: When fishing for steelhead here, only the fish with clipped adipose fin may be kept.

Salmon River $11
Sawtooth National Forest
Sawtooth National Recreation Area
5.1 mi E of Stanley on SR 75. $11. About MD-9/15; 10-day limit. 30 sites (32-ft RV limit). Tbls, toilets, cfga, drkg wtr, coin laundry. Fishing, boating. Elev 6135 ft.

Sheep Trail Campground $10
Sawtooth National Forest
Sawtooth National Recreation Area
9 mi NW of Stanley on SR 21. $10. 6/15-9/15; 10-day limit. 3 sites (may be reserved by a group). Tbls, toilets, cfga, drkg wtr. Fishing, hiking, biking. Elev 6600 ft.

Stanley Lake $6.50
Sawtooth National Forest
Sawtooth National Recreation Area
5 mi N of Stanley on SR 21; 3.5 mi W on FR 455. $6.50 with federal Senior Pass; others pay $13. About MD-LD; 10-day limit. 16 sites (22-ft RV limit). Tbls, toilets, cfga, drkg wtr. Swimming, fishing, boating, waterskiing, hiking. 12 acres.

Stanley Lake Inlet $6.50
Sawtooth National Forest
Sawtooth National Recreation Area
5 mi N of Stanley on SR 21; 6.5 mi W on FR 455. $6.50 with federal Senior Pass; others pay $13. About MD-LD; free rest of year, but no wtr or services; 10-day limit. 15 sites (22-ft RV limit). Tbls, toilets, cfga, drkg wtr. Boating(l), fishing, swimming beach, waterskiing, hiking. 9 acres. Elev 6537 ft.

Sunny Gulch $11
Sawtooth National Forest
Sawtooth National Recreation Area
3.2 mi S of Stanley on SR 75; on Salmon River. $11 about MD-10/31; free rest of year, but no wtr or services; 10-day limit. 19 sites (22-ft RV limit). Tbls, toilets, cfga, drkg wtr. Fishing, picnicking, hiking, horseback riding, boating, interpretive program, visitor center. Elev 6500 ft; 10 acres. Visitor center & horseback rides 3 mi at Redfish Lake; dump 1 mi at Stanley ranger station.

Thatcher Creek $5
Challis National Forest
15 mi NE of Stanley on SR 31. $5. 7/1-9/30; 16-day limit. 5 sites (32-ft RV limit). Tbls, toilets, cfga, drkg wtr. Fishing. Marsh across the road often contains feeding moose, elk, birds.

Tin Cup FREE
Challis National Forest
12 mi NE of Stanley on US 93; 11 mi NW on FR 112; 20 mi N on FR 007 (narrow rd, so RVs over 16 ft not recommended); on Loon Creek. MD-10/15; 16-day limit. 13 sites (RVs under 23 ft). Toilets, cfga, firewood, no drkg wtr. Rockhounding, picnicking, fishing, horseback riding. Elev 5600 ft; 4 acres.

Upper O'Brien $11
Sawtooth National Forest
Sawtooth National Recreation Area
16.9 mi E of Stanley on SR 75; 2 mi E on FR 054; at Salmon River. $11 about 5/15-9/15; free rest of year, but no wtr or services; 10-day limit. 9 sites (22-ft RV limit). Tbls, toilets, cfga, drkg wtr. Fishing. Boat ramp only for rafts, canoes, kayaks. 3 acres. Elev 5730 ft. Must cross narrow bridge to access site; not recommended for large RVs.

SWAN VALLEY (135)

Big Elk Creek $10
Targhee National Forest
1.5 mi E of Swan Valley on US 26; 1.4 mi E on FR 262; on narrow area of Palisades Reservoir. $10. MD-9/12; free but no wtr after 9/12; 14-day limit. 18 sites. Tbls, toilets, cfga, drkg wtr. Fishing, boating(l), swimming, waterskiing, hiking, horseback riding (horse loading ramp). Trailhead. Elev 5700 ft; 20 acres. Snake River.

Blowout $10
Targhee National Forest
15 mi SE of Swan Valley on US 26. $10 during MD-LD; free until closure 10/31, but no wtr; 16-day limit. 30 sites. Tbls, toilets, cfga, drkg wtr. Fishing, boating(ld), swimming, waterskiing. Elev 5700 ft. Palisades Reservoir, Snake River.

Falls Creek $10
Targhee National Forest
4 mi W of Swan Valley on US 26; 2.3 mi S on FR 058. $10 during 5/15-9/15; free 9/15-10/31, but no wtr; 16-day limit. 23 sites (no RV size limit). Tbls, toilets, cfga, drkg wtr. Hiking, fishing, birdwatching. Elev 5400 ft; 18 acres. Palisades Reservoir, Snake River. 60-ft Falls Creek Falls.

Palisades Dam FREE
Bureau of Land Management
US 26 between Swan Valley and Alpine, along Snake River. Free. Several dispersed sites. Tbls, grills, dump, drkg wtr. Fishing, hiking.
Fishing tip: Below the dam, the Snake River offers great fishing for huge sturgeon, smallmouth bass & channel catfish.

TENSED (136)

RV Milepost 382 $11
At 2nd & D Sts, Tensed. $11. All year. 11 sites. Tbls, toilets, cfga, drkg wtr.

TWIN FALLS (137)

Bostetter FREE
Sawtooth National Forest
8 mi E of Twin Falls on SR 50 & US 30; 39 mi S on Rock Creek Rd, FR 538 & FR 526. Free. 6/1-9/15; 16-day limit. 18 sites on 20 acres (RVs under 18 ft). Tbls, toilets, cfga, firewood, piped drkg wtr. Picnicking, fishing, horseback riding. Elev 7160 ft.
Travel tip: Town of Oakley is on National Register of Historic Places because of its many intricate stone and wood buildings erected by pioneers in late 1800s. Near city park is jail cell which once held the noted outlaw, Diamondfield Jack Davis.

Father and Sons $
Sawtooth National Forest
8 mi E of Twin Falls on SR 50 & US 30; 38 mi S on Rock Creek Rd, FR 538 & FR 526. Fees unavailable. 6/1-9/15; 16-day limit. 12 sites. Tbls, toilets, cfga, firewood, piped drkg wtr. Picnicking, fishing, horseback riding. Elev 7100 ft; 13 acres. Stream.

Porcupine Springs FREE
Sawtooth National Forest
8 mi E of Twin Falls on SR 50 & US 30; 30 mi S on Rock Creek Rd (CR G3/FR 515). Free. 6/1-9/15. 5 sites (RVs under 16 ft). Tbls, toilets, cfga, firewood, piped drkg wtr. Picnicking, fishing, horseback riding. 6800 ft; 44 acres. Biking, hiking, horseback riding.

Steer Basin FREE
Sawtooth National Forest
8 mi E of Twin Falls on FR 50 & US 30; 20 mi S on Rock Creek Rd (CRG3/FR515); at Rock Creek. Free. 5/1-10/15; 14-day limit. 5 sites; no RV size limit. Tbls, toilets, cfga, drkg wtr. Fishing, hiking, horseback riding.

VIRGINIA (138)

Hawkins Reservoir FREE
Bureau of Land Management
Pocatello Field Office
10 mi W of Virginia on Hawkins Reservoir Rd. Free. May-Oct; 14-day limit. 10 sites. Tbls, toilets, cfga, no drkg wtr. Fishing, hiking.

VICTOR (139)

Pine Creek $8
Targhee National Forest
5.3 mi W of Victor on SR 31; at Little Pine Creek. $8. 5/15-9/15; 16-day limit. 11 sites (32-ft RV limit). Tbls, toilets, cfga, no drkg wtr. No trash service; pack it out. Hiking, fishing. Elev 6600 ft; 3 acres.

Trail Creek $10
Targhee National Forest
5.5 mi E of Victor on Sr 33; qtr mi S on SR 22, in Wyoming. $10. 5/15-9/15; 16-day limit. 10 sites (35-ft RV limit). Tbls, toilets, cfga, drkg wtr. Fishing, hiking. Elev 6600 ft; 7 acres.

WALLACE (140)

Silver Leaf Motel $5
In Wallace at 416 Sixth St. $5-10 base. 7 sites. Tbls, flush toilets, cfga, drkg wtr, showers, dump, hookups($), pool, coin laundry, CATV. Swimming.

WARREN (141)

Burgdorf
Payette National Forest $8
30 mi W of Warren on Warren Wagon Rd (FR 21) and FR 246; near Burgdorf Hot Springs. Free. 7/1-9/30; 14-day limit. $8. 5 sites (RVs under 22 ft). Tbls, toilets, cfga, firewood, no drkg wtr. Picnicking, hiking, fishing. Elev 6000 ft; 5 acres. Stream. Near private Burgdorf Hot Springs.

WEIPPE CREEK (142)

Lolo FREE
Clearwater National Forest
9 mi E of Weippe Creek on co rd; 10 mi S on FR 100; at Lolo Creek. Free. 5/1-10/15 or until inaccessible; 14-day limit. 5 tent sites. Tbls, toilets, cfga, firewood, no drkg wtr. Picnicking, fishing, berry picking. Elev 2800 ft; 4 acres. On Lewis and Clark National Historic Trail. Capt. Clark & 5 hunters camped here 9/19/1805.

WEISER (143)

Indian Hot Springs $8
6 mi NW of Weiser. $8-$12 base; $15 full hookups. About 12 sites. Tbls, flush toilets, cfga, drkg wtr, showers, spa, hookups($). Swimming.

Justrite FREE
Payette National Forest
12.5 mi N of Weiser on US 95; 11.5 mi N on CR 004; 3.2 mi N on FR 009. Free. 6/1-10/31; 16-day limit. 4 tent sites. Tbls, toilets, cfga, no drkg wtr. Picnicking, fishing, horseback riding. Elev 4200 ft; 1 acre. Stream. Mann Creek Reservoir (12 mi S). Adjacent to Mann Creek.

Lower Spring Creek $8
Payette National Forest
12.5 mi N of Weiser on US 95; 11.5 mi N on CR 009; 5.3 mi N on FR 009. $8 ($5 off-season). 6/1-10/30; 16-day limit. 12 sites (16-ft RV limit). Tbls, toilets, cfga, drkg wtr. Picnicking, fishing, horseback riding. Elev 4800 ft; 10 acres. Mann Creek Reservoir 14 mi S. Note: Camp being renovated at last report; fee status may change.

Mann Creek Campground $8
Bureau of Reclamation
Payette National Forest
18 mi N of Weiser on Hwy 94; at Mann Creek Reservoir. $8. 4/1-10/30; 14-day limit. 14 sites (32-ft RV limit). Tbls, toilets, cfga, drkg wtr. Swimming, boating, fishing, hiking. Owned by Bureau of Reclamation; managed by Payette NF.
Fishing tip: This 283-acre lake is stocked with rainbow trout, crappie and largemouth bass.

Paradise FREE
Payette National Forest
12.5 mi N of Weiser on US 95; 11.5 mi N on CR 009; 3.8 mi N on FR 009. 6/1-10/31; 16-day limit. 4 tent sites. Tbls, toilets, cfga, no drkg wtr. Picnicking, fishing, horseback riding. Elev 4200 ft; 1 acre. Stream.

Spring Creek $8
Payette National Forest
12.5 mi N of Weiser on US 95; 14 mi N on FR 009. $8 during 5/15-10/15; $5 off-season if wtr shut off; 16-day limit. 13 sites (16-ft RV limit). Tbls, cfga, drkg wtr, toilet. Picnicking, fishing, horseback riding. Elev 4800 ft; 10 acres. Mann Creek Reservoir 14 mi S.

Steck Recreation Site $5
Bureau of Land Management
Four Rivers Field Office
22 mi W of Weiser on SR 70 to Olds Ferry Rd; on Brownlee Reservoir. $5 for tents; $8 for RVs. 4/15-10/31; 14-day limit. 38 sites (25-ft RV limit). Tbls, toilets, cfga, drkg wtr, dump. Swimming, picnicking, fishing, boating(ld), hunting, hiking, waterskiing.
Fishing tip: Brownlee considered one of the best smallmouth bass and crappie lakes in Idaho.

WHITE BIRD (146)

Hammer Creek $10
Lower Salmon River Recreation Area
Bureau of Land Management
Cottonwood Field Office
1.5 mi S of White Bird on Hwy 95; 1.5 mi N on co rd; along Lower Salmon River. $10. All year; 14-day limit. 8 sites (24-ft RV limit). Tbls, toilets, cfga, drkg wtr, handicapped facilities. Swimming, boating(l), rafting, fishing. 20 acres; elev 1500 ft. Put-in spot for river floats.

North Fork Slate Creek FREE
Nez Perce National Forest
11 mi S of White Bird on US 95; 10 mi E on FR 354. Free. 6/1-10/1. 5 sites for tents or pickup campers. Tbls, toilets, cfga, firewood, no drkg wtr. Picnicking, fishing, horseback riding. Elev 3000 ft; 2 acres. Stream. Slate Creek Ranger Station (half mi S). Cool place to camp on hot days. Creek-side camping. Pan-size trout.
Travel tip: Visit White Bird Battlefield & Hill 16 mi S of Grangeville on US 95; site of 1877 battle that started the Nez Perce War; self-guided tour maps available at Nez Perce Nat'l Historic Park headquarters, Spalding.

Pittsburg Landing $8
Hell's Canyon
National Recreation Area
Wallowa-Whitman National Forest
17 mi up Deer Creek Rd 493, off Hwy 95 S of White Bird. Access rough & slippery when wet. $8. 28 sites. Tbls, toilets, cfga, drkg wtr. Trailhead for Snake River National Recreation Trail. Boating(l), fishing, hiking.

Rocky Bluff FREE
Nez Perce National Forest
11 mi S of White Bird on US 95; 14 mi NE on FR 233; 1 mi E on FR 641. Adjacent to Gospel Hump Wilderness. 6/1-10/1; 14-day limit. 4 sites. Tbls, toilets, cfga, no drkg wtr. Suitable for tents, pickup campers, mini motorhomes and small trailers; trailers longer than 16 ft have maneuvering difficulty. Picnicking, fishing, Hiking.

Slate Creek Recreation Site $10
Bureau of Land Management
Cottonwood Field Office
8 mi S of White Bird on US 95. $10. All year; 14-day limit. 6 sites (26-ft RV limit). Tbls, toilets, cfga, drkg wtr, handicap facilities. Boating(l), fishing, swimming. Fee for use of dump station. 20 acres.

WINCHESTER (147)

Winchester Lake State Park $12
Qtr mi SW of Winchester, off US 95, following signs. $12 base; $20 with elec/wtr; seniors pay half rate weekdays. All year; 15-day limit. 69 sites up to 60 ft. Flush toilets, cfga, drkg wtr, showrs, dump. Fishing, hiking, biking, boating(l), guided walks.
Fishing tip: The lake is stocked with rainbow trout and also provides excellent fishing for largemouth bass. Electric motors only.

YELLOW PINE (148)

Big Creek Airfield $8
Payette National Forest
50 mi NE of McCall on FR 371 (Big Creek Rd), or 31 mi NE by airplane. $8. 6/15-9/10; free 9/10-10/31; 16-day limit. 4 walk-in tent sites. Tbls, toilets, cfga, drkg wtr. Pack out trash. Elev 5750 ft.

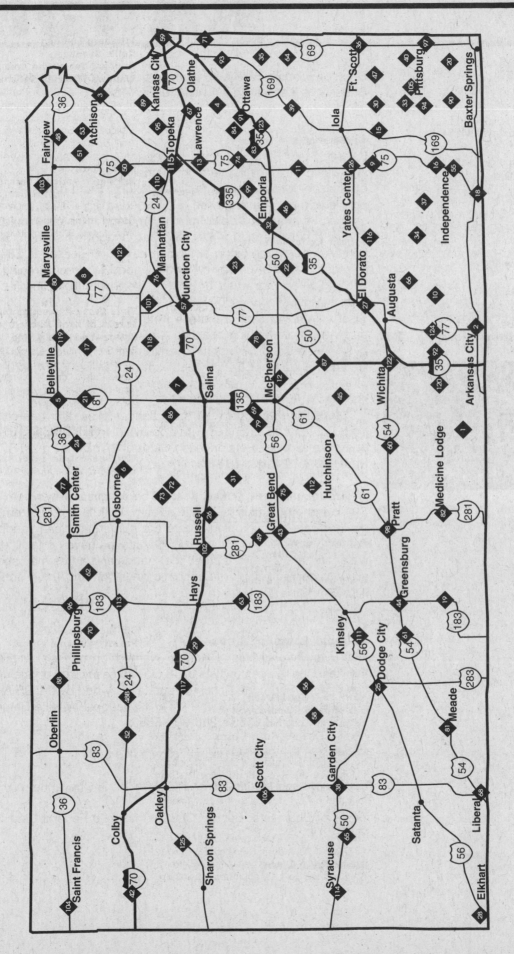

KANSAS

MISCELLANEOUS

Capital:
Topeka

Nickname:
Sunflower State, Jayhawk State

Motto:
Ad Astra Per Aspera (To the Stars Through Difficulties)

Flower:
Sunflower

Tree:
Cottonwood

Bird:
Western Meadowlark

Song:
"Home on the Range"

Internet Address:
www.travelks.com

Dept. of Economic Development, Travel and Tourism Division, I-10 & 110th St near the Kansas Speedway. 800-2KANSAS.

State Parks

Kansas State Parks are among America's best value in overnight camping. Basic charge for overnight camping is only $8.50 in-season ($7.50 off-season) for sites without utility hookups. State parks also charge $4.20 per vehicle per day entry fee ($3.70 during 10/1-3/31). However, we recommend that anyone doing much camping in Kansas should purchase an annual vehicle permit for $19.35 (when bought off-season, $24.35 in-season). A 14-day camping permit purchased off-season is $87.15; $101.15 in-season. Annual camping permits, good for free camping all year, are $152.15 Sites with water or electric are $14.50 ($13.50 off-season); sites with two utility connections are $15.50-16.50; with three utilities, $16.50-17.50. Camping limit, 14 days. Pets on leashes are permitted, but are prohibited from bathing beaches. Unlimited tent camping is available, and overflow sites cost $6. For further information contact: Department of Wildlife and Parks, 512 SE 25th Ave., Pratt, KS 67124-8174; 620-672-5911.

State Fishing Lakes. All state fishing lakes offer free camping; 7 day limit, but may be extended with approval. No sport boats, but only fishing boats are allowed. Pets on leash. Dept of Wildlife & Parks, RR 2, Box 54A, Pratt, KS 67124. 620-672-5911.

Arkansas River Canoe Trail. The Arkansas River from Raymond to Sterling is a beautiful sand-hills stream. With a sand bottom, it is usually shallow enough for tubing. There are numerous clean sandbars for sunbathing, picnicking and camping. Campsites have no facilities or drinking water and are free. For further information and a free map showing campgrounds contact: Dept. of Economic Development, Travel and Tourism Div, 913/296-7091.

National Camping Areas

Flint Hills National Wildlife Refuge. Named for the Flint Hills Region just to the west, the refuge consists of 18,500 acres located on the upstream portion of John Redmond Reservoir and land owned by the US Army Corps of Engineers. Refuge Manager, Flint Hills National Wildlife Refuge, P.O. Box 128, Hartford, KS 66854; 316-392-5553.

Kirwin National Wildlife Refuge, Kirwin, KS 67644.

Bureau of Land Management, P.O. Box 1828, Cheyenne, WY 82001.

Corps of Engineers, Kansas City District, 700 Federal Bldg, Kansas City, MO 64106.

State Rest Areas

Overnight self-contained camping is permitted one night only.

ANTHONY (1)

Anthony City Lake Park $4
1 mi N of Anthony on SR 2; W on access rd. $4 base for primitive unimproved areas; $9 for improved sites with elec. All year; 14-day limit. 47 sites. Tbls, flush toilets, cfga, drkg wtr, elec($), playground. Swimming, fishing, waterskiing, boating(l), horseshoes, gun club, go-cart track, bike trails, sand volleyball, driving range. 153-acre lake; 416 acres. Self-pay stations.

Fishing Tip: Catch channel catfish off the rock jetties using dough bait, sponge balls or worms.

ARGONIA

Argonia River Park $10
S of US 60 at 210 S. Main St; half mi S of town at the Chikaskia River. $10 for RVs with elec; $15 full hookups; $5 tents. All year. 14 RV sites. Tbls, flush toilets, cfga, drkg wtr, dump. Walking trail, fishing.

ARKANSAS CITY (2)

Cowley State Fishing Lake FREE
13 mi E of Arkansas City on US 166; in canyon of Panther Creek. Free. All year; 7-day limit. 10 sites; 84-acre lake. Tbls, toilets, cfga, drkg wtr. Picnicking, fishing boating(rld).

Travel Tip: The famous Cherokee Strip Land Rush Museum is S of town on US 77; commemorates the land rush of 1893 when 100,000 people raced from here for land in Oklahoma. Fee.

Fishing Tip: This lake has some excllent fishing for its size and contains walleye, bass (spotted, smallmouth, largemouth), crappie and catfish. For largemouth, try deep-diving lures and pig-n-jig along the weed edges.

Newman City Park FREE
At Summit & Lincoln in Arkansas City just N of Arkansas River. Free. All year; 3-day limit. 8 sites. Tbls, toilets, cfga, drkg wtr, elec($), dump, playground. Fishing, canoeing.

Walnut City Park $2
At Mill Rd & Hwy 166 in Arkansas City. $2 without hookups; $5 with elec/wtr. All year; 30-day limit. 16 RV sites. Tbls, toilets, cfga, drkg wtr, elec. Boating(l), fishing. Patrolled & lighted.

ATCHISON (3)

Atchison FREE
State Fishing Lake
3 mi N of Atchison on Hwy 7; then follow 318th Rd to Pawnee Rd access. Free. All year; 7-day limit. 15 sites; 66 acre-lake. Tbls, toilets, cfga, drkg wtr. Boating(l), picnicking, fishing.

Fishing Tip: Although small, this lake has a good population of largemouth bass and crappies and plenty of sunfish, channel catfish and some walleye. Try for crappies around sunken brush and off the piers on the E side of lake. Use spinnerbaits around brush for largemouth, and work vertical jigs along the creek channel for walleye.

Ron's Full Hookup RV Park $10
Bean Lake, Missouri
E of Atchison on US 59, then 5 mi S on Hwy 273 to Bean Lake. $10 (weekly, $60, monthly $135). All year. 35 sites with full hookups, including CATV. Boating, fishing.

Warnock Lake City Park $7
Dam 23
US 73 to Price Blvd; then right on gravel rd to park. $7 for RVs, free tent sites. All year; 7-day limit. 16 RV sites with elec; no RV slideouts. Drkg wtr, tbls, cfga, shelters, playground, toilets, dump. Fishing, picnicking, swimming, paddleboating, hiking on nature trail, playground. Dump station at NW corner of Hwy 59 & Woodlawn Ave.

Fishing Tip: Warnock Lake stocked with crappie, largemouth bass, channel catfish and trout (in winter). 66 acres.

Travel Tip: Nearby International Forest of Friendship is dedicated to those contributing to advancement of aviation; trees from all 50 states, US territories & 33 countries; grove includes a tree from George Washington's Mt. Vernon estate; a tree grown from seed taken to the moon.

BALDWIN CITY (4)

Douglas FREE
State Fishing Lake
1.5 mi N of Baldwin on CR 1055; 1 mi E on CR 150 to campground. Free. All year; 7-day limit. 20 sites; 180-acre lake. Tbls, 3 pit toilets, cfga, firewood, drkg wtr, fish cleaning stations 2 floating docks, marina. Picnicking, fishing, hunting, boating(rl). 538 acres.

Travel Tip: Visit Midland Historical Railway in town & travel 6 mi aboard renovated antique diesel-engine train; 1906 depot is on National Register of Historic Places. Fee.

Fishing Tip: Primary fish in this lake are largemouth bass, crappies and bluegills. It also contains flathead, bullhead & channel catfish and white bass. Brush piles, tire and rock reefs provided.

BAXTER SPRINGS

Riverside City Park $10
On E edge of Baxter Springs, S side of Hwy 166 at Spring River. $10 for RV sites with elec. All year. Tbls, flush toilets, cfga, drkg wtr, showers. Fishing, boating(l).

BELOIT (6)

Chautauqua City Park FREE
From Hwy 24 in Beloit, turn S on Hwy 14 through town to park sign on S side of town; at Solomon River. Free. Jan-Oct; 10-day limit. Tbls, flush toilets, cfga, drkg wtr, elec (14 30-amp, 5 50-amp, the rest 20-amp), dump, playground, picnic shelters, pavilion($), pool with waterslide($). Boating(l), fishing, canoeing. Nice, clean park.

Glen Elder State Park $8.50
11 mi W of Beloit on US 24 to Glen Elder (Waconda) Lake. $8 without hookups in-season ($7.50 during 10/1-3/31); $13.50-17.50 with hookups. $2.50 extra charged at sites with new level concrete pads All year; limited facilities in winter (Kanza shower & visitor center may be open in winter); 14-day limit. 420 sites at 12 campgrounds (120 with elec). Tbls, flush toilets, cfga, drkg wtr, showers, elec, dump, fish cleaning station, showers, beach. Boating(lrd), fishing, hiking & biking trails, horseshoes, sand volleyball (at Osage area), softball, hunting, swimming. 13,250 acres with 12,500-acre lake. Here are campgrounds, all with some primitive sites:

Cheyenne -- Primitive sites near shore; 36 wtr/elec sites (12 w/50 amp); shower house & pit toilets.

Kanza -- 66 wtr/elec (28 w/50 amp), shade, shower house & pit toilets; on Manna Cove.

Kaw -- 18 wtr/elec (12 w/50 amp); shower house & pit toilets; pull-through.

Wichita -- Secluded primitive sites, no shade; no facilities.

Comanche -- Primitive sites, shower house & pit toilets, under development.

Arickaree -- Primitive sites, low maintenance, no shade; shower house & pit toilets.

Kiowa -- Primitive low-maintenance sites; no shade; no facilities.

Uskuts -- Primitive low-maintenance sites; no shade; no facilities.

Takota -- Primitive low-maintenance sites; no shade; shower house & pit toilets.

Osage -- Primitive sites near Osage boat ramp; little shade; shower house, pit toilets.

Sioux -- Primitive sites near shore; shower house & pit toilets.

Pawnee -- Primitive sites near lake; no facilities.

Fishing Tip: Waconda lake is well known for its walleye and white bass fishing. Its walleyes are most active in spring; anchor or drift shallow water near dropoffs using jigs tipped with minows or worms or troll with Shad Raps or Hot 'n' Tots. Striped bass are stocked some years, but in 2006, they were replaced with wiper stockings. Rainbow trout provide good put-and-take fishing. In fall, look for crappies around Marina Cove and near the causeway bridge, and concentrate on shoreline areas within the park and off the south bluffs for white bass of 1-3 pounds. During 2007, a creel clerk will collect information about fish harvests and will interview both shore and boat anglers.

Glen Elder FREE
State Wildlife Area
12 mi W of Beloit on US 24. Free. All year; 14-day limit. Primitive undesignated tent camping; RVs limited to developed sites at state park, but wildlife parking areas open to camping the opening weekend of pheasant

season. Toilets, no other facilities. Hiking, biking, horseback riding, hunting, boating(l), fishing. 13,200 acres surrounding 12,500-acre lake.

BENNINGTON (7)

Ottawa State Fishing Lake $5
5 mi N of Bennington and 1 mi E. All year; 7-day limit. $5 for elec sites; non-elec sites free. 121 sites; 148 acres. Drkg wtr, toilets, elec ($5), store. Swimming, boat rental, boating (rl), fishing. 111-acre lake..

Fishing Tip: Best bet is largemouth bass or crappies. Good fishing for channel catfish, and the lake also contains bullhead and sunfish.

BLUE RAPIDS (8)

Riverside Park $3
Chamber of Commerce Park
On Hwys 77/99 in Blue Rapids. Camp free, but $3 donation for elec. 41 sites; 60-ft RV limit. Tbls, toilets, cfga, drkg wtr, dump, playground, pool. Basketball, baseball, swimming, croquet. Tennis courts nearby at 5th & East Aves.

BUFFALO (9)

Wilson State Fishing Lake FREE
1.5 mi SE of Buffalo on US 75. Free. All year; 14-day limit. 20 sites; 110-acre lake. Tbls, toilets, cfga, no drkg wtr. Picnicking, fishing, boating(l).

Fishing Tip: This small lake contains white bass, walleye, spotted bass, largemouth bass and crappie. Catch the spotted bass suspended over dropoffs on crankbaits. The dam face and rocky points which drop off quickly are most productive. Crappie are caught around brush piles and near the bridge.

BURDEN (10)

Burden City Park $3
On W side of Burden. $3 donation requested. All year. Primitive sites; popular among hunters in fall & winter. Tbls, toilets, cfga, drkg wtr, pool. Swimming.

BURLINGTON (11)

Dam Site $10
Corps of Engineers
John Redmond Lake
3 mi N on Hwy 75, 1 mi W on JR access rd. $10 base at 4 no-hookup sites; $15 at sites with elec/wtr. 4/1-10/31; 14-day limit. Free at some sites 11/1-3/31, but no services. 32 sites; 14-day limit. Tbls, flush toilets, showers, cookers, cfga, boat ramp & dock, dump, drkg wtr, group shelters, elec ($). Horseshoes, playground, pavilion. Fishing, boating(ld), hiking, picnicking, swimming (sandy beach), horseback riding. 2-day minimum stay on weekends.

Fishing Tip: Fish the "jumps" for white bass when water is calm; try the Redmond Cove area for crappies, largemouth bass and walleyes, using spinnerbaits and crankbaits around dropoffs & points.

Drake City Park $10
Burlington Dam
On E edge of Burlington along Neosho River. Auire permit at city hall, 301 Neosho St, or police station, 625 S. 3rd St in Kelley Park. $10 ($8 for seniors). Sites include 8 new concrete pads. Tbls, flush toilets, cfga, drkg wtr, elec/wtr, showers. Fishing, hiking.

Kelley City Park $6
On E edge of Burlington, 3rd St, a few blocks S of city dam on Neosho River. Aquire permit at city hall, 301 Neosho St, or police station, 625 S. 3rs St (in the park). $6 ($4 for seniors). RV sites with tbls, flush toilets, showers, cfga, drkg wtr, playground, shelters. 46 acres.

Riverside East $12
Corps of Engineers
John Redmond Lake
3.5 mi N of Burlington on Hwy 75; 1.5 mi W on Embankment Rd following signs. On Neosho River below dam. $12. 4/1-10/31; 14-day limit; 28 days with written permission. 53 sites; 65-ft RVs. Flush toilets, cookers, cfga, elec/wtr hookups. Fishing, boating, hiking. Note: Ticks are a problem on the Rush Hill hiking trail. 2-night minumum stay on weekends.

Fishing tip: Float the Neosho or cast from shore for bass and channel catfish. Try for walleyes along the channel of Otter Creek in the game management area; also good section for crappies and largemouth bass.

Riverside West $8
Corps of Engineers
John Redmond Lake
3.5 mi N of Burlington on Hwy 75; 1.5 mi W on Embankment Rd, following signs. $8 base; $14 with wtr hookups, $15 with elec. Apr-Oct; 14-day limit. 43 sites; 65-ft RVs. Tbls, flush toilets, cfga, drkg wtr, showers, elec($). Boating(l), fishing, hiking. 2-night minimum stay on weekends.

West Wingwall $10
Corps of Engineers
John Redmond Lake
From Hwy 75, W approx 2.5 mi; left down ramp on back side of dam; left again for half mi; below dam. $10. 4/1-10/31; 14-day limit. 6 sites. Tbls, toilets, cfga, drkg wtr. Fishing, boating

Fishing Tip: Fish the "jumps" for white bass particularly along the edges of the main river channel leading to the dam.

CANTON (12)

McPherson FREE
State Fishing Lake
Maxwell State Wildlife Refuge
6 mi N of Canton on CR 304; 2.5 mi W on CR 1771. Free. All year; 7-day limit. 25 sites; 306 acres; 46-acre lake. Tbls, no drkg wtr, cfga, toilets, fishing piers. Picnicking, fishing, hiking, boating(l), nature trails. 260 acres; 46-acre lake.

Travel Tip: Lake is located within the Maxwell Game Preserve, a 2,250-acre midgrass prairie containing 200 bison, 50 elk.

Fishing Tip: Best bet here is to fish for largemouth bass or crappie. The lake also contains catfish and sunfish. When water is cloudy, find bass in 1-4 feet with crankbaits, jigs, spinnerbaits, soft plastics.

CARBONDALE (13)

Osage State Fishing Lake FREE
3 mi S and half mi E of Carbondale on US 56; then half mi S. Free. All year; 7-day limit. 120 undesignated sites; 506 acres; 140-acre lake. Tbls, drkg wtr, cfga, toilets. Picnicking, fishing, hiking, boating(l).

Fishing Tip: Try this lake for walleye, crappie or largemouth bass. It also contains catfish, wipers and sunfish. Shad sides, liver, worms and minnows produce channel cats of up to 15 pounds.

CHANUTE (15)

Santa Fe City Park $3
1 mi S of Chanute on US 169 at 35th & S. Santa Fe Sts. $8 base after 2 nights free. All year; 10-day limit. 30 sites (no RV size limit). Tbls, flush toilets, cfga, drkg wtr, elec (18 30-amp, some 50-amp), showers, playground, dump. Fishing, boating(l), horseshoes.

CHERRYVALE (16)

Mound Valley $10
Corps of Engineers
Big Hill Lake
On E side of dam on the lake. $10 without hookups; $14 with elec; $16 at premium sites with elec; $17 full hookups. 3/30-9/30; 14-day limit. 82 sites (76 with elec, 2 full hookups); 65-ft RVs. Tbls, flush toilets, cfga, drkg wtr, showers, playground, beach. Fishing, boating(l), hiking, swimming.

Timber Hill $8
Corps of Engineers
Big Hill Lake
7 mi E of Cherryvale; 2.5 mi N; 1 mi W. From E side of dam, 3 mi N & W on gravel rds. $8. 3/31-10/30; 14-day limit. 20 primtive sites. Tbls, toilets, cfga, drkg wtr, dump. Boating(dl), fishing, waterskiing, horseback riding trail. Boat ramp fee.

Fishing Tip: Evenings are the best time to fish this lake. Large crankbaits and spinnerbaits produce largemouth bass, and channel catfish are frequently caught after dark in the swimming beach area. Try Rea Bridge and submerged brush for big crappie, and work the daqm face and rocky points early mornings and just before dark for smallmouth bass.

CIMMARON

Cimmaron Crossing City Pk **Free**
From US 50 & SR 23 driving S out of town, park N of Arkansas River, on W side. Free; donations accepted. 5/15-9/15. Mostly dry camping for self-contained RVs; four 15/20-amp elec, but city says no hookups provided. Tbls, flush toilets, cfga, drkg wtr.

CLAY CENTER

Huntress City Park **FREE**
On W side of town on US 24, W of SR 15 (6th St.); E on Court St; Non B St; E on W. Dexter St; RV area on right. Free, but donations requested. Five 30-amp elec/wtr. Tbls, flush toilets at pool, cfga, drkg wtr. Free dump at Clay County Fairgrounds. GPS: N39 22.679, W97 08.194.

Sportsman Wayside Park **FREE**
On W side of town just W of Huntress City Park & E of football field, on S side; on US 24 (low tree limbs at entry; best for small RVs). Free, but donations requested. 3-day limit. Two 15/20-amp elec sites. Tbls, toilets, cfga, drkg wtr. Free dump at Clay County Fairgrounds, 12th & Bridge Sts in SE part of town.

CLIFTON (17)

Berner Memorial City Park **$8**
W of junior high school in Clifton on N side of Hwy 9. $8 for 20-amp elec; $12 for 30-amp. 50 sites. Tbls, flush toilets, cfga, drkg wtr, playgrounds, dump. Ball fields, horseshoes, pool, tennis. GPS: N39 34.0004', W97 17.256.

CLYDE

Clyde City Park **FREE**
From SR 9 at Clyde, N on N. Grant St, then W on Grand Ave to far W end of park; off N end of Perrier, to the right. Free, donations accepted. All year. Several 20 & 30-amp hookups, toilets, cfga, drkg wtr. 2 bathrooms with showers at pool bathhouse. Beautiful park. GPS: N39 35.741', W97 24.261'.

COFFEYVILLE (18)

Walter Johnson Park **$4**
On E side of Coffeyville off Hwys 169 & 166 just S of Verdigris River. $4. All year. 175 sites. Tbls, flush toilets, cfga, drkg wtr, elec. dump, showers. Fishing, recreation center, playground, horseshoe pits, fairground. Park named for noted baseball player who once resided in town.

COLDWATER (19)

Coldwater Lake **$10**
Municipal Park
1.5 mi S of US 160 (N of Coldwater) on US 183; three-fourths mi W on Lake Coldwater Rd. $10 without hookups; $15 with hookups. (monthly rates available) All year. 50 sites (40-ft RV limit). Tbls, flush toilets, showers, cfga, drkg wtr, playground, dump. Fishing, boating(l), swimming. 250-acre lake; 930-acre park.
Fishing Tip: The most popular fish at this lake are wipers and channel catfish. It is restocked annually.

COLUMBUS (20)

VFW City Park **$8**
On E County Rd off Hwy 69 in Columbus. $8. All year; 14-day limit. 10 sites; 60-ft RV limit. Tbls, flush toilets, cfga, 30-amp elec/wtr hookups, dump. Fishing pond

CONCORDIA (21)

Airport Park **FREE**
Concordia City Campground
1.3 mi S of town on SR 9/Sixth St, across from Wal-Mart; pass National Guard tanks airport on entrance rd. Donations solicited; camping free. All year; 7-day limit (register if longer than 24 hrs). 16 sites; 45-ft RVs. Elect (10 with 30 or 50-amp), wtr hookups, tbls, cfga, flush toilets, dump. Picnic shelter & play area next to campground. Pay phone in pilot's lounge behind park. GPS: N39 33.114', W97 39.446'.
Travel Tip: Visit Cloud County Historical Museum in town; county history & artifacts; early farm & kitchen tools, clothing, jewelry, barbed wire, old Bell Telephone switchboard.

COTTONWOOD FALLS (22)

Chase State Fishing Lake **FREE**
3 mi W of Cottonwood on gravel co rd on the left (runs between Cottonwood Falls and Elmdale). Free. All year; 7-day limit. 10 sites. Tbls, toilets, cfga, drkg wtr. Picnicking, fishing, swimming, boating(l). 109-acre lake.
Fishing Tip: Excellent population of smallmouth bass in this lake; use small jigs, spinnerbaits and Rebel crankbaits with light tackle. Also present are white bass, wiper, walleye, spotted bass, saugeye, largemouth and crappie. Find bass along the face of the dam and off rocky points. Search out the mud flats at the lake's upper end for channel catfish. Drift jig-and-worm across the flats and rocky points for walleye and sauger, or toss twister tails along rock structure at night.
Travel Tip: Roniger Memorial Museum at Courthouse Square in town contains private collection of Indian artifacts & hunting trophies; arrowhead collection; Indian exhibit.

COUNCIL GROVE (23)

Canning Creek Cove **$10**
Corps of Engineers
Council Grove Lake
From SR 177 at Council Grove, .1 mi W on US 56; 1.4 mi to spillway; 2 mi NW; 1 mi N. $10 at primitive sites; $15 at elec sites; $16 at sites with elec/wtr ($17 premium locations); $18 wtr & 50-amp elec. 4/1-10/31; 14-day limit. 42 sites (32 with elec); 65-ft RVs. Tbls, flush toilets, cfga, drkg wtr, dump, playground, showers, beach, pavilion, elec($). Swimming, fishing, boating(l), hiking. Boat ramp fee. 2-night minimum stay on weekends.
Fishing Tip: This camp is located strategically for some great crappie fishing; in early spring, Canning Creek produces crappies up to three pounds. Use minnows and small jigs. Sauger stocked at Council Grove periodically.

Custer Park **$7**
Corps of Engineers
Council Grove Lake
3.5 mi N of Hwy 56 on Hwy 177. $7. 3/1-12/31; 14-day limit. 10 sites (no RV size limit). Tbls, toilets, cfga, drkg wtr. Picnicking, boating(l), fishing. Boat ramp fee.
Fishing Tip: Try for sauger in various parts of the lake; they're eating size after first being stocked in 1990. Remember also that this lake produced the state record northern pike of 24 pounds, 12 ounces, caught on a sliver spoon in 1971.

Kansas View **$7**
Corps of Engineers
Council Grove Lake
2 mi N of Council Grove on SR 177; qtr mi W on dam rd. $7 during 4/1-10/31; free rest of yr, but get wtr from Neosha campground & office area. 14-day limit. 5 primitive sites. Tbls, toilets, cfga, no drkg wtr. Fishing, boating.

Kit Carson Cove **$8**
Corps of Engineers
Council Grove Lake
2.5 mi N of Hwy 56 on Hwy 177. $8 at 10 sites without hookups; $14 at 14 sites with elec/wtr during 3/1-12/31 (no wtr after 11/1 except at Neosho campground & near office. 14-day limit. No RV size limit. Tbls, flush toilets, cfga, drkg wtr, elec ($). Boating(l), fishing, hiking trail, picnicking. Boat ramp fee. 18 acres.
Travel Tip: See three unusual sites -- Council Oak Shrine, birthplace of the Santa Fe Trail; Custer Elm, where General Custer camped shortly before his massacre by Sitting Bull; Madonna of the Trail Monument, one of 12 commemorating the National Old Trails Road and paying tribute to pioneer mothers.

Marina Cove   **$8**
Corps of Engineers
Council Grove Lake
2.5 mi NW of Council Grove on paved co rd. $8 at 1 primitive site, $12 at 3 sites with elec during 4/1-10/31; free rest of yr, but get wtr at Neosho campground & office area. 14-day limit. 4 sites (no RV size limit). Tbls, flush toilets, showers, cfga, drkg wtr, elec($), fish cleaning station, marina. Boating(lr), fishing, waterskiing, swimming. Boat ramp fee.

Fishing Tip: Marina Cove and Kit Carson Cove are good producers of early spring crappies up to three pounds and sauger of 1-2 pounds.

Travel Tip: Stop at the Last Chance Store in town; built 1857, it was the last supply stop on the Santa Fe Trail.

Neosho Campground   **$12**
Corps of Engineers
Council Grove Lake
2 mi NW of Council Grove on paved co rd. $12 without hookups, $14 with elec/wtr during 4/1-10/31; some sites free 11/1-3/31. 14-day limit. 8 sites. Tbls, toilets, cfga, drkg wtr, elec($). Swimming, fishing, boating(l), picnicking. Boat ramp fee.

Fishing Tip: Stocked sauger are being caught near camp; they're good eating size.

Travel Tip: See the "Calaboose" on E Main in town; the only jail on the Santa Fe Trail.

Richey Cove   **$11**
Corps of Engineers
Council Grove Lake
From US 56 at Council Grove, 2.8 mi on SR 56/177; on W side. $11 at sites without hookups ($12 premium locations), $15 with elec, $17 with elec/wtr, $20 full hookups during 4/1-10/31; some sites free 11/1-3/31 without hookups but wtr available. 14-day limit. 42 sites (40 with elec); 65-ft RVs. Tbls, flush toilets, cfga, drkg wtr, showers, dump, beach($), elec($), playground. Boating(dl), fishing, swimming, hiking trail. Boat ramp fee. 2-night minimum stay on weekends.

Fishing Tip: Hit this cove area hard during early spring when white bass & crappie are schooling. Also some good catches of largemouth bass are made here.

Santa Fe Trail   **$11**
Corps of Engineers
Council Grove Lake
3 mi NW of Council Grove on paved co rd. $11 at non-hookup sites, $15 with elec, $16 with elec/wtr, $18 full hookups. 4/15-9/30 (free walk-in camping in Oct). 35 sites; no RV size limit. 14-day limit. Tbls, flush toilets, cfga, drkg wtr, elec($). Swimming, fishing, boating(l). Boat ramp fee. 2-night minimum stay on weekends.

COURTLAND (24)

Larsen City Park   **FREE**
Off SR 199 in Courtland near the water tower. S of US 36 on SR 199; 1 blk E of Main St.

on Freedom St. Free courtesy overnight RV parking with two 20-amp elec/wtr. No RV size limit. Tbls, toilets, cfga. GPS: N39 46.944', W97 53.553'.

DODGE CITY (25)

Ford County Lake   **FREE**
State Fishing Lake
7 mi NE of Dodge City off US 283. Free. All year. Spaces for self-contained RVs at 48-acre lake. Fishing, boating(l).

Travel Tip: Visit the Boot Hill Museum on Front St; recreated Dodge City of the 1870s at site of the old cemetery; video presentation about the town's history; 1865 jail; Santa Fe depot; blacksmith shop, schoolhouse, daily entertainment.

Fishing Tip: This lake contains walleye as well as largemouth bass, catfish & sunfish.

DORRANCE (26)

Minooka Park   **$12**
Corps of Engineers
Wilson Lake
From exit 199 on I-70, N 6 mi on SR 231 to park; at S side of lake. During 4/15-9/30, $12 for basic sites & tent sites without hookups; $16 with elec; $18 elec/wtr. Camp free during 10/1-4/14 except at $12 walk-in tent sites, but no wtr, and $8 for elec. Double sites are $24 & $36. All year; 14-day limit. 165 sites; 65-ft RVs. Drkg wtr, showers, cfga, dump, tbls, separate tent area, playground, elec($), fish cleaning staton, lantern hangers. Picnicking, fishing, hiking, swimming (beach), boating(ld), ranger programs, tennis, horseshoes, volleyball. 2-night minimum stay on weekends.

Fishing Tip: Good panfishing on Wilson Lake, but the lake is most famous for striped bass of up to 40 pounds and its excellent population of smallmouth bass. Fish the rock bluffs for smallmouth using light tackle. Hit shoulders of the main channel for stripers; in most areas, it's only 12-18 feet deep. The state record striper, 43 pounds 8 ounces, was caught here in 1988.

EL DORADO (27)

El Dorado State Park   **$8.50**
5 mi E of El Dorado on SR 177; at El Dorado Reservoir. $8.50 without hookups in-season ($7.50 off-season); $13.50-17.50 with hookups. All year; limited facilities in winter; 14-day limit. About 1,100 sites at four campgrounds. Tbls, flush toilets, cfga, drkg wtr, showers, elec($), dump, 2 beaches, marina, amphitheater. Swimming, boating (ld), fishing, hiking & biking trails. 3,800 acres.

Fishing Tip; The 8,000-acre lake contains walleyes, largemouth & smallmouth bass, channel catfish and crappies. Try the fish attractors, sunk 6-18 feet in the standing timber on the west shoreline (they are marked with buoys); also the dam riprap, the railroad right-of-way riprap at N end of the

lake. Catch crappies and largemouth in the standing timbers and around the attractors, smallmouth bass and walleyes at the riprap and the face of the dam, channel and flathead catfish in the old river channels.

ELKHART (28)

Cimarron Recreation Area   **$7**
National Grasslands Park
7.5 mi N of Elkhart on SR 27; 4 mi E on FR 700. $7. All year; 10-day limit. 14 sites (32-ft RV limit). Tbls, toilets, cfga, drkg wtr. Fishing, hiking.

Fishing Tip: Trout were restocked on 11/5/01. Use small spinners, slamon eggs or Power Bait in the recreation area ponds.

ELLIS (29)

Ellis Lakeside   **$7.50**
Municipal Campground
7 blocks S of I-70 in Ellis; 2 blocks E. $7.50 for RV sites during 11/16-4/14 ($15 rest of year); $5 off-season for tent sites ($10 rest of year); limited facilities off-season. 17 sites wtih elec. Tbls, flush toilets, cfga, drkg wtr, showers, dump, elec, fishing pier. Boating(ld), fishing, playground, biking. 2 acres on shore of Big Creek. 100-acre Ellis Lake.

ELSMORE (30)

Bourbon State Fishing Lake   **FREE**
4 mi E of US 59 in Elsmore on co rd to campground. Free/ All year; 7-day limit. 10 sites. Tbls, toilets, cfga, drkg wtr. Picnicking, fishing, boating(l). 103-acre lake.

Fishing Tip: Some good variety is available here: walleye, spotted bass, largemouth bass, crappie and channel catfish. Find bass early and late in the day by casting plastic worms, crankbaits and topwaters close to weedy points, along the face of the dam and near underwater structure.

ELLSWORTH (31)

Kanopolis State Park   **$8.50**
21 mi SE of Ellsworth on SR 141. $8.50 without hookups in-season ($7.50 off-season); $13.50-17.50 with hookups. All year; limited facilities in winter; 14-day limit. About 330 sites at 12 campgrounds; 41 new sites with elec added. Tbls, flush toilets, cfga, drkg wtr, showers, elec($), dump, beaches. Swimming, boating(ld), fishing, hiking trails, biking, horseback riding, volleyball, softball, hunting, nature trails. 3,500-acre lake; 12,500-acre wildlife area.

Fishing Tip: Kanopolis Lake is best known for its white bass and crappie fishing. In spring, try for white bass in the shallows near Bluff Creek or in the Smoky Hill River. Crappie can be caught all year in the Marina or Yankee Run Cove areas and along the face of the dam. Other fish include walleye, saugeye, wiper, largemouth bass and channel catfish. Fish cleaning stations at Buzzard

Bay boat ramp and the South Shore Langley Point ramp.

Travel Tip: Within the park are some special sights: an active prairie dog town, best viewed on warm sunny days; Faris Caves, hand dug to the sandstone cliffs to serve as a school and living quarters.

EMPORIA (32)

Arrow Rock   **$12**
Corps of Engineers
Melvern Lake
26 mi E on I-35 to US 75; then N 4 mi off Olivet exit, W 1 mi, N half mi on lake rd 1; at S side of lake. During 5/1-9/30, $12 at sites without hookups, $16 with elec, $17 wtr/elec. Some sites free 10/1-4/30; cfga & toilets only off-season facilities. 45 sites; 65-ft RVs. Tbls, flush toilets, showers, cfga, drkg wtr, dump, playground, coin laundry, elec($). Fishing, boating(l), hiking, picnicking, horseback riding trail. 2-night minimum stay on weekends.

Fishing Tip: Melvern Lake contains walleye, crappie, channel catfish, flathead catfish, largemouth bass, white bass, striped bass, smallmouth bass, sauger and wiper.

Coeur d'Alene   **$12**
Corps of Engineers
Melvern Lake
26 mi E on I-35 to US 75; then N 5 mi to Melvern Lake exit, 1.5 mi on lake rd; at SE corner of lake. During 5/1-9/30, $12 at sites without hookups; $16 with elec; $19 full hookups. Free 10/1-4/30 at some sites, but only toilets & cfga available. 14-day limit. 60 sites; 50-ft RV limit. Tbls, showers, drkg wtr, beach, dump, coin laundry, elec($), playgrounds, marina. Boating(l), fishing, hiking, picnicking, swimming, 2 nature trails. 450 acres. 2-night minimum stay on weekends.

Fishing Tip: This section of the lake has been producing good catches of quite large walleye; check out the long, sloping points, preferably those that lead into deep water, using crankbaits & jigs tipped with minnows or crawlers. Walleye limits: 5 fish, 18 inches.

Kahola Lake and Park   **FREE**
Flint Hills National Wildlife Refuge
10.5 mi W on US 50, then 10 mi NW. Free all year. Undesignated sites. Fishing, boating, swimming, picnicking, playground.

Travel Tip: Spend some time at the refuge, on self-guided tour (info available at visitors bureau in Emporia); largest remaining tall grass prairie in the US, encompasses 500 million acres.

Sundance Park   **FREE**
Corps of Engineers
Melvern Lake
18 mi E of Emporia on I-35 to Lebo exit, then 8 mi N on co rd; at SW corner of Melvern Lake. Free. All year; 14-day limit. 30 sites. Tbls, toilets, cfga, drkg wtr. Picnicking, fishing, swimming, boating(l), horseback riding.

Fishing Tip: This lake offers excellent crappie fishing. Crappies must be 10 inches, but 50 may be kept.

Turkey Point   **$12**
Corps of Engineers
Melvern Lake
18 mi E of Emporia on I-35 to Lebo exit, then N 10 mi to K170, then E 1 mi to co rd; E 2 mi, then S 1 mi on lake rd 7; at N side of lake. Durin 5/1-9/30, $12 at sites without hookups; $17 with wtr/elec; $18 with wtr/50-amp. Free 10/1-4/30 at some sites, but no elec or wtr. 50 sites (36 with elec); 65-ft RV limit. Cfga, flush toilets, showers, tbls, drkg wtr, elec($), dump, playground, coin laundry. Boating(l), picnicking, fishing, hiking. 2-night minimum stay on weekends.

Fishing Tip: This is excellent location for catching 5-6 pound walleyes; use jigs, working the points leading into deep water. Also keep in mind that the state record sauger was caught here in 1996; it was caught on a jig and minnow and weighed 4.8 pounds.

ERIE (33)

Erie City Park   **$4**
In Erie, follow signs from US 59 to E on Third St. $4 for 4 RV sites with elec/wtr; tent camping free. Tbls, toilets, cfga, no drkg wtr, dump. Swimming, tennis.

FALL RIVER (34)

Damsite   **$6.50**
Corps of Engineers
Fall River Lake
3 mi W of Fall River on Hwy 96; 1.5 mi N on lake access rd; 1.5 mi W. During 4/1-10/31, $6.50 with federal Senior Pass at sites without hookups (others pay $13), $8.50 at sites with elec/wtr (others pay $17), $10 & $10.50 at full-hookup sites (others pay $20 & $21). During 11/1-3/31, sites with elec are $5-$10 (seniors pay half price). 33 sites; 65-ft RVs. 14-day limit. Tbls, flush toilets, cfga, drkg wtr, elec($), dump, showers. Fishing, hiking, boating. 30 acres.

Fishing: Work the nearby dam area as well as the outlet and mud flats forchannel catfish, using shad sides or stink baits.

Rock Ridge Cove North   **$9**
Corps of Engineers
Fall River Lake
3 mi W of Fall River on Hwy 96; 1.5 mi N on access rd; 1.5 mi W. During 4/1-10/31, $9 at 19 primitive sites, $13 at 25 sites with elec. During 11/1-3/31, sites with elec are $5. 14-day limit. 44 sites. Tbls, flush toilets, cfga, drkg wtr, elec($), dump. Boating(l), fishing, hiking nature trail.

Fishing Tip: Use small jigs and spinners in and around this cove for crappies & white bass during early spring. Concentrate on logs and woody debris.

White Hall Bay   **$10**
Corps of Engineers
Fall River Lake
From lake project office at Fall River, 2 mi E, then 1.8 mi N and 4.2 mi NW on gravel rd. During 4/1-10/31, $6.50 with federal Senior Pass at sites without hookups (others pay $13), $8.50 at sites with elec (others pay $17), $10.50 with full hookups (others pay $21). During 11/1-3/31, sites with elec are $5. 33 sites; 65-ft RVs. 14-day limit. Tbls, toilets, cfga, drkg wtr, beach, showers, dump. Swimming, boating(l), fishing.

Fishing Tip: This bay area produces good catches of white bass on white plastic shad lures and spinners. Also try the dam area.

FONTANA (35)

Miami State Fishing Lake   **FREE**
2 mi N & E of Fontana on county rd (5 mi S of Osawatomie). Free. All year; 7-day limit. 16 primitive sites. Tbls, toilets, cfga, no drkg wtr, no trash service. Fishing, boating, hunting.

Fishing Tip: This 118-acre was heavily stocked and also renovated in 2002. It already had a new boat ramp, courtesy dock and parking area as well as added restrooms. More than 250 brush piles were installed underwater, and the lake has been restocked with largemouth bass and redear sunfish.

FORT SCOTT (36)

Gunn City Park   **$4**
NW corner of Fort Scott; at Marmaton River. $4 for tent sites; $8 for RVs. Nov-Mar for RVs (wtr off rest of year). Tbls, toilets, cfga, drkg wtr, one 30-amp elec site. Boating(lr), fishing, picnicking. Dump at fairgrounds.

Fishing Tip: Ponds at this park contain bass, channel catfish, white bass and white crappie. Hook crappie on jigs and minnows near the dam, around fish attractors. Try jigs, spoons and crankbaits around schooling and surfacing shad for white bass.

FREDONIA (37)

Fall River State Park   **$8.50**
17 mi NW of Fredonia on SR 96; 3 mi N on Fall River Rd. $8.50 without hookups in-season ($7.50 off-season); $13.50-17.50 with hookups. All year; limited facilities in winter; 14-day limit. 125 sites at 2 camps (45 with elec). Tbls, flush toilets, cfga, drkg wtr, showers, elec, dump. Swimming beach, boating(ld), canoeing, fishing, fitness trail, canoeing. 917 acres; 2,450-acre lake.

Fishing Tip: Fall River Lake is stocked with largemouth bass, crappie, walleye and white bass. In early spring, catch white bass in Otter Creek and Fall River above the lake.

GARDEN CITY (38)

Concannon   **FREE**
State Fishing Lake
15 mi NE of Garden City. Free. All year; 7-day limit. Primitive camping at 60-acre lake. Tbls, toilets, cfga, no drkg wtr. Fishing, boating(l).

Fishing Tip: The primary game fish at this lake is largemouth bass, but it also contains bullhead & channel catfish and bluegills.

Finney Refuge Pits   **FREE**
State Fishing Area
On S edge of Garden City. Free. All year; 7-day limit. Primitive camping at 5 acres of pits. Tbls, toilets, cfga, no drkg wtr. Fishing. Pits periodically dry up.

Fishing Tip: These waters are stocked with catchable-size rainbow trout as well as containing largemouth bass and channel catfish. The state record redear sunfish (1.69 pounds) was caught from here in 1995 on a jig. Catch trout on small spinners, salmon eggs or Power Bait.

GARNETT (39)

Cedar Valley Reservoir   **$9**
7 mi SW of Garnett at Kentucky & 1500 Rds on 705 acres surrounding the lake. $9 base. All year. Base fee for non-residents at primitive sites; $14 with elec; $16 with elec/wtr. 12 sites with elec. Tbls, toilets, cfga, drkg wtr, hookups($). Fishing, boating. Register at police dispatch office, 131 W. 5th Ave. Boating(l), fishing, hiking, swimming.

Lake Garnett North Park   **$9**
North end of Garnett at Lake Garnett. $9 base. All year. Base fee for non-residents at primitive sites; $14 with elec; $16 elec/wtr. 23 sites with hookups plus designated primitive area. Tbls, toilets, cfga, drkg wtr, hookups($), pool, playground. Fishing, boating(l), shooting range, tennis, basketball, swimming, horseshoes, sand volleyball, golf. 55-acre lake. Register at police dispatch office, 131 W. 5th Ave.

GIRARD (40)

Lake Crawford State Park   **$8.50**
10 mi N of Girard on SR 7. $8.50 without hookups in-season ($7.50 off-season); $13.50-17.50 with hookups. All year; limited facilities in winter; 14-day limit. 114 sites (72 with elec) at 7 campgrounds. Tbls, flush toilets, cfga, drkg wtr, showers, dump, store, beach, marina. Swimming, boating (lrd), fishing, sand volleyball, horseshoes, interpretive nature trail, scuba diving. 439 acres; 150-acre lake.

Fishing Tip: The best year-long fishing here is for channel catfish, crappie and striped bass.

GODDARD (41)

Lake Afton   **$7**
Sedgwick County Park
3 mi S of Goddard on Goddard Rd; 3 mi W on 39th St. $7 base. 4/1-10/31; 14-day limit. Base fee for primitive sites ($6 for seniors); $11 with elec/wtr ($9 seniors); wtr at 16 sites, $1 extra. Weekly & monthly rates available. 180 sites (55-ft RV limit). Tbls, flush toilets, cfga, drkg wtr, elec, showers, 2 dumps, store, playgrounds, 3 fishing piers. Horseshoes, swimming, fishing, boating (ld), shooting range. Open ground fires prohibited. 725 acres; 258-acre lake. $3 recreational permit ($25 annual).

Fishing Tip: Lake Afton yields some of the state's biggest flathead catfish. It also contains crappie, largemouth bass, walleye and channel catfish. To catch big catfish in fall, try shallow water areas with southern exposure. Use minnows and jigs for crappie.

GOODLAND (42)

Sherman   **FREE**
State Fishing Lake
10 mi S of Goodland on KS 27; 2 mi W; 3 mi S to campground. Free. All year; 3-day limit. 12 sites. Tbls, toilets, cfga, drkg wtr. Picnicking, fishing, boating(l). 210 acres. Periodically dry.

Travel Tip: High Plains Museum in town displays pioneer & Indian artifacts and an automated replica of America's first patented helicopter, built 1910. Donations.

Fishing Tip: Not a good fishing lake; it is periodically dry.

GREAT BEND (43)

Cheyenne Bottoms Inlet   **FREE**
State Wildlife Area
6 mi NE of Great Bend. Free. All year; 3-day limit. Undesignated sites. No drkg wtr. Fishing. 2 acres.

Travel Tip: The Cheyenne Bottoms area contains endangered whooping cranes, bald eagles, peregrine falcons, other wildlife in a 41,000-acre marshland. Approximately 500,000 birds nest at nearby Quivira National Wildlife Refuge, 30 mi SE of Great Bend.

GREENSBURG (44)

Kiowa State Fishing Lake   **FREE**
NW corner of Greensburg. Free. All year; 7-day limit. 10 sites; 21 acres. Tbls, drkg wtr, cfga, toilets. Picnicking, fishing, boating(l).

Travel Tip: See the "World's Largest Hand Dug Well & World's Largest Pallasite Meteorite" in town. Well, dug 1887, furnished city's water 50 years; 1,000-pound meteorite found E of town in 1949. Fee to walk down well.

Fishing Tip: This 21-acre lake contains largemouth bass and crappie as well as catfish and sunfish.

HARTFORD (46)

Flint Hills   **FREE**
National Wildlife Refuge
On upstream portion of John Redmond Reservoir. Free. All year. Open camping. No facilities. Hiking, fishing, hunting, boating, waterskiing.

Fishing Tip: Good section of water for spawning walleyes & white bass, spring largemouth and lunker flathead catfish of up to 55 pounds.

Hartford Campground   **FREE**
Corps of Engineers
John Redmond Lake
On SW side of lake, off CR 130 at Hartford. Free. All year; 14-day limit. 10 primitive sites. Tbls, toilets, cfga, drkg wtr. Boating(l), fishing.

Fishing Tip: Good section of water for spawning walleyes & white bass, spring largemouth and lunker flathead catfish.

HIATTVILLE (47)

Elm Creek Lake   **$3**
Bourbon County Park
2 mi N of Hiattville. $3 for tents; $10 with elec. All year; 14-day limit. 10 sites. Tbls, toilets, cfga, drkg wtr; limited facilities in winter. Picnicking, boating(l), fishing, swimming.

HIAWATHA (48)

Brown   **FREE**
State Fishing Lake
7.5 mi E of Hiawatha on US 36; 1 mi S to campground. Free. All year; 7-day limit. 10 sites; 62-acre lake. Tbls, toilets, cfga, no drkg wtr, food. Picnicking, fishing, boating(rl).

Travel Tip: Visit the unusual Davis Memorial at Mount Hope Cemetery; a memorial of John M. Davis includes 11 life-sized Italian marble statues showing Davis & wife at various stages in their lives. Free.

Fishing Tip: Try this lake for saugeye -- a crossbreed of sauger and walleye; also largemouth bass, crappies, channel & flathead catfish. Use tube jigs or minnows around brush for crappie; cast jig-n-pig for bass. The lake's walley are quite small and few of them.

HILL CITY

Graham County Fairgrounds   **FREE**
From jct of US 24 & US 283 in town, about half mi S on US 283, over abandoned railroad tracks; fairground on E side. Free primitive camping, $8 with elec/wtr. All year. Several sites with elec/wtr. Flush toilets, dump (at S entrance).

HOISINGTON (49)

Roadside Park   **FREE**
W edge of Hoisington on US 281 & SR 4. Free. Tbls, toilets, cfga, drkg wtr.

HOLTON (50)

Banner Creek Reservoir   **$6**
Jackson County Campground
1.5 mi W of US 75 on SR 16. $6 base; $14 with hookups. All year. 54 sites. Drkg wtr, cfga, tbls, flush toilets, showers, dump. Boating, fishing, swimming, waterskiing, 5.2-mi hiking & biking trail.
Fishing Tip: Lake is stocked with flathead & channel catfish, largemouth bass, crappie, sunfish & walleye.

Nebo State Fishing Lake   **FREE**
8 mi E of Holton on SR 116; 1 mi S, then half mi W. Free; $5 with elec. All year; 7-day limit. Primitive designated camping area on shore of 38-acre lake. Toilets, cfga, tbls, no drkg wtr, no trash service. Hunting, fishing, boating(lr), picnic area, swimming.
Fishing Tip: The primary gamefish at this small lake is the largemouth bass, although it also contains crappie and channel catfish. For bass, work submerged brush piles with jig or spinnerbaits. Use tube jigs or minnows in the same areas for crappie.

Prairie Lake City Park   **$5**
1.5 mi N & 3.5 mi W of Holton on CR 246. $5 base. All year; 14-day limit. Base fee without elec; $7 with elec. 30 sites. Tbls, toilets, cfga, drkg wtr, elec. Boating(l), fishing, picnicking. Boating & fishing permits ($3.50-$7) needed.
Fishing Tip: This 56-acre lake contains largemouth bass, channel catfish, crappie & bluegill.

HORTON (51)

Mission Lake City Park   **$5**
1 mi N of Horton on US 73; follow signs to just W of fishing pond. $5 base for primitive sites ($110 for season); $7 with elec; free tent camping at nearby Little Mission Lake. All year; limited facilities in winter. 130 sites. Tbls, toilets, cfga, drkg wtr, dump, shelter, elec($ - permit needed). Boating(l), canoeing, fishing, wheel-chair accessible fishing dock, waterskiing. Seasonal rates available. 278 acres; 177-acre lake. GPS: N39 40.472', W95 31.051'.

HOXIE (52)

Sheridan County Fairgrounds   **$10**
From jct of SR 23 (Main St) & US 24 (Oak St), N on SR 23 past W side of Express Deli, then E into fairgrounds; sites are NE behind the building & the deli (no signs for camping). $10. About a dozen sites with 30-amp elec/wtr. Flush toilets, showers, dump. GPS: N39 21.470, W100 26.482.

Sheridan   **FREE**
State Fishing Lake
12 mi E of Hoxie on US 24; .7 mi N. Free. All year. 12 sites. Tbls, toilets, cfga. Picnicking, fishing, boating(l), swimming. 263 acres; 67-

acre lake.
Fishing Tip: Sheridan Lake is primary a panfish lake, with crappie and catfish the most popular species. It also contains wiper, saugeye and largemouth bass. In fall, saugeye of up to 24 inches are caught. Pick up crappie by anchoring near brush piles and casting jigs tipped with minnows.

HURON (53)

Atchison County Lake   **$3**
W of Huron on 326th Rd. $3 daily for 2 days; $1 each additional day; 5-day limit. Tbls, toilets, cfga, drkg wtr. Fishing, boating.
Fishing Tip: This lake stocked with bullhead & channel catfish.

INDEPENDENCE (55)

Card Creek   **$8**
Corps of Engineers
Elk City Lake
From SR 39 at Elk City, 7 mi SE on US 160; 1.3 mi N, then 1.7 mi NW. $8 at 4 primitive sites; $12 at 16 sites with elec. 4/1-10/31; 14-day limit. Some sites free 11/1-3/31 ($11 with elec hookups) but reduced services. Tbls, flush toilets, cfga, drkg wtr, elec($), dump, playground. Boating(ld), fishing, hiking.
Fishing Tip: Try the flats during evenings to catch channel catfish by drifting live shad.

Elk City State Park   **$8.50**
5.5 mi NW of Independence on co rd. $8.50 without hookups in-season ($7.50 off-season); $13.50-17.50 with hookups. All year; limited facilities in winter; 14-day limit. Primitive camping in wildlife area (no trash service). 95 elec/wtr sites; 11 with sewer. Tbls, flush toilets, cfga, drkg wtr, showers, elec($), dump, playground, fishing piers, beach. Swimming, basketball, sand volleyball, boating(ld), fishing, hiking (15-mi trail), 4-mi mountain biking trail, birdwatching. 857 acres; 4,500-acre lake.
Fishing Tip: Catch spawning crappies in the spring from the coves and the connected streams. The white bass run in May provides excellent action in the Elk River. The lake also contains channel & flathead catfish, largemouth bass and saugeye.

Montgomery   **FREE**
State Fishing Lake
3 mi S and 1 mi E of jct of US 75 and US 160 (in Independence) on co rd to campground. Free. All year; 7-day limit. 60 sites; 408 acres; 92-acre lake. Tbls, toilets, cfga, firewood, no drkg wtr. Picnicking, fishing, swimming, boating(rl).
Travel Tip: William Inge Collection is displayed at Independence Community College; records, tapes & books from Pulitzer Prize-winner's collection; Independence native best known for "Picnic," "Splendor in the Grass" and "Come Back Little Sheba."
Fishing Tip: This lake contains walleye,

largemouth bass, crappie, catfish & sunfish. Most fish are small, but channel catfish run to 3 pounds; catch them from shore on doughballs.

Outlet Channel   **$8**
Corps of Engineers
Elk City Lake
7 mi NW of Independence on CR, below dam, W side of spillway. $8 at 15 primitive sites during 4/1-10/31. Free 11/1-3/31 but limited services. 14-day limit. Tbls, flush toilets, cfga, drkg wtr, dump. Boating, fishing, hiking.
Fishing Tip: This lake has a state-wide reputation for its large crappies; use jigs & minnows in spring for best results.

JETMORE (56)

Buckner Valley Park   **FREE**
Pawnee Watershed District
5 mi W of Jetmore on US 156. Free. Primitive sites. Tbls, toilets, cfga, drkg wtr, elec. Horseback riding, fishing, picnicking. At Buckner Creek.

Hodgeman   **FREE**
State Fishing Lake
5 mi E of jct of US 156 and US 283 (in Jetmore); 2 mi S. All year; 7-day limit. Undesignated sites. Tbls, toilets, cfga, drkg wtr. Picnicking. 87 acres. Lake periodically dry; it is stocked with fish when water present. Not enough water in 2001 for stocking.

Jetmore City Lake   **$5**
3 mi W & 1.5 mi S of Jetmore on Spring Creek. $5 for primitive & tent sites; 5 RV sites $9 with elec. 15 sites Tbls, toilets, cfga, drkg wtr, elec. Boating(l), fishing.
Fishing Tip: Channel catfish of nearly 2.5 pounds were stocked late October 2001. Use shad guts & sides, cut bait, liver, worms or stink baits. Wipers up to 8 pounds are caught on surface lures.

JEWELL

Jewell City Park   **FREE**
In Jewell, 2 blks E of SR 14 on SR 28 (Delaware St). Free primitive camping; $5 with four 30/50-amp elec, flush toilets, showers, dump (at NE corner of park), playground. 30-ft & 40-ft RV limit. Nice park (but 6 p.m. tornado test siren sounds). GPS: N39 40.218', W98 09.327'.

JUNCTION CITY (57)

Curtis Creek   **$12**
Corps of Engineers
Milford Lake
2 mi NW of Junction City on SR 57; W on SR 244; 6 mi N on CR 837. $12 at non-hookup sites; $16 with elec; $18 elec/wtr. 4/15-9/30; 14-day limit. 61 sites; 65-ft RVs. Drkg wtr, cfga, flush toilets, tbls, dump, play-

ground, showers, elect($). Boating(l), fishing, swimming, hiking. 2-night minimum stay on weekends.

Fishing Tip: This campground is well situated for the lake's topnotch white bass fishing. Use spoons near both islands and at the mouth of Curtis Creek. For varied action, move around and cover the causeway, Farnum Creek, Military Flats, Madison Creek and School Creek.

Geary State Fishing Lake   FREE
8.5 mi S of Junction City on US 77. Free. All year; 7-day limit. 50 sites. Tbls, toilets, cfga, drkg wtr. Picnicking, fishing, boating(ld). 451 acres.

Travel Tip: Geary County Historical Museum in town contains innovative displays from frontier days; in old Junction City High School; free self-guided tours.

Fishing Tip: Try for smallmouth & largemouth bass or crappies, but the lake also contains walleye as well as flathead and channel catfish. For bass, use jibs near brush or Carolina rigs along rocky ledges and dam.

Milford State Park $8.50
4 mi N of Junction City on US 77; 3 mi W on SR 57. $8.50 without hookups in-season ($7.50 off-season); $13.50-17.50 with hookups. All year; limited facilities in winter; 14-day limit. 5 campgrounds with 222 sites (see below). Tbls, flush toilets, cfga, drkg wtr, showers, hookups($), dump, beach, marina. Swimming, boating(lrd), fishing, hiking, nature trails. 16,000-acre lake.
    Hickory Hollow Camp: 32 full-hookup sites & dump station.
    Cedar Point Camp: 9 primitive sites, 42 sites with elec/wtr; new shower building, dump.
    Prairie View Camp: 20 elec/wtr sites; portable toilets.
    Woodland Hills: 60 primitive sites, 30 sites with elec/wtr; newly renovated shower house.
    Walnut Grove Camp: 30 primitive sites, renovated shower house, basketball court.
    Fishing Tip: In April, catch walleyes along the face of the dam. White bass run upriver and along the dam in May, and crappie spawn along shallow banks. Catch summer walleye and white bass at night, using spoons. Wiper topwater fishing it hot in August, and in September, hook bass feeding on shad in the backs of the creeks. On 11/2/01, a state record blue catfish weighing 36 pounds was caught in Milford Lake.

School Creek $8
Corps of Engineers
Milford Lake
NW of Junction City on SR 57; W on SR 244; 8 mi N on CR 837, then 1 mi E on Luttman Rd. $8 during 4/1-9/30; free rest of yr. 56 sites (30-ft RV limit). Toilets, cfga, drkg wtr, shelter, tbls, playground. Boating (l), fishing, picnicking.
    Fishing Tip: Excellent location for a variety of fishing experiences, ranging from school-

ing white bass and stripers at the mouth of School Creek and along the main river channel to crappies, catfish and largemouth bass in the School Creek section itself.

Timber Creek Park $8
Corps of Engineers
Milford Lake
11 mi N of Junction City on US 77; 2 mi W on SR 82. $8 during 4/15-9/30; free rest of year; 14-day limit. 36 sites (30-ft RV limit). Tbls, flush toilets, cfga, drkg wtr, dump, playground. Fishing, boating.
    Fishing Tip: From camp, boat upstream, fishing the small bays and then the bends of the main river channel. Good smallmouth bass & white bass area; use small jigs & spinnerbaits or crankbaits. State record smallmouth, 6.37 pounds, was caught from Milford Lake on a jig in 1997.
    Travel Tip: Custer House, in town at Ft. Riley is open for tours; named for General George Custer, who served as second in command of the 7th Cavalry when it was formed at Ft. Riley in 1806.

West Rolling Hills $12
Corps of Engineers
Milford Lake
NW on SR 57, then 3 mi W on SR 244. $12 base. Free tent camping area all yr on SW section. Non-hookup sites $12; elec sites $18; 50-amp elec $19. 4/15-9/30. 60 sites; 65-ft RVs. Flush toilets, cfga, dump, tbls, wtr, elec($), hot showers, flush toilets. Boating(l), hiking, fishing, swimming, playground. 2-night minimum stay on weekends.
    Fishing Tip: Try offshore from camp for striped bass, white bass and catfish. Also, hit the rocky shoreline & steep bluffs with light tackle for smallmouth bass. Early spring and fall, use Carolina rigs 10-15 feet near rock ledges.

KALVESTA (58)

Finney State Fishing Lake   FREE
8 mi N, 3 mi W, then 1 mi N of Kalvesta. Free. All year; 7-day limit. Primitive camping at 110-acre lake. Tbls, toilets, cfga, no drkg wtr. Fishing, boating(l).
    Fishing Tip: This lake is stocked with rainbow trout and also contains largemouth bass, channel catfish and sunfish.

KANSAS CITY (59)

Leavenworth   FREE
State Fishing Lake
4 mi N of Kansas City on KS 16; 2 mi E on KS 90 to park (3 mi W and 1 mi N of Tonganoxie). Free. All year; 14-day limit. 20 sites; 331 acres; 175-acre lake. Toilets, tbls, cfga, drkg wtr, dump, playground. Fishing, hiking, boating(lr), swimming.
    Travel Tip: Agricultural Hall of Fame in Kansas City offers nation's largest & most varied collection of agricultural artifacts & honors farmers.
    Fishing Tip: This lake has a rare treat for

fishermen -- a population of wipers (striped bass & white bass) as well as walleye, largemouth bass, crappies, catfish and bluegills. Catch the wipers on slab spoons, the largemouth on plastic worms, crankbaits and spinners.

KINGMAN (60)

Kingman County Fairgrounds $6
In Kingman at W. 1st St, across from Riverside City Park. $6. All year. 94 RV sites (fee, plus $20 deposit for key to hookups); tent camping also avilable. Tbls, toilets, cfga, drkg wtr, elec, dump.

Kingman   FREE
State Fishing Lake
8 mi W of Kingman on US 54. Free. All year; 14-night limit. 60 primitive sites around the lake. Tbls, toilets, cfga, no drkg wtr. Picnicking, fishing, boating(l), nature trail, hunting. 4,242 acres; 144-acre lake. Byron Walker Wildlife Area.
    Fishing Tip: Good fishing is available for walleye, wiper and crappie. The lake also contains channel catfish, northern pike and sunfish. Bass are generally under 2 pounds; northern pike, 18-30 inches. For pike, try spinnerbaits and buzzbaits in the spillway tower area.

Riverside City Park   FREE
E of town on US 54 across from fairgrounds at 100 W. 1st St. Sign says "All night parking for tourists only." Free. Tbls, toilets, cfga, drkg wtr, hookups, dump.

KINGSDOWN (61)

Clark State Fishing Lake   FREE
10 mi S of Kingsdown on SR 94; 1 mi W on co rd to campground. Free. All year; 7-day limit. 65 sites; 1,243 acres. Tbls, toilets, cfga, no drkg wtr. Picnicking, fishing, boating(lr).
    Fishing Tip: 337-acre lake contains a few surprises -- walleye, saugeye and white bass as well as largemouth bass, crappies, channel catfish and bluegills.

KIRWIN (62)

Kirwin National   FREE
Wildlife Refuge
4 mi W and 1 mi S of Kirwin via KS 9 to refuge headquarters. Free. All year; 7-day limit. Free camping at 6 developed campgrounds, designated on a map available from refuge headquarters. Each site has tbls, cfga, pit toilet, drkg wtr (but not at campsites on N side), trash cans. Fishing, boating, picnicking in designated areas; waterskiing, hunting, hiking. 11,000 acres. More information/map contact: Refuge Manager, Kirwin National Wildlife Refuge, Box 125, Kirwin, KS 67644.
    Fishing Tip: Excellent fishing throughout the refuge for channel catfish, largemouth bass and sunfish. Most crappies are caught near fish attractors

LA CROSSE (63)

Grass City Park   **25 cents**
1 mi S of jct SR 4 & US 183 on US 183 in town. 25 cents per hr for elec; primitive camping free. All year; 3-day limit. 3 sites plus tent area. Tbls, flush toilets, cfga, drkg wtr, elec($). Picnicking. Laundry, store nearby.
Travel Tip: Stop at the Barbed Wire Museum in town; it displays barbed wire & tools used for working with it.

LA CYGNE (64)

LaCygne Lake   **$7**
Linn County Park
On Lake Rd, E of Hwy 69; N of power plant. $7 for no hookups; $9 elec; $10 wtr/elec; $11 full hookups. All year. About 100 sites. Tbls, flush toilets, showers, cfga, drkg wtr, elec($), playground, shelter, pool, store. Fishing, boating, swimming.
Fishing Tip: For crappies, cast jigs and minnows around the dam, the outlet gates at the dam, over submerged brush in both 20 feet of water and near shore. Wipers of up to 8 pounds can be caught on lures that imitate gizzard shad; look for schooling and surfacing shad to find the wipers.

LAKIN (65)

Beymer   **$5**
Water Recreation Park
Kearny County Park
2.5 mi S of Lakin on SR 25. $5. 5/1-10/1; 3-day limit. 8 sites. Tbls, flush toilets, drkg wtr, showers, cfga, 30-amp elec. Fishing, swimming, picnicking. Beautiful spot.

LATHAM (66)

Butler State Fishing Lake   **FREE**
2 mi W of Latham and 1 mi N on co rd to campground. Free. All year; 7-day limit. 20 sites. Tbls, toilets, cfga, drkg wtr. Picnicking, fishing, boating(l). 351 acres.
Fishing Tip: This 124-acre lake offers good walleye and largemouth bass fishing as well as crappies, catfish and sunfish. In fall, take crappie off the face of the dam, using minnows or jigs in 10-12 feet. Catch bass along the edges of weeds and around piers in 5-6 feet of water using spinnerbaits, buzz baits and topwater lures.

LAWRENCE (67)

Clinton State Park   **$8.50**
4 mi W of Lawrence at Clinton Reservoir. $8.50 without hookups in-season ($7.50 off-season); $13.50-17.50 with hookups. All year; limited facilities in winter; 14-day limit. About 500 sites (240 elec/wtr). Tbls, flush toilets, cfga, drkg wtr, showers, dump, beach, playground, marina. Swimming, boating (lrd), fishing, winter sports, hiking & mountain biking trails, horseback riding, waterskiing.

Fishing Tip: Find crappie suspended over brush; catch them with minnows and jigs. Look for white bass in the backs of coves.

Douglas County Fairgrounds   **$10**
From Hwy 10 in Lawrence, 2 blocks N on Harper to fairgrounds at 21st St. $10. All year. Tbls, flush toilets, cfga, drkg wtr, showers, hookups.

Hickory/Walnut Camp   **$12**
Bloomington Park Area
Corps of Engineers
Clinton Lake
From Lawrence, 4 mi W on Hwy 40 (6th St); 5 mi left on CR 442 to Stull; 6 mi left on CR 1023; left on CR 6 through Clinton, then follow signs. $12 without hookups; $16 with elec. Sites in Oak Loop with hookups are $10. 5/1-3/30; 14-day limit. 221 sites (94 with elec); 65-ft RVs. Tbls, flush toilets, cfga, drkg wtr, dump, playground, showers, beach. Swimming, hiking, boating(l), biking. Amphitheater, fish cleaning station. Hickory & Walnut Campgrounds have been merged and now utilize one gate station.

Lone Star Lake   **$7**
Douglas County Park
4 mi SW of Lawrence. $7 primitive sites; $12 with elec. 4/1-9/15. 50 sites. Tbls, flush toilets, cfga, drkg wtr, dump, showers, elec($). Boating(l), fishing, picnicking. Fees for boating & fishing

Riverfront Park   **FREE**
Hike Bicentennial Trail in Lawrence. Free. Primitive backpack camping; no facilities. Swimming, ATV activities.

Rockhaven   **$6**
Corps of Engineers
Clinton Lake
4 mi W of Lawrence on US 40; 4 mi S on Co 13, 5 mi SW on CR 458; 1 mi N. $6 self-pay $8 if ranger collects. 4/1-10/31; 14-day limit. 50 sites (9 with wtr hookups). Tbls, toilets, cfga, drkg wtr. Picnicking, swimming, fishing, horseback riding, hiking. Horse or mule camping permitted. 350 acres.

Woodridge   **FREE**
Corps of Engineers
Clinton Lake
5 mi W of Lawrence on US 40, 4 mi W on CR 442; 4 mi S on CR 1023; 1 mi E on CR 2, half mi N on co rd. Free. All year; 14-day limit. Undesignated primitive tent sites on 450 acres. Tbls, toilets, cfga, drkg wtr. Swimming, fishing. Also camp along 4.5-mi hiking trail at fire rings.
Fishing Tip: Near camp, try the shallow rocky flats during summer early mornings for smallmouth bass, using crankbaits such as bass-colored Rebel Deep-Wee R. Smallmouth spawn here in late April or early May.

LIBERAL (68)

Arkalon City Park   **$5**
10 mi NE of US 83 in Liberal on US 54; 2 mi N on county rd. $5 base; $10 with elec. 4/1-10/31; 14-day limit. 35 sites (27 with elec). Tbls, flush toilets, cfga, drkg wtr, elec($), dump, showers. Fishing, horseshoes, nature trails, birdwatching.
Fishing Tip: The park contains 3 lakes & a marsh area, and all fishing areas have been stocked, primarily with catfish. Fishing fees are $3 for 3 days, $8 annually.

Mid-America Air Museum   **FREE**
On W end of Liberal, S of Liberal Airport: N off Hwy 54 onto Western Ave, then left on General Welch Blvd; at Second St. Free overnight RV camping with $5 paid museum admission. No facilities.

Seward County Fairgrounds   **$10**
About 10 mi E of Liberal on US 54. $10. $10. 4/1-10/15. Sites with 20-amp or 30 amp elec; 7 sites with 50-amp full hookups. Flush toilets, showers, drkg wtr, dump.

LINDSBORG (69)

Old Mill Park & Campground   **$5**
McPherson County Park
Across the river on S First St from the Old Mill Museum, 120 Mill St. $5 for non-hookup sites; $7 with elec. Check in at museum office. 24 sites. Tbls, flush toilets, cfga, drkg wtr, elec($). Fishing, canoeing.
Travel Tip: Old Mill Museum exhibits artifacts on native Americans, natural history and area settlement, with special focus on 1870-1910.

LOGAN (70)

Logan City Lake   **FREE**
2.5 mi S of Logan. Camp free, but donations accepted. No facilities. Picnicking, fishing, boating(l), playground.

LOUISBURG (71)

Louisburg-Middlecreek   **FREE**
State Fishing Lake
7 mi S of Louisburg on Metcalf Rd. Free. All year; 7-day limit. 5 sites. Tbls, toilets, cfga, no drkg wtr, no trash service. Boating(l), fishing, hunting. 280-acre lake.
Fishing Tip: This small lake has a large, varied fish population, including walleye, both largemouth & smallmouth bass, saugeye, white bass, channel & flathead catfish and most types of sunfish.

LUCAS (72)

Lucas Campground   **$12**
Corps of Engineers
Wilson Lake
From I-70 exit 206, N 8 mi on Hwy 232 to lake, cross dam, then first left to park; on

N side of lake. During 4/15-9/30, $12 at non-hookup sites; $16 with elec; $18 with wtr/elec, premium sites with wtr/elec and sites with wtr/50-amp; double sites $24 & $35. Walk-in tent sites at Whitetail Ridge are $12 10/1-4/14. 14-day limit. 104 sites; 65-ft RVs. Tbls, showers, flush toilets, cfga, drkg wtr, playground, beach, elec($), pavilion, fish cleaning station. Picnicking, fishing, swimming, boating(ld), hiking.

Fishing Tip: Just off shore from the campground, fish the main river channel for flathead and channel catfish, using minnows, nightcrawlers, shad and crayfish, especially at night. Lots of catfish under a pound.

Travel Tip: Visit the "Garden of Eden" -- started in 1907; a unique display of art using cement, wood, native limestone.

Sylvan $12
Corps of Engineers
Wilson Lake

7 mi S of Lucas on SR 232, below dam on N side of spillway. During 4/15-10/15, $12 at basic sites without hookups, $18 with elec. Sites free 10/16-4/14, with hookups $8. All year; 14-day limit. 28 sites; 65-ft RVs. Tbls, flush & pit toilets, cfga, drkg wtr, playground. Hiking, boating, fishing, horseshoes

Fishing Tip: Good strategic location to try for this lake's huge striped bass, especially near the campground and SE toward the dam. Fish the main river channel with live bait or large jigs with twister tails. Also hit the rocky shallows & bluffs for smallmouth bass, using small jigs & spinnerbaits.

LURAY (73)

Luray Municipal Park   FREE

Along SR 18 in Luray. Free primitive camping; $10 at 2 sites with elec. Tbls, toilets, cfga, drkg wtr, playground, picnic shelter. Horseshoes, basketball. Park also contains oldest house in Russell County, built 1870, rebuilt by the local Lions Club.

LYNDON (74)

Eisenhower State Park $8.50

5 mi S of Lyndon on US 75; 3 mi W on SR 278; at N shore of Melvern Lake. $8.50 without hookups in-season ($7.50 off-season); $13.50-17.50 with hookups. All year; limited facilities in winter; 14-day limit. 190 sites with elec/wtr; numerous primitive sites; 5 campgrounds. Tbls, flush toilets, cfga, drkg wtr, showers, elec, dump, beaches. Swimming, boating(rld), fishing, hiking trail, interpretive trail, horseshoes, volleyball, archery, hunting, horseback riding, naturalist programs. Equestrian camping at Cowboy Campground & N loop of Westpond Camp (4 sites have wtr; 10 have elec). 1,785 acres; 6,930-acre lake.

Fishing Tip: The flats just offshore from the state park usually produce good catches of sauger and walleye. Use jigs and worms in 10-15 feet at dropoffs. Crappie are mostly

small, usually caught near submerged brush. Find smallmouth around rocky points.

Carbolyn Park $12
Corps of Engineers
Pomona Lake

3.8 mi N of Lyndon on US 75; E before bridge. $12 base at sites without hookups; $16 with elec/wtr. 5/1-9/30; 14-day limit. 32 modern sites; 55-ft RV limit. Tbls, flush toilets, showers, cfga, drkg wtr, dump, playground, elec($), pavilion. Boating(l), fishing, picnicking.

Fishing Tip: The state record wiper was caught in this lake in 1993. It weighed 22 pounds. Most of Pomona's wipers are 1-4 pounds. Catch them on spoons, crankbaits and soft plastics that mimic gizzard shad. Look for surfacing shad around 110 Creek and Wolf Creek arms. Best bet is at first light.

Lyndon City Park   FREE

At 10th & Topeka Ave in Lyndon. Free. All year; 7-day limit. 3 sites without hookups. Tbls, flush toilets (summers only), cfga, drkg wtr, playground, pavilion. Restrooms at nearby ball field or at Osage County Sheriff's office a few blocks downtown. Park contains historical 2-story 1870 log house.

LYONS (75)

Lyons Overnight   FREE
Municipal Park

From jct US 56 & 96, half mi S on Hwy 96; half mi W at 500 W. Taylor St. Camp free 5 days; donations suggested. All year. 18 close sites. Tbls, toilets, cfga, drkg wtr, showers, elec($). Picnicking, hiking. Check in at city hall or police station before camping.

MANHATTAN (76)

Pottawatomie County   FREE
State Fishing Lake #2

2.5 mi E of Manhattan on US 24; 2 mi N; 2 mi NW to campground. Free. All year; 7-day limit. 25 sites. Tbls, toilets, cfga, no drkg wtr. Picnicking, fishing, boating(rl). 247 acres; 25-acre lake.

Fishing Tip: This lake is stocked with crappie, largemouth bass, walleye, catfish and sunfish. Bass are small, but numerous; most are under the 15-inch limit. Try for crappie near the north courtesy dock using jigs and minnows. Excellent fishing everywhere for sunfish and bluegill.

Tuttle Creek Cove $12
Corps of Engineers
Tuttle Creek Lake

From dam at project office, 2.5 mi N on CR 897. $12 at sites without elec; $18 elec/wtr. All year; 14-day limit. 56 sites. Tbls, toilets, cfga, drkg wtr, beach, fishing pier, playground. Boating (ld), fishing.

Fishing Tip: In early April, run your boat SE to the dam in order to catch saugeye,

and try the mud flats in May and June, using jigs, minnows and imitation baitfish lures. Cast the jumps for white bass in open water and off rocky points in mid-April. In fall, catch crappie near flooded stumps & debris using jigs and live bait.

Tuttle Creek State Park $8.50

5 mi N of Manhattan on US 24; at base of dam. $8.50 without hookups in-season ($7 off-season); $13.50-17.50 with hookups. All year; limited facilities in winter; 14-day limit. Park's 4 camping areas are outlined below. Tbls, flush toilets, cfga, wtr hookups, showers, dump, beach, playground, marina. Swimming, boating(lrd), fishing, waterskiing, 4-mi hiking & biking trail, waterskiing, windsurfing, sand & mud volleyball, 18-hole disc golf course, wildlife viewing blind. 12,200 acres; 15,800-acre lake. *Fishing Tip:* Park's quarter-mile trout stream is one of only two streams in Kansas stocked all year.

River Pond Park: 514 acres below the dam. 193 sites, 104 with wtr/elec (24 with 50 amp; 16 winterized with frost-free hydrants). 3 boat ramps, dump, 2 shower houses, 2 courtesy docks, playground, fishing pier, fish cleaning station, beach, nature trail.

Spillway Park: 153 acres on E edge of lake, 2 mi N of dam. Random primitive camping (self-pay), boat ramp, marina, shower house, courtesy dock, fish cleaning station.

Fancy Creek Park: Secluded 372 acres at W side of N end of lake. 12 elec sites, primitive sites, drkg wtr nearby, pit toilets, hiking trail, 2 high-water boat ramps, no showers. *Fishing Tip:* Channel catfish angling often is excellent at the N end near Fancy Park.

Randolph Park: At E side of lake on N end; 202 acres. Unlimited random primitive camping, high-water boat ramp, dump, shower house, hiking/equestrian trails

MANKATO (77)

Jewell State Fishing Lake   FREE

1 mi W on US 36; 6 mi S of Mankato on co rd; 2 mi W on co rd. Free. All year; 7-day limit. 10 sites; 57 acres. Tbls, toilets, cfga, drkg wtr. Picnicking, fishing, boating(l).

Fishing Tip: The lake contains largemouth bass, sunfish, wiper and catfish. Most popular fish is channel catfish.

Lovewell State Park $8.50

4 mi E of Mankato on US 36; 10 mi N on SR 14; 4 mi E on co rd; 1 mi S on access rd. $8.50 without hookups in-season ($7.50 off-season); $13.50-17.50 with hookups. All year; limited facilities in winter; 14-day limit. 423 sites (222 with elec) at 4 campgrounds (1 for groups). Tbls, flush & pit toilets, cfga, drkg wtr, showers, elec, dumps, store, beach, playground, marina, lighted fish cleaning station with elec outlets. Swimming, boating(ld), fishing, archery range, sand volleyball, horseshoes, basketball courts. 1,126 acres; 3,000-acre lake.

Fishing Tip: Try for crappies near the fish attractors, and concentrate on the Cedar Point area for white bass and wipers. The lake also contains big channel catfish and walleye. Very little fishing pressure off-season.

Mankato City Park   **FREE**
At W end of town, turn N on South McRoberts St; park on W side, loop rd. Free. All year. Mostly off-level sites with several prs of 15 & 20-amp elec outlets on 3 poles; space for 3-4 medium or large RVs on sides of driveway. Flush toilets, playgrounds, cfga, drkg wtr. Less appealing than other N Kansas parks. GPS: N39 47.172', W98 12.892'.

MARION (78)

French Creek Cove   **$10**
Corps of Engineers
Marion Lake
6 mi W of Marion on US 56; 1 mi N, 1 mi E. During 3/15-11/15, $10 with elec. Some sites free 11/16-4/14, but reduced services. 14-day limit. 20 elec sites. Tbls, toilets, cfga, drkg wtr. Boating(dl), fishing, waterskiing. Fee for boat ramp.

Fishing Tip: This campground is situated near the absolutely best channel catish waters in the lake! Using live shad, worms and varioud prepared baits, fish the flooded Timber of French Creek and near the dam. The creek's humps also are excellent places for catching white bass and wiper.

Marion County Lake Park   **$6**
2 mi E of Marion on US 256; 2 mi S on Airport Rd; half mi W on Lakeshore Dr. $6 base; $12 with elec; free dry camping in overflow area. All year; 14-day limit. 52 sites at Hillsboro Cove & 92 sites at Cottonwood Point, all with elec, wtr shower; 6 sites without hookups at Marion Cove & 12 without hookups at French Creek Cove; primitive camping at Durham Cove and near spillway. Tbls, toilets, cfga, drkg wtr, dump. Fishing, boating(ld), swimming, playground.

Fishing Tip: The state record spotted (Kentucky) bass was caught in this lake in April 1977; it weighed 4 pounds 7 ounces and was caught with a topwater popper on a flyrod. For walleye, try the NE side and in the trees, using jigs and nightcrawlers.

Marion Cove   **$7**
Corps of Engineers
Marion Lake
3 mi W of Marion on US 56, then 2 mi N. During 3/15-11/15, $7; free at some sites rest of year, but reduced services. 14-day limit. 6 non-elec sites. Cfga, drkg wtr, tbls, toilets, beach. Boating(dl), fishing, picnicking, swimming. Boat ramp fee.

Fishing Tip: Try the shallow ater near camp, using spinnerbaits, plastic worms and jig-n-pig for largemouth bass.

MARQUETTE (79)

Riverside Campground   **$12**
Corps of Engineers
Kanopolis Lake
Below SE end of dam at outlet area; at Smoky Hill River. During 5/1-9/30, $12 at primitive sites, $18 with elec. Some sites free during 10/1-4/30, but no wtr, $4 with elec. 40 sites; 65-ft RVs. Tbls, flush toilets, showers, cfga, drkg wtr, elec($), dump, playground. Handicap access. Fishing, boating.

Fishing Tip: Excellent rainbow trout fishing should be available from Riverside Park now. A series of stockings at the seep stream below the dam started in October 2002. Use Power Bait, cheese, corn, small spinners, worms or flies.

Venango   **$12**
Corps of Engineers
Kanopolis Lake
8 mi W on SR 4; 5 mi N on SR 141. During 5/1-9/30, $12 at sites without hookups, $16 with elec, $18 with wtr/elec. Some sites free 10/1-4/30. No wtr during free period, but elec $4. 14-day limit. 205 sites (87 with elec); 65-ft RVs. Tbls, toilets, cfga, drkg wtr, elec($), showers, dump. Fishing, boating(l), swimming beach, playground, motorcycle trail. 2-night minimum stay on weekends.

Fishing Tip: If you camp here during the free off-season, fish rocky areas for the lake's walleyes and saugeye, using jig-n-worm, small shad crankbaits or slab spoons. There are plenty of saugeye over 7 pounds, and off-season is a good time to catch them.

Yankee Run Boldt Bluff   **FREE**
Corps of Engineers
Kanopolis Lake
From dam, 2 mi S on SR 141, 4.9 mi W on gravel road past Langley Point State Park, 3 mi N on gravel road, access E. Free. Primitive, non-designated sites. Toilets, cfga, no drkg wtr. Fishing, boating.

Fishing Tip: This lake contains good concentrations of white bass and wipers, with plenty of wipers in the 5-pound range. Look for both species in the feeder streams; use slab spoons and jigs on the edges of the river channel along Loders and the points around Yankee Run.

MARYSVILLE (80)

Marysville City Park   **FREE**
Just S of Hwys 36 on US 77 in Marysville. Free; 5-day limit. Tbls, flush toilets, cfga, drkg wtr, two 30/50-amp elec plus 20-amp, dump, playground, pool, gazebo, tennis. No camping May 12-14; no parking on grass. GPS: N39 50.254', W96 38.579'.

MEADE (81)

Meade City Park   **FREE**
E side of Meade on KS 54E. Free. All year. 30 undesignated sites. Tbls, flush toilets, cfga,

drkg wtr, playground, pavilion, dump on W side near pool entry (flush wtr only). No wtr or toilets 11/15-4/1.

Travel Tip: Dalton Gang Hideout in Meade, is home of a gang member's sister; only Dalton hideout that's been preserved; restored as it was in 19th Century; Dalton Museum contains Western artifacts.

Meade State Park   **$8.50**
13 mi SW of Meade on SR 23; at Lake Meade. $8.50 without hookups in-season ($7 off-season); $13.50-17.50 with hookups. All year; limited facilities in winter; 14-day limit. 137 sites (32 elec). Tbls, flush toilets, cfga, drkg wtr, showers, elec, dump, beach, playground. Swimming, boating (ld), fishing, hiking, nature trail. 443 acres; 80-acre lake.

Fishing Tip: Largemouth bass and crappie are the best bets here, along with channel catfish and sunfish.

MEDICINE LODGE (82)

Barber State Fishing Lake   **FREE**
At jct of US 160 and US 281; on N edge of Medicine Lodge. Free. All year; 7-day limit. 20 sites. Tbls, toilets, cfga. Picnicking, fishing, boating(l). 77-acre lake.

Fishing Tip: This small lake contains walleye, largemouth bass, crappie and channel catfish.

Medicine Lodge   **$5**
Memorial Peace Park Campground
On E edge of Medicine Lodge on US 160. $5 base for primitive sites; $15 with hookups. 10 sites; 45-ft RVs. 15/20 & 50-amp elec/wtr hookups (no 30-amp), tbls, toilets, cfga, drkg wtr, showers. Dump in town, N on US 281. GPS: N37 16.563', W93 3.438'.

MELVERN (83)

Outlet Park   **FREE**
Corps of Engineers
Melvern Lake
3.5 mi W of Melvern on SR 31, then N below the dam. Free during 11/1-3/31, but no wtr or elec; $17-$20 rest of yr with elec/wtr hookups (holders of federal Senior Pass pay half price). 150 sites; 65-ft RVs. Tbls, flush toilets, cfga, drkg wtr, showers, beach, dump, coin laundry, sewer hookups($), fish cleaning station, horseshoes, softball field, volleyball, 4 nature trails, historical suspension bridge. Fishing, boating(ld), hiking, swimming. Fish stocked in 85-acre pond, but motorboats prohibited.

MICHIGAN VALLEY (84)

110 Mile Park   **FREE**
Corps of Engineers
Pomona Lake
From Michigan Valley, 2 mi W on East 213th St, 1 mi N on S. Shawnee Heights Rd, 1.5 mi W on East 205th St following signs; N side of the lake. Free. All year; 14-day limit. 25 primi-

tive sites. Tbls, toilets, cfga, drkg wtr (except in winter), playground. Picnicking, horse & hiking trail, boating (dl), fishing, nature trail. Group camping available.

Fishing Tip: In spring and summer, fish the bays between this camp and Cedar Park, watching for crappies and white bass chasing schools of shad. Try for crappies at 15 feet in the summer along the contour of the old creek channel. Wipers -- a cross between white and striped bass -- are found in the same areas as white bass and hit lures aggressively.

Cedar Park   **FREE**
Corps of Engineers
Pomona Lake
2 mi W of Michigan Valley on E. 213th St; 1 mi N on S. Shawnee Heights Rd; 3 mi W on 205th St; at N side of lake. Free. All year; 14-day limit. 8 primitive sites. Tbls, toilets, cfga, drkg wtr. Picnicking, fishing, swimming, boating(l). 72 acres.

Fishing Tip: Lake areas near Cedar Park are popular among catfish anglers, and the offshore structure such as submerged trees and brush provide good habitat for largemouth bass and crappies. For channel cats, use cut shad, worms, dough bait and minnows close to fish feeders and at the rock quarry.

Michigan Valley Camp   **$12**
Corps of Engineers
Pomona Lake
1 mi S of Michigan Valley; 1 mi W, on NW side of dam. $12 at sites without hookups; $16 with elec ($18 premium locations). 5/1-9/30; 14-day limit. 87 sites; 65-ft RVs. Drkg wtr, flush toilets, tbls, showers, dump, cfga, picnic shelters, beach, playgrounds. Picnicking, swimming, fishing, boating(l).

Fishing Tip: Campsites are within walking distance of good shoreline fishing. This area is one of the best in the lake for catching big channel catfish on live bait such as nightcrawlers or cut shad. In spring, fish off shore for spawning crappies using bobbers and minnows around submerged brush.

Wolf Creek Campground   **$12**
Corps of Engineers
Pomona Lake
1 mi S of Michigan Valley, then 1 mi W to dam and 1 mi NW; on N side of lake W of Pomona Dam Rd. During 5/1-9/30, $12 without hookups, $16 with elec/wtr. Group camping only rest of year. 14-day limit. 78 sites; 65-ft RVs. Flush toilets, tbls, drkg wtr, showers, dump, picnic shelter, group camp, playground, elec($). Fishing, picnicking, baseball, boating(l).

Fishing Tip: By boat, head north from the park into the creek channels in search of crappies. Focus on submerged brush near shore during April and May; use minnows or jigs with twister-tail grubs. Search out deeper underwater structure in the summer and look for crappies in 15-20 feet along contours, flat areas near drop-offs and around points, drifting minnows early morning and evening.

MINNEAPOLIS (86)

Markley Grove City Park   **$10**
From Hwy 106 at Minneapolis, park is on left after crossing Solomon River bridge. $10. Tbls, toilets, cfga, drkg wtr, elec, shelters, playground, pool, showers. Dump across street at fairgrounds. Fishing, swimming, hunting.

Ottawa   **$5**
State Fishing Lake
7 mi E of Minneapolis on SR 93. $5 elec; free primitive camping. All year; 14-day limit. 120 sites. Tbls, toilets, cfga, drkg wtr, elec($). Boating(l), fishing, hunting.

Fishing Tip: Use spinnerbaits near shoreline cover to catch largemouth bass; try shallow and deep brush piles for crappie. Use shad sides or fresh shad, liver or worms to hook channel catfish.

NEWTON (87)

Harvey County East Park   **$8**
7 mi E of Newton. $8 without hookups ($7 for county residents); $16 with elec ($13 for county residents. 3/1-9/30; 14-day limit. 66 sites. Tbls, flush toilets, cfga, drkg wtr, showers, dump, elec. Fishing, hiking, boating(l), swimming. Tent camping $8 at Camp Hawk Park, 4 mi SW of Newton.

Fishing Tip: Catch walleye and saugeye by trolling plugs or jigging with minnows. The lake also contains channel catfish of up to 8 pounds, largemouth bass up to 6 pounds and white bass.

Harvey County West Park   **$8**
9 mi W of Newton on 12th St to Moundridge Rd. $8 without hookups ($7 for county residents); $16 with elec ($13 for county residents). 3/1-9/30; 14-day limit. 130 sites. Tbls, flush toilets, cfga, drkg wtr, showers, dump, elec, store, playground. Fishing, swimming, biking. 310 acres.

NORTON (88)

Norton State Wildlife Area   **FREE**
3 mi SE of Norton off US 36. Free. All year; 14-day limit. Primitive camping in 7 designated areas. Tbls, toilets, cfga, no drkg wtr, no trash service. Boating(l), fishing, horseback riding & hiking trail, hunting.

Prairie Dog State Park   **$8.50**
4 mi W of Norton on US 36; S on SR 261; at N shore of Sebelius Reservoir. $8.50 without hookups in-season ($7.50 off-season); $13.50-17.50 with hookups. All year; limited facilities in winter; 14-day limit. About 125 undesignated primitive sites, most for tents; 14 designated primitive sites; 16 sites with elec. Tbls, flush toilets, cfga, drkg wtr, showers, elec, dumps, beach. Swimming, boating(ld), fishing, hiking, hunting (in Norton Wildlife Area), 7.5-mi bridle trail. 1,150 acres; 2,000-acre lake.

Fishing Tip: Keith Sebelius Lake has good fishing for wipers, saugeye, largemouth bass, crappie and channel catfish, and it also contains spotted bass, walleye, flathead catfish and blue catfish. Look for largemouth bass near submerged cover and for spotted bass along the dam. This lake produced the state record saugeye (9.81 pounds) in November 1997. Remember that gizzard shad are the primary forage fish; select your lures accordingly.

OSKALOOSA (89)

Longview   **$12**
Corps of Engineers
Perry Lake
5.5 mi W of Oskaloosa on SR 92; 2 mi S on Ferguson Rd; E side of lake. $12 without hookups, $16 with elec. base. 5/1-9/30; 14-day limit. 45 sites (26 with elec); 65-ft RVs. Cfga, tbls, drkg wtr, dump, toilets, showers, elec($), showers, dump. Fishing, boating(ld), picnicking, swimming, hiking. 316 acres. $5 visitor fee charged on weekends & holidays. 2-night minimum stay on weekends.

Fishing Tip: This lake is loaded with fat crappies! Catch them all year around brush piles on tube jigs or minnows. When they're in the shallows chasing shad, use white or yellow twister-tail jigs.

Old Town   **$12**
Corps of Engineers
Perry Lake
6 mi W of Oskaloosa on SR 92; S side before bridge; on E side of lake. $12 without hookups, $16 with elec. 5/1-9/30; 14-day limit. 76 sites on 113 acres; 65-ft RVs. Cfga, flush toilets, drkg wtr, dump, playground, showers, tbls, elec($). Fishing, boating (ld), swimming, hiking, picnicking.

Fishing Tip: Try flat areas with hard bottom for channel catfish, especially at night. In fall and winter, use worms and cut bait near shore. For sauger, bump jigs and minnows along bottom near dropoffs.

OSWEGO (90)

Danny Elliott Park   **$10**
N of town on Commercial St; E on A St over river bridge; on E side of rd. $10 for unreserved sites; $15 for reserved sites; after 2 weeks. 4/1-10/1; 30-day limit (longer with approval). 7 sites for tents, small RVs. Tbls, flush toilets, cfga, showers, drkg wtr. Dump at Kamp Siesta.

Kamp Siesta   **$10**
Labatte County Fairgrounds
1 mi N of US 59 in Oswego on Kansas St, N of fairgrounds. $10 for unreserved sites; $15 for reserved sites. 4/1-10/1; 30-day limit (longer with approva). 30 sites (RVs under 35 ft.). Tbls, flush toilets, cfga, showers, elect($). Store, food, ice, laundry nearby. Fishing, swimming. Pay for site at city offices, 703

Fifth St., on weekdays; evenings or weekends, pay at visitor information center, 515 Commercial.

OTTAWA (91)

Pomona State Park   **$8.50**
14 mi W on SR 68; NW on SR 268; N on SR 368; at S shore of Pomona Reservoir. $8.50 without hookups in-season ($7.50 off-season); $13.50-17.50 with hookups. All year; limited facilities in winter; 14-day limit. 156 sites with elec, some with sewer; numerous primitive sites. Tbls, flush toilets, cfga, drkg wtr, showers, elec($), dump, beach, playground. Swimming, boating(rld), fishing, hiking, horseshoes, volleyball, nature trail. 490 acres.

Fishing Tip: Pomona Lake offers some of the best crappie fishing in Kansas as well as good populations of walleye, white bass and largemouth bass. Pomona has produced state record catfish and wiper. For crappies, focus on submerged brush and other structure.

OXFORD (92)

Napawalla City Park   **$3**
At Oxford (9 mi W of Winfield). $3 base. All year. Base fee for primitive sites; $5 with elec. Limited elec service (25 20/30-amp). Tbls, toilets, cfga, drkg wtr.

PAOLA (93)

Hillsdale State Park   **$8.50**
On W 255th St., Paola (25 mi SW of Kansas City) at Hillsdale Reservoir. $8.50 without hookups in-season ($7.50 off-season); $13.50-17.50 with hookups. All year; limited facilities in winter; 14-day limit. About 200 sites (99 with elec). Tbls, flush toilets, cfga, drkg wtr, showers, dump, shelters, 2 beaches. Boating(l), fishing, hunting, hiking, horseback riding trails, swimming, model airplane flying area. 4,500-acre lake.

Fishing Tip: Walley, largemouth bass, catfish and crappie are plentiful, and excellent habitat is available in the standing timber that was left when the lake was created. In fall, use minnows 10-14 feet deep along the dam to catch crappies. Largemouth bass can nearly always be found in the ends of coves. Cast crankbaits along shallow flats or use jigs with worms or minnows at night to hook walleye.

Lake Miola City Park   **$12**
1 mi N & 1 mi E of Paola. $12 base. 5/1-LD; 14-day limit. Base fee for primitive camping (non-residents); $5 daily elec fee. 54 sites (25 with RV hookups). Tbls, toilets, cfga, drkg wtr, dump, elec($), playgrounds, beach. Boating (l), fishing, swimming, 8 picnic areas, ATV use, volleyball.

PARSONS (94)

Marvel City Park   **$5**
7 blocks E on US 160 from jct with US 59. $5 for 24 RV sites with 30-amp elect; no tents. Tbls, toilets, cfga, drkg wtr, showers, sports field, dump. Walking trail, horseshoes. 58 acres.

Lake Parsons City Park   **$8**
2 mi N of Main St in Parsons on 32nd St; 3 mi W on county rd; 2 mi N, following signs. $8 without elec ($60 annual permit); $12 with elec ($120 annually); tents $5. 4/1-11/1; 10-day limit. 47 sites. Tbls, flush toilets, cfga, drkg wtr, showers, dump, playground, beach. Swimming, fishing, boating (ld). 1,000 acre park; 980-acre lake.

PERRY (95)

Rock Creek   **$12**
Corps of Engineers
Perry Lake
2 mi N of US 24 on CR 1029, then 3 mi W on park rd; W side of lake just above dam. $12 without hookups; $16 with elec; $17 elec/wtr; $18 wtr/50-amp elec. Some primitive camping in designated area. 4/16-10/15; 14-day limit. 141 sites (65 with elec); 65-ft RVs. Drkg wtr, tbls, flush toilets, showers, elec($), dump, fish cleaning stations, playground. Fishing, boating, picnicking, swimming, horseback riding, hiking.

Fishing Tip: The Rock Creek area has a well deserved reputation for producing huge catches of catfish between May and Sept. In the spring, white bass offer fast and furious action, chasing shad in shallow water.

Slough Creek Park   **$12**
Corps of Engineers
Perry Lake
5.5 mi N of Perry on CR 1029; SW on park access rd; E side of lake above dam. $12 without hookups; $16 with elec; $17 at premium sites & wtr/elec sites; $18 with wtr/50-amp elec. 4/16-10/15; 14-day limit. 273 sites (118 with elec); 65-ft RVs. Tbls, flush toilets, dump, showers, elec($), beach, fish cleaning, playground. Fishing, boating (ld), swimming, hiking. $5 visit fee on weekends & holidays. 2-night minimum stay on weekends.

Fishing Tip: Perry Lake contains flathead and channel catfish, sauger, white bass, largemouth bass and walley, but the most sought-after fish is its white crappies. Specimen weighing 1.5 pounds are frequently caught. Sauger, introduced in 1994, are now well over their 15-inch limit.

PHILLIPSBURG (96)

Phillipsburg City Campground   **$10**
About 5 blocks W of US 183 on US 36 at W end of town, turn S on Ft. Bissel Ave & follow signs; small rigs can enter at next entrance. $10. May-Oct. 10 sites. Tbls, flush toilets, cfga, drkg wtr, showers, rec hall, playground, five 30-amp & six 15/20-amp elec/wtr, pool, dump with threaded flush wtr outlet in day-use section. GPS: N39 45.265', W99 20.092'.

PITTSBURG (97)

Big Brutus Visitor Center   **$7**
S of Pittsburg on US 69; W on US 160; S on SR 7; 6 mi W on SR 102, then qtr mi S. Near West Mineral. $7 base for primitive sites for self-contained RVs; $10 with hookups. 10 RV sites. Tbls, cfga, flush toilets, showers, dump, shelter. Exhibits on Big Brutus electric coal shovel. Fishing, hunting, horseback riding.

Lincoln City Park   **$8**
At Hwy 69 bypass & 12th St in Pittsburg. $8 for full hookups. 12 sites. Tbls, flush toilets, cfga, drkg wtr, pool, playground. Fishing, horseshoes, mini-golf, tennis, volleyball, swimming, batting box.

POWHATTAN

Sac & Fox Casino   **FREE**
11 mi S of US 36 on US 75 to casino entrance on E side; RV area at far E end of paved parking lot. Free dry camping, $10 with elec (30 & 50-amp). 12 back-in sites. Drdk wtr, dump. Gambling, golf driving range. GPS at RV sites: N39 41.973', W95 43.586.

PRATT (98)

Pratt County Lake   **$10**
State Fishing Access Site
2.5 mi E of Pratt on SR 54; 1 mi S; at Innenscah River. $10. All year; 5-day limit. 10 sites with elec. Tbls, toilets, cfga, drkg wtr. Boating(l), fishing, picnicking. Adjoins state's Nature Education Center (free), which displays renovated century-old buildings, aquariums, wlidlife mounts. Wtr reported bad tasting. Dump at park on Sixth St.

RANDALL

Randall City Park   **FREE**
S on Main St behind grain elevator complex. Free. 2 sites. 3-day limit. No working elec at last report. Pit toilets in roofless, doorless bldg. GPS: N39 38.352', W98 02.736'.

READING (99)

Lyon State Fishing Lake   **FREE**
5 mi W of Reading on KS 170; 1.5 mi N to campground. Free. All year; 7-day limit. About 100 sites. Tbls, toilets, cfga, firewood, no drkg wtr. Picnicking, boating(l), fishing, swimming. 582 acres; 135-acre lake.

Fishing Tip: Try this lake for walleye, crappies, largemouth bass and channel catfish.

RILEY (101)

Stockdale Park   **$8**
Corps of Engineers
Tuttle Creek Lake
3.5 mi E of Riley on US 24/77; 4.7 mi E on CR 396. During 4/15-9/30, $8 for random camping, $12 at designated sites. Some sites free during rest of year, but no wtr. 14 non-elec sites; 65-ft RVs. Tbls, toilets, cfga, drkg wtr, showers, dump. Boating(l), fishing. 188 acres. 2-night minimum stay on weekends.

Fishing Tip: Excellent channel catfish angling is available just offshore in the old river channel and in the Mill Creek channel just W of the park. Use worms, minnows, shad and crayfish. Also fish Mill Creek's wooded cover and submerged brush piles for crappies, using jigs and live minnows. Try the same areas for largemouth bass.

RUSSELL (102)

Wilson State Park   **$8.50**
20 mi E of Russell on I-70; 8 mi N on SR 232; at S side of Wilson Lake. $8.50 without hookups in-season ($7.50 off-season); $13.50-17.50 with hookups. All year; limited facilities in winter; 14-day limit. About 300 sites (125 elec). Tbls, flush toilets, cfga, drkg wtr, showers, elec, dumps, 2 beaches, store, marina. Swimming, boating(rld), fishing, hiking & biking trails, volleyball, basketball, horseshoes, interpretive programs, mountain biking trail.

Fishing Tip: Campers at this park are well positioned for the lake's excellent walleye fishing, especially in early April, when good numbers are caught off the face of the dam. Try up-lake mud flats during may and June. Jigs, spoons and trolled baits are most effective. Near the park, look for walleyes at submerged islands and river channel dropoffs. The state record walleye of just over 13 pounds was caught from Wilson Lake on a Rapala in 1996.

SABETHA (103)

Sabetha City Lake   **FREE**
5 mi W of Sabetha in Memaha County. Free. Primitive undesignated sites. Toilet, cfga, no other facilities except picnic shelter; no drkg wtr. Fishing at 114-acre lake for largemouth bass & channel catfish. Note: no camping at nearby Pony Creek Lake.

ST. FRANCIS (104)

Roadside Park   **FREE**
Just S of Hwy 36 in St. Francis. Free. Hot showers, tbls, flush toilets, cfga, shelters, drkg wtr, dump.

St. Francis Sandpits   **FREE**
State Fishing Area
1 mi W and 2 mi S of St. Francis. Free. All year; 7-day limit. Primitive camping area.

Tbls, toilet, cfga, no drkg wtr.
Fishing Tip: Fish the sandpits for largemouth bass, bluegill and channel catfish.

ST. MARYS

St. Marys City Park   **$5**
On US 24 NW of Topeka, take 3rd or 6th St 4 blks S to S side of the park. $5. 3-day limit. Three 30/30-amp elec sites. Tbls, flush toilets, cfga, drkg wtr, dump at sewage plant on S side of town. Swimming pool, tennis, horseshoes.

ST. PAUL (105)

Neosho State Fishing Lake   **FREE**
1 mi E of St. Paul on SR 57. Free. All year; 7-day limit. 5 RV sites. Tbls, toilets, cfga, drkg wtr, no trash service. Fishing, boating(l), swimming, picnic area, hunting. 92-acre lake adjacent to Neosho Wildlife Area.

Fishing Tip: Good fishing for largemouth bass and crappie; lake also contains catfish and sunfish. For bass, try jigs, plastic worms, crankbaits and spinnerbaits around brush piles and at dropoffs. Use jigs & minnows in the same areas for crappies. For channel catfish, try shad sides, grasshoppers, shrimp and livers near the three automatic feeders.

SCOTT CITY (106)

Scott State Park   **$8.50**
10 mi N of Scott City on US 83; 3 mi N on SR 95; at Lake Scott. $8.50 without hookups in-season ($7.50 off-season); $13.50-17.50 with hookups. All year; limited facilities in winter; 14-day limit. About 200 sites (60 with elec). Tbls, flush toilets, cfga, drkg wtr, showers, elec($), beach, playground, dump. Swimming, boating (ld), canoeing(r), fishing, hiking, horseback riding, nature trails. Buffalo & elk herds. 1,180 acres.

SEDAN (108)

Old City Lake Park   **$7**
7 mi N of Sedan on SR 99. $7. All year. 10 primitive sites. Tbls, cfga, no drkg wtr. Boating(l), fishing.

Sedan City Park   **$7**
5 mi N of Sedan on SR 99. $7. Al lyear. Tbls, toilets, cfga, drkg wtr, elec, pool, playground. Tennis, swimming.

SILVER LAKE (110)

Shawnee   **FREE**
State Fishing Lake
7 mi N of US 24 in Silver Lake; 2 mi E to campground. Free, but $5 with elec All year; 7-day limit. 50 sites; 135-acre lake. Tbls, toilets, cfga, drkg wtr, dump. Fishing, boating(l).

Fishing Tip: Wipers (a cross between striped and white bass) provide excellent

fishing action in this lake, which also contains largemouth bass, crappie and catfish. The state record rainbow trout (9 pounds) was caught from this lake on a jig in 1982. Most bass are too small to keep. Catfish 12-14 inches are stocked regularly. Crappie average 8-9 inches.

SMITH CENTER

Smith Center City Park   **FREE**
On N side of US 36 at W end of town; gps N39 47.100, W98 47.746. Free. All year; 24-hr limit. Big rigs okay. Tbls, toilets, cfga, drkg wtr. Dump at nearby Peterson Industries, maker of Excel RVs (free factory tours). Elev 1750 ft.

SPEARVILLE (111)

Hain State Fishing Lake   **FREE**
1 mi SW of Spearville on US 56, then right on county rd for 5 mi. Free. All year except during duck season; 7-day limit. Primitive undesignated sites at 53acre lake. No facilities except cfga, tbls; no trash pickup. Fishing, huntiing.

STAFFORD

Staford R-V Hook-Ups (Priv.)   **$8**
W of S. Buckeye St & E Main St on unnamed diagonal street, SE of water tower, 1 blk N of grain silos, following signs. $8 (drop box on shed wall facing sites. Two 30-amp elec/wtr, 4 pr of 15-amp elec, dump, tbls. GPS: N37 57.331', W98 35.875.

STERLING (112)

Sterling Lake   **$7**
City Campground
In south Sterling, from SR 14 (South Broadway Ave), turn E on East Garfield St for several blocks to the lake; entrance on SE corner of lake before railroad tracks. Warning: Use first entrance past the restroom because the second has a large, low limb over the rd. $7 with 30-amp elec & full hookups. 14 sites. Tbls, flush toilets, cfga, drkg wtr, pool, playground, dump. Swimming, beach volleyball, tennis, horseshoes, hiking, fishing. A location for filming of the movie, "Picnic."

STOCKTON (113)

Nicodemus   **FREE**
National Historical Site
About 10 mi W of Stockton on US 24; on S side of of hwy at village of Nicodemus in front of the park. Free. 1-night limit. Paved frontage rd with overnight parking. Drkg wtr, pit toilets, cfga, tbls, 15-amp elec (long cords needed). Site of the last remaining all-black settlements in Kansas.

Rooks State Fishing Lake   **FREE**
Half mi S of Stockton on US 183; 2 mi W; 2

mi S to park. Free. Apr-Oct; 7-day limit. 15 sites. Tbls, toilets, cfga, drkg wtr, firewood. Picnicking, fishing, boating(l). 64 acres. Periodically dry. Ltd facilities in winter.

Travel Tip: Rooks County Historical Museum at the fairgrounds contains valuable & interesting historical artifacts from the area.

Fishing Tip: The primary gamefish in this lake is largemouth bass; it also contains catfish and sunfish.

Stockton City Park   **$10**
From US 183 in center of town, qtr mi W on US 24 (Main St), left into park following signs. All year; 7-day limit. $10. About 5 sites; no RV size limit. 30-amp elec, tbls, flush toilets, showers, drkg wtr, dump. Limited facilities in winter. Swimming pool, ball fields, sand volleyball, disc golf, skateboard park, playground, fitness trail. GPS: N39 26.149, W099 16.844.

Webster State Park   **$8.50**
8 mi W of Stockton on US 24; S on access rd; split between N & S shores of Webster Reservoir. $8.50 without hookups in-season ($7.50 off-season); $13.50-17.50 with hookups. All year; limited facilities in winter; 14-day limit. 178 sites (6 elec, 72 elec/wtr). Tbls, flush toilets, cfga, drkg wtr, showers, elec, dump, beach, playgrounds, fish cleaning station, 2 fishing piers. Swimming, boating (ld), fishing, tennis, ball fields, volleyball, hiking trail, horseshoes, nature trail, hunting.

Travel Tip: The Nearby Nicodemus National Historic Site, 10 mi W, is the only remaining western town established by African-Americans.

Fishing Tip: Webster Lake contains largemouth & smallmouth bass, walleye, crappies, channel catfish, wipers and some white bass. Find crappie around fish attractors; catch them on minnows & jigs. For white bass and wipers, cast jigs from shore near the dam.

Webster   **FREE**
State Wildlife Area
8 mi W of Stockton off US 24. Free. All year; 14-day limit. Primitive camping in 5 designated areas. Toilets, cfga, no drkg wtr, no trash service. Fishing, hunting, boating(l), hiking, horseback riding. Fish cleaning station on N shore; pier at stillng basin. 5,500 acres surrounding 3,800-acre lake.

Fishing Tip: Rainbow trout can always be found in the stilling basin; still fish with Power Baits and salmon eggs or cast small spinners. The trout average 10-14 inches, with some larger.

SYRACUSE (114)

Hamilton State Fishing Lake   **FREE**
3 mi W of Syracuse on US 50; 2 mi N to campground. Free. All year; 7-day limit. Undesignated sites; 432 acres. Tbls, toilets, cfga, no drkg wtr. Picnicking, fishing, boating(l).

Fishing Tip: Primary fish in this lake usually are largemouth bass and channel catfish, with plenty of sunfish and bluegills, but at last report (fall of 2001), the lake was dry.

✪ TOPEKA (115)

Perry Reservoir State Park   **$8.50**
10 mi E of Topeka on US 24; 4 mi N; SW of Perry Lake. $8.50 without hookups in-season ($7.50 off-season); $13.50-17.50 with hookups. All year; limited facilities in winter; 14-day limit. About 350 primitive sites and 124 with elec. Tbls, flush toilets, cfga, drkg wtr, showers, elec, dump, beach, playground. Swimming, boating(ld), fishing, hiking, hunting, mountain biking & equestrian trails, hunting. 1,597 acres.

Fishing Tip: Perry Lake draws fishermen for its crappie and channel catfish angling. Best places for crappie are in Slough Creek, Rock Creek and the Old Town area. For channel catfish, try the mud flats at the upper end of the lake. The Delaware River also offers good catfishing. In the spring, try the white bass runs up the river, and catch white bass in open water on the lake when they chase schools of shad near the surface.

TORONTO (116)

Woodson   **FREE**
State Fishing Lake
From US 54, S on KS 105 to Toronto; 5 mi E on co rd. Free. All year; 7-day limit. 50 sites. Tbls, toilets, cfga, no drkg wtr, dump. Picnicking, fishing, boating(rl). 180-acre lake, also known as Lake Fegan; built during Depressioon by the CCC.

Fishing Tip: This lake has a wide array of fishing opportunity. It contains wiper, walleye, striped bass, spotted bass, largemouth and smallmouth bass, crappie and panfish. But most importantly, the state record black crappie (4 pounds 10 ounces) was caught here on a live minnow in 1957. Channel catfish run to 15 pounds, and wiper up to 4 pounds can be caught in open water around the dam.

WAKEENEY (117)

Cedar Bluff State Park   **$8.50**
8 mi SE of WaKeeney on I-70; 15 mi S on SR 147. $8.50 without hookups in-season ($7.50 off-season); $13.50-17.50 with hookups. All year; limited facilities in winter; 14-day limit. 121 elec sites, numerous primitive sites and the state park system's only group campground. Tbls, flush toilets, cfga, drkg wtr, showers, elec($), dump, beach, 2 fishing piers. Swimming, boating(ld), fishing, hiking, horseshoes, sand volleyball, basketball, frisbee golf, interpretive programs, hunting. 6,000-acre lake.

Fishing Tip: In late summer or early fall, look for crappies at underwater shelfs 24-35 feet deep and close to brush & timber. Use live minnows with jigs or slab spoons. For white bass and wipers, try the mouth of

Spillway Cove, Boy Scout Cove and Church Camp Cove on the north side; use slab spoons.

Cedar Bluff   **FREE**
State Wildlife Area
13 mi S of the I-70 Ogallah exit on SR 147. Free. Primitive caming in 9 designated areas. Toilets, cfga, no drkg wtr. Boating(l), hiking, biking, horseback riding, hunting.

WAKEFIELD (118)

Clay County Park   **$8**
3 blocks S of SR 82 on Dogwood St at Wakefield. $8 for tents; $14 for RVs with elec/wtr. 4/15-10/15. 250 sites (35-ft RV limit). Tbls, flush toilets, cfga, drkg wtr, showers, store, playgrounds, dump. Swimming, fishing, boating(ld), horseshoes, volleyball.

WASHINGTON (119)

Marcon RV Park   **$10**
1 block S of Hwy 36 in Washington. $10-12. 4 sites. Tbls, toilets, cfga, drkg wtr, hookups, dump. Private campground.

Rose Garden RV Camp (Private)   **$12**
2 blocks S of Hwy 36/15 jct at 127 E. 9th St in Washington. $12-14. 9 sites. Tbls, toilets, cfga, drkg wtr, elec.

Rotary Park   **FREE**
Half mi E of Washington on KS 36. Free. All year. Undesignated sites. Tbls, no toilets, well drkg wtr. Picnicking.

Washington   **FREE**
State Fishing Lake
7 mi N of US 36 (in Washington); 3 mi W to campground, just S of Nebraska line. Free. All year; 7-day limit. 20 sites; 352 acres; 111-acre lake. Tbls, toilets, cfga, drkg wtr. Picnicking, fishing, boating(l). 352-acre hunting area.

Washington City Park   **Donation**
2 blocks S of US 36 in Washington at 1100 D St (just past fairgrounds). Donation first 72 hrs, $10 thereafter. All year. 25 sites, some pull-through. 3-day limit in 30 days; longer with permission. Drkg wtr, cfga, hookups, playground, flush toilets, showers, 20 & 30-amp elec, dump by donation. Nature walks, swimming pool, tennis. Arena for horse shows, midget car track. Munchkinland playground has Wizard of Oz theme, poppfield entrance, "emerald castle," tornado slide, witch's castle, monkey trapeze. GPS: N39 48.511', W97 03.262'.

WELLINGTON (120)

Wellington Lake   **$8**
Municipal Recreation Area
5 mi W & 1.5 mi S of Wellington. $8 (includes $4 entry permit) for primitive sites; $11.50

with elec. 2/1-11/30; 30-day limit. Tbls, toilets, cfga, drkg wtr (except in winter), elec($), dump. Boating(lr), fishing, picnicking, swimming, hunting.

Fishing Tip: This lake has a good population of channel catfish; catch them around the feeders using worms and -- believe it or not! -- cat food and dog food. Crappie up to 1.5 pounds are caught on jigs and minnows, and anglers report catches of flathead catfish of 15-30 pounds using bluegills and goldfish or shad. Drift nightcrawlers to find saugeye and walleye up to 4 pounds. Wipers are caught suspended over deep water, chasing shad.

WESTMORELAND (121)

Pottawatomie   **FREE**
State Fishing Lake #1
5 mi N of Westmoreland on KS 99. Free. All year; 7-day limit. 20 sites; 190 acres; 24-acre lake. Tbls, toilets, cfga, drkg wtr, firewood. Picnicking, fishing, boating(l).

Fishing Tip: This lake is stocked with crappie, largemouth bass, catfish and sunfish. Bass weigh 1-5 pounds; crappie are small. Use live bait, livers and cut bait virtually anywhere in the lake for channel catfish.

WICHITA (122)

Cheney State Park   **$8.50**
20 mi W of Wichita on US 54; 5 mi N on SR 251; at Cheney Reservoir. $8.50 without hookups in-season ($7.50 off-season); $13.50-17.50 with hookups. All year; limited facilities in winter; 14-day limit. 185 elec sites, numerous primitive sites. Tbls, flush toilets, cfga, drkg wtr, showers, elec, 4 dumps, beach, marina. Swimming, boating (rld), fishing, hiking. 1,913 acres; 9,537-acre lake.

Fishing Tip: Angling here is excellent for channel catfish and white bass; good for crappie, striped bass and wipers, and fair for walleyes. White bass run upriver in May. Three deepwater fish attractors, marked with buoys, are quite productive when crappie move out of shallow water.

Cheney   **FREE**
State Wildlife Area
20 mi W of Wichita off US 54. Free. All year; 15-day limit. Primitive camping in designated areas. Toilets, cfga, no drkg wtr. Hunting, fishing, hiking, gun safety range; interpretive nature trail

WINFIELD (124)

Cowley County Fairgrounds   **$3**
1 mi W of downtown Winfield on US 160; at Walnut River. $3 base; $6 with elec. 4/1-11/1;15-day limit. 600 sites with 20-amp elec plus limited 30-amp sites. Tbls, elec($), flush toilets, cfga, drkg wtr, dump (near horse barn). Fishing, boating(l). 10.2-acre primitive camping area; 6.5-acre developed area.

Pecan Grove area has 44 acres of primitive camping & some electrical service; Tunnel Mill Park on W 19th has 11.3 acres of primitive camping. Pay at on-site drop box or at city hall.

Winfield City Lake   **$8**
10 mi NE of Winfield. $8. 4/15-11/1; 14-day limit. 80 sites. Tbls, flush toilets, cfga, drkg wtr, showers, elec, beach; $12 full hookups. Fishing, waterskiing, boating(l) hiking, swimming, picnicking, hunting. Daily $4 or $25 annual permit required. Primitive camping $2 with daily ($4) or annual ($30) permit.

Fishing Tip: For crappies, focus on Cowley County #1 Cove or along the rocky bluffs on the S shore. Catch walleye 18-23 inches off rocky points in 6-10 feet, and hook wipers while trolling or drifting at the mouth of Manna Cove and on the roadbed on old Cowley #1 on N side. Nightcrawlers and shad produce flathead catfish up to 14 pounds.

Winfield Island Park   **$3**
N of Winfield. $3. Tbls, toilets, cfga, drkg wtr. Fishing.

WINONA (125)

Logan County   **FREE**
State Fishing Lake
9 mi S of Winona. Free. All year; 7-day limit. Undesignated sites. Tbls, firewood, cfga. Picnicking, fishing. 271 acres; 75-acre lake.

YATES CENTER (126)

Toronto State Park   **$8.50**
12 mi W of Yates Center on US 54; 5 mi S on SR 105. $8.50 without hookups in-season ($7.50 off-season); $13.50-17.50 with hookups. All year; limited facilities in winter; 14-day limit. 145 sites (3 camping areas; 15 full hookup sites, 47 elec). Tbls, flush toilets, cfga, drkg wtr, showers, elec($), dump. Swimming beach, boating(ld), fishing. 1,075 acres; 2,800-acre lake.

Fishing Tip: Both Toronto Lake and the Verdigris River are noted for excellent white bass, white crappie and flathead & channel catfish. Find good catfish by using shad sides on the sunken railroad bed. Try worms, crayfish or spinners around Walnut Creek stumps for largemouth bass. Find white crappie on rocky points and around standing timber, using minnows or white jigs.

Yates Center Reservoir Park   **$4**
3 mi S of Yates Center on Hwy 75; about 3 mi W on 80th RD or 4 mi W on Hwy 54, then 3 mi S on Indian Rd, following signs. $4 (or $22 seasonal permit) daily use fee, includes primitive camping on 500 acres around the lake. Toilets, cfga, drkg wtr. Fishing, boating(l), hiking, hunting.

Fishing Tip: Yates Center Reservoir has an exclllent largemouth bass but a small population of smallmouths, caught most often at the dam area and near rocky points. Walleye are numerous; catch them off ledges and drop-offs. Wiper up to 10 pounds are caught on artificial lures.

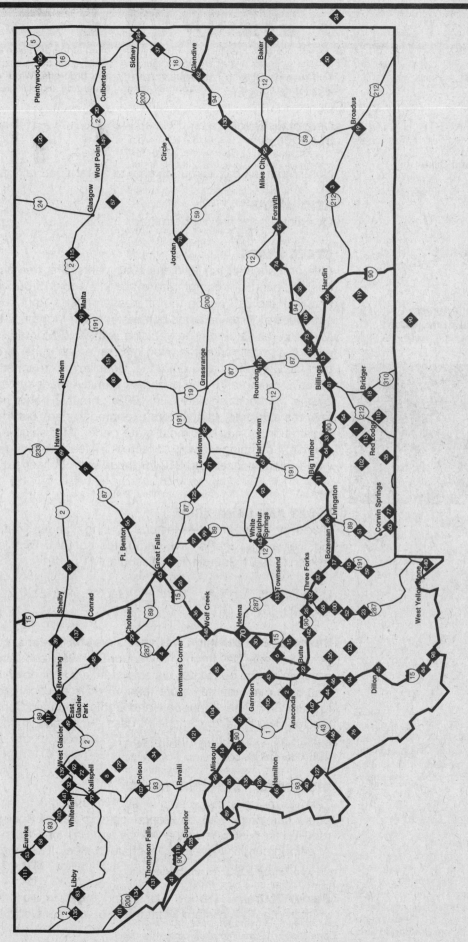

MONTANA

MISCELLANEOUS
Capital:
Helena
Nickname:
Treasure State
Motto:
Oo y Plata (Gold and Silver)
Flower:
Bitterroot
Tree:
Ponderosa Pine
Bird:
Western Meadowlark
Song:
"Montana"

Internet Address:
www.travel.state.mt.us

Toll-free number for travel information: 1-800-VISIT-MT (out of state); 406-444-2654 (in state).

Dept of Fish, Wildlife and Parks, 1420 E 6th Ave, Helena, MT 59620, 406-444-1200.

Note: Montana campgrounds charge a state bed tax of 4.8%.

REST AREAS
Overnight stops are not permitted.

STATE PARKS
Although a few of the Montana state parks offer free primitive camping, in general, overnight camping fees are $12 and $15 during the peak season and $10 and $13 during the off-season (Oct 1-April 30). In addition, daily entry fees of $5 are charged non-residents of Montana at most of the parks. Montana residents driving vehicles with valid Montana license plates can enter the state parks free. Non-residents can either buy an annual passport for $25 or pay a $5 entry fee. Usually, maximum stay at state parks is 14 days during a 30-day period. A primitive park system was established by the Montana legislature in 1993; primitive parks have a minimum of services available, with visitors expected to pack out their own trash. Self-registration is in use at most state parks. At Fishing Access Sites where overnight camping fees are collected, $7 fees are charged all year for those with fishing licenses and $12 for those without licenses. 406/444-3750.

FLOAT AND CAMP TRIPS
Blackfoot River. Activities include hunting, fishing, floating and free camping. For a map that shows campsites contact: Dept of Fish and Game, Region 2, 3201 Spurgin Rd, Missoula, MT 59801.

U.S. Forest Service - Northern Region, PO Box 7669, Missoula, MT 406/329-3511.

Beaverhead/Deerlodge National Forests. The main camping season is from Memorial Day through the Labor Day weekend. Although most campgrounds remain open later, water system are shut down to prevent freezing. Campers may not stay more than 16 days at each campground. At Philipsburg Bay, Pine, Lodgepole and Cable Mountain Campgrounds, all near Georgetown Lake, the limit is 14 days. When this limit is reached, move at least 5 miles to another campsite. 420 Barrett St., Dillon, MT 59725-3572. 406/683-3900.

BITTERROOT NATIONAL FOREST
This 1.6-million-acre forest in west central Montana and east central Idaho offers camping at 18 developed campgrounds. Special use permits are required for float trips on the Selway and Salmon Rivers during the summer. At campgrounds where fees are charged, free off-season camping is permitted. Forest supervisor, 1801 N. 1st St, Hamilton, MT 39840; 406/363-7100.

Custer National Forest. Consisting of 1.2 million acres, this forest is scattered across eastern Montana and western North Dakota. Most of its campgrounds have occupancy periods of 10 days. Generally, its sites have recommended RV limits of about 30 feet. 1310 Main St, Billings, MT 59105. 406-657-6200.

Flathead National Forest

The official camping season is Memorial Day weekend through Labor Day weekend, although most campgrounds remain open to free camping after the regular season. However, water systems are shut down to prevent freeze damage, and trash collection is discontinued. Campers are requested to pack out their own trash during off-season periods. All campground limit stay to 14 days in one location; when this limit is reached, the camper may move a minimum of five miles to another campsite unless special written permission has been given by the appropriate district office. 1935 3rd Ave East, Kallispell, MT 59901. 406/758-5204.

Gallatin National Forest, PO Box 130, Bozeman, MT 59771. 406/587-6701.

Helena National Forest, 2880 Skyway Drive, Helena, MT 59601. 406/449-5201.

Kootenai National Forest. Many of the forest's 40 developed campgrounds are open all year, or when accessible, even though the managed period is generally from June through September. Free off-season camping is permitted in some of the campgrounds where fees are charged during the managed season. Forest Supervisor, 1101 US Highway 2 West, Libby, MT 59923. 406/293-6211.

Lewis and Clark National Forest, 1101 15th St. North, Great Falls, MT 59403. 406-791-7700.

Lolo National Forest, Building 24A, Fort Missoula, Missoula, MT 59801. 406/329-3750.

Bighorn Canyon National Recreation Area. Three developed campgrounds are available -- Afterbay, Horseshoe Bend and Barry's Landing -- in addition to two camps that are accessible only by boat: Medicine Creek and Black Canyon. Free back-country permits are necessary for camping in non-designated areas. Daily entry fees, $5; $30 annual. Box 7458, Fort Smith, MT 59035-7458.

Bureau of Land Management, 500 Southgate Dr, Billings, MT 59101. 406/896-5000.

BUREAU OF RECLAMATION:

Many reclamation projects are managed for recreation by cooperating sister agencies. Pishkun and Willow Creek Reservoirs and Intake Diversion Dam are managed by the Montana Department of Fish, Wildlife and Parks. Gibson Reservoir and Hungry Horse Reservoir are managed by the U.S. Forest Service. Lake Sherburne at Glacier National Park and Bighorn Lake behind Yellowtail Dam are managed by the National Park Service.

BOR's Canyon Ferry Lake property had been administered by the state parks department, but the property and its various camping areas have been returned to the bureau. The BOR is now operating the campgrounds, charging camping fees with no entry fees.

The bureau also directly manages several projects, including Clark Canyon Reservoir and Barretts Park near Dillon; Tiber Reservoir (Lake Elwell) near Chester; Fresno Reservoir near Malta; Anita Reservoir near Pompeys Pillar, and the Huntley Diversion Dam on the Yellowstone River. All those reclamation-administered recreation sites are free for camping and day-use. Vault toilets are provided in all camping areas; drinking water is available at many, and all reservoirs are accessible by concrete boat ramps. Clark Canyon and Tiber feature public concessions that provide on-site gasoline, groceries and other amenities. Bureau of Reclamation, Montana Projects Office, PO Box 30137, Billings, MT 59107-0137; 406/657-6202. For details about camping at Canyon Ferry Lake, contact the Canyon Ferry field office, 7661 Canyon Ferry Rd, Helena, MT 59601.

U.S. Army Corps of Engineers, PO Box 208, Fort Peck, MT 59923; 406/526-3411. The Corps operates campgrounds at Libby Dam and Fort Peck Lake. All sites are free except those at West End Campground and Downstream Campground.

ABSAROKEE (1)

Buffalo Jump   **FREE**
Stillwater River
State Fishing Access Site
21 mi SW of Absarokee on Secondary 419; at Stillwater River. Free. All year; 7-day limit. Primitive undesignated sites on 6.8 acres; 35-ft RV limit. Toilets, cfga, no drkg wtr. Boating, fishing.

Fishing tip: Also known as Nye Bridge, this access area has productive pools, boulder pockets and riffles. Between Absarokee and the Yellowstone, lunker brown trout are frequently caught from the Stillwater. Most fish are 2-4 pounds, but some in excess of 6 pounds are landed quite often.

Castle Rock   **FREE**
Stillwater River
State Fishing Access Site
23 mi SW of Absarokee on Secondary 420; at Stillwater River. All year; 7-day limit. Primitive undesignated sites on 80 acres; 35-ft RV limit. Tbls, toilets, cfga, drkg wtr. Fishing, hiking, boating, swimming. Spectacular scenery, but difficult access.

Fishing tip: Some of the best whitefish angling in the state is available from this section of the Stillwater River. Castle Rock has some excellent shallow riffles and pockets that produce well.

Cliff Swallow   **FREE**
Stillwater River
State Fishing Access Site
10 mi W of Absarokee on Secondary 420; at Stillwater River. All year; 7-day limit. Primitive undesignated sites on 160 acres; 32-ft RV limit. Toilets, cfga, no drkg wtr. Fishing, boating, swimming. Easy access.

Fishing tip: For trout, concentrate first on whitewater breaking around and over boulders. Frequently, those small pools hold big fish. Also look for logjams, deep banks, the inside of riffle-corners and fast water dumping into slow sections. If you don't mind a short drive, try a dirt road access at Thompson's bridge, 1 mi below Absarokee, but ask the landowner's permission.

Moraine   **FREE**
Stillwater River
State Fishing Access Site
24 mi W of Absarokee on Secondary 420; at Upper Stillwater River. Free. All year; 7-day limit. Primitive undesignated sites on 60 acres. Toilets, tbls, cfga, drkg wtr. Fishing, swimming. Difficult access.

Fishing tip: Moraine has outstanding pocket water that holds trout. The upper Stillwater is most suitable for fly fishing, while other sections appeal more to lure and bait fishermen. Try small versions of stonefly imitations such as the Soft Pillow or Bird's Stone. Fish dry or slightly submerged.

Rosebud Isle   **FREE**
State Fishing Access Site
3 mi S of Absarokee on SR 78; 3 mi SW on Secondary 419 to Fishtail; at West Rosebud Creek. Free. All year; 7-day limit. Primitive undesignated sites on 11 acres; 35-ft RV limit. Toilets, cfga, no drkg wtr. Fishing. Difficult access.

ANACONDA (2)

Lost Creek State Park   **FREE**
1.5 mi E of Anaconda on SR 1 to milepost 5; 2 mi N on Secondary 273; 6 mi W on county rd. Free camping, but donations accepted. 5/1-11/30; 7-day limit. 25 primitive sites (23-ft RV limit). Tbls, toilets, cfga, drkg wtr. Fishing, biking, interpretive display. 25 acres. 50-ft Lost Creek Falls. View mountain goats & bighorn sheep.

Racetrack   **FREE**
Deerlodge National Forest
3.1 mi E of Anaconda on MT 1; NW on FR 169. Free. 6/15-9/15; open rest of year, weather permitting, but wtr shut off; 16-day limit. 13 sites (RVs under 23 ft). Tbls, toilets, cfga, drkg wtr. Picnicking; fishing. Elev 6000 ft; 5 acres. Stream. Geological.

Travel tip: 4 mi W to ghost town of Danielsville via very poor motor rd (unsuitable for passenger cars).

Sportsman's Club Park   **$5**
25 mi S of Anaconda on MT 273; 2 mi W on Hwy 43. Free, but $5 donations suggested. 5/15-10/31; 10-day limit. 30 sites. Tbls, toilets, cfga, firewood, drkg wtr, beach, bike trails. Group camping. Swimming, picnicking, fishing, hiking, rockhounding, biking.

Spring Hill   **$10**
Deerlodge National Forest
10.7 mi NW of Anaconda on MT 1. $10. 6/15-9/15; 16-day limit; free rest of year, weather permitting, but no drkg wtr. 15 sites (RVs under 23 ft). Toilets, tbls, cfga, drkg wtr, no trash service. Fishing, hiking. Elev 6400 ft.

Warm Springs   **FREE**
Deerlodge National Forest
10.5 mi W of Anaconda on SR 1; 2.5 mi N on FR 170. Free. About 6/20-9/15; 16-day limit. 6 sites (16-ft RV limit). Tbls, toilets, cfga, drkg wtr. Fishing, hiking. Elev 6500 ft; 2 acres.

ASHLAND (3)

Cow Creek   **FREE**
Custer National Forest
4 mi E of Ashland on US 212; 20 mi S on CR 485; 5 mi W on FR 95; at Cow Creek. Free. 5/15-11/1; 14-day limit. 5 sites; 32-ft RV limit. Tbls, toilets, cfga, no drkg wtr. Hiking, hunting, horseback riding. Fee may be charged.

Holiday Springs   **FREE**
Custer National Forest
5 mi E of Ashland on US 212; 9.5 mi NE on FR 423; E on FR 777; at East Fork Otter Creek. Free. All year; 14-day limit. 3 primitive sites; 30-ft RV limit. No facilities, no drkg wtr. Hiking, horseback riding Elev 3120 ft.

Red Shale   **FREE**
Custer National Forest
6 mi E of Ashland on US 212; at East Fork Otter Creek. Free. MD-11/30; 10-day limit. 14 sites; 32-ft RV limit. Tbls, toilets, cfga, drkg wtr. Hiking, horseback riding, fishing. Elev 3000 ft.

AUGUSTA (4)

Bean Lake   **$7**
State Fishing Access Site
14 mi S of Augusta on SR 434. $7 with fishing license; $12 otherwise. All year; 14-day limit. 25 tent sites; no trailers. Tbls, toilets, cfga, no drkg wtr. Swimming, boating(l), fishing (rainbow trout), hiking. 33-acre lake.

Benchmark   **$6**
Lewis and Clark National Forest
14 mi W of Augusta on CR 235; 16 mi SW on FR 235. $6. Open MD-11/30, but free & no wtr after LD; 14-day limit. 25 sites (35-ft RV limit). Tbls, toilets, cfga, drkg wtr, no trash service. Fishing, hiking. Trailhead for horsemen & backpackers to the Skapegoat Wilderness; feeding troughs , hitching posts. Elev 5200 ft; 19 acres.

Home Gulch   **$6**
Lewis and Clark National Forest
4 mi W of Augusta on Manix St; 17 mi NW on Sun River Canyon Rd; 2 mi W on FR 108; at North Fork of Sun River. $6 during MD-LD; free LD-11/30 but no wtr; 14-day limit. 15 sites (16-ft RV limit). Tbls, toilets, cfga, drkg wtr, no trash service. Fishing, boating (l), nature trails, swimming. Trail into Bob Marshall Wilderness. Grizzly bear country. Elev 4400 ft; 6 acres.

Fishing tip: There's good fishing in the river for rainbow & cutthroat trout.

Mortimer Gulch   **$8**
Lewis and Clark National Forest
4 mi W of Augusta on Manix St; 22 mi NW of Augusta on Sun River Canyon Rd; 4 mi W on FR 108; 3 mi N on FR 8984; near Gibson Reservoir. $8 during MD-LD; free LD-11/30 but no wtr; 14-day limit. 28 sites (22-ft RV limit). Tbls, toilets, cfga, drkg wtr, no trash service. Hiking (trailhead to the Bob Marshall Wilderness). Swimming, boating (l), waterskiing, fishing, horseback riding. Elev 5300 ft; 8 acres.

Fishing tip: Fish for rainbow & cutthroat trout in either the 1,300-acre reservoir or the North Fork of the Sun River. 4WD needed to reach the boat ramp.

Nilan Reservoir   **$7**
State Fishing Access Site
10 mi W of Augusta on county rd. $7 with fishing license; $12 otherwise. All year; 7-day limit. Primitive undesignated sites; 35-ft RV limit. Toilets, cfga, no drkg wtr. Boating(l), fishing. 3.3 acres. GPS: 47.473, -112.52.

South Fork   **$8**
Lewis and Clark National Forest
31 mi W of Augusta on Benchmark Rd (FR

235). $8. MD-11/30, but free & no wtr after LD; 14-day limit. 7 sites (35-ft RV limit). Tbls, toilets, cfga, drkg wtr, no trash service. Fishing, hiking & bridle trails into Bob Marshall Wilderness and Scapegoat Wilderness. Be wary of grizzly bears. Elev 5500 ft; 9 acres.

Wood Lake   **$6**
Lewis and Clark National Forest
24 mi W of Augusta on FR 235 (Benchmark Rd). $6. Open MD-11/30, but free & no wtr after LD; 14-day limit. 9 sites (35-ft RV limit). Tbls, toilets, cfga, drkg wtr. Fishing, swimming, hiking.

Willow Creek Reservoir   **$7**
State Fishing Access Site
5 mi NW of Augusta on Gibson Reservoir Rd (CR 108). $7 with fishing license; $12 otherwise. All year; 7-day limit. Primitive undesignated sites; 35-ft RV limit. Toilets, cfga, no drkg wtr. Boating(l), fishing. Difficult access. 1,396 acres. GPS: 45.555, -112.437.

BAKER (5)

Medicine Rocks State Park   **FREE**
25 mi S of Baker on SR 7 to milepost 10; 1 mi W on county rd. All year; 14-day limit. 12 undesignated primitive sites; 50-ft RV limit. Tbls, toilets, cfga, drkg wtr (5/30-9/1), no trash service. Hiking trail. Group camping area. No metal detectors. 332 acres; elev 3441 ft.

South Sandstone Reservoir   **FREE**
State Fishing Access Site
3.5 mi S off US 12 near milepost 75; then 2.5 mi W on gravel county rd. Free. All year; 7-day limit. Primitive undesignated sites; 55-ft RV limit. Tbls, toilets, cfga, no drkg wtr. Boating(l), fishing, swimming. Difficult access. 581 acres. GPS: 46.333, -104.474.

BASIN (6)

Basin Canyon   **FREE**
Deerlodge National Forest
5 mi N of Basin on I-15; 3 mi NW on FR 172. Free. Elev 5800 ft. MD-9/15; 14-day limit. 2 sites (RVs under 17 ft). Tbls, toilets, cfga, firewood, no drkg wtr. Picnicking; fishing; horseback riding (1 mi). On Basin Creek.

Ladysmith Campground   **FREE**
Deerlodge National Forest
4 mi W of Basin on I-15; 4 mi W on FR 82. Free. Elev 5600 ft. About MD-12/1; 14-day limit. 6 sites. Tbls, toilets, cfga, no drkg wtr. Picnicking; fishing; horseback riding (1 mi).

Merry Widow   **$7.50**
Health Mine & Campground
E of I-15 at exit 156 near Basin; at Boulder River. $7.50 base without hookups; $12 with elec; $15 full hookups. 57 sites. Tbls, flush toilets, cfga, drkg wtr, showers, hookups($), coin laundry, dump. Fishing, birdwatching, horseshoes, mountain biking

Mormon Gulch   **FREE**
Deerlodge National Forest
4 mi W of Basin on I-15; 2 mi W on FR 82. Free. About 6/20-9/15; 16-day limit. Elev 5500 ft. 16 sites on 10 acres (RVs under 17 ft). Tbls, toilets, cfga, firewood, no drkg wtr. Picnicking.

Whitehouse   **FREE**
Deerlodge National Forest
4 mi W of Basin on I-15; 8 mi W on FR 82. Free. 6/15-12/10; 14-day limit. 5 sites (22-ft RV limit). Tbls, toilets, cfga, drkg wtr. Fishing, hiking trails. At Boulder River.

BIGFORK (8)

Swan Lake Compound   **$7**
Flathead National Forest
17 mi S of Bigfork on Hwy 83; at Swan Lake. $7 with federal Senior Pass; others pay $14. 5/15-9/30; 14-day limit. 36 sites (50-ft RV limit). Tbls, toilets, cfga, drkg wtr. Boating, fishing, swimming beach, nearby hiking trails & dump. Elev 3066 ft. Dump in Bigfork.

Fishing tip: The 2,680-acre Swan Lake has good fishing for Cutthroat, rainbow, bull and brook trout, along with kokanee salmon and northern pike. For pike, try the weed beds on the lake's southwest shoreline. The kokanee average about 2 pounds.

BIG SANDY (9)

Paul F. Williams Memorial
Big Sandy City Park   **FREE**
In Big Sandy on US 87. Free overnight. 4/1-11/1. 10 sites, no hookups. Tbls, flush toilets, cfga, drkg wtr, no showers. Well maintained. GPS: N48' 10.752, W110' 06.723.

Cow Island Landing   **FREE**
Missouri River Waterway
Bureau of Land Management
28 mi NE of Judith Landing on Missouri River, BY BOAT. Free. 5/1-9/30; 14-day limit. 5 tent sites. Tbls, toilets, no drkg wtr. Boating; picnicking. 21 acres.

Eagle Creek   **FREE**
Bureau of Land Management
S of Big Sandy. No vehicle access. Free. All year; 14-day limit. Undesignated sites. Toilets, cfga, no drkg wtr.

Hole-in-the-Wall Landing   **FREE**
Missouri River Waterway
Bureau of Land Management
11 mi S of Big Sandy on US 87. S at sign for Upper Missouri Wild & Scenic River to Coal Banks Landing; 21 mi E of Coalbanks Landing on Missouri River, BY BOAT. Free. 5/1-9/30; 14-day limit. 5 tent sites. Log shelters. Tbls, toilets, cfga, no drkg wtr. Boating; picnicking.

Judith Landing   **FREE**
Bureau of Land Management
US 87 at Big Sandy, milepost 79; 44 mi S

on Secondary 236. Free. 5/15-10/15; 14-day limit. 12 sites; 48-ft RV limit. Tbls, no drkg wtr, cfga, toilet. Picnicking; fishing; hiking; boating(l).

Slaughter River Landing   **FREE**
Missouri River Waterway
Bureau of Land Management
14 mi SE of Hole-in-the-Wall Landing on Missouri River, BY BOAT. Free. 5/1-9/30; 14-day limit. 5 tent sites. Tbls, toilets, cfga, no drkg wtr. Boating; picnicking. 42 acres.

BIG SKY (10)

Greek Creek   **$11**
Gallatin National Forest
3 mi E of Big Sky on SR 191S; 9.5 mi N on US 191 (31 mi S of Bozeman); at Gallatin River. $11 during 5/15-9/15; free rest of year, but no wtr or services; 16-day limit. 14 sites; 60-ft RV limit. Tbls, toilets, cfga, drkg wtr, firewood($). Fishing, boating, rafting, kayaking, birdwatching, winter snowmobiling. Elev 5600 ft; 5 acres.

Fishing tip: The river offers excellent fishing for brown & rainbow trout, mountain whitefish and sculpin.

Moose Creek Flat   **$11**
Gallatin National Forest
3 mi E of Big Sky on SR 191S; 7 mi N on US 191 (33 mi S of Bozeman). $11 during 5/15-9/15; free rest of year, but no wtr or services; 16-day limit. 12 sites (16-ft RV limit). Tbls, toilets, cfga, drkg wtr, firewood($). Fishing on Gallatin River. Elev 5700 ft; 6 acres.

Red Cliff   **$11**
Gallatin National Forest
3 mi E of Big Sky on SR 191S; 6.5 mi S on US 191 (48 mi S of Bozeman). $11 during 5/15-9/15; free rest of year, but no wtr or services; 16-day limit. 63 sites (50-ft RV limit). Tbls, toilets, cfga, drkg wtr, elec($4). Fishing, rafting, kayaking on Gallatin River. Elev 6400 ft; 49 acres.

Swan Creek   **$11**
Gallatin National Forest
3 mi E of Big Sky on SR 191S; 8.5 mi N on US 191; 1 mi E on FR 481 (Swan Creek Rd); at confluence of Swan Creek & Gallatin River. $11 during 6/15-9/15; free rest of year, but no wtr or services; 16-day limit. 13 sites; 45-ft RV limit. Tbls, toilets, cfga, drkg wtr. Fishing, hiking, kayaking, rafting. Scenic. Elev 5400 ft; 6 acres.

BIG TIMBER (11)

Aspen Campground   **$5**
Gallatin National Forest
25 mi S of Big Timber on SR 298; 8.5 mi S on CR 212; at Boulder River. $5. All year; 14-day limit; free 10/1-MD, but winter access may be limited by snow. 8 sites; 32-ft RV limit. Tbls, toilets, cfga, no drkg wtr. Fishing, hiking. Elev 4500 ft; 8 acres.

Fishing tip: Catch Yellowstone cutthroat & rainbow trout from Boulder River.

Big Beaver   **FREE**
Gallatin National Forest
25 mi S of Big Timber on MT 298; 8 mi S on CR 212; at Boulder River. Free. Elev 5500 ft. All year; 15-day limit. Winter access may be limited by snow. 5 sites (32-ft RV limit). Tbls, toilets, cfga, no drkg wtr, no trash service. Fishing, horseback riding, hiking, birdwatching.
Fishing tip: Catch Yellowstone cutthroat and rainbow trout in Boulder River.

Big Rock   **FREE**
Boulder River State Fishing Access Site
4 mi S of Big Timber on Upper Boulder River (river mile 5.3). Free. All year; 7-day limit. Tbls, toilets, cfga, no drkg wtr. Primitive camping on 76 acres. Boating, fishing. Difficult access. GPS: 45.793, -109.964.

Boulder Forks   **FREE**
Boulder River State Fishing Access Site
17 mi S of Big Timber off Hwy 298 on Upper Boulder River (stream mile 0.4). Free. All year; 7-day limit. Primitive camping on 72.4 acres. Toilets, cfga, tbls, no drkg wtr. Fishing, boating. Difficult access. Popular. GPS: 45.658, -110.109.

Bratten   **FREE**
Yellowstone River
State Fishing Access Site
16 mi E of Big Timber on I-90; 2 mi E on frontage rd; at Yellowstone River (river mile 434.2). Free. All year; 7-day limit. Primitive camping on 436 acres; 25-ft RV limit. Tbls, toilets, cfga, no drkg wtr. Boating(l), fishing. Difficult site access, but good access to river for floating & fishing. "Clark on the Yellowstone" historic site. GPS: 45.717, -109.63.

Chippy Park   **$5**
Gallatin National Forest
25 mi S of Big Timber on MT 298; 9 mi S on FR 212; at mouth of Boulder Canyon. $5. Elev 5500 ft. All year; 15-day limit. 7 sites (32-ft RV limit). Tbls, toilets, cfga, firewood, drkg wtr (5/25-9/30), no trash service. Rockhounding; picnicking; fishing, hiking. Scenic view. Horseback riding nearby.

East Boulder   **FREE**
Gallatin National Forest
17 mi S of Big Timber on RT 298; E on Boulder Rd 8 mi; at East Fork Boulder River. Free. All year; 14-day limit. 2 open sites; 20-ft RV limit, but RVs not encouraged. Tbls, toilets, cfga, no drkg wtr, no trash service. Fishing, hiking, horseback riding.
Fishing tip: Fishing here is excellent for Yellowstone cutthroat and westslope cutthroat trout.

Falls Creek   **FREE**
Gallatin National Forest
34 mi SW of Big Timber on Hwy 298; 5 mi S on CR 212; at Boulder River. Free. All year;

15-day limit. 8 tent sites. Tbls, toilets, cfga, drkg wtr (5/25-9/30), no trash service. Fishing, hiking.

Grey Bear   **$7**
Yellowstone River
State Fishing Access Site
E of Big Timber to I-90 exit 367, then N to frontage rd and 5 mi W to Yellowstone River. $7 for licensed fishermen; $12 for others. All year; 7-day limit. Developed camping on large open area on 25.7 acres. Toilets, cfga, tbls, no drkg wtr. Boating(l), fishing, hiking, picnicking. Difficult access. GPS: 45.786, -110.066.

Half Moon   **$5**
Gallatin National Forest
12 mi N of Big Timber on US 191; 8 mi W on CR 197; 2 mi W on FR 197; at Timber Creek. $5. All year; 15-day limit. Winter access may be limted by snow. 8 sites (22-ft RV limit). Tbls, toilets, cfga, well drkg wtr, no trash service. Fishing, mountain climbing. Crazy Mountain (only public access E side). Elev 6500 ft; 3 acres.

Hells Canyon   **FREE**
Gallatin National Forest
25 mi SW of Big Timber on SR 298; 14 mi S on CR 212. All year; 15-day limit. 11 sites (16-ft RV limit). Tbls, toilets, cfga, no drkg wtr, no trash service. Fishing, hiking trails, rockhounding. Elev 6000 ft; 5 acres.

Hicks Park   **$5**
Gallatin National Forest
25 mi SW of Big Timber on SR 298; 20 mi S on CR 212; near Boulder Creek. $5. All year; 15-day limit; free during 10/1-MD, but no drkg wtr; winter access limited by snow. 16 sites (RVs under 32 ft due to turns on access rd). Tbls, toilets, cfga, drkg wtr. Fishing, hiking trails. Elev 5500 ft; 5 acres.

Indian Fort   **$7**
Yellowstone River
State Fishing Access Site
E of Big Timber on I-90 to exit 392 at Reedpoint; across bridge to first left; at Yellowstone River. $7 for licensed fishermen; $12 for others. All year; 7-day limit. Primitive camping on 18.7 acres. Tbls, toilets, cfga, no drkg wtr. Boating(l), fishing. Good access. GPS: 45.715, -109.549.

Otter Creek   **FREE**
Yellowstone River
State Fishing Access Site
2 mi N of Big Timber on Hwy 191; 1.5 mi E on Howie Rd; at Upper Yellowstone River (river mile 454). Free. All year; 7-day limit. Primitive camping on 29 acres. Tbls, toilets, cfga, no drkg wtr. Boating(l), fishing. GPS: 45.855, -109.916.

West Boulder   **$5**
Gallatin National Forest
16 mi SW of Big Timber on SR 298 to McLeod; 6.5 mi SW on CR 30; 8 mi SW on

West Boulder Rd. $5. All year; 15-day limit. Free 10/1-MD, but no drkg wtr; winter access limited by snow. 10 sites (20-ft RV limit due to access rd turns). Tbls, toilets, cfga, drkg wtr, no trash service. Good fishing, hiking, horseback riding. Equestrian facilities next to camp.

BILLINGS (13)

Broadview Pond   **FREE**
State Fishing Access Site
25 mi N of Billings on Hwy 3 at N end of Broadview. Free. All year; 7-day limit. Primitive undesignated sites; no facilities, no drkg wtr. Boating(l). Fishing poor in 2007 due to low wtr. 108 acres.

BONNER (14)

Clearwater Crossing   **$7**
Clearwater River
State Fishing Access Site
34 mi E of Bonner on SR 200; 1 mi W of Clearwater Junction (stream mile 3.4). $7 for licensed fishermen; $12 for others. All year; 7-day limit. 6 sites (30-ft RV limit). Tbls, toilets, cfga, no drkg wtr. Boating (no motors), fishing. Canoes can be hand-launched. 19 acres.

Corrick's Riverbend   **$7**
Blackfoot River
State Fishing Access Site
26 mi E of Bonner on Hwy 200 to milepost 26; 7.5 mi W on Ninemile Prairie Rd (stream mile 23). $7 for licensed fishermen; $12 for others. All year; 7-day limit. Developed sites on 32 acres; 25-ft RV limit. Tbls, toilets, cfga, drkg wtr. Fishing, boating(l). Difficult access. No boat motors on Blackfoot River or tributaries.

Monture Creek   **$7**
State Fishing Access Site
39 mi E of Bonner to milepost 39; at Monture Creek. $7 with fishing license; $12 otherwise. All year; 7-day limit. Primitive camping on 112 acres. Tbls, toilets, cfga, no drkg wtr. Fishing. No boat motors. Difficult access.

Ninemile Prairie   **$7**
Blackfoot River
State Fishing Access Site
26 mi E of Bonner on Hwy 200 to milepost 26; 4 mi W on Ninemile Prairie Rd (stream mile 25.1). $7 for licensed fishermen; $12 for others. All year; 7-day limit. 2 developed sites on 14 acres; 25-ft RV limit. Tbls, toilet, cfga, no drkg wtr. Fishing. Boat launching not advised. Difficult access; rough rds.

River Junction   **$7**
Blackfoot River
State Fishing Access Site
39 mi E of Bonner on Hwy 200 to milepost 39; 9 mi SE on county rd (stream mile 52.5). $7 with fishing license; $12 otherwise. All year; 7-day limit. Primitive camping on 179

acres. 6 sites; 25-ft RV limit. Tbls, toilets, cfga, no drkg wtr. Boating(l), fishing. Difficult access; rds very rough. Canoes can be hand-launched; no boat motors on Blackfoot River & tributaries.

Russell Gates Memorial $7
Blackfoot River
State Fishing Access Site
35 mi E of Bonner on SR 200 to milepost 35 (stream mile 40.1). $7 for fishing license holders; $12 for others. All year; 7-day limit. 12 sites (25-ft RV limit). Tbls, toilets, cfga, drkg wtr (no wtr 5/1-9/30). Boating, canoeing (hand launch), fishing. 41 acres.

Thibodeau $7
Blackfoot River
State Fishing Access Site
6 mi E of Johnrud FAS on the Corridor Rd (stream mile 17.7). $7 for licensed fishermen; $12 for others. All year; 14-day limit. Developed sites. Tbls, toilets, cfga, no drkg wtr. Fishing, no boat launch.

Upsata Lake $7
State Fishing Access Site
38 mi E of Bonner on Hwy 200 to milepost 38; 4 mi N on Woodworth Rd. $7 for licensed fishermen; $12 for others. All year; 7-day limit. Primitive sites; 25-ft RV limit. Toilets, tbls, cfga, no drkg wtr. Fishing, boating(l). Catch-and-release fishing for bass. Difficult access. 11 acres.

BOULDER (15)

City Park FREE
On Main St. just off I-15. Free, but $5 donation suggested. 5/1-9/30. 10 sites. Tbls, toilets, cfga, drkg wtr, dump. 5 acres.

Free Enterprise $10
Health Mine Campground
From Hwy 69 in Boulder, follow 2nd Street for 2 mi to top of hill, then follow signs. $10.70 with elec; full hookups $16. 4/1-10/30. 20 sites. Tbls, toilets, cfga, drkg wtr, dump, hookups ($), coin laundry, showers. On side of radon therapy mine. Campers do not have to be mine guests. Elev 5400 ft.

BOZEMAN (17)

Battle Ridge FREE
Gallatin National Forest
21 mi NE of Bozeman on SR 89. Elev 6400 ft; in Bridger Mtns at Battle Ridge Pass. Free. MD-LD; 16-day limit. 13 sites; RV limit 16 ft. Toilets, cfga, tbls, drkg wtr. Pack out trash. Hiking; picnicking. 5 acres. Elev 6500 ft.

Chisolm Campground $11
Gallatin National Forest
18 mi S of Bozeman on Hyalite Canyon Rd; Hyalite Reservoir. $11 during 5/15-9/15; free rest of year, but no wtr or services; 16-day limit. 10 sites; 35-ft RV limit. Tbls, toilets, cfga, drkg wtr. Fishing, hiking, mountain biking nearby, boating (hand launch).

Fishing tip: This 300-acre lake contains Arctic grayling and cutthroat trout.

Fairy Lake FREE
Gallatin National Forest
22 mi NE of Bozeman on MT 293; 6 mi W on FR 74 (Fairy Lake Rd; poor, steep gravel access rd). Free. Elev 7600 ft. 7/1-9/15; 14-day limit. 9 tent sites; 2 acres. Tbls, toilets, cfga, firewood, drkg wtr. Picnicking; fishing; hiking. Geological. Limestone Peaks. Trail to 9,700-ft Sacagawea Peak.

Greycliff $7
Madison River
State Fishing Access Site
23 mi W of Bozeman on SR 84; 6 mi N on Madison River Rd. $7 for licensed fishermen; $12 for others. All year but closed to camping 1/1-MD; 7-day limit. 30 sites; 25-ft RV limit. Tbls, toilets, cfga, drkg wtr. Boating(l), fishing. Difficult access. 552 acres.
Fishing tip: Excellent trout fishing in Madison River. It has the state's highest trout density and is consered Montana's best dry fly fishery. It contains rainbow, brown and Yellowstone cutthroat trout as well as whitefish and Arctic grayling.

Hood Creek $11
Gallatin National Forest
17 mi S of Bozeman on CR 243; 10 mi SE on CR 62; at Hyalite Reservoir. $11 during 5/15-9/15; free rest of year, but no wtr or services; 16-day limit. 18 sites (50-ft RV limit). Tbls, toilets, cfga, drkg wtr. Pack out trash. Boating(l), fishing, mountain biking, hiking. Hand boat launch. Elev 6800 ft; 5 acres.

Langohr $11
Gallatin National Forest
8 mi S of Bozeman on CR 243; 5.5 mi SE on CR 62. $11 during 5/15-9/15; free rest of year, but no wtr or services; 16-day limit. 10 sites (32-ft RV limit). Tbls, toilets, cfga, drkg wtr. Boating, fishing (handicap-accessible fishing trail), picnicking, hiking. Wheelchair-accessible fishing trail & nature walk. Scenic. Elev 6100 ft; 5 acres.
Fishing tip: Good fishing for west slope cutthroat trout.

BRIDGER (18)

Sage Creek $5
Custer National Forest
3 mi S of Bridger on US 310; 22 mi SE on Pryor Mountain Rd; half mi E on FR 50. $5 single sites, $10 double. Elev 5600 ft. MD-LD; 10-day limit. 12 sites; 30-ft RV limit. Tbls, toilets, cfga, firewood, drkg wtr. Rockhounding; picnicking; fishing. High-clearance vehicles recommended. Cave exploring (permit needed). Pryor Mountains contan wild horses, bighorn sheep. Site recently renovated.

BROCKTON (20)

Brockton Community Park FREE
Fort Peck Indian Agency
Qtr mi S of Brockton at the jct of US 2 and MT 404. Free. 5/1-9/15; no limit. 4 sites (RVs under 15 ft). Tbls, cfga, firewood. Dump, store, LP-gas (1 mi). Fishing; picnicking.

BUTTE (22)

Beaver Dam $5
Deerlodge National Forest
7 mi W of Butte on I-90; 18 mi S on I-15; 6 mi W on FR 961. $5. MD-LD; 16-day limit; free rest of year, weather permitting, but no drkg wtr. 15 sites (50-ft RV limit). Tbls, toilets, cfga, drkg wtr, no trash service. Fishing, hiking trails. 6 acres.

Delmoe Lake $8
Deerlodge National Forest
17 mi NE on I-90 from Butte to Homestake Pass exit; follow signs 10 mi on FR 222. $8. MD-9/15; 16-day limit; free rest of year, weather permitting, but no wtr or trash service. 25 sites; 32-ft RV limit. Tbls, toilets, cfga, drkg wtr. Swimming, fishing, hiking, boating, picnicking.

Lowland $5
Deerlodge National Forest
9 mi NE of Butte on I-15; 6 mi W on FR 442; left on FR 9485 for 1.5 mi. $5 during about MD-LD; free rest of yr, weather permitting (but wtr shut off); 14-day limit. 11 sites (RVs under 23 ft). Tbls, toilets, cfga, drkg wtr. Picnic area can be reserved ($). Elev 6400 ft.

CAMERON (23)

Madison River $9
Beaverhead National Forest
23.5 mi S of Cameron on SR 287; SW on CR 8381. $9 during MD-10/15; 16-day limit; free rest of year, weather permitting, but no wtr or trash service. 10 sites (30-ft RV limit). Tbls, toilets, cfga, drkg wtr. Fishing.

West Fork Madison $7
Beaverhead National Forest
23.6 mi S of Cameron on MT 287; qtr mi W on FR 8381. $7 during MD-9/15; 14-day limit. 7 tent sites. Tbls, toilets, cfga, firewood, drkg wtr. Dump (1 mi). Horseback riding; picnicking; fishing (trout).

CAMP CROOK (SD.) (24)

Lantis Spring FREE
Custer National Forest
3 mi W of Camp Crook, South Dakota, on Hwy 20 SE of Ekalaka; 11 mi NW on FR 777. Free. 5/1-11/15; 14-day limit. 10 sites (RVs under 31 ft). Tbls, toilets, cfga, drkg wtr. Pack out trash. Nearby ATV activities, mountain biking.

Wickham Gulch   FREE
Custer National Forest
3 mi W of Camp Crook, South Dakota, on SD 20; 4 mi NE on FR 3049 (about 40 mi E of Ekalaka in the Lone Pine Hills). Free. 5/1-9/15; 14-day limit. 4 sites on 6 acres; 16-ft RV limit. Toilet, cfga, drkg wtr.

CASCADE (26)

Hardy Bridge   FREE
Missouri River
State Fishing Access Site
4 mi S of Cascade on I-15 to Hardy Creek exit 247; 4 mi S on Recreation Rd to Missouri River (river mile 2,179.8). Free. All year; 14-day limit. Primitive camping on 1 acre. Toilets, tbls, cfga, no drkg wtr. Fishing, hiking. To access river on foot, cross railroad tracks. Difficult access to site; RVs not recommended.

Mountain Palace $7
Missouri River
State Fishing Access Site
14 mi S of Cascade to Canyon Exit 244; 1 mi N on Recreation Rd; at Missouri River (river mile 2,180.6). $7 for licensed fishermen; $12 for others. All year; 14-day limit. Undesignated primitive sites on 2.8 acres. Toilets, tbls, cfga, no drkg wtr. Boating(l), fishing, picnicking. Difficult access.

Pelican Point $7
Missouri River
State Fishing Access Site
10 mi S of Cascade on I-15 to Hardy Creek exit 247, then 2 mi N on Frontage Rd; at Missouri River (river mile 2,175.9). $7 for licensed fishermen; $12 for others. All year; 14-day limit. Developed primitive sites on 93.7 acres. Tbls, toilets, cfga, no drkg wtr. Boating(l), fishing. Difficult access.

CHESTER (28)

Island Area   FREE
Lake Elwell (Tiber Reservoir)
Bureau of Reclamation
12 mi S of Chester on Rt 223; follow signs to site. Free. All year; 14-day limit. Primitive undesignated camping area. Toilets, drkg wtr, cfga, dump. Fishing, boating (l). Summer concession nearby with gasoline, supplies, fee campground, marina.

Fishing tip: Good varied fishing on Lake Elwell; try for your choice of perch, walleye, northern pike, catfish. Trout fishing not very good, however.

North Bootlegger   FREE
Lake Elwell (Tiber Reservoir)
Bureau of Reclamation
12 mi S of Chester on Rt 223; follow signs to site. Free. All year; 14-day limit. Primitive undesignated camping area. Toilets, no drkg wtr, cfga. Fishing, boating (primitive launch). Summer concession nearby with gasoline, supplies, fee campground, marina.

Sanford Park   FREE
Lake Elwell (Tiber Reservoir)
Bureau of Reclamation
12 mi S of Chester on Rt 223; follow signs to site. Free. All year; 14-day limit. Primitive undesignated camping area. Toilets, drkg wtr, cfga. Fishing, boating (4WD launch). Summer concession nearby with gasoline, supplies, fee campground, marina.

South Bootlegger   FREE
Lake Elwell (Tiber Reservoir)
Bureau of Reclamation
12 mi S of Chester on Rt 223; follow signs to site. Free. All year; 14-day limit. Primitive undesignated camping area. Toilets, drkg wtr, cfga. Fishing, boating (l). Summer concession nearby with gasoline, supplies, fee campground, marina.

VFW Campgroundq   FREE
Lake Elwell (Tiber Reservoir)
Bureau of Reclamation
12 mi S of Chester on Rt 223; follow signs to site. Free. All year; 14-day limit. Primitive undesignated camping area. Toilets, no drkg wtr, cfga. Fishing, boating (l). Summer concession nearby with gasoline, supplies, fee campground, marina.

Willow Creek   FREE
Lake Elwell (Tiber Reservoir)
Bureau of Reclamation
12 mi S of Chester on Rt 223; follow signs to site. Free. All year; 14-day limit. Primitive undesignated camping area. Toilets, no drkg wtr, cfga. Fishing, boating (l). Summer concession nearby with gasoline, supplies, fee campground, marina.

CHOTEAU (29)

Arod Lake   FREE
State Fishing Access Site
1 mi E of Choteau on CR 221; 6 mi N on CR 220; 5 mi E, then 6.5 mi N on county rds. Free. All year; 7-day limit. Primitive undesignated sites. Tbls, toilets, cfga, no drkg wtr. Boating(l), fishing. 20 acres. Difficult access.

Bynum Reservoir $7
State Fishing Access Site
19 mi NW of Choteau, 7 mi W of Bynum on county rd; 2 mi S on county rd. $7 for licensed fishermen; others pay $12. All year; 7-day limit. Primitive undeveloped sites. Tbls, toilets, cfga, no drkg wtr. Fishing, boating(l). 75 acres.

Cave Mountain $6
Lewis & Clark National Forest
5 mi NW of Choteau on SR 89; 22 mi W on Teton Canyon Rd (FR 144). $6. MD-LD; 14-day limit. 14 sites (22-ft RV limit. Tbls, toilets, cfga, drkg wtr. Fishing, hiking trails. 5 acres.

Choteau Creek City Park $8
E part of Choteau on SR 221; off US 89 and 287. $8. 5/15-10/1; 3-day limit. 35 RV sites,

35 tent sites. Tbls, flush toilets, cfga, drkg wtr, dump. Picnicking, fishing, children's pond, access to river, playground, 9-hole golf course. Elev 4000 ft; 2 acres.

Elko   FREE
Lewis and Clark National Forest
5.5 mi N of Choteau on US 89; 23 mi W on CR 144 (Teton Canyon Rd); 2.5 mi N on FR 144; at Teton River. Free. MD-Thanksgiving, but no services after LD; 14-day limit. 3 sites. Tbls, toilets, cfga, no drkg wtr, no trash service. Hiking, fishing (brook trout). Near Bob Marshall Wilderness.

Eureka Reservoir $7
State Fishing Access Site
4 mi N of Choteau on US 89; 4 mi NW on county rd. $7 for licensed fishermen; others pay $12. All year; 7-day limit. Primitive undesignated sites; 35-ft RV limit. Toilets, cfga, no drkg wtr, no trash service. Boating(l), fishing. Easy access. 35 acres.

Freezeout Lake   FREE
State Wildlife Refuge
10 mi N of Choteau on Hwy 89 (3 mi N of Fairfield). Free. All year; 14-day limit. Primitive undesignated camping on refuge; no facilities, no drkg wtr. Montana's primary staging area for snow geese & tundra swans in spring & fall.

Mills Falls   FREE
Lewis and Clark National Forest
5.5 mi N of Choteau on US 89; 19 mi W on CR 144 (Teton Canyon Rd); 9 mi S on CR 109 & W on FR 109; at South Fork of Teton River. Free. MD-LD; 14-day limit. 4 sites. Tbls, toilets, cfga, no drkg wtr, no trash service. Fishing, hiking trails.

Fishing tip: Brook, rainbow & cutthroat trout are stocked in the South Fork, but their numbers are quite small.

Pishkun Reservoir $7
State Fishing Access Site
17 mi SW of Choteau on county rd. $7 for licensed fishermen; others pay $12. All year; 7-day limit. Primitive undesignated sites. Tbls, toilets, cfga, no drkg wtr. Boating(l), fishing, swimming, hiking, waterskiing. 1,550-acre lake; 1,620-acre site. Difficult access.

Fishing tip: This lake is stocked with rainbow trout, northern pike and kokanee salmon.

West Fork Teton   FREE
Lewis and Clark National Forest
5.5 mi N of Choteau on Hwy 89; 22.7 mi W on CR 144.1; 10 mi N on FR 144.2. Free. MD-LD; 14-day limit. 6 sites. Tbls, toilets, cfga, no drkg wtr, no trash service. Fishing, hiking trails. Trail into Bob Marshall Wilderness.

CLANCY (30)

Park Lake $8
State Fishing Access Site
Helena National Forest
1 mi N of Clancy on CR 426; 5.5 mi W on

FR 4000; 2.1 mi SW on FR 426.1; 5 mi W on FR 4009. $8. MD-9/15; 15-day limit. 22 sites (35-ft RV limit). Tbls, toilets, cfga, drkg wtr. Picnicking, swimming, fishing, boating (no motors; primitive launch); canoeing, hunting, hiking. Elev 6400 ft; 10 acres. Free dispersed camping is available along the roadways nearby.

Fishing tip: Try scenic Park Lake for cutthroat trout and grayling. This is an ideal canoeing lake.

CLINTON (31)

Bitterroot Flat $6
Lolo National Forest
4.9 mi SE of Clinton on I-90 to Rock Creek exit; 23 mi S on rough FR 102. $6 during 5/15-9/30; free rest of year, when accessible, but no drkg wtr; 14-day limit. 15 sites (32-ft RV limit). Tbls, toilets, cfga, firewood, well drkg wtr, no trash service. Picnicking; fishing. Elev 4300 ft.

Dalles $6
Lolo National Forest
4.9 mi SE of Clinton on I-90 to Rock Creek exit; 14.5 mi S on FR 102. $6 during 5/15-9/30; free rest of year, but no wtr or services; 14-day limit. 10 sites (RVs under 32 ft). Tbls, toilets, cfga, firewood, drkg wtr, no trash service. Fishing. Elev 4200 ft.

Garnet Ghost Town FREE
Bureau of Land Management
E of Clinton on I-90 to either the Drummond or Bearmouth exit; follow N side frontage rd to Bear Gulch Rd, about 10 mi W of Drummond or 5 mi E of Bearmouth for about 7.5 mi; take Cave Gulch Rd 4 mi. Camp free at dispersed sites around town; $2 for admission to ghost town. BLM & private preservation group maintain the town, which is Montana's most intact ghost town from the 1890s gold mining period.

Grizzly $6
Lolo National Forest
4.9 mi SE of Clinton on I-90 to Rock Creek exit; 10.6 mi S on rough FR 102 (Rock Creek Rd); 1 mi SE on FR 88 (Ranch Creek Rd). Elev 4200 ft. $6 during 5/15-9/30; free rest of year, but no wtr or services; 14-day limit. 9 sites (RVs under 32 ft). Tbls, toilets, cfga, firewood, drkg wtr, no trash service. Picnicking, fishing, volleyball, horseshoes. Old town of Quigley (3 mi N). Elev 4100 ft.

Harry's Flat $6
Lolo National Forest
4.9 mi SE of Clinton on I-90 to Rock Creek exit; 17.6 mi S on rough FR 102 (Rock Creek Rd). $6 during 5/15-9/30; free rest of year, but no wtr or services; 14-day limit. 18 sites (RVs under 32 ft). Tbls, toilets, cfga, piped drkg wtr, no trash service. Picnicking; fishing. Elev 4300 ft.

Norton $6
Lolo National Forest
4.9 mi SE of Clinton on I-90 to Rock Creek exit; 11 mi S on rough FR 102 (Rock Creek Rd). $6 during 5/15-9/30; free rest of year, but no wtr or services; 14-day limit. 13 sites (16 ft RV limit). Tbls, toilets, cfga, firewood, drkg wtr, no trash service. Picnicking; fishing, hiking trails. Elev 3900 ft; 5 acres.

Siria FREE
Lolo National Forest
4.9 mi SE of Clinton on I-90; 29.2 mi S on FR 102 (rough rd). On Rock Creek. All year; 14-day limit. 4 sites (RVs under 16 ft). Toilets, cfga, firewood, no drkg wtr. Picnicking; fishing. Elev 4500 ft; 5 acres. Elev 4500 ft.

COLUMBIA FALLS (32)

Big Creek $12
Flathead National Forest
21 mi N of Columbia Falls on CR 486; at North Fork of Flathead River. $12 during 5/15-9/30; free rest of yr, but no wtr or trash service; 14-day limit. 22 sites (40-ft RV limit). Tbls, toilets, cfga, drkg wtr. Fishing, boating (l), hiking. 3 mi from Glacier National Park. Elev 3300 ft; 15 acres.

Travel tip: Big Creek Outdoor Education Center of the Glacier Institute is across the road. It focuses on the natural & cultural aspects of Glacier NP, offers field seminars, guided hikes in the park.

Fishing tip: The Flathead River contains cutthroat trout, whitefish, rainbow trout, bull trout, lake trout and northern pike. This campground is one of the major access points for fishermen on the North Fork.

Moose Lake FREE
Dispersed Camping Area
Flathead National Forest
20 mi N of Columbia Falls on CR 486; 17.5 mi W on FR 316 (Big Creek Rd); right on FR 315, then right on FR 5207; at Moose Lake. Free. All year; 14-day limit. 1 site plus others along the road. Tbl, toilet, cfga, no drkg wtr. Fishing, canoeing, berry-picking, hiking. No trash service.

Red Meadow Lake FREE
Dispersed Camping Area
Flathead National Forest
About 42 mi N of Columbia Falls on CR 486; 11.5 mi W on CR 115. Free. All year; 14-day limit. 1 site; 32-ft RV limit. Tbl, toilet, cfga, no drkg wtr, no trash service. Fishing, hiking, canoeing.

Tuchuck FREE
Flathead National Forest
53 mi N of Columbia Falls on FR 210; 10 mi W on FR 114 (4WD or high-clearance vehicles only on FR 114). Free. 6/15-9/1; 14-day limit. 7 sites (RVs under 22 ft). Tbls, toilets, cfga, firewood, no drkg wtr. Fishing; picnicking. Hitch rail for horsemen. Elev 4500 ft; 2 acres.

COLUMBUS (33)

Fireman's Point FREE
Stillwater River
State Fishing Access Site
2 mi SW of Columbus on Hwy 78; half mi W on Countryman Creek Rd; at Stillwater River (river mile 1.9). Free. All year; 7-day limit. Primitive sites. Tbls, toilets, cfga, no drkg wtr. Fishing, hiking, raft slide launch. Difficult access. 162 acres.

Fishing tip: Try the Stillwater for rainbow, brookies and cutthroat trout, but keep in mind this section of the river also produces big northern pike -- up to 20 pounds. This area is the first public fishing spot on the river.

Itch-Ke-Pe City Park FREE
S of Columbus on SR 78 (off I-90 milepost 408); at Yellowstone River (several sites along river). Free, but donations accepted. 4/1-10/31; 10-day limit. 48 sites (no RV size limit). Tbls, flush toilets, cfga, drkg wtr. Fishing, swimming, picnicking. 406-322-4505. GPS: 45.62764, -109.24600.

Swinging Bridge FREE
Stillwater River
State Fishing Access Site
5.3 mi SW of Columbus on Hwy 78; 1 mi S on gravel rd; at Stillwater River. All year; 7-day limit. Tbls, toilets, cfga, no drkg wtr. Primitive camping on 4 acres. Fishing, boating. Difficult access.

Fishing tip: For Stillwater trout, try Mepps, Thomas Cyclones and Panther Martin lures, preferably with gold metal rather than silver or brass. Cast upstream and reel back fast or cast downstream with a slow retrieve.

White Bird FREE
Stillwater River
State Fishing Access Site
6.5 mi S of Columbus on Hwy 78; half mi NW on gravel rd; at Stillwater River (river mile 5.8). Free. All year; 7-day limit. Tbls, toilets, cfga, no drkg wtr. Primitive camping on 22.7 acres. Fishing, hiking, boating (no motors). Difficult access.

Fishing tip: The Stillwater provides great wading action from early July through the rest of summer. Concentrate on the eddies behind boulders. An unmarked river access just below White Bird provides a long stretch of good riffle water.

CONDON (34)

Holland Lake $7
Flathead National Forest
9 mi SE of Condon on SR 83; 3 mi E on FR 44 (Holland Lake Rd). $7 with federal Senior Pass; others pay $14. About 5/15-9/15; 14-day limit. 40 sites (50-ft RV limit). Tbls, toilets, cfga, drkg wtr, dump, beach. Fishing, boating(l), hiking trails, swimming. $3 fee for dump. Elev 3500 ft; 24 acres.

Fishing tip: Try 400-acre Holland Lake for

kokanee salmon, rainbow and cutthroat trout as well as the rare bull trout. Fishing is best in the early spring and late fall. But be aware that the lake is popular among waterskiiers in the summer.

COOKE CITY (35)

Chief Joseph   **$8**
Gallatin National Forest
4.8 mi E of Cooke City on US 212. $8. 6/15-10/31; 16-day limit. 6 sites (42-ft RV limit). Open as overflow or for groups by reservation. Tbls, toilets, cfga, drkg wtr. Picnicking, hiking. Nearby trailhead to Absaroka-Beartooth Wilderness. Ranger programs. Elev 8000 ft. Less than 20 mi to Yellowstone NP. May be closed in 2007 for reconstruction.

Colter   **$8**
Gallatin National Forest
2.3 mi E of Cooke City on US 212 in Wyoming. $8. 7/15-9/30; 16-day limit. 23 sites (48-ft RV limit). Tbls, toilets, cfga, drkg wtr. Fishing, hiking trails along Lady of the Lake Creek. Elev 7900 ft; 15 acres. Closed in 2007 for reconstruction.

Crazy Creek   **$10**
Shoshone National Forest
10.5 mi SE of Cooke City on US 212 in Wyoming. Along Clarks Fork of Yellowstone River. $10. About 6/15-10/20; 14-day limit. 16 sites (32-ft RV limit). Tbls, toilets, cfga, drkg wtr. Fishing, hiking, picnicking. Crazy Lakes trailhead to backcountry lakes in Absaroka-Beartooth Wilderness. Scenic walk to Crazy Creek Falls. Elev 6900 ft.

Fox Creek Campground   **$10**
Shoshone National Forest
7.5 mi SE of Cooke City on US 212 in Wyoming. $10 with federal Senior Pass; others pay $20. 6/1-9/30; 14-day limit. 34 sites with elec (50-ft RV limit). Tbls, toilets, cfga, drkg wtr. Fishing, hiking, boating, picnicking. At Fox Creek and Clarks Fork of Yellowstone River. Elev 7100 ft.

Hunter Peak Campground   **$10**
Shoshone National Forest
14.4 mi SE of Cooke City on US 212; 5 mi S on Hwy 296 in Wyoming. $10. All year; 14-day limit. 9 sites (32-ft RV limit). Tbls, toilets, cfga, drkg wtr. Fishing, hiking, picnicking. Clarks Fork Trailhead nearby has horse facilities. Elev 6500 ft.

Lake Creek   **$5**
Shoshone National Forest
14.4 mi SE of Cooke City on US 212 in Wyoming. $5. 6/1-9/30; 14-day limit. 6 sites (32-ft RV limit). Tbls, toilets, cfga, drkg wtr. Fishing, hiking, picnicking. Elev 6900 ft.

Soda Butte   **$9**
Gallatin National Forest
1.2 mi E of Cooke City on US 212. $9. 7/1-LD; 16-day limit. 21 sites; 48-ft RV limit. Tbls, toilets, cfga, drkg wtr. Pack out trash. Fishing, hiking. Elev 7500 ft; 10 acres.

CRAIG (36)

Craig   **$7**
Missouri River
State Fishing Access Site
At Craig off I-15 on shore of Missouri River, upstream side of bridge (stream mile 2,194). $7 for licensed fishermen; $12 for others. All year; 7-day limit. 8 sites and open area. Tbls, toilets, cfga, drkg wtr (5/1-9/30). Boating(l), fishing, picnicking, wildlife viewing. 2.5 acres. Easy access.

Missouri River   **FREE & $7**
State Fishing Access Sites
Numerous scattered developed and undesignated sites are along 30-mi stretch of Missouri River just E of and parallel to I-15. Most are free, but fees of $7-$12 are charged at some. All year; 7 to 14-day limits in 30-day period. Toilets, cfga, tbls, some with drkg wtr. Boating (many with ramps), fishing, hiking, picnicking. Sites with camping (listed elsewhere) include Hardy Bridge, Craig, Mountain Palace, Pelican Point, Lewis and Clark, Deepdale, Fairweather, Spite Hill, Stickney Creek and Wolf Creek Bridge. Camping is now prohibited at Prewett Creek

Fishing tip: Although best known for its huge channel catfish, shovelnose sturgeon and paddlefish, this section of the Missouri also offers excellent walleye and sauger fishing.

Spite Hill   **$7**
Missouri River
State Fishing Access Site
From I-15 exit 234 at Craig, 5 mi N on Recreation Rd; at Missouri River (river mile 2,189.6). $7 for licensed fishermen; $12 for others. All year; 7-day limit. Developed sites on 13.5 acres; limited space for RVs. Tbls, toilets, cfga, no drkg wtr. Boating, fishing. Difficult access.

Stickney Creek   **$7**
Missouri River
State Fishing Access Site
From I-15 exit 234 at Craig, 4.5 mi N on Recreation Rd; at Missouri River (river mile 2,190.3). $7 for licensed fishermen; $12 for others. 5/1-10/30; 7-day limit. Developed sites on 1 acre. Tbls, toilets, cfga, no drkg wtr. Boating(l), fishing. Difficult access.

CRANE (37)

Gartside Reservoir   **FREE**
State Fishing Access Site
1 mi N of Crane on Hwy 16; 1 mi W on co rd. Free. All year; 7-day limit. Primitive camping on 160 acres. Toilets, tbls, cfga, no drkg wtr, fishing pier. Fishing, boating (no boat motors; hand launch). Easy access.

CUSTER (38)

Captain Clark   **FREE**
Yellowstone River
State Fishing Access Site
8 mi W of Custer on county rd; at Yellow-

stone River (river mile 310.6). Free. All year; 7-day limit. Primitive camping on 266 acres; 40-ft RV limit. Tbls, toilets, cfga, no drkg wtr, fishing pier. Boating(l), fishing. Easy access.

Manuel Lisa   **FREE**
Bighorn River
State Fishing Access Site
6 mi E of Custer on frontage rd off I-94 exit 49 (stream mile 1.8); last access point on Bighorn River, close to mouth of Yellowstone. Free. All year; 7-day limit. Primitive camping on 38 acres. Toilets, cfga, tbls, no drkg wtr. Boating(l), fishing. Moderate access.

DARBY (40)

Alta Campground   **$8**
Bitterroot National Forest
4 mi S of Darby on US 93; 21.5 mi S on CR 473; 6 mi S on CR 96. $8 during MD-LD; free rest of year; 10-day limit. 15 sites; 30-ft RV limit. Tbls, toilets, cfga, drkg wtr (no wtr during free period). Hunting, fishing, hiking, gold panning. On West Fork of Bitterroot River. Nearby Hughes Creek was site of early placer gold mining. Elev 5000 ft; 6 acres.

Travel tip: Hughes Creek was site of early day placer gold mining. Near historical town of Alta and first ranger station in the U.S.

Fishing tip: Good fishing for small cutthroat, rainbow & brook trout in Bitterroot River.

Bear Creek Pass Trailhead   **FREE**
Bitterroot National Forest
7.3 mi N of Darby on US 93; 1.4 mi W on co rd; 17 mi W on FR 429 (dirt mountain rd). Free. 7/15-9/15; 10-day limit. 6 sites (RVs under 33 ft) & 4 hunter camps. Tbls, toilets, cfga, no drkg wtr. Hunting; hiking; picnicking; fishing(1 mi); boating(ld-3 mi). Elev 6200 ft; 2 acres. At the head of Lost Horse Creek. Access point for Selway-Bitterroot Wilderness. Stream.

Deep Creek   **FREE**
Bitterroot National Forest
51 mi SW of Darby at Deep Creek (mountain rd to the area). Free. All year; 14-day limit. 6 sites; 30-ft RV limit. Tbl, toilet, cfga, no drkg wtr, no trash service. Fishing, hiking.

Fales Flat Camp   **FREE**
Bitterroot National Forest
4 mi S of Darby on US 93; 14.4 mi SW on CR 473; 10 mi W on FR 468. Free. 6/1-9/15; 14-day limit. 7 sites. Primarily a group camp with horse facilities at one end. Tbls, toilets, cfga, no drkg wtr, no trash service. Hiking, horseback riding, fishing.

Indian Creek   **FREE**
Bitterroot National Forest
4.1 mi S of Darby on US 93; 14.4 mi SW on CR 473; 36.5 mi W on FR 468; 5 mi N on FR 6223. Free. 6/15-11/30; 14-day limit. 6 sites; 25-ft RV limit. Tbls, toilets, cfga, no drkg wtr. Hiking, picnicking, fishing.

Indian Trees   **$10**
Bitterroot National Forest
4 mi S on US 93; 14 mi SW on CR 473; 37 mi W on FR 468; 5 mi N on FR 6223; at Eat Fork of Bitterroot River. $10. About 5/20-9/30; 14-day limit. 16 sites (50-ft RV limit). Tbls, toilets, cfga, drkg wtr. Hiking, fishing.

Logging Camp   **FREE**
Dispersed Camping Area
Lick Creek Demonstration Forest
Bitterroot National Forest
N of Darby to Lake Como Recreation Area, then N on Lick Creek Interpretive Auto Tour toward Lost Horse Creek; camp just past the Lick Creek bridge on left side of rd. Free. All year; 14-day limit. No facilities except cfga, no drkg wtr. Hiking, fishing.

Paradise   **FREE**
Bitterroot National Forest
4.1 mi S of Darby on US 93; 14.4 mi SW on CR 473; 36.5 mi W on FR 468; 11.4 mi N on FR 6223. All year; 10-day limit. 11 sites (RVs under 26 ft). Tbls, toilets, cfga, firewood, no drkg wtr. Picnicking. Elev 3200 ft; 6 acres. Scenic. Whitewater float trips down Selway River in June.

Raven Creek   **FREE**
Bitterroot National Forest
4.1 mi S of Darby on US 93; 14.4 mi SW on CR 473; 36.5 mi W on FR 468; 2.6 mi N on FR 6223. Free. 6/15-11/26; 14-day limit. 2 sites; 25-ft RV limit. Tbls, toilets, cfga, no drkg wtr. Picnicking; hiking; fishing. Elev 3800 ft; 1 acre. Mountains. Dense forest. Raven Creek. In Selway Canyon.

Rock Creek Horse Camp   **$4**
Lake Como Recreation Area
Bitterroot National Forest
5 mi N of Darby on US 93; 1 mi SW on CR 550; 2 mi W on forest rd. Camp free, but $4 for daily vehicle pass ($20 annually). 5/15-9/15; 14-day limit. 11 sites (40-ft RV limit). Tbls, toilets, cfga, no drkg wtr. Hitch rails, feed troughs. Fishing, hiking, bridle trails.

Rombo   **$8**
Bitterroot National Forest
4 mi S of Darby on US 93; 18 mi SW on CR 473; at West Fork of Bitterroot River. $8. MD-LD; 14-day limit. 15 sites (30-ft RV limit). Tbls, toilets, cfga, drkg wtr. Fishing, hunting, hiking. Elev 4400 ft; 6 acres. Handicap toilet facilities.

Sam T. Billings Memorial   **FREE**
Bitterroot National Forest
4 mi S of Darby on US 93; 13 mi SW on CR 473; 1 mi NW on FR 5631. Free. All year; 14-day limit. 12 sites (30-ft RV limit). Tbls, toilets, cfga, no drkg wtr. Hunting, fishing, horseback riding, picnic area. Elev 4400 ft; 8 acres. Selway/Bitterroot Wilderness Takeoff, half mi. Scenic. Formerly named Boulder Creek Trail Takeoff.

Schumaker   **FREE**
Bitterroot National Forest
7.3 mi N of Darby on US 93; 2 mi W on CR 76; 16 mi W on FR 429; 2.4 mi N on FR 5605. Free. 7/15-9/15; 10-day limit. 6 sites; 55-ft RV limit. Tbls, toilets, cfga, no drkg wtr. Picnicking; fishing(1 mi); boating(I-1 mi). Elev 6600 ft; 7 acres. On Twin Lakes. Access to Selway-Bitterroot Wilderness(1 mi, unsurfaced rd).

Slate Creek   **FREE**
Bitterroot National Forest
4.1 mi S of Darby on US 93; 21.6 mi S on CR 473; 2 mi S on CR 96. Free. Elev 4800 ft. 6/25-9/6; 10-day limit. 4 sites on 6 acres (RVs under 26 ft). Tbls, toilets, cfga, firewood, no drkg wtr. Picnicking; fishing; boating(ld); waterskiing(1 mi). Adjacent to 700-acre Painted Rocks Lake on W fork of Bitterroot River.
Fishing tip: Thousands of cutthroat trout have been planted in Painted Rocks Lake since the mid-1970s, when it was drawn almost dry, and they're now providing good fishing.

Upper Como   **$8**
Lake Como Recreation Area
Bitterroot National Forest
5 mi N of Darby on US 93; 1 mi SW on CR 550; follow signs. $8 during MD-LD; free rest of year; 14-day limit. 11 sites (30-ft RV limit). Tbls, toilets, cfga, drkg wtr. Boating(l), fishing, hiking, cross-country skiing; no wtr during free period. Note: $14 fee for Lower Como Lake camp, plus $2 for hookups ($7 base with federal Senior Pass).

DE BORGIA (41)

Cabin City   **$7**
Lolo National Forest
3 mi SE of DeBorgia on I-90 (exit 22 at Henderson); 2.5 mi NE on Camel's Hump Rd; qtr mi N on FR 353 (Twelvemile Creek Rd). $7. MD-LD; 10-day limit. 24 sites (32-ft RV limit). Tbls, toilets, cfga, drkg wtr. Fishing in Twelvemile Creek, self-guided nature trail, beaver dams in area. Elev 3200 ft; 8 acres.

DEER LODGE (43)

Orofino   **FREE**
Deerlodge National Forest
13 mi SE of Deer Lodge on FR 82 (Boulder Basin Rd) via Champion Pass. Free. About 6/20-9/15; 16-day limit. 10 sites (RVs under 23 ft). Tbls, toilets, cfga, firewood, drkg wtr. Picnicking; hiking; horseback riding. Elev 6500 ft; 3 acres.

DEWEY (44)

Greenwood Bottoms   **FREE**
Big Hole River
State Fishing Access Site
1.5 mi E of Dewey on SR 43 (stream mile 56.5). Free. All year; 7-day limit. Primitive camping on 6 acres. No facilities; no drkg wtr. Boating(l), fishing. Very difficult river access; access rd dangerous, not recommended for RVs.

DILLON (45)

Bannack State Park   **$12**
5 mi S of Dillon on I-15; 21 mi W on secondary rd 278; 4 mi S on county rd. $12 ($10 off-season). All year; 14-day limit. 28 tent/RV sites. Tbls, pit toilets, cfga, drkg wtr. Fishing, picnicking, horseshoes. Visitor center. Elev 5800 ft; 1,154 acres. Visitor center.
Travel tip: Nearby ghost town of Bannack was site of state's first gold discovery (1862); ghost town served as first territorial capital. Main steet is lined with historic log and frame structures. Site is a National Historic Landmark.

Barretts Park   **FREE**
Clark Canyon Reservoir
Bureau of Reclamation
5 mi S of Dillon on I-15. Free. All year; 14-day limit. Primitive undesignated camping area. Toilets, drkg wtr, cfga. Fishing, boating (primitive launch). Concession nearby with gasoline, supplies, fee campground, marina.
Fishing tip: Fish the lake near camp for trophy-size rainbow trout, up to 7 pounds.

Beaverhead   **FREE**
Clark Canyon Reservoir
Bureau of Reclamation
S of Dillon, at reservoir off I-15. All year; 14-day limit. Primitive undesignated camping area. Toilets, drkg wtr, cfga. Fishing, boating (l). Concession nearby with gasoline, supplies, fee campground, marina.
Fishing tip: Beaverhead River produces large numbers of big rainbow & brown trout, caught by fly fishermen who float the river or fish from shore; brush along shore hampers waders, however. Bank access best below Pipe Organ bridge.

Cameahwait   **FREE**
Clark Canyon Reservoir
Bureau of Reclamation
20 mi S of Dillon, at reservoir off I-15. Free. All year; 14-day limit. Primitive undesignated camping area. Toilets, drkg wtr, cfga. Fishing, boating. Concession nearby with gasoline, supplies, fee campground, marina.
Fishing tip: Try for the lake's famous 10-pound brown trout.

Cattail Marsh   **FREE**
Bureau of Reclamation
S of Dillon on I-15 to exit 44 at Clark Canyon; follow Secondary Hwy 324 over the dam; turn right across cattle guard at river fishing access sign. Free. All year; 14-day limit. Tbls, toilets, cfga, drkg wtr. Hiking, fishing, birdwatching. View trout near large spring on W side of hiking trail

Deadman Gulch   **FREE**
Bureau of Land Management
55 mi S of Dillon on I-15; W at Dell exit. Free. All year; 14-day limit. Primitive undesignated sites.

Dinner Station   **FREE**
Beaverhead National Forest
12 mi N of Dillon on I-15; from Apex exit, 12 mi NW on Birch Creek Road. Free. 5/15-9/15; 16-day limit. 8 sites (16-ft RV limit). Toilets (handicapped facilities), cfga, drkg wtr. Picnicking; fishing; boating; hiking. Multi-family picnic area can be reserved. Elev 7500 ft; 5 acres.

Fishing Access   **FREE**
Clark Canyon Reservoir
Bureau of Reclamation
S of Dillon, at reservoir off I-15. Free. All year; 14-day limit. Primitive undesignated camping area. Toilets, drkg wtr, cfga. Fishing, boating (l). Concession nearby with gasoline, supplies, fee campground, marina.

Glen   **FREE**
Big Hole River
State Fishing Access Site
19 mi N of Dillon on I-15 to milepost 85, Glen exit; 6 mi S on frontage rd (stream mile 34.9). Free. All year; 7-day limit. Primitive camping on 9.4 acres; 30-ft RV limit. Toilets, cfga, tbls, no drkg wtr. Fishing, boating(l). Difficult access.

Grasshopper   **$8**
Beaverhead National Forest
4 mi S of Dillon on I-15; 22 mi NW on MT 278; 13 mi N on Hwy 73 (Pioneer Mountain Scenic Byway); half mi N on FR 484. Elev 7000 ft. $8 during MD-LD; 16-day limit; free rest of year, weather permitting, but no drkg wtr or trash service. 24 sites on 9 acres (RVs under 26 ft). Tbls, cfga, toilets, firewood, piped drkg wtr. Picnicking; horseback riding, fishing, boating(l).

Hap Hawkins   **FREE**
Clark Canyon Reservoir
Bureau of Reclamation
S of Dillon, at reservoir off I-15. Free. All year; 14-day limit. Primitive undesignated camping area. Toilets, drkg wtr, cfga. Fishing, boating. Concession nearby with gasoline, supplies, fee campground, marina.

High Bridge   **FREE**
Beaverhead River
State Fishing Access Site
14 mi S of Dillon on I-15 to recreation rd exit; 4 mi S under I-15 bridge (stream mile 23.2). Free. All year; 14-day limit. Primitive camping on 10.3 acres. No facilities, no drkg wtr. Fishing, boating(l). Very difficult access.

Horse Prairie   **FREE**
Clark Canyon Reservoir
Bureau of Reclamation
S of Dillon, at reservoir off I-15. Free. All year; 14-day limit. Primitive undesignated camping area. Toilets, drkg wtr, cfga. Fishing, boating(l). Concession nearby with gasoline, supplies, fee campground, marina.

Lewis & Clark   **FREE**
Clark Canyon Reservoir
Bureau of Reclamation
20 mi S of Dillon, at reservoir off I-15. Free.

All year; 14-day limit. Primitive undesignated camping area. Toilets, drkg wtr, cfga. Fishing, boating. Concession nearby with gasoline, supplies, fee campground, marina.

Lonetree   **FREE**
Clark Canyon Reservoir
Bureau of Reclamation
20 mi S of Dillon, at reservoir off I-15. Free. All year; 14-day limit. Primitive undesignated camping area. Toilets, drkg wtr, cfga. Fishing, boating (primitive ramp). Concession nearby with gasoline, supplies, fee campground, marina.

Price Creek   **$8**
Beaverhead National Forest
2.5 mi S of Dillon on I-15; from exit 58, right on Hwy 278 for 25.2 mi; right on Hwy 73 at Polaris for 16 mi; right on FR 2406 for qtr mi. $8. MD-LD; 14-day limit. 28 sites; 30-ft RV limit. Tbls, toilets, cfga, drkg wtr. Fishing, hiking.

Reservoir Lake   **FREE**
Beaverhead National Forest
19 mi S of Dillon on I-15; 16.8 mi W on MT 324; 10 mi NW on CR 1814; 5 mi N on FR 1813. Elev 7000 ft. Free. 6/1-9/15; 16-day limit. 16 sites on 11 acres (RVs under 16 ft). Tbls, toilets, cfga, firewood, well drkg wtr. Picnicking; swimming; fishing; boating(ld-no motors); horseback riding. Family picnic area can be reserved. Horse loading ramp. Fee for groups.

West Cameahwait   **FREE**
Clark Canyon Reservoir
Bureau of Reclamation
S of Dillon, at reservoir off I-15. Free. All year; 14-day limit. Primitive undesignated camping area. Toilets, drkg wtr, cfga. Fishing, boating. Concession nearby with gasoline, supplies, fee campground, marina.

DIVIDE (46)

Dickie Bridge   **FREE**
Big Hole River Recreation Area
Bureau of Land Management
10 mi W of Divide on Hwy 43. Free. All year; 14-day limit. Open camping for about 8 RVs; 24-ft RV limit. Toilets, cfga, no drkg wtr. Boating, fishing, picnicking, hiking.

Fishing tip: Big Hole River contains huge trout; try large orange salmon flies in spring.

Divide Bridge   **$6**
Bureau of Land Management
2.5 mi W of Divide on SR 43. $6 5/15-10/15; free rest of year; 14-day limit. 25 sites (24-ft RV limit). Toilets (handicap-accessible), cfga, drkg wtr. Picnicking, fishing, boating(l), hiking, backpacking trails. Elev 5400 ft.

East Bank   **FREE**
Big Hole River Recreation Area
Bureau of Land Management
17 mi W of Divide on SR 43. Free. All year; 14-day limit. 5 sites (RVs under 25 ft--no tents). Tbls, toilets, cfga, no drkg wtr. Boating(l), fishing, swimming.

Humbug Spires   **FREE**
Wilderness Study Area
Bureau of Land Management
I-15 S of Divide, Moose Creek exit; 3 mi NE on Moose Creek Rd. Free. All year; 14-day limit. Undesignated sites (24-ft RV limit); 14-day limit. Tbls, toilets, no drkg wtr (RVs under 25 ft). Backpacking trails. 11,175-acre public lands area.

Missouri River   **FREE & $7**
State Fishing Access Sites
Numerous scattered undesignated sites along 30-mi stretch of Missouri River just E of and parallel to I-15. All year; 14-day limit in 30-day period. Toilets, cfga, tbls, no drkg wtr. Boating(ld), fishing, hiking, picnicking. Sites include Big Bend, Dearborn (now $7), Eagle Island, Hardy Bridge, Mid Canon (now $7), Missouri Dunes, Mountain Palace (now $7), Pelican Point (now $7), Lower Smith River, Ulm Bridge, Spite Hill ($7), Stickney Creek ($7), White Bear and Wolf Creek Bridge (now $7).

DRUMMOND (47)

J. H. Mellen   **$10**
Memorial City Park
From I-90 exit 153, S to Frontage Rd, then E to center of Drummond; S (left) on Old Hwy 10A, following signs for city park); cross bridge over Clark Fork River, then left to park entrance. $10. 5/1-10/15. 12 sites. Flush toilets, cfga, drkg wtr, playground. Field report says dump station sealed shut & water faucets locked or broken. Boating(l), fishing.

DUPUYER (48)

Willim Jones   **FREE**
Memorial City Park
On W edge of town. Free. Primitive camping & picnic areas along Dupuyer Creek. Fishing, canoeing.

EAST GLACIER PARK (49)

Summit   **$10**
Lewis and Clark National Forest
13 mi SW of East Glacier on US 2; adjacent to Glacier National Park. $10. MD-LD; 14-day limit. 17 sites (36-ft RV limit). Tbls, toilets, cfga, drkg wtr, no trash service. Hiking trails. Elev 5200 ft; 10 acres. Roosevelt and Slippery Bill Morrison Memorials. Trailhead for Continental Divide National Scenic Trail. Nature trails, fishing. Snowmobiles okay 7/1-4/1.

EKALAKA (50)

Ekalaka Park   **FREE**
Custer National Forest
3.3 mi SE of Ekalaka on MT 323; .8 mi W on co rd; 5.1 mi S on FR 813; rd too narrow for any RV larger than pickup camper or folding trailer. Free. 5/1-11/15; 14-day limit. 10 sites. Tbls,

toilets, cfga, firewood, piped drkg wtr. Picnicking, hunting. Elev 3800 ft; 5 acres. Located in a cool hardwood draw. Pack out trash.

EMIGRANT (51)

Dailey Lake $7
State Fishing Access Site
1 mi E of Emigrant; 4 mi S on Hwy 540; 6 mi SE on co rd. $7 for licensed fishermen; others pay $12. All year; 7-day limit. 35 sites (no RV size limit). Tbls, toilets, cfga, no drkg wtr, shade shelter, fishing pier. Boating(dl), fishing, swimming. Fishing pier for disabled. Easy access.

ENNIS (52)

Bear Creek FREE
Beaverhead National Forest
10 mi S of Ennis on Hwy 287; 10 mi E on Bear Creek Rd. Free. 6/15-11/30; 16-day limit. 12 sites; 28-ft RV limit. Tbls, toilets, cfga, drkg wtr. Hiking, horseback riding. Elev 6350 ft.

Clover Meadows FREE
Beaverhead National Forest
1.5 mi SW of Ennis on Hwy 287; 10 mi S on Varney Rd; 12 mi SW on Call Rd 292; 8 mi S on Gravelly Range Rd. Free. 7/1-9/25; 16-day limit. 1 tent site. Tbl, toilet, cfga, no drkg wtr. Picnic area.

Ennis $7
Madison River
State Fishing Access Site
Qtr mi SE of Ennis on US 287 at Madison River. $7 for licensed fishermen; $12 for others. 5/1-11/30; 7-day limit. 22 sites (25-ft RV limit). Tbls, toilets, cfga, drkg wtr. Boating(l), fishing. Elev 5406 ft; 76.8 acres. Difficult access.
Fishing tip: Most dry fly fishermen seeking Madison River trout like bitch creek nymphs, girdle bugs, yuk bugs, parachute adams, bead-head pheasant tail, sofa pillow, bird's stonefly, elk hair caddis, Royal Wulffs and maribou streamers.

Meadow Lake FREE
State Fishing Access Site
6 mi N of Ennis on US 287 to milepost 55; 2 mi E on county rd. Free. All year; 7-day limit. Primitive undesignated sites; 25-ft RV limit. Tbls, toilets, cfga, no drkg wtr. Fishing, boating(l). 5.5 acres. Easy access.

Riverview $9
Beaverhead National Forest
34 mi S of Ennis on Hwy 287; at the Madison River. $9 during MD-10/15; free rest of year, weather permitting, but no wtr or trash service; 16-day limit. 20 sites; 30-ft RV limit. Tbls, toilets, cfga, drkg wtr. Fishing, hiking. Elev 6000 ft.
Fishing tip: The Madison River offers good fishing for whitefish and both rainbow & brown trout. Try Rooster Tail spinners; gold, silver and black lures, and black Daredevles.

South Madison Recreation Area $4
Bureau of Land Management
26 mi S of Ennis on US 287; turn right at the South Madison Recreation Area sign, and proceed qtr mi to campground. $4. All year; 14-day limit. 11 sites (35-ft RV limit). Tbls, toilets, cfga, firewood, drkg wtr, no trash service. Store. Hiking; hunting; float boating; mountain climbing; picnicking; fishing. Elev 5700 ft; 41 acres.
Fishing tip: There's excellent fishing for brook trout in Madison River. Fishing for Arctic grayling also is catch-and-release for the entire length of the Madison.

Valley Garden $7
Madison River
State Fishing Access Site
Half mi S of Ennis on US 287 to milepost 48, 2 mi N on co rd to Madison River (river mile 48.5). $7 for licensed fishermen; $12 for others. 4/1-11/30; 7-day limit. Undesignated sites (25-ft RV limit) on 143 acres. Tbls, toilets, cfga, no drkg wtr. Fishing, boating(l). Moderate access.
Fishing tip: This is a good base camp for catch-and-release trout fishing on the Madison River. If floating the river, cast slightly upstream, allowing your fly to sink before it begins to drag behind the boat. As soon as it drags, cast again.

Varney Bridge $7
Madison River
State Fishing Access Site
9 mi S of Ennis on US 287; 2 mi W on co rd to Madison River (river mile 59.9). $7 for licensed fishermen; $12 for others. All year; 7-day limit. Undesignated sites (20-ft RV limit). Tbls, toilets, cfga, no drkg wtr. Boating(l), fishing, picnicking, hiking. Elev 5400 ft; 220 acres. Easy access
Fishing tip: The upper Madison River between Quake Lake and Varney bridge is catch-and-release trout fishing with lures only. Bring the fish to net quickly so they can survive to provide sport another day. Below Varney Bridge, brown trout up to four pounds are not uncommon.

West Madison Recreation Area $4
Bureau of Land Management
18 mi S of Ennis on US 287, 3 mi S on BLM rd. $4. All year; 14-day limit. 22 sites (35-ft RV limit). Tbls, toilets, cfga, drkg wtr. Fishing; hiking; picnicking. No trash service. 128 acres, elev 5540 ft.

EUREKA (53)

Big Therriault Lake $5
Kootenai National Forest
7 mi SE of Eureka on US 93; 3.2 mi NE on CR 114; 10.6 mi NE on FR 114; 13 mi W on FR 319; S on FR 7085. $5 during 7/1-9/10; free rest of season (without wtr), but snowed in about 12/15-5/30; 14-day limit. 10 sites on 5 acres (32-ft RV limit). Tbls, toilets, cfga, firewood, drkg wtr. Boating(small boat

launch); picnicking; fishing; hiking. Scenic. Trailhead to Ten Lakes Scenic Area (1.5 mi). Elev 5700 ft.
Fishing tip: Fishing is only fair at both Big and Little Therriault Lakes, although they contain cutthroat trout.

Gateway Boat Camp FREE
Kootenai National Forest
1 mi N of Eureka on MT 93; 1.5 mi W on MT 37; 5.5 mi NW on CR 3392; 1.8 mi N, BY BOAT from Tobacco Plains boat ramp on Lake Koocanusa; on the US-Canada border. Free. Open 6/1-10/15 or when accessible; 14-day limit. 5 tent sites. Tbls, toilets, cfga, firewood, no drkg wtr. Picnicking; fishing; Elev 2500 ft; 3 acres. Pack out all trash. Trail leads from camp to Swisher Lake.
Fishing tip: Lake Koocanusa offers excellent fishing for kokanee salmon and also whitefish, brown trout and rainbows. Below the dam, Kootenai River is a wonderful fishery.

Glen Lake FREE
State Fishing Access Site
6 mi S of Eureka on Hwy 93; 6 mi E on county rd. Free. All year; 14-day limit. About 5 primitive sites. Tbls, toilet, cfga, no drkg wtr. Boating (l), hiking, fishing.

North Dickey Lake $7
Kootenai National Forest
13 mi SE of Eureka on US 93. $7. All year; 14-day limit. 25 sites (32-ft RV limit). Tbls, toilets, cfga, drkg wtr. Swimming beach, fishing, picnicking. Elev 3200 ft; 8 acres.
Fishing tip: Dicky lake contains kamloop & kokanee salmon and mostly small brook trout.

Rock Lake FREE
Kootenai National Forest
1.3 mi SE on CR 854; 1 mi SE on FR 3656; 2.3 mi SE on FR 688; .8 mi SE on FR 3683 (rough rd). Free. 5/15-9/30; 14-day limit. 5 sites (20-ft RV limit). Tbls, toilets, cfga, firewood, no drkg wtr. Picnicking; fishing; boating (carry-in boat launch). Elev 3000 ft; 3 acres.

Rocky Gorge $9
Kootenai National Forest
30 mi SW of Eureka on SR 37; on Lake Koocanusa. $9 during MD-9/30; free rest of year when accessible, but no wtr or services; 14-day limit. 60 sites (32-ft RVs or larger okay). Tbls, toilets, cfga, drkg wtr. Fishing, picnicking, hiking trails, cross-country & downhill skiing, waterskiing. Elev 2470 ft; 25 acres.
Fishing tip: The 46,500-acre lake offers excellent fishing for kokanee salmon, whitefish, rainbow & brown trout.

Swisher Lake FREE
Kootenai National Forest
1 mi S of Eureka on US 93; 3 mi W on SR 37; 5 mi N on county rd. Free. 4/15-11/30; 14-day limit. 4 primitive tent sites. Tbls, toilets,

cfga, no drkg wtr. Fishing, boating(l). Fishing & boating access also on nearby Sophie, Moran, Terault Lake and from the Tobacco Plains day use area at nearby Koocanusa Lake.

FISHTAIL (54)

Emerald Lake   **$9**
Custer National Forest
1 mi W of Fishtail on CR 419; 6 mi SW on CR 425 (West Rosebud Rd); 12 mi S on rutted FR 72. $9. MD-LD; 10-day limit. 32 sites; 30-ft RV limit. Tbls, toilets, cfga, drkg wtr. Fishing (rainbow trout), boating (no motors), picnicking, hiking. Elev 6400 ft; 11 acres.

Pine Grove   **$9**
Custer National Forest
1 mi W of Fishtail on CR 419; 6 mi SW on CR 426; 8 mi S on rough FR 72. $9. MD-9/15; 10-day limit. 46 sites, including large group site; 30-ft RV limit. Tbls, toilets, cfga, drkg wtr. Along West Rosebud Creek. Fishing, picnicking, hiking trail.

FORSYTH (55)

East Rosebud   **$7**
Yellowstone River
State Fishing Access Site
From E exit of I-94 at Forsyth, one-eighth mi N to Yellowstone River (stream mile 235.5). $7 for licensed fishermen; $12 others. 5/1-11/30; 7-day limit (open to fishing all year). 18 sites (25-ft RV limit). Tbls, toilets, cfga, drkg wtr. Boating(l), fishing, nature trail (no signs). Elev 2515 ft; 29 acres. Difficult access.

Far West   **FREE**
Yellowstone River
State Fishing Access Site
10 mi E of Forsyth on I-94; N at exit 102, then E on frontage rd 1 mi; 1 mi N on Hey 446; 1 mi W on county rd; at Yellowstone River (river mile 222.7). Free. All year; 7-day limit. Primitive camping on 33 acres. Tbls, toilets, cfga, no drkg wtr. Boating, fishing; concrete boat launch half mi W of camp. Difficult site access.

Wagon Wheel Campground   **$11**
Qtr mi S of I-94 exit 95 at Forsyth. $11 for primitive sites; $16 full hookups. 20 sites. Tbls, flush toilets, showers, cfga, drkg wtr, hookups($).

West Rosebud   **FREEE**
Yellowstone River
State Fishing Access Site
W of Forsyth on US 12 at S end of Yellowstone River bridge, milepost 270 (stream mile 236.6). Free. All year; 7-day limit. 10 sites. Tbl, toilet, cfga, no drkg wtr. Fishing, boating(l). 11.8 acres. Difficult access.

FORT BENTON (56)

Coal Banks Landing   **FREE**
Missouri River Waterway
Bureau of Land Management
N of Fort Benton, milepost 67, on US 87; 8 mi S on co rd, following signs; or, 8 mi E BY BOAT on Missouri River. Free. 5/1-10/1; 14-day limit. 5 sites; 24-ft RV limit. Toilets, tbls, cfga, drkg wtr. Boating; picnicking, fishing.

FORT PECK (57)

Bear Creek   **FREE**
Fort Peck Lake
Corps of Engineers
11 mi SE of Fort Peck on SR 24; 7 mi W on co rd. Free. All year; 14-day limit. Undesignated primitive camping area. Toilets, tbls, cfga, drkg wtr. Fishing, boating (no ramp), hiking.
Fishing tip: September and October are the best months to fish Fort Peck Lake's Bear Creek for lunker chinook salmon and lake trout. Some of them, returning to the creek where they were stocked in order to spawn, reach up to 30 pounds. The salmon don't reproduce naturally in the lake, so they're stocked -- and more than 200,000 of them were put into the lake in the year 2000, promising good fishing for the next few years. For fall lake trout, troll crankbaits 12-15 feet or jig for them.

Bone Trail   **FREE**
Fort Peck Lake
Corps of Engineers
60 mi SW of Fort Peck on Willow Creek Rd. All year; 14-day limit. 6 primitive sites (16-ft RV limit). Toilets, cfga, no drkg wtr. Boating(l), fishing, swimming.
Fishing tip: Finding walleyes on Fort Peck Lake is difficult because they're known to be especially nomadic. That's because they're always chasing their primary food fish -- the cisco. So experienced anglers tend to do a lot of trolling in order to find fish; then they anchor and cast or drift-fish.

Downstream   **$10**
Fort Peck lake
Corps of Engineers
1 mi E of Fort Peck on SR 117, below dam on Missouri River. $10 without hookups. $12 with elec. About 5/1-10/31; 14-day limit. 74 sites (71 with elec); 65-ft RVs. Tbls, flush toilets, showers, cfga, drkg wtr, elec ($), dump. Picnicking, boating(l), hiking trails, playground, fishing.
Fishing tip: The most popular walley lures at Fort Peck are Shad Raps, Reef Runners, Wally Divers, bottom-bumping spinners with nightcrawlers or leeches, or jig-and-minnow combinations.

Duck Creek   **FREE**
Fort Peck Lake
Corps of Engineers
4 mi SW of Fort Peck on co rd. Free. All year; 14-day limit. Primitive undesignated sites (no RV size limit). Toilets, cfga, no drkg wtr. Boating(l), fishing.
Fishing tip: Duck Creek Bay has numerous shoreline fingers that are productive. Keep in mind that in 1991, Fort Peck Lake produced the state's biggest chinook salmon -- 31.13 pounds. From the lake also was landed the state record 4.88-pound coho salmon in 1973, a record 25.8-pound channel catfish in 1988, an 8.8-pound sauger in 1994, a 15.66-pound saugeye in 1995 and a 16.29-pound walleye in 1995.

Fort Peck Dredge Cuts   **FREE**
State Fishing Access Site
3 mi N of Fort Peck on SR 117; half mi W on gravel rd; easy access. Free. All year; 14-day limit. Primitive open camping; 35-ft RV limit. Tbls, toilets, cfga, no drkg wtr. Boating(ld), fishing. No wake allowed; waterskiing now banned.

McGuire Creek   **FREE**
Fort Peck Lake
Corps of Engineers
41 mi SE of Fort Peck on SR 24; 7 mi W on co rd. Free. All year; 14-day limit. 10 primitive sites (16-ft RV kimit). Toilets, cfga, no drkg wtr. Boating(l; primitive), fishing.
Fishing tip: This area of the lake provides excellent northern pike and smallmouth bass fishing. Cast spoons and shallow-running crankbaits along the edge of weeds for pike, and use spinnerbaits and plastics over and around submerged rocks for bass.

Nelson Creek   **FREE**
Fort Peck Lake
Corps of Engineers
49 mi S of Fort Peck on SR 24; 7 mi W on co rd. Free. All year; 14-day limit. 16 primitive sites (40-ft RV limit). Tbls, toilets, cfga, no drkg wtr, fishing pier. Fishing, boating(l).
Fishing tip: Walleyes begin hitting in mid-May, and while you're trying to catch 12-pounders, keep in mind you might also hook a 15-pound northern pike, sauger of 4-5 pounds or lake trout up to 17.

Rock Creek   **FREE**
State Fishing Access Site
30 mi S of Fort Peck on SR 24; 7 mi W on county rd; at Fort Peck Lake. Free. All year; 7-day limit. Primitive undesignated sites. Tbls, toilets, cfga, no drkg wtr, fish cleaning station. Boating(l), fishing. 5 acres. Moderate access.

Roundhouse Point   **FREE**
Fort Peck Lake
Corps of Engineers
3Below dam on SR 117, across rd from swimming beach. Free. All year; 14-day limit. Primitive undesignated sites. Toilets, cfga, no drkg wtr. Boating(l), fishing, swimming.
Fishing tip: In fall, catch spawning lake trout.

The Pines Campground   **FREE**
Fort Peck Lake
Corps of Engineers
33 mi SW of Fort Peck on co rd; 12 mi mi SW on Willow Creek Rd. Roads impassable when wet. Free. All year; 14-day limit. About 30 primitive sites; 30-ft RV limit. Pit toilets, tbls, cfga, drkg wtr, fishing pier. Swimming; boating(l); fishing; playground. Limited facilities in winter. 200 acres.

Fishing tip: Northern pike are plentiful here and can be caught in shallow water. Use large spoons and Flatfish for trolling, or drift with minnows.

West End Recreation Area   **$10**
Fort Peck Lake
Corps of Engineers
2 mi SW of Fort Peck to SR 24; half mi W, 1 mi S, on W side of dam. $10 (overflow sites $5). 5/1-10/15; 14-day limit. 13 sites; 35-ft RV limit. Flush toilets, cfga, drkg wtr, tbls, elec/wtr hookups, showers. Self-registration. Boating(l), fishing, swimming. 350 acres.

Fishing tip: Near camp, the face of Fort Peck dam is a good place to find lake trout, particularly in May and June. In summer, lakers are in cooler deep water, but in the spring, they can be landed by trolling 15-20 feet deep.

FORTINE (58)

Grave Creek   **FREE**
Kootenai National Forest
2.8 mi NW on US 93; 2.1 mi NE on CR 114; half mi E on FR 7019. Narrow rd to creek. Free. All year, but serviced 5/15-9/10; 14-day limit. 4 sites (20-ft RV limit). Tbls, toilets, cfga, firewood, no drkg wtr. Picnicking; fishing.

Fishing tip: Try the nearby Lolo Creek for some excellent trout fishing.

Little Therriault Lake   **$5**
Kootenai National Forest
2.8 mi NW of Fortine on US 93; 3.2 mi NE on CR 114 (Grave Creek Rd); 13.2 mi W on FR 319; S on FR 7085. $5 during MD-10/15; free rest of year when accessible, but no wtr; 14-day limit. 6 sites (32-ft RV limit). Tbls, toilets, cfga, firewood, drkg wtr. Boating (hand launch); horseback riding; picnicking; fishing(d); hiking. Elev 5800 ft; 1 acre. Trailhead to Ten Lakes Scenic Area(1 mi).

Fishing tip: Fishing is only fair for cutthroat trout at both Big and Little Therriault Lakes.

GALLATIN GATEWAY (59)

Spire Rock   **$9**
Gallatin National Forest
11.4 mi S of Gallatin Gateway on US 191; 3.3 mi E on FR 1321 (Squaw Creek Rd); at Squaw Creek. $9 during 5/15-9/15; free rest of year, but reduced services. 16-day limit. 16 sites (50-ft RV limit). Tbls, toilets, cfga, firewood, no drkg wtr. Picnicking; fishing. Elev 5600 ft; 5 acres. Spanish Peaks Wilderness Area (5 mi W).

GARDINER (60)

Canyon Campground   **$7**
Gallatin National Forest
18 mi N of Gardiner on US 89; at Yellowstone River. $7. All year; 16-day limit. 12 sites; 48-ft RV limit. Tbls, toilets, cfga, no drkg wtr. Pack out trash. Fishing, boating. Less than 20 mi from Yellowstone NP. Boat ramp at nearby Yankee Jim Canyon.

Fishing tip: Fishing in the Yellowstone is excellent for rainbow, brown, goldeye trout, shorthead redhorse and mountain whitefish.

Carbella Recreation Site   **FREE**
Bureau of Land Management
20 mi N of Gardiner on US 89; 1 mi W at Miner. Free. All year; 14-day limit. 20 sites (RVs under 35 ft). Tbls, toilets, cfga, no drkg wtr. Boating (primitive launch), fishing.

Eagle Creek   **$7**
Gallatin National Forest
3 mi NE of Gardiner on FR 493 (Jardine Rd). $7. All year; 16-day limit. 16 sites (48-ft RV limit). Cfga, no drkg wtr, tbls, toilets, corral, horse facilities. Pack out trash. Picnicking, fishing, hiking horseback riding. 2 mi from Yellowstone NP. Elev 6200 ft.

Fishing tip: Try the Yellowstone River, one of America's most famous trout streams, for cutthroat, rainbow & browns. Best bet is to fish from a drifting boat using spinners or flies, although wading & bank fishing can be productive in places too.

Tom Miner   **$7**
Gallatin National Forest
16 mi NW of Gardiner on US 89; 12 mi SW on CR 63; 3.5 mi SW on FR 63. $7. 6/1-10/31; 16-day limit. 16 sites (35-ft RV limit). Tbls, toilets, cfga, drkg wtr. Pack out trash. Petrified forest, hiking, fishing. Elev 6640 ft. Near the remote NW corner of Yellowstone NP.

GLENDIVE (62)

Intake Dam   **$7**
Yellowstone River
State Fishing Access Site
16 mi N of Glendive on SR 16; 3 mi S on county rd; difficult access. $7 for licensed fishermen; $12 for others. All year; 7-day limit. Free 10/1-5/14, but no drkg wtr. Open area; undesignated primitive sites. Tbls, toilets, cfga, drkg wtr. Fishing (paddlefish, catfish, walleye), boating(l), picnicking. 92 acres.

JC West   **FREE**
Municipal Park
Glendive exit from I-94, to town; at 100 W Towne St. Free. 5/1-10/1; 2-day limit. 20 sites (RVs under 25 ft). Pool, wading pool, 4 tennis courts, playground, drkg wtr, dump. Grocery, cafe nearby. Boating(l) nearby. Quiet, next to Yellowstone River.

Makoshika State Park   **$12**
Qtr mi SE of Glendive on Snyder Ave. All year; $12 ($10 off-season). All year; 14-day limit. 22 sites (40-ft RV size limit). Tbls, pit toilets, cfga, drkg wtr. Flush toilets in visitor center. Hiking trails, picnicking, Frisbee golf, interpretive trail. Elev 2069 ft; 11,531 acres. Fossil/dinosaur interpretive displays, shooting range, archery range, wildlife viewing. Badlands nature trail; 12-mile scenic drive (no trailers).

GREAT FALLS (63)

Sluice Boxes State Park   **FREE**
8 mi S of Belt on US 89; half mi W on co rd. Free. All year; 7-day limit. 17 primitive undesignated sites. Toilets, cfga, no drkg wtr. Fishing, hiking trails, interpretive programs, river floating. 1,451 acres.

GREYCLIFF (64)

Pelican   **FREE**
Yellowstone River
State Fishing Access Site
1 mi NE of Greycliff on county rd; at upper Yellowstone River. Free. All year; 7-day limit. Primitive camping on 122 acres. Tbls, toilets, cfga, no drkg wtr. Boating(l), fishing. Difficult access.

HAMILTON (65)

Black Bear   **FREE**
Bitterroot National Forest
3 mi S of Hamilton on US 93; 12.9 mi E on MT 38. Free. 6/1-9/15; 10-day limit. 6 sites (50-ft RV limit). Tbls, toilets, cfga, firewood, no drkg wtr. Hunting; hiking; picnicking; fishing(1 mi).

Blodgett Canyon Trailhead   **FREE**
Bitterroot National Forest
5 mi NW of Hamilton. 5/15-9/15; 5-day limit. 7 sites (45-ft RV limit). Tbls, toilets, cfga, no drkg wtr. Fishing, swimming.

Hannon Memorial   **$7**
Bitterroot River
State Fishing Access Site
20 mi S of Hamilton on Hwy 93 to milepost 27 (stream mile 81.8). $7 for licensed fishermen; others pay $12. All year; 7-day limit. Primitive camping on 57.8 acres. 6 sites; 25-ft RV limit. Toilet, cfga, tbls, no drkg wtr. Boating(l), fishing. One of two areas; second is day use only.

Painted Rocks State Park   **FREE**
17 mi S of Hamilton on US 93; 23 mi SW on Secondary 473; at Painted Rocks Reservoir. Free, but donations accepted. All year; 14-day limit. 25 primitive sites; 25-ft RV limit. Tbls, toilets, cfga, no drkg wtr. Boating(dl), swimming, fishing, biking. 293 acres.

Wally Crawford   **FREE**
Bitterroot River
State Fishing Access Site
S of Hamilton off Hwy 93 at Coms Broke

(stream mile 71.6). Free. All year; 14-day limit. Primitive camping on 1.7 acres. Toilets, tbls, cfga, no drkg wtr. Boating(l), fishing. Difficult access.

HARDIN (66)

Arapooish   **FREE**
Bighorn River
State Fishing Access Site
1 mi NE of Hardin on Hwy 47; 2 mi E on co rd (river mile 40.7). Free. 4/1-10/31; 14-day limit. Primitive camping on 95 acres. Tbls, toilets, cfga, no drkg wtr. Boating(l), fishing, hiking trail. Managed jointly by state & Bighorn County. Access to Bighorn River & Koyama's Pond.

Bighorn   **$7**
Bighorn River
State Fishing Access Site
29 mi S of Hardin on Hwy 313 (stream mile 71.7). $7 for licensed fishermen; $12 for others. All year; 7-day limit. Primitive camping on 112 acres. Tbl, toilet, cfga, no drkg wtr. Fishing, boating(l). Heavily used by outfitters; termination point for upriver floaters.

General Custer   **FREE**
Bighorn River
State Fishing Access Site
13 mi N of Hardin on Hwy 47 (stream mile 24.2). Free. All year; 7-day limit. Primitive undesignated camping on 34 acres. Toilet, cfga, no drkg wtr. Boating(l), fishing. Difficult access.

Grant Marsh   **FREE**
Bighorn River
State Fishing Access Site
7 mi N of Hardin on Hwy 47; 1 mi E on county rd (stream mile 31.7); very difficult access. Free. All year; 7-day limit. Primitive camping; no facilities except toilet, no drkg wtr, no trash service. Boating(l), fishing.

Two Leggins   **FREE**
Bighorn River
State Fishing Access Site
8 mi N of Hardin on Hwy 313 (stream mile 52); on Crow Indian Reservation. Free. All year; 7-day limit. Primitive undesignated camping on 30 acres. Toilet added 2006; no other facilities, no drkg wtr. Boating(l), fishing. Difficult access, but good access to Bighorn River. On Crow Indian Reservation.

HARLOWTON (67)

Chief Joseph City Park   **$3**
W end of town on US 12. $3 base. 4/1-10/31. Base fee for tent sites; $6 for RV sites with no hookups; $8 for RV sites with elec. 8 RV sites; unlimited tent camping. Tbls, flush toilets, cfga, drkg wtr, showers. Hiking trails, fishing pond, picnic shelters, playground.

Deadman's Basin   **FREE**
State Fishing Access Site
20 mi E of Harlowton on US 12 to milepost 120; 1 mi N on co rd. Free. All year; 7-day limit. Undesignated sites. Tbls, toilets, cfga, no drkg wtr. Boating (l), fishing. 101 acres. Difficult access, but popular site.

Selkirk   **FREE**
Musselshell River
State Fishing Access Site
19 mi W of Harlowton on Hwy 13; at Musselshelf River (river mile 338.7). Free. All year; 7-day limit. Primitive sites on 265 acres. Tbls, toilets, cfga, no drkg wtr. Fishing, boating (primitive launch). Moderate access.

Fishing tip: The Mussellshell produces great catches of channel catfish, including fish up to 30 pounds.

HARRISON (68)

Potosi   **FREE**
Beaverhead National Forest
7 mi W of Harrison on Pony Rd; at Pony, go 10 mi S on South Willow Creek Rd. Free. MD-9/15; 16-day limit. 15 sites (22-ft RV limit). Tbls, toilets, cfga, firewood, drkg wtr. Horseback riding; picnicking; fishing. Elev 6200 ft; 3 acres. Scenic. South Willow Creek drainage. Stream.

HAVRE (69)

Bearpaw Lake   **$7**
State Fishing Access
21mi S of Havre on Hwy 234. $7 for licensed fishermen; others pay $12. All year; 7-day limit. Toilets, tbls, cfga, no drkg wtr. Primitive sites on 185 acres. Fishing, hiking, boating (no motors of any type), fishing pier. Easy access.

Beaver Creek   **$5**
Hill County Park
10 mi S of Havre on Hwy 234; on Fifth Ave. $5 daily or $30 annually. All year; 14-day limit. 254 sites. Tbls, toilets, cfga, drkg wtr, dump, rec room, dump. Boating(l), fishing, horseback riding & hiking trails, swimming, canoeing, winter sports. 2 lakes. 10,000 acres along N slope of Bear Paw Mtns; said to be among the nation's largest county parks. Fees not verified for 2007.

Fishing tip: The lower lake contains trout, walleye, perch and northern pike up to 30 pounds. The upper lake contains rainbow and brook trout and smallmouth bass. Miles of creeks also provide excellent fishing.

Fresno Beach   **FREE**
Fresno Reservoir
Bureau of Reclamation
W of Havre on US 2; 2 mi N on co rd; follow signs to site at reservoir. Free. All year; 14-day limit. Primitive undesignated camping area. Toilets, no drkg wtr, cfga. Fishing, boating(l), swimming.

Fishing tip: Each year, wallleyes of up to

10 pounds and northern pike of 20 pounds are caught here.

Fresno Tailwater   **FREE**
Milk River
State Fishing Access Site
11 mi W of Havre on Hwy 2; 1 mi N on Fresno Rd; at Milk River. All year; 7-day limit. Primitive camping on Bureau of Reclamation land adjacent to the fishing site. Tbls, toilets, cfga, no drkg wtr, fishing pier. Boating(l), fishing. 35.6 acres.

Kiehns   **FREE**
Fresno Reservoir
Bureau of Reclamation
W of Havre on US 2; 2 mi N on co rd; follow signs to site at reservoir. Free. All year; 14-day limit. Primitive undesignated camping area. Toilets, no drkg wtr, cfga. Fishing, boating, swimming.

Kremlin   **FREE**
Fresno Reservoir
Bureau of Reclamation
W of Havre on US 2; 2 mi N on co rd; follow signs to site at reservoir. Free. All year; 14-day limit. Primitive undesignated camping area. Toilets, no drkg wtr, cfga. Fishing, boating, swimming.

River Run   **FREE**
Fresno Reservoir
Bureau of Reclamation
W of Havre on US 2; 2 mi N on co rd; follow signs to site at reservoir. Free. All year; 14-day limit. Primitive undesignated camping area. Toilets, no drkg wtr, cfga. Fishing, boating, swimming.

✪ HELENA (70)

Canyon Ferry   **$8**
Bureau of Reclamation
Bureau of Land Management
10 mi E of Helena on US 12/287; 8 mi N on CR 284. $8. Formerly state park; now returned to BOR. 5/1-9/30; 10-day limit. 233 sites at 12 developed camping areas (some free) with 3 commercial marinas, 7 boat docks, 2 boat access areas. Tbls, flush & pit toilets, cfga, drkg wtr. Swimming, boating(), fishing, waterskiing. Elev 3800 ft; 9,000 acres.

Fishing tip: Sample nettings of fish in Canyon Ferry Lake revealed that walleye numbers are increasing fairly rapidly, promising to provide an excllent fishery for years to come.

Coulter   **FREE**
Helena National Forest
2 mi NE of Helena on US 91; 15 mi N on US 15; 2.8 mi E on CR 17; 3.8 mi NE, BY BOAT (on lake) or trail. Free. MD-9/15; 15-day limit. 7 tent sites. Tbls, toilets, cfga, well drkg wtr. Boating(d); waterskiing; hiking; picnicking; fishing; sailing. Elev 3600 ft. Gates of the Mountains Wilder-ness. Limestone rock formation. Nature trails. Gates of the Mountains Wilderness Boat Club Landing 4 mi downriver or launch from the dam.

Cave Bay — $8
Bureau of Reclamation
Bureau of Land Management
E of Helena at milepost 55 on US 287; 10 mi NE on CR 284; on Canyon Ferry Reservoir. $8. All year; 10-day limit. Undesignated sites. Toilets, drkg wtr, cfga. Swimming, picnicking, fishing. Formerly part of Canyon Ferry State Park.

Chinaman's Recreation Area — $8
Bureau of Reclamation
Bureau of Land Management
9 mi E of Helena, milepost 55, on US 287; 10 mi NE on CR 284. $8. 5/1-9/30; 10-day limit. 40 sites. Flush toilets, tbls, cfga, drkg wtr, dump. Boating(l); picnicking; fishing; swimming. Elev 3800 ft. Formerly part of Canyon Ferry State Park.

Court Sheriff — $8
Bureau of Reclamation
Bureau of Land Management
9 mi E of Helena, milepost 55, on US 287; 9 mi NE on CR 284. $8. 5/1-9/30; 10-day limit. 25 sites. Toilets, drkg wtr, tbls, cfga, picnic shelters. Swimming; picnicking, boating (4WD launch). Formerly part of Canyon Ferry State Park.

Cromwell-Dixon — $8
Helena National Forest
17 mi SW of Helena on US 12. $8. MD-9/15; 15-day limit. 15 sites (35-ft RV limit). Toilets, tbls, cfga, drkg wtr. Fishing, hiking trails. Replica Frontier Town nearby. On the continental divide.

Fish Hawk — $8
Bureau of Reclamation
Bureau of Land Management
9 mi E of Helena on US 287; 8 mi NE on Hwy 284 to Yachat Basin; 1 mi S on West Shore Rd. $8. All year; 10-day limit. Undesignated sites. Tbls, toilets, cfga, no drkg wtr. Fishing, boating, picnicking, swimming.

Hellgate Recreation Area — $8
Bureau of Reclamation
Bureau of Land Management
9 mi E of Helena, milepost 55, on US 287; 18 mi NE on CR 284. $8. All year; 10-day limit. 130 sites. Toilets, drkg wtr, picnic shelters. Boating(l); swimming; picnicking. Formerly part of Canyon Ferry State Park.

Jo Bonner — $8
Bureau of Reclamation
Bureau of Land Management
9 mi E of Helena on US 287; 12 mi NE on Hwy 284. $8. All year; 14-day limit. Undesignated sites (no RV size limit). Tbls, toilets, cfga, drkg wtr. Boating(l), fishing. Formerly part of Canyon Ferry State Park.

Kading — $5
Helena National Forest
23.3 mi W on MT 12; 4 mi S on CR 227; 9 mi SW on FR 227. $5 during MD-10/15; free rest of year, but no drkg wtr; 15-day limit. 10 sites (35-ft RV limit). Tbls, toilets, cfga, firewood, piped drkg wtr, no trash service. Berry picking; picnicking; fishing; boating; hiking; horseback riding (corral); hunting. Little Blackfoot River (brook trout). Elev 6100 ft.

Moose Creek — $5
Helena National Forest
10 mi W of Helena on US 12; 4 mi SW on Rimini Rd; at confluence of Tenmile Creek & Moose Creek. $5. MD-9/15; 14-day limit. 9 sites (32-ft RV limit). Tbls, toilets, cfga, drkg wtr, no trash service. Fishing, hiking trails. Elev 5100 ft; 4 acres.

Overlook — $8
Bureau of Reclamation
Bureau of Land Management
E of Helena, milepost 55, on US 287; NE on CR 284 to yacht basin; 1 mi S. $8. All year; 10-day limit. Undesignated sites. Toilets, no drkg wtr. Picnicking. Formerly part of Canyon Ferry State Park.

Ponderosa Recreation Area — $8
Bureau of Reclamation
Bureau of Land Management
9 mi E of Helena, milepost 55, on US 287; 9 mi NE on CR 284. $8. All year; 14-day limit. 49 sites (no RV size limit). Toilets, tbls, cfga, drkg wtr. Boating; swimming; picnicking. Formerly part of Canyon Ferry State Park.

Riverside Recreation Area — $8
Bureau of Reclamation
Bureau of Land Management
9 mi E of Helena, milepost 55, on US 287; 9 mi NE on CR 284 to Canyon Ferry Village; 1 mi NW on FR 224 toward power plant. $6. All year; 14-day limit. Undesignated sites. Toilets, drkg wtr. Boating(l), fishing, picnicking. Formerly part of Canyon Ferry State Park.

Shannon — $8
Bureau of Reclamation
Bureau of Land Management
9 mi E of Helena on US 287 at milepost 55; 8 mi NE on Secondary 284. $8. All year; 14-day limit. Undesignated sites (no RV size limit). Tbls, toilets, cfga, drkg wtr. Fishing, hiking trails. Formerly part of Canyon Ferry State Park.

Tizer Lakes — FREE
State Fishing Access Site
18 mi S of Helena on I-15 at Jefferson City exit; 3 mi SE on gravel rd, then 8 mi E on pack trail. Free. All year; 7-day limit. Undesignated hike-in tent sites in Elkhorn Mountains of Helena NF; difficult access. No facilities. Fishing, hiking. 142 acres.

Vigilante — $5
Helena National Forest
E on Custer Ave 1.3 mi from jct with Montana Ave in Helena; bear left at Y onto York Rd for 24.3 mi; at Trout Creek. $5 during MD-9/15; free rest of year but no wtr or services; 14-day limit. 18 sites. Tbls, toilets, cfga, drkg wtr, no trash service. Hiking trail, fishing, horseback riding, mountain biking.

White Earth Recreation Area — $8
Bureau of Reclamation
Bureau of Land Management
32 mi SE of Helena to Winston, milepost 64, on US 287; 5 mi E on co rd. $8. All year; 10-day limit. 40 sites (no RV size limit). Toilets, drkg wtr. Boating(l), picnicking, fishing. Formerly part of Canyon Ferry State Park.

Wolf Creek Bridge — $7
Missouri River
State Fishing Access Site
35 mi N of Helena on I-15 to Wolf Creek exit 226; 2 mi N on Recreation Rd (stream mile 2,199.5). $7 for licensed fishermen; $12 for others. All year; 7-day limit. Developed sites on 2 acres. Toilets, tbls, cfga, no drkg wtr. Boating(l), fishing. Good access.

York Bridge — $7
State Fishing Access Site
7 mi N of Helena on I-15; 5 mi E on Secondary 453; 4 mi S on Lake Helena Dr; 5 mi E on York Rd (Secondary 280); easy access. $7 for licensed fishermen; $12 others. All year; 7-day limit during 30-day period. 14 sites (30-ft RV limit). Tbls, toilets, cfga, drkg wtr. Boating(l), fishing, picnicking. Dump, phone, store at nearby private campground. 10 acres.

HOBSON (71)

Hay Canyon — FREE
Lewis and Clark National Forest
12 mi W on MT 239; 11.8 mi SW on co rd; 4.4 mi SW on FR 487. Free. Elev 5300 ft. 6/15-LD; 14-day limit. 9 sites (30-ft RV limit). Tbls, toilets, cfga, firewood, no drkg wtr. Fishing; picnicking, 4WD activities, hunting, rockhounding for Yogo sapphires.

Indian Hill — FREE
Lewis and Clark National Forest
12 mi W of Hobson on MT 239; 11.8 mi SW on co rd; 3.1 mi SW on FR 487; at South Fork of Judith River. Free. 6/15-LD; 14-day limit. 7 sites (20-ft RV limit). Tbls, toilets, cfga, firewood, no drkg wtr. Picnicking; fishing; horseback riding, rockhounding for Yogo sapphires.

HUNGRY HORSE (72)

Abbot Bay Boat Launch — FREE
Flathead National Forest
Half mi E of Hungry Horse on US 2; 5 mi S along E side of Hungry Horse Reservoir on FR 38; about 1 mi W on Abbot Bay Rd (FR 5301). Free. 5/15-9/30; 14-day limit. Primitive undesignated sites. Toilets, cfga, no drkg wtr. Pack out trash. Boating(l), fishing, hiking. Elev 3600 ft.

Beaver Creek — FREE
Flathead National Forest
Half mi E of Hungry Horse on US 2, then follow signs for E side of Hungry Horse Reservoir, following FR 38 (Abbot Bay Rd) 54 mi

S, then 8.5 mi E on FR 568; at Spotted Bear River. Free. MD-10/1, but open all year if accessible (call 406-387-3800); 14-day limit. 4 sites; 32-ft RV limit. Tbls, toilets, cfga, no drkg wtr. Fishing, hiking, horseback riding, hunting. Stock loading ramp.

Canyon Creek Boat Ramp   **FREE**
Flathead National Forest
Half mi E of Hungry Horse on US 2; 26 mi S along E side of Hungry Horse Reservoir on FR 38 (Abbot Bay Rd). Free. MD-10/1; 14-day limit. Dispersed primitive camping. Toilets, cfga, no drkg wtr. Fishing, boating(l).

Crossover Boat Ramp   **FREE**
Flathead National Forest
Half Mi E of Hungry Horse on US 2; about 45 mi S along E side of Hungry Horse Reservoir on FR 38. Free. MD-10/1; 14-day limit. Primitive, undeveloped sites near boat launch. Toilets, cfga, no drkg wtr. Fishing, boating(l).

Devil's Corkscrew   **FREE**
Flathead National Forest
Half mi E of Hungry Horse on US 2; about 37 mi S along E side of Hungry Horse Reservoir on FR 38. Free. MD-10/1; 14-day limit. 4 primitive sites; 32-ft RV limit. Toilets, cfga, no drkg wtr. Boating(l), fishing, hiking, mountain biking. Trapper's grave.

Doris Point Campground   **FREE**
Flathead National Forest
8 mi SE of Hungry Horse on FR 895 (on W side of national park). Free. 6/15-9/30; 14-day limit. 18 tent sites. Tbls, toilets, cfga, no drkg wtr. Picnicking, fishing, swimming.

Elk Island   **FREE**
Flathead National Forest
8 mi SE of Hungry Horse on FR 895; 10 mi SE, BY BOAT. Free. 5/15-9/30; 14-day limit. 7 tent sites. Tbls, cfga, firewood, no drkg wtr. Swimming; picnicking; fishing; boating. 7 acres. Pack out trash.

Fire Island Campground   **FREE**
Flathead National Forest
Boat to the island from any launchoing point on Hungry Horse Reservoir. Free. 5/15-9/30; 14-day limit. 4 tent sites in the middle of the lake. Toilets, cfga, no drkg wtr. Pack out trash. Beware of bears.

Graves Bay Campground   **FREE**
Flathead National Forest
35 mi SE of Hungry Horse on FR 895; near W shore of Hungry Horse Reservoir. Free. 6/15-9/30; 14-day limit. 10 sites; 22-ft RV limit. Toilets, cfga, no drkg wtr. Fishing, boating, hiking. Boat access at Lost Johnny Point.

Handkerchief Lake   **FREE**
Flathead National Forest
35 mi SE of Hungry Horse on FR 895; 2 mi NW on FR 897. Free. 6/15-9/30; 14-day limit. 9 sites (RVs under 23). Tbls, toilets, cfga, drkg wtr shut off. Fishing, trails to numerous lakes. Pack out trash. Elev 3500 ft; 4

acres; 32-acre lake. 1 mi to Hungry Horse Reservoir.

Lakeview   **FREE**
Flathead National Forest
24 mi SE of Hungry Horse on FR 895. Free. 6/15-9/30; 14-day limit. 5 sites (RVs under 23 ft). Tbls, toilets, cfga, firewood, no drkg wtr. Pack out trash. Picnicking; fishing. Elev 3600 ft. On Hungry Horse Reservoir. Use boat ramp at Lost Johnny Point.

Lid Creek   **$10**
Flathead National Forest
15 mi SE of Hungry Horse on FR 895; on W shore of Hungry Horse Reservoir. $10 during 5/6-9/30; free rest of year but no wtr or services; 14-day limit. 23 sites (32-ft RV limit). Tbls, toilets, cfga, drkg wtr, no trash service. Picnicking, boating, swimming, fishing, waterskiing, berry picking.

Lost Johnny Camp   **$12**
Flathead National Forest
8.5 mi SE of Hungry Horse on FR 895; near W shore of Hungry Horse Reservoir. $12 during 5/6-9/30; free rest of yr, but no wtr or services; 14-day limit. 5 sites (50-ft RV limit). Tbls, toilets, cfga, drkg wtr, no trash service. Fishing, boating (primitive launch). Elev 3570 ft. 27,750-acre lake.

Lost Johnny Point   **$12**
Flathead National Forest
8.5 mi SE of Hungry Horse on FR 895; near W shore of Hungry Horse Lake. $12 during 5/6-9/30; 14-day limit. 21 sites (40-ft RV limit). Tbls, toilets, cfga, drkg wtr, no trash service. Swimming, fishing, boating(l). Elev 3600 ft; 6 acres.

Peters Creek   **FREE**
Flathead National Forest
Half mi E of Hungry Horse on US 2; about 41 mi S along E side of Hungry Horse Reservoir on FR 38. Free. MD-10/1; 14-day limit. 6 sites; 30-ft RV limit. Toilets, cfga, no drkg wtr. Fishing, boating, hiking.
    Fishing tip: This is a good spot to try for cutthroat and bull trout at Hungry Horse Lake. Also catch whitefish, but release the bulls.

HUNTLEY (73)

Huntley Diversion Dam   **FREE**
Bureau of Reclamation
1 mi W of I-94, Huntley exit, on gravel rd. Free. All year; 14-day limit. Primitive undesignated sites. Tbls, cfga, no toilets, no drkg wtr. Boating (primitive launch), fishing.

HYSHAM (74)

Howrey Island   **FREE**
Bureau of Land Management
25 mi W of Forsyth on I-94; 3 mi N to Hysham; 8 mi W on Rt 311 to bridge. Free. 5/10-10/31; 14-day limit. Undesignated primitive sites

(RVs under 25 ft). No facilities; no drkg wtr. Boating(l), fishing, backpacking trails.

JACKSON (76)

North Van Houten   **FREE**
Beaverhead National Forest
1.5 mi S of Jackson on Hwy 278; 10.5 mi S n Bloody Dick Rd (FR 181). Free. MD-LD; 16-day limit. 3 sites; 20-ft RV limit. Tbls, toilets, cfga, no drkg wtr. Fishing, swimming, canoeing. No trash service; wtr at South Van Houton.

South Van Houten   **FREE**
Beaverhead National Forest
1.5 mi S of Jackson on Hwy 278; 10 mi S on Bloody Dick Rd (FR 181); on S shore of Van Houten Lake. MD-LD; 16-day limit. 3 sites; 30-ft RV limit. Tbls, toilets, cfga, drkg wtr. Swimming, fishing, hiking, canoeing. No trash service.

JARDINE (77)

Bear Creek Campground   **FREE**
Gallatin National Forest
6 mi NE of Jardine; at Upper Bear Creek. Free. 6/15-10/31; 16-day limit. 31 dispersed primitive sites; 21-ft RV limit. Tbls, toilets, cfga, no drkg wtr. Pack out trash. Hiking, fishing, horseback riding, hunting.

Timber Camp   **FREE**
Gallatin National Forest
On Upper Bear Creek, 4 mi NE of Jardine. Free. 6/15-10/31; 16-day limit. Dispersed primitive sites between Yellowstone NP and the Absaroka-Beartooth Wilderness; 35-foot RV limit. Toilets, cfga, no drkg wtr. Fishing, hiking, horseback riding.

JORDAN (78)

Devils Creek   **FREE**
Fort Peck Lake
Corps of Engineers
48 mi NW of Jordan on gravel co rd. Free. All year; 14-day limit. 6 primitive sites (16-ft RV limit). Toilets, cfga, no drkg wtr. Group camping area. Fishing, boating(l).
    Fishing tip: Although Fort Peck Lake is best known for its big walleye, don't forget its smallmouth bass. Devil's Creek holds a good population of bronzebacks. Try spinners, small shad-type crankbaits and Rapalas.

Kamp Katie (Private)
Just off Hwy 200 on S side of Jordan (turn-off is tricky). $10. All year. 10 sites. Tbls, flush toilets, cfga, drkg wtr, showers, elec. Fee not verified for 2007.

KALISPELL (79)

Ashley Lake Camping Area   **FREE**
Flathead National Forest
7 mi W of Kalispell on US 2; 7 mi NW on county rd; 5 mi W on FR 912 to first forest

campground on N shore of Ashley Lake (just W of the state fishing lake site). Free. 5/15-9/30; 14-day limit. Dispersed primitive sites with toilet, cfga, no drkg wtr. Boating, fishing.

Fishing tip: This camp is on the N shore of Ashley Lake, which contains good cutthroat trout, kokanee salmon and yellow perch.

Lions Bitterroot Camp $8

5 mi N of Marion at 1650 Pleasant Valley Rd. $8. 5/1-9/30. 14 RV sites; no hookups. Tbls, toilets, cfga, showers, coin laundry. Swimming area, playground.

McGregor Lake $8
Kootenai National Forest

32 mi W of Kalispell on US 2. $8 during 5/15-9/15; free rest of year when accessible, but no wtr or services; 14-day limit. 22 sites (32-ft RV limit). Tbls, toilets, cfga, drkg wtr. Boating(l), fishing, waterskiing, cross-country & downhill skiing, hiking trails. Elev 3900 ft; 10 acres.

Fishing tip: 5-mile-long McGregor Lake offers good fishing for cutthroat, lake & rainbow trout as well as kokanee salmon & perch.

Spruce Park RV Park $10

3 mi E of Kalispell on Hwy 35, at the Flathead River bridge over the Flathead River. $10 base. All year. 160 sites (100 for RVs). Tbls, flush toilets, cfga, drkg wtr, showers, CATV, hookups($), dump, playground, rec room. Fishing, hiking, birdwatching, horseshoes, boating.

Thompson Chain-of-Lakes $7
State Fishing Access Site

From 35 mi W of Kalispell to 55 mi W of Kalispell on Hwy 2; very difficult access; roads primitive, not recommended for large motrohomes & trailers. $7 for licensed fishermen; others pay $12. All year; 7-day limit. 83 primitive lakeside sites (and 8 group sites) spread over 20 mi along Hwy 2. Tbls, toilets, cfga, no drkg wtr. Fishing, boating(l), hiking. Shoreline access to 18 lakes, including McGregor, Lower Thompson, Middle Thompson, Upper Thompson, Horshoe & Loon. Developed boat ramps at several locations. 4,655 acres.

LANDUSKY (80)

Montana Gulch $4
Bureau of Land Management

Drive approx 4.5 mi N on SR 376 from its jct with SR 191; turn right on gravel country rd toward Landusky for approx 3 mi; turn left at sign to Montana Gulch Campground; qtr mi on BLM graded rd. $4. 5/1-10/31; 14-day limit. 15 sites. Tbls, toilets, cfga, no drkg wtr. Hiking, mountain climbing, snowmobiling, picnicking.

LAUREL (81)

Bluewater Fish Hatchery $7
Bluewater River
State Fishing Access Site

30 mi S of Laurel on Hwy 310 to milepost 32; 9 mi SE on county rd (stream mile 11.5); next to fish hatchery complex. $7 for licensed fishermen; $12 for others. All year; 7-day limit. Developed sites on 91 acres. Tbls, toilets, cfga, no drkg wtr. Fishing, no boat launch. Easy access.

Riverside City Park $10

Half mi S of Laurel on Hwy 212; take I-90 exit 434, then half mi S on US 212, cross Yellowstone River. $10 base. All year. Base fee for no hookups, some small 15-amp elec sites. Eleven 30-amp wtr/elec sites, $15. All year; 7-day limit. Tbls, flush toilets, cfga, drkg wtr, playground, showers. Horseshoe pits, volleyball, fishing, boating(l). Very nice park on Yellowstone River. Free dump at nearby Cenex Convenience Center. Site of German prisoner of war camp during WWII.

LEWISTOWN (82)

Ackley Lake State Park FREE

17 mi W of Lewistown on US 87 to Hobson; 5 mi S on Hwy 400; 2 mi SW on county rd. Free, but donations accepted. All year; 14-day limit. 23 primitive undesignated sites; 24-ft RV limit. Tbls, toilets, cfga, drkg wtr. Boating(l), fishing, swimming. Elev 4336 ft; 160 acres.

Crystal Lake $10
Lewis & Clark National Forest

9 mi W of Lewistown on US 87; 16 mi S on county rd; 8.5 mi S on FR 275. $10. 6/15-LD; 14-day limit. 28 large sites; 22-ft RV limit. Tbls, toilets, cfga, drkg wtr. Fishing, hiking, nature trails. Elev 6800 ft; 14 acres.

Fishing tip: Crystal Lake is a small, shallow lake that can get quite low in summer; use of boat motors (except electric) prohibited. Some rainbow trout are caught.

East Fork Dam FREE
Municipal Park

About 11 mi SE of Lewistown on SR 238 near the US Gypsum plant at Heath. Free. Primitive sites. Tbls, toilets, cfga, drkg wtr. Boating(l), fishing.

Jack Pine Flats FREE
Kootenai National Forest

9 mi SE of Trout Creek on Hwy 200; right on Beaver Creek Rd for about 10 mi (just 3.5 mi from Idaho state line). All year; 14-day limit. Small dispersed camp with about 4 RV sites. Toilets, cfga, no drkg wtr. Hiking, fishing.

James Kipp Recreation Area $12
Bureau of Land Management

65 mi NE of Lewistown on US 191. $12 without dump use ($6 seniors); $15 with dump use ($10 seniors); $60 seasonal without

dump ($30 seniors). 4/1-11/30; 14-day limit. 34 sites (15 for groups) plus 1 floater's tent site. Tbls, toilets, cfga, drkg wtr, fish cleaning station, dump ($10 fee), no trash service. Boating(l), fishing, hiking. Public phone.

Kiwanis Park FREE

1 mi W of Lewistown on Hwy 87 at Hwy 200. Free (donations accepted). All year. Primitive sites. Tbls, pit toilets, cfga, drkg wtr, playground. Park was originally a project of the local Jaycees, then taken over by Kiwanis in 1983.

LIBBY (83)

Alexander Creek FREE
Lake Koocanusa
Corps of Engineers

From dam, 1 mi below on W shore of Kootenai River on FR 228. Free All year; 14-day limit. 2 primitive sites. Tbls, toilets, cfga, no drkg wtr. Boating(l), fishing.

Barron Creek Ramp FREE
Kootenai National Forest

14 mi E of Libby on SR 37; 13 mi N on FR 228; at W shore of Lake Koocanusa. Free. All year, but serviced 5/15-9/10; 14-day limit. 15 dispersed sites (32-ft RV limit). Tbls, toilets, cfga, no drkg wtr, no trash service. Boating(l), fishing, swimming, canoeing.

Blackwell Flats FREE
Lake Koocanusa
Corps of Engineers

From dam, 3 mi below on W shore on Kootenai River on FR 228. Free. All year; 14-day limit. 7 primitive sites. Tbls, toilets, cfga, no drkg wtr. Fishing, boating(l).

Dunn Creek Flats FREE
Lake Koocanusa
Corps of Engineers

From dam, 2.5 mi below on E shore of Kootenai River on SR 37. Free. All year; 14-day limit. 13 primitive sites. Tbls, toilets, cfga, no drkg wtr. Fishing.

Howard Lake $5
Kootenai National Forest

12 mi S of Libby on US 2; 14 mi W on FR 231. $5. MD-10/15; 14-day limit. 9 sites (2 picnic sites); 20-ft RV limit. Tbls, toilets, cfga, drkg wtr, beach. Fishing (rainbow trout), waterskiing, swimming, winter sports. Cabinet Mountain Wilderness Area 3 mi. Elev 4000 ft; 6 acres. Libby Gold Panning Area nearby.

Fireman & Memorial $2
Municipal Park

West end of city on S side of US 2 behind Chamber of Commerce office. $2 for tent sites; $5 for RVs. 4/15-10/1; 5-day limit. 15 sites, 28 ft RV limits. Drkg wtr, flush toilets, tbls, dump.

Lake Creek   FREE
Kootenai National Forest
24.7 mi S of Libby on US 2; 6.9 mi SW on FR 231. Free. All year; 14-day limit. 4 sites (32-ft RV limit). Tbls, toilets, cfga, firewood, piped drkg wtr. Berry picking (huckleberries); picnicking; fishing (trout). Elev 3400 ft; 9 acres. Nice stream. Scenic. Trailhead to Cabinet Mountain Wilderness Area.

Libby Creek   FREE
Recreational Gold Panning Area
Kootenai National Forest
13 mi S of Libby on US 2; 10 mi up Libby Creek Rd (FR 231) to panning area. Free dispersed camping areas. All year; 14-day limit. Toilets, cfga, no drkg wtr, no trash service. Hiking, swimming Developed Howard Campground is 1 mi south. Gold panning area open for recreational panning. Former site of major gold mining operations
  Fishing tip: Don't bother to fish Libby Creek; mine pollution has hurt the trout production.

Loon Lake   FREE
Kootenai National Forest
Half mi N of Libby on MT 37; 17.9 mi N on FR 68; 2.9 mi W on FR 371. Free. All year; 14-day limit. 4 sites (20-ft RV limit). Tbls, toilets, cfga, firewood, no drkg wtr. Boating (hand launch), picnicking, fishing. Elev 3600 ft.
  Fishing tip: Try Loon Lake for smallmouth & largemouth bass, small rainbow trout, some brook trout.

McGillivray $7
Kootenai National Forest
15 mi E of Libby on Hwy 37; 10 mi N on FR 228; near Lake Koocanusa. $7. MD-LD; 14-day limit. 22 sites (32-ft RV limit). Tbls, flush toilets, cfga, drkg wtr, fish cleaning station. Boating(l), fishing, waterskiing, swimming beach, winter sports, rock climbing. Elev 2500 ft; 50 acres.

Yarnell Islands   FREE
Kootenai National Forest
25 mi NE on MT 37; 2 mi SW, BY BOAT. Free. Open when accessible; 14-day limit. 8 tent sites. Tbls, toilets, cfga, firewood, no drkg wtr. Pack out trash. Picnicking; boating; swimming; fishing; waterskiing; hiking. 5 acres. Mountains. On Lake Koocanusa. Libby Dam (6 mi S).

LIMA (84)

East Creek   FREE
Beaverhead National Forest
7.5 mi SW of Lima on CR 179; half mi S on FR 3929; 1.1 mi SE on FR 3930. Free. Elev 6600 ft. 5/15-10/1; 16-day limit. 4 sites (RVs under 16 ft). Tbls, toilets, cfga, firewood, well drkg wtr. Picnicking; hiking.

LINCOLN (85)

Aspen Grove $8
Helena National Forest
7.1 mi E on of Lincoln on SR 200; qtr mi SE on FR 1040; near Blackfoot River. $8. MD-LD; 14-day limit. 20 sites (RVs under 50 ft). Tbls, toilets, cfga, drkg wtr. Fishing, picnicking, excellent birdwatching along river. Elev 4800 ft; 8 acres.
  Fishing tip: This area of the Blackfoot River contains whitefish and rainbow, brook & cutthroat trout.

Copper Creek $8
Helena National Forest
6.5 mi E of Lincoln on SR 200; 8.5 mi NW on FR 330; near Snowbank Lake. $8. MD-LD; 14-day limit. 21 sites (50-ft RV limit). Tbls, toilets, cfga, drkg wtr. Fishing, hiking, mountain biking, horseback riding. Trailhead to Scapegoat Wilderness. This is grizzly bear country. Elev 5300 ft; 3 acres.
  Fishing tip: Fishing is excellent for cutthroat trout at Snowbank Lake. Launch boat by hand; motors prohibitited.

Hooper Municipal Park $10
In town on SR 200 next to library. $10 base. 4/1-10/31. Base rate for primitive sites; wtr/elec sites for $17. 15 sites (25-ft RV limit). Tbls, toilets, cfga, drkg wtr, dump. Hiking trails.

Reservoir Lake   FREE
Dispersed Camping Area
Helena National Forest
1 mi W of Lincoln on SR 200; 9 mi N on FR 4106. Free. 6/15-9/15; 14-day limit. Primitive undeveloped sites; 16-ft RV limit. Tbls, toilets, cfga, drkg wtr. Boating(l), fishing, hiking trail.

LIVINGSTON (86)

Loch Leven $7
Yellowstone River
State Fishing Access Site
9 mi S of Livingston on US 89 to milepost 44; 2 mi E & 4 mi S on Hwy 540; at Yellowstone River $7 for licensed fishermen; $12 for others. All year; 7-day limit. 30 sites (no RV size limit). Tbls, toilets, cfga, drkg wtr. Boating(l), fishing. Good access. 76 acres.

Mallard's Rest $7
Yellowstone River
State Fishing Access Site
13 mi S of Livingston on US 89 to milepost 42; at Yellowstone River. $7 for licensed fishermen; $12 for others. All year; 7-day limit. 20 primitive sites; 30-ft RV limit. Tbls, toilets, cfga, drkg wtr. Boating (l), fishing. Moderate access; steep rd into site.

Paradise   FREE
Yellowstone River
State Fishing Access Site
9 mi S of Livingston on US 89 to milepost 44; 2 mi E, then 4.5 i S on Secondary Hwy

540; at Yellowstone River. Free. All year; 7-day limit. Primitive camping on 2.5 acres; 20-ft RV limit. Toilet, cfga, tbls, no drkg wtr. Boating(l), fishing. Difficult access.

Pine Creek $11
Gallatin National Forest
9 mi S of Livingston on US 89; 2 mi W on CR 540; 2.5 mi W on FR 202 (narrow, steep). $11 during MD-9/30; free in fall until 11/31, but limited services; 16-day limit. Closed to vehicles Dec-May to protect wildlife habitat. 24 sites; 45-ft RV limit. Group sites available. Tbls, toilets, cfga, drkg wtr. Fishing (brook trout), hiking, nature trails. Trailhead for Absaroka-Beartooth Wilderness. Elev 6000 ft; 25 acres.

Shields River   FREE
Gallatin National Forest
28 mi N of Livingston on US 89 to Wilsall; NE on Shields River Rd 24 mi. Free. MD-9/30; 14-day limit. About 6 primitive dispersed sites; 22-ft RV limit. Tbls, toilets, cfga, no drkg wtr, no trash service. Hiking, fishing.
  Fishing tip: This river offers excellent fishing for whitefish and Yellowstone cutthroat. The best fishing is from the mouth to Willow Creek and from Bennett Creek to Lodgepole Creek

Snow Bank $11
Gallatin National Forest
15 mi S of Livingston on US 89; 12 mi SE on CR 486 (Mill Creek Rd); at Mill Creek. $11. MD-LD; 16-day limit. Free in fall until 11/31, but reduced services; closed Dec-May to protect wildlife habitat. 10 sites; 35-ft RV limit. Tbls, toilets, cfga, drkg wtr. Fishing, hiking, picnicking. Elev 5800 ft; 5 acres.
  Fishing tip: Only limited fishing is available for Yellowstone cutthroat and mountain whitefish.

LOGAN (87)

Fairweather   FREE
Missouri River
State Fishing Access Site
From 1 mi W of Logan on Hwy 205, 3 mi N on Logan Trident Rd; 7 mi NE on Clarkston Rd (river mile 2,301.1). Free. All year; 7-day limit. 10 sites; 20-ft RV limit. No facilities except toilet, no drkg wtr. Boating(l), fishing. 852 acres. Difficult access.

LOLO (88)

Chief Looking Glass $7
Bitterroot River
State Fishing Access Site
6 mi S of Lolo on Hwy 93; E on Chief Looking Glass Rd (stream mile 21.4). $7 for licensed fishermen; others pay $12. 5/1-11/30; 7-day limit. Primitive camping on 13 acres; 28-ft RV limit. Tbls, toilets, cfga, drkg wtr. Boating (no motors), fishing. Canoes & rafts can be hand launched.

Lee Creek   **$10**
Lolo National Forest
26 mi W of Lolo on US 12. $10. MD-9/30; 14-day limit. Free during off-season, but no drkg wtr or trash service. 22 sites (34-ft RV limit). Tbls, toilets, cfga, drkg wtr. Fishing, hiking trails, interpretive trail. Elev 4200 ft; 6 acres. Segment of historic Lolo Trail nearby; Lolo Pass Visitor Center 6 mi W; commercial hot springs 1 mi. Cross-country skiing & snowmobiling after 12/1.

LOLO HOT SPRINGS (89)

Jerry Johnson   **$8**
Clearwater National Forest
30 mi W of Lolo Hot Springs on US 12, in Idaho. $8. 6/1-9/15; 14-day limit. 15 sites (22-ft RV limit). Tbls, toilets, cfga, drkg wtr. Fishing, hiking. Elev 3100 ft; 6 acres.

Powell   **$8**
Clearwater National Forest
18 mi W of Lolo Hot Springs on US 12, in Idaho. $8. 6/1-9/30; 14-day limit. 39 sites (32-ft RV limit). Tbls, flush toilets, cfga, drkg wtr. Fishing, hiking.

Wendover   **$8**
Clearwater National Forest
22 mi W of Lolo Hot Springs on US 12, in Idaho. $8. 6/1-9/30; 14-day limit. 27 sites (32-ft RV limit). Tbls, toilets, cfga, drkg wtr. Fishing.

White Sands   **$8**
Clearwater National Forest
22 mi W of Lolo Hot Springs on US 12; 1 mi S on Elks Summit Rd; in Idaho. $8. 6/1-9/15; 14-day limit. 6 sites (32-ft RV limit). Tbls, toilets, cfga, drkg wtr. Swimming, fishing, hiking.

Whitehouse   **$8**
Clearwater National Forest
22 mi W of Lolo Hot Springs on US 12, in Idaho. $8. 6/1-9/15; 14-day limit. 13 sites (32-ft RV limit). Tbls, toilets, cfga, drkg wtr. Fishing.

LOVELL (WY.) (90)

Afterbay   **$5**
Bighorn Canyon
National Recreation Area
42 mi S of Hardin on SR 313; 1 mi NE of Yellowtail Dam. $5. All year; 14-day limit. 29 sites (20-ft RV limit). Tbls, toilets, dump, cfga, drkg wtr. Boating(l), fishing, visitor center, recreational program, nature trails, swimming.
Fishing tip: Walleye fishing at Bighorn Lake has been hot the last couple of years. The growth of walleyes has been fueled by in influx of emerald shiners from Wyoming, and the walleyes are gorging on them.

Horseshoe Bend   **$5**
Bighorn Canyon National
Recreation Area
National Park Service
2 mi E of Lovell on US 14A to Jct 37; 14 mi N. $5. All year; 14-day limit; fee only MD-LD, free rest of year. 54 sites. Tbls, toilets, cfga, drkg wtr, dump. Fishing, boating(r), hiking, campfire talks. Pryor Mtn Wild Horse Range.
Fishing tip: To catch walleyes from Bighorn Lake, you might have to fish deep -- typically in 25 to 50 feet of water. And fish slowly! Use minnows or leeches on jigs.

Medicine Creek Boat-In   **$5**
Bighorn Canyon
National Recreation Area
27 mi N of Lovell, Wyoming, on Hwy 37 to Barry's Landing; 1 mi N of Barry's Landing; access BY BOAT. $5 NRA entry fee; camp free. 5/1-11/1; 14-day limit. 8 tent sites. Tbls. Swimming; picnicking; fishing; boating.
Fishing tip: While you're camped in the NRA, you have a good choice of fish to search out: brown and rainbow trout, mountain whitefish, golden eye, burbot, smallmouth bass and catfish.

Trail Creek   **$5**
Bighorn Canyon
National Recreation Area
2 mi E of Lovell, WY via US 14A, 24 mi N on HWY 37. $5 NRA entry fee; camp free. Open all year; 14-day limit. 7 RV/tent sites, 5 tent sites (16-ft RV limit). Tbls, toilets, cfga, no drkg wtr. Swimming; boat ramp; fishing.
Fishing tip: The Bighorn River averages more than 2,900 trout over 13 inches per mile. One of those caught was a record 16-pound, 2-ounce rainbow.

MALTA (91)

Camp Creek Recreation Site   **$5**
Bureau of Land Management
40 mi SW of Malta on US 191; 7 mi W on county rd (to Zortman). $5. 18 sites (24-ft RV limit). Tbls, toilets, cfga, drkg wtr. Hunting, hiking, picnicking. 20 acres.

Fourchette Creek   **FREE**
Corps of Engineers
Fort Peck Lake
60 mi S of Malta on gravel co rd. Free. All year; 14-day limit. About 44 primitive sites (20-ft RV limit). Tbls, toilets, cfga, no drkg wtr, fishing pier. Fishing, boating(l), swimming.
Fishing tip: Some of the best walleye fishing in the lake is near here. Try the whole section between Forchette Creek and the Hell Creek State Recreation Area.

Nelson Reservoir   **FREE**
Bureau of Reclamation
State Fishing Access Site
18 mi E of Malta on US 2; 2 mi N on co rd. Free. All year; 14-day limit. About 9 undesignated sites. Tbls, toilets, cfga, drkg wtr, 3

picnic areas. Fishing, boating (l), swimming. Managed by BOR.
Fishing tip: This 4,000-acre lake is regarded as the state's best big-walleye waters. It already has produced the state record walleye as well as huge nortnern pike.

Trafton Municipal Park   **$5**
From jct of Hwys 2 & 191, N in Malta to park; at Milk River. $5. All year, but limited facilities in winter; 7-day limit. 25 sites (no RV size limit). Tbls, toilets, cfga, drkg wtr, playground, no showers, dump. Basketball, volleyball, horseshoes, fishing. 6 acres. Also dumps ($) at Westside Conoco & Greens Exxon in town.

MARTIN CITY (92)

Emery Bay   **$12**
Flathead National Forest
6 mi SE of Martin City on FR 38. $12 during 5/6-9/30; free rest of year, but no wtr or services; 14-day limit. 26 sites; 32-ft RV limit. Tbls, toilets, cfga, drkg wtr, no trash service. Boating(l), fishing, swimming. Fee reduced in-season if unable to haul water.

Murray Bay   **$10**
Flathead National Forest
22 mi SE of Martin City on FR 38; at E side of Hungry Horse Reservoir. $10 during 5/6-9/30; free rest of yr, but no wtr or services; 14-day limit. 18 sites (32-ft RV limit). Tbls, toilets, cfga, drkg wtr. Pack out trash. Boating(l), fishing, swimming. Elev 3570 ft; 19 acres.

Spotted Bear   **$10**
Flathead National Forest
55 me SE of Martin City on FR 38 (rough rds); at confluence of Spotted Bear River & North Fork of Flathead River. $10 during 5/6-9/30; 14-day limit. 13 sites (32-ft RV limit). Tbls, toilets, cfga, drkg wtr (only MD-LD), dump. Fishing (cutthroat trout), boating, picnicking, hiking trails. Elev 3700 ft; 5 acres.
Fishing tip: The North Fork is not nearly the fishery of the Middle Fork, and anglers have to work harder for their catches of smaller fish.

MARTINSDALE (93)

Martinsdale Reservoir   **$7**
State Fishing Access Site
1 mi E of Martinsdale on county rd. $7 for licensed fishermen; $12 for others. All year; 7-day limit. Primitive undesignated sites. Tbls, toilets, cfga, no drkg wtr, shelters, no trash service. Fishing, swimming, boating(l), hiking. 339 acres. Boat ramp unusable in 2007 due to low wtr.
Fishing tip: This lake offers good rainbow & brown trout fishing, although it gets heavy fishing pressure all year. Yellowstone cutthroat trout also have been stocked. The best success is trolling spoons and other lures. Daily limits of trout 12 to 16 inches are common.

MELROSE (94)

Browne's Bridge FREE
Big Hole River
State Fishing Access Site
6 mi S of Melrose on I-15's frontage rd (stream mile 32). Free. All year; 7-day limt. Primitive camping on 10.4 acres; 20-ft RV rig limit. Tbls, toilets, cfga, no drkg wtr. Boating(l), fishing. Historic interpretation of bridge. Easy access.

Brown's Lake $7
State Fishing Access Site
8 mi S of Melrose on I-15 to Glen exit, then 12 mi W on county & forest rd. $7 for licensed fishermen; others pay $12. All year; 7-day limit. Tbls, toilets, cfga, no drkg wtr. Primitive sites on 77 acres. Fishing, boating(l). Inaccessible in winter; difficult access other times. Within Beaverhead NF.

Canyon Creek FREE
Beaverhead National Forest
From S of Melrose on US 91, 10.2 mi W on FR 187; 4.5 mi SE on FR 7401 (RVs discouraged due to poor rds). Free. 6/15-9/15; 16-day limit. 3 sites; 18-ft RV limit. Tbls, toilets, cfga, no drkg wtr, no trash service. Hiking, fishing, horseback riding. Horse loading ramp.

Maidenrock $7
Big Hole River
State Fishing Access Site
I-15 at Melrose, milepost 93; 6 mi W & N on co rd (stream mile 41.8). $7 for licensed fishermen; others pay $12. All year; 7-day limit. 30 sites (no RV size limit). Tbls, toilets, cfga, drkg wtr. Boating (primitive launch), fishing. Difficult access; steep access rd. 398 acres.
Fishing tip: Adjoining Big Hole River contains huge trout; try large orange salmon flies in spring.

Salmon Fly $7
Big Hole River
State Fishing Access Site
I-15 at Melrose, milepost 93; 6 mi W & N on co rd (stream mile 38.3). $7 for licensed fishermen; others pay $12. All year; 7-day limit. Primitive sites on 12 acres. Tbls, cfga, no drkg wtr. Fishing, boating(l). Difficult access.

Sportsman Motel & RV Park $12
At Melrose exit of I-15; on Big Hole River. $12 for tents; $18 full hookups. 4/1-12/1. 20 sites. Tbls, flush toilets, cfga, drkg wtr, hookups($), showers, coin laundry. Fishing, boating.

MILES CITY (95)

Big Sky Camp & RV Park $11
From I-94 exit 141 at Miles City, qtr mi W on Hwy 12 (Business 94). $11-$12. Open 4/15-11/1. 48 RV sites plus primitive space for dry camping & tenting. Tbls, flush toilets, cfga, drkg wtr, hookups, dump ($5 non-campers), coin laundry, rec room, pool, playground.

Twelve Mile Dam FREE
Tongue River
State Fishing Access Site
12 mi S of Miles City on Hwy 59; 1 mi SW of Tongue River Rd (Hwy 332) at Tongue River; limited RV access due to tight turn on entrance rd. Free. All year; 7-day limit. Primitive camping on 35 acres; 20-ft RV limit. Tbls, toilets, cfga, no drkg wtr. Boating(l), fishing.

MISSOULA (96)

Big Pine FREE
Fish Creek
State Fishing Access Site
W of Missoula on I-90 at exit 66, then 4.5 mi S on Fish Creek Rd (stream mile 2.5). Free. All year; 7-day limit. 5 primitive sites; 23-ft RV limit. Tbls, toilets, cfga, no drkg wtr. Fishing, no boat launch. Difficult access. 18 acres. Site of huge ponderosa pine.

Forest Grove $7
Clark Fork River
State Fishing Access Site
W of Missoula on I-90 to Tarkio exit 61; 4 mi W on frontage rd to Clark Fork River (river mile 154.8). $7 for licensed fishermen; $12 for others. All year; 7-day limit. Developed sites on 5.6 acres; 20-ft RV limit. Tbls, toilets, cfga, no drkg wtr. Boating(l), fishing. Difficult access.

Forks FREE
West Fork Fish Creek
State Fishing Access Site
W of Missoula off I-90 at exit 60, then S & W on Fish Creek Rd (about 10 mi S of I-90). Free. All year; 7-day limit. 5 sites; 25-ft RV limit. Tbls, toilets, cfga, no drkg wtr. Fishing. Difficult access. 5.8 acres.

Kreis Pond FREE
Lolo National Forest
About 20 mi NW of Missoula on I-90; from Exit 82 at Ninemile, take SR 10 W to Remount Rd; 2.5 mi N to Ninemile Ranger Station, then 3.5 mi NW via Edith Peak & Butler Creek Loop Rds. Free. 4/1-10/31; 14-day limit. 7 sites. Tbls, toilets, cfga, no drkg wtr. Boating, fishing, mountain biking.

River Edge Resort $10
30 mi W of Missoula on I-90 at exit 75; Alberton Gorge. $10 base; $18 full hookups. All year. Tbls, flush toilets, cfga, drkg wtr, showers, hookups($), coin laundry, beach. Biking, swimming, fishing, horseshoes.

MONARCH (97)

Logging Creek $10
Lewis and Clark National Forest
3 mi N of Monarch on MT 89; 10 mi E on FR 839. $10 during MD-9/15; free 9/16-11/30, but no wtr; 14-day limit. 25 sites (22 ft RV limit). Tbls, toilets, cfga, firewood, well drkg wtr, no trash service. Picnicking; fishing. Elev 4600 ft; 8 acres. Scenic. Access rds not suit-

able for large RVs.
Fishing tip: Rainbow & brook trout are plentiful in Logging Creek..

MONIDA (98)

Elk Lake FREE
Beaverhead National Forest
50 mi E of Monida on Red Rock Lake National Wildlife Rd (2e mi W of Henry's Lake, Idaho, via Red Rock Pass. Free. 5/15-10/15; 16-day limit. 2 tent sites. Tbl, toilet, cfga, no drkg wtr.
Fishing tip: Good fishing in Elk Lake for cutthroat, rainbow and lake trout as well as Arctic grayling.

Lower Red Rock Lake FREE
National Wildlife Refuge
From I-15, Monida exit, travel 33 mi E. Free. 6/1-11/1; 14-day limit. Open grassland camping with toilets, cfga, no drkg wtr. Boating(l), fishing, hiking. No motorbikes, no dogs. Lake open for boating from 9/1 to freeze-up.

Upper Red Rock Lake FREE
National Wildlife Refuge
From I-15, Monida exit, travel 33 mi E. Free. 6/1-11/1; 14-day limit. 10 sites. Tbls, firewood, toilets, cfga, drkg wtr. Boating(l); picnicking; fishing; hiking. No motorbikes. No dogs.
Fishing tip: Red Rock Lake is celebrated for its fly-fishing for cutthroat & rainbow trout. Boating is permitted from July 15 to freeze-up.

NEIHART (99)

Aspen $8
Lewis and Clark National Forest
6 mi N of Neihart on US 89; in canyon of Belt Creek. $8 during about MD-10/15; 14-day limit. 6 sites (22-ft RV limit). Tbls, toilets, cfga, drkg wtr, no trash service. Fishing (brook trout), hiking trails. Elev 5200 ft; 5 acres.

Kings Hill $8
Lewis and Clark National Forest
9 mi S of Neihart on US 89. $8 during 6/15-9/15; free but no wtr or services until 11/30. 14-day limit. 16 sites (22 ft RV limit). Tbls, toilets, cfga, drkg wtr, no trash service. Fishing, biking, hiking trails. Winter snowmobiling, skiing. Elev 7300 ft; 9 acres.

Many Pines $10
Lewis and Clark National Forest
4 mi S of Neihart on US 89; at Belt Creek. $10 during MD-9/15; free 9/15-Thanksgiving weekend but no wtr or services; 14-day limit. 22 sites (22-ft RV limit). Tbls, toilets, cfga, drkg wtr. Fishing, hiking trails, biking. Elev 6000 ft; 15 acres.

NORRIS (100)

Harrison Lake **$7**
State Fishing Access Site
10 mi N of Norris on US 287 to Harrison; 5 mi E on co rd. $7 for licensed fishermen; $12 others. All year; 7-day limit. 15 sites (no RV size limit). Tbls, toilets, cfga, no drkg wtr. Boating (4WD launch), fishing. 39 acres.

Red Mountain **$8**
Bureau of Land Management
9 mi E of Norris on SR 84; right at Beartrap Canyon Recreation Areas sign to the camp. $8 during 5/1-12/1; free rest of year, but no wtr. All year; 14-day limit. 11 sites (35-ft RV limit). Tbls, toilets, cfga, firewood, store, drkg wtr. Hunting, picnicking, fishing, hiking, rockhounding, flat boating, mountain climbing. Elev 4485 ft; 20 acres. Madison River. Beartrap Wilderness Area, 3 mi S on BLM rds. Bike trails. High winds & lack of trees make tents inadvisable at times.

NOXON (101)

Bull River Campground **$8**
Kootenai National Forest
6 mi NW of Noxon on US 200. $8. Open 4/15-12/1, but wtr & services available only 5/15-9/10 (free when water is off). 14-day limit. 26 sites (32-ft RV limit). Tbls, flush toilets, cfga, drkg wtr, fish cleaning station. Hiking, waterskiing, boating, picnicking, fishing, swimming. Access to Cabinet Gorge Reservoir. Next to Bull River, near Cabinet Mountains Wilderness and Lake Koocanusa. Bike trails, beach. Elev 2200 ft; 13 acres.

NYE (102)

Woodbine **$7.50**
Custer National Forest
8 mi SW of Nye on SR 419. $7.50 with federal Senior Pass; others pay $15. MD-LD; 10-day limit. 44 sites in 3 loops; 30-ft RV limit. Tbls, toilets, cfga, drkg wtr. Fishing, boating (2-hp motor limit) hiking (trail to Woodbine Falls). Horse loading ramp. Along Stillwater River. Elev 5300 ft; 30 acres. Concession-operated.

Fishing tip: In late June, watch for hatches of medium-size stoneflies and try to match it in order to hook the 2-pound brown trout which feed on them. Our favorite flies are Bird's Stone and Soft Pillow in #8 sizes.

OLNEY (103)

Spring Creek **FREE**
Stillwater State Forest
7.5 mi N of Olney on SR 93, then W toward creek. Free. All year; 14-day limit. 6 primitive undesignated sites. Tbls, toilets, cfga, no drkg wtr, no trash service. Hiking, fishing.

OVANDO (104)

Big Nelson **FREE**
Lolo National Forest
8 mi E of Ovando on SR 200; 11 mi NE on FR 500 (North Fork Blackfoot Rd). 6/15-9/15; 14-day limit. 4 sites (RVs under 17 ft). Tbls, toilets, cfga, no drkg wtr. Boating (cartop boats), fishing, hiking trails, picnic area. 3 acres on Coopers Lake. Elev 4200 ft.

Harry Morgan **$7**
North Fork Blackfoot River
State Fishing Access Site
4 mi S of Ovando on SR 272; at North Fork of Blackfoot River. $7 for licensed fishermen; others pay $12. All year; 7-day limit. Primitive camping on 65 acres; 25-ft RV limit. 4 sites. Tbls, toilets, cfga, no drkg wtr. Boating(l), fishing. Difficult access.

Monture **FREE**
Lolo National Forest
8.9 mi N on Monture Rd (FR 89). Free. 6/15-9/30; 14-day limit. 5 sites (RVs under 22 ft). Tbls, toilets, cfga, firewood, drkg wtr (1 mi). Rockhounding; hiking; picnicking; fishing (1 mi); horseback riding. Elev 4200 ft; 3 acres. Scenic. Scapegoat Wilderness (11 mi, by trail). Bob Marshall Wilderness Area (16 mi, by trail).

PHILIPSBURG (105)

Cable Mountain **$8**
Deerlodge National Forest
15.7 mi S of Phiipsburg off Discovery Basin Rd (FR 65); at North Fork of Flint Creek. $8. About MD-11/1; no fee or services after 9/15 14-day limit. 11 sites (22-ft RV limit). Tbls, toilets, cfga, drkg wtr. Fishing, biking, rockhounding, boating. Elev 6500 ft; 5 acres. Historic. Near Georgetown Lake & Echo Lake.

Copper Creek **FREE**
Deerlodge National Forest
6 mi S of Philipsburg on SR 1; right on SR 38 (Skalkaho Hwy) for 8.5 mi, then 10 mi S on FR 5106 (Middle Fork Rd); qtr mi on FR 80. Free. 6/15-9/30; 16-day limit. 7 sites (22-ft RV limit). Tbls, toilets, cfga, drkg wtr. Fishing, hiking.

Crystal Creek **FREE**
Deerlodge National Forest
6.2 mi S of Philipsburg on MT 10A; 24.5 mi SW on MT 38 (Skalkaho Hwy). Free. 6/15-9/30; 16-day limit. 3 sites (RVs under 17 ft). Tbls, toilets, cfga, firewood, no drkg wtr. Rockhounding; picnicking; fishing (2 mi). Elev 7000 ft; 1 acre. Historic.

East Fork Blacktail **FREE**
Deerlodge National Forest
6 mi S of Philipsburg on SR 1; 6 mi SW on SR 38 (Skalkaho Hwy); 5 mi SE on FR 3; 1 mi SE on FR 9349. Free. 6/15-9/30; 16-day limit. 7 sites (22-ft RV limit). Toilets, cfga, tbls no other facilities; drkg wtr. Fishing. Elev 6000

ft. Access to Anaconda-Pintlar Wilderness Area. On East Fork Creek.

Flint Creek **FREE**
Deerlodge National Forest
8 mi S of Philipsburg on MT 1; qtr mi SE on FR 1090. Free. 5/1-9/30; 16-day limit. 16 sites (RVs under 17 ft). Tbls, toilets, cfga, firewood, no drkg wtr, but nearby. Rockhounding; picnicking; fishing; boating(l-4 mi). Elev 5800 ft; 3 acres. Historic.

Lodgepole **$10**
Deerlodge National Forest
10.7 mi S of Philipsburg on SR 1; NE on FR 9465. $10 during MD-9/15; free but no services 9/16-11/1; 14-day limit; roads not plowed in winter. 31 sites; 32-ft RV limit. Tbls, toilets, cfga, drkg wtr. Fishing, hiking, waterskiing, biking, nature trails, boating(l). Elev 6400 ft; 14 acres.

Philipsburg Bay **$12**
Deerlodge National Forest
9 mi S of Philipsburg on SR 1; 1.5 mi SW on FR 406; half mi SE on FR 9460; at Georgetown Lake. $12 during 5/20-9/15 (opening depends on snow conditions); 14-day limit; free rest of year, weather permitting, but no wtr or trash service. 69 sites; 32-ft RV limit. Tbls, toilets, cfga, drkg wtr. Waterskiing, biking, fishing, swimming, boating(l). Elev 6400 ft; 29 acres.

Piney Bay **$12**
Deerlodge National Forest
9 mi S of Philipsburg on SR 1; 2 mi SW on FR 406. $12 during about 5/20-9/15; 14-day limit; free rest of year, weather permitting, but no wtr or trash service (interior rd not plowed). 48 sites (32-ft RV limit). Tbls, toilets, cfga, drkg wtr. Boating(l), fishing, swimming, waterskiing. Elev 6400 ft; 14 acres.

Spillway **FREE**
Deerlodge National Forest
6 mi S of Philipsburg on SR 1; 6 mi SW on SR 38; 5 mi SE on FR 672 (East Fork Rd); 1 mi on FR 5141. Free. MD-9/30; 16-day limit. 13 sites (22-ft RV limit). Tbls, toilets, cfga, drkg wtr. Boating, fishing, swimming.

Stony Campground **FREE**
Deerlodge National Forest
19 mi W of Philipsburg off Rock Creek Rd (FR 102). Free. 5/15-9/30; 16-day limit. 10 sites; 32-ft RV limit. Fishing, hiking. Camp formerly called Squaw Rock.

PLENTYWOOD (106)

Bolster Dam Campground **FREE**
On N edge of Plentywood. Free, but $10 suggested donation for RVs, $5 tents. All year. 10 back-in RV & tent sites. Tbls, pit toilets, cfga, 30-amp elec, drkg wtr. Boating(l), fishing, canoeing. Elev 2075 ft.

POLSON (107)

Lake Mary Ronan State Park $12
23 mi N of Polson on US 93 to Dayton, then 7 mi NW. $12 in-season; $10 off-season. 5/31-2/28; 14-day limit. 26 RV sites (35-ft RV limit). Tbls, pit toilets, cfga, drkg wtr. Boating(ld), fishing, berry-picking, swimming. Elev 4000 ft; 129 acres.

POMPEYS PILLAR (108)

Anita Reservoir FREE
Bureau of Reclamation
4 mi S of I-94 from Pompeys Pillar exit. Free. All year; 14-day limit. Primitive undesignated sites. No facilities, no drkg wtr. Fishing, boating (primitive hand launch).

RED LODGE (110)

Basin Campground $11
Custer National Forest
1 mi S of Red Lodge on US 212; 7 mi W on FR 71 (West Fork Rd); at West Fork of Rock Creek near Wild Bill Lake. $11. MD-LD; 10-day limit. 30 sites; 30-ft RV limit. Tbls, toilets, cfga, drkg wtr. Fishing, picnicking, hiking, mountain biking. Concessionaire operated. Elev 7340 ft; 10 acres.
Fishing tip: Catch rainbow & brown trout in both the creek and the lake.

Beaver Lodge FREE
Rock Creek
State Fishing Access Site
6 mi N of Red Lodge on Hwy 212 at milepost 72. Free. All year; 7-day limit. Tbls, toilets, cfga, no drkg wtr. Primitive camping on 60 acres. Walk-in fishing. Difficult access. Small, remote site; RVs not recommended.

Bull Springs FREE
Rock Creek
State Fishing Access Site
7 mi N of Red Lodge on Hwy 212; qtr mi E on co rd. Free. All year; 7-day limit. Tbls, toilets, cfga, no drkg wtr. Primitive camping on 32 acres. Fishing. Very difficult access.

Cascade $11
Custer National Forest
1.5 mi S of Red Lodge on US 212; 9.5 mi W on FR 71 (West Fork Rd); at West Fork of Rock Creek. $11 during MD-LD; free rest of year, weather permitting; 10-day limit. 31 sites; 22-ft RV limit. Tbls, toilets, cfga, drkg wtr. Fishing, hiking. Elev 6700 ft. On primary access route into the Absaroka-Beartooth Wilderness. Concessionaire-operated. No horses in camp.

Greenough Lake $11
Custer National Forest
12 mi SW of Red Lodge on US 212 (Beartooth Scenic Byway); 1 mi SW on FR 421 (Rock Creek Rd); at 5-acre Greenough Lake. $11 during MD-LD; free rest of year, weather permitting; 10-day limit. 18 sites; 32-ft RV limit.

Tbls, toilets, cfga, drkg wtr. Fishing, nature trails. Trail leads to popular fishing area (rainbow trou). Elev 7300 ft; 8 acres.

Horsethief Station FREE
Rock Creek
State Fishing Access Site
3 mi W of Red Lodge on Hwy 212; at Rock Creek. Free. All year; 7-day limit. Primitive camping on 84 acres. Tbls, toilets, cfga, no drkg wtr. Fishing. Difficult access.

Limber Pine $11
Custer National Forest
12 mi SW of Red Lodge on US 212; 1 mi SW on FR 421 (Rock Creek Rd); at Rock Creek. $11 during MD-LD; free rest of year, weather permitting; 10-day limit. 13 sites; 32-ft RV limit. Tbls, toilets, cfga, drkg wtr. Fishing (rainbow trout), hiking. Concessionaire-operated. Elev 7400 ft; 16 acres.

M-K Campground $11
Custer National Forest
12 mi S of Red Lodge on US 212; 3.5 mi SW on FR 421; on a ridge above Rock Creek. $11. MD-LD; 10-day limit. 10 sites (30-ft RV limit). Tbls, toilets, cfga, firewood, no drkg wtr, no trash service. Rockhounding; picnicking; fishing. Elev 7500 ft; 5 acres. Scenic.
Fishing tip: Catch rainbow trout in either Rock Creek or nearby Greenough Lake.

Palisades FREE
Custer National Forest
1.5 mi S of Red Lodge on US 212; 1 mi W on FR 71; 1.5 mi W on CR 3010; half mi NW on FR 3010; at Willow Creek. Free. Elev 6400 ft. 6/15-9/15; 10-day limit. 6 sites on 3 acres (16-ft RV limit). Tbls, toilets, cfga, no drkg wtr or trash service. Rockhounding; picnicking; fishing; horseback riding.

Parkside $11
Custer National Forest
12 mi SW of Red Lodge on US 212; half mi SW on FR 421 (Rock Creek Rd). $11 during MD-LD; free rest of year, weather permitting; 10-day limit. 28 sites; 32-ft RV limit. Tbls, toilets, cfga, drkg wtr. Fishing (rainbow trout), hiking. Concessionaire-operated. Elev 7200 ft; 15 acres.

Ratine $11
Custer National Forest
8 mi S of Red Lodge on US 212; 3 mi SW on FR 379 (East Side Rd). $11 during MD-LD; free rest of year, weather permitting; 10-day limit. 6 small sites and large group site (16-ft RV limit); no turn-around for larger rigs. Tbls, toilets, cfga, drkg wtr. Fishing, hiking. Concessionaire-operated. Elev 6400 ft.

Sheridan $11
Custer National Forest
5 mi SW of Red Lodge on US 212; 2 mi SW on FR 379 (East Side Rd); at Rock Creek. $11 during MD-LD; free rest of year, weather permitting; 10-day limit. 8 sites; 16-ft RV limit. Tbls, toilets, cfga, drkg wtr. Fishing, hiking. Concessionaire-operated. Elev 6300 ft.

Water Birch $7
Rock Creek
State Fishing Access Site
9 mi N of Red Lodge on Hwy 212. $5 for licensed fishermen; $12 for others. All year; 7-day limit. Primitive camping on 77 acres. Tbls, toilet, cfga, no drkg wtr. Fishing, boating (primitive hand launch). Difficult access.

REXFORD (111)

Camp 32 FREE
Kootenai National Forest
2.5 mi S of Rexford on Hwy 37; 2 mi SE on FR 856; 1.5 mi SW on FR 7182. Free. 4/15-11/15; 14-day limit. 8 sites; 20-ft RV limit. Tbls, toilets, cfga, no drkg wtr. Fishing, picnicking. On Pinkham Creek. Pinkham Falls nearby--hike upstream.
Fishing tip: Try the good fishing not far away at Lake Koocanusa, where the Corps of Engineers has boat ramps and 3 free campgrounds.

Caribou FREE
Kootenai National Forest
1 mi SW on MT 37; 20.4 mi W on FR 92; at East Fork Yaak River at Caribou Creek. Free. 4/15-11/15; 14-day limit. 3 sites; 32-ft RV limit. Tbls, toilets, cfga, firewood, no drkg wtr. Picnicking; fishing; hiking. Elev 3500 ft. Watch for logging trucks.
Fishing tip: Excellent fishing for trout in the river, but daily limit has been reduced, so beware of limits on the area you fish.

Peck Gulch $9
Kootenai National Forest
Half mi NE & 16 mi SW of Rexford on SR 37; at Lake Koocanusa. $9 during 5/15-9/15; free earlier & later, but no wtr or services; 14-day limit. 22 sites (32-ft RV limit). Tbls, toilets, cfga, drkg wtr (wtr turned off during free period). Fishing, boating(l), biking, swimming. Handicapped facilities. Nearby is Stone Hill climbing area. Elev 2470 ft.

Rexford Bench Complex $10
Kootenai National Forest
7 mi SW of Rexford on SR 37. $10 base. 5/1-10/15. Base fee for camping at boating site (33 sites, free 10/1-5/14), Kamloops Terrace (52 sites, free 5/1-6/1 and 10/1-10/15) or picnic area (for overflow -- 12 sites); regular campground, $10, 80 sites. Free 5/1-5/14 and 10/1-10/15. 32-ft RV limit. Tbls, toilets, cfga, drkg wtr, dump. Swimming, boating(l), fishing, waterskiing, biking, hiking. Elev 2500 ft; 120 acres.

Tobacco River FREE
Kootenai National Forest
2 mi E of Rexford on SR 37 to river; half mi W on forest rd. Free. All year; 14-day limit. 6 sites; 20-ft RV limit. Tbls, toilets, cfga, no drkg wtr. Fishing, hiking, boating.

ROSCOE (113)

East Rosebud Lake   **$9**
Custer National Forest
7 mi SW of Roscoe on CR 177; 6 mi SW on FR 177 (East Rosebud Rd). $9 during MD-9/15; 10-day limit. Free 9/16-5/31, but no wtr or trash service. 14 sites (RVs under 16 ft). Tbls, toilets, cfga, piped drkg wtr. Boating(ld); hiking; waterskiing; picnicking; fishing; mountain climbing. Elev 6200 ft; 12 acres. Scenic. Hiking and riding trail into Beartooth Primitive Area; adjacent to East Rosebud Trailhead.

Jimmy Joe   **FREE**
Custer National Forest
7 mi SW of Roscoe on CR 177; 3 mi SW on FR 177 (East Rosebud Rd). Free. Elev 5600 ft. MD-LD; 10-day limit. 10 sites on 4 acres (RVs under 32 ft). Tbls, toilets, cfga, firewood, no drkg wtr. Rockhounding; picnicking; fishing. 4 acres.

ROUNDUP (114)

Cow Bell Campground   **FREE**
County Park
In Roundup, near fairgrounds. From jct of Main St and E Second, half mi E on E Second. Free, but donationa accepted. 5/15-9/15. 20 sites. Tbls, flush toilets, cfga, firewood, playground, drkg wtr. Dump, LP-gas, ice, laundry, store, swimming pool nearby. Swimming; snowskiing; hunting; rockhounding; hiking; picnicking; fishing; biking; golf nearby. Elev 3279; 20 acres. On Musselshell River. Bike trails. Nature trails. Only campground in the area.

Fishing tip: Try the river's channel catfish; they're plentiful and easy to catch, and you might just hook a 30-pound lunker.

SACO (115)

Cole Ponds   **FREE**
State Fishing Access Site
10 mi NW of Saco on Hwy 243. Free. All year; 7-day limit. Primitive undeveloped sites. Toilets, cfga, tbls, no drkg wtr. Fishing. 190 acres.

ST. MARY (117)

Cut Bank Campground   **$10**
Glacier National Park
15 mi S on US 89; 4 mi W on dirt Cut Bank Rd; at E side of park. $10. MD-LD; 14-day limit (7-day 7/1-8/31). 14 primtive sites (22-ft RV limit; not recommended). Tbls, toilets, cfga, drkg wtr. Hiking, fishing, backpacking. Elev 5500 ft; 2 acres.

St. Mary Lake   **$11.50**
Glacier National Park
1 mi W of St. Mary on Going-to-the-Sun Rd; E side of Glacier NP. $11.59 with federal Senior Pass; others pay $23 during 6/1-9/30; 7-day limit. Reduced fees for primitive camping 4/1-5/24 and 9/24-10/30. Winter camping 11/1-3/30. 148 sites (35-ft RV limit). Tbls, flush toilets, cfga, drkg wtr, dump. Fishing, hiking (paved trail). Elev 4500 ft; 5 acres.

ST. REGIS (118)

Cascade   **$10**
Lolo National Forest
16 mi E of St. Regis on SR 135. $10. MD-10/1; 14-day limit. 12 sites (22-ft RV limit). Tbls, toilets, cfga, drkg wtr, boating (hand launch), fishing, hiking trails, swimming. Extra charge for pets. Cascade National Recreation Trail. Elev 2900 ft.

Slowey   **$10**
Lolo National Forest
7 mi SE of St. Regis on I-90 or US 10; 3 mi W on Dry Creek Rd. On Clark Fork River. $10. About MD-9/30; 14-day limit. 16 sites plus 10 pull-through RV sites. Tbls, toilets, cfga, drkg wtr. Fishing, horseback riding, volleyball, horseshoe pits, sandbox, horse camp facilities. Elev 2800 ft; 14 acres.

Fishing tip: The Clark Fork near St. Regis offers excellent trout fishing, with good populations of rainbow, cutthroat & bull trout. Browns also are common in the upper reaches east of Missoula. Use Panther Martin spinners or dry flies. Rainbows will average 15 inches, browns larger. May best time, just before high-elevation snow melts.

ST. XAVIER (119)

Mallard's Landing   **FREE**
Bighorn River
State Fishing Access Site
5 mi N of St. Xavier on Hwy 313 (stream mile 62.9); Upper Bighorn River access. Free. All year; 7-day limit. Primitive undesignated camping on 43 acres. Toilets, tbls, cfga, no drkg wtr. Fishing, boating(l). Difficult access, but good fishing and floating.

SCOBEY (120)

Lions Campground   **Donations**
From northbound SR 13/Main St, E on SR 5/1st Ave E; N on Timmons St to Railroad Ave; right into park. Free, but $12 donation requested. May-Sept. 10 pull-through RV sites. Tbls, toilets, cfga, drkg wtr, dump, 30/50-amp elec. GPS: N48degrees 47.599, W105degrees 25.203.

SEELEY LAKE (121)

Big Larch   **$10**
Lolo National Forest
1.3 mi NW of Seeley Lake on SR 83; half mi W on FR 2199; on E side of lake. $10 during 5/15-9/30; free rest of year, but no drkg wtr or services; 14-day limit. 50 sites; 32-ft RV limit. Tbls, toilets, cfga, drkg wtr, pay phone. Boating(concrete launch), fishing, swimming, waterskiing, cross-country ski trails, 8 picnic sites, birdwatching, nature & interpretive trails. Near Bob Marshall Wilderness. On E side of lake. Store 1 mi. Elev 3993 ft; 17 acres.

Harpers Lake   **$7**
State Fishing Access Site
13 mi S of Seeley Lake on SR 83. $7 for licensed fishermen; $12 for others. All year; 7-day limit. 14 sites (28-ft RV limit). Tbls, toilets, cfga, no drkg wtr, fishing pier. Fishing, boating (no motors; hand launch). Elev 4000 ft; 100 acres.

Hidden Lake   **FREE**
Lolo National Forest
4 mi S of Seely Lake on SR 83; 7 mi E on FR 349; 1 mi N on unimproved dirt rd. Free. 6/15-9/15; 14-day limit. 2 primitive sites; no facilities, no drkg wtr. Fishing, swimming. No signs to indicate campsites; be careful not to trespass on private land.

Lake Alva   **$10**
Lolo National Forest
13 mi NW of Seeley Lake on Hwy 83; at N end of Lake Alva. $10 during 5/15-9/30; free rest of year, but no wtr or services; 14-day limit. 41 sites plus 2 small group camping areas (12 vehicles maximum). Tbls, toilets, cfga, drkg wtr. Boating(concrete launch), fishing, swimming. 15 mi to Mission Mountain Wilderness. Reservations accepted for small groups. Elev 4100 ft.

Lake Inez   **FREE**
Lolo National Forest
9 mi NW of Seeley Lake on SR 83; at N end of Lake Inez. Free. All year (when snow-free); 14-day limit. 3 primitive open sites. Toilets, cfga, tbls, no drkg wtr, no trash service. Boating(l), fishing, swimming, hiking, waterskiing. Elev 4100 ft.

Lindbergh Campground   **FREE**
Flathead National Forest
18 mi N of Seeley Lake on SR 83; about 4 mi W on FR 79; at Lindbergh Lake. Free. 6/15-9/15; 14-day limit. 7 sites; 20-ft RV limit. Toilets, cfga, no drkg wtr. Boating(l), fishing, hiking, canoeing, mountain biking, hunting.

Fishing tip: Due to its limited spawning areas and low fish production, Lindbergh Lake is not an outstanding fishery. Still, it is stocked annually with small cutthroat trout and kokanee salmon. In summer, anglers catch 12-inch cutthroat and plenty of kokanee. Troll Thomas Cyclones and Mepps spinners 8-20 feet to locate fish.

Owl Creek Packer   **FREE**
Flathead National Forest
21 mi N of Seeley Lake on SR 83; about 3.5 mi S on FR 44; at S side of Holland Lake. Free. 5/15-9/15; 14-day limit. Primitive undesignated sites at trailhead. Tbls, toilets, cfga, drkg wtr. Hiking, boating, fishing, horseback riding. Boat ramp & dump at Holland Campground. Beware of grizzly bears.

River Point $10
Lolo National Forest
3 mi S of Seeley Lake on SR 209; 2 mi NW on CR 70; on W side of lake. $10 during MD-LD; free LD-winter; 14-day limit. 26 sites. Tbls, toilets, cfga, drkg wtr. Swimming, fishing, canoeing on Clearwater River; boating (l-1 mi), 8 picnic sites, horseshoes, sand volleyball. Elec 3933 ft; 8 acres.

Seeley Lake $10
Lolo National Forest
.3 mi S of Seeley Lake on SR 83; 3 mi NW on CR 70; on W side of lake. $10 base. ; 14-day limit. Base fee for regular sites; $10 for lakeside sites. 29 sites; 32-ft RV limit. Tbls, flush toilets, cfga, drkg wtr, pay phone. Boating(l), swimming, waterskiing, fishing. Elev 3993 ft; 11 acres.

SHERIDAN (123)

Balanced Rock FREE
Beaverhead National Forest
About 10 mi E of Sheridan on rough, narrow Mill Creek Rd, following Mill Creek Recreation sign (rd not recommended for RVs). Free. MD-9/25; 16-day limit. 5 sites; 32-ft RV limit. Tbls, toilet, cfga, no drkg wtr, no trash service. Fishing, hiking, birdwatching. Elev 7360 ft.

Branham Lakes FREE
Beaverhead National Forest
About 6 mi E of Sheridan on rough, narrow Mill Creek Rd; rd not recommended for RVs. Free. About 5/1-9/30; 16-day limit. 6 sites (22-ft RV limit. Tbls, toilets, cfga, drkg wtr. Boating(l), fishing, hiking trails. Elev 8800 ft; 3 acres.

Cottonwood FREE
Beaverhead National Forest
10 mi SE of Sheridan on SR 287, then 12 mi S of Alder on CR 248; 11 mi SE on CR 142; 2 mi S on FR 100. Free. MD-11/30; 16-day limit. 10 sites (28-ft RV limit). Tbls, toilets, cfga, no drkg wtr. Fishing, hunting. No trash service.

Mill Creek FREE
Beaverhead National Forest
7 mi E of Sheridan on Mill Creek Rd. Free. MD-9/30; 16-day limit. 10 sites (RVs under 23 ft). Tbls, toilets, cfga, drkg wtr.

SIDNEY (124)

Elk Island FREE
State Fishing Access Site
Wildlife Management Area
29 mi S of Sidney on MT 16, milepost 30; 1 mi E on co rd; limited access for RVs. Free. All year; 14-day limit. 7 sites. Tbls, toilets, cfga, no drkg wtr Picnicking; fishing; boating; hiking.

Seven Sisters FREE
State Wildlife Area
About 10 mi SW of Sidney near Crane; access from Hwy 15 at milepost 41; half mi E on gravel county rd. Free. All year; 14-day limit. Primitive undesignated sites; no facilities, no drkg wtr. 555-acre recreation area.

STANFORD (125)

Dry Wolf $5
Lewis and Clark National Forest
20 mi SW of Stanford on co rd; 6 mi SW on FR 251, following signs. $5 during LD-MD; free rest of yr but no wtr or services; 14-day limit. 25 sites (32-ft RV limit). Tbls, toilets, cfga, drkg wtr, no trash service. Hiking trails, fishing (brook & rainbow trout). On Dry Wolf Creek. Marine fossils in nearby Bandbox Mtns. Elev 5900 ft. This camp was built in 1930 as a Kiwanis Club project; it was improved in 1937 by the WPA & by the NFS in the 1960s.

Thain Creek $5
Lewis and Clark National Forest
15 mi N of Stanford on US 87 to Geyser; turn right & follow signs 25 mi. $5 during MD-LD; free rest of year but no wtr or services; 14-day limit. 16 sites (22-ft RV limit). Tbls, toilets, cfga, drkg wtr, no trash service. Fishing, hiking trails. Elev 4700 ft. Closed by flood damage during early 2007.
Fishing tip: Try for brook & rainbow trout in Thain Creek and Briggs Creek.

STEVENSVILLE (126)

Charles Waters $10
Bitterroot National Forest
2 mi NW of Stevensville on CR 269; 4 mi N on US 93; 2 mi W on CR 22; 1 mi W on FR 1316; on Bass Creek. $10 during MD-9/10; free rest of year, but no wtr or services; 14-day limit. 28 sites; no RV size limit; 5 sites are pullthrough; 1 bicycle site. Drkg wtr, toilets, cfga, tbls. Handicapped facilities. Hiking trails, fishing, hunting, physical fitness trail. Historical area at Stevensville (St. Mary's Mission and Fort Owen, Montana's first white settlement). Access point to Selway-Bitterroot Wilderness. Elev 3200 ft; 12 acres.

Gold Creek FREE
Bitterroot National Forest
Half mi S of Stevensville on CR 269; 10.4 mi SE on CR 372; 3.8 mi S on FR 312. Free. 6/1-9/15; 14-day limit. 5 sites; 40-ft RV limit. Tbls, toilets, cfga, firewood, no drkg wtr. Hiking; picnicking; fishing; hunting. Elev 4800 ft; 3 acres. Poor rd up Burnt Fork Creek.

SULA (127)

Crazy Creek (Upper) $8
Bitterroot National Forest
4.8 mi NW of Sula on US 93; 1 mi SW on CR 100; 3 mi SW on FR 370; on Warm Spring Creek. $8 during 6/1-9/15; free rest of yr but no wtr or services; 14-day limit. 7 sites (RVs under 27 ft); the lower sites are for horse camping with tie racks, watering trough. Tbls, toilets, cfga, firewood, well drkg wtr. Hiking; picnicking; fishing. Elev 5000 ft; 9 acres. Trailhead to Warm Springs Area. Upper loop open to use by hunters; lower loop closed to hunters.

Crazy Creek Horse Camp FREE
Bitterroot National Forest
4.8 mi NW of Sula on US 93; 1 mi SW on CR 100; 2.5 mi SW on FR 370 (half mi before reaching Crazy Creek Campground); along warm Spring Creek. Free. All year; 14-day limit. 5 sites; 26-ft RV limit. Tbls, toilets, cfga, no drkg wtr. Feed bunkers & tie racks for horses. Horseback riding, hiking, fishing.

East Fork Trailhead FREE
Bitterroot National Forest
17 mi NE of Sula; on E fork of Bitterroot River. Free. 6/15-11/30. No improved camping sites. Toilets, stock unloading ramps. Horseback riding (corrals & ramps). Access point for the Anaconda-Pintlar Wilderness.

Jennings Camp FREE
Bitterroot National Forest
1 mi W of Sula on US 93; 10 mi NE on CR 472. Free. 6/15-9/15; 14-day limit. 4 sites (RVs under 21 ft). Tbls, toilets, cfga, firewood, well drkg wtr. Hunting; hiking; picnicking; fishing (1 mi). On E Fork of the Bitterroot River.

Martin Creek $8
Bitterroot National Forest
1 mi N of Sula on US 93; 4 mi NE on CR 472; 12 mi NE on FR 80. Elev 5400 ft. $8 during 6/15-9/15; free rest of yr, but no wtr or services; 14-day limit. 7 sites (50-ft RV limit). Tbls, toilets, cfga, firewood, well drkg wtr. Hunting; picnicking; hiking; fishing (1 mi). On Moose and Martin Creeks.

Spring Gulch $12
Bitterroot National Forest
3 mi NW of Sula on US 93. $12 during MD-9/30; 14-day limit. Free rest of year, but no wtr or services. 11 sites (one reserved for biking tour groups); 50-ft RV limit. Tbls, toilets, cfga, drkg wtr. Fishing, hunting, hiking, swimming.

Warm Springs $8
Bitterroot National Forest
4.7 mi NW on US 93; 1 mi SW on CR 100. $8. MD-LD; 14-day limit; free rest of year. 14 sites; 26-ft RV limit. Tbls, toilets, cfga, drkg wtr, picnic area. Fishing, swimming, hiking, picnicking. Elev 4400 ft; 7 acres.

SUPERIOR (128)

Clearwater Crossing FREE
Lolo National Forest
20.2 mi SE on I-90 to Fish Creek exit 66; 9.2 mi S on FR 343 (Fish Creek Rd); 7.1 mi SW on FR 7750. 6/1-11/30; 14-day limit. 3 tent sites. Tbls, toilets, cfga, no drkg wtr. Picnicking; fishing; swimming; hiking; horseback riding (corrals, stock facilities). Elev 3800 ft;

1 acre. Mountains. Dense forest. Entrance to Upper Fish Creek Recreation Area. Along Fish Creek Rd is the state's largest pine tree.

Diamond Lake FREE
Lolo National Forest
Near Superior, follow I-90's frontage rd 4 mi N to where it crosses south (LaVista), then 10 mi SW on FR 342; 3 mi S on dirt FR 7843; at Diamond Lake. Free. 6/1-9/30; 14-day limit. 4 sites. Tbls, toilets, cfga, no drkg wtr. Overlooks Idaho border. Not recommended for RVs.

Quartz Flat $10
Lolo National Forest
10 mi SE of Superior on I-90 (at rest area). $10. About 5/15-9/30; 14-day limit. 52 sites. Tbls, flush toilets, cfga, drkg wtr. Dump $2 for non-campers. Short walk to Clark Fork River. Self-guided nature trail. Fishing. Elev 2900 ft; 40 acres.

Trout Creek $6
Lolo National Forest
5 miSE of Superior on SR 269; 3 mi SW on FR 257 (Trout Creek Rd). $6. during MD-LD; free rest of year, but no drkg wtr; 14-day limit. 12 sites (30-ft RV limit). Tbls, toilets, cfga, drkg wtr, no trash service. Fishing, boating(l). 6 acres.

SWAN LAKE (129)

Cedar Creek FREE
Swan River State Forest
7 mi S of Swan Lake on Hwy 83; 1 mi W on gravel rd at Cedar Creek. Free. 6/1-10/30; 14-day limit. 12 sites for tents; 12 for truck/folding campers. Tbls, toilets, cfga, firewood. Fishing at Cedar Creek and Swan Lake; picnicking; horseback riding. 2 acres; elev 3500 ft.

Fishing tip: Fishermen can keep just one of the rare bull trout caught from Swan Lake, but it must be killed immediately or else returned to the water. It's illegal to have a live bull trout.

Point Pleasant FREE
Swan River State Forest
8 mi S of Swan Lake on Hwy 209 (Swan Valley Hwy); at Swan River. Free. 6/1-10/30; 14-day limit. 12 sites (RVs under 12 ft). Tbls, toilets, cfga, firewood, no drkg wtr. Fishing; picnicking. 5 acres.

Fishing tip: Swan River can provide some excellent action for rainbow & cutthroat trout, but it's strictly catch-and-release with artificial lures.

Soup Creek FREE
Swan River State Forest
6 mi S of Swan Lake on US 209; 4 mi E on Loop Rd (Gravel rd). Free. 6/1-10/30; 14-day limit. 9 tent sites, 9 RV sites (RVs under 12 ft). Tbls, toilets, cfga, drkg wtr. Picnicking; fishing. Elev 3500 ft; 5 acres.

Van Lake FREE
Plum Creek Timber
From near Swan Lake, E on Hwy 83 near milemarker 54-55, then take Van Lake Rd 3 mi (last half mi rough). Free. Several primitive, undeveloped sites around small, scenic lake. No facilities, no drkg wtr. Boating(l), fishing. Crowded on weekends & holidays.

TERRY (130)

Highway 10 Picnic Area FREE
Municipal Park
7 mi W on US 10. Free. All year. 10 primitive tent sites; 10 primitive RV sites. Tbls, toilets, cfga, drkg wtr. Picnicking; fishing (1 mi). 2 acres beside Yellowstone River.

Fishing tip: Try the Yellowstone River, one of America's most famous trout streams, for cutthroat, rainbow & browns. Best bet is to fish from a drifting boat using spinners or flies, although wading & bank fishing can be productive in places too.

Terry City Park FREE
On US 10 at center of Terry. Free. 6/1-9/1. 20 tent & 20 RV sites. Tbls, flush toilets. Ice, dump, LP-gas, laundry, store nearby. Picnicking; swimming. 4 acres. Swimming pool (extra charge). Playground. River.

Terry RV Oasis $12
From I-94 exit 176, turn left on Yellowstone St; 10 blocks to camp. $12 base. 4/1-11/30. 16 sites. Tbls, flush toilets, showers, drkg wtr, cfga, hookups($), dump.

THOMPSON FALLS (131)

Clark Memorial $5
Lolo National Forest
5 mi E of Thompson Falls on MT 200; 5.4 mi NE on FR 56 (Thompson River Rd). $5. 5/15-10/15. 5 sites (RVs under 16 ft). Tbls, toilets, cfga, no drkg wtr. Picnicking; fishing. Thompson River. Access rd not suitable for long RVs.

Copper King $5
Lolo National Forest
5 mi E of Thompson Falls on MT 200; 4 mi NE on FR 56 (Thompson River Rd); at Thompson River. $5. 6/1-10/15; 14-day limit. 5 sites (RVs under 16 ft). Tbls, toilets, cfga, no drkg wtr. Picnicking; fishing. Access rd not suitable for long RVs.

Fishtrap Lake FREE
Lolo National Forest
5 mi E of Thompson Falls on MT 200; 13 mi NE on FR 56; 14.7 mi NW on FR 516; 1.8 mi W on FR 7593. Free. 6/1-10/15; 14-day limit. 10 sites (32-ft RV limit). Tbls, toilets, cfga, well drkg wtr. Berry picking; picnicking; fishing; rockhounding; waterskiing; boating (ld, qtr mi).

Gold Rush $5
Lolo National Forest
9 mi S of Thompson Falls on FR 352 (E fork of Dry Creek Rd). $5. 6/1-10/15; 14-day limit. 7 sites (32-ft RV limit). tbls, toilets, cfga, drkg wtr. Picnicking, fishing. Motor vehicles not permitted on trails 12/1-5/15 to reduce wildlife disturbance.

Flatiron Ridge FREE
Clark Fork River
State Fishing Access Site
2 mi W of Thompsons Falls off Hwy 200; near Noxon Rapids Lake. Free. All year; 14-day limit. Primitive sites on 18 acres. Tbls, toilets, cfga, no drkg wtr. Boating(l), fishing. Good access.

Thompson Falls State Park $12
1 mi N of Thompson Falls on MT 200; milepost 50; at Noxon Rapids Reservoir. $12. 5/1-9/30; 14-day limit. Designated as primitive park. 17 RV sites (30-ft RV limit). Tbls, pit toilets, firewood, cfga, drkg wtr, shelters. Boating(l); picnicking; fishing; swimming. Elev 2473 ft; 36 acres.

West Fork Fishtrap Creek FREE
Lolo National Forest
5 mi E of Thompson Falls on MT 200; 13 mi NE on FR 56 (Thompson River Rd); 15 mi NW on FR 516 (Fishtrap Creek Rd); 2 mi W on FR 6593. Free. 6/1-10/15. 4 sites (32-ft RV limit). Tbls, toilets, cfga, well drkg wtr. Picnicking; fishing, boating(l). Elev 4200 ft.

THREE FORKS (132)

Missouri Headwaters State Park $12
I-90 at Three Forks, milepost 278; 6 mi N on CR 286; at confluence of Jefferson, Madison & Gallatin Rivers, which create the Missouri River. $12. 5/1-9/30; 14-day limit. Designated as primitive park. 23 RV sites (25-ft RV limit). Tbls, cfga, drkg wtr, pit & flush toilets. Boating(l); picnicking; fishing, hiking trails. Elev 4795 ft; 530 acres. This spot was a campsite for the Lewis & Clark expedition; scenic overlook, historical exhibits.

Fishing tip: The Gallatin & Madison Rivers offer excellent fishing for rainbow trout & brown trout.

TOWNSEND (133)

Deepdale FREE
Missouri River
State Fishing Access Site
4 mi S of Townsend on US 287 to milepost 2, then 1 mi W; at Missouri River (river mile 2,275.9). Free. All year; 7-day limit. Primitive camping on 16 acres. Tbls, toilets, cfga, no drkg wtr. Boating(l), fishing. Easy access.

Gipsy Lake FREE
Helena National Forest
2 mi E of Townsend on US 12; 10 mi N on SR 284; about 15 mi E on Duck Creek Rd (FR 139); about 1 mi S on access rd. Free.

6/15-9/15; 14-day limit. 5 sites; 15-ft RV limit. Toilets, cfga, no drkg wtr, no trash service. Hiking, boating (hand launch), fishing (rainbow trout). Historic gold mines nearby.

Indian Road Recreation Area   **$6**
Bureau of Reclamation
N of Townsend, milepost 75, on US 287 at bridge. $6. All year, 14-day limit. 25 sites (no RV size limit). Drkg wtr, tbls, toilets, cfga. Boating; picnicking, boating(l), fishing. Formerly part of Canyon Ferry State Park.

Indian Creek   **$7**
Broadwater County Campground
State Division of Wildlife & Parks
At Missouri River bridge just N of Townsend on US 287. $7. All year. Undesignated sites. Tbls, toilets, drkg wtr, cfga. Boating(l), picnicking, fishing, swimming.

Silos Recreation Area   **$6**
Bureau of Reclamation
Bureau of Land Management
7 mi N of Townsend on US 287, milepost 70; 1 mi E on county rd. $6. All year; 14-day limit. 80 sites. Drkg wtr, shelters, tbls, cfga. Boating(l); fishing; picnicking. Formerly part of Canyon Ferry State Park.

Skidway   **FREE**
Helena National Forest
23 mi E of Townsend on US 12; turn right at milemarker 22; 2 mi S on FR 4042 (paved but tough access). Free. Elev 6000 ft. 5/15-10/30; 14-day limit. 13 sites (RVs under 16 ft). Tbls, toilets, cfga, firewood, tank drkg wtr. Picnicking; fishing, hiking trails.

Toston Dam   **FREE**
Bureau of Land Management
13 mi S of Townsend on US 287; E to Tosten Dam. All year; 14-day limit. 2 locations, with 5-10 sites each (RVs under 25 ft). Tbls, cfga, toilets, no drkg wtr. Boating(l), fishing.

TROUT CREEK (134)

Big Eddy   **FREE**
Kootenai National Forest
N of Trout Creek on SR 200; on N side of Cabinet Reservoir. Free. All year; 14-day limit. 3 undesignated sites (40-ft RV limit). Tbls, toilets, cfga, no drkg wtr. Boating(l), fishing.

Marten Creek   **FREE**
Kootenai National Forest
7 mi NW of Trout Creek on Marten Creek Rd. All year; 14-day limit. 3 sites (32-ft RV limit). Tbls, toilets, cfga, no drkg wtr. Boating(l), fishing, hiking. At Marten Creek Bay on Noxon Reservoir.

North Shore   **$7**
Kootenai National Forest
2.5 mi NW of Trout Creek on SR 200; half mi E on co rd. $7 during 5/15-9/10; free earlier &

later, but no wtr or services; 14-day limit. 13 sites (40-ft RV limit). Tbls, toilets, cfga, drkg wtr. Swimming; picnicking; fishing; hiking; horseback riding; boating(ld). Elev 2200 ft; 7 acres. On N shore of Noxon Rapids Reservoir. Near Cabinet Mountains Wilderness.

Sylvan Lake   **FREE**
Kootenai National Forest
1 mi W of Trout Creek on Hwy 200; 17 mi N on FR 154 (Vermilion River Rd). 5/15-10/15; 14-day limit. 5 primitive sites; 32-ft RV limit. Tbls, toilets, cfga, no drkg wtr. Boating(l), fishing.
  Fishing tip: There's excellent fishing in both Sylvan Lake and in Miller Lake, just below it.

Willow Creek   **FREE**
Kootenai National Forest
19.4 mi E of Trout Creek on FR 154. Free. All year; 14-day limit. 4 sites (40-ft RV limit). Tbls, toilets, cfga, firewood, no drkg wtr. Picnicking; fishing, hiking, boating(l).

TROY (135)

Bad Medicine   **$8**
Kootenai National Forest
3 mi E on US 2; 18 mi S on SR 56. $8 during 5/15-9/10; free earlier & later, but no wtr or services. 14-day limit. 17 sites (32-ft RV limit). Tbls, toilets, cfga, drkg wtr, 6 picnic sites. Fishing, boating(ld), swimming, hiking trails. Elev 2200 ft; 15 acres.

Dorr Skeels   **FREE**
Kootenai National Forest
3 mi SE of Troy on US 2; 12.5 mi S on SR 56; W to camp; on Bull Lake. Free. All year; 14-day limit. 3 sites; 32-ft RV limit. Tbls, toilets, cfga, no drkg wtr. Fishing, boating(l), waterskiing, swimming, biking, waterskiing.
  Fishing tip: 1,000-acre Bull Lake has good fishing for kokanee salmon, cutthroat & rainbow trout, largemouth bass and perch.

Kilbrennen Lake   **FREE**
Kootenai National Forest
2.7 mi NW of Troy on US 2; 9.8 mi NE on FR 2394. Free. 4/15-11/30; 14-day limit. 7 sites (32-ft RV limit). Tbls, toilets, cfga, firewood, no drkg wtr. Boating; waterskiing; picnicking; good fishing. Beautiful lake.

Pete Creek   **$7**
Kootenai National Forest
7 mi NW of Troy on US 2; 12.8 mi NE on SR 508; 14 mi NE on FR 92; at confluence of Yaak River & Pete Creek. $7 during 5/15-9/10; free earlier & later, but no wtr or services; 14-day limit. 13 sites (32-ft RV limit). Tbls, toilets, cfga, drkg wtr. Fishing (trout), picnicking. Elev 3000 ft; 8 acres.

Red Top   **FREE**
Kootenai National Forest
10.2 mi NW on US 2; 12.8 mi NE on MT 508; 3 mi N on FR 92; at Yaak River. Free. All year;

14-day limit. 5 sites (32-ft RV limit). Tbls, toilets, cfga, firewood, no drkg wtr. Picnicking; fishing. Watch for logging trucks.

Spar Lake   **FREE**
Kootenai National Forest
3 mi SE of Troy on US 2; 8 mi S on Lake Creek Rd; 12 mi on Spar Lake RD (FR 384). Free. About 5/1-11/15; 14-day limit. 8 sites; 32-ft RV limit. Tbls, toilets, cfga, drkg wtr. Fishing, boating(l), hiking, biking, ATV activity.

Whitetail   **$7**
Kootenai National Forest
7 mi NW of Troy on US 2; 12.8 mi NE on SR 508; 10 mi NE on FR 92; at Yaak River. $7 during 5/15-9/10; free rest of year, but no wtr or services; 14-day limit. 12 sites (32-ft RV limit). Tbls, toilets, cfga, drkg wtr. Fishing, boating, hiking trails, mountain biking. Elev 3000 ft; 8 acres.

Yaak Falls   **FREE**
Kootenai National Forest
10 mi NW of Troy on US 2; 6.5 mi NE on MT 508. Free. All year; 14-day limit. 7 sites (32-ft RV limit). Tbls, toilets, cfga, firewood, no drkg wtr. Hiking; picnicking; fishing. Adjacent to scenic Yaak River Falls; easy trail.
  Fishing tip: For the largest rainbow trout, fish the Yaak between the falls and Kootenai River.

Yaak River   **$9**
Kootenai National Forest
7.5 mi NW of Troy on US 2. $9 during 5/15-9/10; free rest of year, but no wtr or services; 14-day limit. 44 sites (32-ft RV limit). Tbls, toilets, cfga, drkg wtr. Hiking, picnicking, fishing, boating, swimming. Yaak & Kootenai Rivers.
  Fishing tip: This is a perfect spot for catching huge rainbow trout in the spring; fish the mouth of the Yaak.

TWIN BRIDGES (136)

Notch Bottom   **FREE**
Big Hole River
State Fishing Access Site
4 mi S of Twin Bridges on SR 41; 10 mi W on co rd (stream mile 17.9). Free. All year; 7-day limit. Primitive camping on 12.3 acres. Toilets, tbls, cfga, no drkg wtr. Boating(l), fishing. Difficult access; not an all-weather rd.

Ruby Reservoir   **FREE**
Recreation Site
Bureau of Land Management
S of Twin Bridges on SR 287 to Alder; S to E shore of Ruby River Reservoir. Free. All year; 14-day limit. 10 sites (35-ft RV limit). Tbls, toilets, no drkg wtr. Boating(l), fishing (trout), swimming, rockhounding for garnets along shore.

VALIER (137)

Lake Frances City Park $7

2 mi E of Valier just off US 44 on Teton Ave (becoming Lake Frances Rd). $7 at primitive sites, $15 at 50 sites with elec. Tbls, toilets, cfga, drkg wtr, playground, dump, beach, fish cleaning station. Boating(ld), swimming, fishing, sailing.

VICTOR (138)

Bear Creek Trailhead FREE
Bitterroot National Forest

10 mi SW of Victor on Bear Creek. Free. All year; 14-day limit. 1 primitive undeveloped site; no facilities. Hiking, fishing. Access point for Selway-Bitterroot Wilderness.

Big Creek Trailhead FREE
Bitterroot National Forest

4 mi NW of Victor on Bear Creek. Free. All year; 14-day limit. 1 primitive undeveloped site; no facilities. Hiking, fishing. Access point for Selway-Bitterroot Wilderness.

WEST GLACIER (139)

Apgar $10
Glacier National Park

2 mi W of West Glacier near park headquarters on Going-to-the Sun Rd. $10 in-season with federal Senior Pass; others pay $20. $10 for primitive camping off-season during 4/1-5/3 and 10/15-11/30. 194 sites (40-ft RV limit). Tbls, flush toilets, cfga, drkg wtr, store, dump. Wtr shut off; self-contained RVs only during winter. Hiking, picnicking, fishing, boating(rl), waterskiing. Golden Eagle Passport or entry fee.

Bowman Lake $7.50
Glacier National Park

32 mi NW of West Glacier on North Fork Rd; 6 mi on dirt rd. $7.50 in-season with federal Senior Pass; others pay $15. $10 for primitive camping off-season prior to 5/25 & after 9/14. All year; 14-day limit (7-day during 7/1-8/31). 48 primitive sites (22-ft RV limit). Tbls, toilets, cfga, drkg wtr. Boating(l), fishing. 5 acres. RVs not recommended. Golden Eagle Passport or entry fee.

Devil Creek $12
Flathead National Forest

45 mi SE of West Glacier on US 2; near Middle Fork of Flathead River. $12 during 5/6-9/30; free rest of year, but no wtr or services; 14-day limit. 14 sites; 40-ft RV limit. Tbls, toilets, cfga, drkg wtr. Fishing, horseback riding, hiking. Elev 4360 ft. Between Glacier National Park and Great Bear Wilderness.

Fishing tip: Trout season begins in May after the water clears from the spring melt. Cutthroat trout will take most mayfly and stonefly patterns; add a trailing nymph for extra appeal.

Kintla Lake $7.50
Glacier National Park

47 mi N of West Glacier on North Fork Rd. $7.50 in-season with federal Senior Pass; others pay $15. $10 off-season for primitive camping prior to 5/25 & after 9/14. 14-day limit (7-day 7/1-8/31). 13 sites (18-ft RV limit, not recommended). Tbls, toilets, cfga, drkg wtr. Boating(l), hiking.

Logging Creek $10
Glacier National Park

About 3 mi W of West Glacier, past Apgar camp, then N on dirt rd along North Fork Flathead River to Logging Creek; RVs not recommended. $10. 7/1-9/8; 7-day limit. 7 sites. Tbls, pit toilets, cfga, drkg wtr. Fishing, hiking. Campground closed in 2007 due to flooding & hazardous trees.

Quartz Creek $10
Glacier National Park

About 3 mi W of West Glacier, past Apgar camp, then N on dirt rd along North Fork Flathead River past Logging Creek Camp; RVs not recommended. $10. 7/1-12/1; 7-day limit. 7 primitive sites. Tbls, toilets, cfga, drkg wtr. Fishing, hiking.

Fishing tip: Quartz Creek produces good catches of 2-pound cutthroat trout and big bull trout (that must be released).

WEST YELLOWSTONE (140)

Beaver Creek $11
Gallatin National Forest

8 mi N of West Yellowstone on US 191; 17.3 mi W on US 287; at E end of Earthquake Lake. $11. 6/15-9/15; 16-day limit. 79 sites; 45-ft RV limit. Tbls, toilets, cfga, drkg wtr. Boating(l), fishing; boat ramp half mi W on US 287; excellent birdwatching. Earthquake site. Elev 6400 ft; 9 acres.

Fishing tip: Both Earthquake Lake and Hebgen Reservoir produce rainbow and brown trout.

Cabin Creek $11
Gallatin National Forest

8 mi N of West Yellowstone on US 191; 14 mi W on US 287; on E end of Earthquake Lake. $11. Open 5/15-9/15; 14-day limit. 15 sites (22-ft RV limit). Tbls, toilets, cfga, drkg wtr. Fishing, boating. Hiking, boating, fishing; boat launch near Beaver Creek Camp. Excellent birdwatching W of camp. Elev 6140 ft.

Travel tip: Visitor center at W end of lake relates story of the 1959 earthquake which collapsed an 80-million-ton dam across the Madison River.

Cherry Creek FREE
Gallatin National Forest

8 mi W of West Yellowstone on US 20; 6 mi N on Hebgen Lake Rd; at Hebgen Lake. Free. MD-10/15; 16-day limit. 12 primitive dispersed sites. Toilets, cfga, no drkg wtr. Fishing, mountain biking on old logging roads winding through forest to the west.

Fishing tip: Catch brown & rainbow trout and Utah chub from Hebgen Lake.

Cliff Point $9
Beaverhead National Forest

8 mi N of West Yellowstone on US 191; 27 mi W on US 287; 6 mi SW on FR 241. $9 during MD-9/15; 16-day limit; free rest of year, weather permitting, but no drkg wtr or trash service. 6 sites (RVs under 17 ft). Tbls, toilets, cfga, firewood, well drkg wtr. Hiking; picnicking; fishing; (good trout fishing); waterskiing; boating (rld-1 mi). Elev 6400 ft; 2 acres. Botanical. Nature trails. Cliff Lake.

Hilltop $8
Beaverhead National Forest

8 mi N of West Yellowstone on US 191; 27 mi W on US 287; 6 mi SW on FR 241. $8 during 5/15-9/15; free rest of year, weather permitting, but no wtr or trash service; 16-day limit. 18 sites (RVs under 23 ft). Tbls, toilets, cfga, firewood, piped drkg wtr. Picnicking; horseback riding; sailing; fishing; waterskiing; boating. Elev 6400 ft; 8 acres. Scenic. Botanical. Wade and Cliff Lakes.

Raynolds Pass FREE
Madison River
State Fishing Access Site

31 mi NW of West Yellowstone on US 287 to milepost 8; half mi S to bridge (river mile 97.7); also walk-in area on E side of US 287. Free. May-Oct; 7-day limit. Primitive camping on 162.5 acres; 25-ft RV limit. Tbls, toilets, cfga, no drkg wtr. Boating(l), fishing. Difficult access.

Spring Creek FREE
Gallatin National Forest

8 mi W of West Yellowstone on US 20; N on Hebgen Lake Rd 9 mi; at Hebgen Lake. MD-10/15; 14-day limit. Undeveloped primitive camping area. No facilities except toilet, cfga. Fishing, boating.

Fishing tip: Try the lake for brown & rainbow trout or chub. Boat ramp is on the opposite side of the lake.

Wade Lake $9
Beaverhead National Forest

8 mi N of West Yellowstone on US 191; 27 mi W on US 287; 6 mi SW on FR 5721. $9 during MD-10/15; 16-day limit; free rest of year, weather permitting, but no wtr or trash service. $16 double occupancy. 30 sites (32-ft RV limit). Tbls, toilets, cfga, firewood, piped drkg wtr. Picnicking; fishing; waterskiing; sailing; boating(lr). Elev 6200 ft; 5 acres. Good trout fishing at Wade Lake.

WHITEFISH (141)

Sylvia Lake FREE
Flathead National Forest

10 mi N of Whitefish on US 93; 23 mi W on FR 538 & FR 113, then about 3 mi S on FR 538B; near scenic Sylvia Lake. Free. 5/6-9/30; 14-day limit. About 3 very small, primitive undesignated sites. Toilets, cfga, no drkg wtr. Fishing, hiking, biking.

Fishing tip: This lake offers good fishing for Arctic grayling and west slope cutthroat trout.

Tally Lake $7
Flathead National Forest
6 mi W of Whitefish on US 93; 15 mi W on FR 113. $7 with federal Senior Pass; others pay $14 during 5/6-9/30; free rest of yr, but no wtr or services; 14-day limit. 39 sites; 40-ft RV limit. Tbls, toilets, cfga, drkg wtr, dump. Fishing, boating(l), swimming, hiking trails. Elev 3400 ft; 23 acres.

Fishing tip: Tally Lake has good populations of kokanee salmon, northern pike and rainbow, cutthroat and brook trout.

Stillwater Lake FREE
Flathead National Forest
23 mi N of Whitefish on US 92; about 1 mi S on FR 10354. Free. 5/6-9/15; 14-day limit. 3 small sites near the lake and Stillwater River. Toilets, cfga, no drkg wtr, no trash service. Boating, fishing, biking. Boat access to river about 1 mi N at state's Spring Creek. Formerly a fee site.

WHITEHALL (142)

Pigeon Creek FREE
Deerlodge National Forest
15.6 mi W of Whitehall on MT 2; 4.6 mi S on FR 668. Free. MD-9/15; 16-day limit. 7 tent sites. Tbls, toilets, cfga, firewood, well drkg wtr. Rockhounding; picnicking; fishing. Elev 5500 ft; 7 acres.

Toll Mountain FREE
Deerlodge National Forest
13 mi W of Whitehall on MT 2; 1.5 mi N on FR 9315. Elev 6000 ft. Free. 5/1-9/15; 16-day limit. 5 sites (22-ft RV limit). Tbls, toilets, cfga, firewood, no drkg wtr. Picnicking; fishing; rockhounding.

WHITE SULPHUR SPRINGS (143)

Camp Baker State Park FREE
Smith River
State Fishing Access Site
17 mi W of White Sulphur Springs on Hwy 360; 9.6 mi N on Smith River Rd. Free. All year; 14-day limit. Primitive camping on 49 acres. Tbls, toilets, cfga, no drkg wtr. Fishing, boating(l). Put-in point for Smith River floats. Difficult access.

Grasshopper Creek $6
Lewis and Clark National Forest
7 mi E of White Sulphur Springs on US 12; 4.2 mi S on FR 211. $6. Elev 6000 ft. 6/1-10/15; 14-day limit. 12 sites (22-ft RV limit). Tbls, toilets, cfga, firewood, well drkg wtr, no trash service. Picnicking; fishing, raspberry-picking, hiking trails. Elev 5700 ft.

Jumping Creek $8
Lewis and Clark National Forest
22 mi NE of White Sulphur Springs on US 89; at Sheep Creek. $8 during 5/30-9/15; free 9/15-Thanksgiving weekend, but no wtr; 14-day limit. 10 sites (22-ft RV limit). Tbls, toilets, cfga, drkg wtr. Fishing (brook & rainbow trout), hiking trails. At jct of Sheep Creek & Jumping Creek. Elev 5700 ft; 10 acres.

Moose Creek $8
Lewis and Clark National Forest
18 mi N of White Sulphur Springs on US 89; 5.5 mi W on FR 119; 3.2 mi N on FR 204. $8. 6/1-9/15. 6 sites (22-ft RV limit). Tbls, toilets, cfga, firewood, well drkg wtr. Fishing (rainbow trout); picnicking, mountain biking, ATV activities, hiking trail.

Newlan Creek Reservoir $7
State Fishing Access Site
7 mi N of White Sulphur Springs on CR 360. $7 for licensed fishermen; others pay $12. All year; 14-day limit. Primitive undesignated sites. Toilets, cfga, no drkg wtr. Boating(l - shallow), fishing, hiking, swimming.

Richardson Creek FREE
Lewis and Clark National Forest
7 mi E of White Sulphur Springs on US 12; 5 mi S on FR 211. Free. Elev 5900 ft. 6/1-10/15; 14-day limit. 3 sites; 16-ft RV limit. Toilets, cfga, no tbls, no drkg wtr.

Smith River State Park FREE
Fort Logan
State Fishing Access Site
17 mi NW of White Sulphur Springs; 2 mi N on Smith River Rd. Free. All year; 14-day limit. Primitive undesignated sites on 215 acres. Tbls, toilets, cfga, no drkg wtr. Fishing. 59-mile river corridor between Camp Baker & Eden Bridge; float permits by lottery.

Spring Creek $10
Lewis and Clark National Forest
26.3 mi E of White Sulphur Springs on US 12; 4.1 mi N on FR 274 (Spring Creek Rd); right for qtr mi at campground sign. $10. MD-12/1; 14-day limit. 10 sites; 22-ft RV limit. Tbls, toilets, cfga, drkg wtr. Fishing (brook trout), hiking, bridle & biking trail. No horses in camp.

WISDOM (146)

American Legion Park FREE
On Hwy 43 on outskirts of Wisdom. Free. Tbls, pit toilets, cfga, drkg wtr. No activities.

Fishtrap Creek FREE
Big Hole River
State Fishing Access Site
23 mi N of Wisdom on SR 43 (stream mile 81.4). Free. All year; 7-day limit. Primitive camping on 82 acres; 28-ft RV limit. Toilets, tbls, cfga, drkg wtr. Boating(l), fishing. Difficult access.

May Creek $7
Beaverhead National Forest
17 mi W of Wisdom on SR 43. $7 during about 6/20-LD; 16-day limit; free rest of year, weather permitting, but no wtr. 21 sites (30-ft RV limit). Tbls, toilets, cfga, drkg wtr, no trash service. Fishing, hiking trails. Elev 6200 ft; 10 acres.

Miner Lake $7
Beaverhead National Forest
19 mi S of Wisdom at Jackson on SR 278; 7 mi W on CR 182; 3 mi W on FR 182. $7 during about 6/20-LD; 16-day limit; free rest of year, weather permitting, but no drkg wtr. 18 sites (20-ft RV limit). Tbls, toilets, cfga, drkg wtr, no trash service. Fishing, boating(l--no motors), hiking trails. Elev 7000 ft; 10 acres.

Mussigbrod $7
Beaverhead National Forest
1.1 mi W of Wisdom on MT 43; 7 mi NW on Lower North Fork Rd; 8.1 mi W on co rd; 2.8 mi NW on FR 573. $7. About 6/20-LD; 16-day limit. 10 sites (30-ft RV limit). Tbls, toilets, cfga, firewood, drkg wtr. Boating(l); picnicking; fishing (no power boats), hiking, horseback riding

Pintler FREE
Beaverhead National Forest
1.1 mi W on MT 43; 14 mi N on co rd; 4.1 mi N on FR 185. Free. 6/15-9/15; 16-day limit. 2 sites (18-ft RV limit). Tbls, toilets, cfga, firewood, well drkg wtr. Picnicking; fishing (cutthroat, rainbow, brook trout); boating; hiking. Elev 6300 ft; 3 acres. Mountains. Lake. Narrow access rd. Within 4 mi of Anaconda-Pintlar Wilderness. Pintler Lake (36 acres).

Steel Creek FREE
Beaverhead National Forest
Quarter mi N on MT 43; 4 mi E on CR 3; 1.3 mi E on FR 90. Free. Elev 6200 ft. About 6/15-LD; 16-day limit. 9 sites (25-ft RV limit). Tbls, toilets, cfga, well drkg wtr. Picnicking; fishing; hiking.

Twin Lakes Campground $7
Beaverhead National Forest
6.8 mi S of Wisdom on MT 278; 7.8 mi W on CR 1290 (Briston Lane Rd); 4.8 mi W on CR 1290; 4.8 mi S on FR 945; 5.8 mi SW on FR 183. Elev 7200 ft. Free after LD, depending upon weather (no wtr). $7 during 6/20-LD; 16-day limit. 21 sites on 13 acres (RVs under 26 ft). Tbls, toilets, cfga, firewood, well drkg wtr. Boating(ld); waterskiing; picnicking; fishing (no power boats). 75-acre lake.

WISE RIVER (147)

Boulder Creek $8
Beaverhead National Forest
12 mi SW of Wise River on Pioneer Mtns Scenic Byway (Hwy 73). $8 during MD-LD; free rest of year, but no drkg wtr or trash service; 16-day limit. 13 sites (30-ft RV limit). Tbls, toilets, cfga, drkg wtr. Fishing, hiking.

Fourth of July $8
Beaverhead National Forest
12 mi SW of Wise River on Pioneer Mtns Scenic Byway (Hwy 73). $8 during 6/15-9/30; 16-day limit; free rest of year, but no wtr or trash service. 5 sites (30-ft RV limit). Tbls, toilets, cfga, drkg wtr. Picnicking, hiking.

Little Joe $8

Beaverhead National Forest
19.6 mi SW of Wise River on Hwy 73 (Pioneer Mtns Scenic Byway). $8 during 6/15-9/30; 16-day limit; free rest of year, weather permitting, but no drkg wtr or trash service. 5 sites; 28-ft RV limit. Tbls, toilets, cfga, drkg wtr. Picnicking, fishing. Elev 7000 ft; 2 acres. River.

Lodgepole $8
Beaverhead National Forest
12.9 mi SW of Wise River on Hwy 73 (Pioneer Mtns Scenic Byway). $8 during MD-LD; 16-day limit; free rest of year, but no drkg wtr or trash service. 10 sites (30-ft RV limit). Tbls, toilets, cfga, drkg wtr. Fishing (brook trout), picnicking. Elev 6400 ft; 2 acres. Scenic.

Mono Creek $8
Beaverhead National Forest
22.8 mi SW of Wise River on Hwy 73 (Pioneer Mtns Scenic Byway). $8 during MD-LD; 16-day limit; free rest of year, but no drkg wtr or trash service. 5 sites (18-ft RV limit). Tbls, toilets, cfga, drkg wtr. Picnicking, fishing. Torrey & Schultz Lakes. Elev 6800 ft; 2 acres.

Seymour   FREE
Beaverhead National Forest
11.2 mi W of Wise River on MT 43; 4 mi N on CR 274; 8 mi NW on FR 934. Free. 6/15-9/30; 16-day limit. 17 sites (18-ft RV limit). Tbls, toilets, cfga, firewood, well drkg wtr. Picnicking; hunting; hiking; fishing. Elev 6700 ft; 7 acres. Stream. Trailhead into Anaconda-Pintlar Wilderness.

Fishing tip: Brook trout in good numbers caught in Seymour Lake.

Willow Campground $8
Beaverhead National Forest
13.4 mi SW of Wise River on FR 484 (Pioneer Mtns Scenic Byway). $8 during 6/15-9/30; 16-day limit; free rest of year, weather permitting, but no drkg wtr or trash service. 5 sites (26-ft RV limit). Tbls, toilets, cfga, drkg wtr. Picnicking, fishing (good brook trout). Scenic area on Wise River. Elev 6600 ft; 3 acres.

WOLF CREEK (148)

Departure Point $10
Holter Lake Recreation Area
Bureau of Land Management
3 mi N of Wolf Creek on Recreation Rd; 8 mi SE on county rd; E side of Missouri River. $10 (sites at dam $6). About 5/15-10/15; 14-day limit. 50 sites (50-ft RV limit). Tbls, toilets, cfga, no drkg wtr. Boating (hand launch), fishing, hiking, picnicking. $2 day-use fee included in site cost.

Holter Lake $10
Holter Lake Recreation Area
Bureau of Land Management
2 mi N of Wolf Creek on Recreation Rd; cross bridge; 3 mi E on co rd. $10 (sites at dam $6). About 5/15-10/15; 14-day limit. 50 sites. Tbls, toilets, cfga, drkg wtr. Swimming, fishing, hiking, boating(ld), waterskiing. Elev 3560 ft; 22 acres. $2 day-use fee included in site cost.

Lichen   FREE
Little Prickly Pear Creek
State Fishing Access Site
12 mi S of Wolf Creek on Little Prickly Pear Creek (stream mile 9.6). Free. All year; 14-day limit. Primitive undesignated camping on 1 acre. Toilets, tbls, cfga, no drkg wtr. Fishing, boating (carry-in launch). Difficult access.

Log Gulch $10
Holter Lake Recreation Area
Bureau of Land Management
3 mi E of Wolf Creek on paved rd to gravel rd; 8 mi on E side of Missouri River. $10 (sites at dam $6). About 5/15-10/15; 14-day limit. 90 sites (50-ft RV limit). Tbls, toilets, cfga, drkg wtr. Beach, swimming, boating(l), fishing. $2 day-use fee included in site cost.

Sleeping Giant   FREE
Wilderness Study Area
Bureau of Land Management
From I-15 exit 234 at Wolf Creek, follow frontage rd to BLM Wood Siding Gulch Rd. Free. All year; 14-day limit. About 40 primitive sites scattered allong the Holter Lake shoreline, and dispersed camping is permitted throughout the WSA. No facilities, no drkg wtr. Hiking, horseback riding, hunting. 11,000 acres.

WOLF POINT (149)

Lewis and Clark   FREE
Missouri River
State Fishing Access Site
6 mi SE of Wolf Point on Hwy 13; at Missouri River (river mile 1,699.9). Free. All year; 14-day limit. Primitive undesignated sites on 51 acres. Toilet, no drkg wtr. Boating(l), fishing, hiking. Difficult access.

WORDEN (150)

Voyagers Rest   FREE
Yellowstone River
State Fishing Access Site
1.5 mi NE of Worden on Hwy 312; 2 mi N on county rd; at Yellowstone River. Free. All year; 7-day limit. Primitive camping on 20 acres. Tbls, toilets, cfga, no drkg wtr. Fishing. Difficult access.

NEBRASKA

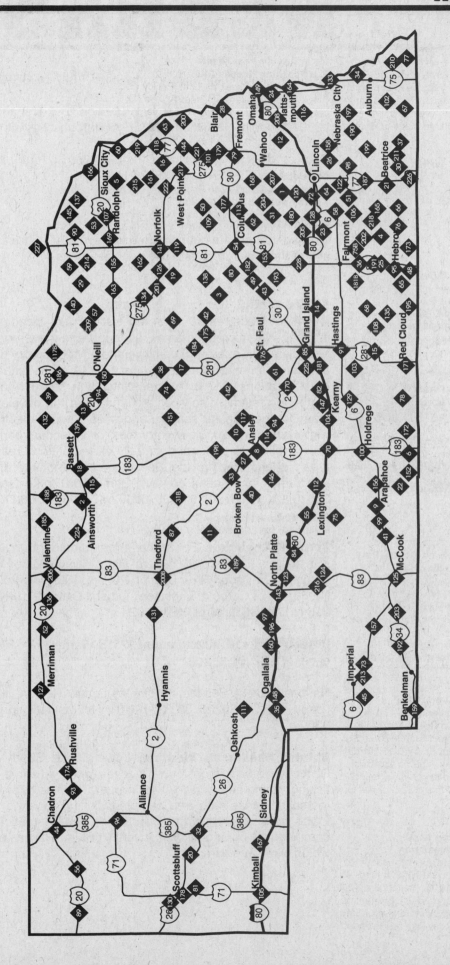

NEBRASKA

MISCELLANEOUS
Capital:
Lincoln
Nickname:
Cornhusker State
Motto:
Equality Before the Law
Flower:
Goldenrod
Tree:
Cottonwood
Bird:
Western Meadowlark
Song:
"Beautiful Nebraska"

Internet Address:
www.visitnebraska.org

Toll-free numbers for travel information: 1-877-NEBRASKA.

Dept of Economic Development, Division of Travel and Tourism, PO Box 98907, Lincoln, NE 68509-8907. E-mail: tourism@visitnebraska.org

Game and Parks Commission, 2200 N 33rd St, PO Box 30370, Lincoln NE 68503. 402/471-0641 or 800/826-PARK.

REST AREAS
Overnight stops are not permitted. RV sanitary stations are not provided at any of the major interstate highway rest areas.

STATE PARKS
Overnight fees are $10-17 in most state park campgrounds and $6-$15 in most state recreation areas, although a few are more and a couple are less. Generally speaking, primitive and off-season dry camping is $6, while developed primitive campsites are $10-11. Sites with electric are $15 at most locations, $17 at others. Water and sewer hookups are $2 each. Water and restroom services are shut off at the developed SRAs after the May-October regular season, and sites without electricity cost $6; sites with electricity, $10. Daily entry fees (or an annual permit) are required all year at all state parks and virtually all recreation areas regardless of the type facilities they provide. Special permits required for RVs over 40 feet. For further information contact: Game and Parks Commission, PO Box 30370, Lincoln, NE 68503-0370. 402-471-0641 or 800/826-PARK.

Corps of Engineers. For further information contact: Corps of Engineers, Kansas City District, 700 Federal Bldg, Kansas City, Mo, 64106; Corps of Engineers, Missouri River District, PO Box 103, Downtown Station, Omaha, NE 68101; or Corps of Engineers, Omaha District, USPO and Court House, 215 N 17th St, Omaha, NE 68102.

Bureau of Land Management, 2515 Warren Ave, PO Box 1828, Cheyenne, WY 82001.

National Forest Service, Rocky Mountain Region, 11177 W. 8TH St., Lakewood, CO 80225; 303/234-4185. Nebraska National Forest, 308-432-0300.

Natural Resources Districts: Lower Platte South Natural Resources District maintains eight public access lakes with free primitive camping, fishing, hiking and wildlife study. Upper Big Blue NRD has four developed recreation areas with free camping, fishing, boating and hiking. Lower Platte North NRD manages Czechland Lake Recreation Area, with its free camping, fishing and hiking. Lower Big Blue NRD has eight reserves, all of which allow free camping.

AGNEW (1)

Meadowlark Lake   **FREE**
Recreational Use Area
Lower Platte South
Natural Resources District
4 mi W of Agnew, then 1 mi N & 1 mi W. Free. All year; 14-day limit. Primitive open camping at 320-acre reserve with 55-acre lake. No facilities except cfga, no drkg wtr. Boating(l), fishing, hiking, hunting.

Fishing tip: The lake contains northern pike, largemouth bass, channel catfish and bluegill. Electric motors only.

AINSWORTH (2)

Calamus   **FREE**
State Canoe Trail
20 mi S of town on SR 7 to river (boat access only). Free primtivie sites. 4/1-10/31; 14-day limit. Tbls, toilets, cfga. Canoeing, fishing. Next public campsite is 17.6 river miles downstream at first county bridge (to camp, make arrangements with landowner). Then 14.2 river mi to primitive camp on N side of river. Then 14.5 river mi to primitive site near US 183 on the Upstream Ranch. Finally, 10.3 river mi to Hannaman Bayou at Calamus Reservoir State Recreation Area.

Ainsworth RV Camper Park   **$7**
From US 20 at E end of Ainsworth, S on N. Richardson Dr; park on E side. $7 for dry camping; $10 with 30/50-amp elec/wtr. All year; 14-day limit. 30 tent & RV sites (30-ft RV limit). Elect, flush toilets, dump, showers, drkg wtr, cfga. Swimming, picnicking. Alternative is Rock County Fairgrounds in Bassett.

Keller Park State Recreation Area   **$6**
4 mi E of Ainsworth on US 20; 7.5 mi N on US 183. $6 at 10 primtive tent sites; $12 at 25 RV sites with elec. All year; 14-day limit. Tbls, toilets, cfga, drkg wtr, dump, shelters. Fishing, hunting, hiking. 196 acres. Limited facilities in winter. Trout ponds. Entry fee 4/1-8/31.

Fishing tip: Four ponds contain largemouth bass, bluegill and channel catfish, and a fifth pond has been stocked with catchable size rainbow trout.

Willow Lake   **FREE**
Wildlife Management Area
20 mi S of Ainsworth on Hwy 181, then 12.5 mi W on Elsmere Rd & 1 mi N. Free. All year; 14-day limit. Primitive camping. Fishing, boting(l). GPS: N42degrees 14.217, W100degrees 04.603.

Fishing tip: This lake contains channel catfish, bullheads, crappie, largemouth bass & yellow perch; 21-inch minimum on bass. Boats limited to 5 mph.

ALBION (3)

Fuller Municipal Park   **$10**
420 W. Market St. $10. 4/1-10/15. 8 RV sites (no tents). Tbls, flush toilets, cfga, drkg wtr, dump, showers, elec, playground, adjoining pool. Swimming, picnicking.

ALEXANDRIA (4)

Alexandria Lakes   **$6**
State Recreation Area
4 mi E of Alexandria on US 81, US 136, or NE 4. $6 without elec, $10 with elec. All year; 14-day limit. 46 sites. Tbls, toilets, cfga, drkg wtr, playground, shelters, dump. Picnicking; swimming; fishing; hunting; hiking; boating (nonpower or elec motor craft). 55 acres with 2 lakes. Near Rock Creek Station State Historic Park.

Fishing tip: In September, catch plenty of channel catfish from the Alexandria Lakes on turkey livers, shrimp and cut bait.

ALLEN (5)

Village of Allen Campground   **N/A**
On N edge of Allen on Hwy 9. Fees unknown. All year. 4 RV sites. Drkg wtr, elec, sewer.

ALMA (6)

Methodist Cove   **FREE**
Corps of Engineers
Harlan County Lake
3 mi E of Alma on US 136; 1.5 mi S on blacktopped co rd; at W end of lake. Free during 9/11-5/14, but no wtr or elec; $10 without hookups during 5/15-9/10 ($14 with elec). All year; 14-day limit. 150 sites (49 with elec); 65-ft RVs. Tbls, flush toilets, showers, cfga, drkg wtr, elec($), dump, playground. Boating(l), fishing, swimming, picnicking. 2-night minimum stay on weekends.

Fishing tip: In early June, catch white bass at night; fish the western third of the lake and in the spillway below the dame for channel catfish up to 12 pounds. In early July, try for wipers up to 12 pounds, especially at night; also try tubing & canoeing river below the dam. The state record wiper, almost 18 pounds, was caught here in 1996.

ANSLEY (8)

Ansley Municipal Park   **FREE**
Hwy 2 near lake at N edge of city. Free. 5/1-9/15; 7-day limit. 6 RV sites plus tent sites. Tbls, toilets, cfga, drkg wtr, elec. Picnicking, fishing, boating(l)

ARAPAHOE (9)

Shady Rest Camp   **$12**
At Hwys 6 & 35 in Arapahoe; 609 Chestnut. $12 base. All year. 10 RV sites. Tbls, drkg wtr, flush toilets, cfga, hookups($), dump, coin laundry.

ARCADIA (10)

Arcadia Garden Club   **Donations**
Village Wayside Park
W edge of village on Hwy 70. Donations requested, but camping free. All year; "reasonable" stay limit. 3 sites with elec. Drkg wtr, elec, pit toilets, cfga, dump, playground. Fishing, swimming.

ARNOLD (11)

Arnold Lake   **$6**
State Recreation Area
0.6 mi S of Arnold on NE 40 or NE 92; on upper reaches of Loup River. $6 at 60 primitive sites; $10 at 20 sites with elec. All year; 14-day limit. Tbls, pit toilets, cfga, drkg wtr, playground. Dump nearby. Picnicking; fishing; hunting; hiking; boating (nonpower or elec motor craft). 10 acres; 22-acre lake. GPS: N41degrees 24.754, W100degrees 11.672.

Fishing tip: Arnold Lake contains bluegill, channel catfish and largemouth, but it is a very weedy lake in summer and difficult to fish.

ASHLAND (12)

Memphis Lake   **$6**
State Recreation Area
8 mi N of Ashland on SR 63, then 1 mi W. $6. All year; 14-day limit. 150 primitive sites; 163 acres. Tbls, pit toilets, cfga, dump, playground, picnic shelters. Fishing, boating(r) (electric motors only), ice skating. Site of old ice plant.

Fishing tip: This shallow 48-acre lake contains crappie, largemouth bass, channel catfish and panfish.

ATKINSON (13)

Atkinson Lake   **$6**
State Recreation Area
Half mi W of jct US 20; half mi S on NE 11 (paved access rds). $6 at 20 primitive sites; $10 at 8 elec sites. All year; 14-day limit. 54 acres. Tbls, pit toilets, cfga, playground, shelters, drkg wtr. Picnicking; swimming; fishing; boating (nonpower or elec motor craft only); hunting. Sites need blocking. Half mi bluebird trail.

Fishing tip: This lake contains bluegill, channel catfish, largemouth bass and northern pike.

AURORA (14)

Pioneer Trails   **FREE**
Recreation Area
Upper Big Blue Natural Resources Dist.
1.2 mi E & 1 mi N of Aurora. Free. All year; 14-day limit. Primitive camping at 45-acre lake. Tbls, toilets, cfga, drkg wtr. Fishing, hiking, hunting, boating.

Streeter Municipal Park   Donations
N side of Aurora on NE 34 (3 mi N of I-80, exit 332). Donations solicited, but camp free. All year (weather permitting); 3-day limit. 20 sites; 18 with hookups (trailers under 27 ft) plus primitive camping area. Tbls, flush toilets, drkg wtr, dump, hookups. Picnicking; swimming (pool nearby), playground, horseshoes.

Travel tip: Stop at the Plainsman Museum at 210 N. 16th; it features an exhibit of hometown boy Harold Edgerton's invention, the strobe light, along with a collection of historic plains memorabilia and an agricultural museum.

AYR (15)

Crystal Lake $6
State Recreation Area
1.5 mi N of Ayr on US 281; at Little Blue River. $6 at 50 primitive sites; $10 at 20 sites with elec. All year; 14-day limit. 50 undesignated and 20 designated sites. Tbls, pit toilets, cfga, drkg wtr, picnic shelters. Picnicking; hunting; hiking; boating (nonpower or elec motor craft); fishing nearby. 33 acres; 30-acre lake.

Fishing tip: This lake's fish population was killed by a winter freeze in 1993, but the lake was restocked and now contains channel catfish, bluegill and largemouth bass.

BANCROFT (16)

Bancroft Municipal Park $6
4 blocks S of 1st National Bank & 2 blocks W; on W edge of Bancroft Park. $6. 5/1-10/15. 5 sites. Wtr & elect hookups, drkg wtr, tbls, cfga, flush toilets, dump, showers, playground.

BARTLETT (17)

Pibel Lake $6
State Recreation Area
9 mi S and 1 mi E of Bartlett on US 281. $6. All year; 14-day limit. About 30 undesignated primitive sites around the lake; 72 acres; 24-acre lake. Tbls, pit toilets, cfga, drkg wtr, playground. Picnicking, fishing, boating (dl--5-hp mtr limit); hunting, hiking.

Fishing tip: You can fish in this lake for largemouth bass, northern pike, channel catfish, bluegill or bullheads.

BASSETT (18)

Rock County Fairgrounds   FREE
SW of city on Hwy 20. 1 block W of US 183 to fairground entrance. Free or donations. All year. 10 RV & tent sites. Flush & pit toilets, cfga, drkg wtr, showers, elect, dump. Swimming, picnicking.

Fishing tip: Try the crappie, largemouth bass and northern pike fishing at 160-acre Twin Lakes Wildlife Management Area SW of Bassett. No boat ramp. Or, consider taking

brown trout from Coon Creek near town.

Travel tip: Fairgrounds contains Rock County Historical Museum with six original buildings, including the Whistle Stop/Chicago Northwestern Depot, 1884 Galloway House and 1897 St. Michael's Catholic Church with pioneer exhibits.

BATTLE CREEK (19)

Municipal Park   Donations
6 blocks S of Main St, E side of Hwy 121. Camp free, but donations encouraged. 5/1-10/15; 3-day limit or prearranged. 1 open site. Flush toilets, cfga, tbl, elec, dump, drkg wtr, playground. Swimming, picnicking. River. Field report says this park hard to find.

BAYARD (20)

Oregon Trail Wagon Train $10
S of Bayard off Hwy 28. $10 without hookups; $18 full hookups. 10 tent sites, 60 RV sites. Tbls, flush toilets, cfga, drkg wtr, showers. Canoeing.

Fishing tip: E of Bayard, Red Willow Creek has some excellent fishing for brown & rainbow trout. W of town, Stuckenhole Creek is stocked with brown & rainbow trout.

BEATRICE (21)

Bear Lake   FREE
Wildlife Management Area
Lower Big Blue Natural Resources District
4 mi N of Beatrice, then 2.5 mi E. Free. All year; 14-day limit. Open primitive camping on 94-acre reserve at 24-acre lake. No facilities, no drkg wtr. Fishing, hunting, hiking. GPS: 40.321454, -96.695138.

Gage County Fairgrounds $10
W Hwys 4 & 136 at Beatrice. $10. All year; 14-day limit (except fair week). 100 sites with elec, wtr; flush toilets, showers, dump.

Travel tip: We've chosen the nearby Homestead National Monument of America as one of the best free attractions in Nebraska. It commemorates the free land idea of the Homestead Act, which led to more than 270 million acres being turned over to individuals. 4 mi W of Beatrice on Hwy 4.

Riverside Municipal Park $9
4 blocks N on Sumner St off Hwy 136 in Beatrice. $9. 4/1-11/1; 30-day limit. 10 open sites with wtr, elec; flush toilets, cfga, tbls, playground, shelter, pool. Boating(l), fishing, swimming, tennis.

Rockford Lake $6
State Recreation Area
7 mi E of Beatrice; 2 mi S to campground. $6 at 77 primitive sites; $12 at 30 elec sites. All year; 14-day limit. 40-ft RV limit. Tbls, pit toilets, cfga, playground, drkg wtr, beach. Picnicking; swimming; fishing; boating; hunting; hiking. Homestead National Monument

nearby. 436 acres. 150-acre lake.

Fishing tip: From this lake, catch saugeye, walleye, largemouth bass, crappie or channel, flathead and bullhead catfish.

BEAVER CITY (22)

Westside City Park $6
From US 283, 4 mi E on SR 89; at 5th & O Sts in Beaver City. $6 ($30 weekly). All year. 4 back-in RV sites with elec. Tbls, flush toilets, drkg wtr, hookups, dump. Swimming.

BEAVER CROSSING (23)

Beaver Crossing City Park   FREE
E Elk St and Martin Ave in Beaver Crossing (2 blocks S & 1 block E of post office). Donations requested, but camp free. All year. 4 RV sites with elec, but numerous other sites. Elec hookups, flush toilets, dump, cfga, drkg wtr, tbls. Swimming.

BELLEVUE (24)

Haworth Municipal Park $7
Hwy 370 & Payne Dr (half mi E of town on SR 370). On Missouri River. $7 tent sites; $15 RV sites. All year; 14-day limit. 129 sites (109 for RVs. Tbls, flush & pit toilets, cfga, drkg wtr, elec, showers, dump. Boating(ld), fishing, tennis courts, ice skating, playground. 75 acres.

BELVIDERE (25)

Centennial City Park   FREE
3 blocks N of Main St; 1 block E. All year; 7-day limit. 2 sites. Tbls, toilets, cfga, drkg wtr.

BENNET (26)

Bennet City Park   FREE
In town off Hwy 2. Free overnight during summer. Undesignated sites. Tbls, toilets, cfga, drkg wtr, playground, sand volleyball. 1.6 acres.

BERWYN (27)

1909 Heritage House $10
At 101 Curran in Berwyn. $10. All year; 14-day limit. 4 RV sites, 4 tent sites. Tbls, drkg wtr, elec.

Berwyn Village Park $5
On Main St N of SR 2 in Berwyn. $5 if elec is used; camping without elec is free. All year; 7-day limit. RVs only; 10 sites. Elec & wtr hookups, tbls, cfga, drkg wtr, flush toilets.

BLAIR (28)

Bob Hardy $12
Municipal RV Campground
From center of town at US 30/Hwy 75, N on

US 75 under RR overpass. $12 for RV sites; $8 for tents. 4/1-11/1; 5-day limit in 14-day period (longer with permission). 8 open RV sites (45-ft back-in) & one 60-ft pull-through. Tbls, flush toilets, showers, cfga, drkg wtr, hookups, dump, playground.

BLOOMFIELD (29)

Bloomfield City Park   **$5**
On W Park St in Bloomfield. $5 without hookups, $10 with elec ($50 weekly, $100 monthly). All year. 6 sites with hookups. Flush toilets, cfga, drkg wtr, showers, new playground equipment in 2006. Horseshoes, basketball, playground.

Knox County Fairgrounds   **$10**
On E edge of town. $10 (weekly rates available). 4/1-11/1. 30 sites. Tbls, flush toilets, cfga, drkg wtr, elec, showers. Owned by City of Bloomfield.

BLUE SPRINGS (30)

Felts Memorial City Park   **FREE**
N at W end of Blue River Bridge, at 104 E Broad St, in Blue Springs. Free. All year; 3-day limit. 5 RV sites & 10 tent spaces. Cfga, drkg wtr. Swimming, fishing, boating(dl).

BRAINARD (31)

Timber Point Lake   **FREE**
Recreational Use Area
Lower Platte South
Natural Resources District
1 mi E, 1 mi S & 1 mi E from S edge of Brainard. Free. Primitive open camping on 160-acre reserve at 29-acre lake. Tbls & portable toilets (Apr-Oct), cfga, no drkg wtr, picnic area. Boating(l), fishing, hunting.
   Fishing tip: The lake is stocked with tiger musky, largemouth bass, channel catfish, bluegill. Electric motors only.

BREWSTER

Uncle Buck's Lodge   **$10**
On E edge of Brewster on Hwy 7, just N of Hwy 91. $10 base; $15 with full hookups. All year. 8 tent sites, 8 RV sites. Tbls, toilets, cfga, drkg wtr, showers.

BRIDGEPORT (32)

Bridgeport State Recreation Area   **$6**
SE on SR 385 from US 26 in Bridgeport; at North Platte River. $6. All year; 14-day limit. About 130 undesignated primitive sites; 199 acres. Tbls, pit toilets, cfga, drkg wtr, dump, playground, beach. Picnicking (shelters), fishing, swimming, boating(ld), hunting, hiking.
   Fishing tips: Several sand pit lakes have been stocked with fish, including rainbow trout in the NW lake and all containing largemouth bass, bluegill, yellow perch and channel catfish. At nearby Greenwood Creek, try for brown trout.

Golden Acres RV Park   **$9**
3 mi N of Bridgeport on Hwy 385. $9 for tent sites; $18 with full hookups. All year. 28 sites. Tbls, flush toilets, cfga, drkg wtr, showers. Hiking, basketball.

BROKEN BOW (33)

Millburn Dam   **FREE**
State Wildlife Management Area
20 mi N off SR 2. Free. All year. 10 sites; 537 acres. Tbls, toilets, cfga, drkg wtr. Picnicking, boating, fishing.
   Travel tip: Custer County Historical Museum at 255 S 10th St displays pioneer life from the 1800s to the present.

Tomahawk Municipal Park   **$ elec**
15th & B Sts, 2 blocks S of Hwy 2; W side of Broken Bow. 25 cents for each 2 hrs of elec; otherwise free. All year; 7-day limit. 10 sites. Water & elect hook-ups($), tbls, cfga, toilets, showers, dump, shelters, playground. Picnicking, tennis, horseshoes, croquet.

BROWNVILLE (34)

Brownville   **$8**
State Recreation Area
Near jct of US 136 and NE 67 at Brownville. $8. All year; 14-day limit. 14 hard-surface primitive sites; 22 acres. Tbls, pit toilets, cfga, drkg wtr. Picnicking; hunting; fishing; hiking; boating(l). On Missouri River, site of historic "Meriwether Lewis" summer programs.

Indian Cave State Park   **$11**
10 mi S of Brownville on Hwy 67; 5 mi E on S-64E. $11 at 130 primitive sites; $15 at 144 elec sites (20 with 50-amp). Modern sites open 5/1-10/31; primitive sites $6 off-season. Tbls, flush toilets, cfga, drkg wtr, showers, dump. Fishing, trail rides, hiking trails, cross-country skiing, backpacking. 2,052 acres. On Missouri River. Restored schoolhouse & general store. Summer programs. Coin laundry. Entry fee 4/1-8/31.

BRULE (35)

Van's Lakeview   **$12**
Fishing Camp (Private)
From Brule, 13 mi NW of I-80 126 on Hwy 26; at Lake Mcconaughy. $12 without hookups. 5/1-10/1. Sites with hookup $20-$28. 100 RV sites, 25 tent sites, 7 open areas. Tbls, flush toilets, cfga, drkg wtr, showers($), dump, store, coin laundry, fish cleaning shed. Fishing, swimming, boating(lr).
   Fishing tip: Catch large catfish from here by drifting minnows in late summer.

BRUNING (36)

Bruning Dam   **FREE**
Wildlife Management Area
Little Blue Natural Resources District
2 mi E of Bruning; 1 mi N; .7 mi E; in Fill-

more County. Free. All year. Undesignated primitive sites. Tbls, toilets, cfga, no drkg wtr. Boating(l), fishing, hunting, picnicking. 250-acre lake.

BURCHARD (37)

Burchard Lake   **FREE**
State Wildlife Management Area
3 mi E of Burchard, then half mi N on NE 65 or 4. Free. All year; 14-day limit. 15 sites. Tbls, toilets, cfga, drkg wtr. Picnicking; swimming; fishing; boating(l). Area closed during waterfowl season except at face of dam. GPS: 40.168589, -96.303055.
   Fishing tip: This 150-acre lake contains largemouth bass (21-inch minimum limit), walleye, channel catfish, bullhead, bluegill. Boating speed 5 mph. SE of Burchard, 7 ponds at Pawnee Prairie WMA offer fishing for largemouth bass, channel catfish and bluegill.

BURWELL (38)

Burwell City Park   **$5**
5 blocks N of City Square on 7th Ave. $5. All year; 3-day limit. 4 RV sites. Tbls, pit toilets, drkg wtr, elec, cfga, dump, playground. No wtr in winter. Fishing, swimming.

Grandpa's on the Calamus   **$10**
6 mi W of Burwell on Calamus Lake Rd. $10. 5/1-10/1. 10 RV sites. Tbls, cfga, drkg wtr, elec.

Calamus Reservoir   **$5**
State Recreation Area
2 mi W of Burwell & 4 mi N on co rds. $6 for primitive camping in open areas of Hannaman Bayou, Valleyview & Nunda Shoals; facilities there include pit toilets, cfga, drkg wtr. 122 modern sites $15 at Homestead Knolls Campground, $14 at Nunda Shoals (or $10 Oct-May with limited facilities); those have flush toilets, showers (except at Nunda), tbls, drkg wtr, elec, dump. Swimming, boating(ld), fishing, winter sports. 11,720 acres on state's newest reservoir. Calamus State Fish Hatchery below dam, open for free tours.
   Homestead Knolls on lake's N shore has 83 hard-surface RV pads with hookups, bathhouse, 2 boat ramps, beach.
   Valleyview Flat offers primtive camping, with only vault toilets and water pump.
   Hannamon Bayou is popular with anglers due to its boat ramp and primitive camping, with drinking water, pit toilets, tbls, cfga.
   Nunda Shoal, midway along the lake's S shore, has developed sites, pit toilets, drkg wtr and a boat ramp.
   Fishing tip: The 5,124-acre lake contains bluegill, channel catfish, crappie, largemouth bass, northern pike, walleye, wiper and perch. Walleye must be at least 18 inches, but only one over 25 inches may be kept daily. Wiper limit 3, with only one fish over 18 inches.

Homestead Knolls Sport Center   **$9**
8 mi NW of Burwell on N side of lake. $9-12. base. 4/1-11/1. 30 sites. Tbls, flush toilets, cfga, drkg wtr, showers, hookups($), dump, coin laundry, store. Fishing.

Fishing tip: Find walleye around sunken trees using nightcrawlers & leeches. In summer, pick up schooling white bass & wipers in open water, and look for northern pike in Dry Creek and Gracie Creek. Gracie also is stocked with rainbow trout.

Kamp Keleo   **$6**
Church Camp
2 mi E & qtr mi S of Hwys 91 & 11 at Burwell; on North Loup River. $6 base; $12 with hookups. All year. 2 RV sites; 10 tent sites, 8 open areas. Hookups, flush toilets, cfga, drkg wtr, showers. Fishing, canoeing(r), tubing(r). Camping by reservation only; 308-346-5083.

Fishing tip: Catch channel catfish to four pounds using shiners, nightcrawlers.

Willow Springs (Private)   **$11**
2 mi E of Burwell on Hwy 91. $11. All year. 60 sites. Tbls, flush toilets, cfga, drkg wtr, showers, dump, coin laundry, hookups($).

BUTTE (39)

Butte City Park   **FREE**
From SR 12, W on Butte St or Center St, on E edge of town; sites at NW corner of park on Eugene St. Camp free, but $5 donation suggested, but no donation box. All year. Undesignated tent & 2 back-in sites for medium-size RVs. Drkg wtr, portable & pit toilets, tbls, cfga, elec, store, LP-gas.

Hull Lake   **FREE**
State Wildlife Management Area
3 mi S of Butte, and 2 mi W via US 281 or SR 11. Free. Open all year; 14-day limit. 10 sites. Toilets, cfga, no drkg wtr. Swimming, fishing. Picnicking. GPS: 42.867402, -98.881073.

Fishing tip: This 5.5-acre lake contains largemouth bass, bluegill, channel catfish.

CALLAWAY (40)

Morgan City Park   **$5**
Morgan & Adams Sts. $5. All year. 30 sites (6 with elec). Tbls, flush & pit toilets, cfga, drkg wtr, elec, showers. Fishing, swimming.

CAMBRIDGE (41)

Medicine Creek RV Park
Cambridge City Park   **Donations**
E edge of Cambridge on Hwy 6 & 34. Donations. All year; 3-day limit. 11 sites for self-contained RVs. Wtr/elec hookups, portable & flush toilets, drkg wtr, showers, cfga, store, dump. Fishing, swimming. (Note: Reader reported showers not available during his visit.) Very nice park.

Fishing tip: To catch largemouth bass

at Medicine Creek Lake in mid-July, use deep-diving crankbaits and plastic worms around lake points and at brushy edges in the mouths of coves.

Medicine Creek   **$6**
State Recreation Area
2 mi W on US 6/34 to Medicine Creek Dam; 8.3 mi N; 1 mi W on Trail 4. $6 in open primitive areas (about 240 sites); 6 non-elec pads $11 (or $6 during 9/16-5/14 with no wtr services); $15 at 70 elec sites ($10 off-season). All year; 14-day limit. Tbls, flush toilets, cfga, showers, dump, playground, 2 fish cleaning stations, beach. Boating(lrd), fishing, picnicking, swimming. On Harry Strunk Lake.

Fishing tip: Long bays of the winding shoreline, along with several small islands, provide excellent habitat for huge crappies. In spring, catch walleye in the shallow water, then follow them to the main lake in June. Top white bass fishing occurs in July & August when the scrappy fighters chase newly hatched shad. Channel catfish and an occasional flathead can be caught in the headwaters.

CEDAR RAPIDS (42)

Mel's Landing   **$5**
Municipal Park
On N edge of Cedar Rapids, on Hwy 52; at Cedar River. $5, All year. 3 RV sites; 10 tent sites. 1 elec hookup. Toilets, tbls, cfga, drkg wtr (shut off in winter), playground. Fishing, swimming, boating(l), canoeing.

CENTRAL CITY (43)

Lone Tree Wayside Area   **FREE**
1 mi W of Central City on S side of NE 30. Free. All year; 1-night limit. Spaces for self-contained RVs. Tbls. Picnicking.

CHADRON (44)

Chadron State Park   **$10**
9 mi S of Chadron on US 385. $10 at 18 non-elec sites; $15 at 70 sites with 30-amp elec. All sites without elec 9/16-5/14, $6. All year; 14-day limit. Tbls, flush toilets, cfga, drkg wtr, elec($4), showers, dump, shelters, pool. Trail rides, swimming, fishing, boating(r), hiking, evening programs, tennis, sand volleyball, mountain biking(r).

Fishing tip: The pond at the park is stocked with put-and-take rainbow trout; no boating, but fishing pier.

J & L RV Park   **$12**
Qtr mi W of Chadron on Hwy 20, at J & L Trailer Court #13. $12. All year. 48 RV sites, 20 tent sites. Tbls, flush toilets, cfga, drkg wtr, dump, showers, coin laundry, elec (elec only in winter).

Fishing tip: Try nearby Chadron City Lake for largemouth bass, trout and channel catfish. No boats allowed on the 27-acre lake. Or, fish for brook & brown trout in Chadron Creek.

Red Cloud   **$5**
Nebraska National Forest
Pine Ridge National Recreation Area
8 mi S of Chadron on US 385 (S of Chadron State Park); turn into camp at picnic ground sign. $5 during 5/19-11/17; free rest of year. 13 sites. Tbls, toilets, cfga, drkg wtr. Hiking, mountain biking, horseback riding nearby.

Roberts Tract Trailhead   **$8**
Nebraska National Forest
Pine Ridge National Recreation Area
8 mi W of Chadron on Hwy 20; 7 mi S on Eleson Rd; 1.5 mi E on Bethel Rd. $8 during 5/19-11/17; free rest of year, but no wtr. 3 tent sites, 1 RV site. Tbls, toilets, cfga, drkg wtr, corrals. Hiking, horseback riding, mountain biking.

Wild Life Campground   **$6-$8**
5-6 mi E of Chadron. $6-$8. All year. 8 RV sites, 6 tent sites. Tbls, pit toilets, cfga, drkg wtr, showers, hookups($). Fishing.

CHAMPION (45)

Champion Lake   **$6**
State Recreation Area
Half mi W of Champion on US 6 or NE 106. $6. All year. 14-day limit. 7 primitive sites. Tbls, pit toilets, cfga, drkg wtr. Picnicking; fishing; hunting; boating (elec mtrs); hiking. On Frenchman Creek. 14 acres. Champion Mill State Historic Park nearby features last working water-powered mill in Nebraska.

CHESTER (48)

Chester City Park   **FREE**
1 blk W of jct of SRs 81/8, on SR 8 in Chester. Low fee after one free night. 4/15-10/31. 2 RV sites & tent spaces. Flush toilets, cfga, drkg wtr, tbls, elec. Basketball, horseshoes, tennis, sand volleyball, golf, ball fields, shelter.

CLARKS (49)

Mormon Trail Wayside Park   **FREE**
1.5 mi S of Clarks on NE 30; 3 mi W on NE 92. Free. All year; 2-day limit. Undesignated sites. Tbls, toilets, cfga, drkg wtr. Picnicking; fishing; hiking.

CLARKSON (50)

Clarkson City Park   **$8**
1 mi N of Clarkson on Hwy 91 Spur (121 Bryan St.). $8. 5/1-10/1; 14-day limit. 20 elec sites; 6 with sewer; 20 tent sites. Tbls, flush toilets, cfga, drkg wtr, hookups($), showers, dump. Swimming pool, lighted tennis court, playground, museum. 5 acres.

CLATONIA (51)

Clatonia Public Use Area **FREE**
Lower Big Blue Natural Resources District
1 mi N of Clatonia. Free. All year; 14-day limit. Primitive open camping on 115-acre reserve at 40-acre lake. Tbls, toilets, cfga, drkg wtr. Fishing, hiking, hunting.

CODY (52)

Cody City Park **FREE**
In town from US 20, N on Cherry St over railroad right-of-way (tracks removed). Free, but $5 donations suggested. 5/1-10/15; 7-day limit. 9 sites with elec (30 & 15-amp); grass & shade for tent sites. Tbls, drkg wtr, flush toilets, showers, dump, pavilion, playground. Very pretty, quiet small park. Mountain time zone.

COLERIDGE (53)

Coleridge Village Park **$5**
NW corner of Coleridge on Nebraska St. $5 donation requested. All year. 4 RV sites. Hookups, dump, flush toilets, drkg wtr, cfga, playground.

COLUMBUS (54)

Columbus Ag Park **$10**
At 822 Fifteenth St, Columbus. $10 base. Apr-Nov. 65 RV sites. Tbls, flush toilets, cfga, drkg wtr, elec, sewer, dump, showers.

Lake North **FREE**
Loup Power District
4 mi N of jct of US 30 and 18th Ave in Columbus on 18th Ave (Monastery Rd). Paved access rds. Free. 5/1-11/1; 7-day limit. 100 tent, 25 RV sites (12 with elec). Tbls, toilets, cfga, playground, drkg wtr. Picnicking; fishing; swimming; boating(l); waterskiing. Sites need blocking. More than 2 mi of beaches at 200-acre lake.
Fishing tip: The lake contains crappie, walleye, channel catfish, carp and drum.

Loup Park **FREE**
Loup Power District
4 mi N of Columbus on 18th Ave; 1.5 mi W on Lakeview Dr (paved access rds). On N & W shores of Lake Babcock. Free. 5/1-11/1; 7-day limit. 120 tent sites, 50 RV sites (28 with elec). Tbls, pit toilets, cfga, drkg wtr, elec hookups, playground. Picnicking; fishing, swimming, boating(l). 40 acres.
Fishing tip: Panfish particularly good on the W tip of Lake Babcock, where waters of Loup Canal flow into it, and quarter mi E at Lake North. The lake also contains channel & flathead catfish. Power boats not allowed.

Powerhouse Park **FREE**
Loup Power District
Half mi E of city limits on US 30; 1.5 mi N on 18th Ave. Free. All year; 7-day limit. 20 tent sites, 6 RV sites (32-ft RV limit). Tbls, pit toilets, cfga, drkg wtr. Picnicking; fishing in Loup Canal; playground. Adjacent to Columbus Powerhouse (free tours available). 4 acres.

Southgate Campground **$12**
At Hwys 81 & 30 S, Columbus. $12. All year. 22 sites with full hookups (elec only during Dec-Mar). Tbls, toilets, cfga, drkg wtr.

Tailrace Park **FREE**
Loup Power District
3 mi E of Columbus on 8th St Rd; 1.5 mi S on co rd. Free. 5/1-11/1; 7-day limit. 20 tent, 6 RV sites. Tbls, pit toilets, cfga, drkg wtr, playground. Picnicking; fishing. Scenic; heavily wooded. Elec lights illuminate park areas at night.

COZAD (55)

Gallagher Canyon **$6**
State Recreation Area
10 mi S of Cozad on NE 21 on US 30; 2 mi E; 1 mi N; 1 mi W on SR 21. $6. All year; 14-day limit. 72 undesignated primitive sites. Tbls, pit toilets, cfga, drkg wtr, playground. Picnicking; swimming; fishing; boating(ld); hunting; hiking. 424-acre irrigation impoundment.
Fishing tip: The lake here contains channel & flathead catfish, crappie, walleye and white bass. A 15-inch minimum limit on walleye is imposed.

Muny Municipal Park **$5**
14th & O Sts, Exit 222. $5. All year. 12 RV sites. Drkg wtr, elec, dump, flush toilets, showers, playground, pool. Swimming, ball fields, exercise trail, horseshoes, volleyball, Frisbee golf. No swimming or showers in winter.

CRAWFORD (56)

City Park Campground **FREE**
From US 20, follow Main St W through town to park entrance; curve right (N) after crossing White Creek in park; elec on power pole near restrooms. Free. All year; overnight limit but no signs or silent ranger. 10 sites (4 with elec). Flush toilets, tbls, drkg wtr, cfga, dump. Picnicking, fishing, swimming pool, playground. Watch for low tree limbs.
Travel tip: On US 20 at W edge of Fort Robinson State Park is Trailside Museum, where free exhibits include a mammoth skeleton, fossils, rocks & minerals.
Fishing tip: Just 3 mi W of Crawford, Soldier Creek has good fishing for brown & rainbow trout. Public access at Fort Robinson.

Fort Robinson State Park **$11**
3 mi W of Crawford on US 20. During 5/15-9/15, $11 at 25 non-elec sites, $15 at 100 sites with 30/50-amp elec, $19 full hookups.
During 9/16-5/14, $6 without elec, $10 with elec (no showers or wtr service). All year; 14-day limit. Tbls, flush toilets, cfga, drkg wtr, showers, dump, shelters, coin laundry. Trail rides, swimming, boating (elec motors), trout fishing, buffalo stew cookouts, rides($), hiking, craft center, biking(r). Restaurant, museums, playground. 11,082 acres.

Soldier Creek Trailhead **$8**
Nebraska National Forest
3.5 mi W of Crawford on US 20; 6 mi N on Soldier Creek Rd. $8 during 5/19-11/17; free rest of year, but no wtr & limited service. 14-day limit. 4 primitive sites. Toilets, cfga, drkg wtr, tbls, corrals. Fishing, hiking trails, hunting, horseback riding trails.

Toadstool Campground **$5**
Nebraska National Forest
Toadstool Geologic Park
4.5 mi N of Crawford on SR 71; 12 mi W on CR 904; left on CR 902 for 1 mi. $5 during 5/19-11/17; free rest of year, but pack out trash; 14-day limit. 6 sites. Tbls, toilets, cfga, no drkg wtr. Hiking, explore rock formations, longest known mammal trackway from Oligocene period. Sod homestead replica.

CREIGHTON (57)

Bruce Municipal Park **$5**
Main St and Douglas Ave in Creighton (W edge of town on Hwy 59). $5. 4/1-10/31. 4 spaces for self-contained RVs. Elec hookups, flush toilets, cfga, drkg wtr, dump. Swimming, boating.

CRETE (58)

Tuxedo Municipal Park **$8**
At Crete, W on 13th St from Hwy 33 to Tuxedo Rd. $8. 4/1-10/15; 10-day limit. 10 RV sites; unlimited tent sites. Tbls, flush toilets, cfga, drkg wtr, elec, dump, showers. Fishing, picnicking.
Fishing tip: Just SE of Crete, try for largemouth bass at the 41-acre Merganser Lake.

Walnut Creek **FREE**
Wildlife Management Area
Lower Big Blue Natural Resources District
2.5 mi NE of Crete. Free. All year; 14-day limit. Primitive camping on 64-acre reserve at 20-acre lake. Toilets, no cfga or tbls, drkg wtr. Hiking, fishing, hunting. GPS:

CROFTON (59)

Bloomfield Campground **$6**
Lewis and Clark Lake
State Recreation Area
6 mi N of Crofton on Hwy 98, 8 mi W on Recreation Rd E. $6 at primitive sites; $15 elec sites ($10 during 9/16-5/14). All year, 14-day limit. Tbls, flush & pit toilets, cfga, drkg wtr, playground, beach. Picnicking; fishing; boating(l), swimming.

Fishing tip: Try for channel catfish along the bluff shoreline of the old river channel. The state record white bass, 5 pounds, was caught from the Gavins Point Tailwaters in 1983. Other fish available include flathead & channel catfish, crappie, paddlefish, smallmouth bass, sauger and walleye. Life jackets must be worn at all times in the tailwater area.

Deep Water Campground　**$6**
Lewis and Clark Lake
State Recreation Area
8 mi N of Crofton; 1 mi W on Recreation Rd E (rd steep & slippery when wet). $6. All year; 14-day limit. Spaces for self-contained RVs. Tbls, toilets, cfga, drkg wtr. Picnicking; fishing; hunting; hiking.
Travel tip: Stop at the national fish hatchery on the N end of the dam and see how gamefish are reared.

Miller Creek Campground　**$6**
Lewis and Clark Lake
State Recreation Area
6 mi N of Crofton on NE 98; 12 mi W; half mi S; 1 mi W to campground. $6. All year; 14-day limit. Primitive undesignated sites. Tbls, pit toilets, cfga, drkg wtr. Picnicking; fishing; boating (lrd); hunting; waterskiing, hiking trail overlooking camping area of the 1804 Lewis and Clark expedition. Low-water boat ramp.
Fishing tip: Late in summer, focus on the W end where the river enters the lake; fish for catfish, walleye & sauger. Watch for schools of shad to find feeding white bass.

Weigand-Burbach Camps　**$6**
Lewis and Clark Lake
State Recreation Area
6 mi N of Crofton on NE 98/121; 5 mi W to campground. $6 at primitive undesignated sites; non-elec sites with camping pads $11; sites with 30/50-amp elec $15 ($10 during 9/16-5/14). All year; 14-day limit. Tbls, flush toilets, cfga, drkg wtr, phone, dump, coin showers, store, playground, beach, marina, fish cleaning station, boat slips, marine fuel, boat pump-out station. Picnicking; swimming; fishing; boating(dl); hunting; waterskiing; hiking. Nature trails.
Fishing tip: Try for walleye, sauger, largemouth & smallmouth bass & crappies around the nearby jetties; they were installed to improve fish habitat. In May & June, catch walleye off the flats at Weigand Creek.

DAKOTA CITY (60)

Cottonwood Cove　**$7.50**
Municipal Park
14th & Hickory Sts in Dakota City at Missouri River. $7.50 without elec; $12 with elec. 5/1-10/1; 14-day limit. 16 sites (10 for RVs). Tbls, flush toilets, cfga, drkg wtr, elec, dump($1 for non-campers). Fishing, boating(lr), canoeing(r), playground, hiking trails, ball fields, soccer, horseshoes. 45 acres.

DANNEBROG (61)

Municipal Park　**$10**
In town. $10 for 4 sites with elec. 5/1-9/30, weather permitting. Tbls, flush toilets, cfga, elec, dump (no wtr hookups). Hiking, picnicking, biking. On Oak Creek. Register with village office in Sherman County Bank building on Mill St or Kerry's Grocery (after 12:30 pm).
Travel tip: The National Liars Hall of Fame is at Eric's Tavern on Mill St. It offers a tribute to famous liars.

DAVID CITY (62)

Butler County Faiorgrounds　**$10**
At 62 L Street, David City. $10. June-Sept. 12 RV sites. Tbls, flush toilets, cfga, drkg wtr, elec, showers.

C & G Trailer Haven　**$9.50**
590 Third St, David City. $9.50 daily ($270 monthly) base. All year. 9 RV sites. Hookups, toilets, drkg wtr, cfga, tbls, dump, coin laundry, store. Fishing, swimming.

David City Campground　**$10**
On S end of David City, Hwy 15 south (camp on NE section of park). $10. 4/1-10/31; 21-day limit. 12 RV sites with elect. Tbls, cfga, flush toilets, dump. Swimming, boating(dl), fishing. Pond, playground, sport field, rec room. 85 acres; 2 lakes. Expansion of the park planned, including pool, running track, lake renovation, trail. Park listed on National Register of Historic Places.

DECATUR (63)

Beck Memorial City Park　**$11**
On East 11th St, Decatur. $11 base. 4/1-10/31; 7-day limit. Base fee for tent sites; $14 for RVs. 45 sites. Tbls, flush toilets, cfga, drkg wtr, hookups, showers, dump, fish cleaning station. Fishing, boating(l), horseshoes, playground.

DENTON (64)

Conestoga Lake　**$6**
State Recreation Area
2 mi N of Denton & 3.5 mi SW of Emerald. $6 at 24 primitive undesignated sites, $12 at 25 sites with 30/50-amp elec. All year; 14-day limit. 40-ft RV limit. Tbls, pit toilets, cfga, drkg wtr, picnic shelters, dump, fish cleaning station. Picnicking, fishing, hunting in season, hiking; boating(dl). 486 acres.
Fishing tip: The 230-acre lake contains bass, walleye & channel catfish. Catch crappies from the dam in June using jigs.

Yankee Hill　**FREE**
State Wildlife Management Area
2.5 mi E & 1 mi S of Denton. Free. All year; 14-day limit. Primitive undesignated sites; limited facilities. Fishing, boatingt(l), hunting.

DESHLER (65)

City Park　**FREE**
S part of Deshler at 4th & Park Sts. From US 136 N of town, S on 1st St to Park St, then E on Park St to 4th St & into the park. Free; donations accepted. All year; 3-day limit. 16 RV sites. Wtr hookups, flush toilets, cfga, drkg wtr, cfga, tbls, showers, dump (at 3rd & Railway, 4 blocks N), elec. Picnicking, boating, swimming pool, tennis, sand volleyball, playground. 10 acres.

DILLER (66)

Diller Municipal Campground　**$7**
In Diller. $7. All year. 7 RV sites. Tbls, flush toilets, cfga, drkg wtr, hookups, dump, playground.

DU BOIS (67)

Iron Horse Trail Lake　**$5**
Nemaha Natural Resources District
Hal mi N & 2 mi W of DuBois in Pawnee County. $5 for 2-day permit; $12 annual permit. All year; 14-day limit. 24 open sites. Pit toilets, tbls, cfga, drkg wtr, beach, playground, beach. Fishing, boating(dl), hiking, swimming, sand volleyball, nature trails.

EDGAR (68)

WPA South Park　**FREE**
At 300 N. C St. in Edgar. Free, but $5 donations requested. All year. 4 RV/tent sites. Tbls, flush toilets, cfga, drkg wtr, elec, sewer, dump, playground, shelters. Tennis, basketball. Rock shelter was built in 1937 by WPA.

ELGIN (69)

Elgin Municipal Park　**FREE**
4 blocks E of jct of Hwys 14 & 70 on North St. Free. 5/5-10/15; 7-day limit. 15 undesignated sites (several primitive). Tbls, flush toilets, cfga, elec, drkg wtr, dump, showers, elec, playground. Swimming, picnicking. Donations accepted. Public phones at nearby Elgin One-Stop on SR 14. GPS: N41.9874, W98.076.

ELM CREEK (70)

Sunny Meadows Campground　**$12**
From I-80 exit 257 at Elm Creek, qtr mi N. $12 ($60 weekly; $210 monthly). All year. 43 RV sites, 3 tent sites. Flush toilets, cfga, drkg wtr, hookups, dump, coin laundry, showers, playground. Fishing.

EMERALD (72)

Pawnee Lake　**$6**
State Recreation Area
2 mi N, 1.5 mi W of Emerald on US 6; 3 mi N of co rd. $6 at 97 sites in open primitive

areas; $11 at 34 designated non-elec sites; $15 at 68 sites with 30/50-amp elec ($10 during 9/16-5/14). All year; 14-day limit. Flush toilets, showers, dump, playground, fish cleaning station, 2 beaches. Boating(drl), swimming, fishing, picnicking, hiking/biking trails. 2540 acres; 740-acre lake. Blue rock area.

Fishing tip: Anglers can catch northern pike, walleye, largemouth bass and catfish from this lake. In early June, pick up white bass on yellow jigs fished around the shoreline. A 10-inch size minimum on crappie is enforced.

ENDERS (73)

Center Dam Area   **$6**
Enders Reservoir
State Recreation Area
Half mi S of Enders at US 6 & SR 61; W 100 ft on US 6. $6 in open primitive areas; $12 with 20/30-amp elec. All year; 14-day limit. Dump, flush toilets, cfga, drkg wtr, coin showers, fish cleaning station. Fishing, boating(l), picnicking.

Fishing tip: Catch your walleye limit in early May by using jig-and-crawler rigs or Lindy nightcrawler rigs. Focus on sandbar areas of around 15 feet.

Church Grove Area   **$6**
Enders Reservoir
State Recreation Area
2 mi S of Enders on US 6. $6 at primitive sites; $12 with elec. All year; 14-day limit. About 160 sites. Tbls, flush toilets, cfga, coin showers, drkg wtr, dump, playground, horseshoes, fish cleaning station. Fishing, boating(lrd), swimming, picnicking. 2,818 acres.

Fishing tip: Try windy points, using jerkbaits, for Enders' fabulous wipers.

ERICSON (74)

Watson Cabins   **Donations**
In Ericson. Donations requested, but camp free. May-Nov. Tbls, pit toilets, cfga, drkg wtr, elec. Boating(l), fishing, swimming.

Fishing tip: Lake Ericson offers good fishing for crappie, northern pike and channel catfish.

EUSTIS (75)

Eustis Municipal Park   **FREE**
From SR 23, S on Hale St, W on Railroad St; S on Main St between 2 huge silos and Kinder Park, cross RR track, then E on Allison St. Free; no stay limit. Primitive camping. Tbls, toilets, cfga, drkg wtr, dump. Tennis, picnicking. GPS: N40.66036, W100.02673.

EXETER

Gilbert City Park RV   **$10**
On Exeter Ave in town. $10. All year; 14-day limit. 2 RV sites on concrete pads. Tbls,

flush toilets, cfga, drkg wtr, playground, elec. Swimming.

FAIRBURY (76)

Crystal Springs Municipal Park   **$8**
1.5 mi SW of town. From US 136, follow Maple St S, following blue camping sign to W. 3rd St & Park Rd; SW of Frontier Fun Park, continue S on Frederick St (CR 2880), then W on Crystal Springs (CR 2880), then N into park. $8 with elec. 5/1-10/15; 14-day limit. 60 sites. Tbls, flush toilets, cfga, drkg wtr, elec, dump, showers, playground. Fishing, swimming, boating. Very pretty park with several lakes, trees, ducks, pelicans.

Rock Creek Station   **$11**
State Historical Park
6 mi E of Fairbury. $11 at non-elec sites; $15 with elec ($10 during 9/16-5/14, but no wtr service). All year; 14-day limit. 25 sites. Tbls, flush toilets, cfga, drkg wtr, dump, showers, playground. Visitor center, exhibits, covered wagon rides, hiking & nature trails. Site of Pony Express station. James Butler Hickok got his name "Wild Bill" there when he killed station agent D.C. McCanless in 1861.

FALLS CITY (77)

Stanton Lake Municipal Park   **$5**
W. 25th St in Falls City. $5 base; $13 full hookups. All year; 14-day per month limit; 5 consecutive days. 10 sites with elec. Tbls, flush toilets, showers, cfga, drkg wtr, dump, sewer. No wtr in winter. Fishing, sand volleyball, playground.

FRANKLIN (78)

South Park   **$8**
Municipal Campground
From US 136, 3 blks S on SR 10/16th Ave; park is on SW quad of SR 10 & J St. $8 (formerly free). All year; 10-day limit. 6 RV sites. Flush toilets, drkg wtr, cfga, tbls, dump, 20/30/50-amp elec. Picnicking. LP-gas, groceries. Boating(l), swimming, fishing. GPS: N40 05.530, W98 57.155.

FREMONT (79)

Christensen Field   **$8**
At 1710 W. 16th St at Ridge Rd in Fremont. $8. All year; 14-day limit. 150 sites. Tbls, pit toilets, cfga, drkg wtr, elec hookups, showers, dump. 55 acres. Senior center, agricultural complex, sports fields

Fremont Lakes   **$11**
State Recreation Area
3 mi W of Fremont on US 30. $11 at 600 non-elec sites; $15 at 212 sites with 20/30-amp elec ($10 during 9/16-5/14). All year; 14-day limit. 600 sites. Tbls, toilets, showers, dump, beaches, coin showers. Swimming, boating(ld), fishing. 666 acres. 20 sandpit lakes.

Fishing tip: Lake No. 5 is a put-and-take carp lake with a daily limit of 10 carp. Other lakes contain catfish, northern pike, crappie, largemouth bass, rock bass and sunfish. Get bass on plastic worms, crappie on minnows. Best lakes usually are 11, 17, 18.

Luther Hormel   **FREE**
Memorial Park
Half mi SW of Fremont. Free. Primitive camping on river; canoe stopover. Tbls, toilets, cfga, drrkg wtr, shelter, nature trail. 167 acres.

Republican River Canoe Trail   **$6**
S of Fremont on US 77 to river (boat access only). $6. 4/1-10/31; 14-day limit. Fishing, picnicking, hiking, canoeing, boating. Canoe trail is 49 mi, from Haran County Lake Dam to Red Cloud. From North Outlet Park, the first leg to Naponee Bridge is 4.7 river mi (no camping available), then 8.1 river mi to Bloomington bridge and another 4.1 river mi to the first primitive camp on N side of river. Next, 3.2 mi to Bislow's Landing access point and 13.2 river mi to the second primitive camp on S side, just E of Riverton. Finally, 15.6 river mi to the primitive camp at Red Cloud, located on S side of river just W of the US 281 bridge.

GENOA (80)

Genoa City Park   **FREE**
3 blocks S of SRs 22 and 39 in Genoa (310 South Park St). Free 3 days; $10 per week thereafter. Apr-Nov. 3 sites with elec (20-amp). Tbls, toilets, cfga, playground, drkg wtr, showers, dump, coin laundry. Picnicking; tennis; softball, shuffleboard, fishing, swimming pool. Extra charge for a/c.

Headworks Park   **FREE**
Loup Power District
6 mi W of Genoa on SR 22. Free. 5/1-11/1; 7-day limit. 12 sites with elec; 25 other RV sites; 25 tent sites. Tbls, toilets, cfga, drkg wtr, playground. Picnicking, boating(l), fishing (in small lake in park or at the Loup Canal nearby). River. Adjacent to entrance of Loup Power District Headquarters, the beginning of the Loup Canal.

Fishing tip: The state record flathead catfish was caught from the Loop Power Canal here in 1988; it weighed 80 pounds.

GERING (81)

Robidoux City RV Park   **$8**
In Gering, half mi S of Hwy 92 on Hwy 71. $6 base. All year. Base fee for tent sites; RV sites up to $24. 35 sites. Tbls, flush toilets, cfga, drkg wtr, coin laundry, showers, dump, hookups($), CATV ($). Swimming, golf.

Wildcat Hills   **$6**
State Recreation Area
10 mi S of Gering on NE 71; not accessible for large RVs. $6. All year; 14-day limit. About

30 undesignated sites on several grass parking areas and along interior trail roads; 705 acres. Tbls, toilets, cfga, drkg wtr, playground, shelters, nature center. Picnicking; hiking; fishing; hunting. Sites need blocking. Nature trails. Game refuge with buffalo, elk.

GIBBON (82)

Windmill   **$11**
State Recreation Area
At NE corner of Gibbon exit from I-80. $11 at 20 primitive sites; $15 at 69 sites with elec ($10 during 9/16-5/14). All year; 2-day limit. Tbls, flush toilets, showers, cfga, drkg wtr, coin laundry, dump, coin showers, shelters, beach. Boating, swimming, fishing. Park features an assortment of antique windmills.

Country Inn & Antiques   **$10**
At exit 285 of I-80, Gibbon. $10 ($250 monthly). All year. 5 RV sites. Elec, drkg wtr, sewer, cfga.

GOTHENBURG (84)

Lafayette Municipal Park   **$10**
2 mi N of I-80 on SR 47 at 27th St. in Gothenburg at Lake Helen. $10 base for tents; $15 RV sites. All year; 14-day limit; limited facilities in winter (bathrooms close 11/1-4/1); no reduced winter rates. 100 tent sites; 51 RV sites. Tbls, flush toilets, cfga, drkg wtr, elec, showers ($5 non-campers), dump. Fishing, swimming. 30 acres. Museum, visitor center, playground. GPS: N40 56.690, W100 09.809.

GRAND ISLAND (85)

George H. Clayton   **$7**
Hall County Park
3 mi N of I-80 on Hwy 281; qtr me E on Schimmer Rd. $7 for tents, $13 for RVs. 4/15-9/30; 3-day limit (extended with permission). 15 tent sites; 19 RV sites (30-ft RV limit). Tbls, flush toilets, 30/50-amp elec, cfga, drkg wtr, showers, dump. Fishing, picnicking, swimming, horseshoes, volleyball, basketball, playground.
Fishing tip: A surprisingly good variety of fishing is available at Grand Island's city Wastewater Pond on Swift Rd, E of Stuhr Rd. The 7.5-acre pond contains largemouth bass and tiger musky as well as bluegill and channel catfish.

Holiday Amoco   **$7.50**
At Grand Island, S Hwy 281 & I-80 exit 312. $7.50. All year. 5 RV sites. Tbls, flush toilets, cfga, drkg wtr, elec, store. Swimming, fishing.
Fishing tip: Grand Island's 83-acre Pier Lake contains largemouth bass, tiger musky and channel catfish.

Mormon Island   **$11**
State Recreation Area
At Grand Island exit from I-80 & US 281. $11

at 4 sites without elec; $15 at 34 sites with 30/50-amp elec. All year; 3-day limit. Tbls, flush toilets, cfga, drkg wtr, coin showers, dump, shelters, beach. Picnicking, boating (no mtrs), swimming, fishing.
Fishing tip: From the SRA, catch walleye, largemouth bass, channel catfish or bluegill. An 8-inch length minimum is enforced for bluegill.

HALSEY (87)

Bessey   **$8**
Nebraska National Forest
2 mi W of Halsey on SR 2. $8 base; $15 for elec sites. All year; 10-day limit. 40 sites, 18 with elec; 30-ft RV limit. Flush toilets, cold showers, cfga, wtr hookups, dump, elec($), pool. No wtr 10/15-MD. Swimming($), boating, canoeing, biking, hiking trails, nature programs, cross-country skiing, hunting, tennis, softball. 3 acres. Group camping available.

Halsey Stockade Camping   **$12**
At Hwy 2 & Main St, Halsey. $12. All year. 6 RV sites. Tbls, flush toilets, cfga, drkg wtr, elec, sewer, dump, showers, store. Fishing, swimming.

Natick Campground   **$8**
Nebraska National Forest
W of Halsey on SR 2 & W of 4-H Camp. $8. All year; 14-day limit. 5 sites. Tbls, toilets, cfga, no drkg wtr, corrals. Hiking, mountain biking, horseback riding.

Whitetail Campground   **$8**
Nebraska National Forest
W of Halsey on SR 2 near Dismal River. $8. All year; 14-day limit. 10 sites. Tbls, toilets, cfga, no drkg wtr, corrals. Hiking, mountain biking, horseback riding.

HARRISON (89)

Gilbert-Baker   **FREE**
Wildlife Management Area
6 mi N of Harrison on access rd near the Wyoming border. Free. All year; 14-day limit. Undesignated sites. Tbls, toilets, cfga, drkg wtr. Picnicking, fishing, hunting. GPS: 42.763629, -103.925777.
Travel tip: 20 mi S on SR 29, see fossil beds formed 19 million years ago at Agate Fossil Beds National Monument.
Fishing tip: For brook trou;t, try the nearby Hat Creek or Monroe Creek (with access at the Gilbert-Baker Wildlife Management Area).

Harrison City Park   **FREE**
From US 20 (Fifth St) & SR 29 (Main St),1 block S on Main to Fourth St; 1.7 mi W on Fourth to sites on N side of park. Donations suggested, but camp free. Open June-Sept; 3-night limit. Two 40-ft back-in sites. Tbls, drkg wtr, flush toilets, showers (in summer at pool), dump (at US 20 & CR 29 at W side

of police station), 20-amp elec. Swimming, picnicking.
Fishing tip: Just NE of town, good brown trout fishing is available at Sowbelly Creek.

HARTINGTON (90)

City Camper Court   **FREE**
In Hartington at jct of Broadway & Felber. Camp free, but donations suggested. 4/15-10/15. 21 sites. Tbls, wtr/elec hookups, cfga, drkg wtr, dump.

HASTINGS (91)

Adams County Fairgrounds   **$9.63**
2 blocks N off the Hwy 6 & Hwy 281 jct. $9.63 with elec; $12.84 elec/wtr; $17.12 full hookups. All year; 10-day limit. 450 sites. Flush toilets, tbls, cfga, drkg wtr, showers, dump (wtr & sewer Apr-Nov). Fishing.

American Legion   **FREE**
Memorial Wayside Area
Half mi N of Hastings on US 281, on N edge of town (paved access rds). Free. All year; 2-day limit. Undesignated sites; 7 acres. Tbls, toilets, cfga, drkg wtr. Picnicking, hiking. Sites need blocking.
Travel tip: At 12th & Denver Sts in Hastings is a colorful fountain of dancing waters, illuminated by spotlights at night.

HAYES CENTER (92)

Hayes Center   **FREE**
State Wildlife Management Area
12 mi NE of Hayes Center on SR 25; at S end of Camp Hayes Lake. Free. All year. 10 sites. Tbls, toilets, cfga, drkg wtr. Boating, swimming, fishing, picnicking. 119 acres. No boat motors. GPS: N40degrees 35.049, W100degrees 55.665.
Fishing tip: The WMA's 50-acre lake contains channel, flathead & bullhead catfish as well as crappie and northern pike.

HAY SPRINGS (93)

Metcalf   **FREE**
State Wildlife Management Area
E edge of Hay Springs, 7 mi N of Hwy 20 on county rd. Free. All year; 14-day limit. Primitive hike-in tent camping in pine forest area. No facilities; no drkg wtr. No vehicles.

Walgren Lake   **$6**
State Recreation Area
2.5 mi E of Hay Springs on NE 20; 2 mi S on NE 87. $6 at 40 primitive sites. All year; 14-day limit. Closed during waterfowl season. 80 acres. Tbls, pit toilets, cfga, drkg wtr, picnic shelters, playground, handicap fishing pier. Picnicking; fishing; hiking; boating(ld -- nonpower or elec mtrs).
Fishing tip: In early June, try for bluegills and catch crappies on small spinners, worms and flies fished behind bobbers. The 50-acre lake also contains walleyes, bass and perch.

HAZARD (94)

Beaver Creek **FREE**
State Wayside Area
1 mi W of Hazard and 1 mi N to campground. Free. All year; 2-day limit. Undesignated sites. Tbls, toilets, cfga, drkg wtr. Picnicking; fishing; playground; hiking boating (non-power craft only).

HEBRON (95)

Riverside Municipal Park **$5**
1 block E of swimming pool; 10th & Holdrege in SE Hebron. From the S, W from US 81 on Howell St; NW on South Ave; W on Holdrege. $5. 5/1-10/31. 15 RV sites. Tbls, flush toilets, cfga, drkg wtr, elec($), showers, dump, pay phone. Fishing. Very good park.

Travel tip: Hebron calls itself the "Capital of the Oregon Trail" and is home to the "World's Largest Porch Swing" in Roosevelt City Park downtown. It seets 16 adults and is in the Guiness Book of World Records.

HEMINGFORD (96)

Box Butte **$6**
State Recreation Area
9.5 mi N of Hemingford on NE 2 (paved). $6-7 at 40 undesignated primitive sites; $11 at 14 sites with elec. All year; 14-day limit. 2,212 acres. Tbls, toilets, cfga, drkg wtr, picnic shelters, playground. Picnicking; swimming; fishing; boating(ld); hunting; hiking.

Fishing tip: At 1,600-acre Box Butte Lake on Niobrara River can be found some of the best panfish action in the state. it has a huge population of rock bass as well as yellow perch and also contains largemouth & smallmouth bass, walleye, crappie and catfish.

HERSHEY (97)

KJ's Korner **$10**
Exit 164 from northbound I-80 at Hershey. $10 for sites without hookups; $12 with wtr hookup; $14 with full hookups. All year. 10 sites. Tbls, flush toilets, cfga, drkg wtr, dump, showers, hookups($), store.

Fishing tip: The nerby Hershey Wildlife Management Area's 53-acre lake offers good fishing for smallmouth & largemouth bass, northern pike, walleye, rock bass and channel catfish.

Morgan's Hide-A-Way **$9**
(Private) Campground
2 mi N of Hershey; 1.5 mi E on Hwy 30; half mi S; .6 mi E. $9. All year. 15 RV sites; 10 tent sites. Hookups, drkg wtr, pit toilets, cfga.

HICKMAN (98)

Hickman City Park **$5**
2nd St, E of Main. $5. All year. Limit, 14 consecutive days, 28 per year; limited facilities in winter. 6 sites with elec; more without hookups. Toilets, cfga, drkg wtr, tbls, shelter, playground gear. Fishing, picnicking, basketball, tennis, volleyball, T-ball.

Stagecoach Lake **$6**
State Recreation Area
1 mi S of Hickman; half mi W. $6 at 50 undesignated primitive sites; $12 at 22 sites with 30/50-amp elec. All year; 14-day limit. Tbls, flush toilets, cfga, drkg wtr, fishing piers. Picnicking; boating(ld); hiking; fishing; hunting. 412 acres; 195-acre lake.

Fishing tip: In early June, anglers here have excellent success with catfish using liver, chubs and nightcrawlers. Some largemouth bass are caught too, and the lake contains northern pike. An 8-inch minimum size on bluegill is enforced.

Wagon Train Lake **$6**
State Recreation Area
2 mi E of Hickman. $6 at 80 primitive sites; $12 at 28 sites with 30/50-amp elec. All year; 14-day limit. Tbls, pit toilets, cfga, drkg wtr, playground, beach, dump. Dog training area. Picnicking; fishing; swimming; boating(ld); hunting. 1,062 acres. 5 hp motor limit. Near state capitol, other points of interest.

Fishing tip: The 315-acre lake has good fishing for walleye & largemouth bass and also contains crappie, flathead & channel catfish.

HOLBROOK (99)

Holbrook City Park **FREE**
W edge of town on Hwys 6 & 34, exit 237. Free. All year; 7-day limit. 5 RV sites. Drkg wtr, pit toilets, cfga, tbls, elec. Picnicking. Pay phone not working, toilets foul in 2004.

HOLDREGE (100)

City Campground **$5**
202 S East Ave at 2nd St in Holdrege. From eastbound US 6 from center of town, S (right) on East St, cross RR tracks to park. $5. All year; 5-day limit. 8 level but short RV back-in sites (40-ft RV limit) on concrete pads. 30/50-amp elec hookups, flush toilets, cfga, dump, drkg wtr, tbls. Picnicking, fishing. Nice small park, but passing trains are noisy. GPS: N40degrees 26.095, W99degrees 22.182.

Travel tip: Visit the National Sod House headquarters at Phelps County Historical Museum; features historical and Indian artifacts, farm equipment and an early bank. N Hwy 183.

HOOPER (101)

Hooper Memorial City Park **FREE**
6 blocks N of Hwy 275 at 500 N Main St. Free. All year; 1-night limit. 3 sites. Flush toilets, cfga, drkg wtr/elec hookups, tbls. Picnicking, swimming.

HUMBOLDT (102)

Humboldt Lake **$10**
City Recreation Park
1 mi S from jct of Hwys 105 & 4; at 1st & Long Branch Sts on N side of lake. $10. Apr-Sept; 2-day limit. 12 sites with elec hookups. Tbls, flush toilets, cfga, drkg wtr, elec, showers, pool($). Free public dump, 2 blocks. Fishing, swimming, tennis, boating(l), horseshoes, playground.

Kirkman's Cove **$5**
Recreation Area
Nemaha Natural Resources District
3 mi NW of Humboldt. $5 for 2-day permit; $12 annual permit. All year. Toilets, cfga, drkg wtr, tbls, beach, playground, outdoor chapel. Fishing, swimming, boating(dl), ball fields, sand volleyball, nature trails, golf. 510-acre area with 160-acre lake.

Fishing tip: This turbid lake offers good fishing for crappie, largemouth bass & walleye.

JUNIATA (103)

Prairie Lake **FREE**
Recreation Area
Little Blue Natural Resources District
3 mi S & qtr mi E of Juniata. Free All year. Primitive undesignated sites. Toilets, cfga, drkg wtr, tbls. Fishing, boating, archery. 124 acres; 36-acre lake.

Roseland Lake **FREE**
Wildlife Management Area
Little Blue Natural Resources District
4.5 mi W & 2.2 mi S of Juniata. Free. All year; 14-day limit. About 7 primitive undesignated sites. Toilets, tbls, drkg wtr. Fishing, picnicking.

KEARNEY (104)

Fort Kearney **$11**
State Recreation Area
Three-fourths mi E & 1 mi N of Ft. Kearney State Historic Park, off SR 10. $11 at 35 pads without elec; $15 at 75 sites with 30/50-amp elec ($10 during 9/16-5/14) All year; 14-day limit. Tbls, flush toilets, cfga, drkg wtr, coin showers, dump, shelters, beach. Swimming, fishing at 8 sandpit lakes, boating(no mtrs) nature trail, hiking/biking trail. 186 acres. Near historic Fort Kearney.

KIMBALL (105)

Gotte Municipal Park **FREE**
On US 30 in city limits; E edge of Kimball. From I-80 exit 20, 1 mi N on SR 71 (S. Chestnut) to center of town traffic light, then E about half mi on US 30 (E. Third St) past Dairy Queen to marked park entrance. Free. Open seasonally; 1-day limit. 10 RV sites (most sites are level), but no signs about RV parking. Tbls, flush toilets, cfga, drkg wtr,

pool, playground. Picnicking; horseshoes, swimming, tennis, skateboard area.

Travel tip: Park contains an obsolete 100-ft Titan I missile, representing the 200 ICBMs once located in the area.

Oliver Reservoir   **$6**
State Recreation Area
8 mi W on US 30. $6 at 175 primitive sites. All year; 14-day limit. 1,187 acres. Pit toilets, tbls, cfga, drkg wtr, beach. Picnicking, fishing, boating(dl), swimming.

Fishing tip: The lake contains largemouth bass, walleye, channel catfish, yellow perch, tiger musky and some rainbow trout. The state record tiger musky was caught here in 1995; it weighed 26 pounds. A 15-inch minimum size for walleye is enforced.

KRAMER (106)

Merganser Lake   **FREE**
Recreational Use Area
Lower Platte South
Natural Resources District
1 mi N & 1 mi E of Kramer. Free. All year; 14-day limit. Primitive open camping on 103-acre reserve at 41-acre lake. Drkg wtr, cfga, no toilets or tbls. Boating(l), fishing.

Fishing tip: The lake is stocked with largemouth bass, channel catfish & bluegill. Electric motors only.

Olive Creek Lake   **$6**
State Recreation Area
1.5 mi SE of Kramer. $6 at 50 undesignated primitive RV/tent sites. All year; 14-day limit. Tbls, pit toilets, cfga, drkg wtr, playground. Picnicking; fishing; hunting; boating (ld - 5 hp limit).

Fishing tip: This 175-acre is very shallow and turbid. Its primary fish are largemouth bass, crappie and channel & flathead catfish.

Tanglewood Lake   **FREE**
Recreational Use Area
Lower Platte South
Natural Resources District
1 mi W of Kramer. Free. All year; 14-day limit. Primitive open camping on 68-acre reserve at 33-acre lake. No facilities except cfga, no drkg wtr. Fishing.

Fishing tip: The lake level fluctuates drastically, and it is not a good fishing lake, containing primarily bullhead catfish.

Wild Plum Lake   **FREE**
Recreational Use Area
Lower Platte South
Natural Resources District
1.5 mi N of Kramer & half mi W. Free. All year; 14-day limit. Primitive open camping on 35-acre reserve at 16-acre lake. No facilities except cfga, no drkg wtr. Boating(l), fishing.

Fishing tip: This lake contains largemouth bass, bluegill and channel catfish. Electric motors only.

LAUREL (107)

Laurel City Park   **Donations**
In Laurel at 3rd & Cedar. Donations appreciated; camp free. All year. 8 sites. Tbls, flush toilets, cfga, drkg wtr, dump, showers, elec. Swimming.

Laurel Lions Club   **Donations**
Municipal Park
600 Wakefield St, at 6th St, on the S edge of Laurel. Donations appreciated; camp free. 4/1-10/1; 14-day limit. 4 sites. Elec/wtr hookups, flush toilets, cfga, drkg wtr, showers, pool. Swimming, tennis.

LAWRENCE (108)

Liberty Cove   **FREE**
Recreation Area
Little Blue Natural Resources District
2 mi W; 2 mi S; qtr mi W of Lawrence on Hwy 4; in Webster County. Free. All year; 14-day limit. Primitive undesignated sites. Toilets, cfga, elec, drkg wtr, tbls. Boating(dl), fishing, swimming, 2.5 mi of hiking trails, bridle trail, arboretum. 247 acres.

Fishing tip: The 36-acre lake is stocked with bass, bluegill, catfish & northern pike.

LEIGH (109)

Centennial Park   **$7**
Main St to dead end; right half mi. $7. Apr-Oct. 12 sites with elec, drkg wtr, toilets, showers, cfga, tbls, playground equipment, dump. Fishing, boating(l), swimming, horseshoes, sand volleyball, pool.

LEWELLEN (111)

Pleasant View Lodge   **$5**
(J's Otter Creek)
On Lake McConnaughey at 1290 Hwy 92 W near Lewellen. $5 base. All year. 16 RV sites. Tbls, pit toilets, cfga, drkg wtr, store, marina, coin laundry. Fishing, boating(lrd).

Fishing tip: Otter Creek offers very good fishing for brown & rainbow trout. Ask the lodge manager for tackle tips.

LEXINGTON (112)

Johnson Lake   **$11**
State Recreation Area
7 mi S of Lexington on US 283. $11 at 94 primitive sites; $15 at 113 sites with 20/30-amp electric ($10 during 9/16-5/14). All year; 14-day limit. Tbls, flush toilets, coin showers, cfga, drkg wtr, dump, shelters, beach, 2 fish cleaning stations. Swimming, boating(dl), fishing. 68 acres. 3 locations: main area on SE side of lake has gravel pads with elec, showers, flush toilets, dump, fish cleaning station, beach; across the lake, South Side Inlet also has gravel pads, elec hookups, modern restrooms, fishing pier, boat ramp, fish cleaning station; North Side Inlet offers

primitive sites, fishing pier, drkg wtr, pit toilets. All areas leased from Central Nebraska Public Power & Irrigation District.

Fishing tip: A new state record tiger musky weighing 33.35 pounds was caught from Johnson Lake in April, 2001. It was more than 48 inches long and was hooked on a Rat-L-Trap lure bought at Lakeshore Marina. It was caught from shore on the fisherman's first cast of the year.

LINWOOD (113)

Camp Moses Merrill (Private)   **$10**
3 mi E of Linwood (9 mi SW of North Bend. $10 for tents; $15 for RVs. 5/1t-10/15. Hookups($), tbls, flush toilets, cfga, drkg wtr, coin laundry, showers, dump. Swimming.

LITCHFIELD (114)

Kamper Korner (Private)   **$12**
N on Main St in Litchfield. $12. 4/15-11/1. 7 RV sites. Hookups, tbls, drkg wtr, dump.

LONG PINE (115)

Long Pine   **$6**
State Recreation Area
1 mi N of Long Pine on US 20. $6 at 20 undesignated primitive sites; $8 at 8 primitive camping pads. All year; 14-day limit. Short sites most suitable for small RVS & pickup campers. Tbls, pit toilets, cfga, drkg wtr. Picnicking; stream trout fishing; swimming; hiking. Scenic canyons. On Long Pine Creek. 154 acres.

Fishing tip: Long Pine Creek has good fishing for brown & rainbow trout.

The Pines   **$6**
at 875 Kyner in Long Pine. $6 for tents; $12 RV sites with elec. All year. 7 sites. Tbls, pit toilets, cfga, drkg wtr, elec($). Fishing swimming.

LOUISVILLE (116)

Louisville Lakes   **$10**
State Recreation Area
Half mi NW of Louisville on SR 50; at S shore of Platte River. $10 at 60 primitive undesignated sites; $11 at 13 non-elec camping pads; $15 at 223 sites with 30/50-amp elec ($10 during 9/16-5/14). All year; 14-day limit Tbls, flush toilets, solar showers, cfga, drkg wtr, dump, shelters, beach. Swimming, boating (elec motors), fishing, hiking, biking, picnicking. 142 acres. Ak-Sar-Ben Aquarium nearby.

Fishing tip: This rec area has 5 sandpit lakes, four of which contain bass, catfish, bluegill, crappie and walleye, with the fifth having carp. The state record yellow bass, 1 pound 7 ounces, was caught from Lake #2 in 1993.

LOUP CITY (117)

Bowman Lake $6
State Recreation Area
Half mi W of Loup City on NE 92; at Loup River. $6. All year; 14-day limit. 12 primitive sites; 22 acres. Tbls, pit toilets, cfga, drkg wtr, playground, shelters. Picnicking; swimming; fishing; hiking; boating (l). 20-acre lake.

Sherman Reservoir $6
State Recreation Area
4 mi E of Loup City; 1 mi N on NE 92; at Oak Creek. $6. All year; 14-day limit. 360 primitive sites around the lake; 4,386 acres. Dump, tbls, flush toilets, cfga, drkg wtr, playground, shelters, coin showers. Picnicking; fishing; swimming; boating(ld); hiking. Store nearby.
Fishing tip: Try walleye near the dam during their spring spawning run. Catch largemouth bass and crappie in the bays, off points and from around underwater cover. White bass can be found everywhere in the lake during summer. Non-boaters can use Fisherman's Bridge, where water and toilets are available. Lake has an 18-inch minimum for walleye, with only 1 fish allowed over 25 inches.

LYNCH

Lynch RV Park & Campground $10
From SR 12 at E end of Lynch,1 block N on 4th St. to city park. $10 for 6 diagonal 50-ft back-in RV sites with 30/50-amp elec/wtr ($4 for tent sites). Flush toilets, cfga, drkg wtr, dump. New park financed by selling stuffed animals.

LYONS (118)

Island Park Municipal Campground $12
1 mi W on Main St in Lyons from jct with US 77. $12. 4/15-10/15. 14 RV sites. Tbls, flush toilets, showers, elec, dump, cfga, wtr hookups, shelter, pool, play field. Swimming, fishing, tennis.

MADISON (119)

Memorial Municipal Park $7
5 blocks N of Hwy 32 on Main St. $7 base. All year; 14-day limit. 6 RV sites, 4 tent sites. Tbls, flush toilets, cfga, drkg wtr, hookups($), showers, dump. Park was in poor condition in 2004, not recommended. Field team says, "worst city park we've ever seen." Most sites full of old, long-term RVs.

Taylor Creek Campground (Private) $8
501 W. 6th St. N. $8 base. All year (weather permitting). 12 sites. Tbls, flush toilets, hookups($), cfga, drkg wtr, showers, dump.

MALCOLM (120)

Branched Oak Lake $6
State Recreation Area
3.5 mi N of Malcolm on SR 34; 5 mi N on SR 79; 4 mi W on Raymond Rd. $6 at 279 primitive sites in open areas; $11 at 33 non-elec modern sites; $15 at sites with 30/50-amp elec; $19 full hookups (elec sites $10 during 9/16-5/14); 287 total sites with hookups. Nine camping sections. Flush toilets, cfga, solar coin showers, dump, drkg wtr, tbls, 2 fish cleaning stations, 2 beaches. Boating (ldr), fishing, swimming, hiking trails, mountain biking trails.
Fishing tip: This lake is stocked with catfish, northern pike, walleye, largemouth bass and tiger musky. In early June, catch wipers on jigs & crawlers, and find catfish in the west end with white perch.

Wildwood Lake FREE
Recreational Use Area
Lower Platte South
Natural Resources District
2 mi N of Branched Oak Lake. Free. All year; 14-day limit. Primitive open camping at 491-acre reserve at 103-acre lake. Tbls, toilets, cfga, drkg wtr. Boating(l), hiking trails, hunting.
Fishing tip: Wildwood Lake has been stocked with largemouth bass, walleye, crappie, bluegill and channel catfish. Electric motors only. Catch-and-release only.

MARTELL (122)

Cottontail Lake FREE
Recreational Use Area
Lower Platte South
Natural Resources District
1 mi N of Martell. Free. All year; 14-day limit. Open primitive camping on 148-acre reserve at 29-acre lake. No facilities except cfga, no drkg wtr. Boating(l), fishing.
Fishing tip: The lake is stocked with largemouth bass, channel catfish & bluegill. Electric motors only.

MAXWELL (123)

Ft. McPherson FREE
State Wildlife Management Area
Near Maxwell, in Lincoln County. Free. All year; 14-day limit. Primitive camping at 30-acre lake. Tbls, toilets, cfga. Fishing (channel catfish, largemouth bass, carp).

MAYWOOD (124)

Maywood Village Park $5
From US 83, about 1 mi E on SR 23 to center of town; N (left) on Commercial for 2 blocks; park on right at end of 2nd block. $5. Open 5/15-9/15; 5-day limit. 3 undesignated RV sites, 3 tent sites. Tbls, flush toilets, cfga, drkg wtr, elec. No fee signs, no silent ranger. On-street parking; need extension cord to reach elec box

MCCOOK (125)

Karrer Municipal Park Donations
At the E edge of McCook on SRs 6/34. 4/1-11/1; 3-day limit. Donations appreciated. 7 RV sites (trailers under 30 ft). Tbls, toilets, 20-amp elec, cfga, drkg wtr, dump, showers, hookups. Picnicking; golf nearby.
Fishing tip: try nearby Hugh Butler Lake for some great wiper action. Catch them in early July suspended off bottom, chasing schools of shad.

Red Willow $6
State Recreation Area
11 mi N of McCook on US 83; 2 mi W on access rd; at Hugh Butler Lake. $6 at 110 sites in open primitive areas; $11 at 50 modern sites without elec; $15 at 45 sites with 20/30-amp elec ($10 during 9/16-5/14) 14-day limit. Tbls, flush & pit toilets, cfga, drkg wtr, dump, beach, store, playground, coin showers, fish cleaning station. Boating(ld), fishing, picnicking, swimming. Longhorn cattle display; prairie dog town near Spring Creek.
Fishing tip: 35 mi of brushy shoreline on this 1,768-acre lake provide lots of great largemouth & smallmouth bass fishing. The tree-filled bays have excellent crappie action in summer; the lake produced state records white & black crappies. White bass, northern pike and walleye also are available, and it has record-size wipers. The state record white crappie, 4 pounds, was caught here in 1980.

MEADOW GROVE (126)

Millstone State Wayside
City Park Donation
Half mi E of Meadow Grove on US 275. Camp free, but donations solicited. All year; 7-day limit. 3 undesignated RV sites. Tbls, pit toilets, cfga, drkg wtr, 15-amp hookups, playground, picnic shelters. Picnicking; hiking. Old millstones.

MERRIMAN (127)

Cottonwood Lake $6
State Recreation Area
Half mi E of Merriman on US 20; half mi S on Park Rd (gravel access rd). $6. All year; 14-day limit. 30 primitive undesignated sites. Tbls, pit toilets, cfga, drkg wtr, playground. Picnicking; swimming; fishing; boating(ld); waterskiing; hiking. Most sites level. 240 acres. Adjacent to Arthur Bowring Sandhills Ranch State Historic Park.
Fishing tip: This lake contains channel catfish, crappie, largemouth bass, northern pike, yellow perch, but heavy vegetation hampers summer fishing.

Shady Spot $10
RV Camp (Private)
1 block N of Hwy 20 on Hwy 61 at Merriman; follow signs. $10 base (weekly rates avail-

able). 5/1-10/1. 6 RV sites. Hookups, drkg wtr, dump. Single 30-amp tested reverse polarity in 2004 field trip.

MINDEN (129)

Bassway Strip **FREE**
State Wildlife Management Area
At I-80, Newark-Minden Interchange. Free. All year. 10 sites. Primitive camping. Drkg wtr, no shower. Swimming, boating, no motors; fishing.

Travel tip: Harold Warp's Pioneer Village is on US 6, 12 mi S of I-80 at the SR 10 exit. It displays a famous collection of pioneer memorabilia tracing man's progress since 1830.

MITCHELL (130)

Scotts Bluff **$10**
County Fairground
At Scotts Bluff Fairgrounds (exits 20 or 22). $10 without hookups, $15 with hookups. All year except fair time (about 8/10-8/17). About 80 RV sites, about 14 tent sites. Tbls, flush toilets, cfga, drkg wtr, elec ($), showers, dump.

Fishing tip: Just NW of Mitchell, try the good brown & rainbow trout fishing at Spotted Tail Creek.

Ziegler Municipal Park **$5**
12th Ave & 12th St in town. $5. All year; 5-day limit. 4 RV sites. Tbls, cfga, drkg wtr, elec.

MULLEN (131)

Dismal River **FREE**
State Canoe Trail
12 mi S of Mullen on SR 97 to river (boat access only). Canoe trail runs from SR 97 bridge to Whitetail Campground in the Nebraska National Forest; 56.5 river miles. Not for novice canoeists; public access quite limited, so arrange camping permission in advance. 4/1-10/31. Primitive tent sites. Tbls, toilets, cfga. Fishing, canoeing. First leg is 15 river mi to Seneca bridge (portage around waterfall required about half way there). Next, 24.2 mi to first public primitive campsite near Nebraska NF (on N side of river about 3 mi E of US 83 bridge). Then 17.3 mi to Whitetail Camp, where overnight fee is $8.

NEBRASKA CITY (133)

Riverview Marina **$6**
State Recreation Area
Access via US 73/75 & SR 2 near Nebraska City; on Missouri River. $6 at 30 primitive sites; $14 at 16 sites with 20/30-amp elec ($10 during 9/16-5/14). All year; 14-day limit. Tbls, flush toilets, cfga, drkg wtr, showers. Fishing, boating(l). 47 acres. Historic Arbor Lodge nearby.

NELIGH (134)

Fred Penn Municipal Park **FREE**
Half mi S of city on Hwy 14 at Wylie Dr. Free. 4/1-10/31; 7-day limit. 14 sites. Toilets, tbls, cfga, drkg wtr. Boating(l), fishing, picnicking, playground.

Fishing tip: Fred Penn Lake is good panfish water. The 8-acre lake also contins largemouth bass and channel catfish. It was renovated in 1994.

Riverside Municipal Park **$5**
S on L St from Hwy 275 in Neligh; follow camping signs around sports fields to RV section near fairgrounds. $5 base. 4/1-10/1; 7-day limit. Base fee for tents; $12 for RVs. 26 sites. Tbls, flush toilets, cfga, 30-amp elec, drkg wtr, showers, pool($), dump. Swimming, fishing, hiking, horseshoes, walking trail.

NELSON (135)

Harbine Park **$5**
At 900 S. Wheeler in Nelson. $5 base. All year; 3-day limit. 2 RV sites. Tbls, flush toilets, cfga, drkg wtr, elec, showers, dump. Swimming.

NENZEL (136)

Steer Creek **$5**
Samuel R. McKelvie National Forest
19 mi S of Nenzel on NE S16F. $5. All year; 14-day limit. 23 sites (RVs under 36 ft). Tbls, toilets, cfga, firewood, drkg wtr. Picnicking; fishing, hunting. 10 acres.

NEWCASTLE (137)

Buckskin Hills **FREE**
State Wildlife Management Area
2 mi W, 3 mi S & half mi W of Newcastle in Dixon County. Free. All year; 14-day limit. Undesignated primitive camping at 75-acre lake. Toilets, cfga, no drkg wtr. Boating(l), fishing.

NEWMAN GROVE (138)

City Park **$6**
E end of Park Ave in Newman Grove. $6. Apr-Oct; no stay limit. 10 sites. Tbls, flush toilets, cfga, drkg wtr, elec, pool, dump. Swimming, tennis, sand volleyball, playground.

NEWPORT (139)

Spring Valley Park **FREE**
1 mi W of Newport on Hwy 20. Free. All year; 1-day limit. Primitive overnight camping. Tbls, toilets, cfga, drkg wtr.

NIOBRARA (140)

Niobrara State Park **$8**
Half mi S of Niobrara; 1 mi W on SR 12. During 5/15-9/15, $8 at tent sites, $15 at 60

RV sites with 30/50-amp elec. During, 9/16-5/14, elec sites are $10 ($6 without elec), but no wtr service. All year; 14-day limit. Tbls, flush toilets, cfga, drkg wtr, shelters, playground gear, coin laundry. Trail rides, swimming pool, boating (l), fishing, hiking & biking trails, handicap fishing bridge.

Fishing tip: The state record sauger, an 8-pounder, was caught from the Missouri River nearby in 1961.

NORFOLK (141)

Elkhorn Wayside **FREE**
1 mi N of Norfolk on US 81 (paved access rds). Free. All year; 2-day limit. Undesignated sites. Tbls, toilets, cfga, drkg wtr, shelters. Bottled gas, flush toilets, showers, ice nearby. Picnicking; hiking. Game and Parks Commission District Office. Most sites are level.

Maskenthine Lake **$5**
City Recreation Area
Lower Elkhorn Natural Resources District
8 mi E of Norfolk on Hwy 275; 2 mi S. $5 for tent sites; $12 for RVs with elec ($14 for 50-amp); $5 overflow. All year; 14-day limit. 25 RV sites plus tent areas. Tbls, pit toilets, cfga, drkg wtr, hookups, dump, showers. Boating (l), fishing, swimming. Arboretum on E side of lake.

Fishing tip: This 98-acre lake contains northern pike, walleye and channel catfish, all stocked annually. Other species include largemouth bass, black crappie and bluegill. Boats are limited to 5 mph.

Ta-ha-zouka Municipal Park **$6**
S of viaduct on US 81 at Norfolk; at 22034 S. 13th St; near Elkhorn River. $6 base for primitive sites; $9 with elec. 4/15-10/15; 4-day limit. 22 sites. Tbls, flush toilets, cfga, drkg wtr, showers, dump. During winter, a few RVs can hook to elec from the roadway for $6.

Fishing tip: Try Skyview Lake's big largemouth bass; they must be 21 inches to keep. The lake also contains crappie, tiger musky, northern pike and walleye.

NORTH LOUP (142)

North Loup Trailer Park **$7**
1 block S of North Loup's main street; E edge of town. $7. 4/15-10/15. 38 sites. Hookups. Monthly rates available.

NORTH PLATTE (143)

Cody Municipal Park **$5**
3 mi N of I-80 on Hwy 83, exit 177. $5. 3/1-10/15; 7-day limit during 30-day period. 39 RV sites. Tbls, flush toilets, cfga, drkg wtr, dump. Swimming, fishing, boating(l).

Fishing tip: North Platte's 26-acre city lake contains largemouth bass, rock bass, walleye and channel catfish.

Lake Maloney $6
State Recreation Area
5 mi S of North Platte on US 83; half mi W on access rd. $6 at 200 sites in open primitive areas; $12 at 56 modern sites with elec. All year; 14-day limit. Tbls, pit toilets, cfga, drkg wtr, dump, showers, 2 fish cleaning stations, 2 beaches. Swimming, fishing, boating(dl), playground. Buffalo Bill's Ranch nearby.
Fishing tip: In early July, catch wipers & white bass at the inlet area.

OAKLAND (144)

Oakland City Park $5
SW edge of Oakland on SR 32. $5. 4/1-11/1. 12 sites. Wtr & elec hookups, flush toilets, cfga, drkg wtr, showers, dump. Swimming pool, picnicking, tennis, basketball, sand volleyball, playground. Large, shady park. 40-acre park contains century-old maple tree, flower garden, picnic areas, shelter.

OBERT (145)

Obert City Park Donations
S side of Hwy 12 in Obert at Main St. Donations requested; camp free. All year. 3 sites. Tbls, pit toilets, cfga, drkg wtr, elec.

OCONTO (146)

Pressey FREE
State Wildlife Management Area
5 mi N of Oconto on NE 21. Free. All year; 14-day limit. 15 undesignated sites. Tbls, toilets, cfga, elec hookups, playground. Picnicking; fishing; swimming. GPS: 41.189599, -99.709811.

ODESSA (147)

Union Pacific $6
State Recreation Area
At Odessa interchange of I-80; 2 mi N. $6. All year; 14-day limit. 5 undesignated primitive sites on 26 acres. Flush toilets, tbls, cfga, drkg wtr. Limited facilities in winter. Boating (electric motors only), fishing, picnicking.
Fishing tip: The 12-acre sandpit lake contains channel catish, rock bass & smallmouth bass. It was renovated in 1994.

OGALLALA (148)

Arthur Bay $6
Lake McConaughy
State Recreation Area
1.5 mi W of jct SR 92/61, 2 mi W of dam on N side of lake. $6. All year; 14-day limit. Open camping. Toilets, tbls, cfga, drkg wtr. 600 undesignated sites. Toilets, cfga, tbls, drkg wtr, coin showers, dump, beaches. Boating(l), fishing, swimming, picnicking, waterskiing.
Fishing tip: The State record coho and kokanee salmon were caught from this lake. Both were hooked in 1971; the coho was almost 6 pounds, the kokanee just over 4.

Cedar Vue $6
Lake McConaughy
State Recreation Area
13 mi W of jct of SR 92/61 just W of Otter Creek. $6 at primitive sites in open areas; $15 at modern sites, with elec ($10 during 9/16-5/14 with limited facilities). All year; 14-day limit. Toilets, tbls, showers, cfga, dump, beach, fish cleaning station, beaches. Boating(ld), fishing, swimming, picnicking, waterskiing, playground.
Fishing tip: Just after ice-out, this area produces very good channel cat fishing. In July, catch walleye here on nightcrawlers, leeches, Rapalas and Thundersticks. Expect good success with wipers of 6-8 pounds.

Eagle Canyon $6
Lake McConaughy
State Recreation Area
15 mi W on US 26 from jct with SR 61; 5 mi N on access rd; on S side of lake. $6. All year; 14-day limit. About 100 undesignated primitive sites. Pit toilets, cfga, drkg wtr, tbls. Boating(l), fishing, swimming, picnicking, waterskiing.
Fishing tip: White bass action can be found all over the lake during the late summer.

Lake Ogallala $6
State Recreation Area
9 mi N of Ogallala on SR 61. $6 at 180 primitive sites; $11 at 20 modern sites without elec; $15 at 62 elec sites ($10 during 9/16-5/14, but no wtr services. All year; 14-day limit. Flush & pit toilets, cfga, tbls, drkg wtr, dump, showers, fish cleaning station. Boating(ld), fishing, swimming, playground, hiking trails. 320-acre lake.
Fishing tip: During early June, catch rainbow trout of 1-6 pounds in the canal and diversion dam on nightcrawlers, olive flies, leech imitations, salmon eggs. In July, try for channel catfish up to 10 pounds on chubs. The state's largest cutthroat trout was caught from here in 1992; it weighed 5 pounds 7 ounces.

Lake View $6
Lake McConaughy
State Recreation Area
7 mi W of Ogallala on US 26 from jct with SR 61. $6. All year; 14-day limit. Open primitive camping. Toilets, cfga, drkg wtr, showers. Boating, swimming, fishing, picnicking, waterskiing.
Fishng tip: This lake holds the state record for the largest walleye -- a 16-pounder caught in 1971.

LeMoyne Bay $6
Lake McConaughy
State Recreation Area
7 mi W of Jct SR 92/61. $6. All year; 14-day limit. Open camping; about 200 undesignated primitive sites. Pit toilets, cfga, drkg wtr, tbls. Groceries, ice. Boating(lrd), swimming, fishing, picnicking, waterskiing.
Fishing tip: From this area in early June,

use crankbaits, nightcrawlers, leeches, Lindy rigs and minnows to catch walleye 15-22 inches.

Little Thunder Campground $6
No Name Bay
Lake McConaughy
State Recreation Area
On W side of No Name Bay, which is on Nor shore along Shore Line Rd just W of Martin Bay. $6 at primitive sites; $11 at pads without elec; $15 at 34 modern sites with elec; $19 at 8 sites with full hookups (elec sites $10 during 9/16-5/14, but no wtr services). All year; 14-day limit. Tbls, flush & pit toilets, cfga, drkg wtr, coin showers. Boating, fishing, swimming.
Fishing tip: The state record walleye of 16 pounds 2 ounces came from this lake. Excellent white bass fishing also is available, and wipers (a cross of white bass & stripers) have been stocked.

Lone Eagle Campground $6
Sandy Beach Area
Lake McConaughy
State Recreation Area
Jct SR 92/61 at Sandy Beach area on N shore of lake. $6 at primtive sites; $11 at modern sites without elec; $15 at 54 30-amp and 14 50-amp elec sites; $19 at 16 full-hookup sites. Elec sites $10 during 9/16-5/14, but no wtr services. All year; 14-day limit. Tbls, flush & pit toilets, coin showers, cfga, drkg wtr, dump. Boating, fishing.

Martin Bay $6
Lake McConaughy
State Recreation Area
N end of Kingsley Dam. $6. All year; 14-day limit. 600 undesignated sites. Toilets, dump, picnic shelter, drkg wtr cfga, tbls, beach, fish cleaning station. Boating(ld), fishing, swimming, picnicking, waterskiing. Playground, groceries. This the lake's most popular camping area.
Fishing tip: During April & May, focus oon the nearby area around the dam for spawning walleye.

Meyer Camper Court $12
Half mi S of Ogallala; qtr mi E of I-80 exit 126. $12 base. All year. 110 sites. Tbls, flush toilets, cfga, drkg wtr, showers, hookups($), coin laundry, dump, store. Swimming.

Ogallala Beach $6
Lake McConaughy
State Recreation Area
5 mi N of Ogallala & 2.5 mi N of Hwy 26/61 jct. $6. All year; 14-day limit. Open primitive camping. Toilets, no drkg wtr, tbls, cfga, beach. Boating, fishing, swimming, picnicking, waterskiing.
Fishing tip: From Ogallala Beach, concentrate on the nearby bays during summer and use light spinning gear for smallmouth bass. Small spinners and crankbaits work best.

Omaha Beach $6
Lake McConaughy
State Recreation Area
15 mi W of jct of SR 92/61 on Hwy 92; on NW side of lake. $6. All year; 14-day limit. Open camping; about 30 undesignated primitive sites. Toilets, cfga, drkg wtr, cfga, store. Boating(l), fishing, swimming, picnicking, waterskiing, playground.

Otter Creek $6
Lake McConaughy
State Recreation Area
11 mi W of jct of SR 92/61 on SR 92. $6. All year; 14-day limit. Open camping; about 400 undesignated primitive sites. Toilets, cfga, drkg wtr, cfga, dump, fish cleaning station. Boating(ld), fishing, swimming, picnicking, waterskiing, playground. Groceries, ice.

Fishing tip: This camping area is perfectly situated for the best walleye fishing in May and June. Try the bays and the lake's upper end. Otter Creek's protected bays are ideal for mooring boats near the campsites.

Sand Creek $6
Lake McConaughy
State Recreation Area
10 mi W of jct of SR 92/61. $6. All year; 14-day limit. Open primitive camping. No facilities except toilets. Boating(l), fishing.

Sandy Beach $6
Lake McConaughy
State Recreation Area
Jct SR 92/61. $6. All year; 14-day limit. Open camping; About 400 primitive sites. Toilets, drkg wtr, tbls, cfga. Boating, fishing, swimming, picnicking, waterskiing.

Spring Park $6
Lake McConaughy
State Recreation Area
9 mi W of jct of SR 92/61 on access rd 9. $6. All year; 14-day limit. Open camping; about 150 undesignated sites. No facilities except toilets, cfga, playground equipment. Boating(l), fishing, swimming, picnicking.

Fishing tip: Catch rainbow trout in June & July by trolling.

Van's $12
Lakeview Fishing Camp
From I-80 exit 126, N out of Ogallala toward the hwy 26-61 interchange; left on Hwy 26 for about 8 mi to campground sign. On Lake McCopnaughy. $12 without hookups; $20-28 with hookups. 5/1-10/1. 100 RV sites. Tbls, flush toilets, showers($), drkg wtr, dump, sewer, beach, cfga, playground, water slide, fish cleaning station. Fishing, swimming, boating(ldr).

OMAHA (149)

Glenn Cunningham Lake $7.50
Municipal Park
96th & State Sts via I-680 North in north-central Omaha. $7.50 base for RV sites without hookups (no stay limit); $7.50 tent sites (no stay limit) $12 with hookups (14-day limit). 5/1-10/15. 58 RV sites. Tbls, flush toilets, cfga, drkg wtr, elec, showers, dump ($1 non-campers). Fishing, swimming, boating(l), bridle trails, windsurfing, hiking, biking trails. 390--acre lake; 1,050 land acres. Closed in 2007 due to lake rehabilitation.

Fishing tip: This 300-acre lake contains largemouth, yellow and white bass in addition to channel catfish & bullheads.

N.P. Dodge Municipal Park $7.50
1 mi N of I-680 & John J. Pershing Dr. $7.50 base for RV sites without hookups; $12 with elec; $7.50 tent sites. 5/15-10/15; 14-day limit. 46 RV sites. Tbls, flush toilets, cfga, drkg wtr, elec($), showers, dump ($1 for non-campers). Boating, swimming, fishing, tennis, horseshoes, bridle trail, bike paths. 445 acres.

O'NEILL (150)

Carney Municipal Park Donations
In the S part of O'Neill on NE 281; or, as you come from the E or W on NE 20, turn S at the stop light (only one in town); go 4 blks; park is approx half blk past the railroad tracks, on the W side of the rd. 3/1-12/1. Donations requested; after 3 days, $10 per night. 4/1-10/1. 21 RV sites, 4 tent sites. Wtr & elec hookups (15 amps), flush toilets, drkg wtr, cfga, dump, showers. Fishing in pond, horseshoes, sports field, playground, biking, sand volleyball.

Goose Lake FREE
State Wildlife Management Area
22 mi S of O'Neill on US 281; 4 mi E to campground. Free. All year; 14-day limit. 10 sites on 349 acres. Tbls, toilets, cfga. Picnicking; fishing; swimming, boating(l).

Fishing tip: This 200-acre lake contains bass, bluegill, northern pike and perch.

ORD (151)

Bussell Municipal Park $10
On 24th & G Sts in town. $10. All year; 3-day limit (longer with permission). 7 RV sites plus tent area. Tbls, pit & flush toilets, drkg wtr, cfga, dump, elec, showers. No wtr in winter. Swimming, fishing, picnicking.

North Loup River Trails $5
8 mi E of Ord. $5 base. 5/1-11/30. 2 RV sites, 25 tent sites. Tbls, pit toilets, cfga, drkg wtr, elec($). Fishing, swimming, horseback riding.

ORLEANS (152)

Orleans City Campground FREE
2 mi S of Orleans on Hwy 136 at Harlan Ave. Free for 1 days, then $10 daily. All year. 8 RV sites. Tbls, drkg wtr, cfga, dump, elec. Picnicking, fishing.

OSCEOLA (153)

City Park FREE
In town on US 81, across from Terry's Drive-In, go N on State St, then E immidiately N of RR tracks to sites; main park with restrooms is farther N. Free. 3-day limit. All year. Undesignated sites & two 35-ft back-in sites with 30-amp elec. Wtr, flush toilets, cfga, tbls, shelter. Tennis, pool, sand volleyball, tennis, playground, ball fields.

OSMOND (155)

Grove Lake FREE
State Wildlife Management Area
W of Osmond on US 20, then 2 mi N in Royal (paved access rds). Free. All year; 14-day limit. 15 sites; 1,600 acres. Tbls, toilets, cfga. Picnicking; fishing; hunting; boating(l); hiking (trails). 5 hp limit.

Fishing tip: The WMA features one of Nebraska's few trout streams. 50-acre Grove Lake coontains crappie, northern pike, largemouth bass and channel catfish.

OXFORD (156)

George R. Mitchell $7
Municipal RV Park
In Oxford at Clark & Central (1 block S of US 136 on Central, then 1 block W on Clark, following camping signs). Free first night, $7 thereafter. All year. 10 sites with elec/wtr (2 with 50-amp). Tbls, pit toilets nearby, cfga, drkg wtr, dump, playground. Fishing (bass, crappie, catfish), disc golf. Park empty during 2004 field trip. Town not thriving.

PALISADE (157)

Smith Trailer Court $10
3 blocks W of Main St. $10. All year. 10 RV sites. Hookups, drkg wtr, dump.

PALMYRA (158)

Palmyra RV Park $10
At Hwy 2 & I St, Palmyra. $10 base; $16 full hookups. All year; no longer a 3-day limit. 16 RV sites. Tbls, flush toilets, cfga, drkg wtr, dump, hookups ($), store.

PARKS (159)

Rock Creek Station $10
State Recreation Area
4 mi N of Parks 1 mi W on US 34. $10 at 10 non-elec sites; $15 at 25 sites with 30/50-amp elec ($10 during 9/16-5/14 but no wtr services. All year; 14-day limit. Tbls, toilets, cfga, drkg wtr. Picnicking; swimming; fishing; boating (nonpower); state fish hatchery nearby.

Fishing tip: The lake contains flathead and channel catfish, largemouth bass, rainbow trout and largemouth bass. Elec motors only on the 50-acre lake.

PAXTON (160)

Ole's Lodge (Private) $10
At I-80 exit 145, Paxton. $10 base. All year. 12 sites. Tbls, flush toilets, cfga, drkg wtr, showers, hookups($), CATV($, coin laundry, store, RV wash bays. Fishing, driving range.

PENDER (161)

Village Campground $5
In Pender at 600 block of Main St. $5. All year; 14-day limit. 6 sites. Hookups, dump, drkg wtr.

PIERCE (162)

Gilman Municipal Park $5
1 block N of Main St in Pierce, on Mill St (Hwy 89). $5. 3/1-11/1; 5-day limit (longer with permission). 4 sites with 30-amp elec; unlimited tent space. Tbls, flush toilets, cfga, drkg wtr, elec, showers (at nearby pool during MD-8/15), shelter, pool. Boating(l), swimming, fishing, sand volleyball, horseshoes. Museum, 14-acre arboretum.
   Fishing tip: 11-acre Bill Cox Memorial Lake contains largemouth bass, bluegill, crappie & catfish.

Willow Creek $6
State Recreation Area
Lower Elkhorn Natural Resources District
2 mi SW of Pierce. $6 at undesignated primitive sites; $11 at 18 designated non-elec sites; $15 at 84 elec sites ($10 during 9/16-5/14). All year; 14-day limit. Tbls, flush toilets, cfga, drkg wtr, coin laundry, showers, dump, beach. Swimming, fishing, horseback/hiking trail, archery, fishing pier.
   Fishing tip: This shallow, 700-acre reservoir contains crappie, bass, catfish, walleye, northern pike and tiger musky.
   Travel tip: Nearby (to the NW), Grove Lake State Wildlife Area has a trout rearing station where visitors can feed the fish.

PLAINVIEW (163)

Chilvers Municipal Park FREE
1 block N of Hwy 20 at Maple. All year. 3 nights free. 4 RV sites with elec. Flush toilets, tbls, drkg wtr, showers, pool. Swimming, picnicking, tennis, playground.

PLYMOUTH (165)

Cub Creek Recreation Area FREE
Lower Big Blue Natural Resources Dist.
3 mi W of Plymout, then 4.5 mi S. Free. All year; 14-day limit. Primitive camping on 85-acre reserve at 40-acre lake. Tbls, toilets, drkg wtr, cfga, shelter. Boating(l), fishing, hiking, hunting.

Leisure Lake FREE
Wildlife Management Area
Lower Big Blue Natural Resources District
3 mi S of Plymouth. Free. All year; 14-day limit. Primitive open camping on 47-acre reserve at 38-acre lake. No facilities, no drkg wtr. Fishing, hunting, hiking.

PONCA (166)

Ponca State Park $11
2 mi N of Ponca on SRs 9 & 12. During 5/15-9/15, $10 at 85 sites without elec ($6 off-season); during Apr-Oct, 72 sites with 30/50-amp elec are $15. All year; 14-day limit. Tbls, flush toilets, showers, cfga, drkg wtr, dump, pool, shelters. Hiking trails, swimming, horseback trail rides, playground. Limited facilities in winter.

PRAGUE (168)

Czechland Lake FREE
Recreation Area
Lower Platte North
Natural Resources District
1 mi N of Prague on Hwy 79. Free. All year; 14-day limit. Open camping on 177 acres at 82-acre lake. Tbls, toilets, cfga. Boating, fishing.

RANDOLPH (169)

City RV Park DONATIONS
In Randolph, 5 blocks S of Hwy 20 & Main St, then 1 block E. Donations requested. All year. 6 RV sites. Elec, wtr, dump. Adjacent to Veteran's Memorial Park with playground, tbls, shelter, sand volleyball, ball fields, pool.

RAVENNA (170)

Buffalo County Recreation Area FREE
1.5 mi E of Ravenna. Free. All year. Primitive undesignated sites. Tbls, toilets, cfga, drkg wtr, playground. Boating(l), fishing. About 100 acres. State parks department plans to renovate & improve this park in the future.
   Fishing tip: This is not a very good fishing lake; it contains carp, bullhead & channel catfish.

RED CLOUD (171)

Bell's Sleepy Valley $11
(Private) Campground
Three-fourths mi N of Hwy 136 on hwy 281 near Red Cloud. $11. All year. 6 RV sites, 3 tent sites. Hookups, tbls, flush toilets, drkg wtr, coin laundry, showers.
   Fishing tip: Nearby Elm Creek contains good populations of brown & rainbow trout, which are stocked three times each year.

REPUBLICAN CITY (172)

Cedar Point $6
Corps of Engineers
Harlan County Lake
Fr Republican City, 3 mi S on CR A at dam, S side. $6 during 5/15-9/15; free rest of year. 14-day limit. 30 primitive sites (30-ft RV limit). Toilets, drkg wtr, cfga, pavilion. Picnicking, hiking, boating(l), beach, snowmobiling, motor bike trail, fishing.
   Fishing tip: Walleye usually spawn on the face of the dam between 4/1 and 4/15, with fishing out in the lake for walleye starting about 3 weeks later.

Gremlin Cove $8
Harlan County Lake
Corps of Engineers
1.5 mi S of Republican City on W side of access rd A. Free during 9/15-5/15; $8 rest of year; 14-day limit. 70 sites (no RV size limit). Tbls, flush toilets, cfga, drkg wtr, beach, playground. Limited facilities during free period. Fishing, swimming, boating(l).
   Fishing tip: Try for white bass in the river about May 1, and catch them at the dam about 2 weeks later. They'll be schooled during June & July. Wipers often school with the white bass.

Hunter Cove FREE
Harlan County Lake
Corps of Engineers
1.5 mi S of Republican City, then 1 mi W of access rd A; at E end of lake. Some sites free during Dec-Mar, but no wtr or elec; $6 during Oct, Nov & Apr (reduced services); $10 without elec & $14 with elec rest of year ($16 at premium sites with elec). All year; 14-day limit. 150 sites (no RV size limit). Tbls, flush toilets, cfga, drkg wtr, showers, dump, fish cleaning station, elec($), playground, coin laundry. Swimming, boating(rl), fishing. 275 acres. 2-night minimum stay on weekends.
   Fishing tip: Boat across the lake after ice out and drift fish for channel catish. Fish the same area for walleye in June, and catch white bass there at night.

North Outlet Area $6
Harlan County Lake
Corps of Engineers
3 mi S of US 136 in Republican City. Free during 9/16-5/14; $6 rest of year. 14-day limit. 30 sites (no RV size limit). Tbls, toilets, cfga, drkg wtr. Limited facilities during free period. Hiking trails, fishing, boating.
   Fishing tip: During a walleye tournament in June 2001, fish averaged 2-4 pounds, with the largest at 9 pounds. In June, catch wipers of 2-4 pounds in the spillway below the dam.

South Outlet Area $6
Harlan County Lake
Corps of Engineers
3 mi S of US 136 on access rd, Republican City. Free during 9/16-5/14; $6 rest of year.

14-day limit. 30 sites (no RV size limit). Tbls, toilets, cfga, drkg wtr, dump. Limited facilities during free period. Fishing, boating, picnicking. 78 acres.

REYNOLDS (173)

Buckley Creek   **FREE**
Recreation Area
Little Blue Natural Resources District
1 mi E & half mi N of Reynolds; in Jefferson County. All year. Primitive undesignated sites. 4 hookups, tbls, toilets, cfga, drkg wtr. Boating(l), golf. Arboretum. 78 acres. This is considered the second-muddiest lake in the world, the mud composed of volcanic ash; no fish can live in it.

RUSHVILLE (174)

Rushville Service & Sports   **$10**
On W end of town, N side of Hwy 20 & S of RR tracks. $10 base. All year. 6 sites with hookups, 5 tent sites. Tbls, toilets, cfga, drkg wtr, sewer, dump. Monthly rates available. Judged drab in 2004 field trip.
Fishing tip: 20 mi S of Rushville, Pine Creek offers good fishing for brown trout.

Smith Lake   **FREE**
State Wildlife Management Area
23 mi S of Rushville on NE 250. All year; 14-day limit. 15 primitive sites; 640 acres. Tbls, toilets, cfga, playground. Picnicking; swimming; fishing; boating (5 hp motor limit).
Fishing tip: This 265-acre lake offers good fishing for walleye, tiger musky, northern pike, largemouth bass and catfish.

ST. EDWARD (175)

City Park Camp Area   **FREE**
3rd & Clark St (1 blk N of SR 39). Camp free 1 day, but donation accepted; $6 thereafter. Apr-Oct; 7-day limit. 3 with elec. Drkg wtr, dump, tbls, flush toilets. Swimming, picnicking. Groceries. GPS: N41.5709, W97.8655.

SANTEE

Mnisose Wicot   **FREE**
(Wandering River) Public Park
In center of town on Veteran's Memorial Dr. Free, but donations accepted. All year. Tbls, flush toilets, cfga, drkg wtr, dump. Fishing.

40-acre park along the Missouri River.

SCHUYLER (177)

Schuyler Park   **$10**
Municipal Campground
S edge of city on Hwy 15. $10. 4/1-10/31; 7-day limit. 35 sites. Elec, drkg wtr, toilets, cfga, tbls, dump. Fishing, swimming.
Fishing tip: Schuyler City Lake, 18 acres, contains bass, crappie, channel catfish & bluegill.

SCOTTSBLUFF (178)

Lake Minatare   **$6**
State Recreation
5 mi N of Scottsbluff on Hwy 71; 6 mi E on gravel rd. $6 at 110 primitive sites in open camping areas around the lake; $15 at 52 gravel 20/30-amp elec sites ($10 during 9/16-5/14 but no wtr services). All year; 14-day limit. Tbls, toilets, cfga, drkg wtr, food, store, dump, shelters, showers, 2 fish cleaning stations, coin laundry, beach. Picnicking; fishing; swimming; boating (ld), waterskiing, sailing. Scottsbluff National Monument nearby. Elev 4126 ft; 769 acres. Playground.
Fishing tip: Minatare is best known for its walleye and wipers, but it has good populations of crappie, white bass and channel catfish too, as well as some smallmouth bass and stripers. A 15-inch minimum limit on walleye is enforced.

Riverside City Campground   **$8**
1 mi W of Broadway on S. Belt Line Hwy. $8 without hookups; $10 wtr/sewer; $15 full hookups. 5/1-9/30; 14-day limit. 43 RV sites with hookups($); 50 tent sites. Tbls, flush toilets, cfga, drkg wtr, showers, dump ($5), elec. Fishing, playground, zoo($), hiking.

SCRIBNER (179)

Dead Timber   **$6**
State Recreation Area
4 mi N of Scribner on US 275 & SR 9; 1.5 mi E; at Elkhorn River. $6 at 25 primitive sites; $12 at 17 sites with 20/30-amp elec. All year; 14-day limit. 42 sites. Tbls, pit toilets, cfga, drkg wtr, playground, shelter. Pack out trash due to budget cuts. Boating (nonpowered or elec mtrs), ski trails, hiking, fishing, playground, canoeing. 200 acres.

Powderhorn   **FREE**
State Wildlife Management Area
4 mi N of Scribner on US 275; adjoins Dead Timbers SRA; on the Elkhorn River (state canoe trail access). All year; 14-day limit. Primitive undesignated camping. Toilets, cfga, no drkg wtr. 289 acres. Hunting, fishing, canoeing.

SEWARD (180)

Arrowhead Campground   **$3-11**
Fuller Public Park
At I-80 exit, Seward. $3-11. All year. 16 sites. Tbls, pit toilets, cfga, drkg wtr, elec, dump.

Blue Valley   **$7**
Municipal Camping Area
Half mi S of Seward on NE 15. $7 for RVs, $5 tents. Open 4/1-11/1; 7-day limit. 10 RV sites, 100 tent sites. Tbls, pit toilets, cfga, drkg wtr, elec hookups, dump. Picnicking; fishing.

Seward County Fairgrounds   **$7**
At 500 N 14th St, Seward. $7. Mar-Oct. 8 RV sites. Tbls, flush toilets, cfga, drkg wtr, elec, dump.

SHELTON (181)

War Axe   **$6**
State Recreation Area
4 mi S of Shelton on access rd, at Shelton Interchange I-80 (Exit 291). $6. All year; 14-day limit. 8 primitive sites. Tbls, flush toilets, cfga, drkg wtr, picnic shelters. Picnicking; fishing, boating (elect mtrs only). 25 acres.
Fishing tip: Good fishing here for largemouth bass and rock bass; also plenty of channel catfish and bluegill as well as big carp.

SHICKLEY

Shickley South Park   **$5**
At 101 N. Market St. near downtown Shickley. $5. All year; 14-day limit. 3 sites. Tbls, toilets, cfga, drkg wtr, elec, coin laundry, playground.

SILVER CREEK (182)

Silver Creek Park   **FREE**
In town with entrances on First St & Vine St, off Hwy 39. From US 30, 1.25 blks on SR 39 (Vine St). Free. May-Oct. Undesignated RV sites; elec installed in 2006 (4 double 15-amp outlets on 2 posts). Tbls, flush toilets, cfga, drkg wtr, playground. Ball fields, horseshoes. Low-cost camping also available at Fisher's Cove private camp S of town. GPS: N41.3150, W97.6621.

SPALDING (184)

Cedar River   **FREE**
State Canoe Trail
Canoe trail with primitive camping sites from Spalding to Fullerton; 53 river miles. Start at Spalding Dam Site campground on the river. First leg to Primrose County bridge on E side & N bank, 14 river mi; no facilities. Then 10.7 river mi to Mel's Landing Municipal Park in Cedar Rapids (see listing for that city). Next, 13 river mi to Belgrade (no facilities), then 17.5 river mi to Powerhouse Park in Fullerton, where park facilities are being built.

City Park   **Donations**
2 blocks S of post office. Donations suggested; camp free. All year; 2-day limit (longer with permission). 14 sites. Drkg wtr, cfga, tbls, elec, flush toilets. Swimming, picnicking, fishing.

Spalding Dam Site   **Donations**
Almost 1 mi S of Spalding on Cedar River. Donations suggested; camp free. All year; 2-day limit (longer with permission). 4 RV sites, 15 tent sites. Hookups, pit toilets, cfga, drkg wtr. Fishing, boating(l), swimming.

SPARKS (185)

A & C Canoe/Camp $3
5 mi S & 2 mi E of Sparks. $3 per person. 5/1-10/15. Tbls, pit toilets, cfga, drkg wtr. Fishing, canoeing(r), swimming.

Grahams' Camp (Private) $5
5 mi S of Sparks. $5 per person (10 yrs & under free). 4/1-11/1. 7 tent sites. Tbls, pit toilets, cfga, drkg wtr, showers. Fishing, swimming.

Rock Barn $3
Canoe Outfitters Camp
W of Springview Hwy 12 & SW. $3 per person for tent sites of dry-camp RVs; no hookups. 5/15-9/15. Tbls, pit toilets, cfga, drkg wtr, showers. Fishing, canoeing(r).

Rocky Ford Campground $5
7 mi S of Valentine & 5 mi E of Sparks. $5 per person. 4/15-9/15. 22 sites. Tbls, flush & pit toilets, cfga, drkg wtr, elec ($8), showers. Fishing, swimming.

Smith Falls State Park $4
3 mi W of Sparks on SR 12; 4 mi S on gravel rd. $4 per person. 4/1-11/30; 14-day limit. 20 tent sites (no RVs). Tbls, toilets, cfga, drkg wtr. State's tallest waterfall nearby on Niobrara River. Hiking, canoeing, fishing, nature programs.

Sparks Store & RV Camp $5
On 102 St in Sparks. $5 base. All year. Base fee for tents; primitive RV sites $10 base without hookups. Pit toilets, drkg wtr, cfga, showers, hookups($), store.

Sunny Brook Camp (Private) $4
5 mi S, 6 mi E of Sparks. $4 per person base for primtive sites; $10 for RVs with elec. All year. 3 tent sites, 20 RV sites, 2 open areas. Elec($), wtr hookup($), tbls, flush toilets, showers, cfga. Fishing, swimming. Horse trails & stables.

SPENCER (186)

City Park $3
Boyd County Fairgrounds
On Logan St (W edge of town). From SR 12, 3 blocks W on Main St, then N on Logan to first fairground entrance. $3 dry camping; $8 with wtr or elec. 4/15-10/1; 8 RV sites plus primitive sites (one 50-amp site). Drkg wtr, flush toilets, cfga, showers. Swimming, picnicking. Groceries.

SPRAGUE (187)

Bluestem Lake $6
State Recreation Area
2.5 mi W of Sprague on NE 33. $6. All year; 14-day limit. 219 primitive sites. Tbls, pit toilets, cfga, drkg wtr, dump, beach. Picnicking, fishing, swimming, hunting, boating(l - 5

mph), archery range. 742 acres.
Fishing tip: The 325-acre lake contains largemouth bass, bluegill, channel catfish, walleye, northern pike and wiper. Daily limit of 3 wiper with only 1 fish over 20 inches.

SPRINGVIEW (188)

Cub Creek Lake FREE
State Fishing Access Lake
8.5 mi W of Springview in Keya Paha County (3 mi N of Jansen). Free primitive camping. Toilets, cfga, no drkg wtr. Boating(ld), fishing, swimming.
Fishing tip: This lake contins bluegills, catfish, largemouth bass, tiger musky, walleye & yellow perch. Electric motors only.

STAPLETON (189)

Stapleton City Park $4
1.5 blks W of Main St on NE 92 or 3rd St in Stapleton (from US 83, W on SR 92/3rd St into town); enter with RV from G St E of park entrance because of trees, then N & W across grass. $4 after 3 free nights (donations suggested). All year. About 4 undesignated sites. Flush toilets, 30-amp elec, drkg wtr, cfga, tbls, playground. Picnicking. GPS: N41degrees 28.841, W100degrees 30.886

STERLING (190)

Sterling Village Park Donations
Corner of Iowa & Lincoln Sts (NE corner of town). Donations suggested; camp free. Open seasonally; 1-day limit. 2 RV sites & tent spaces. Tbls, flush toilets, cfga, elec, drkg wtr, playground, shelter. Tennis courts, sand volleyball, ball field.

STRANG (191)

Strang City Park FREE
On Main St between Sharon & Racine Sts at S end of Strang. Free. Tbls, pit toilets, cfga, drkg wtr, no elec available during 2004 field inspection.

STROMSBURG (193)

Buckley Municipal Park FREE
S edge of Stromsburg on US 81; between confluence of Big Blue River & Prairie Creek; N of city park at camping sign, just S of the RR line. Free for 2 nights; donations accepted. 4/1-10/15; 2-day limit (longer with permission--$8 thereafter); no wtr or restrooms during 10/15-5/1. 12 20/30/50-amp elec sites. Tbls, showers, flush toilets, dump, drkg wtr, firewood, playgrounds. Food, ice, laundry, store nearby. Swimming pool, picnicking, tennis, softball, sports field, sand volleyball, horseshoe complex. Sites on N & W of loop are 30-ft back-ins; 3 sites on E loop handles 45-ft back-ins.

STUART (194)

Stuart Municipal Park $5
1 mi N of Stuart's Main St off US 20. $5. Mar-Nov; 6-day limit. 20 RV sites; no RV size limit. Tbls, flush toilets, cfga, drkg wtr, elec, showers, dump.

SUPERIOR (195)

Lincoln Park FREE
Municipal Campground
From W of town on SR 14, follow camping signs on W. Fourth St. Donations suggested, but camp free. All year; 3-day limit (see city clerk for extension, $5 per day). 20 concrete RV sites. Tbls, flush toilets, cfga, drkg wtr, elec, dump, playground. Horseshoes, sand volleyball. Note: 3-ton bridge weight limit on 4th St from center of town.
Travel tip: Nuckolls County Museum has exhibits about the life of Lady Evelyn Vestey, local person who became one of the richest and most powerful women in the world.

SUTHERLAND (196)

Sutherland Reservoir $6
State Recreation Area
2 mi SW of Sutherland on SR 25. $6. All year; 14-day limit. 85 primitive sites. Pit toilets, cfga, drkg wtr, fish cleaning station, beach. Swimming, fishing, boating(ld). 3,057 acres.
Fishing tip: The state record striped bass, just shy of 65 pounds, was caught from this lake in 1993. it also contains walleye, wiper, white bass and channel catfish. 15-inch minimum for walleye.

Oregon Trail Campground $10
1 mi S of Sutherland off I-80; exit 158. $10 base. 3/15-10/15. 17 sites with hookups; base fee for primitive sites. Tbls, flush toilets, cfga, drkg wtr, hookups($), dump. Fishing, swimming. Private campground.

SYRACUSE (197)

Syracuse South Park $4
Municipal Campground
3rd & Midland Sts on S end of Syracuse. $4 for 40 sites with elec; $8 for 5 sites with full hookups ($30 per week). 5/1-10/15; 14-day limit. Dkg wtr, cfga, tbls, flush & pit toilets, dump, elec. Sand volleyball, horseshoes, playground, ball field, batting cage.

TAYLOR (198)

City RV Tourist Park $4
(Hoops Municipal Park)
From US 281,2 blocks W. on Broadway St (SR91) to 5th St. $4 base with elec; $7 with full hookups. 4/1-11/15. 6 RV sites (no tents). Drkg wtr, elec($).
Fishing tip: Try Horseshoe Bend Lake

12 mi N of Taylor or Gracie Creek Pond on the N side of Calamus Reservoir. Horseshoe Bend, 34 acres, contains channel catfish & largemouth bass. 2-acre Gracie Creek Pond boasts of put-and-take rainbow trout fishing.

TECUMSEH (199)

Wirth Brothers Lake   **$5**
Nemaha Natural Resources District
5 mi N & 1 mi W of Tecumseh. $5 for 2-day permit; $12 annual permit. All year; 14-day limit. 5 open tent sites. Pit toilets, cfga, drkg wtr, tbls. Boating(l), fishing, swimming.
  Fishing tip: From this lake, catch catfish on works and try for the lake's good size largemouth bass. Fish removed from the lake in 2000 & restocked in 2001, beginning with large bass & large bluegill.

TEKAMAH (200)

Pelican Point   **$8**
State Recreation Area
4 mi E of Tekamah, 4 mi N, 1 mi E on co rds. $8. All year; 14-day limit. 17 non-elec sites on 36 acres. Pit toilets, cfga, tbls, drkg wtr. Fishing, picnicking, boating(ld). Missouri River boat access.

Summit Lake   **$6**
State Recreation Area
1 mi S of Tekamah, 3 mi W. $6 at 32 undesignated primitive sites; $8 at 26 designated non-elec sites. All year; 14-day limit. 535 acres. Tbls, pit toilets, cfga, drkg wtr, beach, fish cleaning station. Fishing, boating(dl), picnicking, swimming. 190-acre lake.
  Fishing tip: While camped here, fish for crappie, walleye, wipers, northern pike, largemouth bass or channel catfish.

Tekamah Memorial Park   **$5**
1 block N of S St. in Tekamah. $5. All year. Tbls, toilets, cfga, drkg wtr, elec, sewer, dump. Swimming.

THEDFORD

Thedford City Park   **FREE**
From US 83 & SR 2, W through Thedford to city park sign on W side of town, S side of SR 2. Free, but donations requested. All year. About 4 back-in RV sites with 30-amp elec/wtr. No dump, no restrooms. GPS: N41degrees 58.642, W100degrees 34.942.

TILDEN (201)

Tilden Sunrise Park   **$6**
From US 275 in Tilden, S on Elm St, then E on 2nd St between Walnut & East St. $6. 4/1-11/1; 14-day limit in 30-day period. 3 short back-in RV sites, one for big rigs. Flush toilets, wtr hookups, cfga, dump (hard to use). Fishing. Sign in at city clerk office. Park is maintained by Girl Scouts. Formerly called East City Park.

TOBIAS (202)

Swan Lake Recreation Area   **FREE**
Lower Big Blue Natural Resources District
4 mi E of Tobias and 6 mi N. Free. All year; 14-day limit. Open primitive camping on 195-acre reserve at 95-acre lake. Tbls, toilets, cfga, drkg wtr, shelter. Boating(l), fishing, hiking, hunting. GPS: N40degrees 30.596, W97degrees 15.2595.

TRENTON (203)

Little Nemaha   **FREE**
State Wayside Area
Near NE 34 in Trenton. Free. All year; 14-day limit. Undesignated sites. Tbls, toilets, cfga, drkg wtr. Picnicking; fishing; swimming; boating. Entry permit required.

Swanson Lake   **$6**
State Recreation Area
2 mi W of Trenton on US 34. $6 at 150 primitive sites in open camping areas; $11 at designated non-elec sites; $15 at 54 sites with 20/30-amp elec ($10 during 9/16-5/14 but no wtr services. All year; 14-day limit. Tbls, flush toilets, cfga, drkg wtr, dump, playground, fish cleaning stations. Boating(lrd), fishing, picnicking, swimming. On Swanson Lake at the Republican River; 6,131 acres.
  Fishing tip: Swanson is regarded as one of the best fishing lakes in Nebraska, containing trophy-size northern pike and huge schools of white bass in addition to largemouth & smallmouth bass, walleye and crappie.

ULYSSES (204)

Oxbow Trail Reservoir   **FREE**
Upper Big Blue Natural Resources Dist.
1.5 mi E of Ulysses; entry from S along Spur 12C & from E along CR L. Free. All year; 14-day limit. Primitive camping at S end & NE section of recreation area. Tbls, toilets, cfga, drkg wtr. Hiking, fishing, boating(l).

UTICA (205)

Smith Creek   **FREE**
Recreation Area
Upper Big Blue Natural Resources Dist.
1.2 mi S & 1 mi E of the Utica interchange off I-80. Free. All year; 14-day limit. Primitive camping near 22-acre lake. Tbls, toilets, cfga, drkg wtr. Hiking, fishing (catfish, largemouth bass, bluegill).

VALENTINE (206)

Ballards Marsh   **FREE**
State Wildlife Management Area
20 mi S on SR 83. Free. All year. 10 sites; 939 acres. Primitive camping. Pit toilets, tbls, cfga. Picnicking, hiking. GPS: N2degrees 35.693, W100degrees 32.359.

Big Alkali Lake   **FREE**
State Wildlife Area
12 mi S on US 83, 3 mi W on SR 483. Free. All year; 14-day limit. 10 sites; 880 acres. Primitive camping. Pit toilets, tbls, cfga. Swimming, boating(l), fishing. Primarily a fishing camp.
  Fishing tip: From this 842-acre lake, you can catch largemouth bass, northern pike, crappie, channel catfish, yellow perch and bluegill.

Berry Bridge Campground   **$5**
13 mi E of Valentine. $5 base. 5/15-9/15. 12 sites. Tbls, flush toilets, cfga, drkg wtr, showers, elec($).

Dryland Aquatics   **$3**
18 mi NE of Valentine on Hwy 12. $3 per person. May-Oct. Overnight camping at canoe & kayak outfitter. Tbls, flush toilets, cfga, drkg wtr, showers, playground, elec.

Merritt Reservoir   **$6**
State Recreation Area
25 mi SW of Valentine on paved rd. $6 at 190 undesignated primitive sites; $12 at 28 sites with elec. All year; 14-day limit. 9,000 acres. Tbls, flush toilets, cfga, drkg wtr, shelters, dump, showers, 2 fish cleaning stations. Picnicking; hunting; fishing; boating(rld); hiking; swimming. Wildlife refuges. Wildlife refuges nearby; heart of sandhills.
  Fishing tip: This 2,900-acre lake has 44 miles of shoreline and produces some of the state's best walleye and white bass angling. The state record smallmouth bass, 6 pounds 1.5 ounces, was caught here in 1978, and the state record channel catfish, 41 pounds, was landed in 1985.

Valentine City Park   **$5**
1 mi N of Valentine on NE 20; follow Main St N toward the pine-covered hills and down into the valley. $5. All year; 5-day limit. About 32 undesignated sites; no RV size limit. Tbls, flush toilets (in-season), cfga, showers (in-season), wtr, sewer, playground, free dump at baseball field (N on Green St from fairgrounds, E on Bias St). Picnicking, fishing, horseshoes. A natural park on the banks of Minnechaduza Creek. (Note: A reader said no showers provided during visit. Nice wooded park with stream.) Park escaped wildfire in 2006. N42 53.168, W100 32.795.

VALPARAISO (207)

Red Cedar Lake   **FREE**
Recreational Use Area
Lower Platte South
Natural Resources District
6 mi N & 2 mi W of Valparaiso. Free. All year; 14-day limit. Primitive open camping on 175-acre reserve at 51-acre lake. Portable toilets Apr-Oct, cfga, no drkg wtr. Boating(l), fishing.
  Fishing tip: The lake is stocked with largemouth bass, flathead catfish, saugeye, channel catfish and bluegill. Electric motors only.

VENICE (208)

Two Rivers $6
State Recreation Area
1 mi S & 1 mi W of Venice on SR 92. $6 at 10 primitive sites; $11 at 152 designated sites without elec; $15 at sites with 20/30-amp elec; $17 with elec/wtr hookups. MD-LD; 14-day limit. 5 camping areas. Tbls, flush toilets, showers, cfga, drkg wtr, dump, shelters, 2 fish cleaning stations, beach. Swimming, boating, biking(r), fishing, hiking trail.
   Fishing tip: Catch tiger musky from lakes 1-4; trout from lake #5; largemouth bass and crappie from five lakes; carp & bullhead from Carp Lake.

VERDIGRE (209)

Wildwood Acres Municipal Park $11
From jct of Hwys 14 & 84, W on SR 84, then S into park at camping sign. $11 (tents, $9). 4/1-11/30. 27 sites (many short, back-in). Tbls, flush toilets, cfga, drkg wtr, 30-amp & 15/20-amp elec, dump, showers, pool. Swimming, tennis, basketball, sand volleyball, playground. Field check could not find dump station.

VERDON (210)

Verdon Lake $6
State Recreation Area
Half mi W of Verdon on US 73. $6. All year; 14-day limit. 20 primitive sites; 75 acres. Tbls, pit toilets, cfga, drkg wtr, playground. Picnicking; fishing; hiking; boating (nonpower or elec mtrs), swimming nearby.

VIRGINIA (211)

Wolf-Wildcat FREE
Wildlife Management Area
Lower Big Blue Natural Resources District
6 mi S of Virginia. Free. All year; 14-day limit. Open primitive camping on 160-acre reserve at 42-acre lake. No facilities, no drkg wtr. Fishing, hiking, hunting.

WAUNETA (213)

Wauneta RV Park $5
At Wauneta. $5. All year. 32 RV sites. Tbls, toilets, cfga, drkg wtr, elec, sewer.

WAUSA (214)

Gladstone City Park Donations
At 203 E. Clark, Wausa. Camp free; donation encouraged. 4/15-10/1. 5 RV sites. Tbls, flush toilets, cfga, drkg wtr, dump, elec. Swimming.

WAYNE (215)

Henry Victor $7
Municipal Park
From jct of SR 15 & 35, 1 mi S on SR 15. $7. 3/1-10/31; 5-day limit (longer on request). 12 RV sites with tbls, flush toilets, cfga, drkg wtr, elec, dump, playground.

Lions Camper Park $8
1.5 mi E of Wayne on SR 35 at airport. $8. All year. 6 sites; 4 acres. Dump, tbls, cfga, drkg wtr, phone, no toilets.

WELLFLEET (216)

Wellfleet Lake FREE
Lincoln County Park
Half mi SW of Wellfleet. Free. All year. Primitive camping at 50-acre lake. Toilets, tbls, cfga. Fishing, boating(l); no motors.
   Fishing tip: The lake contains largemouth bass, crappie, channel & flathead catfish.

WEST POINT (217)

Elkhorn River FREE
State Canoe Trail
Half mi W of town on SR 32 to river (boat access only). Free. 4/1-10/31; 14-day limit. Undesignated tent sites. Tbls, toilets, cfga. Fishing. This canoe trail runs 99 river miles, from Norfolk to the Elkhorn Crossing State Recreation Area. Begin S of Norfolk on the E of US 81 at the SE corner of Ta-Ha-Zouka Park. The first leg is 16 river mi to Stanton. Next, 9 river mi to Red Fox Wildlife Management Area near the Pilger bridge; located on the E side of SR 15 on the N side of the river, it has parking & primitive camping. Then float 8 river mi to Wisner River Park, which has good access, camping and toilets. From Wisner to West Point is 16 river mi, where camping and restrooms are available at Riverside Park. Then it's 9 river mi to US 275 bridge, about 500 yards N of Powderhorn WMA with its primitive camping. (Dead Timber State Recreation Area's camping area is a 3-mi drive from the WMA parking lot.) From US 275 bridge to the Scribner is 6 river mi; access on SW side of bridge. Next, 8 river mi to Hooper, then 7 mi to Winslow Hwy 81 bridge; 6 mi to Nickerson; 10 mi to Arlington, and 11 mi to Elkhorn Crossing and its camping. If desired, the float can be continued 32 mi to Schramm SRA or 5 mi farther to Louisville SRA.

Neligh City Park $10
3 blocks W of West Point on Hwy 275; at 400 W. Bridge St. $10. 4/1-10/1. 7 RV sites with elec/wtr; unlimited tent spaces. Tbls, flush toilets, cfga, drkg wtr, dump ($2), elec, showers during pool hours($). Picnicking, fishing, swimming.

WESTERN (218)

Village Park FREE
Half block E of Main St on Sumner St. in Western. Camp free, but donations sug-gested. All year; 7-day limit. 2 sites with elec; 4 sites no elec. Tbls, flush toilets, cfga, drkg wtr, dump, showers, store.

WINNEBAGO (219)

Winnebago Park FREE
Sioux Tribal Agency
7 mi E of Winnebago. Free. All year. 6 sites. Tbls, toilets, cfga, no drkg wtr. Eight free sites with toilets & water also are available at Big Elk Park, 28 mi S of Sioux City in Nebraska; 32 RV hookups there for a fee.

WINSLOW (221)

Winslow Village Park FREE
SE corner of Winslow on Hwy 77. Free. All year. 1 site. Hookups, toilet, cfga.

WISNER (222)

River Park Municipal Park $10
S on corner of First National and Citizens Bank; cross railroad tracks; S one blk; in Wisner (3 blocks S of Avenue E & 10th St); at Elkhorn River. $10. Undesignated RV spaces & 5 RV sites (with elect on site pad); unlimited tent camping. All year. Tbls, flush & toilets, cfga, drkg wtr, dump, elec, pool, 3 playgrounds. Picnicking, boating(l), fishing, basketball, sand volleyball, horseshoes, tennis, swimming.

WOOD LAKE (224)

Wood Lake City Park Donations
3 blks N of NE 20 on Main St, 1 blk E in Wood Lake. Free, but donations requested (no donations box, though). 5/1-9/30; 2-day limit at hookup sites. 2 sites with wtr/elec hookups. No parking inside park except next to 2 wtr/elec hookups. Toilets, pit tbls, cfga, drkg wtr. Not recommended; inconvenient elec, foul toilets during 2004 field trip.
   Fishing tip: For good trout fishing, try the nearby Fairfield Creek. You'll need to hike a fair distance for the best fishing, though. The creek is stocked regularly with brown & rainbow trout.

WOOD RIVER (225)

Cheyenne $6
State Recreation Area
At I-80 Wood River Interchange. $6. All year. 14-day limit. 15 primitive sites; 32 acres with 15-acre pond. Tbls, cfga, flush toilets, drkg wtr. Modern restrooms. Boating (no mtrs), fishing.

WYMORE (226)

Arbor State $7
Municipal Park
9th & M Sts. $7 base. All year; 14-day limit. 20 sites. Tbls, flush toilets, cfga, elec/wtr($) hookups, dump, showers. Swimming, picnicking.

NEBRASKA

Big Indian Recreation Area
FREE
Lower Big Blue Natural Resources Dist.
6 mi S of Wymore on US 77; 2 mi W on Hwy 8. Free. All year. 50 sites. Tbls, toilets, cfga, drkg wtr. Fishing, swimming, boating(ld), playground. 233 acres.

Fishing tip: Try for largemouth bass & channel catfish at the 77-acre Big Indian Lake.

YORK (228)

Bruce L. Anderson **FREE**
Recreation Area (Recharge Lake)
Upper Big Blue Natural Resources Dist.
1.7 mi W of York on 4th St. Free. All year; 14-day limit. Primitive camping near 50-acre lake. Tbls, toilets, cfga, playground, visitor's center, drkg wtr, shelter. Fishing, boating(l), hiking trails.

Fishing tip: Recharge Lake is stocked with bass, bluegill and catfish.

Overland Trail **FREE**
Recreation Area
Upper Big Blue Natural Resources Dist.
2 mi E & 1.5 mi S of York. Free. All year; 14-day limit. Primitive camping in designated areas; no facilities, no drkg wtr. 14.5-acre lake. Hiking, boating(l), fishing.

Y Motel & RV Park **$12**
5.5 mi N of York on Hwy 81, exit 353. $12. All year. 4 RV sites. Hookups($), dump, drkg wtr.

NEVADA

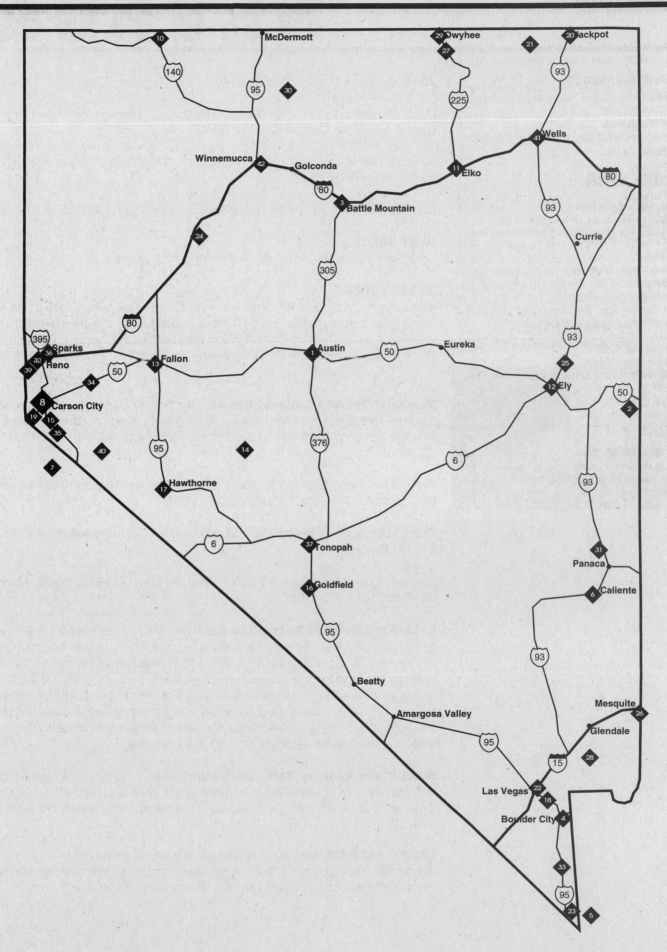

NEVADA

MISCELLANEOUS
Capital:
Carson City
Nickname:
Sagebrush State, Battle Born State,
Silver State
Motto:
All For Our Country
Flower:
Sagebrush
Tree:
Single-Leaf Pinon
Bird:
Mountain Bluebird
Song:
"Home Means Nevada"

Internet Address:
www.travelnevada.com

Toll-free information: 800/NEVADA-8.

Dept of Conservation and Natural Resources, Division of State Parks, Capitol Complex, Carson City, NV 89710. 702-885-4384.

Nevada Commission on Tourism, 401 N. Carson St., Carson City, NV 89701. 800-NEVADA-8.

Dept of Wildlife, 1100 Valley Rd., Reno, NV 89512. 775-688-1500.

REST AREAS
Overnight stops are permitted unless otherwise posted.

STATE PARKS
Annual permits are $50 at most state parks with daily entry fees of $4-6. Base daily camping fees are $10-14 at most parks. Maximum length of stay is 14 days. Dept of Conservation and Natural Resources, Division of State Parks, 901 S. Stewart St., Carson City, NV 89701. 775-684-2777.

Humboldt-Toiyabe National Forest. This combined forest is the largest national forest area outside Alaska. Sections of it are scattered through Nevada and into California. 1200 Franklin Way, Sparks, NV 89431. 775-331-6444.

Refuge Manager, Sheldon National Wildlife Refuge, Sheldon-Hart Mountain Complex, Box 111, Lakeview, OR 97630.

Refuge Manager, Stillwater National Wildlife Refuge, 1000 Auction Rd, Fallon, NV 89406.

Bureau of Land Management, 1340 Financial Blvd, PO Box 12000, Reno, NV 89520. 775-861-6400

Lake Mead National Recreation Area. Vehicle passes are $5 for 5 days or $20 annually. User fees also are assessed against motorized boats entering the park: $10 per boat for 1-5 days; $20 annual pass. Campgrounds are open all year and feature restrooms, water, dump stations, grills, tables and shade. Fees are $12 per site ($6 with federal Senior Pass). Primitive camping, accessible by boat, foot or horseback, is permitted anywhere along the shore outside of developed areas or where otherwise prohibited by signs, limited to 30 days at each site and 90 days per year.

Great Basin National Park. Campsites are $12. Primitive campgrounds are free. An RV dump station is open just inside the park from May to October. Dump fee is $5. 100 reat Basin National Park, Baker, NV 89311. 775-234-7331.

CASINO PARKING. Several of Nevada's gaming towns have casinos which permit free overnight parking. In Laughlin, for example, free overnight parking is permitted at 10 casino lots. No facilities are available.

AUSTIN (1)

Big Creek Campground   **FREE**
Toiyabe National Forest
About 1.5 mi W of Austin, then 11 mi S on Big Creek Rd; FR 002). Free. May-Oct; 14-day limit. 6 sites along the creek; 25-ft RV limit. Fee for group camping. Tbls, toilets, cfga, no drkg wtr. OHV activities, hiking, fishing.
    Fishing tip: This creek is a good place to catch nice size rainbow and native brown trout.

Columbine Campground   **FREE**
Toiyabe National Forest
11 mi SW of Austin; 45 mi on SR 21 to Reese River Guard Station; E on FR 119. Free. May-Oct; 14-day limit. 5 sites. Tbls, toilets, cfga, no drkg wtr. Hiking, horseback riding, fishing, biking.

Hickison Petroglyph   **FREE**
Recreation Area
Bureau of Land Management
24 mi E of Austin on US 50, then gravel access rd, in Central Nevada. Free. All year; 14-day limit. 16 primitive sites (RVs under 55 ft). Tbls, toilets, cfga, picnic shelters, no drkg wtr. Hunting, hiking, picnicking. Elev 6500 ft; 40 acres. Most sites are level pull-through spaces. No fishing. Petroglyphs in the area.
    Travel tip: Austin was silver boom town in 1860s; remains include public buildings, mine dumps, Stokes Castle on hill to SW, 3 frontier churches. At one time, 5,000 prospectors worked town's silver mines.

Kingston   **FREE**
Toiyabe National Forest
12 mi E of Austin on US 50; 14 mi S on Hwy 376; 6 mi NW on FR 20012 (improved gravel rds). Free. 5/15-10/15; 14-day limit. 11 sites (RVs under 22 ft). Tbls, toilets, cfga, no drkg wtr. Mountain climbing; picnicking; fishing (trout); hunting; horseback riding (1 mi); swimming and nonpower boating (2 mi). Elev 7000 ft; 12 acres. Stream. Adjacent to fish and game reservoirs. No off-season camping.

San Juan Campground   **FREE**
Toiyabe National Forest
31 mi S of Austin via SR 722, CR 21 & FR 016. Free. May-Oct; 14-day limit. 19 primitive sites. Tbls, toilets, cfga, no drkg wtr. Fishing, hiking, hunting.

Toquima Caves Campgr   **FREE**
Toiyabe National Forest
W of Austin on US 50 abou;40 mi; about 26 mi S on SR 82, the follow FR 100 to camp. Free. May-Oct; 14-day limit. Tbls, 1 toilet, cfga, no drkg wtr. Explore caves with petroglyphs.

BAKER (2)

Baker Creek   **$12**
Great Basin National Park
5 mi W of Baker on SR 488; 3 mi S on Baker Creek Rd. $12. 5/15-10/30; 14-day limit. 34 sites (16-ft RV limit). Tbls, flush toilets, cfga, drkg wtr. Fishing, hiking trails. Elev 8000 ft; 30 acres.

Lower & Upper Lehman Creek   **$12**
Great Basin National Park
5 mi W of Baker on SR 488, following signs. $12. All year; 14-day limit. 33 total sites (30-ft RV limit). Tbls, toilets, cfga, drkg wtr. Hiking, picnicking. Elev 7300 ft.

Shoshone Area   **FREE**
Primitive Area
Great Basin National Park
Within the park, at end of Snake Creek Rd. Free. May-Oct; 14-day limit. 3 primitive sites. Tbls, toilets, cfga, no drkg wtr. Fishing, hiking.

Snake Creek   **FREE**
Primitive Area
Great Basin National Park
Within the park, along Snake Creek Rd. Free. May-Oct; 14-day limit. 19 primtive sites along the rd. Tbls, toilets, cfga, no drkg wtr. Fishing, hiking.

Strawberry Creek   **FREE**
Primitive Area
Great Basin National Park
Within the park, along Strawberry Creek Rd. Free. May-Oct; 14-day limit. Primitive sites along the road. Tbls, toilets, cfga, no drkg wtr. Fishing, hiking.

Wheeler Peak   **$12**
Great Basin National Park
5 mi W of Baker on SR 488; 12 mi W on FR 10446. $12. 6/1-9/30; 14-day limit. 37 sites (RVs under 17 ft). Tbls, toilets, cfga, drkg wtr. Hiking trails, nature programs. Elev 9900 ft. 22 acres.

BATTLE MOUNTAIN (3)

Mill Creek Recreation Area   **FREE**
Bureau of Land Management
24 mi S of Battle Mountain on US 305; 4 mi on gravel rd. Free. All year; 14-day limit. 11 RV/tent sites; suitable for RVs under 30 ft. Tbls, toilets, cfga, no drkg wtr. Fishing, hiking (half-mi interpretive trail). Site developed by CCC in 1930s.
    Fishing tip: Mill Creek offers good action for German brown, rainbow and brook trout.

BOULDER CITY (4)

Boulder Beach   **$12**
Lake Mead National Recreation Area
6 mi NE of Boulder City on SR 166. $12. All year; 30-day limit. 154 sites. Flush toilets, cfga, drkg wtr, coin laundry, dump. Fish-ing, boating(ldr), waterskiing. 33 acres. Elev 1200 ft.

BULLHEAD CITY (AZ.) (5)

Telephone Cove   **FREE**
Lake Mead National Recreation Area
1 mi N on SR 68 from jct with SR 95 to Katherine Road turnoff; 3 mi W to ranger station. Inquire at ranger station for further instructions. Free. 7-day limit; closed 10/15-3/15. Toilets, cfga, no other facilities. Fishing, boating, swimming. Desert scenery. Elev 500 ft.
    Fishing tip: Make sure to try Lake Mead's striped bass fishing; it's famous. Also good largemouth bass fishing, but stripers better. Try rocky ledges & points, dropoffs and brushy coves for largemouth. Stripers can reach 40 pounds; best time March-Nov, using topwater lures or large jigs 20-50 feet deep; drift frozen anchovies along bottom.

CALIENTE (6)

Beaver Dam State Park   **$10**
6 mi N on US 28; 32 mi on gravel co rd. Elev 5500 ft. $10 (combined entrance, boating & camping, $12). All year; 14-day limit. 33 sites at 3 campgrounds; 20-ft RV limit. 2,032 acres. Tbls, pit & chemical toilets, cfga, drkg wtr (May-Oct). Swimming, fishing, boating (no motors), hiking trails, nature study. RVs over 20 ft not recommended because of road switchbacks. Elev 5000 ft.
    Fishing tip: Fishing is not very good at the park's Schroder Reservoir; it is stocked only once a year -- by helicopter -- with five-inch rainbow trout. Fishing is better in the stream below the dam for small, but naturally populating rainbow. At presstime, the lake was empty due to flood damage of the dam in 2005.

Kershaw-Ryan State Park   **$10**
2 mi S of Caliente on US 93 & SR 317. $10. Campground was redeveloped after being wiped out in a flash flood several years ago; at presstime, it was not yet open for camping. Current facilities include hiking trails, a picnic area, visitor center, restrooms, drkg wtr.

CAMP RICHARDSON, (CA.) (7)

Bayview   **$10**
Lake Tahoe Basin Management
5.3 mi NW on Hwy 89. $10. 6/1-10/15; 1-day limit. 13 sites (22-ft RV limit); 4 acres. Toilets, cfga, tbls, no wtr. Dump 5 mi. Hiking trails. Elev 6800 ft.
    Travel tip: Visit the Lake Tahoe Forest Service Visitor Center, 3 mi N of South Lake Tahoe on Hwy 89; watch trout & kokanee salmon in Taylor Creek through underground viewing chamber.
    Fishing tip: Beautiful Lake Tahoe has excellent fishing for lake trout, rainbow trout & kokanee salmon.

✪ CARSON CITY (8)

Indian Creek   **$10**
Bureau of Land Management
From Carson City, W on US 395 to Hwy 88; right on Hwy 88 across state line into California; at Woodfords, S on Hwy 89 toward Markleeville; follow signs. $10 with federal Senior Pass at RV sites; others pay $20. Walk-tent sites, $14 ($7 with Senior Pass). 5/5-10/9; 14-day limit. 19 RV sites; 30-ft RV limit. Tbls, flush toilets, cfga, drkg wtr, showers, dump. Boating(l), fishing.

DENIO (10)

Big Spring Reservoir   **FREE**
Sheldon National Wildlife Refuge
In the refuge W of Denio off Hwy 140. Free. All year. 12 sites. Toilets, tbls, cfga, no drkg drkg wtr, showers, no trash service. Fishing, hiking, boating. Popular fishing spot.
Fishing tip: Cutthroat & rainbow trout in recent years average 16-20 inches. Anglers should keep their limits because winter kills are likely. Most fishermen use pontoon boats & float tubes.

Onion Valley Reservoir   **FREE**
Bureau of Land Management
9 mi W of Denio on US 140; S 8 mi from Knott Creek turnoff. Free. 6/1-10/30; 14-day limit. 6 primitive sites (RVs not recommended). Tbls, toilets, cfga, no drkg wtr. Hunting, boating, canoeing, fishing, sailboating. Jeep & hiking trails lead to Blue Lake & Little Onion Lake.
Fishing tip: Try for rainbow & brook trout in the reservoir; season from second Sat in June to about 11/15, with 5-trout limit. The trout average 14-15 inches. Nearby Knott Creek Reservoir was restocked with catchable rainbow in 2000 following a winter kill, and a year later they were up to 19 inches.

Sheldon Antelope Refuge   **FREE**
National Wildlife Refuge
27 mi W of Denio on NV 140; 3 mi on gravel rd (Denio is on the Nevada-Oregon border, 87 mi N and slightly W of Winnemucca, NV). Free. Season for all the camps, except Virgin Valley, depends on weather conditions and road conditions. From May-Oct, most roads are usually accessible. Virgin Valley Camp is available all year. 14-day limit. 15 designated campgrounds. All camps, except Virgin Valley Camp, are primitive (RVs under 25 ft). There are no facilities. Natural spring wtr at most campgrounds, restroom facilities and wtr at Virgin Valley Camp. Hunting (all wildlife is protected except those species authorized to be taken during special hunting seasons); rockhounding (max 7 lbs of rock specimens per person; digging and blasting prohibited). Camping is restricted to 18 designated campgrounds shown on a map that can be obtained from Sheldon Antelope Refuge, PO Box 111, Lakeview, OR 97630; or from Refuge Headquarters. Campfires are permitted during times of low fire hazard. Inquire at refuge sub-headquarters for current regulations. Migratory bird hunting is prohibited.

Virgin Valley   **FREE**
Sheldon National Wildlife Refuge
In the refuge W of Denio off SR 140. Free. All year; 14-day limit. 12 sites. Tbls, toilets, cfga, no drkg wtr, no trash service, spring-fed showers, hot springs (pooling at 90 degrees). Hiking, tour opal mines, fishing. Favorable report from 2005 field trip.

ELKO (11)

Jack's Creek   **FREE**
Humboldt National Forest
27 mi N of Elko on NV 225; 33 mi NW on NV 226; 1.4 mi NE on FR 473. Elev 6500 ft. MD-10/15; 16-day limit. 6 sites on 4 acres (RVs under 22 ft). Tbls, toilets, cfga, firewood, drkg wtr. Hunting; picnicking; fishing.
Travel tip: Visit nearby Tuscarora, a former mining camp from 1860s; scenic.

North Wildhorse Reservoir   **$6**
Recreation Site
Bureau of Land Management
68 mi N of Elko on SR 225. $5 during 5/15-11/15; free rest of year but no wtr; 14-day limit. 18 sites (RVs under 25 ft). Tbls, toilets, cfga, drkg wtr, dump. Fishing, boating(ld), swimming, horseback riding. Elev 6500 ft; 40 acres. Ice fishing in winter.

South Fork Canyon   **FREE**
Recreation Area
Bureau of Land Management
5 mi S of Elko on SR 227; 5 mi S on SR 228; W to recreation area. Free. All year; 14-day limit. Primitive camping in canyon; no facilities, no drkg wtr. Popular rafting area.
Fishing tip: South Fork Reservoir is the state's newest lake. It produces rainbow & brown trout of 12-18 inches, with occasional 20-inchers hooked. Summer is good for both smallmouth & largemouth bass, and several channel catfish over 20 pounds were caught in 2001.

South Fork of Owyhee River   **FREE**
Bureau of Land Management
110 mi NW of Elko via SR 225 & 226 to river. Free. 4/1-6/15; 14-day limit. Undesignated primitive sites. No facilities. Kayaking, rafting, hiking, climbing. Check in at Petan Ranch for permission to launch.

South Fork   **$10**
State Recreation Area
8 mi S of Elko on SR 227; 5.5 mi S on SR 228; 3.5 mi S on Lower Fork Rd. $10 (combined entry, camping & boating, $13). 5/1-11/15; 14-day limit. 25 sites; 40-ft RV limit. Tbls, cfga, flush toilets, drkg wtr, dump. Swimming, fishing, boating(l), hunting, waterskiing, hiking. Open camping also available along the W shore.

Wild Horse   **$10**
State Recreation Area
65 mi N of Elko on SR 225. $10 (combined entry, boating & camping, $12). All year; 14-day limit. 33 sites on 120 acres (RVs under 40 ft); on NE shore of Wild Horse Reservoir. Tbls, flush toilets, cfga, drkg wtr, showers, dump. Swimming, boating, fishing, ice fishing, snowmobile trails, nature trails.
Fishing tip: Wild Horse Lake typically produces rainbow trout of 13-17 inches, and some browns also are caught. From June to mid-July and again in September, us worms, corn and powerbaits. After July 1, one bass of at least 15 inches can be kept; use plastic worms and crankbaits. Yellow perch were introduced illegally, and there is no limit to the 9-10 inch fish; use crappie jigs with worms.

Wilson Reservoir   **$4**
Bureau of Land Management
27 mi N of Elko on SR 225; 40 mi W on Hwy 226; at Wilson Reservoir. $4. All year; 14-day limit. 15 sites. Tbls, toilets, cfga, drkg wtr, dump, fishing dock. boating(l - $2) fishing, hiking.
Fishing tip: Stocked rainbow are 12-16 inches, and Wilson also produces excellent natural largemouth bass. Shore fish for trout with worms and powerbait, but action is better using boats or tubes. Bass fishing best from June through August.

Zunino/Jiggs Reservoir   **$2**
Bureau of Land Management
7 mi E of Elko on SR 227; 23 mi S on SR 228. $2 use fee. Open dispersed camping on N & S shores plus 9 sites (30-ft RV limit). All year; 14-day limit. Tbls, toilets (in day-use area), cfga, no drkg wtr. Fishing, picnicking, boating, windsurfing, ice fishing Dec-Feb. Elev 5600 ft.
Fishing tip: This lake has good all-year fishing for rainbow & brown trout and largemouth bass.

ELY (12)

Cherry Creek   **FREE**
Humboldt National Forest
24 mi S of Ely on US 6; 46 mi Son SR 318 to Sunnyside, then 44 mi W on improved gravel & dirt rd; NW on FR 410. Free. Apr-Oct; 14-day limit. 4 undesignated dispersed sites. Toilet, cfga, no drkg wtr. Hiking, fishing, biking.

Cleve Creek   **FREE**
Bureau of Land Management
30 mi SE on US 50; 12 mi N on NV 893; 4 mi W on FR 1043. Elev 6400 ft. 5/16-9/30; 14-day limit. 12 sites; 24-ft RV limit; also dispersed camping along the creek; 20 acres. Tbls, toilets, cfga, firewood, no drkg wtr. Picnicking; fishing; hiking.
Fishing tip: Cleve Creek contains rainbow & brown trout.

Currant Creek   **FREE**
Humboldt National Forest
45 mi SW of Ely on US 6. Free. Elev 6200 ft. 5/16-9/15. 14-day limit. 7 sites (RVs under 16 ft). Tbls, toilets, cfga, firewood, no drkg wtr. Fishing, picnicking, OHV activity, horseback riding, hiking, biking, hunting.

Garnet Hill   **FREE**
Bureau of Land Management
6.4 mi W of Ely on US 50; 1.7 mi E on graded rd; from right fork, 1.4 mi S & W; near Garnet Hill. Free. All year; 14-day limit. 2 primitive areas for tents, small RVs, primarily for rockhounds. Tbls, toilet, cfga, no drkg wtr. Hiking, biking. Find dark red garnets nearby. View open-pit copper mine. Elev 7280 ft.

Goshute Creek   **FREE**
Bureau of Land Management
45 mi N of Ely on US 93 to MP 98.56; 6.9 mi W on Hwy 489; 11 mi N on county rd to sign, then W 1.5 mi (high-clearance vehicles recommended). Free. All yar; 14-day limit. About 20 primitive sites (20-ft RV limit) in 3 areas. Tbls, toilets, cfga, no drkg wtr. Hunting, fishing, hiking, mountain climbing, caving. Bristlecone pine forests, limestone formations. Elev 6230 ft.

Illiapah Reservoir   **FREE**
Recreation Area
Bureau of Land Management
37 mi W of Ely on Hwy 50; 1 mi SE on dirt rd. Free. All year; 14-day limit. 14 primitive sites; no RV size limit. Tbls, toilets, cfga, no drkg wtr. Picnicking, fishing, boating(l).
   Fishing tip: Illiapah Reservoir is stocked with rainbow trout, and plenty of holdover fish of up to 18 inches can be caught, although most average 12-14 inches. Occasional trophy-size brown also are landed. Troll deep water or cast nightcrawlers or powerbaits from shore. In spring, use flies matching nymph patterns.
   Travel tip: Ely is home of the Nevada Northern Railway Museum, which displays large collection of historic rolling stock, including heavy-duty locomotives that hauled copper to the smelter; rides on some summer weekends.

Meadow Valley Camp   **FREE**
Bureau of Land Management
26 mi SE of Ely on US 6/50; 18 mi S on US 93; 17 mi E on SR 322; 1 mi W on paved rd; at S end of Mt. Wilson volcanic calders. Free. All year; 14-day limit. 6 primitive sites (RVs not recommended). Toilet, cfga, no drkg wtr. Fishing, hiking, hunting. Usually gets overflow campers from nearby Spring Valley SP. Elev 5470 ft.
   Fishing tip: Try rainbow trout from nearby Meadow Valley Wash.

Ward Mountain   **$8**
Humboldt National Forest
7 mi SW of Ely on US 6; half mi S on FR 10439. $8. 5/21-9/30; 16-day limit. 17 sites (RVs under 17 ft). Tbls, toilets, cfga, drkg wtr. Hiking, horseback riding, hunting, biking, volleyball, baseball, swing set. Elev 7400 ft; 6 acres.

White River   **$4**
Recreation Area
Humboldt National Forest
37 mi SW of Ely on US 6; 8 Mi W on FR 1163. $4. Elev 7000 ft. 6/1-10/31; 16-day limit. 10 sites on 8 acres. Tbls, toilets, cfga, firewood, no drkg wtr. Hunting; picnicking; fishing; biking.

FALLON (13)

Churchill Beach   **$10**
Lahontan State Recreation Area
18 mi W of Fallon on US 50; on Carson River. $10 (combined camping, boating & entry $15). All year; 14-day limit. 11 developed sites but unlimited camping space on beach (RVs under 31 ft). Tbls, flush toilets, cfga, drkg wtr, dump. Limited facilities in winter. Swimming, fishing, boating(dl), hunting. Elev 4100 ft; 30,000 acres. Bureau of Reclamation project. Ft Churchill (1860) 10 mi W.
   Fishing tip: Walley, white bass and wiper fishing is excellent at Lahontan Reservoir. Action peaks about Memorial Day and remains strong through June. For sport, try the lake's huge carp. The lake has 69 mi of shoreline.

Sand Mountain   **$40**
Recreation Area
Bureau of Land Management
25 mi E of Fallon on US 50; at Sand Springs Pony Express Station and desert study area; camp at base of mountain in open desert (follow signs). 4x4 recommended (Sand Mtn is 2 mi long, 600 ft high). $40 for 7-day permit; $95 annual pass (holders of federal Senior Pass pay half price). 4/1-10/31; 14-day limit. 100 primitive sites, most for tents or self-contained RVs. Tbls, toilets, cfga, no drkg wtr, no wood for campfire. OHV activity, hiking. Self-guided tours of 1860s expess station.

Stillwater   **FREE**
Wildlife Management Area
Anaho Island & Fallon
National Wildlife Refuges
5 mi E of Fallon on US 50; 13 mi on Stillwater Rd. Free. All year. Primitive camping & boating facilities in 24,000-acre WMA. No facilities. Birdwatching, fishing, boating.

GABBS (14)

Berlin-Ichthyosaur State Park   **$12**
23 mi E of Gabbs on SR 844; 7 mi SE on gravel rd. $12. All year;14-day limit. 14 sites (RVs under 26 ft). Tbls, toilets, cfga, drkg wtr (mid-Apr to Oct), dump. Hiking trails, visitor center. Guided tours for fee. Elev 7000 ft; 903 acres.

GARDNERVILLE (15)

Topaz Lake   **$10**
Douglas County Park
20 mi S of Gardnerville on US 395; left at sign; on Topaz Lake. $10 primitive sites; $15 with hookups. All year; 14-day limit. 140 sites; 35-ft RV limit (29 hookup sites, 40 dry sites, numerous undeveloped sites). Tbls, flush toilets, dump, cfga, drkg wtr, showers. Fishing, swimming, boating.
   Fishing tip: Tropy rainbow trout in the four to eight-pound range are caught regularly in the lake.

GOLDFIELD (16)

Goldfield RV Park   **$8**
On 4th St in Goldfield (S of Tonopah). $8 primitive sites, $15 full hookups. Tbls, cfga, drkg wtr, flush toilets, showers, dump. Town has wild burros on the street.

HAWTHORNE (17)

Sportsman's Beach   **$4**
Walker Lake Recreation Area
Bureau of Land Management
16 mi N of Hawthorne on Hwy 95, on W shore of Walker Lake. $4 for primitive sites; $6 developed sites. All year; 14-day limit. About 30 developed sites (30-ft RV limit), plus primitive camping at the Cove, East Shore, Tamarack & Twenty-Mile Beach. Tbls, toilets, cfga, drkg wtr. Fishing, hiking, picnicking, boating (l), waterskiing, swimming beach. Walker Lake has 38,000 acres of water, 15 mi long.
   Fishing tip: Walker is noted for its cutthroat trout. But beware of the giant serpent (named Cecil) that supposedly lives in the lake. Rental boats available; also good fishing from shore.

Tamarack Point   **FREE**
Recreation Site
Bureau of Land Management
18 mi N of Hawthorne on US 95 (W shore of Walker Lake). All year; 14-day limit. 10 sites (RVs under 31 ft). Tbls, toilets, cfga, no drkg wtr. Boating, picnicking, fishing, swimming, hiking, horseback riding, sailing, rockhounding, hunting. Elev 4500 ft. Gillis Range is E of lake. Wassuk Range, with Mount Grant (11,239 ft), is W.

HENDERSON (18)

Callville Bay   **$12**
Lake Mead National Recreation Area
22 mi NE of Henderson on SR 147. $12 base. All year; 30-day limit. 80 sites. Tbls, flush toilets, cfga, drkg wtr, coin laundry. Boating(l), fishing, waterskiing.
   Fishing tip: Although fishing generally slows down in summer at Lake Mead, channel catfish are active all summer, with the best action occurring after dark in the coves.

Las Vegas Bay   **$12**
Lake Mead National Recreation Area
8 mi NE of Henderson on SR 166 (13 mi NW of Boulder City). $12 base. All year; 30-day limit. 89 sites. Tbls, flush toilets, cfga, drkg wtr. Fishing, boating(lr), hiking, waterskiing. 12 acres.

Fishing tip: Huge numbers of shad are reported in Las Vegas Bay, meaning excellent forage in the future for the lake's big striped bass. In summer, watch for surface boils, indicating stripers are chasing schools of shad. Use stick baits such as Zara Spook, Pencil Poppers and shallow-running shad-type lures.

HIGH AMANA (19)

Mount Rose   **$6.50**
Toiyabe National Forest
3 mi NW of High Amana on SR 28; 7 mi NE on SR 431. $6.50 with federal Senior Pass; others pay $13. MD-LD; 14-day limit. 24 sites (16-ft RV limit). Tbls, toilets, cfga, drkg wtr, dump. Hiking. Elev 8900 ft; 11 acres.

JACKPOT (20)

Cactus Pete's RV Park   **$10**
In Jackpot on SR 93. $10 base for overnight parking at "budget" area with hookups; $14 with hookups. All year. 15 budget sites without toilets, showers, but hookups. 52 deluxe sites with tbls, flush toilets, CATV, pool, tennis, store, coin laundry, dump, cfga, drkg wtr, elec, sewer, showers. Golf($). Casinos nearby.

Salmon Falls Creek   **FREE**
Bureau of Land Management
Two access points: 1 mi & 2 mi S of Jackpot. Free. All year; 14-day limit. Primitive dispersed camping along Salmon Falls Creek; no facilities, no drkg wtr. Fishing, hiking, boating. Best floatingg is late Apr through June.

JARBIDGE (21)

Jarbidge Campground   **FREE**
Humboldt National Forest
1.1 mi S of Jarbidge on FR 10062, 62 mi W and S of Hwy 93 from Rogerson, ID. MD-9/30; 14-day limit. 5 sites (RVs under 16 ft). Tbls, toilets, cfga, firewood, piped drkg wtr. Hunting; picnicking; fishing; hiking. Elev 6300 ft; 2 acres. Stream. Near Jarbidge Wilderness.

Fishing tip: Try the rainbow & brown trout, kokanee salmon or largemouth bass at nearby Wildhorse Reservoir.

Pine Creek   **FREE**
Humboldt National Forest
3 mi S of Jarbidge on FR 10062. 64 mi W & S of RT 93 from Rogerson, ID. MD-9/30; 14-day limit. 22 sites (RVs under 25 ft). Tbls, toilets, cfga, firewood, piped drkg wtr. Hunting; picnicking; fishing; hiking. Elev 6600 ft;

2 acres. Pine Creek. Near Jarbidge Wilderness.

Fishing tip: Pine Creek offers good fishing for stocked rainbow trout.

LAS VEGAS (22)

Cold Creek   **FREE**
Recreation Site
Bureau of Land Management
31.5 mi NW of Las Vegas on US 95; 13.5 mi W on paved co rd .2 mi W on dirt road; half mi S on dirt road. Free. Elev 6000 ft. 3/1-11/30; 14-day limit. 6 sites on 160 acres (RVs under 16 ft). Tbls, toilets, cfga, no drkg wtr. Fishing (in season, for small brown trout); picnicking. No hunting.

Oak Creek   **$10**
Red Rock Canyon
National Conservation Area
Bureau of Land Management
18 mi W of Las Vegas strip via W. Charleston Blvd. $10. All year; 14-day limit. 71 sites (including 10 group sites & 24 walk-in tent sites). Also free primitive camping in several backcountry locations. Tbls, toilets, cfga, drkg wtr. Hiking, rock climbing, 13-mile scenic loop drive, mountain biking trails, horseback riding, hunting, caving. Visitor center with desert tortois exhibit. Wild burros nearby.

LOVELOCK (24)

Rye Patch   **$10**
State Recreation Area
22 mi N of Lovelock on I-80; 1 mi W of co rd. $10 (combined camping, entry & boating, $14). River campground below dam has tbls, flush toilets, showers; campground on W side has 25 improved sites; several other undeveloped sites along shoreline. Tbls, flush toilets, cfga, drkg wtr, dump. Picnicking, swimming, waterskiing, nature trails, boating(l), fishing, hunting. Elev 4100 ft; 20,000 acres. Bureau of Reclamation project. Humboldt Trail (1828) nearby.

Fishing tip: 11,000-acre Rye Patch Reservoir provides excellent fishing for wipers, walleye & white crappie. Try in the river immediately below the dam and at the Pitt-Taylor arm. A 12-pound walleye was caught in 2000, and the lake is expected to produce a record wiper. Shore fishing is good for crappie, wipers, white bass, channel catfish, Sacramento perch.

MCGILL (25)

Berry Creek   **FREE**
Humboldt National Forest
5 mi N of McGill on US 93; 1 mi E on SR 496; 3 mi E on FR 67. Free. About MD-10/31; 14-day limit. Primitive undesignated sites. Toilets, cfga, no drkg wtr. OHV activity, hunting, hiking, fishing, biking.

Fishing tip: Berry Creek contains small trout, but they're easy to catch.

East Creek   **$8**
Humboldt National Forest
5 mi N of McGill on Hwy 93; 4 mi E on SR 486; turn at East Creek sign, then 1 mi NE on FR 427; 3.5 mi E on FR 56. $8. 5/16-10/31; 14-day limit. 7 primitive sites; 20-ft RV limit. Tbls, toilets, cfga, no drkg wtr. Fishing, picnicking, hiking, biking, hunting.

Kalamazoo Campground   **FREE**
Humboldt National Forest
5 mi N of McGill on US 93; 4 mi E on SR 486 to East Creek turnoff, then 4 mi on FR 1054 (high clearance vehicles); at Kalamazoo Creek. Free. June-Sept; 14-day limit. 5 sites. Tbls, toilets, cfga, no drkg wtr. Fishing, hiking, hunting, biking. Elev 6900 ft.

Fishing tip: Try tor trout in adjoining Kalamazoo Creek.

Timber Creek   **$8**
Humboldt National Forest
5 mi N of McGill on US 93; 8 mi E on SR 486; 4 mi E on Timber Creek Rd. $6. 6/1-9/30; 16-day limit. 6 sites; 20-ft RV limit. Tbls, flush toilets, cfga, drkg wtr. Hiking, picnicking, fishing. Elev 8200 ft. N of Cave Lake State Park.

Fishing tip: Nearby Cave Lake is a put-and-take trout fishery which is stocked April through October with catchable size rainbow & brook trout.

MESQUITE (26)

Mesquite Park   **FREE**
At S end of town across from Peppermill Casino. Free overnight camping. No further information available.

MOUNTAIN CITY (27)

Big Bend   **$8**
Humboldt National Forest
18 mi S of Mountain City on SR 225; 10.5 mi E on CR 745. $8. 6/16-10/15; 14-day limit. 15 sites & 2 grp sites; 35-ft RV limit. Tbls, toilets, cfga, no drkg wtr. Fishing, hiking. Elev 6900 ft; 8 acres.

Wildhorse Crossing   **$8**
Humboldt National Forest
10 mi SE of Mountain City on SR 225; at Owyhee River. $8. 5/23-10/15; 14-day limit. 20 sites (plus 1 grp site). Tbls, toilets, cfga, no drkg wtr. Fishing. Elev 5900 ft; 12 acres. 5 mi N of Wildhorse Reservoir.

OVERTON (28)

Echo Bay   **$12**
Lake Mead National Recreation Area
30 mi S of Overton on SR 167. $12. All year; 90-day limit. 166 sites. Flush toilets, tbls, cfga, drkg wtr. Boating(lr), fishing, hiking, waterskiing. Elev 1200 ft.

OWYHEE (29)

Mountain View Reservoir   **$5**
Duck Valley Indian Reservation
6 mi N of Owyhee on SR 51. $5 per person. 3/1-10/31. 50 sites (no RV size limit). Tbls, toilets, cfga, drkg wtr. Fishing, boating, swimming.

Sheep Creek Reservoir   **$5**
Duck Valley Indian Reservation
On Hwy 51. $5 per person. 3/1-10/31. 30 sites (no RV size limit). Tbls, toilets, cfga, drkg wtr. Fishing, boating, swimming.
   Fishing tip: This lake provides excellent rainbow trout angling, with some fish up to 10 pounds. Early mornings, try scud pattern flies on slow-sinking line; then switch to leech patterns, damsel nymphs or large attractor patterns.

PARADISE VALLEY (30)

Lye Creek   **$10**
Humboldt National Forest
18 mi N of Paradise Valley on SR 792; 2 mi W on FR 087. $10. (double sites $12). 7/1-10/31; 14-day limit. 14 sites (RVs under 25 ft). Tbls, toilets, cfga, drkg wtr (June-Oct). Fishing, hunting, picnicking. No trash service. Elev 7400 ft.

PIOCHE (31)

Echo Canyon State Park   **$10**
4 mi E & 10 mi S of Pioche. $10 (combined entry, camping & boating $12). All year; 14-day limit. 33 sites; 30-ft RV limit. Tbls, flush toilets, cfga, drkg wtr, dump. Ltd facilities in winter. Fishing, swimming, boating(l), hiking, nature study. Elev 5300 ft; 930 acres; 65-acre lake.
   Fishing tip: Echo Canyon Lake is stocked heavily with rainbow trout, largemouth bass & white crappie. Fishing is slow during summer but picks up in September.

Pioche City Park   **FREE**
S end of town, just off US 93 behind post office. Free overnight camping; donations accepted. 10 sites. Toilets, drkg wtr, showers. Playground, recreation area, swimming.
   Travel tip: See town's famous landmark, the Million Dollar Courthouse, which cost nearly that much to build due to corruption & mismanagement; tours available.

RENO (32)

Lookout   **$6**
Toiyabe National Forest
9 mi W of Reno off I-80 in Dog Valley (gravel entrance rd). $6. 6/1-10/15; 14-day limit. 22 sites (22-ft RV limit). Tbls, toilets, cfga, drkg wtr. Picnicking, hiking, horseback riding, hunting, rockhounding. Fishing in nearby Verdi. Elev 6700 ft.
   Fishing tip: Try the nearby Truckee River

for trophy trout. Rainbow, brown and cutthroat are available from the Verdi all the way to Painted Rock. Cooler water areas (50-65 degrees) produce best.

SEARCHLIGHT (33)

Cottonwood Cove   **$12**
Lake Mead National Recreation Area
14 mi E of Searchlight on SR 164; on Lake Mohave. $12. All year; 30-day limit. 145 sites. Tbls, flush toilets, cfga, drkg wtr, coin laundry, store. Fishing, boating(ldr), hiking, waterskiing. 3 acres.

SILVER SPRINGS (34)

Fort Churchill   **$10**
State Historic Park
8 mi S of Silver Springs on US 95A; 1 mi W on Old Fort Churchill Rd. $10-12. All year; 14-day limit. 20 sites (RVs under 25 ft). Tbls, toilets, cfga, drkg wtr, dump. Fishing. Visitor center. Elev 3600 ft; 1,232 acres. $45 annual entry fee.

Silver Springs Beach   **$10**
Lahontan State Recreation Area
4 mi S of Silver Springs on US 95A; 3 mi on Fir Ave. $10 (combined entry, camping & boating, $15). All year; 14-day limit. 29 sites & unlimited beach sites. Tbls, flush toilets, cfga, drkg wtr, dump; limited facilities in winter. Swimming, boating(dl), fishing, waterskiing. Elev 4200 ft; 31,322 acres.

SONORA JUNCTION (35)

Obsidian   **$8**
Toiyabe National Forest
4 mi S of Sonora Junction off Hwy 395; 4 mi on gravel Little Walker Rd (FR 066). $8. About 6/1-10/15; 14-day limit. 13 sites (RVs under 30 ft). Tbls, toilets, cfga, drkg wtr. Picnicking, hiking, fishing. Elev 7840 ft.

SPARKS (36)

Mt. Rose Campground   **$6.50**
Toiyabe National Forest
9 mi S of Sparks on Hwy 395; 9 mi W on Hwy 431. $6.50 with federal Senior Pass; others pay $13. About 6/15-9/20; 14-day limit. 24 sites; 35-ft RV limit. Tbls, flush toilets, cfga, drkg wtr. Fishing, hiking; trailhead to Mt. Rose Wilderness.

Pyramid Lake Marina   **$9**
Pyramid Lake Paiute Reservation
16 mi N of Sparks on SR 447; left on SR 448 for 18 mi to marina sign; at Pyramid Lake. $9 base. All year; 10-day limit. Base fee for primitive overnight beach parking & tent sites ($74 for 10 days); more for RVs with hookups. 40 RV sites. Tbls, flush toilets, cfga, drkg wtr, dump, coin laundry, store. Fishing (permit $9 daily), boating ($9 daily), waterskiing. Museum at visitors center.
   Fishing tip: Fall & winter fishing for trout is

excellent. During hot weather, fish deep -- up to 85 feet for trout 6-9 pounds, with some trophies landed occasionally. Use green, frog, orange and red Apex, Flatfish and spoons. Only 2 hooks per angler permitted.

TONOPAH (37)

Barley Creek   **FREE**
Toiyabe National Forest
W of Tonopah to SR 376, then 12 mi N; 42 mi N on CR 82, then follow FR 005 to its end at the edge of the wilderness area. Free. Open primitive camping. May-Oct. Tbl, toilet, cfga, no drkg wtr. Hiking, fishing, biking.
   Fishing tip: This creek is stocked with rainbow trout and also contains brown & brook trout. From where Barley and Cottonwood Creek meet, hike upstream on Cottonwood for some excellent brook trout action, although the fish are generally small.

Peavine Campground   **FREE**
Toiyabe National Forest
5 mi E of Tonapah to SR 376, then 32 mi to forest rd; left 9 mi; at Peavine Creek. Free. All year; 14-day limit. 10 sites in open area; 35-ft RV limit. Tbls, toilets, cfga, drkg wtr. Fishing, hiking, horseback riding, hunting, rockhounding. Elev 6700; 6 acres. Peavine Creek. No off-season camping. Primitive camping. Near desert big horn sheep habitat.
   Travel tip: Take driving tour of the active mining districts at Round Mountain & Manhattan; visit the Belmont Courthouse State Historic Monument, located in the ruins of a picturesque 19th Century mining ghost town.

Pine Creek   **FREE**
Toiyabe National Forest
6 mi E of Tonopah on US 6; 13 mi NE on SR 376; 15 mi NE on CR 82; 2.5 mi W on FR 009 (30 mi of improved gravel rd). Free. 5/1-10/15; 14-day limit. 21 sites (35-ft RV limit). Tbls, toilets, cfga, drkg wtr. Horseback riding, picnicking, fishing (trout), hunting, rockhounding, hiking. On E side of Toquima Range next to Pine Creek. No off-season camping. Trailhead portal to Mt. Jefferson Natural Area. Elev 7600 ft; 20 acres. Note: Safe drinking water may not always be available, and when it's not, campis is free.
   Fishing tip: Pine Creek contains brown, brook and rainbow trout.
   Travel tip: stop at Central Nevada Museum in Tonopah; among the state's best small museums; large collection of mining implements.

Saulsbury Wash   **FREE**
Toiyabe National Forest
State Rest Area & Campground
30 mi E of Tonopah on US 6. Free. Elev 5800 ft. All year. 6 sites (RVs under 32 ft). Tbls, toilets, cfga, no drkg wtr. Rockhounding; picnicking. Reader says portable toilets are disgracefully dirty.

VERDI (39)

Hunting Camp #1   **FREE**
Toiyabe National Forest
3 mi NW on FR 027. Free. All year; 14-day
limit. Undesignated primitive area, undeveloped. Toilet, cfga, no drkg wtr. Horses permitted. Primarily a hunter's camp.

Hunting Camp #2   **FREE**
Toiyabe National Forest
3.5 mi NW on FR 027. Free. 4/1-11/1; 14-day
limit. Undesignated primitive area, undeveloped. Toilet, cfga, no drkg wtr. Horses permitted. Primarily a hunter's camp.

Hunting Camp #4   **FREE**
Toiyabe National Forest
NW of Verdi on FR 027. Free. 4/1-11/1; 14-
day limit. Undesignated primitive area, undeveloped. Toilet, cfga, no drkg wtr. Primarily a
hunter's camp.

WELLINGTON (40)

Desert Creek   **FREE**
Toiyabe National Forest
3 mi SW of Bridgeport on SR 338; 7 mi S
on FR 027 (Desert Creek Rd); near Desert
Creek. Free. About 5/1-11/1; 14-day limit. 13
sites. Tbls, toilets, cfga, no drkg wtr. Fishing,
hiking. Also numerous primitive dispersed
sites along the creek.

Wilson Canyon   **FREE**
Dispersed Campsites
Bureau of Land Management
NE of Wellington on SR 208 along the West
Walker River. Free. All year; 14-day limit. Pull-
out areas along W end of canyon. Undesignated primitive sites; no facilities. Hiking,
fishing. Dump ($3) at Bybee's store in Smith.
   Fishing tip: The best trout fishing water on
the West Walker River is next to the highway
in Wilson Canyon.

Wilson Reservoir Camp   **$4**
Bureau of Land Management
25 mi N of Elko on SR 225; 40 mi N & W on
SR 226; 20 mi on graded rd; NE of Wellington; on W shore of Wilson Reservoir. $4 dur-
ing May-Oct; free rest of year; 14-day limit.
15 sites. Tbls, toilets, cfga, drkg wtr (except
during free period), fishing platform. Boating(l
-- $2), fishing, horseback riding, hunting, hik-
ing, biking.
   Fishing tip: This lake produces excellent
catches of rainbow & brown trout and largemouth bass.

WELLS (41)

South Ruby   **$12**
Humboldt National Forest
Ruby Mountains Recreation Area
S of Wells on US 93 & SR 229. $12 during
5/15-LD; $10 LD-10/31; $8 11/1-11/11; free
11/12-5/14. 14-day limit. 35 sites; 22-ft RV
limit. Tbls, toilets, cfga, drkg wtr, dump ($5),

fish cleaning station (MD-LD). Boating, fishing, hunting, picnicking. Adjacent to Ruby
Lake Wildlife Refuge.
   Fishing tip: This natural marsh is famous
for its largemouth bass and trophy-size rainbow trout. Best trout fishing is in spring
before water warms, but bass action is
great all summer; use plastics and live bait.
The refuge's Collection Ditch produces huge
brook and rainbow.

Tabor Creek   **$2**
Bureau of Land Management
30 mi N of Wells on US 93 7 gravel rds. $2
use fee. About 4/15-11/15; 14-day limit. 10
sites. Toilets, cfga, no drkg wtr. Picnicking,
fishing, hiking, mountain biking.
   Travel tip: Drive through the town of
Wells; its old Main St is an authentic 19th
century cow country downtown.
   Fishing tip: Tabor Creek is stocked regularly with rainbow trout.

WINNEMUCCA (42)

Pine Forest   **FREE**
Recreation Area
Bureau of Land Management
75 mi NW of Winnemucca on Hwy 140. Free.
3 primitive dispersed locations at Knott Creek
Reservoir, Onion Reservoir, Blue Lakes. All
year; 14-day limit. Tbls, toilets, cfga, no drkg
wtr. Fishing (trout), hiking. Remote.
   Fishing tip: Knott Creek Reservoir was
restocked with 4,360 catchable rainbow trout
in 2000 following a winter kill, and a yer later,
they'd grown to 19 inches. Only artificial
lures are permitted. Blue Lake is stocked
by helicopter and provides good fishing for
brook & rainbow trout.

239

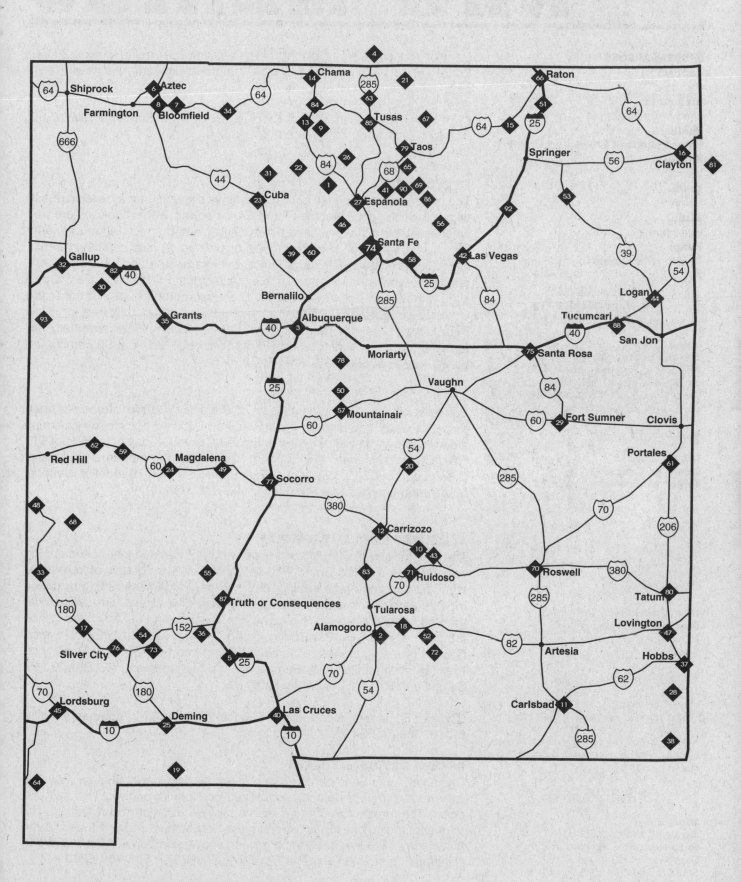

NEW MEXICO

MISCELLANEOUS
Capital:
Santa Fe
Nickname:
Land of Enchantment
Motto:
Crescit Eundo (It Grows as It Goes)
Flower:
Yucca
Tree:
Pinon
Bird:
Roadrunner
Song:
"O Fair New Mexico"

Internet Address:
www.newmexico.org

Dept of Tourism, Lamy Building, 491 Old Santa Fe Trail, PO Box 20003, Santa Fe, NM 87503. 800-545-2070. Internet: enchantment.newmexico. org.

Dept of Game and Fish, Villagra Bldg, PO Box 25112, Santa Fe, NM 87504. 505-827-7911 & 827-7880 or 800-275-3474.

STATE PARKS
The overnight camping fee is $8 for primitive sites, $10 for a developed site with a $4 charge for electricity and $4 for sewer; water hookups are free when available. Primitive sites offer only a cleared space, although some may have trash cans, chemical toilets or parking. Annual camping permits are $180 for state residents ($100 for seniors or disabled); $225 for non-residents; with an annua permit, sites with electric or sewage are $4, and sites with electric and sewer are $8. State campgrounds do not honor the Golden Age Passport. Daily entrance fee is $5 ($40 annual); free for walk-in or bicycles. 14-day camping limit. Pets on leashes are permitted. For further information contact: State Parks Division, 1220 Sout St. Francis Dr., Santa Fe, NM 87505. 888-NMPARKS.

Bandelier National Monument. Most of Bandelier's 29,661 acres are open to backcountry camping all year. Required but free backcountry permits are available at the visitor center in Frijoles Canyon. 7-day entry fees of $12 ($6 daily or $39 annual) are charged. Camping at the monument's Juniper Campground is $12, plus entry fee. Superintendent, Bandelier National Monument, Los Alamos, NM 87544. 505-672-3861

BUREAU OF LAND MANAGEMENT
The BLM in New Mexico offers a wide variety of free and low-cost camping opportunities. The Rio Grand Wild & Scenic River area boasts of free white-water river rafting and camping, and two-day wilderness rafting or canoe trips through scenic sandstone canyons and pine forests are available at the Chama Wild & Scenic River. There is free camping at Mescalero Sands (38 mi E of Roswell), Rio Bonito Camp (7 miles west of Lincoln), Simon Canyon (at Aztec along the San Juan River) and Fort Stantion Recreation Area (65 mi W of Roswell). Bureau of Land Management, PO Box 27115, Santa Fe, NM 87505. 505/438-7400.

Corps of Engineers, Albuquerque District, PO Box 1580, Albuquerque, NM 87103. 505-342-3464.

CARSON NATIONAL FOREST
Carson NF offers free camping at most of its developed sites as well as a large number of undeveloped, dispersed locations throughout its 1,491,000 acres. The forests lakes and streams provide excellent trout fishing. The normal camping season is May through September; snow is found at the timberline until June; frequent afternoon showers in July & August. Carson National Forest, 208 Cruz Alta Rd, Taos, NM 87571. 505-758-6200.

CIBOLA NATIONAL FOREST

Most developed campgrounds in this forest also are free. However, parking permits of $3 daily or $30 annually have been implemented throughout the Sandia Ranger District as part of the national Fee Demonstration Program; those fees apply primarily to picnicking abd group camping sites. 1,625,500 acres. The forest features Indian pueblos, prehistoric ruins, ice caves, lava flows. Good deer hunting; some elk, antelope & turkey. Fishing in Bluewater & McGaffey Lakes. Cibola National Forest, 2113 Osuna Rd NE, Suite A, Albuquerque, NM 87113-1001; 505-346-3900.

GILA NATIONAL FOREST

This forest contains 3,321,000 acres (including 614,200 of the Apache National Forest). This rugged area in SW New Mexico features excellent trout streams and lake fishing in Lake Roberts, Snow Lake and Quemado Lake. It also encompasses the gold mining ghost town of Mogollon and the Gila Cliff Dwellings. Most of its campgrounds are free. Gila National Forest, 3005 E. Camino del Bosque, Silver City, NM 88061. 505-388-8201.

LINCOLN NATIONAL FOREST

The forest has fewer free campgrounds than the other New Mexico national forests. It contains 1,103,400 acres and is a good area for horseback riding, turkey hunting, trout fishing and scenic drives. 1101 New York Ave., Alamogordo, NM 88310. 505-434-7200.

SANTA FE NATIONAL FOREST

Santa Fe NF offers free camping at about half of its developed campgrounds. This forest has 1,587,100 acres and contains the headwaters of the Pecos, Jemez and Gallinas Rivers. Its mountain streams and lakes contain trout. Wilderness backpack and saddle trips have great appeal, and there is whitewater boating on the Rio Chama River. 1474 Rodeo Rd, Santa Fe, NM 87505. 505-438-7840.

ABIQUIU (1)

Rio Chama   **FREE**
Santa Fe National Forest
About 5 mi N of Abiquiu on US 84; about 12 mi W on FR 151 (high-clearance vehicles suggested; rd unusable when wet). Free. 5/1-11/15; 14-day limit. 9 sites; 16-ft RV limit. Tbls, toilets, cfga, no drkg wtr. 2 group sites. Rafting, fishing. At S end of Rio Chama Wilderness.

Fishing tip: The Rio Chama is an excellent trout stream that produces trophy size browns. From El Vado Reservoir, it is a designated wild & scenic river, and it contains rainbow trout and kokanee salmon as well as browns. Best fishing is within several miles of the El Vado dam.

Riana Recreation Area   **$5**
Corps of Engineers
Abiquiu Dam
SW of Abiquiu on US 84; 2 mi SW on SR 96; N on access rd. $5 base (tent sites), RV sites without elec $10, RV sites with elec $14 during 4/10-10/31; 14-day limit. Free 4/10-4/15 and 9/15-10/31 but no services. 54 sites (13 with 50-amp elec); 65-ft RVs. Tbls, flush toilets, cfga, firewood, summer drkg wtr. Boating, waterskiing, swimming, hunting (waterfowl), picnicking, fishing. Elev 6140 ft.

ALAMOGORDO (2)

Oliver Lee   **$10**
Memorial State Park
12 mi S of Alamogordo on US 54, then 4 mi E on Dog Canyon Rd. $10 base. All year; 14-day limit. 48 developed sites (1 with handicap access, 6 with elec); 48-ft RV limit. Tbls, elec($4), cfga, drkg wtr, tbls, showers, flush toilets, dump, visitor center. Nature trails, picnicking. Historical exhibits; restored 19th Century ranchhouse. Elev 4400 ft; 180 acres.

ALBUQUERQUE (3)

Apache Plume Campground   **$8**
Cochiti Recreation Area
Cochiti Lake
Corps of Engineers
50 mi N of Albuquerque on I-25; between community of Cochiti Lake & W side of the lake off SR 22. $8 at primitive sites. Camp is normally closed, used only for overflow. 22 sites, each with shelter. No facilities (use those in adjoining camps). Fishing, swimming, boating, hiking.

Chemisa Campground   **$8**
Cochiti Recreation Area
Cochiti Lake
Corps of Engineers
50 mi N of Albuquerque on I-25; between community of Cochiti Lake & W side of the lake off SR 22. $8 without hookups, $12 with elec. 21 sites with shelters; 65-ft RVs. Concrete tbls, pit toilets, cfga, drkg wtr,

dump, elec($), showers. Fishing, swimming, boating(ld), picnicking, hiking. 3-night minimum stay on holiday weekends.

Fishing tip: The state record spotted bass (4.5 pounds) was caught from Cochiti Lake in 1998 oon a jig with a skirted grub.

Juniper Campground   **$8**
Cochiti Recreation Area
Cochiti Lake
Corps of Engineers
50 mi N of Albuquerque on I-25; between community of Cochiti Lake & W side of the lake off SR 22. $8 for non-hookup sites, $12 with elec. 34 sites; 65-ft RVs. Tbls, flush toilets, cfga, drkg wtr, dump, elec($), showers. Fishing, swimming, boating(ld), picnicking, hiking. 3-night minimum stay on holiday weekends.

Fishing tip: Cochiti Lake has good populations of bass, white bass, crappie, walleye, northern pike and catfish. For rainbow trout, try the stocked Stilling Basin and downstream. Trout 3-5 pounds frequently are landed Nov-Feb. Big rainbows & browns also are caught in winter from the Rio Grande below the Stilling Basin.

Cholla Campground   **$8**
Tetilla Peak Recreation Area
Cochita Lake
Corps of Engineers
50 mi N of Albuquerque on I-25; E side of lake across from Cochiti Park off SR 16. $8 at non-elec sites, $12 with elec. 51 sites, 34 with elec (65-ft RV limit). Tbls, flush toilets, cfga, drkg wtr, showers, dump, elec($). Boating(l), fishing, hiking, picnicking. 5 acres. 3-night minimum stay on holiday weekends.

Coyote Campground   **$8**
Tetilla Peak Recreation Area
Cochita Lake
Corps of Engineers
50 mi N of Albuquerque on I-25; E side of lake across from Cochiti Park off SR 16. $8. 10 sites (7 for tents). Concrete tbls, pit toilets, cfga, drkg wtr. Boating, fishing, hiking, picnicking. 2 acres.

ANTONITO (COLORADO) (4)

Rio de Los Pinos   **FREE**
Carson National Forest
15 mi SW of Antonito, in New Mexico, on US 285. Free. May-Sept; 14-day limit. 4 sites (16' RV limit) plus dispersed camping. Toilets, tbls, cfga, no drkg wtr. Excellent trout fishing at state fishing area nearby. Elev 8000 ft.

Rio de Los Pinos   **FREE**
State Wildlife & Fishing Area
10 mi SW of Antonito on CR C (becomes FR 284 in New Mexico). Free. All year; 14-day limit. Developed & dispersed sites. Trls, toilets, cfga, no drkg wtr. Fishing, hiking, hunting. 850 acres with 1.5 mi of stream trout fishing.

ARREY (5)

Arrey RV Park   **$10**
1 mi S of I-25 from milemarker 59 on Hwy 187 to milemarker 19. $10 RV sites with hookups. 22 sites. Tbls, flush toilets, cfga, drkg wtr, tbls, showers.

AZTEC (6)

Aztec Ruins Road RV Park   **$6**
At 312 Ruins Rd, Aztec. $6 for primitive sites; $15 with full hookups. All year. 30 sites. Tbls, toilets, cfga, drkg wtr, hookups($).

Pine Rivers Area   **$10**
Navajo Lake State Park
13 mi E of Aztec on SR 173; 10 mi E on SR 511. $10 base. All year; 14-day limit. Base fee for 246 developed sites; 50-ft RV limit. Tbls, flush toilets, cfga, drkg wtr, dump, elec($4), playground. Fishing, canoeing, hunting, hiking, boating(ld). Visitor center, exhibits, marina.

Fishing tip: An Albequerque angler, snagging salmon in Navajo Lake in 2000, caught the state record coho -- a four-pounder. 20 years earlier, the lake produced the state record kokanee salmon (three pounds, 10 ounces), and in 1999, a Colorado man fishing with a jig landed the state record smallmouth bass (6 pounds, 14 ounces).

San Juan Area   **$8**
Navajo Lake State Park
17 mi E of Aztec on SR 173. $8 base. All year; 14-day limit. Base fee for primitive sites; 47 developed sites (50-ft RV limit), $10 base. Tbls, flush toilets, cfga, drkg wtr, elec($4), dump. Fishing, hunting, boating. Handicap access sites.

Fishing tip: Fly fishermen from all over the world travel to New Mexico to fish the San Juan tailwaters below Navajo Dam. A 3.75-mi stretch below the dam is special catch-and-release waters the first qtr mi and limits of one 20-inch trout for the remainder. Trout of 15-19 inches are routine. Below that stretch, the fish run smaller.

BLANCO (7)

Buzzard Park   **FREE**
Carson National Forest
43 NE of Blanco on US 64; 17 mi N on FR 310 (rds treacherous when wet). All year; 14-day limit. 4 sites (32-ft RV limit) plus dispersed camping. Toilets, no drkg wtr. Elev 7300 ft. W of Jicarilla Apache Reservation.

Cedar Springs   **FREE**
Carson National Forest
43 mi E of Blanco on US 64; 15 mi S on FR 357 (not recommended for RVs). Free. May-Nov; 14-day limit. 4 primitive sites (32-ft RV limit). Toilets, tbls, cfga, no drkg wtr. Elev 7300 ft. Hunting.

BLOOMFIELD (8)

Angel Peak Recreation Site   **FREE**
Bureau of Land Management
About 10 mi SE of Bloomfield on SR 44 in NW New Mexico; 4 mi E on CR 7175. Free. All year (weather permitting); 14-day limit. 10 sites (35-ft RV limit); 200 acres. Tbls, toilets, cfga, shelters, no drkg wtr. Hiking, rockhounding, picnicking. Elev 6400 ft.

Gallo Wash Campground   **$10**
Chaco Culture
National Historic Park
27 mi S of Bloomfield on SR 44; 29 mi S on SR 57 to N entrance of the monument. Visitor center is 7 mi beyond entrance. Campground is 1 mi from visitor center. $10, plus $8 entry fee for 7 days. All year. 14-day limit. 47 sites (RVs under 30 ft). Group site available for $4 per person (minimum of $40). Tbls, flush toilets, cfga, drkg wtr. Picnicking, hiking. Call the monument. 505-988-7627, about dirt road conditions during stormy weather. Pets in campgrounds but not on trails. 34,000 acres. Limited facilities in winter. 34,000 acres. Park entry fee.

CANJILON (9)

Canjilon Creek   **FREE**
Carson National Forest
10 mi NE of Canjilon on FR 559 and FR 130. Primitive road, very slick when wet. Free. 6/1-9/15; 14-day limit. 4 sites (no trailers). Toilets, tbls, cfga, no trash service, no drkg wtr. Fishing. Elev 9300 ft.

Lower Canjilon Lakes   **$5**
Carson National Forest
7 mi E of Canjilon on SR 110; 4 mi N on FR 129. $5. MD-LD; 14-day limit. 11 sites; 22-ft RV limit. Tbls, toilets, cfga, drkg wtr. Boating(l), fishing, hiking.

Middle Canjilon Lakes   **$5**
Carson National Forest
7 mi E of Canjilon on SR 110; 4 mi N on FR 129. $5. MD-9/30; 14-day limit. 32 sites (22-ft RV limit). Tbls, toilets, cfga, drkg wtr. Boating, fishing, hiking. Elev 9900 ft.

Upper Canjilon Lakes   **FREE**
Carson National Forest
12 mi NE of Canjilon on FR 559 & FR 129. Free. Primitive, undesignated camping area (22-ft RV limit). Tbls, toilets, no drkg wtr. Picnicking, fishing. Elevation 10,100 ft.

CAPITAN (10)

Baca Campground   **FREE**
Lincoln National Forest
About 10 mi E of Capitan on US 380; left on FR 57 for about 7 mi. Free sites on left side of rd for RVs & tents. All year; 14-day limit. Toilets, cfga, sometimes piped spring wtr. Once a CCC camp

Top of Capitan's   **FREE**
Dispersed Area
Lincoln National Forest
2 mi E of Capitan on US 380; left on FR 56 (a rough rd requiring high-clearance 4WD. Wilderness boundary 100 yds N of FR 56; no vehicles allowed. All year; 30-day limit. Primitive tent camping; no facilities, no drkg wtr. Good area for wildlife study.

CARLSBAD (11)

Brantley Lake State Park   **$8**
12 mi N of Carlsbad on US 285, then 4.5 mi E on CR 30. $8 base. All year; 14-day limit. Base fee for 25 primitive sites; 51 developed sites (36 with shelters), $10 base (no RV limit). Tbls, flush toilets, cfga, drkg wtr, elec ($4), dump, showers, playground. Picnicking, boating(ld), fishing, hiking trails, canoeing, birdwatching, waterskiing, sailing. Visitor center with Wild West town of Seven Rivers. Elev 3300 ft; 3,000 acres. Southernmost lake in New Mexico.
Fishing tip: Local anglers expect some big largemouth bass to be produced by Brantley Lake in the near future. Florid-strain bass were introduced in the mid-1990s, and lunkers are already being caught in the eight pound range. The lake also contains spotted bass, white bass, walleye and crappie. Note: in 2007, environmentalists warned about DDT in the lake's fish and recommended catch-and-release only.

Dog Canyon Campground   **$8**
Guadalupe Mountains National Park
10 mi N of US 285; 60 mi SW on SR 137, in Guadalupe Mountains National Park. $8. All year; 14-day limit. 23 sites, plus walk-in tent sites. Limited facilities in winter. Drkg wtr, flush toilets, cfga, tbls. Nature trails. Park entry fee $3 for 7 days.

Pine Springs Canyon   **$8**
Guadalupe Mountains National Park
Frijoe information station is located 55 mi SW of Carlsbad on US 62-180. The campground is 1.5 mi W of the information station. $8. All year; 14-day limit. 19 sites for self-contained RVs; 20 tent sites. Tbls, toilets, drkg wtr, no cfga. Hiking, picnicking. Park entry fee $3 for 7 days.

CARRIZOZO (12)

Three Rivers   **$6**
Lincoln National Forest
24 mi S of Carrizozo on US 54 (18 mi N of Tularosa); turn E on FR 579 at sign that says "Three Rivers Petroglyphic Site and Campground" for 13 mi, follow signs. $6. All year; 14-day limit. 12 sites sites (RVs under 26 ft). Tbls, toilets, cfga, firewood, drkg wtr. Hiking, mountain climbing, picnicking, fishing, horseback riding. Elev 6400 ft; 10 acres. Good cool-weather campground. Trailhead into White Mountain Wilderness. Scenic. Horse corrals. Popular hunting camp.

Fishing tip: From the campground, follow Trail 44 along Three Rivers and catch brook trout all spring, summer & fall.

Valley of Fires Recreation Area   **$12**
Bureau of Land Management
4 mi W of Carrizozo on SR 380 (NW of Alamogordo). $12 base. All year; 14-day limit. Base fee without hookups; $18 with elec. 19 sites (14 with elec). Tbls, flush toilets, cfga, drkg wtr, dump, showers. Hike past 1,000-yr-old lava flow. Visitor center. Elev 6300 ft.

CEBOLLA (13)

Trout Lakes   **FREE**
Carson National Forest
1 mi S of Cebolla on US 84; 9.5 mi NE on FR 125 (primitive rd). 6/1-9/30. 14-day limit. 16 sites (16-ft RV limit). Tbls, toilets, cfga, no drkg wtr. Picnicking, fishing, horseback riding, hiking, biking. 4 acres. Scenic. Primitive rd, not recommended for large RVs. Elev 9300 ft.

CHAMA (14)

Chama Basin   **FREE**
Rio Grande National Forest
4.6 mi SW on SR 17; 7 mi N on FR 121. Free. 5/13-11/15. Undesignated sites. Tbls, cfga, toilets. Hiking, fishing, picnicking.
Fishing tip: The Brazos River E of Chama produces nice catches of rainbow & brown trout, but finding access through private property might be difficult.

CIMARRON (15)

Cimarron Canyon State Park   **$8**
Colin Neblett Wildlife Area
11 mi W of Cimarron on Hwy 64. $8 base. All year; 14-day limit. Base fee for 9 primitive sites; 88 developed sites, $10 base; 30-ft RV limit. Tbls, flush toilets, no elec, cfga, drkg wtr, dump. Picnicking, fishing, hiking trails, winter sports. Elev 8000 ft; 400 acres, part of the 33,116-acre Colin Neblett Wildlife Area.
Fishing tip: This area has 8 mi of premier brown trout & rainbow trout water on the Cimarron River. Typical fish are 10-14 inches.

McCrystal   **$10**
Carson National Forest
From Cerrososo Canyon (off US 64 about 5 mi NE of Cimarron), 20 mi along canyon ; 7 mi on FR 1950. $10. 5/15-10/15; 14-day limit. 60 sites (32-ft RV limit), including 1 group site. Toilets, tbls, cfga, drkg water. Horse facilities at 6 sites. Bridle & hiking trails, hunting, fishing.

CLAYTON (16)

Clayton Lake State Park   **$8**
12 mi N of Clayton on SR 370. $8 base. All year; 14-day limit. Base fee for 4 primitive

sites; 37 developed sites with shelters (7 with elec), $10. 70-ft RV limit. Tbls, flush toilets, cfga, drkg wtr, showers, elec($4), no dump, playground. Boating(dl), fishing, hiking trails, swimming, sailing. Trail overlooks rare 100-million year-old dinosaur trackway. Elev 5040 ft; 417 acres.

Fishing tip: This 175-acre lake regularly produces large rainbow trout, and the last five state record walleyes came from there, including the current record of 16 pounds 9 ounces. It also contains catfish, largemouth bass and bluegills.

CLIFF (17)

Bill Evans   **FREE**
State Fishing Lake
3 mi S of Cliff on US 180; 5 mi SW on FR 809. Free. All year; 14-day limit. Primitive undesignated sites. Tbla, toilets, cfga, no drkg wtr. Boating(l), fishing. No shade.

Fishing tip: This 62-acre lake is stocked with rainbow trout and often provides excellent catches of large smallmouth bass. Elec motors only. It holds the state record for largemouth bass -- a Florida-strain fish.

CLOUDCROFT (18)

Apache   **$11**
Lincoln National Forest
1.2 mi E of Cloudcroft on US 82; 1.5 mi NW on SR 244; 1 mi S on FR 24G. $11. 5/15-9/15; 14-day limit. 26 sites (32-ft RV limit). Tbls, toilets, cfga, drkg wtr, gray water sumps, dump ($5 non-campers), showers ($2). New interpretive trail nearby. Elev 8900 ft; 6 acres.

Deerhead   **$11**
Lincoln National Forest
1 mi S of Cloudcroft on SR 244. $11. 5/15-9/15; 14-day limit. 34 small tent sites. Tbls, toilets, cfga, drkg wtr, gray water sumps. Hiking (trailhead of 21-mi Rim Trail). Elev 8700 ft; 10 acres.

Pines   **$6.50**
Lincoln National Forest
1.2 mi E of Cloudcroft on US 82; half mi NW on SR 244. $6.50 with federal Senior Pass; others pay $13. 5/15-9/15; 14-day limit. 48 sites (16-ft RV limit). Tbls, toilets, cfga, drkg wtr, gray water sumps. Primarily tent area with limited space for RVs. Hiking trail access.

Saddle Mountain   **$6.50**
Lincoln National Forest
1.2 mi E of Cloudcroft on US 82; 1.5 mi NW on SR 44; half mi S on FR 24G. $6.50 with federal Senior Pass; others pay $13. 5/15-9/15; 14-day limit. 17 sites (32-ft RV limit). Tbls, toilets, cfga, drkg wtr, gray water sumps at each site (garden hose needed), showers, dump ($5). New interpretive trail nearby. Elev 9000 ft; 6 acres.

Silver   **$11**
Lincoln National Forest
1.2 mi E of Cloudcroft on US 82; 1.5 mi NW on SR 244; half mi S on FR 24G. $11. 4/15-10/15; 14-day limit. 32 sites (32-ft RV limit). Tbls, toilets, cfga, drkg wtr, gray water sumps at each site (garden hose needed),, dump ($5), showers ($2). New interpretive trail. Weekend ranger programs at amphitheater. Elev 9000 ft.

Silver Overflow   **$9**
Lincoln National Forest
1.2 mi E of Cloudcroft on US 82; 1.5 mi NW on SR 244; qtr mi S on FR 24G. $9. 5/1-10/15; 30-day limit. 52 sites (No RV length limit). Tbls, toilets, cfga, drkg wtr, showers $2 at Silver Camp. Hiking.

Sleepygrass   **$9**
Lincoln National Forest
1.4 mi S of Cloudcroft on SR 130; veer left onto FR 24B. $9. 5/1-10/15; 14-day limit. 45 sites (16-ft RV limit). Tbls, toilets, cfga, drkg wtr. Hiking trail for blind & sighted.

COLUMBUS (19)

Pancho Villa State Park   **$8**
On S edge of Columbus on SR 11. $8 base. All year; 14-day limit. Base fee for 8 primitive sites; 62 developed sites with shelters, $10 base; 48-ft RV limit. Tbls, flush toilets, cfga, drkg wtr, dump, elec($4), showers. Picnicking, hiking. Historical exhibit, desert botanical garden. Visitor center, historic buildings. Elev 4000 ft; 60 acres.

CORONA (20)

Red Cloud   **FREE**
Cibola National Forest
9.5 mi SW of Corona on US 54; 1.5 mi W on FR 161. 6.5 mi NW on FR 399. 4/1-10/31; 14-day limit. 5 sites (RVs under 22 ft). No drkg wtr, no facilities. Picnicking. Elev 7600 ft. 2 acres. Primitive forest environment. This camp was destroyed by fire in 2001 but has been re-opened.

COSTILLA (21)

Cimarron   **$7.50**
Carson National Forest
30 mi SW of Costilla on SR 196; E on FR 1950 past Valle Vidal Unit line to jct with FR 1900; 10 mi S on FR 1950 to FR 1910, then 1 mi to camp. $7.50 with federal Senior Pass; others pay $15 (fee may be reduced if wtr not available). MD-10/1; 14-day limit. 36 sites (32-ft RV limit); horse camping facilities at 6 sites. Tbls, toilets, cfga, drkg wtr, corrals. Fishing, hunting, hiking, horseback riding. Elev 9400 ft.

Fishing tip: From Valle Vidal Unit, follow fR 1950 to Shuree Ponds, special trout waters containing plenty of rainbow trout 15 inches and larger. Stream fishing in the Valle Vidal is catch-and-release, with a ponds limit

of only 2 fish over 15 inches. One pond is reserved for children. The ponds are ideal for float tubes. For variety, try the rainbow, brown and Rio Grande cutthroat trout at Costilla Creek.

COYOTE (22)

Rio Puerco   **FREE**
Santa Fe National Forest
11 mi W of Coyote on NM 96; 9.6 mi S on FR 103. Primitive roadway. Free. May-Oct; 14-day limit. 4 sites (space too small for trailers). Toilets, cfga, no drkg wtr. Fishing, heavily used during hunting season. Elev 8200 ft.

CUBA (23)

Cabezon Peak Recreation Area   **FREE**
Bureau of Land Management
20 mi SW of Cuba via CR 279. Free. All year; 14-day limit. Primitive undesignated camping. No facilities except cfga; no drkg wtr. Biking, hiking, hunting.

Clear Creek   **$10**
Santa Fe National Forest
11.2 mi E of Cuba on SR 126; at th Rio de las Vacas River. $10. 5/15-11/1, depending on snow; 14-day limit. 15 sites (30-ft trailer limit; 35-ft motorhome limit). Tbls, toilets, cfga, firewood, drkg wtr. Picnicking, fishing, hiking trails. Elev 8500 ft. Reconstructed in 2005.

Rio de las Vacas   **$10**
Santa Fe National Forest
12.7 mi E of Cuba on SR 126. $10. 5/30-11/1; 14-day limit. 16 sites. (RVs under 35 ft). Tbls, toilets, cfga, firewood, drkg wtr (but treat it before drinking to be safe). Fishing, picnicking. Elev 8200 ft. 2 acres. Stream. Reconstructed in 2005.

DATIL (24)

Datil Well Campground   **$5**
Bureau of Land Management
.4 mi W of US 60 near Datil in western New Mexico. $5. All year (weather permitting); 7-day limit. 22 sites. Tbls, toilets, cfga, drkg wtr, ice, recreation hall. Store, food nearby. Picnicking, hiking. Elev 7400 ft. 680 acres. Interpretive display. Nature trails.

DEMING (25)

City of Rocks State Park   **$10**
22 mi NW of Deming on US 180; 5 mi E on SR 61. $10. All year; 14-day limit. 52 developed sites (10 with elec); no RV size limit. Tbls, flush toilets, cfga, drkg wtr, showers, elec($4), no dump. Hiking trails. Volcanic rocks, cactus gardens, interpretive exhibits. Elev 5200 ft; 680 acres.

LoW-Hi RV Ranch   **$2.18**
4 mi S on Country Club from I-85 exit at Deming; W on O'Kelley to first driveway on

North; operated by Loners on Wheels. $2.18 base for members at boondock sites ($5.44 non-members). Member rates are $8.64 with elec/wtr & $10.82 full hookups. Mon-members pay $12.99 for elec/wtr; $15.17 full hookups. Weekly & monthly rates available. Tbls, toilets, cfga, drkg wtr, showers($).

Rockhound State Park $10
14 mi SE of Deming on SR 11 and Rd 549. $10 base. All year; 14-day limit. 29 developed sites (27 with elec); 40-ft RV limit. Tbls, flush toilets, cfga, drkg wtr, elec($4), showers, dump. Picnicking, hiking, playground, rockhounding for agates, opals & quartz. Visitor center. Elev 4500 ft; 250 acres.

EL RITO (26)

El Rito Creek FREE
Carson National Forest
5.3 mi NW of El Rito on FR 129. Free. Elev 7600 ft. 4/15-10/15; 14-day limit. 11 sites (RVs under 22 ft). Firewood, tbls, cfga, toilets, no drkg wtr. Picnicking, fishing, horseback riding. Crowded in summer.
Fishing tip: Access El Rito Creek from the campground or from FR 559 N of the El Rito ranger station. Brown trout are plentiful in the lower reaches of the creek, and Rio Grande cutthroat are above Salvador Canyon. Alternative: Take Hwy 111 from El Rito to Rio Vallecitos and its brown trout.

ESPANOLA (27)

Santa Cruz Lake $7
Recreation Area
Bureau of Land Management
13 mi E of Espanola on SR 4 & SR 76. $7 for primitive sites at Overlook Campground; $9 for developed sites at North Lake. All year; 14-day limit. 30 sites (no RV size limit). Tbls, toilets, cfga, drkg wtr. Fishing, boating (l), hiking, canoeing.
Fishing tip: Santa Cruz Lake is stocked regularly with rainbow trout, but it also contains German brown trout & other species. The state record rainbow (31.78 pounds) was caught from here in 1999 on a jig-and-leech.

EUNICE (28)

Stephen Municipal Park FREE
4 mi W of Eunice on SR 176. Free. All year. 3-day limit. About 10 sites. Flush toilets, sheltered picnic units, elec/wtr, dump, playground. Tennis, picnicking, fishing (stocked lake), baseball fields, croquet courts, horseshoes, golf nearby, basketball, nature trails.

FORT SUMNER (29)

Sumner Lake State Park $8
16 mi N of Fort Sumner on US 84. $8 base. All year; 14-day limit. Base fee for 58 primitive sites; 50 developed sites (18 with elec) with shelters, $10 base. 45-ft RV limit. Tbls,

flush toilets, elec($), cfga, drkg wtr, dump, playground, showers, beach. Swimming, boating(l), fishing, waterskiing, sailing, hiking, biking. Elev 4300 ft; 6,667 acres.
Fishing tip: Sumner Lake's 4,600 acres are heavily populated with walleye, crappie, largemouth bass, white bass & spotted bass.

FORT WINGATE (30)

McGaffey $10
Cibola National Forest
7 mi S of Fort Wingate on SR 400. $10 base. 5/15-9/30; 14-day limit. Base fee for tent & RV sites withou;t hookups; $15 for RV sites with hookups. 5/15-9/30; 14-day limit. 29 sites (no RV size limit). Flush toilets, cfga, tbls, drkg wtr, showers. Group sites available by reservation. Fishing, hiking, boating (very small, shallow lake). Elev 8000 ft; 46 acres.

Quaking Aspen $5
Cibola National Forest
6 mi S of Fort Wingate on SR 400. $5. 5/15-9/30; 14-day limit. 19 sites (22-ft RV limit). Tbls, toilets, cfga, drkg wtr. Hunting, fishing, hiking trail. Elev 7600 ft.

GALLINA (31)

Resumidero FREE
Santa Fe National Forest
2.5 mi SE of Gallina on Hwy 96; 6.5 mi S on FR 103; 2 mi W on FR 93. Free. June-Oct; 14-day limit. About 10 undesignated sites. Tbls, toilets, cfga, no drkg wtr, no trash service. Hiking, fishing.

GALLUP (32)

Red Rock State Park $10
City of Gallup
Near Gallup off I-40. $10 without hookups; $15 with wtr hookups; $20 elec/wtr. All year; 14-day limit. 140 sites. Tbls, flush toilets, cfga, drkg wtr, dump, hookups($), playground, store, showers, horse stalls($). Hiking trails, fishing. Visitor center; museum; rodeo arena. $1 discount for AARP, Good Sam, RV clubs.
Fishing tip: Consider a side trip to Whiskey Lake, N of Gallup on the Navajo reservation. Typical catches are rainbow 14-18 inches, but 20-24 inchers are not uncommon. You'll need Navajo fishing & boating permit.

GLENWOOD (33)

Bighorn FREE
Gila National Forest
On N edge of Glenwood at US 180. Free. All year; 30-day limit. 17 sites. Tbls, toilets, cfga, no drkg wtr. Elev 4800 ft.

Pueblo Park FREE
Gila National Forest
25 mi N of Glenwood on US 180; 5.6 mi W

on FR 232 (18 mi SW of Reserve). Apr-Nov; 30-day limit. 6 sites. Tbls, toilets, cfga, spring wtr, no trash service. Hiking, rockhounding. Elev 6150 ft.

GOBERNADOR (34)

Sims Mesa Area $8
Navajo Lake State Park
N of Gobernador on Hwy 527. $8 base. All year; 14-day limit. Base fee for primitive sites; 47 developed sites $10 base; 35-ft RV limit. Tbls, flush toilets, cfga, drkg wtr, dump, showers, playground, elec($4), store. Fishing, waterskiing, boating(ldr), birdwatching, hunting, swimming.

GRANTS (35)

Bluewater Lake State Park $8
28 mi W of Grants via I-40 and SR 412. $8 base. All year; 14-day limit. Base fee for 150 primitive sites; 149 developed sites, $10 base. 45-ft RV limit. Elec($4), tbls, flush toilets, cfga, drkg wtr, dump, playground, store, no showers. Nature trails, fishing, waterskiing, boating(lrd), swimming. Elev 7500 ft; 2,104 acres. Visitor center.

Coal Mine Canyon $5
Cibola National Forest
10 mi NE of Grants on SR 547. $5. 5/15-9/30; 14-day limit. 17 sites (22-ft RV limit). Tbls, flush toilets, cfga, drkg wtr. Picnicking, hiking, nature trail. Elev 7400 ft.

The Narrows FREE
El Mapais National Conservation Area
Bureau of Land Management
E of Grants on I-40, then 18 mi S on Hwy 117. Free. All year; 14-day limit. 3 sites plus dispersed camping area. Tbls, flush toilets, cfga, drkg wtr. Hiking, climbing, biking. El Mapais National Monument nearby (no camping at the monument).

El Morro National Monument $5
42 mi SW of Grants on Hwy 53 at Ramah. $5 plus $3 entry fee for 7 days. All year; free when wtr is off. 9 sites. Tbls, toilets, cfga, drkg wtr. Hiking, museum, visitor center.

Lobo Canyon FREE
Cibola National Forest
10 mi NE of Grants via NM 547 & FR 239 & FR 193. Free. Apr-Oct; 14-day limit. 6 sites (no trailers), 8 picnic sites. Toilets, cfga, no drkg wtr. Hiking, picnicking. Elev 7400 ft.

HILLSBORO (36)

Middle Percha FREE
Gila National Forest
7 mi W of Hillsboro on SR 152; 2 mi N on FR 157. Free. All year; 30-day limit. About 5 primitive dispersed sites. No facilities, no drkg wtr. Hiking, horseback riding. Be aware of private land in the area.

HOBBS (37)

Harry McAdams State Park   **$11**
4 mi NW of Hobbs on SR 18. $11. All year. 47 sites. Tbls, flush toilets, showers, cfga, elec($4), dump, playground, drkg wtr. Fishing ponds open only to children.

JAL (38)

Jal City Park   **FREE**
In town. Free. All year; 3-day limit. 6 sites. Tbls, toilets, cfga, elec, drkg wtr, dump. Fishing.

JEMEZ SPRINGS (39)

Calaveras Campground   **FREE**
Seven Springs Fish Hatchery
7.5 mi N of Jemez Springs on Hwy 4; left on Hwy 126 for 12 mi. Free. May-Nov. Primitive undesignated sites for about 5 RVs. Tbls, toilets, cfga, no drkg wtr. Hiking, hunting, fishing. Fish hatchery about half mi.

Jemez Falls   **$10**
Santa Fe National Forest
15 mi NE of Jemez Springs on NM 4; 1 mi S on FR 133 (primitive roadway). $10. 4/15-11/15; 14-day limit. 52 sites (40-ft trailer limit, 45-ft motorhome limit). Tbls, toilets, cfga, drkg wtr. Picnicking, hiking, fishing. Elev 7900 ft; 2 acres. Scenic. National Recreation Trailhead. Trail access to scenic Jemez Falls & nearby hot springs.

Redondo   **$10**
Santa Fe National Forest
11.3 mi NE of Jemez Springs on SR 4. $10. 4/15-11/15; 14-day limit. 59 sites (30-ft trailer limit, 45-ft motorhome limit). Tbls, toilets, cfga, drkg wtr, amphitheater. 4 hiking trails, nature trail.

San Antonio   **$10**
Santa Fe National Forest
9 mi NE of Jemez Springs on SR 4; 1.5 mi N on SR 126. $10. 4/15-11/15; 14-day limit. 42 sites (35-ft RV limit). Tbls, toilets, cfga, drkg wtr. Swimming, fishing, hiking. Wheelchair access; group sites available. Elev 7800 ft; 10 acres.

Seven Springs   **N/A**
Santa Fe National Forest
9.1 mi NE of Jemez Springs on SR 4; 9.7 mi NW on SR 126; 1.6 mi E on FR 314. Fee charged, but amount unknown; camp being renovated at last report; not open in 2007. Elev 8000 ft. 5/15-9/15; 14-day limit. Sites undetermined. Tbls, toilets, cfga, firewood, drkg wtr. Boating (d; l--5 mi); picnicking, fishing. State fish hatchery 2 mi.

Vista Linda   **$10**
Santa Fe National Forest
5 mi S of Jemez Springs on SR 4; near James River. $10. All year; 14-day limit. 13 improved pull-through sites (40-ft RV limit). Tbls, toilets, cfga, drkg wtr. Hiking.

LAS CRUCES (40)

Aguirre Spring   **$6**
Organ Mountain Recreation Area
Bureau of Land Management
5 mi S of US 70 and 17 me E of Las Cruces. $3 day use fee plus $3 vehicle fee. All year; 14-day limit. 57 sites (RVs under 22 ft). Tbls, toilets, cfga, shelters, no drkg wtr. Hiking, picnicking, horseback riding. Interpretive trails and facilities. Elev 6400 ft; 160 acres.

Leasburg Dam State Park   **$8**
15 mi N of Las Cruces on I-25; from exit 19, W on SR 157; at Radium Springs. $8 base. All year; 14/-day limit. Base fee for 25 primitive sites; 31 developed sites (10 with elec) with shelters, $10 base; 36-ft RV limit. Tbls, flush toilets, cfga, drkg wtr, elec($4), dump, showers, playground. Fishing, hiking trails, kayaking, canoeing. Visitor center. Fort Selden State Monument nearby. Elev 4000 ft; 140 acres.

LAS TRAMPAS (41)

Trampas Diamante   **FREE**
Carson National Forest
1 mi N on Hwy 76; 5 mi SE on FR 207. Free. 5/15-9/30; 14-day limit. 5 sites (RVs under 16 ft). Tbls, toilets, cfga, no drkg wtr. Picnicking, fishing, hiking. Trailhead.

Trampas Trailhead   **FREE**
Carson National Forest
7.8 mi W of Los Trampas on NM 76. Free. May-Sept; 14-day limit. 5 sites (RVs under 17 ft). Toilets, no drkg wtr. Fishing. Elev 9000 ft.

LAS VEGAS (42)

E.V. Long   **$8**
Santa Fe National Forest
16.2 mi NW of Las Vegas on SR 65; .1 mi SW on FR 156; at El Porvenir Creek. $8. Elev 7500 ft. 5/1-11/15; 14-day limit. 21 sites (RVs under 25 ft). Tbls, toilets, cfga, well drkg wtr. Picnicking, fishing, hiking, climbing, hunting.

El Porvenir   **$8**
Santa Fe National Forest
17 mi NW of Las Vegas on SR 65; .7 mi W on FR 261. $8. 5/1-11/15; 14-day limit. 13 sites (32-ft RV limit). Tbls, toilets, cfga, drkg wtr. Fishing, hiking.

McAllister Lake   **FREE**
Waterfowl Area
Las Vegas National Wildlife Refuge
1.5 mi E of Las Vegas on Hwy 104; 6.4 mi on Hwy 281; camp on the S & W sides of lake. 4/1-10/31; 14-day limit. 20 sites. Tbls, toilets, cfga, no drkg wtr. Fishing, boating, birdwatching.
Fishing tip: This very fertile 100-acre lake contains lots of fast-growing rainbow trout, many in the 14-18 inch range and some 20-24 inches. Good float tube water.

Storrie Lake State Park   **$8**
4 mi N of Las Vegas on SR 518. $8 base. All year; 14-day limit. Base fee for 50 primitive sites; 45 developed sites with shelters (21 with elec), $10 base; 35-ft RV limit. Tbls, flush toilets, cfga, drkg wtr, showers, dump, elec($4), playground. Windsurfing, waterskiing, boating(l), fishing. Visitor center with historical displays. Elev 6400 ft; 82 acres.
Fishing tip: This 1,000-acre lake's most popular fish are crappie and rainbow trout.

Villanueva State Park   **$10**
23 mi S of Las Vegas on I-25 to exit 323; 15 mi S on SR 3. $10 base. All year; 14-day limit. 33 developed sites (19 with shelters, 12 with elec); 40-ft RV limit. Tbls, flush toilets, cfga, drkg wtr, elec($4), showers, dump, playground. Fishing, spring canoeing & rafting, nature trails. Visitor center. Old ranching ruins. Elev 6000 ft; 1,679 acres.

LINCOLN (43)

Fort Stanton Recreation Area   **FREE**
Bureau of Land Management
W of Lincoln via US 380 & SR 214. Free. All year; 14-day limit. Primitive undesignated sites. Toilets, tbls, cfga no drkg wtr. Hiking (Rio Bonito Petroglyph Trail), horseback riding, biking, caving, fishing, hunting.

LOGAN (44)

Ute Lake State Park   **$8**
3 mi W of Logan on SR 540; on Canadian River. $8 base. All year; 14-day limit. Base fee at primitive sites; 142 developed sites (77 with elec) with shelters, $10 base; 45-ft RV limit. Tbls, flush toilets, elec($4), cfga, drkg wtr, dump, showers, playground, beach. Swimming, boating(lrd), fishing, nature trails, waterskiing. 2 handicap-access sites. Visitor center. Elev 3895 ft; 1,524 acres.
Fishing tip: Ute Lake, an 8,000-acre reservoir of the Canadian River, offers some of best walleye fishing in the state as well as good fishing for bass, crappie and catfish. The lake also has good white bass fishing.

LORDSBURG (45)

Lower Gila Box   **FREE**
Bureau of Land Management
2 mi NW of Lordsburg on US 70; 14 mi N on Hwy 464; 3.5 mi W on CR A027, then 4.5 mi N on CR A024 from the steel storage tank; camp area not marked. Free. About 12 primitive undesignated sites; no facilities, no trash service. Hiking, canoeing, fishing. Gila River.

LOS ALAMOS (46)

Fenton Lake State Park   **$10**
35 mi W of Los Alamos on Hwy 4. $10 base. All year; 14-day limit. 37 developed sites (2 handicap access; 5 sites with elec); 32-ft RV limit. Tbls, flush toilets, cfga, drkg

wtr, elec($4), playground. Fishing, picnicking, boating(ld), hiking trails, skiing, wheelchair-accessible fishing platforms. Elev 7978 ft; 700 acres.

Fishing tip: Fenton Lake and the Jemez mountain streams are heavily stocked with rainbow trout, and some streams also contain brown trout.

LOVINGTON (47)

Chaparral City Park　　FREE
2 mi SE of truck bypass on SR 82 (S. Commercial St). Free. All year. 15 self-contained sites. Tbls, toilets, cfga, phones. Fishing, tennis, basketball, volleyball, jogging path. 80-acre park.

Fishing tip: Try the largemouth bass in 20-acre Chaparral Lake.

LUNA (48)

Trout Creek　　FREE
Apache National Forest
2.8 mi N of Luna on FR 19; at Trout Creek. Free. All year; 30-day limit. Primitive undesignated dispersed sites along creek. No facilities. Fishing, hunting.

MAGDALENA (49)

Bear Trap　　FREE
Cibola National Forest
26 mi SW of Magdalena via US 60 & FR 549. Free. May-Oct; 14-day limit. 4 sites (20-ft RV limit). Toilets, cfga, no drkg wtr. Hiking, hunting, horseback riding. Elev 8500 ft.

Hughes Mill　　FREE
Cibola National Forest
26 mi SW of Magdalena via US 60 & FR 549. Free. May-Oct; 14-day limit. 2 sites (20-ft RV limit) and dispersed camping with trailead. Toilets, cfga, no drkg wtr. Hiking trail. Elev 8100 ft.

Water Canyon　　FREE
Cibola National Forest
16 mi SE of Magdalena via US 60 & FR 235. Free. All year; 14-day limit. 4 sites (22-ft RV limit); 11 picnic sites. Tbls, toilets, cfga, no drkg wtr. Hiking, biking trail. Elev 6800 ft. Reader says camp is "unkept, tends to be a party spot for young people at night."

MANZANO (50)

Capilla Peak　　FREE
Cibola National Forest
12 mi W of Manzano via NM 55 & FR 245 (rough rd). Free.. May-Sept; 14-day limit. 8 sites (RVs under 17 ft). Toilets, cfga, no drkg wtr. Hiking, horseback riding, hunting. Elev 9200 ft. Reconstructed in 2005.

New Canyon　　FREE
Cibola National Forest
5 mi W of Manzano on SR 55 & FR 245.

Free. Apr-Nov; 14-day limit. 10 sites (22-ft RV limit). Tbls, toilets, cfga, no drkg wtr. Hiking, picnicking, hunting.

Red Canyon　　$7
Cibola National Forest
6 mi W of Manzano on SR 55 & FR 253. $7. Apr-Nov; 14-day limit. 49 sites; 22-ft limit (camp recently refurbished). Tbls, toilets, cfga, drkg wtr. Hiking, hunting, horseback riding. Elev 8000 ft.

MAXWELL (51)

Maxwell Lake Campground　　FREE
Maxwell national Wildlife Refuge
1 mi N of Maxwell on Hwy 455; 2.5 mi W on Hwy 505, then 2 mi N to lake. Free. 3/1-10/31; 14-day limit. Primitive undesignated sites. Tbls, toilets, no drkg wtr, no fires. Fishing, birdwatching, boating(l).

Fishing tip: 450-acre Lake 13 produces rainbow trout between 13 and 34 inches.

MAYHILL (52)

Bear Canyon & Dam　　FREE
Dispersed Area
Lincoln National Forest
S of Mayhill on SR 130, then S on SR 24; after crossing the Rio Penasco, keep to the right onto FR 621 to switchback. Free. All year; 14-day limit. Primitive undeveloped RV area. Tenters can go on to Bear Canyon Dam (no place there for RVs to turn around). No facilities, no drkg wtr. Hiking, hunting.

Fishing tip: Fish Penasco River in the fall & spring for brown and rainbow trout.

Burnt Canyon　　FREE
Dispersed Area
Lincoln National Forest
2 mi E of Mayhill on US 82; 3 mi N on FR 607 (Car Gap Rd); turn right to the curve. Free. All year; 14-day limit. Primitive undeveloped area for 4-5 RVs. Hiking, wildlife study.

Hoosier Canyon　　FREE
Dispersed Area
Lincoln National Forest
S of Mayholl on SR 130, then SE on SR 24; W on FR 521 through Weed & Sacramento to FR 64; follow FR 64 about 6 mi to Hoosier Canyon (FR 5959). Free. All year; 14-day limit. Primitive undeveloped flat camping areas; no facilities, no drkg wtr. Hiking, hunting.

James Canyon　　FREE
Lincoln National Forest
2 mi NW of Mayhill on US 82. Apr-Nov; 14-day limit. 6 sites (RVs under 16 ft). Tbls, toilets, cfga, no drkg wtr, 1 group ramada. Picnicking, fishing. Elev 6800 ft. Botanical.

Miller Flats Road　　FREE
Dispersed Area
Lincoln National Forest
1.5 mi S of Mayhill on SR 130; left onto Miller Flats Rd (FR 212) for about 2 mi; on left is

sign for Bible Canyon; on right is flat, grassy area for free primitive camping. No facilities, no drkg wtr. Hiking, wildlife study.

Prestridge Hill/Hay Canyon　　FREE
Dispersed Area
Lincoln National Forest
S of Mayhill on SR 30, past SR 24 turnoff for about 4 mi; S onto FR 164 for half mi from sign for Wills Canyon; S on FR 541 over Prestridge Hill, intersecting with FR 257 at Hay Canyon. Free. All year; 14-day limit. Primitive undesignated camping in flat areas among trees. No facilities, no drkg wtr. Hiking, hunting, widlife study.

Top of Denny Hill　　FREE
Dispersed Area
Lincoln National Forest
S of Mayhill on SR 130 to southbound SR 24; ascend Denny Hill; cross cattle guard to pull-off. Free. All year; 14-day limit. Primitive undeveloped camping; no facilities, no drkg wtr. Hiking, wildlife study.

MILLS (53)

Mills Canyon　　FREE
Kiowa National Grassland
Cibola National Forest
10 mi SW of Mills, off Hwy 39 on FR 600. Rd is poor for RVs; high clearance vehicles only. Free. All year; 14-day limit. 7 sites (no trailers). Tbls, toilets, cfga, drkg wtr. Picnicking, fishing, hiking, rockhounding. Located in a very scenic canyon in the middle of flat plains; excellent spot for watching cliff-dwelling birds & Barbury sheep.

MIMBRES (54)

Bear Canyon Reservoir　　FREE
State Fishing Area
State Game & Fish Department
Gila National Forest
2 mi N of Mimbres, then W on forest rd; dispersed sites along shore of lake. Toilets, cfga, tbls, no drkg wtr. Fishing, boating(l).

Cooney　　FREE
Gila National Forest
9 mi N of Mimbres on Hwy 36; right on FR 150 about 6 mi, then right on FR 150A. Free. All year; 14-day limit. Primitive undesignated sites; no facilities. Hiling (trailhead for Aldo Leopold Wilderness).

Lower Black Canyon　　FREE
Gila National Forest
22 mi N of Mimbres on SR 35 & FR 150 (high clearance vehicles best). Free. 4/1-11/30; 30-day limit. 3 sites (17-ft RV limit). Tbls, toilets, cfga, no drkg wtr. Fishing (from fish barrier downstream), hiking, horseback riding. Elev 6900 ft; 2 acres. Scenic.

Mesa　　$7
Gila National Forest
3 mi from Mimbres Ranger station at Lake Roberts (30 mi NE of Silver City via SRs 15

& 35). $7. All year; 14-day limit. 24 sites. Tbls, toilets, cfga, drkg wtr. Fishing, boating, hiking.

Fishing tip: Great fishing is available on 72-acre Lake Roberts; elec motors only. Catch rainbow trout in spring & fall, smallmouth bass and channel catfish in summer. Best catches between late March & late May.

Rocky Canyon   FREE
Gila National Forest
4 mi NW of Mimbres on Hwy 35; 13 mi N on FR 150 (high-clearance vehicles suggested). Free. 4/1-11/30; 30-day limit. 2 sites (17-ft RV limit). Tbls, toilets, cfga, no drkg wtr. Hiking, fishing. Favored as fall hunting camp. Elev 7300 ft.

Sapillo Group Camp   FREE
Gila National Forest
9.8 mi NW of Mimbres on SR 61; 6.6 mi W on SR 35; half mi S on FR 606. Free. All year; 30-day limit. 8 dispersed group sites. Toilets, cfga, no tbls, no drkg wtr. Hiking, horseback riding, fishing. Elev 6100 ft; 5 acres. Scenic.

Upper Black Canyon   FREE
Gila National Forest
23 mi N of Mimbres on NM 150 (high-clearance vehicles suggested). Free. 4/1-11/30; 30-day limit. 2 sites (22-ft RV limit). Tbls, toilets, cfga, no drkg wtr. Hiking, fishing. Elev 6900 ft.

Upper End $7
Gila National Forest
12 mi NW of Mimbres on SR 35. $7 during MD-LD; free rest of yr, but no wtr; 7-day limit. 10 sites (32-ft RV limit). Tbls, toilets, cfga, drkg wtr. Fishing, boating(lr nearby), hiking. Elev 6000 ft; 13 acres.

MONTICELLO (55)

Luna Park   FREE
Cibola National Forest
8 mi N of Monticello on FR 139. High clearance vehicles only. Free. Apr-Nov; 14-day limit. 3 sites (20-ft RV limit). Toilets, cfga, no drkg wtr. Hiking, horseback riding, hunting. Odd volcanic rock formations give moon-like appearance to this site. Elev 7400 ft.

Springtime   FREE
Cibola National Forest
10 mi NE of Monticello on FR 139. High-clearance vehicles only. Free. Apr-Nov; 14-day limit. 6 sites with Adirondack shelters. Toilets, cfga, no drkg wtr. Wtr & corral for horses. Hiking, bridle trails. Elev 7400 ft.

MORA (56)

Coyote Creek State Park $8
17 mi N of Mora on SR 434. $8 base. All year; 14-day limit. Base fee at primitive sites; 47 developed sites (12 with shelters, 17 with elec), $10; 35-ft RV limit. Tbls, flush toilets, cfga, drkg wtr, elec($4), showers, playground, dump. Fishing, picnicking, hiking trails. Visitor center. Elev 7700 ft. Recent expansion added 382 acres to 80-acre park.

Fishing tip: N of the state park on SR 434, a state fishing easement along 1.15 mi of Coyote Creek in Guadalupita Canyon provides excellent action for stocked trout. It's called the Harold L. Brock Fishing Area. It has two gravel parking lots and basic toilets.

Morphy Lake State Park $8
4 mi S of Mora on SR 94; 4 mi W on steep dirt rd; accessible by foot, horseback or four-wheel drive. $8 at primitive sites, $10 at 20 developed sites. 4/1-10/31; 14-day limit. No drkg wtr. Tbls, toilets, cfga. Picnicking, boating (elec mtrs), fishing. Elev 7840 ft; 18 acres.

MOUNTAINAIR (57)

Fourth of July Campground $7
Cibola National Forest
23 mi N of Mountainair to Tajique; 8 mi W on FR 55. $7. Apr-Nov; 14-day limit. 25 sites. Tbls, toilets, cfga, drkg wtr. Hiking, horseback riding.

Manzano Mountains State Park $8
16 mi NW of Mountainair on SR 55. $8 base. About 4/15-10/31; 14-day limit. Base fee at primitive sites; 37 developed sites (5 with shelters, 8 with elec), $10 base; 30-ft RV limit. Elec($4), tbls, flush toilets, cfga, drkg wtr, playground, no showers. Nature trails, birdwatching, cross-country skiing. Salinas National Monument nearby. Elev 7200 ft; 160 acres.

PECOS (58)

Mora River   FREE
State Game & Fish Department
14 mi N of Pecos on Hwy 63; at Mora & Pecos Rivers. Free. All year; 14-day limit. About 40 primitive undesignated sites. Tbls, toilets, cfga, no drkg wtr. Fishing.

Fishing tip: This is a good spot for some fine rainbow and brown trout fishing in both streams.

Cow Creek   FREE
Santa Fe National Forest
10 mi NE of Pecos on FR 86 & FR 322. Primitive roadway; possible problems on access rd; check conditions before using. Free. May-Oct; 14-day limit. 5 sites (no trailers). Toilets, cfga, no drkg wtr. Fishing. Elev 8300 ft. Note: This camp was partly destroyed by forest fire and at presstime was undergoing rehabilitation and not operable.

Field Tract $8
Santa Fe National Forest
9 mi N of Pecos on SR 63. $8. 5/1-11/15; 14-day limit. 15 sites (22-ft RV limit). Tbls, flush & pit toilets, cfga, drkg wtr. Some Adirondack shelters. Fishing, hiking. Elev 7400 ft; 5 acres.

Fishing tip: Try the nearby Monastery Lake fishing area on SR 63. It includes a short stretch of the Pecos River and is heavily stocked with rainbow trout. In late summer and early fall, the river produces big brown trout.

Travel tip: Rainbow trout stocked in the lake & river come from the nearby Lisboa Springs State Fish Hatchery -- New Mexico's oldest hatchery. Located 2 mi N of Pecos on SR 63, it is open for visitors to see trout in a display pond and rearing ponds.

Glorieta   FREE
Santa Fe National Forest
12 mi W of Pecos on NM 50; 12 mi NW on FR 375 (primitive roadway). Free. May-Oct; 14-day limit. 5 sites (no trailers). Toilets, cfga, no drkg wtr. Elev 10,000 ft. Hiking; trailhead.

Holy Ghost $8
Santa Fe National Forest
13.2 mi N of Pecos on SR 63; 2.2 mi NW on FR 122. $8. 5/1-11/15; 14-day limit. 24 sites (32-ft RV limit). Tbls, toilets, cfga, drkg wtr. Fishing. 20 acres.

Iron Gate $8
Santa Fe National Forest
18.8 mi N of Pecos on SR 63; 4.2 mi NE on FR 223. $8 (trailhead parking, $2) Elev 9400 ft. 5/1-10/31; 14-day limit. 14 sites (RV rigs under 31 ft). Tbls, toilets, cfga, no drkg wtr. Hiking, picnicking, fishing, horseback riding (4 corrals). 8 acres. Pecos Wilderness.

Jacks Creek $10
Santa Fe National Forest
18 mi N of Pecos on SR 63 to Cowles; 1 mi N on FR 555. $10 (equestrian camping, $12). 5/1-11/15; 14-day limit. 29 sites, newly refurbished; 40-ft RV limit. Tbls, toilets, cfga, drkg wtr, corrals. Hiking, fishing.

Fishing tip: SR 63 provides easy access to a well-stocked section of the Pecos River, with its 14-inch rainbows. Good summer fishing.

Terrero Campground   FREE
Bert Clancy Fish & Wildlife Area
N of Pecos on SR 63 along the Pecos River. Free. All year; 14-day limit. 10 primitive sites. Tbls, toilets, cfga, drkg wtr. Fishing, widlife study, hiking. 2,166 acres.

Fishing tip: The Pecos River here contains both native and stocked rainbow trout.

PIE TOWN (59)

Lester Jackson   FREE
Park & Campground
Small town is 86 mi W of Socorro & 56 mi E of the state line on edge of Gila National Forest on US 60; 1 block N of post office. Free. Undesignated sites on 78 acres. Tbls, toilets, cfga, no drkg wtr.

PONDEROSA (60)

Paliza $10
Santa Fe National Forest
3 mi N of Ponderosa on FR 10. $10. 5/15-9/15; 14-day limit. 26 sites (30-ft RV limit). Tbls, toilets, cfga, drkg wtr. Fishing, hiking, hunting. Elev 5700 ft; 10 acres. Closed for reconstruction until about September 2007.

PORTALES (61)

Oasis State Park $8
7.5 mi NE of Portales off SR 467. $8 base. All year; 14-day limit. Base fee for 10 primitive sites; 23 developed sites (13 with shelters), $10 base. 65-ft RV limit. Tbls, flush toilets, cfga, drkg wtr, dump, elec($4), showers, playground. Picnicking, fishing, hiking trails, birdwatching. Elev 4030 ft; 196 acres; 3-acre pond.

QUEMADO (62)

Armijo Springs FREE
Gila National Forest
20 mi S of Quemado on Hwy 32; left on FR 854 for 6 mi. Free. All year; 14-day limit. Primitive undesignated sites for tents or self-contained RVs. Tbls, toilet, cfga, no drkg wtr. Wtr & corrals for horses. Horseback riding, hunting.

El Caso FREE
Gila National Forest
20 mi S of Quemado on Hwy 32; 4 mi E on Hwy 103; just past E end of Quemado Lake on FR 13. Free. All year; 14-day limit. 22 primitive dispersed sites along rd. Tbls, toilets, cfga, no drkg wtr. Boating(l), fishing at lake.

Juniper Campground $10
Gila National Forest
W of Quemado on US 60; S on SR 32; E on FR 13; on N side of Quemado Lake. $10 without hookups; $15 with RV hookups. 5/1-9/30; 14-day limit. 36 sites; 30 to 42-ft RV limit. Tbls, toilets, cfga, drkg wtr. Boating(l), fishing.
Fishing tip: 131-acre Quemado Lake is the largest lake in Gila NF. It is a very good trout lake and has produced big rainbows even though most of the fishing is from shore. This camp is only 200 yards from the shoreline. Spring & fall are the best times.

Pinon Campground $10
Gila National Forest
W of Quemado on US 60; S on SR 32; E on FR 13; on N side of Quemado Lake one-third mi E of Juniper camps. $10. 5/1-9/30; 14-day limit. 22 sites; 40 ft RV limit. Tbls, toilets, cfga, drkg wtr, dump ($5 non-campers). Fishing, boating(l). Elev 8000 ft.

Quemado Lake FREE
Gila National Forest
23 mi S of Quemado on US 60, SR 32 & FR

13; at 130-acre Quemado Lake. Free. Mar-Nov; 7-day limit. 46 dispersed sites. Tbls, toilets, cfga, no drkg wtr. Fishing, boating(l), horseback riding, hiking, hunting. Elev 7750 ft.

Valle Tio Vinces FREE
Gila National Forest
9 mi E of Quemado on Hwy 60; 19 mi S on FR 214. All year; 14-day limit. 4 sites. Tbls, cfga, no drkg wtr, no toilets. Wtr, troughs & corrals for horses. Bridle trails, hunting. Primarily a horse camp.

QUESTA (63)

Big Arsenic Springs $7
Wild Rivers Recreation Area
Bureau of Land Management
3 mi N of Questa on Hwy 522; left on Hwy 378, follow signs. $7 (two RVs, $10). All year; 14-day limit. $5 for for hike-in tent sites along river. 6 developed sites and designated primitive hike-in river sites. Tbls, toilets, cfga, drkg wtr. Fishing, hiking.
Fishing tip: The Rio Grande contains northern pike, native & German brown trout and rainbows. Special trout fishing regulations are in effect on all river sections within the recreation area.

Cabresto Lake FREE
Carson National Forest
6 mi NE of Questa on FR 134; 2 mi NE on FR 134A (poor access rd); overlooking 15-acre lake. Elev 9500 ft. 5/15-10/31; 14-day limit. 9 sites for tents, pop-ups, vans or pickup campers (no larger RVs due to winding rd). Tbls, toilets, cfga, drkg wtr. Boating (no motors in lake), picnicking, fishing.
Fishing tip: Little Cabresto Lake is one of the few places in New Mexico to catch brook trout, and it also contains other species of trout, with rainbow providing the best action.

Cebolla Mesa FREE
Carson National Forest
8 mi SW of Questa on NM 3 & FR 9. Free. May-Sept; 14-day limit. 5 sites (32-ft RV limit). Toilets, tbls, cfga, no drkg wtr. Fishing, hiking. Trailhead. Elev 7300 ft.
Fishing tip: There is good access to some topnotch Rio Grande brown & rainbow trout from this campground. Large fish are often caught from here.

Columbine $7.50
Carson National Forest
5 mi E of Questa on SR 38. $7.50 with federal Senior Pass; others pay $15. MD-10/1; 14-day limit. 27 sites (32-ft RV limit). Tbls, toilets, cfga, drkg wtr. Fishing, hiking, rockhounding, horseback riding. Columbine Creek, Red River. Elev 7900 ft; 22 acres.
Fishing tip: From Questa to the town of Red River, the Red River is heavily stocked with rainbow trout. There is excellent fishing from Hwy 38, and five campgrounds provide places to stay.

El Aguaje Campground $7
Wild Rivers Recreation Area
Bureau of Land Management
3 mi N of Questa on Hwy 522; left on Hwy 378, follow signs. $7. All year; 14-day limit. $5 for hike-in tent sites along river. 6 developed sites. Tbls, toilets, cfga, drkg wtr. Fishing, hiking.
Fishing tip: The Red River contains rainbow trout stocked by the fish hatchery upstream. Access from Hwy 522 N too Arroyo Hondo.

Goat Hill FREE
Carson National Forest
4 me E of Questa on NM 38; roadside camping with access to Red River. Free. May-Sept; 14-day limit. 6 sites (32-ft RV limit). Toilet, no drkg wtr. Fishing. Elev 7500 ft.

La Bobita FREE
Carson National Forest
6.1 mi E of Questa on NM 38. All year; 14-day limit. Primitive overflow camp open when others nearby are full. Toilets, tbls, cfga, no drkg wtr.

La Junta Campground $7
Wild Rivers Recreation Area
Bureau of Land Management
3 mi N of Questa on Hwy 522; left on Hwy 378, follow signs. $7. All year; 14-day limit. $5 for hike-in tent sites along river. 6 developed sites. Tbls, toilets, cfga, drkg wtr. Fishing, hiking.
Fishing tip: La Junta Creek contains brown, rainbow and small numbers of Rio Grande cutthroat trout.

Little Arsenic Spring $7
Wild Rivers Recreation Area
Bureau of Land Management
3 mi N of Questa on Hwy 522; left on Hwy 378, follow signs. $7. All year; 14-day limit. $5 for hike-in tent sites along river. 4 developed sites. Tbls, toilets, cfga, drkg wtr. Fishing, hiking.

Montoso Campground $7
Wild Rivers Recreation Area
Bureau of Land Management
3 mi N of Questa on Hwy 522; left on Hwy 378, follow signs. $7. All year; 14-day limit. $5 for hike-in tent sites along river. 2 developed sites. Tbls, toilet, cfga, drkg wtr. Fishing, hiking.

Red River FREE
State Trout Hatchery
Carson National Forest
6 mi S of Questa on US 522; W on Hwy 515; sites along road at tbls, shelters, cfga. Free. Drkg wtr & toilets at hatchery. Fishing. Tour hatchery. Open all year.

RADIO (64)

Idlewild $10
Coronado National Forest
SW of Radio on Hwy 80, then 7 mi W on rd to Portal, AZ; 2 mi W on FR 42; must ford stream at one point (impassable in wet weather). $10 during 4/1-10/31; free rest of year. 10 sites. Tbls, toilets, cfga, drkg wtr. Hiking, fishing.

Rustler Park $10
Coronado National Forest
SW of Radio on Hwy 80, then W on rd to Portal, AZ; W on FR 42 & FR 42D toward Chiricahua National Monument; must ford stream at one point (impassable in wet weather); 2.5 mi S on Onion Saddle Rd. $10 when wtr available; free about Dec-Apr. 22 sites; 16-ft RV limit. Tbls, toilets, cfga, drkg wtr. Hiking.

Sunny Flat $10
Coronado National Forest
SW of Radio on Hwy 80, then 7 mi W on rd to Portal, AZ; 3 mi W on FR 42; must ford stream at one point (impassable in wet weather). $10 during 4/1-11/30; free rest of year; 14-day limit. 12 sites; 16-ft RV limit. Tbls, toilets, cfga, drkg wtr. Hiking, fishing.

RATON (66)

NRA Whittington Center $12
S of Raton on US 64; on 52 sq mile property. $12 for primitive camping; $18 at developed RV camp with hookups. Tbls, flush toilets & chemical, cfga, drkg wtr, showers, dump, coin laundry. Shooting range, hunting.

Raton RV Park $8
At 1012 S. Second St., Raton. $8 without hookups; $15 with full hookups. 35 sites. Tbls, flush toilets, cfga, drkg wtr, hookups($), restaurant.

Sugarite Canyon State Park $10
10 mi NE of Raton on SR 526. $10 base. All year; 14-day limit. 40 developed sites (10 with shelters, 12 with elec); 40-ft RV limit. Tbls, elec($4), flush toilets, cfga, drkg wtr, showers, dump. Boating(ld), canoeing, fishing, winter sports, hiking trails. Historical, nature exhibits; visitor center. Elev 7000 ft; 3,600 acres.

RED RIVER (67)

Elephant Rock $7.50
Carson National Forest
2.7 mi W of Red River on SR 38; near Red River. $7.50 with federal Senior Pass; others pay $15. MD-10/1; 14-day limit. 22 sites (18-ft RV limit). Tbls, toilets, cfga, drkg wtr. Fishing, hiking trails, biking. Elev 8300 ft; 2 acres. Fawn Lakes.
Fishing tip: Excellent fishing is available at Red River and nearby Eagle Rock Lake, which is stocked with catchable rainbows.

Fawn Lakes $7.50
Carson National Forest
3.2 mi W of Red River on SR 38. $7.50 with federal Senior Pass; others pay $15. MD-10/1; 14-day limit. 22 sites (32-ft RV limit); refurbished paved loops at 2 small stocked ponds. Tbls, toilets, cfga, drkg wtr. Fishing, hiking, rockhounding, biking. Can be crowded on summer weekends. Elev 8500 ft; 8 acres.
Fishing tip: Fawn Lakes are actually 2 small ponds that have been stocked with rainbow trout.

Junebug $7.50
Carson National Forest
2.2 mi W of Red River on SR 38. $7.50 with federal Senior Pass; others pay $15. MD-10/1; 14-day limit. 20 sites (22-ft RV limit), recently refurbished & sites doubled. Tbls, toilets, cfga, drkg wtr. Fishing, hiking, rockhounding. Near historic Red River mining area. Busy on summer weekends. Elev 8500 ft; 5 acres.

Middle Fork Lake FREE
Carson National Forest
9.7 mi S of Red River on FR 578 (4x4 rd steep, with switchbacks) to lake. 6/1-10/31; 14-day limit. 4 tent sites. Toilet, cfga, no drkg wtr. Fishing, hiking, OHV activity. Elizabethtown mining ghost town.

RESERVE (68)

Ben Lilly FREE
Gila National Forest
5 mi S of Reserve on SR 435; 28.5 mi SE on FR 141; 12.5 mi SW on SR 78; 1 mi W on FR 507. Free. 4/1-11/30; 30-day limit. 7 sites (RVs under 18 ft). Tbls, toilets, cfga, no drkg wtr. Picnicking, fishing, horseback riding. Elev 8100 ft. At N edge of Gila Wilderness.

Dipping Vat $5
Gila National Forest
6 mi S of Reserve on SR 435; 23.5 mi SE on FR 141; 9.5 mi SW on FR 78; 7 mi E on FR 142. $5 for primitive sites during. 5/1-11/15; free rest of yr at lower loop, but no wtr or elec; 30-day limit. 40 sites (20-ft RV limit). Tbls, toilets, cfga, drkg wtr. Fishing (trout), boating(l - elec mtrs only), hiking. Elev 7300 ft; 17 acres.

Dutchmen Spring FREE
Gila National Forest
9 mi N of Reserve on SR 12; 13 mi SE of Apache Creek on FR 94. Free. All year; 14-day limit. Undesignated dispersed camping along FR 94; no facilities, no drkg wtr. Hunting, hiking, horseback riding.

Gilita FREE
Gila National Forest
19.4 mi E of Mogollon on SR 78. From Reserve, take FR 141 & FR 28. Free. 4/1-11/15; 30-day limit. 8 sites (RVs under 18 ft). Tbls, toilets, cfga, drkg wtr. Hiking, horse-

back riding, picnicking, fishing. Elev 8100 ft; 2 acres. Near Gila Wilderness.
Fishing tip: Gilita Creek is a tributary of the Gila River and produces excellent rainbow & brown trout fishing.

Head-of-the-Ditch FREE
Gila National Forest
4 mi W of Luna (NW of Reserve) on Hwy 180 on San Francisco River. Free. Apr-Nov; 15-day limit. 12 primitive sites (30-ft RV limit). Tbls, toilets, cfga, no drkg wtr, no trash service. Rockhounding for agates, fishing, horseback riding. Elev 7150 ft.
Fishing tip: The lower reaches of the San Francisco River provides excellent fish for channel & flathead catfish and smallmouth bass as well as limited trout fishing.

Snow Lake FREE
Gila National Forest
5 mi S of Reserve on Hwy 435; 28.5 mi E on FR 141; 9.5 mi SW on FR 28; 7 mi E on FR 142. All year; 30-day limit. Undesignated dispersed sites near Snow Lake along FR 142. No facilities, no drkg wtr, no trash service. Use facilities at lake. Boating (no mtrs), fishing, hiking.
Fishing tip: Snow Lake regularly produces numerous trout.

Upper Frisco FREE
Gila National Forest
2 mi W of Luna (NW of Reserve). Free. Apr-Nov; 30-day limit. Undeveloped area. No facilities. Elev 7100 ft.

Willow Creek FREE
Gila National Forest
5 mi S of Reserve on SR 435; 28.5 mi SE on FR 6141; 12.5 mi SW on SR 78. Free. 4/1-11/30; 14-day limit. 9 sites (RVs under 18 ft). Tbls, toilets, cfga, no drkg wtr. Hiking, picnicking, fishing (trout), horseback riding. Elev 8000 ft; 2 acres. At northern edge of Gila Wilderness.
Fishing tip: Willow Creek, a tributary of Gila River, is stocked with catchable rainbow trout.

RODARTE (69)

Hodges FREE
Carson National Forest
3 mi E of Rodarte on SR 73; 3 mi S on FR 2116; half mi S on FR 2702. Free. Elev 8200 ft. 5/1-10/31; 14-day limit. 8 sites (RVs under 22 ft). Tbls, toilets, cfga, firewood, no drkg wtr. Picnicking, fishing, horseback riding, hiking, biking, hunting.

Santa Barbara $12
Carson National Forest
2 mi E of Rodarte on SR 73; 6.3 mi E on FR 21162. $12. 6/1-9/30; 14-day limit. 22 sites (32-ft RV limit). Tbls, toilets, cfga, drkg wtr. Fishing, hiking, horseback riding. Corral.
Fishing tip: The Rio Santa Barbara has wild populations of Rio Grande cutthroat

trout on the upper forms. Browns and some cutthroat can be found in the lower sections.

ROSWELL (70)

Bottomless Lakes State Park $10
16 mi SE of Roswell on US 380 & SR 409. $10 base. 2/1-11/30; 14-day limit. Park is actually seven small lakes bordered by red bluffs. 37 developed sites (9 with shelters, 32 with elec). No RV size limit. Tbls, flush toilets, cfga, drkg wtr, elec($4), dump, showers, playground. Boating(lr), fishing, nature trails, picnicking, swimming, scuba diving. Visitor center. Elev 3470 ft; 1,400 acres.

Haystack Mountain $5
OHV Recreation Area
Bureau of Land Management
W of Roswell via US 380. Free camping, but $5 entry fee. All year; 14-day limit. Primitive undesignated camping. No facilities except cfga. Small mound in flat 1,500-acre area attracts OHV enthusiasts. Hunting, biking.

Mescalero Sands $5
North Dunes OHV Area
Bureau of Land Management
35 mi E of Roswell via US 380. Free camping, but $5 entry fee. All year; 14-day limit. Primitive undesignated camping in 3 separate OHV areas; 610 acres. Tbls, toilets, cfga, no drkg wtr. Hiking, OHV activitiy.

RUIDOSA (71)

Argentine/Bonito Trailhead   FREE
Lincoln National Forest
18 mi NW of Ruidoso via SR 48; left on FR 107 to its end, about 5 mi past turnoff to South Fork Camp. Free. All year; 14-day limit. No developed sites. Toilets, cfga, no drkg wtr. Corrals, wilderness area. Horseback riding, hiking trails. Elev 7800 ft.

Cedar Creek   FREE
Dispersed Area
Lincoln National Forest
From near the Smoky Bear ranger station, follow FR 88 to its end (about 4 mi). Free tent camping in forested area along the creek with tents, pickup campers, small trailers. All year; 3-day limit. No facilities, no drkg wtr or trash service.

Eagle Creek   FREE
Dispersed Area
Lincoln National Forest
4 mi N of Ruidosa on SR 48; 3 mi W on SR 532; N on FR 127; free dispersed camping along the creek for a couple mi. All year; 14-day limit. No facilities; no drkg wtr. Fishing, hiking.
  Fishing tip: This stream produces excellent brook and rainbow trout action spring, summer & fall.

Monjeau   FREE
Lincoln National Forest
4 mi N of Ruidoso on SR 48; 1 mi W on SR 532; 5 mi N on FR 117 (last 3 mi rough).Free. About 5/1-11/1, depending on weather & road conditions; 14-day limit. 4 sites (RVs under 17 ft). Tbls, toilets, cfga, no drkg wtr or trash service. Hiking. Wilderness area. Elev 9500 ft.

Oak Grove Campground $6
Lincoln National Forest
4 mi N of Ruidoso on SR 48; 5 mi W on SR 532. Not recommended for RVs over 18 ft due to grades & curves of access rds. $6. About 5/15-9/30; 14-day limit. 30 sites). Tbls, cfga, toilets, no drkg wtr. Elev 8400 ft; 6 acres. Scenic. Quiet mountain setting.

Philadelphia Canyon   FREE
Lincoln National Forest
Follow Hwy 48 to Hwy 37, to Bonita Lake turnoff; watch for signs. Free. All year; 14-day limit. Primitive undesignated sites. No facilities except cfga; no drkg wtr. Hiking, fishing, horseback riding. Corrals.

Pennsylvania Canyon   FREE
Lincoln National Forest
Follow Hwy 48 to Hwy 37, then to Bonita Lake turnoff; watch for signs. Neaar Nogal Canyon. Free. All year; 14-day limit. Primitive undesignated sites; no facilities except cfga; no drkg wtr. Fishing, hiking. Beautiful site not often visited.

Skyline Campground   FREE
Lincoln National Forest
4 mi N of Ruidoso on SR 48; 1 mi W on SR 532; 4 mi NW on gravel FR 117(last 2 mi rough). Free. About 5/1-11/1; 14-day limit. 17 sites (RVs under 17 ft). Tbls, toilets, cfga, firewood, no drkg wtr, no trash service. Picnicking, hiking. Elev 9000 ft; 4 acres. Panoramic views of Eagle Creek Drainage.
  Fishing tip: Consider trying some of the special trout water fishing nearby. Choices are the Rio Ruidosa along US 70 in Ruidosa Downs, from Friedenbloom Dr downstream, and 30-acre Grindstone Lake on Carrizo Canyon Rd. Both produce rainbows of 12-14 inches and browns ranging from 16 to 35 inches.

South Fork $10
Lincoln National Forest
9 mi NW of Ruidosa on SR 48; 1.5 mi W on SR 37; 5 mi SW on FR 107 (pass Bonito Lake, then turn left, continuing 1 mi). $10. 5/15-9/15; 14-day limit. 60 sites (35-ft RV limit). Tbls, flush toilets, cfga, drkg wtr. Wheelchair access. Hiking, fishing, horseback riding. Trail to White Mountain Wilderness.
  Fishing tip: Fishing is good at nearby Bonito Lake between Apr & Nov. Bonito Creek contains brook & rainbow trout.

SACRAMENTO (72)

Alamo Peak Road   FREE
Dispersed Area
Lincoln National Forest
W of Sacramento on Scenic By-Way 6563, then follow Alamo Peak Rd. Free. All year; 14-day limit. Several undeveloped primitive camping areas along the rd. No facilities, no drkg wtr.

Bailey Canyon   FREE
Dispersed Area
Lincoln National Forest
Access S of US 82 on FR 206 at Bailey Canyon; steep rd, not suited to low-clearance vehicles or those towing trailers; several undeveloped camping areas along FR 206. No facilities, no drkg wtr. Restrictions on ORVs.

Bluff Springs   FREE
Dispersed Area
Lincoln National Forest
W of Sacramento on Scenic By-Way 6563, then 4 mi on FR 164. Free. All year; 14-day limit. Primitive undeveloped camping. Toilet, cfga, no drkg wtr. Small waterfall; spring nearby. Popular area.

Dry Canyon   FREE
Dispersed Area
Lincoln National Forest
NW of Sacramento on US 82; between mileposts 5 & 6, turn S on on steep rd to top of Horse Ridge. Free. All year; 14-day limit. Primitive undeveloped camping. Hiking, target shoting.

Horsebuckle Hill   FREE
Dispersed Area
Lincoln National Forest
On ridge W of Sacramento River on West Side Rd (FR 90). Free. All year; 14-day limit. Primitive undeveloped sites; no facilities, no drkg wtr. Spring 1 mi W below rd. Hiking trails.

Karr Canyon   FREE
Dispersed Area
Lincoln National Forest
W of Sacramento on Scenic By-Way 6563; follow FR 63 toward FR 82. Free. All year; 14-day limit. Primitive undeveloped sites in canyon less than 1 mi S & N of Karr Canyon picnic area (rd S of picnic area is rough). No facilities except tbls, cfga, drkg wtr at picnic area.

Sacramento River   FREE
Dispersed Area
Lincoln National Forest
Along the Sacramento River from Thousandmile Canyon to Scott Able Canyon, accessible from FR 537. Marshy Sacramento Lake is near mouth of Thousandmile Canyon, surrounded by numerous undeveloped camping sites; 16-ft RV limit. Some good spots for equestrian camping. Free. No facilities, no drkg wtr.

West Side Road   **FREE**
Dispersed Area
Lincoln National Forest
W of Sacramento to FR 90 (West Side Rd) between US 82 at High Rolls and FR 537 at Hornbuckle Hill (distance of 30.1 mi); N half of rd is gravel, S half is rough & muddy after rains. Free. All year; 14-day limit. Numerous primitive undeveloped campsites along the rd. No facilities, but some drkg wtr sources. Popular in hunting season. Elev 7000 ft.

Wills Canyon Road   **FREE**
Dispersed Area
Lincoln National Forest
Follow Wills Canyon Rd (FR 169) WSW from FR 164, W of its jct with SR 130 (NW of Sacramento); rd can be muddy during winter & after rain. Free. All year; 14-day limit. Numerous primitive, undeveloped sites; several good spots for equestrian camping. No facilities, no drkg wtr. Hiking, horseback riding.

SAN LORENZO (73)

Gallinas Canyon   **FREE**
Gila National Forest
8 mi E of San Lorenzo on Hwy 152 (no RV access). Free. 3/1-11/1; 30-day limit. About 15 dispersed primitive sites. Toilets, cfga, no drkg wtr. Hiking.

Iron Creek   **FREE**
Gila National Forest
12 mi W of Kingston via SR 152. Free. 4/1-11/30; 30-day limit. 15 sites (17-ft RV limit). Tbls, cfga, toilets, no drkg wtr. Hiking, picnicking. Elev 7300 ft; 7 acres. Nature trails. On scenic route between I-25 and US 180.

Railroad Canyon   **FREE**
Gila National Forest
9 mi E of San Lorenzo on Hwy 152; at Railroad Canyon Trailhead. Free. All year; 14-day limit. About 8 primitive undesignated tent sites; no facilities. Hiking.

Wright's Cabin   **FREE**
Gila National Forest
13 mi NE of San Lorenzo on Hwy 152. Free. 4/1-10/31; 30-day limit. 8 walk-in tent sites or Adirondack shelters. Toilet, tbls, cfga, no drkg wtr. Hiking.

✪ SANTA FE (74)

Aspen Basin   **FREE**
Santa Fe National Forest
From Santa Fe, quarter mi N on SR 22; 16 mi NE on SR 475. Free. All year; 14-day limit. 10 RV/tent sites. Tbls, toilets, cfga, no drkg wtr. Hiking, picnicking. Elev 10,300 ft; 5 acres. Scenic. Stream. Pegono Wilderness. Pecos Wilderness jump-off, Trail 254.

Backcountry Camping   **$12**
Bandelier National Monument
16 mi N of Santa Fe on US 84/285; 12 mi W on SR 502; 8 mi SW on SR 4. $12 for 7-day entry fee; camp free. All year; 14-day limit. Get free backcountry permit & directions from visitor center. No facilities. Elev 7000 ft.

Big Tesuque   **FREE**
Santa Fe National Forest
Qtr mi N of Santa Fe on Hwy 22; 12.1 mi NE on SR 475. Free. 5/15-10/31; 14-day limit. 10 sites (no RVs). Toilets, cfga, no drkg wtr. Fishing. Elev 9700 ft.

Black Canyon   **$10**
Santa Fe National Forest
7 mi NE of Santa Fe on Hwy 475 to Hyde Park Rd; tight turn into camp for RVs. $10. 5/15-9/30; 14-day limit. 42 sites (32-ft RV limit). Tbls, toilets, cfga, drkg wtr. Hiking & biking trail, horseback riding. State dump station at nearby Hyde Memorial State Park ($5).

Borrego Mesa   **FREE**
Sante Fe National Forest
N of Santa Fe and 20 mi E of Espanola. SR 76 from Espanola to Chimayo; SR 4 toward Santa Cruz Lake. E on FR 306, from this intersection, 10 mi of unsurfaced rd to campground (rd muddy if wet). Free. All year; 14-day limit. 8 dispersed sites (RVs under 32 ft) with corrals. No drkg wtr or toilets. Tbls, cfga. Hiking, picnicking, fishing. Elev 8400 ft. 3 acres. Ponderosa pine, Douglas fir, and white fir trees. Stream in canyon (half mi, steep access). Campground on mesa. Pacos Wilderness boundary 4.3 mi by good trail.

Hyde Memorial State Park   **$8**
7.5 mi NE of Santa Fe on SR 475. $8 base. All year; 14-day limit. Base fee for 43 primitive sites; 50 developed sites (7 with elec), $10 base; 42-ft RV limit. Elec($4), tbls, flush toilets, cfga, drkg wtr, dump, no showers, playground, restaurant. Hiking trails. Elev 8600 ft; 350 acres.

Juniper Campground   **$12**
Bandelier National Monument
16 mi N of Santa Fe on US 84/285; 12 mi W on SR 502; 8 mi SW on SR 4. $12 (plus $12 entry fee for 7 days or $6 daily). 94 sites. Tbls, flush toilets, cfga, drkg wtr, dump, showers. All year; 14-day limit. Hiking, visitor center, interpretive programs, backpacking.

North Lake Campground   **$9**
Bureau of Land Management
Santa Cruz Lake Recreation Area
20 mi N of Santa Fe on US 84; 13 mi E on Rt 503; right on Rt 596. $9 for developed sites. All year; 14-day limit. 5 sites. Tbls, toilets, cfga, drkg wtr. Boating(l), fishing, hiking. $5 day use fee.

Overlook Campground   **$7**
Bureau of Land Management
Santa Cruz Lake Recreation Area
20 mi N of Santa Fe on US 84; 9 mi E on Rt. 503. $7. All year; 14-day limit. 5 sites. Tbls, toilets, cfga, drkg wtr. Fishing, hiking. $5 day use fee.

SANTA ROSA (75)

Santa Rosa State Park   **$8**
7 mi N of Santa Rosa on access rd via 2nd St. $8 base. All year; 14-day limit; limited facilities in winter. Base fee for 15 primitive sites; 76 developed sites (25 with elec) with shelters, $10 base. 80-ft RV limit. Elec($4), tbls, flush toilets, cfga, drkg wtr, showers, dump. Boating(l), fishing, waterskiing, nature trails, winter sports. Historical & nature exhibits; visitor center. Elev 4650 ft; 500 acres.
Fishing tip: Fishing at Santa Rosa Lake is often quite good and sometimes excellent, depending upon fluctuating water levels. At normal levels, try for black bass, walleye, catfish and panfish. During winter, shore fishing for walleye can be very good in the control tower area

SILVER CITY (76)

Cherry Creek   **FREE**
Gila National Forest
13.2 mi NW of Silver city on SR 15. Free. Elev 7400 ft. 4/1-11/30; 10-day limit. 12 primitive sites (RVs under 17 ft). Tbls, toilet, cfga, no drkg wtr.

Forks Campground   **FREE**
Gila Cliff Dwellings
National Monument
44 mi N of Silver City on SR 15; located near the main Gila Bridge. SR 15 is a 2-lane blacktop that only recently was a rough, winding trail. The trip through this mountainous terrain takes about 2 hrs because of the rd condition; RVs more than 20 ft long should use SR 35 through the scenic Mimbres Valley instead of SR 15. SR 35 is reached from SR 61, N from San Lorenzo, 19 mi E of Silver City on SR 90. Free, but park entry fee charged. All year (except during flood conditions). 25 sites (RVs under 22 ft). Toilets, cfga, tbls, no drkg wtr. Hiking, picnicking, fishing nearby. Cliff dwellings nearby (100-400 A.D.).
Fishing tip: Consider taking a side trip to the small, 63-acre Bill Evans Lake 30 mi NW of Silver City if you're interested in catching huge bass. Stocked with Florida-strain largemouth, the Phelps Dodge impoundment produced two state record fish in the early 1990s, and in 1995, a new record 15-pounder was caught from there on an Augertail lure. The lake also holds the state record for white bass -- a nearly five-pounde caught in 1983.

Grapevine Campground   **FREE**
Gila Cliff Dwellings
National Monument
44 mi N of Silver City on SR 15; located at main Gila Bridge. Because of rd conditions, RVs more than 20 ft should use SR 35 through the scenic Mimbres Valley instead of SR 15. SR 35 is reached from SR 61, N from San Lorenzo, 19 me E of Silver City on SR 90. Free, but park entry fee charged. All year (except during flood conditions). 25 sites

(RVs under 22 ft). Tbls, toilets, cfga, no drkg wtr. Hiking, picnicking, fishing nearby. Cliff dwellings nearby.

Lower Scorpion   **FREE**
Gila Cliff Dwellings
Gila National Forest
44 mi N of Silver City on SR 15 (see other entries for alternative route). Free, but park entry fee charged. All year (except during flood conditions). 10 sites (paved parking area for RVs). Tbls, flush toilets, cfga, dump. Wtr available at trailer dump site except during winter months. Picnicking, hiking, fishing, horseback riding (r, 5 mi). Elev 5700 ft; 5 acres. Access to Gila National Forest Wilderness and Primitive Area. Cliff Dwellings nearby.

McMillan   **FREE**
Gila National Forest
14.7 mi NE of Silver City on SR 15. Free. 4/1-10/31; 30-day limit. 3 sites; 17-ft RV limit. Tbls, toilets, cfga, no drkg wtr. Picnicking, hiking. Elev 6950 ft.

Upper Scorpion   **FREE**
Gila National Forest
45 mi N of Silver City via SR 15. Free. All year; 7-day limit. 10 sites; paved area for RVs. Tbls, toilets, cfga, drkg wtr. Hiking, horseback riding, biking, caving, climbing, hunting, fishing. Half mi from Gila Cliffs.

SOCORRO (77)

San Lorenzo Canyon   **FREE**
Recreaion Area
Bureau of Land Management
NE of Socorro, accessed from Lemitar exit via frontage & county rds. Free. All year; 14-day limit. Primitive dispersed camping throughout east-west canyon. No facilities, no drkg wtr. Sandy arroyo requires caution with vehicles in all weather. Hiking.

TAJIQUE (78)

Tajique   **FREE**
Cibola National Forest
5 mi W of Tajique via NM 55 & FR 55. Free. Apr-Oct; 14-day limit. 6 sites (22-ft RV limit), 2 picnic sites. Tbls, toilets, cfga, no drkg wtr. Fishing, hiking, hunting. Elev 6800 ft.

TAOS (79)

Cuchillo Campground   **FREE**
Carson National Forest
16.6 mi NE of Taos on SR 522 & 150. Free. May-Oct; 14-day limit. 3 primitive sites; 16-ft RV limit. Tbls, toilets, cfga, no drkg wtr. Fishing, hunting, hiking.
Fishing tip: While in the area, drive E to Eagle Nest Lake, which is one of the state's premier kokanee and trout lakes. The 2,000 acrs of water offer 14-inch plus rainbows.

Cuchila del Medio   **FREE**
Carson National Forest
13 mi N of Taos on NM 230 & 150. Free. May-Sept; 14-day limit. 3 sites (RVs under 23 ft). Toilets, no drkg wtr. Fishing, hiking, biking. Elev 7800 ft.

Las Petacas   **$6**
Carson National Forest
4.3 mi SE of Taos on US 64. $6. 4/1-11/15; 14-day limit. 9 sites (RVs under 16 ft). tbls, toilets, cfga, firewood, no drkg wtr. Picnicking, fishing, horseback riding (r, 4 mi). Elev 7400 ft; 2 acres. Historic. Visitor center 4 mi.

Lower Hondo   **FREE**
Carson National Forest
12 mi N of Taos via NM 3 & 150. Free. May-Sept; 14-day limit. 4 sites (22-ft RV limit). Toilets, no drkg wtr. Fishing, hiking, hunting. Elev 7700 ft.

Orilla Verde Recreation Area   **$5**
Bureau of Land Management
12 mi S of Taos on SR 68; W on SR 570, following signs; at Rio Grande River. $5 base. All year; 14-day limit. Base fee for primitive sites; developed sites $7; hookups sites $15. Numerous designated primitive sites & 24 developed sites at 5 campgrounds. Tbls, toilets, cfga, drkg wtr (at developed sites), shelters, handicapped fishing pier. Campgrounds are Taos Junction (4 sites), Petaca (5 sites), Arroyo Hondo (5 sites), Orilla Verde (10 sites) and Pilar (5 sites). Boating, fishing, hiking, nature programs. Swimming not recommended. Petroglyphs. Elev 6000 ft.
Fishing tip: The Rio Grande contains native brown trout, German browns, rainbows and northern pike. The section between Taos Junction bridge to Colorado is designated as special trout waters, with restrictions.

Twining   **FREE**
Carson National Forest
20 mi N of Taos on NM 3 & 150. Free. May-Sept; 14-day limit. 4 sites (22-ft RV limit). Toilets, cfga, tbls, no drkg wtr. Fishing, hiking, horseback riding, biking. Elev 9300 ft.

TATUM (80)

Randolph Rampy City Park   **FREE**
On Hwy 30 on E side of Tatum. Free. All year. 5 sites with hookups, tbls, toilets, cfga, drkg wtr.

TEXLINE (TEXAS) (81)

Thompson Grove   **FREE**
Cibola National Forest
15 mi NE of Texline, Texas, just across NM line. May-Oct. Primitive undesignated area (22-ft RV limit). 10 picnic sites. Tbls, toilets, cfga, drkg wtr.

THOREAU (82)

Ojo Redondo   **FREE**
Cibola National Forest
24.5 mi SE of FR 178; 3.2 mi E on FR 480. Free. All year; 14-day limit. 19 sites (RVs under 23 ft). Tbls, toilets, cfga, firewood, no drkg wtr. Picnicking. Elev 8900 ft. Isolated site.

THREE RIVERS (83)

Three Rivers Petroglyph Site   **$2**
Bureau of Land Management
5 mi E of Three Rivers off SR 54 on gravel co rd. $2 per vehicle entry; camp free at primitive sites; $10 for 2 sites with hookups. All year; 14-day limit. 6 sites. Tbls, toilets, cfga, picnic shelters, drkg wtr (available at picnic sites). Hiking, picnicking. 120 acres. Area has extensive interpretive displays. Carvings made with stone tools (900-1400 A.D.). Site contains more than 500 petroglyphs. Flev 4992 ft.

TIERRA AMARILLA (84)

El Vado Lake State Park   **$8**
17 mi SW of Tierra Amarilla on SR 112. $8 base. All year; 14-day limit. Base fee at primitive sites; 80 developed sites (18 with shelters, 19 with elec), $10 base; 40-ft RV limit. Elec($4), tbls, flush toilets, cfga, drkg wtr, playground, showers, dump. Boating(ld), fishing, swimming, waterskiing, sailing. 5.5-mi scenic trail along Rio Chama River connects with Heron Lake. Elev 6902 ft; 1,728 acres.
Fishing tip: The Rio Chama produced the state record Brown trout many years ago, in 1946; it weighed just over 20 pounds. More recently, in 1999, the record 31-pound lake trout was caught from Heron Lake. Heron, a 6,000-acre lake, often produces 14-20 inch kokanee salmon and 10-20 pound lakers.

Heron Lake State Park   **$8**
11 mi W of Tiera Amarilla on US 64 & SR 95. $8 base. All year; 14-day limit. Base fee at primitive sites. 250 developed sites (54 with elec), $10 base; 35-ft RV limit. Elec($4), tbls, flush toilets, cfga, drkg wtr, dump, showers. Swimming, boating(l), fishing, nature trails, winter sports, sailing. No-wake boating. 5.5 mi-scenic trail along Rio Chama River connects with El Vado Lake State Park.

TRES PIEDRAS (85)

Hopewell Lake   **FREE**
Carson National Forest
20 mi NW of Tres Piedras on US 64. Free. May-Oct; 14-day limit. 6 sites (16-ft RV limit) plus primitive dispersed sites. Toilets, tbls, cfga, no trash service, no drkg wtr. Fishing, boating (electric motors only) on 19-acre lake, hiking, biking, horseback riding. Elev 9800 ft.

Fishing tip: 14-acre Hopewell Lake provides good fishing for brook & rainbow trout.

Laguna Larga   FREE
Carson National Forest
25 mi N of Tres Piedras on US 285, FR 87 & FR 78 (can be very muddy). Free. Primitive road. May-Oct; 14-day limit. 4 sites and dispersed camping around the lake. Toilets, cfga no drkg wtr. Fishing, boating, hiking, hunting, horsebadk riding. Elev 9000 ft.

Fishing tip: From FR 87, try for brown trout and some Rio Grande cutthroat from the Tio Grande River. Be aware, though, that most of the river is through private property.

Lagunitas   FREE
Carson National Forest
10 mi N of Tres Piedras on US 285; 26 mi NW on FR 87; .8 mi NW on FR 87B. Free. 6/1-10/15; 14-day limit. 12 sites (RVs under 17 ft). Tbls, toilets, cfga, piped drkg wtr. Picnicking, fishing, hiking, horseback riding, hunting, biking. Elev 10,400 ft; 5 acres. Scenic. Rd poor during rainy season; beautiful when dry.

Fishing tip: Scenic Lagunitas Lake and several small lakes at the head of Lagunitas Creek offer good fishing for brook & rainbow trout.

TRES RITOS (86)

Duran Canyon $10
Carson National Forest
2 mi NE of Tres Ritos on Hwy 51; 2 mi on FR 76. $10. MD-LD; 14-day limit. 12 sites (22-ft RV limit). Tbls, toilets, cfga, drkg wtr. Fishing, hiking, motorcycling, mountain biking, hunting, OHV activity. Duran Creek. Elev 9000 ft.

La Junta $5
Carson National Forest
Half mi E of Tres Ritos on Hwy 518; 5 mi NE on FR 76. $5. MD-LD; 14-day limit. 8 sites (30-ft RV limit). Tbls, toilets, cfga, no drkg wtr Fishing, hiking.

TRUTH OR CONSEQUENCES (87)

Caballo Lake State Park $8
16 mi S of Truth or consequences on I-25, at Caballo Lake. $8 base. All year; 14-day limit. Base fee at primitive sites; 135 developed sites (44 with shelters, 63 with elec), $10 base. Tbls, flush toilets, showers, dump, cfga, drkg wtr, elec($4), beach, playground, store, beach. Boating (dlr), fishing, picnicking, hiking, waterskiing, swimming. Visitor center, cactus gardens. Bald & golden eagles nest here in winter. Park has 2 cactus gardens. Elev 4180 ft; 5,326 acres.

Fishing tip: Cabello Lake is noted for its fabulous warm-weather white bass fishing, but it also contains Florida-strain largemouth bass as well as smallmouth bass, walleye, crappies and catfish.

Elephant Butte Lake $8
State Park
5 mi N of Truth or Consequences on I-25. $8 base. All year; 14-day limit. Base fee for numerous primitive sites; 132 developed sites (86 with shelters, 98 with elec), $10 base; 40-ft RV limit. Elec($4), tbls, flush toilets, dump, cfga, drkg wtr, playground, showers. Boating(ldr), fishing, hiking, swimming, waterskiing, nature trails. Interpretive exhibits; visitor center. Elev 4407 ft; 24,520 acres.

Fishing tip: Catch big striped bass around Three Sisters, Kettletop, the Jungles and in McRae. Live bait works best, but also jig near bottom with white or silver slab spoon. Try for white bass in north Monticellow near the narrows; troll Tennessee shad oor other crankbaits. The lake also contains largemouth & smallmouth bass, crappie, catfish (blue, channel & flathead), walleye and panfish. The state record blue catfish (33.5 pounds) was caught here in 1999 on a waterdog, and the record longear sunfish of 1.5 pounds was landed in 1985.

Percha Dam State Park $10
21 mi S of Truth or Consequences on I-25; near Arrey. $10 base. All year; 14-day limit. 50 developed sites, 30 with elec; no RV size limit. Tbls, flush toilets, cfga, drkg wtr, playground, showers, elec($4), no dump. Picnicking, fishing, hiking. Along Rio Grande River. Elev 4100 ft; 84 acres.

TUCUMCARI (88)

Conchas Lake State Park $8
32 mi NW of Tucumcari on SR 104. $8 base. All year; 14-day limit. Base fee at primitive sites; 105 developed sites (41 with elec) with shelters, $10 base; 45-ft RV limit. Elec($4), tbls, flush toilets, cfga, drkg wtr, dump, showers, playground, marina. Swimming, boating(lrd), fishing, waterskiing, sailing. Visitor center. Elev 4230 ft; 600 acres.

VADITO (90)

Agua Piedro $12
Carson National Forest
3 mi E of Vadito on SR 75; 7 mi E on SR 3. $12. MD-LD; 14-day limit. 44 sites; 36-ft RV limit (camp recently renovated & enlarged). Tbls, flush toilets, cfga, drkg wtr (wtr tastes of sulphur), horse facilities. Hiking, fishing, biking, hunting, horseback riding, OHV activity. National Recreational Trail available (23 mi long).

Fishing tip: Try the lower section of Angostura Creek for the rare and beautiful Rio Grande and brown trout.

Comales $6
Carson National Forest
3 mi E of Vadito on SR 75; 2.5 mi E on SR 3. $6. Elev 7800 ft. MD-LD; 14-day limit. 10 sites (RVs under 37 ft). Ttoilets, cfga, no drkg wtr, no tbls. Hiking, picnicking, fishing,

horseback riding, mountain biking.

Fishing tip: The best section of Rio Pueblo for catching rainbow & Rio Grande cutthroat trout is above this campground. The Rio Pueblo is one of the most popular trout streams in New Mexico.

Upper La Junta $6
Carson National Forest
3 mi E of Vadito on SR 75; 8.5 E on SR 3; 4 mi N on FR 2761. $6 (but may be free). Elev 9400 ft. 5/1-9/30; 14-day limit. 8 sites on 8 acres (RVs under 16 ft). Tbls, toilets, cfga, firewood, drkg wtr. Hiking, picnicking, fishing. Parking lot for fishermen.

WAGON MOUND (92)

Charette Lakes   FREE
Fishing & Waterfowl Area
State Game & Fish Department
From I-25 about 16 mi N of Wagon Mound, 13 mi W of Colmor exit on Hwy 569. Free. 3/1-10/31; 14-day limit. Primitive undesignated sites at lower lake. Tbls, toilets, cfga, no drkg wtr, no trash service. Fishing, hunting, boating(l), birdwatching.

Fishing tip: The lakes provide good fishing for 10-14 inch rainbows, and anglers catch -- but don't eat -- lots of perch.

ZUNI (93)

Bolton Lake (Dry)
Zuni Pueblo Indian Reservation
1 mi E of Zuni on Hwy 53. $5 first night, $3 thereafter; $15 per season. One-time $5 travel habitat fee also charged. All year. Undesignated sites at dry lake. Tbls, toilets, cfga, no drkg wtr.

Eustace $5
Zuni Pueblo Indian Reservation
1 mi E of Zuni on Hwy 53. $5 first night; $3 thereafter; $15 per season. One-time $5 travel habitat fee also charged. All year. 5 sites. Tbls, toilets, cfga, no drkg wtr. Fishing, picnicking. Fishing fees: $5 first day, $3 additional days, $20 annually. Boating fees: $1 daily or $5 annually.

Nutria Lake No. 2 $5
Zuni Pueblo Indian Reservation
8 mi E of Zuni on Hwy 53; 4 mi N on Hwy 32; 3 mi e on dirt rd. $5 first night; $3 thereafter; $15 per season. One-time $5 travel habitat fee also charged. All year. Undesignated sites (25-ft RV limit). Tbls, toilets, cfga, no drkg wtr. Fishing, picnicking. Fishing fees: $5 first day, $3 additional days, $20 annually. Boating fees: $1 daily or $5 annually.

Nutria Lake No. 4 $5
Zuni Pueblo Indian Reservation
10 mi E on Hwy 53; 11 mi N. $5 first night; $3 thereafter; $15 per season. One-time $5 travel habitat fee also charged. All year. Undesignated sites (RVs under 26 ft). Tbls, toilets, cfga, drkg wtr. Fishing, picnicking.

Fishing fees: $5 first day, $3 additional days, $20 annually. Boating fees: $1 daily or $5 annually.

Ojo Caliente Lake   **$5**
Zuni Pueblo Indian Reservation
14 mi SW of Zuni. $5 first night; $3 thereafter; $15 per season. One-time $5 travel habitat fee also charged. All year. 5 sites (RVs under 26 ft). Tbls, toilets, cfga, no drkg wtr. Fishing, picnicking. Fishing fees: $5 first day, $3 additional days, $20 annually. Boating fees: $1 daily or $5 annually.

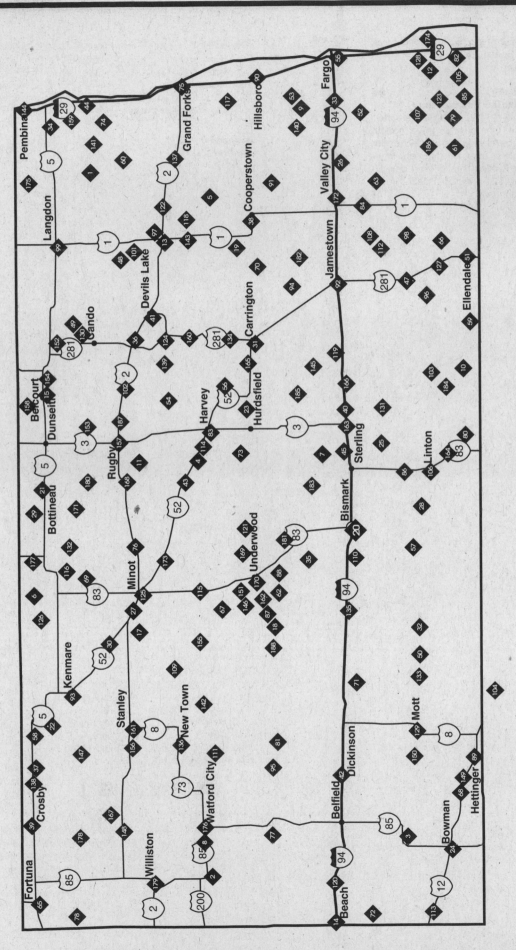

MISCELLANEOUS
Capital:
Bismarck
Nickname:
Peace Garden State
Motto:
Liberty and Union, Now and Forever, One and Inseparable
Flower:
Wild Prairie Rose
Tree:
American Elm
Bird:
Western Meadowlark
Song:
"North Dakota Hymn"

Internet Address:
www.ndtourism.com

Toll-free number for travel information: 1-800-HELLO-ND, ext. 220. Home page: http://www.ndtourism.com

Game and Fish Dept, 100 North Bismarck Expressway, Bismarck, ND 58501. 701/328-6300. E-mail: ccmail.ndgf@ranch.state.nd.us

Parks and Recreation Dept, 1835 Bismarck Expressway, Bismarck, ND 58504; 701/328-5357.

REST AREAS
Overnight stops are not permitted.

STATE PARKS
Camping fees are $5-$14 per night, with most (in modern parks) costing $8 ($5 at Little Missouri & Sully Crek) without electricity and $14 ($8 at Little Missouri & Cross Ranch) with elec during the full-service season, 5/15 through 9/15. Those fees DO NOT now include the $5 daily entrance permit fees ($25 annually; $20 for senior ND residents). Off-season rates are $5 without electricity and $12 with electricity during October, but water may be turned off; the same rates apply during 11/1-5/15, but water is shut off and electric service may not be available. 50-amp service is available in some parks for $2 additional. Pets on leashes are permitted. Primitive parks are Sully Creek and Little Missouri. All others are designated as modern parks. No camping is permitted at The Narrows and Black Tiger Bay Lake Access Areas. Horses are allowed at Ft. Ransom, Little Missouri, Ft. Abraham Lincoln and Sully Creek State Parks; a $5 per-horse user fee is charged. Parks and Recreation Dept, 1600 E. Century Ave, Suite 3, Bismarck, ND 58503; 701/328-5357.

North Dakota Forest Service. First & Brander, Bottineau, ND 58318. 701/228-5422. Camping fees are $7 between Memorial Day and Labor Day. Extra $3 per horse charged for equestrian camping.

Theodore Roosevelt National Memorial Park. A $10 per vehicle entry fee (good for 7 days) is charged from mid-June to Labor Day ($20 annual permit); America the Beautiful passes are accepted. Camping is $10 per day; $1 per horse is charged for horse camping at the South Unit Campground. Wilderness and trailside camping is permitted with a free permit, available at the park's north or south unit ranger stations. PO Box 7, Medora, ND 58645; 701/623-4466.

ADAMS (1)

Adams City Park　　　　$5
N on Park St to Third Ave. $5. 2 RV sites with hookups, drkg wtr, tbls, cfga, dump, toilets, showers. Museum, playground, pioneer log cabin.

ALEXANDER (2)

City Park　　　　FREE
On ND 85 in Alexander. Free. 5/1-9/30; 1-night limit. Policed. 4 primitive sites. Tbls, toilets, cfga, playground. Field report says three 30-amp RV sites (cost unknown) available across street at run-down Ragged Butte Motel.

Sather Lake　　　　FREE
Dakota Prairie Grasslands
16 mi SW of Alexander on Hwy 68. Free. 5/1-10/15; 14-day limit. 8 sites (30-ft RV limit). Tbls, toilets, cfga, no drkg wtr. Swimming, boating(d), fishing (trout & bass in lake).

AMIDON (3)

Burning Coal Vein　　　　FREE
Dakota Prairie Grasslands
2 mi W of Amidon on US 85; 12 mi NW on CR 742; 1.4 mi E on FR 772. Free. All year; 14-day limit. 5 sites. Tbls, toilets, cfga, no drkg wtr. Hiking, berry picking, swimming, boating, fishing. Burning coal vein & columnar juniper tree area nearby. Coal is no longer burning.

Firehouse RV Park　　　　$10
S end of Amidon on US 85. $10 without hookups; $14 full hookups. 10 RV sites with elec & wtr hookups, unlimited tent space. Flush toilets drkg wtr, tbls, cfga, dump, showers. Hiking, hunting, picnicking. Nearby is White Butte (state's highest point) and the Burning Coal Vein. Often described as a ghost town because of its dwindling population, Amidon is the nation's smallest town to hold a county seat.

ANAMOOSE (4)

Anamoose City Park　　　　$5
3 blocks N of jct of US 52 & SR 14, on Main St. $5. 3 designated sites & undesignated sites. Tbls, flush toilets, cfga, drkg wtr, dump, elec, playground. Tennis, horseshoes. Pop. 282.

ANETA (5)

Aneta City Campground　　　　FREE
Half mi N of Aneta on ND 32; half mi W on co rd. Free. 5/15-9/15. 5 RV sites. Tbls, toilets, cfga, no drkg wtr, elec. Picnicking; swimming, basketball, tennis courts, playground.

ANTLER (6)

Antler Memorial Park　　　　FREE
From SR 256 half mi N of Antler (pop. 101), 1 mi E E on 108th St NW; 0.75 mi N on 26th Ave NW. Free. 5/1-11/30; 3-day limit. Sites with tbls, pit toilets, cfga, drkg wtr (hand pump), 20-amp elec. Tours of historic school. GPS: N48 59.503, W101 16.716.

ARENA (7)

Arena　　　　FREE
Wildlife Management Area
1 mi S & half mi E of Arena in Burleigh County. Free primitive camping. All year; 10-day limit. No facilities. Hunting, fishing. 800 acres.

ARNEGARD (8)

Nelson Memorial Park　　　　$7
In Arnegard off SR 85 on Main St. $7. 8 RV sites with hookups (4 pull-through). Drkg wtr, tbls, flush toilets, cfga; elec, dump, showers, playground. Old schoolhouse historical exhibits. Horseshoes, tennis, ball diamonds, basketball. Field report: showers immaculate. Free town golf course close by.

ARTHUR (9)

Arthur City Park　　　　FREE
In Arthur at 4th & 5th St. Free. 4 RV sites with hookups. Drkg wtr, toilets, cfga, tbls. Tennis courts, horseshoes.

ASHLEY (10)

Ashley　　　　FREE
Wildlife Management Area
8 mi NE of Ashley in McIntosh County. Free primitive camping. All year; 10-day limit. No facilities. Hunting. 80 acres.
　Fishing tip: Not far away, try Blumhardt Lake. It's stocked with catchable size rainbow trout. The lake is 10 mi E of Ashley, then 7 mi N and 1.5 mi E.

Coldwater Lake City Park　　　　$8
16 mi E Ashley, then 2 mi S & 1 mi W. $8 with hookups; $5 for tents. 5/15-10/15. 6 sites for dry camping; 15 sites with wtr/elec. Toilets, tbls, cfga, drkg wtr. Fishing, boating(ld).
　Fishing tip: This lake offers excellent fishing for northern pike, walley and perch. An aeration system helps the fish thrive.

Lake Hoskins City Park　　　　$8
3 mi W of Ashley on SR 11; 1 mi N on county rd. $8 with hookups; $5 for tents. 5/15-10/15. 11 sites (6 with elec). Tbls, flush toilets, showers, cfga, drkg wtr, dump. Fishing, hiking, swimming, boating(ld).

BALTA (11)

Balta Dam　　　　DONATIONS
Municipal Recreation Area
1 mi S of Balta. All year. Donations. 20 sites. Tbls, toilets, cfga, elec. Picnicking; fishing; swimming, boating(l). No trash service.
　Fishing tip: The dam area contains northern pike and perch.

Balta　　　　FREE
Wildlife Management Area
Half mi S of Balta in Pierce County. Free primitive camping. All year; 10-day limit. No facilities. 105 acres.
　Fishing tip: The Davis Dam area 3.5 mi SW of Balta contains northern pike & perch.

BARNEY (12)

Barney City Park　　　　FREE
N of ND 13, in Barney. Free. All year. Undesignated sites. Tbls, toilets, cfga, drkg wtr, 2 elec hookups, playground. Tennis, 9-hole golf nearby.

BARTLETT (13)

Black Swan　　　　FREE
Wildlife Management Area
6 mi S of Bartlett in Nelson County. Free primitive camping. All year; 10-day limit. No facilities. Fishing, boating, hunting. 854 acres.

BEACH (14)

Red Rock Campground (Private)　　　　$10
Exit 1 from I-94 at Beach; N to frontage rd; 2 mi E on frontage rd. $10 base. 5/15-10/15. 20 RV sites; tent sites. Elec, tbls, flush toilets, showers, cfga, drkg wtr, dump. Camp formerly named Kittel's Kourt.

BELCOURT (15)

Belcourt Lake　　　　N/A
Turtle Mountain Indian Reservation
1 mi N of Belcourt. Small fee charged. All year. Undesignated sites. Tbls, toilets, cfga, drkg wtr. Picnicking; swimming; fishing; boating(l).

Broken Arrow Resort　　　　N/A
Turtle Mountain Indian Reservation
7 mi N of Belcourt, 1.5 mi W to campground. Fee charged. 5/15-9/30. 10 sites (RVs under 25 ft). Tbls, toilets, cfga, drkg wtr. Picnicking; fishing; swimming; boating(l).

Camp Waupun　　　　N/A
Turtle Mountain Indian Reservation
3 mi N of Belcourt. Fee charged. 5/15-9/30. 15 sites (RVs under 25 ft). Tbls, toilets, cfga, drkg wtr. Picnicking; fishing; swimming; boating(d).

Jarvis Lake Access   **FREE**
Turtle Mountain Indian Reservation
7 mi N of Belcourt, 5 mi W to campground. Free. 5 sites. Tbls, toilets, cfga, drkg wtr. Picnicking; fishing; boating(l). Reservations accepted.

Fishing tip: This lake offers fair fishing for perch, walleye, rainbow trout & northern pike. Fishing permit needed.

Lake Gordon   **N/A**
Turtle Mountain Indian Reservation
6 mi N and 1 mi W of Belcourt. Small fee. All year. Undesignated sites. Tbls, toilets, cfga, drkg wtr. Picnicking; swimming; fishing; boating(l).

BERTHOLD (17)

Centennial Municipal Park   **$5**
In town (pop. 485) at 411 Tyler St NE. $5 donation requested. All year. 6 sites with elec, drkg wtr, toilets, tbls, cfga, dump. Playground, tennis courts. Nearby 9-hole golf course.

BEULAH (18)

Beulah Bay   **$8**
City Recreation Area
From jct of SR 49 & 200, N 15 mi on SR 49; follow signs 1 mi; on S shore of Lake Saka-kawea. $8 primitive sites; $12 at 58 sites with elec; $15 at double-size premium sites with elec. 5/15-9/15; 7-day limit. 35 sites (no RV size limit). Tbls, flush toilets, cfga, drkg wtr, elec ($), shelters, dump, store, new showers, fish cleaning station. Swimming, fishing, boating (ld), playground. Concession with ice, fishing bait, stroller & movie rental.

Beulah Eagles   **$8**
City RV Park
On Hwy 49, S side of Beulah. $8 primitive sites; $10 with elec. 12 RV sites with elec/wtr; tent sites. Tbls, toilets, cfga, drkg wtr, dump.

Dakota Waters Resort (Private)   **$8**
3 mi N of Beulah on SR 49; 13 mi N on CR 21; 1.8 mi W on Beulah Bay Recreation Area Rd, following signs. $8 for primitive sites; $14 with hookups. 23 sites; 18 with elec($). Tbls, flush toilets, showers, cfga, drkg wtr, store, snack bar. Swimming, boating (ld), hunting, fishing. Leased by the Corps of Engineers.

Riverside   **$8**
City Recreation Area
On S side of Beulah E of SR 49. $8 for primitive sites; $12 with elec. 4/1-11/1; 7-day limit. 15 RV sites with elec; numerous tent & non-elec sites. Tbls, toilets, cfga, drkg wtr. Canoeing, fishing, hiking, horseshoes. Knife River. Permit required from parks department at city hall or from Hiway Express service station.

Fishing tip: Try the holes below riffles on the Knife River and catch walleye, sauger, northern pike, crappie.

BINFORD (19)

Centennial Municipal Park   **$5**
3 blocks W of Main St in Binford. $5 base for primitive sites; $6 with wtr; $10 full hookups; free bicycle camping. MD-LD. 6 RV sites. Drkg wtr, flush toilets, elec ($), cfga, tbls, dump. Biking, picnicking.

✪ BISMARCK (20)

General Sibley   **$7**
City Nature Park
Bismarck Parks & Recreation
W of Bismarck on I-94 to exit 157, then left on Divide Ave to just past golf course & YMCA; 5.2 mi S on Washington. $7 for tent sites; $17 for RVs with elec. 4/23-10/28; 30-day limit. Tbls, flush toilets, cfga, drkg wtr, showers, playground, dump. Nature trail, frisbee golf.

Kimball Bottom   **FREE**
Lake Oahe
Burleigh County Park
From Bismarck, 9 mi S on SR 1804, then go SW. Free. Primitive undesignated sites. Drkg wtr, cfga, no toilets. Boating(l), fishing. Formerly Corps of Engineers park.

BOTTINEAU (21)

Black Lake   **FREE**
Wildlife Management Area
7 mi N of Bottineau; 2 mi W. Free primitive camping. All year; 10-day limit. No facilities. Fishing, boating, hunting. 180 acres.

Bottineau City Park   **$8**
E of town on SR 5; 1 blk N on Jay St; W on 10th St & E into park. $8 primitive camping, $12 full hookups with 30-amp elec. 5/15-11/1. 20 sites (no RV size limit at 16 back-in sites). Tbls, flush toilets, cfga, drkg wtr, dump ($2), showers ($2 non-campers), playground, play field. Biking, tennis, picnicking. Future plans are to make sites longer for big rigs & 50-amp. GPS N48 49.334, W100 25.961.

Hahn's Bay Recreation Area   **$7**
Turtle Mountain State Forest
14 mi N of Bottineau on Lake Metigoshe Rd; half mi N; on W side of Lake Metigoshe. $7. 5/1-10/31; 14-day limit. 35 sites (RVs under 26 ft). Tbls, toilets, cfga, drkg wtr, fishing pier. Boating(l), fishing, swimming, hiking trails, winter sports, mountain biking.

Fishing tip: Lake Metigoshe offers good fishing for northern pike and walleye, and there's also crappie, perch & bullherad. Boats available for rent nearby.

Lake Metigoshe State Park   **$5**
14 mi NE of Bottineau. $8 base and $14 with elec during MD-9/30; $5 base and $12 with elec rest of year; 14-day limit. 130 sites (90 with elec/wtr). Tbls, flush toilets, cfga, drkg wtr, dump, showers, playground. Boating(l), fishing, ice skating, picnicking, swimming

beach, hiking trails, cross-country ski trails, nature programs, amphitheatre, snowmobile trails. 1,551 acres.

Long Lake   **FREE**
State Fishing Access Site
1 mi E of Bottineau; 11 mi N; 4 mi E; 1 mi S; 1 mi W. Free. All year; 10-day limit. Primitive undesignated sites; no facilities. Boating, fishing.

Fishing tip: This lake contains walleye, largemouth bass, northern pike and panfish. It's aerated for improved fish survival.

Pelican Lake   **FREE**
State Fishing Access Site
1 mi E of Bottineau; 11 mi N; 6 mi E; 1 mi SW. Free. All year; 10-day limit. Primitive undesignated sites; no facilities. Boating, fishing.

Fishing tip: This isn't the best fishing lake around, but it contains northern pike, perch and bullhead.

Pelican Lake/Sandy Lake   **$7**
Recreation Areas
Homen Mountain State Forest
11 mi N of Bottineau on Lake Metigoshe Rd; 12 mi E on SR 43. $7. 5/1-10/31; 14-day limit. 10 RV sites; tent sites. Tbls, toilets, cfga, drkg wtr. Fishing, boating(l), swimming.

Strawberry Lake   **$7**
Recreation Area
Turtle Mountain State Forest
From jct of SR 14 & SR 5 near Bottineau, N 9.5 mi; 2.5 mi E on SR 43. $7. 5/1-10/31; 14-day limit. 25 sites (RVs under 29 ft). Tbls, toilets, cfga, drkg wtr. Swimming, boating(l), fishing, hiking, horseback riding, swimming, winter sports. Hitching rails & horse trailer parking. 7,500 acres.

Fishing tip: This is primarily a trout lake. Electric motors only. Lake is aerated.

Twisted Oaks   **$7**
Recreation Area
Turtle Mountain State Forest
9.5 mi N of jct of ND 14 and ND 5; 1.5 mi E on ND 43. $7. All year. 15 sites. Tbls, toilets, cfga, drkg wtr. Observation tower. Picnicking, hiking.

BOWBELLS (22)

Bowbells City Trailer Court   **$10**
From SR 5, turn SW on SR 8 (Main St), follow it SW to Railroad St SW (just before RR tracks), then right on Railroad for 2-1/2 blks to trailer court. $5 for tents; $12 at 8 pull-through RV sites with full hookups ($60 weekly, $200 monthly). 5/1-9/30. Tbls, flush toilets, cfga, drkg wtr, shelters, playground. Free dump station in city park at Main & 3rd (pull across the street from the S to use it). City park supposed to have free camping, but no RV sites per 2006 field inspection. 701-377-2608. GPS: N48 48.235, W 102 14.982.

Fishing tip: Nearby Northgate Dam state

fishing area contains walleye, crappie, largemouth bass, smallmouth bass & trout. It is 9.5 mi NW of Bowbells. Free primitive camping & elec hookups.

BOWDON (23)

Bowdon RV Campground **FREE**
Half mi N of ND 200 in Bowdon. Free. 5/1-11/1. 6 RV sites with full hookups. Tbls, toilets, cfga, drkg wtr, showers. Fishing, boating.

BOWMAN (24)

Bowman Haley Campgrond **FREE**
Bowman Dam Marina County Park
11 mi S, 8 mi E & 2 mi S of Bowman; on N shore of Bowman lake near Bowman. Free primitive lakeshore camping; $10 at 35 sites with elec (8 by marina, 27 one mile W). Tbls, cfga, drkg wtr. Toilets, showers for a fee at marina. Boating(l), fishing. Proceeds used by Bowman Haley Anglers Association for conservation, fishing improvement.
Fishing tip: Excellent fishing for walleye, smallmouth bass & northern pike.

Butte View State Campground **$8**
2 mi E of Bowman on US 12. $8 base and $12 with elec. All year; 14-day limit. 50 sites with elec/wtr. Tbls, flush toilets, cfga, drkg wtr, dump, showers, playground. No entry fee.
Fishing tip: Try nearby Kalina Dam for perch & northern pike; no boat ramp available.

BRADDOCK (25)

Braddock Dam **FREE**
2 mi S & half mi W of town. All year. Primitive camping. Toilets, cfga, no drkg wtr. Camping also on grounds of South Central Threshing Bee during the bee. Boating(l), fishing.
Fishing tip: Fishing is good here for northen pike, largemouth bass, walleye and perch.

BUFFALO (26)

City Park **FREE**
In town (pop 226). Free primitive camping. No facilities. Ball diamonds, tennis court, playground.

BURLINGTON (27)

Old Settler's Campground **$10**
Ward County Highway Department
E of Burlington on Park Rd; after 3-day stop, left on Project Rd. $10 base. 5/1-10/1. Base fee for primitive sites; $15 for sites with elec ($18 in Canadian dollars). May-Oct. 28 sites (20 with elec). Tbls, flush toilets, showers, cfga, drkg wtr, playground. Fishing, swimming, biking, volleyball, horseshoes.

CARBURY (29)

Carbury Dam **FREE**
State Fishing Access Site
1 mi S & 1 mi W of Carbury to dam. Free. All year; 10-day limit. Primitive undesignated sites; no facilities. Fishing, boating.
Fishing tip: The dam area contains trout, bluegill and walleye. Idle speed only.

Carbury Lake **FREE**
Recreation Area
Bottineau County Park
3.2 mi N of SR 5 on SR 14; 1 mi W on access rd. 5/1-9/30. 10 sites. Tbls, toilets, cfga, drkg wtr, elec. Boating(l), fishing, swimming. 228-2225.

Dalen Recreation Area **$7**
Turtle Mountain State Forest
7.7 mi N of Carbury on ND 14; 4 mi E to campground. $7. All year. 10 sites (28-ft RV limit). Tbls, toilets, cfga, drkg wtr. Picnicking; snowmobiling.

Homen State Forest **$7**
6 mi E of Lake Metigoshe; encompasses Pelican and Sandy Lakes. $7. All year. Primitive undesignated camping in 4,184-acre forest. Tbls, toilets, cfga, drkg wtr. Birdwatching, fishing, canoeing, hunting.

Strawberry Lake **FREE**
State Fishing Access Site
4 mi N of Carbury on SR 14; 2.5 mi E; half mi S. All year; 10-day limit. Primitive undesignated sites; no facilities. Boating (elec mtrs only), trout fishing.

CARPIO (30)

Carpio City Park **Donations**
2 blks N & 1 blk E off Hwy 52. Donations suggested; camping free. 4/15-10/31; 7-day limit. 7 RV sites plus tent sites. Pit toilets, tbls, cfga, drkg wtr, elec. Playground, picnicking. 7 acres. Upper Souris National Wildlife Refuge, 8 mi E.

CARRINGTON (31)

Carrington City Park **$10**
On US 281 in Carrington. $10. 4/15-10/15. 8 sites. Tbls, flush toilets, cfga, drkg wtr, elec, dump, playground, pool. Swimming, picnicking.

CARSON (32)

City Park **FREE**
S edge of town on SR 21 next to fairgrounds. Free. 5/1-10/31. Undesignated sites. Tbls, toilets, cfga, drkg wtr, playground, pool.

CAVALIER (34)

Icelandic State Park **$5**
5 mi W of Cavalier on SR 5; on N shore of Lake Renwick. $8 base and $14 with elec

during MD-9/30; $5 base and $12 with elec rest of year; 14-day limit. 159 sites. Tbls, flush toilets, cfga, drkg wtr, dump, showers, beach. Boating(l), swimming, fishing, swimming beach, hiking trails, snowmobile & cross-country ski trails, nature programs, playground, amphitheatre, visitor center, historic buildings.

CENTER (35)

Klein Municipal Park **$3**
On E edge of city, E of jct SR 25 & 48. $3 base. 5/1-10/15. 15 sites with hookups. Tbls, flush toilets, drkg wtr, cfga, elec($), dump. Fishing. Indoor pool nearby. Nearby Nelson Lake has good bass fishing. Weekly rate available.

CHURCH'S FERRY (36)

Wild Goose RV Park **$10**
At Church's Ferry, Hwys 2 & 281. $10 base. 15 RV sites (10 elec). Tbls, toilets, cfga, drkg wtr, showers, dump.

COLUMBUS (37)

Columbus City Park **$5**
In Columbus from northbound Main St from SR 5, E on 4th Ave. $5 base with elec, $2 with wtr hookup. 4/15-10/15. Space for up to 9 RVs. Flush toilets, cfga, drkg wtr, tbls, no showers, dump. Golf course, tennis courts, ball diamond, playground, picnic area. Old steam locomotive, veterans memorial. GPS: N48 5.264, W102 46.460.

Short Creek Dam **$5**
Municipal Park
6 mi N of town on SR 5. $5 base; $10 elec. 20 RV sites with elec, tent sites. Tbls, toilets, cfga, drkg wtr, shelter. Boating(l), fishing.
Fishing tip: The Short Creek Dam waters containg a nice variety of fish: walleye, bluegill, perch, northern pike and both smallmouth and largemouth bass.

COOPERSTOWN (38)

City Park **$5**
At 10th & Foster in Cooperstown. $5 tent sites; $8 RV sites without hookups; $9 with elec; $10 full hookups. 5/31-9/30. 6 RV sites, several tent sites. Tbls, flush toilets, cfga, showers, drkg wtr, elec($), dump, store, pool. Swimming, biking, picnicking, horseshoes, playground.

CROSBY (39)

Fairgrounds Campsite **FREE**
Divide County Fairgrounds
About 0.75 mi N of SR 5 on 4th St SE at 1st Ave N. 5/1-9/1. Free; 7-day limit. 5 RV sites with elec/wtr, others with just elec; tent sites. Showers, flush toilets, dump, drkg

wtr. Patrolled. 965-6029. GPS: N48 54.796, W103 17.235.

Long Creek　　　　　　　　**FREE**
Municipal Park
4.5 mi N of Crosby. 6/1-9/30. Undesignated sites. Tbls, toilets, cfga, drkg wtr. Picnicking; swimming; golfing nearby.

Pioneer Village Camping Area　**FREE**
Divide County Historical Society
On SW side of Crosby; from SR 5, N on 103rd St SW to Pioneer Village; RV area is S of he village on 5th St S & 4th Ave W. Free without hookups, $10 with elec/wtr. 5/1-9/15. Up to 20 pull-through RV sites with 30-amp elec; open tent sites. Tbls, flush toilts, cfga, drkg wtr, showers. 9-hole greens course, tennis, ball diamonds, outdoor pool. 19 historic buildings represent frontier life. Patrolled. 3-day threshing show 3rd weekend in July. Beautiful courthouse. GPS: N48 54.522, W103 18.082.

DAWSON (40)

Lee Pettibone　　　　　　　**FREE**
Memorial City Park
Off I-94 on SE edge of Dawson. Free. All year. 5 sites. Tbls, toilets, cfga, drkg wtr.

DEVILS LAKE (41)

East Bay Campground　　　　**$12**
E of Devils Lake on Hwy 2 to rest area, then 5 mi S & 1.5 mi W. $12 for primitive sites; $15 for tent sites; $18 for RVs with elec/wtr hookups. All year. 50 overnight sites. Tbls, toilets, cfga, drkg wtr, beach, dump, coin laundry, showers, fish cleaning station. Boating(lr), store.

Grahams Island State Park　　**$5**
9 mi W of Devils Lake on Hwy 19, then 6 mi S. $8 base and $14 with elec during MD-9/30; $5 base and $12 with elec rest of year; 14-day limit. 44 sites. Tbls, flush toilets, cfga, drkg wtr, dump, showers, playground. Showers at bait shop all year. Marina, Boating(l), swimming beach, fish cleaning station, store, hiking trails, shelters. 1,122 acres.

Shelvers Grove State Park　　**$5**
3 mi SE of Devils Lake on Hwy 2. $8 base and $14 with elec during MD-9/30; closed off-season; 14-day limit. 26 sites. Tbls, flush toilets, cfga, drkg wtr, dump, showers, playground, shelter. Swimming, shoreline fishing, picnicking, hiking. Park was closed in early 2005 due to high water.

DICKINSON (42)

Patterson Lake Recreation Area　**$12**
Bureau of Reclamation
Dickinson Parks & Recreation
3 mi W of Dickinson on US 10 and I-94; 1 mi S (exit 2). $12 for primitive sites; developed sites with hookups, $18. 4/1-9/30; 3-day

limit at modern sites, 7-day at primitive sites. About 20 RV sites with hookups; 40 primitive sites & large tent area. Tbls, flush toilets, cfga, coin showers, drkg wtr, dump, beach house. Fishing, swimming, boating(l), hunting, swimming, horseshoes, tennis, basketball, volleyball, winter sports. 819-acre lake. Entry fee included in campsite cost.

DRAKE (43)

City Park Campground　　**Donations**
In Drake (pop. 479) at Lake & 6th St. Donations suggested; camp free. 20 sites (12 with elec). Tbls, elec($), drkg wtr, flush toilets, tbls, playground, shelter. Picnicking, biking.

DRAYTON (44)

Drayton Dam　　　　　　　**FREE**
Pembina County Recreation Area
2 mi N of Drayton, then E 1 mi to dam of Red River. Free. 5/1-9/30. 12 primitive sites; tent sites. Tbls, toilets, cfga, drkg wtr. Fishing, picnicking. About filled with long-term RVs during 2006 field trip; confronted by drunk men.

Schumacher City Park　　　　**$10**
From I-29 exit 187, E on SR 6; S on Old Hwy 44 (N Main St); 5 blks W on W. Wallace Ave. $10 (tents $7); 5/30-10/31; 7-day limit. 20 RV sites with elec; tent sites. Tbls, toilets, showers, dump, cfga, drkg wtr, pool, playground. Swimming, tennis. GPS: N48 33.953, W97 11.002.

DRISCOLL (45)

Sibley County Park　　　　　**FREE**
Burleigh County Parks
Exit 41 from I-94, 1 mi S to old Rt 10; 1.5 mi W to park. Free. Small park, tbls, drkg wtr, toilets.

EDGELEY (47)

Weaver City Park　　　　　　**$7**
In Edgeley on N end of 2nd St. $7 base with hookups; $10 with A/C ($175-200 monthly). 4/15-11/1. 29 RV sites with elec; tent sites. Tbls, flush toilets, cfga, drkg wtr, elec, sewer, dump, CATV, showers. Fishing, swimming. Swimming pool next to park.

EDMORE (48)

Edmore City Park　　　　　　**$3**
In Edmore on Madison Ave, E of Main St. $3 base; $5 with elec. 6 RV sites (4 with elec/wtr); tent sites. Toilets, water, elec, dump, shelters, playground.

EGELAND (49)

Sportsmen's City Campground　**$5**
In Egeland, 4 blocks S on Range from SR 66; 2 blocks E on 4th Ave; 2 blocks S on

Olmstead St. $5 for tents; $8 for RVs with full hookups. May-Oct. 12 RV sites; open tent sites. Tbls, flush toilets, cfga, drkg wtr, showers, dump, playground. Hunting.

ELGIN (50)

Sheep Creek Dam　　　　　　**FREE**
Grant County Water Resources Dist.
At jct of ND 49 and ND 21; 4 mi S and half mi W of Elgin. Free. 5/1-10/1; 4-day limit. 10 sites (RVs under 26 ft). Tbls, toilets, cfga, drkg wtr, elec, dump, playground, fishing pier. Picnicking; swimming; fishing, boating(l).
　Fishing tip: Fish from the pier or from a boat for bluegills, rainbow trout and bass.

Heart Butte Dam　　　　　　**FREE**
Lake Tschida Recreation Area
Bureau of Reclamation
15 mi N of Elgin on Hwy 49. 5/15-9/15; 14-day limit. Primitive undesignated sites at 6 campgrounds. Tbls, toilets, cfga, drkg wtr, dump. Boating(l), fishing, swimming.
　Fishing tip: This lake has good fishing for crappie, walleye, white bass, northern pile, saugeye and largemouth & smallmouth bass. Idle speed only. Numerous boat launches.

ELLENDALE (51)

Johnson Gulch　　　　　　　**FREE**
Wildlife Management Area
From jct of SR 11 & SR 56 (W of Ellendale), half mi E, then 2 mi S & 2 mi E. Free. All year; 10-day limit. Primitive camping. Toilets, cfga, no drkg wtr. 1,400 acres at largest & best known of several glacial ravines. Hiking, wildlife study.
　Fishing tip: Try Pheasant Lake, 6 mi W of Ellendale, for northern pike, largemouth bass, walleye, crappie and panfish.

Oster Park　　　　　　　　　**$10**
N end of Ellendale. $10 fee, 1-night limit. 3 RV sites with elec; tent sites. Tbls, toilets, cfga, drkg wtr, dump nearby.

ENDERLIN (52)

Enderlin Campground　　　　　**$5**
Patrick Pierce City Park
NE corner of Enderlin. $5. Open 5/1-11/1. 7 RV sites (5 with elec); 13 tent sites. Tbls, flush toilets, cfga, drkg wtr, dump. Fishing, boating.

ERIE (53)

Brewer Lake Campground　　　**FREE**
1 mi S of Erie; 1 mi W; half mi N. Free. All year. 8 RV sites with elec; tent sites. Swimming, fishing.

ESMOND (54)

Buffalo Lake   **FREE**
Benson County Recreation Area
5 mi W of Esmond on SR 19; 2 mi S. Donations suggested; camp free. All year. Open primitive camping; 9 RV sites. Toilets, drkg wtr, elec, cfga, playground. Picnicking, swimming, boating, fishing.

Randy Marthe Esmond
Memorial City Park   **$10**
4 blocks S of SR 19 in Esmond; at W side of school. $10 for full hookups; free overnight RV parking without hookups. Apr-Oct. Tbls, flush toilets, cfga, drkg wtr, showers.

FESSENDEN (56)

City Park Campground   **$8**
Half mi E of SRs 15 & 52 jct. $8. 5/1-10/1. 22 sites (8 with elec). Tbls, flush toilets, cfga, drkg wtr, showers, coin laundry, store, LP-gas, museum. Golf, tennis, wading pool.

FLASHER (57)

Centennial City Camp   **$8**
At 106 S Main. $8 ($50 weekly; $150 monthly). All year. 5 RV sites. Tbls, toilets, cfga, elec/wtr.

FLAXTON (58)

Flaxton Overnite Parking   **$5**
and Municipal Park
Actually 2 nearby parks. Former trailer park (now Flaxton Overnite Parking) is NE from SR 5 on Davis Ave SW, then left on NW Railway St. $5 at 8 RV sites (2 with full hookups), but elec turned off during 2006 visit. 4/1-10/31. Tbls, drkg wtr, dump, coin laundry. Flush toilets & showers 1 block at city park. City park NE of SR 5 on Davis Ave SW, then right on First St at watertower. Free camping, no hookups, tight parking for RVs; flush toilets, showers by donation. GPS for trailer park: N48 53.957, W102 23.675. GPS for city park: N48 53.962, W102 23.574. Depressed town.

FORBES (59)

City Park   **$5**
In town (pop 84) at Main & Fourth Sts. $5. Mid-May to mid-Oct. Primitive, undesignated sites. Elec, tbls, shelters, drkg wtr, cfga, pit toilets. Playground. Nearby are Tviet Shimmin Museum, Johnson Gulf, Whitestone Hill Battlefield, Petroglyphic Rock, Grave of the Unknown Soldier.

FORDVILLE (60)

Fordville Dam   **$10**
City Recreation Area
Grand Forks County
Water Resource District
Half mi S of Fordville; 2 mi E; 1 mi S (N of US & SR 18). $10 at 28 sites with wtr hookups; $14 at 15 sites with elec/wtr. Also tent sites. 5/1-10/1. Tbls, flush toilets, showers, cfga, drkg wtr, dump. Swimming, boating(l), fishing, horseshoes, playground.
Fishing tip: Boating limited to idle speed. Catch northern pike, walleye, crappie, largemouth bass and panfish. The camping area has a fishing pier.

FORMAN (61)

Lions Campground   **$5**
On Hwy 32 at Forman. $5. 4/15-10/15. 4 RV sites with elec; tent sites. Toilets, cfga, drkg wtr, dump, playground, tbls.

Silver Lake   **$10**
Sargent County Recreation Area
6 mi S of Forman on SR 32; 3 mi E on CR 3; half mi S. $10 for RV sites; $5 for tents. 5/1-10/1. 32 wtr/elec sites. Tbls, toilets, showers, cfga, drkg wtr, 8 elec, dump, playground, fishing pier. Picnicking; swimming; fishing; boating(l), horseshoes, basketball, volleyball. 100 acres.

FORT CLARK (62)

Arroda Lake   **FREE**
Wildlife Management Area
1 mi E of Fort Clark in Oliver County. Free primitive camping. All year; 10-day limit. No facilities. Fishing, boating, hunting. 384 acres.

FORT RANSOM (63)

Fort Ransom State Park   **$5**
2 mi N of Fort Ransom. $8 base and $14 with elec during MD-9/30; $5 base and $12 with elec rest of year; 14-day limit. 30 sites (15 with elec/wtr). Tbls, flush toilets, cfga, drkg wtr, dump, showers, horse facilities. Walk-in tent sites available along Sheyenne River; horse camping permitted($). Picnicking, hiking, horseback riding, canoeing(r), snowmobiling. 887 acres.
Fishing tip: Try the Cheyenne River below the Fort Ramsom dam for walleye, northern pike, crapple, smallmouth bass & white bass.

FORTUNA (65)

Skjermo Lake   **FREE**
Municipal Park
7 mi W of town. Free. Primitive undesignated sites. Swimming, picnicking, fishing (perch).

FULLERTON (66)

Fullerton City Park   **$6**
On E edge of Fullerton. $6. 12 RV sites with elec; tent sites. Tbls, toilets, cfga, drkg wtr.

GARRISON (67)

Audubon   **FREE**
Wildlife Management Area
8 mi E of Garrison in McLean County. Free primitive camping. All year; 10-day limit. No facilities. Fishing, boating, hunting. 11,285 acres. Leased from Corps of Engineers.
Fishing tip: At nearby Lake Audubon, try for walleye, smallmouth bass, cisco. Metal boat ramp; electric motors only.

Douglas Creek   **FREE**
State Fishing Access Site
11 mi W of Garrison, then 5 mi S & 4 mi E. Free. All year; 10-day limit. Primitive camping. Tbls, toilets, cfga, drkg wtr. Boating(ld), fishing. 1,980-acre wildlife area.

East Totten Trail   **$10**
Corps of Engineers
Lake Sakakawea
6 mi E of Garrison on SR 37; 2.5 mi S (N on US 83 from Coleharbor, then qtr mi E). $10. All year; 14-day limit. 40 sites ($6 for primitive); 25-ft RV limit. Tbls, toilets, cfga, drkg wtr, elec, fish cleaning station. Wheelchair access. Boating(l), fishing.

Fort Stevenson State Park   **$5**
3 mi S of Garrison on N shore of Lake Sakakawea. $8 base and $14 with elec ($16 with 50-amp) during MD-9/30; $5 base and $12 with elec rest of year; 14-day limit. 145 sites (100 with elec & wtr). Tbls, flush toilets, cfga, drkg wtr, dump, showers, marina, playground, restaurant, store, fish cleaning station. Picnicking, boating(lrd), swimming, fishing, hiking, cross-country ski trails, snowmobiling. North Dakota Fishing Hall of Fame nearby.

Indian Hills Resort   **$10**
Follow Hwy 83 N from Garrison; left on SR 1804/SR 37 to milemarker 204, then 3 mi S on gravel rd. $10 without hookups; $15 with elec; $18 elec/wtr. Tbls, flush toilets, cfga, drkg wtr, showers, dump, fish cleaning station, store. Boating(ld), fishing. This is a state park facility leased to private resort. 80 acres.

Sportsmen's Centennial Park   **$9**
McLean County Park
5 mi E & 3 mi S of Garrison. $9 base. 5/1-10/30. Base fee for primitive sites; $12 with elec. 100 primitive sites plus 18 with elec. Tbls, toilets, cfga, drkg wtr, store, playground, bait store, fish cleaning station, showers. Swimming, fishing, boating(ld), hiking trail, volleyball. Adjacent to de Trobriand Wildlife Management Area.

Steinke Bay   **FREE**
De Trobriand Wildlife Management Area
3 mi E & 2 mi S of Garrison. Free primitive camping. All year; 10-day limit. Toilets, cfga, no drkg wtr. Boating(ld), fishing.

GASCOYNE (68)

Gascoyne Lake City Park   **FREE**
Quarter mi W of Gascoyne on US 12; 1/4 mi N. Free. All year. 10 sites (no hookups). Tbls, toilets, cfga. Picnicking; swimming; fishing; boating(l).

Fishing tip: This lake contains mostly panfish; some northern pike.

GLENBURN (69)

North Municipal Park   **Donations**
In town (pop. 454). Camp free, but donations suggested. RV sites. Tbls, toilets, cfga, drkg wtr, dump. Fishing pond.

GLENFIELD (70)

Glenfield City Park   **FREE**
At SW Jct SR 20 & 200. Free. All year. 16 sites; 4 acres. Tbls, toilets, cfga, drkg wtr. Elec at 5 sites. Tennis court; playground, horseshoes, volleyball, softball. 785-2188

GLEN ULLIN (71)

Memorial Municipal Park   **$4**
Half mi W on Old ND 10. 5/1-10/1. $4 for tent sites; $8 for RVs with elec. 5/15-10/1; 7-day limit. Policed. 49 sites. Tbls, toilets, cfga, drkg wtr, dump, elec, dump. Picnicking, archery, playground. 80 acres.

GOLVA (72)

City Park   **FREE**
In town. Free. Primitive camping. No facilities. Golf course, other recreation opportunities.

GOODRICH (73)

Goodrich City Park   **Donations**
Just off Hwy 200 in town. Donations suggested; camp free. 6/1-10/15; 7-day limit. 10 sites. Tbls, toilets, cfga, drkg wtr, elec, dump, showers. Picnicking, tennis.

GRAFTON (74)

Leistikow   **$10**
Municipal Park Campground
1 block E on 12th St from US 81 in Grafton; 7 blocks N on Cooper Ave; 7 mi W on 5th St. $10 for tent sites; $18 for RVs. 5/1-10/1. 38 RV sites with full hookups; tent area. Tbls, flush toilets, cfga, drkg wtr, showers, dump, playground. Adjacent to sports complex with heated pool, picnic shelters.

GRAND FORKS (75)

Turtle River State Park   **$5**
22 mi W of Grand Forks, off US 2. $8 base and $14 with elec during MD-9/30; $5 base and $12 with elec rest of year while accessi-

ble; tent camping all winter without services; 14-day limit. 125 sites. Tbls, flush toilets, cfga, drkg wtr, dump, showers, playground, store, shelters. Fishing, swimming, snow-mobiling, sledding, ice rink, hiking trails, cross-country ski trails, horseback riding. 784 acres.

Fishing tip: Catchable size rainbow trout are stocked regularly for the state park's fishermen.

GRANVILLE (76)

Buffalo Lodge Lake   **FREE**
McHenry County Park
3 mi N of Granville, 2 mi E, 1 mi N. Free. All year. Primitive undesignated sites. Tbls, toilets, cfga, no drkg wtr. Boating(ld), fishing.

City Park   **$10**
In Granville, 5 blocks W of US 2 (Main St) on 6th St at McHenry Ave (past school buildings). $10. 10 RV sites with 30-amp elec, 10 tent sites. Drkg wtr, foul pit toilets during 2006 field stop, tbls, cfga. Ball fields, rodeo arena, playground, sand volleyball, ball fields, tennis. Patrolled. GPS: N48 15.817, W100 50.969.

GRASSY BUTTE (77)

Summit   **FREE**
Dakota Prairie Grasslands
10 mi N of Grassy Butte on US 85. Free. 6/1-10/31; 14-day limit. 5 sites (30-ft RV limit). Tbls, toilets, cfga, no drkg wtr. Rockhounding. 4 mi S of N Unit of Theodore Roosevelt National Memorial Park.

GRENORA (78)

Sunset Municipal Park   **$5**
SR 50 to Main St in Grenora; 2 blks to park. $5 at last report. 5/15-9/15. 2 sites with elec; 24-ft RV limit. Tbls, flush toilets, cfga, drkg wtr, playground, dump.

GWINNER (79)

City Rest Area   **FREE**
Hwy 13 & 32 on E side of town. Free. Drkg wtr, toilets, cfga, tbls, dump. Picnicking.

HAGUE (80)

City Park   **$5**
On Main St in Hague. $5. 4 RV sites with hookups; tent area. Toilets, showers, tbls, cfga, drkg wtr.

HALLIDAY (81)

Charging Eagle Bay   **FREE**
Fort Berthold Indian Reservation
Lake Sakakawea
14 mi N of Halliday on ND 8; 4 mi W and 4.5 mi NW to campground. 4/1-10/31.

Undesig-nated sites. Tbls, toilets, cfga, firewood, dump, well drkg wtr, showers, store, elec hookup. Swimming; picnicking; fishing; boating(rl; fuel and storage facilities).

Twin Buttes Recreation   **FREE**
Three Affiliated Tribes
Fort Berthold Indian Reservation
15 mi N of Halliday on ND 8; 6 mi E of Twin Buttes School. Free. 5/1-9/30; 14-day limit. 200 sites (RVs under 32 ft). Tbls, toilets, cfga, firewood, drkg wtr. Boating(l); picnicking; fishing; swimming nearby.

HANKINSON (82)

Lakeview Beach City Park   **$8**
1 block S of SR 11 in west Hankinson. $8. 9 RV sites with elec; tent area. Drkg wtr, tbls, cfga, toilets. Ball diamonds, playground, lighted tennis & basketball courts, lighted skating rink, 2-mi hikingbiking-jogging trail.

HARVEY (83)

Lone Tree   **FREE**
State Wildlife Mnagement Area
13 mi S of Harvey. Free. All year; 10-day limit. 3 primitive campgrounds. Tbls, toilets, cfga, drkg wtr, corrals. Hunting on 33,000 acres, fishing in Sheyenne River.

Fishing tip: They Cheyenne contains nice smallmouth bass, walleye, northern pike and crappie.

West Side Municipal Park   **$10**
Just W of Hwys 3 & 52 jct in Harvey. $7 for tents ($35 weekly); $10 with elec ($50 weekly). 5/15-9/15. 17 RV sites, 8 with 30-amp elec & wtr (most on short concrete pads; 2 40-ft RV sites in SW corner); tent area. Tbls, flush toilets, cfga, drkg wtr, dump, showers, heated pool, shelter, playground. Golf, lighted tennis courts, swimming, boating, fishing. 5 acres. GPS: N47 46.391, W99 56.427. Pop. 1,989.

HASTINGS (84)

Clausen Springs   **FREE**
State Fishing Access Site
Just N of Hastings on SR 1, then 1 mi E & half mi N. All year; 10-day limit. Primitive undesignated sites. Recreation area, fishing pier. Boating, fishing.

Fishing tip: Utilize the fishing pier or boat in idle speed to catch perch & largemouth bass.

HAVANA (85)

City Park   **FREE**
In town (pop 148) at end of E Main St. All year. Donationsl accepted. Undesignated sites; 2 RV sites with elec. Tbls, toilets, cfga, drkg wtr. Playground.

HAZELTON (86)

Hazelton Park   **FREE**
Corps of Engineers
Lake Oahe
13 mi W of Hazelton on gravel rd. Free. 4/1-10/31; 14-day limit. 12 primitive sites (30-ft RV limit). No toilets, cfga, no drkg wtr. Boating(l), fishing.

Hazelton City Park   **$2**
In Hazelton at 400 block of Hazel Ave. $2 base. All year. Base fee for primitive tent sites; $8 for RV sites with wtr/elec. 7 RV sites with elec; tent area. Tbls, flush toilets, cfga, drkg wtr, showers, dump, playground. Biking, hiking.

HAZEN (87)

Hazen Bay   **$7**
City Recreation Area
15 mi N on CR 27 on Lake Sakakawea. $7 for primitive sites; $12 with elec. MD-10/31. 20 RV sites (16 with elec); several tent sites. Drkg wtr, toilets, tbls, cfga, elec($), playground, fish cleaning station, 60-ft dock. Boating (ld), fishing, swimming, hiking, group camping area. A new municipal campground, Lewis & Clark RV Park on W. Main St., has RV sites with full hookups for $13 (no tents).

HENSLER (88)

Cross Ranch State Park   **$5**
5 mi SE of Hensler on Hwy 1806; at undeveloped stretch of Missouri River. $8 base and $8 with elec during MD-9/30; $5 base and $18 with elec rest of year; 14-day limit. Wtr until end of Oct unless an early freeze. 70 sites (35-ft RV limit); hike-in backcountry area available. Tbls, flush toilets, cfga, drkg wtr, dump, showers, visitor center & warming house. Hiking, cross-country ski trails, boating(l), picnicking, canoeing(r), fishing. 589 acres.

HETTINGER (89)

Cedar River   **FREE**
National Grasslands
SE of Hettinger, S of Hwy 12. Free. 6,700-acre mixed-grass prairie. Primitive camping permitted, but no developed sites. Wildlife & wildflower photo. Mule, antelope, bird, upland game hunting.

Mirror Lake City Park   **$8**
S of Hettinger on SR 8, then left; at lake. $8 base. 5/1-10/31. Base fee for tent sites; $12 for RV sites (32-ft RV limit). Tbls, flush toilets, showers, cfga, drkg wtr, dump, elec($). 16 sites; 10 with elec/wtr; open tent camping area. Swimming, boating(rl), fishing, hiking, golf, ball fields.
  Fishing tip: Mirror Lake is a good largemouth bass lake, and it also contains trout, northern pike, walleye, crappie & perch. Idle boat speed only.

JAMESTOWN (92)

Lakeside Marina   **$10**
Stutsman County Park
Jamestown Dam
2 mi N of Jamestown on Hwy 20; half mi W. $10 for tents. 5/1-9/15. 48 RV sites; tent area. Tbls, flush toilets, cfga, drkg wtr, elec($), showers, dump, playground. Fishing, boating (ldr), swimming. Extra charge for a/c or elec htr.

Parkhurst/Pipestem Lake   **FREE**
Stutsman County Park
4 mi N of Jamestown on ND 281; 1 mi W on gravel road to campground. All year; 14-day limit. 16 sites (RVs under 24 ft). Tbls, toilets, cfga, firewood, drkg wtr, store. Swimming; picnicking; fishing; boating(ld); golf nearby. On Pipestem Lake.
  Fishing tip: Try this lake's walleye, bluegill, northern pike, crappie and smallmouth bass.

Shady Grove Campground   **$10**
Spiritwood Lake (Private)
10 mi N of Jamestown on Hwy 20; 4.5 mi E. $10 base. 5/1-9/30. 25 RV sites with elec; tent area. Tbls, flush toilets, cfga, drkg wtr, showers, dump. Swimming, fishing, boating(rl).

Smokey's Campsite & Landing   **$10**
Stutsman County Park
10 mi N of Jamestown on Hwy 281; 1.5 mi E (I-94 exit 59). $10 for tents; $15 RVs. 5/1-9/30. 75 RV sites; tent area. Tbls, flush toilets, cfga, drkg wtr, elec ($), store, dump, fish cleaning station. Swimming, boating (ldr), fishing, waterskiing. Entry fee charged.

KATHRYN

Little Yellowstone   **$10**
Barnes County Park
4 mi S & 1 mi E of Kathryn; at Sheyenne River. $10 with hookups. 5/1-10/1. 16 RV sites with elec; tent sites. Tbls, toilets, cfga, drkg wtr, dump. Fishing, swimming, hiking trails, walking bridges.

KENMARE (93)

Kenmare City Campground   **$5**
Off US 52 on NE side of Kenmare. $5 base. 5/1-9/30. Base fee for primitive & tent sites; $10 with hookups ($40 weekly). 30 sites. Tbls, flush toilets, cfga, drkg wtr, showers, elec($), dump. Hiking, swimming, hunting. Weekly or monthly rates available.

KENSAL (94)

Kensal City Campground   **$10**
In town across from city park. $10. All year. 8 RV sites with hookups; tent area. Tbls, toilets, cfga, drkg wtr.

KILLDEER (95)

City Park   **DONATIONS**
2 mi N of jct of ND 200 and ND 22, on gravel access rds. All year. Donations suggested. Policed. 10 sites with 30-amp elec. Tbls, toilets, cfga, drkg wtr, playground, dump, showers.

Little Missouri Bay   **$5**
Primitive State Park
18 mi N of Killdeer on SR 22; 2 mi E on twp rd. $5 base; $8 with elec. All year; 14-day limit; limited winter access. 30 sites (10 with elec). Tbls, vault toilets, cfga, drkg wtr, no showers, group shelters. Horseback riding($), corral, hiking & bridle trails, hiking trails picnicking. 5,748 acres.

KULM (96)

Kulm City Park   **$10**
At SE end of Kulm on 4th Ave (off Hwy 56, last exit into town, next to pool). $10. 5/1-10/31. 8 RV sites with hookups; tent area. Tbls, flush toilets, cfga, drkg wtr, showers, dump. Swimming, picnicking, tennis, horseshoes. Pay fees at Dale's Hardware.

Kulm Edgeley Dam   **$10**
Lamoure County Park
9 mi E of Kulm on Hwy 33; 3 mi N; 1 mi W. $10. All year. 12 RV sites; tent area. Tbls, drkg wtr, cfga, toilets, shelters. Boating(l), fishing, picnicking, hiking.

LAKOTA (97)

Stump Lake   **$8**
Nelson County Recreation Area
12 mi S of Lakota. $8 at primitive sites, $10 at tent sites, $20 with hookups. About 60 RV sites with elec; tent area has lower fees. Tbls, flush toilets, cfga, drkg wtr, showers, dump. Skating, playground, ball fields, tennis, concessions, picnic area.

LAMOURE (98)

Lake LaMoure Campground   **$10**
5 mi S of LaMoure. $10. 5/1-10/15. 12 RV sites with elec, sewer; tent area. Tbls, toilets, cfga, drkg wtr, dump. Fishing, boating(l).
  Fishing tip: The lake contains walleye, largemouth bass, crappie, northern pike, bluegill and bullhead catfish.

LaMoure County   **$10**
Memorial Park
9 mi N of LaMoure near Grand Rapids. $10. 5/15-9/15; 14-day limit. 90 RV sites with elec; tenting area. Tbls, flush toilets, showers, cfga, drkg wtr, dump, playground. Tennis, fishing, hiking.

James River Dam Site   **FREE**
Municipal Park
Half mi W of La Moure on ND 13. Free. 5/1-10/1. Policed. 6 tent, 3 RV sites. Tbls, toilets,

elect, cfga, drkg wtr. Store, food, ice, laundry nearby. Swimming; boating(d); picnicking; fishing; golf nearby.

LANGDON (99)

Mt. Carmel Campground   **$11**
Cavalier County Water Resources Board
9 mi N of Langdon, then 2 mi E; 2 mi N; 1 mi E; on South Fork of Little Pembina River. $11 at primitive sites; $15 with elec/wtr ($55 & $75 weekly). 5/15-9/15. Tbls, toilets, cfga, drkg wtr, fish cleaning station. Fishing, swimming, boating(ld). Daily entry fee $3; $20 seasonal.

  Fishing tip: This 322-acre lake has good fishing for walleye, northern pike, crappie, perch and bluegill.

LAWTON (101)

Centennial City Park   **FREE**
In Lawton (pop. 63). Free. 1 RV site with elec; tent area. Nearby Lawton City Park has 3 free RV sites with elec. For info, 701/655-3641.

LEEDS (102)

Fireman's Memorial Park   **FREE**
In town (pop 678) on Hwy 2. Free. 10 sites. 6/1-9/15. 12 sites (8 with elec). Tbls, flush toilets, cfga, drkg wtr, playground. Grass greens golf course, swim pool, tennis courts, picnicking.

LEHR (103)

City Park Campground   **FREE**
In town (pop 254) at 201 S Main St. Free at last report. All year. 10 sites. Drkg wtr, flush toilets, cfga, tbls, elec. Shelters, playground, store; shuffleboard, tennis, basketball & volleyball courts. Patrolled.

  Fishing tip: At nearby Lehr Dam, fish for northern pike, largemouth, perch or bluegill.

LEMMON (SD.) (104)

North Lemmon Lake   **FREE**
State Fishing Access Site
Five mi N of Lemmon, in North Dakota. Free. All year; 10-day limit. Primitive undesignated sites; no facilities. Fishing.

  Fishing tip: This lake contains trout, largemouth bass, northern pike, walleye, crappie and perch. Idle speed only.

LIDGERWOOD (105)

Lidgerwood Campground   **$10**
On E end of Lidgerwood by tennis courts. $10. 6 RV sites with elec; tent area. Tbls, toilets, cfga, drkg wtr, dump.

LINTON (106)

Badger Bay Campground   **FREE**
Corps of Engineers
Lake Oahe
From Linton, 13 mi W on SR 13; 17 mi N on SR 1804, then W. Free. 6 primitive sites. Toilets, cfga, no drkg wtr. Boating, fishing.

Beaver Creek   **$8**
Corps of Engineers
Lake Oahe
16 mi W of Linton on SR 13; 1 mi S on SR 1804. $8 base; $12 with elec. 5/15-9/15; 14-day limit. 66 sites. Tbls, toilets, cfga, drkg wtr, elec($), playground, dump, showers, fish cleaning station. Boating(l), fishing.

Seeman Municipal Park   **$10**
1 mi E of US 83 on SR 13; half mi S. $10. 4/15-9/15. 52 sites (10 with elec). Tbls, flush toilets, cfga, drkg wtr, elec, showers, playground. Fishing, biking. Policed.

LISBON (107)

Dead Colt Creek   **$5**
Ransom County Recreation Area
5 mi S of Lisbon on SR 32; 1.5 mi E. $5 base for tent sites (with some free sites); $8 for RV sites with hookups. 5/1-9/30. 43 RV sites with hookups; tent area. Tbls, flush toilets, cfga, drkg wtr, showers, dump, shelters, beach, ball fields, playground. Boating(dl), fishing, swimming.

Sandager City Park   **$8**
On Second Ave, NW side of Lisbon. $8 for primitive sites; $12 with hookups. 20 RV sites, 16 with elec; tent area. Drkg wtr, cfga, flush toilets, showers, dump, tbls. Swimming pool, fishing, hiking, boating, horseshoes, playground.

Sheyenne   **FREE**
National Grasslands
E of Lisbon on Hwy 27. 70,000-acre grassland. Primitive camping; no developed sites. Canoeing & fishing on Sheyenne River. Largest population in U.S. of prairie chicken; western white-fringed orchid.

  Fishing tip: Try the Sheyenne River below Lisbon Dam for walleye, northern pike, smallmouth bass, white bass, rock bass and crappie.

Sheyenne River State Forest   **$7**
10 mi NW of Lisbon on CR 13. $7. Primitive undesignated sites. Tbls, cfga, no other facilities. Hiking & snowmobiling trail, fishing, canoeing, hunting. 509 acres. Part of forest hiking trail on National North Country Trail. Fee for camping not usually charged.

LITCHVILLE (108)

City Park   **N/A**
1 block N of water town in Litchville (pop 205). Fee status uncertain; formerly free. 5

RV sites with elec; tent area. Drkg wtr, toilets, tbls, cfga, store. Tennis.

MAKOTI (109)

Makoti Fairgrounds Camp   **$7**
At threshing grounds in Makoti. $7. 80 RV sites; tent area. Tbls, flush toilets, cfga, drkg wtr, elec. Activities nearby.

MANDAN (110)

Fort Abraham Lincoln State Park   **$5**
7 mi S of Mandan on SR 1806. $8 base and $14 with elec during MD-9/30; $5 base and $12 with elec rest of year; 14-day limit. 95 sites (57 with elec/wtr). Tbls, flush toilets, cfga, drkg wtr, dump, showers, amphitheatre, playground. Picnicking, shoreline fishing, hiking, snowmobiling, cross-country ski trails. Visitor center, reconstructed Indian village & infantry post; interpretive & cultural programs. 1,006 acres.

Graner Park Campground   **$12**
Morton County Park
17 mi S of Mandan on SR 1806; at Lake Oahe. $12 for RV sites with elec; primitive camping $3. All year; 14-day limit. About 100 sites (27 with elec). Tbls, toilets, cfga, drkg wtr, dump, playground, fish cleaning station. Boating(l), fishing, hiking. Former Corps of Engineers park.

Sweetbriar Lake   **FREE**
Morton County Park
20 mi W of Mandan off I-94 on CR 84. Free. All year; 14-day limit. Undesignated primitive sites for numerous RVs. Tbls, toilets, cfga, drkg wtr. Boating(l), fishing, hunting. $2 fee may be charged. GPS: N46.87407, W101.27859.

MANDAREE (111)

Lost Bridge Picnic Area   **FREE**
Three Affiliated Tribes
Fort Berthold Reservation
10 mi S of Mandaree on ND 22. Free. 5/1-9/30; 14-day limit. 20 sites (RVs under 32 ft). Tbls, toilets, cfga, firewood, no drkg wtr. Swimming; picnicking; fishing; boating(l).

MARION (112)

City Park Campground   **FREE**
On E side of Marion (pop 214). Free. All year. Undesignated sites with drkg wtr, elec, flush toilets, tbls, cfga, shelters, playground.

MARMARTH (113)

Marmarth City Park   **$5**
7 mi E of the MT/ND State Line on US 12. $5 for elec sites; camp free. 5/1-10/30; 1-day limit. 10 sites. Tbls, flush toilets, cfga, firewood, playground, elec($5). Store, food, laundry nearby. Picnicking; fishing; swim-

ming nearby; tennis; basketball. Little Missouri River within walking distance.

MARTIN (114)

City Park **$7**
In town, half blk off Hwy 52 (pop. 114). $7 or $45 weekly. May-Oct. 12 sites with elec. Drkg wtr, toilets, tbls, playground. Quiet. Register at Someplace Else Bar.

MAX (115)

City Camper Park **$10**
At Flower St & 6th. $10. All year. 4 RV sites with elec. Tbls, toilets, cfga, drkg wtr, dump, 2 shelters. Tennis, playground, horseshoes.

Max Roadside Park **FREE**
On W side of Hwy 83. Free. Primitive sites. Tbls, cfga, drkg wtr.

MAXBASS (116)

Maxbass City Park **N/A**
In town (pop 123). Fee status uncertain. Tbls, toilets, cfga, drkg wtr. 9-hole sand greens golf nearby.

MCVILLE (118)

McVille Dam City Park **$10**
On E edge of town; qtr mi E of downtown on Hwy 15 to just W of dam; at McVille Lake. $10. 25 RV sites, several with elec/wtr; tent sites. Tbls, cfga, flush toilets, elec, sewer, shelters, beach, drkg wtr, no dump. Swimming, fishing, boating. Register at Dean's Standard station at Hwy 15 & Main St. GPS: N47 45.703, W98 10.104.
Fishing tip: The lake area is well stocked with walleye, northern pike, trout, largemouth bass, bluegills. No rough fish.

MEDINA (119)

Medina City Park **$10**
At S side of town (pop 521). $10 tent, $15 for RVs with hookups. 5/1-10/30. 12 RV sites. Toilets, showers, elec, dump, mini shelters, cfga, tbls. Tennis court. Chase Lake, 9 mi NW, is nesting area for white pelicans. 486-3162

MEDORA (120)

Backcountry Camping **$10**
South Unit
Roosevelt National Park
N of Medora at national park. $10 vehicle entry fee for 7 days (or $20 annually); camp free in backcountry. All year; 14-day limit. No facilities.

Buffalo Gap **$6**
National Grasslands
7 mi W of Medora on I-94; N on CR 7263; 1 mi W on FR 726A. $6. MD-LD; 14-day limit. 37 sites (22-ft RV limit). Tbls, flush toilets, cfga, drkg wtr. Hiking trails, fishing. 40 acres.
Fishing tip: South Buffalo Gap Lake has good fishing for largemouth bass, bluegill and trout.

Cottonwood Campground **$10**
South Unit
Roosevelt National Park
6 mi N of I-94 & Medora on paved rd. $10. All year; 14-day limit. 78 sites. Tbls, flush toilets, cfga, drkg wtr. Nature program, visitor center. Limited service in winter. Museum. Entry fee $10 for 7 days.

Red Trail Campground (Private) **$12**
d1.9 mi SE of I-94 exit 24 on service rd; 2 blocks S on E. River Rd. $12 base. 5/15-LD. About 100 sites. Tbls, flush toilets, cfga, drkg wtr, hookups($), coin laundry, store, playground, CATV($).

South Buffalo Gap Lake **FREE**
Buffalo Gap National Grasslands
7 mi W of Medora on I-94 to exit 18 (Buffalo Gap exit), then three-fourths mi S, 1 mi E, half mi N to lake. Free. Primitive dispersed camping; no facilities, no drkg wtr. Fishing, boaitng.
Fishing tip: This lake contains largemouth bass, trout and panfish.

Sully Creek **$5**
State Recreation Area
2.5 mi SE of Medora on gravel rd; $5. MD-9/30; 14-day limit. 33 primitive sites. Tbls, vault toilets, cfga, drkg wtr, corrals. Horseback riding($), canoeing, fishing, hiking trails. 80 acres.

MERCER (121)

Blue Lake **FREE**
Wildlife Management Area
5 mi N of Mercer, then 2.5 mi W & half mi S in McLean County. Free primitive camping. All year; 10-day limit. Fishing. 13 acres.

MICHIGAN (122)

City Park **FREE**
Inquire locally for directions. Free at last report. All year. 4 RV sites. Tbls, flush toilets, cfga, dump, sewer hookup, elect, playground, tennis court.
Fishing tip: Lake Laretta, 3 mi N & 2 mi W of Michigan, contains northern pike & perch but has no boat ramp.

MILNOR (123)

City Park **$10**
In Milnor (pop 716) on SR 13. $10 for sites with no elec ($50 weekly); $15 with elec & wtr; $75 weekly. 8 RV sites with elec. Drkg wtr, flush toilets, showers, tbls, cfga, pool, track. Hiking, jogging, volleyball, tennis, swimming, picnicking. Renovated in 2002.

MINNEWAUKAN (124)

Humphrey Memorial Park **FREE**
On Hwy 281 in Minnewaukan. Donations are requested to help offset costs. Tbls, flush toilets, cfga, drkg wtr, showers, elec, shelter, playground gear. Tennis & basketball across the street. Favorite base camp for hunters.

MINOT (125)

Pat's Motel Camping **$10**
At Minot, Hwy 2 & 52 bypass E. $10 without hookups; $12 with elec; $16 full hookups. 4/1-11/15. 62 sites; 32 with elec. Tbls, flush toilets, cfga, showers, drkg wtr, playground.

MOHALL (126)

Mohall City Campground **$5**
On W edge of Mohall behind ball diamonds. $5 base after 3 days; camp free first 3 days. 5/1-10/31. 10 RV sites, tent sites. Tbls, toilets, cfga, drkg wtr, elec($), new showers, new dump. Swimming, fishing, hunting.

Mouse River **$12**
Renville County Park
15 mi W of Mohall. $8 tents; $12 at RV sites with elec. 75 RV sites, 50 with elec; tent sites, new primitive section. Tbls, flush toilets, cfga, drkg wtr, showers, dump. Fishing, roller skating, volleyball, ball fields, tennis, volleyball, horseshoes, boating(ld).

MONANGO (127)

City Park **$10**
In town (pop. 59). $10. 4 sites & tenting area. Tbls, flush toilets, cfga, drkg wtr, elec, playground. Biking, volleyball, picnicking, playfield.
Fishing tip: Six mi W of Monango, Wilson Dam is a good place to catch northern pike, largemouth bass, perch and catfish.

MOORETON (128)

City Park **FREE**
In town (pop 216). Free primitive sites with drkg wtr, toilets, tbls, playground. 274-8827.

MOTT (129)

American Legion Park **$5**
S side of Mott. $5. May-Oct. 14 sites, 4 with 20-amp elec. Tbls, flush toilets, cfga, drkg wtr, dump. Swimming, fishing, boating. On shore of Cannonball River. Dedicated to military veterans.
Fishing tip: Fish the Cannonball's pools for walleye, sauger, crappie, northern pike and smallmouthbass.

Mott West Side Trailer Court **$5**
In town. $5 for primitive sites; $15 full hookups. Tbls, toilets, full hookups($), cfga, drkg wtr.

MUNICH (130)

City of Munich Park   **FREE**
On ND 20, S edge of Munich (2nd exit S off Hwy 20). Free. 4/1-10/31; 7-day limit. Donations accepted. 10 sites (5 RV sites with full hookups). Tbls, flush toilets, cfga, drkg wtr, playground, showers. Picnicking, ball field, tennis, volleyball.

NAPOLEON (131)

Beaver Lake State Park   **$5**
17 mi SE of Napoleon. $8 base and $14 with elec during MD-9/30; $5 base & $12 with elec rest of year; 14-day limit. 25 sites with elec/wtr available. Tbls, flush toilets, cfga, drkg wtr, dump, showers, playground. Picnicking, fishing, swimming beach, hiking. 200 acres.

City Campground   **$6**
NE corner of Napoleon. $6 for primitive & tent sites, $12 with hookups. All year. 12 sites with hookups, plus 25 tent sites & RV primitive area. Tbls, flush toilets, cfga, drkg wtr, playground.

Fishing tip: Two good fishing lakes are nearby. West Napoleon Lake (2 mi W of town) contains northern pike & perch. Rudolph Lake (14 mi E & 1 mi S), offers the same species; only electric motors are permitted.

NEWBURG (132)

Newburg City Park   **FREE**
In town (pop 141) N of school. Free. 5/1-10/1. 4 sites. Tbls, flush toilets, cfga, drkg wtr, elec. Playground, tennis.

NEW LEIPZIG (133)

City Campground   **$5**
S side of Main in New Leipzig. $5 for sites with elec; $10 full hookups ($35 weekly, $100 monthly). 14 RV sites, 4 with elec; tent camping area. Tbls, toilets, cfga, drkg wtr, dump. Volleyball, picnic area, golf area.

NEW ROCKFORD (134)

North Riverside
Municipal Park   **$5**
N side of New Rockford at jct of SR 15 & US 281. $5 base. 5/1-9/30. 22 sites (13 for RVs with elec). Tbls, toilets, cfga, drkg wtr, elec($), pool, playground, showers. Tennis, fishing, boating, swimming.

NEW SALEM (135)

North Municipal Park   **FREE**
Half mi N of New Salem, three-fourths mi S of I-94, exit 27. Free, but donations accepted. 5/15-9/30; 3-day limit. 15 sites. Tbls, flush toilets, cfga, drkg wtr, 6 elec hookup, firewood. Limited facilities in winter. Store, ice, food, laundry, dump, LP-gas nearby. Picnicking, playground, golf nearby.

NEW TOWN (136)

4 Bears Casino RV Park   **$6**
Three Affiliated Tribes
Fort Berthold Reservation
4 mi W of New Town on Hwy 23. All year; 14-day limit. $6 for primitive sites; $12 with elec. March-Nov. 85 RV sites with elec. Drkg wtr, toilets, store, dump, showers, coin laundry. Swimming, boating(l), fishing.

Antelope Creek   **FREE**
Wildlife Management Area
12 mi NW of New Town in McKenzie County. Free primitive camping. All year; 10-day limit. No facilities. Boating, fishing, hunting. 964 acres. Leased form Corps of Engineers.

Bear Den Recreation Area   **FREE**
Three Affiliated Tribes
Fort Berthold Reservation
W of New Town on ND 23 to jct with ND 22; 12 mi S on ND 22. Free. 5/1-9/30; 14-day limit. 150 sites (RVs under 32 ft). Tbls, cfga, firewood, no drkg wtr. Boating(l); fishing; picnicking; swimming nearby.

New Town City Marina   **$7**
Three Affiliated Tribes
Fort Berthold Reservation
2 mi W of New Town on US 23; on Lake Sakakawea. $7 base. 5/1-10/1. 55 RV sites; open tent sites. Tbls, flush & pit toilets, showers, elec($) cfga, drkg wtr, dump, store, bait, playground, fish cleaning station. Boating(dl), fishing, waterskiing, swimming.

Pouch Point Recreation Area   **$12**
Three Affiliated Tribes
Fort Berthold Reservation
16 mi S of New Town on SR 1804. $12. 11 RV sites with elec; tent camping area. 5/1-10/1. Tbls, cfga, drkg wtr, flush toilets, showers, dump, playground, fish cleaning station. Fishing, swimming, boating(ld).

Van Hook Recreation Area   **$9**
Montrail County Park
6 mi E of New Torn on SR 23; 2 mi S. $9 without elec ($45 weekly); $14 with elec ($70 weekly); $6 for tents ($31.50 weekly). MD-LD. 110 sites, 30 with elec. Tbls, flush & pit toilets, showers, drkg wtr, dump, cfga, playground, fish cleaning station, store. Swimming, fishing, biking, boating(ld). Former Corps of Engineers park.

White Earth Bay   **$5**
Montrail County Park
28 mi NW of New Town on Hwy 1804; 2 mi S, 1 mi E, 3 mi S, 3 mi E. $5. Primitive camping, $3. Tbls, toilets, cfga, drkg wtr, playground. Boating(ld), fishing. Former Corps of Engineers park.

NIAGARA (137)

City Park   **FREE**
In SE corner of Niagara (pop 73). Free. 4 overnight RV sites with elec. Picnic shelter, ballpark. Historic Fort Totten Trail marker 4 mi E on Hwy 2.

NOONAN (138)

Baukol-Noonan Park   **FREE**
Divide County Recreation Area
From SR 5, three mi E of Noonan, go 1 mi S on dirt 102nd Ave NW, then half mi W. Donations suggested; camp free. 12 RV sites with elec; open tent area. Toilets, tbls, cfga, no drkg wtr, no trash service. Fishing, swimming, hiking, boating. GPS: N48 53.678, W102 56.377.

Fishing tip: Electric motors only at the spillway pond, but catch-planted rainbow trout. The East Mine Pond and dam both contain largemouth bass, bluegill & perch.

Noonan Lions City Park   **$10**
From SR 7 at Noonan, S on Main St; park is on E side between Summit Ave & 5th Ave. $10 ($50 weekly; $200 monthly). 5/15-10/15. 7 RV sites with elec; tent camping area. Tbls, toilets, cfga, drkg wtr, dump. GPS: N48 53.197, W103 00.473.

NORTHWOOD

Campbell City Park   **$10**
From Hwy 15, follow Raymond St to park on S end of town. $10 ($16 weekly) at 5 RV sites with elec/wtr. Tbls, flush toilets, cfga, drkg wtr, showers at pool, dump, shelters, playground. Swimming pool, tennis, volleyball, basketball, arboretum. Tree identification on walking path. Reservations recommended.

OBERON (139)

City Park   **FREE**
In town (pop 150). Free primitive sites. Tbls, drkg wtr. Playground, shelter.

PAGE (140)

City Recreation Park   **FREE**
In Page (pop 329) on S side of Main. Free. 8 RV sites with hookups, playground, drkg wtr, tbls, cfga; tent area. Tennis, ball field.

PARK RIVER (141)

Homme Dam   **$5**
Walsh County Park
Follow signs 2 mi W of Park River on SR 17; at S branch of Park River near dam. $5 base; $10 with elec. 4/1-11/1. 19 sites. Tbls, flush toilets, cfga, drkg wtr, showers, elec($2), dump. Boating(l), fishing, canoeing, waterskiing.

Fishing tip: This scenic 200-acre lake contains northern pike, crappie, largemouth bass, walleye, saugeye, perch & bullhead. A fishing pier provides good shoreline access.

PARSHALL (142)

North City Park — **Donation**
Qtr mi S of downtown on Hwy 37, just N of Rock Museum in town. Camp free, but donations accepted. 12 undesignated sites. Sheltered tbls, cfga, drkg wtr, playground, dump.

Parshall Bay — **$9**
Montrail County Recreation Area
2 mi S of SR 23 on SR 37; 10 mi W & S on winding county rd; at Lake Sakakawea. $9-$14. 200 sites; 43 with elec. Tbls, flush toilets, cfga, drkg wtr, elec($), dump, fish cleaning station, showers. Boating(dl), fishing, playground, swimming.

PEKIN (143)

Pioneer City Park — **$5**
On NE side of Pekin (pop 101) at SR 1 & 15. $5 daily or $30 weekly. All year. 10 RV sites with elec; tent sites. Elec, drkg wtr, cfga, tbls, shelters. Boating & fishing nearby.

PEMBINA (144)

Fort Daer Campground — **$10**
Pembina City Recreation Area
On E. Stutsman Street in Pembina. $10. 5/1-10/1. 12 RV sites, tent spaces. Tbls, flush toilets, cfga, drkg wtr, showers, elec, playground, fish cleaning station. Boating(l), fishing, picnicking.

PETTIBONE (145)

City Park — **$5**
In town. $5 without hookups; $10 with elec & wtr. All year. Tent & 8 RV sites with elec. Tbls, flush toilets, showers, cfga, drkg wtr, shelter.

PICK CITY (146)

Lake Sakakawea State Park — **$5**
1 mi N of Pick City. $8 base and $14 with elec during MD-10/31; $5 base & $12 with elec rest of year; 14-day limit. 192 sites. Tbls, flush toilets, cfga, drkg wtr, dump, showers, marina, store, playgrounds, shelters, beach, amphitheatre. Boating(ldr), fishing, picnicking, swimming. Knife River Indian Village National Historic Site nearby.

POWERS LAKE (147)

Lake Park — **FREE**
Municipal Campground
1 mi E & qtr mi E of town at lake. Donations suggested; camp free. 5/1-10/1; 3-day limit. 12 RV sites, 8 with elec($), and several tent sites. Drkg wtr, tbls, flush toilets, cfga, elec($), dump. Swimming, fishing, boating(l), tennis, basketball. Patrolled.
Fishing tip: Fish from a boat or the park's fishing pier for northern pike & perch.

Lonetree Municipal Park — **FREE**
1 mi E of Powers Lake on SR 50; 1 mi S on access rd. Donations suggested; camp free. 5/1-10/1. 38 sites, 12 with elec. Tbls, toilets, cfga, drkg wtr, elec($). Boating(l), swimming, fishing.

Smishek Dam City Park — **$8**
Just NW of town off SR 50. $8. 5/1-10/1; 3-day limit. 30 primitive sites, 30 RV sites with elec. Tbls, toilets, cfga, drkg wtr, elec($), fishing piers. Boating(l), fishing, swimming.
Fishing tip: Try for northern pike, walleye, perch or bluegill.

RAY (148)

Kota-Ray — **$5**
Williams County Park
5 mi S of Ray, then half mi E, 2 mi S. $5 without hookups, $10 with elec. 12 RV sites, tent sites. Tbls, flush toilets, cfga, drkg wtr, elec, fishing dock. Boating(l), fishing.

Lake McLeod City Park — **DONATIONS**
S 2 blks off Hwy 2. All year. Donations. 12 sites. Pit toilets, drkg wtr, tbls, cfga, elec. Swimming; boat ramp; fishing; waterskiing; golf-9 holes; lighted tennis courts; ice skating; snowmobiling; playground. 568-2204

REEDER (149)

Reeder City Campground — **$7**
On SE side of Reeder. $7 base. 5/1-10/1. 10 RV sites, tent sites. Tbls, flush toilets, cfga, drkg wtr, elec($). Tennis, golf, playground.

REGENT (150)

Indian Creek Dam — **FREE**
Hettinger County Park
1.5 mi W of Regent, then 2 mi S, 2 mi W, 3 mi S. Free. Primitive undesignated camping. Toilets, cfga, no drkg wtr. Fishing, hiking, swimming, boating.
Fishing tip: The dam area contains rainbow trout, walleye, bluegill, smallmouth bass. Idle speed only.

RIVERDALE (151)

Deepwater Park — **FREE**
Corps of Engineers
Lake Sakakawea
From Jct US 83, W on SR 37 (17 mi S of Parshall). Free. 17 primitive sites. Drkg wtr, toilets, tbls, cfga, pavilion. Picnicking, boating(l), pier, fishing.

Douglas Creek — **FREE**
Corps of Engineers
Lake Sakakawea
From jct US 83, 2 mi W of Emmet on SR 37, 7 mi S on gravel rd. Free. All year; 14-day limit. 17 primitive sites (25-ft RV limit). All year; 14-day limit. Drkg wtr, toilets, cfga, tbls. Picnicking, boating(l), fishing, hiking, horseback riding.

Downstream — **$10**
Corps of Engineers
Lake Sakakawea
Near Riverdale, below dam, W side of spillway. $10 at primitive sites; $14 with elec. May-Sep; 14-day limit. 118 sites (101 with elec); 65-ft RVs. Tbls, pit & flush toilets, cfga, drkg wtr, showers, dump, pay phone, 2 playgrounds. Wheelchair access. Fishing, boating(l), interpretive programs.

Wolf Creek — **$6**
Corps of Engineers
Lake Sakakawea
2 mi E of Riverdale on Hwy 200; 3 mi N on gravel rd. $6. May-Sep; 14-day limit. 101 sites. Tbls, toilets, cfga, drkg wtr, dump, fish cleaning station. Boating(l), fishing.

ROCK LAKE (152)

Rock Lake City Park — **FREE**
In NW corner of town at Main & Eller (pop 287.) Free. About 8 sites with 4 pr of 20-amp elec outlets. All year. Cfga, drkg wtr, 2 shelters, tbls, playground. GPS: N48 47.612, W99 14.920.

ROLETTE (153)

Rolette RV Park — **$12**
At W end of town next to airport on Hwy 66. $12 (or $200 monthly) for full hookups. Tbls, toilets, cfga, drkg wtr. Swimming pool. Register at Town & Country Tesoro station.

ROLLA (154)

Armourdale Lake — **FREE**
Wildlife Management Area
9 mi E & 1.5 mi N of Rolla in Towner County. Free primitive camping. All year; 10-day limit. No facilities. Fishing, boating, hunting. 23 acres.
Fishing tip: The lake contains walleye, northern pike, perch.

City Park — **$10**
Neameyer Field
From SR 5 in town, SE on 1st St SE or 2nd St SE and go to end, next to Neameyer ball field. $10 for 1-5 nights; $8 thereafter. Pay fees at Bill's Sinclair Service on Main St. 5/1-10/31. Policed, quiet. 12 RV sites (8 with full hookups). Showers, cfga, drkg wtr, dump, pool, shelters, playground, 1 portable toilet. Swimming; picnicking. No silent ranger or fees posted during 2006 field visit.

Turtle Mountain — **N/A**
Indian Reservation
W of Rolla, near the Canadian border. Fees charged for camping at 10-site Sundown Park (toilets, cfga, drkg wtr) and 5-site Wheaton Lake (toilet, cfga, drkg wtr).

ROSEGLEN (155)

White Shield　　　　　　　**FREE**
Recreation Area
Three Affiliated Tribes
Fort Berthold Reservation
8 mi S of Roseglen on CR 7. Free. 4/1-10/31. Abou 200 undesignated campsites. Tbls, toilets, cfga, drkg wtr. Picnicking, hiking.

ROSS (156)

Dakota West RV Park　　　　**$10**
On Hwy 2 in Ross. $10 base. 5/5-9/30. 30 sites (21 with elec). Tbls, flush toilets, showers, cfga, drkg wtr, elec($), coin laundry, store, dump. Private campground.

RUGBY (157)

Rugby Fairgrounds　　　　　**FREE**
Municipal Park
On E 1st St N of grain elevators in Rugby. Free. All year. Policed. 25 sites. Tbls, flush toilets, cfga, drkg wtr, playground.

ST. JOHN (158)

Dion Lake　　　　　　　　　**FREE**
State Game & Fish Department
12 mi W of St. John, in Turtle Mountains. Free. Undesignated sites; 14-day limit. Toilets, tbls, cfga, no drkg wtr. Swimming, fishing, boating (l).
　Fishing tip: This 82-acre lake offers good walleye & saugeye fishing, with walleye of 2-7 pounds quite common. Northern pike 2-5 pounds also are caught, and smallmouth of up to 4 pounds are landed occasionally. Idle boat speed only.

Gravel Lake　　　　　　　　**FREE**
State Game & Fish Department
5 mi W of St. John, in Turtle Mountains. Free. Undesignated primitive sites; 14-day limit. Toilets, tbls, cfga. Swimming, fishing, boating(l).
　Fishing tip: Gravel Lake contains rainbow trout, walleye, saugeye. Electric motors only, or utilize the fishing pier.

Hooker Lake　　　　　　　　**FREE**
Wakopa Wildlife Management Area
State Game & Fish Department
9 mi W of St. John. Free. Primitive, undeveloped campsites. All year; 10-day limit. Toilets, tbls, cfga, no drkg wtr. Trout fishing, canoeing, swimming, boating(l); idle boat speed only.
　Fishing tip: This little-known lake produces rainbow trout of up to 6 pounds and cutthroat trout that average 1-2 pounds.

Lake Upsilon　　　　　　　　**FREE**
State Game & Fish Department
8 mi W of St. John in Turtle Mountains. Free. All year; 10-day limit. Undesignated primitive sites. Toilets, tbls, no drkg wtr. Fishing, boating, swimming.

　Fishing tip: The lake contains trout, bluegill, crappie and produces northern pike to 12 pounds. A fishing pier is on the E side of the lake.

ST. THOMAS (159)

Hager Municipal Park　　　**FREE**
In town (pop 528) 3 blocks W of Main St on 5th St, following blue & white tent camping symbol. Free. Unlimited tent & self-contained RV camping. Tbls, toilets, cfga, drkg wtr, shelters. Lighted ball diamonds, playground, tennis, horseshoes, recreation hill. GPS: N48 37.234, W97 27.526.

SHEYENNE (160)

Hendrickson Municipal Park　**FREE**
1.5 mi W of Sheyenne. Free. All year. 6 sites. Tbls, toilets, cfga, drkg wtr, 6 elec hookups, playground.

Warsing Dam　　　　　　　　**FREE**
Wildlife Management Area
E of Sheyenne on Sheyenne River. Free primitive camping. All year; 10-day limit. No facilities. Boating, fishing. 86 acres.
　Fishing tip: The dam area contains walley, perch & bullhead. If you don't have a boat, try the fishing pier.

STANLEY (161)

Stanley Municipal Park　　**FREE**
On US 2 across from the courthouse, at N edge of Stanley. Free or $25 per week. 5/1-10/1; 5-day limit. Policed. 30 sites (RVs under 18 ft). Tbls, flush toilets, cfga, firewood, dump, elec/wtr hookup (16 sites), drkg wtr, showers, playground. Store, ice, food, laundry nearby. Lake. Picnicking; fishing; swimming; golf nearby; 2 tennis courts. Donations accepted.

STANTON (162)

Sakakawea Park　　　　　　**$5**
On E side of Stanton at Knife River. $5 without elec., $9 with elec. 4 RV sites with elec; also primitive camping area. Drkg wtr, elec, toilets, cfga, tbls, dump. Swimming, fishing, boating, fish cleaning station. New bathrooms with showers. Park with playground, horseshoes, tennis nearby.
　Fishing tip: Launch boat at Missouri River just S of town; catch walleye, northern pike, catfish. At the Knife River, focus on pools below riffles for walleye, sauger, crappie, northern pike and smallmouth bass.

STEELE (163)

Steele Municipal Park　　　**FREE**
3 mi W of Steele on old US 10; S of I-94 Interchange. Free. All year. Policed. 15 sites. Tbls, playground. Picnicking; golf nearby.

STRASBURG (164)

Strasburg City Campground　**FREE**
On N end of Strasburg. Free without hookups; $12 with full hookups ($2 discount for longer than 4 nights. 9 RV sites with elec; tent sites. Drkg wtr, tbls, cfga, flush toilets, showers, dump. Tennis, swimming.

SYKESTON (165)

Lake Hiawatha　　　　　　　**FREE**
Municipal Park
1 mi N of Sykeston at Lake Hiawatha. Free at last report. All year. 10 RV sites (4 with hookups) & tent sites. Tbls, toilets, cfga, drkg wtr, firewood, playground, 2 elec. Store, ice, food, laundry, dump nearby. Swimming; picnicking; fishing; tennis. Policed.
　Fishing tip: The lake contains bullhead catfish, perch and northern pike.

TAPPEN (166)

Alkaline Lake　　　　　　　**FREE**
Wildlife Management Area
11 mi S & 1 mi E of Tappen in Kidder County. Free. All year; 10-day limit. Primitive camping. No facilities. Boating, fishing. 47 acres.

TIOGA (167)

City Park　　　　　　　　　**FREE**
3 mi N of US 2 on ND 40, in Tioga; on NE edge of town. Free at last report. All year; 3-day limit. Policed. Undesignated tent sites; 12 RV sites (8 with elec). Tbls, flush toilets, cfga, firewood, drkg wtr, playground, showers, dump, elec hookup. Swimming; picnicking; fishing; golf nearby.
　Fishing tip: Try for rainbow trout, largemouth bass at Iversoon Dam, 3 mi S of town, then 1 mi W, 8 mi S and half mi E. Or, just N of Tioga, the Tioga Reservoir contains northern pike & perch; it has a metal boat ramp.

Peaceful Valley　　　　　　**$10**
Mobile Home & RV Park
2nd & Dakota St South in Tioga. $10 for sites with 30-amp elec; $15 with 50-amp. 9 RV sites. Tbls, flush toilets, cfga, drkg wtr, sewer.

TOWNER (168)

Towner City Park　　　　　**FREE**
From US 2, 1 blk N on SR 14 (Main St) at Sixth Ave. Free. Spring-fall. 4 free back-in RV sites for big rigs & tent sites. Drkg wtr, tbls, cfga, elec, flush toilets, no showers, dump, playground, shelters. Tennis courts, sand volleyball. GPS: N48 20.467, W100 24.364. Pop. 574, "Cattle Capital of North Dakota."

Towner Recreation Area　　**$7**
Mouse River State Forest
2 mi N of Towner on paved co rd. $7. All year. 8 sites. Tbls, toilets, cfga, firewood, dump,

drkg wtr, playground. Fishing; boating; picnicking; golf nearby.

Vagabond Recreation Area $7
Mouse River State Forest
10 mi N of Towner on paved co rd. $7 All year. Undesignated sites. Tbls, toilets, cfga, firewood, drkg wtr. Snowmobiling; picnicking; fishing.

TURTLE LAKE (169)

Brekken-Holmes $10
City Recreation Complex
1.5 mi N of Turtle Lake. $10 first night; $5 thereafter. All year. 2 sites with elec, numerous primitive sites. Tbls, toilets, cfga, drkg wtr, dump, shelters, softball complex. Boating(ld), fishing.
Fishing tip: Try for rainbow trout, walleye, smallmouth bass, bluegill.

Turtle Lake Municipal Park $10
On E side of Turtle Lake. $10 first night, $5 thereafter. Tent sites; 6 RV sites with elec/wtr. Drkg wtr, cfga, tbls, flush toilets, shelters, dump. Basketball field.

UNDERWOOD (170)

Pioneer City Park FREE
Inquire locally for directions; on E side of town, CR 14. Free. All year. Policed. Undesignated RV sites; 50 tent sites. Tbls, toilets, cfga, playground, no elec. Picnicking, swimming, fishing, boating.

UPHAM (171)

Municipal Park Donations
S of Upham business district on C Ave. Camp free, but donations requested; fee for elec. Tent sites; 12 RV sites, 8 with elec. Drkg wtr, toilets, tbls, cfga. Playgrounds. J. Clark Salyer National Wildlife Refuge nearby. Another location in town being considered for camping; wtr, elec, sewer hookups would be offered. Inquire locally or call 701-768-2839.

VALLEY CITY (172)

Ashtabula Crossing East $12
Corps of Engineers
Lake Ashtabula
15 mi N of Valley City on CR 21, following signs. $12 at 5 walk-in tent sites; $16 at 33 sites with elec ($8 with federal Senior Pass). 5/1-9/30; 14-day limit. 38 sites. Tbls, flush toilets, showers, cfga, drkg wtr, elec($), dump, beach, playground, pavilion, fish cleaning station. Boating(l), fishing, waterskiing, swimming. 34 acres. 2-night minimum stay on weekends.
Fishing tip: There's great fishing in Lake Ashtabula for a variety of species -- walleye, northern pike, white bass, crappie, smallmouth bass, muskie, perch and bluegill. Rental boats are available nearby.

Clausen Springs $10
Barnes County Recreation Area
3 mi W of Valley City; 20 mi S on SR 1; follow signs (15.5 mi SE of Litchville). $10. 5/1-11/1. 56 sites (no RV size limit). Tbls, flush toilets, cfga, drkg wtr, elec, dump. Fishing, boating(d), swimming.
Fishing tip: Fish here for trout, perch or largemouth bass from a boat (idle speed only) or the fishing pier.

Eggert's Landing $7
Corps of Engineers
Lake Ashtabula
12 mi N of Valley City on CR 21. $7 with federal Senior Pass at non-elec sites ($8 at sites with elec); others pay $14 & $16. 5/1-9/30; 14-day limit. 41 sites, 35 with elec; 65-ft RVs. Tbls, flush & pit toilets, cfga, drkg wtr, elec, playground, dump, fish cleaning station, showers, public phone. Fishing, boating(dl), canoeing, hiking, interpretive programs, mountain biking, nature trail, waterskiing. Wheelchair access.

Lake Ashtabula FREE
Baldhill Dam
State Fishing Access Site
10 mi N of Village City. Free. All year; 10-day limit. Primitive undesignated sites; no facilities. Boating(rl), fishing.
Fishing tip: This lake has good fishing, offering northern pike, perch, walleye, white bass, crappie and smallmouth bass. If you don't have your own boat, you can rent one.

Mel Rieman Recreation Area $12
Corps of Engineers
Lake Ashtabula
E side of dam (N of Valley City on CR 21. $12 at non-elec sites; $14 with elec. About 5/1-9/15; 14-day limit. 27 sites, 15 with elec. Tbls, flush toilets, cfga, drkg wtr, showers, elec, playground, beach, fish cleaning station. Handicap access. Boating(l), fishing, swimming, horseshoes.

Moon Lake FREE
State Fishing Access Site
2 mi W of Valley City to SR 1. 5.5 mi S on SR 1; 4 mi W; 2 mi N. Free. All year; 10-day limit. Primitive undesignated sites; no facilities. Fishing for trout, smallmouth bass, catfish.

Municipal Tourist Park $6.50
At 675 E. Main St, I-94 business loop, on E end of Valley City. $6.50 for tent sites; $8.50 base for RV sites; $13.75 with hookups. 5/15-10/15. 18 RV sites (20 with full hookups). Tbls, flush toilets, showers, cfga, drkg wtr, elec ($), dump ($), playground.
Fishing tip: For rainboe trout, try Blumers Lake just S of Valley City.

VELVA (173)

Velva Municipal Park $10
From US 52, N on SR 41 (Main St) under RR, then right on 5th St to 1st Ave W. $10 with

hookups ($50 per week); free tent camping. All year. Policed. Undesignated sites & 20 large back-in RV sites with 30-amp elec/wtr. Tbls, toilets, cfga, drkg wtr, playground, pool, showers at pool. Swimming; picnicking; fishing, tennis. Dump at Cenex station On US 52 W of SR 41. Pop. 1,049. GPS: N48 03.533, W100 55.304.
Fishing tip: Try trout fishing at nearby Velva Sportsmens Pond, in Ward County 10 mi SW of Velva.

WALHALLA (175)

Riverside City Park $10
S side of town off Hwy 32 at 9th St & Riverside Ave on the Pembina River. $10 at tent sites; RV sites $15. 5/15-9/30. Numerous tent sites; 45 RV sites with elec/wtr. Tbls, flush toilets, cfga, drkg wtr, elec/wtr, coin laundry, showers, pool, store, playground, dump. Golf, mini-golf, horseshoes, swimming, tennis, sand volleybal, nature trails. 15 acres.

Tetrault Wood State Forest $7
Half mi S of Walhalla on W side of Hwy 32. $7. All year. Dispersed camping in the forest. No facilities. Pembina River.

WATFORD CITY (176)

CCC Campground FREE
Dakota Prairie Grasslands
14 mi S of Watford City on US 85, then right. Free. All year; 14-day limit. 4 sites. Tbls, toilets, cfga, no drkg wtr, no trash service. Hunting, horseback riding.

City Tourist Park $7
Off SR 23 on E end of Watford City at Cherry Creek. $7 for tents, $10 for RVs with hookups. 5/1-11/15; 14-day limit. 40 sites (8 with 30-amp elec/sewer). Tbls, flush toilets, cfga, drkg wtr, showers, elec, dump, playground. Biking, fishing, picnicking.

McKenzie Bay Marina $8
Watford City Park
E of Watford City on SR 23; 10 mi S on SR 22, then E 18 mi to Lake Sakakawea. $8 base; $12 with elec. 200 sites (27 RV sites, 22 with elec). Tbls, flush toilets, cfga, drkg wtr, showers, dump, fish cleaning station. Swimming, boating(ldr), fishing, waterskiing.

Squaw Creek Campground $10
North Unit
Roosevelt National Park
15 mi S of Watford City on Us 85; 6 mi W. $10. All year; 14-day limit. 50 sites. Tbls, flush toilets, cfga, drkg wtr, dump. Limited facilities in winter. Hiking, scenic drive, nature program. Entry fee $10 for 7 days.

Tobacco Garden $8
Resort & Marina
McKenzie County Park
29 mi NE of Watford City on SR 1806. $8

without elec; $10 with elec. All year. 60 sites with elec. Tbls, toilets, drkg wtr, cfga, dump, showers, store, coin laundry. Boating(ldr), fishing, campfire programs.

Fishing tip: Lake Sakakawea produces excellent catches of walleye, many up to 14 pounds. Use Lindy rigs, jig-and-minnow or jig-and-leech, spinners, crankbaits.

WESTHOPE (177)

Westhope City Park **$10**
On E side of Westhope on SR 6, N on E. 6th St. $10 or $50 weekly, $150 monthly. 8 sites. Tbls, no toilets, cfga, full hookups at each site with four 30-amp & two 50-amp elec. Dump across street. Swimming, hiking. Former mobile home park.

WILDROSE (178)

Municipal Park **$6**
On S. Main St in Wildrose. $6 base. 6 sites. Drkg wtr, toilets, cfga, tbls, elec($), dump. Nearby historic school with golf, tennis, horseshoes. Fees not verified for 2007.

WILLISTON (179)

American Legion Park **Donations**
4 mi W of Williston on Hwy 2/85; 3 mi S on Hwy 85; 4 mi E.. Camp free, but donations suggested. 5/1-9/30. Tent sites; 15 RV sites with elec, plus elec for several more RVs. Tbls, toilets, cfga, drkg wtr, playground. Boating(l), fishing. Near Missouri River. Beautiful park.

Blacktail Dam Campsite **$7**
Blacktail Dam Association
17 mi N of Willison on Hwy 85, 5.5 mi W on CR 10; 1 mi N on access rd. $7 with elec. 5/1-9/1. 32 RV sites with elec. Tbls, flush toilets, cfga, drkg wtr, dump, playground, coin laundry. Swimming boating(l), fishing. Fees not verified for 2007.

Fishing tip: Try for northern pike, walleye, perch, bluegill, smallmouth bass.

Lewis & Clark State Park **$5**
19 mi SE of Williston on Hwy 1804; at Lake Sakakawea. $8 base and $14 with elec during MD-9/30; $5 base & $12 with elec rest of year; 14-day limit. 80 sites. Tbls, flush toilets, cfga, drkg wtr, dump, showers, shelters, marina, store, beach, amphitheatre, fish cleaning station. Nature trail, picnicking, boating(ldr), swimming, fishing, cross-country skiing, snowmobiling.

WILLOW CITY (180)

Willow City Campground **FREE**
In town on Hwy 60 (pop 329). Free. May-Oct. 2 RV sites with elec. Tbls, toilet, cfga, drkg wtr.

WILTON (181)

Wilton City Park **$7**
On Burleigh Rd, E across RR tracks. $7 All year. Policed. Undesignated sites, 4 with elec/wtr. Tbls, toilets, cfga, dump, drkg wtr, playground.

WIMBLEDON (182)

Victory Municipal Park **FREE**
On NE edge of town. Free at last report. All year. Policed. 12 sites (4 RV sites with elec). Tbls, flush toilets, cfga, drkg wtr, playground, dump, sewage, 4 elec hookups. Picnicking.

WING (183)

City Park **FREE**
On W edge of Wing, jct of Hwys 14 & 38. Donations suggested; camp free. 4 RV sites with elec and primitive open sites. Drkg wtr, cfga, tbls, toilets, elec($). Playground, tennis & basketball courts, store.

Lake Mitchell
Burleigh County Park **Donations**
1 mi W of Wing on SR 36; 2 mi N. Donations suggested; camp free. Open primitive camping area. Tbls, toilets, drkg wtr, cfga, beach, fishing pier. Boating, fishing, swimming.

Fishing tip: This lake is limited to electric motors, but it has good fishing for northern pike and perch from shore.

WISHEK (184)

Doyle Memorial **$8**
State Recreation Area and City Park
7 mi SE of Wishek on SR 85. $8 base for primitive sites, $12 with elec. 5/15-9/30; 14-day limit. 20 RV sites with elec, unlimited primitive sites. Tbls, toilets, cfga, drkg wtr, showers, dump, fish cleaning station. Swimming, boating(ld), fishing. Leased from state by city.

WOODWORTH (185)

Woodworth Park **FREE**
In center of Woodworth; follow signs. Free. May-Nov. 15 tent sites; 3 RV sites with elec. Tbls, toilets, cfga, drkg wtr, showers.

WYNDMERE (186)

Gateway Municipal Park **FREE**
At Ash & RR Dr (off 4th St) in Wyndmere. Free. May-Sept. 8 sites with hookups, tent sites. Tbls, cfga, hookups, dump, elec, playground, shelter, sewer. Basketball, volleybll, horseshoes, tennis.

YORK (187)

Village Park **FREE**
Small town (pop. 69) offers free camping. Two sites have wtr, elect. Tbls, cfga. Picnicking.

ZAP (188)

Beaver Bay Recreation Area **$5**
Lake Sakakawea
Zap Park Board
Corps of Engineers
12 mi N of Zap. $5. All year; 14-day limit. Primitive camping. Tbls, toilets, cfga, no drkg wtr. Boating(ld), fishing. Managed by city; owned by corps of engineers.

Beaver Creek **FREE**
Wildlife Management Area
12 mi N of Zap in Mercer County. Free primitive camping. No facilities. Fishing, boating, hunting. 298 acres. Leased from Corps of Engineers.

Zap City Park **$7**
On 3rd Ave N in Zap; W side of town by Spring Creek. $7 daily; $30 weekly; $100 monthly. All year. 18 RV sites (13 with full hookups); 5 sites with elec; tent sites. Tbls, toilets, cfga, drkg wtr, dump. Tennis, picnicking.

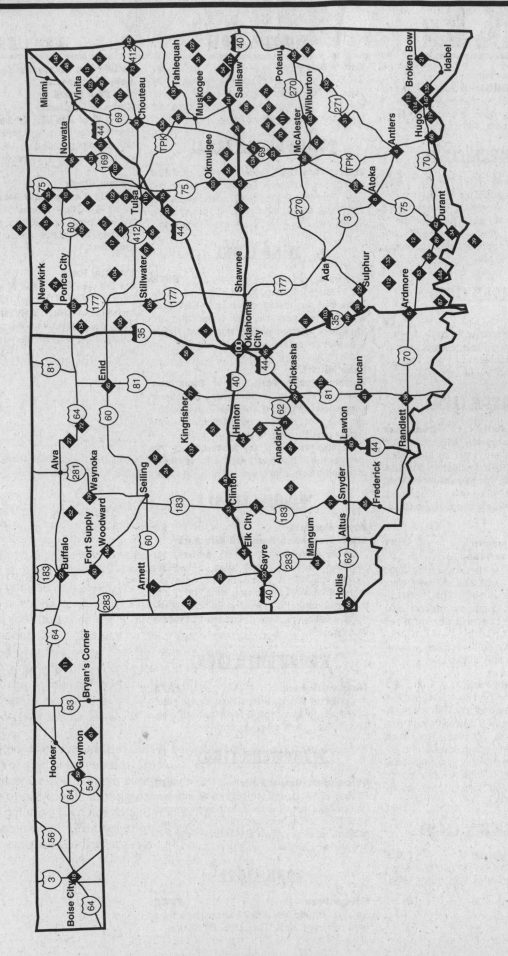

OKLAHOMA

MISCELLANEOUS
Capital:
Oklahoma City
Nickname:
Sooner State
Motto:
Labor Omnia Vincit (Labor Conquers All Things)
Flower:
Mistletoe
Tree:
Redbud
Bird:
Scissortail Flycatcher
Song:
"Oklahoma"

Internet Address:
www.travelok.com

Toll-free number for travel information: 800-652-6552.

Tourism and Recreation Department, PO Box 52002, Oklahoma City, OK 73152. 405-230-9400 or 800-652-6552.

Dept of Wildlife Conservation, 1801 N Lincoln, Oklahoma City, OK 73152; 405-521-3851.

REST AREAS
Overnight stops in self-contained RVs are permitted.

STATE PARKS
Camping with no hookups is available for a small charge at most state parks. Tent and primitive sites are $8; semi-modern sites (with electric and water) are generally $14-16; modern include water, electricity and sewer and are usually $17-19. Preferred sites have higher fees because of locations or desirability. Maximum stay is 14-days. Seniors and disabled campers pay lower rates. Dept of Tourism and Recreation, 800/654-8240.

OTHER STATE CAMPING AREAS
Backpacking Trails. Camping is permitted in most areas along trails. Stream water should be purified before drinking. For further information and a copy of Oklahoma Trails Guide contact Dept of Tourism and Recreation.

The Illinois Wild & Scenic River is Oklahoma's best known Scenic River. Legislation in the 1970s officially designated 70 miles of the river as a Scenic River to protect it for future generations. Free primitive camping is permitted at several public access points along the river; most of those areas have few, if any, facilities. Canoeing is one of the most popular activities on the Illinois. Floaters can enjoy 70 miles of interesting and sometimes challenging stream. The river is one of the few streams in Oklahoma that has clean, clear conditions necessary for smallmouth bass; 68 other species of fish also can be caught. May 1-Oct 1, the Oklahoma Scenic Rivers Commission requires a user fee of $1 per canoe to be paid per trip. Canoes may be rented from numerous outfitters along the Illinois. Most of those outfitters have RV and tent camping facilities available. For a list of outfitters and a map of the Illinois, write to Oklahoma Scenic Rivers Commission, P.O. Box 292, Tahlequah, OK 74465 or call 918/456-3251.

Oklahoma Department of Wildlife Conservation properties. Camping (free) is limited to 14 days except at areas open only to hunter camping for special season. Camping on those areas is limited to two days longer than the period which the hunter/camper is authorized to hunt. Camping is permitted only in areas listed in this chapter. All camping on these properties is primitive; no facilities are provided. Camping areas are meant to accommodate fishermen and hunters using the properties.

Salt Plains National Wildlife Refuge, Route 1, Box 76, Jet, OK 73749.

Tishomingo National Wildlife Refuge, PO Box 248, Tishomingo, OK 73460.

Bureau of Indian Affairs, Eastern Oklahoma Development District, PO Box 1367 , Muskogee, OK 74401; or Bureau of Indian Affairs, Anadarko Area Office, PO Box 368, Anadarko, OK 73005.

OUACHITA NATIONAL FOREST
Located in southern LeFlore County, the forest contains approximately 207,736 acres in Oklahoma. Camping is available without cost except in developed campgrounds. All camping areas are on a first-come, first-served basis, with a 14-day limit. 501-321-5202.

CORPS OF ENGINEERS
In the Tulsa District, camping fees are charged according to three classifications of campgrounds: Class A sites are those having flush toilets, showers, paved roads, sanitary dump stations, designated tent or RV spaces, trash containers and potable water; Class B areas have similar facilities except flush toilets or showers are not provided; Class C areas have basic sanitary facilities, designated tent or RV spaces, trash containers and potable water. Campers are exempt from day-use charges.

ALTUS (2)

Quartz Mountain   **$8**
State Park and Resort
7 mi S of Lone Wolf on SR 44. $8 for self-contained RVs in unimproved areas; $8 for tents. All year; 14-day limit. 92 primitive sites; 33 wtr/elec sites; 20 full-hookup sites. Tbls, toilets, cfga, showers, drkg wtr, dump, store. Swimming, fishing, boating (lr), archery, volleyball, picnic areas, group camps, mini golf, hiking trails, ORV area, golf, paddleboating (r). 4,284 acres. Water slide nearby.

Fishing tip: North Fork of the Red River is a designated trout stream from Altus-Lugert Dam downstream to the low-water dam at SR 44A within this park. Best access is along the N shore. Season: 11/15-3/15.

ANADARKO (3)

Thunderbird Campground   **$12.50**
Indian City USA
2 mi S of Anadarko on SR near Indian City USA. $12.50 for primitive & tent sites; $18 full hookups. Tbls, flush toilets, showers, cfga, drkg wtr, coin laundry, dump, playground. Swimming. Part of the Indian City USA complex.

Randlett City Park   **$8**
On W edge of Anadarko on Oklahoma St. $8 ($4 for senior citizens). All year; 21-day limit. 35 sites. Tbls, toilets, cfga, drkg wtr, pool, playground, elec, dump. Fishing, horseshoes.

ANTLERS (4)

Lake Ozzie Cobb   **FREE**
State Fishing Lake
Dept of Wildlife Conservation
13 mi E of Antlers & NE of Rattan off SR 3. All year. Primitive camping at 116-acre lake. 30-ft RV limit. Toilets, tbls, cfga, no drkg wtr. Fishing, boating(l).

Fishing tip: Considered a good bass lake, Cobb also is known for its crappie, bluegill & channel catfish. The lake produced the state's 18th-largest largemouth -- 12 pounds, 10 ounces, caught in 1989.

ARDMORE (5)

Lake Murray State Park   **$8**
3 mi S of Ardmore on US 77. $8 base. All year; 14-day limit. Base fee for 53 primitive sites. $15 for semi-modern sites; $18 for modern sites; $21, full hookups. 209 elec/wtr sites; 50 full-hookup sites. Tbls, flush toilets, cfga, drkg wtr, showers, dump, store, pool, playground, equestrian facilities. Boating(lr), fishing, swimming, mini golf, biking(r), motorcycling area, golf, airstrip, nature center.

Fishing tip: From the park, boat out to the windy points in early afternoon and cast plastics and crankbaits for smallmouth & largemouth bass. In evenings, look for white bass in shallow cove areas; use silver artificials for them, especially if you see schooling shad.

ARCADIA (6)

Arcadia Lake   **$8**
City of Edmond
2.5 mi E of I-35 on SR 66 or 15th St. $8 base. All year. Base fee off-season for primitive "preferred" sites Mon-Thurs during 12/1-3/30 ($14 in-season; $11.20 for seniors, $7 with federal Senior Pass); higher weekend rates. For primitive non-preferred sites, $10 weekdays in-season and $8 off-season ($15 weekends). Regular "preferred" sites with wtr/elec range from $6.50 off-season for seniors to $24 on weekends in-season. Full hookups are $9 off-season for seniors to $29 on weekends in-season. 39 primitive sites; 55 elec/wtr sites; 10 full-hookup sites. Tbls, toilets, cfga, drkg wtr, dump. Boating(ld), hiking trails.

Fishing tip: This lake has a huge carp population, but it also contains some nice largemouth bass. Concentrate on the rocky points.

ARNETT (7)

Earl's Point/Parker Place   **FREE**
Ellis County
State Wildlife Management Area
6 mi S of Arnett on SR 46; 2 mi W on co rd; 1 mi N on co rd to camps. Free. Two primitive camps for fishermen or hunters only. Part of Ellis County Public Hunting Area, 4,796 acres. Camp only in designated areas; 14-day limit. Fishing at Commission Creek & nearby Lake Lloyd Vincent.

Lake Lloyd Vincent Camp   **FREE**
Ellis County
State Wildlife Management Area
2 mi W of Arnett on SR 51; 5 mi S on co rd to WMA's northern entrance; 2 mi S of camp at spillway of Lake Vincent dam. Free. Toilets, cfga. Boating(l), fishing. Picnic areas on N & S shores of lake. Only fishermen & hunter primitive camping permitted in designated areas; 14-day limit.

North 240   **FREE**
Ellis County
State Wildlife Management Area
2 mi W of Arnett on SR 51; 4.5 mi S on co rd; 2 mi W on co rd to camp. On shore of creek leading into Lake Lloyd Vincent. Free. Only fishermen & hunter primitive camping permitted in designated areas; 14-day limit. Fishing in streams and nearby Lake Vincent.

Virginia Place   **FREE**
Ellis County
State Wildlife Management Area
2 mi W of Arnett on SR 51; 5 mi S on co rd to WMA's north entrance; 1 mi S to camp. On W bank of West Hog Creek. Free. Only fishermen & hunter primitive camping are permitted in designated areas; 14-day limit. Fishing in streams & nearby Lake Lloyd Vincent.

Wilson Place   **FREE**
Ellis County
State Wildlife Management Area
3 mi S of Arnett on SR 46; 1 mi W on co rd; 1.5 mi S on co rd to camp. On W bank of Hog Creek. Free. Only fishermen & hunter primitive camping permitted in designated areas. 14-day limit. Fishing in streams & at nearby Lake Lloyd Vincent.

ATOKA (8)

Atoka Rest Area   **FREE**
Confederate Memorial Museum
1 mi N of Atoka on Hwy 69; near museum. All year; 1-night limit. Free. Primitive undesignated sites for self-contained RVs. Tbls, drkg wtr.

Travel tip: The museum contains exhibits on prehistoric fossils, the Chocktaw Trail of Tears, the Butterfield Stage Line and celebrity Reba McEntire. Free admission.

Boggy Depot State Park   **$8**
11 mi W of Atoka on SR 7; 4 mi S on Park Lane. $8 for self-contained RVs in unimproved areas; $8 for tents; 6 modern sites with full hookups, $18; 20 semi-modern sites with elec/wtr, $15; 65 primitive sites. Tbls, flush toilets, cfga, drkg wtr, dump, showers, shelters. Nature trails, historical area, picnic areas, playground. Fishing.

Fred's Fish Camp   **FREE**
Municipal Park
5 mi N of Atoka on US 69, past Stringtown; half mi W on access rd. Free. Primitive, undeveloped camping area; no facilities. Boating (l), fishing.

Lake Atoka
Wildlife Management Area   **FREE**
12 mi N of Atoka on US 69. Free. All year. 1 designated primitive area; no facilities. At 6,000-acre lake. Fishing, hiking, waterskiing, boating(l).

Fishing tip: This lake is known for its good catfish angling, but it also contains crappies, sunfish and largemouth bass.

McGee Creek State Park   **$8**
18 mi E of Atoka on SR 3; 3 mi N of Farris on McGee Creek Lake. $8 for self-contained RVs; $8 for tents. Primitive camping area and elec/wtr sites. $15 for semi-modern sites; $18 preferred sites. Tbls, flush toilets, cfga, drkg wtr, elec/wtr($), dump, beach. Fishing, boating(l), swimming, waterskiing, equestrian facilities, hiking trails.

Fishing tip: McGee Creek Lake is considered by many anglers to be the best largemouth bass lake in Oklahoma. It consistently produce big bass, and an angler survey in 2000 revealed it gave up more bass per fishing hour than any other lake, edging out Kerr with 88 per cent of its fishermen successf, with a per-angler success rate of just over two bass per day.

Old 43 Landing   **FREE**
Municipal Park
8 mi N of Atoka on US 69, past Stringtown; 2 mi W on SR 43, across lake; qtr mi SE on access rd. Free. Primitive, undeveloped camping area; no facilities. Boating(l), fishing, swimming beach. Lake Atoka.

BARNSDALL (9)

Candy   **FREE**
State Wildlife Management Area
Candy Creek
6 mi SE of Barnsdall on SR 11 to just S of Wolco; E on co rd to WMA entrance. Two parking areas on northbound access rds, and one 1.5 mi from entrance. South entrance E on SR 11 from Avant, then N on CR N3908. Free. Primitive camping for fishermen and hunters only in designated areas; 14-day limit. Stream fishing. 3,658 acres.

Twin Cove   **$8**
Corps of Engineers
Birch Lake
About 4 mi S of Barnsdall. $8. Open 4/1-9/30; 14-day limit. 11 primitive sites. Tbls, toilets, cfga, drkg wtr, beach, playground. Boating (dl), fishing, hiking, waterskiing, swimming, nature trail.
Fishing tip: In spring & fall, try for large-mouth bass in the creek channels at 3-6 feet; catch striped bass on crankbaits, and look for crappies in 10-14 feet using minnows & jigs.

BARTLESVILLE (10)

Johnstone City RV Park   **$5**
On N Cherokee Ave (SR 123), N of Cherokee Bridge near Johnstone Park; contact Bartles-ville police records dept, 110 N. Johnstone. $5 the first night, $4 thereafter. All year; 10-day limit. 6 RV sites. Tbls, toilets, elec, drkg wtr nearby, no dump.

BEAVER (11)

Beaver Dunes State Park   **$8**
1 mi N of Beaver on US 270. $8 for self-contained RVs in unimproved areas; $8 for tents; $19 at 13 semi-modern sites. All year; 14-day limit. 5 primitive sites; 7 semi-modern sites with elec/wtr. Tbls, flush toilets, cfga, drkg wtr, showers, dump, group shelters. Fishing, dune buggy & motorcycle courses, playground, volleyball. 5-acre lake; 377 acres.

BEE (12)

Butcher Pen   **FREE**
Bee Community Park
Lake Texoma, Denison Dam
11 mi SE of Tishomingo on OK 78/22; on Washita River. All year; 14-day limit. 11 sites. Tbls, flush toilets, cfga, drkg wtr. Hunting; picnicking; fishing (sunfish, bass, catfish); boating(rl); waterskiing; tennis/golf/horse-

back riding nearby. Heated fishing dock. Former corps of enginers camp

BERNICE (13)

Bernice State Park   **$8**
Half mi E of Bernice off SR 85A. $8 for self-contained RVs in unimproved areas; $8 for tents; $16 semi-modern sites; $18 preferred sites. All year; 14-day limit. 45 primitive sites; 33 elec/wtr sites. Tbls, flush toilets, showers, drkg wtr, dump. Swimming, boating(l), fishing. Grand Lake O' the Cherokees.
Fishing tip: This lake well known for crappie fishing, and it also produces a log of nice bass. In May, entice big ones from Horse Creek by tossing 10-inch power worms near laydowns in the coves.

BIGHEART (15)

Whippoorwill Unit   **FREE**
Hulah Lake
State Wildlife Management Area
N of Bigheart on SR 99 to WMA's head-quarters; E on access rds. 2 camping areas: one near mouth of Birch Creek, the second at mouth of Cotton Creek, with public boat launch nearby at wildlife development unit. Free. Only fishermen/hunter primitive camp-ing permitted in designated areas; 14-day limit. Lake is 3,600 acres, 62-mi shoreline; WMA is 16,141 acres. Deer & waterfowl hunting excellent. Big catfish.

BINGER (16)

Fort Cobb   **FREE**
State Wildlife Management Area
Fort Cobb Lake
4 mi SW of Binger on SR 142; 4 mi S on SR 146 to Albert; W on co rds. Free. Only fisher-men & hunter primitive camping is permitted in designated areas; 14-day limit. 2,623-acre lake and 3,500-acre WMA boast of some of the best hunting areas in state and excellent fishing. Deer, quail, rabbit, turkey abound, and up to 20 million crows descend on area each winter. Game refuge attracts 60,000 nesting ducks. Boat ramps at Lemmons Area, Fort Cobb State Park and West Side Area.
Fishing tip: The lake offers good fishing for white bass, largemouth bass, walleye, catfish and hybrid striped bass.

BLACKBURN (17)

Blackburn Section   **FREE**
Keystone Lake
State Wildlife Management Area
Arkansas River
4 mi E of Blackburn on co rds to WMA entrance on Arkansas River. W shore NW of Keystone Lake. Free. Hunter & fisherman primitive camping is permitted only within 50 yds of public use rds. WMA is 16,537 acres.

Fishing tip: Use live minnows for striped bass, white bass, largemouth bass & flat-head catfish.

BOISE CITY (18)

Black Mesa State Park   **$8**
23 mi NW of Boise City on SR 325; 8 mi W. $8 for self-contained RVs in unimproved areas; $8 for tents; $15 semi-modern sites; $19 preferred sites. All year; 14-day limit. 21 primitive sites; 34 elec/wtr sites. Tbls, flush toilets, showers, drkg wtr, dump, play-ground, group camp. Fishing, boating(l), pic-nic areas.
Fishing tip: The park's 159-acre Lake Carl Etling produced the state's record north-ern pike a quarter century ago, in 1976. It weighed 36.5 pounds and was 44 inches long. The lake also contains rainbow trout, walleye, hybrid striped bass & white bass. In early 2007, the lake was dry.

Walton RV Park   **$10**
5 blocks N of courthouse in Boise City on US 287. $10. All year. 8 full-hookup sites. Tbls, flush toilets, cfga, drkg wtr, showers, dump.

BRAGGS (19)

Greenleaf State Park   **$8**
3 mi S of Braggs on SR 10. $8 base self-contained RVs & tents in unimproved areas; $16 for semi-modern sites (shared water); $17 semi-modern; $19 semi-modern with 50-amp; $19 modern. 80 primitive sites; 76 elec/wtr sites; 22 full-hook-up sites. Tbls, flush toilets, cfga, drkg wtr, showers, play-ground, dump. Swimming pool, bathhouse, boating(ld), fishing, fishing dock, hiking trails, nature center, naturalist programs.
Fishing tip: Try Greenleaf Lake's white bass fishing. A recent test netting surprised everyone when EVERY white bass caught was more than 12 inches, and the largest fish was 2.4 pounds.

Pumpkin Center Camp   **FREE**
Camp Gruber Public Hunting Area
Gruber State Wildlife Management Area
N of Braggs on SR 10 to WMA entrance; 4 mi E on Hilltop Rd; 4 mi S on North South Rd to camp near Pumpkin Center Pond. Free. Only primitive hunter camping permitted. Camp only in designated areas during open hunting season; 14-day limit. Well known for top deer yields. Fishing at nearby Greenleaf Lake. Combined Gruber & Cherokee Wildlife Management Areas 55,515 acres.

BRISTOW (20)

Northeastern Section   **FREE**
Lake Heyburn
State Wildlife Management Area
9 mi N of Bristow on SR 43; 2 mi E on SR 33; 1 mi S on access rd to WMA entrance (just W of Heyburn State Park). Free. Only fishermen & hunter primitive camping permitted in des-

ignated areas; 14-day limit. 1,070-acre lake noted for bass, catfish, sunfish & crappie fishing. The 4,615-acre WMA is popular for duck, goose, quail and squirrel hunting.

Western Section   FREE
Lake Heyburn
State Wildlife Management Area

7 mi N of Bristow on sR 43; 2 mi E on access rd to WMA entrance. Ask directions to camping area. Free. Only hunter & fishermen primitive camping in designated areas; 14-day limit. Boat ramps at Heyburn State Park, Heyburn Recreation Area & Sheppards Point.

BROKEN BOW (21)

Beavers Bend State Park $8

6 mi N of Broken Bow on US 259; E on US 259A. On Mountain Fork River. $8 for self-contained RVs in unimproved areas; $8 for tents; $15 semi-modern sites; $18 modern & preferred. 68 primitive sites; 110 elec/wtr sites. Tbls, toilets, cfga, drkg wtr, showers, dump, store. Swimming, trout fishing, nature trails, horseback riding, naturalist programs, playgrounds, canoes, hayrides, archery, tennis courts, canoe floats, miniature golf, whitewater float trips, boating(lr), golf, fly fishing clinics, waterskiing, volleyball, biking(r), hay-rides.

Fishing tip: In Jan 2001, a Texas angler fishing in the Mountain Fork River below Broken Bow Lake caught a 9 pound 10 ounce brown trout and set a new state rocord for that species. That section of the river is restricted to barbless hooks. The trout was caught on a Renegade golden spoon. The previous record was a 7-pounder, also caught from the Mountain Fork.

Broken Bow   FREE
State Wildlife Management Area

About 21 mi N of Broken Bow on US 259; 3 mi E on co rds from Herman (just S of Bethel) to lake. WMA is along E shore of Mountain Fork River arm of Broken Bow Lake, adjacent to W edge of McCurtain County Wilderness Area. Free. Hunter & fishermen camping only within 50 yds of designated public rds; 14-day limit. Noted for largemouth bass. Boat ramp at nearby Holly Creek.

Fishing tip: Holly Creek is an excellent area for bass fishermen, often giving up big largemouths in the 10-pound range. Just off the boat ramp in the standing timber is a good place to start, using either spinnerbaits or black jig-and-pig. Then use depth-finders to locate underwaterhumps and ridges 15-25 feet and try jigs or Texas-rigged plastic worms.

Carson Creek Area $8
Hochatown State Park

15 mi N of Broken Bow on US 259; 3 mi E. $8 for self-contained RVs in unimproved areas; $8 for tents; $15 semi-modern sites; $18 modern & preferred. 150 primitive sites; 50 elec/wtr sites; 21 full-hookup sites.

Tbls, flush toilets, cfga, drkg wtr, showers, dump, beach. Group shelter, playground, picnic areas. Boating (ldr), fishing, swimming, waterskiing, golf, hiking trails. On Broken Bow Lake.

Fishing tip: Broken Bow produced the state's biggest largemouth bass, 14 pounds 11 ounces, caught in 1999. It also gave up the state's 13th largest, just short of 13 pounds, in 1991.

Stephens Gap Area $8
Hochatown State Park

15 mi N of Broken Bow on US 259; 3 mi E. On Broken Bow Lake. $8 for self-contained RVs; $8 for tents. Primitive campsites. Tbls, toilets, cfga, drkg wtr. Group shelter. Boating(l), fishing, swimming, waterskiing.

Fishing tip: This lake has an excellent population of big white bass. A recent test netting revealed that 93 per cent of the white bass netted were over 12 inches long. The biggest fish examined was 2.7 pounds.

BUFFALO (22)

Doby Springs City Park $10

W of Buffalo on Hwy 64 at municipal golf course. $10 ($5 for seniors). 18 sites. Tbls, toilets, cfga, drkg wtr, hookups, playground, dump. Fishing, golf, nature trails.

CANADIAN (23)

Arrowhead State Park $8

18 mi S of I-40 on US 69; 20 mi N of McAlester. $8 for self-contained RVs in unimproved areas; $8 for tents; $14 for RV sites with elec/wtr; $17 for modern sites. All year; 14-day limit. 129 primitive sites; 65 elec/wtr sites; 20 full-hookup sites. Tbls, flush toilets, cfga, drkg wtr, showers, dump, group shelters. Groceries, airstrip. Hiking trails, swimming, boating(ld), group camps, enclosed fishing dock, equestrian facilities, golf, picnic areas.

CANTON (24)

Beaver Dam Camps   FREE
Canton Lake
State Wildlife Management Area

2 mi W of Canton on SR 51; 4 mi N on co rd; 3 mi N on co rd; 1 mi N to camp, on S bank of North Canadian River near its entry into Canton Lake. Second camp is 1 mi farther W; third camp is 2 mi W. Free. Only fishermen and hunter primitive camping is permitted. 14-day limit.

Big Bend A $12
Corps of Engineers
Canton Lake

1.8 mi W of Canton on SR 51; 1.5 mi N on SR 58A; 3 mi N to lake. $12 at sites with elec; $17 at sites with wtr/elec hookup (50 amp $18). Some sites free Nov & March but no services. 4/1-10/31; 14-day limit. 45-ft RV limit. Tbls, flush toilets, cfga, drkg wtr, showers, dump, playground, elec($). Fishing, boating(l).

Fishing tip: Drift-fishing can produce good catches from Canton Lake. Drift nightcrawlers near stream channels for walleye, and drift live shad for white bass and stripers.

Big Bend B $12
Corps of Engineers
Canton Lake

1.8 mi W of Canton on SR 51; 1.5 mi N on SR 58A; 3 mi N to lake. $12 at sites with elec; $17 at sites with wtr/elec hookup (50 amp $18). Some sites free Nov & March but no services. 4/1-10/31; 14-day limit. 45-ft RV limit. Tbls, flush toilets, cfga, drkg wtr, showers, dump, playground, elec ($). Fishing, boating(ld).

Blaine Park $8
Corps of Engineers
Canton Lake

Three-fourths mi W of Canon on SR 41; 1.7 mi N on SR 58A, below dam. $8. 4/1-10/31; 14-day limit. Free Nov & March but no services. 16 primitive sites. Tbls, toilets, cfga, drkg wtr, playground, ball field. Boating(l), fishing, swimming, hiking.

Canadian A $12
Corps of Engineers
Canton Lake

0.7 mi W of Canton on SR 51; 1.5 mi N on SR 58A; .8 mi W. $12 during March & Nov, but no wtr; $16 with elec; $17 elec & wtr (50 amp $18) 4/1-10/30 (some sites free 12/1-2/28, but no services. 14-day limit. 77 sites with elec; 65-ft RVs. Tbls, flush toilets, cfga, drkg wtr, showers, dump, elec($). Boating(dl), fishing. 2-night minimum stay on weekends.

Eastern Dam Camp   FREE
Canton Lake
State Wildlife Management Area

4 mi N of Canton on SR 58; 2 mi W on SR 58A to designated camp below dam. Free. Only fishermen and hunter primitive camping is permitted; 14-day limit. Sandy Cove Recreation Area (Corps of Engineers) nearby.

North Canadian River Camp   FREE
Canton Lake
State Wildlife Management Area

17 mi NW of Canton on co rds; N to camp on S bank of North Canadian River. Free. Only fishermen & hunter primitive camping is permitted; 14-day limit.

Western Dam Camp   FREE
Canton Lake
State Wildlife Management Area

Half mi W of Canon on SR 51; 2.2 mi N & NW on SR 58A, then S of Canton dam to camp on E side of Canadian River. Free. Only hunter & fishermen primitive camping permitted; 14-day limit. Nearby Blaine Park has boat ramp, picnic area, toilets.

OKLAHOMA

(continued)

CHATAUQUA (KANSAS) (25)

Hog Pen Units FREE
Hulah Lake State Wildlife Area
3 mi S of Chatauqua on R 99; W on co rds to 7 camping areas. Their general locations are on Caney River arm near Caney River Park; at the mouth of Pond Creek; on Caney River arm at Boulanger Landing; at the state line E of Cedar Creek; at the state line W of Cedar Creek; on Caney Creek arm half mi W of Cedar Creek mouth, and on Caney Creek arm at the mouth of Buck Creek. Free. Only fishermen & hunter primitive camping permitted in designated areas; 14-day limit. Lake is 3,600 acres; 62-mi shoreline; WMA is 16,141 acres. Deer & waterfowl hunting excellent. Big catfish.

Turkey Creek Unit FREE
Hulah Lake State Wildlife Area
2 mi S of Chatauqua on SR 99; 4 mi SE to Turkey Creek arm of Hulah Lake; cross bridge, camp on the right, on E shore of arm. Free. Only fishermen & hunter primitive camping is permitted in designated areas; 14-day limit. Boat launch at Turkey Creek Public Use Area at mouth of Turkey Creek.

CHECOTAH (26)

Gentry Creek Cove $10
Corps of Engineers
Eufaula Lake
9 mi W of Checotah on US 266; S to lake. $10 at primitive sites; $11 at sites with wtr hookup; $14 at 15 sites with elec. 50-ft RV limit. 4/1-10/1; 14-day limit. Flush toilets, tbls, cfga, drkg wtr, showers, dump, beach, elec($). Boating(l), fishing, waterskiing, swimming.

Fishing tip: The state record white bass was caught from Lake Eufaula in October 1984. It weighed 5 pounds 4 ounces.

Holiday Cove FREE
Corps of Engineers
Eufaula Lake
5 mi W of Checotah on I-40 to Sycamore Bay Exit; 2 mi S on SR 150. Free. All year; 14-day limit. 15 primitive sites. Tbls, toilets, group shelter, cfga, drkg wtr. Swimming, boating(l), fishing. 40 acres.

Welch's Camping (Private) $6
4 mi S of Checotah, then qtr mi W. $6 for primitive sites; $9 full hookups ($35 weekly). 27 full hookups; 9 primitive sites. Tbls, flush toilets, cfga, drkg wtr, showers, dump. Fees not verified for 2007.

CHEROKEE (27)

North Spillway Area $8
Great Salt Plains Lake State Park
18 mi E of Cherokee on OK 8/11; 8.5 mi N on jct OK 38A. $8. 14-day limit. 5 tent sites. Tbls, toilets, cfga, drkg wtr. Wtr may be off during free period. Fishing, boating, swim-
ming. Formerly a corps of engineers camp.

Fishing tip: The spillway area produces great catches of saugeye, most often on jigs with nightcrawlers or minnows or on shallow-running crankbaits.

South Spillway Area $9
Great Salt Plains State Park
18 mi E of Cherokee on OK 8/OK 11; 8 mi N on jct OK 38A. $9 for primitive sites; $8 for tent sites; $15 semi-modern sites; $18-19 preferred. All year; 14-day limit. 20 sites. Tbls, toilets, cfga, drkg wtr, showers, dump, elec hookups, food. Hunting; hiking; waterskiing; swimming; boating(l); picnicking; fishing; rockhounding (selenite crystal). 9,300-acre lake; 41-mile shoreline. Formerly a corps of engineers camp.

Fishing tip: Use whole, cut or fresh shad to catch huge catfish in the spillway area. Out in the lake, try jigs, crankbaits or spinnerbaits for hybrid striped bass, white bass, saugeye.

CHEYENNE (28)

Dead Indian Lake FREE
Black Kettle Nationsl Grasslands
11 mi N of Cheyenne at 80-acre national grasslands area. Free. All year; 14-day limit. 12 primitive sites. Tbls, toilets, cfga, drkg wtr, fishing pier. Boating(l), fishing, swimming, wilidlife study, nature trail.

Skipout Lake FREE
Black Kettle National Grasslands
10 mi W of Cheyenne at 60-acre national grasslands area. Free. All year; 14-day limit. Tbls, toilets, cfga, drkg wtr. Boating(l), hunting, fishing, swimming, wildlife study.

CHICKASHA (29)

Lake Burtschi FREE
State Fishing Lake
Dept. of Wildlife Conservation
11 mi SW of Chickasha on SR 92. Free primitive camping. Tbls, toilets, cfga, no drkg wtr. Fishing, boating(l), picnicking.

Fishing: The 180-acre lake features five fishing jetties and two fishing piers. It has good populations of largemouth bass, crappie and channel catfish as well as recently introduced saugeye.

CHOUTEAU (30)

Mazie Landing Resort FREE
4 mi S of Chouteau on US 69; 3 mi E on Mazie Landing Rd. Free. 3/1-11/30. 10 primitive sites (formerly corps of engineers camp). Tbls, toilets, cfga, drkg wtr nearby. Boating(l), fishing.

Fishing tip: We suggest boating from here to Ranger Creek. Cast around the boat docks with small plugs and Texas-rigged worms.

CLAYTON (31)

Clayton Lake State Park $8
5 mi SE of Clayton on US 271. $8 base for self-contained RVs & tents in unimproved areas; $14 for semi-modern sites; $17 modern sites. All year; 14-day limit. 33 primitive sites; 26 elec/wtr sites. Tbls, flush toilets, cfga, drkg wtr, showers, dump, beach. Fishing, swimming, boating(l), playground. 95-acre lake.

Indian Mounds $7
Equestrian Camp
2.5 mi SE of Clayton on US 271; half mi N. $7 per person. All year. Base fee for primitive sites; $8 extra with elec. 125 sites. Tbls, flush toilets, cfga, drkg wtr, elec($), CATV($), playground. Horseback riding(r), hiking, mountain bike trails, turkey & deer hunting, horseshoes.

Nanih Waiya Lake FREE
Gary Sherer
State Wildlife Management Area
NW of Clayton on Sardis Lake Rd, past Sardis Cove Public Use Area, N across bridge; 10 mi W on CR D1606 to village of Counts; 1 mi N of Counts on CR D4170 to WMA entrance; 1.5 mi E on dirt rd to camp area. Free. Camping permitted only during open hunting season, and only within 50 yds of public use rds; 14-day limit. 4 primitive camp locations along Bolen Creek. Fishing, picnicking, boating(l), drkg wtr, toilets. 1,280 acres.

Potato Hills South $8
Public Use Area
Corps of Engineers
Sardis Lake
Half mi N of Sardis Project office on SR 2 NE of Clayton. $8. 4/1-10/31; 14-day limit. 18 primitive sites; 65-ft RVs. Tbls, toilets, showers, cfga, drkg wtr, fishing pier, beach. Fishing, boating(ld), swimming. 2-night minimum stay on weekends.

Fishing tip: This lake is a consistent producer of big largemouth bass: 13.5 pounds in 1994; 13 pounds 1 ounce in 1992; 13 pounds in 1993; 12 pounds 12 ounces in 1991.

Pushmataha FREE
State Wildlife Management Area
SE of Clayton on US 271, pass Clayton Lake State Park, then W following signs. Free. All year; 14-day limit. Primitive camping in designated areas only during hunting seasons. Hunting, hiking.

Sardis Cove Campground $8
Corps of Engineers
Sardis Lake
8 mi SW of the Sardis Project office, and about 4 mi W of Clayton, on Sardis Lake Rd. $8 for 23 basic sites; $12 at 22 sites with elec. Apr-Oct; 14-day limit. Toilets, cfga, drkg wtr, tbls, dump. Fishing, boating(lr), picnicking.

Fishing tip: Catch crappie on minnows by fishing in 12-16 feet of water round standing timber. Try the shallow flats for largemouth bass, using spinnerbaits and black pig-&-jig rigs. Bridge areas and islands also produce well.

CLEVELAND (32)

Cleveland Section   **FREE**
Keystone State Wildlife
Management Area
Arkansas River
2 mi N of Cleveland on SR 99, across bridge to WMA entrance on Arkansas River east shore NW of Keystone Lake. Free. Hunter & fisherman primitive camping is permitted only within 50 yds of public-use rds. Within Osage Indian Reservation. WMA is 16,537 acres.

Feyodi Creek State Park   **$8**
2 mi S of Cleveland on US 64. $8 for self-contained RVs in unimproved areas; $8 for tents. All year; 14-day limit. 37 primitive sites; 19 full-hookup sites. Tbls, flush toilets, cfga, drkg wtr, showers, dump. Hiking trails, swimming, fishing, boating(l), horseshoes, paddleboats(r). Operated by City of Cleveland.

CLINTON (33)

Foss State Park   **$8**
11 mi W of Clinton on SR 73; 2 mi N on SR 44. $8 for self-contained RVs in unimproved areas; $8 for tents; $15 semi-modern sites (paved sites $16); $18 modern & semi-modern. All year; 14-day limit. 22 primitive sites; 67 wtr/elec sites; 10 full-hookup sites. Tbls, flush toilets, cfga, drkg wtr, showers, dump, beach. Fishing, indoor fishing dock, swimming, boating(ld), playground. 1,749 acres.
Fishing tip: For white (sand) bass, use Roadrunner jigs and medium running shad or chrome-and-blue crankbaits. Cast off the points and along face of the dam. Or, use chartreuse slabs along the N shore for white bass and hybrids.

COLBERT (34)

Burns Run East   **$12**
Corps of Engineers
Lake Texoma
5 mi W of Colbert on SR 75A, across dam, W side. $12 at sites with wtr hookups ($10 walk-in 9/16-4/14, wtr available at dump station); $20 at 45 sites with elec/wtr. 4/1-9/15; 14-day limit. 54 sites; 65-ft RVs. Toilets, tbls, cfga, elec($), drkg wtr, dump, showers, pavilion. Swimming, picnicking, boating(l), fishing.
Fishing tip: Try for largemouth bass off the points, 5-10 feet, using spinnerbaits and plastic worms.

Burns Run West   **$12**
Corps of Engineers
Lake Texoma
8 mi N of Denison on SR 75A, across bridge, then 3 mi W. $12 base primitive & tent sites; $20 for sites with elec/wtr; $22 full hookups. 4/1-9/30; 14-day limit. 115 sites; 65-ft RVs. 4/15-9/15; 14-day limit. Tbls, flush toilets, cfga, drkg wtr, dump, showers, elec($), pavilion, beach, playground. Boating(l), fishing, swimming, hiking
Fishing tip: Keep in mind, the state record smallmouth bass was caught from Lake Texoma in February 1996. It weighed 7 1/2 pounds.

COPAN (35)

Skull Creek   **N/A**
State of Oklahoma
Hulah Lake
10 mi W of Copan on SR 10; 1.5 mi N; 1.5 mi W; half mi N on co rds. Fees status uncertain. All year; 14-day limit. 22 sites (no RV size limit). Tbls, toilets, cfga, drkg wtr. Fishing.
Fishing tip: The channel of Skull Creek produces excellent catches of largemouth bass up to 7 pounds.

COOKSON (36)

Cookson Bend   **$10**
Corps of Engineers
Tenkiller Ferry Lake
2 mi W of Cookson on count rd, off SR 100 on E side of lake. $10 at 64 primitive sites; $14 at sites with elec ($15 premium locations); $18 wtr & 50 amp hookup. 1/1-9/30; 14-day limit (primitive sites $7, elec sites $11 during off-season). 131 sites (some pull-through, 7 with 50-amp elec); 65-ft RVs. Pavilion, tbls, flush toilets, cfga, drkg wtr, dump, beach, showers, elec($). Boating(lr), fishing, swimming. 2-night minimum stay on weekends.
Fishing tip: If you like light tackle for bass, rig your spinning outfit with an eighth-ounce Darter Head jig and a blue/green four-inch Zoom French Fry. Cast parallel to shore at steep, rocky banks and points; hop the lure back along bottom.

Elk Creek Landing   **$10**
Corps of Engineers
Tenkiller Lake
3 mi N of Cookson on SR 100; at N end of lake. $10 at 35 sites without elec, $15 at 6 sites with elec during 1/1-9/30 (fees $7 & $11 during 10/1-11/.30); 14-day limit. 41 sites; 65-ft RVs. Tbls, toilets, cfga, drkg wtr, elec($), dump, beach. Wtr may be turned off during winter. Fishing, boating(ldr), swimming. 2-night minimum stay on weekends.

CORDELL (37)

Cordell Reservoir   **$7**
State Fish & Wildlife Conservation Area
Along I-40, SR 152 & Hwy 183 near Cordell;

3 mi N & half mi E of Dill City. $7-$12 for entrance fee and general use permit. Primitive sites. Tbls, toilets, cfga, drkg wtr. $5 of the daily fee is refundable key deposit (fee includes $2 per individual or $5 family general use permit ($1.50 seniors). Fishing, hiking, wildlife study, picnicking.

DAVIS (38)

77 RV Park   **$12**
On SR 77S near Turner Falls Park. From I-35 exit 51, 3 blocks S on SR 77; right on Hanna St. $12 ($15 for 50-amp elec). All year. 14 full hookups, restaurant. Tbls, toilets, cfga, drkg wtr.

DENISON (TEXAS) (39)

Dam Site Area   **$10**
Corps of Engineers
Lake Texoma
5 mi N of Denison on SR 75A; on S side of dam. $10 base during 4/1-10/31 for primitive sites (free rest of year); $16 at sites with wtr/elec. 14-day limit. 27 sites; 65-ft RVs. Tbls, cfga, drkg wtr, flush toilets, showers, elec($), pavilion, dump. Boating(l), fishing. See Durant entry for N side of dam.

DISNEY (40)

Disney State Park   **$8**
At the Pensacola Grand River Dam, E on SR 28. $8 for self-contained RVs in unimproved areas; $8 for tents. 40 primitive sites. Tbls, flush toilets, cfga, drkg wtr, showers, dump. Swimming, fishing, boating(l).

Little Blue State Park   **$8**
SR 28 through Disney, across Spillway; 2 mi S at fire station between flood gates; at SE shore of Grand Lake. $8 for 80 primitive sites. Tbls, toilets, cfga, drkg wtr, playground. Boating, fishing, waterskiing, birdwatching. Boat ramp at Disney State Park. 32 acres.

DUNCAN (41)

Clear Creek Lake   **$8**
Municipal Campground
N of Duncan on US 81; 6 mi E on Plato Rd; 5 mi N on Clear Creek Rd. $8 with elec ($5 for seniors); $2 without elec. All year. 102 sites. Tbls, flush toilets, cfga, showers, drkg wtr, dump, store, snack bar. Swimming, boating (ld), fishing (enclosed dock), waterskiing.

Duncan Lake   **$8**
Municipal Campground
7 mi E of Duncan on Bois D'Arc; 2 mi N on Duncan Lake Rd. $8 with elec ($5 for seniors); $2 without elec. All year. 44 sites. Tbls, flush toilets, cfga, drkg wtr, showers, dump, elec, playground. Boating, fishing(l), waterskiing, swimming, picnicking.
Fishing tip: This lake has heavy underwater cover becuse it was never cleared of trees prior to flooding. Inlets contain big catfish and provide lunker largemouth bass in the spring.

Fuqua Lake   **$8**
Municipal Campground
10 mi N of Duncan on US 81; 18 mi E on SR 29; 3 mi S. $8 with elec ($5 for seniors); $2 wtihout elec. All year. 54 sites. Tbls, flush toilets, cfga, drkg wtr, showers, dump, elec. Fishing, swimming, boating(ld).

Fishing tip; Fuqua Lake is considered one of the best trophy bass lakes in Oklahoma. It has excellent underwater cover

Humphrey's Lake   **$8**
Public Campground
N of Duncan on US 81; 4 mi E on Osage Rd; 3 mi N; .7 mi W. $8 with elec ($5 for seniors); $2 without elec. All year. 44 sites. Tbls, flush toilets, cfga, drkg wtr, dump, store. Boating(ld), fishing (fishing dock).

Fishing tip: Try the inlets for excellent catfish action.

DURANT (42)

Dam Site   **$7**
Corps of Engineers
Lake Texoma
13 mi S of Durant on SR 75; 3 mi W on SR 75A. $7. All year; 14-day limit. 6 sites. Tbls, toilets, cfga, drkg wtr. Fishing, boating. See Dennison entry for S side of dam.

Johnson Creek   **FREE**
Corps of Engineers
Lake Texoma
10 mi W of Durant on US 70, N side of road at causeway. Free during 9/16-4/14 but no services (wtr at dump station); $20 rest of year with wtr/elec. 14-day limit. 53 sites with elec (13 have 50 amp); 65-ft RVs. Flush toilets, cfga, tbls, drkg wtr, elec, dump, showers. Boating(l), fishing, hiking.

Lakeside   **$10**
Corps of Engineers
Lake Texoma
9 mi W of Durant on US 70; 4 mi S on Streetman Rd. $10 at sites with elec during 9/16-4/14 ($12 rest of year); $20 with elec/wtr in-season (holders of federal Senior Pass pay half price). All year; 14-day limit. 139 sites; 65-ft RVs. Flush toilets, cfga, tbls, elec($), showers, playground, dump, pavilion. Boating(l), fishing, hiking, waterskiing.

Platter Flats   **$10**
Corps of Engineers
Lake Texoma
5 mi SW of Durant on US 75; 6 mi W on county rd; on lake. $10 at 44 elec sites & free at 10 non-elec sites during 9/16-4/14 5/1-9/30 (wtr availlable at dump station). During 4/15-9/15, sites without hookups, equestrian sites & sites with wtr are $12; sites without hookups are $10; sites with elec are $16 (holders of federal Senior Pass pay half rate). 83 sites; 65-ft RVs. 14-day limit. Pavilion, tbls, flush toilets, cfga, drkg wtr, elec($). Fishing, boating (l), swimming, horseback riding.

Coy Simmons RV Park   **$12**
3 mi W of Durant on US 70. $12 ($13 & $15 for 30-50 amp elec). 35 sites. Tbls, flush toilets, cfa, drkg wtr, showers, coin laundry, dump, CATV($), hookups. Horseshoes.

Willow Springs Marina   **$10**
9 mi W of Durant on Hwy 70; 1 mi S at sign. $10 for primtve or tent sites; $20 for prime waterfront sites with elec. All year. 13 sites. Tbls, flush toilets, cfga, drkg wtr, dump. Boating(lr), fishing.

DURHAM (43)

Spring Creek Lake   **FREE**
Black Kettle National Grasslands
2 mi S, 4 mi E, 3 mi SE of Durham. 4/11-11/15; 7-day limit. 9 sites (RVs under 25 ft). Tbls, toilets, cfga, drkg wtr. Fishing; swimming; hiking; canoeing; rockhounding.

ELK CITY (44)

Westwood RV Park   **$10**
From I-40 exit 32, follow Bus 40 about 3 mi, then half mi S on Pioneer Rd. $10 base. All year. 112 sites. Tbls, flush toilets, cfga, drkg wtr, hookups($).

ENID (45)

Garfield County Fairgrounds   **$12**
In Enid on 4th St, just N of Willow. $12 fee for all sites. Tbls, flush toilets, cfga, drkg wtr, dump, full hookups.

ENTERPRISE (46)

Damsite East   **$11**
Corps of Engineers
Eufaula Lake
5 mi N of Enterprise on SR 71; on NE side, below dam. $11 during 4/1-10/31; 14-day limit. Free off-season, but no elec or wtr. 10 sites with elec, tbls, flush toilets, cfga, drkg wtr. Boating, fishing.

Damsite South   **$10**
Corps of Engineers
Eufaula Lake
5 mi N of Enterprise on SR 71 (across dam from Damsite East). $10 at 9 primitive RV sites; $11 at 5 tent sites; $16 at 43 sites with elec. 45-ft RV limit. 4/1-10/31; 14-day limit. Pavilion, tbls, flush toilets, cfga, drkg wtr, showers, beach, dump, elec($). Wheelchair access. Fishing, boating (l), swimming, hiking.

EUFAULA (47)

Crowder Point   **$10**
Family Campground (Private)
12 mi S of Eufaula on US 69 at Rock Creek Rd. $10 without hookups; $18 with hookups. All year. 21 sites. Flush toilets, tbls, drkg wtr, cfga, dump, showers, beach, playground. Fishing, boating(ldr), swimming.

Lake Eufaula State Park   **$8**
7 mi S of I-40 on SR 150; N on SR 150; at Lake Eufaula. $8 for self-contained RVs in unimproved areas; $8 for tents; $10 for semi-modern sites Sun-Thurs ($15 Fri-Sat); $12 for modern sites Sun-Thurs ($18 Fri-Sat); preferred sites, $19. All year; 14-day limit. 105 primitive sites; 50 elec/wtr sites; 34 full-hookup sites. Tbls, flush toilets, cfga, drkg wtr, showers, dump, beach. Fishing, swimming, boating(ld), cafe, waterskiing, playground, group camp, hiking trails, nature center, enclosed fishing dock, visitor center, airstrip, putting green, golf, nature trails. 3,401 acres.

Gaines Creek   **FREE**
Corps of Engineers
Eufaula Lake
4 mi S of Eufaula on US 69; 1.5 mi NE on OK 9A; 3 mi S to campground. Free. All year; 14-day limit. 10 sites. Tbls, toilets, cfga. Hiking; boating(l); picnicking; fishing; waterskiing. Near Prague's Kolache Festival.

Highway 9 Landing East   **$10**
Corps of Engineers
Eufaula Lake
9 mi E of Eufaula on SR 9, then N. $10 for 4 basic sites; $16 for 5 sites with elec. 4/1-10/31; 14-day limit. Tbls, toilets, cfga, drkg wtr, elec($), dump. Swimming, boating(l), fishing, playground.

Highway 9 Landing North   **$10**
Corps of Engineers
Eufaula Lake
9 mi E of Eufaula on SR 9, then N. $10-$11 for 2 primitive sites; $16 for 33 sites with elec. 4/1-10/31; 14-day limit. 35 sites. Tbls, flush toilets, pavilion, cfga, drkg wtr, showers, dump, playground, beach, elec($). Wheelchair access. Swimming, boating(l), fishing.

Highway 9 Landing South   **$10**
Corps of Engineers
Eufaula Lake
9 mi E of Eufaula on SR 9, then S. $10 for 3 basic sites; $16 for 27 sites with elec. 4/1-10/31; 14-day limit. Tbls, flush toilets, cfga, showers, drkg wtr, elec($). Boating(l), fishing.

Mill Creek Bay Park   **$7**
Corps of Engineers
Eufaula Lake
6 mi W of Eufaula on SR 9, then 2 mi S. $7. 4/1-10/31; 14-day limit. 12 primitive sites. Pavilion, tbls, toilets, cfga, drkg wtr. Boating(l), fishing.

Mill Creek Unit   **FREE**
Eufaula State Wildlife Management Area
3 mi W of Eufaula on SR 9; 1 mi S, 1 mi E & 1 mi S on co rds. Free. On Mill Creek arm of Eufaula Lake. WMA encompasses the N & S shores of the Mill Creek arm. Lake noted for bass & catfish. Only hunter & fishermen primitive camping permitted in designated

areas; 14-day limit. The Mill Creek Bay facility operated by the U.S Army Corps of Engineers is nearby, also offering free camping and boat ramps. Mill Creek WMA Unit connects with the South Canadian River Unit of Eufaula WMA, where free primitive camping also available to hunters and fishermen in designated areas. That area can best be reached by co rds from Indianola.

Oak Ridge $7
Corps of Engineers
Eufaula Lake
6 mi NE of Eufaula on SR 9A. $7 for 5 primitive sites; $11 for 8 sites with elec. 4/1-10/31; 14-day limit (some sites free off-season, but no wtr or elec). Tbls, toilets, cfga, drkg wtr, elec($). Fishing, boating(l).

FAIRLAND (48)

Twin Bridges State Park $8
7 mi E of Fairland on US 60. $8 for self-contained RVs in unimproved areas; $8 for tents; $15 for semi-modern 30-amp (50 amp $16); $18 modern preferred ($22 for 50-amp preferred). All year; 14-day limit. 90 primitive sites; 63 elec/wtr sites. Tbls, flush toilets, cfga, drkg wtr, showers, dump. Shelters, enclosed fishing dock. Boating(ldr), fishing, horseshoes, volleyball. 63 acres. Primitive camping is $8 on the Spring River Canoe Trails.

FORT COBB (49)

Fort Cobb State Park $8
7 mi N of Fort Cobb on SR 146. $8 for self-contained RVs in unimproved areas; $8 for tents; $15 semi-modern; $18 modern & preferred. 700 primitive sites; 264 elec/wtr sites. Tbls, flush toilets, cfga, drkg wtr, showers, dump, beach. Picnic pavilions, golf course, playground, enclosed fishing dock, 120-person community building. Fishing, boating(l), waterskiing, swimming. 1,872 acres.

Fishing tip: Fort Cobb Lake has hot white bass, hybrid striped bass and walleye fishing from late April through June. Troll around points and drift live bait around the large island on the lake's west side. Or, cast soft-body jigs from the dam for feeding white bass and hybrids.

FORT SUPPLY (50)

Crappie Cove Section $8
Beaver Point Campground
Corps of Engineers
Fort Supply Lake
S on co rd from US 270 just E of Fort Supply; near dam. $8. 4/1-10/31; 14-day limit. 16 sites. Tbls, toilets, cfga, some tbls shelters, no drkg wtr. Fishing, boating(l), hiking. Rest of Beaver Point and all of Wolf Creek Public Use Areas are for day use & lake access; camping is prohibited.

Fishing tip: Crappie Cove is aptly named; its sunken brush piles produce excellent catches of crappie for anglers with the patience to work the slowly with minnows and jigs.

Supply Park $12
Corps of Engineers
Fort Supply Lake
1 mi S of Fort Supply; on W side of dam. $12 base. 4/1-10/31. Base fee for 16 primitive sites; $17 at 96 sites with wtr/elec; $18 with 50 amp. May be free during 11/1-2/28, but no elec or wtr; restrooms closed; no trash service. Tbls, flush toilets, cfga, drkg wtr, showers, dump, playground, fishing berm. Boating(ld), fishing.

Fishing tip: For a break from lake fishing, try the stilling basin below the dam for channel catfish, using stinkbaits and cut bait. Some real monster catfish are landed there.

Western Wolf Creek FREE
Fort Supply
State Wildlife Management Area
4 mi S of Fort Supply on co rd (or N on co rd from Airport Rd W of Woodward). Free. 5 primitive camping areas W of Wolf Creek. Only hunter & fishermen primitive camping permitted in designated areas; 14-day limit. Hunting; shooting range; fishing in river & Fort Supply Lake; boat launch at state park, Cottonwood Point & Supply Park. Picnic areas on E & W sides of Lake. Lake has 26-mile shoreline; WMA is 5,550 acres.

Fishing tip: Where Wolf Creek flows into the lake is packed with log jams and brush, and that's a great place to catch feeding catfish with all kinds of live and cut bait. We prefer using soft crayfish and shrimp there, but others insist on stinkbaits.

FOYIL (51)

Blue Creek Park $12
Corps of Engineers
Oologah Lake
6 mi W of Foyil on SR 28A; 1.2 mi N; 1.5 mi W on gravel rd. $12 for 37 basic sites; $16 for 24 sites with elec. 4/1-9/30; 14-day limit. 65-ft RVs. Tbls, flush toilets, cfga, drkg wtr, showers, elec($), dump. Boating(l), fishing.

Fishing tip: This lake is well known for its huge population of catchable size white bass. A recent test netting revealed 60 per cent of the white bass are over 12 inches. The largest fish netted weighed 2.1 pounds.

Spencer Creek Cove $12
Corps of Engineers
Oologah Lake
11 mi N of Foyil on paved/gravel rds. $12 for 39 basic sites; $16 for 30 sites with elec. 4/1-9/30; 14-day limit. 65-ft RVs. Tbls, flush toilets, cfga, drkg wtr, dump, showers, pavilion. Fishing, boating(l), picnicking. 2-night minimum stay on weekends.

Fishing tip: This is our choice as a convenient campng spot when fishing for crappie and largemouth bass. The standing timber of Spencer Creek provides good cover, and fishing is great in spring and fall. Use minnows & jigs for crappie and plastics & spinnerbaits for bass.

FREEDOM (52)

Alabaster Caverns State Park $8
6 mi S of Freedom on SR 50; half mi E on SR 50A. $8 for self-contained RVs in unimproved areas; $8 for tents; $15 semi-modern sites; $17 modern. 12 primitive sites, 10 semi-modern sites with elec/wtr. Tbls, flush toilets, cfga, drkg wtr, showers, dump, group shelters. Swimming pool, bathhouse, horseshoes, volleyball, hiking trails, playground. Cavern tours May 1-Sept 30 every hour 8-5; Oct 1-Apr 30, every hour 8-4.

GEARY (53)

American Horse Lake FREE
State Fishing Lake
Dept of Wildlife Conservation
1 mi N of Geary on US 270/281; 12 mi W; 1 mi S. Free primitive camping. Toilets, tbls, cfga, drkg wtr. Fishing, boating(l), picnicking. 100 acres.

Fishing tip: The best fishing on this lake is for big bluegills, and there's also fair bass fishing.

GORE (54)

Gore Landing City Park $8
Robert S. Kerr Lake
2 mi E on US 64; 1 mi N. $8. 3/1-LD; 14-day limit. 24 sites (no RV size limit). Tbls, toilets, cfga, drkg wtr. Fishing, boating(l). Formerly a Corps of Engineers park.

Fishing tip: There's excellent shoreline fishing at the dam tailwaters and downstream for smallmouth bass, walleye, white bass, striped bass, trout and catfish.

Sizemore Landing $5
Corps of Engineers
Tenkiller Ferry Lake
From the dam, W side of spillway, 2 mi NW on SR 10A; 9 mi N on SR 10; 4 mi SE. $5. All year; 14-day limit. 32 basic sites (30-ft RV limit). Toilets, cfga, no drkg wtr. Boating(l), fishing, waterskiing.

Snake Creek Cove $10
Corps of Engineers
Tenkiller Ferry Lake
15 mi NE of Gore on SR 100; half mi W to SE side of lake. $10 for 3 basic sites ($7 during 11/1-3/31, but no wtr or gate attendands); $18 at 109 sites with elec (50-amp at 5 sites), but $11 during 11/1-3/31. All year; 14-day limit. 65-ft RVs. Tbls, pavilion, flush toilets, cfga, drkg wtr, showers, dump, playground, beach, elec($). Wheelchair access; 4 handicap sites with sewer. Boating(lr), fishing, swimming. 2-night minimum stay on weekends in-season.

Tenkiller State Park   **$8**
From I-40 at Gore, 10 mi N on SR 100. $8 base for self-contained RVs & tents in unimproved primitive areas; $15 semi-modern sites; $18 preferred semi-modern & modern; $21 preferred modern. All year; 14-day limit. 172 primitive sites; 50 elec/wtr sites; 37 full-hookup sites. Tbls, flush toilets, cfga, drkg wtr, showers, dump, community building, store, restaurant, pool. Swimming, fishing, boating(lr), waterskiing.

GOTEBO (55)

Lake Vanderwork   **FREE**
State Fishing Lake Park
5 mi N & 2 mi E of Gotebo. All year. Primitive undesignated sites; no facilities. Boating, fishing. 135 acres. 580-529-2795.

GRAYSON (56)

Deep Fork Unit   **FREE**
Eufaula Wildlife Management Area
3 mi S of Grayson on SR 52; 1 mi SW on co rd. Only fishermen & hunter primitive camping permitted in designated areas; 14-day limit. WMA encompasses both N & S shorelines of Deep Fork River just W of Eufaula Lake and the Deep Fork arm of Eufaula.

GROVE (57)

Honey Creek State Park   **$8**
1 mi S of Grove on State Park Rd off US 59; at Grand Lake O' The Cherokees. $8 for self-contained RVs in unimproved areas; $8 for tents; $16 for semi-modern 30-amp; $19, semi-modern 50-amp. All year; 14-day limit. 83 primitive sites; 54 elec/wtr sites. Tbls, flush toilets, cfga, drkg wtr, showers, dump, playground, pool. Swimming, fishing, shelters, boating(l), hiking trail.
Fishing tip: This park is in a perfect location for spring anglers hoping to catch good numbers of largemouth bass. Try spinnerbaits around the Honey Creek boat houses. You won't catch many lunkers, but you'll get a lot of action.

Marsh's Wildewood Cove   **$8**
Follow Hwy 127 to Zena; bear left at Zena store, then follow signs. $8 for tents; $13 base for RV sites. Tbls, flush toilets, cfga, drkg wtr, showers, dump, hookups($). Fishing, hiking, swimming, boating(ld).

Snider's Camp (Private)   **$8**
On Lake Rd 6, 1 mi S & half mi E of Honeycreek Bridge near Grove; on Grand Lake O' the Cherokees. $8 base for tent sites; $10 with elec; $15 for full hookup sites. All year. Tbls, drkg wtr, cfga, flush toilets, showers, dump. Entertainment, boating(lr), fishing.
Fishing tip: Northern snowbirds & winter Texans traveling through on their way back home in April should give this lake a try. Fish the big hollow area for bass using Texas-

rigged worms or Carolina lizards. Start at twin bridges, work your way upriver toward the dam. Toss some spinnerbaits at brush, too.

GUTHRIE (58)

Guthrie Lake
City ParkCampground   **$4**
4.5 mi SW of Guthrie; 2 mi W of I-35 on Seward Rd; 1 mi N on Coltrane. $4 base. All year. Base fee for 6 primitive sites; $6 for 6 elec sites. Tbls, toilets, cfga, drkg wtr. Picnicking, boating(l), fishing. 244 acres.

Liberty Lake
City Park Campground   **$4**
4.5 mi SW of Guthrie; 4 mi S to Seward Rd; 3 mi W. $4 base; $6 with elec. 1/15-10/15. 24 primitive sites. Tbls, toilets, cfga, drkg wtr. Picnicking, boating(l).

GUYMON (59)

Beaver River   **FREE**
State Wildlife Management Area
About 15 mi W of Guymon on US 64; S on co rds to management area. Headquarters located on E side of area on N shore of Beaver River. Free. Primitive camping; camp only in designated areas; 14-day limit. Fishing, hunting. 15,600 acres.

No Man's Land City Park   **FREE**
On SR 3 just E of US 54/64; RV parking in lot NE of behind visitor center or behind on grass. Free. All year; 1-night limit. Tbls, flush toilets, cfga, drkg wtr, showers, dump, no elec. Hiking, playground. Don't confuse this park with the day-use Centennial Park at the jct of US 54 & US 412/SR 3.

Panhandle Campground   **$5**
7 mi W of Guymon on US 64. $5 base. All year. 24 sites. Tbls, flush toilets, cfga, drkg wtr, hookups($).

Southwind RV Park   **$9**
1 mi W of Guymon on US 64. $9 base; $19 full hookups. 40 sites. Tbls, flush toilets, drkg wtr, cfga, hookups($), coin laundry, rec room, playground, showers.

HAILEYVILLE (60)

Gaines Creek Unit   **FREE**
Eufaula State Wildlife Management Area
Follow co rds N from Haileyville to Gaines Creek arm of Lake Eufaula and US 270 W 1 mi to Brushy Creek arm. Free. Only fishermen & hunter primitive camping permitted in designated areas; 14-day limit. Hickory Point Recreation Area (Corps of Engineers) also offers free camping, boat launch & toilets at mouth of Gaines Creek.

HARDESTY (61)

Optima Lake   **FREE**
State Wildlife Management Area
3 mi NE of Hardesty on SR 3; 6 mi N on SR 94; turn right just across bridge over North Canadian River. Free. 4 primitive camping areas within 2 mi of WMA's entrance. On N shore of Optima Lake. Only fishermen & hunter primitive camping permitted in designated areas; 14-day limit. Boat ramps, Hooker Point & Prairie Dog Point. Lake, at jct of Coldwater Creek & Beaver River, is 600 acres with good hybrid striper & walleye fishing. WMA is 3,400 acres, known for deer, quail & pheasant hunting.

HEAVENER (62)

Billy Creek   **$8**
Ouachita National Forest
6 mi W of Heavener (W of Bena, Ark) on SR 63; 3 mi N on FR 22. $8. All year; 14-day limit. 11 sites. Tbls, toilets, cfga, drkg wtr, hiking trail. Picnicking, fishing, hiking.

Cedar Lake   **$6**
Equestrian Camp
Ouachita National Forest
10 mi S of Heavener on US 270; 3 mi W on CR 5; 1 mi N on FR 269. $6 base. All year; 14-day limit. Base fee for primitive, undesignated sites with no facilities in original campground. In new section, $12 for sites without elec; $17 for wtr/elec ($11 with federal Senior Pass). 53 sites (44 with wtr/elec). Also about 100 primitive & overflow sites. Tbls, flush toilets, cfga, firewood, piped drkg wtr, showers, dump, hitching posts, accessible mounting stand. Hiking; fishing; swimming; picnicking; boating(ld-1 mi), 75 mi of equestrian trails. 3 acres. Foothills. Note: Regular Cedar Lake Campground has fees of $13-16 with hookups.

Cedar Lake   **$10**
Ouachita National Forest
10 mi S of Heavener on US 270; 3 mi W on CR 5; a mi N on FR 269. $10 base; $15 with elec/wtr; $17 full hookups ($11 with federal Senior Pass). All year; 14-day limit. 87 sites. Tbls, toilets, cfga, drkg wtr, dump. Swimming, boating(l), fishing, boating (l), hiking trails.

Wister Lake   **FREE**
State Wildlife Management Area
2 mi S of Heavener on US 59. Free. WMA encompasses Poteau River below Wister Lake. Hunter & fishermen primitive camping permitted only within 50 yds of public-use rds. Boat dock 3 mi W of US 59 off co rds.
Fishing tip: A little-known tactic is fishing for crappie just below the dam, in VERY shallow water (1 feet deep at times). Schools of crappie gather to feed, and live minnows can be deadly with them.

HENRYETTA (63)

Jim Hall Lake   **FREE**
Municipal Park Campground
Just S of Henryetta, with entry from Main St to Lake Rd; follow signs. Free camping in primitive area; $3 for tents at camping pads, but no services; $5 for RVs not using wtr or elec; $6.50 for RV with wtr and/or elec hookups. Tbls, toilets, cfga, drkg wtr. Boating(l), fishing, fishing piers. 660 acres. Formerly named Lake Henryetta Park.

Nichols Lake   **FREE**
Municipal Park Campground
2 mi S of Henryetta, with entry from Main St to Lake Rd; follow signs. Free. 7 primitive sites. Tbls, toilets, cfga, drkg wtr, covered shelters, playgrounds. Ball fields, volleyball, walking trails, boating(l), swimming, fishing. Municipal golf & tennis nearby. Gates are locked each evening. 225 acres.

HINTON (64)

Red Rock Canyon State Park   **$8**
5 mi S of I-40 on US 281 (exit 101); half mi S of city. $8 for self-contained RVs in unimproved areas; $8 for tents; $15, semi-modern sites; $18, modern sites. 38 primitive sites; 33 with elec/wtr; 5 full hookups. Tbls, flush toilets, cfga, drkg wtr, showers, dump. Swimming pool, playground, volleyball, hiking trails, rock climbing, rappeling, group camp. Rough horse trail. Historical site.

HITCHITA (65)

Headquarters Area   **FREE**
Deep Fork Unit
Eufaula State Wildlife Management Area
1 mi S of Hitchita on co rd; 1 mi W on US 266 to headquarters. Get directions to camping areas. Free. Only fishermen & hunter primitive camping permitted in designated areas; 14-day limit. WMA encompasses both N & S shorelines of most Deep Fork River just W of Eufaula Lake and the Deep Fork arm of Eufaula.

HOLLIS (66)

Lake Hall   **FREE**
State Fishing Lake
Dept of Wildlife Conservation
13 mi N of Hollis in Harmon County. Free primitive camping. No facilities. Boating, fishing(l). 36 acres.

HOMINY (67)

Hominy Section   **FREE**
Keystone State
Wildlife Management Area
Arkansas River
7 mi S of Hominy on SR 99; W on co rds along N shore of Aransas River. 3 WMA entrances in Boston Pool area of Arkansas River E

shore NW of Keystone Lake. Free. Hunter & fisherman primitive camping is permitted only within 50 yds of public-use rds. Within Osage Indian Reservation. WMA is 16,537 acres.

Boar Creek Branch   **FREE**
Skiatook Lake
State Wildlife Management Area
5 mi E of Hominy on SR 20 to WMA entrance on Boar Creek arm of Skiatook Lake. Free. Only fishermen & hunter primitive camping is permitted in designated areas; 14-day limit.
Fishing tip: Fish the creek channels early mornings & evenings for crappie, focusing on brush piles in 10-20 feet of water and using minnows.

Buck Creek Branch   **FREE**
Skiatook Lake
State Wildlife Management Area
5 mi E of Hominy on SR 20; 1.5 mi S on CR D3541; 2 mi E on CR D0451 to WMA's entrance on Buck Creek arm of Skiatook Lake. Free. Only fishermen/hunter primitive camping permitted in designated areas; 14-day limit.
Fishing tip: Buck Creek produces good catches of chanel and blue catfish. Use live goldfish or cut baits.

Bull Creek Branch   **FREE**
Skiatook Lake
State Wildlife Management Area
7 mi E of Hominy on CRs D0410 & D0400 to Bull Creek arm of Skiatook Lake. Free. Only fishermen & hunter primitive camping permitted in designated areas; 14-day limit.
Fishing tip: To catch Bull Creek's largemouth bass in the fall during a combined fishing-hunting outing, cast deep-running crankbaits around the brush piles.

HUGO (68)

Hugo Lake   **FREE**
State Wildlife Management Area
N of Hugo on SR 93. (Wildlife refuge portion, immediately N of lake & encompassing Kiamichi River, is closed to camping.) Free. Only hunter & fishermen primitive camping permitted in designated areas; 14-day limit. Hugo Lake has 13,250 acres and 110 mi of shoreline; WMA has 18,196 acres. Boat lanes provided in uncleared upper half of lake. Noted Florida bass & blue catfish angling. Duck, geese, squirrel, quail, deer and rabbit hunting. Boat ramps at Frazier Point & Rattan Landing.
Fishing tip: The nearby Kiamichi River produced the state's record yellow hybrid bass in 1991; it weighed 2 pounds 5 ounces.

Kiamichi Park   **$9**
Corps of Engineers
Hugo Lake
6.8 mi E of Hugo on US 70; 1 mi N on secondary rd. $9 for 2 basic sites; $14 at sites with elec; $15 with elec/wtr. 3/1-11/30, but

some camping permitted Dec-Feb; 14-day limit. 92 sites. Tbls, pavilion, flush toilets, cfga, drkg wtr, dump, showers, beach, playground, elec($). Fishing, boating (l), swimming. 2-night minimum stay on weekends.

Raymond Gary State Park   **$8**
16 mi E of Hugo on US 70; 2 mi S of Fort Towson on SR 209. $8 for self-contained RVs in unimproved areas; $8 for tents; $15, modern sites. All year; 14-day limit. 100 primitive sites; 10 elec/wtr sites; 10 full-hookup sites. Tbls, flush toilets, cfga, drkg wtr, showers, dump, beach. Playground, swimming, boating(l), fishing. 390-acre lake. 60 acres.

Rattan Landing   **$12**
Corps of Engineers
Hugo Lake
2 mi E of Hugo on US 70; 16 mi N on SR 83; 3 mi W on SR 3. $12. All year; 14-day limit. 13 sites with wtr/elec. Tbls, flush toilets, cfga, drkg wtr. Boating(l), fishing.
Fishing tip: This site is quite popular during March & April during the early sand bass run in the upper Kiamichi River. Fishing from here is regarded as better all year than other parts of the lake.

HULAH (69)

Wah-Sha-She State Park   **$8**
3.5 mi W of Hulah on SR 10; half mi W. $8 for self-contained RVs in unimproved areas; $8 for tents; $15 for semi-modern sites. 112 primitive sites; 46 elec/wtr sites. Tbls, flush toilets, cfga, drkg wtr, showers, dump, beach. Playground, swimming, boating (ld), waterskiing. 275 acres.

INDIANOLA (70)

South Canadian River Unit   **FREE**
Eufaula State Wildlife Management Area
E & W of Indianola on co rds to south shore of South Canadian River arm of Eufaula Lake. WMA encompasses the N & S shorelines of the lake arm. Free. Lake noted for bass & catfish. Only fishermen & hunter primitive camping permitted in designated areas; 14-day limit. The Mill Creek Bay facility operated by the U.S Army Corps of Engineers is nearby (in the next lake arm north, by boat), also offering free camping and boat ramps. The Mill Creek Unit of the WMA connects with the South Canadian River Unit and also offers free primitive camping to hunters and fishermen in designated areas. That area can best be reached by SR 9 and co rds from Eufaula. Public boat access is available just E of Indianola.

JET (72)

Great Salt Plains State Park   **$8**
8 mi N of Jet on SR 38. $8 for self-contained RVs in unimproved areas; $8 for tents; $9 for prime primitive spillway sites; $15, semi-modern sites; $18-19, preferred.

All year; 14-day limit. 108 primitive sites; 63 elec/wtr sites. Tbls, flush toilets, cfga, drkg wtr, showers, dump, beach. Swimming, fishing, boating(l), waterskiing, hiking trails, playground, nature talks, community building. Selenite crystal digging. Three camping areas include Cottonwood Point River Rd area and Sandy Beach area. 840 acres.

Jet Recreation Area   **FREE**
Salt Plains National Wildlife Refuge
3 mi N of Jet on OK 38. Free. 4/1-10/15; 7-day limit. 20 sites (RVs under 20 ft). Tbls, toilets, cfga, firewood, drkg wtr. Hiking; waterskiing; boating(l); swimming; picnicking; fishing. No off-road vehicles. The Salt Plains is a flat expanse of mud, completely devoid of vegetation. 9,300-acre dam has 41-mile shoreline. Crystal digging 4/1-10/15. Nature trails.

KANSAS (73)

Jean Lee RV Park (Priv)   **$12**
From Cherokee Turnpike, N qtr mi on SR 10, then just E on CR 55.3. $12. All year. 16 sites. Tbls, flush toilets, cfga, drkg wtr, hookups.

KAW CITY (74)

Oxbow   **$10**
RV Park & Storage
11 mi E of US 177 on SR 11 to Kaw City, then half mi E of town on N side of rd. $10 base; $14 full hookups. All year. 11 sites. Tbls, flush toilets, cfga, drkg wtr, showers, CATV($), store. Boating, fishing, swimming.

KELLYVILLE (75)

Sheppard Point   **$10**
Corps of Engineers
Heyburn Lake
On N side of lake. $10 base for 17 primitive sites; $14 at sites with elec/wtr ($16 premium locations). 4/1-10/31; 14-day limit. 38 sites; 65-ft RVs. Tbls, flush toilets, cfga, drky wtr, showers, dump, playground, beach. Fishing, boating(l), swimming, nature trail. 2-night minimum stay on weekends.

Sunset Bay   **$7**
Corps of Engineers
Heyburn Lake
6 mi W of Kellyville on co rd. $7 during 4/25-9/25; free rest of year; 14-day limit. 14 primitive sites (no RV size limit). Tbls, toilets, cfga, firewood, drkg wtr, beach. Boating(ld); swimming; picnicking; fishing.

KEOTA (76)

Cowlington Point   **$10**
Corps of Engineers
Robert S. Kerr Lake
2.5 mi W of Keota on Hwy 9; 3 mi N, 2 mi W. $10 for 6 primitive sites; $15 for 32 sites with elec & wtr. All year; 14-day limit. Tbls, flush toilets, pavilion, cfga, drkg wtr, showers,

beach, dump, elec($). Boating(l), fishing.

Fishing tip: This is a good place for catching bass from shore with live bait. Walk the rocky shoreline quietly and work the underwater cover with crayfish, nightcrawlers, plastic worms and crankbaits. Catch white bass in the creeks using shad lures in 5-10 feet of water. Around timbered areas, use cut bait and whole shad for channel catfish.

KINGFISHER (77)

Elmer Lake   **FREE**
State Fishing Lake
Dept of Wildlife Conservation
1 mi N & 2 mi W of Kingfisher. Primitive camping at 60-acre lake. Toilets, cfga, drkg wtr, tbls, shelters. Fishing, boating(l).

Fishing tip: Use the fishing jetties or float the shoreline for big bluegill and good size largemouth bass.

KINGSTON (78)

Buncombe Creek   **$10**
Corps of Engineers
Lake Texoma
4 mi W of Kingston on SR 32; 7 mi S on SR 99; 2 mi E, following signs. $10 during 9/16-4/14 (elec hookups, but wtr only at dump station); rest of year, $16. 54 sites with hookups; 45-ft RV limit. Tbls, flush toilets, cfga, drkg wtr, elec, showers, dump. Boating(l), fishing, hiking.

Caney Creek   **$10**
Corps of Engineers
Lake Texoma
3 mi S of Kingston on Donahoo St (Rock Creek Rd); 2 mi E on Lassiter Rd; 2 mi E & S on gravel rd. $10 at 10 basic sites during 9/16-3/31 ($12 in-season); $18 at 42 sites with elec & wtr in-season. Wtr available only at dump station off-season. All year; 14-day limit. 52 sites; 65-ft RVs. Tbls, flush toilets, cfga, drkg wtr, showers, elec($), beach, playground, dump. Hiking, fishing, boating(l), swimming.

Lake Texoma State Park   **$8**
4 mi E of Kingston on US 70. $8 base for self-contained RVs & tents in unimproved areas; $10 at semi-modern sites; $12 at modern sites, $19 preferred sites. 230 primitive sites; 608 elec/wtr sites; 89 full-hookup sites. Tbls, flush toilets, cfga, drkg wtr, showers, dump, pool, beach. Swimming, fishing, boating(ld), enclosed fishing dock, hiking trail, playground, archery, mini golf, golf, tennis, biking(r), nature center, batting cage, arcade, equestrian facilities, waterskiing, sand volleyball. Airstrip.

LANGLEY (79)

Cherokee State Park Area 1   **$8**
1 mi S of Langley. $8 for self-contained RVs in unimproved areas; $8 for tents. All

year; 14-day limit. Primitive sites. Tbls, flush toilets, cfga, drkg wtr, showers, dump. Boating(l), river swimming. Below Pensacola Dam, world's largest multiple-arch dam.

LAWTON (80)

Collier Landing Municipal Park   **$5**
12 mi NE of Lawton on I-44 to Elgin exit; 1 mi W on SR 277; continue N of Fisherman's Cove Park. On Lake Ellsworth. $5 for primitive tent sites; $9 for RV sites with elec ($5 seniors); $12 preferred sites. 6 sites with shelters. Tbls, toilets, cfga, drkg wtr, elec ($), showers. Boating(l), fishing, swimming.

Fishing tip: Catch blue catfish around windy points on cut shad, and use minnows around Chandler Creek's boat docks for crappie. The state's record blue was caught here in December 1999. It weighed 85 pounds 4 ounces and was 52 inches long.

Doris Campground   **$8**
Wichita Mountains
National Wildlife Refuge
12 mi N of Cache. $8 base. All year; 14-day limit. Base fee for primitive sites; $16 for elec/wtr; walk-in tent camping, $6. 90 sites. All year. Tbls, flush toilets, cfga, drkg wtr, showers, dump. Picnicking, wildlife viewing, boating(ld), fishing, hiking, rock climbing, biking. Open range is home to buffalo, elk, deer, Texas longhorn cattle. Visitor center with interactive displays, theater. $2 showers for non-campers.

Fisherman's Cove Municipal Park   **$5**
12 mi NE of Lawton on I-44 to Elgin exit; 1 mi W on SR 277; 1 mi N. On Lake Ellsworth. $5 for primitive sites; $9 for RV sites with elec ($5 seniors); $12 preferred sites. 30 sites with shelters. Tbls, toilets, cfga, drkg wtr, elec($), showers. Boating(l), fishing, swimming.

Lake Ellsworth City Park   **$5**
W of Lawton on I-44 to exit 53, the 1-4 mi W, following signs. $5 for primitive sites; $9 with elec ($5 seniors); $12 preferred sites. All year (limited services off-season). 41 sites; no RV size limit. Tbls, flush toilets, cfga, drkg wtr, showers, dump, store. Boating(dl), fishing, swimming.

Lake Lawtonka Municipal Park   **$5**
8 mi N of Lawton on I-44; 4 mi W on Hwy 49; 2 mi N on Hwy 58 to Lake Lawtonka. $5 for primitive sites; $9 for RV sites with elec ($5 seniors); $12 preferred sites. 41 sites with shelters; big rigs okay. Tbls, toilets, cfga, drkg wtr, elec($), showers, pavilion, playground, dump. Boating(ld), fishing, canoeing, swimming.

Fishing tip: For largemouth bass, fish the brushpiles and sunken trees in 4-6 feet of water with spinnerbaits and plastic worms.

Trader's Bay
Robinson's Landing (Priv.) **$11**
5 mi N of Lawton on I-44; 3 mi W on SR 49; 5 mi N on SR 58; 1 mi W on Meers Rd; qtr mi S on Lawtonka Rd; on shore of Lawtonka Lake. $11. 4/1-10/31. Tbls, toilets, cfga, drkg wtr, elec, store. Horseshoes, volleyball, canoeing (r), paddleboats(r), game room. Discounts to FMCA.

Fishing tip: This is a good area to catch smallmouth bass. They chase baitfish that are blown into ambush areas over shallow flats with rocky outcroppings. Use chartreuse spinnerbaits and Rapalas for best results. Most schooling smallies are 1-2 pounds, but occasional 3-4 pounders can be caught.

LEXINGTON (81)

Dahlgren Lake **FREE**
Lexington
State Wildlife Management Area
4 mi N of Lexington on US 77 to Slaughterville; 6 mi E on co rd to WMA's entrance and main camping area. SE on co rd to 30-acre Dahlgren Lake. Free. Hunter & fishermen primitive camping permitted only within 50 yds of public-use rds. Boating(l), fishing, hunting. Heisel, Little Buckhead Creeks; Conklin Lake. 9,433 acres. Playground, shelters.

LONGDALE (82)

County Line Camp **FREE**
Canton Lake
State Wildlife Management Area
2 mi N of Longdale on SR 58; 5 mi W on co rd to Dewey/Blaine co line; qtr mi S to camp. On N shore of Canton Lake. Free. Only fishermen & hunter primitive camping permitted in designated areas; 14-day limit. Boating, fishing, hunting.

Headquarters Camp **FREE**
Canton Lake
State Wildlife Management Area
2 mi N of Longdale on SR 58; 6 mi W on co rd into Dewey County; qtr mi S to camp, near WMA headquarters. On N shore of Canton Lake. Free. Only fishermen & hunter primitive camping permitted in designated areas; 14-day limit. Boating, fishing, hunting.

Longdale Camp **FREE**
Canton Lake
State Wildlife Management Area
1.5 mi W of Longdale on Blaine County rd; just NE of Longdale Recreation Area. Free. Only fishermen & hunter primitive camping permitted in designated areas; 14-day limit. Boating (launch at Longdale RA), fishing, hunting.

Longdale Recreation Area **$6**
Corps of Engineers
Canton Lake
2 mi W of Longdale on co rd. $6 at 12 primitive sites; $8 at 37 basic sites; all sites free

11/1-3/28, but no wtr or services. All year; 14-day limit. 40-ft RV limit. Pit toilets, tbls, cfga, drkg wtr, playground, no elec. Fishing, hiking, boating(ld). 2-night minimum stay on weekends.

Northwest Shore Camps **FREE**
Canton Lake
State Wildlife Management Area
2 mi N of Longdale on SR 58; 6.5 mi W on co rd; qtr mi S to camp. Second camp three-fourths mi farther S & qtr mi W. Free. Only fishermen & hunter primitive camping is permitted in designated areas; 14-day limit. Boating, fishing, hunting.

Unwins Cutoff Lake Camps **FREE**
Canton Lake
State Wildlife Management Area
2 mi W of Longdale on SR 58; 11-13 mi W on co rd to 3 camps N of Canadian River at cutoff lake. Free. Only fishermen & hunter primitive camping permitted in designated areas; 14-day limit. Boating, fishing, hunting.

MADILL (83)

Juniper Point **$12**
Corps of Engineers
Lake Texoma
17 mi S of Madill on SR 99, across lake bridge, then E; in Texas. $12 without hookups, $18 with elec/wtr during 4/1-10/31. During 11/1-3/31, some sies free with reduced services. 70 sites; 50-ft RV limit. Tbls, flush toilets, cfga, drkg wtr, showers, dump, elec($). Boating(l), fishing, hiking.

Little Glasses Resort **$12**
4 mi S of Madill on SR 106 to its end. $12 base for primitive sites; $19 full hookups. 84 sites. Tbls, flush toilets, cfga, drkg wtr, dump, showers, store, marina. Boating(ld), fishing.

MANGUM (84)

Sandy Sanders **FREE**
State Wildlife Management Area
W of Mangum on SR 9. Free. All year. Primitive, undesignated sites, but in designated areas; no facilities. On 19,000 acres. Hunting, fishing ponds, hiking, bridle trails, mountain biking. 45 mi of unpaved rds.

MANITOU (85)

Lake Frederick **$6**
Frederick City Park
5 mi E of Manitou on baseline; half mi N. $6 for tents; $9 for sites with elec; $12 elec/wtr hookups ($9 for seniors). All year. Tbls, flush toilets, cfga, drkg wtr, showers, dump. Picnicking, boating (ld) fishing.

MANNFORD (86)

House Creek Branch **FREE**
Cimarron River
Keystone State Wildlife
Management Area
W of Mannford on SR 51 to SR 48; N on sR 48 across Keystone Lake bridge, then W on co rd to WMA entrance on N shore of House Creek. Free. Hunter & fishermen primitive camping is permitted only within 50 yds of public rds.

Keystone State Park **$8**
6 mi E of Mannford on SR 51; half mi N on SR 151. $8 base; $16, semi-modern sites; $21 modern; $22 modern assigned area; $18, preferred. All year; 14-day limit. 61 primitive sites; 40 elec/wtr sites; 40 full-hookup sites. Tbls, flush toilets, showers, drkg wtr, cfga, dump, store, restaurant, playground. Biking(r), boating(l), hiking trails, fitness trail, waterskiing, biking(r).

New Mannford Ramp
$10
Keystone Lake
Mannford City Park
Half mi N of Mannford on county rd; half mi E on access rd. $10 at 12 primitive sites. 36 RV sites with elec, $11 during 11/1-4/1 off-season ($8 for seniors), $17 in-season. Tbls, flush toilets, cfga, drkg wtr, flush toilets, dump, elec($). Boating(l), fishing. This is a former Corps of Engineers park now operated by the city. Call 918-965-4314 for details & fees.

Salt Creek Cove North **$10**
Corps of Engineers
Keystone Lake
2 mi E of Mannford on SR 51; N on access rd. $10 at sites without hookups; $15 with elec; ($16 premium locations); $16 with wtr/elec ($17 premium locations). for 126 sites; 65-ft RVs. 4/1-10/31; 14-day limit. Pavilion, tbls, flush toilets, cfga, drkg wtr, showers, dump, playground, beach. Swimming, boating(l), fishing.

Waterfowl Development Unit **Free**
Cimarron River
Keystone State Wildlife
Management Area
W of Mannford on SR 51 across 1st Keystone Lake bridge just W of SR 48; N & W on access rd to WMA entrance on S shore of Cimarron River, W of main lake. Free. Hunter & fishermen primitive camping is permitted only within 50 yds of public-use rds.

MARIETTA (87)

Hickory Creek **FREE**
State Wildlife Management Area
1.5 mi E of Marietta on SR 32; 6 mi N on SR 77S; 1.5 mi E on county road. Controlled hunt campground. Other entrances to the WMA are on CR D3370, W of Enville; on CR

D3352, W of Enville, and NE of Marietta on CR D2038. In those areas, ask for directions to the designated campsites. Free. Only fishermen & hunter primitive camping is permitted in designated areas; 14-day limit. Hickory Creek Public Use Area, with campsites, boat ramps, picnic tables and toilets, is at the mouth of Hickory Creek just outside the WMA, on SR 32. The WMA encompasses the Hickory Creek arm of Lake Texoma.

Love Valley **FREE**
State Wildlife Management Area
Along N shore of Lake Texoma from where I-35 crosses into Oklahoma from Texas, NE to point where Hickory Creek empties into the lake at SR 32. Includes Brown's Spring, Crow Bottom, Hog Pen areas. Free. Hunter & fishermen primitive camping permitted only within 50 yards of public-use rds.

MCALESTER (88)

Elm Point **$7**
Corps of Engineers
Eufaula Lake
18 mi E of McAlester on SR 9; 6 mi N on SR 71. $7 for 3 basic sites; $11 for 14 sites with elec. Free 11/1-2/28, but no wtr or elec. All year; 14-day limit. No RV size limit. Tbls, flush toilets, cfga, drkg wtr, elec($), beach. Fishing, boating(l), swimming.

Hickory Point Park **FREE**
Corps of Engineers
Eufaula Lake
From McAlister/Jct US 69, 4 mi E on SR 31, 6 mi E, go N before bridge. Free. All year; 14-day limit. 10 sites. Tbls, toilets, cfga, drkg wtr. Fishing, boating(l), swimming.

Highway 31 Landing **FREE**
Corps of Engineers
Eufaula Lake
5 mi NE of US 270 on SR 31; N side. Free. All year; 14-day limit. Primitive undesignated sites. No facilities. Fishing, boating, hiking.

Juniper Point Park **FREE**
Corps of Engineers
Eufaula Lake
From jct with US 270 at McAlester, 5 mi N on US 69; 1 mi E; 3 mi N. Free. All year; 14-day limit. 21 sites. Tbls, toilets, cfga, drkg wtr., pavilion. Boating, fishing.

Rock Creek RV Park **$12**
14 mi N of McAlester on US 69; Qtr mi W on Rock Creek Rd. $12. All year. 36 sites. Tbls,flush toilets, cfga, drkg wtr, hookups. Fishing, boating(l).

MOUNTAIN PARK (91)

Great Plains State Park **$8**
2 mi N of Mountain Park; 2 mi W on US 487 on Lake Tom Steed. $8 base for self-contained RVs & tents in unimproved areas; $15, semi-modern sites; $16, preferred semi-

modern (50-amp); $18, modern; $19, preferred semi-modern with 50-amp. All year; 14-day limit. 10 primitive sites; 46 elec/wtr sites; 14 full-hookup sites. Tbls, flush toilets, cfga, drkg wtr, showers, dump, beach, playground, store. Swimming, fishing, boating(dl), hiking trails, waterskiing.

Fishing tip: Fish the brushpiles and underwater structures for crappie, using jigs and minnows. If you have a boat, work chartreuse curly-tail lures slowly off rocks near the dam for saugeye.

Mountain Park **FREE**
State Wildlife Management Area
Tom Steed Reservoir
10 mi N of Mountain Park on US 183; qtr mi E to camp. Second camp 1 mi farther on US 183; half mi W on co rd; half mi S on co rd. Free. Only fishermen & hunter primitive camping permitted in designated areas; 14-day limit. Great Plains State Park nearby. Tom Steed Reservoir is 6,400 acres & 31-mi of shoreline. Bluegill, channel catfish & bass fishing. WMA is 5,000 acres, with hunting for waterfowl & dove.

NEW PRUE (93)

Walnut Creek State Park **$8**
Turner Turnpike, Bristow exit, SR 48 to SR 51; cross Keystone Dam to SR 64; 1 mi to New Prue, then 13 mi to 209 West Ave. $8 for self-contained RVs in unimproved areas; $8 for tents; $15, semi-modern 30-amp; $16, semi-modern 50-amp; $18, modern & preferred 30-amp; $22, preferred modern 50-amp. All year; 14-day limit. 84 primitive sites; 78 elec/wtr sites. Tbls, flush toilets, cfga, drkg wtr, showers. Swimming, fishing, boating(l), waterskiing, playground, grocery. 1,429 acres.

NEWKIRK (94)

Kaw State **FREE**
Wildlife Management Area
9 mi E of Newkirk on co rd; 2 mi s; 3 mi 3 to two Little Beaver Creek entrances. Continue 4 mi E to another east branch (Beaver Creek) entrance. 3 mi W of Newkirk on co rd to western branch (Arkansas River) entrance. East branch encompasses Little Beaver Creek & Beaver Creek; W branch encompasses Arkansas River N of Kaw Lake & Bear Creek arm. Free. Only fishermen & hunter prim. camping permitted in designated areas; 14-day limit. New lake has 17,000 acres & 169-mi shoreline; Kaw WMA has 16,254 acres. Excellent fishing & hunting. Duck, deer, geese, wild turkey. Free camping area at Traders Bend has boat ramp within Arkansas River section; Bear Creek Cove camp area also has ramp.

Fishing tip: The Beaver Creek areas are consistently good producers of crappie, and the best successes are with jig-and-minnow rigs. Concentrate on sunken brush.

NORMAN (95)

Clear Bay Area **$8**
Lake Thunderbird State Park
13 mi E of Norman on SR 9. $8 base for self-contained RVs & tents in unimproved areas; $10 at primitive assigned sites; $16 at semi-modern sites ($17 if paved); $17 modern sites; $19-21 modern preferred. All year; 14-day limit. 100 primitive sites; 161 elec/wtr sites. Tbls, flush toilets, cfga, drkg wtr, showers, dump. Pavilions, swimming beach, game room, grocery, boating(lrd), fishing, waterskiing, cafe, ice, horse rental, ski rental.

Indian Point Area **$8**
Lake Thunderbird State Park
11 mi E of Norman on Alameda Dr. $8 base for self-contained RVs & tents in unimproved areas. $10 at primitive assigned sites; $16 at semi-modern sites ($17 if paved); $17 modern sites; $19-21 modern preferred. All year; 14-day limit. 120 primitive sites; 77 elec/wtr sites. Tbls, flush toilets, cfga, drkg wtr, showers. Pavilions, swimming beach, archery, picnic areas, boating(ld), fishing, fishing dock, waterskiing.

NOWATA (96)

Big Creek Ramp **FREE**
Corps of Engineers
Oologah Lake
5.1 mi E of Nowata on US 60; 2 mi N on SR 28; 1 mi W on access rd. Free. All year; 14-day limit. 16 sites. Tbls, toilets, cfga, drkg wtr. Boating(l), picnicking, fishing.

Fishing tip: Try Big Creek's channel for white bass in the spring and fall. Use white jigs 10-15 feet deep. This creek also produces good channel catfish action on worms and livers.

Verdigris River Camp **$10**
Oologah Lake
State Wildlife Management Area
5 mi E of Nowata on US 60; cross bridge, then 2 mi N on 1st co rd and W 1 mi to camp at mouth of Vertigris River. $10. 7 sites. Toilets, cfga, drkg wtr. WMA boat launch 8 mi S on lake at Lightning Creek.

Fishing tip: In May, fish this area for bass using spinnerbaits with white blades. Focus on sunken trees.

OILTON (97)

Oilton/Lagoon Creek Sections **FREE**
Keystone State Wildlife
Management Area
Cimarron River
1 mi N of Oilton on SR 99; turn E just across bridge to WMA's western entrance on N shore of Cimarron River. Or, continue 2 mi N on SR 99, then E on co rd to parking area on N shore of Lagoon Creek. Free. Hunter and fishermen primitive camping permitted only within 50 yds of public-use rds.

OKLAHOMA

OKAY (98)

Wahoo Bay Public Use Area   **FREE**
Corps of Engineers
Fort Gibson Lake
3 mi E of Okay on SR 16, then 4 mi E. Free. All year; 14-day limit. 16 primitive sites. Tbls, toilets, cfga, no drkg wtr. Boating(ld), fishing.

OKEMAH (99)

Okemah City Lake   **$10**
8 mi N of Okemah. $10 with elec/wtr; $4 primitive. All year. 13 sites. Elec/wtr hookups, cfga, drkg wtr, tbls, showers, dump. Handicap access. Picnicking, boating(ld), fishing.

❑ OKLAHOMA CITY (100)

Lake Stanley Draper   **$8**
Park and Marina
Between Midwest Blvd & Post Rd from SE 74th to SE 134th in Oklahoma City; E on I-240 to Sooner Rd exit, then S to 104th St & E to lake. $8. All year. Primitive camping. Tbls, toilets, cfga, drkg wtr. Boating(l), fishing, OHV activity, canoeing(r), paddleboating(r), boating(ldr).

Okie RV Park (Private)   **$9**
Off I-40 between Douglas & Post at 9824 SE 29th St, Midwest City. $9 for full hookups ($63 weekly; $250 monthly); $8 for primitive sites. 150 sites. Tbls, flush toilets, cfga, drkg wtr, showers.

OKMULGEE (101)

Okmulgee State Park   **$8**
6 mi W of Okmulgee on SR 56. $8 base. All year; 14-day limit. Base fee for 54 primitive sites; $16, semi-modern sites; $19 for 1 accessible modern site. 46 elec/wtr sites. Tbls, flush toilets, cfga, drkg wtr, showers, dump. Playground, shelter, fishing, boating(l), hiking trails, waterskiing.

Okmulgee   **FREE**
State Wildlife Management Area
Deep Fork River
1 mi W of Okmulgee on co rd to WMA's E entrance. Second entrance from there, 2 mi N & 1 mi W on co rds to WMA's northern headquarters. S headquarters & entrances at Lions Point area off SR 56. Free. Camp only in the public hunting portion of WMA N & E of the Deep Fork River. Only fishermen & hunter primitive camping permitted in designated areas; 14-day limit. 9,700 acres.

OOLOGAH (102)

Sunnyside Ramp   **FREE**
Oologah Lake
City of Talala Park
4 mi E of Talala (town is N of Oologah on US 169) on co rds. Free. All year; 14-day limit. 8 sites. Tbls, toilets, cfga, drkg wtr. Hunting, waterskiing, fishing, swimming, picnicking, boating(l). Note: Leased by Corps of Engineers to City of Talala; fee status uncertain for 2007.

Fishing tip: Oologah Lake produced the state's largest flathead catfish in 1998. It weighed 71 pounds and was 49 inches long.

PAULS VALLEY (103)

Lake R.C. Longmire   **$5**
Municipal Camping Area
11 mi E of Pauls Valley on Hwy 19; 3 mi S. $5. All year; 14-day limit. Primitive camping. Tbls, toilets, cfga, drkg wtr. Fishing, boating(l), hunting. 935-acre lake. Favored winter nesting place for bald eagles.

Fishing tip: Lake Longmire is a desgnated trophy bass lake and has been stocked with Florida-strain largemouth bass since 1990.

Pauls Valley City Lake   **$5**
1.5 mi E of Pauls Valley on Hwy 19; half mi N; half mi W. $5 without hookups; $10 with elec & wtr; $12 full hookups ($2 seniors discount). All year; 14-day limit. No tents around pavilion. 8 full-hookup sites; 12 with wtr/elec. Tbls, flush toilets, showers, drkg wtr, cfga, dump, pavilion. Picnic areas, boating(ld), fishing, fishing dock. 750-acre lake.

PAWNEE (104)

Pawnee City Lake   **$10**
1 mi N of Pawnee on SR 18. $10 with hookups; $6 for tents. All year. 150 sites. Tbls, toilets, cfga, drkg wtr, elec. Boating(l), fishing, swimming, waterskiing -- fees charged. Pistol range, archery, picnic area.

PAWHUSKA (105)

Bluestem Lake   **$6**
6 mi W of Pawhuska on SR 60. $6 at non-elec sites; $15 with elec. All year. 15 primitive sites, 4 sites with elec. Tbls, toilets, cfga, drkg wtr. Boating(ld), fishing. 762-acre lake. Boating fee.

Lake Pawhuska Campground   **$6**
2 mi W of Pawhuska on US 60, then 2 mi S. $6 at 6 primitive sites; $15 with elec. Tbls, toilets, cfga, drkg wtr, handicap dock, dump. Boating(ld), fishing (state trout license required). Boating fee.

Osage Hills State Park   **$8**
11 mi Ne of Pawhuska on US 60. $8 for self-contained RVs in unimproved areas; $8 for tents; $$15, semi-modern sites. 35 primitive sites; 20 elec/wtr sites. Tbls, flush toilets, cfga, drkg wtr, showers, dump. Swimming pool, tennis & volleyball courts, playground, bathhouse, fishing, boating(l), group camp, hiking trails.

Fishing tip: 96-acre Lake Pawhuska is designated as trou water, and the city's fishing fees are waived during trout season, 11/1-3/15.

PERRY (106)

Lake Perry   **$4.25**
Oklahoma State University
1 mi W of Perry; 1 mi S on Perry Lake Rd. $4.25. All year. Primitive camping for self-contained RVs. Toilets, cfga, drkg wtr, concession area. Boating(lr), fishing($2), swimming. Fee for boating, $3.14.

PONCA (107)

Coon Creek Cove   **$8**
Corps of Engineers
Kaw Lake
4 mi N of Ponca City , then 6 mi E on SR 11; 1 mi N & 2 mi E. $8 for 12 basic sites; $16 for 54 sites with wtr & elec. 3/1-11/30; 14-day limit. 55-ft RV limit. Tbls, flush toilets, cfga, drkg wtr, fishing pier, showers, dump, elec($). Boating(l), fishing. 2-night minimum stay on weekends.

Fishing tip: From this campground, focus on sunken brush in Coon Creek for crappie, then move out to Ponca Cove and the Burbank Landing areas for white bass, using spoons and spinners.

McFadden Cove   **$12**
Corps of Engineers
Kaw Lake
7 mi E of Ponca City, on N side of lake. $11. 3/1-11/30; 14-day limit. 15 sites with elec. Tbls, flush toilets, cfga, drkg wtr, elec, pavilion. Fishing, boating(l).

Fishing tip: Catch Kaw Lake's walleye by using crankbaits and jigs on windy, sandy points.

Sandy Park   **$12**
Corps of Engineers
Kaw Lake
9 mi E of Ponca; half mi below dam, E side. $12. 4/1-10/31; 14-day limit. 12 sites with elec. Tbls, flush toilets, cfga, drkg wtr, beach. Swimming, fishing, boating(l).

Fishing tip: Boat to the nearby coves in search of white bass. Using a depth-finder, look for valleys and channels 10-15 feet deep and catch the white bass on 1-ounce white-and-blue Sooner Slab lures.

PORUM (108)

Dutchess Creek Unit   **FREE**
Eufaula State Wildlife Management Area
NW of Porum on SR 2 and co rds to Dutchess Creek section of Eufaula Lake. Southbound co rds lead to camping areas inside the WMA. Free. Only fishermen & hunter primitive camping permitted in designated areas; 14-day limit. WMA encompasses the N and most of the S shorelines of the Dutchess Creek arm.

Fishing tip: Shore fish from here with minnows for crappie, concentrating on brushy structure close to creek channels.

Porum Landing   **$11**
Corps of Engineers
Eufaula Lake
6 mi E of Porum on SR 150. $11 for 8 basic sites; $16 for 37 sites with elec. 4/1-9/30; 14-day limit. 65-ft RVs. Tbls, flush toilets, cfga, drkg wtr, showers, elec($), beach, pavilion, dump. Boating(l), swimming, fishing.

Fishing tip: Crappie fishermen, use jigs with minnows around brush and the boat docks in mornings and evenings.

QUINTON (111)

James Collins   **FREE**
State Wildlife Management Area
S & SW of Quinton on SR 31 to Featherstone; S on co rd to entrance of WMA & camping area. Free. Only fishermen & hunter primitive camping permitted in designated areas; 14-day limit. Hunting, stream fishing (Ash Creek, Jones Creek, Elm Creek). 20,913 acres.

RAVIA (112)

Washita Arm   **FREE**
Tishomingo
Texoma State Wildlife Management Area
2 mi SW of Ravia on SR 12. Free. Primitive campground just inside S boundary of WMA on S shore of Washita River arm of Texoma Lake. Only fishermen & hunter primitive camping permitted in designated areas; 14-day limit. No facilities. 10,126 acres.

Fishing tip: Washita River consistently produces good catches of channel catfish of up to 10 pounds. The state's record fish was hooked here in June 1974; it weighed 30 pounds and was 39 inches long.

RINGOLD (113)

Turkey Creek   **FREE**
Pine Creek Lake
State Wildlife Management Area
2 mi from Ringold on co rd. Free. Fishermen & hunter primitive camping permitted only within 50 yds of public-use rds; 14-day limit.

Fishing tip: Turkey Creek provides good fishing all year for bass, crappie and white bass. If you have a boat, troll crankbaits at the creek's mouth around points. From shore, focus on brushy areas for crappies and cast into the creek channel for catfish.

RUFE (114)

Pine Creek Branch   **FREE**
Pine Creek Lake
State Wildlife Management Area
S and E of Rufe on co rds. Free. Fishermen & hunter primitive camping permitted only within 50 yds of public-use rds; 14-day limit. Fishing in Pine Creek area of lake. 10,280 acres.

RUSH SPRINGS (115)

Lake J.W. Taylor Campground   **$2**
1 mi S of Rush Springs on US 81; 1 mi E. $2 base. All year. Base fee for 30 primitive sites; $7 for 25 sites with elec/wtr. Tbls, flush toilets, cfga, drkg wtr, showers, dump. Picnicking, boating(ld), fishing.

SALINA (116)

Lake Shore   **$8**
RV & Recreation Park
1.2 mi S of Salina on SR 82; private camp. $8 base. 4/1-10/31. Base fee for 20 primitive & tent sites; $17 for RV hookup sites. Tbls, flush toilets, cfga, showers, drkg wtr. Boating(l), fishing, picnicking.

Fishing tip: Try the rip-rap along the Saline Creek shore at Hudson Lake. Toss crankbaits and bump them along bottom to pick up smallmouth & white bass.

Snowdale State Park   **$8**
6 mi E of Pryor on SR 20, or 2.5 mi W of Salina on SR 20. $8 for self-contained RVs in unimproved areas; $8 for tents; $15, semi-modern sites. All year; 14-day limit. 66 primitive sites; 18 elec/wtr sites. Tbls, flush toilets, cfga, drkg wtr, elec ($), showers, dump, beach, playground. Fishing, beach, boating(l), waterskiing, volleyball.

SALLISAW (117)

Brushy Lake State Park   **$10**
8 mi N of US 64 on Marble City Rd; 1 mi W. $10 for self-contained RVs; $10 for tents; $15 for semi-modern RV sites with elec/wtr. Primitive camping. 28 sites. Tbls, toilets, cfga, drkg wtr, showers. Fishing, boating.

Short Mountain Cove   **$10**
Corps of Engineers
Robert S. Kerr Lake
11 mi W of Sallisaw on Hwy 59; 1 mi W. $10 at 3 basic sites without wtr and at all open sites during 10/1-3/31; $15 at 32 sites with wtr/elec during 4/1-9/30. 14-day limit. 55-ft RV limit. Tbls, toilets, cfga, drkg wtr, dump, elec($). Boating(l), fishing, hiking, swimming. 2-night minimum stay on weekends.

Fishing tip: For bass, find rip-rap areas and fish them slowly with plastic worms and live bait. Also keep in mind, this lake produced the state's record sauger -- a 5-pounder in 1981.

Super 8 Motel RV Park   **$10**
At I-40 exit 308, behind Super 8 Motel. $10. All year. 14 sites. Tbls, flush toilets, showers, cfga, drkg wtr, hookups, store, restaurant, pool.

SAND SPRINGS (118)

Appalachia Bay   **$8**
Corps of Engineers
Keystone Lake
12 mi W of Sand Springs on US 64; 1.5 mi SW on co rd. $8. 4/1-10/31; 14-day limit. 18 very primitive sites (no RV size limit). Tbls, toilets, cfga, drkg wtr, beach. Boating (l), fishing, swimming.

Cowskin Bay South   **FREE**
Corps of Engineers
Keystone Lake
10 mi SE of Sand Springs on US 64; 1.5 mi N on access rd. Free. All year. 14-day limit. 30 sites (no RV size limit). Tbls, toilets, cfga, drkg wtr, dump. Boating(l), fishing.

Washington Irving Cove South   **$10**
Corps of Engineers
Keystone Lake
Near Sand Springs, 4 mi W on SR 64 & SR 51 jct; 1 mi E. $10 at 2 basic sites; $16 wtr/elec ($17 premium locations). 4/1-10/31; 14-day limit. 41 sites; 65-ft RVs. Tbls, flush toilets, cfga, drkg wtr, elec($), beach, dump, showers, playground. Boating(l), fishing, hiking, swimming.

SAWYER (119)

Lake Schooler   **FREE**
State Fishing Lake
Dept of Wildlife Conservation
7 mi N of Sawyer. Primitive camping on 35-acre lake. No facilities. Fishing, boating(l).

Fishing tip: This lake provides good crappie, sunfish and channel catfish angling. It was built by the WPa in the 1930s.

SAYRE (120)

Sayre City Park   **$12**
Half mi S from city stoplight. $12. All year. 85 RV sites with hookups. Tbls, flush toilets, cfga, drkg wtr, elec, showers, dump, mini-golf, ball fields, playground. 3 stocked fishing ponds surrounded by lighted walking trail. Store & restaurant nearby. Picnic areas.

SKIATOOK (122)

Bull Creek Peninsula   **$8**
Corps of Engineers
Skiatook Lake
10.8 mi W on SR 20; 3.7 mi NE; 1 mi E. $8. All year; 14-day limit. 41 basic sites. Tbls, toilets, cfga, no drkg wtr. Limited facilities in winter. Boating(ld), fishing.

Fishing tip: This area provides some excellent hybrid white bass action in spring, summer and fall. Troll artifical shad in the creek channels along brush lines.

SPAVINAW (123)

Spavinaw State Park   **$8**
Directly off SR 20 & SR 82 jct. $8 base for tents & self-contained RVs in unimproved areas; $15, semi-modern sites. All year; 14-day limit. 30 primitive sites; 26 elec/wtr sites. Tbls, flush toilets, cfga, drkg wtr, showers, dump, playground, beach. Swimming, boating, fishing. 35 acres.

STIDHAM (124)

North Canadian River Unit   FREE
Eufaula State Wildlife Management Area
2 mi W of Stidham on co rd; 1 ml N to management area. Get directions to camping areas. Free. Only fishermen & hunter primitive camping permitted in designated areas; 14-day limit. Management area encompasses both N & S shorelines of 12-mile section of the North Canadian River arm of Eufaula Lake.

Fishing tip: Huge blue catfish are caught in this area using live bait such as shad. Most flatheads are caught on cut bait, and channel catfish are plentiful can can be caught easily with nightcrawlers, shrimp and crayfish.

STIGLER (125)

Lake John Wells City Park $3
1 mi E of Stigler; 1 mi S. $3 base. All year. Base fee for 10 primitive sites; $5 for 10 elec sites. Tbls, toilets, cfga, drkg wtr. Boating(l), fishing, picnicking.

STILLWATER (126)

Lake McMurtry Park $6
Stillwater City Park
4 mi W of Stillwater on SR 51; 5 mi N on Redlands Rd. $6 base. All year. Base fee for 20 primitive sites, 4 with wtr hookups; $12 for 20 elec/wtr sites. Tbls, flush toilets, cfga, drkg wtr, dump, store. Picnicking, fishing (enclosed fishing dock), boating.

Fishing tip: The primary fish in this lake are largemouth & sand bass, crappie, catfish.

Lake Carl Blackwell $8
Oklahoma State University
7 mi W of Stillwater on SR 51; 2 mi N on SR 51C. $8 base. All year; 14-day limit. Base fee at 25 primitive sites Mon-Thurs ($10 Sat-Sun); $12 at sites with elec Mon-Thurs ($15 Fri-Sat); $20-22 with elec/wtr. Toilets, cfga, drkg wtr, elec($), showers, dump, playground, store. Horseshoes, fishing, boating(ld), swimming, horseback riding (stables), hiking trails, archery range.

Fishing tip: This is a good lake for southbound snowbirds to try in the fall. Catch crappie, white bass (Okies call them sand bass) and saugeye in the shallows. Troll crankbaits for the saugeye. Catfish are caught on cut baits and stinkbait. Find suspended largemouth with crankbaits.

Payne County Expo Center $10
3 mi E of Sixth & Perkins Rd on Hwy 51. $10. All year. 10-15 sites with wtr/elec. Tbls, flush toilets, cfga, drkg wtr, dump, elec. Restrooms open only during expo's working hours.

STILWELL (127)

Adair State Park $8
Half mi E of Stilwell on SR 51. $8 base; $16 for semi-modern sites. 20 primitive sites, 6 elec/wtr sites. Tbls, toilets, cfga, drkg wtr, group shelters, playground. Fishing pond, picnic areas, paddleboats(r). Fees uncertain for primitive sites; they are operated by a university.

Fishing tip: Stilwell City Lake isn't known for its plentiful white bass population, but a recent test netting there revealed that all of the white bass netted were larger than 12 inches, and the biggest fish was 2.5 pounds.

STRINGTOWN (128)

Atoka   FREE
State Wildlife Management Area
5 mi N of Stringtown on US 69; E on gravel co rd. Site 1 is just inside the WMA boundary, at the Missouri-Kansas-Texas railroad crossing; site 2 is 2.5 mi farther W on co rd; qtr mi S on Ridge Road South (rd open only Sept-Jan). Free. Primitive camping areas only for fishermen & hunters in designated areas; 14-day limit. Bluestem Lake. 6,440 acres.

McGee Creek   FREE
State Wildlife Management Area
10 mi E of Stringtown on co rd, through Stringtown WMA S on CR D4010 to WMA's entrance and headquarters. Free. Primitive fishermen & hunter camping permitted at 2 areas, except that camping is limited to hunters during specified seasons; 14-day limit. Fee area has sites with wtr/elec & primitive sites. 3 boat ramps, 3 comfort stateions with showers, fishing pier, beach, 15 picnic sites, playground. 8,900 acres.

Stringtown   FREE
State Wildlife Management Area
8 mi E of Stringtown on co rd to main camping. Free. Camping is permitted only during open hunting season & only at campground or within 50 yds of public use rds. Fishing at nearby Fugate Lake (70 acres).

SULPHUR (129)

Arbuckle Public Hunting Area   Free
State Recreation Area
1 mi W of Sulphur on OK 7; 3 mi S on Point Rd. Free. All year; 1-night limit. Primitive sites. Fishing; hunting.

Fishing tip: Arbuckle Lake produced the state's record grass carp in 1998. It weighed an enormous 64 pounds as was 46 inches long! In summer, watch for sandies (white bass) surfacing in schools near the dam.

Buckhorn $7
Chickasaw National Recreation Area
6 mi S of Sulphur on Hwy 177; 3 mi W following signs. $7 with federal Senior Pass at non-utility sites (others pay $14); $10 with federal Senior Pass at sites with hookups (others pay $20); $11 with federal Senior Pass at premium utility sites (others pay $22). All year; 14-day limit. 184 sites. Tbls, flush toilets, cfga, drkg wtr, store, dump. Fishing, swimming. Handicap access.

Cold Springs $12
Chickasaw National Recreation Area
1 mi E of Sulphur on Hwy 7, following signs. $12 for primitive sltes. MD-LD; 14-day limit. 63 sites. Tbls, flush toilets, cfga, drkg wtr, coin laundry, store, restaurant. Swimming, fishing, hiking. Handicap access.

Guy Sandy $12
Chickasaw National Recreation Area
3 mi SW of Sulphur on Hwy 7, following signs. $12. MD-LD; 14-day limit. 40 primitive sites. Tbls, toilets, cfga, drkg wtr. Swimming, fishing. Handicap access.

Point $7
Chickasaw National Recreation Area
6 mi SW of Sulphur on Hwy 7, following signs. $7 with federal Senior Pass at non-utility sites (others pay $14); $10 with federal Senior Pass at sites with hookups (others pay $20). All year; 14-day limit. 52 sites. Tbls, flush toilets, cfga, drkg wtr. Fishing, swimming, hiking. Handicap access.

Rock Creek $12
Chickasaw National Recreation Area
2 mi W of Sulphur on Hwy 7, following signs. $12 for primitive sites; $20 at 1 site with elec/wtr ($10 with federal Senior Pass). All year; 14-day limit. 106 sites. Tbls, flush toilets, cfga, drkg wtr, dump, coin laundry, store, restaurant. Swimming, fishing. Handicap access.

TAHLEQUAH (130)

Arrowhead Resort $12
14 mi N of Tahlequah on Hwy 10 (12 mi S of US 412). On Illinois River. $12 base for primitive sites; $18 with elec; $24 full hookups. Tbls, flush toilets, cfga, drkg wtr, dump. Fishing, floating, volleyball, swimming.

Buck Ford   FREE
Public Access Area
Oklahoma Scenic Rivers Commission
32 mi N of SR 51/US 62 bridge on SR 10; at Illinois River. Free primitive camping. Toilets, drkg wtr. Boating(l), fishing. Canoe access at about 28-mi pt on Illinois Wild & Scenic River.

Carters Landing $7
Corps of Engineers
Tenkiller Ferry Lake
11 mi S of Tahlequah on OK 82; at upper

Illinois River, about 2.5 mi from lake. $7 for 15 basic sites; $11 for 10 sites with elec/wtr. All year (reduced fees in winter); 14-day limit. RVs under 30 ft. Tbls, flush toilets, cfga, firewood, drkg wtr. Swimming; picnicking; fishing; boating(rld).

Fishing tip: The river here is an excellent place in the spring to catch spawning crappies. Look for small pea-gravel banks and shallow willow trees.

Cherokee State Park   **$8**
12 mi S of Tahlequah on SR 82, on Tenkiller Lake. $8 base self-contained RVs & tents in unimproved areas; $15, semi-modern sites; $26, modern. All year; 14-day limit. 53 primitive sites; 92 elec/wtr sites. Tbls, flush toilets, cfga, drkg wtr, elec ($), showers, dump. Swimming beach, fishing, boating(l), waterskiing, softball, horseshoes, volleyball.

Cherokee   **FREE**
State Wildlife Management Area
5 mi S of Tahlequah on US 62 to Zeb; S on co rd to Zeb entrance to Cherokee Public Hunting Area; S on Burnt Cabin Rd 5 mi to camp (3.5 mi S of WMA headquarters). Free. Only fishermen & hunter primitive camping permitted; camp only in designated areas; 14-day limit. No camping in game management (refuge) portion. Combined Cherokee and Gruber WMA is 55,515 acres. Fishing at nearby Greenleaf Lake.

Chewey Bridge   **FREE**
Public Access Area
Oklahoma Scenic Rivers Commission
36 mi N of SR 51/US 62 bridge on SR 10; 2 mi E on Chewey Rd to bridge. Free primitive camping. Toilets, drkg wtr. Boating(l), fishing. Canoe access at about 20-mi pt on Illinois Wild & Scenic River.

Diamondhead Resort (Private)   **$12**
2 mi E & 5 mi N of Tahlequa on SR 10. $12 base. All year. Base fee for primitive sites; $15 with elec/wtr. 22 sites with hookups; 250 primitive sites. Tbls, flush toilets, showers, cfga, store, dump. Float trips, picnicking, canoeing(r), volleyball, basketball, horseshoes.

Echota   **FREE**
Public Access Area
Oklahoma Scenic Rivers Commission
2 mi N of SR 51, US 62 bridge on SR 10. Free primitive camping. Toilets, drkg wtr. Boating (l), fishing. Canoe access at 50-mi marker on Illinois Wild & Scenic River.

Elephant Rock Nature Park   **$5**
2 mi from Tahlequah on Hwy 62E; 1.7 mi N on Hwy 10; across from Scenic River Commission bldg. $5 per person. All year; 21-day limit. Tbls, flush toilets, cfga, drkg wtr, showers. Hiking, rafting.

Falcon Floats (Private)   **$5**
1 mi N of Hwy 51 on Hwy 10 near Tahlequa; on Illinois River. $5 base. All year. Primitive sites. Showers, volleyball court, cfga, drkg

wtr. Float trips($), canoeing(r), kayaking(r), boating(ld), swimming beach, playground. Tent rentals.

Fishing tip: The state record striped bass was caught from the upper Illinois River in June 1996. It weighed 47 1/2 pounds.

Hanging Rock Camp (Private)   **$3**
3 mi E of Tahlequah on US 62, on Illinois River. $3 base. Mar-Oct. Base fee per person for 20 primitive sites; $12 for 6 RV sites with hookups. Tbls, flush toilets, cfga, drkg wtr, showers, store, restaurant. Picnic areas. Boating (l), canoe float trips, volleyball. 15 acres.

Horseshoe Bend   **FREE**
Corps of Engineers
Tenkiller Ferry Lake
From Tahlequah, 4 mi S on US 62, 4 mi S on SR 82, 5 miles E. Free. All year; 14-day limit. No designated sites; primitive camping area on river for small RVs & tents. Toilets, no drkg wtr. Fishing, boating(l), picnicking. Not an official campground.

Indian Village RV Park   **$12**
3 mi S of Tahlequah on Willis Rd at Hwy 62; behind Phillips 66. $12 if paid in advance; $15 otherwise. Full-hookup sites, tbls, flush toilets, cfga, drkg wtr, no showers. 10 minutes from Illinois River.

No Head Hollow   **FREE**
Public Access Area
Oklahoma Scenic Rivers Commission
3 mi N of SR 51, US 62 bridge on SR 10. Free primitive camping. Toilets, drkg wtr. Boating(l), fishing. Canoe access at 50-mi marker on Illinois Wild & Scenic River. Note: 10 mi of river between No Head & Echota Public Access Areas are only about 1 mi apart by road.

Peavine Hollow   **FREE**
Public Access Area
Oklahoma Scenic Rivers Commission
30 mi N of SR 51/US 62 bridge on SR 10. Free primitive camping. Toilets, drkg wtr. Canoe access at about 40-mi point on Illinois Wild & Scenic River. Boating (l), fishing.

Petit Bay   **$10**
Corps of Engineers
Tenkiller Ferry Lake
4 mi S of Tahlequah on US 64; 4.6 mi S on SR 82; 2 mi S to Petit; 1 mi SE to W side of lake. $10 for 21 basic sites; $14 with elec; $18 full hookups, 5 with 50-amp. 1/1-9/30; 14-day limit. 93 sites; 65-ft RVs. Pavilion, tbls, flush toilets, cfga, drkg wtr, showers, dump, beach, elec($). Wheelchair access. Boating (l), fishing, swimming.

Peyton's Place (Private)   **$12**
10 mi NE of Tahlequah on SR 10, on Illinois River. $12 for tent camping; $20 at 10 RV sites with full hookups. Tbls, flush toilets, cfga, drkg wtr, showers. Canoe, raft rentals, canoe float trips.

Riverside Park   **FREE**
Public Access Area
Oklahoma Scenic Rivers Commission
Just S of SR 51/US 62 bridge on W side of Illinois River. Free primitive camping. Toilets, drkg wtr. Canoe access at about 52-mi point on Illinois Wild & Scenic River. Boating(l), fishing.

Round Hollow   **FREE**
Public Access Area
Oklahoma Scenic Rivers Commission
34 mi N of SR 51/US 62 bridge on SR 10. Free primitive camping. Toilets, drkg wtr (not recommended). Boating(l), fishing. Canoe access at about 26-mi pt on Illinois Wild & Scenic River. Heavy nighttime use of pay phone by travelers. Summer campfire programs on Sat.

Sparrow Hawk Camp (Private)   **$10**
5 mi NE of Tahlequah on SR 10; qtr mi E on Ben George Rd, on Illinois River. $10 for tents; $16-20 for 66 RV sites with elec/wtr. Apr-Oct. 200 primitive sites. Tbls, flush toilets, cfga, showers, drkg wtr, dump, store, playground. Picnic areas, boating, volleyball. Canoe & raft rentals.

Standing Rock Landing   **FREE**
Corps of Engineers
Tenkiller Lake
9 mi S of Tahlequah on SR 82. Free. All year; 14-day limit. 10 sites (RVs under 30 ft). Toilets, tbls, cfga, drkg wtr. Hiking (trail), waterskiing, scuba diving, boating(l), picnicking, fishing. Local residents keep park clean.

Stunkard   **FREE**
Public Access Area
Oklahoma Scenic Rivers Commission
33 mi N of SR 51/US 62 bridge on SR 10. Free primitive camping. Toilets, drkg wtr. Boating(l), fishing. Canoe access at about 27-mi pt on Illinois Wild & Scenic River.

Todd   **FREE**
Public Access Area
Oklahoma Scenic Rivers Commission
From SR 51/US 62 bridge, E on SR 51 2 mi; N on access rd to Todd PAA. Or, boat/canoe access downstream from No Head Hollow Public Access Area, or upstream from Echota Public Access. Free primitive camping. Toilets, drkg wtr. Boating (l), fishing. Canoe access at about 48 mi point on Illinois Wild & Scenic River.

Turner Ford   **FREE**
Public Access Area
Oklahoma Scenic Rivers Commission
6 mi S of SR 51/US 62 bridge. Free primitive camping (no facilities). Boating(l), fishing.

War Eagle Resort   **$12**
2 mi E & 5 mi N of Tahlequah on SR 10. $10 base. All year. Base fee for primitive sites; $20 with elec/wtr. 100 primitive sites, 30 with elec/wtr. Tbls, flush toilets, cfga, drkg wtr, showers, dump, store. Picnic areas, float trips, volleyball, basketball, canoe rentals.

Watts Public Access Area   **FREE**
Oklahoma Scenic Rivers Commission
36 mi N of SR 51/US 62 bridge on SR 10; about 10 mi E on Chewey Rd to US 59; N on US 59 to Watts bridge (adjacent to Lake Frances Resort). Free primitive camping. Toilets, drkg wtr. Boating(l), fishing. Canoe access at beginning of Illinois Wild & Scenic River canoe route.

TALALA (131)

Rogers County Section   **FREE**
Oologah Lake
State Wildlife Management Area
E of Talala on CR E0352 to island campground. Deer hunting by archery only; shotgun hunting with pellets only. Also access via US 169 N from Talala 3 mi, then E across bridge to management area along E shore of Oologah Lake. Free. Hunter/fishermen camping permitted only within 50 yds of public-use rds; 14-day limit. WMA encompasses Spencer Creek arm of lake.

TALIHINA (132)

Downtown City RV Park   **FREE**
At Dallas & First Sts in downtown Talihina. All year. Undesignated sites; 35-ft RV limit. No facilities.

Emerald Vista   **FREE**
Ouachita National Forest
7.2 mi NE of Talihina on US 271; E on Hwy 1. Primitive camping. Tbls, toilets, cfga, no wtr.

Homer L. Johnson Sector   **FREE**
Ouachita State
Wildlife Management Area
4 mi E of Talihina on SR 1; 9-12 mi NE & E on FR 1005. Free. 7 camps. Primitive camping within 50 yds of public-use rds; follow rules of Ouachita National Forest when camping outside this sector in the WMA.

Lake Carl Albert   **FREE**
Municipal Campground
Qtr mi W of Talihina on SR 1; 1 mi N on SR 82, then W following signs. Free. All year. Primitive undesignated sites; 40-ft RV limit. Flush toilets, cfga, drkg wtr. Boating(l), fishing, hiking. 918-567-2194

Lake Nanih Waiya   **FREE**
State Fishing Access Site
12 mi S of Talihina on US 271; 2 mi W following signs. All year. Primitive undesignated sites; 30-ft RV limit. Tbls, toilets, cfga, no drkg wtr. Boating(l), fishing, hiking.

Talimena State Park   **$8**
7 mi N of Talihina on SR 271. $8 for self-contained RVs in unimproved areas; $8 for tents; $16, semi-modern sites. 15 primitive sites; 10 sites with elec/wtr. Flush toilets, cfga, drkg wtr, showers, dump, equestrian facilities. Playground, fishing. 20 acres.

Winding Stair   **$10**
Ouachita National Forest
7.2 mi NE of Talihina on US 271; 18 mi E on Hwy 1. $10. Free in Apr, Oct & 2 wks in Nov; 14-day limit. 26 sites (RVs under 23 ft). Tbls, flush toilets, cfga, drkg wtr. Fishing, boating, swimming.

TISHOMINGO (133)

Blue River Public Hunting   **FREE**
and Fishing Area
Dept of Wildlife Conservation
3 mi E of Tishomingo on Ok 78; 8 mi N to campground. Free. All year. Sites (RVs under 20 ft). Tbls, toilets, cfga. Hunting; picnicking; fishing. River. Trout fishing in winter.

Fishing tip: The Blue River here is a designated trout stream, with bank fishing & wading popular. Season: 11/1-3/15.

Headquarters   **FREE**
Tishomingo Wildlife Refuge
3 mi SE of Tishomingo on SR 78 on Lake Texoma. Camp is on S shore of lake's Washita arm. Free primitive camping only in designated areas for hunters & fishermen; 14-day limit. 20 sites. Tbls, toilets, cfga, hydrant drkg wtr. Boating (d). Closed for boating 10/1-3/1.

Nida Point   **FREE**
Tishomingo Wildlife Refuge
10 mi SE of Tishomingo. Free primitive camping for hunters and fishermen in designated areas. All year; 14-day limit. No facilities..

Pennington Creek Park   **$5**
City of Tishomingo
Lake Texoma, Denison Dam
On the W side of Tishomingo; S and E half mi on OK 99. $5 for tent sites; $15 for RV sites with hookups. All year; 14-day limit. 19 sites. Tbls, flush toilets, cfga, drkg wtr, dump ($5 non-campers). Store, ice, food, laundry nearby. Boating(rl); picnicking; fishing; hunting; waterskiing; tennis, golf, horseback riding nearby. Heated fishing dock. Former corps of engineers camp. 580-371-2369.

TONKAWA (134)

Ray See City Park   **FREE**
500 S Main St in Tonkawa, 3 mi off I-35. Free. All year; 3-day limit. Policed. 10 sites. Tbls, toilets, cfga, dump, phone, playground. Water fill tap. Swimming; picnicking. Register at police station 1 block S, 1 block E of stop light. Very nice park.

VALLIANT (135)

Pine Creek Cove   **$10**
Corps of Engineers
Pine Creek Lake
7 mi N of Valliant. $10 for 1 basic site; $15 for 40 sites with wtr & elec; 65-ft RVs. 4/1-9/30; 14-day limit. Tbls, toilets, cfga, drkg wtr, nature trails, dump, elect($) beach, showers,

playground, ball field. Fishing, boating(l), hiking, swimming.

WAGONER (136)

Afton Landing   **$10**
Corps of Engineers
Chouteau Lock & Dam 17
5 mi W of Wagoner on SR 51; SE before bridge. $10 for 2 primitive sites; $15 for 20 sites with elec. All year; 14-day limit. Tbls, flush toilets, showers, cfga, drkg wtr, dump, elec($). Fishing, boating(l).

Blue Bill Point Park   **$11**
Corps of Engineers
Fort Gibson Lake
From SR 51 at Wagoner, 6 mi N on US 69, then 3 mi ENE. $11 base for 9 primitive sites; $16 for 40 sites with elec/wtr ($17.50 amp). 3/13-9/30; 14-day limit. 43 sites; 65-ft RVs. Tbls, flush toilets, cfga, drkg wtr, hookups($), showers, dump. Fishing, boating(ld).

Flat Rock Creek   **$10**
Corps of Engineers
Fort Gibson Lake
8 mi N of Wagoner on US 69; 3 mi E. $10 for basic sites; $14 elec; $15 elec/wtr. 3/13-9/30; 14-day limit. 38 sites; 65-ft RVs. Tbls, toilets, cfga, showers, drkg wtr, dump, elect($). Boating(l), fishing, picnicking.

Long Bay Marina   **$5**
4.5 mi E of Wagoner on Hwy 51; 1 mi N on Long Bay Rd; at Fort Gibson Lake. $5 tent sites; $10 RV sites with hookups. All year. 14 sites. Tbls, flush toilets, cfga, drkg wtr, store. Boating(ld), fishing.

Rocky Point   **$11**
Corps of Engineers
Fort Gibson Lake
4 mi NE of Wagoner n US 69; 3 mi E, then 1 mi N on co rd. $11 base for 5 primitive sites; $15 at sites with elec; $16 elec/wtr; $18 full hookups. 3/13-9/30; 14-day limit. 63 sites; 65-ft RVs. Pavilion, tbls, flush toilets, showers, drkg wtr, cfga, dump, beach. Boating(l), fishing, swimming.

Sequoyah Bay State Park   **$8**
5 mi S of Wagoner on SR 16; 5 mi E on Grey Oaks Rd, on Fort Gibson Lake. $8 for self-contained RVs in unimproved areas; $8 for tents; $15, semi-modern sites with 30-amp ($17 with 50-amp); $18, preferred with 30-amp ($19 with 50-amp). All year; 14-day limit. 110 primitive sites; 77 elec/wtr sites. Tbls, flush toilets, cfga, drkg wtr, showers, dump. Shelters, group shelter, tennis courts, swimming, boating(ld) waterskiing, indoor fishing dock, grocery, picnic areas. Five new monuments depict chiefs from civilized tribes.

Fishing tip: The park has good shoreline fishing for largemouth bass, crappie, white bass & catfish.

OKLAHOMA

Sequoyah State Park $8

8 mi E of Wagoner on SR 51. $8 for self contained RVs in unimproved areas; $8 for tents; $15, semi-modern sites; $16, sem-modern preferred; $19, modern & preferred. All year; 14-day limit. 178 primitive sites; 151 elec/wtr sites; 28 full-hookup sites. Tbls, flush toilets, cfga, drkg wtr, showers, dump. Grocery, swimming, fishing, archery, riding stables, boating(l) waterskiing, playground, hiking trails, shelters. Site of a state water-fowl refuge; deer, wild turkey, fox, other wildlife. 2,853 acres at peninsula on Fort Gibson Lake.

Taylor Ferry South $11
Corps of Engineers
Fort Gibson Lake

6 mi E of Wagoner on SR 51. $11 for 7 basic sites without hoookups; $16 at sites with elec ($17 for 50 amp. 3/13-9/30; 14-day limit. wtr; $14-$15 for 19 sites with elec; $16 for 99 sites; 65-ft RVs. Tbls, flush toilets, cfga, drkg wtr, showers, beach, nature trail, elect ($). Swimming, boating(l), fishing, picnicking.

WATONGA (137)

Roman Nose State Park $8

8 mi N of Watonga on SR 8A on Lake Watonga & Lake Boecher. $8 for self-contained RVs in unimproved areas; $8 for tents; $15, semi-modern ($16 with 50-amp); $18, semi-modern preferred ($19 with 50-amp); $21, modern ($22 with 50-amp). All year; 14-day limit. 45 primitive sites; 31 elec/wtr sites; 4 full-hook-up sites. Tbls, flush toilets, cfga, drkg wtr, showers, dump. Swimming pool, playground, boating(ldr), fishing, riding stables, tennis, volleyball, picnic areas, biking(r), golf, mini golf.

Fishing tip: Lake Watongs is a designated trout water, with the best shore access on the W side of the lake. Season: 11/1-3/15.

WAURIKA (138)

Lake Jap Beaver   FREE
State Fishing Lake
Dept of Wildlife Conservation

4.5 mi NW of Waurika in Jefferson County. Free primitive camping at 65-acre lake. Toilets. Fishing, boating(l).

Moneka Park North $8
Corps of Engineers
Waurika Lake

6 mi N of Waurika on Hwy 5. $8. 3/1-10/31; 14-day limit. 38 basic sites. Tbls, toilets, cfga, drkg wtr. Boating, fishing, swimming, nature trail.

Wichita Ridge $8
Corps of Engineers
Waurika Lake

7 mi N of Waurika Lake Project Office (which is 5 mi N of Waurika on Hwy 5). $8 for 16 basic sites & 1 site with wtr hookup; $12 for 8 sites with elec & 12 sites with wtr & elec. Self-deposit fee system. All year; 14-day limit. No RV size limit. Toilets, drkg wtr, cfga,

tbls, elec($). Boating(ld), fishing, swimming, hiking & horse trail nearby.

Fishing tip: Waurika doesn't have many large trophy bass, but it contains extremely big catfish and is known for its crappie and hybrid striped bass.

WAYNOKA (139)

Little Sahara State Park $8

4 mi S of Waynoka on US 281. $8 for self-contained RVs in unimproved areas; $8 for tents; $16 for semi-modern sites. All year; 14-day limit. 24 primitive sites; 21 sites with elec/wtr. Tbls, flush toilets, cfga, drkg wtr, showers, dump. ORV trails, concession stand, group camp. 1,520 acres of dunes.

WEATHERFORD (140)

Crowder Lake $6
University Park
Southwestern Oklahoma State University

8 mi S of Weatherford on SR 54; 2 mi E & 1 mi S on county rd; half mi W on park rd. $6 for 3 primitive sites; $16 for 5 RV siteswith elec/wtr. Seniors get $2 discount. Tbls, toilets, cfga, dump, showers, picnic area. Boating(ld), fishing, bait vending machine, horseshoes.

WEBBER FALLS (141)

Brewer Bend $10
Corps of Engineers
Webber Falls Lake

2 mi W of Webber Falls on US 64; 3 mi N & 2 mi NW. $10 for 8 basic sites; $15 for 34 sites with wtr/elec (reduced rates 11/1-3/31). Tbls, flush toilets, cfga, drkg wtr, showers, beach, dump. Boating(l), fishing.

Fishing tip: Try the tailwaters below the dam for striped bass, white bass, walleye, northern pike, crappie.

WEST SILOAM SPRINGS (142)

Natural Falls State Park $8

3 mi W of West Siloam Springs on US 412. $8 for tent sites; $16 for semi-modern sites; $18, modern & preferred. Tbls, flush toilets, cfga, drkg wtr, dump. Walking paths, board-walks, picnic area.

WILBURTON (143)

Robbers Cave State Park $8

5 mi N of Wilburton on SR 2. $8 for self-con-tained RVs in unimproved areas; $8 for tents; $15, semi-modern sites; $18, modern & pre-ferred. 40 primitive sites; 30 elec/wtr sites; 11 full-hookup sites. Tbls, flush toilets, cfga, drkg wtr, showers, dump. Equestrian camp-ground; equestrian trails. Hiking trails, swim-ming pool, bathhouse, grocery, playground, fishing, boating, cafe, group camp, paddle

boats, canoes, miniature golf, horseshoes, volleyball. Lake Wayne Wallace (94-acres).

Fishing tip: 1.5 mi of the Fourche River through the park is a designated trout stream. Bank access is good. Season: 11/1-3/15.

Wayne Wallace Lake   FREE
State Fishing Access

6 mi N of Wilburton on SR 2; W on Ash Creek Rd. All year; 14-day limit. Primitive undesig-nated sites; no facilities. Fishing, boating(l).

Yourman   FREE
State Wildlife Management Area

8 m S of Wilburton, E of Hwy 2. Walk-in access only except for designated camping & parking areas. Free. All year; 14-day limit. Camping for hunters or fishermen in desig-nated areas. No facilities, no drkg wtr.

WILLIS (144)

Fobb Bottom   FREE
Texoma State Wildlife Management Area

W of Willis on co rds (just W of SR 99 at Texas border). On N shore of Lake Texoma at Willis Bridge & across lake from Juniper Point Public Use Area. Free. Fisherman & hunter camping allowed only within 50 yds of public roads. Boat ramps at Juniper Point, across the lake in Texas, and at Briar Creek SW of Madill. 2,273 acres.

WISTER (145)

Lake Wister State Park $8

2 mi S of Wister on SR 270. $8 base for self-contained RVs & tents in unimproved areas; $16 for semi-modern sites; $19, mod-ern. All year; 14-day limit. 100 primitive sites; 80 elec/wtr sites; 17 full-hookup sites. Tbls, flush toilets, cfga, drkg wtr, showers, dump, store. Nature trail, swimming pool, playground, fishing, canoeing(r), biking(r) boating(lr), waterskiing, group camp, cafe.

Fishing tip: While everyone else is casting Wister's shoreline for bass, catch largemouth by working plastics slowly off deep points.

WOODWARD (146)

Boiling Springs State Park $8

1 mi N of Woodward on SR 34; 5 mi E on SR 34C. $8 for self-contained RVs in unimproved areas; $8 for tents; $15, semi-modern sites; $19, modern. All year; 14-day limit. 12 primi-tive sites; 21 elec/wtr sites; 10 full-hookup sites Tbls, flush toilets, cfga, drkg wtr, show-ers, dump. Group camps, swimming pool, fishing, playground, hiking, golf nearby.

Eastern Wolf Creek Camps   FREE
Fort Supply
State Wildlife Management Area

4 mi W of Woodward on Airport Rd; N on co rd. Free. 3 primitive camping areas on E side of Wolf Creek. Only hunter & fishermen primi-tive camping permitted in designated areas;

14-day limit. Hunting; shooting range; fishing in river & Fort Supply Lake; boat launch at state park, Cottonwood Point & Supply Park. Picnic areas on E & W sides of lake. Lake has 26-mile shoreline; WMA is 5,550 acres. See Fort Supply entry for more camp areas.

WRIGHT CITY (147)

Little River   **$10**
Corps of Engineers
Pine Creek Lake
6 mi N of Wright City on SR 98; 8.5 mi W on SR 3, then SE. $10 for 28 basic sites; $15 at sites with elec & wtr, $18 full hookups. 4/1-9/30; 14-day limit. 89 sites; 65-ft RVs. Pavilion, tbls, flush toilets, cfga, drkg wtr, showers, elec($), playground, dump, beach. Baseball, hiking, fishing, boating(l). 2-night minimum stay on weekends.

Lost Rapids   **$8**
Corps of Engineers
Pine Creek Lake
6 mi N of Wright City on SR 98; 6 mi W on SR 3, then S. $8 for 14 basic sites; $13 for 16 sites with elec & wtr. All year; 14-day limit. 65-ft RVs. Tbls, flush toilets, cfga, drkg wtr, dump, playground, elec ($). Boating(l), fishing. 2-night minimum stay on weekends.

Turkey Creek Landing   **$8**
Corps of Engineers
Pine Creek Lake
6 mi N of Wright City on SR 98; 8.5 mi W on SR 3; SE to Little River Park, then half mi W on SR 3; half mi N to Burwell; half mi W & 2 mi N on secondary rds; 1.5 mi E on secondary rd. $8 for 22 basic sites with wtr hookups; $13 for 8 sites with elec/wtr. All year; 14-day limit. Tbls, toilets, cfga, drkg wtr, dump, playground. Boating(l), fishing.

WYANDOTTE (148)

Sycamore Valley Recreation Area   **$6**
2 mi S of Hwy 60 on Hwy 10. $6 per person. 5/1-10/1. 150 sites. Tbls, flush toilets, cfga, drkg wtr, showers, hookups($), playground, store, pool. Swimming, fishing, tennis, volleyball, basketball, mini-golf, volleyball, horseshoes, nature trail.

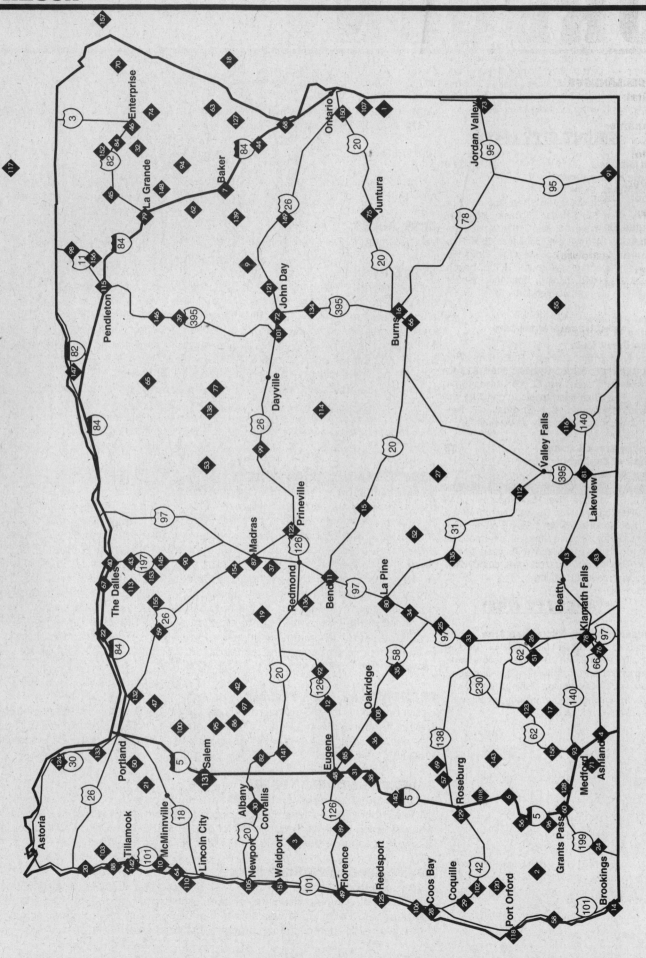

OREGON

MISCELLANEOUS
Capital:
Salem
Nickname:
Beaver State
Motto:
The Union
Flower:
Oregon Grape
Tree:
Douglas Fir
Bird:
Western Meadowlark
Song:
"Oregon, My Oregon"

Internet Address:
www.traveloregon.com

Toll free number for travel information: 1-800-547-7842.

Dept of Transportation, Parks and Recreation Division, 525 Trade St SE, Salem, OR 97310. 503-378-6305 or 800-542-5687.

Tourism Division, 775 Summer St. NE, Salem, OR 97310.

Fish and Wildlife Dept, PO Box 59, Portland, OR 97207; 503-229-5400 or 800-ASK-FISH.

REST AREAS
Vehicles may not park in rest areas more than 14 hrs in a 24-hr period.

STATE PARKS
Pets on leashes are permitted. RV limit usually 30 feet, with a 10-day limit in any 14-day period during summer months. For purposes of our listings, we have included only those state parks with primitive campsites that have overnight fees of $12 or less. Typically, primitive sites are $8 in-season, $5 off-season; tent sites are $14-$17 during the summer and $10-13 off-season. Sites with electricity are generally $16-$23 during the summer and $12-$16 in the winter. Full-hookup sites are $16-$22 during the summer and generally $16-$17 off-season. Fees vary according to region and individual campground. In addition, premium sites with river or lake views are $2 extra at a few parks. Hiker-biker camping is $4 per person where available. Primitive horse campsites have the same fees as other primitive sites plus $1.50 per horse. Oregon State Parks, 725 Summer ST NE, Suite C, Salem, OR 97301. 800-551-6949.

DESCHUTES NATIONAL FOREST
Several campgrounds where free camping had been offered previously (due to cutbacks in federal support funds) now have fees of about $6. A few years ago, many of the forest's campgrounds were turned over to concessionaires to be administered and, as a consequence of that and the implementation of new county "room taxes," fees increased. Off-season fees are not charged at forest campgrounds, but most of those facilities are closed to camping during the off-season. Anyone desiring to camp in the off-season should check with the respective ranger district to determine which camping areas are open for use. Deschutes is among the Oregon National Forests participating in the national fee demonstration program. During the period of the program, $5 will be charged daily (or $30 annually) for Northwest Forest Passes to visit some recreation areas. Visitors must pay those fees in order to camp overnight at numerous campgrounds where free camping otherwise was permitted. 1001 SW Emkay Dr., Bend OR 97702. 541-383-5300.

FREMONT NATIONAL FOREST
All but one of this forest's campgrounds are now free. Fees are charged at East Bay. The Fremont and Winema National Forests are now combined administratively, but they each operate their own set of campgrounds. 1301 South G St., Lakeview, OR 97630. 541-947-2151.

MALHEUR NATIONAL FOREST
All of this forest's campgrounds were free, but with participation in the Demonstraton Fee Program, $5-7 fees are now collected ar formerly free camps. Malheur is now managing some of the Ochoco National Forest campgrounds. 431 Patterson Bridge Rd., John Day, OR 97845. 541-575-3000.

MOUNT HOOD NATIONAL FOREST
A year-around playground with a cluster of resort communities, five wilderness areas featuring a superb hiking trail system, excellent fishing and camping and several ski areas. Mount Hood was among the Oregon National Forests participating in the national fee demonstration program, but campgrounds which were assigned

fees of $5 daily or $30 annually under that program are now $10 per night. The program virtually eliminated free camping at most easy-access campgrounds, and now fees at those sites have doubled. 16400 Champion Way, Sandy, OR 97055. 503-668-1700. Email at infoctr@mthood.org

OCHOCO NATIONAL FOREST

Small, developed campgrounds, usually close to small streams, are found throughout the forest. About half have overnight camping fees of $6-$8, and the rest are free. Rockhounding is popular, and forest roads lead to several sites containing semi-precious quartz-family stones such as thunder eggs, agates, jasper, limb casts and petrified wood. Three wildernesses and three special management units provide many opportunities for backcountry hiking, camping and horseback riding. There are more than 120 miles of summer hiking, horseback riding and mountain bike trails. Forest Supervisor, Ochoco National Forest, 3160 NE Third St., Prineville, OR 97754. 541-475-9272.

ROGUE RIVER-SISKIYOU NATIONAL FOREST

Small camping fees are charged at most of the forest's developed campgrounds; they generally range from $6 to $10. The forest is participating in the Pacific Northwest's fee demonstration program, but campgrounds are relatively unaffected. Most campgrounds are closed after Labor Day or operated on a limited basis through October for hunting season; they open by Memorial Day each year. In 2007, the two forests blended their nine ranger districts into five. Forest Supervisor, Rogue River National Forest, PO Box 520, Medord, OR 97501-0209. 541-858-2200.

SIUSLAW NATIONAL FOREST

The section of Siuslaw National Forest along the Oregon coast offers exciting diversion. For hikers, try three wilderness areas: Drift Creek Wilderness E of Waldport and N of Alsea River; Cummins Creek Wilderness, 4 mi S of Yachats next to the Cape Perpetua Scenic Area (primitive, no-trace camping permitted); Rock Creek Wilderness, 10 mi S of Yachats, with its difficult and limited access. Cape Perpetua Visitor Center (547-3289) is open daily during summer months. Forest Supervisor, Siuslaw National Forest, 4077 SW Research Way, Corvallis, OR 97339. 541-750-7000.

OREGON DUNES NATIONAL RECREATION AREA

The Oregon Dunes is within (and administered by) Siuslaw National Forest. The dunes area stretches along 40 miles of Oregon's Central Coast and has about a dozen federal campgrounds open for winter use. All have fees higher than $12.

UMATILLA NATIONAL FOREST

The forest has several campgrounds with low-cost sites available, as well as hundreds of primitive, undeveloped sites for which overnight camping fees are not charged. The forest is participating in the national recreation fee demonstration program, requiring $5 daily passes or $30 annual passes at some recreational sites. A Forest Supervisor, Umatilla National Forest, 2517 SW Hailey, Pendleton, OR 97801. 541-278-3716.

UMPQUA NATIONAL FOREST

Low-cost camping is available at several developed campgrounds, with fees ranging from $6 to $12 per night. Some of those campgrounds are completely closed during the off-season, but others are open without drinking water and services. There are no fees during the off-season for those that are open. Forest Supervisor, Umpqua National Forest, 2900 Stewart Pkwy, Roseburg, OR 97470. 541-672-6601.

WALLOWA-WHITMAN NATIONAL FOREST

The forest's campsite fee schedule is based upon the services available, with classifications ranging from "very primitive" (no water, low use) and "primitive" (no water, moderate use) to "modern" (high use with water, electricity, sewers and showers). Most fee campgrounds are classified as "primitive, moderate use" and have drinking water available but no hookups or showers. Fees for those are generally $8-14. Union Creek and Anthony Lakes campgrounds are closed off-season; all others are open but are not maintained with services such as water or trash removal. Forest Supervisor, Wallowa-Whitman National Forest, PO Box 907, Baker City, OR 97814. 541-523-6391.

WILLAMETTE NATIONAL FOREST
Many of the forests developed campgrounds are now operated by concessionaires. Most fees are $6-$12. Forest Supervisor, Willamette National Forest, 211 East 7th Ave, Eugene, OR 97401; or PO Box 10607, Eugene, OR 97440. 541-465-6521.

WINEMA NATIONAL FOREST
The Fremont and Winema National Forests are combined Fees at Winema's 12 developed campgrounds are generally $6-$13, but about half of the campgrounds are free. 1301 South G St., Lakeview, OR 97630. 541-947-2151.

Bureau of Land Management, PO Box 2965, Portland, OR 97208.

NORTH UMPQUA RIVER area of Oregon, managed by the Roseburg District of the Bureau of Land Management and the National Forest Service, is considered by many outdoorsmen to be one of the finest steelhead and trout angling rivers in the nation. The river is restricted to fly fishing upstream from the fish hatchery water intake at Rock Creek. RV and tent campers have numerous opportunities for free and low-cost camping. The nearest RV sanitary stations to the North Umpqua area are at the Douglas County Fairgrounds in Roseburg and at the Forest Service campground at Diamond Lake.

ROGUE RIVER NATIONAL RECREATION TRAIL
The Rogue River Trail from Grave Creek to Illahe is in the heart of the National Wild and Scenic Rogue River Canyon. One of the most interesting ways to experience the canyon is by taking a backpacking trip on the trail, which follows the north bank of the river as it winds its way toward the Pacific Ocean. Grave Creek, the eastern trailhead, is about 30 miles downriver from the town of Grants Pass. Free and low-cost campgrounds are located strategically all along the trail. Sites are managed by the Bureau of Land Management and Siskiyou National Forest.

LOWER DESCHUTES RIVER NATIONAL BACKCOUNTRY BYWAY
The Bureau of Land Management's Prineville District manages almost 50 per cent of the land in the river corridor extending from Pelton Reregulation Dam to the river's confluence with the Columbia River. Along the path are numerous free and low-cost campgrounds (see entries under Maupin and Madras). At boat-in sites (both state and federal), camping is permitted for up to four nights, and each site may be re-occupied only after three nights of absence have elapsed. Vehicles are limited to 28-foot lengths on the byway roads.

Popular activities include whitewater rafting, kayaking, drift and jet boating, bank fishing, swimming, hiking, mountain bike riding and sightseeing. Between June 1 and Oct. 15, fires, charcoal and candles are prohibited. The rest of the year, fires may be built or charcoal burned in a metal fire pan with sides at least two inches high. Fire rings are not permitted, and cutting or gathering live or dead wood is prohibited; pack out ashes and charcoal.

LOWER CROOKED RIVER NATIONAL BACKCOUNTRY BYWAY
The BLM's Prineville District also manages lands in this section. Favorite activities are camping, fishing, hiking, picnicking, boating and sightseeing. The river corridor is within the ceded lands of the Confederated Tribes of the Warm Springs Indian Reservation. Fires are prohibited June 1-Oct. 15 and, during the rest of the year, fire rings are prohibited.

U.S. ARMY CORPS OF ENGINEERS
Low-cost camping is available at Cottage Grove Lake, Dorena Lake and Fall Creek Lake, while free camping is offered at Fall Creek, Lake Umatilla, Lake Wallula and Lost Creek Lake.

ADRIAN (1)

Slocum Canyon Camp FREE
Bureau of Land Management
Vale District
8 me S of Adrian on Hwy 201, following Leslie Gulch/Succor Creek National Back Country Byway signs; rd steep & narrow, not recccmended for large RVs. Free. 4/1-11/1; 14-day limit. 12 primitive undesignated sites along Owyhee Reservoir. Toilets, cfga, no drkg wtr. Fishing, boating(l), swimming, waterskiing.

AGNESS (2)

Illahe $5
Siskiyou National Forest
4.9 mi N of Agness on CR 375. $5 during 5/1-10/1; free rest of year but no wtr service; 14-day limit. 14 sites (22-ft RV limit). Tbls, flush & pit toilets, cfga, drkg wtr. Swimming, boating, fishing. 20 acres.

ALSEA (3)

Alsea Falls $10
Bureau of Land Management
Salem District
7 mi SE of Alsea on South Fork Alsea Rd. $10. 5/15-9/30; 114-day limit. 16 sites (30-ft RV limit). Tbls, toilets, cfga, drkg wtr, 22 picnic sites. Fishing, hunting, rockhounding, swimming, hiking. 40 acres.

Mary's Peak $10
Siuslaw National Forest
7 mi NE of Alsea on SR 34; 4 mi NW on FR 30; 3 mi N on FR 3010. $10. 5/15-10/1; 14-day limit. 6 sites (small RVs & tents only). Tbls, toilets, cfga, drkg wtr. Scenic. Hiking, picnicking, berry picking.

ASHLAND (4)

Beaver Dam $5
Rogue River National Forest
25 mi NE of Ashland on Dead Indian Hwy; 1.5 mi N on FR 37; at Beaver Dam Creek. $5 (2nd RV, $2). 5/7-11/15; 14-day limit. 4 sites; 16-ft RV limit. Tbls, toilet, cfga, no drkg wtr, no trash service. Fishing, hiking, picnicking. Elev 4500 ft.

Daley Creek $5
Rogue River National Forest
25 mi NE of Ashland on FR 25 (Dead Indian Hwy); 1.6 mi N on FR 37. $5 (second RV, $2). 5/7-11/15; 14-day limit. 8 sites (RVs under 19 ft). Tbls, toilets, cfga, no drkg wtr or trash service. Fishing, picnicking, hiking. At Beaver Dam & Daley Creeks. Elev 4500 ft.

Hyatt Lake Recreation Area $12
Bureau of Land Management
Medford District
16 mi SE of Ashland on SR 66; 5 mi E of East Hyatt Lake Rd. $12 on Mon-Thurs; $15 Fri-Sun; $10 equestrian. About 5/1-11/1. 14-day limit. 47 RV sites (40-ft RV limit) and 7 walk-in tent sites (for 1-3 tents). Tbls, flush toilets, cfga, drkg wtr, showers, dump, fish cleaning station. Fishing, swimming, boating(ld), volleyball, horseshoes, playground. Nearby lodges offer meals, boat rentals.
Fishing tip: Hyatt Lake is stocked with trout and also contains smallmouth bass.

Mount Ashland FREE
Klamath National Forest
12.1 mi SE of Ashland on I-5; 1.1 mi W on CR 993; 9.1 mi W on CR 1151; 4.8 mi W on FR 40S01. Free. 7/1-10/31. 6 sites (RVs under 16 ft). Tbls, toilets, cfga, no drkg wtr. Picnicking; mountain climbing; hiking. Elev 6600 ft; 1 acre. Ski bowl (.5 mi). Geological. Mountain summit (1.5 mi). Maintained by Rogue River National Forest.

Wrangle FREE
Rogue River National Forest
11 mi SE of Ashland on I-5; 15 mi W on FR 20; 10 mi SW on FR 392. Free. 6/1-10/30; 14-day limit. 5 tent sites. Tbls, toilets, cfga, drkg wtr. Picnicking; hiking; horseback riding (no stables). Elev 6400 ft; 2 acres. Historical community kitchen, tbls & shelter built by CCC. Scenic. Mount Shasta. Elev 6400 ft.

AZALEA (6)

Devils Flat $6
Umpqua National Forest
From I-5, 18.2 mi E of Azalea on CR 36 (Cow Creek Rd). Alternative route: From ranger station at Tiller, 1.5 mi S on CR 1 to Callahan Rd 3230, then 7 mi to FR 32; turn right for 2 mi to campground. FR 32 becomes CR 36 the last mi. $6. 5/1-10/31; 14-day limit. 3 sites (RVs under 23 ft). Tbls, toilets, cfga, no drkg wtr. Picnicking; hiking. Elev 2100 ft; 2 acres. Cow Creek Falls Trail makes qtr mi loop along Cow Creek Falls. Trout in stream. Dump station 26 mi at Canyonville.

BAKER (7)

Deer Creek FREE
Wallowa-Whitman National Forest
About 23 mi SW of Baker City on SR 7; N on CR 656, then N on FR 6550; 4 mi N on CR 6530 (gravel). Free. 5/15-10/31; 14-day limit. 8 tent sites. Tbls, toilets, cfga, no drkg wtr, no trash service. Fishing, hiking, gold panning.

Lake Fork $5
Hells Canyon Nat. Recreation Area
Wallowa-Whitman National Forest
4 mi N of Baker City in I-84; 62 mi E on Hwy 86; 8 mi N on FR 39; left on access rd; at Lake Fork Creek. $5. 6/1-11/30; 14-day limit. 10 sites; 22-ft RV limit. Tbls, toilets, cfga, drkg wtr. Fishing, hiking, boating.

Millers Lane FREE
Wallowa-Whitman National Forest
24 mi SW of Baker City on SR 7; just past Phillips Lake, go 2 mi S on Hudspath Lane, then 3.5 mi SE on FR 2220 (gravel); on S shore of Phillips Lake. Free. 5/1-11/15; 14-day limit. 7 sites (20-ft RV limit). Tbls, toilets, cfga, no drkg wtr, no trash service. Boating(l), fishing, hiking, swimming.

Southwest Shore $8
Wallowa-Whitman National Forest
24 mi SW of Baker City on SR 7; just past Philips Lake, go 2 mi S on Hudspath Lane, then 2.5 mi SE on FR 2220 (gravel); on S shore of Phillips Lake. $8. 5/1-11/15; 14-day limit. 18 sites (24-ft RV limit). Tbls, toilets, cfga, no drkg wtr, no trash service. Fishing, boating(l), swimming, waterskiing, hiking.

BATES (9)

Lower Camp Creek FREE
Malheur National Forest
16.5 mi NW of Bates on FR 5930; 1.5 mi S on FR 1036. Elev 3700 ft. 6/15-11/1. 6 primitive undeveloped sites (RVs under 32 ft). Toilets. Fishing. Pack out trash.

BEAVER (10)

Rocky Bend Campground FREE
Siuslaw National Forest
13 mi SE of Beaver (S of Tillamook) via CR 858 (Blaine Rd); at the Nestucca River. Free. All year; 14-day limit. 6 sites (RVs under 16 ft). Toilets, tbls, cfga, no drkg wtr, no trash service. Hiking, fishing, clamming, swimming.
Fishing tip: Try the Nustucca River for trout and salmon.

BEND (11)

Big River $6
Deschutes National Forest
17 mi S of Bend on US 97; 5 mi W on CR 42. $6. 4/15-10/31; 14-day limit. 9 RV sites (26-ft RV limit), 2 tent sites. Tbls, toilet, cfga, no drkg wtr. Boating(l), picnicking, fishing. On Deschutes River. Elev 4150 ft.
Travel tip: We've selected the nearby Lava Butte Geological Area as one of the best free attractions in Oregon. Focal point is a 500-ft cinder cone volcano which erupted about 6,000 years ago. Automated tremors and dramatic visual displays are among exhibits at the visitor center. 10 mi S of Bend on US 907.

Bull Bend $6
Deschutes National Forest
26.8 mi S of Bend on US 97; 8 mi W on CR 43; 2 mi S on FR 4370. $6. 4/15-10/31; 14-day limit. 12 sites; 30-ft RV limit. Tbls, toilets, cfga, no drkg wtr. Picnicking, fishing, boating(l), swimming, canoeing, rafting. On the Deschutes River. Elev 4300 ft.
Fishing tip: The state's best population of stream brown trout are in the Deschutes below Wickiup Reservoir. It also contains rainbow & brook trout, whitefish and small coho & kokanee salmon from the lake.

Cinder Hill $10
Newberry National Volcanic Monument
Deschutes National Forest
23.5 mi S of Bend on Hwy 97; 17.6 mi E on CR 21; half mi N on FR 2100-700; at East Lake. $10 (premium site, $12). 5/1-9/30; 14-day limit. 110 sites; 30-ft RV limit. Tbls, pit & flush toilets, cfga, drkg wtr. Boating(l), fishing, hiking, swimming, birdwatching, biking, canoeing. Forest pass required for trailhead parking.

Fishing tip: East Lake provides exceptional trout fishing. It contains kokanee & Atlantic salmon, rainbow & brown trout. Its average depth is more than 67 feet.

Cow Meadow $6
Deschutes National Forest
44.7 mi SW of Bend on CR 46; half mi E on FR 40; 2 mi S on FR 4000-970; on N end of Crane Prairie Reservoir at Deschutes River. $6. Open 5/15-10/31; 14-day limit. 21 sites (26-ft RV limit). Tbls, toilets, cfga, drkg wtr. Picnicking, fishing, boating(l - small boats only). Elev 4500 ft; 8 acres.

Fishing tip: Crane Prairie Lake is one of the state's best producers of rainbow trout, which average growing two inches each summer. Numerous trout 4-9 pounds are caught, and the lake's largest was more than 19 pounds.

Cultus Corral Horse Camp $5
Deschutes National Forest
43 mi SW on CR 46 (Cascade Lakes Hwy); right on FR 4630 for qtr mi. $5. About MD-10/31; 14-day limit. 11 RV sites; 30-ft RV limit. Tbls, toilets, cfga, drkg wtr, horse corral, stalls. Fishing, boating, hiking, horseback riding. Near Cultus Lake. Elev 4450 ft.

Fishing tip: Stocked rainbow trout, including large holdover fish and some brook trout are caught near the mouth of Winopee Creek at Cultus Lake. Also try the SW corner of the lake using power bait or worms, and work the shelves along the NW shoreline.

Cultus Lake $12
Deschutes National Forest
43.5 mi SW of Bend on CR 46 (Cascade Lakes Hwy); 2 mi W on FR 4635; may travel by boat to E shore of lake. $12 (premium lakeside sites, $14). About MD-9/30; 10-day limit. 55 RV/tent sites; 30-ft RV limit. Tbls, toilets, cfga, drkg wtr. Swimming, boating(rl), fishing, waterskiing. Elev 4700 ft; 7 acres.

Fishing tip: Cultus Lake produces trophy 10-pound lake trout (mackinaw), and in 1996, a 17.5-pounder was caught there. Best times are May-June and Sept-Oct. Troll flashers with Flatfish or crankbaits near dropoffs.

Cultus North Shore Coves $5
Deschutes National Forest
46 mi SW of Bend on Cascade Lakes Hwy; 2 mi W on FR 4635; boat-in or hike-in to N shore of Cultus Lake. Camp free, but $5 daily (or $30 annual) forest parking pass required at boat ramp. About MD-9/30; 14-day limit. 15 tent sites. Toilet, cfga, no drkg wtr. Fishing, hiking, boating, waterskiing.

Deschutes Bridge $6
Deschutes National Forest
39 mi SW of Bend on CR 46 (Cascade Lakes Hwy); half mi E on FR 4270; at upper Deschutes River. $6. 5/1-9/30; 14-day limit; free 9/30-11/15. 12 sites (30-ft RV limit). Tbls, toilets, cfga, drkg wtr. Fishing, picnicking, boating(l), bird watching. Elev 4650 ft.

Fishing tip: Use nightcrawlers & salmon eggs in the Deschutes for rainbow & brook trout, steelhead and whitefish.

Devils Lake $5
Deschutes National Forest
28.7 mi W of Bend on CR 46 (Cascade Lakes Hwy). Free with forest's annual $30 parking permit; otherwise $5 for daily forest parking pass. 6/15-9/30; 14-day limit. 9 walk-in tent sites. Tbls, toilets, cfga, no drkg wtr, horse facilities. Fishing, boating, hiking, canoeing, horseback riding. Access point to Three Sisters Wilderness via Elk-Devils Trail or Wickium Plains Trail. House route via Katsuk Pond Trail to Quinn Meadow Horse Camp. Elev 5450 ft.

Fishing tip: This clear, scenic lake produces mainly stocked rainbow trout of 8-11 inches, although it also contains small brookies. Use light tackle and either cast Rooster Tails or Mepps spinners or still-fish worms and salmon eggs.

East Lake $12
Newberry National Volcanic Monument
Deschutes National Forest
23.5 mi S of Bend on Hwy 97; 16.6 mi E on CR 21; at East Lake. $12 (premium lakeside sites, $14). 5/15-10/31; 14-day limit. 29 sites; 26-ft RV limit. Tbls, flush & pit toilets, cfga, drkg wtr. Boating(l), fishing, hiking, swimming, biking, birdwatching.

Fishing tip: East Lake consistently produces brown trout over 10 pounds, and the lake record is 22.5 pounds. The lake also contains plenty of catchable-size rainbows. Use crankbaits, flashers with worms and dark woolly worms & nymphs.

Elk Lake $10
Deschutes National Forest
33.1 mi W of Bend on CR 46 (Cascade Lakes Hwy); on N end of Elk Lake. $10 (premium sites, $12). About MD-9/30; 7-day limit. 23 sites (22-ft RV limit). Tbls, toilets, cfga, drkg wtr. Swimming, boating(lr), fishing, hiking trails. Elev 4900 ft; 7 acres.

Fishing tip: This is a very clear, cold lake which produces small but tasty kokanee salmon, maninly at the S end near the lava flow. Use nightcrawlers, salmon eggs, periwinkles.

Fall River $6
Deschutes National Forest
15 mi S of Bend on US 97; 12 mi W on CR 42. $6. 4/15-10/31; 14-day limit. 10 sites (22-ft RV limit). Toilets, cfga, no drkg wtr, tbls. Picnicking, fishing, boating(no mtrs), hiking. Elev 4000 ft. Fishing.

Fishing tip: Fall River is a beautiful 8-mile-long stream through the forest and is well known for its flyfishing. Submerged logs provide good cover for stocked rainbows and native brookies.

Travel tip: Tumalo Falls, a 97-foot waterfall that drops into an eaily reached canyon, is among the best free atractions of Oregon. It's in Deschutes National Forest, 13 mi W of Bend from Galveston Ave.

Hot Springs $10
Deschutes National Forest
Newberry National Volcanic Monument
23.5 mi S of Bend on Hwy 97; 17.2 mi E on CR 21. $10. 6/30-9/30; 14-day limit. 52 sites; 26-ft RV limit. Tbls, toilets, cfga, drkg wtr. Fishing, hiking, swimming, birdwatching, biking. Near East Lake. Elev 6400 ft. Monument entry fee charged.

Fishing tip: This lake contains huge brown trout, numerous rainbow, brook trout, kokanee & Atlantic salmon.

Irish and Taylor FREE
Deschutes National Forest
44 mi SW of Bend on CR 46; .8 mi W on FR 4635; 2.3 mi SW on FR 4630; 7 mi W on FR 600 (high-clearance vehicle needed). Free. 7/1-9/15; 14-day limit. 6 tent sites. Toilets, no drkg wtr, no tbls. Picnicking; fishing; boating(no motors). Elev 5700 ft; 4 acres. Little Cultus Lake(5.5 mi). Near Pacific Crest Trail.

Fishing tip: Use a float tube at Irish Lake and fly fish with dry mosquitoes, midges and small Adams patterns. Focus on shaded spots for stocked brook, rainbow & cutthroat trout.

Lava Lake $10
Deschutes National Forest
36 mi SW of Bend on CR 46 (Cascade Lakes Hwy); 1 mi E on FR 500. $10 (premium sites $12). About 5/1-10/31; 14-day limit. 43 sites (30-ft RV limit). Tbls, toilets, cfga, drkg wtr, showers, dump. Fishing, boating(ldr), hiking trails. Elev 4800 ft; 11 acres.

Fishing tip: Formed when a lava flow created a dam, Lava Lake is fed by springs, not streams. It contains whitefish, brook & rainbow trout. Use cheese, power bait, Flatfish, flashers, green spinners.

Little Cultus Lake $8
Deschutes National Forest
44.5 mi SW of Bend on CR 46 (Cascade Lakes Hwy); N mi NW on FR 4635; 2 mi SW on FR 4630; 1 mi W on FR 4636. $8. About MD-10/31; 14-day limit. 20 sites; 30-ft RV limit. Tbls, toilets, cfga, drkg wtr. Picnicking, swimming, fishing, boating(l), waterskiing. 9 acres.

Fishing tip: 175-acre Little Cultus Lake offers good fishing for rainbow & brook trout, with stocked rainbows averaging 11-17 inches. Troll flashers with trailing nightcrawlers. Top lures are gold Thomas or yellow Roostertail. The best bank fishing is from the N shore with bobbers & worms, spinners, spoons or marshmallow & worm fished near bottom.

Little Fawn $8
Deschutes National Forest
31 mi SW of Bend on CR 46 (Cascade Lakes Hwy); 2 mi SE on FR 470; at Elk Lake. $8. About MD-9/30; 14-day limit. About 20 undesignated sites; 30-ft RV limit. Tbls, toilets, cfga, drkg wtr. Boating, fishing, hiking, swimming, windsurfing.

Fishing tip: Besides small (7-10 inch) kokanee, Elk Lake produces brook trout that average about 12 inches, with some in the 2-3 pound range. Still-fish worms, troll with gold flashers and worms or fly-fish with black flies.

Little Lava Lake $8
Deschutes National Forest
38.4 mi SW of Bend on CR 46 (Cascade Lakes Hwy); 0.7 mi E on FR 4600; 0.4 mi E on FR 4600-520; on Little Lava Lake. $8. About 5/1-10/31; 14-day limit. 12 sites (26-ft RV limit). Tbls, toilets, cfga, drkg wtr. Boating (rentals, dock, launch nearby), fishing, hiking.

Fishing tip: Little Lava Lake, source of the Deschutes River, produced the state record brook trout in 1980; it weighed 9 pounds 6 ounces. The 130-acre lake offers good fishing for planted rainbow trout averaging 6-12 inches. Troll or fish from shore N of the boat ramp.

Mallard Marsh $6
33 mi W of Bend on CR 46; 1.9 mi N on FR 4625; on Hosmer Lake. $6. About MD-10/31; 14-day limit. 15 sites (26-ft RV limit). Tbls, toilets, well drkg wtr. Picnicking, fishing, boating(l). Elev 4900 ft.

Fishing tip: Fly fish for rainbow trout & Atlantic salmon in Hosmer Lake. No other method allowed! The salmon are stocked annually, and the lake also contains big brook trout. All salmon must be realeased, so barbless hooks are required. The water is so clear, you can see the fish swimming.

North Twin Lake $6
Deschutes National Forest
17.5 mi S of Bend on US 96; 19 mi W on CR 42; 2 mi SW on FR 4260. $6. 4/15-10/31; 14-day limit. 19 sites; 30-ft RV limit. Tbls, toilets, cfga, no drkg wtr. fishing, boating, swimming.

Fishing tip: 112-acre North Twin Lake contains stocked rainbow trout and illegally introduced bullhead catfish. Trout average 8-12 inches and are plentiful. Try the W shore using red salmon eggs, power baits or marshmallows & worms suspended just off bottom. Troll Roostertails or Panther Martins slowly. Good lake for float tube fishing.

Point Campground $10
Deschutes National Forest
33 mi SW of Bend on CR 46 (Cascade Lakes Hwy). $10 (premium sites $12). About MD-10/31; 14-day limit. 10 sites (26-ft RV limit). Tbls, toilets, cfga, drkg wtr. On shore of Elk Lake. Fishing, hiking, boating(l).

Fishing tip: Catch sall kokanee salmon or brook trout at S end of Elk Lake using night-crawlers, salmon eggs, periwinkles or gold flashers with worms.

Quinn Meadow Horse Camp $12
Deschutes National Forest
30 mi W of Bend on CR 46 (Cascade Lakes Hwy); qtr mi SE on FR 450. $12. 6/15-9/30; 14-day limit. 24 sites (30-ft RV limit). Tbls, toilets, cfga, drkg wtr, horse stalls. Horseback riding trails, hiking trails, fishing. Elev 5100 ft; 5 acres. Reservations required; 877-444-6777.

Reservoir $6
Deschutes National Forest
57 mi W of Bend on CR 46; 2 mi E on FR 44. $6. About 5/1-9/30; 14-day limit. 26 sites (30-ft RV limit). Tbls, toilets, cfga, no drkg wtr. Fishing, boating(l), hiking. Elev 4400 ft; 1 acre. on S shore of Wickiup Reservoir.

Fishing tip: Spring and summer fishing for kokanee salmon has been excellent in recent years at Wicklum Reservoir. The fish aren't large, but they're plentiful.

Sand Springs FREE
Deschutes National Forest
21.2 mi E of Bend on US 20; 18.6 mi SE on CR 23. Free. Elev 5100 ft. 5/15-10/30. 3 sites on 3 acres (RVs under 31 ft). Toilets, cfga, no tbls, no drkg wtr.

Sheep Bridge $6
Deschutes National Forest
17.5 mi S of Bend on US 97; 19 mi W on CR 42; half mi SW on FR 4260; half mi W on FR 070. $6. 4/15-10/31; 14-day limit. 23 sites; 30-ft RV limit. Tbls, toilets, cfga, drkg wtr. Picnicking; fishing, boating (l). On Deschutes River at entrance to Wickiup Reservoir.

Fishing tip: Kokanee salmon in the lake scatter early in the season, then school in June. In spring, focus on shallow flats, then on river channel as the water warms. Daily limit is 25 kokanee. Good numbers of brown trout also are available.

Soda Creek FREE
Deschutes National Forest
26.2 mi W of Bend on CR 46; at Sparks Lake. Free. 5/1-10/15; 14-day limit. 10 RV/tent sites; 30-ft RV limit. Tbls, toilets, cfga, no drkg wtr. Hiking, fly fishing, boating (no mtrs), hiking trails.

Fishing tip: Once stocked with brook trout that are now up to 18 inches, Sparks Lake is being developed into cutthroat trout waters.

South Campground $6
Deschutes National Forest
33 mi W of Bend on CR 46; 1.2 mi N on FR 4625. $6. About MD-10/31; 14-day limit. 23 sites (26-ft RV limit). Tbls, toilets, cfga, no drkg wtr. Picnicking, fishing, boating (l). Elev 4900 ft.

Fishing tip: It's fly fishing only at Hosmer Lake, which is stocked with rainbow trout.

Sparks Lake Trailhead $5
Deschutes National Forest
31 mi W of Bend on CR 46; S side of rd. Camp free with $30 annual forest pass; $5 daily otherwise. 5/30-10/15. Boat-in dispersed camping. Tbls, toilets, no drkg wtr. Hiking, fly fishing, boating (no motors). Scenic. Elev 5000 ft.

Fishing tip: Fish this lake by canoe or small boat, and you'll catch plenty of brook trout (and a few cutthroat) up to 18 inches. The south pool and channel between the two lake sections are best producers. Use Mickey Finn flies as well as caddis, Adams and humpy patterns.

Swamp Wells Horse Camp FREE
Deschutes National Forest
4 mi S of Bend on US 97; 5.4 mi SE on CR 18; 5.8 mi S on FR 1810; 3.2 mi SE on FR 1816. Free. 5/150-10/30; 14-day limit. 6 primitive sites (30-ft RV limit). Tbls, cfga, toilets, no drkg wtr. Hiking trails, horseback riding. Nearby Arnold Ice Cave lava tubes.

Todd Creek $5
Trailhead & Horse Camp
Deschutes National Forest
24 mi W of Bend on CR 46; 0.6 mi S on FR 4600-390. $5 daily or $30 annual forest pass. Primitive undesignated camping area. Toilets, cfga, no drkg wtr. Horseback riding, hiking, mountain biking.

Todd Lake Trailhead $5
Deschutes National Forest
24 mi W of Bend on CR 46; .4 mi NE on FR 370; .3 mi NW on trail. Hike in. Free for those with $30 annual forest pass; $5 daily otherwise. 7/1-9/15; 14-day limit. 11 tent sites. Tbls, toilets, cfga, no drkg wtr. Hiking; picnicking; fishing; mountain climbing; canoeing, boating(no motors); horseback riding. Access point to Three Sisters Wilderness. Elev 6200 ft; 10 acres. Scenic.

Fishing tip: Todd Lake has good brook trout fishing, especially early in the year. Stocked annually, they average 8-10 inches, but holdover fish are up to 15 inches. It's a good lake for flyfishing with a tube rig.

West Cultus $5
Deschutes National Forest
44.3 mi SW of Bend on CR 46; 1.5 mi W on FR 3635; 2.5 mi across Cultus Lake by boat or trail (on W shore). Camp free with $30 annual forest pass; $5 daily otherwise. 6/1-9/15; 14-day limit. 12 tent sites. Tbls, toilet, cfga, no drkg wtr. Picnicking, fishing, hiking, boating, swimming.

Fishing tip: For lake trout, troll flashers with Flatfish or crankbaits near dropoffs. Just after ice-out, try the shallows with dragonfly or leech patterns.

Wyeth $6
Deschutes National Forest
26 mi S of Bend on US 97; 8 mi W on FR 43; 1 mi S on FR 4370; at Deschutes River below Wickiup Reservoir. $6. 4/15-10/31; 14-day

limit. 3 sites; 26-ft RV limit. Tbls, toilet, cfga, no drkg wtr, horse facilities. Picnicking, fishing, horseback riding, boating(l). Elev 4300 ft; 2 acres.

Fishing tip: Although fishing in this section of the Deschutes cn be fabulous for rainbow & brown trout, the rainbow must be released unharmed. This area is managed as a spawning and recruitment area for Wickiup Reservoir fish.

BLUE RIVER (12)

Box Canyon Horse Camp   **FREE**
Willamette National Forest
3.5 mi E on US 126; 27 mi S on FR 19. Free. 4/15-11/15; 14-day limit. 14 sites (RVs under 22 ft). Tbls, toilets, cfga, no drkg wtr. Picnicking, hiking, horseback riding.

Cougar Creek   **$8**
Willamette National Forest
3.5 mi E of Blue River on SR 126; 1 mi S on FR 19 (Aufderheide Dr), keeping left; from stop sign, go 1.5 mi on FR 1900-410, then turn right; make immediate right into camp. $8. 5/10-9/11; 14-day limit. 2 sites. Tbls, toilets, cfga, no drkg wtr. Fishing, hiking. Elev 1200 tt.

Cougar Crossing   **$10**
Wilamette National Forest
3.5 mi E of Blue River on SR 126; 9.5 mi S on FR 19 (Aufderheide Rd). $10. Managed 5/10-12/31; reduced fees & services off-season. 14-day limit. 12 sites; 40-ft RV limit. Tbls, portable toilets, cfga, no drkg wtr. Hiking, swimming, fishing. At jct of South Fork of McKenzie River & S end of Cougar Reservoir.

Delta   **$12**
Willamette National Forest
3.5 mi E of Blue River on SR 126; qtr mi S on FR 19, then FR 400 to camp; at McKenzie River. $12. About 4/15-10/30; 14-day limit. 38 sites (40-ft RV limit). Tbls, toilets, drkg wtr, cfga, gray water sumps. Picnicking, fishing, hiking. 16 acres.

French Pete   **$12**
Willamette National Forest
3.5 mi E on SR 126; S on FR 19, on right side of dam. $12. 5/10-9/15; 14-day limit. 17 sites (40-ft RV limit). Tbls, toilets, cfga, drkg wtr, gray water sumps. 3 acres.

Frissell Crossing   **$10**
Willamette National Forest
3.5 mi E of Blue River on SR 126; 23 mi S on FR 19; at South Fork of McKenzie River. $10. About 5/15-9/15; 14-day limit. 12 sites (40-ft RV limit). Tbls, toilets, cfga, drkg wtr. Built 1934 by CCC. 2 acres; elev 2600 ft.

Homestead   **FREE**
Willamette National Forest
3.5 mi E of Blue River on US 126; 22 mi S on FR 19; on South Fork of McKenzie River. Free. All year; 14-day limit. 7 sites; 32-ft RV

limit. Tbls, toilets, cfga, no drkg wtr, no trash service. Fishing, swimming, boating, hunting, picnicking. Near Cougar Reservoir.

Lookout Campground   **$8**
Willamette National Forest
3.5 mi E of Blue River on SR 126; 3 mi N on FR 15. $8. 4/20-9/30; 14-day limit. 20 sites; 40-ft RV limit. Tbls, toilets, cfga, drkg wtr, gray wtr sump. Boating(l), fishing. On NE shore of Blue River Reservoir.

Red Diamond   **$10**
Willamette National Forest
3.5 mi E of Blue River on SR 126, then follow FR 19 for 15 mi. $10. About 5/15-9/15; 14-day limit. 3 sites; 32-ft RV limit. Tbls, portable toilet, cfga, no drkg wtr. Fishing, hiking.

Slide Creek   **$7**
Willamette National Forest
3.5 mi E of Blue River on SR 126; 11.6 mi S on FR 19; 1.5 mi N on FR 500. $7 with federal Senior Pass; others pay $14. Managed 5/10-9/15; 14-day limit. 16 sites (40-ft RV limit). Tbls, toilets, cfga, drkg wtr. Boating, fishing, hiking. 3 acres.

Sunnyside Camp   **$12**
Willamette National Forest
3.5 mi E of Blue River on SR 126; 9.5 mi S on FR 19; left on FR 1900-500 for qtr mi; on SE side of Cougar Reservoir. $12. About 5/15-9/15; 14-day limit. 13 sites; 36-ft RV limit. Tbls, toilets, cfga, no drkg wtr. Fishing, boating, hiking. Steep entrance rd; large RVs not recommended.

BLY (13)

Corral Creek Forest Camp   **FREE**
Fremont National Forest
13 mi SE of Bly on SR 140; left on FR 3660 for 13 mi; right on FR 34 for one-eight mi, then left on FR 012. Maintained 5/15-10/15; 14-day limit. 6 sites. Tbls, toilets, cfga, no drkg wtr, no trash service. Box-style horse stalls. Birdwatching, hiking, horseback riding, fishing.

Deming Creek Trailhead   **FREE**
Fremont National Forest
1 mi E of Bly on SR 140; left on Campbell Rd for half mi, then 4 mi on FR 34; left on FR 335 for 2 mi; follow FR 018 for 2.7 mi to trailhead. Free. 6/15-10/15; 14-day limit. Undesignated dispersed sites; no facilities, no drkg wtr. Hiking, horseback riding, fishing, birdwatching. Accesses Gearhard Mountain Wilderness.

Horseglade Trailhead   **FREE**
Fremont National Forest
3.5 mi W of Bly to Ivory Pine County Rd, then continue 12 mi NE; 1.5 mi W on FR 27; at Five Mile Creek. Free. Maintained 6/1-10/30; 14-day limit. 2 sites. Tbls, toilets, cfga, no drkg wtr. Birdwatching, fishing, hiking.

Lofton Reservoir   **FREE**
Fremont National Forest
13 mi SE of Bly on SR 140; 7 mi S on FR 3715; 1.3 mi NE on FR 013. Free. 5/1-10/31; 14-day limit. 26 sites (22-ft RV limit). Tbls, toilets, cfga, drkg wtr, gray water dump, accessible fishing pier. Boating(l; no motors), fishing, birdwatching, swimming. On Little Lofton Lake. 8 acres. Elev 6200 ft.

Fishing tip: Lofton Reservoir is stocked each year with both catchable size and trophy size rainbow trout.

BROOKINGS (14)

Alfred A. Loeb State Park   **$12**
10 mi NE of Brookings off US 101; near Chetco River. $12 for 48 sites with elec off-season; $16 during 5/1-9/30; 10-day limit. 40-ft RV limit. Tbls, flsuh toilets, showers, cfga, drkg wtr, beach. Swimming, boating, birdwatching, nature programs, fishing. Three-fourths mi hike to nation's northern-most redwood grove.

First Camp   **$5**
Siskiyou National Forest
5.6 mi SE of Brookings on US 101; 6.3 mi NE on CR 896; E on FR 1107 just before Winchuck Campground; at Winchuck River. $5 at self-service fee station; $8 if collected by ranger. 5/15-9/15; 14-day limit. Tbls, cfga, toilets. Fishing, swimming, floating.

Little Redwood   **$10**
Siskiyou National Forest
Half mi S of Brookings on US 101; 7.5 mi NE on CR 784; 6 mi NE on FR 1376. On the Cheto River. $10. 5/15-9/30; 14-day limit. 12 sites (16-ft RV limit). Tbls, toilets, cfga, drkg wtr, grey wtr dumps. Fishing (good trout), swimming, hiking trail. 2 acres.

Ludlum Recreation Area   **$10**
Siskiyou National Forest
5.6 mi SE of Brookings on US 101; 6.3 mi NE on CR 896; 1 mi E on FR 1107, then 2 mi on FR 1108; at Wheeler Creek & Winchuck River. $10. 5/15-10/15; 14-day limit. 7 sites. Tbls, toilets, cfga, drkg wtr. Hiking, swimming, fishing. New campground.

Miller Bar   **$5**
Half mi S of Brookings on US 101; 7.5 mi NE on CR 784 (becomes FR 1376); 2 mi past forest boundary; at the Cheto River. $5 at self-service fee station; $8 if ranger collects. 5/15-10/15; 14-day limit. Undesignated RV/ tent sites. Tbls, toilets, cfga, no drkg wtr. Fishing, swimming, floating.

Nook Bar   **$5**
Siskiyou National Forest
Half mi S of Brookings on US 101; 7.5 mi NE on CR 784 (becomes FR 1376); 3 mi past forest boundary; at the Cheto River. $5 at self-service fee station; $8 if ranger collects. 5/15-10/15; 14-day limit. Undesignated RV/ tent sites. Tbls, toilets, cfga, no drkg wtr. Fishing, swimming, floating.

Redwood Bar $5
Siskiyou National Forest
Half mi S of Brookings on US 101; 7.5 mi NE on CR 784 (becomes FR 1376); 6 mi past forest boundary, just past Little Redwood Camp; at the Cheto River. $5 at self-service fee station; $8 if ranger collects. 5/15-10/15; 14-day limit. Undesignated RV/tent sites. Tbls, toilets, cfga, no drkg wtr (but planned). Fishing, swimming, floating, hiking.

South Fork Camps $5
Siskiyou National Forest
Half mi S of Brookings on US 101; 7.5 mi NE on CR 784 (becomes FR 1376); 8 mi past forest boundary, just past Redwood Bar Camp; at the South Fork of Cheto River. $5 at self-service fee station; $8 if ranger collects. 5/15-10/15; 14-day limit. Upper & Lower South Fork Campgrounds. Undesignated RV/tent sites. Toilets, cfga, no drkg wtr. Fishing, swimming, floating, hiking.

Winchuck $10
Siskiyou National Forest
5.6 mi SE of Brookings on US 101; 6.3 mi NE on CR 896; 1 mi E on FR 1107; at Winchuck River. $10. 5/15-9/15; 14-day limit. 15 sites. Tbls, toilets, cfga, drkg wtr. Swimming, fishing. 5 acres. Handicap access.

BROTHERS (15)

Pine Mountain FREE
Deschutes National Forest
10 mi W on US 20; 7 mi S on FR 2017. Free. 5/15-10/30. 3 sites (RVs under 31 ft). Tbls, toilets, cfga, no drkg wtr. Picnicking, birdwatching. Elev 6200 ft; 2 acres. Qtr mi S of Pine Mountain Observatory.

BURNS (16)

Chickahominy Reservoir $8
Bureau of Land Management
Burns District
34 mi W of Burns on US 20 (5 mi W of Riley); on N side of hwy. Free or variable rates during Oct-Mar; $8 rest of year; 14-day limit. 28 sites; 35-ft RV limit. Tbls, toilets, cfga, drkg wtr. Boating(ld), fishing, fish cleaning station. No wtr during free period. Elev 4300 ft; 20 acres. Ice fishing in winter.
Fishing tip: This 530-acre lake has some great trout fishing. Stocked heavily, the trout grow quickly in the fertile water. Use bait (salmon eggs, nightcrawlers, power bait), fished near bottom, or leech and minnow pattern lures.

Crystal Crane $12
Hot Springs Campground
25 mi SE of Burns on Hwy 78; milepost 25.5. $12 for self-contained RVs or tents; $16 for RV sites with elec/wtr; $18 full hookups. 7 sites; 60-ft RV limit. Tbls, flush toilets, showers, cfga, drkg wtr, hookups($), hot pond. Horse corral & exercise area.

Harney County Fairgrounds $10
On S. Egan in Burns. $10 for tents; $12 for RVs. Tbls, toilets, cfga, drkg wtr, showers, elec, dump.

Idlewild $7
Malheur National Forest
17 mi N of Burns on US 395. $7. 5/15-10/15; 14-day limit. 23 sites (32-ft RV limit). Tbls, toilets, cfga, drkg wtr. Picnicking, fishing. Elev 5300 ft. 18 acres. Excellent stop for US 395 travelers.

Mann Lake FREE
Bureau of Land Management
Burns District
78 mi SE of Burns on SR 78; 22 mi S on Fields-Denio Rd (Harney CR 201); at Mann Lake. Free. All year; 14-day limit. Primitive undesignated sites; no facilities except cfga; 35-ft RV limit. Fishing, boating, swimming, hiking. Tents not recommended because of high winds. Elev 4200 ft.
Fishing tip: This lake has some great fishing and contains huge lahontan cutthroat trout with a minumum length limit of 16 inches. Biggest handicap her is battling the strong wind. Only artificial lures are allowed.

Riley Store Camping $5
29 mi W of Burns on US 20. $5 for tent sites; $8 for RVs without hookups; $12 with hookups. Tbls, toilets, cfga, drkg wtr, showers, store. Fees not verified for 2007.

Yellow Jacket $7
Malheur National Forest
1 mi S of Burns on US 20; 32 mi NW on FR 47; 4 mi E on FR 37; half mi S on FR 3745. $7. 5/15-10/15; 14-day limit. 20 sites (22-ft RV limit). Tbls, toilets, cfga, drkg wtr. Hunting, fishing, boating(l; no motors). Elev 4800 ft. Adjacent to Yellow Jacket Reservoir.
Fishing tip: Most planted rainbows here are 8-15 inches, but some run up to 20 inches. Both float-tubers and shore anglers enjoy success with streamers, nightcrawlers and salmon eggs. Summer is quite productive for fly fishermen, although spring and fall produce the best catches.

BUTTE FALLS (17)

Fourbit Ford $10
Rogue River National Forest
9.3 mi SE of Butte Falls on CR 30; 1.2 mi NE on FR 3065. $10 (2nd RV, $5). 5/15-10/31; 14-day limit. 7 tent sites. Tbls, toilets, cfga, drkg wtr. Fishing. Secluded, on Fourbit Creek.

Snowshoe FREE
Rogue River National Forest
9.3 mi SE of Butte Falls on FR 30; 4.8 mi NE on FR 3065. Free. 5/1-10/31. 5 sites. Tbls, toilets, cfga, firewood, well drkg wtr. Picnicking; fishing (3 mi). Elev 4000 ft; 3 acres.

Whiskey Springs $10
Rogue River National Forest
9.3 mi SE of Butte Falls on CR 30; qtr mi E on FR 3317. $10 (2nd RV $5). 5/15-10/30; 14-day limit. 36 sites (30-ft RV limit). Tbls, toilets, cfga, drkg wtr. Fishing, hiking trails. Elev 3200 ft; 40 acres.

CAMBRIDGE (IDAHO) (18)

Copperfield Park $10
Idaho Power Company
Hwy 71 from Cambridge to Oxbow, Oregon; right on OR 86. $10 tent sites ($5 Nov-Mar); $16 RVs ($8 Nov-Mar). All year; 14-day limit. 62 sites (50-ft RV limit). Tbls, flush toilets, cfga, drkg wtr, dump, elec($), showers. Hiking, fishing.

Hells Canyon Park $10
Idaho Power Company
Hwy 71 from Cambridge toward Brownlee Dam; right just before crossing Snake River Bridge; half mi N. $10 base. All year; 14-day limit. Base fee for tents; $16 for RVs Apr-Oct; $8 for RVs & $5 tents rest of year. 24 RV sites (40-ft RV limit) & 30 tent sites. Tbls, flush toilets, showers, drkg wtr, dump, elec($). Handicap access. Fishing, hiking, boating(ld), hunting.

McCormick Park $10
Idaho Power Company
28 mi N of Cambridge on Hwy 71 to Snake River; follow signs (on Idaho side of Oxbow Reservoir). $10 base. All year; 14-day limit. Base fee for tent sites; RV sites $16 Apr-Oct; $8 for RVs & $5 for tents rest of yr. 34 sites (30-ft RV limit). Tbls, flush toilets, showers, drkg wtr, cfga, elec/wtr, dump. Fishing, swimming, boating (ld). 12 acres.

Woodhead Park $10
Idaho Power Company
Hwy 71 from Cambridge toward Brownlee Dam; half mi before reaching dam. $10 base. All year; 14-day limit. Base fee for tent sites; $16 for RVs Apr-Oct; $8 for RVs & $5 tents rest of year. 124 sites; 40-ft RV limit. Tbls, flush toilets, drkg wtr, elec, showers, cfga, dump. Handicap access. Hiking, fishing, boating. 65 acres.

CAMP SHERMAN (19)

Candle Creek $10
Deschutes National Forest
10 mi N of Camp Sherman on FR 12; 1.6 mi N on FR 1200-980; on Candle Creek at Metolius River. $10. 4/15-10/15; 14-day limit. 10 RV/tent sites (RVs under 25 ft). Tbls, toilets, cfga, no drkg wtr. Picnicking; fly fishing; hiking trails. Elev 2600 ft.
Fishing tip: This river contains bull trout, but only hatchery rainbow, kokanee salmon & whitefish may be caught. Follow trails from the campground & along the river, wading and bank fishing only with flies and barbless hooks.

Canyon Creek $10
Deschutes National Forest
5 mi N of Camp Sherman on FR 1420; on W side of Metolius River. $10. 4/15-10/15; 14-day limit. 7 sites (RVs under 21 ft). Tbls, toilets, cfga, no drkg wtr. Picnicking; fly fishing; hiking.

Jack Creek $10
Deschutes National Forest
2 mi N of Camp Sherman on FR 1420; 3 mi NW on FR 12; half mi W on FR 1230. $10. 4/15-10/15; 14-day limit. 11 sites (40-ft RV limit). Tbls, toilets cfga, no drkg wtr. Picnicking; fishing; hiking. Elev 3100 ft.

Jack Lake Trailhead $5
Deschutes National Forest
2 mi N of Camp Sherman on FR 1420; 3 mi W on FR 12; 1.7 mi NW on FR 1230; 6.2 mi NW on FR 1234. Free for those with $30 annual forest pass; $5 daily otherwise. 6/15-10/15; 14-day limit. 2 tent sites. Tbls, toilet, cfga, no drkg wtr, horse facilities. Picnicking, fishing, hiking. Trailhead into Mt Jefferson Wilderness.

Riverside $10
Deschutes National Forest
2 mi S of Camp Sherman on FR 900; on Metolius River. $10. 4/15-10/15; 7-day limit. 16 walk-in tent sites. Tbls, toilets, cfga, drkg wtr. Fishing, hiking trails. Concessionaire operated.

CANNON BEACH (20)

Saddle Mountain $9
State Natural Area
E from Cannon Beach on US 26 to Necanicum Junction; 8 mi N on park entrance rd. $9 ($6 off-season). 10-day limit in any 14-day period. 10 primitive tent sites; RVs restricted to parking area. Tbls, flush toilets, cfga, drkg wtr. Picnicking, hiking trail. Rare plants. 2,922 acres.

CARLTON (21)

Alder Glen $10
Bureau of Land Management
Salem District
21 mi W of Carlton on Nestucca access rd; or, off US 101, 18 mi NE of Alder Glen. $10. About 4/6-11/30; 14-day limit. 10 sites on 5 acres (RVs under 27 ft). Tbls, toilets, cfga, drkg wtr. Hunting, fishing, swimming.

Dovre $10
Tillamook Resource Area
Bureau of Land Management
Salem District
14 mi W of Carlton on Nestuca access rd. $10. About 4/6-11/30; 14-day limit. 9 sites (RVs under 25 ft). Tbls, toilets, cfga, drkg wtr, shelter. Swimming, picnicking, fishing.

Fan Creek $10
Bureau of Land Management
Tillamook Resource Area
Salem District
16 mi W of Carlton on Nestucca access rd. All year; 7-day limit. $10. 11 sites (RVs under 25 ft). Tbls, toilets, cfga, drkg wtr. Swimming, picnicking, fishing.

CASCADE LOCKS (22)

Cascade Locks $10
City Marine Park
Half mi E of Cascade Locks on I-84; half mi E on exit 42. $10. All year; 14-day limit. 45 sites (32-ft RV limit). Flush toilets, tbls, cfga, drkg wtr, dump, showers, playground. Picnicking, swimming, boating(l), fishing.

Eagle Creek $10
Columbia River Gorge
National Scenic Area
Mt. Hood National Forest
2 mi W of Cascade Locks on I-84; from Bonneville exit, under hwy, up hill through picnic area. $10. About 5/15-10/15; 14-day limit. 20 sites (20-ft RV limit). Tbls, flush toilets, cfga, drkg wtr. Swimming, fishing, hiking (Eagle Creek Trail to Wahtum Lake, connects to Pacific Crest Trail), biking. 5 acres. Built in 1945, this is considered the first forest service campground in America. It features the first restroom with flush toilets built by the forest service.

Herman Creek Horse Camp $8
Columbia River Gorge
National Scenic Area
Mt. Hood National Forest
1.5 mi E of Cascade Locks on I-84. $8. About 5/1-10/15; 14-day limit. 7 sites (22-ft RV limit). Tbls, toilets, cfga, drkg wtr. Horse facilities. Dump & showers nearby. Hiking, fishing, boating, biking.

Wyeth Campground $10
Columbia River Gorge
National Scenic Area
Mt. Hood National Forest
7 mi E of Cascade Locks on I-84 to Wyeth exit; half mi W on county rd. $10. About 4/1-10/15; 14-day limit. 14 sites (30-ft RV limit). Flush toilets, tbls, cfga, drkg wtr. Swimming, hiking, fishing. 18 acres. Site of CCC camp in 1930s.

CAVE JUNCTION (24)

Bolan Lake $5
Siskiyou National Forest
Half mi S of Cave Junction on US 199 to O'Brien; 8 mi SE on CRs 5560; 7 mi SE on FR 48; 6 mi E on FR 4812. $5. Elev 5400 ft. 6/15-LD; 14-day limit. 12 sites on 3 acres (RVs under 16 ft). Tbls, toilets, cfga, no drkg wtr. Self-service site. Swimming; picnicking; fishing; boating(ld); hiking trail to Bolan Lake Trail.

Fishing tip: 12-acre Lake Bolan is stocked

with brook & rainbow trout; no outboard motors permitted.

Cave Creek $10
Siskiyou National Forest
16 mi E of Cave Junction on SR 46; 1 mi S on FR 4032 (narrow, curving rd not recommended for large RVs). $10. MD-LD; 14-day limit. 18 sites. Tbls, toilets, cfga, drkg wtr. Oregon Caves National Monument 4 mi. Hiking, fishing. Elev 2900 ft; 10 acres.

Grayback Campground $8
Siskiyou National Forest
12 mi E of Cave Junction on SR 46 (Oregon Caves Hwy); at Sucker Creek. $8 without hookups for holders of federal Senior Pass ($10 with hookups); others pay $16 & $20. MD-LD; 14-day limit. 39 sites (1 with hookups); 22-ft RV limit. Tbls, flush toilets, cfga, drkg wtr, grey wtr dumps. Swimming, fishing, hiking (1-mi loop trail). Oregon Caves National Monument 10 mi. Built by CCC in 1930s.

CHEMULT (25)

Corral Springs FREE
Winema National Forest
2.7 mi N of Chemult on US 97; 1.9 mi W on FR 9774 (Corral Springs Rd). Free. 5/15-10/15; 14-day limit. 6 sites (RVs up to 50 ft). Tbls, toilets, cfga, firewood, no drkg wtr. Mountain biking, hunting. Elev 4900 ft; 2 acres. Mosquitoes abound. Historic (explorer John C. Fremont probably camped there).

Digit Point $9
Winema National Forest
1 mi N of Chemult on US 97; 12 mi W on FR 9772 (Miller Lake Rd). $9. MD-9/15; 14-day limit. 64 sites (30-ft RV limit). Tbls, flush toilets, cfga, drkg wtr, dump. Swimming, fishing, boating(l), hiking, waterskiing. On Miller Lake. Elev 5600 ft; 10 acres.

Fishing tip: This lake is known for its brown trout fishing. It also contains rainbow trout and is somewhat over-populated with small kokanee salmon. Browns, however, feed on the kokanee and grow quite large, although averaging 16-18 inches. Troll shiny lures at 30-60 feet in summer.

Jackson Creek FREE
Winema National Forest
24.5 mi S of Chemult on US 97; 22.1 mi NE on CR 676 (Silver Lake Rd); 5.3 mi SE on FR 49. Free. 5/1-11/15; 14-day limit. 12 sites (RVs under 22 ft). Tbls, toilets, cfga, firewood, no drkg wtr. Picnicking; fishing. Elev 4600 ft; 3 acres. Yamsay Mountain Crater (10 mi).

Scott Creek FREE
Winema National Forest
24 mi S of Chemult on Hwy 97; 3 mi W on FR 66; 1.5 mi N on Sun Pass Rd; 2 mi W on FR 2310. Free. 6/1-10/15; 14-day limit. 6 sites. Toilets, tbls, cfga, no drkg wtr. Hunting, hiking. Elev 4700 ft.

OREGON

Walt Haring Snopark   **FREE**
Winema National Forest
Half mi N of Chemult on Miller Lake Rd (FR 9772) (half mi W of US 97). Free. All year; 14-day limit. 5 sites. Tbls, toilets, cfga, drkg wtr, dump. In winter, camp is starting point for skiing & snowmobile activities.

CHILOQUIN (26)

Head of the River   **FREE**
Winema National Forest
5 mi NE of Chiloquin on CR 858 (Sprague River Rd); 20 mi NE on Williamson River Rd; 1 mi N on FR 4648. Free. Elev 4400 ft. 6/1-10/15; 14-day limit. 5 sites (RVs under 32 ft). Tbls, toilets, cfga, firewood, no drkg wtr. Fishing.

Williamson River   **$6**
Winema National Forest
5.5 mi N of Chiloquin on US 97; 1 mi NE on FR 9730. $6. 6/1-10/31; 10-day limit. 7 RV sites (32-ft limit), 3 tent sites. Tbls, toilets, cfga, drkg wtr. Good trout fishing. Coin laundry.

Fishing tip: From its mouth upstream to Kirk bridge, Williamson River has excellent fishing for large, wild redband rainbow trout; fishing peaks during July, August and Sept. The section upstream from the bridge has good fishing for redbands too, and brook trout have been introduced there.

CHRISTMAS VALLEY (27)

Green Mountain Camp   **FREE**
Bureau of Land Management
Lakeview District
About 8 mi N of Christmas Valley on county & BLM rds following signs; near Green Mountain summit. All year; 14-day limit. About 4 primitive undesignated sites. Tbls, cfga, no toilets, no drkg wtr. Elev 5100 ft.

COOS BAY (28)

Charleston Marina RV Park   **$12**
From Charleston exit of US 101 at Coos Bay, 9 mi W on Cape Arago Hwy; after crossing Charleston-South Slough Bridge, go 2 blks N on Boat Basin Dr, then E 1 blk on Kingfisher Dr. $12 for tent sites; $21-23 for RV sites with hookups. All year. 110 sites. Tbls, flush toilets, cfga, drkg wtr, CATV, showers, coin laundry, dump, marina, playground. Boating(ldr), fishing, hiking, clamming, swimming.

Nesika   **$10**
Coos County Park
21 mi E of Eastside on county rds (about 5 mi W of Gold and Silver Falls State Park); at East Fork of Millicoma River. $10. 5/16-9/30; 10-day limit. 20 primitive sites. Toilets, cfga, no drkg wtr (tbls in picnic area). Fishing, swimming, hiking, picnicking. 77 acres.

Rooke-Higgins   **$10**
Coos County Park
12 mi E of Eastside on county rds, along North Fork of Coos River; at Millicoma River. $10. 5/16-9/30; 10-day limit. 20 primitive sites. Toilets, cfga, no drkg wtr. Swimming, boating(l), fishing. 26 acres.

COQUILLE (29)

Bear Creek   **FREE**
Bureau of Land Management
Coos Bay District
26 mi SE of Coquille on OR 42. Free. All year; 14-day limit. 17 sites on 26 acres (RVs under 16 ft). Tbls, toilets, cfga, firewood, drkg wtr. Picnicking; fishing; swimming; hiking.

Frona   **$10**
Coos County Park
9 mi NE of Coquille to Fairview; 9 mi E on Coos Bay Wagon Rd; at East Fork of Coquille River. $10. 5/16-9/30; 10-day limit. 15 primitive sites (scattered). Toilets, tbls, cfga, no drkg wtr. Fishing, rockhounding. 77 acres.

Ham Bunch   **$10**
Cherry Creek, Coos County Park
9 mi NE of Coquille to Fairview; 7 mi E on Coos Bay Wagon Rd; at Cherry Creek. $10. 5/16-9/30; 10-day limit. 10 primitive sites. Tbls, toilets, cfga, no drkg wtr. Fishing, wading pool, rockhounding. 2 acres.

Laverne   **$10**
Coos County Park
N to Fairview, then 5 mi N on county rds; at North Fork of Coquille River. $10 without hookups, $12 with hookups during 10/1-5/15; $11 without hookups & $16 with hookups during 5/16-9/30. 10-day limit. 76 sites. Tbls, flush toilets, cfga, drkg wtr, showers($), portable dump, elec($). Swimming, playground, fishing, volleyball, horseshoes. 350 acres.

Park Creek   **FREE**
Bureau of Land Management
Coos Bay District
24 mi E of Coquille on Middle Cove Rd. Free. All year; 14-day limit. 15 shaded sites; 8 acres. Tbls, toilets, cfga, drkg wtr. Picnicking; fishing; hunting; berry picking. Park Creek & Middle Creek. Myrtlewood grove.

COTTAGE GROVE (31)

Crawfish Lake Dispersed   **FREE**
Umpqua National Forest
From Cottage Grove Ranger Station, 17 mi E on Row River Rd 2400; stay to the right on Brice Creek Rd 2470 for 4.1 mi; right on Adams Mtn Rd 2240 (FR 2234) for 8 mi to trailhead on left. Half mi trail descends steeply from trailhead to lake shore. Free. 2 primitive tent sites; cfga, no other facilities. Fishing (cutthroat trout), picnicking, hiking. Dump 17 mi NW at Boyd's Market in Culp

Creek. Recreational gold panning permitted along Brice Creek.

Pine Meadows   **$9**
Corps of Engineers
Cottage Grove Lake
Approx 7 mi E of Cottage Grove on CR 2700 (London Rd); follow signs to Pine Meadow Campground; from lake, primitive area is approx quarter mi S of Pine Meadow Campground. $9 for 15 primitive sites, $15 for 92 RV sites ($4.50 & $7.50 with federal Senior Pass). 5/15-9/15; 14-day limit. 65-ft RVs. Tbls, toilets, cfga, drkg wtr, playground, beach, dump, showers, pier. Swimming; boating(l); fishing; picnicking nearby. 2-night minimum stay on weekends.

Schwarz Campground   **$6.50**
Corps of Engineers
Dorena Lake
Exit 174 off I-5, E of Cottage Grove 5.2 mi; 4 mi E of information center on Row River Rd; take Y (Gov't Rd) to right. Park on left. $6.50 with federal Senior Pass; others pay $13. About 5/1-9/30; 14-day limit. 78 sites; 65-ft RVs. Dump, drkg wtr, solar hot showers, flush toilets. Lots of room. Fishing, swimming, boating, hiking trails. 2-night minimum stay on weekends.

COUNCIL (32)

Black Lake   **FREE**
Wallowa-Whitman National Forest
40 mi N of Council on FRs 002, 105, 112 (steep, gravel; no RVs). Free. May-Oct; 14-day limit. 4 tent sites. Tbls, toilets, cfga, no drkg wtr. Fishing, hiking.

CRATER LAKE (33)

Lost Creek Campground   **$10**
Crater Lake National Park
From the main Rim Drive, approx 3 mi SE on Branch Rd (follow signs toward "The Pinnacles"). $10. 7/1-9/1 (depending on the weather); 14-day limit. 16 tent sites. Toilets, cfga, drkg wtr. Store (Rim Village). Gas near park headquarters. Hiking; fishing (no fishing license required in park); no hunting. Elev 5972 ft. Grayback Motor Nature Rd begins here. $10 entry fee charged for 7 days but proposed to increase to $20.

CRESCENT (34)

Boundary Springs   **FREE**
Dispersed Camp
Deschutes National Forest
2 miS of Crescent on Hwy 97; 6 mi on FR 9768; 1 mi on FR 9768-600. Free. All year; 14-day limit. 4 primitive sites; 50-ft RV limit. Toilet, cfga, no tbls, no drkg wtr, no trash service.

Crescent Creek $11
Deschutes National Forest

8.2 mi W of Crescent on CR 61. $11. 5/15-10/31; 14-day limit. 10 sites (50-ft RV limit). Tbls, toilets, cfga, drkg wtr. Boating(lr), fishing, swimming. Elev 4500 ft.

Fishing tip: Crescent Creek is only lightly fished, and this stretch of stream has the best fishing. It contains naturally producing rainbow & brown trout as well as whitefish. Rainbows must be returned (bait is not allowed). To catch browns, fish streamers around the undercut banks.

Cy Bingham $5
Klamath County Park

Half mi W of Crescent on Crescent Cutoff Rd. $5. 5/1-10/31; 14-day limit. 10 sites. Tbls, toilets, cfga, drkg wtr. 2.5 acres.

East Davis Lake $9
Deschutes National Forest

9 mi W of Crescent on CR 61; 6.5 mi N on FR 46; 1.5 mi W on FR 855. $9 (premium sites $11). About 4/15-10/31; 14-day limit. 30 sites (24-ft RV limit). Tbls, toilets, cfga, drkg wtr. Hiking, fly fishing, boating, swimming.

Fishing tip: Davis Lake is one of the most popular fly fishing lakes in the Northwest. It produces numerous trophy rainbow trout, although most fish are in the 2-5 pound range. The lake also contains largemouth bass, which were introduced illegally in 1995. Only fly fishing is permitted, even for the bass.

Lava Flow South FREE
Deschutes National Forest

8.8 mi W of Crescent on CR 61; 7.7 mi N on CR 46; 1.8 mi N on FR 4600-850. Free. Open only 9/1-12/31 for wildlife protection, although a few sites at N end are not in the closure area; 14-day limit. 6 sites (22-ft RV limit). Tbls, toilets, cfga, no drkg wtr, no trash service. Boating(l), fishing, bird watching, waterskiing, windsurfing, swimming, sailing. On E shore of Davis Lake. Lava formation. Elev 4400 ft. Due to fire destruction of campsites on Davis Lake in 2003, this campground will eventually be developed into a fee area with 25 sites.

Fishing tip: Boat or float tube needed to reach the best areas because lakeshore is primarily reeds, grass, muddy bottom. Boat ramp on NE corner of lake my be closed due to nesting eagles; use primitive ramp at West Davis Camp. 3,906-acre lake.

CRESCENT LAKE (35)

Crescent Lake $6.50
Deschutes National Forest

2.7 mi SW of Crescent Lake on FR 60. $6.50 with federal Senior Pass ($7.50 at premium sites; others pay $13 & $15. 5/15-10/15; 14-day limit. Free in fall before weather closes access. 47 sites (22-ft RV limit). Tbls, toilets, cfga, drkg wtr. Swimming, boating(ld), fishing, waterskiing, hiking trail into Diamond

Peak Wilderness and to Odell Lake. 20 acres. Elev 4850 ft.

Fishing tip: June, July & Aug are best times to catch trout. Before July, use Flatfish & crankbaits. After July, use downriggers to catch them deep. An effective way to catch trout from Crescent Lake is top drop bait off the underwater ledges near Contorta Point.

Odell Creek $11
Deschutes National Forest

1.5 mi NW of Crescent Lake on SR 58; half mi SW on FR 2317. $11. 5/15-10/15; 14-day limit. Free in fall before weather closes access. 22 sites (22-ft RV limit). Tbls, toilets, cfga, no drkg wtr. Boating(lr), fishing, hiking trails to other lakes, windsurfing. Elev 4800 ft; 10 acres. On shore of Odell Lake.

Fishing tip: Average depth of Odell Lake is 132 ft, so lake trout (mackinaw) & bull trout thrive. The 3,562-acre lake also contains rainbow trout, kokanee salmon & whitefish. Odell Creek is catch-and-release, and fishing is restricted to flies and lures.

Pebble Bay Boat-in Camp FREE
Deschutes National Forest

5.4 mi NW of Crescent Lake on SR 58 to Princess Creek Campground; BOAT across Odell Lake to S shore. Free. 6/1-9/30; 14-day limit. 2 sites. Tbls, toilets, cfga, no drkg wtr. Picnicking, fishing, swimming boating, mountain climbing, hiking. Elev 4800 ft.

Princess Creek $12
Deschutes National Forest

5.5 mi NW of Crescent Lake on SR 58. $12 (premium lakeside sites $14). 5/15-10/15; 14-day limit. Free in fall before weather closes access. 46 sites (22-ft RV limit). Tbls, toilets, cfga, no drkg wtr. Fishing, swimming, waterskiing, boating. Elev 4800 ft; 20 acres. On E shore of Odell Lake.

Fishing tip: Oregon's last 2 state record lake trout were caught here. Current record, 40 pounds 8 inches, was caught in 1984. Bull trout are listed as threatened and therefore cannot be caught. Lake open late Apr to 10/31.

Spring $6.50
Deschutes National Forest

8 mi SW of Crescent Lake on FR 60; NE on FR 260. $6.50 with federal Senior Pass (premium sites $7.5); others pay $13 & $15. 6/10-10/15; 14-day limit. Free in fall before weather closes access. 68 sites (30-ft RV limit). Tbls, toilets, cfga, drkg wtr. Swimming, fishing, waterskiing, hiking. On S shore of Crescent Lake. Elev 4800 ft; 18 acres.

Fishing tip: Crescent Lake contains kokanee salmon, mountain whitefish and lake, rainbow and brown trout.

Summit Lake FREE
Deschutes National Forest

7.3 mi SW of Crescent Lake on CR 60; 6.7 mi on FR 6010 (high-clearance vehicles suggested). Free. 7/1-9/30; 14-day limit. 3 sites (RVs under 22 ft). Tbls, toilets, cfga, no drkg

wtr, no trash service. Picnicking; swimming; fishing; boating; mountain climbing; hiking. Elev 5600 ft; 3 acres. Access to Pacific Crest Trail (200 yds). On N shore of Summit Lake. Diamond Peak Wilderness(1 mi).

Sunset Cove $6.50
Deschutes National Forest

2.5 mi NW of Crescent Lake on SR 58. $6.50 with federal Senior Pass; others pay $13. 4/30-10/31; 14-day limit. Free in fall before weather closes access. 20 sites (30-ft RV limit). Tbls, toilets, cfga, drkg wtr, fish cleaning station. Boating(rl), fishing, waterskiing, hiking, windsurfing. On SE shore of Odell Lake.

Fishing tip: Open late Apr to 10/31, Odell Lake contains kokanee salmon, whitefish, rainbow, lake & bull trout.

Trapper Creek $6.50
Deschutes National Forest

7 mi NW of Crescent Lake on Hwy 58; 1.7 mi SW on FR 5810. $6.50 with federal Senior Pass; (premium lakeside sites $7.50); others pay $13 & $15. 6/1-10/15; 14-day limit. Free in fall before weather closes access. 32 sites (30-ft RV limit). Tbls, toilets, cfga, drkg wtr. Fishing, boating, swimming, hiking, berry picking. E shore of Odell Lake.

Fishing tip: Fishing not allowed within 200 ft of the mouth of Trapper Creed 9/1-10/31. Catch trout & salmon by trolling, jigging, still fishing, fly fishing or casting spinners and lures. The best baits are corn, worms, crayfish and salmon eggs.

Whitefish Horse Camp $6.50
Deschutes National Forest

8 mi SW of Crescent Lake on FR 60. $6.50 with federal Senior Pass for 14 sites with 2 horse stalls; $7.50 with Senior Pass for 3 sites with 4 stalls; others pay $13 & $15, respectively. 6/1-10/15; 14-day limit. Free in fall before weather closes access. 17 sites; equestrians only. Tbls, toilets, cfga, drkg wtr. Equestrian facilities. Reservations required (877-444-6777). At W end of Crescent Lake. Swimming, hiking trails. 30 acres. Concessionaire operated.

Fishing tip: Crescent Lake is a popular fishing lake for kokanee salmon, rainbow, brown and lake trout. Lake trout are typically 5-10 pounds, with an occasional 30-pounder landed. The lake's record is a 30-pound laker caught in 1993.

CULP CREEK (36)

Boy Scout Camp FREE
Umpqua National Forest

4.3 mi SE of Culp Creek on CR 2400; about 6 mi E on CR 2470 (Brice Creek Rd); left on spur rd 2200-767, drive or wade across Brice Creek; not suggested for low-clearance vehicles. Also small site on rd side of creek below Brice Creek Rd. Free. All year; 14-day limit. Primitive undesignated sites. No facilities except cfga. Fishing, swimming, hiking.

Cedar Creek **$6**
Umpqua National Forest
4.3 mi SE of Culp Creek on CR 2400; 4.6 mi SE on CR 2470; .1 mi N on FR 448. $6. Open all year but managed 4/15-11/30; 14-day limit. 8 sites (16-ft RV limit). Tbls, toilet, cfga. no drkg wtr, gray water sumps. Picnicking, hiking, fishing, swimming. 3 waste water sumps. Brice Creek. Gold panning, swimming, hiking on Crawfish Trail (1 mi E). Dump 10 mi W at Boyd's Market, Culp Creek. Moderate use on weekends.

Emerald Pool **FREE**
Dispersed Area
Umpqua National Forest
4.3 mi SE of Culp Creek on CR 2400; 2.4 mi SE on CR 2470 (Brice Creek Rd); right on FR 2200-124 for 1.5 mi. Free. All year; 21-day limit. Primitive camping areas along rd near swimming hole known as Emerald Pool. No facilities except cfga. Swiming, fishing, picnicking. 50 acres.

Gleason's Cabin **FREE**
Dispersed Area
Umpqua National Forest
4.3 mi SE of Culp Creek on CR 2400; 4 mi SE on CR 2470; left on FR 2200-737 through large flat area. Rd spur not recommended for RVs. Trails along Brice Creek to several other primitive tent sites. Free. No facilities. Gold panning, fishing, swimming.

Hobo Dispersed Camp **FREE**
Umpqua National Forest
4.3 mi SE of Culp Creek on CR 2400; 7.5 mi SE on CR 2470 (Brice Creek Rd); on both sides of rd. Free. 5/25-9/30; 1-day limit. 2 undeveloped sites for 2-4 RVs; 16-ft RV limit. Tbl, toilet, cfga. Picnicking, hiking. Above Brice Creek. Used by day-use swimmers & picnickers. Adams Mountain Way Trail half mi W on S side of FR 2470. Gold panning. Dump 12 mi W at Boyd's Market, Culp Creek.

Lund Park **$6**
Umpqua National Forest
4.3 mi SE of Culp Creek on CR 2400 (Row River Rd); 6.3 mi E on CR 2470 (Brice Creek Rd). $6. Managed 5/25-9/30, but open all year; 14-day limit. 3 sites on 6 acres & 2 dispersed sites (RVs under 16 ft). Tbls, toilets, cfga, no drkg wtr. Store, gas (4 mi). Picnicking; berry picnicking; swimming; fishing. Brice Creek. Dump station 11 mi W at Boyd's Market, Culp Creek.
Travel tip: Park is a point of interest along the historic Tour of the Golden Past auto tour. It once was stopover for miners traveling from Cottage Grove to the Bohemia mining area; in early 1900s, it was site of post office, hotel, dam, power house, other buildings. Only power house foundation remains. Adams Mountain Way Trail nearby. Recreational gold panning permitted.

Mineral Camp **FREE**
Umpqua National Forest
12 mi SE of Culp Creek on CR 2460; at

Sharps Creek. Free. MD-9/30; 14-day limit. 2 tent sites. Tbls, toilets, cfga, no drkg wtr. Hiking, picnicking, rockhounding. Hardscrabble Grade nearby. Once a stopover place for miners before starting up steep grade to the Bohemia Mining Area.

Rujada **$8**
Umpqua National Forest
4.3 mi E of Culp Creek on CR 202; 2 mi NE on FR 2143; .1 mi S on FR 2148; on terrace above Laying Creek. $8. MD-9/30; 14-day limit. 11 sites (RVs under 22 ft); 10 picnic sites. Tbls, flush & pit toilets, cfga, elec in restrooms, piped drkg wtr, 4 waste water sumps. Picnicking, berry-picking, swimming, fishing, horseshoe pits. Elev 1200 ft; 9 acres. Flat grass area for field games. Swordfern Trail. Dump at Boyd's Market, Culp Creek.

Saddle Camp Shelter **FREE**
Umpqua National Forest
10.5 mi SE of Culp Creek on CR 2460 (Sharps Creek Rd); right on BLM Clark Creek Rd 22-1-12 for .7 mi; left across bridge to FR 23 for 5.1 mi; left on FR 2358 for 2.5 mi; hike Bohemia National Recreation Trail 1.5 mi E from trailhead. Free. All year; 14-day limit. Shelter is 3-sided pole & shake structure 12x15 ft (cira 1930); contains elevated bunk, tbls, firepit. Boil wtr before drinking. Hiking, hunting.

Sharps Creek **$8**
Bureau of Land Management
Eugene District
5 mi S of Culp Creek on Sharps Creek County Rd. $8. 5/15-10/15; 14-day limit. 10 sites. Tbls, toilets, cfga, drkg wtr. Swimming, fishing. 1200 acres.

Twin Rocks Shelter **FREE**
Umpqua National Forest
10.5 mi SE of Culp Creek on CR 2460 (Sharps Creek Rd) to end of paved section; continue on 4.7 mi (rough & steep); right on CR 2358 for 3 mi to Bohemia National Recreation Trail; hike 1 mi S along trail. Free. All year; 14-day limit. 3-sided pole & shake shelter (circa 1930s) 12x12 ft with firepit & 4 elevated bunks. No other facilities. Hiking, berrypicking, hunting.

CULVER (37)

Monty **$12**
Deschutes National Forest
20 mi W of Culver on CR 63; 10 mi W on CR 64 (rough rd); at Metolius River. $12. 5/15-10/15; 14-day limit. 20 sites (20-ft RV limit). Tbls, toilets, cfga, no drkg wtr. Fishing, hiking, boating at Lake Billy Chinook. Elev 2000 ft; 10 acres. No access to campground 1/1-5/15 to protect bald eagles. Campground closed 10/1-5/15 because noise from campground has been shown to cause nesting failures.
Fishing tip: The Deschutes River nearby holds good numbers of brown and rainbow trout as well as whitefish.

CURTIN (38)

Pass Creek Park **$11**
Douglas County Park
Off I-5 exit 163 at Curtin. $11 without hookups, $14 with full hookups off-season Nov-Apr; $13 & $16 in-season. All year; 10-day limit. Tbls, flush toilets, cfga, drkg wtr. showers, playground, coin laundry. Fishing, hiking.

DALE (39)

Driftwood **FREE**
Umatilla National Forest
From SR 395 near Dale, 5 mi NE on FR 55; on shore of North Fork of John Day River. Free. 6/1-11/1; 14-day limit. 5 sites (45-ft RV limit). Tbls, toilets, cfga, no drkg wtr. Fishing, hiking, boating. Elev 2500 ft.

Gold Dredge **FREE**
Umatilla National Forest
7 mi E of Dale on FR 5506; access via Hwy 244; at North Fork of John Day River. Free. May-Oct; 14-day limit. 6 sites; 3 picnic sites. Tbls, toilets, cfga, no drkg wtr. Hunting, fishing, trail bikes. Elev 4300 ft.

Olive Lake **$5**
Umatilla National Forest
1 mi NE on US 395; half mi SE on FR 55; 26.3 mi SE on FR 10; qtr mi SW on FR 420. $5 (group sites $10). 6/1-9/30; 14-day limit. 23 sites (RVs under 32 ft). Tbls, toilets, cfga, firewood, no drkg wtr. Picnicking; fishing; berry picking; horseback riding; boating(l); swimming. Elev 6000 ft; 11 acres. Area not fully developed. Scenic.
Fishing tip: 160-acre Olive Lake has excellent underwater fish-holding structure, including sunken logs.

Oriental Creek **FREE**
Umatilla National Forest
12 mi E of Dale on FR 5506; access via Hwy 395; not recommended for RVs. Free. May-Oct; 14-day limit. 4 primitive sites. Tbls, toilets, cfga, no drkg wtr. Hunting, fishing, wilderness access.

Welch Creek **$5**
Umatilla National Forest
1 mi N of Dale to FR 55; left for 1 mi, then right on FR 10 for 13 mi. $5. Apr-Oct; 14-day limit. 5 sites. Tbls, toilet, cfga, no drkg wtr. Fishing, hunting. Desolation Creek. Elev 4200 ft.

THE DALLES (40)

Albert Philippi Camp **FREE**
Lake Umatilla
Corps of Engineers
On E side of the John Day River, 3.5 mi upstream from LePage Park; boat access only. Free. Primitive undesignated tent sites. Tbls, toilets, cfga, showers, drkg wtr. Hiking, fishing, boating.

Deschutes River   **$8**
State Recreation Area
12 mi E of The Dalles on I-84; exit 97 to Celilo, then 5 mi S on Hwy 206. $8 for 25 primitive sites ($5 off-season); $12 for 33 sites with elec off-season ($16 in-season). All year; 10-day limit in 14-day period. 30-ft RV limit. Tbls, flush toilets, cfga, drkg wtr, no showers. At Deschutes River near Columbia River. Fishing, rafting, boating, hiking, bridle trail, biking trail.

Giles French Park   **FREE**
Lake Umatilla
Corps of Engineers
Below dam of Lake Umatilla, on Oregon side. Free. Primitive undesignated sites. All year; 14-day limit. Tbls, toilets, cfga, drkg wtr. Boating(l), fishing.

LePage Park   **$12**
Lake Umatilla
Corps of Engineers
From John Day dam, 9 mi E on I-84 to exit 114, then S. $12 for 5 tent sites, weekends only; $17-18 for 22 RV sites with elec ($8.50 & $9 with federal Senior Pass). 4/1-10/31; 14-day limit. 55-ft RV limit. Tbls, toilets, cfga, drkg wtr, showers, dump, beach. Fishing, boating(l). 2-night minimum stay on weekends.

Memaloose State Park   **$12**
11 mi W of The Dalles on I-84; at Columbia River. $12 off-season 67 tent sites ($16 in-season); 43 full hookup sites $16 off-season, $20 in-season. 10-day limit. 110 sites; 40-ft RV limit. Tbls, flush toilets, cfga, drkg wtr, dump, showers. Nature programs, interpretive displays.

Quesnel Park   **FREE**
Lake Umatilla
Corps of Engineers
3 mi E of LePage Park. Free. All year; 14-day limit. Toilets, cfga, no drkg wtr. Boating(l), fishing.

DETROIT (42)

Big Meadows Horse Camp   **$7**
Willamette National Forest
27 mi SE on SR 22; left for 2 mi on FR 2267 (Big Meadows Rd); left 1 mi on FR 2257. $7 with federal Senior Pass; others pay $14. About 5/15-9/15; 14-day limit. 9 sites; 50-ft RV limit. Tbls, toilets, cfga, drkg wtr, horse corrals, loading ramp, stock water trough. Horseback riding, hiking.

Breitenbush   **$12**
Willamette National Forest
10 mi NE of Detroit on FR 46. $12. About 5/15-9/30; 14-day limit. 30 sites (24-ft RV limit). Tbls, toilets, cfga, drkg wtr. Free or reduced-fee camping during winter, but no drkg wtr or trash pickup; pack out trash. Fishing, swimming, hiking.

Fishing tip: Native brook trout in Breitenbush lake run small, and they dominate the trout population, but good ranbows can be caught by working weed beds mornings and evenings. Neighboring Olallie Lake produces bigger trout, 4-10 pounds.

Cleator Bend   **$12**
Willamette National Forest
9 mi NE of Detroit on FR 46. $12. About 5/15-9/30; 14-day limit. 30 sites (24-ft RV limit). Tbls, toilets, cfga, drkg wtr. Fishing in Breitenbush River, hiking, picnicking.

Elk Lake   **FREE**
Willamette National Forest
4.5 mi NE of Detroit on FR S46; 7 mi N on FR 4696; 9.5 mi NW on FR 2209; half mi SW on FR 430. Free. All year; 16-day limit. 12 tent sites. Tbls, toilets, no drkg wtr, cfga, no trash service. Boating(l; poor), fishing. 10 acres. The forest planned to charge $6 at this site in 2007.

Humbug   **$12**
Willamette National Forest
5 mi NE of Detroit on FR 46. $12. About 5/15-9/30; 14-day limit. 22 sites (22-ft RV limit). Tbls, toilets, cfga, drkg wtr. Fishing, hiking, picnicking. On Breitenbush River. 15 acres. May-June, rhododendrons are spectacular.

Marion Forks   **$10**
Willamette National Forest
16 mi SE of Detroit on SR 22. $10. MD-9/30; 14-day limit. 15 sites (24-ft RV limit). Tbls, toilets, cfga, drkg wtr. Fishing, hiking, picnicking. On Marion Creek. Marion Forks Fish Hatchery, NFS guard station, restaurant nearby.

Piety Island   **FREE**
Willamette National Forest
1 mi SW of Detroit BY BOAT Free. All year; 16-day limit (ltd facilities in winter). 20 tent sites. Tbls, toilets, cfga, no drkg wtr. Swimming, boating(rl), fishing, water skiing. Middle of Detroit Lake.

Riverside   **$12**
Willamette National Forest
13 mi SE of Detroit on SR 22. All year; 14-day limit. $12. Free or reduced-fee camping during winter until snow falls, but no drkg wtr or trash service; pack out trash. 37 sites (24-ft RV limit). Tbls, toilets, cfga, drkg wtr. Fishing, picnicking, hiking. North Santiam River.

Santiam Flats   **$12**
Willamette National Forest
2 mi E of Detroit on Hwy 22. $12 during 4/15-9/30; free or reduced fees rest of year, but no services. 32 sites. All year; 7-day limit. Tbls, toilets, cfga, no drkg wtr. Fishing, swimming, boating.

Fishing tip: Stocked rainbow trout are the primary fish at nearby Detroit lake, although many anglers go after the plentiful bullhead catfish. The lake also contains some brook & cutthroat trout. Troll flashers with a weight and worm trailer for the 10-16 inch rainbows.

Whispering Falls   **$12**
Willamette National Forest
7 mi E of Detroit on SR 22. $12. About 5/15-9/30; 14-day limit. 16 sites; 30-ft RV limit. Tbls, flush toilets, cfga, drkg wtr. Hiking, fishing, picnicking.

DUFUR (43)

Eightmile Crossing   **$10**
Mount Hood National Forest
12 mi SW of Dufur on CR 1; 4.3 mi W on FR 44; half mi N on FR 4430. $10. 6/1-10/15; 14-day limit. 21 sites (30-ft RV limit). Tbls, toilets, cfga, no drkg wtr. Fishing, hunting, picnicking. Elev 4200 ft.

Fifteen Mile   **$5**
Mount Hood National Forest
2 mi S of Dufur on OR 197; 14 mi W on CR 118; 9 mi W on FR 205. $5 daily pass or $30 annually. Elev 4600 ft. 9/1-9/10. 3 sites (RVs under 17 ft). Tbls, toilets, cfga. Picnicking; horseback riding (5 mi).

Knebal Springs Horse Camp   **$10**
Mount Hood National Forest
12 mi SW of Dufur on CR 1; 4.3 mi SW on FR 44; 4 mi NW on FR 105; 1 mi SW on FR 16. $10. 7/1-9/10; 14-day limit. 8 sites (RVs under 23 ft). Tbls, toilets, cfga, firewood, drkg wtr. Horseback riding; picnicking.

Lower Crossing   **$10**
Mount Hood National Forest
12 mi SW of Dufur on CR 1; 4 mi W on FR 44; 1 mi N on FR 167. Elev 3800 ft. $10. 7/1-9/10; 10-day limit. 4 sites (RVs under 16 ft). Tbls, toilets, cfga, no drkg wtr. Hunting; picnicking; fishing; horseback riding (5 mi).

Pebble Ford   **$10**
Mount Hood National Forest
12 mi SW of Dufur on CR 1; 5 mi W on FR 44; half mi S on FR 131. $10. 7/1-9/10; 14-day limit. 3 sites (16-ft RV limit). Tbls, toilets, cfga, no drkg wtr. Picnicking, hunting. Elev 4000 ft. 1 acre.

Underhill Site   **$10**
Mount Hood National Forest
Follow directions to Eightmile Crossing; continue W on FR 44 to FR 44, then to Underhill camp. $10. 7/1-9/10; 14-day limit. 2 primitive sites; 18-ft RV limit. Tbls, toilet, cfga, no drkg wtr, no trash service. Hiking. If fee box not available, no fee will be charged.

DURKEE (44)

Bassar Diggins Camp   **FREE**
Bureau of Land Management
Vale District
9 mi S of Durkee on Hwy 84; follow signs on dirt rd to Lookout Mountain. Free. 5/1-11/1; 14-day limit. About 3 primitive undesignated sites. Toilets, cfga, tbls, drkg wtr. Rockhounding. Primarily a hunter camp.

ELGIN (45)

Minam State Recreation Area　　**$8**
15 mi NE of Elgin off SR 82; at Wallowa River. $8 for 12 primitive sites. Apr-Oct; 10-day limit. 21 primitive sites. Tbls, toilets, cfga, drkg wtr. Boating(l), fishing, birdwatching.

ENTERPRISE (46)

Buckhorn Springs　　**FREE**
Hells Canyon Nat. Recreation Area
Wallowa-Whitman National Forest
3 mi S of Enterprise on Hwy 82; 32 mi N on CR 772; 10 mi NE on FR 46. Free. 6/1-11/15; 14-day limit. 6 sites. Tbls, toilets, cfga, no drkg wtr. Berrypicking.

Coyote　　**FREE**
Wallowa Whitman National Forest
3 mi E of Enterprise on SR 82; 21.5 mi N on CR 799; 19 mi N on FR 46. Free. 5/15-11/30; 10-day limit. 30 sites (22-ft RV limit). Tbls, toilets, cfga, no drkg wtr. Picnicking. 8 acres. Space available for large groups.

Dougherty Springs　　**FREE**
Hells Canyon Nat. Recreation Area
Wallowa Whitman National Forest
15 mi N of Enterprise on OR 3; 12 mi NE on FR N201; 10 mi E on FR 431; 10 mi NE on FR N437. Free. Elev 5100 ft. 6/1-12/1; 14-day limit. 12 sites (RVs under 22 ft). Tbls, toilets, cfga, no drkg wtr. Self-service sites. Berrypicking.

Vigne　　**$5**
Wallowa Whitman National Forest
3 mi E of Enterprise on SR 82; 21.5 mi N on CR 799; 6.5 mi N on FR 46; 11 mi E on FR 4625. $5. 4/15-11/30; 10-day limit. 7 sites (22-ft RV limit). Tbls, toilets, cfga, drkg wtr. Fishing, picnicking. Elev 3500 ft; 6 acres.

ESTACADA (47)

Alder Flat　　**FREE**
Mount Hood National Forest
25.8 mi SE of Estacada on Hwy 224; three-fourths mi W on Trail 574. Free. 4/23-9/30; 14-day limit. 6 tent sites. Tbls, toilets, cfga, no drkg wtr. Fishing, picnicking. Elev 1300 ft; 4 acres.

Breitenbush Lake　　**FREE**
Mount Hood National Forest
27 mi SE on OR 224; 28.6 mi S on FR S0046; 8.4 mi E on FR 4220 (access rd is primitive and unmaintained; difficult for RVs and passenger cars). Free. Elev 5200 ft. 6/15-9/20; 14-day limit. 14 sites. Tbls, toilets, cfga no drkg wtr. Picnicking; fishing; swimming; boating (no motors); hiking trails.

Carter Bridge　　**$7**
Mount Hood National Forest
About 15 mi SE of Estacada on SR 224; at Clackamas River. $7 with federal Senior Pass; others pay $14. 5/15-9/15; 14-day limit. 16 sites; 28-ft RV limit. Tbls, toilets, cfga, drkg wtr. Fishing (catch & release steelhead & salmon), hiking.

Hideaway Lake　　**$7**
Mount Hood National Forest
27 mi SE of Estacada on Hwy 224; 7.5 mi E on FR 57; 3 mi N on FR 58; 5.5 mi NW on FR 5830. $7 with federal Senior Pass; others pay $14. 6/15-9/15; 14-day limit. 9 sites; 16-ft RV limit. Tbls, toilets, cfga, no drkg wtr. Hiking, fishing. Elev 4500 ft.

Highrock Springs　　**FREE**
Mount Hood National Forest
27 mi SE of Estacada on Hwy 224; 7.5 mi E on FR 57; 10.5 mi NE on FR 58. Free. 6/15-9/20; 14-day limit. 6 sites; 16-ft RV limit. Tbls, toilets, cfga, drkg wtr. Fishing, picnicking. Elev 4400 ft; 1 acre.

Horseshoe Lake　　**$10**
Mount Hood National Forest
27 mi SE of Estacada on OR 224; 21.8 mi S on FR S46; 8.2 mi SE on FR S806; 8.3 mi S on FR 4220 (rough rd). $10. 6/15-9/20; 14-day limit. 6 sites (16-ft RV limit). Tbls, toilets, cfga, firewood, no drkg wtr. Hunting; picnicking; fishing; hiking; berry picking; boating (rl-3 mi; no motors); horseback riding (1 mi).

Lower Lake　　**$8**
Mount Hood National Forest
27 mi SE of Estacada on OR 224; 21.8 mi S on FR S46; 8.2 mi SE on FR S806; 4.5 mi S on FR 4220. $8. 6/15-9/20; 14-day limit. 8 sites; 16-ft RV limit. Tbls, toilets, cfga, firewood, no drkg wtr. Store, gas (1 mi). Picnicking; berry picking; horseback riding; boating(rl); fishing (1 mi). Elev 4600 ft; 2 acres.

Milo McIver State Park　　**$8**
4 mi W of Estacada on Springwater Rd; at the Clackamas River. $8 for 9 primitive sites ($5 off-season); $13 for 44 sites with elec off-season ($17 in-season). 10-day limit. Tbls, flush toilets, cfga, dump, showers, drkg wtr, dump. Boating(l), fishing, hiking trail, nature programs, bridle trail, biking trail.

North Arm　　**$12**
Mount Hood National Forest
SE of Estacada on Hwy 224, past Indian Henry & Alder Flat Camps to FR 57; E on FR 57; N on FR 58 past FRs 5830, 5850 & 5860; S on FR 5890, then S on 5890-012; at Timothy Lake. $12. MD-LD; 14-day limit. 8 sites; 16-ft RV limit. Tbls, toilets, cfga, no drkg wtr. Boating, fishing, hiking. Elev 3200 ft.

Olallie Meadows　　**$8**
Mount Hood National Forest
27 mi SE of Estacada on OR 224; 21.8 mi S on FR S46; 8.2 mi SE on FR S806; 1.4 mi S on FR 4220. $8. 6/15-9/20; 14-day limit. 4 sites (16-ft RV limit). Tbls, toilets, cfga, firewood, no drkg wtr. Berry picking; picnicking; boating (rld-4 mi); fishing (1 mi). Elev 4500 ft; 1 acre. Spring.

Paul Dennis　　**$7**
Mount Hood National Forest
27 mi SE of Estacada on SR 224; 21.7 mi S on FR 46; 8.2 mi SE on FR 4690; 6.3 mi S on FR 4220. $7 with federal Senior Pass; others pay $14. 7/1-10/15; 14-day limit. 17 sites (16-ft RV limit). Tbls, toilets, cfga, drkg wtr. Boating (lr -- no motors), fishing, hiking. Elev 5000 ft; 4 acres.

Peninsula　　**$10**
Mt. Hood National Forest
27 mi SE of Estacada on SR 224; 21.7 mi S on FR 46; 8.2 mi SE on FR 4690; 6.5 mi S on FR 4220. $10. 7/1-10/15; 14-day limit. 35 sites (24-ft RV limit). Tbls, toilets, cfga, drkg wtr. Fishing, boating(lr -- no motors), swimming, hiking. Elev 4900 ft; 10 acres.

Raab　　**$7**
Mt. Hood National Forest
27 mi SE of Estacada on SR 224; 4 mi SE on FR 46; 1 mi SE on FR 63. $7 with federal Senior Pass; others pay $14. 5/15-9/15; 14-day limit. 27 sites; 22-ft RV limit. Tbls, cfga, no drkg wtr, toilets (get wtr at Two Rivers Picnic Area, 1 mi). Fishing, hiking, horseback riding.

Rainbow　　**$7**
Mt. Hood National Forest
27 mi SE of Estacada on SR 224. $7 with federal Senior Pass. 5/15-9/15; 14-day limit. 17 sites (16-ft RV limit). Tbls, toilets, cfga, drkg wtr. Swimming, hiking, fishing. 3 acres.

Ripplebrook　　**$7**
Mount Hood National Forest
26.5 mi SE of Estacada on SR 224. $7 with federal Senior Pass; others pay $14. MD-LD; 14-day limit. 13 sites (16-ft RV limit). Tbls, toilets, cfga, drkg wtr. Fishing, hiking. On Oak Grove Fork of Clackamas River.

Riverford　　**$7**
Mount Hood National Forest
27 me SE of Estacada on SR 224; 3.5 mi S on FR 46. $7 with federal Senior Pass. About 4/20-9/20; 14-day limit. 8 sites; 16-ft RV limit. Tbls, toilets, cfga, no drkg wtr (get wtr at Two Rivers Picnic Area). Rockhounding, fishing.

Round Lake　　**FREE**
Mount Hood National Forest
27 mi SE of Estacada on Hwy 224; 3.6 mi S on FR 46; 12.4 mi SE on FR 63; 6.7 mi SE on FR 6370; hike half mile to sites. Free. 6/15-9/20; 14-day limit. 6 sites; 26-ft RV limit. Tbls, toilets, cfga, no drkg wtr. Swimming, fishing, picnicking.

Shellrock Creek　　**$12**
Mount Hood National Forest
27 mi SE of Estacada on SR 224; 7.5 mi E on FR 57; half ml N on FR 58. $12 during 6/15-10/10; free rest of year, but no services; 14-day limit. 8 sites; 16-ft RV limit. Tbls, toilets, cfga, no drkg wtr, no trash service. Fishing, hiking, hunting. Elev 2200 ft.

Triangle Lake   **$7**
Equestrian Camp
Mount Hood National Forest
27 mi SE of Estacada on SR 224; 21.7 mi S on FR 46; 8.2 mi SE on FR 4690; S on FR 4220. $7 with federal Senior Pass; others pay $14. 5/15-9/15; 14-day limit. 8 sites; 30-ft RV limit. Tbls, toilets, cfga, no drkg wtr. Horseback riding, hiking.

EUGENE (48)

Hult Pond   **FREE**
Dispersed Campsites
Bureau of Land Management
Eugene District
28 mi NW of Eugene (5 mi N of Horton) off SR 36 on gravel rd. All year; 14-day limit. Primitive undesignated sites along S & W shores of Hult Reservoir. Free. Tbls, portable chemical toilets in summer, tbls, cfga, no drkg wtr. Fishing, hiking, boating (no motors). Primitive boat launch. Within the Upper Lake Creek Special Recreation Management Area (15,000 acres acquired from Willamette Industries in 1995). Primitive dispersed camping permitted throughout the area off poorly defined rds (access to many only by horse, hiking or biking)

FLORENCE (49)

Baker Beach   **$10**
Siuslaw National Forest
About 6 mi N of Florence at end of Baker Beach Rd. $10. 5 sites primarily for equestrian campers. Tbls, toilets, cfga. Hiking & bridle trails to beach & forest; fishing.
Fishing tip: From camp, hike by trail to Lily Lake, which contains cutthroat trout. Use a canoe or float tube because shoreline is very brushy. Catch-and-release with artificial lures only.

Driftwood II   **$10**
Oregon Dunes
National Recreation Area
7 mi S of Florence on US 101; 1.5 mi W on Silcoos Dune & Beach Access Rd. $10 with federal senior pass for 2007 & 2008; others pay $20. All year; 14-day limit. 69 sites; 40-ft RV limit. Tbls, flush toilets, cfga, drkg wtr. Swimming, hiking, fishing. OHV access. 2-night minimum stay on weekends.
Fishing tip: Try the Silcoos River for striped bass, rainbow trou; steelhead, salmon.
Travel tip: We've selected Florence's Heceta Head Lighthouse as one of the best free attractions in Oregon. Built in 1894, it is still in operation and is one of America's most photographed lighthouses. 11 mi N of Florence within Devil's Elbow State Park (entry fee for park).

FOREST GROVE (50)

Elk Creek Campground   **$5**
Tillamook State Forest
About 27 mi NW of Forest Grove via Hwy 47 (Nehalem Rd), then W on Hwy 6 (Wilson River Hwy); at the Wilson River. $5. MD-10/31; 14-day limit. 15 walk-in tent sites. Tbls, toilets, cfga, drkg wtr. Hiking, fishing.

Gales Creek Campground   **$10**
Tillamook State Forest
About 10 mi NW of Forest Grove on Hwy 8 (Gales Creek Rd), then W on Wilson River Rd; at Gales Creek stream. $5 for 4 walk-in tent sites; $10 for 19 drive-to sites. MD-10/31; 14-day limit. Tbls, toilets, cfga, drkg wtr. Hiking, fishing.

Stagecoach Horse Camp   **$5**
Tillamook State Forest
About 10 mi N of Forest Grove on Hwy 47 (Nehalem Rd), then W on Hwy 6 about 30 mi; near historic Wilson River Wagon Road Trail. $5. All year; 14-day limit. 11 sites with horse corrals. Tbls, toilets, cfga, no drkg wtr. Hiking, horseback riding.

FORT KLAMATH (51)

Jackson F. Kimball   **$8**
State Recreation Site
3 mi N of Fort Klamath on Hwy 232. $8 ($5 off-season). 4/15-10/31; 10-day limit in 14-day period. 10 primitive sites (45-ft RV limit). Tbls, toilets, cfga, no drkg wtr. Near Wood River. Hiking, fishing, picnicking, canoeing.
Fishing tip: Brown trout provide just fair fishing action early in the year after season opens in late May, but fishing generally gets better as the summer progresses. Redband rainbow trout provide additional summer action.

FORT ROCK (52)

Cabin Lake   **FREE**
Deschutes National Forest
9.8 mi N of Fort Rock on FR 18. Free. 5/1-10/15; 14-day limit. 14 sites (RVs under 31 ft). Tbls, no toilets, no drkg wtr, cfga. Birdwatching. Elev 4550 ft. Toilets were vandalized and will not be replaced. This seldom-used, secluded campground will be allowed to deteriorate.

China Hat   **FREE**
Deschutes National Forest
22.7 mi N of Fort Rock on FR 18. Free. Elev 5100 ft. 5/1-10/15; 14-day limit. 14 sites (RVs under 31 ft). Tbls, toilets, drkg wtr, cfga. Hiking, birdwatching, OHV activity

FRENCHGLEN (55)

Fish Lake Recreation Site   **$8**
Bureau of Land Management
Burns District
From Hwy 205 at Frenchglen, 17 mi E on Steens Mountain Rd (gravel). $8 during 7/1-10/31; free rest of year; 14-day limit. 23 sites (35-ft RV limit). Tbls, toilets, cfga, drkg wtr. Swimming, fishing, hunting, hiking, birdwatching, boating(ld). 25 acres. Limited parking for large RVs; average site 20 ft, but 3 longer than 30.

Frenchglen Hotel   **FREE**
State Wayside Park
At Frenchglen on US 20 near Frenchglen Hotel State Heritage Site. Free. 1 night limit. 3/1-12/1. 1 primitive site. Toilet, cfga, tbls, no drkg wtr.

Jackman Park Recreation Site   **$6**
Bureau of Land Management
Burns District
From Hwy 205 at Frenchglen, 19 mi E on Steens Mountain Rd (gravel); 2 mi E of Fish Lake camp. $6. 7/1-10/1; 14-day limit. 6 sites (35-ft limit, but RVs not recommended). Tbls, toilets, no drkg wtr, cfga. Fishing, hiking, hunting, birdwatching. Elev 8100 ft.

Page Springs Recreation Site   **$8**
Bureau of Land Management
Burns District
From Hwy 205 at Frenchglen, SE 3 mi on Steens Mountain Rd (gravel); at Blitzen River. $8 during May-Oct; free rest of year; 14-day limit. 36 sites (35-ft RV limit). Tbls, toilets, cfga, drkg wtr. Fishing, hiking, hunting, nature trail, birdwatching. Elev 4200 ft; 8 acres.
Fishing tip: The remote, scenic Blitzen River is well known for its redband rainbow trout fishing. Restricted to fly flishing, it is at its best in summer and fall. The best areas are the five miles above Page Springs, by trail. It has plenty of small rainbow, but also some 5-pounders.

South Steens   **$6**
Bureau of Land Management
Burns District
10 mi S of Frenchglen on SR 205; 18 mi E on Steens South Loop Rd (Steens Mountain Back Country Byway). $6 during 5/1-11/1; free rest of year; 14-day limit. 36 sites; 35-ft RV limit. Tbls, toilets, cfga, drkg wtr, hitching bars at 15 sites. Hiking, fishing, horseback riding, hunting.

GLENDALE (56)

Tucker Flat   **FREE**
Bureau of Land Management
Medford District
20 mi W of Glendale on Cow Creek Rd; 5 mi W on Mule Creek Rd; 14 mi SW on Marial Rd. Free. 5/1-10/31; 14-day limit. 10 primitive tent sites (small RVs okay). Tbls, firewood, cfga, toilets, no drkg wtr. Swimming; fishing nearby. River permit needed if floating 5/15-10/15. Remote. Roads are one lane, curvy, not recommended for RVs.

GLIDE (57)

Beaver Pond   **FREE**
Dispersed Camp
Umpqua National Forest
From North Umpqua Ranger Station at Glide, 23 mi E on Hwy 138; Steamboat Creek Rd

38 for 9 mi; FR 3816 for 4 mi; FR 3816-200 S for 4 mi. Free. Primitive dispersed camping area at 2-acre pond; no facilities. Rainbow & eastern brook trout fishing (small boat recommended). Rds 38 & 3816 often have heavy logging traffic.

Bradley Ridge Trailhead   FREE
Umpqua National Forest
24 mi E of North Umpqua Ranger Station at Glide to FR 4713 (on left about half mi E of Island Campground); follow FR 4713 (Jack Creek Rd) 3.5 mi; 3 mi on FR 4713-100; 3 mi on FR 120; 1 mi on FR 130 to trailhead. Free. Undeveloped camping areas. Trail (1.75 mi) open to foot, horse, bicycle and motorcycle traffic. Rock overhang where Umpqua Indians lived; Dog Creek Indian caves. Trail borders & enters Limpy Rock Research Natural Area.

Cavitt Creek Falls $8
Recreation Site
Bureau of Land Management
Roseburg District
7 mi E of Glide on Little River Rd; 3 mi S on Cavitt Creek Rd. $8 (2nd RV, $3). About 5/15-9/30; 14-day limit. 10 sites (20-ft RV limit) & 14 picnic sites. Tbls, toilets, cfga, drkg wtr. Swimming (at base of 10-ft waterfall), fishing.

Cavitt Lake   FREE
Dispersed Camp
Umpqua National Forest
From North Umpqua Ranger Station at Glide, qtr mi W on Hwy 138; Little River Rd 17 for 2.6 mi; New Bridge Rd (Cavitt Creek Rd) FR 25 to FR 763 & follow 763 to its end. Sign on Cavitt Creek Rd points way. Total distance, 21 mi. Free. Dispersed primitive camping area; no facilities. Lake just being formed. Fishing.

Cinderella Springs   FREE
Dispersed Camp
Umpqua National Forest
From North Umpqua Ranger Station at Glide, qtr mi W on Hwy 138; Little River Rd 17 for 28 mi; FR 2715 for 2.5 mi; FR 4720 for 1.5 mi. Free. Dispersed primitive camping area. Log tbls, cfga, flat area for RVs, no toilet, no drkg wtr (spring wtr may be boiled). Wildlife & flowers plentiful. Fishing, hunting, berrypicking.

Coolwater $6
Umpqua National Forest
15.5 mi SE of Glide on CR 17. Along Little River. $6. Maintained 5/20-10/31; 14-day limit. 7 sites (24-ft RV limit). Tbls, toilets, cfga, drkg wtr. Fishing, hiking, swimming. Waterfall nearby.

Cougar Bluffs Shelter   FREE
Dispersed Area
Umpqua National Forest
From North Umpqua Ranger Station at Glide, 27 mi E on Hwy 138; right for 7 mi on FR 4714 (Apple Creek Rd); right for 1 mi on FR

2703; right for 3 mi on FR 600; right about 1 mi on FR 630; hike qtr mi to shelter. Free. Spring-fall; 14-day limit. Shelter (circa 1920s) with tbl & firering; space for tent. Toilet, cfga, drkg wtr (boil before using). Hunting, hiking, horseback riding.

Cultus Lake   FREE
Dispersed Area
Umpqua National Forest
From North Umpqua Ranger Station at Glide, qtr mi W on Hwy 138; Little River Rd 17 for 7.5 mi; Cavitt Creek Rd (CR 82) for 5 mi; it becomes FR 25; FR 25 7.5 mi; right on FR 2500-425 for 3.7 mi; right on FR 2500-480 for half mi to Cultus Creek. Cultus Lake is short walk across flat area. Free. Dispersed camping area; no facilities. Inflatable boat recommended for fishing due to brush & marsh. Hunting, hiking, nature photography.
Fishing tip: This large, deep lake produces big mackinaw trout of 20 pounds. It also contains rainbow & brook trout, but those average 6-11 inches and sometimes larger because the mackinaw feed on them. Troll Rapalas and Flatfish, and use a downrigger to get summer lakers.

Emile Shelter   FREE
Dispersed Area
Umpqua National Forest
13.1 mi E of Glide on CR 17; half mi E on FR 27; 8.5 mi N on FR 2703. On Little River. Free. 6/15-10/31; 14-day limit. 1 large RV site; 2 small ones (RVs under 22 ft). 1 camping shelter. Tbls, toilets, cfga. Picnicking, fishing, hunting, hiking. Elev 4000 ft; 1 acre. Mountains. Stream. Old trail shelter on site. 1 mi from Emile Big Trees.

Fuller Lake   FREE
Dispersed Camp
Umpqua National Forest
From North Umpqua Ranger Station at Glide, 23 mi E on Hwy 138; Steamboat Creek 38 for 10 mi; Spur 3817 for 3 mi; FR 3850 for 9 mi; left on FR 3810 for qtr mi; Spur 380 for 1 mi to trailhead. Hike half mi on Trail 1543 to lake & shelter. Free. Dispersed primitive 3-sided trail shelter; no facilities. Brook & rainbow trout in lake. Solitude. Fuller Lake Trail, nearby Bulldog Rock Trail.

Grassy Ranch Camp   FREE
Umpqua National Forest
From North Umpqua Ranger Station at Glide, 23 mi E on Hwy 138; Steamboat Creek 38 for 9 mi; FR 3817 for 3 mi; FR 3850 for 9 mi; right on FR 3810 for 0.7 mi; right on Spur 370 for qtr mi. Free. Undeveloped dispersed camp on W side of Boulder Creek drainage. No facilities. Berrypicking, hunting, hiking, photography.

Grotto Falls Dispersed Area   FREE
Umpqua National Forest
From North Umpqua Ranger Station at Glide, qtr mi W on Hwy 138; 16.5 mi on Little River Rd 17; left on FR 2703 for 3 mi; 2 mi on FR 2703-150; hike Grotto Falls Trail 1503. Free.

All year; 14-day limit. 1 tent site. Tbl, toilet, cfga, no drkg wtr. Hiking, picnicking.

Hemlock Lake $8
Umpqua National Forest
16.5 mi E of Glide on CR 17; 15.5 mi E on FR 27; half mi S on FR 495. $8. Maintained 6/1-10/31; 14-day limit. 13 sites (RVs under 35 ft). Tbls, toilets, cfga, no drkg wtr. Swimming, boating(l), fishing, hiking trail. 28-acre lake. Elev 4400 ft.

Hemlock Meadows Boat Ramp $8
Umpqua National Forest
From North Umpqua Ranger Station at Glide, 154 mi W on Hwy 138; 32 mi on Little River Rd 17; boat ramp is half mile from Hemlock Lake Campground around E arm of 28-acre lake. $8. 6/1-10/31; 14-day limit. 1 site (35-ft RV limit). Tbl, toilet, cfga, no drkg wtr. Boating (no mtrs), fishing, hiking trails, swimming.

Hi Si Pond Dispersed Area   FREE
Umpqua National Forest
From North Umpqua Ranger Station at Glide, 23 mi E on Hwy 138; 3 mi on Steamboat Creek Rd 38; left for 8 mi on FR 3806. Free. Spring-fall; 14-day limit. Primitive undesignated sites. No facilities. Fishing, hunting.

Illahee Flat Dispersed Area   FREE
Umpqua National Forest
From North Umpqua Ranger Station at Glide, 29 mi E on Hwy 138; left on FR 4760 for 2 mi; qtr mi on Spur 039 to gazebo. Free. Spring-fall; 14-day limit. Primitive undesignated camping near covered gazebo. No facilities except cfga. Hiking.

Lake in the Woods $10
Umpqua National Forest
17 mi E of Glide on CR 17; 11 mi E on FR 27. $10. MD-10/1; 14-day limit. 11 sites (35-ft RV limit). Tbls, flush & pit toilets, cfga, drkg wtr. Fishing, hiking, boating. On 4-acre Lake in the Woods. Hike to Yakso or Hemlock Falls.

Limpy Sump   FREE
Dispersed Area
Umpqua National Forest
From North Umpqua Ranger Station at Glide, qtr mi W on Hwy 138; 28 mi on Little River Rd 17; 1.5 mi on FR 2715; 154 mi on FR 4720, then either follow FR 200 or continue on FR 2715 past FR 4720 and left on FR 210. Free. Summer-fall; 14-day limit. Primitive undesignated site. Tbl, cfga, no toilet, no drkg wtr. Youtkut Pillars rock formation about half mi S on FR 2715. Hiking, fishing, hunting, berrypicking.

Millpond $8
Bureau of Land Management
Roseburg District
4 mi E of Glide on Hwy 138; 5 mi N on Rock Creek Rd. $8. About 5/15-10/15; 14-day limit. 12 sites (30-ft RV limit). Tbls, flush & pit toilets, cfga, drkg wtr. Swimming, horseshoes, picnicking, hiking (nature trail). 20 acres.Free fish hatchery nearby.

Reynolds Shelter   **FREE**
Dispersed Area
Umpqua National Forest
From North Umpqua Ranger Station, 23 mi E on Hwy 138; Steamboat Creek Rd 38 for 9 mi; FR 3817 for 3 mi; FR 3850 for 8 mi; left on Spur 366 for qtr mi. Free. May-Oct; 14-day limit. Undeveloped primitive area. 3-sided toilet, cfga, spring wtr (boil before using). Popular berrypicking. Hunting, photography, hiking.

Rock Creek Recreation Site   **$8**
Bureau of Land Management
Roseburg District
4 mi E of Glide on Hwy 138; 8.5 mi N on Rock Creek Rd. $8. About 5/15-10/30; 14-day limit. 17 sites (30-ft RV limit). Tbls, toilets, cfga, drkg wtr. Fishing (at North Umpqua River), picnicking, rafting, hiking. 12 acres. Free fish hatchery nearby.

Susan Creek   **$11**
Bureau of Land Management
Roseburg District
11 mi E of Glide on Hwy 138. $11. About 5/1-10/30; 14-day limit. 31 sites (35-ft RV limit). Tbls, flush toilets, showers, cfga, drkg wtr. Fishing on North Umpqua River, hiking, picnicking, rafting, kayaking.

Twin Lakes East Trailhead   **FREE**
Umpqua National Forest
From North Umpqua Ranger Station at Glide, 33 mi E on Hwy 138 to Marsters Bridge; cross bridge, turn right on FR 4470 for 10 mi. Trail 1500 connects with Twin Lakes Loop Trail at 1 mi. Lakes & shelter about qtr mi past jct. Area renowned for serenity & beauty. Free. Shelter & 6 tent sites at Big Twin Lake; rustic log tbls, cfga, toilet. 1 tent site at Little Twin Lake. 1-mile loop trail connects lakes. Wildflowers, hiking trails, grotto caves, fishing for brook trout, canoeing, photography.

Twin Lakes West Trailhead   **FREE**
Umpqua National Forest
From North Umpqua Ranger Station at Glide, qtr mi W on Hwy 138 to Little River Rd 17; after 20 mi it becomes gravel FR 27; continue on it to FR 2715 about 3 mi E of Lake in the Woods Campground; left on FR 2715 for 8 miles to jct with FR 2715-530, then left to the trailhead. Free. Site details at Twin Lakes East entry.

White Creek   **$6**
Umpqua National Forest
13.1 mi E of Glide on CR 17; 4 mi E on FR 27; 2 mi E on FR 2792; at Little River. $6. 5/20-9/30; 14-day limit. 4 sites. Tbls, toilets, cfga, well drkg wtr. Picnicking; fishing; swimming (no lifeguards); hiking. Sandy beach. Elev 1600 ft; 1 acre. Mountains. White Creek. Central parking area with walk-in sites. Grotto Falls Trail, Overhang Trail. Limited parking lot for RVs. Excellent sandy swimming beach for children. Grotto Falls Trail, Overhang Trail. RV dump 19 mi NW at Forest Ranch Mobile Park (2 mi E of Glide on Hwy 138) and 38 mi W at Douglas County Fairgrounds.

Williams Creek   **$6**
Umpqua National Forest
From North Umpqua Ranger Station at Glide, 14 mi E on Hwy 138 to FR 4710 (just past Susan Creek Falls Trailhead); left 4 mi; FR 4710-480 to camp 5.3 mi. FR 4710-480 not maintained for low-clearance vehicles. Also, walk-in access available off Hwy 138, two mi W of Steamboat at the mouth of Williams Creek. $6. 6/1-9/10; 14-day limit. Self-service period 9/11-5/31. Not recommended for trailers. 3 rustic sites w/tables; tent or RV parking in grassy clearing. Toilets, cfga, no drkg wtr. Swimming in secluded stream pool. North Umpqua & Mcdonald hiking trails. Boating, picnicking. Wtr 9 mi E at Susan Creek campground. Dump 21 mi W at Forrest Ranch Mobile Park or 50 mi E at Diamond Lake Campground.

Fishing tip: There's great steelhead fishing (flies only) in the North Umpqua River, and access to the Williams Creek fish passage.

Willow Flats Sump   **FREE**
Dispersed Camp
Umpqua National Forest
From North Umpqua Ranger Station at Glide, qtr mi W on Hwy 138; Little River Rd 17 for 16.5 mi to Coolwater Campground; left onto FR 2703 for 7.9 mi; FR 4711 qtr mi; FR 4711-750 for 3.3 mi; right at FR 4711-835 for half mi. Free. June-Oct; 14-day limit. Undeveloped primitive camping area. Toilet, log tbl, cfga, no drkg wtr. 2-acre trout lake. Hunting, fishing, swimming, hiking, berry-picking, photography.

Wolf Creek   **$10**
Umpqua National Forest
12 mi SE of Glide on CR 17. $10. 5/20-9/30; 14-day limit. 8 sites (30-ft RV limit). Tbls, flush toilets, cfga, drkg wtr, gray water sumps. On Little River. Fishing, picnicking, horseshoes, volleyball, swimming.

Wright Creek Campground   **$6**
Umpqua National Forest
From North Umpqua Ranger Station at Glide, 17.5 mi E on Hwy 138; right on Wright Creek Rd 4711 to camp just across bridge at Wright Creek. $6. All year; 14-day limit. 2 sites, toilet, no drkg wtr, tbls or cfga. Fox and Mott segments of North Umpqua Trail. Fly fishing only.

GOLD BEACH (58)

Elko Dispersed Camp   **FREE**
Siskiyou National Forest
SE of Gold Beach on CR 635, then follow FR 3680 and FR 11503 (10 mi total). Free. All year; 14-day limit. 3 sites. Toilet, cfga, no drkg wtr. Elev 3000 ft.

Foster Bar   **$5**
Siskiyou National Forest
30 mi E of Gold Beach on Agness-Gold Beach Rd; right on Illahe-Agness Rd for 3 mi.

$5. All year; 14-day limit. 8 sites. Tbls, flush toilets (portable toilets Nov-May), cfga, drkg wtr, drinking fountain, pay phone. Hiking, boating(l), fishing & tubing in Rogue River. Former dispersed site is now a developed campground.

Game Lake   **FREE**
Dispersed Camp
Siskiyou National Forest
Follow CR 635 from Gold Beach, then FR 3680 to camp. 5/1-11/1; 14-day limit. 3 primitive undesignated sites. Toilet, cfga, no drkg wtr. Fishing, hiking.

Lobster Creek   **$5**
Siskiyou National Forest
4.2 mi NW of Gold Beach on CR 375; 5.6 mi NW on FR 333; at Rogue River. $5. All year; 14-day limit. 6 sites (22-ft RV limit). Tbls, toilets, cfga, no drkg wtr. Boating(l), fishing, swimming, picnicking, rockhounding. Scenic.

Oak Flat   **FREE**
Dispersed Camp
Siskiyou National Forest
Follow CR 545 E from Gold Beach along Rogue River, then S on CR 450 to camp. Free. 5/1-11/1; 14-day limit. 15 primitive dispersed sites. Toilet, cfga, no drkg wtr. Horse corral. Hiking, horseback riding. Access to Illinois River Trail 1161. Elev 3000 ft.

Fishing tip: The Illinois River is closed to fishing 4/1-5/25. Below Pomeroy Dam, it is open to catch-and-release steelhead & trout fishing May 26, using artificial flies and lures. The rest of the Illinois and its tributaries are closed to fishing.

Quosatana   **$10**
Siskiyou National Forest
1 mi N of Gold Beach on US 101; 4.2 mi NE on CR 595; 10 mi NE on FR 33. $10. All year; 3-day limit. 43 sites (32-ft RV limit). Tbls, flush toilets, cfga, drkg wtr, dump, grey wtr dumps, fish cleaning station. Boating(l), fishing, hiking trail. On Rogue River.

Wildhorse Dispersed Camp   **FREE**
Siskiyou National Forest
Follow CR 595 E along Rogue River, then FR 3318 to camp. Free. 5/1-11/1; 14-day limit. 3 primitive undesignated sites. Toilet, cfga, no drkg wtr. Fishing, hiking. Solitude. Scenic.

GOVERNMENT CAMP (59)

Barlow Creek   **$10**
Mount Hood National Forest
2 mi E of Government Camp on US 26; 4.5 mi N on Hwy 35; 4.2 mi SE on FR 3530. $10. Elev 3100 ft. 5/1-10/1; 14-day limit: 3 sites. Tbls, toilets, cfga, firewood, no drkg wtr. Picnicking; hunting; fishing; horseback riding & hiking (1 mi).

Barlow Crossing   **$10**
Mount Hood National Forest
2 mi E of Government Camp on US 26; 4.5 mi N on OR 35; 5.2 mi SE on FR 3530 (dirt

rd). $10. Elev 3100 ft. 5/15-10/1; 14-day limit. 6 sites. Tbls, toilets, cfga, firewood, no drkg wtr. Picnicking; fishing; horseback riding (1 mi); hiking (2 mi).

Cove Campground $12
Mount Hood National Forest
15 mi SE of Government Camp on US 26; 8 mi S on FR 42; at Timothy Lake. $10. 5/12-LD; 14-day limit. 10 walk-in tent sites. Tbls, toilets, cfga, no drkg wtr (available at Pine Point camp). Fishing, boating, hiking. Elev 3200 ft. Site of 1930s CCC camp.

Devils Half Acre FREE
Mount Hood National Forest
2 mi E of Government Camp on US 26; 4.5 mi N on OR 35; 1 mi E on FR 3530 (dirt rd). Free. 5/15-10/1; 14-day limit. 2 small sites. Tbls, toilets, cfga, firewood, no drkg wtr. Picnicking; horseback riding & hiking (1 mi). Elev 3600 ft; 1 acre. Stream. Nature trails (1 mi).

Grindstone FREE
Mount Hood National Forest
2 mi E of Government Camp on US 26; 4.5 mi N on OR 35; 3 mi SE on FR 3530 (dirt rd). Free. 5/15-10/1; 14-day limit. 3 primitive sites. Tbls, toilets, cfga, firewood, no drkg wtr. Picnicking; fishing; hunting; hiking (3 mi). On Barlow Creek.

Meditation Point $5
Mount Hood National Forest
15 mi SE of Government Camp on US 26; 8 mi S on FR S42; 6 mi W on FR S57. Hike in or boat in, 1 mi. $5 daily permit or $30 annually. 5/15-10/1; 14-day limit. 5 tent sites. Tbls, toilets, cfga, firewood, no drkg wtr. Picnicking; fishing; swimming; boating; hiking; horseback riding (1 mi). Elev 3200 ft; 1 acre.

Summit Lake $12
Mount Hood National Forest
15 mi SE on OR 26; 13 mi S on FR 42; 1 mi SE on FR S601; 1 mi W on FR 141. $12. 5/30-10/1; 14-day limit. 5 sites; 16-ft RV limit. Tbls, toilets, cfga, firewood, no drkg wtr. Picnicking; boating; swimming. Elev 4000 ft; 3 acres. Mountains.

White River Station $5
Mount Hood National Forest
2 mi E of Government Camp on US 26; 4.5 mi N on OR 35; 7 mi NE on FR 3530. $5 daily NW pass or $30 annually. 5/15-10/1; 14-day limit. 5 sites; 32-ft RV limit. Tbls, toilets, cfga, no drkg wtr. Picnicking; fishing; horseback riding (1 mi); hiking (3 mi).

GRANTS PASS (60)

Bear Camp Pasture FREE
Siskiyou National Forest
From 35 mi NW of Grants Pass on I-5; take Merlin exit 61, follow Merlin-Galice Rd to Bear Camp Rd 23; then 19 mi to camp. Free. About 6/15-10/15; 14-day limit. Primitive undesignated sites. Tbls, toilets, cfga, no drkg wtr.

Big Pine $5
Siskiyou National Forest
3.4 mi N of Grants Pass on I-5; 12.4 mi NW on Merlin-Galice Rd; 12.8 mi SW on FR 25. $5. MD-Oct; 14-day limit. 12 sites (RVs under 22 ft). Tbls, toilets (handicap access), cfga, firewood, grey wtr dumps. Elev 2400 ft; 15 acres. 12.5 mi SW of Rogue River. Fishing, hiking, play field, blind interpretive trail. Site of the world's tallest Ponderosa pine tree.

Meyers Camp FREE
Siskiyou National Forest
From 35 mi NW of Grants Pass on I-5, take Merlin exit 61; follow Merlin-Galice Rd 12 mi; l3ft on FR 25 for 11 mi. Free. All year; 14-day limit. Primitive undesignated sites. Tbls, toilet, cfga, no drkg wtr.

Sam Brown $5
Siskiyou National Forest
3.4 mi N of Grants Pass on I-5; 12.4 mi NW on Merlin-Galice Rd; 13.7 mi SW on FR 25. $5. MD-LD; 14-day limit. 29 sites (32-ft RV limit). Tbls, toilets, cfga, drkg wtr, solar shower, picnic shelter (reservations). Hiking & horseback trails, fishing.

Sam Brown Horse Camp $5
Siskiyou National Forest
3.4 mi N of Grants Pass on I-5; 12.4 mi NW on Merlin-Galice Rd; 13.7 mi SW on FR 25. $5. May-Oct; 14-day limit. 7 sites. Tbls, toilets, cfga, drkg wtr, corrals. Hiking, horseback riding, fishing.

Secret Creek $5
Siskiyou National Forest
35 mi NW of Grants Pass, exit 61 off I-5 to Merlin-Galice Rd for 19 mi (from Hwy 199 on FR 25, Onion Mt. Lookout Rd, it is about 37 mi). $5. All year; 14-day limit. 4 sites. Tbls, toilets, cfga, no drkg wtr. Handicap access.

Spalding Pond $5
Siskiyou National Forest
15 mi SW of Grants Pass on US 199; 7 mi NW on FR 25; 5 mi W on FR 2524. $5. May-Oct; 14-day limit. 4 sites. Tbls, toilet, cfga, drkg wtr. Fishing, swimming, hiking. Near historical mill site.
Fishing tip: The pond here is stocked annually with rainbow trout. Best fishing is spring to early summer. Fishing platforms provided.

Tin Can $4
Siskiyou National Forest
3.4 mi N of Grants Pass on I-5; 5 mi from Merlin-Galice Rd on way to Big Pine CG (16 mi NW of Merlin); at Taylor Creek. $4. All year; 14-day limit. 5 tent sites. Tbls, toilet, cfga, no drkg wtr. Near Taylor Creek Trail.

Valley of the Rogue State Park $12
12 mi E of Grants Pass at I-5 exit 45B; at the Rogue River. $12 for 21 tent sites off-season ($16 in-season). Sites with hookups, $16-20. All year; 10-day limit. Flush toilets, tbls, cfga, drkg wtr, showers, playgrounds, dump. Boating(l), fishing, bike trail, hiking trail, nature programs.

Whisky Creek FREE
Bureau of Land Management
Medford District
N of Grants Pass on I-5; take Merlin exit, drive 23 mi W on Merlin-Galice Rd; cross Grave Creek Bridge to boat ramp, then hike 3 mi on Rogue River Trail or float downstream (float permit needed 5/15-10/15). Free. 3 tent sites, tbl, cfga, toilet at mouth of Whisky Creek, qtr mi from historic Whisky Creek Cabin (oldest known mining cabin still standing in lower Rogue River Canyon, circa 1880).

HAINES (62)

Anthony Lakes $8
Wallowa-Whitman National Forest
17 mi NW of Haines on SR 411; 7 mi W on FR 73. $8; $12 RV sites. 7/1-10/31; 14-day limit. 21 tent sites, 16 RV/tent sites. Tbls, toilets, cfga, drkg wtr, grey wtr dumps. Fishing, hiking (trailhead), boating, swimming, winter sports. Elev 7100 ft; 13 acres.

Grande Ronde Lake $5
Wallowa-Whitman National Forest
17 mi NW of Haines on SR 411; 8.5 mi W on FR 73; half mi NW on FR S438; qtr mi W on FR S438B. $5. 7/1-9/15; 14-day limit. 8 sites (16-ft RV limit). Tbls, toilets, cfga, drkg wtr. Boating(ld), trout fishing, swimming. Elev 6800 ft. Trail to site of Aurelia Mine.

Mud Lake $5
Wallowa-Whitman National Forest
17 mi NW of Haines on SR 411; 7.3 mi W on FR 73. $5. 7/1-9/15; 14-day limit. 5 RV sites (16-ft limit), 3 tent sites. Tbls, toilets, cfga, drkg wtr. Swimming, boating(rl), hiking trails, trout fishing. Elev 7100 ft.

HALFWAY (63)

Duck Lake FREE
Hells Canyon Nat. Recreation Area
Wallowa-Whitman National Forest
9.2 mi E of Halfway on SR 86; 13 mi N on FR 39; 5,8 mi W on FR 66; .7 mi N on FR 398. High-clearance vehicles only. Free. 7/1-9/15. 2 tent sites. Tbl, toilet, cfga, no drkg wtr. Fishing, boating, hiking, picnicking. Self-service site.

Fish Lake $5
Wallowa-Whitman National Forest
5 mi N of Halfway on CR 733; 18.6 mi N on FR 66. $5. 7/1-10/31; 10-day limit. 15 sites (RVs under 22 ft). Tbls, toilets, cfga, firewood, piped drkg wtr. Picnicking; swimming; fishing; boating(ld). Elev 6600 ft; 12 acres. Stream. Self-service site.

Lake Fork $5
Wallowa-Whitman National Forest
Hells Canyon National Recreation Area
9.2 mi E of Halfway on Hwy 86; 8.3 mi N on

FR 39. $5. 6/1-11/30; 14-day limit. 10 sites (22-ft RV limit). Tbls, toilets, cfga, drkg wtr. Fishing. Along Lake Fork Creek. Trail 10 mi to Fish Lake, then on to other lakes.

McBride   **FREE**
Wallowa-Whitman National Forest
6 mi NW of Halfway on Hwy 413; 2.5 mi W on FR 7710. Free. 5/15-10/31; 10-day limit. 11 sites (16-ft RV limit). Tbls, toilets, cfga, drkg wtr. Fishing, hiking. Brooks Ditch.

Tunnel Launch   **FREE**
Bureau of Land Management
Vale District
23 mi NE of Halfway on SR 86. Free. All year; 14-day limit. Undeveloped camping area. No facilities, no drkg wtr. Rockhounding, boating(l), fishing.

Twin Lakes   **FREE**
Hells Canyon Nat. Recreation Area
Wallowa-Whitman National Forest
5 mi N of Halfway on CR 733; 24 mi N on FR 66. Free. 7/1-9/15; 10-day limit. 6 tent sites. Tbls, toilet, cfga, no drkg wtr. Hiking, fishing (Twin Lakes). Elev 6500 ft.

HEBO (64)

Castle Rock   **FREE**
Siuslaw National Forest
4.7 mi SE of Hebo on OR 22. Free. All year; 10-day limit. 4 walk-in tent sites. Tbls, toilets, cfga, firewood, well drkg wtr. Pack out trash. Picnicking; fishing.

Hebo Lake   **$10**
Siuslaw National Forest
Qtr mi E of Hebo on Hwy 22; 5 mi E on FR 14. $10. 4/15-10/15; 14-day limit. 15 sites (18-ft RV limit). Tbls,toilets, cfga, drkg wtr. Boating (no motors), fishing, hiking.

South Lake Campground   **FREE**
Siuslaw National Forest
13 mi off Hwy 22 at Little Hebo/Coast Range Summit. Travel FR 2234 to FR 2282, then N to FR 2210 & FR 14 jct; left on FR 14 to FR 1428 & follow signs. Free. All year, weather permitting; 14-day limit. Primitive sites. Toilets, cfga, no drkg wtr, no trash service.
   Fishing tip: South Lake is stocked with trout; no boat motors.

HEPPNER (65)

Anson Wright Memorial   **$10**
Morrow County Park
26 mi S of Heppner on Hwy 207. $10 for tents; $15 for partial RV hookups; $18 full hookups. 5/1-11/30; 10-day limit. 12 sites (30-ft RV limit). Tbls, flush toilets, showers, cfga, drkg wtr, dump. Fishing, playground, hiking trails, rockhounding. The only public park within 25 miles, it is often full. Elev 3400 ft; 15 acres.

Bull Prairie   **$7**
Umatilla National Forest
32 mi SW of Heppner on SR 207; 3.5 mi E on FR 2039. $7 with federal Senior Pass; others pay $14 during 5/15-10/15; free rest of year, but no wtr or trash service; 16-day limit. 28 sites (32-ft RV limit). Tbls, toilets, cfga, drkg wtr, dump. Boating(l), fishing, swimming, hiking. Elev 4000 ft.
   Fishing tip: This beautiful 28-acre lake contains brook & rainbow trout as well as bluegills. It is 4 mi from the campground.

Cutsforth Forest   **$10**
Morrow County Park
20 mi SE of Heppner on Willow Creek County Rd. $10 for tents; $15 for partial hookups; $18 full RV hookups. 5/15-11/30; 10-day limit. 38 sites (30-ft RV limit). Tbls, flush toilets, showers, cfga, drkg wtr, dump. Fishing, playground, hiking trails. Elev 4000 ft; 15 acres.

Morrow County Fairground   **$10**
In town, on SR 74. $10. All year. Undesignated sites in open area for self-contained RVs with elec; $8 without elec. Tbls, toilets, cfga, drkg wtr.

Penland Heppner Lake   **FREE**
Umatilla National Forest
26 mi SE of Heppner off FR 21; access via Hwy 207 & FR 53. Free. 5/1-10/31; 14-day limit. 17 sites; 5 picnic sites. Tbls, toilets, cfga, no drkg wtr. Hunting, fishing, boating, swimming. Elev 4950 ft.
   Fishing tip: Catch rainbow trout or bluegill from Penland Lake; electric motors only. Springtime lake access may be hampered by muddy rds, especially FR 2103.

HINES (66)

Alder Spring   **FREE**
Dispersed Camping
Ochoco National Forest
1 mi S of Hines on US 20; 12 mi NW on CR 127; 26.5 mi NW on FR 41; just E of Delintment Lake. Free. 5/15-9/15; 14-day limit. Primitive undesignated sites. Tbls, toilets, cfga, no drkg wtr. Managed by Malheur NF.

Buck Springs   **FREE**
Ochoco National Forest
1 mi S of Hines on US 20; 12 mi NW on CR 127; 26.5 mi NW on FR 41; SW of Delintment Lake off FR 4545. Free. 5/15-9/15; 14-day limit. About 8 primitive undesignated sites. Tbls, cfga, toilets, no drkg wtr. Managed by Malheur NF.

Delintment Lake   **$8**
Ochoco National Forest
1 mi S of Hines on US 20; 12 mi NW on CR 127; 26.5 mi NW on FR 41; 5 mi W following signs; at W side of Delintment Lake. $8. 5/15-9/15; 14-day limit. 26 sites (32-ft RV limit). Tbls, toilets, cfga, drkg wtr, fishing pier. Swimming, boating(l), fishing. Elev 5600 ft. 11 acres. Managed by Malheur NF.

Fishing tip: This lake is stocked with rainbow trout, providing good bank, pier and boat fishing; some fish are large, holdovers from earlier stockings, while the average catches are of those 10-14 inches. Bait angling is most successful.

Doe Springs   **FREE**
Ochoco National Forest
1 mi S of Hines on US 20; 12 mi NW on CR 127; 26.5 mi NW on FR 41; SW of Delintment Lake off FR 4515. Free. 5/15-9/15; 14-day limit. Primitive undesignated sites. Tbls, cfga, toilets, no drkg wtr. Managed by Malheur NF.

Donnelly Camp   **FREE**
Ochoco National Forest
1 mi S of Hines on US 20; 12 mi NW on CR 127; 26.5 mi NW on FR 41; E of Delintment Lake off FR 45. Free. 5/15-9/15; 14-day limit. Primitive undesignated sites. Tbls, cfga, toilets, no drkg wtr. Managed by Malheur NF.

Emigrant   **$6**
Ochoco National Forest
1 mi S of Hines on US 20; 20 mi NW on CR 127; 9.7 mi W on FR 43; left on FR 4340 then turn on FR 4340-050; along Emigrant Creek. $6. 6/1-10/15; 14-day limit. 6 sites (32-ft RV limit). Tbls, toilets, cfga, drkg wtr. Swimming, fly fishing, picnicking. Elev 5400 ft. Managed by Malheur NF.
   Fishing tip: Emigrant Creek provides good trout fishing in spring & early summer.

Falls   **$6**
Ochoco National Forest
1 mi S of Hines on US 20; 25 mi NW on CR 127; 8.5 mi W on FR 43; half mi NW on FR 4300-50. $6. 5/15-9/15; 14-day limit. 6 sites (30-ft RV limit). Tbls, toilets, cfga, drkg wtr. On Emigrant Creek. Fishing, hunting, swimming, hiking. Waterfalls nearby. Elev 5300 ft. Managed by Malheur NF.

Pendleton Springs   **FREE**
Ochoco National Forest
1 mi S of Hines on US 20; 12 mi NW on CR 127; 26.5 mi NW on FR 41; NE of Delintment Lake off FR 43. Free. 5/15-9/15; 14-day limit. Primitive undesignated sites. Tbls, cfga, toilets, no drkg wtr. Managed by Malheur NF.

Tip Top Springs   **FREE**
Ochoco National Forest
1 mi S of Hines on US 20; 12 mi NW on CR 127; 26.5 mi NW on FR 41; near Delintment Lake off FR 41. Free. 5/15-9/15; 14-day limit. Primitive undesignated sites. Tbls, cfga, toilets, no drkg wtr. Managed by Malheur NF.

HOOD RIVER (67)

Kingsley Reservoir   **$10**
Hood River County Park
W of Hood River: Binns Hill to Kingsley Rd, W of country club at Oak Grove Junction. $10. 20 sites. Toilet, tbls, cfga, no drkg wtr. Fishing, boating(l), biking & hiking trails. Elev 3200 ft.

HUNTINGTON (68)

Spring Recreation Site $5
Bureau of Land Management
Vale District

6 mi NE of Huntington on co rd from I-84 exit 5; at Brownlee Reservoir. $5. 4/1-10/30; 14-day limit. 35 undesignated sites (30-ft RV limit). Tbls, toilets, cfga, drkg wtr, fish cleaning station. Boating(l), fishing, hunting. 20 acres.

IDLEYLD PARK (69)

Apple Creek $7
Umpqua National Forest

22.5 mi E of Idleyld on Hwy 138; near North Umpqua River. $7. 5/20-10/31; 14-day limit. 8 sites (RVs under 23 ft). Tbls, toilets, cfga, no drkg wtr, gray water waste sump. Hiking on segments of North Umpqua National Recreation Trail. Whitewater boating. Self-service 11/1-5/19. Dump station 25 mi W at Forrest Ranch Mobile Park, 35 mi E at Diamond Lake Campground. Wtr 4 mi E at Dry Creek store.

Fishing tip: Fly fishing only (for steelhead) allowed on North Umpqua River.

Bogus Creek $11
Umpqua National Forest

On SR 138 near Idleyld Park; at North Umpqua River. $11. 5/20-10/15; 14-day limit. 15 sites; 35-ft RV limit. Tbls, flush toilets, cfga, drkg wtr, gray water sump. Fishing, picnicking, rafting, hiking. Major launch site for whitewater boaters.

Boulder Flat $8
Umpqua National Forest

31.7 mi E of Idleyld Park on SR 138. $8. 5/1-10/15; 14-day limit. 11 sites (24-ft RV limit). Tbls, toilets, cfga, no drkg wtr, gray water waste sump. Boating, good fly fishing fishing, hiking. At North Umpqua River & Boulder Creek. Adjacent to major launch point for whitewater boaters.

Bunker Hill Campground $7
Umpqua National Forest

49.4 mi E of Idleyld Park on Hwy 138; 5 mi N on FR 2610 (Lemolo Lake Rd) across dam; right on FR 2610-999 for half mi; on NW shore of Lemolo Reservoir. $7. 5/15-10/31; 14-day limit. 8 sites; 22-ft RV limit. Tbls, toilets, cfga, no drkg wtr. Waterskiing, hiking trails. Elev 4150 ft.

Fishing tip: This 420-acre lake contains rainbows, eastern brook trout, kokanee salmon and large native brown trout. Most browns are 11-14 inches.

Canton Creek $8
Umpqua National Forest

18 mi E of Idleyld Park on SR 138; half mi NE on FR 38. $8. 5/20-10/15; 14-day limit. 5 sites (22-ft RV limit). Tbls, toilets, cfga, drkg wtr, gray water sump. Swimming, hiking trails. At jct of Canton & Steamboat Creeks; no fishing.

Clearwater Falls $7
Umpqua National Forest

46.2 mi E of Idleyld Park on Hwy 138; qtr mi E on FR 4785. $7. 6/1-10/31; 14-day limit. 12 sites (25-ft RV limit). Tbls, toilets, cfga, no drkg wtr. Along Rogue-Umpqua Scenic Biway corridor. Whitehorse Falls viewpoint.

Eagle Rock $10
Umpqua National Forest

30 mi E of Idleyld Park on SR 138 (14 mi SE of Steamboat). $10 (double sites, $12). 5/20-9/15; 14-day limit. 25 sites (30-ft RV limit). Tbls, toilets, cfga, drkg wtr, gray water sump. Fishing, hiking, picnicking.

East Lemolo $7
Umpqua National Forest

49.4 mi E of Idleyld Park on Hwy 138; 3.2 mi N on FR 2610; 2.3 mi NE on FR 400. $7. 5/15-10/30; 14-day limit. 10 sites (RVs under 23 ft). Tbls, toilets, cfga, no drkg wtr. Fishing, swimming, boating, waterskiing, hiking trails. Dump at nearby Diamond Lake & Broken Arrow campgrounds.

Fishing tip: On the SE shore of Lemolo Reservoir, this is a favorite camp for fishermen after kokanee salmon, brook, rainbow & brown trout.

Horseshoe Bend $12
Umpqua National Forest

About 35 mi E of Idleyld Park on SR 138 (10 mi E of Steamboat). $12. 5/20-9/30; 14-day limit. 24 sites (35-ft RV limit). Tbls, flush toilets, cfga, drkg wtr, gray water sump. Fishing, rafting, hiking, picnicking. Major launch point for whitewater boating is near the camp entry.

Inlet $7
Umpqua National Forest

49.5 mi E of Idleyld Park on Hwy 138; 3.2 mi N on FR 2610; 2.7 mi NE on FR 2610-400; at Lemolo Reservoir. $7. 5/15-10/30; 14-day limit. 14 sites (RVs under 23 ft). Tbls, toilets, cfga, no drkg wtr. Swimming, boating, fishing, waterskiing. Elev 4160 ft.

Fishing tip: The lake contains kokanee salmon, brook, rainbow, brown trout.

Island $8
Umpqua National Forest

19.3 mi E of Idleyld Park on SR 138. Along Umpqua River. $8. 5/1-10/31; 14-day limit. 7 sites (RVs under 24 ft). Tbls, toilets, cfga, no drkg wtr, gray water sump. Fly fishing (steelhead), boating, rafting, swimming, rafting, hiking.

Kelsay Valley Horse Camp $7
Umpqua National Forest

50.4 mi E of Idleyld Park on SR 138; 4.7 mi NE on FR 60; qtr mi E on FR 6000-958. $7. 5/15-9/30; 14-day limit. 16 sites (RVs under 21 ft). Tbls, toilets, cfga, no drkg wtr. Picnicking, hiking, hunting. Elev 430 ft; 1 acre. Mountains, stream. Primitive hunter camp near Lemolo Lake. Camp accommodates horse riders and serves as trailhead for North

Umpqua Trail, connecting to Lucille Lake Trail, Tolo Creek Trail, Pacific Crest Trail.

Poole Creek $11
Umpqua National Forest

4.5 mi N of Idleyld Park on FR 2610 (Lemolo Lake Rd) from Hwy 138; at mouth of Poole Creek on W shore of Lemolo Lake. $11. 5/15-9/30; 14-day limit. 59 sites (35-ft RV limit). Tbls, toilets, cfga, drkg wtr, beach. Swimming, boating(l), fishing. NW forest pass needed for boat ramp.

Scaredman Creek FREE
Bureau of Land Management
Roseburg District

39.5 mi NE of Idleyld Park on OR 138 to Steamboat; 3 mi N on Canton Creek Rd. Free. 5/1-10/31; 14-day limit. 9 sites (RVs under 40 ft). Tbls, toilets, cfga, drkg wtr. Swimming; picnicking. 10 acres. Motorbikes prohibited. Site named by hunters afraid of the quantity of wolves. Popular fall hunting site. No fishing at Canton Creek. Elev 1360 ft.

Steamboat Falls $7
Umpqua National Forest

18 mi NE of Idleyld Park on OR 138; 5.5 mi NE on FR 232; half mi SE on FR 2432. $7. 6/1-12/1; self-service 12/2-5/31; 14-day limit. 10 sites (RVs under 24 ft). Tbls, toilets, cfga, no drkg wtr. Picnicking; swimming. Elev 1400 ft; 4 acres. Steamboat Creek; stream closed to all fishing. View steelhead trout jump falls in summer. Wtr 6 mi W at Canton Creek Campground.

Toketee Lake $7
Umpqua National Forest

35.2 mi E of Idlewyld Park on SR 138; 1.5 mi NE on FR 34. $7. All year; 14 day limit. 33 sites (RVs under 31 ft). Tbls, toilets, cfga, no drkg wtr. Swimming, boating(l), fishing. 6 acres.

Fishing tip: 80-acre Toketee Lake boasts of a good population of brown & rainbow trout.

Whitehorse Falls $7
Umpqua National Forest

42.4 mi E of Idleyld Park on Hwy 138. Along Clearwater River. $7. 6/1-10/31; 14-day limit. 5 sites; 25-ft RV limit. Tbls, toilets, cfga, no drkg wtr.

IMNAHA (70)

Sacajaewa FREE
Wallowa-Whitman National Forest

17.2 mi SE of Imnaha on FR N163; 5.3 mi E on FR N38; 1.6 mi E on FR S114. Elev 6800 ft. 7/1-11/30. 3 tent sites. Tbls, toilets, cfga, firewood, piped drkg wtr. Picnicking; fishing.

Saddle Creek FREE
Hells Canyon Nat. Recreation Area
Wallowa-Whitman National Forest

19.7 mi SE of Imnaha on FR 4240. 7/1-11/30; 14-day limit. 7 walk-in tent sites. Tbls, toilets, cfga, no drkg wtr. Area meant for day use, but serves as free overnight spot. Elev 6800 ft.

JACKSONVILLE (71)

Carberry   **$8**
Rogue River National Forest
8 mi SW of Jacksonville on SR 238; 18 mi S on CR 10. Walk to sites on SW shore of Applegate Reservoir. $8. 5/1-10/30; 14-day limit. 10 walk-in tent sites. Tbls, toilets, cfga, well drkg wtr. Fishing, hiking.
Fishing tip: Applegate Lake's boat launches can become inaccessible during low-water periods. The lake is known for its good smallmouth bass angling, and in 2001, it also was stocked with rainbow trout.

French Gulch Boat Ramp   **FREE**
Rogue River National Forest
8 mi SW of Jacksonville on SR 238 to Ruch; left on Upper Applegate Rd (CR 859) for 15 mi to Applegate Lake; left on CR 959, across dam, then .3 mi to boat ramp. Free. All year; 14-day limit. 2 RV sites. No facilities, but toilets at adjacent French Gulch Trailhead. Site of decommissioned French Gulch campground. Boating(l), fishing.

Harr Point Camp   **FREE**
Rogue River National Forest
8 mi SW of Jacksonville on OR 238 to Ruch; left on Upper Applegate Rd (CR 859) for 15 mi; left on CR 959, crossing the dam & 3 mi farther; right on FR 100 for half mi to Squaw Arm parking area; hike qtr mi along PayetteTrail or boat to site; on E shore of Applegate Lake. Free. 5/1-9/30; 14-day limit (open rest of yr with reduced maintenance). 5 tent sites. Tbls, toilets, cfga, no trash service. Picnicking; fishing; swimming; boating; hiking.

Hart-Tish Park   **$10**
Rogue River National Forest
8 mi SW of Jacksonville on SR 238; 15 mi SW on FR 10. $10. 4/15-10/31; 14-day limit. Open space for self-contained RVs & 5 walk-in tent sites. Tbls, flush toilets, cfga, drkg wtr, fish cleaning station. Boating(l), fishing, swimming, hiking.Elev 2000 ft. On Applegate Lake.

Jackson Campground   **$8**
Rogue River National Forest
8 mi SW of Jacksonville on SR 238; 9 mi SW on CR 10; 1 mi SW on FR 1095; across the river from Flumet Flat Campground. $8. 5/1-9/30; 14-day limit (reduced rates rest of year). 12 sites (large trailers not recommended due to tight corners & short sites). Tbls, flush toilets, cfga, drkg wtr. Fishing, boating, hiking.

Squaw Lakes   **$10**
Rogue River National Forest
8 mi SW of Jacksonville on SR 238; 14 mi SW on CR 10; 8 mi SE on FR 1075. $10; free 11/1-5/15 but no wtr or services. All year; 14-day limit. 17 tent sites (no trailers). Tbls, toilets, cfga, drkg wtr. Swimming, fishing, boating(l), hiking trails. Elev 3000 ft; 85 acres.
Fishing tip: Lower Squaw Lake contains cutthroat trout, largemouth bass, yellow perch & black crappie; Upper Squaw has good fishing for cutthroat trout.

Tipsu Tyee Camp   **FREE**
Rogue River National Forest
8 mi SW on OR 238; 16 mi SW on CR 859; hike in or boat in; at Applegate Lake. Free. 5/15-9/30; 14-day limit. 5 tent sites. Tbls, toilets, cfga, no drkg wtr. Picnicking; fishing; swimming; boating (l-2 mi); hiking. Elev 2100 ft; 3 acres. Mountains. Lake.

Watkins   **$8**
Rogue River National Forest
8 mi SW of Jacksonville on SR 238; 17 mi S on CR 10. On SW shore of Applegate Reservoir. $8. 5/1-9/30 (free rest of year, but no wtr or trash service); 14-day limit. 14 walk-in tent sites. Tbls, toilets, cfga, well drkg wtr. Fishing, hiking, boating(ld).

JOHN DAY (72)

Canyon Meadows   **FREE**
Malheur National Forest
10 mi S of John Day on US 395; 9 mi SE on FR 15; 5 mi NE on FR 1520. Free. 5/15-10/30; 14-day limit. 5 sites (15-ft RV limit). Tbls, cfga, toilets, drkg wtr. Boating(l; no motors), fishing, hiking, swimming. Elev 5100 ft.

Wickiup   **FREE**
Malheur National Forest
10 mi S of John Day on US 395; 8 mi SE on FR 1541. Free. 5/15-11/1; 14-day limit. 9 RV sites (16-ft RV limit), 4 tent. Tbls, toilets, cfga, no drkg wtr. Fishing in Wickiup Creek. Elev 4300 ft.

JORDAN VALLEY (73)

Antelope Reservoir   **FREE**
Bureau of Land Management
Vale District
10 mi SW of Jordan Valley on US 95; follow signs 1 mi SE to site. Free. All year; 14-day limit. 4 sites. Tbls, toilets, cfga, no drkg wtr. Boating(l), fishing. Elev 4318 ft.

Birch Creek   **FREE**
Bureau of Land Management
Vale District
8 mi N of Jordan Valley, then W on Cow Creek Rd, following Jordan Craters signs; follow BLM's Owyhee River access signs 28 mi; high-clearance vehicles recommended; rd may be impassible when wet. Free. All year (depending on rd conditions); 14 day limit. 5 primitive sites. Toilets, tbls, cfga, no drkg wtr. River floating, hiking, hunting, fishing.

Cow Lakes   **FREE**
Bureau of Land Management
Vale District
5 mi S of Jordan Valley on US 95; follow signs NW on Danner Loop Rd to site. Free. All year; 14-day limit. 10 sites. Tbls, toilets, cfga, no drkg wtr. Boating(l), fishing, hiking. Elev 4338 ft.

Rome Launch   **FREE**
Bureau of Land Management
Vale District
32 mi SW of Jordan Valley on US 95; S at Owyhee River & BLM boat launch sign. Free. 3/1-12/1; 14-day limit. 5 sites. Tbls, toilets, cfga, drkg wtr (no firewood). Boating(l), fishing, hiking.

Three Forks   **FREE**
Bureau of Land Management
Vale District
15 mi SW of Jordan Valley on US 95; 35 mi S on Three Forks Rd; high-clearnace vehicles suggested; rd may be impassible when wet. Free. All year; 14-day limit. Undeveloped camping area; 4 sites. Toilet, cfga, tbls, no drkg wtr. Fishing, hiking, canoeing, river floating.

JOSEPH (74)

Blackhorse   **$8**
Hells Canyon Nat. Recreation Area
Wallowa-Whitman National Forest
7.5 mi E of Joseph on Hwy 350; 29 mi S on FR 39; at Imnaha River. $8. 5/15-10/31; 14-day limit. 16 sites; 30-ft RV limit. Tbls, toilets, cfga, no drkg wtr (available at nearby Ollokot Camp), grey wtr dumps. Fishing, boating, swimming.

Coverdale   **$5**
Wallowa-Whitman National Forest
1 mi S of Joseph on SR 82; 7.3 mi E on Hwy 350; 28.8 mi SE on FR 39; 4 mi S on FR 3960. $5. 6/15-11/15; 14-day limit. 11 sites (32-ft RV limit). Tbls, toilets, cfga, no drkg wtr. Fishing, hiking. Elev 4300 ft; 4 acres.

Ollokot   **$8**
Hells Canyon Nat. Recreation Area
Wallowa-Whitman National Forest
7.5 mi E of Joseph on Hwy 350; 30 mi S on FR 39; at Imnaha River. $8. 5/15-10/31; 14-day limit. 12 sites; 30-ft RV limit. Tbls, toilets, cfga, drkg wtr. Fishing, hiking, boating. Note: drkg wtr was not available in 2006; status unknown for 2007.

Evergreen Group Camp   **FREE**
Hells Canyon Nat. Recreation Area
Wallowa-Whitman National Forest
1 mi S of Joseph on Hwy 82; 7.7 mi E on Hwy 350; 28.8 mi S on FR 39; 8 mi SW on FR 3960. Free. 6/1-11/30; 14-day limit. Primitive undesignated sites (RVs under 32 ft). Tbls, toilets, cfga, no drkg wtr. Swimming, fishing. Elev 4500 ft.

OREGON

Hidden   **$6**
Hells Canyon Nat. Recreation Area
Wallowa-Whitman National Forest
7.5 mi E of Joseph on Hwy 350; 29 mi S on FR 39; at Imnaha River. $6. 5/15-10/31; 14-day limit. 10 sites. Tbls, toilets, cfga, drkg wtr. Fishing, boating, hiking.

Hurricane Creek   **$6**
Wallowa-Whitman National Forest
11 mi N of Joseph on OR 82; 1.9 mi W on Co Hwy 774; qtr mi SW on FR S218A. $6. 5/15-10/31; 10-day limit. 8 sites (RVs under 16 ft). Tbls, toilets, cfga. Self-service site. Fishing; picnicking. Elev 4800 ft. S end of camp rd not recommended for low-clearance vehicles.

Indian Crossing   **$6**
Wallowa-Whitman National Forest
Hells Canyon National Recreation Area
1 mi S of Joseph on SR 82; 7.3 mi E on SR 350; 28.7 mi S on FR 39; 8.7 mi SW on FR 3960. On Imnaha River. $6. 6/15-11/15; 14-day limit 14 sites (32-ft RV limit). Tbls, toilets, cfga, drkg wtr. Fishing, hiking trails, horseback riding. Horse facilities. Elev 4500 ft; 16 acres.

Lick Creek   **$6**
Hells Canyon Nat. Recreation Area
Wallowa-Whitman National Forest
7.5 mi E of Joseph on Hwy 350; 15 mi S on FR 39; at Lick Creek. $6. 6/1-11/30; 14-day limit. 12 sites; 30-ft RV limit. Tbls, toilets, cfga, drkg wtr. Fishing, boating, hiking.

JUNTURA (75)

Chukar Park Recreation Site   **$5**
Bureau of Land Management
Vale District
3 mi NW of Juntura on Beulah Reservoir Rd. $5. 4/15-11/30; 14-day limit. 18 sites (28-ft RV limit). Tbls, toilets, cfga, drkg wtr. Hunting, fishing. On North Fork of Malheur River. 80 acres; elev 3100 ft.

KENO (76)

Keno Reservoir Recreation Area   **$12**
Pacific Power Company
1 mi W of Keno on SR 66. $12. MD-9/15; 14-day limit. 25 sites. Tbls, flush toilets, cfga, drkg wtr, public phone, dump. Fishing, boating(ld), picnicking, hiking, horseshoes.

Klamath River Camp   **FREE**
Bureau of Land Management
Lakeview District
14 mi W of Keno on SR 66; 6 mi S on Klamath River Rd to John C. Boyles substation site, then 1 mi S. Free. 5/15-10/15; 14-day limit. 4 primitive sites. Toilets, cfga, no drkg wtr. Boating(l), fishing.

Fishing tip: The Klamath from Keno Dam downstream to Boyle Dam is open to trout fishing during 1/1-7/1 and 10/1-12/31. There's some great fishing for redband rainbow trout.

Surveyor Campground   **FREE**
Bureau of Land Management
Lakeview District
14 mi NW of Keno (7 mi S of Lake of the Woods). Free. 5/1-10/31; 14-day limit. 5 sites. Tbls, toilets, cfga, drkg wtr. Wheelchair access.

Fishing tip: Take that short drive to the lake for its kokanee, brown trout and largemouth bass fishing, as well as for its stocked rainbows.

Topsy Recreation Area   **$7**
Bureau of Land Management
Lakeview District
6 mi W of Keno on SR 66; 1 mi S on Topsy Rd. (SW of Klamath Falls). $7 if wtr is available; free if no water. $4 for 2nd RV. 5/15-11/15; 14-day limit. 15 sites (no RV size limit); 12 picnic sites. Toilets, drkg wtr, gray water dump. Fishing, swimming, hiking, boating(l), water skiing, hunting. On John C. Boyles Reservoir. Elev 3800 ft.

KIMBERLY (77)

Big Bend   **$5**
Bureau of Land Management
Prineville District
John Day River System
2 mi E of Kimberly on the rd to Monument. $5. All year; 14-day limit. 4 sites. Tbls, toilets, cfga, no drkg wtr. Fishing, boating, hiking. Along North Fork of John Day River.

Lone Pine   **$8**
Bureau of Land Management
Prineville District
John Day River System
1 mi E of Kimberly on the rd to Monument. $8. All year; 14-day limit. 8 sites. Tbls, toilets, cfga, no drkg wtr. Fishing, hiking, boating. Along North Fork of John Day River.

Muleshoe   **$5**
Bureau of Land Management
Prineville District
John Day River System
2 mi E of Service Creek along Hwy 207/19. $5. All year; 14-day limit. 10 sites. Tbls, toilets, cfga, no drkg wtr. Fishing, hiking, boating. On main stem of John Day River.

KLAMATH FALLS (78)

Collier Memorial State Park   **$11**
30 mi N of Klamath Falls on US 97; at the Williamson River and Spring Creek. $11 for tent sites off-season ($15 in-season); $13-17 with hookups. 10-day limit. Tbls, flush toilets, cfga, drkg wtr, showers, horse corrals, dump. Hiking & bridle trails.

Fishing tip: Legal-size rainbow trout are stocked in Spring Creek throughout the summer.

Eagle Ridge   **$5**
Klamath County Park
15 mi W of Klamath Falls off Hwy 140; at 17300 Eagle Ridge Rd; at Upper Klamath Lake, on W side at Shoalwater Bay. $5. All year. 6 sites. Tbls, toilets, cfga, drkg wtr. Boating, fishing, boating(l). Elev 4139 ft. Fee not verified for 2007.

Fourmile Lake   **$11**
Winema National Forest
33 mi NW of Klamath Falls on SR 140; 5.5 mi N on FR 3661. $11. 6/1-LD; 14-day limit. 25 sites (22-ft RV limit). Tbls, toilets, cfga, drkg wtr. Swimming, boating(l), fishing. Elev 5800 ft; 14 acres.

Fishing tip: Kokanee salmon are plentiful in Fourmile Lake, and brook trout fishing is good too. Planted lake trout are about 18".

Hagelstein   **$5**
Klamath County Park
9 mi N of Klamath Falls on US 97. $5. 4/15-11/30; 14-day limit. 10 sites. Tbls, flush toilets, cfga, wtr. Swimming; picnicking; fishing; boating(l); waterskiing; hiking. 3 acres on Upper Klamath Lake. Elev 4139 ft. Fee not verified for 2007.

Hunter Camp Development   **FREE**
Klamath County Parks
The county has set 28 pit toilets at free hunter campsites throughout the county, and cfga have been established by the users. No other facilities, no drkg wtr. Hunting, fishing. Fee not verified for 2007.

Klamath County Fairgrounds   **$12**
Just off SRs 140/39 at S. Sixth St. in Klamath Falls. $12 for sites with elec/wtr; $15 full hookups. All year. Tbls, flush toilets, cfga, drkg wtr, showers, dump (no wtr hookup during winter).

Malone Springs   **FREE**
Winema National Forest
25 mi NW of Klamath Falls on SR 140; 5 mi on Westside Rd, then on FR 3459. Free. 5/15-9/30; 14-day limit. 2 tent sites. Tbl, toilet, cfga, no drkg wtr. Boating, fishing, canoe trail. Unimproved boat ramp.

Odessa   **FREE**
Winema National Forest
21.5 mi NW of Klamath Falls on SR 140; 1 mi NE on FR 3639. Free. 5/15-9/30; 14-day limit. 5 sites. Tbls, toilets, cfga, no drkg wtr. Fishing, boating(l).

Petric Park   **$5**
Klamath County Park
29 mi from Klamath Falls on Hwy 427; at Wood River. $5. All year. Primitive undesignated sites. Toilets, cfga, no drkg wtr. Boating(l), fishing. Fees not verified for 2007.

LA GRANDE (79)

Birdtrack Springs   **$8**
Willowa-Whitman National Forest
W of LaGrande on I-84 to exit 252; 6 mi W on Hwy 244. $8. 6/1-10/15; 14-day limit. 26 sites. Tbls, toilets, cfga, drkg wtr. Nature study, hiking trails, birdwatching, fishing.

Hilgard Junction State Park **$8**

8 mi W of LaGrande on Starkey Rd; at Grande Ronde River. $8 in-season for 18 primitive sites; $6 off-season. 10-day limit in 14-day period. 18 primitive sites; 30-ft RV limit. Tbls, toilets, cfga, drkg wtr, dump. Oregon Trail interpretive display. Rafting, boating, fishing, hiking.

Moss Springs **$5**
Wallowa-Whitman National Forest

15 mi E of LaGrande on Hwy 237; 1.5 mi SE of Cove on CR 237; 8 mi E on FR 6220. $5. 6/15-10/15; 14-day limit. 12 tent sites. Tbls, toilets, cfga, no drkg wtr (except for horses), horse loading ramp, corrals. Hiking, horseback riding.

N. Fork Catherine Creek **FREE**
Wallowa-Whitman National Forest

24 mi SE of LaGrande on Hwy 203 (past Union); 4 mi E on FR 7785 (last 6 mi gravel). Free. 6/1-10/15; 14-day limit. 6 sites. Tbls, toilets, cfga, no drkg wtr. Fishing, hiking, horseback riding (loading ramp).

Red Bridge State Wayside **$8**

16 mi SW of LaGrande on SR 244; at Grande Ronde River. $8 ($5 off-season) for 20 primitive sites. 10-day limit. Tbls, toilets, cfga, drkg wtr. Fishing.

River Campground **FREE**
Wallowa-Whitman National Forest

8.1 mi NW of La Grande on I-84; 12.6 mi SW on OR 244; 10.9 mi S on FR 51. Free. Elev 3800 ft. 5/15-11/20. 6 sites (RVs under 22 ft). Tbls, toilets, cfga, firewood, well drkg wtr. Self-service sites. Picnicking; berry picking; fishing; horseback riding.

Spool Cart **$5**
Wallowa-Whitman National Forest

8.1 mi NW of LaGrande on I-84; 13 mi SW on Hwy 244; 7 mi S on FR 51. $5. MD-9/30; 14-day limit. 16 sites (22-ft RV limit). Tbls, toilets, cfga, no drkg wtr. Fishing, hiking. Grande Ronde River.

Spring Creek **$5**
Wallowa-Whitman National Forest

About 16 mi NW of LaGrande on I-84 to exit 248, then 1 mi on FR 21. $5. 5/15-11/15; 14-day limit. 4 sites. Tbls, toilets, cfga, no drkg wtr. Birdwatching, mountain biking.

West Eagle Meadow **$5**
Wallowa-Whiteman National Forest

46 mi SE of LaGrande on Hwy 203, FR 77 & FR 7755. $5. 5/15-11/15; 14-day limit. 24 tent sites (6 equestrian). Tbls, toilets, cfga, no drkg wtr (except for horses). Fishing, picnicking, hiking, horseback riding.

LA PINE (80)

Chief Paulina Horse Camp **$12**
Newberry National Monument
Deschutes National Forest

5 mi N of La Pine on US 97; 13 mi E on CR 21. $12 for 2-horse stalls; $14 for 4-horse stalls. 6/1-10/31; 14-day limit. 14 equestrian sites; 25-ft RV limit. Tbls, toilets, cfga, no drkg wtr. Bridle trails, hiking. Near Paulina Lake in Newberry National Volcanic Monument. Elev 6400 ft. Entry fee required.

Crane Prairie **$10**
Deschutes National Forest

2.5 mi NW of LaPine on US 97; 20 mi W on FR 42; 4 mi N on FR 4270. $10 (premium lakeside sites $12). About 5/1-10/31; 14-day limit. 146 sites; 30-ft RV limit. Tbls, toilets, cfga, drkg wtr. Boating(lr), fishing, hiking. Two fish cleaning stations. On Crane Prairie Reservoir. Elev 4400 ft; 10 acres. Multi-family sites $5 for 3rd & subsequent vehicle.

Fishing tip: Crane Prairie Lake contains rainbow trout up to 19 pounds, brook trout, mountain whitefish, kokanee salmon, largemouth bass and crappie.

Gull Point **$12**
Deschutes National Forest

2.5 mi W of LaPine on CR 42; S on FR 4262. $12 (premium sites $14). About 5/1-10/15; 14-day limit. 81 sites (30-ft RV limit). Tbls, flush & pit toilets, cfga, drkg wtr, dump, 2 fish cleaning stations. Boating (ldr), fishing, hiking, swimming, waterskiing. On N shore of Wickiup Reservoir. $3 dump for non-campers.

Fishing tip: Wickiup produces some of the best fishing in central Oregon and is well known for brown trout of 5-8 pounds, with some over 20 pounds. Biggest trout caught early in the season; a 26-pounder was caught on opening day in 1998 on a rainbow-colored Rapala.

McKay Crossing **$6**
Deschutes National Forest

5 mi N of LaPine on US 97; 5 mi E on CR 21; 2.7 mi E on FR 2120; at Paulina Creek. $6. About 4/15-10/15; 14-day limit. 10 sites (22-ft RV limit). Tbls, toilets, cfga, no drkg wtr. Picnicking, hiking, fishing, boating. Elev 4750 ft.

North Cove Boat-In Camp **FREE**
Deschutes National Forest

5 mi N of LaPine on US 97; 12.9 mi E on CR 21 to Pauline Lake; boat across lake to sites. Free. May-Oct; 14-day limit. 6 tent sites. Toilet, cfga, no tbls, no drkg wtr. Fishing, boating, hiking.

North Davis Creek **$8**
Deschutes National Forest

2.5 mi N of LaPine on US 97; 11 mi W on CR 42; 9 mi W on CR 42; 4 mi S on CR 46 (Cascade Lakes Hwy). $8. About 4/15-9/30; 14-day limit. 15 sites (22-ft RV limit). Tbls, toilets, cfga, drkg wtr. Boating(ld), fishing, hiking. On Wickiup Reservoir.

Fishing tip: To catch Wickiup's giant brown trout, use plugs or other lures that imitate fleeing baitfish. The lake also contains rainbow & brook trout, Kokanee & coho salmon and whitefish.

Paulina Lake **$12**
Newberry National Volcanic Monument
Deschutes National Forest

5 mi N of La Pine on US 97; 12.9 mi E on CR 21; at Paulina Lake. $12 (premium lakeside sites $14). 6/1-10/31; 14-day limit. 69 sites. Tbls, flush & pit toilets, cfga, drkg wtr, dump nearby. Boating(l), fishing, hiking, swimming, birdwatching, biking. Forest pass ($) needed for trailhead access. Elev 6350 ft. Entry fee to monument.

Fishing tip: This 250-ft deep lake produces huge brown trout, including the state record 27-pounder caught in 1993. A 35-pound brown was caught there in 1965, but it was not a legal record because it was netted after it broke another fisherman's line. The state record kokanee salmon was caught here in 1989; it weighed four pounds, 2 ounces.

Prairie Campground **$10**
Deschutes National Forest

5 mi N of La Pine on US 97; 3 mi SE on CR 21; at Paulina Creek. $10. 4/15-10/15; 14-day limit. 16 sites (32-ft RV limit). Tbls, toilets, cfga, drkg wtr. Fishing, biking, hiking trails, horseback riding. Elev 4300 ft.

Pringle Falls **$6**
Deschutes National Forest

2.4 mi NE of La Pine on US 97; 7.2 mi W on CR 43; three-fourths mi NE on FR 4330-500; at Deschutes River below Wickiup Reservoir. $6. 4/15-10/31; 14-day limit. 7 sites; 26-ft RV limit. Tbls, toilets, cfga, no drkg wtr. Fishing, canoeing on Deschutes River. Pringle Falls nearby. Elev 4300 ft.

Quinn River **$10**
Deschutes National Forest

2.5 mi NE of LaPine on US 97; 10 mi W on CR 43; 10 mi W & 4 mi N on CR 46 (Cascade Lakes Hwy); at Crane Prairie Reservoir. $10 (premium sites, $12). 5/1-9/30; 14-day limit. 41 sites (30-ft RV limit). Tbls, toilets, cfga, drkg wtr. Hiking, fishing, boating(l). Elev 4400 ft; 20 acres.

Fishing tip: Crane Prairie contains big rainbow trout, brook trout, mountain whitefish, kokanee salmon, largemouth bass, black crappie. For trout, fish the channels with power bait, worms, dragonfly nymphs or marshmallows with worms.

Rock Creek **$10**
Deschutes National Forest

2.5 mi NE of LaPine on US 97; 10 mi W on CR 43; 10 mi W on CR 42; 2.5 mi N on CR 46 (Cascade Lakes Hwy). $10 (premium sites $12). 5/1-10/15; 14-day limit. 31 sites (22-ft RV limit). Tbls, toilets, cfga, drkg wtr, fish cleaning station. Boating(l), fishing. On Crane Prairie Reservoir 50 mi SW of Band. Elev 4450 ft; 13 acres.

Fishing tip: Crane Prairie observers claim the illegally introduced bass, bluegill and crappie have hurt the trout population. Bass up to 9 pounds are caught, and both the bluegill and crappie are in the jumbo class.

West South Twin $10
Deschutes National Forest

2.5 mi N of LaPine on US 97; 11 mi W on CR 43; 5 mi W on CR 42; 1.5 mi S on FR 4260; at Wickiup Reservoir. $10 (premium sites $12). About 5/1-10/15; 14-day limit. 24 sites (22-ft RV limit). Tbls, flush toilets, cfga, drkg wtr, horse facilities. Fishing, boating(ldr), hiking, horseback riding, waterskiing.

Wickiup Butte $5
Deschutes National Forest

2.5 mi NE of LaPine on US 97; 10 mi W on CR 43; 3.5 mi SW on FR 4380; 2.3 mi SW on FR 4260. On Wickiup Reservoir. $5. About 4/15-9/30; 14-day limit. 8 sites. Tbls, toilets, cfga, no drkg wtr. Picnicking, boating, fishing, waterskiing.

Fishing tip: For Wickiup's trout and salmon, use spinners, lures such as Rapalas, gold or bronze minnow imitations, dark spinners. Fish the points and ledges, trolling or jigging.

LAKEVIEW (81)

Can Springs Forest Camp FREE
Fremont National Forest

2.5 mi N of Lakeview on Hwy 395; 8 mi E on Hwy 140; left on FR 3615 for 11.5 mi; right on FR 3720 for 4 mi. Free. Maintained 6/1-10/15; 14-day limit. Primitive undesignated sites. Tbls, cfga, toilets, no drkg wtr. Birdwatching, hiking, mountain biking, horseback riding. Elev 6300 ft.

Clear Springs Forest Camp FREE
Fremont National Forest

3 mi W of Lakeview on Hwy 140; right on CR 2-16 for 5 mi; left on CR 2-16A (becomes FR 28) for 19 mi; after crossing Dairy Creek, left on FR 047 for 4 mi to pull-off marked "Clear Springs." Free. Maintained 5/15-10/31; 14-day limit. Primitive sites. Tbls, cfga, toilets, drkg wtr, no trash service. Fishing, hiking.

Cottonwood Recreation Area FREE
Fremont National Forest

24 mi W of Lakeview on SR 140; 8 mi NE on FR 3870 (surfaced rd). Maintained 6/1-10/15; 14-day limit. 21 sites (RVs under 32 ft). Tbls, toilets, cfga, drkg wtr, no trash service. Good fishing, hiking, boating(no motors), birdwatching, swimming, horseback riders, mountain biking. 12 mi of trails Popular among fishermen. Elev 6100 ft.

Dead Horse Creek FREE
Forest Camp
Fremont National Forest

3 mi W of Lakeview on Hwy 140; right on CR 2-16 for 5 mi; left on CR 2-16A (becomes FR 28) for 19 mi; after crossing Dairy Creek, left on FR 047 for 3 mi; just past Deadhorse Creek is unmaked rd to campsites. Free. Apr-Nov; 14-day limit. 4 sides. Toilets, cfga, no drkg wtr, no trash service. Fishing in Dairy Creek. Elev 5400 ft.

Fishing tip: A special treat here is catching wild redband rainbow trout from Dairy Creek.

Deep Creek Forest Camp FREE
Fremont National Forest

5.4 mi N of Lakeview on US 395; 6.5 mi E on SR 140; 6.1 mi S on FR 391. Free. Maintained 6/1-10/15; 14-day limit. 6 sites. Tbls, toilets, cfga, no drkg wtr, no trash service. Fishing, hunting. Elev 5600 ft. Good rds.

Dog Lake FREE
Fremont National Forest

5 mi W of Lakeview on OR 140; 7 mi S on CR W60; 13 mi W on FR 4017 (gravel rd). Free. Maintained 6/1-10/15; 14-day limit. 8 sites (RVs under 16 ft). Tbls, toilets, cfga, piped drkg wtr. Hunting; picnicking; fishing; boating(l). Elev 5100 ft; 4 acres. Good gravel rds.

Fishing tip: This lake is a popular all-year fishing lake for largemouth bass, crappie and perch.

Dismal Creek Forest Camp FREE
Fremont National Forest

3 mi N of Lakeview on Hwy 395; right on Hwy 140 for 8 mi; right on FR 3615 for half mi, then right on Old Hwy 140 for 1.4 mi; left on FR 3915 for 15 mi; left at jct with FR 4015, staying on FR 3915 for 1 mi. Free. Maintained 6/1-10/15; 14-day limit. 3 sites. Tbls, cfga, toilets, no drkg wtr. Fishing, birdwatching, hiking. Elev 5600 ft.

Drews Campground FREE
Lake County Park

2 mi SE of Drews Reservoir on CR 4812. Free. All year. 5 primitive sites. Tbls, toilets, cfga, no drkg wtr. Fishing, hiking, boating(l).

Drews Creek FREE
Fremont National Forest

10 mi W of Lakeview on SR 140; 4.5 mi S on CR 1-13 & 1-11; 4 mi W on CR 1-13; right on CR 1-11D & FR 4017 for 6 mi. Free. Maintained 6/1-10/15; 14-day limit. 5 sites. Tbls, toilets, cfga, drkg wtr, no trash service. Fishing, hiking, horseshoes, ball field. Elev 4900 ft.

Fishing tip: Try Drews Reservoir, 2 mi (boating, fishing & waterskiing); paved bike lane to lake.

Goose Lake $12
State Recreation Area

14 mi S of Lakeview off SR 395. $12 for 48 elec sites off-season ($16 in-season). 10-day limit. Flush toilets, tbls, cfga, drkg wtr, dump, showers. Fishing, boating(l), birdwatching.

Holbrook Reservoir FREE
Forest Camp
Fremont National Forest

25 mi W of Lakeview on Hwy 140; left on FR 3715 for 6 mi; right on FR 3817 to picnic area entrance. Free. Maintained 5/15-10/15; 14-day limit. Primitive undesignated sites. Tbls, toilets, cfga, no drkg wtr. Boating(l), fishing, birdwatching, swimming. Elev 5400 ft.

Fishing tip: Holbrook is stocked annually with fingerling, legal-size and trophy-size rainbow trout. Angling is quite good here.

Mud Creek Forest Camp FREE
Fremont National Forest

2.5 mi N of Lakeview on US 395; 6.5 mi E on SR 140; 6.1 mi N on FR 3615. Free. Maintained 6/1-10/15; 14-day limit. 7 sites (16-ft RV limit). Tbls, toilets, drkg wtr, cfga. Hunting, good fishing. Elev 6600 ft. Scenic drive.

Overton Reservoir FREE
Forest Camp
Fremont National Forest

2.5 mi N of Lakeview on US 395; 6.5 mi E on SR 140; 12.5 mi N on FR 3615; left on FR 3624 for 2 mi; right on FR 011 to pond. Free. Maintained 6/1-10/15; 14-day limit. Primitive undesignated sites. Toilets, tbls, cfga, no drkg wtr. Elev 6600 ft.

Fishing tip: Pond has been stocked with rainbow trout.

Twin Springs Forest Camp FREE
Fremont National Forest

2.5 mi N of Lakeview on Hwy 395; 8 mi E on SR 140; half mi N on FR 3615; right on Old Hwy 140 for 1.4 mi; left on FR 3915 for 3 mi; left on FR 3910 for 2 mi to camp entrance sign. Free. Maintained 6/1-10/15; 14-day limit. 3 sites. Tbls, toilets, cfga, drkg wtr. Hiking, birdwatching. Elev 6300 ft.

Willow Creek FREE
Fremont National Forest

5.5 mi N of Lakeview on US 395; half mi E on SR 140; 10 mi S on FR 391. Free. Maintained 6/1-10/15; 14-day limit. 8 sites (22-ft RV limit). Tbls, cfga, toilets, no drkg wtr, no trash service. Fishing, birdwatching. Elev 5800 ft; 5 acres.

LEBANON (82)

Waterloo Campground $9
Linn County Park

From jct of Hwys 20 & 34 in Lebanon, 5.7 mi E on Hwy 20 to Waterloo turnoff, then 1 mi N on Gross Rd. $9 without hookups, $12 with wtr/elec for seniors off-season 9/4-5/23; others pay $16 off-season, $18 in-season. 4/1-11/1. 110 sites; 60-ft RV limit. Tbls, flush toilets, cfga, drkg wtr, hookups($), playground. Fishing, hiking, swimming.

LORELLA (83)

Gerber Reservoir $7
Bureau of Land Management
Lakeview District

10 mi E of Lorella on East Longell Valley Rd; gravel rd to site (or, S on gravel rd from Bly). $7. 5/15-11/15; 14-day limit. 50 sites (30-ft RV limit). Tbls, toilets, cfga, drkg wtr. Boating(dl), fishing, swimming, hiking. 80 acres.

LOSTINE (84)

Shady $6
Wallowa-Whitman National Forest

7 mi S of Lostine on CR 551; 10.1 mi S on FR 8210. $6. Elev 5400 ft. 6/15-11/1; 10-day

limit. 12 sites (RVs under 22 ft). Tbls, toilets, cfga, firewood, no drkg wtr. Self-service sites. Swimming; fishing; picnicking. On Lostine River.

Two Pan $6
Wallowa-Whitman National Forest
7 mi S of Lostine on CR 551; 10.8 mi S on FR 8210. On Lostine River. $6. Elev 5600 ft. 6/15-11/1; 10-day limit. 8 sites (RVs under 16 ft). Tbls, toilets, cfga, firewood, no drkg wtr. Self-service sites. Picnicking; swimming; berry picking; horseback riding (2 mi).

Williamson $6
Wallowa-Whitman National Forest
7 mi S of Lostine on CR 551; 4 mi S on FR 8210. On Lostine River. $6. Elev 5000 ft. 6/15-11/1; 10-day limit. 9 sites (RVs under 16 ft). Tbls, toilets, cfga, firewood, no drkg wtr. Self-service sites. Swimming; picnicking; fishing; horseback riding (4 mi).

LOWELL (85)

Bedrock $10
Willamette National Forest
2 mi N of Lowell on CR 6220; 10 mi E on CR 6240; 4 mi on Fall Creek Rd (FR 18). $10. About MD-9/15; 14-day limit. 21 sites (36-ft RV limit). Tbls, toilets, cfga, drkg wtr. Swimming, fishing, hiking. Access to Fall Creek National Recreation Trail and the Jones Trail.

Big Pool $12
Willamette National Forest
2 mi N of Lowell on CR 6220; 10 mi E on CR 6240; 1.5 mi on FR 18 (Fall Creek Rd). $12. About MD-9/15; 14-day limit. 5 sites (24-ft RV limit). Tbls, toilets, cfga, drkg wtr. Swimming, fishing, hiking.

Dolly Varden $10
Willamette National Forest
2 mi N of Lowell on CR 6220; 10 mi E on CR 6240; E on Fall Creek Rd (FR 18). $10. About MD-9/15; 14-day limit. 5 tent sites (every site on shore of Fall Creek). Toilets, cfga, no drkg wtr. Fishing, swimming, hiking. Fall Creek National Recreation Trail.

Puma Creek $12
Willamette National Forest
2 mi N of Lowell on CR 6220; 10 mi E on CR 6240; 6.5 mi E on FR 18. $12. About MD-9/15; 14-day limit. 11 sites (30-ft RV limit). Tbls, toilets, cfga, drkg wtr. Swimming, fishing, hiking trails. 10 acres.

Winberry $8
Willamette National Forest
2 mi N of Lowell on CR 6220; half mi E on CR 6240; 5.8 mi SE on CR 6245; 3.5 mi SE on FR 191. $8. About MD-LD; 14-day limit. Higher fee for site with A-frame shelter. 6 sites (RVs under 16 ft). Tbls, toilets, cfga, firewood, drkg wtr. Hunting; picnicking; fishing. At Winberry Creek & North Blanket Creek.

MADRAS (87)

Haystack Reservoir $8
Ochoco National Forest
Crooked River National Grasslands
9.3 mi S of Madras on US 97; 3.3 mi SE on Jericho Lane; half mi N on FR 9605. In Crooked River National Grassland. $8. 5/15-9/15; 14-day limit. 24 sites (32-ft RV limit). Tbls, flush toilets, cfga, drkg wtr. Fishing, swimming, waterskiing, hiking, boating(l). Elev 2900 ft; 5 acres. Rehabilitation of campsites planned.

Fishing tip: This cold-water lake averages only 27 feet deep, and it offers a variety of fishing: kokanee salmon, largemouth bass, rainbow & brown trout, crappie, bullhead and bluegills. Kokanee are now averaging 12-15 inches, and the daily catch limit is 25. One bull trout of at least 24 inches can be kept.

Jefferson County Fairgrounds $7
In town at Madison & M Sts. $7 without hookups; $15 full hookups. All year; 14-day limit. 660 sites (55-ft RV limit). Tbls, flush toilets, cfga, drkg wtr, elec($), sewer($), wtr hookups ($), showers. Picnicking. Fees not verified for 2007.

Skull Hollow FREE
Dispersed Camp & Trailhead
Ochoco National Forest
SE of Madras on Hwy 26; right on Lone Pine Rd for 2.5 mi, then right on FR 5710; poor access. Free. All year; 14-day limit. 40 primitive sites. Toilets, no drkg wtr, no tbls, no cfga. SE of Haystack Reservoir. Elev 3000 ft.

South Junction $8
Bureau of Land Management
Prineville District
Lower Deschutes River System
29 mi N of Madras on US 97; left on gravel rd near intersection of US 97 & US 197 at sign, "BLM Recreation Site." $8 Sun-Thurs; $12 Fri-Sat. All year; 14-day limit. 11 sites. Tbls, toilets, cfga, no drkg wtr. Hunting, boating(l), fishing, rafting, swimming. Elev 2900 ft.

Travel tip: Rockhounding for thunder eggs N of Madras is among the best free attractions in Oregon.

Trout Creek $8
Bureau of Land Management
Prineville District
Lower Deschutes River System
3 mi N of Madras on US 97; 7 mi NW on gravel rd; E side of Deschutes River. $8 Sun-Thurs; $12 Fri-Sat. All year; 14-day limit. 21 sites (35-ft RV limit). Tbls, toilets, cfga, no drkg wtr. Fishing, hiking, rafting, boating(l), hunting, summer interpretive programs. 11 acres.

MANZANITA (88)

Nehalem Bay State Park $8
3 mi S of Manzanita Junction, off US 101. $8 for primitive/overflow sites; $16-20 for RV sites wtih hookups ($5 off-season); $12 for equestrian sites off-season ($16 in-season); sites with hookups $16-20. About 300 sites. Tbls, flush toilets, cfga, showers, drkg wtr, elec($), dump, beach, playgrounds. Swimming, boatiing, bike trail, hiking trail, crabbing, fishing.

MAPLETON (89)

Clay Creek $10
Bureau of Land Management
Eugene District
15 mi SE of Mapleton on SR 126, then S on Siuslaw River Rd; follow signs. $10. 5/15-11/30; 14-day limit. 21 sites. Tbls, toilets, cfga, drkg wtr. Hunting, fishing, swimming, horseshoes. $5 for extra vehicle.

Whittaker Creek $10
Bureau of Land Management
Eugene District
14 mi SE of Mapleton SR 126; S on Siuslaw River Rd. $10 (2nd RV, $5). 5/15-11/30; 14-day limit. 31 sites. Tbls, toilets, cfga, drkg wtr. Boating(l), fishing, swimming, hunting, hiking. 10 acres; elev 1300 ft.

MAUPIN (90)

Bear Springs $12
Mt. Hood National Forest
25 mi W of Maupin on SR 216 (24 mi SE of Government Camp) at Indian Creek. $12. 5/12-LD; 14-day limit. 21 sites (32-ft RV limit). Tbls, toilets, cfga, drkg wtr. Fishing, hiking, picnicking.

Beavertail Recreation Site $8
Bureau of Land Management
Prineville District
Lower Deschutes River System
17 mi NE of jct of Hwy 216 and Deschutes River Rd at Sherars Falls. All year; 14-day limit. $8 Sun-Thurs; $12 Fri & Sat. 15 sites (30-ft RV limit). Tbls, toilets, cfga, drkg wtr, cold showers. Boating(l), fishing, rafting, hiking.

Blue Hole $8
Bureau of Land Management
Lower Deschutes River System
Prineville District
From US 197 in Maupin, N on paved Lower Access Rd along Lower Deschutes River; pass Oasis CG & Grey Eagle day-use area. $8 Sun-Thurs; $12 Fri & Sat. All year; 14-day limit. 1 site. Tbls, toilets, cfga, no drkg wtr. Boating, fishing, swimming, rafting. Wheelchair-accessible fishing ramp & toilets. Reservations available for physically handicapped individuals or groups (395-2270).

Clear Creek Crossing $10
Mount Hood National Forest
25 mi W of Maupin on Hwy 216; 3 mi N on FR 2130. $10. 5/15-10/1; 14-day limit. 7 sites; 16-ft RV limit. Tbls, toilets, cfga, firewood, no drkg wtr. Picnicking; fishing; horseback riding/hiking (1 mi).

Devil's Canyon **$8**
Bureau of Land Management
Prineville District
Lower Deschutes River System
N into Maupin on US 197, first left on gravel Upper Access Rd for 4 mi; pass Wapinitia, Harpham Flat & Long Bend camps. $8 Sun-Thurs; $12 Fri & Sat. All year; 14-day limit. 4 sites. Tbls, toilets, cfga, no drkg wtr. Boating, swimming, fishing, hunting. Elev 980 ft.

Harpham Flat **$8**
Warm Springs Reservation
Bureau of Land Management
Lower Deschutes River System
Prineville District
3.5 mi N of Maupin along Lower Deschutes River on gravel Lower Access Rd. (RVs not recommended on rough rd). $8 Sun-Thurs; $12 Fri & Sat. All year; 14-day limit. 9 sites. Tbls, toilets, cfga, drkg wtr. Fishing, boating(l), rafting, picnicking. Owned by Confederated Tribes of the Warm Springs Reservation; operated by BLM. Upgrading of site planned.

Hunt Park **$10**
Wasco County Fairgrounds
2 mi SW of Maupin on US 197, on Fairgrounds Rd. $10-12. 150 RV sites (no size limit); 50 tent sites. Drkg wtr, tbls, flush toilets, showers, dump, elec($). Hiking trails, bike trails, tennis nearby.

Jones Canyon **$8**
Bureau of Land Management
Prineville District
Lower Deschutes River System
NE of Maupin on Deschutes River Rd (Upper Access Rd) from jct with Hwy 216; pass Oasis, Blue Hole, White River, Twin Springs & Oakbrook camps; at Jones Canyon Creek. $8 Sun-Thurs; $12 Fri & Sat. All year; 14-day limit. 10 sites. Tbls, toilets, cfga, no drkg wtr. Boating (l), fishing, rafting, hiking.

Keeps Mill **$10**
Mount Hood National Forest
24 mi W of Maupin on OR 216; 3 mi N on FR 2120 (RVs not recommended). $10. 14-day limit. 5 tent sites (no RVs). Tbls, toilets, cfga, firewood, no drkg wtr. Picnicking; fishing; horseback riding/hiking (1 mi). Elev 2600 ft.

Longbend **$8**
Bureau of Land Management
Prineville District
Lower Deschutes River System
N into Maupin on US 197, first left on gravel Upper Access Rd for 4 mi; pass Wapinitia & Harpham Flat camps. $8 Sun-Thurs; $12 Fri & Sat. All year; 14-day limit. 4 sites. Tbls, toilets, cfga, no drkg wtr. Boating(l), swimming, fishing, hunting. Elev 980 ft.

Macks Canyon Recreation Site **$8**
Bureau of Land Management
Prineville District
Lower Deschutes River System
24 mi NE of Maupin on Deschutes River Rd.

(Upper Access Rd) from jct with Hwy 216. $8 Sun-Thurs; $12 Fri & Sat. All year; 14-day limit. 17 sites (30-ft RV limit). Tbls, toilets, cfga, drkg wtr, cold showers. Boating(l), fishing, rafting, hiking.

McCubbins Gulch **$10**
Mount Hood National Forest
24.5 mi NW of Maupin on OR 216; 1 mi E on FR 2110. $10. 5/1-10/1; 14-day limit. 15 sites (RVs under 26 ft). Tbls, toilets, cfga, firewood, no drkg wtr. Primitive 10 acres. Picnicking; fishing, ORV use.

Oak Springs **$8**
Bureau of Land Management
Prineville District
Lower Deschutes River System
From US 197 in Maupin, N on paved Lower Access Rd along Lower Deschutes River; pass Oasis & Blue Hole camps. $8 Sun-Thurs; $12 Fri & Sat. All year; 14-day limit. 7 sites. Tbls, toilets, cfga, no drkg wtr. Boating, fishing, swimming, rafting.

Oasis Flat **$8**
Bureau of Land Management
Prineville District
Lower Deschutes River System
From US 197 in Maupin, N on paved Lower Access Rd along Lower Deschutes River. $8 Sun-Thurs; $12 Fri-Sat. All year; 14-day limit. 10 sites and 2 group sites (16 or 24-person capacities). Tbls, toilets, cfga, no drkg wtr. Boating, fishing, swimming, rafting.

Rattlesnake Canyon **$8**
Bureau of Land Management
Prineville District
Lower Deschutes River System
About 22 mi NE of Maupin on Deschutes River Rd (Upper Access Rd) from jct with Hwy 216; pass Oasis, Blue Hole, White River, Twin Springs, Oakbrook, Jones Canyon & Gert Canyon camps. $8 Sun-Thurs; $12 Fri & Sat. All year; 14-day limit. 8 sites. Tbls, toilets, cfga, no drkg wtr. Boating, fishing, rafting, hiking.

Twin Springs **$8**
Bureau of Land Management
Prineville District
Lower Deschutes River System
NE of Maupin on Deschutes River Rd (Upper Access Rd) from jct with Hwy 216; pass Oasis, Blue Hole, White River camps & cross Elder Creek. $8 Sun-Thurs; $12 Fri & Sat. All year; 14-day limit. 7 sites. Tbls, toilets, cfga, no drkg wtr. Boating, fishing, rafting, hiking.

Wapinitia **$8**
Bureau of Land Management
Prineville District
Lower Deschutes River System
N into Maupin on US 197, first left on gravel Upper Access Rd for 3 mi. $8 Sun-Thurs; $12 Fri & Sat. All year; 14-day limit. 6 sites. Tbls, toilets, cfga, no drkg wtr. Boating(l), swimming, fishing, hunting. Elev 2900 ft.

White River **$8**
Warm Springs Reservation
Bureau of Land Management
Lower Deschutes River System
From US 197 in Maupin, N on paved Lower Access Rd along Lower Deschutes River; pass Oasis CG, Grey Eagle day-use area, Blue Hole & Oak Springs camps. $8 Sun-Thurs; $12 Fri & Sat. All year; 14-day limit. 3 sites. Tbls, toilets, cfga, no drkg wtr. Boating, fishing, swimming, rafting. Site owned by Confederated Tribes of Warm Springs Reservation, managed by BLM's Prineville District.

MCDERMITT (91)

Willow Creek Hot Springs **FREE**
Bureau of Land Management
Vale District
From US 95 N of McDermitt, W on White Horse Rd approx 40 mi, then 2.5 mi S. Free. Undeveloped primitive area with hot spring; 4 sites. No facilities except cfga; no drkg wtr. 14-day limit. Wilderness camping in Pueblo Mountains. Hunting, fishing, hiking.

MCKENZIE BRIDGE (92)

Alder Springs **FREE**
Willamette National Forest
7 mi E of McKenzie Bridge on Hwy 126; 8 mi E on Hwy 242 (narrow & steep). Free. MD-9/30; open off-season without services; 14-day limit. 6 tent sites. Tbls, toilet, cfga, no drkg wtr. Hiking.

Lakes End **FREE**
Willamette National Forest
13.2 mi NW of McKenzie Bridge on SR 126; 3.3 mi NW on FR 730; 1.7 mi N BY BOAT on Smith Reservoir. Free. Abou 4/15-10/30; 10-day limit. 17 tent sites. Tbls, toilets, cfga, no drkg wtr. Fishing, boating, picnicking.

Limberlost **$10**
Willamette National Forest
E of McKenzie Bridge on Hwy 126, then follow Hwy 242 to camp. $10. Abou;4/15-9/30; 14-day limit. 12 sites; 16-ft RV limit. Tbls, toilets, cfga, no drkg wtr. Fishing.

McKenzie Bridge Camp **$12**
Willamette National Forest
3 mi W of McKenzie Bridge on SR 126. $12. About 4/14-9/30; 14-day limit. 20 sites (40-ft RV limit). Tbls, toilets, cfga, drkg wtr. Boating(l), fishing, hiking. Elev 1400 ft.

Olallie **$12**
Willamette National Forest
11 mi NE of McKenzie Bridge on SR 126. $12 (one loop free off-season, but no wtr or services). About 4/15-9/30; 14-day limit. 17 sites (50-ft RV limit). Tbls, toilets, cfga, drkg wtr. Fishing, picnicking, hiking, horseback riding. Pacific Crest Trail & Olallie Lake nearby. Elev 4500 ft; 11 acres. At jct of Olallie Creek & McKenzie River.

Fishing tip: Annually stocked with rainbow trout, Olallie Lake consistently produces good catches of 10-12 inch fish, but it also provides trout up to 12 pounds. Fish rocky points with power baits, worms, salmon eggs.

Scott Lake **FREE**
Willamette National Forest
3.5 mi E of McKenzie Bridge on SR 126; 14.5 mi NE on SR 242; half mi SW on FR 1532; then walk in to tent sites. Free. 5/1-10/24; 10-day limit. 20 tent sites. Tbls, toilets, cfga, no drkg wtr. Boating, fishing, swimming, picnicking.

Trail Bridge **$10**
Willamette National Forest
13.2 mi NE of McKenzie Bridge on SR 126; qtr mi SW on FR 730. $10. About 4/15-9/30; 10-day limit. Free rest of year, but no wtr or services. 46 sites, including 19 RV sites; (45-ft RV limit). Tbls, toilets, cfga, drkg wtr. Boating, fishing, boating(l). Elev 2000 ft; 19 acres.

MEDFORD (93)

Cantrall-Buckley Lake **$10**
Jackson County Park
18 mi W of Medford on SR 238; 1 mi S on Hamilton Rd, following signs; at Applegate River. $10 (or $8 for seniors). All year; 14-day limit. 25 sites (25-ft RV limit). Tbls, flush toilets, showers, drkg wtr, cfga, playground. Horseshoes, fishing, swimming, playground, ball field, picnicking.
   Travel tip: This is a great locale for rockhounds. Search around Medford for moss and dendritic agate, jaspers, milky chalcedony.

Fire Glen **FREE**
Lost Creek lake
Corps of Engineers
From jct with Takelma Dr NE of Medford, 3.6 mi NE on SR 62 across Peyton Bridge; .8 mi W on Lewis Rd, then SW; hike or boat to sites. Free. All year; 14-day limit. Undesignated primitive sites limited to 4 tents & 8 people. Toilets, cfga, no drkg wtr. Hiking trails, fishing, boating.
   Fishing tip: Some of the best fishing in this lake is for stocked rainbow trout and native smallmouth bass. The Rogue River above the lake opens for trout fishing about May 28. The North Fork of the Rogue is stocked with catchable size trout each May.

Four Corners **FREE**
Lost Creek Lake
Corps of Engineers
From jct with SR 62 NE of Medford, 1.4 mi N on Takelma Dr; half mi N on logging rd; E side; hike or boat to sites. Free. All year; 14-day limit. Primitive undesignated sites limited to 4 tents & 8 people. Toilets, cfga, no drkg wtr. Hiking trails, fishing, boating.

Joseph H. Stewart **$12**
State Recreation Area
35 mi NE of Medford on SR 62; at Lost Creek Reservoir. $12 off-season for sites with elec ($16 in-season); $10 off-season for tent sites ($14 in-season). 148 sites. with elec off-season ($15 during 5/1-9/30). Open Mar-Nov; 10-day limit. 40-ft RV limit. Tbls, flush toilets, cfga, drkg wtr, dump, showers, beach. Swimming, boating(l), hiking trail, fishing, evening programs, biking trail.

Willow Prairie **$8**
Rogue River National Forest
31.5 mi E on SR 140; 1.5 mi N on FR 37; 1 mi W on FR 3738. $8. 5/15-10/31; 14-day limit. 10 RV sites (16-ft RV limit); 4 corrals at each site. Tbls, toilets, cfga, drkg wtr, horse troughs. Primarily a horse camp, in use since the 1950s. Fishing, boating, 19 mi of bridle trails.

MEDICAL SPRINGS (94)

Boulder Park **$8**
Wallowa-Whitman National Forest
SE of Medical Springs on Hwy 203, then NE on FRs 67, 77 & 7755 (gravel last 14 mi). $8. 6/1-11/1; 14-day limit. 8 sites. Tbls, toilets, cfga, no drkg wtr. Fishing, hiking, horseback riding. Corrals.

Tamarack **$5**
Wallowa-Whitman National Forest
5.5 mi SE of Medical Springs on FR 7735; 10.2 mi E on FR 7720; qtr mi E on FR 77. $5. 6/1-10/31; 10-day limit. 24 sites (22-ft RV limit). Tbls, toilets, cfga, drkg wtr. Fishing, hiking.

Two Color **FREE**
Wallowa-Whitman National Forest
5.5 mi SE on FR 67; 10.2 mi E on FR 77; 1.2 mi NE on FR 7755. Free. 6/15-9/30; 10-day limit. 14 sites (22-ft RV limit). Tbls, drkg wtr, cfga, toilets. Fishing. Elev 4800 ft. 4 acres.

MEHAMA (95)

Shady Cove **$8**
Willamette National Forest
29 mi NE of Mehama on Little North Santiam Rd. $8. All year; 14-day limit. Free rest of year. 12 sites. Tbls, toilets, cfga, no drkg wtr. Fishing, swimming, hiking. At Battle Creek & Scenic Creek. Elev 1600 ft.

MERLIN (96)

Ennis Riffle **$5**
Josephine County Park
NW of Merlin on Merlin-Galice Rd; along Rogue River just S of Galice. $5. All year; 2-day limit. Tbls, toilets, cfga, no drkg wtr. Fishing, rafting.

MILL CITY (97)

Fishermen's Bend **$12**
Bureau of Land Management
Salem District
2 mi W of Mill City on Hwy 22; on S side of rd. $12 for back-in sites; $22 for pull-through sites ($6 & $11 with federal Senior Pass). 39 sites (40-ft RV limit). Tbls, flush toilets, cfga, drkg wtr, group shelter, 12 picnic sites, showers. 162 acres. Boating(l), fishing, rafting, hiking trails, swimming. Adjacent to North Santiam River. Visitor center.

MILTON-FREEWATER (98)

Bone Springs **FREE**
Umatilla National Forest
9.2 mi S of Milton-Freewater on SR 11; 17.5 mi E on SR 204; 16.3 mi E on FR 64; NE on FR 360. Free. Primitive, undeveloped area, popular as hunting camp. Usually free of snow from July through October. No facilities except pit toilet.

MITCHELL (99)

Barnhouse **FREE**
Ochoco National Forest
13 mi E of Mitchell on US 26; 5 mi S on FR 12. Free. 5/1-9/15; 14-day limit. 6 sites. Tbls, toilets, cfga, no drkg wtr.

Big Springs Rustic Camp **FREE**
Ochoco National Forest
13 mi E of Mitchell on US 26; 18 mi S on FR 12; 8 mi W on FR 4270; cattle guard at camp entrance. Free. 5/1-9/15; 14-day limit. 6 primitive sites. Tbls, toilets, cfga, no drkg wtr.

Cottonwood Pit **FREE**
Ochoco National Forest
13 mi E of Mitchell on US 26; 15 mi S on FR 12; qtr mi W to access rd, FR 4274-080. Free. 5/1-9/15; 14-day limit. 3 sites. Tbls, toilets, cfga, no drkg wtr.

MOUNT VERNON (101)

Magone Lake **$10**
Malheur National Forest
9 mi N of Mount Vernon on US 395; 8 mi NE on FR 1036; 2 mi N on FR 1219. Free. Services MD-LD 14-day limit. 20 sites (RVs under 22 ft). Tbls, toilets, cfga, firewood, piped drkg wtr. Swimming; picnicking; fishing; boating (ld); hiking. Elev 5100 ft. Geological.
   Fishing tip: Magone is stocked with trout each spring, but by summer, most of the biggest ones are caught. Excellent place for teaching kids to fish for trout, though.

MYRTLE CREEK (101B)

Millsite Municipal Park **$6**
Near I-5 exit 108 in Myrtle Creek, on 4th St. next to South Umpqua River. $6 for dry

camping; $15 with hookups. 11 RV sites (45-ft RV limit), several tent sites. Tbls, flush toilets, cfga, drkg wtr, showers($1), dump ($3). Nature trail, ball fields, music Thurs nights in summer.

MYRTLE POINT (102)

Bennett $5
Coos County Park
8 mi E of Myrtle Point on Sitkum Rd to Gravel Ford; half mi N along North Fork Coquille River. $5. 5/1-10/31. 18 primitive sites. Tbls, toilets, cfga, wading pool. Rockhounding, hiking, fishing. 4 acres.

NEAHKAHNIE BEACH (103)

Nehalem Falls Campground $10
Tillamook State Forest
About 2 mi S of Neahkahnie Beach on US 101, then 1.3 mi E on Hwy 53; 1 mi S on Miami Foley Rd; 7 mi E on Foss Rd to milepost 7; at Nehalem River near Nehalem Falls. $5 for 4 walk-in tent sites; $10 for 14 drive-to sites; 1 group site ($25). All year; 14-day limit. Tbls, toilets, cfga, drkg wtr, beach. Hiking trail, swimming, fishing.

Oswald West State Park $10
N off US 101 at Neahkahnie Beach; qtr mi foot trail (wheelbarrows provided). $10 off-season for 30 walk-in primitive tent sites ($14 in-season). Tbls, flush toilets, cfga, drkg wtr, beach. Swimming, fishing, picnicking, hiking. 2,509 acres.

NORTH BEND (106)

North Spit Recreation Area FREE
Bureau of Land Management
Coos Bay District
Northbound from North Bend on US 101, just N of McCullough Bridge outside North Bend, watch for signs to "Oregon Dunes/Horsfall Beach); use left lane at base of incline & follow Transpacific Hwy; cross rail tracks near Weyerhaeuser plant, then bear right over second sent of tracks; turn left past Horsfall Beach rd & on to the BLM boat ramp (ramp is 6 mi from Hwy 101 on Transpacific Hwy). Southbound on US 101, look for rd heading W through the waters of the Bay as you approach North Bend. All year; 14-day limit. Undesignated sites. Tbls, flush toilets, cfga, drkg wtr, info exhibits, phone. Boating(l), fishing, clamming, crabbing, beachcombing, hiking. Sand dunes, wetlands. Watch commercial ships from strip of land between ocean & the bay. Three 4WD sand rds open to public.

NYSSA (107)

Lake Owyhee State Park $8
33 mi SW of Nyssa off SR 201. $8 for 25 primitive sites (not available off-season); $12 off-season for 31 sites with elec ($16 in-season); $14 in-season for 8 tent sites ($10 off-season). 10-day limit. Tbls, flush toilets, cfga, drkg wtr, dump, showers. Boating(l), fishing, swimming, birdwatching.

Succor Creek
State Natural Area FREE
30 mi S of Nyssa off SR 201. Free. 4/15-10/31; 10-day limit in 14-day period. 19 primitive sites (28-ft RV limit). Tbls, flush toilets, cfga, drkg wtr. Hiking, picnicking. Elev 2600 ft; 1910 acres.

OAKRIDGE (108)

Black Canyon $7
Willamette National Forest
6 mi W of Oakridge on SR 58. $7 with federal Senior Pass; others pay $14. About 5/1-9/30; 14-day limit. Higher fee for waterfront sites. 72 sites (38-ft RV limit). Tbls, toilets, cfga, drkg wtr. Swimming, boating(l), fishing, hiking, interpretive trails. On Middle Fork of Willamette River. Lookout Point Lake nearby.

Blair Lake $8
Willamette National Forest
1 mi E of Oakridge on CR 149; 8 mi NE on FR 24; 7.5 mi NE on FR 1934 (rough, narrow); 1.5 mi E on FR 733, then access on FR 741. $8. MD-9/24; 14-day limit. 7 tent sites. Tbls, toilets, cfga, drkg wtr. Fishing, boating (no motors), swimming, hiking, mountain biking. Elev 4800 ft.
Fishing tip: This small 35-acre lake has a large population of brook & rainbow trout and is restocked regularly. The fish are easy to find because the lake is only 20 ft deep.

Blue Pool $12
Willamette National Forest
8.7 mi SE of Oakridge on SR 58. $12. About 5/15-9/24; 14-day limit. 24 sites (22-ft RV limit). Tbls, flush & pit toilets, cfga, drkg wtr. Fishing, swimming in Salt Creek. Picnic area at creek has 5 stoves built by CCC in 1930s. Half mi to public hot springs (no facilities). Elev 2000 ft; 15 acres.
Fishing tip: Salt Creek flows into and out of Gold Lake. The lake is strictly for babless flyfishing. The section of river just below the lake is closed to fishing to protect lake spawners. Use waders below that point, and fish the sunken logs for rainbows and brookies.

Campers Flat $10
Willamette National Forest
2.2 mi SE of Oakridge on OR 58; .5 mi SE on CR 360; 20 mi S on FR 21. $10. About MD-9/24; 14-day limit. 5 sites (RVs under 19 ft). Tbls, toilets, cfga, firewood, well drkg wtr. Picnicking, fishing, hiking trails. On Middle Fork of Willamette River. Mountain biking nearby.
Fishing tip: Fishing is good, with easy access. Catch rainbow & cutthroat trout or large suckers.

Hampton Campground $10
Willamette National Forest
10 mi W of Oakridge on SR 58 on shore of Lookout Point Lake. $10. About MD-9/15; 14-day limit. 4 sites; 36-ft RV limit. Tbls, toilets, cfga, drkg wtr. Boating(l), fishing, picnicking, hiking.

Harralson Horse Camp $10
Willamette National Forest
25 mi SE of Oakridge on SR 58 to Waldo Lake Rd (FR 5897), then 10.5 mi on FR 5897. $10. July-Sept when snow-free. 6 sites; 30-ft RV limit. Toilet, cfga, tbls, no drkg wtr; dump near Islet camp. Tether horses at North Waldo Campground; water them near there off Waldo Lake Trail. Hiking, horseback riding, biking.

Indigo Lake Hike-In FREE
Oregon Cascades Recreation Area
Willamette National Forest
2.2 mi E of Oakridge on SR 58; half mi SE on CR 360 (Kitson Springs Rd); 32 mi S on FR 21; turn on FR 2154 for 10 mi to Timpanogas Lake Campground; park at end of the spur rd with the hiker symbol; hike 1.9 mi to lakeside camp. Free. July-snowfall. 5 tent sites. Toilet, cfga, no wtr, no trash service. Fishing, hiking, swimming. Elev 5900 ft.

Indigo Springs FREE
Willamette National Forest
2.2 mi E of Oakridge on SR 58; half mi SE on CR 360; 26 mi S on FR 21. Free. Abou MD-9/30; 16-day limit. 3 sites (16-ft RV limit). Tbls, toilets, cfga, no drkg wtr. Hiking, hunting, picnicking. Section of Oregon Central military wagon trail.

Kiahanie $10
Willamette National Forest
2 mi E of Oakridge on SR 58; 19.3 mi N of Westfir on FR 19 (Aufderheide Scenic Byway). $10. About MD-10/1; 14-day limit. 19 sites (24-ft RV limit). Tbls, toilets, cfga, drkg wtr. Fishing, hiking, picnicking. 15 acres.
Fishing tip: The North Fork Wild & Scenic River is not stocked & contains only native fish. Fishing is restricted to flies.

Larison Cove #5
Canoe-In Campground
Willamette National Forest
2.2 mi E of Oakridge on SR 58; half mi SE on CR 360; 3 mi S on FR 21 to parking lot & canoe access on FR 2106; at Larison arm of Hills Creek Reservoir. Camp free with $30 annual NW forest pass; $5 daily otherwise. 4 tent sites. Tbls, toilet, cfga, no drkg wtr. Canoeing (no boats), fishing, hiking.

Opal Lake FREE
Willamette National Forest
2.2 mi SE of Oakridge on SR 58; half mi SE on CR 360; 32.5 mi S on FR 21; 11 mi E on FR 2154, following signs to Timpanogas; after passing access rd to Summit Lake, take FR 399 left, then FR 398 left to Opal Lake trailhead; hike qtr mi to camp. Free. About

6/1-9/30; 16-day limit. 1 hike-in tent site. Toilet, cfga, no drkg wtr or tbl; no trash service. Hiking, fishing, hunting.

Packard Creek $7
Willamette National Forest
2.2 mi SE of Oakridge on SR 58; half mi SE on CR 360; 7 mi SE on FR 21; at Hills Creek Reservoir. $7 with federal Senior Pass; others pay $14; higher fee for lakeside sites. MD-LD; 14-day limit. 33 sites (28-ft RV limit). Tbls, toilets, cfga, drkg wtr, gray water sumps. Swimming, boating(ld), fishing, playground.

Sacandaga $8
Willamette National Forest
2.2 mi SE of Oakridge on SR 58; half mi SE on CR 360; 23 mi S on FR 21. $8. MD-9/24; 16-day limit. 17 sites (24-ft RV limit). Tbls, toilets, cfga, no drkg wtr. Hiking, fishing, hunting. On Middle Fork of Willamette River.

Salmon Creek Falls $12
Willamette National Forest
1 mi SE of Oakridge on SR 58; 4 mi NE on FR 24. $12. About 5/1-10/15; 14-day limit. 15 sites (20-ft RV limit). Tbls, toilets, cfga, drkg wtr. Fishing (Salmon Creek); next to Salmon Creek Waterfall. 9 acres.

Sand Prairie $12
Willamette National Forest
2.2 mi SE of Oakridge on SR 58; half mi SE on CR 360; 12 mi S on FR 21. $12. About 5/24-9/24; 16-day limit. 21 sites (28-ft RV limit). Tbls, flush & pit toilets, cfga, drkg wtr. Fishing, hiking (along 40-mi Middle Fork Trail). Middle Fork of Willamette River. 14 acres.

Secret Campground $10
Willamette National Forest
2.2 mi SE of Oakridge on SR 58; half mi SE on CR 360; 19 mi S on FR 21; at Middle Fork of Willamette River. $10. About MD-9/24; 14-day limit. 6 sites; 24-ft RV limit. Tbls, toilets, cfga, no drkg wtr. Fishing, hiking, biking.
   Fishiung tip: Trout fishing in this section of the Middle Fork is only fair.

Skookum Creek $8
Willamette National Forest
NW of Oakridge on SR 58 to Westfir, then 35 mi N on FR 19 to FR 1957; follow FR 1957 4 mi to camp. $8. About MD-10/15; 14-day limit. 9 walk-in tent sites. Tbls, toilets, cfga, drkg wtr, no trash service. Fishing, horseback riding, hiking.

Taylor Burn Forest Camp FREE
Willamette National Forest
25 mi SE of Oakridge on SR 58; 11 mi on Waldo Lake Rd (FR 5897), then 1.3 mi on FR 5898 and 7 mi on FR 514 (unimproved & not recommended for trailers or low-clearance vehicles). Free. About MD-10/15; 14-day limit. Toilets, cfga, no drkg wtr. Fishing, hiking. Wildflowers in summer. Elev 5200 ft.

Timpanogas Lake $8
Willamette National Forest
2.2 mi SE of Oakridge on OR 58; half mi SE on CR 360; 38.4 mi SE on FR 211; 3 mi S on FR 250. $8. 6/15-10/30; 16-day limit. 10 sites (RVs under 25 ft). Tbls, toilets, cfga, firewood, well drkg wtr. Swimming; picnicking; fishing; boating(d; no motors); hunting; hiking. Elev 5200 ft; 7 acres.
   Fishing tip: This lake often produces excellent catches of cutthroat & brook trout.

PACIFIC CITY (110)

East Dunes Camping Area $10
Siuslaw National Forest
Sand Lake Recreation Area
8.5 mi N of Pacific City on CR 871; near Sandbeach Campground. $10. All year. 49 RV sites on paved area; no length limit. Tbls, flush toilets, cfga, drkg wtr, beach. OHV area. $10 entry permit required on MD, July 4 & LD weekends.

West Winds Camping Area $10
Siuslaw National Forest
Sand Lake Recreation Area
8.5 mi N of Pacific City on CR 871; just N of Sandbeach Campground. $10. All year. 40 RV sites on paved area; no length limit. Tbls, flush toilets, cfga, drkg wtr, beach. OHV area. $10 entry permit required on MD, July 4 & LD weekends.

Woods Park $10
Tillamook County Park
N of Pacific City, off US 101 on Sandlake Rd in community of Woods. $10 at undesignated sites, $15 back-in sites. All year. 7 sites. Tbls, pit toilet, cfga, drkg wtr, shelter. Fishing, swimming. Day-use fee charged.

Whalen Island $10
Tillamook County Park
5 mi N of Pacific City on Sandlake Rd; at 3 Capes. $10. All year; limited facilities offseason. 30 undesignated sites. Tbls, flush toilets, cfga, drkg wtr, dump ($10 non-campers). Fishing, swimming, boating.

PAISLEY (112)

Campbell Lake FREE
Fremont National Forest
1 mi W of Paisley on SR 31; left on Mill St, which becomes FR 33 at the Y; 22.6 mi W on FR 33; stay right at the T & follow FR 28 for 11 mi; left on FR 33 for 2 mi. Free. Maintained 7/1-10/31; 14-day limit. 16 sites (22-ft RV limit). Tbls, toilets, cfga, drkg wtr, no trash service. Fishing, boating(l; no motors), hunting, swimming. Elev 7200 ft; 4 acres. Trails to Dead Horse Lake. Camp usually full holidays & weekends
   Fishing tip: Campbell Lake is stocked with rainbow trout.

Chewaucan Crossing FREE
Fremont National Forest
1 mi W of Paisley on SR 31; left on Mill St (becomes FR 33 at "Y"); stay to left for 8.5 mi to trailhead sign. Free. Apr-Oct; 14-day limit. 5 sites. Tbls, toilets, cfga, no drkg wtr, no trash service. Hiking, fishing, birdwatching.
   Fishing tip: It's good fishing in the Chewaucan River here for rainbow & brook trout. Focus on backwaters, weedy banks, pools and shallow riffles. There are holdover stocked rainbow trout (stocking is now discontinued) and native redband rainbows.

Dairy Point FREE
Fremont National Forest
1 mi W of Paisley on SR 31; left on Mill St to Y; 20 mi W on CR 28 & FR 33; 2 mi S on FR 28; SE on FR 3428; along Dairy Creek. Free. 4/15-10/15 (maintained 5/15-10/31); 14-day limit. 4 sites (some suitable for groups). Tbls, toilets, cfga, drkg wtr. No trash service. Fishing (rainbow trout), picnicking, horseshoes, birdwatching. Sites full holidays & most weekends.

Deadhorse Lake FREE
Fremont National Forest
1 mi W of Paisley on SR 31; left on Mill St to Y, then 20 mi W on FR 33; 11 mi S on FR 28; left on gravel FR 033 for 3 mi. Maintained 7/1-10/31; 14-day limit. 9 sites (22-ft RV limit); 7 group sites. Tbls, toilets, cfga, drkg wtr, no trash service. Boating (l; no motors), good fishing; hiking loop trails connect with Deadhorse Rim & Campbell Lake & accesses Dead Cow Trail, Lakes Trail system. Elev 7400 ft; 9 acres. Grassy & pebble beaches. Full most holidays & weekends.
   Fishing tip: Each year, Deadhorse Lake is stocked with about 5,000 legal-size and trophy size rainbow trout as well as fingerling brook trout.

Hanan/Coffeepot Trailhead FREE
Fremont National Forest
1 mi N of Paisley on SR 31; left on Mill St to Y, then continue on FR 3315 for 18 mi; Hanan Trail directional sign is on the W side of the rd just past milepost 18; turn W into trailhead. Free. Maintained 6/1-10/15; 14-day limit. Rustic undesignated sites; no facilities, no drkg wtr. Adequate RV turn-around. Birdwatching, hiking on historic trail.

Happy Camp FREE
Fremont National Forest
1 mi N of Paisley on SR 31; left on Mill St to Y, then 20 mi SW on FR 33; 2.4 mi S on FR 28; 1 mi W on FR 047; along Dairy Creek. Free. 5/15-10/31; 14-day limit. 9 sites (16-ft RV limit). Tbls, toilets, cfga, drkg wtr, no trash service. Trout fishing, horseshoes, birdwatching. Elev 5200 ft. Three 1930s-era CCC-built picnic shelters.

Jones Crossing Forest Camp FREE
Fremont National Forest
Half mi N of Paisley on SR 31; left on Mill St to Y; 9 mi farther on FR 33; along Chewau-

OREGON

can River. Free. 4/15-10/31; 14-day limit. 8 primitive sites. Tbls, cfga, toilet, no drkg wtr, no trash service. Fishing, birdwatching. Elev 4810 ft. Park 100 ft from river's edge.

Fishing tip: There's good fishing for rainbow & brook trout in the river. Wild redband rainbow offer special action.

Lee Thomas FREE
Fremont National Forest
1 mi N of Paisley on SR 31; left on Mill St to Y, then right on FR 3315 for 18 mi; right on FR 28 for half mi; right on FR 3411 for 5 mi; along North Fork of Sprague River. Free. 4/15-11/1 (maintained 6/1-10/31); 14-day limit. 8 sites (16-ft RV limit). Tbls, toilets, cfga, drkg wtr, no trash service. Hunting, fishing, birdwatching, picnicking. Elev 6200 ft; 3 acres. Good to fair rds. Popular fall hunt camp.

Fishing tip: Try the North Fork for rainbow trout.

Marster Spring FREE
Fremont National Forest
1 mi W of Paisley on Hwy 31; 7.1 mi S on Mill St, which becomes FR 33 at the Y (stay to the left; good gravel rd). Maintained 5/15-10/15; 14-day limit. 10 large sites. Tbls, toilets, cfga, drkg wtr, no trash service. Fishing, birdwatching, hunting. Elev 4700 ft; 4 acres.

Fishing tip: There's good fishing on Chewaucan River for rainbow & brook trout.

Pike's Crossing FREE
Recreation Area Forest Camp
Fremont National Forest
12 mi N of Paisley on SR 31; left on fR 29 (Government Harvey Rd) for 10 mi to jct with FR 2910 & Summer Lake viewpont; stay on FR 29 for 2 more mi; at T with FR 28, stay to the right for 3.6 mi; stay left at Y jct with FR 30 for 3 mi on FR 30 to sign for Pike's Crossing; along Paradise Creek & Sycan River. Free. 5/15-10/15; 14-day limit. 4-6 sites. Toilet, cfga, no drkg wtr, no tbls, no trash service. Fishing, birdwatching. Quiet, secluded.

Fishing tip: Try for native brook & rainbow trout from both Paradise Creek and Sycan River. Work downed trees, undercut banks and wide pools, using stealth because all the trou are native; some are up to 20 inches.

Rock Creek Forest Camp FREE
Fremont National Forest
11 mi N of Paisley on SR 31; left on FR 29 (Government Harvey Rd) for 10 mi to jct with FR 2901 & Summer Lake viewpoint; stay on FR 29 for 2 more mi; at T jct with FR 28, go left for half mi; along Sycan River. Also, for 3 mi on FR 28 after Rock Creek turnoff, there are several dispersed camping areas in meadows & trees along river. Free. 5/15-10/15; 14-day limit. 4-6 primitive sites. Toilets, cfga, no tbls, no drkg wtr, no trash service. Trout fishing, birdwatching. Hanan/Sycan Trailhead nearby. Quiet, secluded.

Sand Hill Crossing FREE
Fremont National Forest
1 mi W of Paisley on Hwy 31; left on Mill St to the Y; right on FR 3315 for 18 mi; 1 mi S on FR 28; 8 mi W on FR 3411. Free. 4/15-10/31 (maintained 6/1-10/31); 14-day limit. 5 sites (16-ft RV limit). Tbls, toilets, cfga, drkg wtr, no trash service. Fishing, swimming (Sprague River), hiking, birdwatching. Elev 6100 ft.

Slide Lake Forest Camp FREE
Fremont National Forest
Half mi N of Paisley on SR 31; left on Mill Street to Y; stay to right on FR 3315 for 6 mi; 9 mi N on Fr 3360 to Slide Lake trailhead sign; from parking area, hike half mi SW on trail to lake. Free. 5/15-10/15; 14-day limit. 1-3 primitive tent sites. No facilities except cfga; no drkg wtr, no trash service. Trout fishing, birdwatching, hiking (Slide Lake Trail follows abandoned rd, offers excellent scenery). Elev 5980 ft.

Upper Jones Forest Camp FREE
Fremont National Forest
Half mi N of Paisley on SR 31; left on Mill St to Y; stay to left on FR 33 for 9.5 mi; unmarked sits in trees, off to left, along Chewaucan River. Free. 4/15-11/1; 14-day limit. 2 sites. No facilities except cfga, no drkg wtr, no trash service. Rainbow & brook trout fishing, birdwatching.

PARKDALE (113)

Cloud Cap Saddle Camp $10
Mount Hood National Forest
8 mi S of Parkdale on CR 428; 11.7 mi W on FR 3512. $10. 7/1-9/15; 14-day limit. 4 tent sites. Tbls, toilets, cfga, firewood, drkg wtr. Hiking; picnicking; mountain climbing. Elev 6000 ft; 1 acre. Starting point for climbing Mount Hood on Timberline Trail. Historic area.

Gibson Prairie Horse Camp $10
Mount Hood National Forest
2 mi NE on CR 428; 3 mi N on OR 35; 15 mi SE on FR 17. $10. Elev 3900 ft. 5/15-10/15; 14-day limit. 4 sites (RVs under 17 ft). Toilets, cfga, no drkg wtr. Horseback riding; equestrian camp.

Kinnikinnick Campground $10
Mount Hood National Forest
8 mi S of Parkdale on SR 35; SW on FR 3512 to FR 2840, then hike to Laurance Lake. $10. 5/15-9/15; 14-day limit. 20 tent sites. Tbls, toilets, cfga, no drkg wtr. Fishing, boating(l), hiking. Elev 3000 ft.

Rainy Lake FREE
Mount Hood National Forest
6 mi N of Parkdale on CR 281; 10 mi W on FR N205. Free. 4 tent sites. Tbls, toilets, cfga, no drkg wtr. Swimming; picnicking; fishing; berry picking; boating(5 mi). Elev 4100 ft; 3 acres. Secluded Lake (qtr mi).

Routson $10
Hood River County Park
20 mi S of Parkdale on Hwy 35. $10. 4/1-11/1. 20 undesignated sites for self-contained RVs. Tbls, flush toilets, cfga, drkg wtr. Boating, swimming, fishing, waterskiing, fishing, hunting. Elev 2600 ft; 200 acres.

Sherwood $10
Mount Hood National Forest
11 mi S of Parkdale on SR 35. $10. MD-9/30; 14-day limit. 14 sites (16-ft RV limit). Tbls, toilets, cfga, drkg wtr. Fishing, hiking (East Fork & Tamanawas Falls Trails). Elev 3000 ft; 4 acres.

Tilly Jane $10
Mount Hood National Forest
8 mi S of Parkdale on SR 35; 11 mi W on FR 3512. Walk in to camp. $10. 7/1-9/30; 14-day limit. 14 walk-in tent sites. Tbls, toilets, cfga, no drkg wtr. Hiking trails, picnicking. Elev 5700 ft.

Wahtum Lake $10
Mount Hood National Forest
6 mi N of Parkdale on Hwy 281; 5 mi SW on CR N22; 5 mi W on FR 13; 8 mi NW on FR 1310. $10. 6/15-9/15; 14-day limit. 5 sites. Tbls, toilets, cfga, no drkg wtr. Swimming, fishing, boating.

PAULINA (114)

Frazier Rustic Camp FREE
Ochoco National Forest
3.5 mi E on CR 112; 2.2 mi N on CR 113; 10 mi E on CR 135; 6.3 mi E on FR 58; 1.1 mi NE on FR 5800-500; cattle guard at entrance. Elev 5000 ft. 5/15-9/15. 10 sites on 7 acres (RVs under 22 ft). Tbls, toilets, cfga, firewood, no drkg wtr. Picnicking; horseback riding (1 mi).

Mud Springs FREE
Horse Camp & Trailhead
Ochoco National Forest
Take left fork 3 mi E of Paulina to FR 58. 6/1-9/15; 14-day limit. 6 sites. Tbls, toilets, cfga, no drkg wtr. 9 steel horse pens Hiking, bridle trails.

Sugar Creek $8
Ochoco National Forest
3.5 mi E of Paulina on CR 380; 6.5 mi N on CR 113; 1.7 mi E on FR 58. $8. 5/1-12/1; 14-day limit. 17 sites (32-ft RV limit). Tbls, toilets, cfga, drkg wtr. Swimming, fishing, hiking, picnicking. Half mi loop trail along Sugar Creek. Elev 4100 ft; 2 acres. Seasonal closures possible due to roosting bald eagles.

Wolf Creek Forest Camp $6
Ochoco National Forest
3.5 mi E of Paulina on CR 380; 6.5 mi N on CR 113; 1.5 mi N on FR 42. $6. 5/15-9/15; 14-day limit. 10 sites (20-ft RV limit). Tbls, toilets, cfga, drkg wtr. Fishing. Elev 4100 ft; 3 acres.

Wolf Creek Industrial   **FREE**
Ochoco National Forest
3.5 mi E of Paulina on CR 380; 6.5 mi N on CR 113; N on FR 42 to first left after Rd 3810 jct (access rd 4200-860, not signed); S of Wolf Creek Forest Camp & E of Wolf Creek bridge. Free. 6/1-9/15; 14-day limit. 6 sites; 20-ft RV limit. Tbls, toilets, cfga, no drkg wtr.

Wolf Creek Overflow   **FREE**
Ochoco National Forest
3.5 mi E of Paulina on CR 380; 6.5 mi N on CR 113; 1.5 mi N on FR 42, then half mi on FR 3810 to camp's access, FR 3810-541 (not signed). Free. 3 sites; 20-ft RV limit. Tbls, toilet, cfga, no drkg wtr.

PENDLETON (115)

Umatilla Forks   **$5**
Umatilla National Forest
32 mi E of Pendleton on CR N32; half mi SE on FR 32; access via Hwy 11 & I-84; between South Fork & North Fork of Umatilla River. $5. MD-10/15; 10-day limit. 15 sites (RVs under 23 ft); 16 picnic sites. Tbls, toilets, cfga, drkg wtr. Fishing, nature trails, hunting, horse trail, trail bikes, wilderness access. 5 acres.

PLUSH (116)

Hot Springs Campground   **FREE**
Hart Mountain
National Wildlife Refuge
29 mi NE on gravel rds. Free. 5/1-10/31; 14-day limit. 12 primitive sites (20-ft RV limit). Tbls, toilets, cfga, drkg wtr. Picnicking, fishing, hiking.

POMEROY (WA.) (117)

Alder Thicket   **FREE**
Umatilla National Forest
10 mi S of Pomeroy on Hwy 128; at fork, continue staight to FR 40, then 3.5 mi to camp. Free. 5/15-11/15; 14-day limit. 5 sites (15-ft RV limit). Tbls, toilets, cfga, no drkg wtr (wtr at Clearwater lookout, 6 mi on FR 40). Hiking.

Big Springs   **FREE**
Umatilla National Forest
10 mi S of Pomeroy on Hwy 128; at fork, continue straight to FR 40; pass the forest boundary & continue 9 mi to Clearwater lookout tower, then left on FR 42 for 3 mi; left on FR 4225 to camp. Free. 5/15-11/15; 14-day limit. 8 tent sites. Tbls, toilets, cfga, no drkg wtr (get wtr at Clearwater tower). Hiking, hunting.

Teal Spring   **FREE**
Umatilla National Forest
10 mi S of Pomeroy on Hwy 128; at fork, continue straight to FR 40 within the forest & on 9 mi to Clearwater lookout tower; camp's turnoff is half mi on right. Free. 6/1-11/15; 14-day limit. 5 sites. Tbls, toilets, cfga, no

drkg wtr. Camp popular with OHV enthusiasts.

Tucannon Campground   **FREE**
Umatilla National Forest
17 mi S of Pomeroy on CR 101; 4 mi SW on FR 47; S on FR 160 to camp. Free. 5/15-11/15; 14-daylimit. 13 sites; 16-ft RV limit. Tbls, toilets, cfga, no drkg wtr.
Fishing tip: Several ponds are stocked with trout and provide excellent fishing opportunities.

Wickiup Campground   **FREE**
Umatilla National Forest
10 mi S of Pomeroy on Hwy 128; at fork, continue straight to FR 40 for about 17 mi; at Troy Junction, turn on FR 44 for 3 mi to jct with FR 43. Free. 6/15-10/15; 14-day limit. 5 sites; 16-ft RV limit. Tbls, toilets, cfga, no drkg wtr. Hiking, hunting.

PORT ORFORD (118)

Butler Bar   **FREE**
Siskiyou National Forest
3 mi N of Port Orford on US 101; 7.4 mi SE on CR 208; 11.2 mi SE on FR 5325; at Elk River. Free. All year; 14-day limit. 7 sites (RVs under 16 ft). Tbls, toilets, cfga, firewood, drkg wtr in summer. Swimming; picnicking; fishing; berry picking, hiking. Elev 600 ft; 4 acres. Elk River Fish Hatchery (11 mi W). Signed for user management.

Cape Blanco State Park   **$12**
N mi N of Port Orford off US 101. $12 for 53 sites with elec off-season ($16 in-season); $10 off-season for 8 equestrian sites ($14 in-season). All year; 10-day limit. Tbls, flush toilets, cfga, drkg wtr, showers, beach, store, dump. Boating, horseback riding, fishing, birdwatching, hiking trail, swimming. Lighthouses, historic homes.

Edson Creek Park   **$5**
Bureau of Land Management
Coos Bay District
4.4 mi N of Port Orford on Hwy 101; 4.5 mi E on Sixes River Rd; bear S just before Edson bridge. $5. All year; 14-day limit. 25 primitive sites along creek & 4 group sites. Tbls, toilets, cfga, drkg wtr. Swimming, fishing, picnicking, boating(l).

Humbug Mountain State Park   **$12**
6 mi S of Port Orford on US 101. $12 off-season for 33 sites with elec ($16 in-season); $10 off-season for 63 tent sites ($14 in-season); $4 for hiker-biker sites. 10-day limit. Tbls, flush toilets, cfga, drkg wtr, dump, showers, beach. Swimming, fishing, windsurfing, hiking trail, evening programs.

Laird Lake   **FREE**
Siskiyou National Forest
3 mi N of Port Orford on US 101; 7.5 mi SE on CR 208; 15.5 mi SE on FR 5325. All year; 14-day limit. 4 primitive sites. Toilets, tbls,

cfga, no drkg wtr. Fishing, birdwatching.
Fishing tip: This 5-acre lake is stocked with rainbow trout.

Sixes River   **$8**
Bureau of Land Management
Coos Bay District
4.4 mi N of Port Orford on US 101; 11 mi E on Sixes River Rd (gravel). $8. All year; 14-day limit. 19 sites (RVs under 30 ft). Tbls, toilets, cfga, dump, no drkg wtr, firewood. Elev 400 ft; 20 acres. Trout fishing in river. Sluice for gold by permit.

Sunshine Bar   **FREE**
Siskiyou National Forest
19 mi E of Port Orford on FR 5325; at Elk River. Free. All year; 14-day limit. 7 sites. Tbls, toilets, cfga, no drkg wtr. Fishing, swimming.

POWERS (120)

Buck Creek   **FREE**
Siskiyou National Forest
About 30 mi SE of Powers via FRs 3300 & 3348. Free. All year; 14-day limit. 2 primitive sites. Tbls, toilets, cfga, no drkg wtr. Recently refurbished. On Powers-Glendale bike route.

Daphne Grove   **$8**
Siskiyou National Forest
4.2 mi SE of Powers on CR 219; 10.5 mi S on FR 333. $8 during MD-LD; free rest of year but no wtr; 14-day limit. 14 sites (30-ft RV limit). Tbls, toilets, cfga, drkg wtr, grey wtr dumps. Fishing, swimming, hiking trails. On South Fork of Coquille River. Near Azalea Lake (1-mi hike). 11 acres.
Fishing tip: Tiny (2-acre) Azalea Lake is stocked with brook & rainbow trout.

Eden Valley Campground   **FREE**
Siskiyou National Forest
33 mi SE of Powers via FRs 3300 & 3348. Free. All year; 14-day limit. 11 sites along Powers-Glendale bike route. Tbls, toilets, cfga, no drkg wtr. Biking.

Island Campground   **$6**
Siskiyou National Forest
17 mi S of Powrs on FR 3300; at South Fork of Coquille River. $6 during MD-10/15; free rest of year; 14-day limit. 5 sites. Tbls, toilets, cfga, no drkg wtr. Swimming, fishing.

Lockhart Campground   **FREE**
Siskiyou National Forest
22 mi SE of Powers via FRs 3300 & 3348; on Powers-Glendale bike route. Free. All year. 1 primitive site. Toilet, cfga, tbl. Fishing, biking.

Myrtle Grove   **FREE**
Siskiyou National Forest
4.2 mi SE of Powers on CR 90; 4.5 mi S on FR 33; at South Fork Coquille River. All year; 14-day limit. 5 sites. Tbls, toilet, cfga, no drkg wtr. Signed for user management. Swimming; picnicking; fishing.

Peacock Campground   **FREE**
Siskiyou National Forest
22 mi SE of Powers via FRs 3300, 3348 & 3358; on Powers-Glendale bike route. Free. All year; 14-day limit. 1 primitive site. Toilet, cfga, tbl. Fishing, biking.

Pioneer Campground   **FREE**
Siskiyou National Forest
28 mi SE of Powers via FRs 3300, 3348 & 5000; on Powers-Glendale bike route. Free. All year; 14-day limit. 1 primitive site. Toilet, cfga, tbl. Fishing, biking.

Rock Creek   **$8**
Siskiyou National Forest
4.2 mi SE of Powers on CR 90; 13 mi S on FR 33; 1.3 mi SW on FR 3348-080. $8 during MD-10/15; free rest of year but no wtr; 14-day limit. 7 tent sites. Tbls, toilets, cfga, drkg wtr. Swimming, picnicking, fishing, berry picking, hiking. Elev 1200 ft; 2 acres.

Powers County Park   **$10**
Coos County
N end of Powers (18 mi S of Myrtle Point). $10 without hookups, $12 with hookups during 10/1-5/15; $11 without hookups & $16 with hookups during 5/16-9/30; 10-day limit. 70 sites. Tbls, flush toilets, showers($), elec($), wtr hookups($), cfga, portable dump. Fishing, boating(l -- no motors), swimming, canoeing, tennis courts, horseshoes, volleyball, basketball, softball field, hiking trails, playground. Covered shelters, coin-operated stoves. On South Fork of Coquille River. 93 acres.

Squaw Lake   **FREE**
Siskiyou National Forest
4.2 mi SE of Powers on CR 90; 12.6 mi S on FR 33; 4.6 mi SE on FS 321; 1 mi E on FR 3348-080. Free. All year; 14-day limit. 6 dispersed sites (21-ft RV limit). Tbls, toilets, cfga, no drkg wtr. Picnicking; fishing. Elev 2200 ft; 2 acres. Stream. Coquille River Falls National Recreation Area nearby.

Fishing tip: 3-acre Squaw Lake contains stocked rainbow trout.

Wooden Rock Creek   **FREE**
Siskiyou National Forest
About 30 mi SE of Powers via FRs 3300, 3348 & 5000; on Powers-Glendale bike route. Free. All year; 14-day limit. 1 site. Tbl, toilet, cfga, no drkg wtr. Biking, fishing.

PRAIRIE CITY (121)

Crescent Campground   **FREE**
Malheur National Forest
17 mi SE of Prairie City on CR 62. Free. 6/1-11/1; 14-day limit. 4 sites. Tbls, toilets, cfga, no drkg wtr. Fishing, hiking. Elev 5200 ft.

Dixie Camp   **$5**
Malheur National Forest
7 mi SE of Prairie City on SR 26; half mi N on FR 1220. $5. 6/1-11/1; 14-day limit. 11 sites (22-ft RV limit). Tbls, toilets, cfga, drkg wtr.

Hunting, berry-picking. Elev 5300 ft at Dixie Summit. Bridge Creek nearby.

Elk Creek   **FREE**
Malheur National Forest
8.3 mi SE of Prairie City on CR 14; 16 mi SE on FR 130; 1.3 mi S on FR 16. Free. 5/15-11/15. 5 sites (RVs under 32 ft). Toilets, cfga, no drkg wtr. Fishing. Elev 5100 ft; 1 acre. N fork Malheur River.

Little Crane   **FREE**
Malheur National Forest
8.3 mi SE of Prairie City on CR 14; 16 mi S on FR 13; 5.7 mi S on FR 16. Free. Elev 5000 ft. 6/1-11/10; 14-day limit. 5 sites (RVs under 16 ft). Tbls, toilets, cfga, no drkg wtr. Picnicking; fishing.

Middle Fork   **$5**
Malheur National Forest
11.5 mi NE of Prairie City on SR 26; 5 mi NW on CR 20. $5. 6/15-11/1; 14-day limit. 10 sites (22-ft RV limit). Tbls, toilets, cfga, no drkg wtr. Fishing on Middle Fork of John Day River. Elev 4200 ft.

North Fork Malheur   **FREE**
Malheur National Forest
8.3 mi SE of Prairie City on CR 14; 16 mi SE on FR 13; 2 mi S on FR 16; 2.7 mi S on FR 1675. Free. 5/15-11/15; 14-day limit. 5 sites. Tbls, toilets, cfga, no drkg wtr. Fishing. Elev 4900 ft.

Slide Creek   **FREE**
Malheur National Forest
6.6 mi S of Prairie City on CR 60; 2.1 mi FR 1428. 6/1-11/15. 3 sites (RVs under 22 ft). Tbls, toilets, cfga, no drkg wtr. Picnicking; fishing; hiking; hunting; horseback riding (corral).

Strawberry   **$6**
Malheur National Forest
6.5 mi S of Prairie City on CR 60; 4.5 mi S on FR 6001. $6. 6/1-10/15; 30-day limit. 12 sites (22-ft RV limit). Tbls, toilets, cfga, drkg wtr. Boating, fishing, hiking trails. Strawberry Mountain Wilderness is nearby. Elev 5700 ft. On Strawberry Lake, near Strawberry Falls.

Fishing tip: Fish Strawberry Lake with a float tube, although you can catch fish from shore too. Rainbows & brook trout reproduce naturally. Use bait or cast lures & flies.

Trout Farm   **$6**
Malheur National Forest
8.3 mi SE of Prairie City on CR 14; 6.9 mi S on FR 14. $6. 5/1-11/15; 14-day limit. 6 sites (21-ft RV limit). Tbls, toilets, cfga, drkg wtr. Good trout fishing pond; picnicking.

PRINEVILLE (122)

Allen Creek Horse Camp   **FREE**
Ochoco National Forest
25 mi E of Prineville on US 26 to Ochoco Ranger Station; 19 mi NE on Rd 22; just past Walton Lake. Free. 5/15-10/1; 14-day limit. 5

sites. Tbls, toilets, cfga, no drkg wtr. Corrals. Hiking & bridle trails.

Fishing tip: Allen Creek provides fair trout fishing early in the year.

Antelope Flat Reservoir   **$8**
Ochoco National Forest
29 mi SE of Prineville on SR 380; 9 mi S on FR 17; 1.3 mi S on FR 1700. $8. 5/15-11/15; 14-day limit. 25 sites (32-ft RV limit). Tbls, toilets, cfga, drkg wtr. Swimming, boating(l), fishing, canoeing. Elev 4600 ft. 20 acres.

Fishing tip: Fishing here is best from spring until mid-summer. Low water conditions during the summer often hamper fishing efforts, and boat launching is difficult. The lake contains trout up to 18 inches.

Biggs Springs   **FREE**
Ochoco National Forest
25 mi E of Prineville on US 26 to Ochoco Ranger Station; 14 mi SE on FR 42; 5 mi S on FR 4215. Free. 5/15-10/1; 14-day limit. 3 sites. Tbls, toilets, cfga, no drkg wtr. Picnicking.

Castle Rock   **$8**
Bureau of Land Management
Prineville District
Lower Crooked River System
12 mi S of Prineville on SR 27 (Crooked River Hwy). $8. All year; 14-day limit. 6 sites. Tbls, toilets, cfga, no drkg wtr. Boating, swimming, fishing. Elev 2960 ft.

Travel tip: This area is a rockhounder's paradise. The chamber of commerce provides directions to points of geological interest and to public lands where agate, agatized jasper, petrified wood and thunber eggs can be found.

Chimney Rock Recreation Site   **$8**
Bureau of Land Management
Prineville District
Lower Crooked River System
14 mi S of Prineville on SR 27 (Crooked River Hwy). $8. All year; 14-day limit. 16 sites. Tbls, toilets, cfga, drkg wtr. Fishing, hiking, picnicking. Elev 3100 ft; 10 acres.

Cobble Rock   **$8**
Bureau of Land Management
Prineville District
Lower Crooked River System
14.5 mi S of Prineville on SR 27 (Crooked River Hwy). $8. All year; 14-day limit. 15 sites. Tbls, toilets, cfga, no drkg wtr. Fishing, hiking, picnicking, boating.

Cottonwood   **FREE**
Ochoco National Forest
25 mi E of Prineville on US 26 to ranger station; 35 mi on FR 42; 9 mi N on FR 12. Free. 5/15-9/15; 14-day limit. 6 sites. Tbls, toilets, cfga, no drkg wtr. Picnicking. Elev 5700 ft.

Cyrus Horse Camp   **FREE**
Crooked River National Grassland
16 mi NE of Prineville on US 26 to FR 7130; left on FR 5650, then 1.3 mi to camp. Free.

All year; 14-day limit. 5 sites. Tbls, toilets, cfga, no drkg wtr. Horse corrals. Bridle trails

Deep Creek   **$8**
Ochoco National Forest
16.7 mi E of Prineville on US 26; 8.5 mi NE on CR 123; 23.6 mi SE on FR 42; .1 mi S on FR 42G; at N Fork of Crooked River. $8. Elev 4200 ft. 5/15-10/1. 6 sites on 2 acres (RVs under 22 ft). Tbls, toilets, cfga, firewood, drkg wtr. Picnicking; fishing.

Fishing tip: The Crooked River consistently produces big trout and is considered a world-class fishery. It contains inland redband rainbow trout, smallmouth bass and whitefish.

Devil's Post Pile   **$8**
Bureau of Land Management
Prineville District
Lower Crooked River System
14 mi S of Prineville on SR 27 (Crooked River Hwy). $8. All year; 14-day limit. 7 sites. Tbls, toilets, cfga, no drkg wtr. Fishing, hiking, picnicking, boating.

Double Cabin   **FREE**
Ochoco National Forest
48 mi SE of Prineville on Hwy 380 to FR 17; left on FR 16; left on FR 1600-350. Free. 5/15-9/15; 14-day limit. 5 sites (equestrian camping allowed). Tbls, toilets, cfga, no drkg wtr. Fishing, hiking, horseback riding.

Dry Creek Horse Camp   **FREE**
Ochoco National Forest
17 mi NE of Prineville on US 26; left on Mill Creek Rd; 2.5 mi on FR 3370 to FR 3370-200. Free. 4/5-11/28. 5 sites. Tbls, toilets, cfga, no drkg wtr. 18 horse corrals. Hiking & horseback riding trails. Roads not suitable for large RVs.

Elkhorn   **FREE**
Ochoco National Forest
37 mi SE of Prineville on Hwy 380 to FR 16; NW of Antelope Reservoir. Free. 5/15-9/15; 14-day limit. 4 sites. Tbls, toilets, cfga, no drkg wtr. Picnicking.

Lone Pine   **$8**
Bureau of Land Management
Prineville District
Lower Crooked River System
13 mi S of Prineville on SR 27 (Crooked River Hwy). $8. All year; 14-day limit. 8 sites. Tbls, toilets, cfga, no drkg wtr. Fishing, hiking, picnicking, boating.

Lower Palisades   **$8**
Bureau of Land Management
Prineville District
Lower Crooked River System
13.5 mi S of Prineville on SR 27 (Crooked River Hwy). $8. All year; 14-day limit. 15 sites. Tbls, toilets, cfga, no drkg wtr. Fishing, hiking, picnicking, boating.

Ochoco Divide   **$12**
Ochoco National Forest
30.8 mi NE of Prineville on US 26; .1 mi SE on FR 1207. $12. 5/15-10/1; free rest of year (weather permitting); 14-day limit. 28 sites (32-ft RV limit). Tbls, toilets, cfga, firewood. No wtr in free period. Picnicking; rockhounding; fishing (2 mi). Separate walk-in site for hikers or bicycle riders. Elev 4700 ft; 10 acres.

Ochoco Forest Camp   **$12**
Ochoco National Forest
25 mi E of Prineville on US 26, adjacent to ranger station at Ochoco Creek. $12. 5/1-10/1; 14-day limit. 6 sites. Tbls, toilets, cfga, drkg wtr. Fishing, hiking, picnicking. Elev 4000.

Fishing tip: Fishing is just fair for small rainbow trout, but catchable-size fish are always stocked in this section of the creek prior to the opening of trout season. Daily bag limit is 5 trout.

Prineville Reservoir   **$12**
State Park
7 mi E of Prineville on US 26. $12 off-season for 23 tent sites ($16 in-season); sites with elec, $16-20. 10-day limit in 14-day period. 30-ft RV limit. Tbls, flush toilets, cfga, drkg wtr. Fishing, boating (dl), picnicking, birdwatching, evening programs, hiking trails. Elev 3100 ft; 10 acres.

Fishing tip: Prineville Reservoir (formerly named Ochoco Lake) contains rainbow and cutthroat trout, smallmouth & largemouth bass, catfish & crappie. Focus on the areas above Jasper Boint and Bear Creek downstream from the state park.

Poison Butte   **$8**
Bureau of Land Management
Prineville District
Lower Crooked River System
14.5 mi S of Prineville on SR 27 (Crooked River Hwy). $8. All year; 14-day limit. 5 sites. Tbls, toilets, cfga, no drkg wtr. Fishing, hiking, picnicking, boating.

Salter's Cabin Group Cmp   **FREE**
Ochoco National Forest
SE of Prineville on SR 380 to CR 112 (Izee Hwy), then 3.5 mi to CR 113 (Beaver Creek Rd); turn at left fork onto CR 113 for 7.5 mi; 1.2 mi on FR 42 to camp sign & access rd 4200-865. Free. 6/1-9/15; 14-day limit. 1 group site. Tbls, toilets, cfga, no drkg wtr. 1 horse corral. Hiking, horseback riding.

Scotts Camp   **FREE**
Ochoco National Forest
25 mi E of Prineville to ranger station; 22 mi NE on FR 22. Free. 5/1-10/1; 14-day limit. 3 sites. Tbls, toilets, cfga, drkg wtr. Picnicking.

Stillwater   **$8**
Bureau of Land Management
Prineville District
Lower Crooked River System
12.5 mi S of Prineville on SR 27 (Crooked

River Hwy). $8. All year; 14-day limit. 10 sites. Tbls, toilets, cfga, no drkg wtr. Fishing, hiking, picnicking, boating.

Walton Lake   **$7**
Ochoco National Forest
16.7 mi E of Prineville on US 26; 8.5 mi NE on CR 123; 6.2 mi NE on FR 1222. $7 with federal Senior Pass at RV sites ($5 for tents); others pay $14 & $10 during 5/10-10/1; free rest of year (weather permitting); 14-day limit. 30 sites (RVs under 32 ft). Tbls, toilets, cfga, drkg wtr, beach, fishing pier. Picnicking; rockhounding, boating(l), hiking, swimming. Elev 5000 ft; 15 acres.

Fishing tip: Fishing here is quite good for rainbow trout, which are stocked 3 times each summer. Some of the stocked fish are up to 2 pounds. Only electric motors are allowed.

Whistler Forest Camp   **FREE**
Ochoco National Forest
30 mi NE of Prineville on McKay Rd to FR 27, to FR 2700-500. Free. 6/1-9/1; 14-day limit. 2 sites. Tbls, toilets, cfga, no drkg wtr. Corrals. Hiking & bridle trails. Also known as Whistler Spring.

White Rock Forest Camp   **FREE**
Ochoco National Forest
25 mi E of Prineville on US 26; left on FR 3350 for 5 mi, then right on FR 300 to end. Free. 6/1-9/1; 14-day limit. Primitive undesignated sites. Tbls, toilets, cfga, no drkg wtr. Hiking, picnicking.

Wildcat   **$8**
Ochoco National Forest
9.2 mi E of Prineville on US 26; 11 mi NE on FR 33. $8. 5/1-9/15; 14-day limit. 17 sites (32-ft RV limit). Tbls, toilets, cfga, drkg wtr. Fishing, hiking trails. On E fork of Mill Creek; trailhead to Mill Creek Wilderness. 11 acres; elev 3700 ft.

Wildwood   **FREE**
Ochoco National Forest
20 mi E of Prineville on US 26; 8 mi E on FRs 22 & 2210. Free. 6/1-9/1; 14-day limit. 5 sites. Tbls, toilets, cfga, no drkg wtr. Hiking, hunting, picnicking.

Wiley Flat   **FREE**
Ochoco National Forest
34 mi SE of Prineville on Hwy 380; 9.8 mi S on FR 16; 1 mi W on FR 400. Free. 5/15-9/15. 5 sites (RVs under 32 ft). Tbls, toilets, cfga, firewood, no drkg wtr. Picnicking; fishing (2 mi); horseback riding (1 mi). Elev 500 ft; 3 acres. Facilities not maintained regularly.

PROSPECT (123)

Abbott Creek   **$10**
Rogue River National Forest
6.7 mi N of Prospect on SR 62; 3.7 mi NW on FR 68. $10. 5/15-10/30; 14-day limit. 25 sites (20-ft RV limit). Tbls, toilets, cfga, drkg wtr. Fishing. 7 acres. Elev 3100 ft.

Big Ben   **FREE**
Rogue River National Forest
14.1 mi S of Prospect on co hwy; 8.2 mi NE on FR 344; .8 mi SE on FR 3317. Free. All year; 14-day limit. 2 small sites. Tbls, toilets, cfga, no drkg wtr. Picnicking; fishing; hiking. Elev 4000 ft.

Hamaker   **$10**
Rogue River National Forest
12 mi N of Prospect on SR 62; 11 mi N on SR 230; half mi SE on FR 6530; half mi S on FR 900. $10. 5/15-10/15; 14-day limit. 10 sites (30-ft RV limit). Tbls, toilets, cfga, drkg wtr, grey wtr dump. Fishing, hiking trails. Elev 4000 ft; 3 acres.

Huckleberry Mountain   **FREE**
Rogue River National Forest
17.4 mi E of Prospect on OR 62; 4.1 mi S on FR 311. 5/15-10/15; 14-day limit. 25 sites (RVs under 22 ft). Tbls, toilets, cfga, well drkg wtr. Picnicking; fishing, berry-picking. Elev 5400 ft; 10 acres. Crater Lake National Park (21 mi E).

Imnaha   **$6**
Rogue River National Forest
2.7 mi SE of Prospect on co hwy; 8 mi SE on FR 3317. $6. Elev 3800 ft. 5/15-10/31. 4 sites. Tbls, toilets, cfga, no drkg wtr. Fishing; picnicking. Some structures built by CCC in the 1930s.

Mill Creek   **$6**
Rogue River National Forest
2 mi N of Prospect on Hwy 62; 1 mi E on FR 30. $6. 5/15-10/15; 14-day limit. 10 sites (25-ft RV limit). Tbls, toilets, cfga, no drkg wtr. Fishing, hiking, hunting.

Natural Bridge   **$6**
Rogue River National Forest
9.9 mi N of Prospect on OR 62; 1 mi W on FR 3106. $6. 5/15-10.15; 14-day limit. 17 sites (RVs under 32 ft). Tbls, toilets, cfga, no drkg wtr. Store, ice, gas, snack bar (2 mi). Picnicking; fishing. Elev 3200 ft; 4 acres. Upper Rogue River. Crater Lake National Park (25 mi). Visitor center at Crater Lake. Geological point of interest.

River Bridge   **$6**
Rogue River National Forest
4 mi No of Prospect on Hwy 62; 1 mi N on FR 6210. $6. 5/15-10/15; 14-day limit. 11 sites. Tbls, toilets, cfga, no drkg wtr. Fishing, hiking (Upper Rogue River Trail passes site).

South Fork   **$6**
Rogue River National Forest
21 mi SE of Prospect on CR 37; on South Fork of Rogue River. $6. 5/15-10/30; 14-day limit. 6 sites (16-ft RV limit). Tbls, toilets, cfga, drkg wtr. Fishing, hiking. Trails east to Sky Lakes Wilderness Area. Elev 4000 ft. Camp was once called Lower South Fork.

Union Creek   **$11**
Rogue River National Forest
10.7 mi N of Prospect on SR 62. $11 without hookups, $19 with hookups (holders of federal Senior Pass get reduced rate). All year; 14-day limit. 78 sites (no RV limit at full-hookup sites). Tbls, toilets, cfga, drkg wtr, community kitchen. Fishing, hiking trails (Upper Rogue River Trail nearby). Elev 3200 ft; 14 acres.

RANIER (124)

Hudson-Parcher   **$12**
Columbia County Park
1 mi NW of Ranier; turn off US 30 onto Larson Rd, then one-third mi to park. $12 base for sites without hookups during 12/1-4/30 ($15 with full hookups); $14 & $18 during 5/1-11/30. Tbls, flush toilets, cfga, drkg wtr, hookups($), dump, playground. Horseshoes, birdwatching, boating, fishing, windsurfing.

REEDSPORT (125)

Fawn Creek   **FREE**
Bureau of Land Management
Coos Bay District
Qtr mi N of Reedsport on US 101; 25 mi E on Smith River Rd; no sign at site, just old rd that paralels main rd along river. Free. All year; 14-day limit. 2 primitive sites. Tbls, cfga, no toilets or drkg wtr. Undevelop setting along river with small boat ramp for acess to confluence of Fawn Creek & Smith River. Boating, fishing, hiking, swimming.

Smith River Falls   **FREE**
Bureau of Land Management
Coos Bay District
Qtr mi N of Reedsport on US 101, 28 mi NE on Smith River Rd. Free. All year; 14-day limit. 8 sites. Tbls, toilets, cfga, dump, no drkg wtr. Picnicking; berry picking; swimming; fishing (1 mi).

Umpqua Lighthouse State Park   **$12**
6 mi S of Reedsport off US 101; at Lake Marie. $12 off-season for 24 tent sites ($16 in-season); sites with elec, $16-20. 40-ft RV limit. Tbls, flush toilets, showers, cfga, drkg wtr. Fishing, boating.

Vincent Creek   **FREE**
Bureau of Land Management
Coos Bay District
Qtr mi N of Reedsport on US 101; 35 mi NE on Smith River Rd just prior to Smith River Falls area. Free. Primitive area; 6 sites. Toilets, cfga, tbls, no drkg wtr. 1-day limit. Swimming, hiking, berry picking, picnicking.

William M. Tugman State Park   **$12**
8 mi S of Reedsport on US 101; at Eel Lake. $12 off-season for 115 sites with elec; $16 during 5/1-9/30; $4 for hiker-biker sites; 10-day limit. 40-ft RV limit. Tbls, flush toilets, dump, showers, cfga, drkg wtr, dump. Biking trail, boating(l), fishing, swimming.

Fishing tip: Try the brush-lined shore and steep drop-offs at Eel Lake for largemouth bass up to 5 pounds. The lake also contains crappie, stocked rainbow trou; steelhead, coho salmon (coho must be released). For those without a boat, a fishing dock is near the boat ramp.

Windy Cove   **$12**
Douglas County Park
4 mi S of Reedsport on Hwy 101, then qtr mi SW on Salmon Harbor Dr; at Winchester Bay. $12 without hookups, $15 with full hookups off-season (Nov-Apr); $14 & $18 in-season. All year; 10-day limit. 40 sites; 50-ft RV limit. Tbls, flush toilets, cfga, drkg wtr, showers. Fishing, crabbing, boating, duning, whale watching.

RICHLAND (127)

Eagle Forks   **$5**
Wallowa-Whitman National Forest
10 mi NW of Richland on FR 7735 (gravel). $5. 6/1-10/15; 14-day limit. 7 sites (21-ft RV limit). Tbls, toilets, cfga, drkg wtr. Fishing, hiking, gold panning.

Harry N. Hewitt Memorial   **$11**
Baker County Park
8 mi from Richland on Hwy 86. $11 without hookups $14 with hookups. Apr-Nov. 38 sites. Tbls, flush toilets, cfga, drkg wtr, fish cleaning station. Fishing, boating(l), birdwatching.

Fishing tip: This park is on Brownlee Pool, the convergence of the Snake and Powder Rivers, and the pool offers good fishing for rainbow trout, smallmouth & largemouth bass and crappie.

ROGUE RIVER (128)

Elderberry Flat   **FREE**
Bureau of Land Management
Medford District
20 mi NE of Rogue River on East Fork Evans Creek Rd; 8 mi N on West Fork Evans Creek Rd. Free. Elev 3000 ft. 5/1-9/30; 14-day limit. 9 sites (4 next to creek); 40-ft RV limit. Toilets, cfga, no drkg wtr. Fishing; hunting; picnicking; berry picking; swimming in creek. ATV & motorcycle trails.

ROSEBURG (129)

Amacher Park   **$11**
Douglas County Park
5 mi N of Roseburg, off I-5 at Winchester exit 129; on the North Umpqua River. $11 for sites without hookups; $14 with full hookups. All year; 10-day limit. 10 tent sites, 20 RV sites. Tbls, toilets, cfga, drkg wtr, hookups($), showers. Playground, fishing, boating(l). Dump at Stanton Park ($5).

Broken Arrow   **$11**
Umpqua National Forest
80 mi E on SR 138 from I-5 exit 120 at

Roseburg; FR 4795 to camp on S shore of Diamond Lake. $11. 5/15-9/15; 14-day limit. 147 sites (35-ft RV limit). Tbls, flush toilets, showers, drkg wtr, dump, graywater sumps. Swimming, fishing, hiking, biking, boating(rld). Crater Lake National Park, Mount Thielsen Wilderness, Mount Bailey nearby. Elev 5200 ft. $12 for two vehicles on site.

Fishing tip: During 2001, more than 40,000 catchable-size rainbow trout were stocked in Diamond Lake; some were 2-pound fish.

Diamond Lake $12
Umpqua National Forest
78 mi E on SR 138 from I-5 exit 120 at Roseburg; turn at sign for Diamond Lake Resort & follow rd to campground. $12 base. 5/15-9/15; 14-day limit. Base fee for interior sites; lakeshore sites $18. 238 sites (35-ft RV limit). Tbls, flush toilets, showers, cfga, drkg wtr, dump, grey wtr dumps. Boating(lrd), fishing, hiking, swimming.

Stanton Park $11
Douglas County Park
Off I-5 exit 99, 19 mi S of Roseburg at Canyonville; at South Umpqua River. $11 without hookups, $14 with full hookups off-season (Nov-Apr); $13 & $16 in-season. All year; 10-day limit 47 sites. Tbls, flush toilets, cfga, drkg wtr, showers, hookups($), playground, dump ($5). Hiking, fishing.

Thielsen View $11
Umpqua National Forest
80 mi E on SR 138 from I-5 exit 120 at Roseburg; S on FR 4795; on W shore of Diamond Lake. $11. 5/15-9/31; 14-day limit. $14 for two vehicles on site. 60 sites (35-ft RV limit). Tbls, toilets, cfga, drkg wtr. Boating(ldr), fishing, waterskiing, picnicking. Scenic view of Mt. Thielsen. Access to Pacific Crest National Scenic Trail.

Whistler's Bend $12
Douglas County Park
15 mi E on SR 138; N on Whistler's Bend Rd; at North Umpqua River. $12 during May-Oct, $10 off-season. All year; 10-day limit except 15 days during winter. 23 sites (30-ft RV limit). Tbls, flush toilets, showers, cfga, drkg wtr, no hookups. Fishing, rafting, boating(l), playground. 176 acres. Dump at Stanton Park ($5).

✪ SALEM (131)

Elkhorn Valley Recreation Site $10
Bureau of Land Management
Salem District
25 mi E of Salem on SR 22; 9 mi NE on Elkhorn Rd. $10. 5/15-9/21; 14-day limit. 23 sites (18 ft RV limit). Tbls, toilets, cfga, drkg wtr. Swimming, hiking, fishing.

Silver Falls State Park $12
26 mi E of Salem on SR 214; at Silver Creek. $12 off-season for tent & equestrian sites ($16 during 5/1-9/30); RV sites with elec, $16 & 20. 10-day limit. 110 sites. Tbls, flush toilets, cfga, drkg wtr, dump, showers, visitor center. Bike trail, hiking trail, bridle trails, swimming, birdwatching, evening programs.

SANDY (132)

Camp Ten $10
Mount Hood National Forest
E of Sandy on Hwy 26, then S on FR 42, across part of Warm Springs Indian Reservation, and S on FR 4220 to camp; at Olallie Lake. $10. 7/1-10/15; 14-day limit. 10 sites; 16-ft RV limit. Tbls, toilets, cfga, no drkg wtr. Fishing, hiking. Elev 5000 ft.

SCAPPOOSE (133)

Big Eddy $12
Columbia County Park
NW of Scappoose on Scapoose-Veronica Rd, then 7 mi N on Hwy 47. $12 during 12/1-4/30 for sites without hookups; $15 with elec & wtr; $14 & $18 rest of year. 10% senior discount. Tbls, flush toilets, cfga, drkg wtr, dump. Canoeing, birdwatching, fishing, boating(l).

Camp Wilkerson $12
Columbia County Park
16 mi NW of Scappoose on Scappoose-Veronia Rd; right on Hwy 47 for 2.5 mi; right on Apiary Rd for 6 mi. $12 during 12/1-4/30; $14 rest of year. 10% senior discount. Flush toilets, cfga, drkg wtr, open play areas, hiking trails. Adirondack shelters. 280 acres.

J.J. Collins Memorial $12
Columbia County Park
2 mi upstream from the Gilbert River boat ramp (7 mi from confluence of Columbia River & Multnomah Channel; on Coon Island. $12 off-season; $14 during 5/1-11/30. 10% senior discount Toilets, tbls, cfga, no drkg wtr. Fishing, boating, hiking trails, birdwtching, horseshoes.

Scaponia $9
Columbia County Park
13 mi W of Scappoose on Scappoose-Veronia Rd. $9 during 5/1-11/30; $6 rest of year. 10% senior discount. Primitive camping at 7-acre wayside. Tbls, toilets, cfga, drkg wtr. Fishing, hiking.

Scappoose RV Park $12
Columbia County Park
1 mi N of Scappoose on US 30; three-fourths mi E on West Lane Rd; left on Honeyman Rd; next to Scappoose Industrial Airpark. $12 without hookups during 12/1-4/30 ($15 with hookups); $14 & $18 rest of year. Tbls, flush toilets, cfga, drkg wtr, hookups($), dump, playground. Horseshoes.

SENECA (134)

Big Creek $5
Malheur National Forest
20.5 mi E of Seneca on FR 16; half mi N on FR 162E. $5. 5/15-11/15; 14-day limit. 15 sites (RVs under 31 ft). Tbls, toilets, cfga, firewood, well drkg wtr. Picnicking; fishing. Elev 5100 ft; 4 acres. On edge of Logan Valley.

Murray Campground FREE
Malheur National Forest
21 mi W of Seneca via FR 16 on FR 1600/924. Free. 5/15-11/30; 30-day limit. 5 sites. Tbls, toilets, cfga, no drkg wtr. Fishing, hiking, hunting.

Parish Cabin $6
Malheur National Forest
12 mi E of Seneca on FR 16. $6. Services MD-LD; 30-day limit. 20 sites (32-ft RV limit). Tbls, cfga, toilets, drkg wtr, grey wtr dumps. Fishing at Little Bear Creek.

Starr $4
Malheur National Forest
9 mi N of Seneca on US 395. $4. 5/10-11/1; 30-day limit. 8 sites (25-ft RV limit). Tbls, toilets, cfga, no drkg wtr. Elev 5100 ft. 7 acres.

SILVER LAKE (135)

Alder Springs Forest Camp FREE
Fremont National Forest
Half mi W of Silver Lake on SR 31; left on CR 4-11 (becoming FR 27) for 13 mi; right on FR 021 for 1.5 mi. Free. 6/1-12/1; 14-day limit. 3 sites. Toilets, cfga, no drkg wtr or tbls, no trash service. Hunting. Historic, tiered water troughs made from dug out logs.

Antler Trailhead FREE
Fremont National Forest
Half mi W of Silver Lake on SR 31; left on CR 4-11 (becoming FR 27) for 9 mi; right on FR 2804 for 2.5 mi; left on FR 7645 for 5 mi; left on FR 036 about 2.3 mi; right on Fr 038 for half mi. Free. May-Nov; 14-day limit. 5 sites. Tbls, toilets, cfga, drkg wtr, corrals, hitching rails. Hiking, horseback riding, mountain biking.

Bunyard Crossing FREE
Rustic Forest Camp
Fremont National Forest
6 mi S of Silver Lake on CR 4-12 (becoming FR 28); 1 mi on FR 28; right on FR 2917 for 1 mi (west); right on FR 413 just before bridge. Free. 5/1-12/1; 14-day limit. 3 sites. Tbls, toilets, cfga, no drkg wtr. Hiking, birdwatching, fishing at Silver Creek. Wildflowers in season.

Duncan Reservoir FREE
Bureau of Land Management
Lakeview District
5 mi E of Silver Lake on OR 31; S 1 mi on Lake County RD 4-14; 4 mi S on BLM 6197. Free. All year, subject to winter clo-

sure. 5 sites. Toilets. Fishing, hunting, hiking, boating(l). Ice fishing in winter, but access variable.

East Bay Campground $8
Fremont National Forest

From forest's office at Silver Lake, qtr mi E on Hwy 31; right on FR 28 for 13 mi; right on FR 014. $8. 5/1-11/15; 14-day limit. 17 sites. Drkg wtr, tbls, toilets, cfga, fishing pier. Boating(l), fishing, hiking, swimming, birdwatching.

Lower Buck Forest Camp FREE
Fremont National Forest

1 mi N of Silver Lake on SR 31; 10 mi W on CR 4-10; left on FR 2804 for 2 mi; after second cattle guard, left on FR 015 for 1 mi. Free. 5/1-12/1; 14-day limit. 5 sites. Tbls, toilets, cfga, no drkg wtr. Fishing. Elev 5000 ft.

Silver Creek Marsh FREE
Fremont National Forest

1 mi W of Silver Lake on SR 31; left on CR 4-11, then 9.7 mi S on FR 27; qtr mi SW on FR 2919. Free. 5/1-11/15; 14-day limit. 17 sites. Tbls, toilets, cfga, drkg wtr, no trash service. Fishing, picnicking, hiking, horseback riding, mountain biking, birdwatching. Quiet, secluded. Elev 5000 ft. On Thompson Reservoir. Overflow area for Thompson camp. Corrals, hitching rails, watering troughs.

Thompson Reservoir FREE
Fremont National Forest

1 mi W of Silver Lake on SR 31; left on CR 4-11, then 13.6 mi S on FR 287; 1 mi E on FR 3204. Free. 5/1-11/15; 14-day limit. 19 sites (22-ft RV limit). Tbls, toilets, cfga, drkg wtr. Swimming, boating(l), fishing. 8 acres. 2,179-acre lake.

Trapper Spring FREE
Forest Camp
Fremont National Forest

NW of Silver Lake on SR 31; 10 mi W on CR 4-10; 4 mi N on FR 2516; left on fR 2780 for 8 mi; left on FR 146 at Trapper Spring sign. Free. 5/15-10/31; 14-day limit. 2 primitive sites. Tbl, cfga, toilet, no drkg wtr, no trash service. Hiking.

Upper Buck Forest Camp FREE
Fremont National Forest

NW of Silver Lake on SR 31; 10 mi W on CR 4-10; left on FR 2804 for 4 mi. 5/1-12/1; 14-day limit. 6 primitive sites. Tbls, toilets, cfga, no drkg wtr. Fishing, wildlfower viewing, birdwatching.

SISTERS (136)

Black Pine Springs FREE
Dispersed Camping
Deschutes National Forest

8.2 mi S of Sisters on FR 16. Free. 6/15-10/15; 14-day limit. About 4 sites (RVs under 16 ft). All facilities removed; no drkg wtr. Elev 4350 ft.

Cold Springs $12
Deschutes National Forest

4 mi W of Sisters on SR 242. $12. 5/1-10/15; 14-day limit. 23 sites (40-ft RV limit). Tbls, toilets, cfga, drkg wtr. Hiking, fishing, picnicking. Elev 3400 ft; 12 acres.

Cow Creek Horse Camp FREE
Deschutes National Forest

1.7 mi W of Sisters on Hwy 242. Free. 6/15-10/15; 14-day limit. 4 sites. Tbls, toilet, cfga, no wtr except for horses. Corrals. Hiking & bridle trails.

Driftwood $12
Deschutes National Forest

17 mi S of Sisters on FR 16 (Elm St); at Three Creek Lake. $12. 6/15-10/15; 14-day limit. 5 RV sites, 12 tent sites; not good sites for RVs, but 30-ft RV limit. Tbls, toilets, cfga, drkg wtr. Fishing, hiking, boating (elec mtrs). Elev 6600 ft.

Fishing tip: Small, 28-acre Three Creek Lake is easy to fish from shore, but boat angling produces better. It contains planted rainbow trout and self-sustaining brook trout of 8-15 inches. Typical fish are 10 inches.

Indian Ford $10
Deschutes National Forest

5 mi NW of Sisters on US 20. $10. 5/1-10/15; 14-day limit. 25 sites (22-ft RV limit). Tbls, toilets, cfga, no drkg wtr. Fishing (Indian Ford Creek), birdwatching. Elev 3200 ft; 9 acres.

Lava Camp Lake FREE
Deschutes National Forest

14.6 mi W of Sisters on SR 242; 1 mi SE on FR 900; near McKenzie Pass; Mckenzie Hwy restricts RV length to 35 ft. Free. Elev 5200 ft. 6/15-10/15; 14-day limit. 10 RV/tent sites (RVs under 22 ft); 2 tent sites; 7 acres. Tbls, toilets, cfga, no drkg wtr. Picnicking, swimming, fishing, hiking. Three Sisters Wilderness access.

Round Lake Dispersed FREE
Deschutes National Forest

12.4 mi NW of Sisters on Hwy 20; 1 mi N on FR 12; 5.5 mi W on FR 1210; at Suttle Lake. Free. All year; 14-day limit. 4 sites. No facilities except cfga, no drkg wtr. Fishing, boating. All facilities were remoed after the camp was severely damaged by fire. Dispersed camping is still available.

Fishing tip: Good to fair fishing is available all year at Suttle Lake. Try for brown trout early and late in the day along the north shore. Kokanee salmon fishing is at its best during the summer; daily bag limit is 25 fish.

Three Sisters City Park $10

Qtr mi E of Sisters on US 20. $10 (seniors $9; hikers & hikers $5 per tent). 5/15-10/15; 14-day limit. 60 sites. Tbls, toilets, cfga, drkg wtr, dump ($5 non-campers). Fishing.

Three Creeks Horse Camp $12
Deschutes National Forest

17 mi S of Sisters on FR 16 (Elm St); N of

Three Creek Lake. $12. 6/15-10/15; 14-day limit. 9 sites (4 stalls per site); 30-ft RV limit. Tbls, toilets, cfga, no drkg wtr. Picnicking, fishing, swimming, horseback riding.

Fishing tip: Popular among local fishermen in July, Three Creek Lake has trout that respond to most lures and baits. We suggest using dark nymphs and wooly buggers or dry fly fishing with cahill, gnat and Adams patterns.

Three Creeks Lake $12
Deschutes National Forest

18 mi S of Sisters on FR 16. $12. 5/1-10/15; 14-day limit. 12 sites (40-ft RV limit). Tbls, toilets, cfga, no drkg wtr. Picnicking, swimming, boating(lr), fishing, hiking. On SE shore of Three Creek Lake. 6 acres; elev 6400 ft.

Fishing tip: No boat motors on Three Creeks Lake. On E shore near the primitive boat ramp, a store rents small boats. Trout are stocked each spring, and bait fishermen catch them near the dam on NE corner. Later, try still fishing deep water along the cliffs on the S end.

Three Creeks Meadow $12
Deschutes National Forest

17 mi S of Sisters on FR 16 (Elm St); N of Three Creek Lake. $12. 6/15-10/15; 14-day limit. 11 sites; 40-ft RV limit. Tbls, toilets, cfga, no drkg wtr. Picnicking, boating, swimming, fishing. Elev 6300 ft; 12 acres. Horse camp adjoining. No camping in the meadow.

Fishing tip: Biggest fish are usually caught from Three Creek Lake along the cliffs on the S end. Also, troll near the dam, near the boat ramp and along the S end with spinners & crankbaits. W shoreline very popular with trolling fishermen.

Whispering Pine Horse Camp $12
Deschutes National Forest

6 mi W of Sisters on SR 242; 5 mi S on FR 1018; 3 mi on FR 1520. $12. 5/15-10/15; 14-day limit. 9 sites (4 box stalls per site); 30-ft RV limit. Tbls, toilets, cfga, no drkg wtr. Picnicking, fishing, horseback riding.

SPRAY (138)

Fairview FREE
Umatilla National Forest

2.5 mi E of Spray on Hwy 19; 11.5 mi N on Hwy 207; half mi W on FR 400. Free. 5/1-10/30; 14-day limit. 5 sites (RVs under 17 ft). Tbls, toilets, cfga, no drkg wtr. Hunting.

SUMPTER (139)

McCully Forks FREE
Wallowa-Whitman National Forest

3 mi NW of Sumpter on CR 410. $5.. 5/15-10/31; 14-day limit. 6 tent sites. Tbls, toilets, cfga, no drkg wtr. Gold panning, fishing, hiking.

Union Creek $12
Wallowa-Whitman National Forest
8 mi SE of Sumpter on SR 7; on N shore of Phillips Lake. $12 base. 5/15-10/15; 14-day limit. Base fee for tent area; $15 elec hookups, $16 full hookups (holders of federal Senior Pass pay less). 58 sites (22-ft RV limit). Tbls, flush toilets, cfga, drkg wtr, hookups($), showers, dump, grey wtr dumps. Fishing, hiking, boating(l), swimming, waterskiing. Concessionaire-operated.

SUTHERLIN (140)

Tyee Recreation Site $8
Bureau of Land Management
Roseburg District
11 mi W of Sutherlin on SR 138; turn across Bullock Bridge; then right half mi. $8. About MD-10/1; 14-day limit. 15 sites (25-ft RV limit), 11 picnic sites. Tbls, toilets, cfga, drkg wtr, shelter. Fishing. 15 acres, on main stem of Umpqua River.

SWEET HOME (141)

Fernview $10
Willamette National Forest
23 mi E of Sweet Home on US 20; at Boulder Creek & Santiam River. $10. 5/1-10/30; 14-day limit. 11 sites (22-ft RV limit). Tbls, toilets, cfga, drkg wtr. Fishing, hiking trails. 5 acres.

House Rock $10
Willamette National Forest
26.5 mi E of Sweet Home on US 20; SE on FR 2044; at Sheep Creek & South Santiam River. $10. 5/1-11/1; 14-day limit. 17 sites; 22-ft RV limit. Tbls, toilets, cfga, drkg wtr. Hiking (loop trail), fishing, swimming. Historic House Rock & Old Santiam Wagon Road.

Lost Prairie $10
Willamette National Forest
40 mi E of Sweet Home on US 20. $10. About MD-10/30; 14-day limit. 10 sites (24-ft RV limit). Tbls, toilets, cfga, drkg wtr. Fishing, hiking. Elev 3300 ft; 5 acres on Hackleman Creek.

Sunnyside Park $9
Foster Lake & Dam
Linn County Park
At Sweet Home on E end of Foster Lake. $9 without hookups for seniors during 9/4-5/23 ($12 with elec/wtr); $11 for seniors in-season without hookups ($13 with wtr/elec). Non-seniors pay $13 off season without hookups ($16 with elec/wtr), $15 in-season without hookups & $18 with elec/wtr. All year. 162 sites. Tbls, cfga, toilets, drkg wtr, hookups($). Floating(l), fishing, skiing. Camp built by Corps of Engineers.

Trout Creek $10
Willamette National Forest
18.6 mi E of Sweet Home on US 20. $10. 5/1-11/1; 14-day limit 24 sites (36-ft RV limit). Tbls, toilets, cfga, drkg wtr. Fishing, hiking. On Santiam River. 14 acres.

Whitcomb Creek $10
Linn County Park
9 mi NE on Quartzville Rd from US 20 at Sweet Home. $10 for seniors; others pay $13. All year; 10-day limit. 39 sites. Tbls, toilets, cfga, drkg wtr, no hookups. Swimming, fishing, boating(ld), hiking.

Yellowbottom Recreation Site $8
Bureau of Land Management
Salem District
From U.S. 20 just E of Sweet Home, 22 mi NE on Quartzville Rd. $8. 5/15-9/30; 14-day limit. 12 RV sites (drive-through, 28-ft limit); 21 tent sites. Tbls, toilets, cfga, drkg wtr, 6 picnic sites. Fishing, swimming, hiking, rockhounding. On Quartzville Creek. 16 acres.

Yukwah $10
Willamette National Forest
19 mi E of Sweet Home on US 20. $10. 5/1-10/30; 14-day limit 20 sites (28-ft RV limit). Tbls, toilets, cfga, drkg wtr. Fishing, hiking. Santiam River. 15 acres.

TILLAMOOK (142)

Browns Camp $10
OHV Staging Area
Tillamook State Forest
E of Tillamook on Hwy 6 (Wilson River Hwy) to about 2 mi from the road's summit. $10. Mar-Nov; 14-day limit. 29 sites. Tbls, toilets, cfga, drkg wtr. OHV trail access, unloading ramp. Popular staging area for OHV activity.

Diamond Mill FREE
OHV Camping Area
Tillamook State Forest
E of Tillamook on Hwy 6 (Wilson River Hwy) to milepost 23, then 2 mi to camp. Free. All year; 14-day limit. Primitive dispersed sites. Toilets, cfga, no drkg wtr. Large, undeveloped staging area for OHV activities.

Jones Creek Campground $10
Tillamook State Forest
About 23 mi E of Tillamook on Hwy 6 (Wilson River Hwy); at the Wilson River. $5 for 9 walk-in tent sites, $10 for 29 drive-to sites. MD-10/31; 14-day limit. Toilets, tbls, cfga, drkg wtr. Fishing, swimming, nature study, hiking, hunting.

Jordan Creek $5
OHV Staging Area
Tillamook State Forest
E of Tillamook on Hwy 6 (Wilson River Hwy) to milepost 18 at community of Jordan Creek, then 2.2 mi on Jordan Creek Rd to staging area. $5. Mar-Nov; 14-day limit. 6 primitive sites. Tbls, cfga, toilet, no drkg wtr. Staging area for OHV activities.

Keenig Creek FREE
Tillamook State Forest
18 mi E of Tillamook on Hwy 6 (Wilson River Hwy). Free. All year; 14-day limit. 15 tent sites. Tbls, toilets, cfga, drkg wtr. Fishing, hiking, hunting.

Kilchis River Park $10
Tillamook County Park
About 10 mi NE of Tillamook off US 101 (just W of Idaville) at end of Kilchis Rd. $10. May-Sept. 34 sites. Tbls, pit toilets, cfga, drkg wtr, dump (non-campers pay $10), playground. Fishing, swimming, volleyball, ball field, hiking, horseshoes.

Trask River Park $10
Tillamook County Park
1.5 mi E of Tillamook on Hwy 6; 10 mi SE on Trask River Rd to nearly its end. $10. May-Sept. 60 rustic sites. Tbls, toilets, cfga, drkg wtr, dump (non-campers pay $10). Fishing, hiking.

TILLER (143)

Boulder Annex FREE
Umpqua National Forest
Qtr mi SE of Tiller on SR 227; 6.2 mi NE on CR 46; 7.8 mi NE on FR 28, just past main Boulder Creek Campground; entry on left (deadend rd, no turnaround). Camp free, but donations accepted. All year, but maintained 5/20-10/1; 14-day limit. 4 small sites (RVs not recommended). Tbls, toilets, cfga, no drkg wtr, no trash service. Trout fishing, hiking. Closed early in 2007 due to tree hazards.

Boulder Creek $6
Umpqua National Forest
Quarter mi SE of Tiller on OR 227; 6.2 mi NE on CR 46; 7.7 mi NE on FR 28. $6. 5/1-10/31; 14-day limit. 8 sites (22-ft RV limit). Tbls, toilets, cfga, no drkg wtr (pump inoperable). Picnicking; fishing; swimming. Gray water waste sumps. Along picturesque section of South Umpqua River, shady & secluded. Good trout fishing; hiking.

Camp Comfort $6
Umpqua National Forest
Quarter mi SE of Tiller on OR 227; 6.2 mi NE on CR 46; 17.9 mi NE on FR 28; 2 mi NE on FR 2739. $6. 5/1-10/31; 14-day limit. 5 sites; 22-ft RV limit. Tbls, toilets, cfga, one open shelter. Picnicking; swimming; fishing; hiking. Trail from CCC Shelter to confluence of Black Rock Fork & Castle Rock Fork (beginnings of South Umpqua River).

Cover $6
Umpqua National Forest
Qtr mi SE of Tiller on CR 1; 5 mi NE on CR 46; 11.8 mi E on FR 29. Along Jackson Creek. $6. 5/20-10/31; 14-day limit. 7 sites; 22-ft RV limit. Tbls, toilets, cfga, no drkg wtr, grey water sumps. Fishing, hiking. Only developed campsite on Jackson Creek. Heavy use during fall hunting season.

Dumont Creek $6
Umpqua National Forest
Qtr mi SE of Tiller on CR 1; 6.2 mi NE on CR 46; 5.4 mi NE on FR 28. $6. 5/1-10/31; 14-day limit. 5 sites; 16-ft RV limit. Tbls, toilets, cfga, drkg wtr. Fishing, swimming. South Umpqua River.

Skookum Pond   **FREE**
Umpqua National Forest
24 mi NE of Tiller on FR 2924-200. Camp free, but donations accepted. 5/20-10/31; 14-day limit. 3 tent sites. Tbls, toilet, cfga, no drkg wtr. Hiking, fishing.

South Umpqua Falls   **$6**
Picnic Ground
Umpqua National Forest
Qtr mi SE of Tiller on SR 227; 6.2 mi E on CR 46; NE on FR 28 to South Umpqua Falls; no camping at picnic area, but at undeveloped area just downstream & across rd. $6. All year; 14-day limit. 5 sites; 35-ft RV limit. No facilities, no drkg wtr.

Threehorn   **$6**
Umpqua National Forest
12.7 mi SE of Tiller, on CR 1. $6. All year; 14-day limit. 5 sites (RVs under 22 ft). Tbls, toilets, cfga, drkg wtr (pump inoperable in 1996). Shady, forested setting. Picnicking, hiking, photography.

3C Rock Picnic Ground   **FREE**
Umpqua National Forest
5 mi SE of Tiller Ranger Station on CR 46; at South Umpqua River boat ramp. No camping at picnic area, but at undeveloped area downstream from scaling station. Camp free, but donations accepted. All year; 14-day limit. No facilities, no drkg wtr. Fishing, hiking, boating(l). Waterfall upstream from boat ramp.

TYGH VALLEY (145)

Little Badger   **$10**
Mount Hood National Forest
8 mi W of Tygh Valley on CR/FR 27; left on FR 2710 for 1 mi. $10. 6/15-9/15; 14-day limit. 3 sites; 16-ft RV limit. Tbls, toilets, cfga, no drkg wtr. Fishing, hiking, horseback riding.

UKIAH (146)

Bear Wallow Creek   **$5**
Umatilla National Forest
10 mi E of Ukiah on Hwy 244. $5 (group site $10). 5/15-11/1; 14-day limit. 7 sites (RVs under 32 ft); 8 picnic sites. Tbls, toilets, cfga, no drkg wtr. Hunting, fishing. Qtr mi interpretive trail.

Big Creek Meadows   **FREE**
Umatilla National Forest
22 mi SE of Ukiah on FR 52; access via Hwy 244. Free. May-Oct; 14-day limit. 3 sites. Tbls, toilets, cfga, no drkg wtr. Hunting, fishing, hiking, wilderness access. ATV trails nearby. Elev 5100 ft.

Divide Wells   **FREE**
Umatilla National Forest
20 mi W of Ukiah on FR 5327-290; access via Hwy 395. Free. May-Oct; 14-day limit. 8 sites & 3 group sites. Tbls, toilets, cfga, no drkg wtr. Hunting, trail bike riding. Popular among elk hunter groups. Elev 4700 ft.

Drift Fence   **FREE**
Umatilla National Forest
7 mi SE of Ukiah on FR 52; access via Hwy 244. Free. May-Oct; 14-day limit. 5 small sites, 1 group site. Tbls, toilets, cfga, no drkg wtr. Hunting. Improvements planned. Elev 4250 ft.

Frazier   **$5**
Umatilla National Forest
18 mi E of Ukiah on SR 244; half mi S on FR 5226; qtr mi E on FR 20. $5 (group sites $10). 6/1-11/1; 14-day limit. 16 sites (32-ft RV limit). Tbls, toilets, cfga, no drkg wtr. Popular big-game hunting site. Fishing, trail bikes. Elev 4300 ft; 10 acres.

Lane Creek   **$5**
Umatilla National Forest
10.5 mi E of Ukiah on Hwy 244. $5 (group site $10). 5/15-11/1; 14-day limit. 6 sites (RVs under 45 ft); 4 picnic sites; 1 group site. Tbls, toilets, cfga, no drkg wtr. Hunting, fishing.

North Fork John Day   **$5**
Umatilla National Forest
36 mi S of Ukiah on FR 52 (Blue Mountain Scenic Byway; access via Hwy 244; on North Fork John Day River. $5. May-Oct; 14-day limit. 17 sites (22-ft RV limit). Tbls, toilets, cfga, no drkg wtr; horse handling facilities at adjacent trailhead. Hunting, fishing, wilderness access.

Pearson Woods Camp   **FREE**
Umatilla National Forest
22 mi NE of Ukian on FR 5400, off Hwy 244. Free. May-Oct; 14-day limit. 4 primitive sites. Toilet, cfga, no drkg wtr. Remnants of a lumber camp still exist.

Toll Bridges   **$5**
Umatilla National Forest
17 mi S of Ukiah on FR 10; at Desolation Creek. $5. May-Oct; 14-day limit. 7 sites. Tbls, toilets, cfga, drkg wtr. Fishing, hiking. Elev 3800 ft.

Ukiah-Dale Forest   **$8**
State Scenic Corridor
SW of Ukiah on US 395 about 3 mi; at Camas Creek. $8 ($6 off-season). 4/15-10/27; 10-day limit in 14-day period. 27 primitive sites (40-ft RV limit). Tbls, flush toilets, cfga, drkg wtr. Elev 3000 ft.
Fishing tip: The North Fork of John Day River and Camas Creek offer excellent fishing for trout, steelhead & salmon.

Winom Creek Campground   **FREE**
Umatilla National Forest
22 mi SE of Ukiah off FR 52; access rd too narrow, winding for large RVs. Free. May-Oct. 5 sites; 3 group sites. 2 shelters, toilets, cfga, no drkg wtr. Primarily an OHV & equestrian camp; staging area for S end of an OHV complex. Built as joint effort by state dept. of transportation, Umatilla NF and Northwest Trailriders.

UMATILLA (147)

Sand Station Recreation   **FREE**
Lake Wallula
Corps of Engineers
10.5 mi E of Umatilla on US 730. Free. All year; 14-day limit. About 15 undesignated primitive sites. Tbls, toilets, cfga, no drkg wtr. Beach. Swimming, boating, fishing.

UNION (148)

Catherine Creek State Park   **$8**
8 mi SE of Union on SR 203. $8 for 20 primitive sites ($5 off-season). 10-day limit in 14-day period. 30-ft RV limit. Tbls, toilets, cfga, no drkg wtr. Picnicking, fishing, horseshoes, hiking trail. 160 acres.

UNITY (149)

Eldorado Forest Camp   **FREE**
Wallowa-Whitman National Forest
10 mi E of Unity on Hwy 26; 3 mi S on FR 1680. Free. 5/1-9/15; 14-day limit. 6 sites (28-ft RV limit. Tbls, toilets, cfga, no drkg wtr. Fishing, hiking. East Camp Creek. Self-service.

Elk Creek Forest Camp   **$6**
Wallowa-Whitman National Forest
5.5 mi SW of Unity on CR 1300; 2 mi SW on FR 1159. $6. Elev 4400 ft. 6/1-9/15; 10-day limit. Undesignated sites. Tbls, toilets, cfga, firewood, no drkg wtr. Berry picking; picnicking, fishing. Self-service.

Long Creek Forest Camp   **FREE**
Wallowa-Whitman National Forest
9 mi S of Unity on FR 1680. Free. 5/1-9/15; 14-day limit. Primitive undesignated sites (28-ft RV limit). Tbls, toilets, cfga, no drkg wtr. Fishing, hiking. Long Creek Reservoir. Self-service.

Mammoth Springs   **FREE**
Wallowa-Whitman National Forest
9 mi W of Unity on Hwy 600, FR 6005 & FR 2640 (gravel last 5 mi). 5/1-9/15; 14-day limit. 2 sites (28-ft RV limit). Tbsl, toilet, cfga, no drkg wtr. Fishing, hiking. Self-service.

Oregon   **$6**
Wallowa-Whitman National Forest
10.5 mi NW of Unity on US 26. $6. 4/28-9/15. 11 sites (28-ft RV limit). Tbls, toilets, cfga, wtr. Hiking; picnicking; fishing. Elev 5000 ft. Self-service.

South Fork   **$6**
Wallowa-Whitman National Forest
5.5 mi SW of Unity on CR 1300; 1 mi SW on FR 6005. $6. 5/28-9/15; 10-day limit. 14 sites (28-ft RV limit). Tbls, toilets, cfga, drkg wtr. Fishing. Self-service.

Stevens Creek   **$6**
Wallowa-Whitman National Forest
7 mi SW on CR 6005. $6. 6/1-9/15; 10-day

limit. Undesignated sites. Tbls, toilets, cfga, firewood, no drkg wtr. Picnicking; berry picking. Self-service.

Wetmore $6
Wallowa-Whitman National Forest
8.2 mi NW of Unity on US 26. 5/28-9/15; 10-day limit. $6. 16 sites (28-ft RV limit). Tbls, toilets, cfga, drkg wtr. Hiking (nature trails), picnicking, fishing. Yellow Pine Handicap Trail.

Yellow Pine $6
Wallowa-Whitman National Forest
9.2 mi NW of Unity on US 26. $6. 5/28-9/15. 21 sites (28-ft RV limit). Tbls, toilets, cfga, drkg wtr, firewood. Hiking (nature trails); picnicking; fishing. Yellow Pine Handicap Trail.

VALE (150)

Bully Creek Park $10
Malheur County Park
5.8 mi W of Vale on Graham Blvd; NW on Bully Creek Rd. $10. 4/15-11/15. 33 sites (55-ft RV limit). Tbls, flush toilets, drkg wtr, cfga, showers, hookups, dump. Fishing, boating(l), swimming, picnicking.

Twin Springs FREE
Bureau of Land Management
Vale District
3.5 mi W of Vale on US 20; 34 mi S on Dry Creek Rd; high-clearance vehicles only. Free. 5/1-10/30; 14-day limit. Open only during dry road conditions. 5 primitive sites. Tbls, toilets, cfga, no drkg wtr. Fishing, hiking, hunting.

WALDPORT (151)

Canal Creek $7.50
Siuslaw National Forest
7 mi E of Waldport on SR 34; 4 mi S on FR 1462 -- narrow, winding, not recommended for large RVs). $7.50 with federal Senior Pass; others pay $15. 5/15-10/1; 14-day limit. 11 sites. Tbls, toilets, cfga, drkg wtr. Fishing, picnicking. Shelter, play area.

WALLOWA (152)

Boundary FREE
Wallowa-Whitman National Forest
5 mi S on CR 515; 1.9 mi S on FR 040. On Bear Creek. Free. 6/15-11/1; 10-day limit. 8 tent sites (RVs under 16 ft). Tbls, toilets, cfga, firewood, no drkg wtr. Self-service sites. Swimming; fishing; berry picking. Near Eagle Cap Wilderness. Backpack trailhead.

WAMIC (153)

Badger Lake $10
Mount Hood National Forest
6 mi SW of Wamic on CR 226; 11 mi SW on FR 408; 10 mi NW on FR 339; 5 mi NW on FR 140. $10 ($5 NW pass in parking lot). Elev 4400 ft. 7/1-9/10; 10-day limit. 4 tent sites. Tbls, toilets, cfga, firewood, no drkg

wtr. Swimming; picnicking; fishing; boating(l; no motors); berry picking. Area beyond dam is Badger Creek Wilderness; no motorized transportation allowed.

Bonney Crossing $10
Mount Hood National Forest
6 mi W of Wamic on CR 226; 1 mi W on FR 48; qtr mi W on FR 4810; 1.2 mi NW on FR 4811. $10. 4/15-10/15; 14-day limit. 8 sites; 16-ft RV limit. Tbls, toilets, cfga, no drkg wtr. Boating, fishing. Elev 2200 ft.

Bonney Meadows $10
Mount Hood National Forest
6 mi W of Wamic on CR 226; 14 mi SW on FR 48; 2 mi N on FR 4890; 4 mi N on FR 4891. $10. 7/1-9/10; 14-day limit. 6 sites (16-ft RV limit). Tbls, toilets, cfga, no drkg wtr. Berry-picking, fishing.

Boulder Lake $10
Mount Hood National Forest
6 mi SW of Wamic on CR 226; 12.2 mi SW on FR 408; 5.7 mi N on FR 446; half mi W on Trail 463. $10 during 7/1-9/10; free rest of yr, but no services; 14-day limit. 10 hike-in tent sites. Tbls, toilets, cfga, firewood, no drkg wtr. Swimming; picnicking; fishing; boating(no motors). Elev 4600 ft; 2 acres.

Camp Windy FREE
Mount Hood National Forest
6 mi W of Wamic on CR 226; 14 mi SW on FR 48; 2 mi N on FR 4890; 5.5 mi N on FR 4891, past Bonney Meadow Campground, then 1 mi NE on FR 3550. Free. 7/1-LD; 14-day limit. 3 hike-in tent sites. Tbls, toilets, cfga, no drkg wtr. Hiking, berry-picking. Elev 5200 ft.

Forest Creek $10
Mount Hood National Forest
6 mi W of Wamic on cR 226; 12.5 mi SW on FR 48; 1 mi SE on FR 4885; qtr mi S on FR 3530. $10. 6/1-10/15; 14-day limit. 8 sites (16-ft RV limit). Tbls, toilets, cfga, no drkg wtr. Hiking, fishing.

Post Camp $10
Mount Hood National Forest
6 mi SW of Wamic on CR 226; 11 mi SW on FR 408; 2 mi NW on FR 339; .7 mi W on FR 468. $10 during 7/10-9/10; free rest of yr, but no services; 14-day limit. 4 sites (RVs under 16 ft). Tbls, toilets, cfga, firewood, no drkg wtr. Picnicking; fishing; horseback riding (5 mi).

WARM SPRINGS (154)

Mecca Flat $8
Lower Deschutes River System
Bureau of Land Management
Prineville District
2 mi off Hwy 26 near Warm Springs; poor access rd. $8 Sun-Thurs; $12 Fri & Sat. All year; 14-day limit. 10 sites. Tbls, toilets, cfga, no drkg wtr. Fishing, hiking, boating, picnicking.

WELCHES (155)

McNeil $12
Mount Hood National Forest
1 mi E of Welches on US 26; 4.7 mi NE on CR 18; E on FR 1825. $12. 5/15-9/15; 14-day limit. 34 sites (22-ft RV limit). Tbls, toilets, cfga, no drkg wtr. Hiking, fishing, biking.

WESTON (156)

Target Meadows $10
Umatilla National Forest
17.5 mi E of Weston on SR 204; one-third mi E on FR 64; 22 mi N on FR 6401; 0.6 mi NE on FR 50. $10. 6/15-9/30; free rest of year, but no wtr or services. 14-day limit. 20 sites (22-ft RV limit); 6 picnic sites. Tbls, toilets, cfga, drkg wtr. Nature trails, hunting. Elev 5100 ft; 20 acres.

Woodland $5
Umatilla National Forest
17.5 mi E of Weston on Hwy 204. $5. 7/1-10/15; 14-day limit. 7 sites (RVs under 23 ft); 2 picnic sites. Tbls, toilets, cfga, no drkg wtr. Hunting. Elev 5200 ft.

Woodward $10
Umatilla National Forest
17.5 mi E of Weston on SR 204. $10. 7/1-10/15; 14-day limit. 18 sites (22-ft RV limit). Tbls, toilets, cfga, drkg wtr, dump. Hunting, hiking, trail bikes. No public access to adjoining private lake. Elev 4950 ft; 15 acres.

WHITE BIRD (IDAHO) (157)

Pittsburg Landing $8
Wallowa-Whitman National Forest
Hells Canyon National Recreation Area
19 mi SW of White Bird on CR 493 (steep, gravel rd). $8. 35 sites. Tbls, toilets, cfga, drkg wtr. Fishing, hiking, boating.

WHITE CITY (158)

North Fork $8
Rogue River National Forest
28.1 mi E of White City on Hwy 140; half mi S on FR 37. $8. 5/1-11/15; 14-day limit. 9 sites (24-ft RV limit). Tbls, cfga, toilets, no drkg wtr. Swimming, boating, fishing.

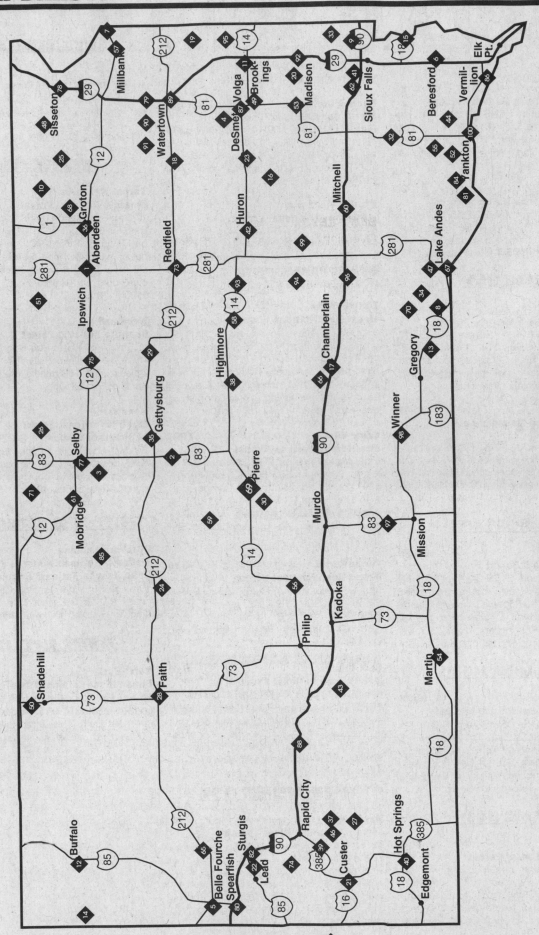

MISCELLANEOUS
Capital:
Pierre
Nickname:
Coyote State, Sunshine State
Motto:
Under God the People Rule
Flower:
American Pasque
Tree:
Black Hill Spruce
Bird:
Ringnecked Pheasant
Song:
"Hail, South Dakota"

Internet Address:
www.travelsd.com

Toll-free number for travel information: 1-800-S-DAKOTA.

Department of Tourism and State Development, Capitol Lake Plaza, Pierre, SD 57501-5070; 605-773-3301. E-mail: sdinfo@state.sd.us

Dept of Game, Fish & Parks, 523 East Capitol, Pierre, SD 57501; 605-773-3391.

REST AREAS
Overnight stops are not permitted.

STATE PARKS
Overnight fees are $6 for a basic campsite with pit toilets; $8 for modern non-electric sites ($15 at Custer SP) and modern equestrian sites with flush toilets and showers and electrical hookups available; $10 for non-electric sites at "preferred" sites (which are modern sites with high occupancy rates); $16 at "prime" sites (waterfront electrical sites at Chief Whie Crane and Lewis & Clark Parks). Electrical hookups are $4 extra (not available at Custer). Daily entrance fee is $3 per person ($5 per vehicle) or $23 annual per vehicle (Custer entry is $12 per vehicle in-season and $6 off-season). Some camping fees are reduced when water systems and comfort stations are winterized; self-registration may be required at such times. Pets on leashes are permitted. Fees listed here do not include entry fees. For further information contact Dept of Game, Fish & Parks, 523 E. Capitol, Pierre, SD 57501; 605-773-3391.

LAKESIDE USE AREAS
Approximately 40 state-operated LUAs provide easy access to lakes and rivers. Nearly all have boat ramps & docking facilities, and most offer picnicking and primitive camping facilities. Camping is free at some sites, but basic camping fees, and in some cases entry fees, were levied at many of them beginning in 1999. At about a dozen LUAs, both $6 camping fees and state park permits ($5 daily or $23 annual) are required, and at some, just the entry permits are necessary.

BLACK HILLS NATIONAL FOREST
Camping is permitted throughout the National Forest outside of developed campgrounds, except at signed locations around Pactola, Sheridan, Roubaix, Bismark and Deerfield Lakes. Open fires are not permitted in the South Dakota portion of the forest. Fires must be built in grates in campgrounds and picnic area; or built safely in a stove, charcoal grill or other similar container. At forest service-operated campgrounds, fees are charged from the end of May through about Labor Day. During the off-season, fees are not collected at those camps, but drinking water is shut off and trash pickup is not provided; pack out your own trash. No free off-season periods are offered at the campgrounds operated by concessionaires.

ABERDEEN (1)

Melgaard City Park   **$12**
1.8 mi E on Melgaard Rd from US 281 at Aberdeen; N on Lloyd St. $12 tent sites; $18 for RV sites with hookups. 4/1-11/1. 16 sites. Tbls, flush toilets, showers, cfga, drkg wtr, hookups($), dump, playground. Tennis, volleyball, horseshoes, picnicking.

Mina   **$10**
State Recreation Area
11 mi W of Aberdeen on US 12; at Mina Lake. $10 base for non-elec sites. All year; 14-day limit. 36 modern sites ($14 with elec). Tbls, elec($4), flush toilets, cfga, drkg wtr, beach, playgrounds, shelter, showers, dump, fishing pier, beach. Reduced fee in winter, but limited faciilities. Swimming, boating(dl), fishing, hiking, picnicking. Assessible fishing pier.

Fishing tip: Mina Lake is regarded as one of the best crappie lakes in northeastern South Dakota; also good populations of walleye, northern pike, bass, perch.

Richmond Lake   **$10**
State Recreation Area
10 mi NW of Aberdeen off US 12. $10 base. All year; 14-day limit. 24 modern sites. Tbls, flush toilets, cfga, drkg wtr, beach, playground, shelter, elec ($4), showers, beach. Reduced fee in winter, but limited facilities. Swimming, boating(l), picnicking, hiking, fishing, bridle trail, winter sports, canoeing.

Wylie City Park Campground   **$12**
N of town qtr mi N of US 281 & CR 15 jct. $12 tent sites; $18-19 RV sites with hookups. 3/1-11/1. 90 sites. Tbls, flush toilets, cfga, drkg wtr, showers, dump, beach, showers, hookups($). Jogging track, waterslide, lakes, zoo, paddleboats, volleyball, horseshoes, playground. 210-acre park.

Travel tip: Wylie Park contains Storybook Land, one of the state's best free attractions. Designed for children, it features fairy tale characters in real-life settings. Open daily 10-9 Apr-Oct.

AGAR (2)

Sutton Bay   **$5**
Lakeside Use Area
12 mi W and 4 mi NW of Agar on SR 1804. Camp free, but $5 entry fee. All year. Primitive undesignated sites. Pit toilet, tbls, shelters, cfga, no drkg wtr. Picnicking, boating(l), fishing. 18 acres. Former Corps of Engineers facility.

AKASKA (3)

LeBeau Lakeside Use Area   **FREE**
4 mi S & 7 mi W of Akaska. Free. All year; 5-day limit. Primitive camping. Toilets, cfga, no drkg wtr. Fishing.

Swan Creek   **$12**
State Recreation Area
9 mi W of Akaska off US 83; on Missouri River. $12. All year; 14-day limit. 23 elec sites. Tbls, flush toilets, cfga, drkg wtr, showers, dump, shelter, elec. Fishing, picnicking, boating, canoeing. Handicap access to restrooms.

Walth Bay   **$5**
State Lakeside Use Area
From Akaska, 3 mi N, 2.5 mi W, 1.5 mi S. 15 free primitive sites, but $5 daily entry fee. Cfga, toilets, no drkg wtr. Boating(l), fishing.

ARLINGTON (4)

Lake Poinsett   **$10**
State Recreation Area
12 mi N of Arlington on US 81; 2 mi E on county rd. $10 base. All year; 14-day limit. Base fee for preferred non-elec sites; $14 with elec. 112 sites (108 with elec). Tbls, flush toilets, cfga, drkg wtr, dump, elec($4), playground, beach, showers. Fishing, boating(l), canoeing, hiking, swimming, junior naturalist program, interpretive program.

Maxwell City Park   **FREE**
From US 81, W on US 14 (Elm St); N on Main St to dirt access rd, left into park entrance. Free without hookups; $5 with 20/30-amp elec. 5/30-9/14. 12 sites. Flush toilets at nearby laundromat, tbls, firewood. Wtr & elect hookups, dump. Register at city hall, half blk W. Pop. 992. Loud fright trains nearby. GPS: N44 21.898, W97 08.042.

BELLE FOURCHE (5)

Bearlodge Campground   **$6**
Black Hills National Forest
W of Belle Fourche on SR 34, connecting to Wyoming SR 24; between Aladdin & Hulett, WY. $6. All year; 14-day limit. 8 sites; 25-ft RV limit. Tbls, toilets, cfga, no drkg wtr. Fishing, hiking. Elev 4700 ft.

Fishing tip: At Orman dam, try for walleyes between the boat launch and Gander Point in 8-22 feet; use purple or green spinners with nightcrawlers or leeches.

BERESFORD (6)

Union Grove State Park   **$8**
11 mi S of Beresford via I-29. $8 base. All year; 14-day limit. Base fee for modern non-elec sites; $12 wtih elec. 25 sites (17 with elec). Tbls, flush toilets, cfga, drkg wtr, no dump, elec($4), showers, playground, shelter. Bridle trail, hiking, picnicking, interpretive programs. Arboretum with 180 species of trees & shrubs. 499 acres.

Windmill Campground (Private)   **$11**
From exit 47 of I-29 at Beresford, half mi E & half mi S on 13th St. $11 base. 4/1-11/1. 52 RV sites, 12 tent sites. Tbls, flush toilets, showers, cfga, drkg wtr, hookups ($), store, pool, coin laundry, dump, store, playground. Swimming (pool), rec hall.

BIG STONE CITY (7)

Rearing Ponds   **FREE**
Water Access Site
4 mi N of Big Stone City off SR 109. Free. All year. Primitive camping. Toilets, cfga, no drkg wtr. Boating(l), fishing.

BONESTEEL (8)

South Scalp Creek   **FREE**
State Lakeside Use Area
4 mi S of Bonesteel on US 18; 11 mi NE on gravel rd. Free. All year. Primitive sites (RVs under 26 ft). Tbls, cfga, drkg wtr, shelters. Boating(l); picnicking, fishing. Fish cleaning table. Former Corps of Engineers campground.

BRANDON (9)

Big Sioux   **$10**
State Recreation Area
1.5 mi SW of Brandon off I-90. $10 base. All year; 14-day limit. Base fee for 13 preferred sites ($14 with elec at 50 sites). Tbls, pit toilets, cfga, drkg wtr, shelter, playground, shelter; no dump. Archery, bridle trail, hiking, canoeing (l), fishing, boating, interpretive program, cross-country skiing, volleyball, equestrian area.

BRITTON (10)

Britton City RV Park   **FREE**
On N end of Main St in Britton, 2 blks N of swimming pool by the tennis courts. Free first 3 nights; $7 per night for next 7 nights; $10 thereafter. Tbls, toilets, cfga, drkg wtr, hook-ups. Contact Britton city hall; 803 - 8th Ave.

BROOKINGS (11)

Sexauer City Park   **$10**
At Brookings, 2 mi W of I-29 on Sixth St; half mi N on Western Ave. $10. 5/1-10/15; 7-day limit. 16 sites. Tbls, flush toilets, cfga, drkg wtr, showers, dump, elec, playground.

Travel tip: McCrory Gardens, often described as the prettiest 70 acres in South Dakota, is among the top ten small botanical gardens in the nation. Admission is free. On Sixth St at South Dakota State University campus in Brookings.

BUFFALO (12)

Picnic Springs   **FREE**
Custer National Forest
26 mi NE of Buffalo on US 85; 4.2 mi W on CR 7330; 2 mi S on co rd; 1.6 mi W on FR 114. Free. 5/1-11/15; 10-day limit. 15 sites (RVs under 31 ft); tbls, toilets, cfga, firewood, piped drkg wtr. Picnicking, hiking. Elev 3300

ft; 3 acres. Campground in the scenic north cave hills. Eagles, falcons, hawks in rim-rocks.

Reva Gap　　　　　　　　　　　**FREE**
Custer National Forest
1 mi S of Buffalo on US 85; 19 mi E on SD 20. Free. 5/1-11/15; 10-day limit. 4 sites (RVs under 22 ft); tbls, toilets, cfga, firewood, drkg wtr. Store/gas (4 mi). Picnicking. Elev 3600 ft; 13 acres. Colorful castle rock formations nearby.

BURKE (13)

Burke City Park　　　　　　　　**$10**
From N of the SR 47 & US 18 jct in Burke, 3 blocks N on CR 22 following City Park sign; entrances on CR 22 & 7th St.. $10. All year, 7-day limit. 5 RV sites with 30-amp elec/wtr; 40-ft RV limit; back-in sites. Tbls, flush toilets, showers, playground. Elec, wtr, sewer hookups. Dump at convenience store. Horseback riding; picnicking; swimming, fishing, golf nearby. Lake.

Burke Lake　　　　　　　　　　　**$6**
State Recreation Area
2 mi E of Burke off US 18. $6. All year; 14-day limit. 16 basic sites. Tbls, pit toilets, cfga, no drkg wtr, playground, beach; no hookups, no dump. Limited facilities in winter. Picnicking, fishing, swimming, boating, hiking.

CAMP CROOK (14)

Lantis Spring　　　　　　　　　**FREE**
Custer National Forest
3 mi W of Camp Crook, on gravel SR 20 extension (SE of Ekalaka, Montana); 2.8 mi N on Capitol Rock Rd; 1.7 mi E on CR 3049; right at fork for 1.2 mi. In Montana. Free. 5/1-11/15; 15-day limit. 10 undesignated sites (RVs under 22 ft). Tbls, toilets, cfga, drkg wtr. Hiking.

Wickham Gulch　　　　　　　　**FREE**
Custer National Forest
3 mi W of Camp Crook on SR 20 gravel extension; 3 mi N on Capitol Rock Rd (CR 3049); 1.5 mi on CR 3060. Free. May-Sept; 14-day limit. 5 primitive sites. Tbls, toilets, cfga, drkg wtr, no trash service. Hunting, hiking, mountain biking. Near Capitol Rock National Natural Area.

CANTON (15)

Newton Hills State Park　　　　**$10**
6 mi S of Canton off US 18. $10 base. All year; 14-day limit. Base fee for preferred non-elec RV sites, tent sites & equestrian sites; $14 with elec. 118 sites (108 with elec). Tbls, flush toilets, cfga, drkg wtr, elec ($4), playground at Horse Thief Camp, showers, dump, shelter. Equestrian facilities, canoeing, fishing, hiking, bridle trails, picnicking, junior naturalist program, interpretive program, cross-country ski trails.

Travel tip: Newton Hills SP hosts summer concerts and a folk festival on weekends.

CARTHAGE (16)

Redstone Park
Carthage City Park　　　　　　　**$10**
On W end of Main St. in Carthage at the Red-stone River. $10. Overnight sites with elec. Tbls, toilets, cfga, drkg wtr. Fishing, hiking.

Lake Carthage　　　　　　　　　**$6**
State Lakeside Use Area
Half mi NE of Carthage on NE side of lake. $6 for primitive sites; $10 for 13 sites with elec. Tbls, toilets, cfga, shelters, drkg wtr, beach. Swimming, picnicking, fishing, boating(ld), playground, waterskiing.

Fishing tip: The state record pumpkin-seed sunfish was caught from Lake Carthage in 1970; it weighed 12 ounces.

CHAMBERLAIN (17)

Elm Creek　　　　　　　　　　　**FREE**
Lakeside Use Area
Lake Francis Case
From Chamberlain, I-90, exit 265, 18 mi S of Chamberlain. Free. 21 primitive sites. May-Oct; 14-day limit. Toilets, cfga, no drkg wtr. Boating(l), fishing. This park was a Corps of Engineers facility; now managed by the state.

Fishing tip: The state record tiger musky (35 pounds) was caught from Lake Francis Case in March 2001.

CLARK (18)

Bailey Lake　　　　　　　　　　**FREE**
Lakeside Use Area
9 mi N; 1 mi W; half mi S of Clark off US 212. Free. All year. Free primitive camping. Tbls, toilets, cfga, no drkg wtr. Picnicking, boating, fishing.

Dickinson City Park　　　　　　**FREE**
In Clark (32 mi W of Watertown). Free camping with elec hookups, toilets, cfga, drkg wtr.

CLEAR LAKE (19)

City Park　　　　　　　　　　　**$10**
On N edge of Clear Lake. $10. 5/1-10/1. 10 sites with hookups; 12 for self-contained RVs (no RV size limit). Tbls, flush toilets, showers, cfga, drkg wtr, elec, dump, playground. Coin laundry, restaurant, grocery.

Ulven City Park　　　　　　　　**$8**
1.5 mi E of Clear Lake on US 77/SR 22. $8 all sites. 4/1-10/1. 22 sites (10 with elec); no RV size limit. Tbls, toilets, tbls, cfga, elec. Fishing, boating(d), golf course. Wtr & dump nearby; plans in 2007 were to expand wtr lines to sites.

Fishing tip: Summertime produces good

catches of walleye from Clear Lake. Try fishing 12 feet deep with jigs or spinners & crawlers. When water is murky, don't neglect areas very close to shore.

COLMAN (20)

Coleman City Park　　　　　　　**$10**
On Hwy 34, E edge of Colman. $10. Tbls, toilets, cfga, drkg wtr, showers, elec.

CUSTER (21)

Echo Valley Park (Private)　　　**$12**
4 mi N on US 385 from jct with US 16 in Custer; half mi E on Echo Valley Rd. $12 base. 5/15-10/15. Base fee for tent sites; $23 elec/wtr. 12 RV sites. Tbls, flush toilets, cfga, drkg wtr, hookups($), pool, showers, dump, horse facilities. Horseback riding, swimming, hiking trails.

DESMET (23)

Washington City Park　　　　　**$8**
Third St & Harvey Dunn Ave in DeSmet. $8 at non-elec sites; $9 with elec. 40 sites. Tbls, flush toilets, showers, cfga, drkg wtr, elec($). Volleyball, horseshoes, 9-hole golf; Father DeSmet Me-morial. Patrolled. 605/854-3731. Reservations okay.

EAGLE BUTTE (24)

Foster Bay　　　　　　　　　　　**FREE**
Lakeside Use Area
Lake Oahe
3 mi W of Eagle Butte on US 212; 22 mi S on SD 63. Free. All year; 14-day limit. 20 primitive sites (RVs under 30 ft); tbls, no toilets, cfga, drkg wtr. Picnicking, fishing, swimming, boating(l). Former Corps of Engineers park; now managed by the state.

EDEN (25)

Buffalo South　　　　　　　　　**FREE**
Lakeside Use Area
4 mi E & half mi SE of Eden off SR 25. Free. All year. Primitive camping. Toilets, cfga, no drkg wtr. Boating(ld), fishing.

EUREKA (26)

Eureka Municipal Park　　　　　**$5**
On SR 10 in Eureka; at Lake Eureka. $5. 16 sites. Tbls, flush toilets, cfga, drkg wtr, showers, elec, playground, rec hall, beach, dump. Swimming, fishing, boating(l).

FAIRBURN (27)

French Creek Camp　　　　　　**FREE**
Buffalo Gap National Grasslands
10.5 mi E of Fairburn on US 79. Free. 5/30-9/15. 8 primitive sites. Tbls, toilets, cfga, drkg wtr. Picnicking.

FAITH (28)

Durkee Lake City Park **FREE**
3 mi S of Faith on SD 73. Free. All year. 50 sites. Tbls, toilets, cfga, dump, firewood, drkg wtr. Swimming, picnicking, fishing, boating(l); golf nearby. Lake.

Faith City Park **$5**
On Main St in Faith. $5. All year. 10 sites. Tbls, flush toilets, cfga, drkg wtr, elec, dump, playground.

FAULKTON (29)

Lake Faulkton **FREE**
Lakeside Use Area
2.5 mi W of Faulkton on US 212; half mi S. Free. All year; 5-day limit. 4 undeveloped campsites, but camping is allowed. Toilets, cfga, drkg wtr, shelters, playground, dump, covered picnic tbls. Picnicking, fishing, boating(ld).

FORT PIERRE (30)

Fischer's Lilly City Park **$10**
From SE 83, E on Cedar St; left on Casey Tibbs; right on Ash; on S side of Bad River. $10. May-Nov weather permitting; no stay limit. 12 RV sites with 20/30/50-amp elec & wtr. Tbls, pit toilets, cfga, drkg wtr, no showers, basic dump (no flush water). This park was site of the Lewis & Clark's first encounter with the Teton Sioux. GPS: N44 21.027, W100 22.151.

FREEMAN (32)

Fensel's Motel Camping **$10**
On Hwy 81 at Freeman. $10. All year. 5 sites with elec/wtr; showers available.

Freeman City Park **$10**
From US 81 NE of town, exit W just S pof John Deere plant on 278th St; S on Wipf St, right into park. Do not follow N. Walnut St off E 1st St; it dead-ends at ballfield. $10 at 6 paved sites with 30/50-amp elec; $6 without hookups. Tbls, flush toilets, cfga, drkg wtr, showers, shelters. Access not great for big rigs; low hanging limbs. GPS: N3 21.331, W97 25.960.

GARRETSON (33)

Palisades State Park **$10**
6.5 mi N of Garretson; 3 mi E & 1 mi S of Corson exit of I-90. $10 base. All year; 14-day limit. Base fee for preferred non-elec sites & tent sites; $14 with elec. 35 preferred sites, 16 with elec; 13 tent sites. Tbls, flush toilets, cfga, drkg wtr, elec ($4), showers, no dump, shelters, playground, amphitheater, fish cleaning station. Fishing, boating(l), hiking, picnicking, junior naturalist program, interpretive program, volleyball, horseshoes.
Travel tip: Stop at the nearby Devil's Gulch Historic Site, a rocky chasm where Jesse James eluded a posse in 1876 following the famous Northfield, Minnesota, bank robbery. He forced his horse to leap over the 20-foot chasm.

Split Rock City Park **$4**
NW end of Garretson on SR 11; along Split Rock River. $4 tent sites; $6 RV sites. 38 primitive camping at WPA-built park. Tbls, toilets, cfga, drkg wtr, playground. Dump nearby. Canoeing, fishing, volleyball, boating(l).

GEDDES (34)

North Wheeler **$6**
State Recreation Area
7 mi W of Geddes on paved rd; 8 mi S on gravel rd to Lake Francis Case. $6 for basic sites; $10 with elec. 22 sites (15 with elec); 25-ft RV limit. Pit toilets, cfga, drkg wtr. Fishing, boating(l). Formerly a Corps of Engineers park; now managed by the state.

GETTYSBURG (35)

City Park **FREE**
On Main St, 5 blocks S of SD 212 in Gettysburg. Free. 5/1-10/31; 3-day limit. 15 sites; tbls, flush toilets, cfga, showers, drkg wtr, 6 elec hookups ($ -- free first night). Store, food, dump nearby. Swimming, picnicking, golf nearby.

Dodge Draw **FREE**
Lakeside Use Area
5 mi W of Gettysburg on US 212; 9 mi N on US 83; 10 mi NW off US 83. Free. All year. Primitive undesignated sites. Toilets, cfga, no drkg wtr. Boating(l), fishing. 25 acres.

East Whitlock **$6**
Lakeside Use Area
12 mi W & 3 mi N of Gettysburg off US 212. $6. All year; 7-day limit. Primitive camping; undesignated sites. Toilets, cfga, drkg wtr. Boating (ld), fishing. Self-registration. $5 daily or $20 annual entry fee charged.
Travel tip: Nearby is the Whitlock Salmon and Imprinting Station, where salmon eggs are fertilized; free tours in the fall.

Forest City **FREE**
Lake Oahe Water Access Site
19 mi W of Gettysburg on US 212, on W side of Lake Oahe. Free. All year; 14-day limit. 7 primitive undesignated sites (RVs under 30 ft); tbls, toilets, cfga, firewood, no drkg wtr. Picnicking, fishing, boating(ld).

West Whitlock **$8**
State Recreation Area
12 mi W of Gettysburg on US 212, 10 mi W on gravel rd to campground. $8 base for modern non-elec sites; $12 with elec. All year; 14-day limit. 100 sites (87 wtih elec). RVs under 30 ft. Tbls, flush toilets, cfga, drkg wtr, elect ($4), playground, dump, showers, shelter, beach. Picnicking, fishing, boating (ld), hiking, swimming, junior naturalist program, interpretive program & trails.
Fishing tip: Early spring is good time for shoreline northern pike fishing; 36-pounder caught from shore in 1993.

GROTON (36)

Amsden Dam **$6**
Lakeside Use Area
6 mi E of Groton on US 12; 5.5 mi S; 1 mi E to campground. $6. All year; 5-day limit. No developed campsites, but camping allowed. Tbls, toilets, cfga, drkg wtr. Swimming, picnicking, fishing, boating(l).
Fishing tip: The state record muskie (40 pounds) was caught from Amsden Dam in April 1991.

Groton City Park **FREE**
3 blks S off US 12 on N Main St in Groton. Fee for elec; camp free. 4/15-11/1; 3-day limit. 12 sites (4 with elec). Tbls, flush toilets, cfga, drkg wtr. Picnicking, tennis, pool. Donations welcome but not required.

HERMOSA (37)

The Bunkhouse **$10**
At 14530 Lower Spring Creek Rd. $10 for self-contained RVs at bed & breakfast facility. Equestrian accommodations, $5 per horse.

HIGHMORE (38)

City Park **$8**
In the center of Highmore on US 14. $8. 4/1-10/15. 10 sites, 6 with elec. Toilets, tbls, cfga, drkg wtr, playground.

HILL CITY (39)

Custer Trail **$12**
Black Hills National Forest
12 mi NW on CR 17 to N shore of Deerfield Lake. $12 & $14 ($6 & $7 with federal Senior Pass). MD-LD; 10-day limit; 16 sites; 50-ft RV limit. Tbls, toilets, cfga, drkg wtr. Fishing, boating(ld), swimming, hiking, bridle trail, mountain biking. Elev 5900 ft.
Fishing tips: The state record brook trout of 46.75 inches was caught from Deerfield Lake in 1994. It was hooked on a Rapala.

Ditch Creek **$7.50**
Black Hills National Forest
12 mi NW of Hill City on CR 17; 7 mi W on CR 110; 4 mi S on FR 291. $7.50 with federal Senior Pass; others pay $15. All year; 10-day limit. 13 sites; 60-ft RV limit. Tbls, toilets, cfga, drkg wtr. Fishing, hiking, mountain biking.

HOT SPRINGS (40)

Angostura   **$10**
State Recreation Area
10 mi SE of Hot Springs off US 18. $10 base. All year; 14-day limit. Base fee for non-elec preferred sites; $14 with elec. 168 sites at four campgrounds (145 elec). Tbls, flush toilets, cfga, drkg wtr, dump, elec($4), showers, playground, shelters, fish cleaning stations, fishing pier, marina. Fishing, picnicking, swimming, boating (lr), hiking, junior naturalist program, interpretive program. 1,125 acres. 4 handicap-accessible sites. Angostura Reservoir.
Travel tip: The remains of several mammoths and other prehistoric creatures can be seen at the Mammoth Site, open all year along the Hwy 18 by-pass in Hot Springs.

Elk Mountain   **$12**
Wind Cave National Park
10 mi N of Hot Springs on US 385. $5-10. 4/1-10/31; 14-day limit. $12 during 5/15-9/15; $6 rest of year, but no wtr & reduced services. 14-day limit. 75 sites. Tbls, flush toilets, cfga, drkg wtr, visitor center. No wtr during free period. Picnicking, hiking, nature trails, cave tours($), nature programs.

Kemo Sabay Campground   **$10**
N of Hot Springs on Hwy 385. $10 for tents, $25 full hookups. 5/1-10/1. 20 RV sites plus 100 tent sites. Tbls, flush toilets, cfga, drkg wtr, showers ($3 non-campers), dump ($5 non-campers), playground, hookups($).

Shep's Canyon   **FREE**
State Water Access Area
6 mi S & 5 mi E of Hot Springs off SR 71. Free. All year; 14-day limit. Primitive undesignated sites. Tbls, toilet, cfga, no drkg wtr. Boating(l), fishing.

HUMBOLDT (41)

Larry Pressler City Park   **FREE**
From I-90, exit 379, N 100 yds on Hwy 19, E on paved rd to water tower, 4 blks S. Free. Spring-fall. Primitive undesignated site at outer perimeter of park, flush toilets, tbls, cfga, pavilion, drkg wtr. Basketball hoop, tennis courts, playground, horseshoes.

HURON (42)

Huron Memorial Park   **$12**
At Huron, half mi S of SR 14 on Jersey Ave. $12 without hookups; $1 full hookups. 4/1-11/1. 24 sites with hookups. Tbls, flush toilets, showers, cfga, drkg wtr, dump, playground, hookups ($). Fishing, horseshoes, boating(l), picnicking, golf, exercise trail, cross-country skiing. 66-acre park.

James River Unit #1   **FREE**
Lakeside Use Area
14 mi N; 1 mi W; half mi N of Huron off SR 37. Free. All year; 5-day limit. Undeveloped camping; 4 primitive sites. Tbls, cfga. Fishing, picnicking.
Fishing tip: The state record channel catfish (56 lbs 8 oz) was caught from the James River in 1949. The state's largest flathead catfish, 60 pounds, 8 ounces, was landed there in 2004.

James River Unit #2   **FREE**
Lakeside Use Area
15 mi N; 1 mi W; half mi N of Huron off SR 37. Free. All year; 5-day limit. Undeveloped camping; 4 primitive sites. Tbls, toilets, cfga. Fishing, boating(ld), picnicking.

Lake Byron Northwest   **FREE**
Lakeside Use Area
15.5 mi N of Huron on SD 37. Free. All year; 5-day limit. All year; 5-day limit. Undeveloped camping. Tbls, toilets, cfga, drkg wtr. Fishing, boating(ld), swimming, picnicking.

Spink County Dam   **FREE**
Lakeside Use Area
21 mi N; 1 mi W of Huron off SR 37. Free. All year; 5-day limit. Undeveloped camping; 4 sites. Tbls, toilets, cfga. Fishing, boating(ld), picnicking.

IRENE (44)

Lake Merindahl   **FREE**
Lakeside Use Area
4 mi W of Irene on SR 46; 3 mi S; half mi W. All year. Free primitive camping. No facilities. Boating (l), fishing.

KEYSTONE (46)

Hanna   **$7.50**
Black Hills National Forest
8 mi SW of Keystone on US 85; 2.2 mi S on FR 17. $7.50 with federal Senior Pass; others pay $15 (free walk-in tent camping after LD). MD-LD; 10-day limit. 13 sites (55-ft RV limit). Tbls, toilets, cfga, drkg wtr. Elev 5600 ft; 3 acres. Near Spearfish Canyon.

LAKE ANDES (47)

Pease Creek   **$12**
State Recreation Area
Fort Randall Dam
15 mi W of Lake Andes on SR 50; 1 mi S and 1 mi W on gravel rd. $12 for 23 sites with elec; $10 for 5 equestrian sites, no elec. All year; 14-day limit. RVs under 26 ft. Tbls, flush toilets, cfga, drkg wtr, showers, dump, fish cleaning station. Picnicking, fishing, boating (ld), beach. Formerly a Corps of Engineers park; now managed by the state. 874 acres.

White Swan   **FREE**
Lakeside Use Area
Lake Francis Case
12 mi W of Lake Andes off SR 50. Free primitive undesignated sites. May-Oct; 14-day limit. Toilets, tbls, cfga, no drkg wtr, shelters. Picnicking, boating (ld), fishing. Formerly a Corps of Engineers park, this facility now is operated by the state.

LAKE CITY (48)

Clear Lake   **FREE**
Lakeside Use Area
4 mi E of Lake City of SD 10. Free. All year; 5-day limit. No developed campsites, but camping is allowed. Tbls, toilets, cfga, no drkg wtr. Swimming, picnicking, fishing, boating(ld).

Fort Sisseton   **$8**
State Historical Park
10 mi SW of Lake City off SR 10. $8 base. All year; 14-day limit; limited facilities in winter. 15 modern sites; $12 with elec.14 sites (10 with elec) & 3 tent sites. Tbls, flush toilets, cfga, drkg wtr, showers, no dump. Visitor center (MD-LD). 45 acres. Frontier army outpost built in 1864; among nation's best preserved forts. Hiking trails, interpretive program, picnicking, guided walking tour of fort, canoeing(r), boating(l).

Four-Mile/Bullhead   **FREE**
Water Access Site
2.5 mi W of Lake City on SR 10; 1 mi S; half mi W. All year. Free primitive camping. Toilets, cfga, no drkg wtr. Boating(l), fishing. Roy Lake.

Roy Lake State Park   **$10**
3 mi W of Lake City on SR 10; 2 mi S. $10 base for tent and non-elec sites at two campgrounds; $14 with elec in western campground. All year; 14-day limit. 102 sites (88 with elec). Tbls, flush toilets, cfga, drkg wtr, elec ($4), playground, dump, showers, shelter, fish cleaning station, beaches, waterskiing beach. Fishing, swimming, boating(l), hiking, junior naturalist program, interpretive program, snowmobile trail, cross-country ski trail.

LAKE PRESTON (49)

Lake Thompson   **$10**
State Recreation Area
On NE shore of Lake Thompson. $10 base. All year; 14-day limit. Base fee for modern preferred non-elec sites; $14 with elec. 103 sites. Tbls, flush toilets, cfga, drkg wtr, showers, dump, beaches, shelter, playground. Boating(ld), fishing, swimming, waterskiing, fish cleaning station. This new campground was opened in 2001 on the state's largest natural lake.
Fishing tip: Lake Thompson is an excellent walleye lake. Best catches in summer are on jigs tipped with minnows or leeches. Most northern pike are caught by walleye fishermen trolling crankbaits.

SOUTH DAKOTA

LEMMON (50)

Hugh Glass　　　　　　　　**FREE**
State Lakeside Use Area
14 mi S of Lemmon on SR 73, opposite shore of Shadehill Reservoir from Shadyhill SRA, where sites are $13. Free. All year. 13 primitive sites. Tbls, toilets, cfga, no drkg wtr. Fishing, boating(l). 5,000-acre lake.

Llewellyn Johns　　　　　　**$10**
State Recreation Area
12 mi S of Lemmon on SR 73. $10 for 10 basic sites with elec. All year; 14-day limit. Tbls, pit toilets, cfga, drkg wtr, elec, no showers, no dump, playground. Fishing. 114 acres.

LEOLA (51)

Leola City Park　　　　　　**FREE**
N of Leola at Leola Dam. Free for 3 days; $1 daily thereafter. All year. 20 sites; limited elec hookups; tbls, toilets, cfga, well drkg wtr. Picnicking, boating(l).

LESTERVILLE (52)

Lesterville　　　　　　　　**FREE**
Lakeside Use Area
12 mi S of Lesterville off SR 52. All year. Free primitive camping. Tbls, toilets, cfga, no drkg wtr. Boating(l), fishing, picnicking.

MADISON (53)

Lake Herman State Park　　　**$10**
2 mi W of Madison on US 34. $10 base. All year; 14-day limit. Base fee for preferred non-elec sites; $14 with elec. 72 sites. Tbls, flush toilets, cfga, drkg wtr, playground, shelters, dump, elec ($4). Fishing dock, boating(l), swimming, bridle trail, picnicking, swimming, junior naturalist program, jogging & exercise trail, interpretive program. 1,350-acre lake.
Fishing tip: Lake Herman has good population of walleyes, but action was slow in recent years and fish were small. Best bet for shore fishermen is casting crappie jigs.

Walker's Point　　　　　　**$10**
State Recreation Area
2 mi SE of Madison; 2 mi S & 5 mi E off SR 19. $10 base. All year; 14-day limit. Base fee for preferred tent & non-elec sites; $14 with elec. 43 sites. Tbls, flush toilets, cfga, drkg wtr, elec($4), playground, dump, accessible fishing dock. Boating(l), fishing, canoeing, interpretive program. 41 acres.

MARTIN (54)

Brooks Memorial　　　　　　**FREE**
Municipal Park
At 602 First Ave in Martin. Donations accepted; camp free. Primitive open sites. Tbls, flush toilets, cfga, drkg wtr, elec. Swimming, biking.

MENNO (55)

Frederick P. Huber　　　　　**FREE**
Memorial Campground
Lake Menno City Park
1 mi W, 1.5 mi N & half mi W of Menno on lake built in 1995. Free, but $5 donation is suggested; 7-day limit. 9 sites. Elec, toilets, tbls, drkg wtr. Panfish fishing, boating at 40-acre lake. Boat ramp, picnic shelters.

MIDLAND (56)

The Country Place (Private)　**$10**
12 mi N on SR 63 from I-90 exit 170 to US 14 at Midland, then qtr mi E on US 14. $10 base; $19 full hookups. 25 RV sites & 5 tent sites. Tbls, flush toilets, cfga, drkg wtr, hookups($), showers, coin laundry, store, pool, dump, playground. Modem hookups. Swimming.

MILBANK (57)

Hartford Beach State Park　　**$10**
15 mi N of Milbank on SR 15. $10 base. All year; 14-day limit. Base fee for tent area and non-elec RV sites; $14 with elec. 49 sites. Tbls, flush toilets, cfga, drkg wtr, elec($4), dump, playground, shelter, showers, accessible fishing dock, beach. Picnicking, fishing, hiking trails, boating(l), swimming, canoeing, cross-country skiing, junior naturalist program, interpretive program.

MILLER (58)

Crystal City Park　　　　　**FREE**
On 7th St W of SD 14 in Miller. Free, but donations accepted. 5/1-9/30; 3-day limit. 32 sites with elec hookups; tbls, flush toilets, cfga, drkg wtr, dump, playground. Picnicking. Tenters allowed in the more primitive area.

Lake Louise　　　　　　　　**$10**
State Recreation Area
14 mi NW of Miller on US 14. $10 base. All year; 14-day limit. Base fee for non-elec modern sites; $14 with elec. 39 sites in three campgrounds. Tbls, flush toilets, elec ($4), cfga, drkg wtr, showers, playground, shelter, dump, beach. Swimming, boating(l), fishing, hiking trails, canoeing, interpretive program. Accessible fishing dock.
Fishing tip: Lake Louise is regarded as a topnotch panfish and bass lake.

MISSION RIDGE (59)

Minneconjou Park　　　　　**FREE**
Lakeside Use Area
Lake Oahe
From Mission Ridge, NW on gravel rd. Free primitive undesignated sites. No toilets, cfga, no drkg wtr. Boating(l), fishing. Former Corps of Engineers Park; now managed by the state.

MOBRIDGE (61)

Indian Creek　　　　　　　**$12**
State Recreation Area
2 mi SE of Mobridge on US 12, then 1.5 mi S. $12. All year; 14-day limit. 124 elec/wtr sites in 2 campgrounds. Tbls, flush toilets, showers, cfga, drkg wtr. Fishing, boating(lr), hiking. Fish cleaning station. 307 acres. Formerly Corps of Engineers campground, now managed by state.

MONTROSE (62)

Lake Vermillion　　　　　　**$10**
State Recreation Area
Near Montrose, 5 mi S of I-90 exit 374. $10 base. All year; 14-day limit. Base fee for preferred sites; $14 with elec. 66 sites. Tbls, flush toilets, cfga, drkg wtr, dump, showers, elec ($4), playground, shelter, waterskiing beach, swimming beach, fish cleaning station. Boating (l), fishing, hiking, picnicking, swimming, interpretive program. 512-acre lake.
Travel tip: The Great Plains Zoo and Delbridge Museum in nearby Sioux Falls features a children's zoo, penguin pool, primate building, bird of prey aviary, and American wild dog and Asian cat habitats.
Fishing tip: Shoreline fishing for crappies pays off with crappie jigs and minnows. Best fishing in the evenings.

NEWCASTLE (WY.) (64)

Beaver Creek　　　　**FREE and $10**
Black Hills National Forest
18 mi N of Newcastle on US 85; 6 mi E on FR 811. $10 during MD-LD; free rest of year but no wtr or trash service; 10-day limit. 8 sites (45-ft RV limit). Tbls, toilets, cfga, drkg wtr. Fishing, picnicking.

Moon Campground　　　　　**$10**
Black Hills National Forest
10 mi SE of Newcastle on US 16; 15 mi N on FR 117. $10. Elev 6400 ft. 6/1-11/30; 10-day limit. 3 sites (RVs under 30 ft); tbls, toilets, cfga, no drkg wtr.

Redbank Spring　　　　　　**$10**
Black Hills National Forest
14 mi NE of Newcastle. $10. All year; 10-day limit. 5 sites (40-ft RV limit). Tbls, toilets, cfga, drkg wtr. Fishing. Elev 6600 ft.

NEWELL (65)

Little Bend　　　　　　　　**$5**
Lakeside Use Area
Lake Oahe
26 mi W of Onida on gravel Rd. Camp free, but $5 daily (or $20 annual) entry permit. All year; 14-day limit. 13 sites. Tbls, toilets, cfga, no drkg wtr. Boating(l), fishing, swimming, waterskiing. 365 acres.

Newell Lake   FREE
Lakeside Use Area
8 mi N of Newell on SR 79; right for 2 mi. Free. All year; 14-day limit. Primitive undesignated sites. Toilets, cfga, no drkg wtr, no trash service. Fishing, boating(l), swimming.

PICKSTOWN (67)

South Shore $6
Lakeside Use Area
Fort Randall Dam
3 mi W of Pickstown on US 181/18. $6. May-Sep; 14-day limit. 10 primitive sites; 25-ft RV limit. Tbls, toilets, cfga, drkg wtr. Fishing, boating(l). Formerly free Corps of Engineers park. $5 daily or $20 annual entry pass also required.

Spillway   FREE
Lakeside Use Area
Fort Randall Dam
At Pickstown, half mi below dam. Free. May-Sept; 14-day limit. 6 primitive sites. Tbls, toilets, cfga, no drkg wtr. Boating(l), fishing. This park formerly managed by Corps of Engineers; now operated by the state.

Whetstone Bay $5
Lakeside Use Area
Fort Randall Dam
23 mi W of Pickstown on SR 46; 13 mi W on US 18; exit N on paved rd. Camp free, but $5 daily or $20 annual entry pass required. All year; 14-day limit. 30 primitive sites; 25-ft RV limit. Toilets, drkg wtr, cfga. Boating(l), fishing. Fish cleaning table. Formerly free Corps of Engineers park.

PIERPONT (68)

Pierpont Lake City Park   FREE
2 mi S of Pierpont at NW shore Lake Pierpont on SD 27. Free. All year. 50 sites; tbls, toilets, cfga, drkg wtr, dump. Picnicking. Very rustic.

☆ PIERRE (69)

Bush's Landing $5
Lakesude Use Area
24 mi N of Oahe Dam on SR 1804. Camp free, but $5 daily or $20 annual entry permit required. All year; 14-day limit. Toilets, cfga, no drkg wtr. Boating(l), fishing.

Chantier Creek   FREE
Lakeside Use Area
15 mi N of Oahe Dam on SR 1806. Free. All year; 14-day limit. Primitive camping; no facilities, no drkg wtr. Boating(l), fishing.

Cow Creek $8
State Recreation Area
15 mi NW of Pierre on SR 1804. $8 for 40 basic non-elec sites. All year; 14-day limit. Tbls, pit toilets, cfga, drkg wtr, showers, fish cleaning station. No hookups. Boating(l),

fishing. Formerly Corps of Engineers campground; now managed by state.

De Grey   FREE
Lakeside Use Area
20 mi E of Pierre on SD 34; 1 mi S to campground. Free. All year; 14-day limit. 10 primitive sites (RVs under 25 ft); tbls, toilets, cfga, firewood, no drkg wtr. Picnicking, boating(ld), fishing.

East Shore $5
Lakesude Use Area
About 3 mi N of Oahe Dam on SR 1804. Camp free, but $5 daily or $20 annual entry permit required. All year; 14-day limit. Toilets, cfga, no drkg wtr. Boating(l), fishing.

Joe Creek   FREE
Lakeside Use Area
20 mi E of Pierre on SR 34; 10 mi S on co rds. Free. All year; 14-day limit. Camping area (about 6 sites) with shelters, tbls, drkg wtr, cfga, toilets. Boating(l), fishing, picnicking.

North Bend   FREE
Lakeside Use Area
31 mi E of Pierre on SD 34; 4 mi S. Free. All year. 10 sites. Pit toilets, tbls, cfga, no drkg wtr. Picnicking, boating(l), fishing.

Okobojo Point $8
State Recreation Area
17 mi NW of Pierre off SR 1804; from E end of dam, 9 mi NW on SR 1804; 2.5 mi W on gravel rd. $8. All year; 14-day limit. 17 modern non-elec sites. Pit toilets, cfga, showers, drkg wtr, tbls, fish cleaning station. Fishing, boating(l), picnicking. Formerly free campground of Corps of Engineers; now managed by state. 160 acres.

West Bend $8
State Recreation Area
26 mi E of Pierre on SR 34. $8 base. All year; 14-day limit. Base fee for non-elec sites in Campground #1 and Lower Campground; $12 with elec. 126 sites. Tbls, flush toilets, cfga, drkg wtr, showers, elec ($4), dump, playground, shelter. Fishing, hiking trails, boating(l), canoeing, bridle trail, interpretive program. 154 acres.

West Shore $5
Lakeside Use Area
Lake Oahe
From Pierre, NW on SR 1806, N near the dam. Camp free, but $5 daily or $20 annual entry permit required. All year; 14-day limit. Primitive undesignated sites. No toilets, cfga, no drkg wtr. Boating(l), fishing. Forme Corps of Engineers camp; now managed by state.

PLATTE (70)

Buryanek $8
State Recreation Area
18 mi W & 2.5 mi N of Platte, off SR 44. $8 for modern sites; $12 with elec. 44 sites. Toilets, tbls, cfga, drkg wtr, showers, play-

ground, beach, fish cleaning station. Swimming, boating(l), fishing. Dump at nearby Snake Creek SRA.

Platte Creek $8
State Recreation Area
8 mi W of Platte on SR 44; 8 mi S on SR 1804; at Lake Francis Case. $8 base. All year; 14-day limit. Base fee for non-electric modern sites; $12 with elec. 54 sites. Tbls, flush toilets, cfga, drkg wtr, showers, dump, playground, shelter, store, fish cleaning station. Fishing, boating(l), hiking trail, junior naturalist program, interpretive program, birdwatching.
    Travel tip: During winter, eagles roost at nearby Fort Randall Dam in one of the nation's largest concentrations of bald and golden eagles. They can be seen other times soaring in search of food.
    Fishing tip: Platte Creek has good population of walleyes. In summer, catch them 14-20 feet deep on white or orange & white jigs tipped with minnows or crawlers.

Snake Creek $10
State Recreation Area
14 mi W of Platte on SR 44; at Lake Francis Case. $10 base for 92 modern non-elec sites; $14 with elec. All year; 14-day limit. 115 sites in 2 campgrounds. Tbls, flush toilets, cfga, drkg wtr, shelter, showers, dump, playground, fish cleaning station. Boating(l), fishing, hiking trails, swimming, junior naturalist program, interpretive program, birdwatching, volleyball.
    Fishing tip: This park is a good base for walleye fishermen. Try shallows during April, May & June with jig & minnow. In summer, spinner rig tipped with nightcrawler in deeper water. Try the second major bay past Red Rock. Best fishing is at night for walleye and striped bass.

POLLOCK (71)

Lake Pocasse Public Park $5
Follow SR 1804 qtr mi E of Pollock. $5. May-Sept; 14-day limit. 13 primitive sites. Toilets, tbls, cfga, drkg wtr, dump, playground. Fishing, boating.

Shaw Creek   FREE
Lakeside Use Area
Lake Oahe
From Pollock, 6 mi S on SR 1804, 2 mi W, 1 mi S. Free. All year; 14-day limit. Primitive undesignated sites. Toilets, cfga, no drkg wtr. Boating(l), fishing. Former Corps of Engineers park; now managed by the state.

West Pollock   FREE
Lakeside Use Aree
Lake Oahe
From Pollock, 1 mi S, 2 mi W. Free primitive camping. All year. Drkg wtr, no toilets, cfga. Boating(l), fishing. Former Corps of Engineers park; now managed by the state.

REDFIELD (73)

Fisher Grove State Park **$8**
7 mi E of Redfield on US 212. $8 base. All year; 14-day limit. Base fee for non-elec sites; $11 with elec. 28 modern sites (19 with elec). Tbls, flush toilets, cfga, drkg wtr, showers, dump, elec($3), shelter, playground. Swimming, canoeing, boating(l), fishing, hiking trails, interpretive program. Historic site.

Hava Rest City Park **FREE**
Quarter mi W of Redfield on SD 212. Free. All year; 5-day limit. 10 sites, elec hookups, tbls, toilets, cfga, drkg wtr, picnic shelter. Picnicking.

ROCHFORD (74)

Black Fox Campground **$10**
Black Hills National Forest
6 mi W of Rochford on FR 231. $10 All year; 10-day limit. 9 sites (50-ft RV limit). Tbls, toilets, cfga, drkg wtr. Fishing, hiking. Elev 5900 ft.

Castle Peak Campground **$10**
Black Hills National Forest
3.5 mi SW of Rochford on FR 17; 1 mi S on FR 187; 3 mi E on FR 181. $10. MD-LD; 10-day limit. 9 sites (RVs under 40 ft). Tbls, toilets, cfga, drkg wtr. Fishing, picnicking, hiking, mountain biking.

ROSCOE (75)

Roscoe City Park **FREE**
On Third Avenue North in Roscoe. Donations suggested; camp free. 5/15-10/1; 3-day limit. Tbls, flush toilets, cfga, drkg wtr, dump, elec, playground. Picnicking.

SELBY (77)

Lake Hiddenwood **$6**
State Recreation Area
2 mi E of Shelby; 3 mi N on US 18/83. $6 base. All year; 14-day limit. Base fee for non-elec sites; $10 with elec. 14 basic sites (7 with elec). Tbls, pit toilets, cfga, drkg wtr, elec ($4), playground, shelter, no showers, no dump, beach. Fishing, boating(l), hiking trails, swimming.

SOUTH SHORE (79)

Round Lake **FREE**
Lakeside Use Area
1 mi E of South Shore off SR 20. Free. All year; 5-day limit. Undeveloped camping; 6 sites. Tbls, toilets, cfga. Fishing, boating(ld), picnicking.

SPEARFISH (80)

Rod and Gun **$7.50**
Black Hills National Forest
1 mi E of Spearfish on US 14A; 13 mi S on US 14; 2.5 mi SW on FR 222. $7.50 with federal Senior Pass; others pay $15. MD-LD; 10-day limit. 7 sites (50-ft RV limit). Tbls, toilets, cfga, drkg wtr (no wtr during free period). Fishing, picnicking, hiking. Elev 5500 ft. Stream. Site of "Dancing With Wolves" movie.

Timon **$7.50**
Black Hills National Forest
1 mi E of Spearfish on US 14A; 13 mi S on US 14; 4 mi SW on FR 222. $7.50 with federal Senior Pass; others pay $15. MD-LD; 10-day limit. 7 sites (RVs under 60 ft). Tbls, toilets, cfga, drkg wtr (no wtr during free period). Fishing, hiking trails, mountain biking trail. Elev 6000 ft. Stream. In Spearfish Canyon.

SPRINGFIELD (81)

Springfield **$8**
State Recreation Area
1 mi E of Springfield on SR 37. $8 base. All year; 14-day limit. Base fee for modern non-elec sites; $12 with elec. 21 sites (20 with elec). Tbls, flush toilets, cfga, drkg wtr, showers, dump, elec ($4), shelter, playground. Swimming, boating (ld), fishing, picnicking, canoeing. Fishing dock.

Sand Creek **$6**
Lakeside Use Area
1 mi N & 3 mi E of Springfield off SR 37. $6. All year; 7-day limit. 10 primitive sites. Toilets, cfga, drkg wtr, shelter. Boating(ld), fishing. 45 acres.

STURGIS (82)

Alkali Creek Trailhead **$6**
Bureau of Land Management
Fort Meade Recreation Area
3 mi SW of Sturgis. $6. 5/15-9/30; 14-day limit. 6 sites. Tbls, toilets, cfga, drkg wtr. Fishing, hiking. 15 acres.

Alkali Creek Horse Camp **$8**
Bureau of Land Management
Fort Meade Recreation Area
3 mi SW of Sturgis; follow signs from exit 34 of I-90 about 1 mi. $8. 5/15-9/30; 14-day limit. 6 sites. Tbls, toilets, cfga, drkg wtr. Equestrian use only. Closed during Sturgis motorcycle rally. 11 acres.

Bear Butte State Park **$6**
4 mi E of Sturgis on SR 34/79; 3 mi N on SR 79. $6. All year; 14-day limit. 16 primitive sites. Tbls, pit toilets, cfga, drkg wtr, no showers, no elec, no dump, playground, shelter. Bridle trail, boating, fishing, hiking trail, interpretive program. Horse camp sites $8.

Glencoe Campresort (Priv) **$8**
3 mi E of Sturgis on SR 34. $8 base. 5/1-10/1. Base fee for tent sites ($5 without use of showers); $12 for RV sites ($15 with use of showers). About 700 sites. Tbls, chemical & flush toilets, cfga, drkg wtr, showers, hookups. Weekly, monthly rates available. Geared to annual motorcycle rally.

SUNDANCE, (WY.) (83)

Cook Lake Recreation Area
Black Hills National Forest **$6.50**
20 mi N of Sundance on US 16 and FRs 838, 841, 843 & 842. $6.50 & $8.50 with federal Senior Pass; others pay $13 & $17. All year; 10-day limit. Free during LD-MD if weather permits, but no wtr or trash service. 34 sites; 45-ft RV limit. Tbls, toilets, cfga, drkg wtr. Boating, fishing, mountain biking, hiking, canoeing. Elev 4400 ft.

Reuter Campground **$11**
Black Hills National Forest
5 mi NW of Sundance. 2 mi W on US 14; 3 mi on FR 838. $11. All year; 10-day limit. Free during LD-MD if weather permits, but no wtr or trash service. 24 sites; 45-ft RV limit. Tbls, toilets, cfga, drkg wtr. Boating, fishing, hiking.

TABOR (84)

Tabor **$6**
Lakeside Use Area
6 mi S of Tabor off SR 52. $6. All year; 7-day limit. 10 primitive sites. Tbls, cfga. Fishing, boating (ld). 221 acres.

TIMBER LAKE (85)

Little Moreau **FREE**
State Recreation Area
6 mi S of Sturgis. All year; 14-day limit. 5 primitive sites. Toilets, tbls, firewood, drkg wtr. Limited facilities in winter. Boating(l), fishing, swimming, playground, shelter, canoeing. On Cheyenne River Indian Reservation. Lots of wildlife. 160 acres.

VERMILLION (86)

Clay County **FREE**
State Recreation Area
4 mi W of Vermillion off SR 50. Free. 5/1-9/30; 5-day limit. 15 sites. Tbls, toilets, cfga, drkg wtr. Hiking, fishing, boating(l). Missouri River.

Lions Trailer Park **FREE**
City Park
On Princeton at SD 50, on W side of Vermillion. Free. 4/1-11/1; 3-night limit. 15 sites, some with wtr & elec hookups, tbls, flush toilets, cfga, firewood, dump, showers($). Tennis, softball, picnicking; swimming, fishing, golf nearby.

VOLGA (87)

Oakwood Lakes State Park **$10**
At Volga, 10 mi N of US 14. $10 at non-elec sites; $14 with elec. All year; 14-day limit.

135 sites ($130 with elec. Tbls, flush toilets, cfga, drkg wtr, elec ($4), dump, showers, beach, playground, shelter, fishing pier. Fishing, hiking, bridle trail, swimming, boating (l), junior naturalist program, interpretive program, cross-country ski trail.

Travel tip: McCrory Gardens in nearby Brookings is among the top small botanical gardens in the U.S. It includes 14 formal theme gardens; free.

WALL (88)

Arrow Campground (Priv)   **$11**
At Wall, follow Business Loop 90 from I-90 exit 109 or 110. $11 base. 5/1-10/15. Base fee for tent sites; full hookups $21.50. 72 RV sites, 40 tent sites. Tbls, flush toilets, elec($), drkg wtr, CATV($), coin laundry, showers, cfga, playground, store, modem hookup($), pool. Near Wall Drug.

Cedar Pass Campground   **$8**
Badlands National Park
8 mi S of I-90 on SR 240 Badlands Loop; westbound exit 131 Cactus Flat; 30 mi E of I-90 on SR 240. $8 in winter; $10 in summer. All year; 14-day limit. 110 sites. Tbls, toilets, cfga, drkg wtr, dump, visitor center. Nature program, museum. Park entry fee charged, good for 7 days.

Sage Creek Primitive   **$10**
Badlands National Park
12 mi W of Pinnacles Ranger Station (on US 16A) on Sage Creek Rd. Camp free, but $10 park entry permit for 7 days. All year; 14-day limit. 15 sites (20-ft RV limit). Toilets, cfga, tbls, no drkg wtr. Hiking trails.

WATERTOWN (89)

RV Dump Station
Free dump station is available, along with water for cleaning & refilling tanks, at Glacial Lakes Tourism Association, on Hwy 212 W, next to Lions Park picnic area (across from swimming pool). Also free Glacial Lakes vacation guide, maps & travel info.

Northwest Pelican Lake   **$6**
Lakeside Use Area
4 mi W & 2 mi S of Watertown off US 212. $6. All year; 7-day limit. 6 primitive sites. Toilets, cfga, drkg wtr. Boating(ld), fishing. 50 acres.

Sandy Shore   **$10**
State Recreation Area
5 mi W of Watertown on US 212. $10 base. All year; 14-day limit. Fase fee for preferred tent sites & non-electric RV sites; $14 with elec. 20 sites. Tbls, flush toilets, cfga, drkg wtr, showers, elec ($4), dump, playground, shelter, beach. Swimming, boating(l), canoeing fishing, interpretive program.

Travel tip: Bramble Park Zoo in Watertown is home to hundreds of birds and animals from around the world; open MD-Ld on SR 20. Watertown World Wildlife Museum on

US 212 features 350 displays and more than 100 mounted animals.

WAUBAY (90)

Pickerel Lake   **$10**
State Recreation Area
10 mi N of Waubay off US 12. $10 at non-elec sites; $14 with elec. 77 sites (61 with elec). Tbls, flush toilets, cfga, drkg wtr, showers, elec ($4), dump, shelter, playground, fishing dock, beach. Swimming, boating(l), fishing, hiking, junior naturalist program, interpretive program. Accessible fishing dock.

Southside Blue Dog Lake   **FREE**
City Park Campground
2 campgrounds half mi apart on the S side of Blue Dog Lake. Free. All year. 20 sites, toilets, cfga, pumped wtr, some elec hookups, shelters. Boating(ld), fishing, playground,/ sports field, swimming.

Fishing tip: The state record white bass (4 lbs 6 oz) was caught from Blue Dog Lake in May 1999.

Enemy Swim   **FREE**
Water Access Site
6 mi N of Waubay off US 12. All year. Free primitive camping. Toilets, cfga, no drkg wtr. Boating(ld), fishing.

South Blue Dog   **FREE**
Lakeside Use Area
Half mi N of Waubay off US 12. Free primitive camping. Tbls, toilets, cfga, drkg wtr. Picnicking, swimming, boating(ld), fishing. Shelters, playground.

WEBSTER (91)

Municipal Park   **FREE**
In Webster at jct Hwys 25 & 12. Free. All year. Drkg wtr, elec hookups, dump, cfga. Picnicking.

WENTWORTH (92)

West Brent   **FREE**
Lakeside Use Area
5 mi S of Wentworth on SR 34. All year. Free primitive camping; 5-day limit. Toilets, no drkg wtr. Boating(l), fishing.

WESSINGTON (93)

Rosehill   **FREE**
Lakeside Use Area
9 mi S of Wessington, then 3 mi W on gravel rd following signs (S & E of Vayland). Free. All year; 41-day limit. Primitive undesignated sites. Tbls, toilets, cfga, drkg wtr. Boating(l), fishing, swimming, hunting.

WESSINGTON SPRINGS (94)

City Park   **FREE**
1 block N of SD 34 in Wessington Springs. Free. All year; 3-day limit. 20 sites. Tbls, cfga,

drkg wtr, toilets, 2 elec hookups, flush toilets at swimming pool half blk N. Swimming, picnicking., tennis, nature trail.

WHITE (95)

Lake Hendricks   **FREE**
Lakeside Use Area
9 mi E, 3 mi N of White off SR 30. Free. All year; 5-day limit. Undeveloped camping; 15 sites. Tbls, toilets, cfga, drkg wtr. Fishing, boating(ld).

WHITE LAKE (96)

A-A-A I-90 Camping   **$5**
Half mi S of I-90 exit 296. $5-10. 5/1-11/15. 18 sites. Tbls, flush toilets, showers, drkg wtr, cfga, hookups($).

WHITE RIVER (97)

White River Municipal Park   **FREE**
On S side of town off US 83; from US 83, 4 blks E on S 4th St; S on Brock St; E on S side of ballfield. Free. All year; 14-day limit. 12 narrow back-in sites on a circular drive; 48-ft RV limit. (Best site for large rig is in far SE corner, allowing easy back-in.) All sites bordered by phone pole stumps that could block slide-outs. Best RV parking in W section by ballfield. Tbls, toilets, cfga, drkg wtr. Fairgrounds, ball park, fishing. GPS: N43 33.894, W100 44.496.

WINNER (98)

Country Club Motel & RV Park   **$10**
On Hwy 18W, on W side of Winner. $10 base. All year. 29 sites. Hookups($).

WOONSOCKET (99)

Twin Lakes   **FREE**
Lakeside Use Area
6 mi S, 3 mi W of Woonsocket off SR 34. Free. All year; 5-day limit. Undeveloped camping; 8 primitive sites. Tbls, toilets, drkg wtr, cfga. Fishing, boating(ld), picnicking, swimming.

YANKTON (100)

Chief White Crane   **$10**
State Recreation Area
Near Yanktown, E of Lewis & Clark Lake dam on downstream side off SR 52. $10 base. All year; 14-day limit. Base fee at 2 tent sites; $14 at 144 RV sites with elec; $16 at 36 prime waterfront sites. 146 sites. Tbls, flush toilets, cfga, drkg wtr, dump, showers, playground. Handicap access. Former Corps of Engineers camp now managed by state. Fishing, boating (l).

Fishing tip: Catch walleyes near the park by casting plugs and jigging with spinners. Nice size catfish caught on stinkbaits.

Kelley's Cove   **FREE**
Lakeside Use Area
3 mi NE of Yankton off US 81. All year. Free primitive camping. No facilities. Fishing.

Nebraska Tailwaters   **$12**
Corps of Engineers
Lewis & Clark Lake
2 mi S of Yankton on US 81; 4 mi W on SR 121; along the Nebraska bank of the Missouri River. $12 base. 5/15-9/30; 14-day limit. 43 sites (32 with elec). Base fee for primitive sites; $14 with elec. Tbls, flush & pit toilets, cfga, drkg wtr, showers, dump. Fishing, boating(l), picnicking. This campground was closed early in 2007 for reconstruction. Check status before visiting there.

Fishing tip: Lewis & Clark Lake holds the state record for rock bass (2 lbs) and smallmouth bass (6 lbs 2 oz), and the state record flathead catfish (56 lbs 8 oz) was caught in 1998 from the Missouri River just outside Yankton.

Vacation Village (Private)   **$6**
At 496 West Hwy 52, Yankton. $6-14, depending upon length of stay & facilities. 25 sites. Tbls, flush toilets, cfga, CATV($), drkg wtr, hookups($).

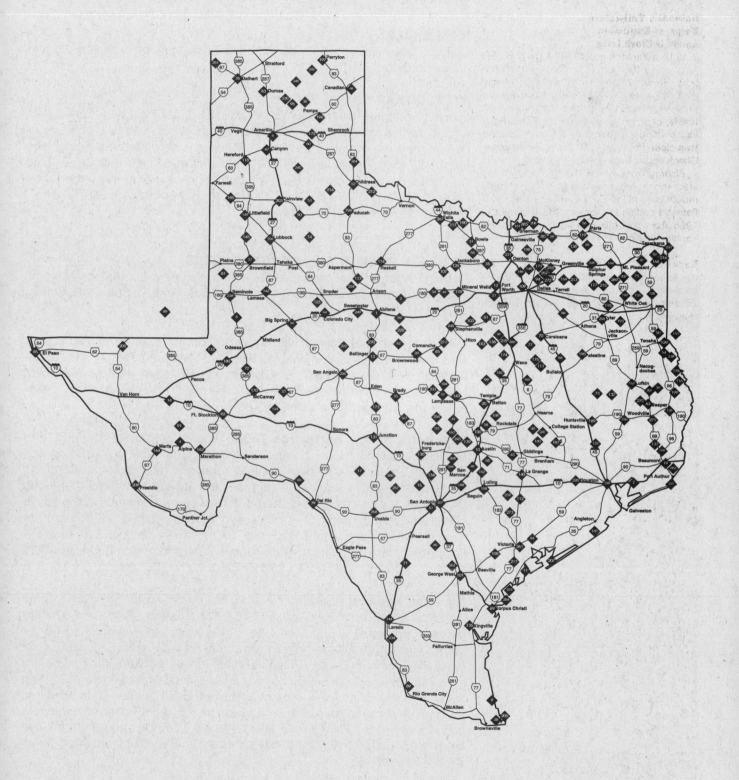

TEXAS

MISCELLANEOUS
Capital:
Austin
Nickname:
Lone Star State
Motto:
Friendship
Flower:
Bluebonnet
Tree:
Pecan
Bird:
Mockingbird
Song:
"Texas, Our Texas"

Internet Address:
www.traveltx.com

Parks and Wildlife Dept, 4200 Smith School Rd, Austin, TX 78744. 1-800-792-1112 or 512-389-4800.

REST AREAS
One-day overnight parking is permitted at Texas state picnic areas and rest areas; no tents.

STATE PARKS
Camping fees are $4-$16 per night, plus $1-5 per person entrance fees (or $60 annual permit good at all state parks). Activity use fees of $2-5 per person also are charged. Pets on leashes are permitted. Camping fees are $5-12 for primitive sites; $8-12 if water is at or near the site; $12-20 with water and electricity; $18-22 with full hookups. For further information contact: Parks and Wildlife Dept, 4200 Smith School Rd, Austin, TX 78744. 512-389-4800 or 800/792-1112.

NATIONAL FORESTS AND NATIONAL PARKS
Angelina National Forest, Davy Crockett National Forest, Sabine National Forest or Sam Houston National Forest, 415 S. First St, Suite 110, Lufkin, TX 75901. 936-639-8588.

Angelina National Forest has numerous primitive, undeveloped campsites scattered along the shores of Lake Sam Rayburn and the banks of the Angelina, Neches, Attoyac and Ayish Rivers. The sites are heavily used at various times of the year by fishermen. The forest does not have an inventory of the sites and their locations, however.

Amistad National Recreation Area, A joint project of the U.S. and Mexico, Amistad impounds waters of the Rio Grand just below its confluence with Devils River It covers 64,900 acres and extends 74 miles up the Rio Grande, 24 miles up the Devils River and about 14 miles up the Pecos River. Amistad has four designated primitive camprounds along the lake's shoreline. Daily camping fees of $4 and $8 are charged. All boats must have a lake use permit of $4 per day, $10 for three days or $40 annually. Shoreline camping is permitted anywhere except for developed aras. 4121 Highway 90 West, Del Rio, TX 78840-9350. 830-775-7491.

Big Bend National Park. Access from Marathon via US 385, from Alpine via SR 118, and from Presidio via US 67, FM 170 and SR 118. A $20 entry fee is charged that is good for 7 days (free admission with federal Senior Pass); annual pass $40. Camping fees are $14 ($7 with Senior Pass) at developed campgrounds. Primitive camping at numerous backcountry roadside sites is available by permit; all are listed in this edition. Starting in 2007, backcountry permits cost $10 per trip. No showers are available at developed campgrounds, but campers may use coin-operated showers and laundry at the Rio Grande Village Store. Campgrounds and primitive areas are usually full during holiday periods. Big Bend National Park, Texas 79834; 915/477-2251.

Guadalupe Mountains National Park, HC 60, Box 400, Salt Flat, TX 79847-9400; 915/828-3251. Free backcountry camping by permit; developed campgrounds are $8 per night. A 7-day $3 per person entry fee is charged.

Muleshoe National Wildlife Refuge, Box 549, Muleshoe, TX 79347.

Lake Meredith National Recreation Area, PO Box 1460, Fritch, TX 79036. No entry fees are charged; camping is free at primitive sites. Daily boat launch fees are $4 ($10 for 3 days, $40 annually).

Padre Island National Seashore. There is primitive camping on North, South, Malaquite, Little Shell and Big Shell beaches. Little Shell and Big Shell beaches are accessible only by 4-wheel drive vehicles. Camping is prohibited in grasslands (watch for rattlesnakes) and on dunes. Most areas have chemical toilets and trash cans. Malaquite Beach has water and showers; water is also available at the ranger station. A $10 entry fee is charged, good for 7 days (or $20 annually). Padre Island National Seashore, PO Box 181300, Corpus Christi, TX 78480-1300. 361-949-8173.

Corps of Engineers, Fort Worth District, PO Box 17300, Fort Worth, TX 76102; Corps of Engineers, Galveston District, PO Box 1229, Galveston, TX 77553; Corps of Engineers, New Orleans District, PO Box 60267, New Orleans, LA 70160; or Corps of Engineers, Southwestern Division, 1200 Main St, Dallas, TX 75202.

Bureau of Land Management, USPO and Federal Bldg, PO Box 1449, Santa Fe, NM 87501.

ABILINE (1)

Abilene State Park   **$8**
19 mi S of Abilene on US 83; 8 mi W on FM 613 to Buffalo Gap; 5 mi SW on FM 89. $8 base. All year; 14-day limit. Base fee for 3 tent sites with tbls, cfga (wtr nearby); $48 weekly and $4 during 12/1-2/28). $10 for 12 tent sites with wtr ($60 weekly & $5 during 12/1-2/28). $10 for 35 RV sites with elec/wtr but no tbls or cfga (rough overflow area); $5 off-season. $15-18 for modern RV sites with hookups (half price off-season). Tbls, flush toilets, showers, cfga, drkg wtr, dump, playground, pool, concessions. Picnicking, swimming, fishing, boating, hiking trail. State longhorn cattle herd. Lake Abilene nearby. $2 per person activity fee.

Johnson City Park   **FREE**
From I-20, Farm 600 N 6.6 mi; Farm 1082 E 6 mi. On Lake Fort Phantom Hill. All year; 48-hr limit. 5 sites. Flush toilets, tbls, cfga, no drkg wtr. Fishing, picnicking, boating (l at E end of dam). 37 acres.

Seebee City Park   **FREE**
From I-20, Farm 600 N 3.2 mi; E on local rd. On Elm Creek. All year; 48-hr limit. 4 sites. Flush toilets, drkg wtr, cfga, tbls. Fishing, boating(l), picnicking. 40 acres.

ALBANY (2)

Fort Griffin State Park   **$10**
15 mi N of Albany on US 283. $10 for 5 walk-in tent sites; $12 for RV sites with wtr; $15 for elec/wtr sites. All year; 14-day limit. Tbls, flush toilets, cfga, drkg wtr, showers, dump, playgrounds, interpretive displays, picnic areas, historic buildings, amphitheater (weekend programs in summer), group shelter, longhorn herd. Ruins of frontier fort.

Webb City Park   **$7.50**
In town; quarter mi NW on Railroad St from US 180. All year. $7.50. All year. 20 sites with elec/wtr hookups. Tbls, cfga, flush toilets, shelters, dump. Pool, playground, ball field. Swimming, picnicking.

ALPINE (4)

Elephant Mountain   **FREE**
State Wildlife Management Area
26 mi S of Alpine on SR 118. Free. All year except for short-term closures; 14-day limit. Primitive undesignated camping. No facilities; no drkg wtr. Birdwatching, hiking, hunting, nature trails. Registration required. Chihuahuan Desert environment. Opportunity to view desert bighorn sheep May-Nov. State Limited Public Use Permit required.

AMARILLO (6)

Interstate Motel & Campground   **$8**
Exit I-40 at Coulter, N to traffic light, then W half block. $8 base. All year. Base fee for tent sites; $12 for RVs with full hookups. Showers, flush toilets, drkg wtr.

Longhorn Trailer & RV Camp   **$10**
From I-40 exit 60, 1 mi W on south access rd. $10. All year. Full hookups, tbls, flush toilets, cfga, drkg wtr.

Rosita Flats Cycle Area   **FREE**
Lake Meredith
National Recreation Area
N of Amarillo on US 87/287 to Canadian River Bridge; E on dirt rd designated for off-road vehicles and motorcycle use. Free. All year; 14-day limit. Primitive undesignated sites. Toilets, cfga, no tbls, no drkg wtr. Horseback riding, OHV use.

ANAHUAC (7)

Cedar Hill   **$5**
Chambers County Park
4 mi N of I-10 on FM 563 to Lake Charleston Rd. $5 for 15 walk-in tent sites. All year; 14-day limit. Pit toilets, cfga, no drkg wtr. Nature trail. Formerly operated by Corps of Engineers.

Double Bayou   **$5**
Chambers County Park
From I-10 near Anahuac, 4 mi S on SR 61; 7 mi S on FM 562; half mi W on Eagle Ferry Rd; on East Fork of Double Bayou. $5 for tent & primitive sites. All year; 14-day limit. 30-acre open camping area. Flush toilets, tbls, cfga, drkg wtr, playground, ball field. Fishing. Trees filled with Spanish moss.

East Galveston Bay   **FREE**
Anahuac National Wildlife Refuge
10 mi S of Anahuac on SR 61 & CR 562; 3 mi E on co rd to gravel wildlife refuge entry rd; half mi SW on Cross Rd; 5 mi S on Windmill Rd. Free. All year; 3-day limit. Camp only along shore of East Galveston Bay. No facilities except toilets. Camping is not encouraged by wildlife service. Wildlife observation, fishing, waterfowl hunting, hiking. Poisonous snakes, fire ants, alligators, mosquitoes.

Fort Anahuac   **$5**
Chambers County Park
From I-10 near Anahuac, S 4 mi on SR 61; then 7 mi on Farm 562; half mi on Eagle Ferry Rd. At Trinity Bay on East Fork of Double Bayou. $5 tent & primitive sites; $10 with wtr & elec. All year; 14-day limit. 8 hookup sites; 40-acre primitive area. Flush toilets, concrete tbls, shelters, 3 ball fields, lighted fishing pier. Swimming; picnicking; fishing; boating(l); playground; golf nearby; crabbing; birdwatching. Judge Oscar Nelson Boardwalk on E bank of Trinity River.

James H. Robbins Memorial   **$5**
Chambers County Park
From I-10 near Anahuac, 4 mi S on SR 61; 22 mi S on FM 562; 1 mi S on Smith Point Rd; 1.6 mi NW on Hawkins Camp Rd; on Galveston & East Bays. $5. All year; 14-day limit. 10-acre open camping area. Flush toilets, cfga, tbls, no drkg wtr. Fishing, boating(l), birdwatching. Observation tower. Access to East Trinity Bay & East Galveston Bay.

Job Beason Park   **$5**
Chambers County Park
From I-10 at Anahuac, 11 mi S on FM 563; 4.7 mi S on Eagle Rd; half mi W on Bayshore Rd; on Double Bayou. $5. All year; 14-day limit. 12-acre open camping area. Tbls, flush toilets, cfga, drkg wtr, playground. Boating(l), fishing.

McCollum Park   **$5**
Chambers County Park
5 mi SW of Anahuac on Farm 565 from I-10; 3 mi S on Farm 2354. On Trinity Bay. $5. All year; 14-day limit. 10-acre open camping area (by reservations only -- 713-383-2011). Tbls, flush toilets, cfga, drkg wtr, shelters. Playground. Fishing, picnicking.

White Memorial   **$5**
Chambers County Park
From I-10 at Anahuac, .1 mi S on SR 61; on White's & Turtle Bayous. $5. All year; 14-day limit. 15 sites & open 85-acre camping area. Flush toilets, cfga, drkg wtr, tbls, shelters, elec, cold showers. Hiking trails, swimming, fishing, boating (l), crabbing.

Winnie-Stowell   **$5**
Chambers County Park
From I-10 at Anahuac, 1 mi S on SR 124; .1 mi E on LeBlanc Rd. $5 base. All year; 14-day limit. Base fee for primitive & tent sites; $10 with wtr/elec. 10 RV sites & 30-acre open camping area. Flush toilets, tbls, cfga, drkg wtr, elec, playground, pavilion, ball field, dump.

ANDREWS (8)

Florey Park   **$5**
Andrews County Park
9.6 mi N on US 385 from SR 87; 1 mi E on local rd. $5 for 252 primitive & tent sites; $10 for 200 sites with hookups. All year; 7-day limit. 252 sites. Tbls, cfga, flush toilets, drkg wtr, dump, elec($), sewer($). Community center. Tennis, basketball, volleyball, croquet courts, playground.

Prairie Dog Town   **FREE**
Chamber of Commerce RV Park
In Andrews, on TX 115/176; 7 blks W of US 385. All year; 3-day limit. 6 RV sites with elec/wtr hookups; 10 tent-trailer sites, free. Tbls, toilets, cfga, dump, drkg wtr. Swimming; picnicking; fishing; golfing. Prairie dog town.

✪ AUSTIN (10)

Canyon of the Eagles   **$10**
Lake Buchanan
Lower Colorado River Authority
From Austin, follow FM 1431 to Hwy 29; E on Hwy 29, then left on FM 690 to dam; N

on Cr 114; left on CR 2341 for 20 mi. $10 for primitive sites; $12 sites with wtr; $20 for full hookups. All year; 14-day limit. 23 RV sites plus tent area. Tbls, flush toilets, cfga, drkg wtr, showers, dump, beach, fishing pier. Fishing, hiking trails, swimming, boating(l). Per-person entry fee.

Grelle $5
Primitive Recreation Area
Lower Colorado River Authority
From I-35 S of Austin, travel W on SR 71; 1 mi N on Spur 191 to Spicewood; right on CR 404 1 mi; left on CR 412 (gravel) for half mi; on upper S side of Lake Travis, E of Starcke Dam. Camp free, but $5 daily or $50 annual entry permit required. All year; 5-day limit. Primitive tent camping at metal fire rings; 400 acres. Toilets, no other facilities; no drkg wtr or trash service. Hiking trail, fishing.

McKinney Falls State Park $12
7 mi SE of Austin on US 183; 2 mi W on Scenic Loop. $12 base. All year; 14-day limit. Base fee for 8 walk-in sites with cfga, tbls, wtr nearby; $16 for 81 RV sites with wtr/elec. Tbls, flush toilets, cfga, drkg wtr, showers, dump, playgrounds, picnic areas, amphitheater, interpretive displays. Hiking & biking trail, swimming, fishing, birdwatching, nature trails. Golf nearby. 2 waterfalls at Onion Creek. $4 per person entry fee.

Muleshoe Bend $5
Primitive Recreation Area
Lower Colorado River Authority
From I-35 S of Austin, travel W on SR 71; 4.5 mi N on CR 404; right on CR 414 for 1.5 mi; right just prior to Ridge Harbor entrance for 1 mi; after pavement ends, continue .3 mi to entrance; on upper S shore of Lake Travis, E of Starcke Dam. Camp free, but $5 daily (or $50 annual) entry fee. All year; 5-day limit. Primitive camping at metal fire rings. Toilets, tbls. Bridle & hiking trail, fishing. 1,000 acres.

AUSTWELL (11)

Wilson Heard City Park $12
At entrance to city. $12 base. All year. Base fee for RV sites with 20-amp elec; $14 for 30-amp elec; $15 for 50-amp. 9 sites. Tbls, flush toilets, showers, cfga, drkg wtr, playground. Volleyball, walking trail, baseball, picknicking.

BALLINGER (13)

Ballinger City Park $3
From SR 158, two blocks E on Crosson St. On Elm Creek. $3 primitive sites; $9 with elec & wtr. All year; 3-day limit. 19 sites. Tbls, flush toilets, cfga, drkg wtr, elec, dump, cold showers. Swimming (pool), fishing, playground.

Concho Park $10
O.H. Ivie Reservoir
Colorado River Municipal Water District
S of Ballinger on US 83 toward Paint Rock; E on FM 1929 (Ray Stoker Hwy) about 17 mi; left on dirt access rd to lake. $10 base. All year; 14-day limit. Base fee for tent sites; $14 for RVs with elec. 29 sites. Tbls, flush toilets, showers (for RVs), cfga, drkg wtr. Boating(l), fishing.

Fishing tip: O.H. Ivie Lake has a large population of Florida largemouth bass, and locals believe the lake record will be broken annually for a few years. This is a deep, clear lake, so use Texas and Carolina rigs and deep runners to reach the big bass.

BALMORHEA (14)

Balmorhea State Park $11
Qtr mi N of Balmorhea on FM 3078. $11 base. All year; 14-day limit. Base fee for 6 sites with wtr; $14 for 16 sites with wtr/elec; $17 for 12 sites with wtr, elec, CATV. Tbls, flush toilets, cfga, drkg wtr, showers, dump, playgrounds, pool, concessions. Fishing, group trips. San Solomon Springs, Fort Davis National Historic Site, McDonald Observatory nearby. Boating & fishing at Lake Balmorhea (3 mi). Park built by CCC in 1930s. Park features a 77,000-square-foot artesian spring pool with constant 72-76 degree temperatures; ideal for swimming, scuba diving. $5 per person entry fee Oct-Apr; $7 May-Sept.

BANDERA (15)

Hill Country $8
State Natural Area
From FM 681, 8.5 mi SW on FM 1077; 2 mi SW on gravel rd. $8 for 3 primitive, designated backpacking camp areas 1.5-3.5 mi from trailhead parking; $10 for the Bar-O developed primitive equestrian area (14 portable stalls, water trough, wash area, cfga, chemical toilet, night security light); $10 for 3 walk-in tent sites on West Verde Creek with tbls, cfga, nearby toilets; $8 for 3 walk-in sites in Comanche Bluff area & 4 walk-in sites in Capita Falls area, all with tbls, cfga & nearby toilets; $15 for developed Trail Head Equestrian Camp with corral & picket line, wtr for horses, tbls, cfga, chemical toilets, 36-mi trail system. No drkg wtr. Equestrian trail, hiking trails, mountain biking, swimming, fishing. Horse rental. Primarily an equestrian camp. Park open only Fri-Sun during Dec-Jan; rest of year, camping every day. Off-site horse rentals near park entrance. 23 designated multi-use trails open to backpacking, horseback riding, mountain biking, making up 36 miles (4 mi limited to horses & hikers). 5,400 undeveloped area. $3 per person entry for overnight use.

BARKSDALE (17)

LedgeWater Campground $5
9.1 mi N of Barksdale on W side of Hwy 55. $5 base. All year. Base fee per person off-

season; $10 per person MD-LD for primitive sites. $10 off-season for sites with elec/wtr; $20 in-season. 13 sites. Tbls, flush toilets, cfga, drkg wtr, showers, dump. Hiking & biking trails, volleyball, basketball, horseshoes, washers, swimming.

BASTROP (18)

Bastrop State Park $10
1 mi E of Bastrop on SR 21; access from Park Rd 1 from Buescher State Park. $10 base. All year; 14-day limit. Base fee for 50 backpack sites on loop trail; $12 for 7 walk-in tent sites with tbls, fire ring, mounted grill, nearby wtr; $12 for 16 drive-to tent sites; $15-17 for RV sites with hookups. Tbls, flush toilets, cfga, drkg wtr, showers, dump, pool, golf pro shop, dining hall, playground. Swimming, hiking trail, nature trails, fishing, golf, group trips. 5,926 acres. $4 per person entry fee. Note: park usually closed parts of Feb & Mar to protect endangered Houston toad.

Buescher State Park $12
10 mi SE of Bastrop on SR 71; NE on FM 153. $12 base. All year; 14-day limit. Base fee for 25 sites with wtr; $15 for 32 RV sites with wtr/elec. Tbls, flush toilets, cfga, drkg wtr, dump, 4 screened shelters, picnic areas, playgrounds, pavilion, recreation hall, showers, store. Hiking trails, fishing, swimming, boating (no motors). 1,000 acres. $4 per person entry fee.

North Shore Park $10
Lake Bastrop
Lower Colorado River Authority
N of Bastrop on SR 95; right on FM 1441 for 2.5 mi; right into park; on N shore of lake. $10 for primitive sites; $15-17 wtr/elec; $20 full hookups. $3 entry fee. 16 sites. Tbls, toilets, cfga, drkg wtr, showers, dump, boat ramp ($), dock, fishing pier. Fishing, boating, picnicking, swimming, horseshoes, volleyball. 900-acre lake. $3 entry fee; $2 seniors.

South Shore Park $10
Lake Bastrop
Lower Colorado River Authority
N of Bastrop, follow FM 352 N from SR 21; on S shore of Lake Bastrop. $10 for primitive sites; $15-17 with elec; $20 full hookups. All year; 14-day limit. 38 sites. Flush toilets, cfga, drkg wtr, showers, dump, pavilion, playground, fish cleaning station, fishing pier, observation deck. Fishing, boating(ld), waterskiing, canoeing, hiking, mountain biking, swimming, volleyball. 900-acre lake. $3 entry fee; $2 seniors.

BEAUMONT (19)

Big Thicket   FREE
National Preserve
NW of Beaumont on US 69/287 to visitor center. Free primitive backcountry camping in designated areas & on sandbars by permit. Hiking, fishing, canoeing, ranger programs.

BELTON (20)

Iron Bridge Park   **FREE**
Corps of Engineers
Belton Lake
10 mi NW of SR 317 on SR 36; 1 mi NE on Iron Bridge Rd. Free. All year; 14-days. 30-acre camping area. 5 sites. Tbls, toilets, cfga, shelters, drkg wtr. Boating (l), fishing, swimming.

Owl Creek Park   **FREE**
Corps of Engineers
Belton Lake
Fr Jct SR 317, 6.5 mi NW on SR 36, across lake bridge, 1 mi W at "y," go S. Free. All year; 14-day limit. 10 sites plus undesignated camping on 47 acres. Toilets, tbls, cfga, drkg wtr. Swimming, fishing, boating(l).

Westcliff Park   **$10**
Corps of Engineers
Belton Lake
N of Belton, 3.7 mi NW on FM 439 from jct with SR 317; qtr mi NW, then NE. $10 base without hookups; $16 with elec; 65-ft RVs. All year; 14-day limit. 31 sites (27 with wtr/elec). Tbls, flush toilets, cfga, drkg wtr, showers, dump, beach, elec ($), picnic shelters. Boating(l), fishing, swimming. 2-night stay required on weekends; 3 nights for holiday weekends.

White Flint Campground   **$9**
Corps of Engineers
Belton Lake
5.5 mi NW of SR 317 on SR 36, across bridge. $9 with federal Senior Pass at 13 sites with 50-amp elec; others pay $18; $30 at 12 screened sites ($15 with Senior Pass); 60-ft RV limit. All year; 14-day limit. Flush toilets, covered tbls, cfga, drkg wtr, dump. Swimming, fishing, boating(l), picnicking. 2-night minimum stay on weekends.

Winkler Park   **$8**
Corps of Engineers
Belton Lake
From SR 317, 5.8 mi NW on SR 36 to W side of Leon River bridge; 2 mi N on local rd past White Flint Park. $8. All year; 14-day limit. 15 sites with wtr hookups; 35-ft RV limit. Tbls, toilets, cfga, drkg wtr, shelter, no elec. Swimming, fishing, boating. 128 acres.

Fishing tip: This campground is popular among fishermen, and many winter campers come hoping to catch a record size flathead catfish (they call them yellow cats).

BENBROOK (21)

Holiday Park   **$10**
Corps of Engineers
Benbrook Lake
8 mi SW of Benbrook on US 377; 2 mi E on Park Rd. $10 base. All year; 14-day limit. Base fee without hookups; $20 with elec/wtr hookups, $30 with 50-amp & wtr ($10 & $15 with federal Senior Pass). 105 sites (34 no hookups); 65-ft RVs. Tbls, flush toilets, cfga, drkg wtr, elec ($), dump, showers. Horseback riding, boating(l), fishing, golf, hiking. Fishing pier. 2-night minimum stay on weekends.

Mustang Creek Point   **$10**
Corps of Engineers
Benbrook Lake
Near Benbrook, 6.9 mi SW of I-20 on US 377; 3.5 mi SE on FM 1187; 2 mi N on Plover Rd (CR 1042); adjacent to Mustang Park Bear. $10. 4/1-9/30; 14-day limit. 9 primitive covered-table sites, plus open camping on 3 acres, including lakeshore. Toilets, cfga, drkg wtr. Fishing, boating(l), picnicking.

Rocky Creek   **$10**
Corps of Engineers
Benbrook Lake
S of Benbrook on US 377; 7 mi SE on FM 1187; N on CR 1089; S on CR 1150. $10. 4/1-9/30; 14-day limit. 11 sites. Tbls, flush toilets, cfga, dump, drkg wtr, dump. Boating(l); picnicking; fishing; marina; swimming.

BEND (22)

Barefoot Camp & RV Park   **$5**
3 mi E of Bend on Colorado River. $5 per person for primitive sites; $20 with full hookups. Jan-Oct. 38 sites plus primitive area. Tbls, flush toilets, cfga, drkg wtr. Tubing, swimming, fishing, boating. At a working cattle ranch.

BIG LAKE (23)

Reagan County Park   **$5**
San Patricio County
Utah Ave N in Big Lake. $5 donation for wtr & elec hookup; primitive camping free. All year; 3-day limit. 62 sites. Tbls, toilets, cfga, dump, drkg wtr, elec. Swimming, picnicking, fishing, softball, bike trails, tennis, playground, volleyball.

BIG SPRING (24)

Big Spring State Park   **$10**
From Big Spring, follow Bus 20 to exit 174; turn right on FM 700 to park. $10. All year; 14-day limit. Tbls, flush toilets, cfga, drkg wtr, no showers, playground, store. Scenic walking route, nature trail. Seasonal interpretive center with Indian artifacts & fossils. 382 acres. $2 per person entry fee.

Moss Creek Lake City Park   **$9**
7.2 mi E of US 87 on I-20; 2.9 mi S & 2.7 mi E on Moss Lake Rd. $9 base (includes entrance fee). Base fee primitive sites; $12 for elec/wtr; $15 full hookups ($100 annually for entry, boat launch & camping). All year; closed 12/15-1/15. 15 RV sites with elec; 40 primitive sites. Tbls, flush toilets, cfga, drkg wtr, store. Hiking, picnicking, fishing, boating(ld), fishing piers. Shelters, playground.

Fishing tip: Find crappies in Lake Moss around structures such as submerged trees and brush piles. Use minnows or jigs. Best bet for white bass is around the mouths of creeks in the spring, also on jigs or small spinners. Often, crappies and white bass can be caught in the same area on the same bait.

BLUM (26)

Kimball Bend Park   **FREE**
Corps of Engineers
Whitney Lake
Fr Blum/Jct FM 933, 6 mi SW on SR 174 across bridge, go NW. All year; 14-day limit. 11 sites plus 129-acre open area. Toilets, tbls, cfga, drkg wtr. Swimming, fishing, boating(l).

Fishing tip: Whitney Lake is one of the few bodies of water in Texas where striped bass reproduce naturally. Ask at local marinas for tips on where and how to catch them while you're there.

BONHAM (29)

Bonham State Park   **$12**
2 mi SE of Bonham on SR 78; 2 mi SE on FM 271; access Park Rd 24. $12 for tent sites; $15 for RV sites with hookups. All year; 14-day limit. Tbls, flush toilets, cfga, drkg wtr, showers, dump, picnic areas, playgrounds, pavilion. Swimming, boating(ldr), fishing (lighted pier), mountain biking & hiking trail. 261 acres. $3 per person entry fee.

Lake Bonham Recreation Area   **$6**
City of Bonham Park
2.5 mi NE of Bonham on FM 898 & FM 3; on Lake Bonham. $6 base. Apr-Sept. Base fee for tent sites; $15 for RV sites with elec/wtr ($12 for seniors over 65). 81 sites on 1,500-acre lake; 30-day limit. Most sites have access to wtr/elec. Tbls, flush toilets, cfga, drkg wtr, showers, dump, playground, concession bldg. Golf, mini golf, fishing, swimming, boating(l$). Boat permits $8 annually.

BORGER (30)

Huber City Park   **FREE**
At S city limits of Borger on TX 207 at TX 152. Free, but donation requested. All year; 3-day limit. 10 sites. Tbls, flush toilets, cfga, wtr, dump, elec. Golf, swimming; picnicking; fishing; hunting; boating(r); horseback riding/rental; tennis. 17 acres.

BOWIE (31)

A-1 RV Park   **$10**
At jct of Fruitland Rd & East Frontage Rd. at Bowie. $10. All year. Tbls, toilets, cfga, drkg wtr, hookups.

Pelham City Park   **$8**
In Bowie at Pelham St & Bus 81/287. $8 with elec/wtr. All year; 7-day limit. 10 sites. Flush

toilets, cfga, drkg wtr, showers, dump, pool, playground.

Selma City Park   FREE
3.5 mi SW of Bowie on TX 59; 3.6 mi on FM 2583; on W side of Amon Carter Lake; roads rough. Free primitive camping; $8 for RVs with elec. All year. 40 sites with elec/wtr); 40-acre open camping area. Tbls, flush toilets, cfga, dump, drkg wtr, cold showers, shelters. Boating(lr); picnicking; fishing. New 5-year plan aims at renovating this park. Work includes area for 4-wheel and motorcycle activities, dock & restroom repair, creation of swimming beach, expanion of RV area. Note: late in 2006, this park had signs posted warning of unsafe drinking water, and park was closed.

BRADY (33)

Brady Lake Park $5
From US 87 near Brady, 4.5 mi W on FM 2028; on Brady Lake. $4 base. All year; 90-day limit. Base fee for primitive tent sites; $20 for sites with wtr/elec ($250 monthly). 28 sites. Tbls, flush toilets, cfga, drkg wtr, shelters, dump, showers, pavilion, store, marina, bathhouse, playground, bait. Fishing, picnicking, swimming, boating (lr), waterskiing, volleyball.

Richards City Park $3
Follow US 87 in Brady to Memory Lane; on Brady Creek. $3 for sites with wtr; $4.50 for sites with elec; $7.50 for sites with elec/wtr. All year; 9-day limit. 295 sites (about 45 full-hookup sites & 150 primitive sites). Tbls, flush toilets, cfga, drkg wtr, showers, hook-ups($), dump nearby, pavilion, playground, rodeo arena, concession stand. Tennis, soccer, biking trails.

BRECKENRIDGE (34)

Hubbard Creek Lake Dam   FREE
West Central Texas
Municipal Water District
At lake's dam near Breckenridge. Free primitive camping at dam. Tbls, toilets, cfga, no drkg wtr. Boating(l), fishing, swimming, waterskiing.

Fishing tip: Hubbard Creek Lake is a good bass lake, with the record fish weighing 12.6 pounds.

Lake Daniel City Park   FREE
6 mi S of Breckenridge on Hwy 183; at Lake Daniel. Free. 7 primitive sites. Tbls, toilets, cfga, no hookups or wtr. Boating(l), fishing, picnicking, no swimming. 950-acre lake.

BROADDUS (36)

Harvey Creek $3
Angelina National Forest
San Augustine County Park
3.5 mi SW of Broaddus on SR 83; 5 mi SW on SR 2390. On Sam Rayburn Lake. $3. All year; 14-day limit. 42 sites (22-ft RV limit). Tbls, toilets, cfga, no drkg wtr. 4 picnic sites, pavilion($). Boating(l), fishing. $3 day use fee (or $25 annually) for boat launch area. All national forest permits honored. Camping closed in 2007 due to hurricane damage.

Fishing tip: Take the kids fishing in Harvey Creek -- or leave the kids in camp and go yourself. Fish around structure and the hydrilla beds for bluegills, using worms, crickets and small spinner jigs.

Powell Park Marina $10
Sam Rayburn Lake Concession
9 mi E of Broaddus on FM 83; 11 mi S on FM 705; on S end of lake. $10 base. All year. Base fee for primitive sites; $16 with elec/wtr; $18 full hookups. Tbls, flush toilets, cfga, drkg wtr, showers, cafe, store, coin laundry, fishing pier. Fishing, boating(ld), horseshoes, volleyball.

Townsend $3
Angelina National Forest
San Augustine County Park
4 mi SE of Broaddus on Hwy 103; 3 mi S on SR 1277; 1 mi W on FR 2923. $3. All year; 14-day limit. 18 sites. Tbls, cfga, drkg wtr, toilets, shelter($). 9 picnic sites. Boating(l), fishing, waterskiing. On Sam Rayburn Lake. $3 day use fee (or $25 annually) for boat launch area. All national forest permits honored.

BROWNFIELD (37)

Coleman   FREE
Terry County Park
From jct US 62 & Reppto St., 1 blk E on Reppto; 1 blk S on First St. Watch for park entry signs off First & Second Sts. Donations accepted, but camp free. All year; 4-day limit. 14 sites. Elec, wtr, flush toilets, dump, cfga. Swimming pool, tennis court nearby.

BROWNSVILLE (38)

Brazos Island State Park   FREE
1 mi NE on Hwy 48; 22 mi E on Hwy 4. On Gulf of Mexico. Free. All year. Undesignated sites. Tbls, toilets, cfga, no drkg wtr. Swimming, fishing.

BROWNWOOD (39)

Festival City Park $8
From jct of US 67/US 84 & US 377 in Brownwood, 4 mi S on US 377, then E (left) on FM 3064 (Morris Sheppard Dr) to Burnett Dr.; half mi E on Milam Dr. On South Willis Creek at Camp Bowie Sports Complex. $8. All year; 3-day limit. 5 sites with elec. Tbls, flush toilets, drkg wtr, cfga. Swimming pool, picnicking, fitnes park, vintage military equipment.

Lake Brownwood State Park $12
16 mi NW of Brownwood on SR 279; 6 mi E on Park Rd 15. $12 for tent sites; $15-25 for RV sites with hookups. All year;

14-day limit. Tbls, flush toilets, cfga, drkg wtr, dump, showers, store, picnic areas, fish cleaning station. Fishing (lighted pier), boating(l), swimming, hiking & nature trails, paddleboating(r), waterskiing, birdwatching. $3 per person entry.

Fishing tip: For summer panfish, catch white bass up to 2 pounds in 15-20 feet on shad and jigs; use minnows and jigs for crappies in the same area or a little deeper.

BRYAN (40)

Lake Bryan City Park $8
At 8200 Sandy Point Rd; on shore of Lake Bryan. $8 base. All year; 7-day limit. Base fee for tent sites; $15 for RVs with elec/wtr. Tbls, flush toilets, cfga, drkg wtr, showers, dump, beach. Biking, fishing, boating(l), hiking, swimming, picnicking.

BRYANS MILL (41)

Thomas Lake Camp   FREE
Cass County Park
Wright Patman Lake Area
NE of Bryans Mill on co rd to Thomas Lake just W of Wright Patman Lake. Free. All year; 14-day limit. Primitive undeveloped camping area. Toilets, no other facilities. Boating(l), fishing.

BURNET (42)

Inks Lake State Park $8
9 mi W of Burnet on SR 29; access S on Park Rd 4. $8 for backpack sites; $12 for 50 sites with wtr hookups; $18 for 137 RV sites with hookups. All year; 14-day limit. Tbls, flush toilets, cfga, drkg wtr, showers, dump, playgrounds, picnic areas, amphitheater, store, coin laundry. Swimming, fishing (2 lighted piers), boating(lr), canoeing(r), golf, hiking trails, scuba diving, waterskiing, biking. 1,201 acres. $5 per person entry fee.

BURTON (43)

Nails Creek Unit $6
Lake Somerville State Park
NW of Burton on FM 1697; access via FM 180. $6 for 50 hike-in tent sites without wtr; $10 for 16 primitive walk-in sites & 10 equestrian sites with wtr; $15 for 40 RV sites with hookups. Tbls, flush toilets, cfga, drkg wtr, showers, dump, picnicking areas, shelters, interpretive shelter. Boating(ld), hiking trails, bridle trails, fishing, waterskiing, picnicking. See Lyons entry. $3 per person entry fee.

CADDO (44)

Possum Kingdom $7
State Park
18 mi N of Caddo on Park Rd 33 off US 180. $7 for 20 walk-in tent sites; $12 for 55 primitive sites with wtr; $14 for 40 RV sites

with wtr/elec; $17-20 for premium sites with hookups; $6 for overflow primitive sites. All year; 14-day limit. Tbls, flush toilets, cfga, drkg wtr, showers, dump, playgrounds, picnic areas, store, longhorn herd, fish cleaning facilities. Boating (ldr), fishing (lighted pier), swimming, waterskiing, canoeing (r), paddleboating (r), biking. 19,800-acre lake. $4 per person entry fee.

Fishing tip: Fishing not very good in Possum Kingdom Lake in recent years; lake was restocked. Contains largemouth bass, striped bass, crappies, catfish.

CALLIHAM (45)

Calliham Unit   **$11**
Choke Canyon State Park
11 mi W of Calliham on SR 72. $11 for walk-in tent sites; $16 for 40 RV sites with hookups. All year; 14-day limit. Tbls, flush toilets, cfga, drkg wtr, dump, showers. Picnicking area with shelters; beach, bathhouse, store. Boating(l), fishing, hiking trails, nature trails, hunting, birdwatching. See Three Rivers entry.

CANADIAN (46)

Gene Howe   **FREE**
State Wildlife Management Area
2 mi N of Canadian on Hwy 60; 6 mi E on FM 2266. Free. All year except about 12/8-10 & 4/13-15; 14-day limit. Primitive undesignated camping. Drkg wtr, cfga, no other facilities. Registration & permit required. Hunting, horseback riding (3/15-8/31), nature trails, fishing, hiking, biking, auto tour. 5,821 acres.

Lake Marvin   **Free**
Black Kettle National Grasslands
Cibola National Forest
Half mi N of Canadian on US 83; 11 mi E on FM 2266 (Formby Rd). Free. All year; 14-day limit. 22 sites. Tbls, toilets, cfga, drkg wtr. Birdwatching, hiking, fishing, boating. Store. Entry fee may be charged.

CANYON (47)

Canyon Municipal Park   **$5**
On N end of town just off I-27. $5. All year. Tbls, toilets, cfga, drkg wtr, elec, dump.

CANYON CITY (48)

Canyon Park   **$8**
Corps of Engineers
Canyon Lake
3.2 mi NW of Canyon City on SR 306, then SW. $8 during Sun-Thurs; $12 Fri-Sat. 4/1-9/30; 14-day limit. 150 primitive tent sites; no RVs permitted. Tbls, toilets, cfga, drkg wtr, dump, beach. Handicap access. Fishing, boating(l), swimming.

Fishing tip: For big catfish, try the canyons and cuts for foraging flatheads and

blues; channel cats hang out near channels and ledges.

North Park   **$8**
Corps of Engineers
Canyon Lake
1.2 mi NW of Canyon City on FM 306; 1 mi SE. $8 during Sun-Thurs; $12 Fri-Sat; . 3/1-10/31; 14-day limit. 19 primitive tent sites; no RVs permitted. Tbls, toilets, cfga, drkg wtr. Fishing, boating (no ramp).

Palo Duro Canyon State Park   **$12**
12 mi E of Canyon City on SR 217; access on Park Rd 5 to Palo Duro Creek. $12 for primitive equestrian sites (including 10 equestrian); $20 for 79 RV sites with hookups. All year; 14-day limit. Tbls, flush toilets, cfga, drkg wtr, showers, dump, playgrounds, picnic areas, interpretive displays, miniature railroad, longhorn herd, amphitheater (summer productions of "Texas"), store. Extensive hiking trails, swimming, horseback riding(r), recreation programs, biking. $4 per person entry fee.

CARLSBAD (NM.) (49)

Dog Canyon Campground   **$8**
Guadalupe Mountains National Park
From Carlsbad, 10 mi N of US 285, 60 mi SW on SR 137. $8. All year; 14-day limit. 9 tent & 4 RV sites. Tbls, flush toilets, no cfga, drkg wtr; limited facilities in winter. No entry fee. Hiking. Backcountry sites nearby at several locations accessible by foot or horseback.

Pine Springs Canyon   **$8**
Guadalupe Mountains National Park
Frijole information center is 55 mi SW of Carlsbad on US 62-180; camp 1.5 mi W of info station. $8. All year; 14-day limit. 41 sites. Tbls, toilets, drkg wtr, no cfga, no dump. Hiking, picnicking.

CARTHAGE (50)

Dotson Road Crossing   **FREE**
Panola County Park
9 mi W of Carthage on Hwy 315; 3 mi S on FM 1971. Free. Primitive sites. tbls, cfga, drkg wtr. Fishing, boating(ldr).

Fishing tip: Just 12 mi SW of Carthage via FM 10 is Murvaul Lake, one of the state's best catfish lake and a good place to catch large bass. The lake's record fish include a 76-pound flathead catfish and a 14.55-pound largemouth.

CEDAR HILL (53)

Cedar Hill State Park   **$7**
3 mi W of Cedar Hill on FM 1382; on SE shore of Joe Poole Lake. $7 for primitive overflow sites & hike-in tent sites; $20 for 355 RV sites with hookups. All year; 14-day limit. Tbls, flush toilets, cfga, drkg wtr, showers, dump, playgrounds, beach. Mountain

biking trails, swimming, boating(l), fishing (lighted jetties), hiking trails. Historic William Penn homestead. North Texas Mountain Bike Trail. $5 per person entry fee.

CENTER (54)

Boles Field   **$6**
Sabine National Forest
6 mi S of center on SR 87; 1.5 mi E on FM 417; bear right at Y onto FM 2694 for 5.5 mi. $6. All year; 14-day limit. 20 sites. Tbls, flush toilets, cfga, showers, drkg wtr (10 shared spigots), elec. Hiking, horseback riding. Camp built by CCC in 1930s; location of competitive fox hunts in November.

Ragtown   **$5**
Sabine National Forest
Sabine River Authority of Texas
13 mi SE of Center on SR 87; 6.5 mi E on SR 139; E 4 mi on SR 3184; 1.5. mi E on FR 132. $5. 4/1-12/15; 14-day limit. 24 sites (22-ft RV limit). Tbls, flush toilets, cfga, drkg wtr, dump, showers. Boating(l--open all yr), fishing, hiking trails.

CHICO (55)

Wise County Park   **$5**
1 mi W of Chico on FM 1810; 3 mi S on FM 2952; 1 mi W on County Park Rd. $5 for primitive sites; $20 with hookups. All year. 100 sites. Tbls, toilets, cfga, drkg wtr, dump ($5), cold showers. Fishing, swimming, boating(l).

Fishing tip: Lake Bridgeport is among the best places in Texas to catch flathead catfish. 40-pounders are common on trotlines in the sloughs and creeks of the north end near Wise Park, so try tightline fishing there.

CHICOTA (56)

Lamar Point   **$7**
Corps of Engineers
Pat Mayse Lake
Near Chicota from FM 1499, N on FM 1500. $7. All year; 14-day limit. 9 sites. Tbls, toilets, cfga, drkg wtr, dump, beach. Swimming, boating(l), fishing, dump. Limited facilities in winter.

Fishing tip: If you'd like to try for this lake's hybrid bass, use the same bates and techniques you'd use for white bass.

Pat Mayse East   **$6.50**
Corps of Engineers
Pay Mayse Lake
Three-fourths mi W of Chicota on FM 197; S on CR 88. $6.50 with federal Senior Pass; others pay $13. All year; 14-day limit. 26 sites with wtr/elec. Tbls, flush toilets, cfga, drkg wtr, dump, beach. Boating(l), fishing, swimming.

Pat Mayse West $10
Corps of Engineers
Pay Mayse Lake
2.3 mi W of Chicota on FM 197, then S on gravel rd. $10 at 10 non-hookup sites; $15 at 83 sites with elec/wtr ($7.50 with federal Senior Pass). 65-ft RVs. All year; 14-day limit. Tbls, flush toilets, cfga, drkg wtr, elec($), beach, dump. Fishing, swimming, boating(l). Limited facilities in winter. 2-night minimum stay on weekends.

Sanders Cove $10
Corps of Engineers
Pay Mayse Lake
S of Chicota on FM 906, across dam on S side. $10 at 4 non-elec sites; $15 at 88 sites with wtr & elec ($7.50 with federal Senior Pass). All year; 14-day limit. Tbls, pavilion, flush toilets, elec($), beach, showers, dump, cfga, drkg wtr. Fishing, swimming, boating(l). Limited facilities in winter. 2-night minimum stay on weekends.

CHILDRESS (57)

Childress City Park $10
Qtr mi N on Main St from courthouse. $10. All year; 3-day limit. 20 sites. Tbls, flush toilets, cfga, drkg wtr, shelter, elec. Pool, playground, tennis, ballfields. Historical marker for Goodnight Trail (extension of famous cattle trail). On tributary of Groesbeck Creek.

CIRCLEVILLE (58)

Pecan Grove Unit FREE
Granger State Wildlife
Management Area
6 mi E of Circleville on FM 1331 to below the dam; at Granger Lake. All year; 14-day limit. Primitive undesignated sites; no facilities, no drkg wtr. Fishing, hiking, biking, hunting, boating. Permit required.

Taylor Campground $12
Corps of Engineers
Granger Lake
From Circleville at SR 95, 9 mi NE on FM 1331, then NW to park. $12. 3/1-9/30; 14-day limit. 48 sites with wtr/elec (4 doubles for $18) & some wilderness sites (50-ft RV limit). Tbls, flush toilets, showers, cfga, drkg wtr, dump, elec. Hiking trail, fishing, boating(l). Launch fee for non-campers. 2-night minimum stay on weekends.
Fishing tip: Best time for crappies in Granger Lake is January through mid-Feb. Try entire SE shoreline from lower end of Taylor Park to just above Wilson H. Fox Park. For white bass, fish outside the impoundment on Willis Creek between mid-Feb and mid-Apr. Best bet for bass is in up-river wooded areas.

CISCO (59)

Lake Cisco City Park FREE
4 mi N of Cisco off SR 6. Free. All year. Primitive camping without facilities at 445-acre lake. No drkg wtr. Fishing, boating, mini-golf, rockhounding.
Fishing tip: Excllent structure provides very good largemouth bass fishing. Fall is best to fish this lake for bass, but there's good crappie action in the spring and summer using jigs and minnows. Catch catfish around Sandy Creek. Water very clear, so use light line.

CLARENDON (60)

Lakeside Marina $10-12
Greenbelt Lake
Greenbelt Municipal
and Industrial Water Authority
3 mi N of Clarendon on SR 70; left on CR N. $10-12. All year. 55 RV sites, $10 with elec (wtr available) at Sandy Creek area; $12 with elec/wtr at Kincaid Park. Tbls, flush toilets, cfga, drkg wtr. Boating(l), fishing, hiking, waterskiing. $2 per person access fee charged daily; boat access $2.
Fishing tip: This 2,600-acre lake is well known for its bass fishing. Use plastic worms, spinnerbaits, crankbaits. Focus on sunken trees, vegetation, drop-offs, ledges. Also catch walleyes along the dam and around rock and sand points or drop-offs. Schools of white bass often can be found in open-water areas of the lake's arms.

Primitive Shoreline Camping $2
Greenbelt Lake
Donley County Park
3 mi N of Clarendon on SR 70; camp in undesignated areas around the lake. Camp free, but $2 per person daily permit required. Tbls, cfga, toilets, no drkg wtr. Boating(l), fishing.
Fishing tip: About 60% of the lake shoreline is accessible to bank fishing. Carol Creek and Kelly Creek offer especially good crappie fishing from shore; both are no-wake boat areas. Fish the flooded timber in spring and fall and along the dam's rip-rap in summer. Use jigs and minnows.

COLEMAN (62)

Elm Creek Village $5
6 mi S of Coleman on SR 206; 4.5 mi W on US 67; 13.8 mi S on FM 503; 6.5 mi W on FM 1929; near Kennedy Recreation Area. $5 base. All year. Base fee for activities fee including primitive camping; no facilities. $16 for RVs with elec/wtr; $20 full hookups. Tbls, flush toilets, cfga, drkg wtr, dump, showers. Fishing, boating(l), waterskiing.

Kennedy Recreation Area $5
Colorado River Municipal Water District
6 mi S of Coleman on SR 206; 4.5 mi W on US 67; 13.8 mi S on FM 503; 6.5 mi W on FM 1929; on O.H. Ivie Reservoir. $5 base. All year; 7-day limit. Base fee for primitive camping. 29 sites with hookups($); 70-acre primitive area. Tbls, toilets,cfga, no drkg wtr, dump, bait, snack bar, store. Swimming, fishing, boating(l). Annual permit available.

Padgitt Recreation Area $5
Colorado River Municipal Water District
6 mi N of Coleman on SR 206; 4.6 mi W on US 67; 11 mi S on FM 503; 7 mi W on FM 2134; on O.H. Ivie Reservoir. $5. All year; 7-day limit. 15 primitive sites. Tbls, toilets, cfga, no drkg wtr. Boating(l), fishing, swimming.

Press Morris City Park $10
14 mi N of Coleman on US 283; 2 mi W on CR 1274. $10 base for primitive sites; $15 for RV sites with elec; $20, full hookups. All year; 14-day limit. 56 primitive sites; 13 with hookups. Tbls, toilets, cfga, drkg wtr, elec. Swimming; picnicking; fishing; boating (ld); hiking; waterskiing; biking trails.

COLMESNEIL (63)

Lake Tejas Campground $5
Colmesneil School District
1 mi E of Colmesneil on N side of FM 256. $5 base. 5/15-LD. Base fee for primitive sites; $15 with hookups & developed shelter areas. 35 sites. Tbls, cfga, drkg wtr, toilets. Fishing($), pedalboat rental, swimming($), hiking trails, games ($). Concession.

COLORADO CITY (64)

Fisher City Park FREE
From I-20, 9 mi S on SR 208; 3 mi W on local rd. On 1,560-acre Champion Lake. Free. $20 deposit required for gate key. Fees may be re-implemented in the future. All year; 14-day limit. 23 sites (28-ft RV limit). Tbls, flush toilets, cfga, drkg wtr, elec (may not be available), shelters. Bike area, fishing, swimming, boating(ldr). See Ruddick entry.

Lake Colorado City State Park $12
11 mi SW of Colorado City on CR 2836. $12 for 34 primitive sites with wtr; $15 for 69 sites with elec/wtr; $20 for 9 premium pull-through sites with elec/wtr. All year; 14-day limit. Tbls, flush toilets, cfga, drkg wtr, showers, dump, playgrounds, picnic areas. Fishing, swimming, boating(l), waterskiing, nature trail. $4 per person entry fee.
Fishing tip: Summer is a good time to catch channel catfish up to 19 pounds at this lake. Use cut perch, shrimp or crawfish or cheese bait while fishing at night.

Ruddick Public Park FREE
From I-20 near Colorado City, 14 blocks S on SR 208; 5 blocks E on 7th St; on Lone Wolf Creek. Free. 90 primitive sites. ; $7.50 for 7 wtr & elec sites; $10 for 40 sites with full hookups. All year; 14-day limit. Tbls, flush toilets showers (Apr-Sept), shelters, cfga, pool, playground, amphitheater. Volleyball, swimming, fishing (seniors and children only), biking & nature trails. Fees previously were $7.50 for sites with wtr/elec & $10 for full hookups, but until electrical problems are resolved, the park will operate without fees.

TEXAS

COMANCHE (65)

Comanche City Park   **$8**
On W edge of Comanche just S of Hwy 67/377 West. $8 for sites with wtr/elec; $15, full hookups. All year. 40 sites. Flush toilets, tbls, cfga, drkg wtr, elec, no showers, playground, pool. Jogging track, hiking trails, soccer, swimming.

CORPUS CHRISTI (69)

Bird Island   **$5**
Padre Island National Seashore
SE of Corpus Christi on Hwy 358 to headquarters; SE on Park Rd 22, then W to campground. Camp free, but $5 daily or $10 annual use fee plus park entrance fee. Primitive sites; tbls, toilets, cfga, no drkg wtr. Fishing, swimming, beachcombing.

Labonte City Park   **FREE**
Exit I-37 at Nueces River Park exit; follow signs. Camp free by permit for 3 days & 2 nights; second permit may be issued; no more permits for 1 month. Primitive sites, no hookups. Tbls, toilets, cfga, drkg wtr, visitor center. Fishing, hiking, picnicking.

Lake Corpus Christi State Park   **$10**
35 mi NW of Corpus Christi on I-37; 4 mi S on SR 359; N on FM 1068. $10 for 60 sites with wtr hookups; $16 for 23 sites with elec/wtr; $18 for full hookups. All year; 14-day limit. Tbls, flush toilets, cfga, drkg wtr, showers, dump, playgrounds, picnic areas, pavilion, fish cleaning shelters. Fishing (lighted piers), boating(rd), canoeing(r), birdwatching, swimming. 21,000-acre lake. $4 per person entry fee.
Fishing tip: Although this lake has good populations of fish, catching them is usually tough; ask locals for advice on where to go and lures to use.

Malaquite Beach   **$8**
Padre Island National Seashore
SE of Corpus Christi on Hwy 538 to headquarters; SE on Park Rd 22 to visitor center area. $8. All year. 42 sites. Tbls, toilets, cfga, drkg wtr, rinse showers, dump. Swimming, fishing, beachcombing, shelling. $10 weekly entry fee.

North Beach   **$10**
Padre Island National Seashore
SE of Corpus Christi on Hwy 358 to headquarters; SE on Park Rd 22 to beach access rd. Camp free, but $10 weekly entry fee. All year. 45 sites. Tbls, toilets, cfga, no drkg wtr. Swimming, fishing, beachcombing, shelling, picnicking.

Padre Island Balli Park   **$10**
Nueces County
From Park Rd 53, 2.8 mi SW on Park Rd 22; qtr mi E on local rd. On Gulf of Mexico. $10 base. All year; 3-day limit. Base fee for primitive camping; $18 for 66 sites with elec

& wtr. 60 tent sites; 40-acre beach primitive area with cold rinse shower. Flush toilets, showers, tbls, bathhouse, laundry, snack bar, dump & wtr fill ($4). Swimming, fishing (1,200-foot lighted pier with tackle shop), boating.

South Beach   **$10**
Padre Island National Seashore
SE on Hwy 358 from Corpus Christi to headquarters; SE on Park Rd 22 to end. Camp free, but $10 weekly entry fee. All year. 45 sites. Tbls, toilets, cfga, no drkg wtr. Swimming, fishing, beachcombing, shelling, picnicking.

CORSICANA (70)

Richland Creek   **FREE**
State Wildlife Management Area
25 mi S of Corsicana on US 287; 2 mi S on FM 488. Free. All year; 14-day limit. Primitive designated campsites; no facilities, no drkg wtr. Hunting, biking, fishing, hiking. Horseback riding. Use permit required. 13,796 acres.

COTULLA (71)

Chaparral   **FREE**
State Wildlife Management Area
12 mi S of Cotulla (about 100 mi SW of San Antonio); 8 mi W on FM 133. Free. 4/1-8/31; 14-day limit. Primitive sites. Tbls, flush toilets, showers, cfga, drkg wtr. Birdwatching, hiking, driving & walking nature trails, hunting, biking. 15,200 acres.

CRANE (72)

Crane County Campground   **FREE**
Half mi N of Crane on US 385; half mi W on Airport Rd. free. All year; 3-day limit. 5 sites (25-ft RV limit). Toilets, cfga, free elec & wtr. Picnicking; golf nearby.

CROCKETT (73)

Mission Tejas State Park   **$8**
20 mi NE of Crockett on SR 7; at Weches. $8 for 2 sites with wtr hookups; $10 for 10 RV sites with wtr/elec; $12 for 10 sites with full hookups ($70 weekly Dec-Feb). All year; 14-day limit. Tbls, flush toilets, cfga, drkg wtr, showers, playgrounds, pavilion, picnic areas, dump. Historical features. Hiking trails, biking, fishing, nature trail. $2 per person entry fee.

Ratcliff Lake   **$10**
Davy Crockett National Forest
20 mi NE of Crockett on SR 7; half mi N on FR 520 (1 mi W of Ratcliff). $10 base. All year; 14-day limit. Base fee for primitive sites ($5 with federal Senior Pass); $15 for elec/wtr ($10 with federal Senior Pass). 77 sites. Tbls, flush toilets, cold showers, cfga, drkg wtr, dump, amphitheater, shelter, beach, snack

bar. Swimming, picnicking, fishing, boating(l--elec mtrs), hiking, ca-noeing(r). Trailhead to 20-mile 4-C Hiking Trail. Forest's only developed campground. $3 day-use fee.

CROSBYTON (74)

Campground #1   **$4**
White River Water Authority
13.5 mi S of US 82 on FM 651; 8.6 mi E & S on FM 2794; on White River Lake. $4 (includes $2 daily entry permit per person). 20 primitive sites; 25-ft RV limit. All year; 7-day limit. Tbls, flush toilets, cfga, drkg wtr. Fishing, boating(l), swimming. Boat permit $2.
Fishing tip: White River Lake produces good catches of bass; the lake's record is 8.69 pounds

Campground #2   **$4**
White River Water Authority
13.5 mi S of US 82 on FM 651; 8.6 mi E & S on FM 2794; 1.5 mi NE on local rd; on White River Lake. $4 (includes $2 daily entry permit per person); $7 with wtr & elec hookups. 35 sites; 25-ft RV limit. All year; 7-day limit. Tbls, flush toilets, cfga, drkg wtr. Fishing, boating, swimming. $2 boat permit.

Campground #3   **$4**
White River Water Authority
13.5 mi S of US 82 on FM 651; 7.2 mi E & S on FM 2794; N on Lake Rd; on White River Lake. $4 (includes $2 daily entry permit per person). No hookups. 25 primitive sites; 25-ft RV limit. All year; 7-day limit. Tbls, flush toilets, cfga, drkg wtr. Fishing, boating(l), swimming. Boat permit $2.

Campground #4   **$4**
White River Water Authority
13.5 mi S of US 82 on FM 651; 7.2 mi E & S on FM 2794; N on Lake Rd 5 mi past Campground #3; on White River Lake. $4 (includes $2 daily entry permit per person). Primitive undesignated sites; no facilities. All year; 7-day limit. Fishing, boating, swimming.

City Park   **FREE**
Crosbyton Overnite RV Parking
Crosbyton Chamber of Commerce
US 82 at E city limit. Free. All year; 2-day limit; $10 thereafter. 8 sites. Toilets, drkg wtr, basic dump (no flush), cfga, elec. Pool($), playground. Field check in 2004 revealed open grounds on 3 elec outlets. Restrooms closed in winter.

DAINGERFIELD (75)

Daingerfield State Park   **$12**
2 mi E of Daingerfield on SR 49. $12 for 30 sites with elec/wtr; $18 for 10 sites with full hookups. All year; 14-day limit. Tbls, flush toilets, cfga, drkg wtr, showers, dump, playgrounds, picnic areas, bathhouse, store. Handicap access. Swimming, fishing (pier), boating(lrd), canoeing, hiking trail. 551 acres on Lake Daingerfield. Entry fee $2 per person.

DALHART (76)

Rita Blanca Lake $3
Dallam County & City Park
1 mi S on US 87 from jct with US 54; 1.5 mi SW on FM 281. On Rita Blanca Lake. $3 base without hookups; $12 full hookups. 31 sites plus 1,000-acre primitive area. All year; 14-day limit. Tbls, toilets, cfga, drkg wtr, dump, elec($). Groceries, ice, snack bar, picnic shelters. Fishing, boating(l), bike trail, horseshoes, softball, playground. Park now operated by city of Dalhart.

DAWSON (77)

Brushy Prairie Park FREE
Corps of Engineers
Navarro Mills Lake
4.3 mi E of Dawson on SR 31; 4 mi N on FM 667; left for 2 mi on FM744; 2 mi S on FM 1578, then left on access rd. Free. All year; 14-day limit. 10 sites. Tbls, toilets, cfga, no drkg wtr. Boating(l), fishing, picnicking.

Pecan Point $8
Corps of Engineers
Navarro Mills Lake
3.5 mi NE of Dawson on SR 31; 3.2 mi N on FM 667; SW on FM 744; SE on FM 1578. $8 without hookups; $10 with wtr & 50-amp elec. 4/1-9/30; 14-day limit. 35 sites (30 without hookups); 65-ft RVs. Pavilion, tbls, toilets, cfga, drkg wtr, dump, elec($). Boating (l), fishing. $4 dump fee for non-campers.

Wolf Creek Park $12
Corps of Engineers
Navarro Mills Lake
Near Dawson, from FM 639, 2.2 mi SW on FM 744; 2 mi SE on FM 1578. $12 base. 4/1-9/30; 14-day limit. Base fee for non-elec sites; $14 with elec; $24 double non-elec ($7 & $12 with federal Senior Pass). 72 sites (22 non-elec). Pavilion, tbls, flush toilets, cfga, drkg wtr, showers, elec($), dump. Boating(l), fishing.

DECATUR (78)

Black Creek Lake Park $2
Caddo/LBJ National Grasslands
7 mi N of US 380 on Farm 730; 1.9 mi W on local rd. On Black Creek Lake. $2 use fee. All year; 14-day limit. Open camping on 2 acres (about 7 sites). Tents or small RVs. Toilets, cfga, no drkg wtr. Fishing, boating(l); no swimming or shooting.
Fishing tip: Catches from this 35-acre lake include a 12-pound largemouth bass and a 29-pound blue catfish.

Tadra Point Trailhead Camp $4
Caddo/LBJ National Grasslands
10 mi N of Decatur on FM 730; W on CR 2461 (Cottonwood Cemetery Rd); bear right at fork on CR 2690 for 3 mi, then 3 mi left on FR 900. $4 use fee. 20 primitive sites. All year; 14-day limit. Pit toilets, cfga, tbls, no drkg wtr. Bike & bridle trails, boating(l), fishing.

DEL RIO (79)

Amistad National Recreation Area
3 mi N of Del Rio on US 90 W to National Park Service headquarters bldg. Camping restricted to 5 designated areas along shoreline below maximum flood pool level. Boating; fishing; swimming; scuba diving; waterskiing; hunting. Dump & drkg wtr at Diablo East. Headquarters bldg (also has wtr) open M-F, 8 am to 5 pm, all year; 9 am to 6 pm weekends (Nov-Mar, 8 am to 5 pm). Interpretive programs; schedules available at headquarters. Donation boxes are provided at the free camping areas, with funds earmarked for education and facilities improvements. $4 daily lake use fee charged for boats.

Devils River $6
State Natural Area
43 mi N of Del Rio on US 277; 22 mi W on Dolan Creek Rd. $6 plus $2 per person activity use fee. 7 primitive sites for tents or self-contained RVs. No facilities, no trash service; drkg wtr nearby. Also 4 primitive canoe sites, $6. Pictographs, hiking trail, guided hikes & tours($). 19,988 acres. Nearest service station, 25 mi. Entry fee $3 per person.
Fishing tip: Remember that a Mexican fishing license is required if you fish in the portion of Lake Amistad that is in Mexico. The Devils River area is one of the lake's best sections for big catfish; use cut baits, worms or shrimp.

Governor's Landing $8
Amistad National Recreation Area
9 mi E of Del Rio on US 90 to Amistad Dam; N on dirt rd. Follow rd along railroad. Go under Hwy 90 bridge to campground. $8. All year; 15-day limit. 15 sites (RVs under 29 ft). Tbls, toilets, cfga, drkg wtr. Store. Dump nearby. Fishing, swimming, boating, waterskiing, scuba diving. Very popular. Has roped off swim area, fishing docks, and amphitheater.
Fishing tip: The dam area is a good place to find smallmouth bass -- particularly the rocky areas. Use small crankbaits, small spinnerbaits and crayfish.

North Highway 277 $4
Amistad National Recreation Area
9 mi N of Del Rio on US 277. 3.5 mi on Hwy 90 W to US 277; turn off, travel N over San Pedro Bridge 1 mi; turn right to campground. $4. All year; 15-day limit. 17 sites. Flush toilets, tbls, cfga, no drkg wtr. Dump nearby. Picnicking; fishing; swimming; boating; waterskiing.
Fishing tip: After a rain, fish near the creeks and arroyos for catfish, using nightcrawlers and crayfish. Catfish bite best in this lake when high winds muddy the shallows; at those times, try shorline flats or wind-swept points. In winter, fish 80-100 feet where the Rio Grande channel drops off.

Rock Quarry $2
Organized Campground
Amistad National Recreation Area
By reservation only. $2 per person per day. All year; 7-day limit. Tbls, cfga, toilets, 1 large site with a shelter. Within 5 miles, Diablo East Marina, Ranger Station. Dump, water, gas supplies. Fina station on Hwy 90 W. Picnicking; fishing; swimming; hiking; waterskiing; boating; canoeing; rockhounding; scuba diving. Pets on leash. This campground has to be reserved. Designated for at least 32 persons. Reserve by calling 830-775-7491 or in person at park headquarters on Hwy 90 at Del Rio.

San Pedro Flats $4
Amistad National Recreation Area
6 mi W of Del Rio on US 90 to Spur 454, N on dirt rd. $4. All year; 14-day limit. 35 sites (RVs under 29 ft). Tbls, toilets, cfga, no drkg wtr. Within 5 mi: Diablo East sanitary dump; Diablo East Marina. Picnicking; fishing; swimming; boating; waterskiing. Boats can be launched when lake is up.
Fishing tip: In Amistad, walleye congregate near the dam rip-rap and on the edges of deep water during late winter and early spring. San Pedro Canyon contains excllent populations of catfish; use cut baits, shrimp or nightcrawlers.

San Pedro Organized Camp $2
Amistad National Recreation Area
By reservation only. $2 per person per day. All year; 7-day limit. Tbls, cfga, toilets, 1 large site with shelter. Within 5 mi: Diablo East Marina, Ranger Station. Water, dump. Picnicking; fishing; swimming; hiking; waterskiing; boating; canoeing. Available for groups of 20-plus. Reserve by calling 830-775-7491 or in person at park headquarters on Hwy 90 at Del Rio.

Seminole Canyon $10
State Historical Park
42 mi NW of Del Rio on US 90; E of Pecos River (9 mi W of Comstock). $10 for 8 sites with wtr; $14 for 23 sites with elec/wtr hookups. All year; 14-day limit. Tbls, flush toilets, cfga, drkg wtr, dump, showers, interpretive displays, canyon tours, store. Picnicking, hiking trail. Indian pictographs, mountain biking. Judge Roy Bean Visitor Center at Langtry. Entry fee $3 per person.

Spur 406 $4
Amistad National Recreation Area
20 mi W of Del Rio on US 9; 4 mi S on Spur 406. $4. All year; 14-day limit. 8 sites (RVs under 29 ft). Flush toilets, no drkg wtr, dump, cfga. Fishing; swimming; boating; waterskiing; boat ramp. This campground is more isolated than the others.
Fishing tip: This area produces good catches of panfish and provides a lot of fun for kids. Use simple cane poles and live bait such as worms, crickets and grubs.

DENISON (80)

Damsite Area $10
Corps of Engineers
Lake Texoma
4 mi N of Denison on SR 75-A; on Texoma & Red River above and below dam. $10 for 7 non-elec sites; $16 for 20 sites with wtr & elec; $8 with federal Senior Pass. Free primitive camping 11/1-3/31. 14-day limit. 65-ft RVs. Pavilion, tbls, flush toilets, cfga, drkg wtr, elec($), showers, dump. Elec & wtr may be off during free period. Boating(l), fishing, picnicking.

Fishing tip: For excellent blue and channel catfish angling, try Texoma's Pecan and Soldier Creeks, drifting cut baits. Or, ask locals for directions to a place called "Slick 'Em Slough," where blues and yellows of 10 pounds or more hang out.

Eisenhower State Park $12
Near Denison from SR 75A, 2 mi N on FM 1310 & Park Rd 20; on Lake Texoma. $12 for 34 tent sites & 11 overflow sites; sites with hookups, $14-17 (higher on holiday weekends). Seniors pay $8-9 for hookup sites during 11/1-2/28. All year; 14-day limit. 179 total sites. Tbls, flush toilets, cfga, drkg wtr, showers, dump, playgrounds, picnic areas, store. Fishing (piers), boating(ldr), multi-purpose trail, minibike trail, mountain bike trails, swimming, nature program. 457 acres. $3 per person entry fee.

Fishing tip: Although best known as a largemouth and striped bass lake, Texoma has an excellent population of smallmouth bass. Search for them around rock ledges, gravel bars and sandy and rocky beaches. Use small, crayfish-color crankbaits and spinnerbaits.

DOUGLASVILLE (82)

Jackson Creek FREE
Corps of Engineers
Wright Patman Lake
From SR 8 at Douglasville, 4.1 mi E on SR 77; 1.5 mi N on FM 2791; 3 mi N. Free. All year; 14-day limit. 10 sites (25-ft RV limit). Tbls, toilets, cfga, drkg wtr. Fishing, boating (l).

DUMAS (83)

Blue Creek Bridge Public Use Area $4
Lake Meredith
National Recreation Area
S of Dumas on US 87/287; E 15.6 mi on Farm 1913; E 2.5 mi on local rd. Camp free, but $4 daily boat fee. All year; 14-day limit. Undeveloped backcountry camping area. Toilets, cfga, no drkg wtr. Boating, fishing, horseback riding. Off-road vehicles okay.

Fishing tip: In 2000, a new lake record bass, 11.61 pounds, was caught; then it was broken that fall when a California fly fisherman hooked a 14.14-pounder from the stilling basin below the dam. Locals claim the lake is full of bass 5-10 pounds.

Blue East Boat-In Camp $4
Lake Meredith
National Recreation Area
S of Dumas on US 87/287; E 15.6 mi on FM 1913; E 2.6 mi on local rd to Blue West PUA; launch boat for access across bay to Blue East. Camp free, but $4 daily boat fee. Primitive tent camping; no facilities. Boating, fishing.

Blue West Public Use Area $4
Lake Meredith
National Recreation Area
S of Dumas on US 87/287; E 15.6 mi on Farm 1913; E. 2.6 mi on local rd. Camp free, but $4 daily boat fee. All year; 14-day limit. Undeveloped canyon rim camping area; about 40 sites. Toilets, cfga, no drkg wtr, shelters, dump. No firewood. Boating(l), fishing, picnicking.

Chimney Hollow Public Use Area $4
Lake Meredith
National Recreation Area
S of Dumas on US 87/287; 15.6 mi E on FM 1913; E 2 mi on local rd. Camp free, but $4 daily boat fee. All year; 14-day limit. Undeveloped shoreline camping. Toilets, cfga, tbls, no drkg wtr. Fishing, boating. Dump, boat ramp at nearby Blue West PUA.

Plum Creek $4
Lake Meredith
National Recreation Area
Approx 19 mi on TX 152 from Dumas; 3 mi on TX 1913 to Plum Creek Rd. Camp free, but $4 daily boat fee. All year; 14-day limit. 15 primitive backcountry sites. Tbls, toilets, no drkg wtr. Dump. Hunting; picnicking; fishing; boating(ld); waterskiing; bank fishing. Shallow-wtr launching ramp. Horse rails, pens.

Sandy Point Boat-in Camp $4
Lake Meredith
National Recreation Area
Approx 19 mi on TX 152 from Dumas; 3 mi on TX 1913 to Plum Creek Rd; from Plum Creek PUA, boat NE on lake to Sandy Point. Camp free, but $4 daily boat fee. All year; 14-day limit. Primitive undeveloped tent camping; no facilities. Boating, fishing.

Texoma City Park FREE
500 W First Street in Dumas (US 87 N). Free. Spring-Fall; 1-day limit. 24 RV sites, some without hookups. Tbls, cfga, toilets, elec, wtr, dump. Picnicking; swimming; biking, rec hall. Donations accepted.

Yerby's MH & RV Park $12
Qtr mi E on 16th St from jct with US 87/287; at 16th & Meredith in Dumas. $12 base. All year. 44 RV sites with hookups; no tents. Tbls, toilets, cfga, drkg wtr.

EDNA (84)

Lake Texana State Park $10
6 mi E of Edna on SR 111; on Lake Texana. $10 for 55 sites with wtr hookups; $15 for 86 sites with elec/wtr (seniors get $2 discounts Mon-thurs). All year; 14-day limit. Tbls, flush toilets, cfga, drkg wtr, showers, dump, playgrounds, picnic areas, pavilion. Fishing (lighted piers), swimming, boating(lr), canoeing(r), sailboating, hiking, birdwatching. $3 per person entry fee.

Mustang Wilderness Campground $1
Lavaca-Navidad River Authority
8 mi E of Edna on US 59 to Ganado; 1 mi on Loop 521; 2.2 mi S on FM 1593; half mi on CR 249; on Lake Texana. $1 per person (honor system). 28 primitive tent sites. No facilities except cfga; site access by trail or boat. Hiking, fishing, swimming, boating(l).

EL PASO (85)

Arvey Park (Private) $12
Near El Paso, from I-10 exit 30, 4 mi N on Lee Trevino Dr; three-fourths mi E on Montana Ave. $12 base without hookups; $14 for wtr & elec; $15 full hookups. 42 sites. Tbls, cfga, drkg wtr, no restrooms.

Franklin Mountains State Park $8
In El Paso, N on US 84 from I-10; left on Loop 375. $8 for 5 self-contained RV sites & 5 walk-in tent sites. All year; 14-day limit. Tbls, pit toilets, cfga, drkg wtr, store, cfga, tbls. Hiking & bridle trails, rock climbing, ranger tours($). Entry fee $4 per person.

Hueco Tanks $12
State Historical Park
35 mi E of El Paso on US 62 & US 180; 8 mi N on FM 2775, following signs. $12 for 3 sites with wtr; $14 for 17 sites with wtr/elec ($16 for 50 amp). All year; 14-day limit. Tbls, flush toilets, drkg wtr, showers, dump ($5), amphitheater, picnic areas. Rock climbing, trails, guided weekend tours. 3500 Indian pictographs. Solid fuels prohibited; only containerized fuel cooking permitted. $4 per person entry fee.

EUSTACE (86)

Purtis Creek State Park $6
3 mi N of Eustace on FM 316. $6-10 for hike-in tent sites & overflow camping; $16 for 59 RV sites with elec/wtr. All year; 14-day limit. Tbls, flush toilets, cfga, drkg wtr, showers, dump, playground, picnic area, fish cleaning shelter, store. Boating(ld), fishing (lighted piers), hiking trail, swimming, canoeing. $5 per day boating fee (50-boat maximum). $2 per person entry fee.

FAIRFIELD (88)

Fairfield Lake State Park $6
6 mi NE of Fairfield on FM 488; E on FM 2570; access on Park Rd 64. $6 for hike-in tent

sites (closed Dec-Feb); $12 for 35 premium waterfront sites with wtr, tbls, cfga (closed 12/1-2/10); $18-22 for 100 RV sites with hookups. All year; 14-day limit. Tbls, flush toilets, cfga, drkg wtr, showers, dump, playgrounds, picnic areas, amphitheater, dining hall. Fishing (lighted pier), boating(l), nature program, waterskiing, swimming, nature trail. 1,460 acres. $4 per person entry fee.

Fishing tip: Try an unusl fishing adventure by going after Fairfield Lake's saltwater redfish (or red drum), a species that's been successfully introduced into the lake and is providing excellent angling, with plenty of fish in the 10-15 pound area. The state record is a 23-pounder caught in 1993.

Travel tip: View wintering bald eagles each Sat during Nov-Feb by boarding a 2-level tour boat that cruises the lake sections where the eagles feed.

FALCON HEIGHTS (89)

Falcon State Park   **$4**
3.5 mi SW of Falcon Heights on FM 2098; N on Park Rd 46. $4 base. All year; 14-day limit. Base fee for 54 walk-in sites with wtr nearby, cfga, tbls; $12 for 31 pull-through sites with wtr/elec; $14-18 wtih full hookups. Tbls, flush toilets, cfga, drkg wtr, showers, dump, playgrounds, picnic areas, rec hall, fish cleaning shelters. Fishing, boating(l), waterskiing, swimming, birdwatching, nature programs, 3-mi circular hiking & biking trail, 1-mi nature trail. On 87,000-acre Falcon Reservoir. $2 per person entry fee.

Fishing tip: In summer, fish for bass off rocky points using chartreuse and watermelon plastic worms rigged Carolina-style.

FLOYDADA (90)

Wayne Russell   **FREE**
Municipal RV Park
In town at First St (US 70) and Taft St on N sice of Floydada. Camp free 3 nights; $5 thereafter. 5-day limit, but may be extended with permission. 32 sites (16 full hookups). Tbls, flush toilets & showers at pool house, cfga, drkg wtr, dump, pool($). Swimming, tennis, baseball, playground.

FORT DAVIS (91)

Davis Mountains State Park   **$6**
4 mi W of Fort Davis on SR 118 (30 mi NW of Alpine). $6 for primitive hike-in tent sites; $9 for 33 primitive sites with wtr (some shared); $15-20 for RV sites with hookups. All year; 14-day limit. Tbls, flush toilets, cfga, drkg wtr, showers, dump, playgrounds, interpretive displays, picnic areas, amphitheater, restaurant. Hiking trails, recreation program, horseback riding, mountain biking. 1,860 acres on Keesey Creek. N half of park is a designated special use area, the Limpia Canyon Primitive Area, with fees; it includes 10 mi of backcountry hiking trails with primitive campsites & a bird banding station. Note:

water pressure regulator needed for water hookup. $3 per person entry fee.

Overland Trail Campground   **$10**
1 mi S of jct of Hwys 17 & 118 on Main St. $10 base for primitive sites; $17 for vans & cabovers with hookups; $19-21 full hookups. 27 sites. Tbls, flush toilets, cfga, drkg wtr, CATV($), showers, coin laundry. Good Sam discounts.

FORT STOCKTON (92)

A & M Camper Park   **$10**
2 blocks N of Bus I-10 on Gatlin St, E end of Fort Stockton. $10 ($50 weekly, $160 monthly). Tbls, flush toilets, showers, cfga, drkg wtr, elec, CATV. Small, quiet park.

Comanche Land RV Park (Private)   **$12**
At Fort Stockton, I-10 exit 257 E on North Service Rd, next to golf course. $11.95 for 57 sites with full hookups. 20 sites. Tbls, flush toilets, showers, cfga, drkg wtr.

I-10 RV Park (Private)   **$10**
At Fort Stockton, half mi off I-10 (exit 259). $10. All year. 30 sites with full hookups. Tbls, flush toilets, showers, cfga, drkg wtr.

FRISCO (94)

Hidden Cove Park   **$8**
The Colony Lake Parks
6 mi E on Hwy 121 from jct with I-35E; 5 mi N on FM 423; 3.1 mi W on Hackberry Rd, following signs. $8 for undesignated tent sites; $10 for designated sites; $16 with elec/wtr; $23 full hookups. All year. 50 sites. Tbls, hookups($), flush toilets, cfga, drkg wtr, playground, showers, dump. Entry fee charged.

FRITCH (95)

Bates Canyon Public Use Area   **$4**
Lake Meredith
National Recreation Area
6 mi W & SW of Fritch on TX 136; 3 mi on Alibates Rd to jct; right fork to camping area. Camp free, but $4 daily boat fee. All year; 14-day limit. Primitive shoreline camping. Tbls, toilets, cfga, no drkg wtr. Boating(l), fishing.

Cedar Canyon   **$4**
Lake Meredith
National Recreation Area
6 mi NE of Fritch and 3 mi W of Sanford; take marked co rds from either Fritch or Sanford. Camp free, but $4 daily boat fee.All year; 14-day limit. Semi-developed with random shoreline camping. Flush toilets, cfga, dump, drkg wtr. Boating; waterskiing; hunting. Deep wtr launching ramp, courtesy dock. Opportunity for camping varies with the lake level.

Fritch Fortress Public Use Area   **$4**
Lake Meredith
National Recreation Area
E of Fritch on Eagle Blvd; N on co rd to camp-

ground. Camp free, but $4 daily boat fee. All year; 14-day limit. 10 undeveloped canyon rim sites. Tbls, shelters, toilets, drkg wtr. No firewood. Picnicking; fishing; boating(ld); waterskiing; hunting. Deep wtr launching ramp, courtesy dock. Store, amphitheater.

Harbor Bay   **$4**
Lake Meredith
National Recreation Area
2 mi NW of Fritch on TX 136. Camp free, but $4 daily boat fee. All year; 14-day limit. Undeveloped primitive shoreline camping; dump nearby. Tbls, toilets, cfga, shelters, dump. Boating(ld).

McBride Canyon   **$4**
Lake Meredith
National Recreation Area
6 mi W & SW of Fritch on TX 136; 3 mi on Alibates Rd to jct; left-hand fork to undeveloped backcountry camping area. Camp free, but $4 daily boat fee. All year; 14-day limit. Tbls, toilets, cfga, no drkg wtr. Dump. Hunting; picnicking; fishing; waterskiing. No lake access.

Travel tip: McBride is the closest campground to Alibates Flint Quarries National Monument. Daily tours available at 10 and 2 MD-LD; entrance to the monument is by guided tour only.

Mullinaw Creek   **$4**
Lake Meredith
National Recreation Area
6 mi W & SW of Fritch on TX 136; 3 mi on Alibates Rd to undeveloped backcountry camping area. Camp free, but $4 daily boat fee. All year; 14-day limit. Tbls, toilets, cfga, no wtr. Dump at McBride Canyon. Hunting, picnicking, fishing, waterskiing, horseback riding (corrals).

Sanford-Yake Public Use Area   **$4**
Lake Meredith
National Recreation Area
1 mi E of Fritch on TX 136; 4 mi N on TX 687; W to campground. Camp free, but $4 daily boat fee. All year; 14-day limit. 40 sites, some with shade shelters. Flush toilets, tbls, cfga, drkg wtr, snack bar. Store, food, ice nearby. Dump. Picnicking; boating; waterskiing; hunting; fishing. Deep wtr launching ramp and courtesy dock, dry land boat storage.

GATESVILLE (99)

Faunt Leroy City Park   **FREE**
In Gatesville on 7th Street South, 2 blocks S of courthouse; on the Leon River. Free RV sites with elec/wtr for 2 days; $15 per day thereafter; 14-day limit. 8 RV sites; 3 primitive tent sites. Flush toilets, cold showers, cfga, drkg wtr, dump, playground. Volleyball, fishing.

GEORGETOWN (100)

Cedar Hollow Camp   **FREE**
The Good Water Trail
Corps of Engineers
Georgetown Lake
4 mi W of I-35 at Georgetown via FM 2388. 16-mi primitive hiking & camping trail around upper end of lake; Cedar Hollow between mileposts 4 & 5. Hike-in or boat-in. Free primitive tent camping. All year; 14-day limit. Sites have lantern stand, cfga, toilet, no drkg wtr. Boating, fishing. Note: fee at boat launch.

Sawyer Camp   **FREE**
The Good Water Trail
Corps of Engineers
Georgetown Lake
4 mi W of I-35 at Georgetown via FM 2388. On Gold Water Trail between mileposts 6 & 7. Access by boat or hike-in. Free primitive tent camping. All year; 14-day limit. Sites have lantern stand, cfga, toilets, no drkg wtr. Boating, fishing. Note: fee at boat launches.

Tejas Camp   **$6**
Corps of Engineers
Georgetown Lake
NW of lake project office at SR 2338 & FM 3405, about 5 mi W on FM 3405; SE on CR 258. $6 for 12 primitive tent sites & 3 walk-in or boat-in sites. Tbls, toilets, cfga, drkg wtr. Hiking, boating, fishing.

Walnut Springs Camp   **FREE**
The Good Water Trail
Corps of Engineers
Georgetown Lake
4 mi W of I-35 at Georgetown via FM 2388. On Gold Water Trail between mileposts 14 & 15. Access by boat or hike-in. Free primitive tent camping. All year; 14-day limit. Sites have lantern stand, cfga, toilets, no drkg wtr. Boating, fishing. Note: fee at boat launches.

GEORGE WEST (101)

Smith's Trailer Village   **$12**
13.9 mi S on US 281 from jct with I-37; 1.3 mi N on access rd. $12. All year. 36 sites. Tbls, flush toilets, cfga, drkg wtr, elec, showers, rec hall, coin laundry.

GILMER (102)

Yamboree Park   **$10**
Barnwell Mountain Recreational Area
Texas Motorized Trails Coalition
On US 271 North at Gilmer. $10 for TMTC members ($15 for non-members). All year; 10-day limit. 76 sites. Tbls, toilets, cfga, drkg wtr, elec($), dump. Honesty payment box.

GLEN ROSE (103)

Dinosaur Valley State Park   **$12**
1 mi W of Glen Rose on US 67; 4.5 mi N on FM 205. $12 for backpack sites; $25 for 46 RV sites with elec/wtr. All year; 14-day limit. Tbls, toilets, cfga, drkg wtr, dump, showers, pavilion, playgrounds, exhibits, amphitheater. Fishing, boating, swimming, hiking trails, museum, summer interpretive programs, horseback riding. Visible dinosaur tracks; Texas longhorn herd. Park features 2 fiberglass dinosaur models built for New York World's Fair of 1964. $5 per person entry fee.

GOLDTHWAITE (104)

Goldthwaite Municipal Park   **FREE**
At US 183 & SR 16 in Goldthwaite. All year. 6 sites. Tbls, flush toilets, cfga, drkg wtr, playground, pool. Swimming, lighted sand volleyball court, washer pitching court. 50-ft deep lake was hand-dug in 1885 to provide wtr for railroad

GOLIAD (105)

Goliad State Park   **$8**
1 mi S of Goliad on US 183. $8 base. All year. Base fee for 14 sites with wtr; sites with hookups, $13-15. Tbls, flush toilets, cfga, drkg wtr, dump, showers, playgrounds, picnic areas, interpretive displays, museum, historical buildings, dining hall. Fishing, boating, mountain biking, nature trail, swimming. Entry fee $3 per person.

GRAHAM (107)

Firemen's Municipal Park   **$12**
4 blocks W on 5th St from SR 16. All year; 5-day limit. $12. 28 sites with elec/wtr; 55-ft RV limit. Dump, shelters, cfga, drkg wtr, tbls, flush toilets. Bike trails, playground, nature trails, hiking trails, fishing, picnicking.

Kindley City Park   **$10**
7 mi NW of Graham on US 380 at Lake Graham Bridge; on Lake Graham. $10. All year; 5-day limit. 27 sites. Tbls, flush toilets, cfga, wtr, elec. Swimming; picnicking; fishing; boating (l).

Lake Eddleman City Park   **$12**
1.6 mi N of Graham on US 380 from SR 16. On Lake Eddleman. $12. All year; 14-day limit. 12 RV sites, 12 RV sites. Tbls, flush toilets, cfga, drkg wtr, elec, lighted fishing pier, dump. Fishing, picnicking, bike trails, boating(l).

GRAPEVINE (109)

Murrell Park West   **FREE**
Corps of Engineers
Grapevine Lake
4.5 mi N of Grapevine on SR 121 and FM 2499; qtr mi W. Free.. 3/1-10/31; 14-day limit. 36 primitive tent sites. Toilets, cfga, drkg wtr. Swimming, picnicking, fishing, boating(l), hiking. 425-acre camping area.

GROESBECK (111)

Public Use Area #2   **FREE**
Brazos River Authority
11.3 mi SE of SR 164 on Farm 937; 3.6 mi N & E on Farm 3371 to E side of Lake Limestone. Free. All year; 14-day limit. Primitive 25-acre camp area. Tbls, cfga, no drkg wtr. Fishing, boating(l).
Fishing tip: Early in the year, look for crappies in he upper sections of the lake.

Public Use Area #3   **FREE**
Brazos River Authority
11.3 mi SE of SR 164 on Farm 937; 5 mi N & E on Farm 3371 to E side of Lake Limestone. Free. All year; 14-day limit. Primitive 17-acre camp area. Tbls, toilets, cfga, no drkg wtr. Fishing, boating(l).

Public Use Area #4   **FREE**
Brazos River Authority
6.7 mi N of US 79 on Farm 1146; local rd 1.8 mi W to E end of dam. On Lake Limestone. Free. All year; 14-day limit. Primitive 10-acre camp area. Tbls, toilets, cfga, no drkg wtr. Fishing, boating(l).
Fishing tip: Lake Limestone contains good populations of largemouth bass, including some giant Florida fish.

HALLETTSVILLE (112)

Hallettsville City Park   **$10**
Off US 77 in Hallettsville; follow signs. $10. All year; 3-day limit. Fee for developed sites (17 with elec & wtr); undesignated sites free. Tbls, toilets, cfga, cold showers. Phone. Dump. Golf, tennis, picnicking, playground.

HAMLIN (113)

City Park   **FREE**
5 blocks W from center of town on S. Central Ave; 6 blocks SW on 5th St; 1 block E on SW Ave. Free/ All year; 7-day limit. 13-acre primitive camp area. Drkg wtr, cfga. Playground, ball field, pool, tennis courts, volleyball court.

South Park   **Free**
Municipal Park
3.5 mi S of US 83 on FM 126; half mi E on local rd. All year. Free camping, but $1/person fishing permit. 50-acre primitive camp area. Cfga, drkg wtr. No toilets. Fishing, boating(l).

HASKELL (114)

Haskell City Park   **$9**
At Haskell, 6 blocks S of US 380 on Ave C. $9. All year. First night free. 10 sites (25-ft RV limit). Tbls, flush toilets, full hookups, cold showers, cfga, dump, pool, playground. Swimming, tennis, fishing. 24 acres.

HAWKINS (115)

Lake Hawkins $7
Wood County Park
Sabine River Authority
At Hawkins, 3 mi W on US 80 from FM 14; 1 mi N on FM 3440. $7 base. 4/1-10/31; 14-day limit. Base fee for primitive tent sites; $9 for 8 tent sites with elec & wtr; $12 for RV sites ($9 for seniors). 41 RV sites & 150 primitive sites. Tbls, flush toilets, cfga, drkg wtr, showers, dump ($2), elec ($), playground, game room, beach. Boating (l), fishing, horseshoes, swimming, 1.5-mi nature trail. 800-acre lake.

Fishing tip: Largemouth bass can be caught from Lake Hawkins most of the year on plastic worms, craw-worms, jigs, spinnerbaits and crankbaits. The lake's spotted bass prefer rocky habitats and feed on crawfish.

HEMPHILL (116)

Indian Mounds $4
Sabine National Forest
Sabine River Authority of Texas
6 mi E of Hemphill on SR 83; 2 mi S on FR 115; 5 mi E on FR 128; 1 mi E on FR 130. $4. 3/1-10/15; 14-day limit. 38 sites. Tbls, toilets, cfga, drkg wtr. Boating(l), fishing. On shore of Toledo Bend Lake.

Fishing tip: For white bass, fish the main lake river, channel sand bars, road beds, sloughs and points at 16-20 feet using small spoons and Rinky Dink tail spinners. Watch for schooling fish.

Lakeview $3
Sabine National Forest
Sabine River Authority of Texas
9 mi S of Hemphill on SR 87; 5 mi NE on SR 2928; 4.2 mi SE on FR 120. $3. 3/1-10/15; 14-day limit. 10 primitive sites. Tbls, toilets, cfga, drkg wtr. Boating, fishing. 20 acres. On shore of Toledo Bend Lake. Trailhead for Trail-Between-the-Lakes. Boat ramp in poor condition.

Fishing tip: For mid-summer bass, try crawdad-colored crankbaits in 14-18 feet at the grass flats and off points or use one-ounce Cyclone jigs at the edge of hydrilla.

Willow Oak $4
Sabine National Forest
Sabine River Authority of Texas
10.5 mi N of Hemphill on SR 87; E on FR 116. $4. All year; 14-day limit. 11 sites (22-ft RV limit). Tbls, toilets, cfga, drkg wtr. Fishing, boating(l). Closed temporarily in 2007 due to bridge work.

HENRIETTA (117)

Hapgood Ctiy RV Park $7
From westbound US 287, half mi N on Spur 512. $7. All year; 14-day limit. 12 RV sites with hookups. Tbls, flush toilets, cfga, drkg wtr, dump, playground, horseshoes.

HEREFORD (118)

Hereford RV Sites FREE
In town at Herford Aquatic Center. Free. All year; 1-day limit. 5 sites. Tbls, toilets, cfga, drkg wtr, elec/wtr hookups, dump nearby. Pond, walking track, YMCA nearby.

HONEY GROVE (119)

Bois-D'Arc Unit $8
State Wildlife Management Area
Caddo National Grasslands
10 mi N of Honey Grove on FM100; within the national grasslands. $8 or $4 with Federal Senior Pass. All year; 14-day limit. Primitive undesignated camping on 16,150 acres. Toilets, drkg wtr, cfga. Hunting, fishing, hiking, horseback riding.

Coffee Mill Lake Park $4
Caddo/LBJ National Grassland
10.5 mi N from US 82 on Farm 100; 3.5 mi W on local rd. $4 ($2 with federal Senior Pass). All year; 14-day limit. 2-acre primitive camping area, 13 sites. Toilets, cfga, drkg wtr. Fishing, boating(l), waterfowl hunting, hiking No swimming.

East Lake Crockett $2
Caddo National Grassland
From US 82 near Honey Grove, 10.5 mi N on FM 100; W to NE shore of Lake Crockett. $2 use fee. All year; 14-day limit. 4 tent sites; no RVs. Tbls, toilets, cfga, no drkg wtr, fishing pier. No horses allowed. Boating(l), fishing, hiking, picnicking.

West Lake Crockett $4
Caddo National Grassland
From US 82 near Honey Grove, 10.5 mi N on FM 100; 3.5 mi W on local rd at NW. shore of Lake Crockett. $4. All year; 14-day limit. 12 sites. Toilets, drkg wtr. Fishing, waterfowl hunting, boating(l), no swimming, hiking. Note: Restroom burned by vandals, and until replaced, camping fees are not being charged.

HOUSTON (120)

Lake Houston City Park $7
30 mi NE of Houston on US 59; exit to FM 1485 at New Caney; E to Baptist Encampment Rd, then S. $7 for 24 hike-in & walk-in tent sites ($5 overflow, $6 equestrian). Tbls, cfga, lantern posts, central wtr, nearby showers. Hiking, interpretive trails, mountain biking. Formerly a state park. Entry fee $3 per person.

Fishing tip: For summertime bass, try areas near the pump station with yellow-and-white spinnerbaits and 6-8 feet near dropoffs around brush piles.

Spring Creek FREE
Harris County Park
11.5 mi NW on FM 149 from FM 1960; 1 mi W on Brown Rd; at Spring Creek. Free. All year; 7-day limit (reservations 7 days in advance required); 281-353-4196). 8 RV sites with elec/wtr; 4 large tent areas (75-person capacity each). Tbls, cfga, flush toilets, drkg wtr, elec($), dump. Fishing, playground, tennis. 114 acres. Note: Improvements in 2007 (including sewer lines) probably mean fees to be charged.

HUNTSVILLE (122)

Huntsville State Park $12
6 mi S of Huntsville on I-45; access on Park Rd 40. $12 for 94 sites with wtr hookups; $16 for 58 sites with wtr/elec; $8 overflow. All year; 14-day limit. Tbls, flush toilets, cfga, drkg wtr, dump, showers, playgrounds, picnic areas, group shelter, store, fish cleaning table, store, rec hall. Horseback riding (guided), picnicking, mini golf, canoeing(r), paddleboating(r), boating(ldr), nature & hiking trails, bike path, mountain biking trails, swimming, fishing (lighted piers), interpretive programs. Lake Raven. $4 per person entry fee.

IRA (123)

Bull Creek Park $5
Colorado River Municipal Water District
4.9 mi W of Ira on FM 1606; 2.6 mi W on FM 2085; 1.9 mi N on FM 1298; 3.2 mi W on FM 1610; 2 mi S on local rd; on Lake J.B. Thomas. $5. All year; 7-day limit. Primitive camping; 65 and over & under 17 free. Tbls, toilets, cfga, no drkg wtr. Swimming, fishing, picnicking, boating(l).

Sandy Beach Park $5
Colorado River Municipal Water District
4.9 mi W of Ira on FM 1606; 4 mi W on FM 2085; on Lake J.B. Thomas. $5. All year; 7-day limit. Primitive camping; over 64 & under 18 free. Primitive open area. Tbls, toilets, cfga, no drkg wtr. Swimming, boating, fishing, picnicking.

South Side Park $5
Colorado River Municipal Water District
4.9 mi W of Ira on FM 1606; 2.6 mi W on FM 2085; .6 mi W & 1.8 mi S on FM 1298; on Lake J.B. Thomas. $5. All year; 7-day limit. Primitive camping; over 64 & under 18 free. 100-acre primitive camping area. Tbls, flush toilets, cfga, no drkg wtr. Swimming, fishing, boating(l), picnicking.

White Island Park $5
Colorado River Municipal Water District
From FM 2085 west of Ira, 3.1 mi S on FM 1298; 2.2 mi W on local rd; on Lake J.B. Thomas. $5. All year; 7-day limit. Primitive camping; over 64 & under 18 free: 5-acre primitive area. Tbls, toilets, cfga, no drkg wtr. Swimming, fishing, boating(l), picnicking.

IRAAN (124)

Alley Oop City Park $10
On US 190 in Iraan. $10. All year; 7-day limit. 10 sites. Tbls, flush toilets, cfga, drkg wtr,

elec, playground, pool, dump. Swimming, tennis. Fee not verified for 2007.

JACKSBORO (125)

Fort Richardson   **$5**
State Historical Park
On US 281 in Jacksboro. $5 for hike-in tent sites; $16-24 for RV sites with hookups. Tbls, flush toilets, cfga, drkg wtr, showers, dump, interpretive displays, reconstructed fort, museum, picnic areas. Fishing, nature trails, volleyball, horseshoes, hiking trail, bike & equestrian trail, swimming. $3 per person entry fee.

JASPER (126)

Angelina-Neches/Dam B   **FREE**
State Wildlife Management Area
11 mi W of Jasper on US 190; in forks of Angelina-Neches Rivers & B.A. Steinhagen Reservoir.. Access by boat from public ramps at Bevlport, the Walnut Ridge and Cherokee Units of Martin Dies Jr State Park, and the Magnolia Ridge Campground of Corps of Engineers. All year; 14-day limit. Primitive undesignated camping at seculuded sections of either the state park or COE property (permit needed for latter). No facilities; no drkg wtr. Boating, fishing, swimming, hunting, waterskiing.

Ebenezer Campground   **$9**
Corps of Engineers
Sam Rayburn Lake
15 mi NW of Jasper on SR 96; 8 mi N on FM 255; cross dam, 1 mi N on entrance rd; on S shore of lake. $9 for 20 sites without elec; $15 with elec. All year; 14-day limit. 30 sites (RVs under 50 ft), plus 44-acre primitive camping area. Tbls, toilets, cfga, drkg wtr, dump, beach. Swimming; picnicking; fishing; boating. Horse camping permitted. Dump & beach fees for non-campers.

Hen House Ridge   **$8**
Martin Dies Jr. State Park
13 mi W of Jasper on US 190; E side of B.A. Steinhagen Lake, S side of US 190. $8 base. All year; 14-day limit. Base fee for 67 sites with wtr hookups during 12/1-2/28 ($10 rest of year); $13 for wtr/elec during 12/1-2/28 ($15 rest of year). Tbls, flush toilets, cfga, drkg wtr, dump, screened shelters, fish cleaning table, beach, showers, store. Swimming, boating (lrd), fishing, hiking trails, playground, birdwatching, canoeing(r), nature program. Lighted fishing piers. $2 entry fee for overnight use. Note: Walnut Ridge sites unavailable at presstime due to Hurricane Rita damage.
Fishing tip: At Steinhagen Lake, striped bass to 10 pounds can be caught routinely on topwater lures, spinnerbaits and crankbaits below the dam in 25-35 feet. In the same area, fish for white bass with topwaters and jigging spoons.

Twin Dikes Campground   **$12**
Corps of Engineers
Sam Rayburn Lake
7.3 mi N of Jasper on US 96; 3.3 mi W on R 255, then N; on S shore of lake. $12 base. All year; 14-day limit. Base fee for non-hookup sites; $16 with elec, $18 with 50 amp & full hookups. Holders of federal Senior Pass pay $6, $8 & $9. 44 sites (15 non-hookup). 60-ft RV limit. Pavilion, tbls, flush toilets, cfga, drkg wtr, dump. Boating(l), fishing, swimming. Boat ramp & dump fees for non-campers. 2-day minimum stay on weekends.

JEFFERSON (128)

Alley Creek   **$12**
Corps of Engineers
Lake O' the Pines
NW of Jefferson on SR 49; 7 mi W on FM 729 past FM 726, then S following signs. $12 tent sites; $18 with wtr elec, $20 wtr & 50-amp (premium sites $22). Holders of federal Senior Pass pay $6, $9, $10 & $11. 3/1-9/30; 14-day limit. 64 sites (15 for tents) plus 12-site group area; 65-ft RVs. Pavilion($), tbls, flush toilets, cfga, drkg wtr, elec($), beach, dump, showers. Boating(ld), fishing, swimming, hiking. 2-night minimum stay on weekends.
Fishing tip: In spring, use Carolina rigs, Rat-L-Traps and soft jerkbaits to catch bass.

Brushy Creek   **$10**
Corps of Engineers
Lake O' the Pines
NW of Jefferson on SR 49; W on FM 729; S on FM 726 past dam, then right following signs. $10 base. 3/1-11/30; 14-day limit. Base fee for primitive tent sites; $12 for premium tent sites; $14 for tent sites with wtr/elec; $18 for RV sites with wtr/elec (premium RV sites $22 & $24. 103 sites (37 for tents); 65-ft RVs. Tbls, flush toilets, cfga, drkg wtr, elec($), showers, beach, dump, playground. Boating(l), swimming, fishing, hiking. 2-night minimum stay on weekends.
Fishing tip: The channel of Brushy Creek is a great place to fish for bass and stripers in the fall, using spinnerbaits; in winter, try plastics and deep-diving crankbaits.

Buckhorn Creek   **$12**
Corps of Engineers
Lake O' the Pines
NW of Jefferson on SR 49; W on FM 729; 2.4 mi S on FM 726, then right following signs. $12 base. 3/1-9/30; 14-day limit. Base fee for primitive tent sites; $16-24 for RV sites with hookups. 96 sites (58 with wtr/elec). 65-ft RVs. Tbls, flush toilets, cfga, drkg wtr, elec ($), dump, showers, playground. Fishing, hiking, boating(l). 2-night minimum stay on weekends.

Cedar Springs Park   **FREE**
Corps of Engineers
Lake O' The Pines
16 mi NW of Jefferson on TX 49 to Avinger; 14 mi SW on TX 155; 1 mi SE on co rd. Free.

All year; 14-day limit. 28 sites; 48 acres. Tbls, toilets, cfga, drkg wtr, dump. Picnicking; fishing; boating(l), hunting during season in undeveloped areas. Historical site.

Hurricane Creek   **FREE**
Corps of Engineers
Lake O' The Pines
From intersection of US 59 and TX 49; 3.3 mi NW on TX 49; 5.45 mi W along Farm Market 729. Free. All year (limited facilities during winter); 14-day limit. 23 sites (camp only in designated areas). Tbls, toilets, cfga, drkg wtr. Swimming; picnicking; fishing; hunting in the undeveloped areas during hunting season. No firearms in developed public use areas.

Johnson Creek   **$12**
Corps of Engineers
Lake O' the Pines
NW of Jefferson on SR 49; 5 mi W on FM 729 past FM 726, then S. $12 base. All year; 14-day limit. Base fee for primitive tent sites; $14 tent sites with wtr/elec; RV sites with hookups $18-24. 85 sites (73 with wtr/elec); 65-ft RVs. Pavilion($), amphitheater, tbls, flush toilets, cfga, drkg wtr, elec ($), beach, dump, showers, playground. Boating (ld), fishing, hiking, swimming. 2-night minimum stay on weekends.

JOAQUIN (129)

North Toledo Bend   **FREE**
Sabine River Authority of Texas
State Wildlife Management Area
4.7 mi S of Joaquin on FM 139; 1.7 mi E on FM 2572; adjacent to Toledo Bend Reservoir. Free. All year; 14-day limit. Primitive designated campsites; no facilities, no drkg wtr. Hiking, hunting, fishing, horseback riding. 3,650 acres. Use permit required.

JOHNSON CITY (130)

Pedernales Falls State Park   **$10**
14 mi E of Johnson City on FM 2766 (45 mi W of Austin). $10 for hike-in tent sites; $20 for 69 RV sites with elec/wtr. All year; 14-day limit. Amphitheater, toilets, cfga, drkg wtr, picnic areas, playgrounds, dump, showers, store. Fishing, canoeing, swimming, hiking trail, nature trail, biking, mountain biking, tubing. $3 per person entry fee for overnight use.

JUNCTION (131)

Schreiner City Park   **FREE**
US 290 at Lake Junction in town. Free up to 3 days. All year; 7-day limit. 15-acre primitive camping area. Flush toilets, cfga, drkg wtr, playground, pool, ball field. Swimming, fishing, boating(l). Sightseeing (scenic views).

South Llano River State Park   **$10**
4 mi S of Junction on US 377. $10 for walk-in tent sites; $15 for 58 RV sites with elec/wtr.

All year; 14-day limit. Tbls, flush toilets, cfga, drkg wtr, showers, dump. Mountain biking, canoeing, fishing, birdwatching, tubing, hiking, picnicking, swimming. 2,700 acres. $2 per person entry fee for overnight use.

KENNARD (132)

Piney Creek Horse Camp   **FREE**
Davy Croxkett National Forest
From W of Kennard on SR 7, 2.5 mi S on Hwy 415; right for half mi on CR 4625. Free. All year; 14-day limit. Primitive sites. Tbls, chemical toilets, cfga, no drkg wtr, hitching posts, stock pond. Hiking trails, horseback riding.

KERMIT (133)

Winkler County Park   **$10**
10 mi NE of Kermit on SR 115 to RR-874. $10 (pay to treasurer at courthouse). All year; 10-day limit. Tbls, toilets, cfga, drkg wtr, elec, pool. Very popular dune buggy and OHV site.

KERRVILLE (134)

Kerrville-Schreiner City Park   **$9**
Half mi S of Kerrville on SR 173. $9 base ($13 with elec/wtr, $15 full hookups). All year; 14-day limit. Tbls, flush toilets, cfga, drkg wtr, showers, dump, playground, lighted fishing piers. Boating(l), fishing, hiking trails. Former Corps of Engineers park. Daily or annual entry fee.

KINGSVILLE (135)

Seawind RV Resort
Kaufer-Hubert Memorial Park   **$10**
3.7 mi N of FM 771 on US 77; 11.4 mi E on FM 628; on Baffin Bay. $10 for tent & boondock sites; $16-20 with hookups. All year. 134 sites. Tbls, flush toilets, cfga, drkg wtr, rec room, coin laundry, store, shelters, bird observation tower, fishing pier, beach, playground, fitness course. Horseshoes, swimming, jogging trail, fishing, boating(l). 10% discount for AARP members.

KOPPERL (136)

Plowman Creek   **$10**
Corps of Engineers
Whitney Lake
1 mi S of Kopper on FM 56; at NW side of lake. $10 for sites with wtr 10/1-2/28; $12 rest of year (sites with elec $14-16). All year; 14-day limit. 38 sites (12 without elec); 45-ft RV limit. Toilets, cfga, drkg wtr, tbls, showers, dump. Fishing, boating(l). Boat ramp fee for non-campers. 2-day minimum stay on weekends.
Fishing tip: For the best channel catfish angling on Lake Whitney, try to White Bluff area, using nightcrawlers, shrimp, chicken livers or crawfish.

KOUNTZE (137)

Indian Springs Camp   **$10**
8 mi N of Kountze on Hwy 69; left on Post Oak Rd for 1 mi; right on Holland Rd about three-fourths mi; right on Holland Cemetery Rd. $10 base. All year. Base fee for tent sites; wilderness tent sites $12; $15 for RV or tent sites with elec/wtr; $20 full hookups. 50-ft RV limit. Tbls, flush toilets, drkg wtr, cfga, showers, modem hookup($), coin laundry, dump ($5). Fishing, canoeing(r).

LADONIA (138)

Ladonia Unit   **FREE**
State Wildlife Management Area
Caddo National Grasslands
4 mi W of Ladonia on SR 34. Within the national grasslands. Free. All year; 14-day limit. No permits or registration required. Primitive undesignated camping on 16,150 acres. Hunting, fishing, hiking, horseback riding.

LAGO VISTA (139)

Turkey Bend   **$5**
Primitive Recreation Area
Lower Colorado River Authority
8 mi W of Lago Vista on FM 1431 (NW of Austin); 1.8 mi S on Shaw Dr; on N side of Lake Travis, E of Starcke Dam. Camp free, but $5 entry fee ($50 annually). All year; 5-day limit. Primitive tent camping at metal fire rings. No toilets, drkg wtr or trash pickup. 400 acres. Horseback/hiking trail; trailhead parking; boating, fishing. 2 mi of shoreline.

LA GRANGE (140)

Lake Fayette Park   **$10**
Lower Colorado River Authority
Off Hwy 71 at Fayette Power Project Lake. $10 for primitive sites; $16-17 for RV sites with elec. All year; 14-day limit. Tbls, flush toilets, cfga, drkg wtr, showers, dump. Fishing, boating(l), hiking. Per-person entry fee charged.
Fishing tip: Although Fayette Lake is full of good bass, it has a slot limit of 14 to 34 inches, and only one bass over 24 inches can be kept.

Northside City Park   **FREE**
At 900 W. Hanacek Lake in LaGrange. Free. All year. Primitive undesignated camping. Tbls, toilets, cfga, drkg wtr, fishing pier. Volleyball, fishing, boating(l). On the Colorado River.

Oak Thicket   **$10**
Fayette Power Project
Lower Colorado River Authority
Off Hwy 71 on N end of Fayette Power Project Lake. $10 for primitive sites; $16-17 for RV sites with elec. All year; 14-day limit. 20 RV sites. Tbls, flush toilets, cfga, drkg wtr,

showers, dump, beach, playground, pavilion, lantern posts, fishing pier. Swimming, fishing, boating(l). 2,400-acre lake. Entry fee $4 per person; $3 seniors.

Park Prairie   **$10**
Fayette Power Project
Lower Colorado River Authority
9 mi E of SR 71 on Fayette Power Project Lake. $10 for tent sites. All year; 5-day limit. 2 acres of primitive camping. Tbls, toilets, cfga, drkg wtr, showers, beach, fishing pier. Fishing, boating(ld), swimming, volleyball, horseback riding, bike trail, nature trail. Entry fee $4 per person, $3 seniors.
Fishing tip: 2,420-acre lake produces excellent catches of largemouth bass and catfish. Lake records include 12.25-lb bass & 65-lb blue catfish.

Plum Access Point   **$5**
Colorado River
Lower Colorado River Authority
8 mi W of LaGrange on Hwy 71; right for 2.25 mi on Prairie Valley Rd (CR 448) to access rd. Camp free, but $5 access fee. All year; 1-day limit. Overnight camping only for river traffic or by special permit. Primitive undesignated sites. Tbls, toilet, cfga, no drkg wtr. Fishing, boating(l).

LAKE JACKSON (141)

Wilderness Park   **FREE**
On SR 332 at Buffalo Camp Bayou. Free primitive camping with permission from city parks department (297-4533). Tbls, toilets, cfga. Interpretive loop trail, hiking trail, fishing on Brazos River. 482 acres.

LAMESA (142)

Forest Park   **FREE**
City Park
.5 mi S of US 180 on TX 137; at 9th St & Bryan Ave. All year; 4-day limit. 40 free primitive sites; no fee for about 10 elect sites. Toilets, drkg wtr, dump, elec. Picnicking; softball; playground.

LAMPASAS (143)

Colorado Bend State Park   **$7**
W of Lampasas on FM 580 to Bend; 4 mi S on gravel rd following signs; on Colorado River. $7 & $12 for hike-in tent sites; $14 for 15 RV sites for tents and self-contained RVs. 30-ft RV limit. Tbls, pit toilets, cfga, drkg wtr, rinse cold-wtr spigot. Swimming, fishing, boating(l), hiking, tours ($), mountain biking. 5,328 acres. Undeveloped caves, Gorman Falls. $4 per person entry fee.

LAREDO (144)

Lake Casa Blanca $12
International State Park
6 mi E of Laredo on US 59; 1 mi N on Lake Casa Blanca Rd. $12 for 66 RV sites with elec/wtr. All year; 14-day limit. Tbls, flush toilets, cfga, drkg wtr, showers, dump, playground, pavilions, store. Fishing, swimming, boating(lr), golf, hiking, mountain biking. $4 per person entry fee.

LEVELLAND (145)

Levelland-Hockley FREE
City-County Park
1 mi S of Levelland on US 385. Free. All year; 3-day limit. 7 sites. Drkg wtr, elec & wtr hookups, dump. Picnicking.

LEWISVILLE (146)

Lake Park $8
Lewisville City Park
Near Lewisville, 3 mi E on FM 407E (Lake Park Rd) from US 35E, following signs. $8 for seniors with wtr/elec ($16 for all others); $9 for seniors at premium sites ($18 all others) $10 for tent sites ($5 for seniors). All year; 14-day limit. 119 sites. Tbls, flush toilets, cfga, drkg wtr, showers, dump, elec. Fishing, boating (ld), swimming. On land leased from the Corps of Engineers.

LITTLE ELM (148)

Little Elm City Park FREE
8.2 mi W of SR 289 on FM 720; on Lewisville Lake. Free. Primitive camping on 70 acres. Tbls, toilets, cfga, drkg wtr, pavilion($), playground. Boating(l), fishing, swimming.

LITTLEFIELD (149)

Waylon Jennings Municipal Park FREE
At US 385 & 15th St (1 mi N of Hwy 84) in Littlefield. Free. All year; 4-day limit. 10 small sites after park's downgrading. Tbls, drkg wtr, dump. Picnicking; horseshoes; baseball; golf nearby. Donations accepted.

LIVINGSTON (150)

Lake Livingston State Park $10
1 mi S of Livingston on US 59; 4 mi W on FM 1988; half mi N on FM 3126; access on Park Rd 65. $10 base. All year; no length-of-stay limit. Base fee for 26 sites with wtr hookups; $15 for 69 sites with elec/wtr; $18-25 for full hookups. Tbls, flush toilets, cfga, drkg wtr, dump, showers, playgrounds, picnic areas, amphitheater, store, pool, observation tower. Fishing, boating(d), swimming, hiking & nature trails. 635 acres on 84,000-acre lake. $3 per person entry fee.
Fishing tip: Summer fishermen should use spinnerbaits for bass; Charlie Slabs, Hellbenders and spoons in the main lake for stripers and white bass; minnows for crappies, and prepared baits for catfish.

Wolf Creek Park $10
Lake Livingston
Trinity River Authority
W of Livingston, across lake on US 190; S on SR 156, then 3 mi E on FM 224. $10 for primitive sites with wtr; $14 tent site with wtr & elec; $17 RV sites with hookups; overflow, $9. Add $1 per person to the fees. 104 sites. 3/1-11/31. Tbls, flush toilets, cfga, drkg wtr, hookups($), showers, coin laundry, playgrounds, pavilion, mini golf. Swimming, picnicking, boating(l), fishing, waterskiing. Daily or annual entry fee charged.
Fishing tip: Lake Livingston provides some of the state's best catfishing, and it's not unusual for anglers to land their day's limit of 50 channel cats. The state record flathead, at 114 pounds, was caught from Livingston in 1976, and a 78-pound blue cat was landed in 1981. Fish the dam's tailrace by casting against the dam from shore

LLANO (151)

Black Rock Park $10
Lower Colorado River Authority
From SR 16 near Llano, 3 16.1 mi on SR 29; 4 mi N on SR 261. On Lake Buchanan. $10 primitive sites; $15-17 with elec/wtr; $20 full hookups. All year; 14-day limit. 40 sites & primitive area. Tbls, flush toilets, cfga, drkg wtr, dump, playground, cold showers. Fishing, boating(l), hiking, wading. Scenic. 2 sites & toilets for handicapped. Park was recently renovated. $3 entry fee ($2 seniors).. Note: Park sometimes reaches vehicle capacity and closes on weekends.

Enchanted Rock $10
State Natural Area
Near Llano, 18 mi N of Fredericksburg on FM 965. No vehicle camping; tents only. $10 base. All year; 14-day limit. Base fee for 3 hike-in primitive areas; $15 for walk-in tent sites with wtr nearby. Flush toilets, tbls, cfga, showers, drkg wtr. No vehicle camping or RVs permitted. Group day-use picnic area. Hiking trails, birdwatching, rock-climbing.

LOGANSPORT (LA.) (153)

Converse Bay FREE
Recreation Site #4
Sabine River Authority of Texas
Toledo Bend Reservoir
From US 84 near Logansport, 20.1 mi S on SR 191 to SR 174/Rec Site 4 Rd between mileposts 55 and 56; half mi W on Rec Site 4 Rd (immediately across from SR 174) to the park. Free. All year; 14-day limit. Primitive undesignated sites; large parking area, large wooded area for tents & picnicking. Tbls, cfga, toilets, playground, beach. Boating(l), fishing, swimming.
Fishing tip: For Toledo Bend's big bass in Jan-Feb, slow roll a spinnerbait in the deep grass areas at Converse and San Patrico, keeping the lure just over the top and along the edge of the hydrilla. On warm winter days, use the same spinnerbait in shallow water of coves or try a RinkyDink in river bends or creek channels. An alternative is jigging spoons about 30 feet deep.

Oak Ridge FREE
Recreation Site #2
Sabine River Authority of Louisiana
Toledo Bend Reservoir
From US 84 near Logansport, 8.1 mi S on SR 191; 1.7 mi W on Circle Dr from corner convenience store; right for half mi on access rd. $10 at RV sites without hookups & primitive tent sites; $15 at tent sites on RV pad with elec; $15 at RV sies with elec/wtr; $20 full hoookups. Seniors with federal Senior Pass pay $7.50, $11.25, $11.25 & $15, respectively. All year; 14-day limit; gate locked at 9 pm. In 2003, 19 RV sites were added to the park's primitive camping area. Tbls, cfga, drkg wtr, toilet, playground, beach, dump ($5 non-campers). Swimming, fishing, boating(l).
Fishing tip: The Oak Ridge section of Toledo Bend is a good place for catching big bass on bright colored spinnerbaits during March & April. Also use three-fourths-ounce Rat-L-Traps on the flats and shallow ridges; alternate with a slowly retrieved black jig-and-pig or Carolina-rig lizard. If the water is up in the bushes, try jigs & spinnerbaits there.

Wilderness Area FREE
Recreation Site #3 & 3A
Sabine River Authority of Louisiana
Toledo Bend Reservoir
From US 84 near Logansport, 14.4 mi S on SR 191; 2.1 mi W on Coker Worsham Rd; right for 1.1 mi on dirt Locust Rd, then left for 1.5 mi. Rough roads; passenger cars not recommended. Free. All year; 14-day limit. Primitive wilderness camping; no facilities. Hand boat launch, boating, fishing.

LONE OAK (154)

Pawnee Inlet Unit FREE
Sabine River Authority of Texas
Tawakoni Wildlife Management Area
2 mi W of Lone Oak on FM 1571. Free. All year; 14-day limit. Primitive designated campsites. No facilities, no drkg wtr. Fishing, hunting, horseback riding, hiking. Access permit required.

Wind Point Park $12
Sabine River Authority of Texas
W of Lone Oak on FM 1571, then 4.5 mi S; at 6553 State Park Rd 55 on Lake Tawakoni. $12 base. All year. Base fee for primitive tent sites ($14 with wtr & elec); $16 for RV sites ($14 during 11/1-3/1). 159 sites. Flush toilets, tbls, cfga, drkg wtr, showers, store, coin laundry, playground, lighted fishing pier. Swimming, fishing, boating(l), mini-bike area,

tennis, nature trail. Operated by concessionaire.

Fishing tip: For bass in this lake, focus on the areas around piers, boat houses, vegetation and submerged trees, using spinnerbaits, jigs and plastic worms. Catch crappies near the bridge pilings and submerged brush piles using minnows or jigs.

LONGVIEW (155)

Fun Wheeler Park   **FREE**
On Ned Williams Rd off Hwy 149 S near Longview. Free. All year on weekends. Free primitive camping; $10 for tent sites with elec; $15 for sites with elec/wtr. Tbls, toilets, cfga, drkg wtr. 900-acre area caters to ATV users; weekend admission $10 per ATV and $10 per person; special event weekens cost more.

LUBBOCK (156)

Buffalo Springs Lake   **$12**
Near Lubbock, 4 mi E on E 50th St from Loop 289. $12 base for tents; $18 with elec & wtr; $24 full hookups. All year; 14-day limit. 162 sites. Tbls, flush toilets, cfga, drkg wtr, showers, dump, elec ($), sewer($), rec hall, playground, beaches. Boating (ld), fishing, bike trails, nature trail, swimming, horseshoes. 225-acre lake. Crappie house.

Samuel W. Wahl   **$7**
City Recreation Area
About 60 mi S of Lubbock on US 84, through Justiceburg; exit on FM 2458, then E on FM 3519 to Lake Alan Henry and 2 mi W of the John T. Montford Dam. $7 Mon-Thurs; $10 Fri-Sun. Park also charges $6-8 daily entry fee or $50 annually ($30 for seniors). All year. Primitive undeveloped camping area on 580 acres. Tbls, cfga, toilets, no drkg wtr. Hiking, boating(l), fishing, picnicking. Future plans include RV sites with hookups. 2,880-acre lake.

Fishing tip: This Lubbock water-supply lake has a good population of largemouth bass, white bass and crappies. Catch bass on Texas-rigged worms or pig-and-jig in heavy brush along creek channels. Shoreline access is very limited, but kids can catch panfish from the fishing dock. Lake's record bass, 12.41 pounds.

LUFKIN (157)

Alabama Creek   **FREE**
Wildlife Management Area
13 mi W of Lufkin on Hwy 94; 4 mi S on FM2262; in Davy Crockett National Forest. Free. All year; 14-day limit. Primitive camping at designated sites. Toilets, cfga, no drkg wtr. Hiking, fishing, biking, hunting, horseback riding.

Bannister   **FREE**
State Wildlife Management Area
25 mi E of Lufkin on SR 103; 3 mi S on FM

1277 to FR 300; information station on E side of jct; in San Augustine National Forest. Free. All year; 14-day limit. No registration or permits required. Primitive designated camping. No facilities; no drkg wtr. Hunting, hiking, fishing, biking, auto tour, horseback riding.

LULING (158)

Ben's RV Park (Private)   **$9**
Near Luling, N 3 mi on US 183 from I-10 exit 632. $9-11 base. All year. 17 sites. Tbls, flush toilets, cfga, drkg wtr, showers, elec.

Palmetto State Park   **$10**
6 mi S of Luling off US 183; 2 mi W on Park Rd 11 (21 mi SE of Lockhart). $10-12 for tent sites with wtr; $14-16 for RV sites with hookups; $8 for overflow area. 41 sites. All year; 14-day limit. Tbls, flush toilets, cfga, drkg wtr, showers, dump, playgrounds, picnic areas, rec hall, fishing pier, store. Birdwatching, canoeing, fishing, tubing, rafting, biking. Numerous wildlfowers & plants. San Marcos River. $3 per person entry fee.

LUMBERTON (159)

Village Creek State Park   **$7**
In Lumberton, on Alma Dr (off US 96); at Neches River. $7 for walk-in tent sites; $15 for 25 sites with wtr/elec. All year; 14-day limit. Tbls, flush toilets, cfga, drkg wtr, showers, dump. Swimming, hiking, canoeing(r), picnicking, bike trails, boating(l). 942 acres. $2 per person entry fee.

LYONS (160)

Birch Creek Unit   **$6**
Lake Somerville State Park
7.6 mi SW of Lyons on FM 60; 4.3 mi S on Park Rd 57. $6 base. All year; 14-day limit. Base fee for primitive hike-in or equestrian sites on trail (no drkg wtr); $10 for walk-in tent sites with wtr and for 10 equestrian sites with wtr; $15 for RV sites with elec/wtr. Tbls, flush toilets, cfga, drkg wtr, showers, dump, shelters, picnic areas, interpretive shelter. Picnicking, waterskiing, fishing (pier), swimming, boating(ldr), canoeing (r), hiking trails, bridle trails. See Burton entry. $3 per person entry fee.

Fishing tip: The tailrace below Lake Somerville is a prime area for shoreline catfish angling.

MADILL (161)

Cross Timbers Trail   **FREE**
Corps of Engineers
Lake Texoma
Trail begins at West Juniper Campground at S end of US 377 bridge crossing the Red River. From first restroom at campground, continue down the paved road to the trailhead. Trail winds westward along shore of Lake Denison for 2.5 mi to Cedar Bayou Resort, then 1.5 mi to Lost Loop Camp (with a 2-mi loop trail); 1

mi to 5-Mile Camp; 1 mi NW to Eagles Roost, then 2.5 mi to Paw Paw Creek Resort and 2 mi beyond. Minimal hills and obstacles. Wtr & toilets at Juniper Camp and Cedar Bayou. Free primitive camping by permit from the Corps of Engineers office at the dam. Ideal trip for new hikers & backpackers.

Juniper Point   **$12**
Corps of Engineers
Lake Texoma
17 mi S of Madill on SR 99, across lake bridge, then E. $12 for 26 primitive sites (some free Nov-March but reduced facilities); $18 for 44 sites with wtr & elec; 50-ft RV limit. All year; 14-day limit. Tbls, flush toilets, cfga, drkg wtr, elec($), showers, dump. Hiking, swimming, fishing, boating(l).

MARATHON (162)

Black Gap   **FREE**
State Wildlife Management Area
58 mi S of Marathon on US 385 & FM 2627. Free. All year except for short-term closures; 14-day limit Primitive camping in designated areas. Registration, permits required. No facilities; no drkg wtr. Hunting, hiking, fishing, biking, auto tour, horseback riding (3/1-8/31). 105,708 acres. Rio Grande River.

Chisos Basin   **$7**
Big Bend National Park
69 mi S of Marathon on US 385; 3 mi W on park rd; 7 mi SW. $7 with federal Senior Pass; others pay $14. All year; 14-day limit. 60 sites (24-ft RV limit). Tbls, flush toilets, cfga, drkg wtr, dump, shelters. Horseback riding, hiking, nature programs. $20 weekly entry fee (free with Senior Pass).

Cottonwood Campground   **$7**
Big Bend National Park
69 mi S of Marathon on US 385; 13 mi W on park rd; 22 mi SW to Castolon; half mi W. On Rio Grande River. $7 with federal Senior Pass; others pay $14. All year; 14-day limit. 35 sites. Tbls, toilets, cfga, drkg wtr, no dump. Fishing, picnicking, hiking trails. $20 weekly entry fee (free with Senior Pass).

Marathon Motel & RV Park   **$10**
Half mi W of Marathon on Hwy 90. $10 base. All year. Base fee for primitive sites; $18 full hookups. 31sites. Flush toilets, showers, CATV($), hookups ($). Historic motel built in early 1940s, recently renovated.

Rio Grande Village Campground   **$7**
Big Bend National Park
69 mi S of Marathon on US 385; 20 mi SE. $7 with federal Senior Pass; others pay $14. All year; 14-day limit. 100 sites. Tbls, flush toilets, cfga, drkg wtr, dump, coin laundry. Fishing, hiking. Note: full hookups at higher fees available from concessionaire. $20 weekly entry fee (free with Senior Pass).

Backcountry Camping $10
Big Bend National Park

70 mi S of Marathon on US 385. All year; 14-day limit. Free primitive camping at numerous backcountry roadside sites (most requiring high-clearance or 4x4 vehicles); $10 backcountry permit required. Obtain backcountry permit from visitor centers. No facilities or services at most sites. Showers($), coin laundry at Rio Grande Village Store at SE side of park. Park entry fee $20 weekly or $40 annually; free with federal Senior Pass. The following backcountry sites are accessible by vehicle, listed by access roads:
Access via Old Ore Rd, 27-mile backcountry road along western flank of Dead Horse Mountains; recommended for high-clearance vehicles.

Candelilla $10
Primitive Roadside Campsite
Big Bend National Park

On Old Ore Rd, 1.1 mi from its S end near Rio Grande Village or 25.4 mi from the Dagger Flat Auto Trail; 0.1 mi W of Old Ore Rd. $10 backcountry permit. 2 sites for 8 persons. High-clearance vehicles usually recommended, but passenger cars okay if rd is in good condition. 4x4 needed following rains. No shade. Small cul-de-sac site.

Ernst Basin $10
Primitive Roadside Campsite
Big Bend National Park

On Old Ore Rd, 10 mi from main paved rd to Rio Grande Village; 16.4 mi from N end at the Dagger Flat Auto Trail; no rock sign, so watch for turn-off S of Willow Tank turn-off. High clearance recommended, 4x4 needed after rain because several washes must be crossed. Access rd usually good. $10 backcountry permit. 1 site for 2 vehicles; no horses. Poor shade; protection from N by low hill. 8-mi hike to ruins of an ore discharge terminal.

Ernst Tinaja $10
Primitive Roadside Campsite
Big Bend National Park

Near S end of Old Ore Rd. Site #2 is 3.6 mi from the main paved rd; access rd to Site #1 is 4.5 mi from paved rd & on qtr mi access rd; 21.5 mi from Dagger Flat Auto Trail. $10 backcountry permit. 2 sites. Site #1 for 2 vehicles of 10 people; Site #2 for 1 vehicle of 6 people. No horses permitted. High-clearance vehicle highly recommended. No shade, but Site #1 is protected from wind by low hills. Excellent panoramic view of Chisos Mtns from Site #2. Do not swim or bathe in nearby tinajas; water not potable.

McKinney Spring $10
Primitive Roadside Campsite
Big Bend National Park

On Old Ore Rd, 7.3 mi from Dagger Flat Auto Trail (19 mi from main paved rd and 2 mi N of Roy's Peak Vista campsite); 50-yd access rd. High clearance highly recommended, 4x4 after rain. $10 backcountry permit. 1 site for 2 vehicles; 4 horses permitted. No shade. Excellent scenery. In a valley near McKinney Spring creekbed. Easy cul-de-sac turn-around.

La Noria $10
Primitive Roadside Campsite
Big Bend National Park

On Old Ore Rd, 4.9 mi from main paved rd to Rio Grande Village (half mi past Ernst Tinaja turn-off); 21 mi from Dagger Flat Auto Trail. High clearance recommended, 4x4 after rain. $10 backcountry permit. 2 sites for 6 persons each; no horses. No shade, but both sites protected by low hills. Good scenery. Warning: Wash N of the Ernst Tinaja turn-off is sandy & deep. After rain, a tinaja 2 mi N in a ravine collects wtr & attracts wildlife; wtr not potable.

Roy's Peak Vista $10
Primitive Roadside Campsite
Big Bend National Park

On Old Ore Rd, 9.3 mi from Dagger Flat Auto Trail (17 mi from main paved rd to Rio Grande Village); short, rutted access rd on W side is quite rough. High clearance recommended, 4.4 needed after rain. $10 backcountry permit. 1 large site for 2 vehicles; on cul-de-sac with good turn-around. No shade, some protection by low hills surrounding site. Old ranch site remains nearby.

Telephone Canyon $10
Primitive Roadside Campsite
Big Bend National Park

On Old Ore Rd, 14 mi from main paved rd to Rio Grand Village; 12.5 mi from Dagger Flat Auto Trail. Very rough qtr-mi access rd on E side of Old Ore Rd. High-clearance highly recommended; 4x4 may be needed following rain. $10 backcountry permit. 2 sites for 3 vehicles & 18 persons. Horses permitted at Site #2. Exposed sites, no shade. Primitive Telephone Canyon hiking trail from Site #2 through Dead Horse Mtns.

Willow Tank $10
Primitive Roadside Campsite
Big Bend National Park

On Old Ore Rd, 10.1 mi from the main paved rd to Rio Grande Village (16.3 mi from Dagger Flat Auto Trail); on W side of short access rd. $10 backcountry permit. High clearance vehicle recommended, 4x4 after rain. No shade in winter; scrub shade in summer, but not for parking or tents. Near natural spring. Good wildlife site.

Acess via River Road, a remote 51-mile route that parallels the park's southern boundary & the U.S. border. Parts of roadway follow the Rio Grande, but most is some distance from the river, especially near Mariscal Mountain. The western end of the road is quite rough and much of it impassable following a rain. Approximate driving time between Castolon and Rio Grand Village is 5 hours:

Black Dike $10
Primitive Roadside Campsite
Big Bend National Park

Via River Rd, 10.7 mi from W end near Castolon or 43.3 mi from E end near Rio Grande Village; high-clearance vehicle required, 4x4 after any rain; short access rd. $10 backcountry permit. 1 site for 2 vehicles & 10 persons; no horses permitted. Good shade. River access by 1-minute walk by by trail through heavy brush. Good fishing. Secure belongings while asleep or absent. Area frequented by passers-by and Mexican residents.

Buenos Aires $10
Primitive Roadside Campsite
Big Bend National Park

Via River Rd, 4.4 mi from W end near Castolon or 49.6 mi from E end near Rio Grande Village; qtr mi access rd. High-clearance vehicle required, 4x4 after any rain. Access rd to Site 2 sometimes impassable. $10 backcountry permit. 2 sites for 3 vehicles & 16 persons; 10 horses permitted. On small hill overlooking Rio Grande floodplain, but no river access. Minimal shade at Site 2. Secure belongings when sleeping or absent. Area frequented by passers-by and Mexican residents.

Dominguez Trailhead $10
Primitive Roadside Campsite
Big Bend National Park

Via River Rd, 22.7 mi from W end near Castolon or 31.3 mi from E end near Rio Grande Village. High-clearance vehicles required, 4x4 after any rain. $10 backcountry permit. 1 sites for 2 vehicles; 4 horses permitted. No shade, but site protected from wind by low hills. No access to river. Vehicles may be parked at nearby Dominguez Spring trailhead; from there, 7-mile rugged trail leads into Sierra Quemada toward a rock house & several unreliable springs. Secure valuables while sleeping or absent.

Elephant Tusk $10
Primitive Roadside Campsite
Big Bend National Park

Via River Rd 21 mi from its E end & 29 mi from W end; take Black Gap Rd for 3 mi N. High-clearance vehicle required, 4x4 after any rain. Black Gap Rd is not maintained and is very rough. $10 backcountry permit. 1 small site near E side of rd across from Elephant Tusk trailhead; no horses. Gravel ground cover, no shade. Scenic. Secure all belongings while sleeping or absent.

Fresno $10
Primitive Roadside Campsite
Big Bend National Park

Via River Road East, 18.6 mi from jct with main park rd; watch for Fresno turnoff to the N; it's easy to miss. High-clearance vehicles required, 4x4 after any rain. Access rd usually in good contidion. $10 backcountry permit. Gravel base, no shade. Good views of Sierra del Carmen Mtns in Mexico and historic Mariscal Mine. Secure belongings while sleeping or absent.

Travel tip: Nearby Mariscal Mine once produced one-fourth of the nation's mercury; operated 1904-1943. Now a National Register Historic Site. Remains of the mine can be visited. Park provides free brochure. Allow half day for visit.

Gauging Station   **$10**
Primitive Roadside Campsite
Big Bend National Park
Via River Rd, 14.2 mi from W end near Castolon or 38.8 mi from E end near Rio Grande Village; half mi access rd. High-clearance vehicles required, 4x4 after any rain. $10 backcountry permit. 1 site. Excellent shade. River access by short trail through heavy brush. Fishing popular. Secure belongings while sleeping or absent. Area frequented by passers-by and Mexican residents.

Gravel Pit   **$10**
Primitive Roadside Campsite
Big Bend National Park
Via River Road East, 1.8 mi from jct with main park rd to Rio Grande Village; 1.4 mi access rd; high clearance vehicles required. $10 backcountry permit. 4 sites for total of 10 vehicles & 41 persons. Sites 1-3 have gravel base, no shade; Site 4 has sandy base, shade from large tree. Horses permitted at Sites 1-2. Riverbank steep, accessible by foot, but boat launch difficult. Safeguard belongings while asleep or away from site.

Jewel's Camp   **$10**
Primitive Roadside Campsite
Big Bend National Park
Via River Rd, 24.6 mi from W end near Castolon or 29.4 mi from the E end near Rio Grande Village. High-clearance vehicle required, 4x4 after any rain. Access rd usually in poor condition with ruts & mud. $10 backcountry permit. 2 sites for 5 vehicles & 20 persons; 4 horses per site permitted. Site 1 in grassland desert, no shade; Site 2 some shade under low mesquite trees. Good view from Site 1. River access by walking to rd's end 7 through river vegetation or via steep bluff near site; no boat access. Keep belongs secure to prevent theft. Area frequented by passers-by & Mexican residents.

Johnson Ranch   **$10**
Primitive Roadside Campsite
Big Bend National Park
Via River Rd, 15.6 mi from W end near Castolon or 38.4 mi from E end near Rio Grande Village; qtr mi access rd. High-clearance vehicles required, 4x4 after any rain. $10 backcountry permit. 2 sites for 4 vehicles & 18 persons; 6 total horses permitted. Scenic 5-minute walk to Johnson house ruins. River access by following cow trails through thick riverside brush; best access from Site 2. Secure belongings while asleep or absent. Nearby remnants of historic structures. In 1929, Army Air Corps developed landing field; no artifact collecting permitted.

La Clocha   **$10**
Primitive Roadside Campsite
Big Bend National Park
Via River Road East, 2.6 mi from jct with main park rd; 0.7-mi access rd. High-clearance vehicle required, 4x4 after any rain. $10 backcountry permit. 2 sites for 4 vehicles & 20 persons; 2 horses permitted at Site #2. Partial shade, sandy base at Site 2; no shade, gravel base at Site 1. River access by foot from Site 1; boat launching possible from Site 2. Secure belongings while sleeping or absent.

Loop Camp   **$10**
Primitive Roadside Campsite
Big Bend National Park
Via River Rd, 23 mi from W end near Castolon or 31 mi from E end near Rio Grande Village; sites just off Loop Camp access rd. High clearance vehicles required, 4x4 after any rain. $10 backcountry permit. 2 sites for 5 vehicles & 20 persons; 4 horses permitted each site. Sites just above river, with foot trail access down a steep bluff. Minimal shade. Secure belongings while sleeping or absent; area frequented by passers-by and Mexican residents.

Solis   **$10**
Primitive Roadside Campsite
Big Bend National Park
Vid River Road East, 13.7 mi from jct with main park rd. Sites 1-2 along access rd; Sites 3-4 on 1.4-mi access rd with deep, soft sand requiring 4x4. High clearance vehicles required, 4x4 after any rain. $10 backcountry permit. 4 sites for 10 vehicles & 54 persons. Gravel base at Sites 1-2. River access for Sites 3-4 from nearby boat launch. Boating, fishing, hiking. Secure belongings while sleeping or absent.

Talley   **$10**
Primitive Roadside Campsite
Big Bend National Park
Via River Road East, 23.2 mi from jct with main park rd. High clearance required, 4x4 after any rain. Site 1 is close to River Rd; other sites about 6 mi on access rd. $10 backcountry permit. 4 sites for total of 9 vehicles & 36 persons; no horses. Sites 1-2 have gravel base, no shade; Sites 3-4 minimal shade, sandy base. Excellent scenery. Access to river from boat launch near Sites 3-4. Theft a recurring problem, so safeguard valuables & take precautions against vehicle damage. Primitive Mariscal Rim hiking trail starts here.

Woodson's   **$10**
Primitive Roadside Campsite
Big Bend National Park
Via River Rd, 28 mi from W end near Castolon or 26.3 mi from E end near Rio Grande Village; access rd usually in poor condition with deep ruts & mud. At sandy river bank. High-clearance vehicles required, 4x4 after any rain. $10 backcountry permit. 2 sites for 5 vehicles & 20 persons; no horses. Minimal

shade. Easy river access & good fishing. Secure belongings while sleeping or absent. Nearby remains of historic structures. Artifact collecting prohibited.

Access via Glenn Springs Road, which begins 5 mi E of Panther Junction and skirts the E side of the Chison Mtns toward Pine Canyon and Juniper Canyon before bouncing over a rough section to the tiny desert oasis of Glenn Springs. Glenn Springs Rd and all campsite rds are rough & rutted, recommended for high-clearance vehicles only, and after a rain, road conditions can deteriorate fast. Many arroyos to cross, requiring 4x4. Five camping areas available:

Glenn Springs   **$10**
Primitive Roadside Campsite
Big Bend National Park
Via Glenn Spring Rd, 8.8 mi from jct with the main park rd to Rio Grande Village; S of Juniper Cnyon Rd, Glenn Spring Rd is extremely rough for half mi over solid bedrock; caution & slow speed are critical. Site 1 is qtr mi along the very rough Black Gap Rd, which is not maintained; Site 2 is on the Glenn Spring Rd just past the historic area. $10 backcountry permit. 2 sites for 2 vehicles; 4 horses permitted at Site 2. Nearby historic remains of Glenn Springs community from early 1900s; brochure available at park headquarters.

Juniper Canyon   **$10**
Primitive Roadside Campsite
Big Bend National Park
Via Glenn Spring Rd, 7.1 mi from jct with the main park rd to Rio Grande Village; 5.5-mi access rd ends at the Dodson/Juniper Canyon trailhead. Section of Glenn Springs Rd before campsite turnoff is very rough and should be driven slowly wtih caution. $10 backcountry permit. 2 small sites for 2 vehicles; 4 horses permitted at Site 2. Minimal shade. No river access. Hikers using Dodson/Juniper Canyon Trails park near Site 2. Secure valuables while sleeping or absent.

Nugent Mountain   **$10**
Primitive Roadside Campsite
Big Bend National Park
Via Glenn Springs Rd, 1.1 mi from jct with the main park rd to Rio Grande Village; qtr mi access rd. $10 backcountry permit. 2 small, adjacent sites for 4 vehicles & 12 persons; 4 horses permitted at each site. No shade, minimal ground cover. Scenic.

Pine Canyon   **$10**
Primitive Roadside Campsite
Big Bend National Park
Via Glenn Springs Rd, 2.6 mi from jct with the main park rd; 4.4 mi access rd, ending at Site #4. $10 backcountry permit. 4 sites for 7 vehicles & 22 persons; horses permitted at Sites 1-2. No shade. Good view of Chisos Mtns; very scenic area. From Site 4, trail continues up-canyon, ending at high pour-off that becomes a beautiful waterfall following

rains. No river access. Hikers using Pine Canyon Trail often park near Site 4. Secure valuables while sleeping or absent.

Rice Tank $10
Primitive Roadside Campsite
Big Bend National Park

Via Glenn Springs Rd, 4.3 mi from jct with the main park rd; sites along E side of rd. No shade, no river access. $10 backcountry permit. 2 adjoining sites for 4 vehicles. Sites adjoin old earthen tank used in the 1920s to hold wtr for livestock; also old corral and loading chute.

Access via Paint Gap Hills Rd, which is about 6 mi W of the Panther Junction Visitor Center. Road is generally in good condition and accessible all year by all vehicles. One camping area:

Pine Gap Hills $10
Primitive Roadside Campsite
Big Bend National Park

Site 1 is 1 mi from pavement; Sites 2-3 are about 2 mi; Site 4 is within the gap about 2.5 mi from pavement. High-clearance vehicle needed for access to Site 3. $10 backcountry permit. 4 sites for 6 vehicles & 20 persons; 2 horses permitted at Site 1. Poor to moderate shade, no river access. Dripping Spring and an old ranch site at end of rd beyond Paint Gap.

Access via Old Maverick Road, a 13-mi improved gravel rd connecting the park's western entrance and the Santa Elena Canyon Trailhead. Although sometimes bumpy, the road is generally well maintained and accessible all year to all vehicles. Two sites in the middle of beautiful desert scenery:

Chimneys West $10
Primitive Roadside Campsite
Big Bend National Park

Via Old Maverick Rd, 6.6 mi from S end & 6.3 mi from N end; qtr mi access rd can be washed out by rain. $10 backcountry permit. 1 site. No shade, no river access, but excellent desert scenery. Secure belongings when sleeping or absent.

Terlingua Abaja $10
Primitive Roadside Campsite
Big Bend National Park

Via Old Maverick Rd, 2.8 mi from S end & 10 mi from N end; 1.7 mi on access rd, which can wash out during rain. $10 backcountry permit. 4 sites for 8 vehicles & 32 people; horses permitted. No shade. Excellent views of Mesa de Anguila and desert scrub terrain. Easy 5-minute access to Terlingua Creek for fishing; wtr not potable. Ruins of old farming community nearby.

Access via Grapevine Hills Rd, which begins 3.3 mi W of the Panther Junction Visitor Center. One camping area:

Grapevine Hills $10
Primitive Roadside Campsite
Big Bend National Park

Via Grapevine Hills Rd; some rough spots, but rd is accessible to Sites 2-3; Site 1 (Government Spring) is 100 yds from pavement; Sites 2-3 are 4r mi from pavement; high-clearance vehicle necessary for access to Sites 4-5, which are 7.2 mi from pavement at end of access rd. $10 backcountry permit. 5 sites for 11 vehicles & 44 persons; horses permitted at first 3 sites. No shade. Government Spring near Site 1; Grapevile Spring near Sites 4-5. Grapevile Hills Hiking Trail about 7 mi from pavement; it is 1.1 mi, ending at a spectacular balanced rock formation. Site 1 is large site with horse corral that may be reserved.

Access via Croton Springs Rd, which is 9 mi W of Panther Junction Visitor Center. Road is generally in good condition and accessible all year to all vehicles. Road is closed beyond the camping area due to erosion. One camping area:

Croton Springs $10
Primitive Roadside Campsite
Big Bend National Park

1 mi dirt rd access from Croton Springs Rd. $10 backcountry permit. 2 adjoining sites for 4 vehicles & 10 persons; 2 horses permitted at each site. No shade. Good scenery. Croton Spring & Wash are short walk from sites. Spring is reliable source of wtr for wildlife.

MARBLE FALLS (163)

Camp Creek FREE
Primitive Recreation Area
Lake Travis
Lower Colorado River Authority

About 6 mi E of Marble Falls on FM 1431; 1 mi W on CR 343 to N shore of Lake Travis (gravel rd may be impassable when wet). Free. All year; 10-day limit. Primitive camping in 5-acre waterfront park operated by Burnet County and in larger conservation area (by permit). Tbls, cfga, toilets, no drkg wtr. Trash service. Boating(l), fishing, hiking trails. Info center. 500 acres.

Shaffer Bend FREE
Primitive Recreation Area
Lake Travis
Lower Colorado River Authority

About 7 mi E of Marble Falls on FM 1431 to Smithwick community; 1 mi S on CR 343A to N shore of Lake Travis. Free. All year; 10-day limit. Primitive camping; prime spots with metal fire rings. No toilets, drkg wtr or trash service. Boating, fishing.

MARFA (164)

Apache Pines RV Park $12

1.3 mi W on US 90 from jct with Hwy 17 at Marfa. $12. All year. 14 sites; full hookups. Tbls, flush toilets, cfga, drkg wtr, CATV, dump.

MARLIN (165)

Falls on the Brazos $4
Falls County Park

3 mi W of Marlin on SR 7; on Brazos River. $4 base. All year. Base fee for primitive sites; $9.50 for RV sites with elec/wtr. 12 tent sites; 6 RV sites. Tbls, flush toilets, cfga, drkg wtr, elec($), dump, store, pavilions($). Fishing, hiking, boating. Weekly & monthly rates available.

MARSHALL (166)

Caddo Lake State Park $8

15 mi NE of Marshall on SR 43; 1 mi E on FM 2198 (1 mi N of Karnack). $8 for 20 small tent/RV sites with wtr; $12 for 18 RV sites with wtr/elec; $18 for 8 full hookups. All year; 14-day limit. Tbls, flush toilets, cfga, drkg wtr, showers, dump, screened shelters, playgrounds, picnic areas, interpretive displays, rec hall. Hiking & nature trails, fishing (pier), boating(lr), canoeing(r), swimming, waterskiing. $2 per person entry fee ($1 for Texas seniors).

Fishing tip: In summer, fish for bass around lilypads with frogs and black shad worms; take crappies at 6-10 feet with minnows.

Caddo Lake FREE
State Wildlife Management Area

13 mi N of Marshall on Hwy 43; right for half mi on FM2198 to Caddo Lake State Park entrances on left or continue 14 mi on Hwy 43 to public boat ramp at bridge crossing Caddo Lake. Boat to WMA. No registration or permits required. Free. All yaer; 14-day limit. Primitive undesignated tent sites. No facilities; no drkg wtr. Hiking, hunting, fishing, boating. Biking & auto tour of WMA also available.

Martin Creek Lake State Park $6

25 mi S of Marshall on SR 43; S on FM 1716 (3 mi SW of Tatum). $6 for hike-in tent sites; $12 for 60 RV sites with elec/wtr; $15 for 6 sites with 50-amp elec/wtr. All year; 14-day limit. Tbls, flush toilets, cfga, drkg wtr, showers, dump, store, picnic areas, playground, beach. Fishing (pier), swimming, boating(l), biking, mountain bike trail, canoeing(r), hiking, waterskiing, interpretive programs, birdwatching. $2 per person entry fee.

Fishing tip: In summer fish at night for bass using blue fleck plastic worms & 10-inch black neon worms.

Mom & Pop's RV Park $12

On US 59 between Marshall & Jefferson; at 8796 Hwy 59 N. $12 base. All year. 44 sites. Tbls, flush toilets, cfga, drkg wtr, showers, rec hall, hookups($).

MASON (167)

Garner Seaquist Ranch   **$5**
6 mi W of Mason on SR 29. $5 base. All year. Base fee for primitive sites; $15 for wtr/elec sites. Tbls, toilets, cfga, drkg wtr. For $10 per person, hunt for topaz, the Texas state gem. Pay fee at Nu-Way Grocery in Mason.

MAUD (168)

Big Creek Landing   **$10**
S of Maud near the end of FM 2624 on CR 1207; at Wright Patman Lake. $10-$12. All year. 28 sites. Tbls, flush toilets, cfga, drkg wtr, hookups. Boating(l), fishing. Leased from Corps of Engineers.

Kelly Creek Landing   **$12**
8 mi S of Maud on FM 2624; on shore of Wright Patman Lake. $12. All year. 75 sites. Tbls, flush toilets, cfga, drkg wtr, hookups($), showers, dump, playground, store. Fishing, boating. Leased from Corps of Engineers.
Fishing tip: The best time for catching crappies in Wright Patman is winter through spring. Use minnows, small jigs and spinnerbaits.

Intake Hill   **FREE**
Corps of Engineers
Wright Patman Lake
From dam, jct US 59, off SR 2148, go SW. Free. All year; 14-day limit. 24 sites on 20 acres. 1 toilet, tbls, cfga, drkg wtr, dump, marina, lantern hangers. Boating(l), picnicking, fishing, swimming.
Fishing tip: This lake's shoreline produces excellent catches of largemouth bass all year. Use plastic worms, jigs and spinnerbaits. The best period for white bass is January through April.

Malden Lake   **$8**
Corps of Engineers
Wright Patman Lake
From jct of US 67 and TX 8; 4.8 mi S on TX 8 to campground. $8 with federal Senior Pass; others pay $16 ($18 with 50-amp). All year; 14-day limit. 39 sites with wtr/elec; 55-ft RV limit. Tbls, toilets, cfga, drkg wtr. Limited facilities in winter. Picnicking; fishing; boating (l); swimming in designated areas; hunting in undeveloped areas during hunting season. No firearms in developed public use areas. 2-day minimum stay on weekends.

MCCAMEY (170)

Santa Fe City Park   **FREE**
Jct of Hwy 385 & US 67, 5 blocks E. All year. 4 sites. Tbls, toilets, cfga, wtr & elec hookups, dump, playground. Picnicking. Rare pecan & elm trees in camp. Obtain permit from city hall.

MCKINNEY (171)

Erwin City Park   **$1**
From Hwy 380 West at McKinney, N on FM 1461; 1 mi E on CR 164; qtr mi N on CR 1006. $1 per person. All year. Overnight primitive camping at 11 fire rings throughout the park. Toilets, drkg wtr (closed 11/1-2/27). Register at community center.

MCLEAN (172)

Country Corner RV Park   **$11**
From I-40 exit 142, turn right; follow signs. $11. All year. 10 sites with hookups. Toilets, tbls, cfga, drkg wtr, playground, store.

MENARD (173)

Stockpen Crossing City Park   **$6**
1 mi W of Menard on FM 2092; on S side of San Saba River. $6 for tents; $15 for RVs wtih elec/wtr; $20 full hookups. All year. Tbls, cfga, firewood, hookups. Fishing, hiking.

MEXIA (175)

Fort Parker State Park   **$10**
7 mi S of Mexia on SR 14; access on Park Rd 28; on Navasota River. $10 for 10 sites with wtr & 5 overflow sites; $15 for 25 sites with elec/wtr hookups; $4 for hike-in tent sites. Tbls, flush toilets, cfga, drkg wtr, dump, showers, playgrounds, picnic areas, pavilion, store. Hiking trail, nature trails, swimming, canoeing(r), fishing, boating(lrd). Reconstructed fort. Old Fort Parker State Historical Park (1 mi S); Confederate Reunion Grounds SHP (6 mi SW). $2 per person entry fee.
Travel tip: Nearby is Old Fort Parker State Historical Park, a replica of the fort erected in 1833 by Elder John Parker and other settlers from Illinois for protection from Indians.

MILAM (176)

Red Hills Recreation Area   **$6**
Sabine National Forest
From SR 21 near Milam, 3 mi N on SR 87; 1 mi E on FR 116; on Red Hills Lake. $6 base. 5/1-10/1; 14-day limit. Base fee for primitive sites; $10 with elec. 28 sites. Tbls, flush toilets, cfga, cold showers, drkg wtr, shelter, dump, elec($), bathhouse. Swimming($), fishing, hiking, biking trails, nature trails.
Fishing tip: After the spring spawn on Toledo Bend in April, bass are tough to find. Forget about shallow-water casting in May & June and concentrate on the main lake points, starting with a Carolina rig and french fry; chartreuse for muddy water, white for clear water. Slow your retrieve to a crawl. Also fish around pepper grass with a chug bug or Cyclone buzzbait early in the day.

MINEOLA (177)

Lake Holbrook   **FREE**
Wood County Park
3.6 mi W of SR 37 on US 80; 1 mi W on Old US 80; quarter mi N on local rd. On Lake Holbrook. Free. All year; 15-day limit. 10 sites, plus 40-acre primitive area. Toilets, cfga, tbls, dump, no drkg wtr. Summer snack bar; playground. Fishing, swimming, boating(l), scenic views.

MINERAL WELLS (178)

Lake Mineral Wells State Park   **$10**
3 mi E of Mineral Wells on US 180 (45 mi W of Fort Worth). $10 base. All year; 14-day limit. Base fee for 20 primitive hike-in sites on 2-mi trail (no cfga); $12 for 11 sites with wtr & 20 equestrian sites with wtr; $18-20 for sites with wtr/elec; $6 overflow. Tbls, flush toilets, cfga, drkg wtr, showers, dump, playgrounds, picnic areas. Boating(lr), fishing (piers), swimming, rock climbing, hiking & nature trails, horseback riding, canoeing(r). $5 per person entry fee.

MONTICELLO (181)

Monticello Park   **$7**
Titus County Park
1.3 mi SE on US 271 from jct with I-30; 8 mi SW on FM 127; 1.4 mi SE on FM 21; between Monticello Lake and Lake Bob Sandlin. $7 with elec/wtr, plus $2 per person entry fee. All year; 14-day limit. 28 RV sites plus primitive area. Flush toilets, cfga, drkg wtr, dump, showers, dump. Fishing, boating(l).
Fishing tip: This 2,000-acre lake is a "hot water" reservoir that produces trophy bass; its largest was a 14-pounder caught in 1980. It produces more bass per acre than any other lake in Texas and offers good all-year fishing. Water temperature seldom drops below 65 degrees.

MOODY (182)

Mother Neff State Park   **$5**
1.5 mi S of Moody on SR 236; access via Park Rd 14; at Leon River. $5 base. All year; 14-day limit. Base fee for 3 primitive hike-in sites near small pond (Sept-May only; toilets & wtr 1 mi); $10 for 15 sites with wtr ; $15 for 6 sites with wtr/elec. Tbls, flush toilets, showers, cfga, drkg wtr, dump, playground, picnic areas, pavilion, rec hall. Hiking, fishing & canoeing (Leon River). Tabernacle. First Texas state park. $2 per persn entry fee.

MORGAN (183)

Steele Creek Park   **FREE**
Corps of Engineers
Whitney Lake
7 mi E of Morgan on TX 927; 1 mi S on TX 56; 2 mi S on co rd. All year; 14-day limit. 21 sites (10 with wtr hookups). Tbls, toilets,

cfga, drkg wtr. No drkg wtr Nov-March. Swimming; picnicking; fishing; boating(rl).

MOUNT VERNON (184)

Dogwood Park $10
Franklin County Water District
From I-30, S 1 mi on SR 37; 7.8 mi SE on FM 21; 2.5 mi S on FM 3007. $10 for undeveloped primitive sites. All year; 14-day limit. Flush toilets, cfga, drkg wtr, elec. 10-acre park on S side of 3,400-acre Lake Cypress Springs dam. Swimming, fishing (big bass & catfish), boating(l).

Harris RV Park $10
From jct of Hwy 37 & Hwy 21 near Mount Vernon, follow Hwy 21 to CR 4110; turn left on CR 4110 at Glade Branch Baptist Church for 200 yds. $10 ($40 weekly or $150 monthly) for RV sites with elec. Tbls, flush toilets, cfga, drkg wtr, hookups($), coin laundry, pool, showers. Discount for SKP.

Overlook Park $10
Franklin County Water District
Lake Cypress Springs
From I-30, S 1 mi on SR 37; 3.2 SE mi on FM 21; 4.6 mi on FM 2723. $10. All year; 14-day limit. Primitive camping. Drkg wtr, flush toilets. 16-acre area. Fishing, swimming, boating(l).

Walleye Park $10
Franklin County Water District
Lake Cypress Springs
From I-30, S 1 mi on SR 37; 3.2 SE mi on FM 21; 2 mi SE on FM 2723; 3 mi on local rd. $10 for RV sites off-season (Nov-Feb); $15-20 rest of year; $10 for for primitive tent sites. All year; 14-day limit. 66 RV sites with elec & wtr; primitive sites. Tbls, flush toilets, showers, cfga, drkg wtr, dump, shelters. Boating(l), fishing, volleyball. 89 acres. Fishing pier.

MULESHOE (185)

Muleshoe FREE
National Wildlife Refuge
20 mi S of Muleshoe on TX 214; 2.25 mi W on Caliche Rd to headquarters. Free overnight primitive campsites in the recreation area. Tbls, toilets, cfga, drkg wtr. Register at refuge headquarters. Hiking, nature trail. No hunting or boating. One of a chain of refuges in the Central Flyway, a wintering area for migratory waterfowl.

NAVASOTA (187)

Al McDonald
City of Navasota RV Park $10
W side of Navasota on SR 105. $10. All year; 14-day limit. 10 sites with full hookups. Tbls, flush toilets, showers, cfga, pavilion.

NEW BRAUNFELS (188)

Guadalupe River State Park $12
27 mi W of New Braunfels on Hwy 46; right on Park Rd for 3 mi; on the Guadalupe River. $12 base. All year; 14-day limit. Base fee for walk-in tent sites with wtr; $14-19 with hookups. 105 sites. Flush toilets, cfga, drkg wtr, tbls, hookups($), dump, showers, playgrounds. Fishing, boating, hiking, birdwatching, canoeing, tubing, swimming. $6 per person entry fee.

NEW WAVERLY (189)

Cagle Recreation Area $10
Sam Houston National Forest
From I-45 exits 102 or 103 near New Waverly, 5 mi W on FM 1375; turn at Cagle sign; on Lake Conroe. $10 with federal Senior·Pass; others pay $20. All year; 14-day limit. 47 sites; 45-ft RV limit. Tbls, flush toilets, showers, cfga, drkg wtr, dump, lantern post. Boating(l), fishing, 2-mi hiking trail. Senior fee expected to increase in 2007 due to elec cost.

Kelley Pond FREE
Sam Houston National Forest
11 mi W of New Waverly on TX 1375; half mi S on FR 204; half mi W on FR 271. Free. All year; 14-day limit. 8 primitive sites (21-ft RV limit). Toilets, cfga, tbls, no drkg wtr. Picnicking; fishing; hiking. Elev 300 ft; 6 acres. Heavily used by off-road vehicle enthusiasts. In a pine-hardwood forest.

Sam Houston National Forest FREE
State Wildlife Management Area
3 mi W of New Waverly on FM 1375 to NF ranger station. Free. All year; 14-day limit. Primitive undesignated sites; no facilities. Fishing, hiking, horseback riding, biking. 161,154 acres.

Stubblefield Lake $10
Sam Houston National Forest
11 mi W of New Waverly on SR 1375; 3 mi NW on FR 215. $10. All year; 14-day limit. 28 sites (22-ft RV limit). Tbls, flush toilets, cfga, drkg wtr, cold showers, shelter. Boating, fishing, hiking trails, designated motorcycle areas. 36 acres. On N end of Lake Conroe.

NOCONA (190)

Boone Park FREE
North Montague County Water District
5 mi N of Nocona on TX 103; 3 mi on FM 2634; 3.9 mi N on FM 2953 to Oak Shores; 0.4 mi S to sign, "Public boat ramp"; turn right on nameless rd; half mi to park (rough rds). On Lake Nocona. Free. All year; 15-day limit. Undesignated RV & tent sites. Tbls, toilets, cfga. Swimming; picnicking; fishing; boating (l). Reader says toilets at all these camps quite dirty.

Fishing tip: 1,470-acre lake contains good populations of bass, sand bass, crappies, catfish and tiger muskies.

Joe Benton Park FREE
North Montague County Water District
From FM 103, E 3 mi on FM 2634; 1.2 mi NE on FM 2953. Free. All year; 21-day limit. Open RV & tent camping. Toilets, tbls, shelters, cfga, no drkg wtr. Swimming, fishing, boating(ld). On 1,470-acre Lake Nocona.

Weldon Rob Memorial Park FREE
North Montague County Water District
From FM 103, E 3 mi on FM 2634; three-fourths mi SE to sites. Free. All year; 21-day limit. Open RV & tent camping. Toilets, cfga, tbls, shelters, no drkg wtr. Also new section with full hookups but no tbls or shelters, $10. On Lake Nocona. Swimming, fishing, boating(l), playground.

OVERTON (193)

Overton City Park $10
From SR 135 in Overton, W on West Henderson St; S on Meadowbrook Dr, then local rd W; on Overton City Lakes. $10 ($50 monthly). All year; 30-day limit. 30 sites. Tbls, flush toilets, cfga, drkg wtr, hookups, dump, pool, playground, community center. Fishing, boating, swimming, golf, volleyball, tennis.

PADUCAH (194)

Matador FREE
State Wildlife Management Area
7 mi N of Paducah on US 83/62; 2.5 mi W on FM 3256. Free. All year except about 12/1-3 & 3/18-20, 3/25-27; 14-day limit. Two primitive designated camping areas W of WMA headquaarters. Toilets, no drkg wtr, no firewood (use camp stoves). Primarily used by hun-ters. Hiking, hunting, fishing, biking, horseback riding, auto tour. Registration & permit required. 28,183 acres.

PALESTINE (195)

Gus Engeling FREE
State Wildlife Management Area
21 mi NW of Palestine on US 287 (or 38 mi SE of Corsicana). Free. All year except for short-term closures; 14-day limit. Primitive undesignated camping; registration required. No facilities, no drkg wtr. Hiking, hunting, birdwatching, nature trails, auto tour.

Rusk-Palestine State Parks $6
2 mi E of Palestine on US 84. $6 base. All year; 14-day limit. Base fee for 12 primitive sites with wtr in Palestine SP; $11 for 39 sites with elec/wtr ($70 weekly); $15 for 32 full-hookup sites. Tbls, flush toilets, cfga, drkg wtr, playground, picnic area. Basketball (two courts at Rusk), birdwatching, canoeing(r). Depot of historic Texas State Railroad to Rusk. $2 per person entry fee.

PAMPA (196)

Hobart Street Park **FREE**
1 block N of US 60 on SR 70. Free. All year; 24-hour limit. 10 RV sites & tent area. Wtr & elec hookups, cfga, tbls, toilets, dump, shelter. Playground, tennis, volleyball, softball. Another camp area, 6 acres.

Pampa City Recreation Park **$8**
From Pampa, 3 mi E of SR 10 on US 60. $8 Sun-Thurs; $10 Fri & Sat. All year; 14-day limit. 25 RV sites & free tent camping in designated areas. Tbls, flush toilets, cfga, drkg wtr, dump, showers, playground, elec. Fishing, boating(l). GPS: N35 32.018, W100 55.959.

PERRYTON (197)

Whigham City Park **FREE**
In town at US 83 and Farm 377. Free. All year; 3-day limit. 5 sites. Wtr/elec hookups. Tbls, toilets, cfga, dump. Tennis & basketball courts, playground. Grocery, laundry.

Wolf Creek Park **$6**
Ochiltree County
12 mi SE of Perryton off US 83; 5 mi E on CR 25 to Lake Fryer. $6 for tents; $8 for primitive RV sites; $15 for RVs with full hookups (also, $1 fee is charged on the first night). 5/1-LD. 94 sites with hookups on 700 acres. Toilets, tbls, cfga, drkg wtr, elec, dump, showers. Fishing, boating(l), hiking, swimming, picnicking.
    Travel tip: The Museum of the Plains on the N end of Perryton features artifacts from The Buried City -- a nearby pre-Columbian site thought to have been active between 800 and 1500. The museum also contains bones of woolly mammoths, mastadons and prehistoric camels. Other exhibits include old bottles, a sofa foutain from the '50s and early ranch artifacts.

PILOT POINT (198)

Isle du Bois Unit
Ray Roberts Lake State Park **$12**
Between Pilot Point & Sanger, 10 mi E of I-35 on FM 455; at S end of Ray Roberts Lake. $12 base. All year; 14-day limit. Base fee for 53 developed hike-in tent sites with tbls, cfga, lantern post; $12 for 14 equestrian sites with wtr; $20 for 115 sites with elec/wtr hookups. Tbls, flush toilets, cfga, drkg wtr, showers, dump, pavilion, store, picnicking area, beach, fish cleaning facility, playgrounds. Biking, swimming, boating(l), fishing (lighted pier), horseback riding, hiking, mountain biking, birdwatching. See Sanger entry. $5 per person entry fee; $3 for Texas seniors.
    Fishing tip: In summer, use shad-pattern topwaters early in the day just off primary lake points, then switch to Carolina-rig plastic worms fished deeper along drop-offs during sunlight hours.

PINELAND (199)

Moore Plantation **FREE**
State Wildlife Management Area
E of Pineland on FM 1, then 3 mi E on FM 2426; info station on N side of rd. Free. Oct-Jan; 14-day limit; in Sabine National Forest. Primitive designated campsites; no facilities, no drkg wtr. Fishing, hunting, hiking, horseback riding, biking.

Rayburn Park **$8**
Corps of Engineers
Sam Rayburn Lake
Near Pineland, 8 mi W of US 96 on Farm 83; 11.7 mi S on Farm 705; 1 mi W on Farm 3127; .8 mi S on Spur 3127; on N shore of lake. $8 with federal Senior Pass at elec/wtr sites ($9 at premium sites with 50 amp); others pay $16 & $18. Sites without elec, $11. All year; 14-day limit. 75 sites (24 with hookups); 65-ft RVs. Pit & flush toilets, shelters, showers, drkg wtr, cfga, dump, playground. Fishing, boating(l). 2-night minimum stay on weekends.
    Fishing tip: Crappies at Sam Rayburn are mostly caught on live minnows or jigs. Fish the edges of the hydrillas 4-16 feet deep in the spring. In summer, try structure and baited holes in 16-35 feet of water. Try the tributaries in February and March for both crappies and bass.

PINE SPRINGS (200)

Backcountry Camping **FREE**
Guadalupe Mountains National Park
Hike to designated backcountry sites after obtaining free permit from visitor center or ranger station. All year; 14-day limit. 10 primitive sites; no facilities, no trash service. No fires; fuel stoves permitted. Hiking, fossil research. 7-day, $3 per person park entry fee.

PITTSBURG (202)

Lake Bob Sandlin State Park **$6**
8 mi N of Pittsburg on SR; E on FM 21; S to park. $6 for 2 primitive walk-in tent sites; $12 for 66 RV sites with elec/wtr ($77 weekly); $16 for 9 premium RV sites with elec/wtr. All year; 14-day limit. Tbls, flush toilets, cfga, drkg wtr, showers, dump, playground, picnic areas, shelter, bathhouse. Hiking, fishing (pier), swimming, boating(l), in-line skating, mountain biking. View eagles during winter. 640 acres; 9,460-acre lake. $2 per person entry fee.
    Fishing tip: To catch nice bass from Lake Sandlin, use spinnerbaits or plastic worms and jigs along the flooded grass beds. Best colors are chartreuse and purple.

PLAINVIEW (203)

Ollie Liner Center RV Park **$10**
At Plainview, 6 mi S of Columbia St from I-27; half block E. $10 base. All year; 7-day limit.

44 sites. Tbls, toilets, cfga, drkg wtr, dump, elec. No tents.

PORT ARANSAS (204)

Mustang Island State Park **$8**
14 mi S of Port Aransas on Park Rd 53. $8 for 300 primitive beach sites (chemical toilets, drkg wtr & rinse showers); $16 for 48 RV sites with wtr/elec, showers, site shelters. Tbls, flush toilets, cfga, drkg wtr, dump, showers, store. Swimming, fishing, mountain biking, birdwatching, hiking. 3,703 acres. $4 per person entry fee.

Port Aransas Beach **FREE**
Municipal Park
Park along the beach on Mustang Island from the south jetty through Port Aransas Beach to the Kleberg County line S of Bob Hall pier. Free with the purchase of a $12 annual vehicle sticker from city hall (710 W. Avenue A). All year; 3-day limit in tent or pop-up; RVs permitted between markers 27 & 34. Toilets, cfga, no other facilities except trash cans. Beach games, swimming, surfing, shelling.

Port Aransas **$10**
Nueces County Park
From SR 361 ferry landing in Port Aransas, take Cotter St. to park at tip of Mustang Island. $10 for primitive beach sites; $18 with wtr/elec. 75 RV sites & primitive open beach camping (with cold rinse shower). All year; 3-day limit. Flush toilets, showers, bathhouse, dump & wtr fill ($4), drkg wtr. Swimming, fishing (lighted pier). Patrolled.

PORT O'CONNOR (207)

Matagorda Island State Park **$6**
From state park docks in Port O'Connor, ride ferry to island (fee charged). $6 for primitive beach tent camping. 200 tent sites. Tbls, toilets, cfga, drkg wtr, beach, store, showers. Swimming, hiking, mountain biking, fishing, boating(d).

Matagorda Island **FREE**
State Wildlife Management Area
From state park docks in Port O'Connor, ride ferry to island (fee charged). Free. All year; 14-day limit. Primitive designated campsites; no facilities, no drkg wtr. Toilets, wtr, showers available at visitors center. Hiking, hunting, fishing. For registration instructions, call 361-983-2215.

POTTSBORO (208)

Preston Bend Recreation Area **$12**
Corps of Engineers
Lake Texoma
6.4 mi N of Pottsboro on SR 120. $12 base. 4/1-10/30; 14-day limit. Base fee without elec; $16 at 26 sites with wtr/elec. 38 sites; 65-ft RVs. Tbls, flush toilets, cfga, drkg wtr, dump, beach, showers. Fishing, boating(l), swimming.

PRESIDIO (209)

Big Bend Ranch State Park $3
4 mi SE of Presidio to Fort Leaton State Historical Park for area N of gravel FM 170; or just E of Lajitas at Barton Warnock Environmental Education Center for area S of FM 170. $3 per-person activity fee for 10 primitive tent sites along roads within park; numerous backcountry tent camping areas on Rancherias Loop Trail. Pit toilets at Madera Canyon & Grassy Banks; no other facilities, no wtr. Fishing, swimming, hiking, interpretive programs, birdwatching. Botanical gardens, museum. 268,495 acres. Waterfalls, pictographs. Park rd along Rio Grande River. Pay user fees either at the education center or at Fort Leaton SP (4 mi E of Presidio on FM 170).

Ocotillo Unit FREE
Las Palomas Wildlife Management Area
36 mi NW of Presidio on FM 170; continue 1 mi N of Ruidosa on FM 170. Free. All year; 14-day limit. Primitive undesignated camping. No faiclities, no drkg wtr. Hunting. Registration & permit required.

PRINCETON (210)

Lakeland $8
Corps of Engineers
Lavon Lake
6.8 mi E of Princeton on US 380; 4.1 mi S on SR 78, then W on access rd. $8. 4/1-9/30; 14-day limit. 32 primitive tent sites. Tbls, toilets, cfga, drkg wtr, no dump. Boating(l), fishing.

Lavonia Park $9
Corps of Engineers
Lavon Lake
3 mi E of Princeton on Hwy 78; half mi W on CR 486, then follow signs to E side of dam. $9 with federal Senior Pass at 38 RV sites with wtr/elec; others pay $18. Tent sites $10. 2/14/9/29; 14-day limit. 53 sites; 60-ft RV limit. Tbls, flush toilets, cfga, drkg wtr, showers, dump, elec($). Boating(l), fishing. 2-night minimum stay on weekends.

PROCTOR (211)

Promontory Park $8
Corps of Engineers
Proctor Lake
9 mi SW of Proctor on US 377; 5.5 mi N on SR 16; 4.2 mi SE on FM 2318 (about 7 mi N of Camanche). $8 base. Open 3/16-9/30; 14-day limit. Base fee without elec; $16 for wtr/elec; $20 at premium sites with 50-amp. 88 sites, 68 with hookups. Pavilion, tbls, cfga, drkg wtr, flush toilets, elec($), dump, showers, shelters. Boating(ld), fishing. 2-night minimum stay on weekends.

QUANAH (212)

Copper Breaks State Park $7
13 mi S of Quanah on SR 6. $7 base. 3/1-11/30; 14-day limit. Base fee for 6 primitive hike-in sites; $10 for 21 sites with wtr (including 10 equestrian); $6 for overflow camping; $20 for 25 sites with elec/wtr (50-amp available). Tbls, flush toilets, cfga, drkg wtr, showers, dump, playgrounds, picnic areas, amphitheater (June productions), fishing pier, beach, store. Swimming, nature trail, hiking trail, equestrian trail, interpretive displays, boating(ld), fishing, paddleboats(r). Equestrian area has 2 tying rails. Longhorn herd. $2 per person entry fee.

Fishing tip: Nearby Lake Pauline (5 mi E of Quanah off US 287) produces good catches of crappie and largemouth bass. The record Florida-strain bass is 9 pounds.

QUINLAN (213)

Caddo Creek Unit FREE
Sabine River Authority of Texas
Tawakoni Wildlife Management Area
1.5 mi N of Quinlan on SR 34. Free. All year; 14-day limit. Primitive designated campsites. No facilities, no drkg wtr. Fishing, hunting, horseback riding, hiking. Access permit required.

Duck Cove Unit FREE
Sabine River Authority of Texas
Tawakoni Wildlife Management Area
1 mi E of Quinlan on FM 35; 7 mi S on FM 751; 1 mi W on CR 3827. Free. All year; 14-day limit. Primitive designated campsites. No facilities, no drkg wtr. Fishing, hunting, horseback riding, hiking. Access permit required.

QUITAQUE (214)

Caprock Canyons State Park $8
4 mi N of Quitaque off SR 86 on FM 1065. $8 base. All year; 14-day limit. Base fee for backpack areas; $12 for 40 walk-in developed sites and for 12 developed equestrian sites; $14 for 9 sites in Lake Theo area with wtr nearby; $11 for overflow; $15-20 for 35 sites with hookups. Visitor center, dump, swimming, boating(l), playground, bridle trails, mountain bike trails, hiking trails, fishing, interpretive displays. $3 per person entry fee.

QUITMAN (215)

Lake Quitman FREE
Wood County Park
From SR 37, qtr mi W on SR 154; 4.8 mi N on FM 2966; 1 mi E on Lake Quitman Rd. Free primitive camping; $15 for RVs with elec. All year; 15-day limit. 12 RV sites & free 25-acre primitive area maintained by county. Flush toilets, cfga, drkg wtr, elec($). Flush toilets but no drkg wtr in primitive area (10-day limit). Boating(rl), fishing, swimming. Scenic.

Oak Ridge Resort $8
4 mi N of Quitman at 2919 SR 154; on SW shore of Lake Fork. $8 base. All year. Base fee for tent sites; $25 for RV sites with elec/wtr. Tbls, flush toilets, showers, cfg, drkg wtr, dump ($2), hookups($). Boating(l), fishing. $2 launch fee.

Fishing tip: Lake Fork has been the hottest bass lake in Texas for several years. The current lake record is 18.8 pounds, and many veteran anglers believe the lake will produce the next world's record largemouth.

REDWATER (216)

Clear Springs $8
Corps of Engineers
Wright Patman Lake
4 mi NE of Redwater on US 67, then S. $8 with federal Senior Pass at 87 sites with elec/wtr ($9 with 50-amp); others pay $16 & $18. Tent sites, $10. All year; 14-day limit. 102 sites; 65-ft RVs. Tbls, flush toilets, cfga, drkg wtr, pavilion, elec($), beach, playground, dump, showers. Fishing, boating(l), swimming. 2-night minimum stay on weekends.

REFUGIO (217)

Jeter City RV Park $12
2 blocks W of US 77 at S end of Refugio, next to Lions/Shelly Park. $12 with hookups ($70 weekly). All year. 15 sites. Tbls, flush toilets, showers, cfga, drkg wtr, hookups. Fishing, playground.

RIO VISTA (219)

Ham Creek Park FREE
Johnson County Park
From SR 174, SW 8.4 mi on FM 916. On Brazos River. Free. 12 sites. All year; 14-day limit. Drkg wtr, toilets, cfga. Swimming, fishing, boating (l). Park is mostly closed. Future plans call for total redevelopment by the U.S. Army Corps of Engineers, then management by the county.

RISING STAR (220)

Rising Star City RV Park $10
On SR 36, 4 blocks W of downtown traffic light. $10. All year. Full hookups, tbls, flush toilets, cfga, drkg wtr, no showers, playground gear, half-mi walking trail. Volleyball, baseball, tennis.

ROBERT LEE (222)

Coke County Park $12
1 block N on TX 158 on TX 208; 3 blocks E on Austin St in Robert Lee. $12 (monthly, $300). All year; 3-day limit. 30 sites. Toilets, cfga, elec/wtr hookup. Store. Swimming; picnicking; fishing; boating (r); golf; tennis; hiking. Recreation hall. Bike trails.

Paint Creek Recreation Area **$5**
Colorado River Municipal Water District
From Robert Lee, 7.8 mi W of SR 208 on SR 158; half mi N & E on local rd; on E.V. Spence Reservoir. $5 base. All year; 7-day limit. 28 sites with hookups($). 100-acre primitive area. Tbls, flush & pit toilets, cfga, drkg wtr, dump, bait, shelters, marina. Swimming, boating(l). Concessionaire-operated.

Fishing tip: E.V. Spence Lake is best known for its huge striped bass. More than 40 of the state's biggest stripers were caught here, including the lake's record 35-pounder, caught in 1988.

Lakeview Park **$5**
Colorado River Municipal Water District
NW of Robert Lee to E.V. Spence Lake Dam; camp on N shore of lake above dam. $5. All year; 7-day limit. Primitive camping in open area. Tbls, toilets, cfga, drkg wtr, dump. Swimming, boating(l), fishing. Hookups at marinas, $18.

Fishing tip: Try the base of the sandstone and red clay bluffs on the upper end of Spence lake for channel catfish.

Rough Creek Park **$5**
Colorado River Municipal Water District
About 6 mi NW of Robert Lee on SR 208; S & W on access rd. $5. All year; 7-day limit. Primitive camping per person; over 64 & under 18 free. Primitive open area. Tbls, toilets, cfga, drkg wtr, dump. Swimming, boating(l), fishing. Hookups at marina, $18.

Wildcat Creek Recreation Area **$2**
Colorado River Municipal Water District
From Robert Lee, 4.5 mi W of SR 208 on SR 158; .6 mi N & E on local rd; on E.V. Spence Reservoir. $2 base. All year; 7-day limit. Base fee for primitive camping per person; over 64 & under 18 free; full hookups at marina, $18. 8 sites with hookups($). Pavilions($), shelters($), tbls, flush toilets, cfga, drkg wtr, showers($), bait, store, snack bar. Swimming, boating(l), fishing. Concessionaire-operated.

ROCKPORT (223)

Goose Island State Park **$10**
8 mi N of Rockport on SR 35; access via Park Rd 13. $10 for 25 walk-in tent sites; $15-18 for 102 RV sites with hookups; $7 overflow for RVs. All year; no time limit. 218 sites. Tbls, flush toilets, cfga, drkg wtr, showers, dump, playgrounds, picnic areas, pavilion. Fishing (lighted pier), boating (l), waterskiing, swimming, hiking, birdwatching. $3 per person entry fee for overnight.

ROTAN (224)

Rotan City RV Park **FREE**
On Hwy 92 (Sammy Bauth Ave) across from football field; from S into town on Hwy 70, turn right on Sammy Bauth Ave at traffic light. Free one night, $6 thereafter. All year. 6 RV sites with wtr/elec; no showers or toilets. Pool, playground, golf course, walking trail.

SABINE PASS (225)

Sabine Pass Battleground **$8**
State Historical Park
1.5 mi S of Sabine Pass on FM 3322. $8 base. All year; 14-day limit. Base fee for 10 primitive sites; $15 for 7 RV sites with elec/wtr. Tbls, flush toilets, cfga, drkg wtr, dump, no showers. Picnicking, fishing, crabbing, boating (l). $2 donation suggested for boat ramp. $2 per person entry fee. Campsites closed at presstime in 2007 due to damage by Hurricane Rita.

Sea Rim State Park **$10**
10 mi S of Sabine Pass on SR 87 (24 mi SW of Port Arthur). $10 base. All year; 14-day limit. Base fee for for 10 sites with wtr; $15 for 20 RV sites with elec/wtr; $8 overflow. Tbls, flush toilets, cfga, drkg wtr, showers, dump, observation blinds, interpretive displays. Picnicking, nature trail, boating(l), hunting, canoeing(r), beachcombing, nature trail, kayaking, birdwatching, swimming, fishing. This park was closed by Hurricane Rita but is expected to re-open in August 2007.

SAN ANGELO (226)

Middle Concho Park **$5**
4 mi S of San Angelo on Hwy 584; 4 mi S & W on Red Bluff Rd; on Lake Nasworthy. $5. All year; 14-day limit. Primitive camping area. Tbls, pit toilets, cfga, drkg wtr. Swimming, fishing, boating(ld). 600 acres. Not a city park.

San Angelo State Park **$8**
Follow FM 2288 S from US 87. $8 for 200 backpack and primitive sites; $18 for 71 sites with wtr/elec hookups and for10 equestrian sites with hookups. All year; 14-day limit. Tbls, flush & chemical toilets, showers, cfga, drkg wtr, dump, store. Swimming, fishing, hiking, boating(dl), waterskiing, mountain biking.

Spring Creek Park **$5**
Follow Knickerbocker Rd from San Angelo to lake bridge; turn on Fisherman's Rd. $5. All year; 14-day limit. Primitive sites. Pit toilets, cfga, drrkg wtr, dump. Tennis, volleyball. Not a city park.

Twelve-Mile Recreation Area **$5**
Twin Buttes Reservoir
12 mi W of San Angelo on Hwy 67; at 12-Mile boat ramp. $5 access fee. Primitive camping; no facilities. Boatig(ld), fishing. Not a city park.

Twin Buttes Park **$5**
5 mi W of San Angelo on US 67; S on access rd to NW shore of Twin Buttes Reservoir. $5. All year; 14-day limit. Primitive camping; pit toilets, cfga, drkg wtr. Boating(l), fishing. not a city park.

SAN ANTONIO (227)

Calaveras Lake Park **$4**
San Antonio River Authority
About 17 mi S of San Antonio on US 181, then 3 mi NE on Loop 1604. $4 per person ($2 seniors & children). Primitive camping. Tble, toilets, cfga, drkg wtr, store, fishing piers. Boating(lr), fishing, hiking, nature trail.

Fishing tip: Fed by Calaveras, Hondo and Chupaderas Creeks, this 3,500-acre lake is best known for its channel catfish, but it also contains blue catfish, hybrid striped bass, red drum and largemouth bass. Using plastic worms & crankbaits, try for bass in the bullrushes and along the rip-rap near the dam.

Victor Braunig Lake **$4**
San Antonio River Authority
About 17 mi S of San Antonio; take exit 130 from I-37. $4 per person ($2 seniors & children). Primitive camping. Tbls, toilets, cfga, drkg wtr, store, fish cleaning station. Boating(l), fishing. 1,350-acre lake.

Fishing tip: A power plant lake with quite fertile water, Braunig Lake is warm all year and has good numbers of catfish that can be caught from shore with nightcrawlers, cheese baits, crawfish and cut bait. Local fishermen use surf-casting rigs to reach deeper water. The lake also is stocked with saltwater redfish.

SAN FELIPE (228)

Stephen F. Austin **$12**
State Historical Park
2.5 mi N of San Felipe on FM 1458; access via Park Rd 38. $12 base. All year; 14-day limit. Base fee for 39 sites with wtr hookups; $15-20 for sites with elec hookups. Tbls, flush toilets, cfga, drkg wtr, showers, dump, pool, playgrounds, picnic areas, shelter, store, historic buildings. Swimming, hiking trail, fishing, golf. Brazos River. 664 acres. $3 per day entry fee.

SANFORD (230)

Bugbee Canyon **$4**
Lake Meredith
National Recreation Area
Take TX 687 from Sanford across Sanford Dam to Bugbee Rd; on Bugbee Rd to campground (difficult access). Camp free, but $4 daily boat fee. All year; 14-day limit. Semi-developed shoreline sites. Tbls, toilets, no drkg wtr. Hunting; waterskiing; fishing. Nestled within a narrow canyon. Opportunity for camping varies with the lake level.

Spring Canyon **$4**
Lake Meredith
National Recreation Area
2 mi N of Sanford on Farm 1319. Camp free, but $4 daily boat fee. All year; 14-day limit. Undeveloped camping area. Toilets, cfga, no drkg wtr. Fishing, swimming, waterskiing, hunting. Camping opportunity varies with lake level. Handicap fishing pier.

SANGER (231)

Johnson Branch Unit   **$6**
Ray Roberts Lake State Park
N of Sanger on I-35 to exit 483; 7 mi W on FM 3002. $6 for 33 primitive hike-in sites (closed until further notice); $12 for 50 developed walk-in sites; $20 for 104 sites with elec/wtr. All year; 14-day limit. Tbls, flush toilets, cfga, drkg wtr, showers, dump, playgrounds, beach, fish cleaning station. Fishing, boating(l), swimming, biking, mountain biking, birdwatching (eagles in winter), hiking. See Pilot Point entry. $5 per person entry fee.

Fishing tip: Ray Roberts Lake is a very good crappie lake; look for them in 20-30 feet of water during summer. Use TailHummers and small Rat-L-Traps for white bass; slabs and crankbaits for hybrid stripers.

SAN SABA (233)

Joe Ragsdale RV Park   **$4**
Mill Pond City Park
In San Saba at Mill Pond Park. $4 for tents; $11 for RVs with hookups. Tbls, flush toilets, cfga, drkg wtr, CATV, dump, pool, pavilion, playground. Swimming, basketball, running track, nature trails. 71-acre park soon to be enlarged. Weekly, monthly rates available.

SAN YGNACIO (234)

River Ranch   **$12**
RV Park & Fishing Camp
1 mi N of San Ygnacio on US 83; at 4506 N Hwy 83. $12. All year. 46 sites with hookups. Tbls, flush toilets, cfga, drkg wtr, showers, rec hall, coin laundry, dump. Fishing, boating.

SEMINOLE (236)

Gaines County Park   **$4**
8 mi N of Seminole on US 385. $4. All year; 5-day limit. 8 RV sites. Tbls, flush toilets, showers, cfga, drkg wtr, dump, playground, rec hall, elec. Very nice park. 50-amp service to be added.

SHELBYVILLE (238)

English Bay Marina   **$5**
1.3 mi E of Shelbyville on FM 417; 9.3 mi E on Hwy 2694; 4.8 mi S on Hwy 139 to FM 3184; follow signs; at Toledo Bend Reservoir. $5 for primitive tent sites; $7 for basic RV or tent sites; $10 for RV sites with elec ($150 per month). 20 RV sites, plus primitive camping on 13 acres. Tbls, toilets, cfga, drkg wtr. Boating(l), fishing. Covered fishing pier & baited bream area.

Fishing tip: Fish the lake's humps and ridges next to deep-water sloughs, using diving crankbaits or plastic worms. Early mornings, try topwater plugs, buzzbaits or spinnerbaits at grass beds close to deep water.

Use shallow and diving crankbaits where you see schooling bass chasing shad.

Haley's Ferry   **$2**
Sabine National Forest
Sabine River Authority of Texas
12 mi E of Shelbyville on FM 2694; 1 mi on FM 172; 2 mi E on FM 100-A. On Toledo Bend Reservoir. $2 use fee. All year; 14-day limit. Undeveloped primitive area with 4 tbls, boat ramp. No camping in the parking area, but numerous dispersed spots nearby. Toilet at boat ramp.

Fishing tip: For summer panfish, use crickets or worms in grass beds at 18-22 feet for bream; catch crappies at night on shiners over baited brush piles.

SHINER (239)

Green Dickson City Park   **$10**
On US 90A at the W edge of Shiner; follow signs half mi N to campground on Ave B. $10. All year. 20 RV sites; no RV limit. Tbls, toilets, cfga. Hiking, picnicking, fishing ponds, golfing, tennis, softball. Pay at town hall. 148 acres.

SILVERTON (240)

Lake Mackenzie Park   **$3**
Mackenzie Municipal Water Authority
4 mi W of Silverton on SR 86/207; 7 mi N on SR 207. $3 base. All year. Base fee for primitive RV and tent camping (or $50 annual primitive camping permit); RV sites with hookups, $15 or $75 weekly. 36 primitive sites, 25 hookup sites. Tbls, flush toilets, cfga, drkg wtr, cold showers, elec/wtr hookups, playground, shelter, 2 dump stations, store. Nature trail, fishing, boating(l - $2), swimming, waterskiing, store. $3 per person entry fee or $50 annual family pass.

SOMERVILLE (241)

Big Creek Park & Marina   **$12**
Somerville Lake
NW of Somerville on SR 36 to Lyons; 4 mi W on FM 60, then S on R 4; on N end of lake. $12 for primtive sites; $20 for RVs with wtr & elec; $25 with 50 amp. All year; 14-day limit. 120 RV sites & 50 acres for tent camping. Tbls, flush toilets, cfga, drkg wtr, showers, elec($). Hiking, boating(l), swimming, waterskiing. Formerly Corps of Engineers facility; now concession-operated.

Fishing tips: Big Creek is well known for its large catfish and plentiful white bass.

Rocky Creek   **$9**
Corps of Engineers
Somerville Lake
SE of Somerville on SR 36; 4.5 mi W on FM 1948. Holders of federal Senior Pass pay $9 at non-elec sites, $10 at elec/wtr sites, $11 with 50-amp; others pay $18, $20 & $22. Off-season (1/1-2/28), regular fees are $14, $16 & $18. 201 sites (82 with wtr/elec); 65-ft RVs.

All year; 14-day limit. Pavilion, tbls, flush toilets, cfga, drkg wtr, showers, dump, elec ($), playground. Fishing, boating(l), swimming, waterskiing. 2-night minimum stay on weekends.

Welch City Park   **$8**
From SR 36 near Somerville, three-fourths mi W on Thornberry Dr to dam; turn right on the dam; camp behind headquarters complex on NE end of Somerville Lake. $8 for primitive sies; $20 for RV sites with hookups. All year; 14-day limit. 40 sites. Pit & flush toilets, cfga, drkg wtr, elec($), showers. Fishing, boating (l), swimming, waterskiing, Entry fee.

Yegua Creek   **$8**
Corps of Engineers
Somerville Lake
SE of Somerville on SR 36; 2 mi W on FM 1948. Holders of federal Senior Pass pay $8 for sites with wtr hookup, $10 with wtr/elec during 3/1-9/30 and $9 during 10/1-2/28. Others pay $16, $20 & $18, respectively. All year; 14-day limit. 82 sites; 65-ft RVs. Tbls, flush toilets, cfga, drkg wtr, showers, playground, elec($), 4WD trails. Hiking, swimming, fishing, boating(l), waterskiing, OHV area, nature trail. 2-night minimum stay on weekends.

SPEARMAN (242)

Palo Duro Reservoir   **$8**
Palo Duro River Authority
N of Spearman on Hwy 15; furn on FM 3214 across the dam to N entrance. $8 base. All year; 14-day limit. Base fee for primitive sites (includes $2 per person entry fee); $12 for sites with elec (including one $2 entry fee). Annual family entry fee, $30; annual individual entry, $15. Two campgrounds, one with 26 RV sites with hookups, the other with 11 hookups. Tbls, toilets, cfga, drkg wtr. Fishing, boating(l), hiking. $2 boat ramp fee.

Fishing tip: Good bank fishing for crappies using minnows or catch catfish on stink baits. Lake also contains walleyes (2 million released in April 2001), smallmouth and Florida-strain largemouth bass. Lake records are 9-pound walleyes and bass.

SPICEWOOD (243)

Krause Springs   **$8**
Private Park
Off SR 71 at Spricewood; turn on Spur 191, then right on CR 404; follow signs; at the Cypress River. $8 per person ($5 children) plus admission fee. All year. 24 RV sites & tent area. Tbls, flush toilets, cfga, drkg wtr, pool. 32 springs in the campground. Hiking, swimming.

STARTZVILLE (244)

Cranes Mills   **$8**
Corps of Engineers
Canyon Lake
2.8 mi N of Startzville. $8 during Sun-Thurs;

$12 Fri-Sat. All year, with limited sites open 10/1-2/28; 14-day limit. 46 primtive tent sites; no RVs permitted. Tbls, toilets, cfga, drkg wtr, showers. Boating(l), fishing, picnicking. Fishing dock. Launch fee.

STEPHENVILLE (245)

Stephenville City Park   **$10**
From south loop of US 377/67/281, N on Graham St (SR 108) qtr mi across Bosque River. $10 for seniors; $15 all others. All year; 7-day limit. 10 RV sites with wtr & elec; 50 primitive sites. Drkg wtr, flush toilets, cfga, group pavilions, elec ($), dump. Horseshoes, volleyball, softball, shuffleboard, nature trails, swimming pool.

STINNET (246)

Stinnet City Park   **FREE**
On Broadway Street, 1 block W of TX 136 and TX 2097, in Stinnet. Free. All year; 3-day limit. 8 sites for self-contained vehicles. Toilets, cfga, pool, playground. Ice, groceries. Tennis, volleyball, swimming.

SULPHUR SPRINGS (248)

South Sulphur Unit   **$8**
Cooper Lake State Park
N of Sulphur Springs on SR 19; W on FM 71; N on FM 3505; on S side of Cooper Lake. $8 base. All year; 14-day limit. Base fee for 15-site primitive walk-in, overflow area and equestrian overflow; $14 for 87 sites with elec/wtr; $18 for 15 equestrian sites with elec/wtr. Tbls, flush toilets, cfga, drkg wtr, showers, dump, shelters, playground, fish cleaning stations, store, lighted fishing piers, beach. Biking, hiking, bridle trails, boating(l), waterskiing, fishing piers, swimming. $3 per person entry fee.
Fishing tip: This relatively new lake (built 1991) has become a major big bass lake. During the spring and summer, every section of it produces fish on lizards, spinnerbaits and jigs. In the fall and winter, fish areas close to deep water with jig-and-pigs, spnnerbaits and plastic worms 10 to 13 inches long.

SWEETWATER (249)

Bo's Bait & Grub   **$8-10**
Public Park
5 mi S on FM 1856 from jct with I-20; 1 mi E on FM 2035; on Lake Sweetwater. $8-10. Mar-Oct. About 100 sites. Flush toilets, cfga, drkg wtr, playground, dump. Fishing, boating(ld). Marina.
Fishing tip: Sweetwater Lake's channel catfish are easiest to find near the mouths of Bitter and Cottonwood Creeks, as well as on the shallow flats. Use nightcrawlers, chicken livers, shrimp or stinkbaits..

Lake Sweetwater City Park   **$10**
From I-20 near Sweetwater, 3.6 mi S on FM 1856; half mi E on FM 2035; at Lake Sweet-

water. $10 for 19 sites with elec/wtr; $15 for 7 lakefront sites. Tbls, flush toilets, cfga, drkg wtr, playground, dump. Fishing, boating(l), swimming. Concessionaire operated.
Fishng tip: Don't neglect this lake's panfish. It has an excellent population of sunfish and crappies in the same areas most anglers fish for bass. Use crickets, worms, mealworms and small jigs.

Lake Trammell   **$2**
Nolan County Park
From I-20, S 4 mi on SR 70; 2.8 mi W on FM 1809; 1.2 mi S to camp; on Lake Trammell. Formerly free, now $2 per day, $3 for 3 days or $10 annually. All year. Primitive 300-acre camping area. Flush toilets, cfga, drkg wtr, tbls. Biking & bridle trail, fishing, boating(l), nature trails. Park is owned by the City of Sweetwater.

TEXARKANA (250)

Atlanta State Park   **$12**
S of Texarkana on US 59 to Atlanta, then 7 mi W on FM 96; 2 mi N on FM 1154 to Park Rd 2; on Wright Patman Lake. $12 for 44 sites with elec (6 are 50-amp); seniors pay $7 Oct-March. $14 for 17 sites with full hookups; seniors pay $9 Oct-March. $10 for 5 primitive sites. All year; 14-day limit. 3 camping areas. Flush toilets, drkg wtr, hookups($), tbls, cfga, dump, playgrounds, fish cleaning shelter, beach. Special rates Oct-Mar for seniors. Fishing, boating(l), waterskiing, sand volleyball, basketball, horseshoes, hiking trails, nature trails, swimming, biking. No entry fee for campers.

TEXLINE (251)

Thompson Grove   **FREE**
Cibola National Forest
15 mi NE of Texline. Free. May-Oct. Primitive undesignated area (22-ft RV limit). 10 picnic sites. Tbls, toilets, cfga, drkg wtr.

THE COLONY (252)

Stewart Creek City Park   **$10**
The Colony Lake Park
2.1 mi N on FM 423 from SR 121 jct; 2 mi W on local rd. On E shore of Lake Lewisville. $10 tent camping with annual vehicle pass, $15 without pass; $13 RV camping with annual pass, $18 without pass (non-resident permit $25-40 monthly). 14-day limit. 40-acre camping area. Toilets, cfga, drkg wtr, tbls, shelters, dump, playground, beach. Fishing, swimming, boating (ld), volleyball, horseshoes. 30 acres.

THREE RIVERS (253)

South Shore Unit
Choke Canyon State Park   **$11**
4 mi W of Three Rivers on SR 72. $11 base. All year; 14-day limit. Base fee for hike-in

developed tent areas on N shore with tbls, cfga, lantern posts, no toilets or wtr; $16 for sites with wtr/elec. Tbls, flush toilets, cfga, drkg wtr, showers, dump, picnic area with shelters, playgrounds, store, pool. Swimming (rinse showers), boating (l), fishing, birdwatching (birding trails), baseball, volleyball, shuffleboard, tennis. $3 per person entry fee. South Shore open only for day use in 2007; closed for repairs.
Fishing tip: Catch largemouth bass to 9 pounds from Choke Canyon Lake in midsummer by using pearl and watermelon flukes and plastic worms along the outer edges of grass beds in the lower end of the lake.

Tips City Park   **$12**
From US 281, half mi W on SR 72; on Frio River. $12 for RV sites with hookups; $5 for primitive tent sites. All year; 14-day limit. Weekly monthly rates available. 20 primitive sites; 8 sites with hookups. Tbls, flush toilets, cfga, drkg wtr, showers, dump. Fishing, basketball, volleyball, picnicking. Reservations accepted, 361-786-4324.

TOW (254)

Cedar Point   **FREE**
Primitive Recreation Area
Lake Buchanan
Lower Colorado River Authority
Just E of Tow on FM 3014; at Lake Buchanan. Free. All year; 10-day limit. Primitive undeveloped camping. Toilet, cfga, no drkg wtr, no tbls. Boating(l), fishing, birdwatching, hiking trails.

TYLER (256)

Tyler State Park   **$12**
8 mi N of Tyler on FM 14. $10 for 37 tent sites with wtr; $12 for 37 tent sites with wtr; $16-20 for RV sites with hookups; $14 for overflow in group area. All year; 14-day limit. Tbls, flush toilets, cfga, drkg wtr, showers, dump, playgrounds, picnic areas, interpretive displays, store. Fishing (pler), boating(rdl), nature trails, minibike trail, swimming, paddleboating(r), canoeing(r). $3 per person entry fee.
Fishing tip: Best bet for summer bass is with Carolina-rig watermelon french fries & plastic worms. Catch crappies with minnows at brush piles.

UVALDE (258)

Garner State Park   **$10**
31 mi N of Uvalde off US 83 (half mi N of Concan). $10 base. All year; 14-day limit. Base fee for 149 sites with wtr; premium sites with water hookups $12 during LD-MD ($15 rest of year); sites with elec/wtr $15--20. Tbls, flush toilets, cfga, drkg wtr, screened shelters, showers, dump, playgrounds, picnic areas, group shelter, store, coin laundry. Biking & nature trails, swimming, fishing, mini golf, boating(r - no motors), tubing(r).

Frio River. Note: Premium sites are in the old Garner Park; 14-day limit is not enforced off-season, LD-MD. $4 per person entry fee for overnight.

VANDERPOOL (260)

Lost Maples   **$8**
State Natural Area
5 mi N of Vanderpool on FM 187 (48 mi W of Kerrville); on shore of Sabine River. $8 base. All year; 14-day limit. Base fee for 40 primitive hike-in sites on trails (with pit toilets); $15 for 30 RV sites with wtr/elec. Tbls, flush toilets, cfga, drkg wtr, showers, dump, playgrounds, picnic areas, interpretive displays, museum, store. Nature trail, hiking trails, swimming, fishing, biking, birdwatching (best in spring). $3 per person entry fee for overnight.

VICTORIA (261)

Spring Creek RV Park   **$12**
4.5 mi N of Victoria on Hwy 87N; right on Raab Rd for 2 blocks. $12. All year. 31 sites. Tbls, flush toilets, cfga, drkg wtr, hookups($), showers, coin laundry.

Victoria City RV Park   **$8**
At Victoria, 2 mi N on Vine St from Red River jct. $8 base. All year; 7-day limit. Base fee for seniors; $12 for others ($60 weekly). 18 pull-through sites; no tents. Tbls, flush toilets, cfga, drkg wtr, hookups, dump. Boating(l), fishing. Guadalupe River. Next to Riverside Park with hiking & biking trails, zoo.

VIDOR (262)

Claiborne West   **$3**
Orange County Park
Sabine River Authority
From I-10 near Vidor, exit 864 to N access rd, then 2 mi E; on Cow Bayou. $3 for primitive camping. All year. 433 acres. Tbls, flush toilets, cfga, drkg wtr, playground, amphitheater. Tennis, canoeing, softball, nature trails, exercise trail, fishing pond, picnicking (shelters). Cypress totem pole.

WELLINGTON (264)

Pioneer Park   **$10**
Collingsworth County
7 mi N of Wellington on US 83 (18 mi S of Shamrock); on Salt Fork of the Red River. $10. All year. 32 sites. Tbls, flush toilets, cfga, drkg wtr, elec, dump. Group shelter, pavilion, 4 small, 1 large covered picnic areas, playground. Restrooms maintained by non-profit group. Patrolled. Recent expansion included fishing pond, exercise stations, covered picnic areas, walking trails, 12 more RV sites.

WHITESBORO (265)

Big Mineral Camp   **$10**
Lake Texoma Concession
From US 377 near Whitesboro, 1.5 mi E on FM 901; 2.5 mi E on local rd. $10 base. All year; 14-day limit. Base fee for primitive sites; $12 for RV sites with elec; $15 for sites with elec/wtr; $18 for full-hookup sites. Senior discounts. 111 sites. Tbls, flush toilets, showers, cfga, drkg wtr, dump, snack bar, shelters($), store. Fishing dock, boating(ldr), volleyball, waterskiing, jet ski(r).

WHITNEY (266)

Cedar Creek   **FREE**
Corps of Engineers
Whitney Lake
4.5 mi N'W of Whitney on FM 933; 2.2 mi SW & SE on FM 2604; on E side of lake. Free. All year; 14-day limit. 20 sites. Tbls, toilets, cfa, drkg wtr. Boating (l), fishing.

Lake Whitney State Park   **$9**
3 mi W of Whitney on FM 1244. $9 base. All year; 7-day limit. Base fee for 71 sites with wtr ($32 weekly Nov-Feb); $14-15 for 66 sites with hookups ($49-56 weekly Nov-Feb); $6 for persons sleeping under their airplanes on landing strip. Tbls, flush toilets, cfga, drkg wtr, showers, dump, playgrounds, picnic areas, airstrip, rec hall. Fishing, boating(l), swimming, minibike trail, hiking trails, birdwatching. 15,700-acre lake; park is 955 acres. $3 per person entry fee.

Lofers Bend East   **$10**
Corps of Engineers
Whitney Lake
5.7 mi S of Whitney on SR 22, then W; on E end of dam. $10 without elec 10/1-2/28 ($14 with elec); $12 without elec 3/1-9/30 ($16 with elec); 14-day limit. 68 sites (62 with wtr/elec); 45-ft RV limit. Pavilion($), tbls, flush toilets, cfga, drkg wtr, elec ($), beach, playground, showers, dump. Fishing, boating(l), swimming. 2-night minimum stay on weekends.

Lofers Bend West   **$12**
Corps of Engineers
Whitney Lake
5.7 mi S of Whitney on SR 22, then W; on E end of dam on SR 22; follow signs to park. $12 for water-only sites; $16 with elec; $20 for 50 amps. 4/1-9/30; 14-day limit. 68 sites. Tbls, flush toilets, cfga, drkg wtr, showers, dump, elec($), playground. Boating(l), fishing. 2-night minimum stay on weekends.

McGown Valley   **$10**
Corps of Engineers
Whitney Lake
2.4 mi NW of Whitney on FM 933; 4 mi SW on FM 1713. $10 with wtr 10/1-2/28 ($12 rest of year); $14-30 with elec. All year; 14-day limit. 54 sites. Pavilion, tbls, flush toilets, cfga, drkg wtr, elec ($), beach, playground, showers, dump. Boating(l), fishing, swimming.

Riverside   **FREE**
Corps of Engineers
Whitney Lake
At Whitney Dam, downstream on SR 22 (W side of river). Free. All year; 14-day limit. 5 primitive sites. Tbls, 1 toilet, cfga, no drkg wtr, fishing platform. Fishing, boating.

Soldiers Bluff   **FREE**
Corps of Engineers
Whitney Lake
6.5 mi S of Whitney on SR 22. Free. All year; 14-day limit. 14 sites, some with wtr. Tbls, 1 toilet, cfga, drkg wtr. No drkg wtr Nov-March. Swimming; picnicking; fishing. Controlled access park; gates locked between 10 p.m. and 6 a.m., with exit lane but no vehicle entry during those hours.

Walling Bend Park   **FREE**
Corps of Engineers
Whitney Lake
1 mi SE of Whitney on TX 933; 10 mi SW on TX 22; 1 mi N on TX 56; 2 mi E on TX 2841. Free. All year; 14-day limit. 10 sites. Tbls, 2 toilets, cfga, drkg wtr. No drkg wtr Nov-March. Swimming; picnicking; fishing; boating(rl).

WICHITA FALLS (267)

Lake Arrowhead State Park   **$7**
8 mi S of Wichita Falls on US 281; 6 mi E on FM 1954. $7 base. All year; 14-day limit. Base fee for primitive walk-in group area for 8 persons (one cfga, 300 yds to wtr & toilets); $10 for 19 sites with wtr; $20 for 52 sites with wtr/elec (4 for equestrians); $5 overflow. Tbls, flush toilets, cfga, drkg wtr, showers, dump, playgrounds, equestrian area, picnic areas, pavilion, store, fish cleaning shelters. Waterskiing, fishing, boating (dl), swimming. 13,500-acre lake. 300-acre horseback area with wtr & toilets. $2 per person entry fee.

Fishing tip: Fish around derricks at 20 feet for suspended crappies, using yellow and red jigs and minnows. Catch summer white bass on RoadRunners near sandbars at dawn or dusk.

Wichita River Bend   **$10**
Municipal Park
In Wichita Falls at 300 Central Freeway (Texas Tourist Information exit of I-44); on Big Wichita River. $10. All year; 72-hr limit in 2-week period. 28 sites. Tbls, wtr/elec hookups, cfga, dump. Nature trails. No reservations.

WIMBERLY (268)

Resort RV Park   **$10**
at Woodcreek
2.5 mi W of Wimberly on FM 2325; half mi N on CR 220; 1 mi NW on Woodacre Dr, following signs. $10 primitive sites; $15 with elec/wtr for tents; $20 full hookups. All year. 43 sites. Tbls, flush toilets, cfga, drkg wtr, showers, dump, playground. Rec field, horseshoes, swimming.

WINNSBORO (269)

Lake Winnsboro North　　　**FREE**
Wood County Park
Sabine River Authority
5 mi S of Winnsboro on SR 37; at park sign, follow CR 4890 W half mi to lake. $6 base. All year; 15-day limit. Base fee for tents; $12 for 15 designated RV sites with hookups. Flush toilets, cfga, tbls, drkg wtr, snack bar, store. Boating (lr), fishing, picnicking, swimming. Secluded, uncrowded. Free primitive camping with toilets, cfga, but no drkg wtr, on upper end of lake.

　Fishing tip: This 806-acre lake offers good bass and crappie fishing. The lake's record bass was 10 pounds; crappie, 3.19 pounds.

Winnsboro City Park　　　**$12**
At Winnsboro, from SR 36, E on FM 515, then N on access rd. $12 for seniors; all others, $15. All year; 15-day limit ($10 nightly for 2 weeks or longer). 42 sites. Tbls, flush toilets, cfga, drkg wtr, elec, dump, concrete pads. Swimming, fishing.

WINTERS (270)

W. Lee Colburn City Park　　　**$11**
S mi N on SR 153 from US 83; 1 mi N on CR 167; on Elm Creek Reservoir. $11. All year; 10-day limit. 14 sites. Tbls, flush toilets, cfga, drkg wtr, elec, dump, playground, store, fishing pier, pavilion, dump. Volleyball, fishing.

WOODVILLE (271)

Campers Cove Park　　　**FREE**
Corps of Engineers
B. A. Steinhagen Lake
15 mi W of US 96 on US 190; 3.5 mi S on FM 92; half mi E on local rd. Free. 4/1-9/30; 14-day limit. 25 sites. Toilets, tbls with canopies, cfga, drkg wtr. Fishing, boating(dl), picnicking.

　Fishing tip: In summer, catch largemouth bass up to 7 pounds from Steinhagen Lake by casting Carolina-rig plastic worms, white Rat-L-Traps and crankbaits around structure in 30-35 feet. In the same areas, try for crappies at 15-20 feet on minnows and jigs.

Magnolia Ridge　　　**$10**
Corps of Engineers
B.A. Steinhagen Lake
12.1 mi E of Woodville on US 190; 1 mi NW on FM 92, then NE. $10 without elec during 10/1-3/31 ($12 rest of year); $16 with elec/wtr during 10/1-3/31 ($18 rest of year). 14-day limit. 41 sites (34 with elec/wtr); 65-ft RVs. Tbls, flush toilets, cfga, drkg wtr, showers, dump, elec($). Boating(l), fishing, hiking. 2-night minimum stay on weekends.

Sandy Creek　　　**$12**
Corps of Engineers
B.A. Steinhagen Lake
14.1 mi NE of Woodville on US 190, across lake; 1.4 mi S on FM 777; 2 mi SW on count rd. $12 at sites without elec; $16 elec/wtr; $18 50-amp. All year; 14-day limit. 72 sites (66 with wtr/elec). Tbls, toilets, cfga, drkg wtr, elec($), dump. Boating(l), volleyball, fishing. 2-night minimum stay on weekends.

WYLIE (272)

East Fork Campground　　　**$10**
Corps of Engineers
Lavon Lake
1 mi N of Wylie on FM 2514; E on dam rd. $10 at 12 tent sites; $16 at 50 RV sites with elec/wtr. All year; 14-day limit. 55-ft RV limit. Tbls, flush toilets, cfga, drkg wtr, showers, dump, elec($). Boating(l), fishing. 2-night minimum stay on weekends.

YOAKUM (273)

Hub City RV Park　　　**$12**
1.1 mi E of US 77A on FM 3475; part of city park. $12 ($10 for seniors); $8 for primitive sites. All year; 14-day limit. 30 RV sites. Tbls, flush toilets, cfga, drkg wtr, hookups, CATV, pool, playground, golf course, exercise stations, showers, pavilion, jogging trail. Fishing, swimming, horseshoes, volleyball.

ZAVALLA (275)

Bouton Lake　　　**FREE**
Angelina National Forest
7 mi E of Zavalla on Hwy 63; 7 mi S on FR 303 to Bouton Lake. Free. All year; 14-day limit. 7 primitive sites. Tbls, toilets, cfga, no drkg wtr; dump at Caney Creek Camp. Fishing, boating, hiking on Sawmill Trail. W end of lake privately owned. 12-acre lake.

　Fishing tip: Largemouth bass from Bouton Lake tested with high levels of mercury.

Boykin Springs　　　**$6**
Angelina National Forest
11 mi E of Zavalla on SR 63; 2.5 mi S on FR 313. $6. All year; 14-day limit. 36 sites; 24-ft RV limit. Tbls, flush toilets, cfga, drkg wtr, showers, beach($). Fishing, boating (no motors), hiking trails. Trout lake. Closed in 2007 due to hurricane damage.

　Fishing tip: Largemouth bass in Boykin Springs Lake tested with high levels of mercury.

Caney Creek Recreation Area　　　**$6**
Angelina National Forest
From US 69 at Zavalla, 4.8 mi E on SR 63; 5.2 mi E on FM 2743; 1 mi N on FR 336; on Sam Rayburn Lake. $6. All year; 14-day limit. 123 sites. Tbls, flush toilets, cfga, drkg wtr, showers, shelter, campfire theater. Fishing, boating(l), swimming, waterskiing. Closed at presstime in 2007 due to hurricane damage.

Letney　　　**FREE**
Angelina National Forest
20 mi SE of Zavalla on SR 63; 3 mi E on SR 255; 2 mi N on FR 335. On Sam Rayburn Lake. Free. All year; 14-day limit. Primitive camping area; no facilities. Now open to free use. Fishing, boating, picnicking.

Sandy Creek　　　**$3**
Angelina National Forest
17.5 mi SE of Zavalla on SR 63; 3 mi N on FR 333. $3. All year; 14-day limit. 15 sites (22-ft RV limit). Tbls, cfga, drkg wtr, flush toilets. Boating(l), fishing, swimming. 15 acres. Fee reduced from $6 in 2007 due to limited services because of hurricane.

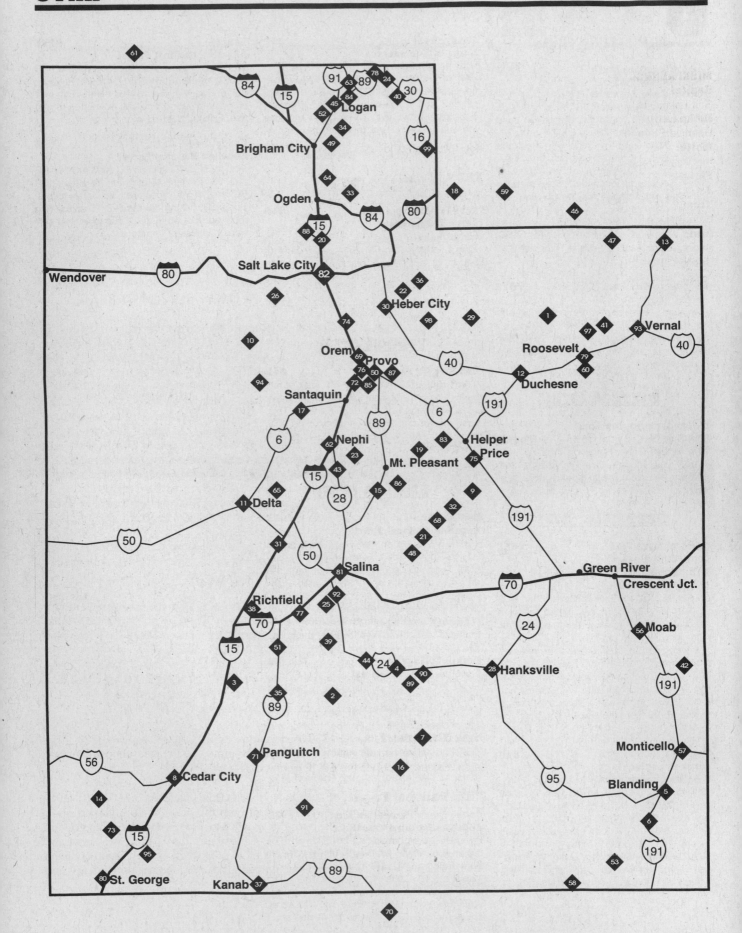

UTAH

MISCELLANEOUS
Capital:
Salt Lake City
Nickname:
Beehive State
Motto:
Industry
Flower:
Sego Lily
Tree:
Blue Spruce
Bird:
Seagull
Song:
"Utah, We Love Thee"

Internet Address:
www.utah.com

Dept of Natural Resources, Division of Parks and Recreation, 1594 W. North Temple, Salt Lake City, UT 84114; 801-322-3770.

Utah Office of Tourism, Council Hall, Capitol Hill, Salt Lake City, UT 84114-1396; 801-538-1030. Offers information about accommodations, campgrounds, rockhounding, fall color, hiking, nightlife and culture.

REST AREAS
Overnight stops are not permitted.

STATE PARKS
At most parks, overnight fees are now $15-21, with $9 charged for primitive sites, $12 with flush toilets, $15 with flush toilets and showers or electric, $18 with flush toilets, showers and electric and $21 for full hookups. Entry fees are $3-9 daily, less for seniors (annual pass $70). Dept of Natural Resources, Division of Parks and Recreation, 1594 W North Temple, Salt Lake City, UT 84114; 801-322-3770.

Ashley and Wasatch-Cache National Forests. Camping is permitted throughout the forests. Activities include backpacking, camping and trout fishing. There is also some fall hunting for moose, elk and deer. Black bears are common. For further information contact: Ashley National Forest, Ashton Energy Center, 355 North Vernal Ave., Vernal, UT 84078 (435-789-1181); or Wasatch National Forest, 3285 East 3300 South, Salt Lake City, UT 84109 (801-4666411).

Ashley National Forest has numerous undeveloped areas that are available for free camping. Fees at most developed sites are terminated when water systems are closed to prevent freezing; timings on those closing dates vary from year to year. After the water is turned off, the sites remain open free until they are not accessible because of weather conditions. Flaming Gorge National Recreation Area is in the northeast part of the forest on Flaming Gorge Reservoir, which extends almost 90 miles into Wyoming. A Flaming Gorge recreation pass is required except at developed campgrounds; it is $2 daily, $5 for 16 days and $20 annually. Visitor centers are at Red Canyon and Flaming Gorge Dam.

Wasatch-Cache National Forest. At all campsites where seasonal fees are charged, free off-season camping is permitted at all sites following the managed season until snowfalls block access and facilities are closed.

Fishlake and Manti-LaSal National Forests. Permits are not required for camping and hiking. Forest Supervisor, Fishlake National Forest, 115 E. 900 North, Richfield, UT 84701 (435-896-9233); or Forest Supervisor, Manti-LaSal National Forest, 599 W Price River Dr, Price, UT 84501 (435-637-2817).

Fishlake NF has 3,000 acres of lakes and reservoirs, several campgrounds, and several picnic areas and boating sites. Manti-LaSal National Forest consists of three mountain blocks located in three different state travel regions.

Manti-LaSal National Forest campground fees are typically $8-$10.

Dixie National Forest, 1789 Wedgewood Lane, Cedar City, UT 84720 (435-865-3700). The largest national forest in the state, it occupies almost 2 million acres. Its campgrounds are $8-12 per night.

Uinta National Forest, 88 W. 100 North, PO Box 1428, Provo, UT 84601 (801-342-5100). Most campgrounds are free between the times water is turned off in October and the sites are closed for the winter. Most of the forest's campgrounds now have camping fees of $12 or $14. Equestrians may camp with horses at Blackhawk, Currant Creek, Whiting and Unit C of Box Lake; each camp contains open stalls and nearby water, and loading docks are provided at Currant Creek and Blackhawk.

Sawtooth National Forest, 2647 Kimberly Rd, E., Twin Falls, ID 83301 (208-737-3200).

Arches National Park. Entrance fee $10 per vehicle or $5 per person for 7 days. Annual passes, $25 (good for entry to Arches, Canyonlands, Hovenweep & Natural Bridge). Located 25 miles south of I-70 just off US 191 and five miles north of Moab, it features the greatest concentration of natural stone arches in the world -- more than 1,800. A 21-mile paved road leads visitors to major points of interest. Camping is $15 per night in summer, less when water is off during 11/1-3/15. PO Box 907, Moab, UT 84532 (435-719-2299).

Bryce Canyon National Park. Entrance fee $25 per vehicle for 7 days or $30 annually. Campiing is $10per night; backcountry camping, $5. Bryce Canyon NP, PO Box 640201, Bryce Canyon, UT 84764-0201.

Canyonlands National Park. Entrance fee $10 per vehicle for 7 days or $25 for annual pass (good for entry to Arches, Canyonlands, Hovenweep & Natural Bridge); camping is $10 & $15. 36 miles northwest of Moab via SR 313. Canyonlands NP, Moab, UT 85432 (435-719-2313).

Capitol Reef National Park, HC 70, Box 15, Torrey, UT 84775 (435-425-3791). Entrance fee, $5 per vehicle for 7 days. Capitol Reef charges $10 at Fruita Campground in the park, but free camping is permitted along the Fremont River outside the eastern boundary of the park on Hwy 24. On Scenic Byway SR 24 two hours southwest of Green River. Hiking trails lead to natural bridges, hidden canyons and ancient Indian petroglyphs.

Zion National Park, Springdale, UT 84767 (435-772-3256). Entrance fee $25 per vehicle for 7 days; $40 for annual pass. Camping is $16 (free at Lava Point). Due to growing number of visitors and limited road system, RVs entering the east or south entrances are charged $15 for escort service through the narrow Long Tunnel.

Cedar Breaks National Monument, 2390 W. Hwy 56, Suite 11, Cedar City, UT 84720. 435-586-9451. Entrance fee $4 per person for 7 days. Campground fees $14 late May through mid-October, free off-season.

Dinosaur National Monument, 4545 Highway 40, Dinosaur, CO 81610 (970-374-3000). Two campgrounds are located near the visitor center. Park entry fees are $10 per vehicle for 7 days, $20 annually; camping fees are free to $12.

Natural Bridges National Monument, HC 60, Box 1, Lake Powell, UT 84533 (435-692-1234). Visitor center and primitive campground are open all year. Entrance fee $6 per vehicle. Annual passes for Natural Bridges, Canyonlands and Arches are accepted; they are $25.

Glen Canyon National Recreation Area. Fee collections are lake-wide, with entrance and boating fees collected at Lees Ferry, Wahweap, Bullfrog, Halls Crossing and Hite. Entry fees (for 7 days) are $15 per vehicle and $16 per boat; season passes, $30. Camping fees are now collected at Bullfrog North & South, Farley Canyon, Hite and Stanton Canyon primitive areas; none has facilities except pit toilets. Shoreline camping outside those areas is free, but campers must have self-contained RVs or portable toilets.

Utah State Office, Bureau of Land Management, 324 S. State, Salt Lake City, UT 84111 (801-539-4001).

ALTONAH (1)

Bridge **$8**
Ashley National Forest
12 mi NW of Altonah on CR 119; 2.6 mi N on FR 119. $8. 5/15-10/1; 14-day limit. 5 sites; 16-ft RV limit. Tbls, toilets, cfga, drkg wtr. Picnicking, fishing, horseback riding and rental(1 mi). Elev 7700 ft; 2 acres.

Reservoir **$5**
Ashley National Forest
12 mi NW of Altonah on CR 119; 5.4 mi N on FR 119; near Yellowstone Reservoir & Yellowstone River. $5. 5/15-10/1; 14-day limit. 4 sites on 3 acres; 15-ft RV limit. Tbls, toilets, cfga, drkg wtr. Picnicking; fishing, hiking.

Swift Creek **$8**
Ashley National Forest
12 mi NW of Altonah on CR 119; 7.5 mi N on FR 119; at jct of Swift Creek & Yellowstone River. $8-10. 5/15-10/1; 14-day limit. 11 sites. Tbls, toilets, drkg wtr, cfga. Fishing. Elev 8100 ft; 15 acres.

Yellowstone **$8**
Ashley National Forest
12 mi NW of Altonah on CR 119; 2.5 mi N on FR 119. $8. 5/15-10/1; 14-day limit. 11 sites; 22-ft RV limit. Tbls, cfga, drkg wtr, toilets. Fishing, biking, hiking, hunting, OHV activity. Elev 7700 ft; 7 acres.

ANTIMONY (2)

Otter Creek Reservoir **FREE**
Recreation Area
Bureau of Land Management
4 mi NW of Antimony on SR 22. Free. All year; 14-day limit. Dispersed camping scattered around reservoir; 25-ft RV limit. No facilities, no drkg wtr. Fishing, boating, OHV activities. Elev 6400 ft.

BEAVER (3)

Anderson Meadow **$10**
Fishlake National Forest
Qtr mi N of Beaver on US 91; 10 mi E on SR 153; 8 mi SE on FR 137. $10. 6/15-LD; 14-day limit. 10 sites (30-ft RV limit). Tbls, toilets, cfga, drkg wtr. Fishing, boating, hiking, horseback riding, ATV activities.

Big John Flat **FREE**
Dispersed Site
Fishlake National Forest
16 mi E of Beaver on SR 153; 3 mi N on FR 123 (narrow rd, not recommended for RVs, after Big John Flat). Free. June-Oct; 16-day limit. Primitive undesignated sites. Toilets, cfga, no drkg wtr. Hiking. Elev 10,000 ft.

Indian Creek **FREE**
Dispersed Site
Fishlake National Forest
7 mi N of Beaver on paved rd through Manderfield; 10 mi E on FR 119. June Oct;

16-day limit. Primitive undesignated sites along Indian Creek and at Manderfield Reservoir. No facilities, no drkg wtr. Hiking, fishing. Elev 6500-7500 ft.

Kents Lake **$10**
Fishlake National Forest
Qtr mi N of Beaver on US 91; 10 mi E on SR 153; 5 mi SE on FR 137. $10. 6/1-10/31; 14-day limit. 28 sites; 60-ft RV limit. Tbls, toilets, cfga, drkg wtr. Boating(l), fishing (50-acre lake), picnicking, hiking (no trails).
Fishing tip: Middle Kents Lake contains rainbow & brook trout. Small boats only; hand carry to lake.

LeBaron Reservoir **$3**
Fishlake National Forest
10 mi SE of Beaver on SR 153; 13 mi SE ongravel FR 137. $3. 6/15-10/1; 16-day limit. Primitive undesignated sites. Toilets, cfga, no drkg wtr, no tbls. Fishing, hiking, OHV activity, biking, boating. Elev 9900 ft.

Little Cottonwood **$12**
Fishlake National Forest
6 mi E of Beaver on SR 153. $12. MD-LD; 14-day limit. 14 sites (2 handicap-access); 40-ft RV limit. Tbls, flush toilets, cfga, drkg wtr. Fishing (accessible fishing walkway), picnicking, bridle trail nearby.

Little Reservoir **$10**
Fishlake National Forest
Quarter mi N of Beaver on US 91; 10 mi E on Hwy 153. $10. 5/1-10/30; 14-day limit. 8 sites (40-ft RV limit). Tbls, toilets, cfga, drkg wtr. Swimming, fishing, boating, picnicking. 1 handicap-access site. 3-acre Little Reservoir.
Fishing tip: This tiny lake contains both rainbow & brown trout and occasionally produces some big fish. Accessible fishing trail & fishing piers.

Lousy Jim Dispersed Site **FREE**
Fishlake National Forest
About 15 mi E of Beaver on SR 153; W on FR 124. Free. June-Oct; 16-day limit. Primitive undesignated sites in about 3 areas. Toilet, no other facilities; no drkg wtr. Near Merchant Valley Dam. Ellev 8800 ft.

Mahogany Cove **$8**
Fishlake National Forest
12 mi E of Beaver on UT 153. $8. 5/1-10/30; 14-day limit. 7 sites on 7 acres (RVs under 25 ft). Tbls, toilets, cfga, firewood, drkg wtr. Picnicking; fishing (1 mi to Beaver River); hunting. Elev 7700 ft; near Beaver Canyon. Whole campground can be reserved for $50 per night.

Merchant Valley **FRE**
Dispersed Site
Fishlake National Forest
About 16 mi E of Beaver on SR 153; at jct of Merchant Creek & Three Creeks. Free. June-Oct; 16-day limit. Primitive undesignated sites. No facilities, no drkg wtr. Fishing in

nearby Beaver River, Merchant Valley Dam, Three Creeks Reservoir.

Puffer Lake Dispersed Site **FREE**
Fishlake National Forest
About 22 mi E of Beaver on SR 153. Free. June-Oct; 16-day limit. Primitive undesignated sites. Spring wtr, tbls, toilet. Fishing, boating (r).

Timid Springs/Big Flat **FREE**
Dispersed Camping Area
Fishlake National Forest
About 24 mi E of Beaver on SR 153. June-Oct; 16-day limit. Primitive undesignated sites. Toilet, cfga, drkg wtr 1 mi S near Big Flat Ranger Station.

BICKNELL (4)

Sunglow **$7**
Fishlake National Forest
.7 mi SE of Bicknell on CR 24; 1.3 mi NE on FR 1431. $7. 5/15-10/30; 14-day limit. 5 sites. Tbls, toilets, cfga, firewood, piped drkg wtr. Hiking, rockhounding, mountain biking, nature trails. Elev 7500 ft.

BLANDING (5)

Devils Canyon **$10**
Manti-LaSal National Forest
9.5 mi NE of Blanding on SR 191. $10. 4/1-11/1; 16-day limit. 33 sites (30-ft RV limit). Tbls, toilets, cfga, drkg wtr (winter shut off in winter). Hiking.

Farley Canyon **$6**
Glen Canyon National Recreation Area
4.4 mi S on Hwy 95 from the Hite jct. $6. All year; 14-day limit. Primitive sites. Toilets, cfga, no drkg wtr. Swimming, fishing, boating(l).

Hite Campground **$6**
Glen Canyon National Recreation Area
60 mi W of Blanding on UT 95. $6. All year; 14-day limit. 6 sites (RVs under 20 ft). Tbls, toilets, cfga, boat sanitary station at marina. Store, food nearby. Swimming; fishing; boating(lr); picnicking.

Nizhoni **$7**
Manti-LaSal National Forest
18 mi N of Blanding on Johnson Creek-Dry Wash Rd. $7. About 5/18-10/1; 16-day limit. 21 sites; 40-ft RV limit. Tbls, toilets, cfga, drkg wtr. Swimming. Relatively new wheelchair-accessible sites. Trail to Anasazi cliff dwellings.

Natural Bridges **$10**
National Monument
38 mi W of Blanding via UT 95 and UT 275 (paved rds). $10 (plus daily or annual entry fee)). All year (but snow not cleared in winter); 14-day limit. 13 sites (26-ft RV limit). Tbls, cfga, toilets, drkg wtr at visitor center (quarter mi from campground). Campfire circle

with ranger-led slide programs from MD-9/15. En-trance fee to national monument from mid-May to mid-Oct; Golden Eagle/Age Passports honored. Pets (not on trails).

BLUFF (6)

Sand Island   **$10**
Bureau of Land Management
2 mi SW of Bluff on Hwy 163, S at sign, down easy hill to San Juan River. $10 during 3/1-10/1; free rest of year; 14-day limit. 27 tent sites. Tbls, chemical toilets, no water. Good boat ramp, rafting.

BOULDER (7)

Deer Creek   **$4**
Bureau of Land Management
Grand Staircase/Escalante Nat. Mon.
6 mi SE of Boulder on Burr Trail. $4 during 5/1-11/30; free rest of year. 14-day limit. 7 sites sites. Tbls, toilets, cfga, no drkg wtr. Fishing, hiking, biking. Elev 5800 ft.

CEDAR CITY (8)

Cedar Canyon   **$12**
Dixie National Forest
21 mi E of Cedar City on SR 14. $12. Managed 6/11-LD; free rest of year, but no wtr; 14-day limit. 12 sites; 24-ft RV limit. Tbls, toilets, cfga, drkg wtr. Hiking. Elev 8100 ft. Cedar Breaks NM nearby.

Duck Creek   **$12**
Dixie National Forest
28 mi E of Cedar City on SR 14. $12. 6/11-LD; 14-day limit. 87 sites (35-ft RV limit). Tbls, flush toilets, cfga, drkg wtr, dump ($3 for non-forest campers). Hiking, fishing, summer interpretive programs. Visitor center. Elev 8600 ft.

Navajo Lake   **$12**
Dixie National Forest
25 mi E of Cedar City off SR 14. $12 at 16 RV or tent sites, $10 at 7 walk-in tent sites. 6/11-LD; 14-day limit. 24-ft RV limit. Tbls, flush toilets, cfga, drkg wtr. Swimming, boating(l-$2), fishing, hiking, waterskiing. Elev 9200 ft; 21 acres.

Spruces   **$12**
Dixie National Forest
25 mi E of Cedar City on SR 14; 3 mi SW on FR 33; at Navajo Lake. $12 at 23 RV/tent sites, $10 at 5 tent sits; $15 with wtr/sewer; 24-ft RV limit. 6/11-LD; 14-day limit. Tbls, toilets, cfga, drkg wtr. Swimming, fishing, boating (l), waterskiing.

Te-Ah   **$12**
Dixie National Forest
28 mi E of Cedar City on SR 14; 7 mi on Navajo Lake Rd; near Navajo Lake. $12. 6/11-LD; 14-day limit. 42 sites (24-ft RV limit). Tbls, flush toilets, cfga, drkg wtr, dump.

Swimming, boating(l), fishing, waterskiing, hiking. Elev 9200 ft; 12 acres.

CLEVELAND (9)

San Rafael Bridge   **$8**
Bureau of Land Management
25 mi SE of Cleveland on co rd. $8. All year; 14-day limit. 4 sites (RVs under 36 ft). Tbls, toilets, cfga, no drkg wtr. Picnicking, fishing, hiking, horseback riding, hunting, OHV activity, biking. Also free dispersed camping at San Rafael Swell Recreation Area nearby.

CLOVER (10)

Clover Spring Campground   **$4**
Bureau of Land Management
5 mi W of Clover off Hwy 199. All year; 14-day limit. 12 sites (24-ft RV limit). Tbls, toilets, cfga, no drkg wtr. 1 group site. Horse troughs, tie-ups, unloading ramps. Popular trailhead for hikers, equestrians. Fishing, hiking. Elev 6000 ft.

DELTA (11)

House Range   **FREE**
Recreation Area
Bureau of Land Management
40 mi W of Delta on US 50. Free. Primitive dispersed camping throughout the area. No facilities, no drkg wtr. Rockhounding at Antelope Springs trilobite beds, biking, caving, hiking, horseback riding, hunting, OHV activity.

DUCHESNE (12)

Avintaquin   **$5**
Ashley National Forest
31.5 mi SW of Duchesne on SR 33; 1.2 mi W on FR 147. $5. MD-10/1; 16-day limit. 11 sites; 16-ft RV limit. Tbls, toilets, cfga, no drkg wtr. Hunting. Elev 8800 ft; 15 acres.

Riverview   **$8**
Ashley National Forest
21 mi N of Duchesne on SR 87, then follow FR 119 about 10 mi to camp; on Yellowstone River. $8 during about 5/15-10/1; free rest of year, but no wtr after 11/1. 19 sites; 20-ft RV limit. Tbls, cfga, toilets, drkg wtr. Fishing, hiking.

Moon Lake   **$10**
Ashley National Forest
14 mi N of Duchesne on UT 87; 12 mi N on UT 134; 5.3 mi NW on CR 131. $10. 5/15-10/1; 16-day limit. 56 sites (RVs under 23 ft). Tbls, toilets, cfga, firewood, piped drkg wtr. Swimming; picnicking; fishing; boating; horseback riding. Elev 8100 ft; 20 acres. Lake. Trail to wilderness nearby.

Starvation Lake State Park   **$9**
4 mi NW of Duschesne on US 40. $9 at 4 secluded primitive campgrounds; $15 at

developed sites. All year; 14-day limit. 74 sites; 40-ft RV limit. Tbls, flush toilets, cfga, drkg wtr, showers, dump, fish cleaning station, no elec. Fishing, boating, swimming. 3,500-acre lake.

Upper Stillwater   **$10**
Ashley National Forest
N of Duchesne on SR 87 to Mountain Home, then 19 mi NW on local rd which becomes FR 134. $10. 5/15-10/1; 16-day limit. 19 sites; 16-ft RV limit. Tbls, flush toilets, cfga, drkg wtr. Fishing, hiking.

DUTCH JOHN (13)

Antelope Flat   **$7**
Ashley National Forest
Flaming Gorge National Recreation Area
5.5 mi NW of Dutch John on US 191; 4.9 mi NW on FR 145; half mi W on FR 343. $7 with federal Senior Pass; others pay $14. About 5/15-9/15; 16-day limit. Parking lot open for camping until wtr turned off. 122 sites; 45-ft RV limit. Toilets, cfga, tbls, drkg wtr, dump. Swimming, boating(l), fishing.

Arch Dam Overflow   **$6**
Ashley National Forest
Flaming Gorge NRA
6.5 mi NE of Dutch John on US 191. $6. 5/15-9/15; 16-day limit. 40 RV sites (35-ft RV limit), 60 tent sites. Tbls, cfga, toilets, drkg wtr. Boating, fishing.

Bridge Hollow   **$5**
Browns Park Recreation Mgt. Area
Bureau of Land Management
Vernal District
7 mi N of Dutch John on US 191 at Wyoming line; 10 mi E on Clay Basin Rd; 5 mi S in Jessee Ewing Canyon; 1 mi W; follow signs to Browns Park at Green River. $5. All year; 14-day limit. 13 sites. Tbls, toilets, cfga, drkg wtr. Rafting, hiking, fishing. Raft ramp.

Browns Park   **FREE**
State Wildlife Area
E of Dutch John along Green River to Colorado line, then SE on CO 318 to CR 10; W to Beaver Creek Unit. To reach Cold Spring Mountain Unit, continue on CR 318 to CR 110; W to access rd; S to property. Free. All year; 14-day limit during 45-day period. Primitive campsites. No facilities. Big-game hunting, fishing, picnicking. Elev 8700 ft. 2 mi of Beaver Creek.

Cold Spring Mountain Area   **FREE**
Bureau of Land Management
E of Dutch John along Green River to Colorado line, then SE on CO 318 to CR 10N and CR 72. Lower portion of mountain accessible in Browns Park. Follow signs to camping areas. Free. All year; 14-day limit. Primitive camping at 5 camp areas. Pit toilets; 3 areas have fire rings. Hunting, hiking, backpacking, photography, fishing in Beaver Creek. Top of mountain wet until mid-June, restricting vehicle use.

Crook Campground   **FREE**
Browns Park
National Wildlife Refuge
E of Dutch John along Green River to Colorado line, then SE on CO 318, nearly to access rd to Lodore Hall National Historic Site; turn right on gravel tour rd 1 mi. Free. All year; 14-day limit during 45-day period. 20 sites for tents of self-contained RVs. No facilities or drkg wtr. Wtr nearby at Subheadquarters and refuge headquarters. Hiking, hunting, fishing, sightseeing. Swing bridge across Green River. Bridge under capacity for RVs; okay for cars & light trucks.

Diamond Breaks   **FREE**
Wilderness Study Area
Bureau of Land Management
E of Dutch John along Green River to Colorado line, then SE on CO 318 and W of Browns Park National Wildlife Refuge. Free. All year; 14-day limit. Primitive camping; no facilities. Photography, nature study, viewing wildlife, day hikes, backpacking. Scenic mountainous area. Solitude. Adjacent to north end of Dinosaur National Monument. Spectacular views into Canyon of Lodore. 36,000 acres.

Douglas Mountain   **FREE**
Bureau of Land Management
E of Dutch John along Green River to Colorado line, then SE on CO 318 to CR 12 and CR 10 (through Greystone) and CR 116 (Douglas Mountain Blvd dirt, poorly maintained). Free. All year; 14-day limit. Primitive camping. No facilities. Deer & elk hunting, sightseeing, hiking, backpacking, horseback riding. Good views to north from Douglas Mountain Blvd. High-clearance vehicles recommended. Scenic: pine forests, red sandstone outcrops.

Gates of Lodore   **$8**
Dinosaur National Monument
E of Dutch John along Green River to Colorado line, then SE on CO 318 and 4 mi SW on unpaved rds. $8 during 4/15-10/15; free rest of year, but no wtr; 15-day limit. 17 sites (30-ft RV limit). Tbls, toilets, cfga, wtr faucets. Boating (concrete launch--whitewater running craft only; special rafting permit required); fishing; picnicking; no swimming (cold water & dangerous currents). Elev 5600 ft; 6 acres. River. N portal to Lodore Canyon. Pets on leash. $10 entry fee.

Gooseneck Boat-In Camp   **FREE**
Ashley National Forest
Flaming Gorge NRA
5 mi SW of Dutch John on UT 260; 1.3 mi NW on FR 183; .1 mi N on FR 391; 8.5 mi W, by boat; on SE arm of Flaming Gorge Reservoir. Free. MD-LD; 14-day limit. 6 tent sites. Tbls, toilets, cfga, no drkg wtr. Hunting; picnicking; fishing; swimming; sailing; waterskiing; boating(d). Elev 6100 ft; 3 acres.

Indian Crossing   **$5**
Bureau of Land Management
7 mi N of Dutch John on US 191 at Wyoming line; 22 mi E on Clay Basin Rd (graded, steep

dirt rd); at Green River. $5. All year; 14-day limit. 22 sites. Tbls, toilets, cfga, drkg wtr, dump. Swimming, boating(l), fishing, hiking, picnicking, biking, hunting. Historic homesteader buildings. Elev 5700 ft.

Irish Canyon   **FREE**
Bureau of Land Management
E of Dutch John along Green River to Colorado line, then SE on CO 318, then 4 mi N through Irish Canyon on Moffat County Rd 10N (gravel rd) for 8 mi. Free. All year; 14-day limit. 3 sites (30-ft RV limit). Tbls, cfga, toilet, no drkg wtr. Picnicking, wildlife viewing, hunting, hiking, sightseeing. 14,400 acres.
Travel tip: Interpretive exhibit, Indian petroglyphs near canyon entrance via short trail. Ponds, wild horse herd at Sand Wash Basin. Vermillion Badlands. Very scenic route with steep, colorful canyon walls.

Rocky Reservoir   **FREE**
Recreation Site
Bureau of Land Management
E of Dutch John along Green River to Colorado line, then SE on CO 318; left on SR 10N for about 15 mi; left (W) on CR 72; follow signs. Free. All year; 14-day limit. 3 primitive RV sites. Toilet, fire rings, no drkg wtr, no tbls. Hunting, hiking, sightseeing, picnicking.

Swinging Bridge Camp   **FREE**
Browns Park
National Wildlife Refuge
E of Dutch John along Green River to Colorado line, then SE on CO 18 almost to access to Lodore Hall National Historic Site and access rd to Crook campground; right on gravel tour 2 mi. Free. All year. 15 sites for tents or self-contained RVs. Cfga, shade trees; no drkg wtr or other facilities. Wtr nearby at Subheadquarters and refuge headquarters. Hiking, hunting, fishing, sightseeing. Next to swinging bridge across Green River. Bridge under capacity for RVs, okay for cars and trucks. Boating on Butch Cassidy pond (no motors) & Green River.

West Cold Spring   **FREE**
Wilderness Study Area
Bureau of Land Management
E of Dutch John along Green River to Colorado line, then SE on CO 318 to N side of Browns Park. Free. All year; 14-day limit. Primitive undesignated camping. No facilities. Hunting, backpacking, scenic viewing, fishing, trail hiking. Beaver Creek Canyon. 17,000 acres.

ENTERPRISE (14)

Honeycomb Rocks   **$7**
Dixie National Forest
5 mi W of Enterprise on CR 120; 5 mi SW on FR 6; at Enterprise Reservoir. $7. 5/4-9/16 (may open earlier if weather permits); 14-day limit. 21 RV sites; 24-ft RV limit. Tbls, cfga, toilets, drkg wtr (high sodium content). Swimming, fishing, boating(l), waterskiing, rafting, kayaking. Elev 5700 ft.

EPHRAIM (15)

Lake Hill   **$8**
Manti-LaSal National Forest
8.5 mi SE of Ephraim on SR 29. $8. 6/1-9/25; 16-day limit. 11 sites. Tbls, toilets, cfga, drkg wtr (no wtr after 9/15). Fishing, hiking trails.

ESCALANTE (16)

Blue Spruce   **$7**
Dixie National Forest
17 mi N of Escalante on FR 153 (Hells Backbone Rd); at Pine Creek. $7. MD-LD; 14-day limit. 6 sites; 18-ft RV limit. Tbls, toilets, cfga, drkg wtr. Fishing, picnicking. Elev 7800 ft.

Calf Creek   **$7**
Bureau of Land Management
15 mi E of Escalante on SR 12 (44 mi S of Torrey). $7. 4/15-11/30; 14-day limit. 14 sites (25-ft RV limit). Tbls, toilets, cfga, drkg wtr. Fishing, 3-mi trail to scenic 125-ft waterfall. Elev 5400 ft; 22 acres.

Pine Lake   **$9**
Dixie National Forest
13 mi E on SR 12 from jct with Hwy 89; about 11 mi N on John's Valley Rd (FR 22), then 6 mi E on FR 132 (Clay Creek Rd). $9. 5/19-9/9; 14-day limit. 33 sites (45-ft RV limit). Tbls, toilets, cfga, drkg wtr, no trash service. Swimming, boating(l), fishing, waterskiing, hiking.

Posey Lake   **$8**
Dixie National Forest
16 mi N of Escalante on gravel FR 153; at S side of Posey Lake. $8. 5/19-9/9; 14-day limit. 22 sites; 24-ft RV limit. Tbls, toilets, cfga, drkg wtr, fish cleaning station, no trash service. Fishing, hiking, canoeing, boating(ld). Elev 8200 ft.

EUREKA (17)

Sand Mountain   **$8**
Little Sahara Recreation Area
Bureau of Land Management
19 mi S of Eureka on US 6; right on BLM rd, following signs. $8 or annual $75 Little Sahara pass. All year; 14-day limit. 300 sites (40-ft RV limit). Tbls, toilets, cfga, drkg wtr. Popular off-road vehicle camp.

EVANSTON (WY.) (18)

Bear River   **$10**
Wasatch National Forest
30.5 mi S of Evanston on SR 150. $10 plus special district parking fee ($3 daily, $6 weekly or $25 annually). May-Oct; 7-day limit. 4 sites; 16-ft RV limit. Toilets, cfga, drkg wtr, toilets. Fishing. Elev 8400 ft.

Beaver View   **$10**
Wasatch National Forest
30 mi S of Evanston on SR 150. $10 plus special district parking ($3 daily, $6

weekly or $25 annually). 6/15-10/15, but no wtr after LD; 7-day limit. 18 sites; 22-ft RV limit. Toilets, cfga, tbls, drkg wtr. Fishing. Elev 8900 ft.

Christmas Meadows   **$12**
Wasatch National Forest
29.5 mi S of Evanston on SR 150; 4 mi S on FR 059. $10 plus special district parking fee ($3 daily, $6 weekly or $25 annually). 6/15-10/30, but no wtr after LD; 14-day limit. 11 sites (22-ft RV limit). Tbls, toilets, cfga, drkg wtr. Hiking, fishing, horseback riding. Horse loading facilities. Trailhead to High Uintas Wilderness.

East Fork Bear River   **$10**
Wasatch National Forest
30 mi S of Evanston on SR 150. $10 plus special district parking fee ($3 daily, $6 weekly or $24 annually). June-Oct; 7-day limit. 7 sites; 20-ft RV limit. Tbls, toilets, cfga, drkg wtr. Fishing, hiking.

Hayden Fork   **$10**
Wasatch National Forest
About 30 mi S of Evanston on SR 150. $10 plus special district parking fee ($3 daily, $6 weekly or $25 annually). 6/15-9/15; 14-day limit. 9 sites (26-ft RV limit). Tbls, toilets, cfga, drkg wtr. Fishing, hiking.

Lyman Lake   **$8**
Wasatch National Forest
30 mi S of Evanston on SR 150; 17 mi on FR 088; half mi on FR 635. $8. 6/15-10/30, but no wtr after LD; 14-day limit. 10 sites (16-ft RV limit). Tbls, toilets, cfga, drkg wtr. Fishing.

Stillwater   **$12**
Wasatch National Forest
33 mi S of Evanston on SR 150. $12 plus special district parking fee ($3 daily, $6 weekly or $25 annually). 5/30-10/15, but no wtr after LD; 14-day limit. 21 sites. Toilets, cfga, tbls, drkg wtr. Fishing. Elev 8500 ft.

Sulphur   **$12**
Wasatch National Forest
32.3 mi S of Evanston on SR 150; at Hayden Fork of Bear River. $12 plus special district parking fee ($3 daily, $6 weekly or $25 annually). 6/15-10/15, but no wtr after LD; 14-day limit. 21 sites; 22-ft RV limit. Drkg wtr, toilets, cfga, toilets; no wtr after LD. Fishing, hiking trails. Elev 9000 ft.

Wolverine Trailhead   **$8**
Wasatch National Forest
37 mi S of Evanston on SR 150, FR 057 & FR 323; near Stillwater Fork of Bear River. $8 plus special district parking fee ($3 daily, $6 weekly or $25 annually). June-Oct; 14-day limit. 6 sites; 16-ft RV limit. Tbls, toilets, cfga, no drkg wtr. Fishing, hiking, biking, horseback riding, OHV activity.

FAIRVIEW (19)

Flat Canyon   **$8**
Manti-LaSal National Forest
12 mi E on SR 31; 4 mi E on SR 26. $8. 6/21-LD; 16-day limit. 13 sites (30-ft RV limit). Tbls, toilets, cfga, drkg wtr. Boating(l), fishing, hiking. Elev 8900 ft. Closed in 2007 for hazardous tree removal.

Gooseberry Reservoir   **$5**
Manti-LaSal National Forest
9 mi E of Fairview on SR 31. $5. 6/1-9/26; 16-day limit. 16 sites (25-ft RV limit). Tbls, toilets, cfga, drkg wtr. Fishing, hiking. Just to S are 10 more sites at Gooseberry Campground; 25-ft RV limit.

FARMINGTON (20)

Bountiful Peak   **$10**
Wasatch National Forest
Half mi N of Farmington on co rd; 8.8 mi E on FR 007 (narrow, steep, winding route). $10. 7/1-9/15; 7-day limit. 39 sites; 20-ft RV limit. Tbls, toilets, cfga, drkg wtr. Hunting, fishing.

Sunset   **$8**
Wasatch National Forest
4 mi NE of Farmington on FR 007. $8. 7/1-LD; 7-day limit. 12 sites. Tbls, toilets, cfga, drkg wtr. 8 acres; elev 6500 ft. Fishing, picnicking, hiking, horseback riding, mountain biking.

FERRON (21)

Ferron Canyon   **FREE**
Manti-LaSal National Forest
9 mi W of Ferron on FR 22; at Ferron Creek. Free. May-Oct; 16-day limit. 3 sites. Tbls, toilets, cfga, no drkg wtr. Fishing.

Ferron Reservoir   **$7**
Manti-LaSal National Forest
28 mi W of Ferron on FR 22. $7. 6/22-9/26; 16-day limit. 32 sites. Tbls, toilets, cfga, drkg wtr. Fishing, boating(l). Elev 9500 ft; 17 acres.

Twelve Mile Flat   **$7**
Manti-LaSal National Forest
11 mi W of Ferron on FR 022. $7. 6/24-10/31; 16-day limit. 16 sites. Tbls, toilets, cfga, drkg wtr (no wtr after 9/15). Wtr system can run dry if more than 5 gallons used at once. Biking, hiking. Farther W, FR 022 becomes a 4x4 rd into Grove of the Aspen Giants Scenic Area.

FREEDOM (23)

Maple Canyon   **$8**
Manti-LaSal National Forest
W of Freedom on Maple Canyon Rd. $8. MD-10/31; 16-day limit. 12 sites. Tbls, toilets, cfga, no drkg wtr. Hiking, biking.

GARDEN CITY (24)

Limber Pine Trailhead   **FREE**
Cache National Forest
8.4 mi W of Garden City on US 89. Jul-Sept; 14-day limit. Undesignated sites. Toilets, no drkg wtr or tbls. Hiking trails. Elev 7800 ft.

Sunrise Campground   **$7.50**
Cache National Forest
8.2 mi SW of Garden City on US 89; at Bear Lake. $7.50 with federal Senior Pass; others pay $15. 6/110-LD; 7-day limit. 27 sites; 20-ft RV limit. Tbls, toilets, cfga, drkg wtr. Fishing, hiking, OHV activity.

GLENWOOD (25)

Big Lake Dispersed Site   **FREE**
Fishlake National Forest
From Main St in Glenwood, E on Center St to fish hatchery; 3 mi S on county rd; 8 mi E on FR 068 to Big Lake. Free. May-Oct; 16-day limit. Primitive undesignated sites. Toilet (on S end of lake), cfga, no drkg wtr, no trash service. Fishing, hunting, picnicking, boating.

GRANTSVILLE (26)

Boy Scout   **$8**
Wasatch National Forest
Quarter mi W of Grantsville on US 40; 4.7 mi S on Hwy 138; 3.5 mi SW on CR 45; 1.8 mi SW on FR 171. $8 during 5/1-10/1 ($30 for entire campground); free rest of yr when access open; 7-day limit. 5 sites; 20-ft RV limit. Tbls, toilets, cfga, no drkg wtr. Fishing, picnicking. RVs not recommended.

Cottonwood   **$8**
Wasatch National Forest
Quarter mi W of Grantsville on US 40; 4.7 mi S on SR 138; 3.5 mi SW on CR 45; 3.5 mi W on FR 171. $8 during 5/1-10/15; free rest of yr when access open; 7-day limit. 2 primitive sites; 20-ft RV limit. Tbls, toilets, cfga, no drkg wtr. Fishing, picnicking, hunting. RVs not recommended.

Intake   **$8**
Wasatch National Forest
Quarter mi W of Grantsville on US 40; 4.7 mi S on CR 138; 3.5 mi SW on CR 45; 4.5 mi SW on FR 171. $8. Elev 6300 ft. 5/1-10/1; 7-day limit. 4 tent sites; 3 acres. Tbls, toilets, cfga, firewood, no drkg wtr. Hunting; picnicking; fishing; rockhounding. Archeological interest.

Loop Campground   **$8**
Wasatch National Forest
Quarter mi W of Grantsville on US 40; 4.7 mi S on CR 138; 3.5 mi SW on CR 45; 3.8 mi SW on FR 80171. Elev 7800 ft. $8 during 5/1-10/1; free rest of yr when access open; 7-day limit. 5 sites on 5 acres. Tbls, toilets, cfga, no drkg wtr. Rockhounding; hunting; picnicking; fishing; horseback riding (1 mi). Archeological interest.

Lower Narrows $8
Wasatch National Forest
Quarter mi W of Grantsville on US 40; 4.7 mi S on CR 138; 3.5 mi SW on CR 45; 2.4 mi SW on FR 171. $8. 5/1-10/1; 7-day limit. 4 tent sites. Tbls, toilets, cfga, no drkg wtr. Fishing, picnicking.

Upper Narrows $8
Wasatch National Forest
Quarter mi W of Grantsville on US 40; 4.7 mi S on Hwy 138; 3.5 mi SW on CR 45; 2.6 mi SW on FR 171. $8. 5/1-10/1; 7-day limit. 8 sites. Tbls, toilets, cfga, no drkg wtr. Fishing, picnicking. RVs not recommended.

HANKSVILLE (28)

Lonesome Beaver Campground $4
Bureau of Land Management
23 mi S of Hanksville on rough mountain rd. $4. 5/1-10/31; 14-day limit. 5 tent sites on 5 acres. Tbls, toilets, cfga, drkg wtr. Picnicking. Elev 8000 ft; high-clearance vehicles recommended.

McMillan Spring $4
Bureau of Land Management
28 mi SW of Hanksville on Hwy 24; left for 31 mi on Notom-Bullfrog Rd; high-clearance vehicles suggested. $4 5/1-11/30; 14-day limit. 10 sites. Toilets, tbls, cfga, drkg wtr. Hiking, picnicking. Elev 8400 ft.

Starr Springs $4
Bureau of Land Management
25 mi S of Hanksville on SR 95; 17.5 mi S on SR 276; right on co rd, following signs; not recommended for large RVs. $4. 4/1-10/31; 14-day limit. 27 sites. Tbls, toilets, cfga, drkg wtr. Hiking trails.

HANNA (29)

Aspen Grove $10
Ashley National Forest
2.5 mi N on FR 144 from SR 35 near Hanna; at North Fork of Duchesne River. $10. About MD-LD. 28 sites; 16-ft RV limit. Tbls, toilets, cfga, drkg wtr. Hiking, horseback riding, fishing.

Hades $10
Ashley National Forest
5 mi NW of Hanna on SR 36; 6 mi NW on FR 144; at Duschesne River. $10. MD-LD. 17 sites; 16-ft RV limit. Tbls, toilets, cfga, drkg wtr. Fishing. Elev 7100 ft; 15 acres.

Iron Mine $10
Ashley National Forest
5 mi NW of Hanna on SR 36; 7.5 mi NW on FR 144. $10. MD-LD. 27 sites. Tbls, toilets, cfga, drkg wtr. Fishing. Elev 7200 ft.

Yellow Pine $10
Ashley National Forest
19.5 mi NE of Hanna on FR 134. $10 during MD-LD. 14-day limit. 29 sites; 16-ft RV limit. Tbls, flush toilets, cfga, drkg wtr. Fishing.

HEBER CITY (30)

Aspen Grove $7
Uinta National Forest
34 mi SE of Heber on US 40; 7 mi on FR 090; past dam, at E arm of Strawberry Reservoir. $7 with federal Senior Pass; others pay $14. 5/12-11/1; 14-day limit. 60 sites. Flush toilets, cfga, drkg wtr, tbls, fish cleaning station. Boating(l), fishing, hiking, horseback riding, biking.

Currant Creek $7
Uinta National Forest
45 mi SE of Heber on US 40 to Currant Creek Junction; 17 mi N on FR 083; at SW side of Currant Creek Reservoir. $7 with federal Senior Pass; others pay $14. MD-LD; 14-day limit. 99 sites; 40-ft RV limit. Flush toilets, tbls, cfga, drkg wtr, playground, fishing pier, fish cleaning station, dump. Boating(l), fishing, mountain biking, bridle trails, hiking. Managed jointly with Bureau of Reclamation.

Fishing tip: This lake offers excellent fishing for stocked rainbow, brown & cutthroat trout.

Hope $6.50
Uinta National Forest
SW of Heber City on US 189 past Mt Timpanogos Wilderness; 6 mi S on FR 027 (Squaw Peak Rd, narrow, winding). $6.50 with federal Senior Pass; others pay $13. MD-10/31; 14-day limit. 24 sites; 20-ft RV limit. Tbls, toilets, cfga, drkg wtr. Biking, hiking, hunting. Elev 6600 ft.

Lodgepole Campsite $7
Uinta National Forest
18 mi SE of Heber City on US 40; at W side of rd. $7 with federal Senior Pass; others pay $14. MD-LD; 14-day limit. 49 sites; no RV size limit. Tbls, flush toilets, cfga, drkg wtr, dump. Nature trail, mountain biking.

Renegade Point $7
Uinta National Forest
23 mi SE of Heber City on US 40; about 8 mi S on FR 131 to its end; at Strawberry Reservoir. $7 with federal Senior Pass; others pay $14. 5/12-11/1; 14-day limit. 66 sites; 40-ft RV limit. Tbls, flush toilets, cfga, drkg wtr. Fishing, boating(l), hiking, biking.

Fishing tip: Try the shallow Meadows area of Strawberry Lake for big rainbow and cutthroat trout. Good shore fishing here too.

Soldier Creek $7
Uinta National Forest
Bureau of Reclamation
33 mi SE of Heber City on US 40; 3.5 mi S on FR 480; at Strawberry Reservoir. $7 with federal Senior Pass; others pay $14. 5/12-10/30; 14-day limit. 166 sites. Flush toilets, cfga, drkg wtr, tbls, marina, store, fish cleaning station, dump. Boating(lr), fishing. Managed jointly with Bureau of Reclamation.

Strawberry Bay $7
Uinta National Forest
23 mi SE of Heber City on US 40; about 5 mi S on FR 131; at Strawberry Reservoir. $7 with federal Senior Pass; others pay $14 ($10 surcharge for elec). May-Oct for most sites; all year with elec; 14-day limit. 345 sites; 40-ft RV limit. Tbls, flush & pit toilets, cfga, drkg wtr, dump (fee for non-forest campers), fish cleaning station, marina, store. Fishing, boating(ldr), biking, hiking. Visitor center nearby.

HOLDEN (31)

Maple Hollow FREE
Fishlake National Forest
1 mi S of Holden on SR 91; 8 mi SE on FR 098. Free, but fee for group camping. MD-LD; 14-day limit. 11 tent sites; no space for RVs. Tbls, toilets, cfga, drkg wtr. Picnicking, fishing, hiking.

HUNTINGTON (32)

Forks Of Huntington Canyon $7
Manti-LaSal National Forest
18 mi NW of Huntington on Hwy 31. $7. 6/1-9/15; 16-day limit. 5 sites (RVs under 21 ft). Tbls, toilets, cfga, drkg wtr. Fishing, picnicking.

Old Folks Flat $10
Manti-LaSal National Forest
22 mi NW of Huntington on Hwy 31. $10. MD-LD; 16-day limit. 9 sites; 30-ft RV limit. Tbls, toilets, cfga, drkg wtr. Fishing, picnicking, hiking. Ghost town.

HUNTSVILLE (33)

Botts Campground $12
Wasatch National Forest
South Fork Recreation Complex
6 mi E of Huntsville on SR 39 on bend in river. $8. 6/1-9/30; 7-day limit. 8 sites; 20-ft RV limit. Tbls, toilets, cfga, no drkg wtr. Fishing, hiking.

Jefferson Hunt $12
Wasatch National Forest
2 mi S of Huntsville on SR 39. $12. 6/1-9/30; 7-day limit. 29 sites (40-ft RV limit). Tbls, toilets, cfga, drkg wtr, dump. Fishing, boating, waterskiing. Handicap access. Elev 5000 ft; 9 acres.

Magpie $12
Cache National Forest
South Fork Recreation Complex
6 mi E of Huntsville on SR 39. $12. 5/15-9/15; 7-day limit. 7 sites (40-ft RV limit). Tbls, toilets, cfga, drkg wtr. Swimming, fishing, hiking.

The Maples FREE
Cache National Forest
10 mi S of Huntsville on UT 226; 2 mi NW on FR 122. Free. 6/1-10/31; 7-day limit. 26 sites (20-ft RV limit). Tbls, toilets, cfga, no drkg wtr.

UTAH

Upper Meadows   **$12**
Cache National Forest
South Fork Recreation Complex
8 mi E of Huntsville on SR 39. $12. 5/15-10/31; 7-day limit. 8 sites (20-ft RV limit). Tbls, toilets, cfga, drkg wtr. Fishing, hiking. Elev 5200 ft.

Willows   **$7**
Cache National Forest
South Fork Recreation Complex
8 mi E of Huntsville on SR 39. $7 with federal Senior Pass; others pay $14. 5/15-9/15; 7-day limit. 12 sites (20-ft RV limit). Tbls, toilets, cfga, drkg wtr. Swimming, hiking, fishing. Elev 5300 ft; 6 acres.

HYRUM (34)

Friendship   **$10**
Cache National Forest
8.4 mi E of Hyrum on SR 242; 3.5 mi NE on FR 055. $10 during 5/15-9/15; free rest of yr when access open; 7-day limit. 6 rustic sites (20-ft RV limit). Tbls, toilets, cfga, no drkg wtr. Fishing, hiking.

Pioneer Campground   **$10**
Cache National Forest
9 mi E of Hyrum on US 101; turn at sign for Pioneer Camp; at Blacksmith Fork River. $10. 5/17-9/10; 7-day limit. 18 sites; 20-ft RV limit. Tbls, toilets, cfga, drkg wtr. Mountain biking, fishing.

Shengar   **$6**
Wasatch National Forest
8.4 mi E of Hyrum on SR 242; 4.2 mi NE on FR 20055. $6 during 5/15-10/31; free rest of yr when access open; 7-day limit. 3 sites; 20-ft RV limit. Tbls, toilets, cfga, no drkg wtr. Fishing, hiking, picnicking. Formerly called Spring Campground.

JUNCTION (35)

City Creek   **FREE**
Fishlake National Forest
.1 mi N on US 89; 5.3 mi NW on UT 153; 1 mi NE on FR 131. Elev 7600 ft. 5/21-10/30; 14-day limit. 5 sites on 3 acres; 24-ft RV limit. Tbls, toilets, cfga, piped drkg wtr. Hiking trails, bridle trails, fishing; hunting, mountain biking.

KAMAS (36)

Beaver Creek   **$11**
Wasatch National Forest
8 mi E of Kamas on Mirror Lake Scenic Byway (SR 150). $11. 6/15-10/15; 14-day limit. 11 sites; 25-ft RV limit. Tbls, toilets, cfga, drkg wtr. Trails for dirt bikes, motorcycles & ATV activities. Fishing, mountain biking.

Butterfly   **$12**
Wasatch National Forest
14 mi NE of Kamas on SR 150; at Butterfly Lake. $12. About 7/1-10/15; 7-day limit. 20 sites (30-ft RV limit). Tbls, toilets, cfga, drkg wtr, horse loading ramp at trailhead. Fishing, hiking. Elev 10,300 ft; snow possible in summer.

Cobble Rest   **$12**
Wasatch National Forest
19.5 mi E of Kamas on SR 150; at Provo River canyon. $12. MD-LD; 7-day limit. 18 sites (30-ft RV limit). Tbls, toilets, cfga, drkg wtr. Fishing. Elev 8500 ft; 5 acres.

Crystal Lake Trailhead   **FREE**
Wasatch National Forest
26 mi E of Kamas on SR 150; 2 mi NW on FS rd. Free. July-Oct; 14-day limit. 10 sites. Toilets, no drkg wtr, no tbls. Hiking & horse trails. Elev 10,000 ft.

Lower Provo   **$10**
Wasatch National Forest
12 mi SE of Kamas on SR 150; near Provo River. $10. MD-LD & through deer season; 7-day limit. 10 sites; 40-ft RV limit. Tbls, toilets, cfga, drkg wtr. Hiking, fishing, mountain biking. Elev 7400 ft.

Shady Dell   **$12**
Wasatch National Forest
17 mi E of Kamas on SR 150; at Provo River. $12. MD-LD & through deer season; 7-day limit. 20 sites; 25-ft RV limit. Tbls, toilets, cfga, drkg wtr. Fishing. Elev 8040 ft.

Shingle Creek   **$10**
Wasatch National Forest
9.5 mi E of Kamas on SR 150. $10. MD-LD & through deer season; 7-day limit. 21 sites (25-ft RV limit). Tbls, toilets, cfga, drkg wtr. Hiking, fishing. Elev 7400 ft; 15 acres.

Taylors Fork   **$10**
Wasatch National Forest
7.5 mi E of Kamas on SR 150. $10. MD-LD & through deer season; 7-day limit. 11 sites; 25-ft RV limit. Tbls, toilets, drkg wtr, cfga. Fishing, hunting, motorcycle & ATV trails. Elev 7600 ft.

Upper Provo River   **FREE**
Wasatch National Forest
21 mi E of Kamas on SR 150. Free. June-Oct; 14-day limit. 5 sites. Toilets, tbls, cfga, no drkg wtr. Fishing, hunting. Elev 9200 ft.

Washington Lake   **$12**
Wasatch National Forest
25 mi E of Kamas on SR 150, then N to Washington Lake. $12. 7/1-LD; 7-day limit. 39 sites. Tbls, toilets, cfga, drkg wtr. Fishing, boating(l), hiking, horseback riding.

Yellow Pine   **$6**
Wasatch National Forest
6 mi E of Kamas on SR 150. $6. MD-LD & through deer season; 7-day limit. 33 sites (50-ft RV limit). Tbls, toilets, cfga, no drkg wtr. Fishing, hiking trails. 11 acres.

KANAB (37)

Paria Movie Set Camp   **FREE**
Bureau of Land Management
35 mi E of Kanab on Hwy 89. 5/1-11/1; 14-day limit. Free. Primitive undesignated camping area; 3 tent sites. Tbls, toilets, cfga, no drkg wtr. Picnicking.

Ponderosa Grove Campground   **$5**
Bureau of Land Management
8 mi N of Kanab on US 89; about 7 mi W on Hancock Rd; just N of Coral Pink Sand Dunes. $5. May-Nov; 14-day limit. 8 sites; 24-ft RV limit. Tbls, toilets, no drkg wtr.

White House Trailhead Camp   **$5**
Bureau of Land Management
About 35 mi E of Kanab on US 89; accessible by dirt rd (RVs not recommended). $5. All year; 14-day limit. 5 tent sites. Tbls, toilets, cfga, no drkg wtr. Northernmost trailhead into Paris Canyon-Vermillion Cliffs Wilderness.

KANOSH (38)

Adelaide Campground   **$10**
Fishlake National Forest
6 mi E of Kanosh on FR 106; at Corn Creek. $10. 5/15-9/15; 14-day limit. 8 sites. Tbls, flush toilets, cfga, drkg wtr, amphitheater. Fishing, hiking, hunting. Elev 5500 ft.

KOOSHAREM (39)

Box Creek Lakes   **FREE**
Dispersed Camping
Fishlake National Forest
About 5 mi S of Koosharem on SR 62, then 1 mi N of Greenwich, turn W onto dirt rd toward Box Creek Canyon; follow FR 069 away from the creek up the mountain to Upper & Lower Box Lakes. Free primitive, undesignated sites. No facilities, no drkg wtr. All year; 14-day limit; vehicle access during summer & fall. Fishing, hiking.

Fishing tip: Good fishing for rainbow & brook trout is the primary reason for camping here. Use flies, lures or bait.

LAKETOWN (40)

Eastside Unit   **$9**
Bear Lake State Park
10 mi N of Laketown. $9. All year; 14-day limit. 6 primitive sites with pit toilets, cfga, drkg wtr (at South Eden Camp), tbls. Boating(l), fishing, swimming. Elev 5900 ft.

LAPOINT (41)

Paradise Park   **$5**
Ashley National Forest
8.8 mi NW on FR 104 from CR 121 near Lapoint. $5 during 7/1-9/25; free rest of year. 16-day limit. 15 sites (25-ft RV limit). Tbls, toilets, cfga, no drkg wtr. Fishing, boating(l). Paradise Park Reservoir.

LA SAL (42)

Buckeye Campground   **FREE**
Manti-LaSal National Forest
From LaSal, E on FR 072, across state line into Colorado; at 90-acre Buckeye Reservoir. Free. June-Sept; 16-day limit. 5 tent sites. Tbls, toilets, cfga, no drkg wtr. Biking, fishing, hiking, horseback riding. Colorado fishing license needed to fish.

LEVAN (43)

Chicken Creek   **FREE**
Manti-LaSal National Forest
6 mi SE of Levan on Chicken Creek Canyon Rd (FR 101). Free. 6/1-LD; 16-day limit. 12 sites. Tbls, toilets, cfga, drkg wtr. Fishing. This site is in Uinta NF, administered by Manti-LaSal NF.

Painted Rocks Unit   **$9**
Yuba State Park
15 mi S of Levan just off Hwy 28; on E side of lake. $9. All year; 14-day limit. 20 undesignated primitive sites. Pit toilets, cfga, drkg wtr, tbls, no showers. Boating (!), fishing, swimming, waterskiing. Primitive camping also on north, west & east beaches for $9; camp with showers, flush toilets, dump, drkg wtr for $15 at Oasis Unit; boat-in tent camping at Eagle View (East Beach) for $9 ($15 with boat dock).

LOA (44)

Elkhorn   **FREE**
Fishlake National Forest
12.5 mi NE of Loa on SR 72; 7.5 mi SE at Elkhorn cutoff (FR 062). 6/15-10/31; 14-day limit. 6 sites; 22-ft RV limit. Tbls, toilets, cfga, drkg wtr. Hunting, fishing, hiking, horseback riding, OHV activity, mountain biking. Fee for group camping. Elev 9300 ft.

Frying Pan   **$10**
Fishlake National Forest
13 mi NW of Loa on SR 24; 16 mi NE on SR 25; 3 mi N of Fish Lake. $10. MD-9/30; 14-day limit. 11 sites (22-ft RV limit). Tbls, toilets, cfga, drkg wtr. Fishing, OHV activity, hunting, horseback riding, hiking, mountain biking, waterfowl viewing. Elev 9000 ft.

Fishing tip: Fish Lake has excellent rainbow trout angling -- recovered after several years of decline. For lake trout (mackinaw), deep troll with white-and-red lures. Bait fish at the N and S sections and along the E shoreline. Popular shore fishing areas are Twin Creeks S to Doctor Creek; use worms, power bait & cheese for trout.

Piute   **$8**
Fishlake National Forest
13 mi NW of Loa on SR 24; 15 mi NE on SR 25; qtr mi W of Johnson Reservoir. $8. MD-9/30; 60-day limit. 48 RV sites in open setting. Toilets, cfga, no drkg wtr, no tbls; showers at Mackinaw Camp. Boating(l), fishing, hiking trails, OHV trails nearby, horseback riding.

LOGAN (45)

Bridger   **$12**
Cache National Forest
5.7 mi E of Logan on US 89. $12. 5/17-9/10.; 7-day limit. 10 sites (20-ft RV limit). Tbls, toilets, cfga, drkg wtr. Fishing. Elev 5000 ft.

Guinavah-Malibu   **$7.50**
Cache National Forest
8 mi E of Logan on US 89. $7.50 with federal Senior Pass; others pay $15. 5/18-LD; 7-day limit. 35 sites (25-ft RV limit). Tbls, flush toilets, cfga, drkg wtr. Hiking, fishing. Elev 5200 ft; 38 acres.

Lewis M. Turner   **$12**
Cache National Forest
12.7 mi N of Logan on US 89; half mi W on FR 141. $12. 5/30-9/15; 7-day limit. 10 sites (20-ft RV limit). Tbls, flush toilets, cfga, drkg wtr. Elev 6300 ft; 6 acres.

Lodge   **$10**
Cache National Forest
11.5 mi E of Logan on US 89; 1.2 mi SE on FR 047; in right fork of Logan Canyon. $10. 5/17-9/10; 7-day limit. 10 sites (20-ft RV limit). Tbls, toilets, cfga, drkg wtr. Fishing.

Preston Valley   **$10**
Cache National Forest
7.8 mi E of Logan on US 89; at Logan River. $10. 5/17-9/10; 7-day limit. 18 sites; 20-ft RV limit. Tbls, flush toilets, cfga, drkg wtr. Fishing.

Red Banks   **$10**
Cache National Forest
27.7 mi NE of Logan on US 89; at Logan River. $10. 5/30-9/18; 7-day limit. 12 sites (20-ft RV limit). Tbls, toilets, cfga, drkg wtr. Fishing.

Spring Hollow   **$6.50**
Cache National Forest
6.3 mi E of Logan on US 89; at Logan River. $6.50 with federal Senior Pass; others pay $13. 5/18-10/12; 7-day limit. 12 sites; 20-ft RV limit. Tbls, cfga, toilets, drkg wtr. Fishing, picnicking, hiking, interpretive trail. Elev 5100 ft.

Tony Grove Lake   **$7.50**
Cache National Forest
22 mi NE of Logan on US 89; 7 mi W on Fr 003. $7.50 with federal Senior Pass. 6/12-9/11; 7-day limit. 37 sites. Tbls, flush & pit toilets, cfga, drkg wtr. Hiking, horseback riding, boating, fishing.

Wood Camp   **$10**
Cache National Forest
12.4 mi NE of Logan on US 89. $10 during 5/15-10/31; free rest of yr when access open; 7-day limit. 6 sites (RVs under 21 ft). Tbls, toilets, cfga, no drkg wtr. Fishing, picnicking.

LONETREE (WYMOING) (46)

Henry's Fork Trailhead   **FREE**
Wasatch National Forest
8 mi S of Lonetree, Wy, on Cedar Basin Rd; 15 mi W on FR 58 to jct with FR 77 at Henry's Fork Creek. 6/1-10/15; 14-day limit. 7 sites; 20-ft RV limit. Toilets, cfga, no drkg wtr. Hunting, horse trails, hiking trails, fishing. Elev 9600 ft.

MANILA (47)

Browne Lake   **$9**
Ashley National Forest
Flaming Gorge NRA
14 mi S of Manila on UT 44; 3 mi W on FR 218; half mi W on FR 364; 3 mi W on FR 221. $9 at developed sites; free in dispersed areas. 6/1-10/1; 16-day limit. 8 tent sites. Tbls, toilets, cfga, firewood, no drkg wtr, no trash service. Boating(d); fishing; picnicking; hunting. Elev 8200 ft; 4 acres.

Carmel/Navajo Cliffs   **$9**
Ashley National Forest
Flaming Gorge NRA
3 mi S of Manila on SR 44. $9. 5/15-9/15; 16-day limit. 13 sites. Tbls, toilets, cfga, no drkg wtr. Fishing. Visitor center with interpretive displays.

Deep Creek   **$9**
Ashley National Forest
Flaming Gorge NRA
14 mi S of Manila on SR 44; 3 mi W on FR 218; 4.5 mi SE on FR 539. $9. All year; 16-day limit. 17 sites; 30-ft RV limit. Tbls, toilets, cfga, no drkg wtr, no trash service. Fishing. 8 acres. Carter Creek. Ute Tower.

Kingfisher Island   **$10**
Ashley National Forest
Flaming Gorge NRA
7.2 mi SE of Manila on SR 44; half mi NE on FR 10092; 2.3 mi NE by boat. $10 during 5/17-9/12; free rest of year; higher fees at improved sites. 16-day limit. 8 tent sites. Tbls, toilets, cfga, no drkg wtr. Fishing, boating(ld). Elev 6100 ft. On Flaming Gorge Lake.

Spirit Lake   **$9**
Ashley National Forest
14 mi S of Manila on SR 44; 3 mi W on FR 218; half mi W on FR 364; 14 mi W on FR 221. $9. 6/1-10/1; 16-day limit. Open free after managed season to accommodate hunters. 24 sites (30-ft RV limit). Tbls, toilets, cfga, no drkg wtr. Fishing, boating(r), picnicking, hiking. 11 acres. Elev 10,000 ft.

MANTI (48)

Manti Community   **$8**
Manti-LaSal National Forest
7 mi E of Manti on Manti Canyon Rd (FR 045). $8. MD-10/31; 16-day limit. 9 sites. Tbls, toilets, cfga, drkg wtr. Fishing, biking, hiking. When group site #1 is not reserved, it is available for $15.

MANTUA (49)

Box Elder   **$7.50**
Cache National Forest
2 mi S of Mantua on county rd; near Mantua River. $7.50 with federal Senior Pass. 5/118-10/14; 7-day limit. 26 sites (30-ft RV limit). Tbls, flush toilets, cfga, drkg wtr. Fishing. Elev 5200 ft; 11 acres.

Willard Basin   **FREE**
Wasatch National Forest
4 mi S of Mantua on FR 84; 12 mi W on FR 841. Free. Elev 9000 ft. 6/1-9/30; 7-day limit. 4 tent sites on 3 acres (no RVs). Tbls, toilets, cfga, no drkg wtr. Picnicking; horseback riding; OHV activity; hiking; mountain biking.

MAPLETON (50)

Whiting Campground   **$7**
Uinta National Forest
4 mi E of Mapleton, up Maple Canyon on FR 025. $7 with federal Senior Pass; others pay $14. 5/1-11/1; 14-day limit. 25 sites (3 equestrian). Tbls, flush toilets, cfga, drkg wtr, cfga (no wtr after LD). Hiking, mountain biking. Elev 5400 ft.

MARYSVALE (51)

Piute State Park   **$9**
12 mi S of Marysvale on US 89; 1 mi E. $9. All year; 14-day limit. Primitive undesignated sites on 40 acres. Tbls, pit toilets, cfga, no drkg wtr. Fishing, hiking, boating(ld), swimming. On N shore of 3,360-acre Piute Reservoir.

MENDON (52)

Maple Bench Trailhead   **FREE**
Wasatch National Forest
1 mi S of Mendon on UT 23; 1 mi SW on co rd; 2 mi SW on CR 86. Free. Elev 6000 ft. 6/15-9/10. Undesignated sites (no RVs), no facilities.

MEXICAN HAT (53)

Goosenecks State Park   **FREE**
Located 4 mi N of Mexican Hat on Hwy 261; 3 mi SW. Camp free, but 5-day park pass required for entry. All year; 14-day limit. 4 sites; 30-ft RV limit. Tbls, toilets, cfga, no drkg wtr. Picnicking. OHV & mountain biking trails nearby

Johns Canyon   **FREE**
Slickhorn Canyon
Bureau of Land Management
Dirt rd along N rim of San Juan River from Goosenecks State Reserve, off SR 261. Or, by dirt rd off SR 261 to upper end. Free. All year; 14-day limit. Informal camping along access rds. Drkg wtr scarce; spring wtr in tributary of Trail Canyon. Hiking, picnicking, fishing. 60,710 acres.

MILFORD (55)

Rock Corral Campground   **FREE**
Bureau of Land Management
Qtr mi from Milford on Hwy 21, follow signs on local rd for about 9 mi. Free. 5/1-10/31; 14-day limit. 3 sites. Tbls, toilet, cfga, no drkg wtr. Hiking, climbing, hunting. Elev 7000 ft.

MOAB (56)

Arches National Park   **$10**
Backcountry Camping
5 mi N of Moab on US 163 to visitor center. Campsites (do not camp in washes) are free. Hiking. $10 entrance fee into park for 7 days from March-Oct. Backcountry hikers should inform park rangers about trip plans. In backcountry, stay away from washes and other areas prone to flash flooding.

Big Bend   **$10**
Bureau of Land Management
Moab District
2 mi N of Moab on US 191; 6 mi NE on SR 128; at Colorado River. $10. All year; 14-day limit. 22 sites. Tbls, toilets, cfga, no drkg wtr, beach. Fishing, swimming, boating.

Colorado River   **FREE**
Bureau of Land Management
From Colorado border to Moab; 67.5 river miles. Upstream river access by unpaved rds at Westwater, near border, and from Cisco. Land access from unmapped 4WD trails. Downstream, SR 128 follows S bank 30 mi from Dewey bridge to Moab. Whitewater rafting section, some canoe and boat stretches. Free. All year; 14-day limit. River campsites for rafters; informal camping at landings and along secondary rds. Fishing, boating, rafting, hiking, picnicking. BLM Grand Resources Office, Sand Flat Rd, P.O. Box M, Moab, UT 84532.

Devil's Garden   **$7.50**
Arches National Park
5 mi N of Moab on US 163 to Park Entrance, 18 mi NE of visitor center. $7.50 with federal Senior Pass; others pay $15. Also $10 entrance fee for 7 days. 53 sites (RVs under 30 ft). Tbls, flush toilets, cfga, pull-through spaces, drkg wtr. Picnicking; hiking. Wtr shut off during free season. 7-day limit.

Dewey Bridge   **$10**
Bureau of Land Management
Moab District
2 mi N of Moab on US 191; 28.7 mi N on SR 128; at Colorado River. $10. All year; 14-day limit. 7 sites. Tbls, toilets, cfga, no drkg wtr. Fishing, boating.

Diamond Canyon   **FREE**
and Flume Canyon
Bureau of Land Management
N of I-70 about 10 me W of Colorado border; take improved rd N along Westwater Creek. 4WD access routes farther S. Free. All year; 14-day limit. Undesignated campsites on access rds. No facilities. Hiking, backpacking.

Drinks Canyon Camping Area   **$5**
Bureau of Land Management
Moab District
2 mi N of Moab on US 191; 6.2 mi N on SR 128; at Colorado River. $5. All year; 14-day limit. 17 primitive sites. Tbls, toilets, cfga, no drkg wtr. Elev 4000 ft.

Echo Camping Area   **$5**
Bureau of Land Management
Moab District
From US 191 N of Moab, 8 mi N on Kane Creek Rd. $5. All year; 14-day limit. 9 sites. Tbls, toilets, cfga, no drkg wtr. Biking, hiking climbing. Elev 4100 ft. Petroglyphs, natural bridge nearby.

Goldbar Camping Area   **$10**
Bureau of Land Management
Moab District
2 mi N of Moab on US 191; 10.2 mi N on SR 128. $10. All year; 14-day limit. 8 primitive sites. Tbls, toilets, cfga, no drkg wtr. Elev 4000 ft.

Fisher Towers Recreation Site   **$10**
Bureau of Land Management
23 mi N of Moab on SR 128, then E on Fisher Towers Rd; no large RVs. $10. May-Oct; 14-day limit. Tbls, toilets, cfga, no drkg wtr. Rock climbing, hiking. Elev 4200 ft.

Goose Island   **$10**
Bureau of Land Management
Moab District
2 mi N of Moab on US 191; 1.4 mi N on SR 128; at Colorado River. $10. All year; 14-day limit. 18 developed sites; 36-ft RV limit. Tbls, toilets, cfga, no drkg wtr. Fishing.

Hal Canyon   **$10**
Bureau of Land Management
Moab District
2 mi N of Moab on US 191; 6.6 mi N on SR 128; at Colorado River. $10. All year; 14-day limit. 11 sites; 24-ft RV limit. Tbls, toilets, cfga, no drkg wtr. Fishing.

Hamburger Rock   **$6**
Bureau of Land Management
Monticello District
S of Moab on US 191 to Needles section of

Canyonlands National Park entrance rd SR 211, then about 20 mi W to Lockhart Rd; camp is just up the rd to the right. $6. All year; 14-day limit. 8 sites. Toilet, cfga, no drkg wtr. Biking, hunting, OHV activity.

Hittle Bottom   **$10**
Bureau of Land Management
2 mi N of Moab on US 191; 22.5 mi N on SR 128. $10. All year; 14-day limit. 10 sites. Tbls, toilets, cfga, no drkg wtr. Fishing, boating(l). Elev 4000 ft.

Hunter Canyon/
Spring Camping Area   **$5**
Bureau of Land Management
Moab District
From US 191 N of Moab, 7.8 mi N on Kane Creek Rd; at Colorado River. $5. All year; 14-day limit. 13 sites (including 4 walk-in sites). Tbls, toilets, cfga, no drkg wtr. Hiking, biking.

Jaycee Campground   **$10**
Bureau of Land Management
Moab District
3 mi N of Moab on US 191; 4.2 mi S on SR 279; near Colorado River. $10. All year; 14-day limit. 7 developed walk-in tent sites. Tbls, toilets, cfga, no drkg wtr. Fishing, hiking, biking, 4x4 action, rock climbing.

Kings Bottom Camping Area   **$5**
Bureau of Land Management
Moab District
From US 191 N of Moab, 2.8 mi N on Kane Creek Rd; at S side of Colorado River. $5. All year; 14-day limit. 7 primitive tent sites. Tbls, toilets, cfga, no drkg wtr. Hiking, biking.

Moonflower Canyon Camping Area   **$5**
Bureau of Land Management
Moab District
From US 191 N of Moab, 3 mi N on Kane Creek Rd. $5. All year; 14-day limit. 8 walk-in tent sites. Tbls, toilets, cfga, no drkg wtr. Petroglypys & Pritchett Natural Bridge nearby.

Negro Bill Canyon Camping Area   **$5**
Bureau of Land Management
Moab District
2 mi N of Moab on US 191; 3 mi N on SR 128. $5. All year; 14-day limit. 17 primitive tent sites. Tbls, toilets, cfga, no drkg wtr. Hiking & biking trails.

Oak Grove   **$10**
Bureau of Land Management
Moab District
2 mi N of Moab on US 191; 6.9 mi N on SR 128. $10. All year; 14-day limit. 7 sites. Tbls, toilets, cfga, no drkg wtr. Fishing.

Oowah Lake   **$6**
Manti-LaSal National Forest
S of Moab on US 191; turn left & follow signs to Ken's Lake/LaSal Mountain Loop Rd; Pass the Pack Creek Ranch, turn right and continue on Loop Rd past end of pavement

to Oowah Lake; turn right and follow rd to camp (rd not plowed, so snow may delay season). $6. 6/1-10/31; 14-day limit. 6 tent sites. Tbls, toilets, cfga, drkg wtr. Hiking, horseback riding.

Sand Flats Recreation Area   **$10**
Bureau of Land Management
Grand County Parks
3 mi E of Moab on Sand Flat Rd. $10. All year; 14-day limit. 124 sites. Tbls, toilets, cfga, no drkg wtr. Mountain biking on 10-mi Moab Slickrock Bike Trail & 4x4 trails.

Squaw Flat   **$7.50**
Canyonlands National Park
40 mi S of Moab on US 163; 45 mi W on UT 211 (paved rds). $7.50 with federal Senior Pass; others pay $15. 26 sites (RVs under 28 ft). Tbls, toilets, cfga, drkg wtr (available off-season at the ranger station about 3 mi from the campground). Picnicking, rock climbing, hiking, interpretive talks, biking, horseback riding.

Warner Lake   **$10**
Manti-LaSal National Forest
6.5 mi SE of Moab on US 191; 7.3 mi SE on Ken's Lake/LaSal Mountain Loop Rd to end of pavement; 7 mi NE on FR 062; 5 mi NE on FR 063. $10. 5/18-10/1; 16-day limit. 27 sites (40-ft RV limit). Tbls, toilets, cfga, drkg wtr. Fishing, hiking. Elev 9400 ft; 10 acres.

Upper Big Bend Camping Area   **$5**
Bureau of Land Management
Moab District
2 mi N of Moab on US 191; 8.1 mi N on SR 128. $5. All year; 14-day limit. 8 tent sites. Tbls, toilets, cfga, no drkg wtr.

MONTICELLO (57)

Anticline Overlook   **FREE**
Canyon Rims Recreation Area
Bureau of Land Management
22 mi N of Monticello on US 191 to Canyon Rims entrance, then 32 mi NW on gravel rd. Free. All year; 14-day limit. 2 sites. Toilets, cfga, no drkg wtr. Hiking, sightseeing. View Cane Creek Anticline (arched up layers of rock), evaporation ponds of Texasgulf potash mine. Also, Arches National Park.

Buckboard   **$8**
Manti-LaSal National Forest
6.5 mi W of Monticello on FR 105. $8. 5/15-10/1; free rest of year, but no wtr; 16-day limit. 13 sites. Tbls, toilets, cfga, drkg wtr. Fishing, horseback riding, biking, OHV activity.

Dalton Springs   **$10.**
Manti-LaSal National Forest
5 mi W of Monticello on FR 105. $10. 5/15-10/30; 16-day limit. 16 sites (30-ft RV limit). Tbls, toilets, cfga, drkg wtr. Fishing, swimming, hunting. 5 acres. Elev 8200 ft.

Hatch Point Campground   **$10**
Canyon Rims Recreation Area
Bureau of Land Management
22 mi N of Monticello on US 191 to Canyon Rims entrance, then 25 mi on gravel rd toward Anticline Overlook. $10 during 4/15-10/15; $8 rest of year, but no wtr; 14-day limit. 10 sites (25-ft RV limit). Tbls, drkg wtr, toilets, cfga. Hiking, biking, wildlife viewing. Nearby Needles Overlook offers spectacular view of Canyonlands National Park; Anticline Overlook; Island in the Sky & Colorado River; 4WD trails.

Newspaper Rock   **FREE**
Bureau of Land Management
13 mi N of Monticello on US 191; 13 mi W on SR 211; across the road from Newspaper Rock State Park. Free. All year; 14-day limit. 14 sites. Tbls, toilets, cfga, no drkg wtr. Biking, climbing. Indian rock panel writing nearby.

Wind Whistle Campground   **$10**
Canyon Rims Recreation Area
Bureau of Land Management
22 mi N of Monticello on US ;191 to Canyon Rims entrance, then 6 mi on gravel rd toward Anticline Overlook. $10 during 4/15-10/15; $8 rest of year, but no wtr; 14-day limit. 15 sites; 30-ft RV limit. Tbls, drkg wtr, toilets, cfga. Hiking, wildlife viewing, biking. Nearby Needles Overlook offers spectacular view of Canyonlands National Park; Anticline Overlook; Island in the Sky & Colorado River; 4WD trails.

MONUMENT VALLEY (58)

Mitten View   **$10**
Monument Valley Tribal Park
Navajo Parks & Recreation Department
24 mi NE of Kayenta, AZ, off US 163. $10 during summer; $5 in winter. All year; (primitive only Oct-Apr) 14-day limit. 99 sites (36-ft RV limit). Tbls, flush toilets, showers($), cfga, drkg wtr, dump, museum, visitor center. Guided hikes. 100 acres. Fee to enter tribal park. Primitive camping also available at the Wildcat Trailhead half mi N of visitor center.

MOUNTAIN VIEW (WY.) (59)

Bridger Lake   **$12**
Wasatch National Forest
7 mi SW of Mountain View on Wyoming SR 410; 16.5 mi S on FR 72; half mi S on FR 126. $12. 6/1-10/15, but no wtr after LD; 14-day limit. 30 sites; 20-ft RV limit. Toilets, cfga, drkg wtr. Fishing, hunting, hiking trails, canoeing, biking. Handicap access. Elev 9300 ft.

China Meadows   **$8**
Wasatch National Forest
7 mi SW of Mountain View on WY 410; 18.4 mi S on FR 72; S of China Lake. $8. About 7/1-10/15, but no wtr after LD; 14-day limit. 9 sites; 20-ft RV limit. Toilets, cfga, no drkg wtr. Fishing, hunting, boating(l). Elev 10,000 ft.

Deadhorse Trailhead   **$6**
Wasatch National Forest
7 mi SW of Mountain View on WY 410; 19.4 mi S on FR 4072. $6 during 7/1-9/30; free rest of year when access open; 14-day limit. 4 sites. Toilets, cfga, no drkg wtr. Hiking trails, hunting, horse trails. Trailhead into High Vintas Wilderness. Horse loading dock.

East Fork of Blacks Fork Trailhead
Wasatch National Forst   **FREE**
S of Evanston on SR 410; SW on FR 073 past Meeks Cabin Lake to end of rd at Blacks Fork Trail on branch of Blacks Fork River. 8 sites; 20-ft RV limit. Tbls, toilets, cfga, no drkg wtr, horse loading ramps. Hiking, fishing, horseback riding.

Hoop Lake   **$10**
Wasatch National Forest
26.6 mi SE of Mountain View on Hwy 414; 3.2 mi S on CR 264; 6.5 mi SE on FR 58. $10. 6/15-10/30, but no wtr after LD; 14-day limit. 44 sites (25-ft RV limit). Tbls, toilets, cfga, drkg wtr (no wtr after LD). Fishing, boating(l), hiking, horseback riding.

East Marsh Lake   **$12**
Wasatch National Forest
7 mi SW of Mountain View on WY 410; 17.8 mi S on FR 72. $12. 6/1-10/15, but no wtr after LD; 14-day limit. 38 sites in 2 aras; 20-ft RV limit. Toilets, cfga, drkg wtr. Hiking, hunting, horse trails, fishing, canoeing. Elev 9400 ft.

Meeks Cabin   **$8**
Wasatch National Forest
S of Mountain View on SR 410; W on FR 073. $8. 6/15-10/30, but no drkg wtr after LD; 14-day limit. 24 sites (20-ft RV limit). Tbls, toilets, cfga, drkg wtr. Swimming, fishing. Elev 8700 ft; 12 acres.

Quarter Corner   **FREE**
Wasatch National Forest
23 mi S of Mountain View on Hwy 414 and FR 017; at Quarter Corner Lake and several small lakes. Free. June-Sept; 14-day limit. 3 sites; 25-ft RV limit. Tbls, toilets, cfga, no drkg wtr. Fishing, hiking, mountain biking, OHV activity.

Stateline   **$12**
Wasatch National Forest
7 mi S of Mountain View on WY 410; 8.2 mi on Uinta CR 246; 5.5 mi on FR 072. $12. 6/1-10/15; 14-day limit. 41 sites (25-ft RV limit). Tbls, toilets, cfga, drkg wtr. Fishing, boating, hiking.

MYTON (60)

Desolation Canyon/   **FREE**
Gray Canyon
Bureau of Land Management
42 mi S of Myton on local rds to Sand Wash Ranger Station; camp along Green River. Free. All year; 14-day limit. Open camping; no facilities. Permits required within Uintah & Ouray Indian Reservations.

Pariette Wetlands   **FREE**
Bureau of Land Management
1 mi W of Myton on US 40 to Sand Wash-Green River access turnoff; 1.7 mi S to Nine Mile-Sand Wash jct; left & follow signs 23 mi (slippery in wet weather). Free. Mar-Nov; 14-day limit. Dispersed camping around ponds complex; no facilities, no drkg wtr. Hiking, fishing, hunting, boating, canoeing in wetlands. Elev 4700 ft.

Sand Wash Recreation Area   **FREE**
Bureau of Land Management
1 mi W of Myton on US 40 to Sand Wash-Green River access turnoff; 1.7 mi S ot Nine Mile-Sand Wash jct; left for 18 mi (slippery when wet). Free. Mar-Nov; 14-day limit. Primitive sites for Green River floaters in Labyrinth Canyon.

NAF (IDAHO) (61)

Clear Creek   **FREE**
Sawtooth National Forest
5.9 mi S of Naf on FR 60006, in Utah. Free. 6/1-9/30; 7-day limit. 10 sites (RVs under 24 ft). Tbls, toilets, cfga, drkg wtr. Fishing.

NEPHI (62)

Cottonwood   **FREE**
Uinta National Forest
6 mi E of Nephi on UT 11; 6 mi N on FR 015. 5/15-10/31; 14-day limit. 18 primitive, undeveloped sites. No facilities. Hunting; picnicking; fishing;horseback riding. Elev 6400 ft; 9 acres. Located near Mt Nebo. Site not recommended for tourist use.

Jericho Campground   **$8**
Little Sahara Recreation Area
Bureau of Land Management
22 mi W of Nephi on US 6 & 50; 3 mi W of visitor center; 5 mi SW of visitor center on BLM rd. $8 or annual $75 Little Sahara pass. All year; 14-day limit. 41 sites. Tbls, flush toilets, cfga, drkg wtr. Nature program. Free camping Nov-Apr, but no wtr except at visitor center.

Oasis   **$8**
Little Sahara Recreation Area
Bureau of Land Management
22 mi W of Nephi on US 6 & 50; 3 mi W to visitor center; 5 mi SW of visitor center. $8 (free Nov-Apr, but no wtr except at visitor center); or annual $75 Little Sahara pass. All year; 14-day limit. 114 sites (40-ft RV limit). Tbls, flush toilets, cfga, drkg wtr. Nature program. Elev 5000 ft; 42 acres. Popular off-road vehicle camp.

Ponderosa   **$7**
Uinta National Forest
5 mi E of Nephi on SR 132, then about 3 mi N on Mount Nebo Loop Rd. $7 with federal Senior Pass; others pay $14. 5/15-11/1; 14-day limit. 23 sites. Tbls, toilets, cfga, drkg wtr (no wtr after LD). Fishing, hiking, horseback riding.

White Sands   **$8**
Little Sahara Recreation Area
Bureau of Land Management
22 mi W of Nephi on US 6 & 50; 3 mi W to visitor center; 1 mi N of visitor center on BLM rd. $8 or annual $75 Little Sahara pass. All year; 14-day limit. 99 sites (40-ft RV limit). Tbls, flush toilets, cfga, drkg wtr. Nature program. 37 acres. Free camping Nov-Apr, but no wtr except at visitor center.

NORTH LOGAN (63)

Green Canyon   **FREE**
Wasatch National Forest
E on Rd. 1900 from North Logan to Green Canyon, then about 2 mi on forest rd. Free. All year; 14-day limit. 6 sites. Tbls, toilets, cfga, no drkg wtr. Hiking, horseback riding, biking.

NORTH OGDEN (64)

North Ogden Canyon   **FREE**
Trailhead Camp
Wasatch National Forest
2 mi E of North Ogden on North Ogden Canyon Rd. Free. Jul-Oct; 7-day limit. Undesignated sites. Toilets, no tbls, no drkg wtr. Hiking trails, horse & trail bike trails. Elev 6200 ft.

OAK CITY (65)

Oak Creek   **$10**
Fishlake National Forest
3.5 mi SE on SR 135; 1 mi E on FR 089. $10. 5/15-9/15; 14-day limit (no wtr after Sept). 19 family sites, 4 group sites. Tbls, flush toilets, cfga, drkg wtr, shelter, amphitheater. Fishing, hiking, horseback riding, biking. Groups can reserve whole campground.

ORANGEVILLE (68)

Indian Creek   **$6**
Manti-LaSal National Forest
7.2 mi NW of Orangeville on SR 29; 12.2 mi N on FR 040. $6. 6/30-9/15; 16-day limit. 29 sites. Tbls, toilets, cfga, drkg wtr. Fishing. Elev 9000 ft; 43 acres.

Joes Valley   **$8**
Manti-LaSal National Forest
17.5 mi NW of Orangeville on SR 29. $8. 5/11-10/1; 16-day limit. 50 sites (30-ft RV limit). Tbls, flush toilets, cfga, drkg wtr. Fishing, waterskiing, boating(l). Manageed jointly with Bureau of Land Management.

   Fishing tip: This 1,170-acre reservoir contains splake, rainbow & cutthroat trout.

OREM (69)

Mount Timpanogos **$6.50**
Uinta National Forest
NE of Orem on US 189, then left on turnoff to Sundance ski area for about 3 mi. $6.50 with federal Senior Pass; others pay $13. MD-10/30; 14-day limit. 27 sites; 30-ft RV limit. Tbls, toilets, cfga, drkg wtr. Hiking trails. Elev 6800 ft. $3 daily user fee (or $10 for 14 days, $25 annually).

PAGE (ARIZONA) (70)

White House Trailhead **$5**
Bureau of Land Management
35 mi W of Page on Hwy 89. $5. 4/1-11/1; 14-day limit. 5 primitive sites; 22-ft RV limit; 3 tent sites. Tbls, toilets, cfga, no drkg wtr. On Paria River. Elev 4600ft.

PANGUITCH (71)

King Creek **$10**
Dixie National Forest
26 mi SE of Panguitch off Hwy 12. $10. 5/15-LD; 14-day limit. 37 sites; 45-ft RV limit. Tbls, flush toilets, cfga, drkg wtr, dump. Swimming, boating(l), fishing, hiking trails, waterskiing, ATV trail. Elev 8000 ft; 18 acres. Tropic Reservoir & East fork of Sevier River.

North Campground **$10**
Bryce Canyon National Park
7 mi S of Panguitch on US 89; 13 mi E on SR 12; 2 mi S on SR 63; just E of park headquarters. $10 (plus $25 entry fee for 7 days or $30 annually). All year; 14-day limit. 107 sites. Tbls, flush toilets, cfga, drkg wtr, dump (showers at Sunset Point). Hiking, horseback riding.

Panguitch Lake North **$12**
Dixie National Forest
16 mi SW of. Panguitch on SR 143. $12. 6/11-LD; 14-day limit. 39 sites (35-ft RV limit). Tbls, flush toilets, cfga, drkg wtr, dump, coin laundry. Hiking, fishing, boating, swimming. Elev 8400 ft.
Fishing tip: This lake has good fishing for rainbow, brown & brook trout.

Panguitch Lake South **$10**
Dixie National Forest
19 mi SW of Panguitch on FR 36. $10. 6/11-LD (free rest of yr, but no wtr or services); 14-day limit. 19 sites (including 1 non-trailer RV site & 18 tent sites). Tbls, drkg wtr, flush toilets, cfga, coin laundry, groceries. Boating(l), swimming, fishing, hiking trails, bike trails. 13 acres.

Red Canyon **$12**
Dixie National Forest
10 mi SE of Panguitch on Hwy 12. $9. 5/15-10/1; 14-day limit. 37 sites (45-ft RV limit. Tbls, flush toilets, cfga, drkg wtr, coin showers, dump ($2). Hiking trails, ATV activity, horseshoes, volleyball. Visitor center.

Sunset Campground **$10**
Bryce Canyon National Park
7 mi S of Panguitch on US 89; 13 mi E on SR 12; S on SR 63 to park headquarters, then 2 mi S. $10 (plus $25 entry fee for 7 days or $30 annually). 4/15-11/30; 14-day limit. 111 sites. Tbls, flush toilets, cfga, drkg wtr (showers at Sunset Point; dump at North Campground). Hiking, horseback riding.

White Bridge **$12**
Dixie National Forest
12 mi SW of Panguitch on SR 143; at Panguitch Creek. $12. 6/11-LD; 14-day limit. 28 sites (24-ft RV limit). Tbls, flush toilets, cfga, drkg wtr, dump. Hiking, fishing, swimming, biking. Elev 7900 ft.

PAYSON (72)

Blackhawk Campground **$7**
Uinta National Forest
16 mi SE of Payson on Nebo Loop Rd (FR 015); 2 mi S on FR 015. $7 with federal Senior Pass; others pay $14. MD-11/1; 14-day limit. 12 sites; 35-ft RV limit. Tbls, toilets, cfga, drkg wtr (no wtr after LD), dump, horse loading ramp (no wtr after LD). Bridle & hiking trails, mountain biking, fishing.

Maple Bench **$7**
Uinta National Forest
5 mi E of Payson on Nebo Loop Rd. $7 with federal Senior Pass; others pay $14. MD-10/1; 14-day limit. 10 sites (35-ft RV limit). Tbls, toilets, cfga, drkg wtr. Fishing, hiking trail. Handicap access. Half mi N of tiny Maple Lake (canoeing, fishing).

Payson Lakes **$7**
Uinta National Forest
12 mi SE of Payson on Nebo Loop Rd, then SW following signs. $7 with federal Senior Pass; others pay $14. MD-11/1; 14-day limit. 82 sites; 45-ft RV limit. Tbls, flush toilets, cfga, drkg wtr (no wtr after LD), corrals. Paved loop nature trail among 3 lakes. Horseback riding, fishing, swimming, hiking.

PINE VALLEY (73)

Blue Spring **$12**
Dixie National Forest
Pine Valley Recreational Complex
About 1 mi E of Pine Valley, near reservoir. $12. 5/4-9/15; 14-day limit. 17 sites; 45-ft RV limit. Toilets, tbls, cfga, drkg wtr. Fishing, floating, rafting, kayaking, hiking trail, OHV activities, horseback riding.

Equestrian Campground **$8**
Dixie National Forest
Pine Valley Recreational Complex
2 mi E of Pine Valley; near Pine Valley Reservoir. $8 for tent sites; $10 for RV sites without horse stalls; $12 for RV sites with stalls. 5/4-9/30; 14-day limit. 14 sites. Tbls, flush & pit toilets, cfga, drkg wtr, 4-way corral, dump 5 mi. Fishing, horseback riding, ATV activities. Good turn-around for large RVs.

North Juniper Park **$12**
Dixie National Forest
Pine Valley Recreation Complex
Just E of Pine Valley. $12. 5/4-10/1; 14-day limit. 11 sites; 45-ft RV limit. Tbls, toilets, cfga, drkg wtr. Dump 5 mi on Pine Valley Rd. Fishing, hiking.

Pines Campground **$12**
Dixie National Forest
Pine Valley Recreation Complex
Just E of Pine Valley about qtr mi past Juniper Park entrances. $12. 5/4-9/16; 14-day limit. 13 sites; 45-ft RV limit. Tbls, toilets, cfga, drkg wtr, dump 5 mi. Fishing, floating, rafting, kayaking, hiking.

South Juniper Park **$12**
Pine Valley Recreation Complex
Just E of Pine Valley; turn right just after entry to North Juniper Park. $12. 5/4-10/1; 14-day limit. 7 sites; 45-ft RV limit. Toilets, tbls, cfga, drkg wtr, dump 5 mi. Fishing, hiking.

PLEASANT GROVE (74)

Granite Flat **$6.50**
Uinta National Forest
14 mi NE of Pleasant Grove on SR 144, up American Fork Canyon, then FR 85 (North Fork Rd) past Tibble Fork Reservoir to camp. $6.50 with federal Senior Pass; others pay $13. MD-9/30; 14-day limit. 44 single sites. Tbls, flush toilets, cfga, drkg wtr. Horse transfer station & loading ramps nearby. Fishing, horseback riding, hiking, hunting. User fee of $3 daily, $10 for 14 days, $25 annually.
Fishing tip: Try the fishing at nearby Tibble Fork Lake; accessible fishing piers are provided; boat motors prohibited.

Little Mill Campground **$6.50**
Uinta National Forest
10 mi NE of Pleasant Grove on SR 92; at American Fork River. $6.50 with federal Senior Pass; others pay $13. 5/15-10/30; 14-day limit. 74 sites; 30-ft RV limit. Tbls, flush toilets, cfga, drkg wtr. Fishing, hiking. Visitor center nearby. Closed for renovation until summer of 2008.

Timpooneke Campground **$6.50**
Uinta National Forest
14.1 mi NE of Pleasant Grove on SR 92. $6.50 with federal Senior Pass; others pay $13. MD-10/30; 14-day limit. 27 sites; 30-ft RV limit. Tbls, toilets, cfga, drkg wtr. Hiking trail, horseback riding, hunting, mountain biking. User fee of $3 daily, $10 for 14 days, $25 annually.

PRICE (75)

Price Canyon Recreational Area **$10**
Bureau of Land Management
9 mi N of Price on US 50/6; turn left at entrance sign; 3 mi up mountain to site. Avoid open, exposed areas, as lightning

frequently strikes ridgetops. $10. Free mid-Oct to mid-Apr; 14-day limit. 18 sites (35-ft RV limit). Tbls, toilets, cfga, drkg wtr. Wildlife viewing, Price Canyon overlook, Bristlecone Ridge Hiking Trail.

PROVO (76)

Hope   **$6.50**
Uinta National Forest
6 mi N of Provo on US 189 to Squaw Peak Rd; 5 mi S on FR 027. $6.50 with federal Senior Pass; others pay $13. MD-10/31; 14-day limit. 24 sites (45-ft RV limit). Tbls, toilets, cfga, drkg wtr.

Tinney Flat   **$7**
Uinta National Forest
S of Provo on I-15 to exit 248 at Santaquin, then E on FR 014 about 9 mi; at Santaquin River. $7 with federal Senior Pass; others pay $14. MD-11/1; 14-day limit. Flush toilets, cfga, drkg wtr (no wtr after LD), cfga. 13 sites; 45-ft RV limit. Fishing, hiking trails.

RICHFIELD (77)

Castle Rock Campground   **$12**
Fremont Indian State Park
21 mi SW of Richfield on I-70. $12. All year; 14-day limit. 31 sites; 30-ft RV limit. Tbls, flush toilets, cfga, drkg wtr, no showers, no dump. Horseback riding, museum of Anasazi Indian culture, picnicking, boating, fishing. In Fishlake National Forest, managed by state. Visitor center & museum. 889 acres; elev 5900 ft.

RICHMOND (78)

High Creek   **FREE**
Wasatch National Forest
2 mi NE of Richmond on US 91; 4 mi E on co rd; 2 mi E on FR 048. Free. Elev 5000 ft. 6/15-9/15; 7-day limit. 3 sites on 3 acres (RVs under 21 ft). Tbls, toilets, cfga, no drkg wtr. Picnicking; fishing; horseback riding (1 mi). Elev 5200 ft.

High Creek Trailhead   **FREE**
Wasatch National Forest
2.2 mi N of Richmond on US 91; 3.3 mi NE on co rd; 1 mi E on FR 48. Free. 5/15-10/30. Open camping area for loading and unloading horses. Toilets, tbls, drkg wtr. Hiking, picnicking, horseback riding, fishing.

ROOSEVELT (79)

Uinta Canyon   **$5**
Ashley National Forest
9.5 mi N of Roosevelt on Hwy 121; 12 mi NW on co rd; 2.5 mi NW on FR 118; at Uinta River. $5. MD-LD; 14-day limit. 24 sites (22-ft RV limit). Tbls, toilets, no drkg wtr, cfga. Fishing, picnicking. Elev 7600 ft; 15 acres.

Wandin   **$5**
Ashley National Forest
9.5 mi N of Roosevelt on UT 121; 12 mi NW on co rd; 4 mi NW on FR 10118. $5 during MD-LD; free rest of year; 14-day limit. 7 sites; 15-ft RV limit. Tbls, toilets, cfga, firewood, no drkg wtr. Hunting; picnicking; fishing; horseback riding/rental (1 mi). Elev 7700 ft.

ST. GEORGE (80)

Baker Reservoir Dam   **$6**
Bureau of Land Management
24 mi N of St. George on Hwy 18. $6 single sites, $12 at four double sites. 19 sites, some for big rigs. All year; 14-day limit. 10 sites; 24-ft RV limit. Tbls, toilets, cfga, no drkg wtr. Fishing, hiking.

Gunlock State Park   **$9**
15 mi N of St. George on US 18; at 240-acre Gunlock Lake. $9. All year; 14-day limit. Primitive undesignated sites (30-ft RV limit); no facilities, no drkg wtr. Swimming, hiking, picnicking. 549 acres.

Quail Creek State Park   **$12**
14 mi NE of St. George on SR 9. $12. All year; 14-day limit. 23 sites; 35-ft RV limit. Tbls, flush toilets, cfga, drkg wtr. No dump or showers. Swimming, boating, fishing, picnicking. Handicap access. Elev 3300 ft.

Red Cliffs   **$8**
Bureau of Land Management
15 mi NE of St. George (4.5 mi SW of Leeds) on I-15; 1.5 mi W on Frontage Rd & BLM rd. $8. All year; 14-day limit. 10 sites (25-ft RV limit). Tbls, toilets, cfga, drkg wtr.

Virgin River Gorge Camp   **$8**
Bureau of Land Management
Arizona Strip District
20 mi SW of St. George on I-15, in Arizona, at Cedar Pockets interchange. Adjacent to the Virgin River and Arizona's Cedar Pockets Rest Area. All year; no time limit. $8. 115 sites for RVs, tents. Toilets, drkg wtr, cfga, tbls. Scenic overlook, interpretive trail, 2 river access trails. Fishing, hiking, picnicking.

SALINA (81)

Clear Creek Dispersed Site   **FREE**
Fishlake National Forest
34 mi E of Salina on I-70 to Exit 89; 1.5 mi W on frontage rd; S on FR 016 to Clear Creek. Free. May-Oct; 16-day limit. Primitive undesignated sites. Some cfga, no other facilities, no drkg wtr, no trash service. Hunting, fishing, picnicking.

Duncan Mountain   **FREE**
Dispersed Recreation Site
Fishlake National Forest
18 mi SE of Salina on I-70; from exit 71, five mi E on paved rd to Accord Lakes; 200 yds W off pavement, then N on FR 007 through private land to forest boundary; camp on

plateau of open areas & pines after small dugway. Free. May-Oct; 16-day limit. Primitive undesignated sites. Some cfga, no other facilities, no drkg wtr, no trash service. Hunting, picnicking. Heavily used during deer & elk seasons. 2 mi past the Accord Lakes turnoff, then S, camp in the Jolley Mill area. From Lizonbee Spring, access to Salina Flats roadless area (26,000 sq acres of non-motorized recreation).

Gooseberry Reservoirs   **FREE**
Dispersed Recreation Sites
Fishlake National Forest
7.5 mi SE of Salina on I-70; 12 mi S on Gooseberry Rd; take numerous spur rds to various locations: Twin Ponds, Cold Spring, Salina Reservoir, Farnsworth Reservoir, Harves River Reservoir, Browns Hole, Niotche Creek, Oak Ridge; Gooseberry Rd is quite rough. May-Oct; 16-day limit. Free. Primitive undesignated sites. Some cfga; toilets at Twin Ponds, Cold Spring, Oak Ridge & Salina Reservoir; no drkg wtr, no trash service. Trout fishing, hunting, boating, hiking trails (part of Great Western Trail) open to OHVs & horses.

Lost Creek Reservoir   **FREE**
Dispersed Recreation Site
Fishlake National Forest
7.5 mi SE of Salina on I-70; 20 mi S on Gooseberry Rd; 1 mi W on FR 058 to Lost Creek Reservoir; numerous pullouts & spur rds for camping. Free. May-Oct; 16-day limit. Some cfga, no other facilities, no drkg wtr, no trash service. Fishing, hunting, boating (no mtrs), hiking, horseback riding, mountain biking, OHV use. Area is a plateau at 9800 ft.

Maple Grove   **$10**
Fishlake National Forest
11 mi NW of Salina on Hwy 50; 3 mi W on FR 101. $10. 5/15-9/15; 14-day limit. 20 sites (22-ft RV limit). Tbls, drkg wtr, toilets, cfga. Fishing, picnicking, hunting, hiking trails, mountain climbing. Scenic; elev 6400 ft.

Old Woman Plateau   **FREE**
Dispersed Recreation Site
Fishlake National Forest
34 mi SE of Salina on I-70 to Exit 89; 4 mi W on frontage rd to FR 011 (Old Woman Plateau Rd); N under freeway to site. Free. May-Oct; 16-day limit. Primitive undesignated sites. Some cfga, no other facilities, no drkg wtr, no trash service. Hunting, picnicking. Area is seldom used.

Red Creek Dispersed Site   **FREE**
Fishlake National Forest
34 mi SE of Salina on I-70 to Exit 89; 2.5 mi W on frontage rd; S on FR 141 to Red Creek. Free. May-Oct; 16-day limit. Primitive undesignated sites. Some cfga, no other facilities, no drkg wtr, no trash service. Hunting, picnicking.

Rex Reservoir   **FREE**
Dispersed Site
Fishlake National Forest
7.5 mi SE of Salina on I-70; 4 mi S on Goose-berry Rd; 1 mi W on FR 037 (Soldier Canyon Rd); 6 mi S on FR 050 (Rex Reservoir Rd). Free. May-Oct; 16-day limit. Primitive undes-ignated sites. Some cfga, no other facilities, no drkg wtr, no trash service. Fishing at Rex Reservoir & nearby Lost Creek, Little Lost Creek, Lost Creek Reservoir, Seven-mile Creek, Johnson Reservoir, Fish Lake & Gooseberry Reservoir; hunting; boating; hik-ing. Elev 7200 ft.

Salina Creek Dispersed Site   **FREE**
Fishlake National Forest
18 mi SE of Salina on I-70; from exit 71, qtr mi E on paved rd, then turn N on FR 009 to Salina Creek bottom area. Free. May-Oct; 16-day limit. Some cfga, no other facilities, no drkg wtr, no trash service. Trout fishing in lower sections of Salina Creek, hunting, hik-ing trails, horseback riding. Access to Salina Flats roadless area with its 26,000 sq acres of non-motorized walk-in camping. Note: better access than Gooseberry Reservoirs; view of a wide area of beaer ponds.

Water Hollow   **FREE**
Dispersed Site
Fishlake National Forest
10.5 mi SE of Salina on I-70 (5 mi past Gooseberry Rd exit) to turnoff (not a formal exit) signaled by break in guard rail; turn sharply, reversing directions, through gate, then N under freeway; many sites after about 4 mi. Free. May-Oct; 16-day limit. Primitive undesignated sites. Some cfga, no other facilities, no drkg wtr, no trash service. Hunting, picnicking, hiking trails, horseback riding.

Willow Creek   **FREE**
Dispersed Site
Fishlake National Forest
3 mi N of Salina on US 89; 7 mi E on gravel rd to forest boundary. Free. May-Oct; 16-day limit. Primitive undesignated sites. Some cfga, tbls; no other facilities; no drkg wtr or trash service. Picnicking, trout fishing, hunt-ing, hiking trails, horseback riding.

✪ SALT LAKE CITY (82)

Rockport State Park   **$9**
45 mi E of Salt Lake City on SR 32, near Wanship. $9 for primitive sites at 5 camp-grounds; $18 for developed sites at Juniper Campground; 40-ft RV limit. Tbls, toilets, cfga, drkg wtr, showers. Hiking, biking, fish-ing, swimming, boating.

SCOFIELD (83)

Fish Creek Trailhead   **FREE**
Manti-Lasal National Forest
3.8 mi N of Scofield on FR 08; 1.5 mi W on FR 123. 6/15-9/10; 9-day limit. 7 tent sites

(no RVs). Tbls, toilets, cfga, no drkg wtr. Hunting, fishing, horseback riding, hiking, hunting. Elev 7000 ft; 2 acres. Near Scofield Reservoir. Access requires pickup or 4-wheel drive vehicles. Fish Creek National Recre-ation Trail.

Madsen Bay Unit   **$12**
Scofield State Park
4 mi N of Scofield, off Hwy 96, on N end of lake. $12. May-Nov; 14-day limit. 40 sites; 35-ft RV limit. Tbls, flush toilets, cfga, drkg wtr, dump, showers, fish cleaning station. Picnicking, boating(l), fishing, swimming, waterskiing. 2,800-acre lake. Developed sites at Mountain View Unit, $15.

SMITHFIELD (84)

Smithfield Canyon   **$10**
Wasatch National Forest
5 mi NE of Smithfield on co rd. $10. 5/15-9/15; 7-day limit. 7 sites (25-ft RV limit). Tbls, toilets, cfga, drkg wtr. Fishing, picnicking, hiking.

SPANISH FORK (85)

Diamond   **$7**
Uinta National Forest
10 mi S of Spanish Fork on Hwy 89; 6 mi NE on FR 029; at Diamond Creek. $7 with fed-eral Senior Pass; others pay $14. 4/1-11/1; 14-day limit. 59 sites (75-ft RV limit). Tbls, toilets, cfga, drkg wtr. Fishing.

Palmyra   **$7**
Uinta National Forest
3.2 mi E of Spanish Fork on SR 147; 9 mi SE on US 50; 5.3 mi NE on FR 092 (Diamond Fork Rd); at Little Diamond Creek. $7. 5/15-10/31; 14-day limit. 11 sites (50-ft RV limit). Tbls, toilets, cfga, drkg wtr. Fishing.

SPRING CITY (86)

Spring City Campground   **$6**
Manti-LaSal National Forest
About 5 mi E of Spring City on FR 036; near Sawmill Creek. $6. May-Oct; 14-day limit. 6 sites. Tbls, toilets, cfga, drkg wtr. Fishing. Elev 7500 ft.

SPRINGVILLE (87)

Balsalm Campground   **$7**
Uinta National Forest
About 12 mi E of Springville on SR 79, which becomes FR 058, to end of pavement; at Right Fork of Hobble Creek. $7 with federal Senior Pass; others pay $14. MD-LD; 14-day limit. 24 sites; 30-ft RV limit. Flush toilets, tbls, drkg wtr, cfga. Fishing, hiking trails, mountain biking, horseback riding.

Cherry Campground   **$7**
Uinta National Forest
About 6 mi E of Springville on SR 79, which becomes FR 058; at Right Fork of Hobble

Creek. $7 with federal Senior Pass; others pay $14. MD-11/1; 14-day limit. 24 sites; 35-ft RV limit. Flush toilets, tbls, drkg wtr, cfga (no wtr after LD). Fishing, hiking trails.

SYRACUSE (88)

Antelope Island State Park   **$12**
9 mi W of Syracuse over 7.5-mi causeway to island. $12 (includes Davis County causeway & wildlife fee). All year; 14-day limit. 30 sites; 65-ft RV limit. Tbls, cfga, drkg wtr, dump, pit & flush toilets. Fishing, boating (l), swimming, picnicking, hiking trails, biking, horseback riding, birdwatching. Largest island on Great Salt Lake. Marina, visitor center, pavilion, herd of 600 bison. 28,463 acres; elev 4200 ft.

TEASDALE (89)

Lower Bowns Area   **FREE**
Fishlake National Forest
22 mi SE of Teasdale on SR 12. Free. All year; 14-day limit. Primitive open camping near 37-acre Lower Bowns Reservoir. Toilet, cfga, no drkg wtr, no trash service.
   Fishing tip: The small Lower Bowns Res-ervoir contains plenty of rainbow & cutthroat trout; power boats not allowed.

Oak Creek   **$9**
Fishlake National Forest
20 mi SE of Teasdale on SR 12. $9. 5/15-10/31; 14-day limit. 8 sites; 25-ft RV limit. Tbls, toilets, cfga, drkg wtr. Fishing. Elev 8800 ft.

Pleasant Creek   **$9**
Fishlake National Forest
18 mi SE of Teasdale on SR 12. $9. MD-9/15; 14-day limit. 19 sites (25-ft RV limit). Tbls, toilets, cfga, drkg wtr. Fishing.

Single Tree   **$10**
Fishlake National Forest
14 mi SE of Teasdale on SR 12. $10 base. 5/15-10/31; 14-day limit. 26 sites (32-ft RV limit). Tbls, flush & pit toilets, cfga, drkg wtr. Fishing, hiking trail.

TORREY (90)

Backcountry Camping   **FREE**
Capitol Reef National Park
12 mi E of Torrey on UT 24 to visitor center. Campsites (do not camp in bottoms of drain-ages). Hiking. Obtain free permit, map, and information from the visitor center or park ranger ($5 entry fee). Spring and fall are ideal times for backcountry hiking and camping because of the mild temps. Insects can be a problem in June and July. Flash floods occur July-Sept.

Cathedral Valley Campground   **$5**
Capitol Reef National Park
23 mi E of Torrey on UT 24, then 28 mi N; rd often impassable. Camp free, but $5 entry fee. All year; 14-day limit. 5 tent sites. Tbls, toilets, cfga, no drkg wtr.

Cedar Mesa Campground   **$5**
Capitol Reef National Park
35 mi S of park's visitor center on Notom-Bullfrog Rd. Camp free, but $5 entry fee. All year; 14-day limit. 5 sites. Tbls, toilets, cfga, no drkg wtr.

Fruita Campground   **$10**
Capital Reef National Park
11 mi E of Torrey on U-24; 1.4 mi S of U-24. $10 during 4/1-11/30; free rest of year. 71 sites. Tbls, drkg wtr, cfga, toilets. Visitor center nearby. Picnicking, hiking. Museum, historical schoolhouse and other exhibits nearby. Hiking trails. Scenic drive. Pets on leash. Restrooms during the fee season, pit toilets during the free season.

TROPIC (91)

Backcountry Camps   **$5**
Bryce Canyon National Park
NW of Tropic on SR 12; S on SR 63 through Bryce Canyon to S part of park. $5 permit required. Spring-fall; 3-day limit per site; 14 days total. 12 tent sites. No facilities except cfga, tbls. Hiking, sightseeing. Backcountry permit required; entry fee $25 for 7-day visit. Wtr, camp store at North and Sunset campgrounds. Primary backcountry areas are Under-the-Rim Trail, 22 mi from Bryce Point to Rainbow Point, with 8 sites, and Riggs Spring Loop Trail (8.8 mi round trip) from Rainbow Point, 4 sites.

VERMILLION (92)

Koosharem Reservoir   **FREE**
Bureau of Land Management
30 mi S of Vermillion on SR 24. Free. All year; 14-day limit. Primitive undesignated sites. Tbls, toilets, cfga, no drkg wtr. Fishing, boating, hiking, OHV activity. Elev 7000 ft.

Fishing tip: The lake is stocked with trout.

VERNAL (93)

Book Cliffs Recreation Area   **FREE**
Bureau of Land Management
Access from I-70 or 60 mi S of Vernal on paved & gravel rds. Free. All year; 14-day limit. Primitive undesignated sites. No facilities, no drkg wtr. Fishing, hiking, horseback riding, hunting, OHV activities, biking, climbing. 455,000-acre wild area. Elev 5000-8200 ft.

Bull Canyon, Willow Creek   **FREE**
Skull Creek
Wilderness Study Areas
Bureau of Land Management
E of Vernal on US 40 into Colorado; N on co rds. Areas N of highway, S of Dinosaur National Monument. Free. All year; 14-day limit. Accessible earlier and later in spring & fall than higher-elevation areas. Primitive backcountry camping; no facilities. Scenic viewing, hiking, backpacking, viewing wild-life, photography, horseback riding. 39,000 acres in the three areas. Colorful canyons, sandstone cliffs, rock outcrops. Archaeological sites (protected by law). Bull Canyon WSA can be viewed from Dinosaur Monument's Plug Hat picnic area.

Cliff Ridge   **FREE**
Hang Gliding Area
Bureau of Land Management
30 mi E of Vernal on US 40; N at Dinosaur NM headquarters near Dinosaur, Colorado; at the Blue Mountain Plateau. Free. May-Sept; 14-day limit. Primitive campground; no facilities, no drkg wtr. Hang gliding, biking, hiking, horseback riding, OHV activity, hunting. Exhibits.

Cross Mountain   **FREE**
Wilderness Study Area
Bureau of Land Management
E of Vernal on US 40 into Colorado nearly to Elk Springs, then NW on Deerlodge Park Rd to parking area at Yampa River at SE end of Dinosaur National Monument. Hike in to canyon rim or backcountry. Free. All year; 14-day limit. Primitive hike-in backcountry camping. No facilities. Hiking, backpacking, photography, hunting, fishing, scenic viewing. Numerous side canyons allow for exploration and boulder scrambling. Yampa River kayaking for experts. Spectacular view of canyon from 1000-ft height at rim. Big horn sheep, mountain lion, deer, elk, golden eagle, bald eagle. S end of mountain excellent for day hikes; N end good for backpacking & camping.

Travel tip: Take a comparatively easy rafting trip on the Yampa River from Deerlodge Park at E end of Dinosaur National Monument; raft through the Yampa River Canyon with its 1,000-foot walls.

Dry Fork   **FREE**
Bureau of Land Management
15 mi NW of Vernal in Dry Fork Canyon. 4/1-11/1; 14-day limit. Free. Primitive undesignated camping area; 5 tent sites. Tbls, cfga, no drkg wtr, no facilities.

East Park   **$8**
Ashley National Forest
20 mi N of Vernal on US 191; 9 mi NW on FR 018 (Red Cloud Loop Rd); right on FR 020 (East Park Campground Rd) for 1 mi; at East Park Reservoir. $8 during June-Sept; free rest of year, but no wtr. 21 sites; 25-ft RV limit. Tbls, toilets, cfga, drkg wtr. Fishing, hiking.

Green River Campground   **$12**
Dinosaur National Monument
13.4 mi W of Vernal on US 40; 6.5 mi N from Jensen on SR 149 to Quarry Visitors Center, then 5 mi E. $12. 4/15-10/15; 14-day limit. About 100 sites; 35-ft RV limit. Tbls, flush & pit toilets, cfga, drkg wtr. Hiking trails. $10 entry fee. In off-season, use Split Mountain Campground.

Iron Springs   **FREE**
Ashley National Forest
25 mi NW of Vernal off Hwy 191. 5/25-10/31; 16-day limit. Free. Primitive undesignated camping area. Tbls, toilets, cfga, drkg wtr. Fishing, hiking, picnicking.

Kaler Hollow   **FREE**
Ashley National Forest
20 mi N of Vernal on SR 44; 11.5 mi NW on FR 018. Free. 6/1-10/31; 14-day limit. 4 tent sites & undesignated RV sites (25-ft RV limit). Tbls, toilets, cfga, no drkg wtr. Fishing. Elev 8900 ft.

Oaks Park   **$5**
Ashley National Forest
20 mi N of Vernal on SR 44; 14 mi NW on FR 18; 1 mi N on FR 24. $5 during 6/1-10/31; free rest of year; 14-day limit. 11 sites. Tbls, toilets, cfga, no drkg wtr. Fishing, boating. At S shore of Oaks Park Reservoir. 7 acres; elev 9200 ft.

Ouray   **FREE**
National Wildlife Refuge
15 mi SW of Vernal on US 40; 13 mi S on SR 88 following signs. Free. All year. Primitive camping on 11,483 acres; no facilities. River fishing for catfish. Boating, rafting.

Pelican Lake   **FREE**
Recreation Area
Bureau of Land Management
15 mi SW of Vernal on US 40; 7 mi S on SR 88; turn right on rd marked for Bandlett, for 2 mi; turn left on marked rd toward boat ramp & camping. Free. All year; 14-day limit. 13 informal sites, some with tbls. Toilets, no drkg wtr; 25-ft RV limit. Boating(l), fishing. No swimming. 840 acres of water.

Red Fleet State Park   **$11**
12 mi N of Vernal, off Hwy 191. $12. All year; 14-day limit. 38 sites; 35-ft RV limit. Tbls, flush toilets, cfga, drkg wtr, dump, no showers, beach. Swimming, boating(l), fishing, picnicking. Fish cleaning station. Dinosaur trackway dating 200 million years.

Rainbow Park   **FREE**
Dinosaur National Forest
13.4 mi E of Vernal on US 40; 4 mi N from Jensen on Sr 149; 4.8 mi NW on Brush Creek Rd, then 2.2 mi N on unmarked rd & 13.8 mi on Island Park Rd; roads rough, not recommended for RVs. Free. All year; 14-day limit. 2 sites. Tbls, toilets, cfga, no drkg wtr. Fishing, boating(l), rafting. On Green River. No winter maintenance on dirt rd.

Red Springs   **$11**
Ashley National Forest
30 mi N of Vernal on SR 44. $11. MD-9/31; 14-day limit. 13 sites (25-ft RV limit). Tbls, toilets, cfga, drkg wtr. Fishing, boating.

Split Mountain Camp   **FREE**
Dinosaur National Monument
13.4 mi E of Vernal on US 40; 6.5 mi N from Jensen on SR 149 to Quarry Visitors Center,

then 4 mi E on SR 149. Free for individual camping in winter but no wtr; group camping only in-season. All year; 14-day limit. 35 sites; 35-ft RV limit. Tbls, 1 pit toilet in winter, cfga, drkg wtr, showers. Boating(l), fishing, rafting, nature trail. $10 monument entry fee.

Steinaker State Park $12
7 mi N of Vernal on Hwy 191. $12. All year; 14-day limit. 31 sites; 35-ft RV limit. Tbls, flush toilets, cfga, drkg wtr, dump, beaches, no showers. Boating(l), fishing, waterskiing, swimming. Handicap access. Group pavilions.

VERNON (94)

Little Valley FREE
Uinta National Forest
1 mi SE of Vernon on UT 36; 5 mi S on co rd; 4 mi SE on FR 052; half mi W on FR 06. Elev 7000 ft. 5/1-10/31; 10-day limit. 6 sites. Tbls, toilets, cfga, firewood, no drkg wtr. Rockhounding; picnicking; fishing.

Simpson Springs $2
Bureau of Land Management
30 mi W of Vernon on gravel co rd (30 mi W of Faust). $2. 4/1-10/31; 14-day limit. 14 sites on 40 acres (RVs under 30 ft). Tbls, toilets, cfga, no drkg wtr. Picnicking; fishing. Corral & horse wtr qtr mi W; no horses in campground.

VIRGIN (95)

Lava Point Primitive Camp FREE
Zion National Park
Approx 35 mi(last 2 mi are gravel rds) from park's S entrance on UT 9, just E of Virgin. Approx 20 mi N on Kolob Reservoir Rd (last mi is gravel); right at Lava Point Rd; 1.5 mi to campground. Camp free, but $25 entry fee for 7 days. Late May through late Oct, depending on snow conditions; 14-day limit. 6 sites; 19-ft RV limit. No drkg wtr. Hiking Area is inaccessible by vehicle during winter. Pets, but not on trails or in bldgs.

WHITEROCKS (97)

Pole Creek Lake $5
Ashley National Forest
8 mi N of Whiterocks on CR 121; 13.5 mi NW on FR 117. $5. Elev 10,200 ft. 7/1-9/10; 16-day limit. 18 sites; 22-ft RV limit. Tbls, toilets, cfga, firewood, no drkg wtr. Hunting; picnicking; fishing; horseback riding (1 mi). Elev 10,200 ft.

Whiterocks $8
Ashley National Forest
8.2 mi N of Whiterocks on CR 121; 5.2 mi N on FR 492. $8 during 5/15-9/15; free rest of year; 16-day limit. 21 sites (RVs under 26 ft). Tbls, toilets, cfga, drkg wtr. Fishing. Elev 7400 ft; 13 acres.

WOODLAND (98)

Mill Hollow $7
Uinta National Forest
12 mi SE of Woodland on SR 35; S on FR 054; at Mill Hollow Reservoir. $7 with federal Senior Pass; others pay $14. 6/15-9/15; 14-day limit. 28 sites; 40-ft RV limit. Tbls, toilets, cfga, drkg wtr. Fishing, boating (no mtrs), hiking (loop trail). Late or early snowfall may shorten season. Campground closed for renovation until summer of 2009.

WOODRUFF (99)

Birch Creek $2
Bureau of Land Management
10 mi W of Woodruff on US 39. $2. 5/1-11/1; 14-day limit. 4 walk-in tent sites, plus dry RV camping in parking lot; 20-ft RV limit. Tbls, toilets, cfga, no drkg wtr. Picnicking; fishing, hiking, boating.

Little Creek Campground $2
Bureau of Land Management
10 mi N of Woodruff on SR 16 to Randolph; about 3 mi W of Randolph on FR 058 to N side of 25-acre Little Creek Reservoir. $2. All year; 14-day limit. 10 sites. Tbls, toilets, cfga, drkg wtr, ramadas. Boating, fishing, snow sports, hunting, biking. Elev 6380 ft.

Monte Cristo $12
Cache National Forest
20 mi E of Woodruff on Walton Canyon Rd. $12. 7/1-9/15; 7-day limit. 44 sites; 25-ft RV limit. Tbls, toilets, cfga, drkg wtr. Hunting, snowmobile trails. Elev 8400 ft.

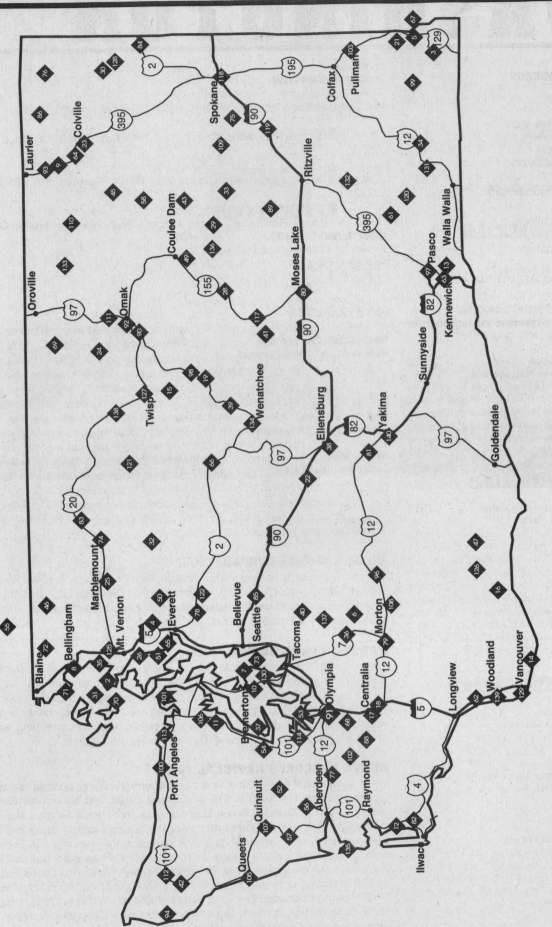

WASHINGTON

MISCELLANEOUS

Capital:
Olympia
Nickname:
Evergreen State
Motto:
Alki (By and By)
Flower:
Western Rhododendron
Tree:
Western Hemlock
Bird:
Willow Goldfinch
Song:
"Washington, My Homeland"

Internet Address:
www.experiencewashington.com

For travel information: 800-544-1800.

Washington State Tourism, PO Box 42500 Olympia, WA 98504-2500.

State Parks and Recreation Commission, PO Box 42650, Olympia, WA 98504-2650.

Dept of Fish & Wildlife, 600 Capitol Way North, Olympia, WA 98501. 360-902-2200.

Dept of Natural Resources, Public Lands Office, PO Box 47001, Olympia, WA 98504. 360-902-1004.

REST AREAS
Overnight stops are not permitted.

STATE PARKS
Overnight camping fees are $12-31 with a 10-day limit in the summer and, among the parks that are open all year, 20 days between Oct. 1 and April 30. Pets on leashes are permitted. Fees do not change during the winter. Park entry fees are now charged: $5 daily or $50 annually. Primitive sites (without amenities) are $12-14. "Standard" sites (available at most parks) are $17-22; they have no hookups but offer a campstove, picnic table, nearby running water, sink waste, trash disposal and flush toilets; most accommodate RVs. "Utility" sites are $22-31 and offer hookups such as water, sewer and electricity. The rates have put most state parks beyond the guidelines of this book and therefore are no longer listed here. Most parks with standard or utility sites have hot showers. At certain popular destination parks, an additional $1 per site surcharge is made between April 1 and Sept. 30. A "natural investment" permit is required at state parks for launching boats and for non-campers to use park dump stations; the permit is $5 daily or $50 annually. Washington State Parks, PO Box 42650, Olympia, WA 98504-2650. The park information line is 360-902-8844.

BOISE CASCADE CORPORATION
The Boise Cascade timberlands in Washington are open for hunting (deer, elk, bird), fishing (salmon, trout, whitefish, walleye, northern pike, bass or panfish), horseback riding, canoeing and snowmobiling. For further information contact: Boise Cascade Corporation, PO Box 51, Yakima, WA 98901.

TAHUYA MULTIPLE USE AREA
There are 33,000 acres of state-owned land in this peninsula recreational area with a number of lakes, creeks and rivers. Eleven recreational sites offer 61 camps, 20 picnic areas and 13 mi of trails. Both the Tahuya River and Green Mountain Horse Camps have facilities. Many of the 68 lakes are stocked with rainbow trout, steelhead and sea run cutthroat. There are 14 public accesses to fishing waters. Dept of Natural Resources, PO Box 47001, Olympia, WA 98504.

NORTH CASCADES NATIONAL PARK
Entry to the park is free and free backcountry camping permits are available at ranger stations. Camping is $12 at Colonial Creek and Newhalem Creek Campgrounds, $10 at Goodell Creek Campground and free at Gorge Lake and Hozomeen Campgrounds. Hunting and trapping are prohibited. Bears are commonly seen in backcountry areas. Pets are prohibited in the backcountry. There are three units to the park -- North Cascades National Park, Ross Lake National Recreation Area and Lake Chelan National Recreation Area. A Northwest Forest Pass ($5 daily or $30 annually) is required for parking anywhere along the North Cascades NP portion of the Cascade River or at certain trailheads within the Ross Lake NRA. For further information contact: Superintendent, North Cascades National Park, 810 State Route 20, Sedro Woolley, WA 98284.

LAKE CHELAN NATIONAL RECREATION AREA

About 2,000 acres of this 55-mile-long lake are in the recreation area. There are 20 free camping areas (ask the park ranger for a map and detailed directions). Boaters using docks on Lake Chelan must purchase a dock site pass for $5 daily or $40 annually. Superintendent, Lake Chelan National Recreation Area, North Cascades National Park, 810 State Route 20, Sedro Woolley, WA 98284.

ROSS LAKE NATIONAL RECREATION AREA

Vehicles can reach this area from the north, through Canada to Hozomeen, which is 40 miles west of Hope, British Columbia, on Silver-Skagit Rd. Access to Ross Lake from the south is limited to trail and water routes. The 3.5-mile Diablo Lake Trail begins near the Diablo Lake Resort and goes to Ross Dam. There is boat and trail access from the dam to specific sites along Ross Lake. The resort should be contacted in advance to ensure the availability of boats and to determine charges for water taxi transportation. The Seattle City Light tugboat also provides access to Ross Lake. There are 122 camping sites, including 15 boat-access camping areas on Ross Lake, many of which have docking facilities. Pets are not allowed. Drinking water is piped and treated. There are no RV hookups or dump stations. Pit toilets and tables are provided. Boat launching ramps are provided. All refuse should be packed out. Superintendent, Ross Lake National Recreation Area, North Cascades National Park, 810 State Route 20, Sedro Woolley, WA 98284. 360-856-5700.

Olympic National Park, 600 E Park Ave, Port Angeles, WA 98362; 360-565-3130. Entry fees ($15 for 7-day periods; $30 annually) are now collected at Elwha, Heart O[the Hills, Hurricane Ridge, Hoh, Sol Duc and Staircase entrance stations from May through September or later. Although most campgrounds have 21-ft RV length limits, the major campgrounds each have a few sites which will accommodate larger RVs. Backcountry permits are required for all trail and beach camping.

Lake Roosevelt National Recreation Area, 1008 Crest Drive, Coulee Dam, WA 99116; 509-633-9441. This park has 25 campgrounds scattered around Roosevelt Lake, with a total of more than 600 sites. Some are accessible only by boat. Fees are now charged at nearly all campgrounds accessible by vehicle, even during the off-season. Overnight fees are $10 during 5/1-9/30 ($5 for seniors & disabled) and $5 during 10/1-4/30 ($2.50 for seniors and disabled). Boat launch fees are $6 for 7 days or $40 annually.

Mount Rainier National Park, 55210 238th Ave East, Ashford, WA 98304. Six developed campgrounds (fees $8-$15; one free) offer nearly 600 campsites. In addition, the park has numerous backcountry trailside camping area, accessible by free permit after payment of 7-day ($15) or annual ($30) entry fees.

Corps of Engineers, Seattle District, PO Box C-3755, Seattle, WA 98124, 206/764-3440; or Corps of Engineers, Walla Walla District, Bldg 602, City-County Airport, Walla Walla, WA 99362, 509/522-6717.

Bureau of Land Management, Spokane District Office, East 4217 Main Ave., Spokane, WA 99202.

Colville National Forest. Although the forest participates in the Recreational Fee Demonstration Program, northwest forest passes are not needed at any campgrounds, and only at four trailheads and one boat launch. However, several campgrounds that had been free now have $6 fees assigned. 765 S. Main St., Colville, WA 99114. 509/684-7000.

GIFFORD PINCHOT NATIONAL FOREST

Fee campgrounds are usually left open for free camping after the managed season ends. However, services are discontinued, and campers must pack out their trash and leave a clean camp. The forest has almost unlimited camping opportunities for dispersed camping throughout the forest. Camping in the same developed campground for more than 14 consecutive days is prohibited; at dispersed sites, a

21-day limit is enforced, and staying at any combination of developed or dispersed sites longer than 45 days in a calendar year is prohibited. About half of the forest's campgrounds now have fees of $15-16 and therefore do not qualify for inclusion in this book. Two-night minimum stays are required on weekends; three nights on holiday weekends. Gifford Pinchot National Forest, 10600 NE 51st St., Vancouver, WA 98668; 360-891/5000.

MOUNT BAKER-SNOQUALMIE NATIONAL FORESTS

38 developed campgrounds operate from Memorial Day through Labor Day weekends. Most charge fees of $12-$16. Some campgrounds remain open through September, and a few are open until mid-October. Overnight camping is not permitted at developed picnic sites. Free dispersed camping is permitted anywhere else in the forest, but user fees of $5 per day (or $30 annually) per vehicle are charged at various trailheads, picnic areas and three rustic areas. 21905 64th Avenue West, Mountlake Terrace, WA 98043. 425-775-9702 or 800-627-0062.

OKANOGAN NATIONAL FOREST

Fees are now charged for overnight parking and camping on land west of the Okanogan River. A one-night or annual pass is necessary for camping outside many developed sites, parking at most trailheads and camping at developed campgrounds. Those passes replace fees formerly charged in developed campgrounds and convert formerly free campgrounds into fee sites. The northwest forest passes are $5 per night or $30 annually. Purchase of a season's pass permits the holder to camp without charge in the specified areas. 1240 South Second Ave., Okanogan, WA 98841.

OLYMPIC NATIONAL FOREST

Coho Campground is the only forest camp with an RV waste disposal station. It is a fee campground located 38 miles north of Montesano. Be watchful of logging traffic on forest roads. All of the forest's 14 developed campgrounds have fees; free rustic camps have limited facilities, with water usually not available. As part of the national Fee Demonstration Program, northwest forest passes are required at many locations; they are $5 daily or $30 annually. Olympic National Forest, 1835 Black Lake Blvd, SW, Olympia, WA 98512-5623. 360-956-2402.

UMATILLA NATIONAL FOREST has hundreds of primitive, undeveloped sites

available to campers without charge as well as several campgrounds with low-cost sites, most in Oregon. 541/278-3716.

WENATCHEE NATIONAL FOREST

Good free, dispersed camping opportunities (outside established campgrounds) are available at lower elevations in the Naches Ranger District; no facilities are available at those locations. Dispersed campers may travel established roads and camp in established camp spots; all litter must be removed. Throughout the forest, more than 150 campgrounds and picnic sites are provided. All campgrounds in the Chelan District are for tent camping; no RVs permitted. A totally new fee structure was implemented in that district a few years ago. Ten developed campgrounds which formerly were free now have fees of up to $12 per night. Also, $5 daily fees ($30 annually) northwest forest pass fees are now charged for formerly free dispersed camping in the South Fork Tieton area and in the peninsula area between Tieton Road 1200 and Rimrock Lake. Wenatchee, like the other national forests of the Northwest, is participating forest-wide in the national Recreation Fee Demonstration Program. 215 Melody Lane, Wenatchee, WA 98801. 509/664-9200.

ANACORTES (2)

Griffin Bay Recreation Site   **FREE**
San Juan Island
Dept of Natural Resources
About 20 mi W of Anacortes by non-motorized boat; S of Friday Harbor on SE side of island. All year; 14-day limit. 1 site; 3 picnic sites. Toilet, cfga, tbl, no drkg wtr. Fishing, boating (mooring buoys provided for non-motorized boats). San Juan National Historic Park nearby. Ideal for 2-person kayak team; seldom used.

James Island State Park   **$12**
About 10 mi W of Anacortes by boat (E of Decatur Island on Rosario Strait). $12. 5/1-9/1; 10-day limit. 13 primitive tent sites. Toilets, cfga, no drkg wtr, no trash service. Fishing (salmon, bottomfish), swimming, boating. Mooring buoys ($) on E side of island; dock on W side.

Moran State Park   **$12**
Ferry from Anacortes to Orcas Island, then 11 mi on Horseshoe Hwy. $12 base. All year; 10-day limit. Limited facilities in winter (20-day limit). Includes 5 campgrounds and primitive area. 15 primitive sites & 115 tent sites at $12; 136 standard sites at $17 (45-ft RV limit). Tbls, flush toilets, showers, drkg wtr, cfga, no hookups, dump. 5 freshwater lakes, 30 mi of hiking trails, 4 waterfalls. 3 of the campgrounds at Cascade Lake, with fishing, swimming, boating(lr), windsurfing(r), picnic area, shelter, interpretive display. 4th campground at Mountainlake, which has good trout fishing, boating(rl). 5,000 acres of forest; 1,800 ft of shoreline.

Saddlebag Island State Park   **$12**
2 mi NE of Anacortes (E of Guemes Island) by boat. $12. All year; 10-day limit. 5 primitive tent sites; 1 toilet, cfga, no drkg wtr. Hiking, beachcombing & crabbing, fishing for sal-mon, bottomfish. 23.7 acres.

Strawberry Island   **FREE**
State Recreation Site
Dept of Natural Resources
About 10 mi NW of Anacortes by boat (west of Blakeley Island); on W side of island. 3 free primitive tent sites; no overflow space. Tbls, toilets, no drkg wtr. Fishing, boating. Dangerously rocky shore area, currents.

ANATONE (3)

Fields Spring State Park   **$12**
4.5 m S of Anatone on SR 129. $12 base. All year; 10-day limit. Limited facilities in winter (20-day limit). 20 standard sites at $17 (30-ft RV limit); 20 primitive RV/tent sites at $10. Tbls, cfga, drkg wtr, flush toilets, handicap facilities, showers, dump ($5 non-campers). Skiing. One-mi hike up 4,500-ft Puffer Butte to view Idaho/Oregon/Washington and the Grande Ronde & Snake River basins. 150 variety of wildflowers.

ASOTIN (5)

Seven Sisters Spring   **FREE**
Umatilla National Forest
24 mi SW of Asotin on CR 104; 4 mi SW on FR N812; 1 mi E on FR N800. Free. 6/15-11/15; 14-day limit. Dispersed camping area; 3 sites. Toilets, firewood. Picnicking. 1 mi E of Wenatchee guard station. Accessible via Cloverland Rd and Anatone.

ASHFORD (6)

Sunshine Point   **$10**
Mount Rainier National Park
7 mi E of Ashford on SR 706 to just inside Nisqually entrance at SW corner of park. $10. All year; 14-day limit. 18 sites. Tbls, toilets, cfga, drkg wtr. Fishing in adjacent Nisqually River.

BAINBRIDGE ISLAND (7)

Fay Bainbridge State Park   **$12**
From Poulsbo on Hwy 305, cross Agate Pass bridge; after 3 mi, turn left on Day Rd for 2 mi, then left for 2 mi on Sunset Dr NE; at NE end of Bainbridge Island. $12 at 10 primitive tent sites; 26 utility sites at $23 (some sites handle RVs larger than 30 ft). All year; 10-day limit. Handicap facilities, tbls, flush toilets, showers, cfga, drkg wtr, dump. Boating(l), fishing, nature trails. Limited facilities in winter. 297 acres. On Puget Sound; access to Seattle via Winslow Ferry. 17 acres.

BELLINGHAM (8)

Clark Island State Park   **$10**
About 7 mi W of Bellingham by boat (2 mi NE of Orcas Island). $12. All year; 10-day limit. 8 primitive tent sites. Toilets; no drkg wtr, no trash service. Fishing, boating (buoys for mooring), swimming beaches, beachcombing, clamming, scuba diving. 55 acres.

Doe Island State Park   **$12**
About 10 mi SW of Bellingham by boat (SE of Orcas Island). $12. All year; 10-day limit. 5 primitive tent sites. Toilets, cfga, no drkg wtr. Fishing, boating (buoys for mooring). Rocky shoreline.

Jones Island Marine State Park   **$12**
About 18 mi W of Bellingham by boat (1 mi W of the SW tip of Orcas Island). $12. 4/1-9/30; 10-day limit. 21 primitive tent sites. Tbls, toilets, cfga, drkg wtr (Apr-Sept). Fishing, boating (buoys for mooring). Excellent for small-boat camping. (GPS 48.6181, -123.0466.)

Matia Island State Park   **$12**
About 7 mi W by boat (2.5 mi NE of Orcas Island) BY BOAT. $12. 5/1 9/1; 10-day limit. 6 primitive tent sites near dock. 1 toilet, no tbls or wtr, no trash service. Fishing, boating(d). Boat buoys for mooring. 145 acres, but only 5 acres open to public. (GPS 48.7492, -122.8483.)

Obstruction Pass   **FREE**
State Recreation Site
Orcas Island
Dept of Natural Resources
About 20 mi W of Bellingham by boat, or take ferry from Anacortes, to Orcas Island; then drive or bike & hike about 3 mi to camp; at SE end of island on W side of Deer Point. Free. All year; 14-day limit. 9 primitive sites; 2 picnic sites. Tbls, toilets, cfga, no drkg wtr. Fishing, boating (2 mooring buoys), hiking.

Patos Island State Park   **$12**
About 10 mi NW of Bellingham by boat (4 mi NW of Sucia Island). $12. All year; 10-day limit. 7 primitive tent sites. Toilets, cfga, no other facilities, no drkg wtr, no trash service. Hiking trails, excellent salmon & bottom fishing. Boat buoys for mooring. Wildflowers bloom Apr-June along a 1,5-mi loop hiking trail. (GPS 48.6186, -123.1660)

Point Doughty   **FREE**
State Recreation Site
Orcas Island
Dept. of Natural Resources
About 20 mi W of Bellingham by boat, or take ferry from Anacortes, to Orcas Island, then drive or bike to NE shore. Free. All year; 14-day limit. 2 sites. Tbls, toilet, cfga, no drkg wtr. Boating, fishing.

Posey Island State Park   **$12**
About 20 mi from Bellingham by small boat; at N end of Roche Harbor, most accessible by canoe or kayak from San Juan Island. $12. All year; 1-night limit. 2 primitive tent sites; toilet, cfga, no drkg wtr, no trash service. Boating, fishing. (GPS 48.6186, -123.1660.)

Stuart Island Marine State Park   **$12**
About 23 mi W of Bellingham by boat (NW of San Juan Island) on N side of Stuart. $12. 5/1-9/1; 10-day limit. 22 primitive tent sites. Tbls, cfga, toilets, no drkg wtr. Fishing, boating. Good mooring areas. (GPS 48.6755, -123.1988.)

Sucia Island State Park   **$12**
About 6 mi NW of Bellingham by boat (2.5 mi N of Orcas Island). $12. All year; 10-day limit. 55 primitive tent sites at 6 sections, picnic shelter, tbls, toilets, no drkg wtr. Fishing, boating, crabbing, clamming, interesting geological formations, scuba diving. (GPS 48.7528, -122.9133.)

Turn Island State Park   **$12**
About 21 mi W of Bellingham by boat; just E of Friday Harbor & San Juan Island. $12. 13 primitive tent sites. Tbls, cfga, toilets, no drkg wtr. Hiking, fishing, boating. 2 nice beaches; foot trails. (GPS 48.5339, -122.9742.)

BOYDS (9)

Davis Lake   **FREE**
Colville National Forest
Half mi S of Boyds on US 395; 3 mi W on

CR 460; 4 mi N on CR 465; 5 mi W & N on CR 480/FR 80. Free. MD-LD; 14-day limit. 4 sites. Tbls, toilets, cfga, no drkg wtr, no trash service. Fishing, boating(l), canoeing.

Fishing tip: This small lake contains planted rainbow trout. Try silver Swedish Pimples and Powerbaits.

BREMERTON (10)

Aldrich Lake FREE
State Recreation Site
Tahuya State Forest
Dept. of Natural Resources
S of Bremerton 10 mi on SR 3 to Belfair, then 3.5 mi SW on SR 300; right on Belfair-Tahuya Rd for 7.7 mi; right on Tee Lake-Dewatto Rd for 2.3 mi; left on Hobas Way for 1.6 mi. Free. 4/15-9/15; 14-day limit. 4 sites, 4 picnic sites. Tbls, toilets, cfga, drkg wtr. Fishing, boating (hand launch).

Camp Spillman FREE
State Recreation Site
Tahuya State Forest
Dept of Natural Resources
S of Bremerton 10 mi on SR 3 to Belfair, then 3.5 mi SW on SR 300; right on Belfair-Tahuya Rd for 1.9 mi; right on Elfendahl Pass Rd for 2.6 mi; left on Goat Ranch Rd Rd for .7 mi. All year; 14-day limit. Free. 6 sites, 4 picnic sites. Tbls, toilets, cfga, drkg wtr, group shelter. Hiking trails; horseback trails; picnicking; fishing; motorcycle trails; mountain biking. On Tahuya River. Seasonal opening considered.

Green Mountain Horse Camp FREE
Green Mountain State Forest
Dept of Natural Resources
SW of Bremerton SR 3; after Silverdale, 3.1 mi W on Newberry Hill Rd; left for 2 mi on Seabeck Hwy; right on Holly Rd for 4 mi; left on Tahuya Lake Rd 1 mi; left on Green Mtn Rd for 2.7 mi to jct, then left 1 mi. On Green Mountain. Free. Camping only Sat-Sun during June-Sept. 12 sites, 2 picnic sites. Tbls, toilets, cfga, drkg wtr, horse facilities. Picnicking; hiking trails; horseback trails.

Kammenga Canyon FREE
State Recreation Site
Tahuya State Forest
Dept. of Natural Resources
10 mi SW of Bremerton on SR 3 to Belfair, then 3.5 mi SW on SR 300; right on Belfair-Tahuya Rd for 1.9 mi; right on Elfendahl Pass Rd for 2.3 mi to Elfendahl Pass Staging Area; half mi farther N on Elfendahl Pas Rd, then left to camp. Free. All year; 14-day limit. 2 sites. Tbls, toilets, cfga, no drkg wtr. Motorcycling, mountain biking, horseback riding. May be closed seasonally.

Tahuya River Horse Camp FREE
Tahuya State Forest
Dept of Natural Resources
10 mi SW of Bremerton on SR 3 to Belfair, then 3.5 mi SW on SR 300; turn right on Bel-

fair-Tahuya Rd for 3.2 mi, then right on Spillman Rd for 2.1 mi; left 1 mi to camp. Free. 8 sites, 1 picnic site. Tbls, sites, cfga, drkg wtr, horse facilities. Hiking, horseback ridng. This camp is available only by reservation now. Call 360-825-1631.

Toonerville Recreation Site FREE
Tahuya State Forest
Dept of Natural Resources
10 mi SW of Bremerton on SR 3 to Belfair, then 3.5 mi SW on SR 300; turn right on Belfair-Tahuya Rd for 1.9 mi, then right on Elfendahl Pass Rd 2.3 mi; pass jct with Goat Ranch Rd; camp on left. Free. All year; 14-day limit. 4 sites, 2 picnic sites. Tbls, toilets, cfga, no drkg wtr. Picnicking; hiking trails; motorbike trails; horse trails. Accommodates the handicapped.

Twin Lakes FREE
State Recreation Site
Tahuya State Forest
Dept of Natural Resources
S of Bremerton 10 mi on SR 3 to Belfair, then 3.5 mi SW on SR 300; right on Belfair-Tahuya Rd for 1.9 mi; right on Elfendahl Pass Rd for 2.6 mi; left on Goat Ranch/Twin Lakes Rd for 1.8 mi; turn right, half mi to camp. On Twin Lakes. Free. 4/15-10/31; 14-day limit. 6 small, walk-in primitive tent sites, 3 picnic sites. Tbls, toilets, cfga, no drkg wtr. Boating (hand launch); picnicking; fishing; mountain biking, hiking.

BRINNON (11)

Collins $10
Olympic National Forest
2 mi S of Brinnon on US 101; 4.7 mi W on FR 2510. $10. 5/15-9/15; 14-day limit. 10 RV & 6 tent sites (21-ft RV limit). Drkg wtr, tbls, toilets, cfga. Swimming, fishing, hiking trails. 4 acres on Duckabush River. Berries in Jul. 4 acres. Pack out trash.

Elkhorn $10
Olympic National Forest
1 mi NW of Brinnon US 101; 10 mi west on Dosewallips River Rd. $10. 5/15-LD; 14-day limit. 20 sites (21-ft RV limit). Toilets, cfga, drkg wtr, tbls. Fishing, hiking, hunting. Scenic. River. 4 acres. Closed in early 2007; road washed out since 2004.

Seal Rock $12
Olympic National Forest
2 mi N of Brinnon on US 101; at famous Seal Rock. $12. Early Apr to mid-Oct. 41 sites (21-ft RV limit). Tbls, flush toilets, cfga, drkg wtr. 100 ft of beachfront. Swimming, fishing, picnicking, nature trails, clamming, oyster gathering, shrimping offshore in spring.

BRUCEPORT (12)

Bush Pioneer Campground $7
Pacific County Park
S on US 101 from Bruceport at town of Bay Center. $7 base. MD-LD. Base fee for primi-

tive tent sites; $5 for bicycle-campers; $10 for primitive RV sites. 10-15 sites. Tbls, flush toilets, cfga, drkg wtr, showers. Picnicking, hiking trails.

Bruceport Campground $7
Pacific County Park
US 101 at Willapa Bay, 5 mi S of South Bend. $7 base. MD-LD. Base fee for primitive tent sites; $5 for bicycle-camping; $10 for primitive RV sites; $12 with one utility hookup; $15, full hookups. 25 sites. Tbls, flush toilets, cfga, drkg wtr, showers. Picnicking, hiking trails to beach (no swimming). Near clamming beaches.

BURBANK (13)

Charbonneau Park $8
Corps of Engineers
Lake Sacajawea
8.3 mi E of Burbank on Hwy 124; 2 mi N on Sun Harbor Dr. $8 base. Base fee for overflow sites & boat-in camping. 54 RV sites with wtr/elec are $18 ($20 premium locations); 15 full-hookup sites are $22 (reduced fees with federal Senior Pass). 60-ft RV limit. 4/1-9/30; 14-day limit. Tbls, flush toilets, cfga, drkg wtr, elec($), full hookups($), dump, showers. Boating(dl), fishing, picnicking, waterskiing. 34 acres. 2-night minimum stay on weekends.

Fishhook Park $8
Corps of Engineers
Lake Sacajawea
15 mi E of Burbank on Hwy 124; 4 mi N on Page Rd. $8 for boat camping by tent (2-day limit per space, 120 sites); 61 total sites; 45-ft RV limit. Tent sites $14; primitive RV sites $16 ($7 & $8 with federal Senior Pass). Sites with hookups, $20-22. 5/1-LD; 14-day limit. Pavilion, marine dump, tbls, flush toilets, cfga, drkg wtr, dump, showers, beach, playground. Fishing, boating(ld), waterskiing, swimming. 29 acres.

Matthews Campground FREE
Corps of Engineers
Lake Sacajawea
26 mi E of Burbank on Hwy 124; 8.6 mi N to Clyde, then left for 15.2 mi N on Lower Monumental Rd; left 1 mi before the dam, then 1 mi E. Free. All year; 14-day limit. Primitive undesignated sites. Tbls, toilets, cfga, no drkg wtr. Boating(l), fishing.

Walker Park FREE
Corps of Engineers
Lake Sacajawea
26 mi E of Burbank on Hwy 124; 8.6 mi N to Clyde; 4 mi NW on Lower Monumental Rd; 9.2 mi W on Wooden Rd. Free. All year; 14-day limit. Primitive undesignated sites. Tbls, toilets, cfga, no drkg wtr. Boating(l), fishing.

WASHINGTON

400

CAMAS (14)

Dougan Creek Campground **FREE**
Yacolt Burn State Forest
Dept of Natural Resources
From SR 14 at Camas, N on SR 140 about 5 mi to Washougal River Rd; right 7.5 mi; bear left, then right next 1.3 mi; bear left for 6 mi to camp. Free. 4/1-10/31; 14-day limit. 7 sites. Tbls, toilets, cfga, drkg wtr. Picnicking. Accommodates handicapped.

CARLTON (15)

Foggy Dew **$5**
Okanogan National Forest
4 mi S of Carlton on Hwy 153; 1.1 mi S on CR 1029; 4.1 mi W on FR 4340. $5. All year; 14-day limit. 13 sites (no size limit). Tbls, toilets, cfga, no drkg wtr. No trash service in winter. Fishing, hiking, biking trails, winter sports. Access to motorbike use area. Watch for rattlesnakes.

CARSON (16)

Crest Horse Camp **FREE**
Gifford Pinchot National Forest
4.9 mi NW of Carson on CR 135; 1 mi NW on CR 139; 10.2 mi NW on FR 65; 2.4 mi on FR 60. Free. 6/15-9/30; 14-day limit. 3 tent sites. Tbls, toilets, cfga, firewood, no drkg wtr. Hiking; picnicking; horseback riding. Trailhead for Cascade Crest Trail.

Falls Creek Horse Camp **FREE**
Gifford Pinchot National Forest
9 mi W on CR 135; 1.5 mi E on FR 405; 12.5 mi N on FR 65. Fee. 6/15-9/30; 14-day limit. 6 sites (RVs under 16 ft). Tbls, toilets, cfga, firewood, no drkg wtr. Picnicking; berry picking; fishing; horseback riding. Stream. Trailhead for Indian Haven Area and Indian Race Track. Historical.

CHEHALIS (18)

Rainbow Falls State Park **$12**
18 mi W of Chehalis on SR 6. $12 for 6 primitive tent sites (3 for equestrians); 37 standard sites (no hookups) at $17; 8 hookup sites, $23 (60-ft RV limit). All year; 10-day limit. Tbls, flush toilets, cfga, drkg wtr, showers, dump. Nature trails, playground, fishing (river sturgeon), waterskiing. Swinging bridge over Chehalis River. 139 acres.

CHELAN (19)

Antilon Lake **FREE**
Dispersed Camp
Wenatchee National Forest
5.8 mi NW of Chelan on SR 150; follow Manson Rd N to Wapato Lake Rd; right on Upper Joe Creek Rd, then N on Grade Creek Rd (FR 8200) to N end of Antilon Lake. Camp free except $5 on July Fourth & MD weekends. 5/1-10/31; 14-day limit. About 3 primitive undesignated tent sites. No facilities except toilet. Boating, fishing. Camp is sometimes badly littered.
Fishing tip: This scenic 96-acre lake offers some fine brown trout fishing, but it also contains an enormous population of pan-size pumpkinseed sunfish. The adjoinining pond extension contains very aggressive native browns, but you'll need a float tube to fish for them.

Big Creek **$5**
Wenatchee National Forest
3.1 mi W of Chelan on US 97; 16 mi NW on CR 10 (South Lakeshore Rd) to Twenty-Five Mile Creek State Park boat launch; about 10 mi NW on Lake Chelan by boat; on S shore. $5 daily or $40 annually for federal dock pass during 5/1-9/30; free rest of year but no services; 14-day limit. 4 tent sites. Tbls, toilets, cfga, no drkg wtr. Swimming; picnicking; fishing; boating(d); sailing; waterskiing. Shelter on site; dock with capacity for 4 boats. Boat launches at Twenty-Five Mile Creek. Waterfall 300 yds upstream.

Boiling Lake **FREE**
Wenatchee National Forest
3.1 mi W of Chelan on US 97; 16 mi NW on CR 10 (South Lakeshore Rd) to Twenty-Five Mile Creek State Park boat launch; about 17 mi NW on Lake Chelan by boat to Prince Creek Camp; then hike N along Prince Creek trail, SE along Middle Fork trail past Cub Lake to Boiling Lake. Free. 5/1-9/30; 14-day limit. 3 tent sites. Tbls, 2 unsheltered toilets, cfga, no drkg wtr. Fishing, hiking.

Corral Creek **$5**
Wenatchee National Forest
3.1 mi W of Chelan on US 97; 16 mi NW on CR 10 (South Lakeshore Rd) to Twenty-Five Mile Creek State Park boat launch; about 10.5 mi NW on Lake Chelan by boat; on S shore. $5 daily or $40 annual dock permit during 5/1-9/30; free rest of year but no services; 14-day limit. 2 tent sites. Tbls, toilets, cfga, firewood, no drkg wtr. Picnicking; boating (floating dock for 6 boats); fishing; swimming; waterskiing; sailing. Boat launches at Twenty Five Mile Creek.

Cub Lake **FREE**
Wenatchee National Forest
3.1 mi W of Chelan on US 97; 16 mi NW on CR 10 (South Lakeshore Rd) to Twenty-Five Mile Creek State Park boat launch; about 17 mi NW on Lake Chelan by boat to Prince Creek Camp; then hike N along Prince Creek trail, SE along Middle Fork trail to Cub Lake. Free. 3 tent sites. Unsheltered toilet, cfga, no tbls, no drkg wtr. Fishing, hiking.

Deer Point **$5**
Wenatchee National Forest
21.7 mi NW of Chelan by boat or ferry (or, ferry from Manson or Fields Point Landing). $5 daily or $40 annual dock permit during 5/1-9/30; free rest of year. 4 tent sites. Tbls, toilets, cfga, no drkg wtr. On Chelan lake. Fishing, boating (floating dock for 8 boats), swimming. Boat launches available at Twenty-Five Mile Creek.

Domke Falls **$5**
Wenatchee National Forest
3.1 mi W of Chelan on US 97; 16 mi NW on CR 10 (South Lakeshore Rd) to Twenty-Five Mile Creek State Park boat launch; about 20.5 mi NW on Lake Chelan by boat; on S shore. $5 daily or $40 annual dock permit during 5/1-9/30; 14-day limit. 3 tent sites. No drkg wtr. Toilets, cfga, tbls. Fishing, boating; floating dock for 6 boats. Scenic falls. Boat launches at Twenty-Five Mile Creek.

Domke Lake **FREE**
Wenatchee National Forest
40 mi NW of Chelan (23 mi from Twenty-Five-Mile Creek State Park) by boat (or, ferry from Manson or Fields Point Landing) to Lucerne; from trailhead, hike 2.5 mi on Trail 1280. Free. 5/1-10/31; 14-day limit. 6 tent sites. Tbls, toilets, cfga, no drkg wtr. Fishing, hiking. Trail past Domke Lake into Glacier Peak Wilderness. End of Domke Lake National Recreation Trail.
Fishing tip: 271-acre Domke Lake contains nice rainbow & cutthroat trout.

Graham Harbor **$5**
Wenatchee National Forest
30 mi NW of Chelan BY BOAT from Twenty-Five Mile Creek State Park. $5 daily or $40 annual dock permit during 5/1-9/30; free rest of year; 14-day limit. 5 tent sites. 4 tbls, 5 cfga, 2 toilets, no drkg wtr. Floating dock for about 10 boats. Good shelter from downlake wind, but none from uplake wind. Hiking, fishing, boating.

Graham Harbor Creek **$5**
Wenatchee National Forest
31 mi NW of Chelan by boat From Twenty-Five Mile State Park (or, ferry from Mansion or Fields Point Landing). $5 daily or $40 annual dock permit during 5/1-9/30; free rest of year. 4 tent sites. Tbls, toilets, cfga, no drkg wtr. Fishing, hiking, boating; dock for 6 boats. Shelter on site.

Grouse Mountain **FREE**
Wenatchee National Forest
3.1 mi W of Chelan on US 97; 16 mi NW on CR 10 (South Lakeshore Rd) to Twenty-Five Mile Creek State Park; 11 mi W on FR 5900. Free. 7/1-9/30; 14-day limit. 4 tent sites. Tbls, toilets, cfga, no drkg wtr (available at Grouse Mountain Spring). Hiking, picnicking.

Grouse Mountain Springs **FREE**
Wenatchee National Forest
3.1 mi W of Chelan on US 97; 16 mi NW on CR 10 (South Lakeshore Rd) to Twenty-Five Mile Creek State Park; 11.2 mi W on FR 5900. Free. 7/1-9/30; 14-day limit. 1 tent site. Tbl, cfga, toilet, drkg wtr. Hiking, picnicking.

Handy Springs   **FREE**
Wenatchee National Forest
3.1 mi W of Chelan on US 97; 16 mi NW on CR 10 (South Lakeshore Rd) to Twenty-Five Mile Creek State Park; 18 mi W on FR 5900. Free. 7/1-9/30; 14-day limit. 1 tent site (no RVs). Tbls, toilets, cfga, firewood, no drkg wtr. Trailhead for Devil's Backbone ORV Trail.

Hatchery   **FREE**
Wenatchee National Forest
40 mi NW of Chelan (23 mi from Twenty-Five-Mile Creek State Park) by boat (or, ferry from Manson or Fields Point Landing) to Lucerne; from trailhead, hike 3 mi S on Trail 1280. Free. 6/1-10/31; 14-day limit. 2 tent sites. Tbls, toilets, cfga, firewood, no drkg wtr. Boating(r-1 mi), swimming, picnicking; fishing.

Junior Point   **FREE**
Wenatchee National Forest
3.1 mi W of Chelan on US 97; 16 mi NW on CR 10 (South Lakeshore Rd) to Twenty-Five Mile Creek State Park; 15 mi W on FR 5900. Free. 7/1-9/30; 14-day limit. 5 tent sites. Tbls, cfga, toilet, no drkg wtr. Site of old fire lookout; great view. Hiking, picnicking.

Lucerne   **$5**
Wenatchee National Forest
40 mi NW of Chelan (23 mi from Twenty-Five-Mile Creek State Park) by boat (or, ferry from Manson or Fields Point Landing) to Lucerne next to forest service station. $5 daily or $40 annual dock permit during 5/1-9/30; free rest of year; 14-day limit. 2 tent sites. Tbls, toilets, cfga, wtr nearby. Boating (dock for 11 boats), fishing, waterskiing.

Mitchell Creek   **$5**
Wenatchee National Forest
3.1 mi W of Chelan on US 97; 16 mi NW on CR 10 (South Lakeshore Rd) to Twenty-Five Mile Creek State Park boat launch; about 3 mi SE on Lake Chelan by boat; on N shore. $5 daily or $40 annual dock permit during 5/1-9/30; free rest of year; 14-day limit. 6 tent sites. Tbls, toilets, cfga, shelter, shelter, no drkg wtr. Boating (dock for 17 boats), fishing, waterskiing. Popular picnic area.

Moore Point   **$5**
Wanatchee National Forest
43 mi NW of Chelan (26 mi from Twenty-Five-Mile Creek State Park) by boat; on N shore of Lake Chelan. Hike S or N along lakeshore trail. $5 daily or $40 annual dock permit during 5/1-9/30; free rest of year; 14-day limit. 4 boat-in or hike-in tent sites. Shelter, cfga, no toilets, no drkg wtr. Boating (dock for 3 boats), fishing, waterskiing. Busy on weekends.

Prince Creek   **$5**
Wenatchee National Forest
3.1 mi W of Chelan on US 97; 16 mi NW on CR 10 (South Lakeshore Rd) to Twenty-Five Mile Creek State Park boat launch; about 17 mi NW on Lake Chelan by boat; on NW

shore. Hike in from N along lakeshore trail. $5 daily or $40 annual dock permit during 5/1-9/30; free rest of year; 14-day limit. 6 tent sites. Tbls, toilets, cfga, no drkg wtr. Boating (floating dock for 3 boats), fishing, waterskiing. Popular boat-in camp. Trailhead for backpacking to Boiling Lake, Cub Lake.

Ramona Creek   **$5**
Wenatchee National Forest
3.1 mi W of Chelan on US 97; 16 mi NW on CR 10 (South Lakeshore Rd) to Twenty-Five Mile Creek State Park; 3 mi W on FR 5900 to FR 8410 access rd. $5 daily or $30 annual NW forest pass. 5/1-9/30; 14-day limit. 8 tent sites. Tbls, toilets, cfga, no drkg wtr. Fishing, hiking.

Refrigerator Harbor   **$5**
Wenatchee National Forest
39 mi NW of Chelan (22 mi from Twenty-Five-Mile Creek State Park) by boat. Or, hike 1 mi S from Lucerne after taking ferry from Manson or Fields Point Landing to Lucerne. $5 daily or $40 annual dock permit during 5/1-9/30; free rest of year; 14-day limit. 4 tent sites. Tbls, toilets, cfga, no drkg wtr. Boating(d), fishing, waterskiing. Good downlake wind protection, but no protection from uplake wind.

Safety Harbor   **$5**
Wenatchee National Forest
3.1 mi W of Chelan on US 97; 16 mi NW on CR 10 (South Lakeshore Rd) to Twenty-Five Mile Creek State Park boat launch; about 8 mi NW on Lake Chelan by boat; on N shore; or hike about 3 mi S from FR 3001. $5 daily or $40 annual dock permit during 5/1-9/30; free rest of year; 14-day limit. 2 tent sites. Toilet, cfga, no tbls, no drkg wtr. Boating (year-round dock for 6 boats), fishing, waterskiing. Good shelter from uplake & downlake wind.

South Navarre   **FREE**
Wenatchee National Forest
5.8 mi NW of Chelan on SR 150; follow Manson Rd N to Wapato Lake Rd; right on Upper Joe Creek Rd, then N on Grade Creek Rd (FRs 8200/3007) about 38 mi. Free. 5/1-10/31; 14-day limit. Tbls, cfga, toilets, no drkg wtr (except for horses). Hiking, horseback riding.

Stewart   **FREE**
Wenatchee National Forest
40 mi NW of Chelan (23 mi from Twenty-Five-Mile Creek State Park) by boat (or, ferry from Manson or Fields Point Landing) to Lucerne; from trailhead, hike 3 mi S on Trail 1280, just past Hatchery Campground. Free. 6/1-10/31; 14-day limit. Undesignated sites with two tbls, 1 cfga, 1 toilet, no drkg wtr. Hiking, boating, swimming, picnicking, fishing.

Surprise Lake   **FREE**
Wenatchee National Forest
39 mi NW of Chelan (22 mi from Twenty-Five-Mile Creek State Park) by boat to Meadow

Creek outlet on Lake Chelan (on N shore opposite Refrigerator Harbor Camp); hike about 4 mi NW to Surprise Lake. Free. 3 tent sites. No facilities except cfga. Fishing, hiking.

CLARKSTON (21)

Silcott Road Camp   **FREE**
6.6 mi W of Clarkston on WA 12; N on Silcott Rd; across Snake River bridge. Free. All year; 14-day limit. 30 sites. Boating(dl); fishing; swimming. No shade. Park on graded gravel lot near site of ghost town.

CLE ELUM (22)

29 Pines Camp   **FREE**
Boise Casdade Corp.
From I-90 exit 86, about 6 mi N on Hwys 970 & 97; left on Teanaway River Rd, along the North Fork Teanaway River to end of pavement; camp on the left. Free. Long RV/tent sites. Tbls, toilets, cfga, no drkg wtr. Biking, fishing, hiking trails.

Beverly   **$5**
Wenatchee National Forest
4 mi SE of Cle Elum on SR 10; 4.2 mi NE on SR 970; 13 mi N on Teanaway Rd & North Fork Teanaway; 4 mi NW on FR 9737. $5. MD-9/30; 14-day limit. 16 sites (RVs under 22 ft). Tbls, toilets, cfga, no drkg wtr. Fishing; picnicking; hiking; horseback riding (1 mi). Horse and motorcycle trail nearby. On North Fork of Teanaway River.

Cle Elum River   **$11**
Wenatchee National Forest
11.2 mi NW of Cle Elum on SR 903; 8.3 mi NW on CR 903. $11. MD-10/1 (weather permitting); 14 day limit. 23 sites. Tbls, toilets, cfga, drkg wtr. Fishing, hunting, hiking, group camping.

Crystal Springs   **$11**
Wenatchee National Forest
20.3 mi NW of Cle Elum on I-90; half mi NW on FR 212. $11 during MD-9/15; free rest of yr, but no wtr or trash service; 14-day limit. 25 sites (22-ft limit). Tbls, toilets, cfga, drkg wtr, community kitchen. Fishing, berrypicking, mushrooming, picnicking. Keechelus & Kachess Lakes nearby. 8 acres.
   Fishing tip: 2,56--acre Keechelus Lake has excellent shoreline fishing access on the N side, and fishing is at its best during the heat of summer. The lake contains kokanee salmon, dolly varden, rainbow trout and bull trout. Road noise from the freeway can be somewhat distracting.

Fish Lake   **FREE**
Wenatchee National Forest
22 mi NW of Cle Elum on WA 903/CR 903 & Salmon La Sac Rd; 11 mi NE on narrow, unpaved FR 43301 (not recommended for RVs). Free. MD-10/1; 14-day limit. 3 sites. Tbls, toilets, cfga, no drkg wtr. Berry picking; picnicking; fishing; boating (1 mi); hiking.

Fishing tip: Popular, slough-like 63-acre Fish Lake contains mainly brook trout and some rainbows.

Icewater Creek **$11**
Wenatchee National Forest
12 mi SE of Cle Elum on I-90; .7 mi S from Thorp exit; 12 mi NW on CR/FR 33 (Taneum Rd). $11. 5/15-11/15; 14-day limit. 17 sites. Tbls, toilets, cfga, no drkg wtr. Fishing, picnicking, hunting, horseback riding, hiking, motorcycling.

Indian Camp **FREE**
State Recreation Site
Dept. of Natural Resources
From Exit 85 of I-90 at Cle Elum, 6.9 mi E on SR 970; left on Teanaway Rd for 7.3 mi; left on West Fork Teanaway Rd for half mi; right on Middle Fork Teanaway Rd for 3.9 mi. Free. All year; 14-day limit. 6 sites. Tbls, toilets, cfga, no drkg wtr, hitching rails. Horseback riding, hiking, mountain biking.

Ken Wilcox Campgroud **$5**
(Haney Meadows)
Wenatchee National Forest
12 mi NE of Cle Elum on SR 970; N on US 97 to Swauk Pass; 8 mi E on FR 9712. Camp free with $30 annual NW forest pass; $5 daily otherwise. 6/15-10/31. 19 sites. Tbls, toilets, cfga, no drkg wtr, horse tethers, council area, horse loading ramps. Hunting, hiking, horseback riding.

Liberty Recreation Site **FREE**
Bureau of Land Management
12 mi NE of Cle Elum on SR 970; N on US 97 to Swauk Pass; E on Liberty Rd. Free. All year; 14-day limit. Primitive dispersed camping in cottonwood grove on right side of rd (surrounded by forest service ORV trails). No facilities. Fishing, hiking, ORV activities.

Mineral Springs **$11**
Wenatchee National Forest
12 mi E of Cle Elum on US 970; 6 mi N on US 97. $11 during MD-9/15; 14-day limit. 7 sites (22-ft limit). Tbls, toilets, cfga, drkg wtr. Coin laundry, groceries nearby. Fishing, berry-picking, hunting. Rockhounding nearby. Elev 2700 ft; 6 acres.

Owhi **$8**
Wenatchee National Forest
From I-90 exit 80 near Cle Elum, 4 mi N on Bullfrog Rd; 19 mi N on Hwy 903; 5 mi W on FR 46; 1 mi on FR 4616, then left onto Spur Rd 113. $8. 6/15-10/15; 14-day limit. 22-walk-in tent sites. Tbls, toilets, cfga, no drkg wtr. Boating(l), fishing, hiking.

Red Mountain **$8**
Wenatchee National Forest
19.5 mi NW of Cle Elum on WA 903 & Cle Elum Valley Rd. 903, about 1 mi N of Cle Elum Lake. $8 during 5/25-9/30, weather permitting; 14-day limit. 10 sites on 2 acres (RVs under 16 ft). Tbls, toilets, cfga, no drkg

wtr. Reduced service. Berry picking; fishing; picnicking; horseback riding (2 mi); swimming, boating, waterskiing (3 mi).

Fishing tip: Cle Elum Lake contains rainbow, cutthroat, kokanee, dolly varden, eastern brook trout, whitefish and burbot as well as some mackinaw up to 20 pounds. Roostertail-type spinners do quite well with trout.

Red Top **$5**
Wenatchee National Forest
10 mi E of Cle Elum on SR 970; 8 mi N on US 97; about 8 mi NW on FR 9702 (to nearly end of rd). Camp free with $30 annual NW forest pass; $5 daily otherwise. 5/15-10/15; 14-day limit. 3 sites (22-ft RV limit). Tbls, toilet, cfga, no drkg wtr. Picnicking, hiking, hunting, . Fire lookout.

South Fork Meadows **$5**
Wenatchee National Forest
25 mi S of Cle Elum off South Fork-Taneum Rd (FR 3300). Camp free with $30 annual NW forest pass; $5 daily otherwise. All year; 14-day limit. 3 sites. Tbls, toilet, cfga, no drkg wtr. Hiking, fishing.

Swauk **$11**
Wenatchee National Forest
10 mi E of Cle Elum on SR 970; 17 mi N on US 97. $11. 4/15-9/15; 14-day limit. 23 sites (22-ft RV limit). Tbls, toilets, cfga, no drkg wtr, community kitchen, swings. Horseshoes, baseball, hiking trail, hunting, fishing, group sports.

Tamarack Spring **FREE**
Wenatchee National Forest
12 mi SE of Cle Elum on I-90; .75 mi S from Thorp exit; 12.5 mi on CR/FR 33 past Taneum Campground; 5 mi S on FR 3330; 1.5 mi E on FR 3120; at forest boundary Free. 5/15-11/15; 14-day limit. 3 sites. Tbl, toilet, cfga, no drkg wtr except for horses. Hunting, hiking, horseback riding, motorcycling.

Taneum Junction **$5**
Wenatchee National Forest
12 mi SE of Cle Elum on I-90; .7 mi S from Thorp exit; 8 mi NW on CR/FR 33 (Taneum Rd). Camp free with $30 annual NW forest pass; $5 daily otherwise. 5/15-11/15; 14-day limit. Group site for about 15 RVs & 75 people. Tbls, toilets, cfga, no drkg wtr. Fishing, hunting, motorcycling, horseback riding.

COLVILLE (23)

Big Meadow Lake **FREE**
Colville National Forest
1 mi E of Colville on SR 20; 20 mi N on Aladdin Hwy; 6 mi E on Meadow Creek Rd. Free. MD-LD; 14-day limit. 16 sites. Tbls, toilets, cfga, no drkg wtr. Boating(l), hiking (wheelchair access), fishing.

Douglas Falls Grange Park **FREE**
Dept of Natural Resources
From SR 20 on E side of Colville, N 1.9 mi on Aladdin Rd; left for 3 mi on Douglas Falls

Rd, then left into park. Free. All year; 14-day limit. 8 sites; 6 picnic sites. Tbls, toilets, cfga, drkg wtr. Baseball field, horseshoes, scenic waterfalls. Mill Creek.

Gillette **$12**
Colville National Forest
20 mi E of Colville on Hwy 20; half mi E on CR 200. $12. 5/15-9/30; 14-day limit. 30 sites. Tbls, toilets, cfga, drkg wtr. Boating(l), fishing, hiking.

Flodell Creek **FREE**
State Recreation Site
Dept of Natural Resources
From jct with US 395 at Colville, 19.4 mi E on SR 20; right on two-lane gravel rd for .3 mi; left to camp entrance. Free. All year; 14-day limit. 8 sites. Tbls, toilets, drkg wtr, cfga. Motorcycle trails, fishing, picnicking, hiking, hunting.

Little Twin Lakes **FREE**
Colville National Forest
12.5 mi E of Colville on WA 20; 4.5 mi NE on CR 4915; half mi N on FR 9413; 1 mi N on fR 150. Free. MD-9/15; 14-day limit. 20 sites (RVs under 16 ft); camp on both sides of lake. Tbls, toilets, cfga, firewood, drkg wtr. Boating(dl); picnicking; fishing; hiking trails. 3800 ft. High-clearance vehicles only. 20 acres.

Rocky Lake **FREE**
State Recreation Site
Dept of Natural Resources
From jct with US 395 in Colville, take SR 20 E 6 mi; turn right for 3.2 mi on Artman-Gibson Rd; right for half mi on one-lane gravel rd; stay left for one-tenth mi, then go 2 mi to camp. Free. Seasonal use for camping; 14-day limit. 7 sites, 1 picnic site. Tbls, toilets, cfga, drkg wtr. Boating (hand launch), fishing.

Sherry Creek **FREE**
State Recreation Site
Dept. of Natural Resources
From jct with US 395 at Colville, 23.8 mi E on SR 20; right for half mi on gravel rd. Free. All year; 14-day limit. 2 sites. Tbls, toilets, cfga, no drkg wtr. Fishing.

Starvation Lake **FREE**
State Recreation Site
Dept. of Natural Resources
From jct with US 395 at Colville, 10.5 mi E on SR 20; right on gravel rd for qtr mi; left at next jct for half mi. Free. All year; 14-day limit. 6 sites. Tbls, toilets, cfga, no drkg wtr, fishing pier. Fishing, boating (hand launch). Moose sighted frequently.

Williams Lake **FREE**
State Recreation Site
Dept of Natural Resources
1.5 mi W of Colville on US 395; 13.7 mi N on Williams Lake Rd; turn left and immediately left again to camp. Free. All year; 14-day limit. 8 sites; 2 picnic sites. Tbls, toilets, cfga,

drkg wtr. Fishing, hiking, mountain biking. Interpretive site.

CONCONULLY (24)

Cottonwood   **$5**
Okanogan National Forest
2.1 mi NW of Conconully on CR 2361/FR 38; along Salmon Creek. $5. All year; 14-day limit. 4 sites (22-ft RV limit). Tbls, toilets, cfga, no drkg wtr. Fishing. Elev 2700 ft. This camp was closed early in 2007 due to 2006 fire.

Kerr   **$5**
Okanogan National Forest
2 mi NW of Conconully on FR 2361; 2 mi NW on FR 38. $5. All year; 14-day limit. 13 sites (22-ft RV limit) & 2 group sites. Tbls, toilets, cfga, no drkg wtr, no trash service. Fishing, swimming, boating. 4 mi N of Conconully Lake on Salmon Creek. Elev 3100 ft; 3 acres. Closed early in 2007 due to 2006 fire.

Oriole   **$5**
Okanogan National Forest
2.6 mi NW of Conconully on CR 2361/FR 38; left 1 mi on FR 38-026; along Salmon Creek. $5. All year; 14-day limit. 10 sites (22-ft RV limit). Tbls, toilets, cfga, no drkg wtr. No trash service in winter. Fishing, hiking. Closed early in 2007 due to 2006 fire.

Salmon Meadows   **$5**
Okanogan National Forest
8.5 mi NW of Conconully on CR 2361/FR 38. $5. All year; 14-day limit. 7 sites (22-ft RV limit). Tbls, toilets, cfga, no drkg wtr, community kitchen. No trash service in winter. Hiking trails, horseback riding (corral), birdwatching, historical exhibit. Closed early in 2007 due to 2006 fire.

Sugarloaf   **$5**
Okanogan National Forest
From Forest Service Work Center at Conconully, 5 mi N on CR 4015, past Conconully Lake to Sugarloaf Lake. $5. All year; 14-day limit. 4 sites. Tbls, toilets, cfga, no drkg wtr. No trash service in winter. Fishing, boating, hiking. Closed early in 2007 due to 2006 fire.

Tiffany Spring   **FREE**
Okanogan National Forest
From Conconully State Park at Conconully, 1.5 mi SW on CR 2017 (becomes FR 42); 21 mi NW on FR 37 (becoming FR 39); 8 mi NE on FR 39. All year; 14-day limit. Free. 6 sites (RVs under 16 ft). Tbls, toilets, cfga, firewood, no drkg wtr, no trash service. Picnicking, fishing, bridle trails, hiking. Near Tiffany Lake. Closed early in 2007 due to 2006 fire.

CONCRETE (25)

Boulder Creek   **$12**
Mt. Baker-Snoqualmie National Forest
9.5 mi N of Concrete on CR 25; 5.5 mi N on CR 11. $12 in 2007 & 2008 unless wtr

becomes available; then fee will be $16. MD-LD; 14-day limit. 8 sites (22-ft RV limit). Tbls, toilets, cfga, no drkg wtr. Reservations available. Fishing, berrypicking. 5 acres. 2-day minimum stay on weekends.

Camp Kulshan   **$7**
Puget Sound Energy Company
10 mi N of Concrete on CR 25 or Baker Lake Rd; right from Baker Lake Rd at sign pointing to upper dam; about 1 mi; campground is at left. $7. Apr-Oct or until closed by snow; 14-day limit. 79 sites. Tbls, toilets, cfga, dump, wtr hookups; no wtr in winter. Picnicking; fishing; boating(ld). Baker Lake. Mount Baker (10,778 ft elev).
Fishing tip: There's good fishing here in May & June for kokanee salmon, and also again in the fall. During July, rainbow trout fishing is excellent. Try the mouth of Noisy Creek with small rainbow-color lures such as a Rapala.

Cathedral Camp   **FREE**
High Camp
Railroad Camp
Mazama Park Horse Camp
Mt. Baker Recreation Area
Mt. Baker-Snoqualmie National Forest
9.5 mi N of Concrete on CR 25; 10 mi N on Baker Lake Rd; about 10 mi NW on FR 13 to Mt. Baker RA Trailhead; hike or ride by horseback NW by trail to one of 4 backpacker camps. Free. All year. Designated tent sites; no campfires permitted. Hiking, snowmobiling, fishing.

Maple Grove   **FREE**
Mount Baker-Snoqualmie National Forest
9.6 mi N of Concrete on CR 25; 2.4 mi N on FR 11; 2 mi E on FR 1118; 1 mi N BY FOOT OR BOAT, on Baker Lake. Free. 5/15-9/15 or until closed by snow; 14-day limit. 5 tent sites. Tbls, Toilets, cfga, no drkg wtr. No trash service in winter. Fishing, boating, hiking.

Park Creek   **$12**
Mt. Baker-Snoqualmie National Forest
9.5 mi N of Concrete on CR 25; 7.4 mi NE on FR 11; .1 mi NW on FR 1144. $12 in 2007 & 2008 unless water becomes available; then fees will be $18. MD-LD; 14-day limit. 12 sites (22-ft RV limit). Tbls, toilets, cfga, no drkg wtr. Fishing, boating nearby on Baker Lake. Hiking trails. 2-day minimum stay on weekends.

Rasar State Park   **$12**
6 mi E of Concrete on SR 20; 1 mi S on Russell Rd; 12 mi E on Cape Horn Rd; along Skagit River. $12 at three walk-in tent sites; $17 for 18 standard sites; $23 for 22 sites with elec & wtr. All year; 10-day limit. Tbls, toilets, cfga, drkg wtr, dump. Hiking, fishing, fall eagle watching, interpretive programs. 169 acres.

Sauk   **$5**
Skagit County Park
Just N of the Lower Government bridge on the Concrete-Sauk Valley Rd. $5. 5/1-10/31; 14-

day limit. Primitive overnight sites at 30-acre park. Tbls, cfga, no drkg wtr, no services. Hiking.

COULEE CITY (28)

Banks Lake Fish Camp   **FREE**
State Dept. of Fish & Wildlife
11.8 mi N of Coulee City on WA 155 (6.5 mi S of Grand Coulee Dam); on E shore of Banks Lake. No designated sites; room for 20 RVs on large, flat gravel area (no size limit). Tbls, toilets, cfga. Boating(l); hunting; picnicking. Beach. Geological interest.
Fishing tip: Excellent fishing for walleye, bass, perch, whitefish, kokanee salmon & rainbow trout. The kokanee are quite plentiful but get little fishing pressure. Rainbow trout are up to 5 pounds, and largemouth bass fishing is excellent. Lots of whitefish too.

CRESTON (29)

Hawk Creek   **$10**
Lake Roosevelt National Recreation Area
14 mi NE of Creston on paved road. $10 during 5/1-9/30; $5 rest of year; 14-day limit. 21 sites (RVs under 16 ft). Tbls, toilets, cfga, drkg wtr. Boating(ld); fishing; picnicking. Near Roosevelt Lake.
Fishing tip: This is a good place for a base camp if you're after Roosevelt Lake's rainbow trout & kokanee salmon. Only kokanee with clpped adipose fin can be kept. Try Roostertails in the creek and under the waterfalls for 15-17 inche rainbows.

CYPRESS ISLAND (31)

Cypress Head   **FREE**
State Recreation Site
Dept of Natural Resources
From Anacortes or Edison, access by boat only; at E tip of island. Float provided for offloading only. Free. 9 tent sites; 7 picnic sites. Tbls, toilets, cfga, no drkg wtr. 5 buoys.

Pelican Beach   **FREE**
State Recreation Site
Multiple Use Area
Dept of Natural Resources
From Anacortes or Edison, access by boat only. Free. 8 tent sites; 3 picnic sites. Tbls, toilets, cfga, no drkg wtr. 1.2 mi hike to Eagle Cliff (trail closed 2/1-7/15). 6 boat buoys. Group shelter. Hiking trails, beach. Dock for offloading.

DARRINGTON (32)

Bedal   **$12**
Mt. Baker-Snoqualmie National Forest
22 mi S of Darrington on FR 20. $12 in 2007 & 2008 unless water becomes available; then fee with be $16. MD-LD; then free until closed by snow; 14-day limit. 18 sites (22-ft RV limit); 6 acres. Tbls, toilets, cfga, no drkg wtr. Fishing, hiking, picnicking. 2-day minimum stay on weekends.

Buck Creek $12
Mt. Baker-Snoqualmie National Forest
7.5 mi N of Darrington on SR 530; 15.2 mi SE on FR 26 along Suiattiei River. $12 in 2007 & 2008 unless water becomes available; then fee will be $16. MD-LD; 14-day limit. 29 sites (30-ft RV limit). Tbls, toilets, cfga, no drkg wtr. Nature trails, fishing. 2-day minimum stay on weekends.

Clear Creek $12
Mt. Baker-Snoqualmie National Forest
2.3 mi SE of Darrington on FR 20; quarter mi SE on FR 3205; on Sauk River at jct with Clear Creek. $12 in 2007 & 2008 unless water becomes available; then fee with be $16. MD-LD; 14-day limit. 12 secluded sites (RVs under 22 ft). Tbls, toilets, cfga, firewood, no drkg wtr, no trash pickup (pack litter out). Hunting; hiking; picnicking; fishing. 4 acres. Frog Lake Trailhead.

French Creek FREE
Mount Baker-Snoqualmie National Forest
8.1 mi W of Darrington on WA 530; .8 mi S on FR 2010. Free. 5/1-9/30; 14-day limit. Undeveloped primitive sites. No facilities. Picnicking; fishing (2 mi). Elev 700 ft; 12 acres. Suitable for dispersed camping.

Texas Wand FREE
Mount Baker-Snoqualmie National Forest
6.2 mi N of Darrington on co hwy; 6 mi NW on FR 3334. Free. 5/30-10/31; 10-day limit. Undeveloped primitive area; no facilities. Picnicking; fishing.

Whitechuck Trailhead $5
Mt. Baker-Snoqualmie National Forest
10.1 mi SE of Darrington on FR 22 (Mountain Loop Hwy); 10 mi SE on FR 23 to end at Kennedy Hot Springs area. Free with $30 annual NW forest pass or $5 daily. Undeveloped primitive camping; no facilities. Fishing, hiking.

DAVENPORT (33)

Fort Spokane $10
Lake Roosevelt National Recreation Area
25 m N of Davenport on SR 25. $10 during 5/1-9/30; $5 rest of year. 14-day limit. 67 sites (26-ft RV limit). Tbls, flush toilets, cfga, drkg wtr, dump, amphitheater. Some handicap facilities. Boating(ld), fishing, playground, swimming. 22 acres.

Porcupine Bay Campground $10
Lake Roosevelt National Recreation Area
19 mi N of Davenport on SR 25. $10 during 5/1-10/30; $5 rest of year; 14-day limit. 32 sites (20-ft RV limit). Tbls, flush toilets, cfga, drkg wtr, beach, dump, fish cleaning station. Swimming, boating(ld), fishing, volleyball.

DAYTON (34)

Godman FREE
Umatilla National Forest
14 mi SE of Dayton on CR 118; 11 mi S on FR 46 (Kendall Skyline Rd). Free. 6/15-10/15; 14-day limit. 5 sites; 16-ft RV limit. Tbls, toilets, cfga, no drkg wtr. Hunting, fishing, hiking, biking. Horse facilities, bitching rails, feed mangers & spring at Godman Trailhead. Elev 5600 ft; 9 acres. Good view of Wenaha Wilderness. Accessible via E Touchet Rd or Kendall Skyline Rd.

EDISON (35)

Lily Lake FREE
State Recreation Site
Dept of Natural Resources
From I-5 Exit 20 at Edison, N half mi on Samish Lake Rd, then left on Barrel Springs Rd for 1 mi; right on SW-C-1000 Rd for 1.5 mi to Blanchard Hill Trailhead. Hike 3.2 mi, then go left half mi to camp. Free. 6 tent sites. Tbls, cfga, no drkg wtr. Horse trails, hiking trails, lake. Toilets removed in 2004; may be closed to camping. It also has been closed to camping at times to protect the cherry harvest.

Lizard Lake FREE
State Recreation Site
Dept of Natural Resources
From Blanchard Hill Trailhead (see Lily Lake entry), hike 3.2 mi, then go right three-fourths mi to camp. Free. 3 tent sites, tbls, cfga, no drkg wtr. Horse & hiking trails, lake. Toilets removed in 2004; may be closed to camping eventually.

ELBE (36)

Beaver Creek FREE
State Recreation Site
Elbe/Tahoma State Forest
Dept. of Natural Resources
6.3 mi E of Elbe on SR 706; 2.3 mi S on Stoner Rd (keep right) to second jct; left fork for 1.9 mi. Free. All year; 14-day limit. 6 sites, 6 picnic sites. Tbls, toilets, cfga, no drkg wtr. Hiking, mountain biking, horseback riding.

Cougar Rock $12
Mount Rainier National Park
12 mi E of Elbe on Hwy 706 to park entrance, then 11 mi to campground; at SW corner of park (2.3 mi N of Longmire). $12 off-season; $15 about 6/15-LD; 14-day limit. 173 sites; 35-ft motorhome limit, 27-ft trailer limit. Tbls, flush toilets, cfga, drkg wtr, dump, store. Fishing, hikng, recreation program.

Elbe Hills ORV Trailhead FREE
Elbe/Tahoma State Forest
Dept of Natural Resources
E of Elbe 6.3 mi on SR 706; left on paved & gravel Stoner Rd for 3.7 mi (keep right); left 0.1 mi to trailhead. Free. All year; 14-day limit. 6 sites; 5 picnic sites. Toilets, cfga, tbls, no drkg wtr. Group shelter, 4x4 trails.

Memorial Trailhead FREE
State Recreation Site
Elbe/Tahoma State Forest
Dept. of Natural Resources
From Beaver Creek camp, continue on main rd for 2.3 mi to gated rd on left; 1.6 mi to trailhead. Free. 3/19-9/1; 14-day limit. 6 sites, 3 picnic sites. Tbls, toilets, cfga, no drkg wtr. Hiking, mountain biking, horseback riding on 50 mi of trails.

Sahara Creek Horse Camp FREE
Elbe/Tahoma State Forest
Dept. of Natural Resources
5.3 mi E of Elbe on SR 706; left to camp. Free. All year; 14-day limit. 18 sites, 9 picnic sites. Tbls, toilets, cfga, drkg wtr, horse facilities. Horseback riding, mountain biking, hiking on 50 mi of trails. This site might be closed to camping.

ELDON (37)

Hamma Hamma $10
Olympic National Forest
1.7 mi N of Eldon on US 101; 6.5 mi W on FR 25. $10. 5/15-9/15; 14-day limit. 15 RV sites (21-ft limit); 3 tent sites. Tbls, toilets, cfga, drkg wtr. Swimming, fishing, hiking trails. On Hamma Hamma River. 5 acres.

Lena Creek $10
Olympic National Forest
1.7 mi N of Eldon on US 101; 8 mi W on FR 25. $10. 5/15-9/15; 14-day limit. 13 sites (21-ft RV limit). Tbls, toilets, cfga, drkg wtr. Swimming, fishing, hiking trails (to Lena & Upper Lena Lakes). 7 acres on Hamma Hamma River.

Lena Lake FREE
Olympic National Forest
1.7 mi N of Eldon on US 101; 8 mi W on FR 25; 3 mi N on Trail 810 from Lena Creek. Free. All year; 14-day limit. 29 hike-in tent sites. Toilets, cfga, no drkg wtr. Hiking, picnicking, fishing, mountain climbing, swimming. Elev 700 ft; 7 acres. Nature trails. Adjacent to Lena Lake.

ELLENSBURG (38)

Lion Rock Spring FREE
Wenatchee National Forest
23 mi N of Ellensburg on CR/FR 35. Free. 6/15-10/15; 14-day limit. 3 tent sites (no trailers). All year; 14-day limit. Tbls, cfga, toilets, benches, no drkg wtr (except horses). Picnicking, hiking, hunting. Elev 6300 ft; 1 acre. Scenic. Horse and motorcycle trails near site.

Manastash $5
Wenatchee National Forest
25 mi W of Ellensburg on CR/FR 3100 & FR 3104. Camp free with annual $30 NW forest pass; $5 daily otherwise. All year; 14-day limit. About 14 primitive undesignated sites. Tbls, toilets, cfga, no drkg wtr except for

horses; hitching posts. Hiking, horseback riding. This camp replaces the old Buck Meadows camp.

Quartz Mountain — FREE
Wenatchee National Forest
33 mi W of Ellensburg on CR/FR 3100; near end of rd. Free. MD-9/30; 14-day limit. 3 sites (22-ft RV limit). Tbls, toilet, cfga, no drkg wtr. Picnicking, hiking horseback riding, motorcycling.

Riders Camp — $5
Wenatchee National Forest
25 mi W of Ellensburg on CR/FR 3100. Camp free with annual $30 NW forest pass; $5 daily otherwise. All year; 14-day limit. Primitive undesignated sites. No facilities except cfga; no drkg wtr except at creek for horses. Hiking, horseback riding.

Roza Campground — $2
Bureau of Land Management
18 mi S of Ellensburg on SR 821; along Yakima River. Free 10/16-5/14; $2 rest of year (or $15 season pass); 7-day limit. 7 primitive sites. Tbls, toilets, cfga, no drkg wtr. Fishing, boating(l), horseback riding, canoeing, rafting, hiking, hunting.

Lmuma Campground — $2
Bureau of Land Management
13 mi S of Ellensburg on SR 821; along Yakima River. Free 10/16-5/14; $2 rest of year (or $15 season pass); 7-day limit. 12 sites. Tbls, toilets, cfga, no drkg wtr. Boating(l), fishing, canoeing, rafting, hiking, hunting, horseback riding. Formerly named Squaw Creek.

Umtanum Campground — FREE
Bureau of Land Management
9 mi S of Ellensburg on SR 821; along Yakima River. Free. All year; 7-day limit. Primitive undesignated sites. Toilets, cfga, no drkg wtr. Boating(l), fishing, canoeing, hiking, rafting, kayaking, horseback riding, hunting.

ENTIAT (39)

Big Hill Dispersed Camp — FREE
Wenatchee National Forest
1.4 mi SW of Entiat on US 97; 25.2 mi NW on Entiat River Rd (FR 51/CR 371); 11 mi NE on Shady Pass Rd (FR 5900); 4.2 mi NW on FR 298; 1.5 mi N on FR 298A. Free. 7/15-9/30; 14-day limit. 1 tent site. Tbl, toilet, cfga, firewood, no drkg wtr. Shelter on site. Picnicking; horseback riding (1 mi). Elev 6800 ft; 1 acre.

Cottonwood — $8
Wenatchee National Forest
1.5 mi SW of Entiat on US 97; 25.2 mi NW on CR 371; 12.7 mi NW on FR 317. $8. MD-10/15; camp free in fall after wtr is shut off; 14-day limit. 2 small RV & 23 tent sites. Tbls, toilets, cfga, drkg wtr. Fishing, hiking & horseback trails. Departure point for Glacier Peak Wilderness.

Fox Creek — $8
Wenatchee National Forest
1.5 mi SW of Entiat on US 97; 25.2 mi NW on CR 371; 1.8 mi NW on FR 317. $8. MD-10/15; camp free in fall after wtr is shut off; 14-day limit. 16 sites (23-ft RV limit). Tbls, toilets, cfga, drkg wtr. Fishing, picnicking, hiking. Elev 2300 ft.

Lake Creek — $8
Wenatchee National Forest
1.5 mi SW on US 97; 25.2 mi NW on CR 371; 3 mi NW on FR 317. MD-10/15; camp free in fall after wtr is shut off; 14-day limit. $8. 18 sites (RVs under 23 ft). Tbls, toilets, cfga, drkg wtr. Fishing, picnicking, hiking trails, horseback riding.

Mad Lake Dispersed — FREE
Wenatchee National Forest
1.4 mi SW of Entiat on US 97; 10 mi NW on CR 371; 2.2 mi NW on FR 2710; 9 mi SW on FR 2615. Free. 7/15-9/30; 14-day limit. 3 tent sites (no trailers). Tbls, toilets, cfga, firewood. Picnicking; fishing.

North Fork — $7
Wenatchee National Forest
1.5 mi SW of Entiat on US 97; 25.2 mi NW on CR 371; 8.3 mi NW on FR 317. $7. MD-10/15; camp free in fall after wtr is shut off; 14-day limit. 1 small RV site (22-ft limit); 8 tent sites. Tbls, toilets, cfga, drkg wtr. Entiat River fishing.

Pine Flat — $5
Wenatchee National Forest
1.4 mi SW of Entiat on US 97; 10 mi NW on CR 371/FR 51 (Entiat River Rd); 3.7 mi NW on FR 5700. $5. 4/15-11/1; 14-day limit. 7 sites (RVs under 22 ft). Toilets, cfga, firewood, no drkg wtr. Horseback riding; picnicking; fishing. Elev 1900 ft; 9 acres. River.

Shady Pass — FREE
Dispersed Camp
Wenatchee National Forest
1.4 mi SW of Entiat on US 97; 25.2 mi NW on CR 371 (Entiat River Rd); 9 mi NE on Shady Pass Rd (FR 5900). Free. 7/15-9/30; 14-day limit. Primitive undesignated sites. Tbls, cfga, no toilet, no drkg wtr.

Silver Falls — $9
Wenatchee National Forest
1.5 mi SW of Entiat on US 97; 25.2 mi NW on CR 371; 5.5 mi NW on FR 317. $9. MD-10/15; 14-day limit. 31 sites (22-ft RV limit). Tbls, toilets, cfga, drkg wtr. Fishing, hiking trails. At Silver Creek & Entiat River. Half-mi hike to Silver Falls.

Three Creek — $3
Wenatchee National Forest
1.4 mi SW of Entiat on US 97; 25.2 mi NW on CR 371 (Entiat River Rd); 10.5 mi NW on FR 317. $3 5/15-11/1; 14-day limit. 3 tent sites. Tbls, toilets, cfga, firewood, no drkg wtr, no trash service; limited maintenance. Elev 2900 ft; 2 acres.

ENUMCLAW (40)

Corral Pass — $5
Mount Baker-Snoqualmie National Forest
31 mi SE of Enumclaw on US 410; 6 mi E on FR 7174. Camp free with $30 annual NW forest pass; $5 daily otherwise. 7/1-11/15; 14-day limit. 20 tent sites. Tbls, toilets, cfga, no drkg wtr. Horse ramp, berry-picking. 15 acres; elev 5600 ft.

Sand Flats Trailhead — $5
Mount Baker-Snoqualmie National Forest
33 mi SE of Enumclaw on Hwy 410; left on FR 7190 (Crystal Mountain Blvd) for 4 mi, then right on FR Spur 510. Camp free with $30 annual NW forest pass; $5 daily otherwise. All year; 14-day limit. Undesignated sites, used primarily by horse campers. Tbls, toilets, cfga, no drkg wtr except for horses. Hitching rails. Hiking, picnicking, horseback riding.

White River — $12
Mount Rainier National Park
43 mi SE of Enumclaw on SR 410 in NE corner of park. $12. 6/15-9/15; 14-day limit. 112 sites (20-ft RV limit). Tbls, flush toilets, cfga, drkg wtr. Hiking, fishing, recreation program. Elev 4400 ft; 25 acres.

EPHRATA (41)

Oasis City Park — $12
1.5 mi N of Ephrata on SR 28. $12 base. All year. 68 sites. Tbls, flush toilets, cfga, drkg wtr, dump, phone, CATV, hookups($), showers. Heated pool, playground, mini golf($), store, LP-gas, coin laundry, nature program, fishing ponds. 35 acres.

FORKS (42)

Bear Creek Recreation Site — FREE
Olympic Experimental State Forest
Dept of Natural Resources
NW of Forks on US 101 at milepost 206, on Soleduck River, just outside Olympic National Forest. Free. All year; 7-day limit during 30-day period at all regional campgrounds. 10 sites. Toilets, tbls, cfga, no drkg wtr. Hiking, fishing.

Coppermine Bottom — FREE
State Recreation Site
Olympic Experimental State Forest
Dept of Natural Resources
From milepost 147 on US 101 S of Forks, go N on Hoh-Clearwater Mainline Rd (paved) 12.6 mi; then right 1.5 mi on gravel, 1-lane C-1010. Camp on left. Free. All year; 7-day limit during 30-day period at all regional campgrounds. 9 sites. Toilets, tbls, cfga, no drkg wtr, shelter. Hand boat launch, fishing.

Cottonwood Recreation Site — FREE
Olympic Experimental State Forest
Dept of Natural Resources
From between mileposts 177 & 178 S of

Forks, go W off US 101 on Oil City Rd (paved) 2.3 mi. Turn left on H-4060 (gravel), then 1 mi to camp. Free.7-day limit during 30-day period at all regional campgrounds. 9 sites. Toilets, tbls, cfga, no drkg wtr. Boating, fishing, hiking. Hand boat launch. On Hoh River.

Hoh Oxbow   **FREE**
State Recreation Site
Olympic Experimental State Forest
Dept of Natural Resources
From between mileposts 176 and 177 S of Forks, go E off US 101 between rd and river. Free. 7-day limit during 30-day period at all regional campgrounds. 8 sites. Toilets, tbls, cfga, no drkg wtr. Hand boat launch, fishing. On Hoh River.

Hoh Rain Forest Campground   **$12**
Olympic National Park
14 mi S of Forks; 1.8 m N on Hoh River Bridge, 17.9 mi E on paved rd along Hoh River. Narrow, winding rds (watch out for logging trucks). $12. All year; 14-day limit. 88 sites (21-ft RV limit). Tbls, toilets, cfga, drkg wtr. Nature program, hiking trails, fishing. Roosevelt elk in vicinity of trails. Hoh River Trail (18 mi)leads to climb of Mount Olympus (highest peak in Olympic region). Ranger station provides information and backcountry use permits all year. Rd passes through one of the finest examples of rain forest. 35 acres.

Klahanie   **$5**
Olympic National Forest
5 mi E of US 101 via paved FR 29, on S fork of Calawa River. $5. All year; 14-day limit. 8 sites; 21-ft RV limit. Toilets, no drkg wtr, no trash service. Hiking, fishing.

Klahowya   **$12**
Olympic National Forest
20 mi NE of Forks on US 101. $10 base. Only sites 21-55 are free; sites 1-20 are $12. 55 sites (34 free); 30-ft RV limit. Tbls, flush toilets, cfga, drkg wtr. Fishing, boating(l), biking trails. 32 acres. On Soleduck River. Site name means "welcome" in Chinook.

Minnie Peterson   **FREE**
Bert Cole State Forest
Dept of Natural Resources
From between mileposts 178 & 179 S of Forks, go E off US 101 on Hoh Rain Forest Rd 5 mi. Camp on left. Free. All year; 7-day limit during 30-day period at all regional campgrounds. 8 sites; 1 picnic site. Tbls, toilets, cfga, no drkg wtr. Fishing. On Hoh River.

Mora Campground   **$12**
Olympic National Park
2 mi N of Forks on US 101; 12 mi W (rd to campground paved but narrow; open all year) on LaPush Rd, then Mora Rd. Follow signs. $12. All year; 14-day limit. 94 sites (21-ft RV limit). Tbls, flush toilets, cfga, drkg wtr, dump. Hiking, picnicking, fishing (salmon,

no license required in park); observation of sea and bird life; nature programs. Elev, sea level. Boat launch at public fishing access, 3 mi W. Hiking to Lake Ozette on the N. Wilderness Beach (18.5 mi), but check with ranger regarding tide tables, as some portions can be crossed only at low tide. 40 acres.

South Fork Hoh   **FREE**
State Recreation Site
Olympic Experimental State Forest
Dept of Natural Resources
From milepost 176 at US 101 S of Forks, E on Hoh Mainline Rd (paved) 6.6 mi, then left on H-1000 Rd (gravel, two lanes, then 1 lane) 7.4 mi. Camp on right. Free. All year; 7-day limit during 30-day period at all regional campgrounds. 3 sites. Tbls, toilets, cfga, no drkg wtr. On South Fork of Hoh River.

Upper Clearwater   **FREE**
State Recreation Site
Olympic Experimental State Forest
Dept of Natural Resources
From milepost 147 on US 101 S of Forks, 12.9 mi N on Hoh-Clearwater Mainline Rd (paved); right 3.2 mi on gravel, 1-lane C-3000 Rd to camp entrance on right. Free. All year; 7-day limit during 30-day period at all regional campgrounds. 9 sites. Toilets, no drkg wtr, tbls, cfga, shelter. Hand boat launch, fishing.

Willoughby Creek   **FREE**
State Recreation Site
Olympic Experimental State Forest
Dept of Natural Resources
From between mileposts 178 & 179 S of Forks, go E off US 101 on Hoh Rain Forest Rd 3.5 mi. Free. Camp on right. All year; 7-day limit during 30-day period at all regional campgrounds. 3 sites. Toilets, tbls, cfga, no drkg wtr. Fishing. On Hoh River. Rustic, small streamside sites.

FORT SPOKANE (43)

Detillon   **FREE**
Lake Roosevelt National Recreation Area
6 mi NE of Fort Spokane, BY BOAT. Free. All year; 14-day limit. 12 tent sites (no RVs). Tbls, toilets, cfga, drkg wtr, no trash service. Swimming; picnicking; fishing; boating(d). Along shore of Spokane River.

Enterprise   **FREE**
Lake Roosevelt National Recreation Area
10 mi N on Hwy 25; then by boat to site. Free. All year; 14-day limit. 13 primitive tent sites. Tbls, cfga, toilet, no wtr. Swimming, picnicking, fishing, boating. At Wilmont Creek.

GIFFORD (45)

Gifford Campground   **$10**
Lake Roosevelt Nat Recreation Area
2 mi S of Gifford on SR 25. $10 during 5/1-9/30; $5 rest of year. 42 sites (20-ft RV limit). Tbls, toilets, cfga, drkg wtr, dump. Boating,

fishing, swimming, waterskiing. On Franklin Roosevelt Lake. Flush toilets operate about 4/15-10/15.

GLACIER (46)

Hannegan Pass   **FREE**
Mt. Baker-Snoqualmie National Forest
12.4 mi E of Glacier on SR 542; 4 mi E on FR 32. Free. 5/15-9/15; 14-day limit. Undeveloped primitive camping area; toilet, cfga, no drkg wtr. Hiking, fishing. Trailhead to Mount Baker Wilderness. On Ruth Creek.

GLENWOOD (47)

Bird Creek   **FREE**
State Recreation Site
Dept of Natural Resources
W qtr mi from Glenwood post office to Bird Creek Rd. then 0.9 mi; turn left over cattle guard on Bird Creek Rd (K-3000) for 1.2 mi, then right on gravel S-4000 Rd for 1.3 mi; left on K-4000 rd, staying left for 2 mi. Free. All year; 14-day limit. 8 sites; 2 picnic sites. Toilets, tbls, cfga, no drkg wtr. E of Mt. Adams Wilderness Area.

Island Camp   **FREE**
State Recreation Site
Dept of Natural Resources
Follow directions to Bird Creek Recreation Site, but continue on K-3000 Rd 1.4 mi; left on K-4200 Rd for 1.1 mi; left qtr mi to camp. Free. All year; 14-day limit. 6 sites. Toilets, tbls, cfga, group shelter, no drkg wtr. Lava tubes, blow holes, stream. Snowmobiling, boatng, fishing. On Bird Creek.

GRAND COULEE (49)

Spring Canyon   **$10**
Lake Roosevelt National Recreation Area
3 mi E of Grand Coulee on SR 174. $10 during 5/1-9/30; $5 rest of year; 14-day limit. 87 sites; 26-ft RV limit. Tbls, flush & pit toilets, cfga, drkg wtr, fish cleaning station, dump. Swimming area, boating(dl), waterskiing fishing, nature trails, hiking trails. 7 acres.
Fishing tip: This is a good camp for bank fishing for smallmouth bass and rainbow trout. Try small spinners and bait such as nightcrawlers & marshmallows.

Steamboat Rock State Park   **$12**
12 mi S of Grand Coulee on Hwy 155; at N end of Banks Lake. $12 base. All year; 10-day limit; reservations available in summer. 44 primitive sites at Jones Bay (no wtr available); 36 primitive sites (no wtr) at Osborn Bay; 12 primitive boat-in sites with wtr. 100 utility sites ($23) with full hookups; 50-ft RV limit. Tbls, toilets, cfga, drkg wtr, dump, showers. Swimming, boating(lr), fishing, hiking trails, waterskiing; store; horse trails in nearby Northup Canyon. 3,523 acres.

GRANITE FALLS (50)

Beaver Plant Lake   **FREE**
Sultan-Pilchuck State Forest
Dept of Natural Resources
N from E side of Granite Falls on Mountain Loop Hwy (SR 92) 15.2 mi; right on FR 4020 Rd for 2.6 mi; right on FR 4021 Rd for 2 mi to West Bald Mountain and Ashland Lake Trailheads, then hike 2.1 mi to camp. Free. 6 tent sites. Tbls, toilets, cfga, no drkg wtr. Hiking trails.

Boardman Creek   **$12**
Mt. Baker-Snoqualmie National Forest
16.5 mi E of Granite Falls on CR 92/FR 7; 4 mi S on FR 3015; .5 mi S on Trail 704. $12 in 2007 & 2008 unless water becomes available; then fee will be $18. MD-LD; 14-day limit. 8 sites (no RV size limit). Tbls, toilets, cfga, no drkg wtr, no trash service. Picnicking; fishing. Elev 3100 ft; 3 acres.

Boardman Lake Dispersed   **$5**
Mt. Baker-Snoqualmie National Forest
15 mi NE of Granite Falls on CR 92/FR 7. Free with $30 annual NW forest pass; $5 daily otherwise. 6/1-10/31; 10-day limit. Undeveloped primitive sites; no facilities, no drkg wtr. Hiking, fishing, picnicking. 3 acres.

Chokwich Dispersed Camp
FREE
Mt. Baker-Snoqualmie National Forest
30.1 mi E of Granite Falls on CR 92/FR 7; 4.6 mi NE on FR 20. Free. 5/30-9/10; 14-day limit. Undeveloped primitive sites; no facilities. Picnicking, fishing.

Coal Lake Dispersed Camp   **$5**
Mt. Baker-Snoqualmie National Forest
25.5 mi E of Granite Falls on CR 92/FR 7; 4.4 mi N on FR 3006. Free with $30 annual NW forest pass; $5 daily otherwise. 6/1-10/1; 10-day limit. Undeveloped primitive sites; no facilities. Picnicking; fishing. Elev 2800 ft; 2 acres.

Cutthroat Lake   **FREE**
Sultan Pilchuck State Forest
Dept of Natural Resources
Hike 4.5 mile to campsite from East Bald Mountain Trailhead. To reach trailhead, from Granite Falls, 18 mi NE on SR 92; at Red Bridge Camp, S on FR 4030, following Mallardy Ridge signs; trailhead at end of rd. (Route from Sultan possible, but more complicated). Free. All year; 14-day limit. 10 tent sites; tbls, toilets, cfga, no drkg wtr. Ponds, hiking trails, good trout fishing.

Dicksperry Dispersed Camp
FREE
Mt. Baker-Snoqualmie National Forest
21.1 mi E of Granite Falls on CR 92/FR 7. Free. 5/30-9/10; 10-day limit. Undeveloped primitive area. No facilities. Hiking; swimming; picnicking; fishing; boating. Nature trails; geological.

Haps Hill Dispersed   **FREE**
Mt. Baker-Snoqualmie National Forest
30.5 mi E of Granite Falls on CR 92/FR 7; 2.5 mi S on co rd. Free. 6/15-10/31; 10-day limit. Undeveloped primitive sites; no facilities. Swimming; picnicking; fishing. Elev 2500 ft.

Lower Ashland Lake   **FREE**
Sultan-Pilchuck State Forest
Dept of Natural Resources
Hike 3 mi from Ashland Lakes Trailhead (see Beaver Plant entry). Free. 6 tent sites. Tbls, toilets, cfga, no drkg wtr. Hiking trails.

Monte Cristo   **FREE**
Mt. Baker-Snoqualmie National Forest
30.3 mi E of Granite Falls on CR 92/FR 7; 4.1 mi hike SE on FR 2963 (old Monte Cristo rd). Free. 5/15-9/30; 10-day limit. 8 undeveloped primitive tent sites; tbls, toilets, cfga, no drkg wtr. Mountain climbing; hiking; fishing. Elev 2800 ft; 2 acres. Stream. Scenic.

Mount Pilchuck   **$5**
Mt. Baker-Snoqualmie National Forest
12 mi E of Granite Falls on Mountain Loop Hwy; pass Verlot Public Services Center; right on Mount Pilchuck Rd (FR 42) for 6.9 mi. Free with $30 NW forest pass; $5 daily otherwise. All year; 14-day limit. 5 tent sites. Toilet, cfga, no drkg wtr.

Old Trail Dispersed   **FREE**
Mt. Baker-Snoqualmie National Forest
30.5 mi E on CR 92/FR 7. Free. 5/15-10/31; 10-day limit. Undeveloped primitive site; no facilities. Picnicking; fishing; swimming. Elev 1500 ft; 1 acre. River.

Perry Creek Dispersed   **$5**
Mt. Baker-Snoqualmie National Forest
16.1 mi E of Granite Falls on CR 92/FR 7. Free with $30 annual NW forest pass; $5 daily otherwise. 5/30-9/10; 10-day limit. Undeveloped primitive area; no facilities. Picnicking; fishing. Stream.

Red Bridge   **$12**
Mt. Baker-Snoqualmie National Forest
18.1 mi E on CR 92/FR 7. $12 in 2007 & 2008 unless water available; then fee will be $18. MD-LD or until closed by snow; 14-day limit. 16 sites (RVs under 32 ft). Tbls, toilets, cfga, no drkg wtr, no trash service. Picnicking, fishing. On South Fork of Stillaguamish River. 2-day minimum stay on weekends.

River Bar Dispersed   **FREE**
Mt. Baker-Snoqualmie National Forest
18 mi E of Granite Falls on CR 92/FR 7. Free. 5/30-9/30; 14-day limit. Undeveloped primitive sites; no facilities. Fishing.

Road Camp Dispersed   **FREE**
Mt. Baker-Snoqualmie National Forest
16.4 mi E of Granite Falls on CR 92/FR 7. Free. 5/1-10/1. Undeveloped primitive area; no facilities.

Sauk River Dispersed   **FREE**
Mt. Baker-Snoqualmie National Forest
30.5 mi E of Granite Falls on CR 92/FR 7; 4 mi S on co rd. Free. 6/110/31; 10-day limit. Undeveloped primitive sites; no facilities. Swimming; fishing; picnicking. Elev 2600 ft; 1 acre.

Silvertop Dispersed   **FREE**
Mt. Baker-Snoqualmie National Forest
30.5 mi E of Granite Falls on CR 92/FR 7; 2.7 mi S on co rd. Free. 6/1-10/31; 10-day limit. Undeveloped primitive sites; no facilities. Picnicking; swimming; fishing. Elev 2500 ft; 1 acre. Stream.

Sloan Creek Dispersed   **FREE**
Mt. Baker-Snoqualmie National Forest
30.1 mi E on CR 92/FR 7; 7 mi NE on FR 20; 6.6 mi SE on FR 49. Free. 6/1-10/31; 10-day limit. Undeveloped primitive sites; no facilities, no drkg wtr. Fishing.

South Fork Dispersed   **FREE**
Mt. Baker-Snoqualmie National Forest
30.1 mi E of Granite Falls on CR 92/FR 7; 4.4 mi NE on FR 20. Free. 5/30-9/10; 14-day limit. Undeveloped primitive sites; no facilities. Fishing, picnicking.

Twin Falls Lake   **FREE**
Sultan-Pilchuck State Forest
Dept. of Natural Resources
Hike 4.5 mi from Ashland Lakes Trailhead (see Beaver Plant entry). Free. 5 tent sites. Tbls, toilets, cfga, no drkg wtr. Hiking trails, trout fishing. Secluded.

Upper Ashland Lake   **FREE**
Sultan-Pilchuck State Forest
Dept. of Natural Resources
Hike 2.5 mi from Ashland Lakes Trailhead (see Beaver Plant entry). Free. 6 tent sites. Tbls, toilets, cfga, no drkg wtr. Hiking trails, fishing.

Twin Bridges Dispersed   **FREE**
Mt. Baker-Snoqualmie National Forest
30.3 mi E of Granite Falls on CR 92/FR 7; 1.1 mi S on FR 2963. Free. 6/1-9/10; 14-day limit. Undeveloped primitive area; no facilities. Fishing; picnicking. River.

White Deer Dispersed   **FREE**
Mount Baker-Snoqualmie National Forest
30.5 mi E of Granite Falls on CR 92/FR 7; 3 mi N on FR 322. Free. 5/30-10/31; 10-day limit. Undeveloped primitive area. No facilities. Swimming; picnicking; fishing.

GREENBANK (51)

Rhododendron   **FREE**
State Recreation Site
Dept. of Natural Resources
9.1 mi N of Greenbank to jct of WA 525 and 20; watch for "Rhododendron Park" sign, follow narrow entrance rd (not labeled). On Whidby Island. (Narrow, rough access). Free.

6 sites (pull-through spaces). Tbls, toilets, cfga, drkg wtr. 4 picnic sites. Scenic.

GRISDALE (52)

Wynoochee Falls   **FREE**
Dispersed Camping
Olympic National Forest
8 mi N of Wynoochee Lake on FR 2312; hike to camp; no motor vehicle access. 5/1-9/30; 14-day limit. 12 primitive hike-in tent sites behind wildlife gate. Toilets, cfga, no drkg wtr. Hunting, fishing, hiking. At Wynoochee River.

HOME (53)

Joemma Beach State Park   **$12**
1.3 mi S of Home on Longbranch Rd; right on Whiteman Rd for 2.3 mi; right on Bay Rd for 1 mi; at SE Kay Peninsula. $12 for 19 primitive tent sites; $12 for boat-in and 2 hiker/biker sites. All year; 10-day limit. Tbls, toilets, cfga, drkg wtr. Boating(ld), fishing, crabbing. 122 acres.

HOODSPORT (54)

Big Creek   **$10**
Olympic National Forest
9 mi NW of Hoodsport on SR 119; .1 mi W on FR 24. $10. 5/15-9/15; 14-day limit. 25 sites (30-ft RV limit). Tbls, toilets, cfga, drkg wtr, dump, handicap facilities. Swimming nearby, boating (l), hiking trails, fishing. Near Lake Cushman. 30 acres.

Elk Lake   **$5**
Olympic National Forest
Hwy 101 to FR 24 10 mi N of Hoodsport; 1.25 mi to FR 2480; 5.5 mi to FR 2401; 2.5 mi to lake. Camp free with $30 annual NW forest pass; $5 daily otherwise. All year; 14-day limit. Primitive undeveloped camping area. One toilet. Hiking, fishing.

Jefferson Lake   **$5**
Olympic National Forest
10 mi N of Hoodsport on Hwy 101; 1.25 mi on FR 24; 5.5 mi on FR 2480; 3.5 mi W of Elk Lake on FR 2401. Camp free with $30 annual NW forest pass; $5 daily otherwise. All year; 14-day limit. Primitive undeveloped camping area. No facilities. Hiking, fishing.

Lilliwaup Creek   **FREE**
State Recreation Site
Hood Canal State Forests
Dept of Natural Resources
11 mi N of Hoodsport on US 101; 5.5 mi W on Jorsted Creek Rd (FR 24); left on 1-lane gravel rd for 6.6 mi. Free. 5/15-9/15 & during first week of rifle deer season. 6 sites. Tbls, cfga, drkg wtr, toilets. Fishing.

Melbourne   **FREE**
State Recreation Site
Hood Canal State Forests
Dept. of Natural Resources
N on US 101 from Hoodsport to Jorsted Creek Rd (FR 24), then W 5.5 mi; left 1.8 mi on gravel, 1-lane rd. Keep left 0.7 mi to camp. Free. 4/23-9/15; 14-day limit. 6 sites. Toilets, cfga, tbls, no drkg wtr. On Melbourne Lake, near Lake Cushman.

Staircase   **$12**
Olympic National Park
16 mi NW of Hoodsport on Skokomish River Rd. $12. All year; 14-day limit. 56 sites (21-ft RV limit) Flush toilets, cfga, drkg wtr, tbls. Hiking trails, fishing. On Staircase Rapids on North Fork, Skokomish River near Lake Cushman. Trails to backcountry. Camp was closed early in 2007 due to forest fire.

HOPE (BRITISH COLUMBIA) (55)

Hozomeen   **FREE**
Ross Lake Nat. Recreation Area
North Cascade National Park
2 mi W of Hope and 39 mi S on Silver Skagit Rd. Free. 6/15-9/1; 14-day limit. 122 sites (22-ft RV limit). Tbls, toilets, cfga, drkg wtr. Swimming, fishing, boating(l), hiking.

HOQUIAM (56)

Graves Creek   **$12**
Olympic National Park
39 mi N of Hoquiam; 18.6 mi on Quinault River Valley Rd (S Shore Lake Quinault Rd); 1st 7 mi paved, then gravel rd (gravel portion may be closed in winter by snow; narrow). $12. All year; 14-day limit. 30 sites (21-ft RV limit). Tbls, toilets, cfga, drkg wtr. Fishing (no license required in park), boating, swimming, picnicking, hiking. Trails. Rd passes through town of Quinault and US Forest Service Lake Quinault Recreation Area; rd winds up valley to a dense stand of rain forest that begins beyond point where Quinault river branches.

July Creek   **$12**
Walk-In Camp
Olympic National Park
41 mi N of Hoquiam on US 101; 3.9 mi on paved rd. $12. All year; 14-day limit. 29 tent sites. Tbls, toilets, cfga, drkg wtr. Hiking, fishing (Washington State license and Indian reservation fisher permit required). Rain forest beyond upper level of Lake Quinault. 1.9-mi Quinault Ranger Station provides info and backcountry permits.

North Fork Campground   **$10**
Olympic National Park
41 mi N of Hoquiam on US 101; 18.2 mi on paved and gravel rd (paved first 8 mi; closed in winter by snow; not suitable for large RVs). $10. All year; 14-day limit. 7 sites (RVs under 22 ft). Toilets, cfga, no wtr. Hiking; fishing (WA State license and Indian Reservation Fishing Permit required). Park entrance fee $15 for 7 days. Rain forest beyond upper level of Lake Quinault.

HUMPTULIPS (57)

Campbell Tree Grove   **FREE**
Olympic National Forest
8 mi N of Humptulips FR 22; 14 mi N on FR 2204; on W. Fork of Humptulips Rd. Free. MD-12/15; 14-day limit. 11 sites (16-ft RV limit). Toilets, tbls, cfga, drkg wtr. Fishing, hiking, hunting, berry-picking.

HUNTER (58)

Hunters Park   **$10**
Lake Roosevelt National Recreation Area
2 mi E of Hunter on access rd from SR 225. $10 during 5/1-9/30; $5 rest of year; 14 day limit. 39 sites (26-ft RV limit). Tbls, flush toilets, cfga, drkg wtr, dump, outside shower station. Boating(ld), fishing, swimming, waterskiing. 12 acres on Franklin Roosevelt Lake.

IONE (60)

Edgewater   **$12**
Colville National Forest
1 mi S of Ione on SR 31; qtr mi E on CR 9345; 2 mi N on CR 3669. 5/15-9/30; 14-day limit. Free from LD until access rd closed; $12 about MD-LD. 20 sites (24-ft RV limit). Toilets, cfga, drkg wtr, tbls. Boating(l), fishing, waterskiing. Pend Oreille River.

Lake Gillette   **$12**
Colville National Forest
S of Ione on Hwy 31 to Tiger; 11 mi SW on Hwy 20; half mi E on CR 200; on shore of Lake Gillette. $12. 5/15-9/15; 14-day limit. 14 sites (32-ft RV limit). Tbls, toilets, cfga, drkg wtr, dump. Handicap facilities. Fishing, boating(l), hiking.

Lake Leo   **$12**
Colville National Forest
S of Ione on Hwy 31 to Tiger; 7 mi SW on Hwy 20. $12. 5/15-9/15; 14-day limit. 8 sites (16-ft RV limit). Tbls, toilets, cfga, drkg wtr. Boating(l), fishing, hiking.

Lake Thomas   **$12**
Colville National Forest
S of Ione on Hwy 31 to Tiger; 11 mi SW on Hwy 20; 1 mi E on CR 200. $12. 5/15-9/15; 14-day limit. 16 sites (16-ft RV limit). Tbls, toilets, cfga, drkg wtr. Swimming, biking, boating, fishing, waterskiing, hiking trails. Store. Elev 3200 ft; 7 acres.

Noisy Creek   **$12**
Colville National Forest
Half mi S of Ione on Hwy 31; 9 mi NE on Sullivan Lake Rd (CR 9345); at S end of Sullivan Lake. $12. 5/12-9/24 (reduced services & no trash pickup after 9/10). Primitive overflow meadow open all year; no fee, no services. 14-day limit. 19 sites. Tbls, toilets, cfga, drkg wtr. Swimming area, boating(l), trailhead for Lakeshore Trail. Elev 2600 ft; 8 acres.

KAHLOTUS (61)

Devils Bench   **FREE**
Corps of Engineers
Lake Herbert G. West
6 mi S of Kahlotus on Devils Canyon Rd. Free. All year; 14-day limit. Primitive undesignated sites. Toilets, cfga, no drkg wtr. Fishing, boating(ld).

KETTLE FALLS (64)

Canyon Creek   **$6**
Colville National Forest
3.5 mi NW of Kettle Falls on US 395; 11 mi W on WA 20; quarter mi S on FR 136. $6. 5/25-10/30; 14-day limit. 12 sites (RVs under 32 ft). Tbls, toilets, cfga, firewood, no drkg wtr. Picnicking; hiking; fishing. Elev 2200 ft; 5 acres. Interpretive center nearby.

Cloverleaf Camp   **$10**
Lake Roosevelt National Recreation Area
.8 mi W of Kettle Falls; 23 mi S on WA 25 (2 mi S of Gifford). $10 during 5/1-9/30; $5 rest of year; 14-day limit. 9 shaded tent sites (parking area for RVs). Tbls, toilets, cfga, changing house, drkg wtr. Boating(ld); waterskiing; picnicking; fishing; hunting. Roosevelt Lake. Sandy beach. Sheltered bay roped off for swimming (floating raft).

Colville River   **FREE**
Lake Roosevelt National Recreation Area
.8 mi W of Kettle Falls on US 395; 3.7 mi S on WA 25. Access rd is unmarked; watch on right for gravel rd located just before white guard rail. Rough, narrow, steep, but short (approx 200 yards) access rd. Free. All year; 14-day limit. Undesignated sites; room for 10 RVs. No facilities. Hunting; fishing (in Roosevelt Lake). Large area amidst a grove of evergreens.

Evans   **$10**
Lake Roosevelt National Recreation Area
1 mi S of Evans on SR 25; on Roosevelt Lake. $10 during 5/1-9/30; $5 rest of year; 14-day limit. 43 sites (26-ft RV limit). Tbls, flush toilets, cfga, drkg wtr, dump. Boating(l), fishing, hiking, swimming, waterskiing. 16 acres.

Haag Cove   **$10**
Lake Roosevelt National Recreation Area
12 mi W of Kettle Falls on CR 3. $10 during 5/1-9/30; $5 rest of year; 14-day limit. 16 sites (RVs under 26 ft). Tbls, toilets, cfga, drkg wtr. Boating(d); swimming; picnicking; fishing.

Kamloops   **$10**
Lake Roosevelt National Recreation Area
7 mi W of Kettle Falls; N on US 395 (where Kettle River enters Roosevelt Lake). $10 during 5/1-9/30; $5 rest of year; 14-day limit. 17 tent sites (no RVs). Tbls, toilets, cfga, drkg wtr. Swimming; hunting; picnicking; fishing; boating(d). Raft. Caution: deep wtr. At Kamloops Island.

Kettle Falls   **$10**
Lake Roosevelt National Recreation Area
3 mi W of Kettle Falls on US 395. $10 during 5/1-9/30; $5 rest of year; 14-day limit. 76 sites; 26-ft RV limit Tbls, flush toilets, cfga, drkg wtr, dump. Playground, fishing, boating(ld), swimming, waterskiing. 22 acres.

Kettle River   **$10**
Lake Roosevelt National Recreation Area
13 mi NW of Kettle Falls, on US 395. $10 during 5/1-9/30; $5 rest of year; 14-day limit. 13 sites. Tbls, flush toilets, cfga, drkg wtr, marina, store. Fishing, swimming area, picnicking.

Lake Ellen   **$6**
Colville National Forest
3.5 mi NW of Kettle Falls on US 395; 4 mi S on WA 20; 4.5 mi SW on CR 3; 5.5 mi SW on FR 412/2014. $10. 5/25-10/30; 14-day limit. 15 sites on 4 acres (RVs under 22 ft). Tbls, toilets, cfga, firewood, no drkg wtr. Fishing; picnicking; boating(ld), swimming.

Marcus Island   **$10**
Lake Roosevelt National Recreation Area
4 mi N of Kettle Falls, on WA 25. $10 during 5/1-9/30; $5 rest of year; 14-day limit. 27 sites (RVs under 20 ft). Tbls, pit toilets, cfga, drkg wtr. Store nearby. Swimming; picnicking; fishing, boating(d). On Roosevelt Lake.

North Gorge   **$10**
Lake Roosevelt National Recreation Area
20 mi N of Kettle Falls on WA 25. $10 during 5/1-9/30; $5 rest of year; 14-day limit. 12 sites. Tbls, toilets, cfga, drkg wtr. Picnicking; fishing; boating(ld), waterskiing. On Franklin Roosevelt Lake.

Sherman Creek   **FREE**
Lake Roosevelt National Recreation Area
3 mi S of Kettle Falls on Hwy 20. ACCESSIBLE BY BOAT ONLY. Free. All year; 14-day limit. 6 primitive tent sites. Tbls, toilets, cfga, drkg wtr. Fishing, boating, picnicking. In Sherman Creek Wild-life Habitat Management Area.

Snag Cove   **$10**
Lake Roosevelt National Recreation Area
7 mi N of Kettle Falls on US 395; right on Northpoint-Flat Creek Rd for 7.5 mi. $10 during 5/1-9/30; $5 rest of year; 14-day limit. 9 sites. Tbls, toilets, cfga, drkg wtr. Boating(ld), fishing.

Trout Lake   **FREE**
Colville National Forest
3.5 mi NW of Kettle Falls on US 395; 5.5 mi W on SR 20; 5 mi N on FR 020. Free. 5/25-10/30; 14-day limit. 4 sites. Tbls, toilets, cfga, no drkg wtr. Boating, swimming, fishing.

LANGLEY (65)

Island County Fairgrounds   **$10**
Near downtown Langley at 819 Camano Ave. $10 without hookups; $15 with hookups. All year except during fair, about 8/10-8/25. 45 sites. Flush toilets, showers, elec/wtr($), no dump.

LEAVENWORTH (66)

Alder Creek Horse Camp   **FREE**
Wenatchee National Forest
15.9 mi NW of Leavenworth on US 2; 4 mi N on SR 207; 1 mi E on CR 22; right on FR 62 past Fish Lake to camp. Free. 5/1-10/15; 14-day limit. Group camp for horsemen. Tbls, toilets, cfga, no drkg wtr, no trash service. Horseback riding, hiking, fishing.

Alpine Meadows   **$7**
Wenatchee National Forest
15.9 mi NW of Leavenworth on US 2; 4 mi N on SR 207; 1 mi E on CR 22; 19 mi NW on Chiwawa River Rd 6200. $7. 6/15-10/15; 14-day limit. 4 sites; 20-ft RV limit. Tbls, toilets, cfga, no drkg wtr. Fishing, hiking.

Atkinson Flat   **$7**
Wenatchee National Forest
15.9 mi NW of Leavenworth on US 2; 4 mi N on WA 207; 1 mi E on CR 22; 15 mi NW on FR 6100/62/311(Chiwawa River Rd). $7. 6/15-10/15; 14-day limit. 7 sites on 1 acre (RVs under 31 ft). Tbls, toilets, cfga, firewood, no drkg wtr. River. Mountain climbing; picnicking; fishing.

Blackpine Creek Horse Camp   **$11**
Wenatchee National Forest
Half mi SE of Leavenworth on US 2; 2.9 mi S on CR 71; 15 mi NW on Icicle Rd. $11 during 5/15-10/30; free rest of year; 14-day limit. 10 sites; 60-ft RV limit. Tbls, toilets, cfga, drkg wtr (no wtr or trash service during free period), horse facilities. Trailhead into Alpine Lakes Wilderness. Horse trails, fishing. At Black Pine Creek near Icicle Creek.

Bridge Creek   **$12**
Wenatchee National Forest
Half mi SE of Leavenworth on US 2; 2.9 mi S on CR 71; 5.5 mi NW on FR 7600 (Icicle Rd). $12 during 4/15-10/31; free rest of year but no wtr or trash service; 14-day limit. 6 sites (19-ft RV limit). Tbls, toilets, cfga, drkg wtr. Fishing, hiking, picnicking. Along Icicle Creek & Bridge Creek.

Chatter Creek   **$12**
Wenatchee National Forest
Half mi SE of Leavenworth on US 2; 2.9 mi S on CR 71; 12.5 mi NW on FR 7600 (Icicle Rd). $12 during 5/1-10/31; free rest of year; 14-day limit. 12 sites (22-ft RV limit). Tbls, toilets, cfga, drkg wtr. Fishing, hiking. Along the Icicle and Chatter Creeks.

Chiwawa Horse Camp   **$7**
Wenatchee National Forest
15.9 mi NW of Leavenworth on US 2; 4 mi N on WA 207; 1 mi E on CR 22; 13 mi NW on FR 6100/62/311 (Chiwawa River Rd). $7. 5/1-10/15; 14-day limit. 21 sites (pull-through spurs). Tbls, toilets, cfga, drkg wtr, horse facilities. Hiking, fishing, horseback riding.

Deep Creek   **FREE**
Wenatchee National Forest
15.9 mi NW of Leavenworth on US 2; about 4 mi N on SR 207; right at state park toward Midway; left on FR 6100 for 4 mi; 2 mi SE on FR 6200. Free. 5/1-10/1; 14-day limit. 3 sites (30-ft RV limit). Tbls, toilets, cfga, no drkg wtr, no trash service. Hiking, fishing.

Deer Camp   **FREE**
Wenatchee National Forest
15.9 mi NW of Leavenworth on US 2; about 4 mi N on SR 207; right at state park toward Midway; left on FR 6100 for 4 mi; 2 mi SE on FR 6200; left for 2 mi on FR 2722. Free. 5/1-10/1; 14-day limit. 3 sites (30-ft RV limit). Tbls, toilets, cfga, firewood, no drkg wtr. Picnicking. 1 acre.

Eightmile   **$6.50**
Wenatchee National Forest
Half mi SE of Leavenworth on US 2; 2.9 mi S on CR 71; 4 mi NW on FR 7600 (Icicle Rd). $6.50 with federal Senior Pass; others pay $13 during 4/15-10/31; free walk-in camping rest of year, but no wtr or trash service; 14-day limit. 45 sites (50-ft RV limit). Tbls, toilets, cfga, drkg wtr. Fishing, hiking, picnicking. Along Icicle & Eightmile Creeks.

Finner Creek   **$7**
Wenatchee National Forest
15.9 mi NW of Leavenworth on US 2; 4 mi N on WA 207; 1 mi E on CR 22; 11.5 mi NW on FR 6100/62/311 (Chiwawa River Rd). $7. 5/1-10/15; 14-day limit. 3 sites (30-ft RV limit). Tbls, toilets, cfga, drkg wtr, no trash service Fishing, hiking. Along Chiwawa River next to Rock Creek Guard Station.

Glacier View   **$12**
Wenatchee National Forest
20 mi N of Leavenworth on US 2 to Coles Corner; 3.5 mi N on SR 207; 1.5 mi W on CR 290; on SW shore of Lake Wenatchee. $12 during 5/1-10/15; free rest of yr, but no wtr or trash service; 14-day limit. 23 sites (30-ft RV limit), including 16 walk-in tent sites on lake shore. Tbls, toilets, cfga, drkg wtr. Boating(l - $4), fishing, swimming, waterskiing, hiking.

Goose Creek   **$7**
Wenatchee National Forest
Quarter mi E of Leavenworth on US 2; 17.5 mi N on WA 209; 3.2 mi N on FR 2746. (Icicle Rd). $7 during 5/1-10/15; free rest of yr, but no wtr or trash service; 14-day limit. 29 sites on 2 acres (no RV size limit). Tbls, toilets, cfga, firewood, drkg wtr. Fishing; picnicking. Stream. Motorcycle trail access.

Grasshopper Meadows   **FREE**
Wenatchee National Forest
15.9 mi NW of Leavenworth on US 2; 10.5 mi N on WA 207; 8 mi NW on FR 6400 (White River Rd). Free. 5/1-10/31; 14-day limit. 5 sites (30-ft RV limit). Tbls, toilets, cfga, firewood, no drkg wtr. Berry picking; picnicking; fishing. Elev 2000 ft; 2 acres. River.

Ida Creek   **$12**
Wenatchee National Forest
Half mi SE of Leavenworth on US 2; 2.9 mi S on CR 71; 10 mi NW on FR 7600 (Icicle Rd). $12 during 5/1-10/30; free rest of year, but no wtr or trash service; 14-day limit. 10 sites; 30-ft RV limit. Tbls, toilets, cfga, drkg wtr. Fishing, hiking. Handicap toilets.

Johnny Creek   **$12**
Wenatchee National Forest
Half mi SE of Leavenworth on US 2; 2.9 mi S on CR 71; 8 mi NW on FR 7600 (Icicle Rd). $12 during 5/1-10/15; free rest of year; 14-day limit. 65 sites; 50-ft RV limit. Tbls, toilets, cfga, drkg wtr. Fishing, hiking, picnicking. Handicap toilets.

Lake Creek   **FREE**
Wenatchee National Forest
15.9 mi NW of Leavenworth of US 2; 8.4 mi N on Hwy 207; 10.5 mi W on FR 6500/6504. Free. 5/1-11/1; 14-day limit. 8 sites. Tbls, toilets, cfga, no drkg wtr. Fishing, berry-picking.

Little Wenatchee Ford   **FREE**
Wenatchee National Forest
15.9 mi NW of Leavenworth of US 2; 8.4 mi N on Hwy 207; 15.5 mi W on FR 6500/6504. Free. 5/1-11/1; 14-day limit. 3 small sites (tents, tent campers or pickup campers). Tbls, toilets, cfga, no drkg wtr, no trash service. Hiking.

Meadow Creek   **FREE**
Wenatchee National Forest
15.9 mi NW of Leavenworth on US 2; 4 mi NE on WA 207; 1 mi E on CR 22; 2.4 mi NE on FR 6100/62/311; 2.1 mi NW on FR 2815. Free. 5/1-10/31; 14-day limit. 4 sites (30-ft RV limit); 1 acre. Tbls, toilets, cfga, firewood, no drkg wtr. Fishing; picnicking. River.

Napeequa   **FREE**
Wenatchee National Forest
15.9 mi NW of Leavenworth on US 2; 10.5 mi N on WA 207; 5 mi NW on FR 6400 (White River Rd). Free. 5/1-10/31; 14-day limit. 5 sites (RVs under 32 ft). Tbls, toilets, cfga, no drkg wtr. Hiking; berry picking; picnicking; fishing. User operated. Elev 2000 ft; 2 acres. Entrance to Glacier Peak Wilderness. Twin Lakes Trail.

Nason Creek   **$7**
Wenatchee National Forest
20 mi N of Leavenworth on US 2 to Coles Corner; 3.5 mi N on SR 207; qtr mi W on CR 290; on Nason Creek near Lake Wenatchee. $7 with federal Senior Pass; others pay $14.

5/1-10/15; 14-day limit. 73 sites. Tbls, flush toilets, cfga, drkg wtr. Elec outlets in restrooms. Boating, fishing, dump, coin laundry.

Nineteen Mile   **$7**
Wenatchee National Forest
15.9 mi NW of Leavenworth on US 2; 4 mi N on WA 207; 1 mi E on CR 22; 18 mi NW on FR 6100/62/311(Chiwawa River Rd). $7. 6/15-10/15; 14-day limit. 4 sites (30-ft RV limit). Tbls, toilets, cfga, no drkg wtr, no trash service. Fishing, hiking. Chiwawa River.

Phelps Creek   **$7**
Wenatchee National Forest
15.9 mi NW on US 2; 4 mi N on WA 207; 1 mi E on CR 22; 21 mi NW on FR 6100/62/311. Camp free with $7. 6/1-10/15; 14-day limit. 7 sites plus 6 sites in equestrian section; 30-ft RV limit. Tbls, toilets, cfga, firewood, horse unloading ramp, corral, parking, no drkg wtr. Mountain climbing; picnicking; fishing; horseback riding. Elev 2800 ft; 4 acres. River. Entrance to Glacier Peak Wilderness. Pets. Corral, horse unloading ramp, parking.

Riverbend Campground   **$7**
Wenatchee National Forest
15.9 mi NW of Leavenworth on US 2; 4 mi N on WA 207; 1 mi E on CR 22; 12 mi NW on FR 6100/62/311. $7. 6 sites (30-ft RV limit). Tbls, toilets, cfga, no drkg wtr, no trash service. Hiking, fishing. Chiwawa River.

Rock Creek   **$7**
Wenatchee National Forest
15.9 mi NW of Leavenworth on US 2; 4 mi N on WA 207; 1 mi E on CR 22; 12.5 mi NW on FR 6100/62/311 (Chiwawa River Rd); next to Chiwawa Horse Camp. $7. 5/1-11/1; 14-day limit. 4 sites (30-ft RV limit). Tbls, toilets, cfga, no drkg wtr, no trash service. Fishing, hiking.

Rock Island   **$12**
Wenatchee National Forest
Half mi SW of Leavenworth on US 2; 3 mi S on CR 71; 13.3 mi NW on FR 7600. $12 during 5/1-10/31; free rest of year; 14-day limit. 10 RV sites (22-ft limit); 12 tent sites. Tbls, toilets, cfga, drkg wtr. Fishing, hiking trails, berry-picking. On Icicle Creek. Elev 2900 ft; 10 acres. Handicap toilets.

Schaefer Creek   **$7**
Wenatchee National Forest
15.9 mi NW on US 2; 4 mi N on WA 207; 1 mi N on CR 22; 14 mi NW on FR 6100/62/311 (Chiwawa River Rd). $7. 5/1-10/115; 14-day limit. 10 sites (30-ft RV limit); 1 acre. Tbls, toilets, cfga, firewood, no drkg wtr. River. Fishing; picnicking.

Soda Springs   **FREE**
Wenatchee National Forest
15.9 mi NW of Leavenworth of US 2; 8.4 mi N on Hwy 207; 7.5 mi W on FR 6500. Free. 5/1-11/1; 14-day limit. 5 sites. Tbls, toilets, cfga, firewood, no drkg wtr. Hiking; picnicking; fishing; berry picking. User operated.

Elev 2000 ft; 2 acres. Stream. Nature trails. Soda spring on site. Little Wenatchee River. No trailer turnaround.

Theseus Creek FREE
Wenatchee National Forest
15 mi NW of Leavenworth on US 2; 8.4 mi NW on WA 207; 10 mi W on FR 6500. Free. 5/1-10/31; 14-day limit. 3 sites on 1 acre (RVs under 31 ft). Tbls, toilets, cfga, firewood, no drkg wtr. Fishing; picnicking.

Tumwater $7
Wenatchee National Forest
10 mi NW of Leavenworth on US 2. $7 with federal Senior Pass; others pay $14. MD-10/15; 14-day limit. 84 sites; 50-ft RV limit. Tbls, flush toilets, cfga, drkg wtr. Fishing; picnicking, hiking. Handicap access.

White Pine FREE
Wenatchee National Forest
24.9 mi NW of Leavenworth on US 2; half mi W on FR 266. Free. 5/1-10/31; 14-day limit. 5 RV/tent sites on 2 acres. Tbls, toilets, cfga, firewood, no drkg wtr. Store/gas (1 mi). Berry picking; picnicking; fishing; horseback riding (1 mi).

White River Falls FREE
Wenatchee National Forest
15.9 mi NW of Leavenworth on US 2; 10.5 mi N on WA 207; 9 mi NW on FR 6400 (White River Rd). Free. 5/1-10/31; 14-day limit. 5 tent sites (no trailer turnaround). Tbls, toilets, cfga, firewood, no drkg wtr. Berry picking; picnicking; fishing; hiking; user operated. Elev 2100 ft; 2 acres. River. Entrance to Glacier Park Wilderness.

LEWISTON (IDAHO) (67)

Blyton Landing FREE
Corps of Engineers
Lower Granite Lake
20 mi W of Lewiston on CR 9000 (North Shore Snake River Rd). Free. All year; 14-day limit. Primitive undesignated sites. Tbls, toilets, cfga, no drkg wtr. Boating(ld), fishing.

Fishing tip: Lower Granite is a good smallmouth bass lake, but fishing in the Snake River above the pool is quite often better. Try slowly retrieved jigs.

Nisqually John Landing FREE
Corps of Engineers
Lower Granite Lake
15 mi W of Lewiston on CR 9000. Free. All year; 14-day limit. Primitive undesignated sites. Tbls, toilets, cfga, no drkg wtr. Boating(ld), fishing.

Wawawai Landing FREE
Corps of Engineers
Lower Granite Lake
28 mi W of Lewiston on N shore of Snake River Rd. Or 19 mi SW of Pullman, WA, on Wawai Rd. Free. All year; 14-day limit. 9 sites; 24-ft RV limit. Tbls, toilets, cfga, no

drkg wtr, playground. Volleyball, hiking trails, fishing, boating(ld). 68 acres.

LITTLEROCK (68)

Fall Creek Recreation Site FREE
Capitol State Forest
Dept of Natural Resources
NW of Littlerock on Waddell Creek Rd; turn right for 1.4 mi, then left fork (C-Line Rd) about 2 mi; turn left onto C-4000 Rd for 2.5 mi, then right after qtr mi to camp; on Fall Creek. 4/1-10/31; 14-day limit. 8 sites. Drkg wtr, toilets, cfga, horse facilities, no trash service. Fishing; picnicking; 80 mi of horse, hiking, mountain biking trails. Facilities accommodate handicapped.

Margaret McKenny FREE
Capitol State Forest
Dept of Natural Resources
3 mi NW of Littlerock along Waddell Creek Rd. Free. 4/1-10/31; 14-day limit. 25 sites. Toilets, tbls, cfga, drkg wtr. Horse ramp. Hiking trails, picnicking, fishing; 80 mi of horse trails, mountain biking. Mima Mounds nearby. This campground is subject to being closed due to funding.

Middle Waddell FREE
Capitol State Forest
Dept of Natural Resources
4.2 mi NW of Littlerock along Waddell Creek Rd. Free. 4/1-10/31; 14-day limit. 24 sites. Toilets, tbls, cfga, drkg wtr. Motorcycle, mountain biking, horse and hiking trails, fishing. On Waddell Creek. Subject to closing due to funding.

Mima Falls Trailhead FREE
Capitol State Forest
Dept of Natural Resources
1 mi NW of Littlerock on Waddell Creek Rd; turn left on Mima Rd for 1.3 mi; turn right on Bordeaux Rd for .7 mi; right on Marksman Rd about .9 mi; turn left qtr mi to site. Free. 4/1-10/31; 14-day limit. 5 sites. Toilets, tbls, drkg wtr, no trash service. Horse ramp. Horse trails, mountain biking, hiking trails; trail to scenic Mima Falls. Subject to closing due to funding.

Mount Molly FREE
Capitol State Forest
Dept of Natural Resources
NW of Littlerock on Waddell Creek Rd; turn left for 1.4 mi; take left fork (C-Line Rd) about 1 mi. Free. All year; 14-day limit. 10 sites. Toilets, cfga, tbls, no drkg wtr. Motorcycle trails.

LOOMIS (69)

Chopaka Lake FREE
State Recreation Site
Loomis State Forest
Dept of Natural Resources
2.1 mi N from Loomis grocery on Loomis-Oroville Rd (CR 9425); left on Toats Coulee

Rd for 1.4 mi; right onto steep one-lane rd for 3.4 mi; stay left for 1.7 mi; turn right 2 mi to camp. On Chopaka Lake. All year; 14-day limit. 16 sites. Toilets, cfga, drkg wtr, tbls, fishing platform. Fishing; boating(l). Accommodates the handicapped.

Fishing tip: Fly fishing only at this lake. Fishing is often quite slow. Best bet is to use a small boat or float tube. The lake also contains smallmouth bass.

Cold Springs FREE
State Recreation Site
Loomis State Forest
Dept of Natural Resources
2.1 mi N from Loomis grocery on Loomis-Oroville Rd (CR 9425); left on Toats Coulee Rd for 5.6 mi to upper Toats Coulee Camp; then OM-T-1000 Rd 2.1 mi; turn right on Cold Creek Rd (gravel) for half mi; stay right; go 1.8 mi; stay left; go 2.3 mi to picnic area then half mi to camp. Free. All year; 14-day limit. 5 sites, 2 picnic sites. Toilets, tbls, cfga, no drkg wtr. Horse facilities. Hiking trails, horse trails, mountain biking.

Long Swamp $5
Okanogan National Forest
2.1 mi N of Loomis on Loomis-Oroville Rd (CR 9425); 21 mi N & W on CR 4066 & FR 39. All year; 14-day limit. Free with $30 annual NW forest pass; $5 daily otherwise. 2 sites; 1 acre. Tbls, toilets, cfga, no drkg wtr. No trash service in winter. Stream. Picnicking, hiking & horse trails. Trailhead. Adopted & maintained by the Backcountry Horsemen. Elev 5500 ft. Closed early in 2007 due to 2006 fire.

North Fork Nine Mile FREE
Loomis State Forest
Dept of Natural Resources
2.1 mi N from Loomis grocery on Loomis-Oroville Rd (CR 9425); left on Toats Coulee Rd for 5.6 mi to upper Toats Coulee Camp; then OM-T-1000 Rd 2.5 mi. Free. 11 sites, 3 picnic sites. Tbls, toilets, cfga, drkg wtr.

Palmer Lake FREE
State Recreation Site
Loomis State Forest
Dept of Natural Resources
8.5 mi N from Loomis grocery (keep right) on Loomis-Oroville Rd (CR 9425); on N shore of Palmer Lake. Free. All year; 14-day limit. 6 lakeside sites. Toilets, tbls, cfga, no drkg wtr. Fishing, hiking, boating (hand launch), picnicking, rockhounding, beach access. View cougar, bighorn sheep, eagles. Watch out for rattlesnakes.

Touts Coule FREE
Loomis State Forest
Dept of Natural Resources
2.1 mi N from Loomis grocery on Loomis-Oroville Rd; left on Toats Coulee Rd for 5.5 mi to lower camp; continue .1 mi to upper camp; at Toats-Coulee Creek. Free. 9 sites, 3 picnic sites. Tbls, picnic area, toilets, cfga, game racks, no drkg wtr.

Touts Junction   **FREE**
Loomis State Forest
Dept. of Natural Resources
2.1 mi N from Loomis grocery on Loomis-Oroville Rd; left on Toats Coulee Rd for 5.5 mi to lower camp; at Toats-Coulee Creek. Free. Primitive undesignated sites; used primarily as a fall hunting camp. Toilets, tbls, cfga, no drkg wtr.

LOPEZ (70)

Spencer Spit State Park   **$12**
E side of Lopez Island. Accessible by Anacortes ferry. $12 base. 3/15-10/30; 10-day limit. Base fee for 7 primitive hiker/biker and boat-in sites; $12 for primitive drive-to tent sites; $17 for standard tent sites. Primitive sites have cfga, nearby drkg wtr & toilets; standard sites have campstove, drkg wtr, cfga, tbls, trash disposal, flush toilets, no hot showers. Fishing, 1 mi beach; good clamming, biking, swimming, beachcombing, canoeing. 130 acres.

LUMMI ISLAND (71)

Lummi Island   **FREE**
State Recreation Site
Dept. of Natural Resources
Ferry or boat access from Lummi Indian Reservation S of Ferndale. Free. 5 primitive tent sites. Tbls, toilets, cfga, no drkg wtr. Beach access. 1 mooring buoy.

LYNDEN (72)

Berthusen City Park   **$12**
1 block W of Hwy 12 on Badger Rd in Lynden. $12 base; $18 with hookups. All year. Tbls, flush toilets, showers, cfga, drkg wtr, dump, kitchen buildings($). Picnicking, multi-use area, playground, garden, hiking, tractor club display; museum nearby. Campground is part of 236-acre homestead willed to town by the late Lida and Hans Berthusen.

MANCHESTER (73)

Blake Island State Park   **$12**
Boat access only; in Puget Sound 3 mi W of Seattle. $12 base. All year; 7-day moorage limit. Limited facilities in winter. 51 primitive tent sites at $12; canoe sites $12. Portable disposal service; flush & pit toilets, cfga, drkg wtr, tbls. Fishing, boating, moorage, scuba diving, swimming, clamming. 476 acres.

MARBLEMOUNT (74)

Big Beaver   **FREE**
North Cascade National Park
(Ross Lake NRA)
22 mi NE of Marblemount on WA 20; 4 mi by trail or boat from dam. Free. 6/1-11/1; 14-day limit. 7 tent sites. Tbls, toilets, cfga, no drkg wtr. Picnicking; fishing; swimming; boating(d).

Cascade Islands Campground   **FREE**
Skagit County Park
2.5 mi E of Marblemount; at Cascade River. Free primitive undesignated sites. No facilities, no drkg wtr. Fishing.

Cat Island   **FREE**
North Cascade National Park
(Ross Lake NRA)
22 mi NE of Marblemount on WA 20; 14.5 mi by trail or boat from dam. Free. 6/1-11/1; 14-day limit. 6 tent sites. Tbls, toilets, cfga, no drkg wtr. Picnicking; fishing; swimming; boating(d).

Community Club Park   **FREE**
Skagit Conty Park
In Marblemount across from the fire hall at riverside. Free undesignated camping at 2-acre park. No facilities, no drkg wtr. Fishing, rafting. Closed at last report.

Green Point   **FREE**
North Cascade National Park
(Ross Lake NRA)
22 mi NE of Marblemount on WA 20; 3 mi by boat or trail from dam. Free. 6/1-11/1; 14-day limit. 10 tent sites. Tbls, toilets, cfga, no drkg wtr. Swimming; fishing; boating(d).

Lightning Creek   **FREE**
North Cascade National Park
(Ross Lake NRA)
22 mi NE of Marblemount on WA 20; 13.5 mi by boat or bridle trails. Free. 6/1-11/1; 14-day limit. 9 tent sites. Tbls, toilets, cfga, no drkg wtr, firewood. Swimming; boating; picnicking; fishing.

Little Beaver   **FREE**
North Cascade National Park
(Ross Lake NRA)
22 mi NE of Marblemount on WA 20; 17 mi by boat from dam. Free. 6/1-11/1; 14-day limit. 7 tent sites. Tbls, toilets, cfga, no drkg wtr. Swimming; picnicking; boating(d); fishing.

Marble Creek   **$12**
Mt. Baker-Snoqualmie National Forest
8 mi E of Marblemount on CR 3528; 1 mi S on FR 1530 (.6 mi of access rd is narrow and winding). $12 in 2007 & 2008. 5/15-9/15 or until closed by snow; 14-day limit. 24 sites (RVs under 32 ft). Tbls, toilets, cfga, firewood, no drkg wtr. Mountain climbing; hunting; hiking; picnicking; fishing. Elev 900 ft; 40 acres. River. Geological. Scenic. Adjacent to Cascade River. Co-sponsored by Seattle City Light. 2-day minimum stay on weekends.

Mineral Park   **$12**
Mount Baker-Snoqualmie National Forest
15 mi E of Marblemount on CR 3528 (Cascade River Rd); campground is on the right; quarter mi farther on the right, across the bridge, is more of the same campground (narrow and winding rd). $12 in 2007 & 2008.

5/15-9/15 or until closed by snow; 14-day limit. 22 sites. Tbls, toilets, cfga, no drkg wtr. Picnicking; hunting; hiking; mountain climbing; fishing. Elev 1400 ft; 7 acres. Scenic. Co-sponsored by Seattle City Light. 2-day minimum stay on weekends.

MEDICAL LAKE (75)

Backcountry Camping   **FREE**
Pend Oreille River Canyon
Bureau of Land Management
N of Metaline Falls to Boundary Dam on both sides of Pend Oreille River; free primitive camping only on BLM lands. All year; 14-day limit. No facilities. Boating, fishing, hiking.

METALINE FALLS (76)

East Sullivan   **$12**
Colville National Forest
8 mi NE of Metaline Falls on CR 9345; 1 mi S on FR 22 (Sullivan Creek Rd); at N end of Sullivan Lake. $12. 5/26-9/9; 14-day limit. 38 sites (55-ft RV limit). Tbls, toilets, cfga, drkg wtr, dump. Swimming beach & dock, boating(l), hiking trails, picnic area, fishing. Public airstrip; pilots & passengers may camp free at edges of airstrip in return for maintaining strip/fence; tbls, cfga provided.

Mill Pond   **$12**
Colville National Forest
8 mi NE of Metaline Falls on CR 9345; 1 mi NW of ranger station. $12. 5/26 9/9; 14-day limit. Free camping from 9/10 until snow closes access rd; no trash service, wtr during free period; pack out trash. 10 sites. Tbls, drkg wtr, cfga, toilets. Boating(carry-in access; no gas motors). Handicap interpretive trail & picnic area, 1.5-mi hiking trail, fishing. 5 acres.

West Sullivan   **$12**
Colville National Forest
8 mi NE of Metaline Falls on CR 9345; 1 mi S on FR 22 (Sullivan Creek Rd); at N end of Sullivan Lake across rd from ranger station. $12. 5/26-9/9; 14 day limit. 10 sites (25-ft RV limit). Tbls, flush & pit toilets, cfga, drkg wtr, dump (at East Sullivan entry). Picnic shelter, swimming change house, swimming beach, boating(l), picnic area, hiking trails, fishing. Public airstrip; pilots & passengers may camp free at edges of airstrip in return for maintaining strip/fence; tbls, cfga provided.

MONTESANO (77)

Chetwoot   **FREE**
Olympic National Forest
12 mi N of Montesano on Wynooche Valley Rd; 21 mi N on FR 22; 2.5 mi N on FR 2294; half mi E on Trail 878. Hike in or boat in only. Free. On Lake Wynoochee. Spring-fall; 14-day limit. 8 tent sites. Tbls, toilets, cfga, no drkg wtr. Hiking; waterskiing; boating; picnicking; fishing; swimming. Nature trails. Elev 1000 ft.

Coho   **$12**
Olympic National Forest
From approx 1 mi W of Montesano, 35 mi
N on Wynoochee Valley Rd & FR 22; bear
left on FR 22 at jct, then right on FR 2294
for 1 mi. $12 (walk-in tent sites, $10). 5/15-
9/15l; 14-day limit. 46 sites (36-ft RV limit); 1
walk-in group site for 12 persons. Drkg wtr,
tbls, flush toilets, cfga, dump. Boating(l), fishing, hunting, swimming, picnicking, hiking.
Wynoo-chee Lake Shore Trail 12 mi around
lake from camp; Working Forest Nature Trail;
vista overlook. 8 acres.

MORTON (79)

Winston Creek   **FREE**
State Recreation Site
Dept of Natural Resources
10 mi W of Morton on US 12 between mileposts 82-83; S 3.6 mi on Winston Creek Rd;
left on Longbell Rd 1 mi (portions of rd are
rough). Free. All year; 14-day limit. 11 sites.
Tbls, toilets, cfga, drkg wtr. Hiking; picnicking. Status uncertain for 2007. Nearby Alder
Lake Campground was closed permanently.

MOSES LAKE (80)

Potholes State Park   **$12**
25 mi SW of Moses Lake on Hwy 170. $12
base. All year; 10-day limit. Base fee for
primitive RV/tent sites; utility sites $23 (50-ft
RV limit). Primitive sites have cfga, nearby
drkg wtr & toilets; utility sites have campstove, drkg wtr, cfga, tbls, trash disposal,
flush toilets, showers. Dump. Boating(l), fishing, waterskiing. 640 acres.
Fishing tip: Potholes Lake is highly
regarded for its rainbow trout, largemouth &
smallmouth bass and walleye fishing. Nearby
Moses Lake offers fast trout action with fish
up to 17 inches as well as good angling for
largemouth bass and walleye. Crappie fishing at both lakes is rather poor.

NACHES (81)

Bumping Crossing   **FREE**
Wenatchee National Forest
4.3 mi W of Naches on US 12; 28.5 mi N on
SR 410; 10 mi S on FR 2000; at Bumping
River. Free. All year; 14-day limit. 12 sites;
16-ft rV limit. Tbls, toilets, cfga, no drkg wtr.
Fishing, hiking.

Clear Lake North   **$10**
Wenatchee National Forest
35.6 mi W of Naches on US 12; .9 mi S on
CR 1200; half mi S on FR 1200. $10. 5/1-
10/31; 14-day limit. 34 sites on 33 acres (RVs
under 22 ft). Tbls, toilets, cfga, drkg wtr 1 mi
at boat launch. Picnicking; fishing; boating(l-
1 mi; r-3 mi). Elev 3100 ft.
Fishing tip: This 265-acre lake contains
plenty of rainbow trout. It's a great place for
shore fishing with kids; they can catch lots
of trout, 6-12 inches. Use green powerbait
eggs.

Clear Lake South & Boat Landing   **$10**
Wenatchee National Forest
35.6 mi W of Naches on US 12; 1 mi S on
FR 1200; .7 mi S on FR 1312. $10 at camp-
ground. Some dispersed sites that were
previously free but now are $5 daily or $30
annually. 5/1-10/31; 14-day limit. 22 sites
on 21 acres (RVs under 22 ft). Tbls, toilets,
cfga, drkg wtr. Picnicking; fishing; boating(l).
Elev 3100 ft.

Crow Creek   **$7**
Wenatchee National Forest
4.3 mi W of Naches on US 12; 24.5 mi N on
SR 410; 2.5 mi NW on FR 1900; half mi W on
FR 1902; on Naches River. $7. 4/15-11/15;
14-day limit. 15 sites; 30-ft RV limit. Tbl, toilets, cfga, no drkg wtr. OHV activities, hiking,
fishing, hunting.

Dog Lake   **$5**
Wenatchee National Forest
About 47 mi W of Naches on US 12 (past
Rimrock Lake) nearly to forest's W boundary
(or 22 mi NE of Packwood). $5 daily or $30
annually. 5/15-11/1; 14-day limit. 11 sites;
20-ft RV limit. Tbls, toilets, cfga, dump, no
drkg wtr. Boating(l.), fishing, hiking.
Fishing tip: Dog Lake produces best in
mid-summer. Use orange-and-yellow powerbait or marshmllow with worms to catch
rainbow & brook trout of 7-15 inches. For
variety, nearby Rimrock Lake offers good
fishing for 8-11 inch kokanee salmon, and it
contains rainbows up to 16 inches.

Halfway Flat   **$10**
Wenatchee National Forest
4.3 mi W of Naches on US 12; 21 mi N on
SR 410; 3 mi NW on FR 1704; at Naches
River. $10. 5/15-11/15; 14-day limit. 9 sites
for large RVs. Tbls, toilets, cfga, no drkg wtr.
Hiking, fishing, OHV activities.

Jayhawk Flat   **FREE**
Wenatchee National Forest
22 mi W of Naches on US 12; about 9 mi SW
on FR 12 (just past South Fork Camp). Free.
All year; 14-day limit. No facilities except
cfga; no drkg wtr. Note: Numerous dispersed, free camping areas exist in the area.

Kaner Flat   **$10**
Wenatchee National Forest
4.3 mi W of Naches on SR 12; 24.3 mi NW
on SR 410; 2.2 mi on FR 19. $10. 5/15-9/30;
14-day limit. Handicap-accessible. 41 sites
(includes 6 double sites, 1 triple); 30-ft RV
limit. Tbls, toilets (1 flushing), cfga, drkg wtr.
Old campsite for wagon trains traveling Old
Naches Trail. Fishing, hiking trails. Near Little
Naches River. Popular motorcycle area. Elev
2678 ft; 64 acres.

Peninsula   **$5**
Wenatchee National Forest
22. mi W of Naches on US 12; 3 mi S on
FR 12; 1 mi W on FR 1382; on Rimrock
Lake. $5 daily or $30 annually for NW for-
est pass. 4/15-11/15; 14-day limit. 19 sites;

20-ft RV limit. Tbls, toilets, cfga, no drkg wtr.
Boating(l), fishing, swimming, hiking.
Fishing tip: Beside rainbow trout up to
16 inches, 2,530-acre Rimrock Lake has
an excellent population of kokanee salmon,
which usually run 8-11 inches.

South Fork Tieton   **$5**
Wenatchee National Forest
22 mi W of Naches on US 12; about 8 mi SW
on FR 12 (Tieton Reservoir Rd); on South
Fork of Tieton River. $5. About 5/15--9/15;
14-day limit. 15 sites (20-ft RV limit). Tbls,
toilets, cfga, no drkg wtr. Fishing, swimming.
Note: Numerous dispersed camping opportunities are in the vicinity.

South Fork Bay   **$5**
Dispersed Camping
Wenatchee National Forest
22 mi W of Naches on US 12; about 8 mi
SW on FR 12 (in same vicinity as South Fork
Camp). Camp free with $30 annual NW for-
est pass; $5 daily otherwise. All year; 14-day
limit. No facilities except cfga; no drkg wtr.

White Pass Lake   **$5**
Wenatchee National Forest
About 50 mi W of Naches on US 12 (past
Rimrock Lake) nearly to forest's W boundary;
right on FR 498 to Leech Lake (19 mi NE of
Packwood). $5 daily or $30 annually for NW
forest pass. 6/1-11/15; 14-day limit. 16 sites;
20-ft RV limit. Tbls, toilets, cfga, no drkg wtr,
dump. Boating(l), fly fishing, hiking.
Fishing tip: Leech Lake is fly fishing only,
and it produces excellent catches of 8-16
inch brook trout each summer. No motors on
the lake. Use either a Hare's Ear or a Royal
Wulff. During evenings, focus on the inlet and
outlet creeks. If a damsel fly hatch is on, use
an adult damsel for great success.

NASELLE (82)

Snag Lake Recreation Site   **FREE**
Dept. of Natural Resources
From milepost 3 on SR 4 (W of Naselle), N
about 1 mi on C-Line (a 2-lane gravel rd that
goes uphill whIle right fork goes to Naselle
Youth Camp); turn right on C-4000 Rd for 1.4
mi, then left on C-2600 Rd (gravel, 1-lane) for
.6 mi; right on C-2620 Rd for qtr mi. Free. All
year; 14-day limit. 4 sites. Tbls, toilets, cfga,
no drkg wtr. Hiking, 3 picnic sites.

Tunerville Recreation Site
Dept. of Natural Resources
From jct of SR 401 & SR 4 N of Naselle, 3.5
mi E on SR 4; 8.5 mi NE on Salmon Creek
Rd (after 6.5 miles, rd becomes gravel and
is 5900 Rd; when rd forks, stay left). All year;
14-day limit. 3 primitive sites. Toilets, tbls,
cfga, no drkg wtr. Hiking, horseback riding.

Western Lakes   **FREE**
State Recreation Site
Dept of Natural Resources
From milepost 3 on SR 4, N about 1 mi on
C-Line (a 2-lane gravel rd that goes uphill

while right fork goes to Naselle Youth Camp); turn right on C-4000 Rd for 1.4 mi, then left on C-2600 Rd (gravel, 1-lane) for 1 mi; right on WA-WT-8520 Rd qtr mi to site. Free. All year; 14-day limit. 3 primtive tent sites. Toilets, cfga, tbls, no drkg wtr. Hiking trails, 3 picnic sites.

NEWHALEM (83)

Colonial Creek   **$12**
Ross Lake National Recreation Area
North Cascade National Park
10 mi E of Newhalem on SR 20. $12. Free 10/1-3/31 or until rds closed by snow; fee rest of year. 162 sites (18 open all year); 14-day limit. 32-ft RV limit. Tbls, flush toilets, cfga, drkg wtr, dump; no wtr during free period. Boating, hiking, picnicking, fishing. No park entry fee. On shore of Diablo Lake & Skagit River. Co-sponsored by Seattle City Light. 28 acres.

Fishing tip: 910-acre Diablo Lake contains planted rainbow trout.

Goodell Creek   **$10**
Ross Lake National Recreation Area
North Cascade National Park
Half mi W of Newhalem on SR 20. $10. All year; 14-day limit. 21 sites (22 ft RV limit). Tbls, toilets, cfga, drkg wtr, dump. Fishing, boating, hiking. 4 acres.

Newhalem Creek   **$12**
Ross Lake National Recreation Area
North Cascade National Park
W end of Newhalem on SR 20. $12. 6/15-9/15; 14-day limit. 111 sites; 32-ft RV limit. Tbls, flush toilets, cfga, drkg wtr, dump. Handicap facilities. Visitor center. Fishing, boating, hiking. 22 acres.

NEWPORT (84)

Pioneer Park   **$12**
Colville National Forest
Half mi NE of Newport on US 2; 2 mi N on CR 9305. $12. 5/15-9/15; 14-day limit. 17 sites (22-ft RV limit). Tbls, toilets, cfga, drkg wtr. Boating(l), fishing, waterskiing. On Box Canyon Reservoir. 5 acres.

Pend Oreille County Park   **$10**
Pend Oreille County
15 mi W of Newport on US 2; W of Rt 211 turnoff for Sacheen Lake. $10. MD LD. 36 sites. Tbls, flush toilets, showers; cfga, drkg wtr. Hiking trails, picnicking.

NORTH BEND (85)

Mine Creek Recreation Site   **FREE**
Dept of Natural Resources
From I-90 Exit 34 E of North Bend, N half mi on 468 Ave SE; right on SE Middle Fork Rd (paved & gravel for 4 mi, then left to camp. Free. All year; 14-day limit. 13 sites; 3 picnic sites. Toilets, cfga, tbls, no drkg wtr.

NORTHPORT (86)

Sheep Creek   **FREE**
State Recreation Site
Dept of Natural Resources
1 mi N of Northport on SR 25 (cross Columbia River); left on gravel Sheep Creek Rd for 4.3 mi; right into campground. Free. 5/15-10/31; 14-day limit. 11 sites; 8 picnic sites. Toilets, tbls, drkg wtr, cfga, group shelter. Fishing, hiking. Interpretive site, stream viewing platform.

Upper Sheep Creek   **FREE**
Dept. of Natural Resources
1.2 mi upstream on Sheep Creek Rd from Sheep Creek Campground. Free. All year; 14-day limit. 2 sites. Tbls, toilets, cfga, no drkg wtr.

OAKVILLE (88)

North Creek Recreation Site   **FREE**
Capitol State Forest
Dept of Natural Resources
From SR 12 about 2.7 mi W of Oakville, go E on D-Line Rd 3.9 mi; along Cedar Creek. Free. 4/1-10/31; 14-day limit. 5 sites. Toilets, cfga, drkg wtr. Hiking trails; picnicking; fishing, mountain biking (only on road).

Sherman Valley   **FREE**
Capitol State Forest
Dept of Natural Resources
From SR 12 about 2.7 mi W of Oakville, go E on D-Line Rd 6.4 mi. Free. 4/1-10/31; 14-day limit. 7 sites. Toilets, cfga, drkg wtr. Hiking, fishing; picnicking; fishing, mountain biking (on road only). On Porter Creek. Canoe launch N of Oakville.

ODESSA (89)

Lakeview Ranch Rec Area   **FREE**
Bureau of Land Management
2.5 mi N of Odessa on SR 21; 4.5 mi W on Lakeview Ranch Rd; at Pacific Lake. Free. All year; 14-day limit. 5 sites. Tbls, toilets, cfga, no drkg wtr, corrals. Horseback riding, hiking, mountain biking, OHV use, fishing, boating. 5300 acres.

Odessa Tourist Park   **FREE**
In town. Free. Small park with primitive overnight sites. Tbls, toilets, cfga, drkg wtr. Golf, pool nearby. Free RV camping with hookups provided for golfers at the Odessa Golf Course.

OKANOGAN (90)

American Legion City Park   **$3**
On Hwy 20 N of town. $3 base. Bikers/walkers, $3; motorized vehicles, $5. All year. 35 sites (no RV size limit); no hookups. Tbls, flush toilets, cfga, drkg wtr, coin showers. Fishing, boating. On Okanogan River, next to Okanogan County Historical Museum. Dump nearby at Flying J service station (free).

Leader Lake Recreation Site   **FREE**
Loup Loup State Forest
Dept of Natural Resources
From US 97 at Okanogan, W 8.4 mi on SR 20 to Leader Lake Rd (paved, one lane); turn right, half mi to camp; at Leader Lake. Free. All year; 14-day limit. 16 sites, 2 picnic sites. Tbls, toilets, cfga, no drkg wtr, fishing platform. Boating(l), fishing.

Fishing tip: This 159-acre lake contains plenty of chunky rainbows as well as bass. The trout average 12 inches.

Rock Creek   **FREE**
Loup Loup State Forest
Dept of Natural Resources
From jct with US 90 at Okanogan, W 9.8 mi on SR 20 to Loup Loup Canyon Rd (dirt, 2 lanes), then 3.9 mi and left into camp. On Loup-Loup Creek. Free. All year; 14-day limit. 6 sites, 4 picnic sites. Toilets, tbls, cfga, drkg wtr, shelter.

Rock Lakes Recreation Site   **FREE**
Loup Loup State Forest
Dept of Natural Resources
From jct with US 90 at Okanogan, W 9.8 mi on SR 20 to Loup Loup Canyon Rd (dirt, 2 lanes) for 4.7 mi; left on Rock Lakes Rd for 5.8 mi, then left qtr mi to camp. On Rock Lakes, near Buck Mountain. Free. All year; 14-day limit. 8 sites. Toilets, tbls, cfga, no drkg wtr. Hiking trail; picnicking; fishing. Accommodates the handicapped.

Sportsman's Camp   **FREE**
Loup Loup State Forest
Dept. of Natural Resources
From jct with US 97 at Okanogan, 14.9 mi W on SR 20; right on Sweat Creek Rd for 1 mi. Free. All year; 14-day limit. 6 sites. Tbls, toilets, cfga, no drkg wtr, shelter.

OMAK (92)

Carl Precht RV Park   **$11**
Eastside Municipal Park
Qtr mi E of Omak on SR 155; on Okanogan River. $11 for tents; $16 for RVs; winer rate $7. All year; 7-day limit. 68 sites. Tbls, flush toilets, showers(50 cents), elec, wtr, sewer, dump, coin laundry, visitor center. Heated pool (2-blk walk), tennis courts, playground. Fishing, swimming, boating. 76 acres.

ORIENT (93)

Pierre Lake   **$6**
Colville National Forest
3.8 mi E of Orient on CR 4134; 3.2 mi N on CR 4013. $6. 5/25-10/30; 14-day limit. 15 sites on 8 acres (RVs under 32 ft). Tbls (10 picnic sites), toilets, cfga, firewood, no drkg wtr. Picnicking; hiking; fishing; swimming; waterskiing; boating(ld).

OZETTE (94)

Ozette Campground $12
Olympic National Park
21 mi from Ozette on Hoko-Ozette Rd. $12. All year; 14-day limit. 15 sites; 21-ft RV limit. Tbls, toilets, cfga, drkg wtr. Boating, fishing, hiking.

PACKWOOD (96)

Ohanapecosh $12
Mount Rainier National Park
7 mi NE of Packwood on US 12; 5 mi N on Hwy 123 to park entrance; camp next to visitor center. $12 off-season; $15 about 6/15-LD; 14-day limit. 188 sites; 32-ft motorhome limit, 27-ft trailer limit. Tbls, flush toilets, cfga, drkg wtr, dump. Fishing, exhibts at visitor center, hiking.

Soda Springs FREE
Gifford Pinchot National Forest
8.9 mi NE of Packwood on US 12; 5.5 mi W on FR 45 & FR 4510. Free. 5/15-9/15; 14-day limit. 8 tent sites. Tbls, toilets, cfga, firewood, no drkg wtr. Hiking; picnicking; fishing. Elev 3200 ft; 4 acres. Stream. Trailhead to Cougar Lake. Summit Area. No horses; ride horses from trailhead at end of FR 4510.

Summit Creek FREE
Gifford Pinchot National Forest
8.9 mi NE of Packwood on US 12; 2.1 mi N on FR 45 & FR 4510. Free. 6/15-9/5; 14-day limit. 6 primtive tent or pickup camper sites. Tbls, toilets, cfga, firewood, no drkg wtr. Picnicking; fishing. Elev 2400 ft; 2 acres. Stream. Rough driveway into campground.

PASCO (97)

Hood Park $8
Corps of Engineers
Lake Wallula
4 mi SE of Pasco on US 12 across Snake River; qtr mi NE of SR 124. $8 for boat camping by tent & for overflow area (90 sites). 69 RV sites, $18-20 (65-ft RV limit); holders of federal Senior Pass pay $9 & $10. 4/1-9/30; 14-day limit. Pavilion, amphitheater, horseshoes, handicap facilities, picnicking, public use areas, elec($), basketball court, swimming beach, playground, showers, flush toilets, tbls, cfga, drkg wtr, campfire programs, dump. Fishing, boating(l). 2-night minimum stay on weekends.
Fishing tip: If you have an Oregon fishing license, boat to the cliffs area in that state and catch big steelhead on dark purple Wiggle Wart Magnums. Or troll crankbaits and Manistee Trollers along the cliffs.

Lake Emma FREE
Corps of Engineers
Lake Sacajawea
E of Pasco on Pasco-Kahlotus Hwy, then 3 mi on Murphy Rd; 1 mi S on Page Rd. Free. All year; 14-day limit. Primitive undesignated sites. No facilities, no drkg wtr. Boating(l), fishing.

McNary FREE
Habitat Management Area
State Dept of Fish & Game
10 mi SE of Pasco on US 395. Free. All year; 14-day limit. 24 primitive sites; no facilities. Fishing in Columbia River or at wildlife refuge, hunting, hiking, boating(l). Adjoins McNary National Wildlife Refuge between Walla Walla and Snake Rivers.
Fishing tip: Try the two ponds in the railroad fill area NW of McNary Reservoir. Mound Pond (34 acres) and Yellepit Pond (36 acres) contain good smallmouth & largemouth bass as well as crappie and yellow perch.

Windust Park $8
Corps of Engineers
Lake Sacajawea
4 mi SW of Kahlotus on Pasco-Kahlotus Rd, exit 5; 2 mi S & E on Burr Canyon Rd. $8 for boat-in camping; $12 for 24 primitive RV/tent sites. 4/1-9/30; 14-day limit. 40-ft RV limit. Tbls, flush toilets, cfga, drkg wtr, playground. Handicap facilities, picnicking, beach, playground, dump. Fishing, swimming, boating. 2-night minimum stay on weekends.

POMEROY (99)

Alder Thicket FREE
Umatilla National Forest
10 mi S of Pomeroy on Hwy 128; at fork, continue staight to FR 40, then 3.5 mi to camp. Free. 5/15-11/15; 14-day limit. 5 sites (15-ft RV limit). Tbls, toilets, cfga, no drkg wtr (wtr at Clearwater lookout, 6 mi on FR 40). Hiking. Designated mushroom camp.

Big Springs FREE
Umatilla National Forest
10 mi S of Pomeroy on Hwy 128; at fork, continue straight to FR 40; pass the forest boundary & continue 9 mi to Clearwater lookout tower, then left on FR 42 for 3 mi; left on FR 4225 to camp. Free. 5/15-11/15; 14-day limit. 8 sites. Tbls, toilets, cfga, no drkg wtr (get wtr at Clearwater tower). Hiking, hunting.

Teal Spring FREE
Umatilla National Forest
10 mi S of Pomeroy on Hwy 128; at fork, continue straight to FR 40 within the forest & on 9 mi to Clearwater lookout tower; camp's turnoff is half mi on right. Free. 6/1-11/15; 14-day limit. 5 sites. Tbls, toilets, cfga, no drkg wtr. Camp popular with OHV enthusiasts.

Tucannon Campground FREE
Umatilla National Forest
17 mi S of Pomeroy on CR 101; 4 mi SW on FR 47; S on FR 160 to camp. Free. 5/15-11/15; 14-daylimit. 13 sites; 16-ft RV limit. Tbls, toilets, cfga, no drkg wtr. Picnicking; fishing; hiking; hunting. Elev 1600 ft; 11 acres. River. Site also accessible via country road from Dayton. Very popular campground.
Fishing tip: Several small, state-managed ponds are stocked with rainbow trout each spring. Big Four pond, fly fishing only, gets surplus rainbow brood stock and contains some hefty fish. At times, fishing is tremendous, especially at Blue, Rainbow & Carrel lakes. Use worms and garlic marshmallows on bottom.

Wickiup Campground FREE
Umatilla National Forest
10 mi S of Pomeroy on Hwy 128; at fork, continue straight to FR 40 for about 17 mi; at Troy Junction, turn on FR 44 for 3 mi to jct with FR 43. Free. 6/15-10/15; 14-day limit. 5 sites; 16-ft RV limit. Tbls, toilets, cfga, no drkg wtr. Hiking, hunting.

PORT ANGELES (100)

Altaire $12
Olympic National Park
9 mi W of Port Angeles on US 101; 4 mi S on Olympic Hot Springs Rd. $12. May-Sept; 14-day limit. 30 sites, suitable for small RVs (21-ft RV limit). Portions of rd closed by snow in winter. Tbls, flush toilets, cfga, drkg wtr. Fishing (no license required), hiking, picnicking. Mountain goats & elk can sometimes be seen on rocks across river in late winter & early spring. Handicap access restrooms.

Deer Park $10
Olympic National Park
6 mi E of Port Angeles on US 101; 18 mi S (gravel access rds). $10. 5/30-9/30; 14-day limit. 14 tent sites (no RVs). Tbls, toilets, cfga, drkg wtr. Picnicking. Elev 5400 ft. Views of Strait of Juan de Fuca, inner Olympic Mountains, and Mount Baker. Alpine wildflower display in summer. No park entrance fee.

Elwha $12
Olympic National Park
9 mi W of Port Angeles on US 101; 3 mi S on Olympic Hot Springs Rd; rd suitable for small RVs; part of rd closed in winter. $12. All year; 14-day limit. 40 sites (21-ft RV limit). Tbls, flush toilets, cfga, drkg wtr, picnic shelter, naturalist program. Fishing (no license required), hiking, picnicking. Mountain goats & elk can sometimes be seen on rocks across river in late winter & early spring. Handicap-access restrooms.

Fairholm $12
Olympic National Park
17.9 mi W of Port Angeles on US 101; 10.7 mi N on North Shore Rd; .1 mi to campground; rds are steep. $12. All year; 14-day limit. 87 sites; 21-ft RV limit. Tbls, flush toilets, cfga, drkg wtr, nature program, nature trails, store. Swimming, boating(l), fishing (no license required), hiking. Lake Crescent nestled between high, forested peaks and is the largest lake in the park. 35 acres. Handicap-access restrooms.

Lyre River   **FREE**
Recreation Site
Dept of Natural Resources
4 mi W of Port Angeles on WA 101, to jct with WA 112; 14.7 mi N to campground sign, right half mi to fork in rd; left fork (gravel rd) to campground. Free. All year; 14-day limit. 11 sites (RVs under 22 ft). Tbls, toilets, cfga, drkg wtr, shelter. Picnicking; hiking, Fishing. On Lyre River. Secluded sites, renovated in 2001.

Heart o' The Hills   **$120**
Olympic National Park
From &S 101 at Race St., .8 mi inside E city limits of Port Angeles, 5.4 mi S on Hurricane Ridge Rd (paved, often closed by snow in winter). $12. All year; 14-day limit. 105 sites (21-ft RV limit). Tbls, flush toilets, cfga, drkg wtr. Hiking, picnicking, nature program. Elev 1807. Trail to Mount Angeles (6400 ft). Elev 1807 ft; 35 acres.

PORT TOWNSEND (101)

Chimacum Park   **$12**
Jefferson County Park
About 5 mi S of Port Townsend on SR 20; SE on Four Corners Rd to Chimacum; on Rhody Dr. next to the Tri-Area Community Center. $12. All year; 7-day limit. 8 sites on 7.95 acres. Tbls, toilets, cfga, drkg wtr.

Jefferson County Fairground   **$10**
In Port Townsend on 49th Ave at Kuhn St. $10 base for open area without hookups & for elec/wtr; $15 for full hookups. All year; 7-day limit. 80 sites. Tbls, flush toilets, cfga, drkg wtr, dump (free for campers; $2 for non-campers), showers. Horse track, sports field.

PORTER (102)

Porter Creek   **FREE**
State Recreation Site
Capitol State Forest
Dept of Natural Resources
From SR 12 in Porter, 3.4 mi NE on Porter Creek Rd, then half mi to camp on B-line Rd. Free. 4/1-10/31; 14-day limit. 16 sites. Toilets, cfga, drkg wtr, no tbls, horse ramps. Hiking & horse trails; motorcycle trails; picnicking; fishing.

QUEETS (105)

Queets   **$10**
Olympic National Park
5 mi E of Queets on US 101; 13.5 mi NE on gravel rd along Queets River (open all year; RVs not recommended). $10. 6/1-9/30; 14-day limit. 20 sites (15-ft RV limit). Tbls, toilets, cfga. Fishing (no license required in park); picnicking. Elev 290 ft. No park entrance fee. Roosevelt elk often seen in abandoned homestead fields in Rain Forest. Queets Campground Trail. Queets ranger station (1.5 mi) provides information and backcountry

use permits summer and fall; closed winter. Campground closed in 2007 due to storm damage of access roads.

QUILCENE (106)

Dosewallips   **$12**
Olympic National Park
9 mi S of Quilcene at Brinnon on Hood Canal on US 101; 15.4 mi W along Dosewallips River on rd that is narrow and paved 6 mi, and gravel 9 mi (closed by snow in winter); upper end of rd is steep and not suitable for RVs. $12. June-Sept; 14-day limit. 30 sites (RVs not recommended). Tbls, flush toilets, showers, cfga, drkg wtr. Fishing (no license required in park); picnicking. Dosewallips ranger station provides info and backcountry use permits (summer only). In 2007, only walk-in camping available because Dosewallips Rd washed out.

Falls View   **$10**
Olympic National Forest
4 mi SW of Quilcene on US 101. $10. 5/15-9/15; 14-day limit. 30 sites (21-ft RV limit). Tbls, flush toilets, cfga, drkg wtr. Hiking, fishing. 6 acres.

Lake Leland Campground   **$12**
Jefferson County Park
About 6 mi N of Quilcene on Hwy 101. $12 in 2007, raising to $15 in 2008 & $18 in 2009. All year; 7-day limit. 22 sites on 2.6 acres. Tbls, toilets, cfga, no drkg wtr, beach. Swimming, boating(l), fishing.

Mt. Walker Viewpoint   **FREE**
Olympic National Forest
6 mi SW of Quilcene on Mt. Walker Rd. Free. All year; 14-day limit. Undeveloped primitive camping area. Toilets, no other facilities. Views of Olympics and Puget Sound.

Quilcene Campground   **$12**
Jefferson County Park
In Quilcene next to the Quilcene Community Center on Hwy 101. $12. All year; 7-day limit. 13 sites. Tbls, toilets, cfga, drkg wtr, playground. Tennis.

QUINAULT (107)

Falls Creek   **$12**
Olympic National Forest
3 mi from US 101 on CR 5 to Quinault Lake. $12 for 10 walk-in tent sites; $15 for drive-to sites (16-ft RV limit). 5/15-9/15; 14 day limit. Tbls, flush toilets, cfga, drkg wtr. Picnicking, fishing, hiking, boating(l), swimming. 5 acres. Concessionnaire-operated.

Gatton Creek   **$12**
Olympic National Forest
3.5 mi from US 101 on CR 5 to Quinault Lake. $12. 5/15-10/15; 14-day limit. 15 walk-in tent sites. Overnight RVs in parking area no longer permitted. Tbls, toilets, cfga, no drkg wtr. Picnicking, fishing, hiking. 5 acres.

Willaby   **$12**
Olympic National Forest
1.5 mi N of Quinault on CR 5; at Quinault Lake. $12 for tent sites; $15 for RV sites ($7.50 with federal Senior Pass). 34 sites; 16-ft RV limit. Tbls, toilets, cfga, drkg wtr. Fishing, hiking, boating(l).

RANDLE (108)

Cat Creek   **FREE**
Gifford Pinchot National Forest
3.1 mi S of Randle on SR 131; 15.7 mi SE on FR 23; 6.1 mi SE on FR 21. Free. 5/15-9/30; 14-day limit. 5 sites (RVs under 16 ft). Tbls, toilets, cfga, firewood, no drkg wtr. Picnicking; fishing; berry picking. Elev 3000 ft; 1 acre. Cat Creek Guard Station (half mi). Cispus River.

Chain-of-Lakes   **$12**
Gifford Pinchot National Forest
3.1 mi S on SR 131; 28.9 mi SE on FR 23; 1.2 mi N on FR 2329; 1 mi N on FR 022. $12. 6/15-10/30; 14-day limit. 3 sites (RVs under 17 ft). Tbls, toilets, cfga, firewood, no drkg wtr. Picnicking; fishing; boating; swimming; hiking; canoeing. Elev 4400 ft; 3 acres. Rolling hills. Lake. 3 mi N of Mount Adams Wilderness Area. Trailhead for Trail 116 to Keenes Horse Camp.

Council Lake   **FREE**
Gifford Pinchot National Forest
3.1 mi S of Randle on SR 131; 28.9 mi SE on FR 23; 1 mi SW on FR 2334. Free. 7/1-9/15; 14-day limit. 7 sites (16-ft RV limit). Tbls, toilets, cfga, no drkg wtr. Boating(d), fishing, hiking, berry-picking. Elev 4300 ft; 2 acres. Excellent view. Mount Adams Wilderness 2 mi. Carry-in boat launch.

Horseshoe Lake   **FREE**
Gifford Pinchot National Forest
3.1 mi S of Randle on SR 131; 28.9 mi SE on FR 23; 6.8 mi NE on FR 2329; 1.3 mi NW on FR 078. 6/15-9/30; 14-day limit. 10 poorly defined sites (RVs under 16 ft). Free. Tbls, toilets, firewood, cfga, no drkg wtr. Boating (d); picnicking; fishing; berry picking; swimming, hiking. Elev 4200 ft; 3 acres, picturesque. 2 mi NW of Mount Adams. About 12 mi of gravel rd to camp.

Keenes Horse Camp   **FREE**
Gifford Pinchot National Forest
3.1 mi SE of Randle on SR 131; 28.9 mi SE on FR 23; 6 mi SE on FR 2329; qtr mi W on FR 073; at Spring Creek. Free. 6/15-9/30; 14-day limit. 6 scattered dispersed sites (RVs under 22 ft). Toilets, cfga, no drkg wtr. Mountain climbing; horseback riding; picnicking; fishing. Elev 4300 ft. 2.4 mi NW of Mount Adams Wilderness. Corral, wtr for horses.

Killen Creek   **FREE**
Gifford Pinchot National Forest
3.1 mi S of Randle on SR 131; 28.9 mi SE on FR 23; 7 mi SE on FR 2329; qtr mi W on

FR 073. Free. 6/1-10/30; 14-day limit. 8 sites (RVs under 22 ft). Tbls, toilets, cfga, no drkg wtr. Mountain climbing; hiking; picnicking; fishing, berrypicking. Elev 4400 ft; 4 acres. Trailhead for climbing Mount Adams N face. Stream. Pick huckleberries 8/15-9/15.

Olallie Lake $12
Gifford Pinchot National Forest
3.1 mi S of Randle on SR 131; 28.9 mi SE on FR 23; 1 mi SW on FR 2334. $12. 6/1-10/30; 14-day limit. 5 sites (RVs under 23 ft). Tbls, toilets, cfga, firewood, no drkg wtr. Boating(no motors); picnicking; fishing; berry picking. Elev 3700 ft; 3 acres. Scenic. Excellent view of Mount Adams. Canyon Ridge Trail.

REARDAN (109)

Long Lake Campground FREE
Dept of Natural Resources
14.2 mi N on SR 231 from jct with US 2 at Reardon; right on Long Lake Dam Rd (US 291) for 4.7 mi, then right to site along Spokane River. Free. All year; 14-day limit. 9 sites; 8 picnic sites. Tbls, toilets, cfga, drkg wtr, shelter. Picnicking, fishing, hiking, boating(l). Pictographs nearby.

REPUBLIC (110)

Boulder/Deer Ceek $5
Colville National Forest
N of Republic on SR 21 to Curlew; CR 61 to Boulder Deer summit. $5. MD-LD; 14-day limit. 7 sites plus 2 group areas. Tbls, toilets, cfga, no drkg wtr. Fishing, hiking.

Long Lake $8
Colville National Forest
7 mi S of Republic on SR 21; 8 mi SW on FR 53; 1.5 mi S on FR 400. $8. 5/15-9/15; 14-day limit. 12 sites. Tbls, toilets, cfga, drkg wtr. Swimming, boating(l), fishing. Elev 3200 ft; 4 acres.

Ferry Lake $6
Colville National Forest
7 mi S of Republic on SR 21; 6 me SW on FR 53; 1 mi N on FR 5330; N on forest rd to camp. $6. 5/15-9/15; 14-day limit. 9 sites (22-ft RV limit). Tbls, toilets, cfga, drkg wtr. Fishing, boating(ld).

Sherman Pass Overlook $6
Colville National Forest
Half mi E of Republic on SR 21; 20 mi E on SR 20. $6. 5/25-9/30; 14-day limit. 9 sites (24-ft RV limit). Tbls, toilets, cfga, no drkg wtr. 7 picnic sites. Near highest pass in Washington. Hiking.

Swan Lake $10
Colville National Forest
7 mi S of Republic on SR 21; 8 mi SW on FR 53. $10. 5/15-9/15; 14-day limit. 25 sites (32-ft RV limit). Tbls, toilets, cfga, drkg wtr. Swimming, boating(l), fishing, nature trails, hiking. Elev 3600 ft; 6 acres.

Ten Mile $6
Colville National Forest
10 mi S of Republic on SR 21. $6 MD-LD; 14-day limit. 9 sites. Tbls, cfga, no drkg wtr, toilets, no trash service. Hiking, fishing.

Thirteen Mile FREE
Colville National Forest
13 mi S of Republic on SR 21. Free. MD-LD; 14-day limit. 4 ssites. Tbls, toilets, cfga, no drkg wtr. Hiking, fishing.

RIVERSIDE (111)

Crawfish Lake FREE
Okanogan National Forest
17.7 mi E of Riverside on CR 9320 (becomes FR 30 for 2 mi); right 1 mi on FR 30-100 access rd. Free. 5/15-9/15; 14-day limit. 19 sites (32-ft RV limit) & 4 group sites. Tbls, toilets, cfga, no drkg wtr (boil wtr from Balanced Rock Spring), no trash service. Boating(l), fishing, swimming, picnicking.

Fishing tip: This lake contains good brook and rainbow trout. Lots of action with small brookies on Roostertail spinners, even from shore.

SAPPHO (112)

Bear Creek FREE
State Recreation Site
Department of Natural Resources
2 mi E of Sappho on US 101. Free. All year; 14-day limit. 14 sites; 40-ft RVs. Tbls, toilets, cfga, no drkg wtr. Fishing, boating(l).

Beaver Lake Waysides FREE
N on SR 112; follow signs toward Neah Bay or Burnt Mountain. 5 mi to lake. Several waysides. No facilities.

Tumbling Waters Camp FREE
Rainier Timber Company
At jct of US 101 & SR 112 at crossroads of Sappho. Free. All year. 10 sites. Tbls, toilets, cfga, drkg wtr. Soleduck River.

SEQUIM (113)

Dungeness Forks $10
Olympic National Forest
4 mi SE of Sequim on US 101; 4.5 mi S on CR 9537; 3 mi S on FR 2958. $10. 5/15-9/15; 14-day limit. 10 tent sites. Tbls, toilets, cfga, drkg wtr. No trash pickup; pack out trash. Fishing, hunting, picnicking. At jct of Dungeness & Greywolf Rivers. 6 acres.

East Crossing $8
Olympic National Forest
8 mi S of Sequim on FR 2909; 2 mi S on FR 2950. $8 during MD-LD; $5 rest of yr, but no drkg wtr; 14 day limit. 9 tent sites. Tbls, toilets, cfga, drkg wtr. Hiking, fishing, picnicking, hunting. Greywolf Trailhead nearby. On Dungeness River. Fee not verified for 2007.

South Sequim Bay RV Park $9.25
5 mi E of Sequim on US 101; qtr mi N on Old Blyn Hwy. $9.25 base. All year. Base fee for field parking of self-contained RVs & for tent & RV sites with wtr, toilets, showers; $10.75 with elec; full-hookup sites $15.50. 30 sites. Tbls, flush toilets, cfga, drkg wtr, phone, showers, dump. Fishing, hiking, swimming.

SHELTON (114)

Brown Creek $10
Olympic National Forest
7.5 mi N of Shelton on US 101; 5.3 mi NW on Skokomish Valley Rd; 8.7 mi N on FR 23; cross bridge on FR 2353 to FR 2340, then qtr mi E. $10. All year; 14-day limit. 20 sites (21-ft RV limit). Tbls, toilets, cfga, drkg wtr. Swimming, fishing, hiking trails. 6 acres. Pack out trash.

Laney Camp Dispersed FREE
Olympic National Forest
Located in the Upper South Fork Skokomish Recreation Area near Church Creek. Free. All year; 14-day limit. 10 primitive tent sites. No facilities. Hunting, fishing, hiking. Closed in early 2007; road washed out in 2004.

LeBar Creek Horse Camp $10
Olympic National Forest
6 mi N of Shelton on US 101; left on Skokomish Valley Rd for 5.6 mi; at FR 23 "Y," bear right for 9.5 mi; bear right at FR 2353 "Y" for half mi, then left at next "Y" for three-fourths mi. $10. All year; 14-day limit. 13 sites; 28-ft RV limit. Tbls, toilets, cfga, no drkg wtr, no trash service. Horse facilities. Hiking, fishing, horseback riding. Camp built by volunteers.

Oxbow Dispersed Camp FREE
Olympic National Forest
1 mi N of Shelton on US 101, then 15 mi NW of US 101 on FR 23. Free. All year; 14-day limit. 30 primitive tent sites; no facilities. Hunting, fishing, hiking.

Pine Lake FREE
Olympic National Forest
Located in the Upper South Fork Skokomish Valley. Free. May-9/30; wildlife gate prevents vehicle access in winter. Primitive undeveloped camping area. No facilities. Hunting, fishing, hiking.

Spider Lake $5
Olympic National Forest
22 mi NW of Shelton to Brown Creek on FR 23, then 7 mi W on FR 23. Camp free with $30 annual NW forest pass; $5 daily otherwise. All year; 14-day limit. Primitive undeveloped camping area. No facilities. Fishing, hunting, hiking.

SOAP LAKE (117)

Smokiam Campground $10
Soap Lake City Park
Off SR 17 in town. $10 base without hookups & tent sites ($9 seniors); $20 with hookups

($18 seniors). All year. 48 RV sites. Tbls, flush toilets, cfga, drkg wtr, showers($), hookups($). Two beaches. Swimming, fishing, boating(ld), playground. Medicinal mineral water in lake.

SPOKANE (118)

Dragoon Creek   **FREE**
State Recreation Site
Dept of Natural Resources
From N side of Spokane, 10.2 mi N on US 395 from US 2 jct; left on Dragoon Creek Rd for half mi to camp entrance. Free. All year; 14-day limit. 22 sites; 5 picnic sites. Tbls, toilets, cfga, drkg wtr. Picnicking, fishing.

SPRAGUE (119)

Fishtrap Lake   **FREE**
Boat-in & Hike-in Camping
Bureau of Land Management
NE of Sprague on Old State Hwy, then E on local rd to N end of lake. Launch boat or hike to primitive shoreline spots; no facilities. Area closed to all types of vehicles. Free. Hiking, boating, fishing, cross-country skiing. Get free camping permit at BLM district office, 1103 North Fancher, Spokane, WA 99212.

STARBUCK (120)

Ayer Boat Basin   **FREE**
Corps of Engineers
Lake Herbert G. West
About 8 mi NW of Starbuck on SR 261 to Lyons Ford Rd (just before Snake River bridge); left on Lyons Ford about half mi; right on gravel county rd, NE to Ayer Junction. Free. All year; 14-day limit. 20 primitive sites (40-ft RV limit). Toilets, tbls, cfga, no drkg wtr. Boating(l), fishing.

Riparia   **FREE**
Corps of Engineers
Lake Herbert G. West
1 mi E of Starbuck on SR 261; N on Riveria Rd to Little Goose Dam; 3 mi W of dam on North Shore Rd. Free. All year; 14-day limit. Primitive undesignated sites; 40-ft RV limit. Tbls, toilets, cfga, no drkg wtr. Fishing, boating.

STEHEKIN (121)

Bridge Creek   **FREE**
Lake Chelan Nat Recreation Area
North Cascades National Park
16 mi NW of Stehekin on unpaved co rd; hike-in, bus-in. Free. 6/15-11/1; 14-day limit. 7 sites (no RVs). Tbls, toilets, cfga, firewood. Fishing; picnicking. Stream.

Harlequin   **FREE**
Lake Chelan Nat Recreation Area
North Cascades National Park
5 mi NW of Stehekin on unpaved road; hike-in, bus-in. Free. 5/11-11/30; 14-day limit. 7 sites (no RVs). Tbls, toilets, cfga, firewood. Fishing; picnicking. Stream.

Weaver Point   **FREE**
Lake Chelan Nat Recreation Area
North Cascades National Park
Boat access from Stehekin, or hike-in. Free. 6/1-11/30; 14-day limit. 13 sites (no RVs). Tbls, toilets, cfga, firewood. Store/ice nearby. Fishing; boating(l); picnicking.

SULTAN (122)

Big Greider Lake   **FREE**
Sultan-Pilchuck State Forest
Dept. of Natural Resources
From Greider Lake Trailhead (see Little Greider entry), hike 3 mi to campsite. Free. 6/15-10/15; 14-day limit. 5 tent sites, tbls, toilets, cfga, no drkg wtr. Hiking trails, fishing.

Boulder Lake Campground
FREE
Sultan-Pilchuck State Forest
Dept. of Natural Resources
From Greider Lake Trailhead (see Little Greider entry), stay right on SLS-7000 Rd about 1.1 mi to Boulder Lake Trailhead, then hike 3.3 mi to campground. Free. 6/15-10/15; 14-day limit. 9 tent sites, tbls, toilets, cfga, no drkg wtr. Hiking trails, fishing.

Little Greider Lake   **FREE**
Sultan-Pilchuck State Forest
Dept. of Natural Resources
From E of Sultan half mi at US 2, go N on Sultan Basin Rd 13.8 mi; continue straight (middle branch) on SLS-4000 Rd about 8.7 mi to trailhead, then hike 2.5 mi to campsite. Free. 6/15-10/15; 14-day limit. 9 tent sites, tbls, toilets, cfga, no drkg wtr. Hiking trails, trout fishing in lake.

Olney Park   **FREE**
Weyerhaeuser Company
(and Dept of Natural Resources)
6 mi N of Sultan, on Sultan Basin Rd (gravel access rds). On Olney Creek. Free. 14-day limit. 8 sites (RVs under 35 ft). Toilets, no drkg wtr. Hunting; picnicking; fishing; hiking.

TONASKET (125)

Beaver Lake   **$6**
Okanogan National Forest
20.1 mi E of Tonasket on SR 20; 11 mi NE on FR 32; 3.3 mi NW on FR 3245. $6. All year; 14-day limit. 11 sites (22-ft RV limit). Tbls, toilets, cfga, no drkg wtr. Boating(l), fishing, swimming, hiking, hunting.

Bonaparte Lake Resort   **$10**
and Campground (Private)
21 ml E on Hwy 20 from jct wlth US 97 near Tonasket; 6.2 mi N on Bonaparte Lake Rd. $10 base for tents; RVs $15 & $18. All year; limited facilities in winter. 50 sites. Tbls, flush toilets, cfga, drkg wtr, wtr/elec hookups($), sewer($), showers, dump, coin laundry, LP-

gas, store. Swimming, boating(ldr), fishing, horseshoes, hiking trails.
Fishing tip: The lake here is stocked with kokanee salmon and rainbow, mackinaw and brook trout.

Lyman Lake   **FREE**
Okanogan National Forest
12.6 mi E of Tonasket on WA 20; 13 mi SE CR 9455; 2.4 mi S on FR 3785; qtr mi NW on FR 30-500 access rd. Free. 5/15-9/15; 14-day limit. 4 sites on 4 acres (RVs under 32 ft). Tbls, cfga, no drkg wtr, no trash service. Fishing. Little Lyman Lake.

Whitestone Lake   **FREE**
Public Hunting & Fishing Area
State Department of Fish & Wildlife
In Tonasket on WA 97; W on 3rd, across Okanogan River Bridge; 10.9 mi N on Many Lakes Recreation Area Rd to the first fishing area with large paved parking area on Whitestone Lake. There are other parking areas like this on the lake; but this is the only one that allows overnight parking. 3-day limit. Undesignated sites (room for 15 RVs). Toilets, cfga, no drkg wtr. Boating(r); picnicking; fishing.
Fishing tip: This 173-acre warmwater lake offers excellent fishing for largemouth bass. Crappie have been edged out by illegally introduced sunfish & perch, though.

TROUT LAKE (126)

Cultus Creek   **$5**
Gifford Pinchot National Forest
5.5 mi SW of Trout Lake on SR 141 to Ice Cave; 12.5 mi mi NW on FR 24. $5. All year; 14-day limit. 51 sites; 32-ft RV limit. Tbls, toilets, cfga, drkg wtr. Fishing, nature trails, hiking, berry picking. Elev 4000 ft; 28 acres. Lightly used except during huckleberry season.

Forlorn Lakes   **$5**
Gifford Pinchot National Forest
5.5 mi S W of Trout Lake on SR 141; 6.5 mi W on FR 24, FR 60 & FR 6040 (7 mi of gravel rd). $5. All year; 14-day limit. Series of small camping areas near isolated, picturesque lakes; 8 defined sites, 25 total; 18-ft RV limit. Tbls, some toilets, cfga, no drkg wtr. Poor fishing (lakes quite shallow), boating. Very popular, crowded on weekends.

Huckleberry Access   **FREE**
Gifford Pinchot National Forest
23 mi W of Trout Lake on SR 141, FR 24, FR 30 & FR 30-580 (also 41 mi N of Carson on Wind River Hwy, FR 30 & FR 30-580). Free. All year; 14-day limit. 3 sites (32-ft RV limit). Toilets, tbls, cfga, no drkg wtr. Hiking. Elev 4300 ft.

Lewis River Horse Camp   **$5**
Gifford Pinchot National Forest
1.4 mi W of Trout Lake on SR 141; 18 mi NW on FR 88; 7-1/5 mi N on FR 32; 5.1 mi NW on FR 3241. $5. 6/15-9/30; 14-day limit.

9 poorly defined sites. Tbls, toilets, cfga, firewood, no drkg wtr. Horseback riding; picnicking; fishing; swimming. Elev 1500 ft; 2 acres. Scenic. On Upper Lewis River. 15 mi of gravel rd. Self-service. Waterfalls.

Little Goose Horse Camp   FREE
Gifford Pinchot National Forest
5.5 mi SW of Trout Lake on WA 141 to Ice Cave; 10.1 mi NW on FR 24; access rough, not recommended for RVs. Free. 7/1-10/31; 14-day limit. 28 sites on 15 acres (RVs under 19 ft). Tbls, toilets, cfga, firewood, piped drkg wtr. Reduced services. Berry picking; picnicking; fishing; horseback riding (1 mi). Sites next to dusty gravel rd. Elev 4000 ft. Wtr available only early in season.

Morrison Creek   FREE
Gifford Pinchot National Forest
Qtr mi SE of Trout Lake on SR 141; 2 mi N on CR 17; 3.5 mi N on FR 80; 6 mi N on gravel FR 8040; access rough, not recommended for RVs. Free. 7/1-9/30; 14-day limit. 12 tent sites. Tbls, toilets, cfga, firewood, no drkg wtr. Mountain climbing; picnicking; horseback riding (1 mi). Elev 4600 ft; 3 acres. On Mount Adams Trailhead. Reduced service.

Saddle   FREE
Gifford Pinchot National Forest
5.5 mi SW of Trout Lake on SR 141; 18.3 mi NW on FR 24; 1.3 mi N on FR 2480 (poor, narrow access). Free. 7/1-10/15; 14-day limit. 12 rough sites (RVs under 16 ft). Tbls, toilets, cfga, firewood, no drkg wtr. Self-service. Berry picking; horseback riding; picnicking. Elev 4200 ft; 5 acres. In Sawtooth Huckleberry area.

Smokey Creek   FREE
Gifford Pinchot National Forest
5.5 mi Sw of Trout Lake on SR 141; 8.8 mi NW on FR 24. Free. 6/15-10/31; 14-day limit. 3 sites (22 ft RV limit) along gravel FR 24. Toilets, cfga, firewood. Hiking trail. Mainly used during berry season.

South   FREE
Gifford Pinchot National Forest
5.5 mi Sw of Trout Lake on SR 141; 18.3 mi NW on FR 24; .3 mi E on FR 2480 (poor dirt rd). Free. 6/15-9/30; 14-day limit. 8 sites on 2 acres (RVs under 19 ft). Tbls, toilets, cfga, firewood, well drkg wtr. Reduced services. Berry picking; horseback riding; picnicking. Secluded. Elev 4000 ft.

Tillicum $5
Gifford Pinchot National Forest
5.5 mi SW of Trout Lake on SR 141; 19 mi NW on FR 24. $5. 7/15-10/15; 14-day limit. 32 sites (18-ft RV limit). Tbls, toilets, cfga, drkg wtr. Nature trails, huckleberry area. A few good sites & several poor ones on 25 acres.

Trout Lake Creek $5
Giffort Pinchot National Forest
5 mi NW of Trout Lake on SR 141, FR 88 & FR 8810-011. $5. All year; 14-day limit. 21 sites (28-ft RV limit). Tbls, toilets, cfga, no drkg wtr. Fishing, hiking.

Twin Falls   FREE
Gifford Pinchot National Forest
1.4 mi W of Trout Lake on WA 141; 16.3 mi NW on FR 88; 5.2 mi N on FR 24. Free. 5/15-9/30; 14-day limit. 8 sites (RVs under 17 ft). Tbls, toilets, cfga, firewood, no drkg wtr. Self-service. Horseback riding; picnicking; fishing. Elev 2700 ft; 4 acres. Upper Lewis River.

Wicky Shelter   FREE
Gifford Pinchot National Forest
Half mi N on WA 141; 1 mi N on WA 17; 3.5 mi on FR 8000; 1.5 mi N on FR 8040. Free. 6/15-9/30; 14-day limit. 1 site; log shelter for self-service groups. Tbls, toilets, cfga, firewood. Picnicking; fishing; hiking. Elev 4000 ft; 1 acre. Rolling hills. Dense forest. Stream.

TWISP (127)

Blackpine Lake $8
Okanogan National Forest
11 mi W of Twisp on CR 9114; 8 mi S on FR 43. $8. All year; 14-day limit. No wtr or trash service in winter; pack out trash. 23 sites. Tbls, toilets, cfga, drkg wtr. Boating(l), fishing, 2 floating docks, nature trail, swimming, hiking.

J.R. $5
Okanogan National Forest
11.5 mi E of Twisp on SR 20. $5. All year; 14-day limit. 6 sites (16-ft RV limit). Tbls, toilets, cfga, drkg wtr (no wtr or trash service in winter). Fishing, hunting, hiking, biking, winter sports, picnic area. On Frazier Creek. Closed early in 2007 due to Tripod fire.

Loup Loup $8
Okanogan National Forest
12.5 mi E of Twisp on SR 20; 1 mi N on FR 42. $8. No wtr or trash service in winter. 25 sites (22-ft RV limit). Tbls, toilets, cfga, no drkg wtr. Biking, hiking, horse trails, hunting, group picnic area, access to mountain-bike trails. Elev 4200 ft. 20 acres. Winter sports activity. Good location for large groups; picnic area. Closed early in 2007 due to Tripod fire.

Mystery $5
Okanogan National Forest
10.8 mi W of Twisp on CR 9114; 7.2 mi NW on FR 44 (Twisp River Rd). $5. All year; 14-day limit. 4 sites. Tbls, toilets, cfga, no drkg wtr or trash service. Fishing, hiking, picnicking, biking. On North Ford of Twisp River. Elev 2800 ft.

Poplar Flat $8
Okanogan National Forest
10.7 mi W of Twisp on CR 9114; 9.5 mi NW on FR 44. $8. All year; 14-day limit. No wtr or trash service in winter. 16 sites (21-ft RV limit). Tbls, toilets, cfga, drkg wtr, commu-nity kitchen. Fishing, bike & hiking trails. On Twisp River. Trails to small backcountry lakes & to Lake Chelan National Recreation Area.

Roads End $5
Okanogan National Forest
10.8 mi W of Twisp on CR 9114; 14.4 mi NW on FR 44 (Twisp River Rd) & FR 4440. $5. All year; 14-day limit. Tbls, toilets, cfga, firewood, no drkg wtr or trash service. Picnicking; fishing. Elev 3600 ft; 2 acres. Gilbert Historical Site (1 mi E). Trailhead to backcountry & North Cascades National Park.

South Creek $5
Okanogan National Forest
10.8 mi W of Twisp on CR 9114; 11.3 mi NW on FR 44 (Twisp River Rd); off gravel FR 4440 by river. $5. All year; 14-day limit. 4 small sites (16-ft RV limit). Tbls, toilets, cfga, firewood, no drkg wtr or trash service. Picnicking; fishing; horseback riding. On North Fork of Twisp River. Trailhead to Lake Chelan National Recreation Area & North Cascades National Park. Elev 3100 ft; 2 acres.

Twisp River Horse Camp $5
Okanogan National Forest
22.6 mi NW of Twisp via FR 4420, 4430 and 4435 to its end. All year; 14-day limit. Free with $30 annual NW forest pass; $5 daily otherwise. 12 sites. Tbls, toilets, cfga, no drkg wtr or trash service. Primarily a horse camp; loading ramp, hitch rails, feed stations. Access to Twisp River, South Creek & Scatter Creek trails.

War Creek $5
Okanogan National Forest
10.8 mi W of Twisp on CR 9114; 3.3 mi W on FR 44. $5. All year; 14-day limit. No wtr or trash service in winter. 10 sites (22-ft RV limit). Tbls, toilets, cfga, drkg wtr. Fishing (Twisp River), hiking trails, picnicking. Trailheads nearby. Picnic area. Rattlesnakes occasionally seen.

USK (128)

Browns Lake $10
Colville National Forest
6.5 mi NE of Usk on CR 3389; 3 mi N on FR 5030. $10. 5/25-9/10; 14-day limit. 18 sites (24-ft RV limit). Tbls, toilets, cfga, no drkg wtr. Boating(l- no motors), fly fishing, mountain bike trail, hiking trails. 22 acres.

Panhandle $12
Colville National Forest
15 mi N of Usk on CR 9325. $12. 5/25-9/10; 14-day limit. 13 sites (32-ft RV limit. Tbls, toilets, cfga, drkg wtr. Swimming, boating(l), fishing. On Pend Oreille River. 20 acres.

South Skookum Lake $12
Colville National Forest
7.5 mi NE of Usk on CR 3389. $12. 25 sites (32-ft RV limit). Tbls, toilets, cfga, drkg wtr. Boating(l), fishing, hiking, swimming, water-skiing. 15 acres.

VANCOUVER (129)

Battleground Lake State Park   **$12**
19 mi NE of Vancouver on SR 503; 3 mi E. $12 base. All year; 10-day limit. 15 primitive hike-in tent sites at $12; 25 standard sites at $17; $23 at six sites with hookups; 50-ft RV limit. Primitive sites have cfga, nearby drkg wtr & toilets, showers, dump. Primitive equestrian camping area. Swimming beach, fishing, boating(l), scuba diving, hiking trails, bridle trails. 280 acres.

Fishing tip: Good fishing for stocked rainbow trout, with typical fish being 10-12 inches and brood stock running 20-26 inches. To those are added brook trout and cutthroat each May. The lake also contains largemouth bass. Troll or cast red-and-white Mepps, black Panther Martins or white Roostertails.

Cold Creek Recreation Site   **FREE**
Yacolt Burn State Forest
Dept of Natural Resources
From I-5 Exit 9 at Vancouver, 5.5 mi E on NE 179th St, then right on SR 503 for 1.5 mi; left on NE 159th St for 3 mi; right on 182nd Ave for 1 mi; left on NE 139th (L-1400 Rd) about 8 mi; left on L-1000 Rd for 3.2 mi; left 1 mi on L-1300 Rd to camp; at Cold Creek. Free. All year; 14-day limit. 6 sites. Picnic area, tbls, toilets, cfga, drkg wtr, group picnic shelter. Fishing, hiking trails, motorcycling, horseback riding. Campground closed except for limited permit use.

Paradise Point State Park   **$12**
20 mi N of Vancouver off US 99 & I-5. $12 base. All year; 10-day limit. Limited facilities in winter (20-day limit). $12 base for primitive sites; $17 for standard sites; $23 at 20 utility sites with hookups (40-ft RV limit). Primitive sites have cfga, nearby drkg wtr & toilets; standard sites have campstove, drkg wtr, cfga, tbls, trash disposal, flush toilets, showers, beach. Dump. Swimming, boating(l), fishing, nature trails. East Fork Lewis River. 88 acres.

VASHON ISLAND (130)

Lisabeula County Park   **FREE**
Vashon Park District
Washington Water Trails System
On W side of island just S of mid-island at Colvos Passage. Free. Limited open tent camping for users of canoes, kayaks, other human-powered watercraft. Tbls, toilets, no drkg wtr, no fires, no trash service. 5.5 acres.

Wingehaven Park   **FREE**
Vashon Park District
Washington Water Trails System
On NE side of Vashon Island, about 1 mi S of Dolphin Point on Puget Sound. Free. Limited open tent camping for users of canoes, kayaks, other human-powered watercraft. Tbls, toilets, no drkg wtr, no fires, no trash service. 12 acres.

WAITSBURG (131)

Lewis & Clark Trail State Park   **$12**
4 mi E of Waitsburg on US 12 (24 mi E of Walla Walla). $12 base. All year; 10-day limit (20-day limit in winter). $12 for 15 primitive sites available all year; $17 for 24 standard sites (available 4/1-9/15); 28-ft RV limit. Tbls, flush toilets, showers, cfga, drkg wtr, dump, beach. Swimming, fishing. 37 acres.

WASHTUCNA (132)

Palouse Falls State Park   **$12**
17 mi SE of Washtucna on SR 261. $12. All year; 10-day limit. Limited facilities in winter (20-day limit). 10 primitive sites with cfga, nearby drkg wtr & toilets. View of 198-ft Palouse Falls; scenic, shady picnic area. 105 acres.

WAUCONDA (133)

Beth Lake   **$6**
Okanogan National Forest
8.5 mi SE of Wauconda on SR 20; N at exit to Bonapaarte Recreation Area (CR 4953, becoming FR 32 for 7 mi). $6. All year; 14-day limit. 15 sites (32-ft RV limit). Tbls, toilets, cfga, no drkg wtr. Boating, swimming. Hiking trails on Clackamas Mtn & Fir Mtn areas.

Bonaparte Lake   **$8**
Okanogan National Forest
2 mi W of Wauconda on SR 20; 5 mi N on CR 4953; half mi N on FR 32. $8. All year; 14-day limit. 28 sites (32-ft RV limit) plus 3 walk-in tent sites & group sites. Tbls, flush & pit toilets, cfga, no drkg wtr. Swimming, boating(l), fishing, hiking, picnicking (8 sites).

Lost Lake   **$8**
Okanogan National Forest
2 mi W of Wauconda on SR 20; 5 mi N on CR 4953; 4 mi NE on FR 32; 6 mi NW on FR 33. $8. All year; 14-day limit. 19 sites (32-ft RV limit) plus group area. Tbls, flush & pit toilets, cfga, no drkg wtr. Boating(l), swimming, fishing, picnicking (13 sites), amphitheater.

WENATCHEE (134)

Daroga State Park   **$12**
18 mi N of Wenatchee on SR 97; on E shore of Columbia River. $12 for 17 walk-in or boat-in or bike-in tent sites; 25 RV utility sites for $23 with wtr & elec. 3/9-10/9; 10-day limit. Tbls, flush toilets, cfga, drkg wtr, showers, dump, beach, shelters. Swimming, fishing, volleyball, tennis, soccer, biking, jet skiing, waterskiing, sailing, windsurfing, hiking. 90 acres.

WESTPORT (135)

Twin Harbors State Park   **$12**
3 mi S of Westport on SR 105; on Pacific coast. All year; 10-day limit (20-day limit in winter). $12 for primitive tent sites; 253 standard tent sites at $17; 49 RV utility sites at $23 (35-ft RV limit, but most RV sites are small, close together). Primitive sites have cfga, nearby drkg wtr & toilets; standard sites have campstove, drkg wtr, cfga, tbls, trash disposal, flush toilets, showers. Dump. Fishing, beachcombing, nature trail. 172 acres.

WILBUR (136)

Jones Bay Campground   **$10**
Lake Roosevelt Nat Recreation Area
Half mi NW of Wilbur on SR 174; right for 6.2 mi; just before milepost 99, right on unmarked rd for 2 mi; veer left on Gollehon Rd for 2 mi, then veer left again on Hanson Harbor Rd for 3.5 mi; right at Y for 3 mi. $10 during 5/1-9/30; $5 rest of year. 9 sites. Pit toilets, tbls, cfga, no drkg wtr. Fishing, boating(l).

Keller Ferry   **$10**
Lake Roosevelt National Recreation Area
14 mi N of Wilbur on SR 21. $10 during 5/1-9/30; $5 rest of year; 14-day limit. 55 sites (16-ft RV limit). Tbls, flush toilets, cfga, drkg wtr, dump, fish cleaning station. Fishing, boating, swimming area, hiking. On shore of Franklin Roosevelt Lake.

WILKESON (137)

Evans Creek ORV Camp   **$5**
Mt. Baker-Snoqualmie National Forest
3.5 mi SE of Wilkeson on Hwy 165 & FR 7920. Free with $30 annual NW forest pass; $5 daily otherwise. 6/15-11/15; 14-day limit. 34 sites. Tbls, toilets, cfga, drkg wtr. Picnicking, no fishing. Take-off point for off-road vehicle trails. Near Mt. Rainier National Park

Ipsut Creek   **$8**
Mount Rainier National Park
18 mi SE of Wilkeson in NW corner of park on Fairfax Forest Reserve Rd. $8. 5/15-9/15; 14-day limit. 30 sites. Tbls, toilets, cfga, no drkg wtr. Free 9/10-5/10 if snow permits access. Fishing, hiking, recreation program. Since early 2005, site has been closed to drive-in camping due to flooding; walk-in camping okay.

Mowich Lake Campground   **FREE**
Mount Rainier National Park
17 mi SE of Wilkeson at the end of mostly unpaved SR 165. Free. All year; 14-day limit. About 30 undesignated walk-in tent sites (50-yard walk). Tbls, toilets, no drkg wtr, no cfga (fires prohibited). Hiking, fishing.

WINTHROP (138)

Ballard   **$5**
Okanogan National Forest
13.2 mi NW of Winthrop on SR 20; 6.9 mi NW on CR 1163; 2.1 mi NW on FR 5400 (Lost River Rd). $5 during 4/15-11/15; free rest of year; 14-day limit. 6 sites (28-ft RV limit). Toi-

lets, tbls, cfga, no drkg wtr or trash service. Fishing, hiking. Access to Robinson Creek, West Fork Methow & Lost River/Monument Creek trails.

Buck Lake   **$5**
Okanogan National Forest
6.6 mi N of Winthrop on W Chewuch Rd; 2.8 mi N on FR 51; 2.5 mi NW on FR 5130 at FR 5130-100; on Buck Lake. $5 during 4/15-11/15; free rest of year; 14-day limit. 9 sites (20-ft RV limit). Tbls, toilets, cfga, no drkg wtr or trash service. Fishing, boating (l - small boats), hiking, mountain biking, picnicking. Good fishing early in year; lake stocked.

Camp 4   **$5**
Okanogan National Forest
6.6 mi N of Winthrop on W Chewuch Rd (CR 1213); 11.3 mi N on FR 51; along Chewuch River. $5. All year; 14-day limit. 5 sites on 2 acres (2 for RVs under 16 ft, but trailers not recommended). Tbls, toilets, cfga, no drkg wtr, no trash service in winter. River. Picnicking; fishing.

Chewuck   **$8**
Okanogan National Forest
6.6 mi N of Winthrop on W Chewuch Rd (CR 1213); 8.6 mi NE on FR 51; along Chewuch River. $8. All year; 14-day limit. Open, undeveloped area with 4 sites (2 with 35-ft RV limit). Tbls, toilets, cfga, no drkg wtr, no trash pickup (pack litter out). Hunting; picnicking; fishing; hiking. Elev 2200 ft; 2 acres. Watch out for rattlesnakes.

Early Winters   **$5**
Okanogan National Forest
10 mi W of Winthrop (near Mazama) on SR 20. $5 during 4/15-11/15; free rest of year; 14-day limit. 6 sites (3 with 24-ft RV limit). Tbls, toilets, cfga, drkg wtr (no wtr or trash service in winter). Fishing, hiking (trail S to Cedar Falls). Info center nearby. Early Winter Creek. Closed in early 2007 by Cedar Creek fire.

Falls Creek   **$5**
Okanogan National Forest
6.6 mi N of Winthrop on CR 1213; 5.3 mi N on FR 51. $5. All year; 14-day limit. 7 sites (3 with 18-ft RV limit). Tbls, toilets, cfga, no drkg wtr. Fishing, swimming. Near Pasayten Wilderness. Hike qtr mi to scenic falls.

Flat   **$5**
Okanogan National Forest
6.6 mi N of Winthrop on W Chewuch Rd (CR 1213); 2.8 mi N on FR 51; 3.5 mi NW on FR 383 & FR 5130; along 8 Mile Creek; easy access for RVs. $5 during 4/15-11/15; free rest of year; 14-day limit. 12 sites (36-ft RV limit; lower level is dead-end). Tbls, toilets, cfga, no drkg wtr or trash service. Fishing, mountainbiking, hiking. Elev 2858 ft.

Harts Pass   **$5**
Okanogan National Forest
13.2 mi NW of Winthrop on SR 20; 6.9 mi

NW on CR 1163; 12.5 mi NW on FR 5400 (Lost River Rd, narrow & winding with steep side cliffs; closed to RVs). $5 during 4/15-11/15; free rest of year; 14-day limit. 5 tent sites. Tbls, toilets, cfga, no drkg wtr. No trash service in winter. Hiking (Pacific Crest Trail nearby; on edge of Pasayten Wilderness). Elev 6198 ft.

Honeymoon   **$5**
Okanogan National Forest
6.6 mi N of Winthrop on W Chewuch Rd (CR 1213); 2.8 mi N on FR 51; 8.9 mi NW on FR 383 & FR 5130. $5 during 4/15-11/15; free rest of year; 14-day limit. 6 sites (3 with 18-ft RV limit). Tbls, toilets, cfga, no drkg wtr. No trash service in winter. Fishing, picnicking. Along 8 Mile Creek. Named after honeymoon spot of forest ranger & wife.

Klipchuck   **$8**
Okanogan National Forest
14.5 mi W of Winthrop on SR 20; 1.2 mi NW on FR 300. $8 during 4/15-11/15; free rest of year; 14-day limit. 46 sites (5 with 34-ft RV limit). Tbls, toilets, cfga, drkg wtr (no wtr or trash service during winter). Fishing, hiking, picnicking. Elev 3000 ft; 20 acres. Watch for rattlesnakes. Group camping possibility.

Lone Fir   **$8**
Okanogan National Forest
21 mi W of Winthrop on SR 20. $8 during 4/15-11/15; free rest of year; 5-day limit. 27 sites (5 with 20-ft RV limit). Tbls, toilets, cfga, drkg wtr. (No wtr or trash service during winter). Fishing, hiking, picnicking. Elev 3640 ft; 13 acres. Along Early Winters Creek near Cutthroat Lake trailhead. Good overnight for bicyclists.

Meadows   **$5**
Okanogan National Forest
13.2 mi NW of Winthrop on SR 20; 6.9 mi NW on CR 1163; 12.5 mi NW on FR 5400 (Lost River Rd); 1 mi S on FR 500. Lost River Rd is narrow & winding with steep side cliffs, closed to RVs. $5 during 4/15-11/15; free rest of year; 14-day limit. 14 tent sites. Tbls, toilets, cfga, no drkg wtr; no trash service in winter. Hiking; horseback riding; picnicking; rockhounding. Elev 6200 ft; 10 acres. Botanical. Scenic trail. Pine meadows. Access to Pacific National Scenic Trail.

Nice   **$5**
Okanogan National Forest
6.6 mi N of Winthrop on CR W Chewuch Rd (CR 1213); 2.8 mi N on FR 51; 3.8 mi NW on FR 5130; along 8 Mile Creek. $5 during 4/15-11/15; free rest of year; 14-day limit. 3 sites (16-ft RV limit; no turnaround). Tbls, toilets, cfga, no drkg wtr, no trash service. Fishing, picnicking. Good spot for group camping.

River Bend   **$5**
Okanogan National Forest
13.2 mi NW of Winthrop on SR 20; 6.9 mi NW on CR 1163; 2.5 mi NW on FR 5400; half mi W on FR 060. $5 during 4/15-11/15;

free rest of year; 14-day limit. 5 sites (24-ft RV limit). Tbls, toilets, cfga, no drkg wtr. No trash service in winter. Fishing, hiking trails. On Methow River.

Ruffed Grouse   **$5**
Okanogan National Forest
6.6 mi N of Winthrop on W Chewuch Rd; 2.8 mi N on FR 51; 8.9 mi NW on FR 383 & FR 5130. $5 during 4/15-11/15; free rest of year; 14-day limit. 4 sites (35-ft RV limit. Tbls, toilets, cfga, no drkg wtr or trash service. Fishing, hiking, biking. Good area for group camping.

WOODLAND (139)

Lake Merrill   **FREE**
State Recreation Site
Yacolt Burns State Forest
Dept of Natural Resources
23 mi E of Woodland on SR 503, then N 5.5 mi N on Cougar Rd; left on FR 81 for 4.7 mi; left on access rd. 11 sites. Free. Tbls, toilets, cfga, drkg wtr. Boating(l), fishing. Near Mount St. Helens. Subject to flooding winter & spring. Note: This campground was closed indefinitely in 2004 due to eruption danger from Mt. St. Helen volcano.

Fishing tip: Fly fishing only in this lake, where boat motors are prohibited. This is a trophy trout lake, but all fish larger than 15 inches must be released. Try woolly-buggers and leeches, and match the hatches with dry flies. Most rainbows are 10-16 inches; browns of 17-24 inches occasionally.

Rock Creek Recreation Site   **FREE**
Yacolt Burn State Forest
Dept of Natural Resources
From I-5 Exit 9 S of Woodland, follow 179th St E 5.5 mi; right on SR 503 for 1.5 mi, then left on NE 159th St for 3 mi; right on 182nd Ave for 1 mi; left on NE 139th (L-1400 Rd) about 8 mi; left on L-1000 Rd for 3.2 mi; left 1.3 mi; left on L-1200 Rd for qtr mi. Camp on right. Free. All year; 14-day limit. 19 sites; 6 picnic sites. Toilets, tbls, cfga, drkg wtr, group shelter. Horse facilities, horse trails, hiking trails. Fishing, hiking, horseback riding. All barrier-free except hiking trail.

Woodland Camp   **FREE**
State Recreation Site
Dept of Natural Resources
From I-5 Exit 21 at Woodland, E 0.1 mi on SR 503 to East CC St., then right to just S of bridge; right on CR 1 for qtr mi; left on CR 38 for 2.5 mi; left to camp. Free. All year; 14-day limit. 10 sites; 5 picnic sites. Tbls, toilets, cfga, drkg wtr, playground equipment, handicap access. May be closed in 2007 except for limited permit use.

YAKIMA (140)

Ahtanum Camp   **FREE**
Ahtanum Multiple Use Area
Dept of Natural Resources
S on I-82 at Yakima for 2 mi to Union Gap;
W on Ahtanum Rd to Tampico; W on A-2000
(Middle Fork) Rd 9.5 mi. Free. All year; 14-
day limit. 18 sites. Toilets, cfga, tbls, drkg
wtr. Fishing; snowmobile trails. On Ahtanum
Creek. Snopark permit required in winter.

Clover Flats   **FREE**
Ahtanum Multiple Use Area
Dept of Natural Resources
S on I-82 at Yakima for 2 mi to Union Gap;
W on Ahtanum Rd to Tampico; W on A-2000
(Middle Fork) Rd 18.7 mi (gravel, one lane).
Camp on left. Beyond 5.8 mi, rd is very steep
(12-13 per cent grade). Free. All year; 14-day
limit. 9 sites. Toilets, cfga, drkg wtr, tbls.
Trails to Goat Rocks Wilderness.

Green Lake   **FREE**
Ahtanum Multiple Use Area
Dept. of Natural Resources
S on I-82 at Yakima for 2 mi to Union Gap;
W on Ahtanum Rd to Tampico; W on A-2000
(Middle Fork) Rd 9.5 mi to Ahtanum Camp;
then North Fork Ahtanum Rd (A-3000) 8 mi;
right on 9-3800 Rd for half mi. Free. All year;
14-day limit. 6 sites. Tbls, toilets, cfga, no
drkg wtr. Fishing. Area often is littered badly.
   Fishing tip: This lake has fair fishing for
small rainbow trout (7-9 inches), but some
fish in the 15-18 inch range are landed too.
Use powerbaits from shore or by boat.

Snow Cabin   **FREE**
Ahtanum Multiple Use Area
Dept of Natural Resources
S on I-82 at Yakima for 2 mi to Union Gap;
W on Ahtanum Rd to Tampico; W on A-2000
(Middle Fork) Rd 9.5 mi to Ahtanum Camp;
then North Fork Ahtanum Rd (A-3000) 7
mi. Free. All year; 14-day limit. 8 sites. Tbls,
toilets, cfga.

Tree Phones   **FREE**
State Recreation Site
Ahtanum Multiple Use Area
Dept of Natural Resources
S on I-82 at Yakima for 2 mi to Union Gap;
W on Ahtanum Rd to Tampico; W on A-2000
(Middle Fork) Rd 9.5 mi to Ahtanum Camp;
then continue 5.8 mi and left into camp. Free.
All year; 14-day limit. 14 sites; 4 picnic sites.
Toilets, tbls, cfga, horse facilities, group
shelter, no drkg wtr, horse mountain ramp.
Horseback riding trails; snowmobile trails;
motorcycling; mountain biking. Middle Fork
of Ahtanum Creek.

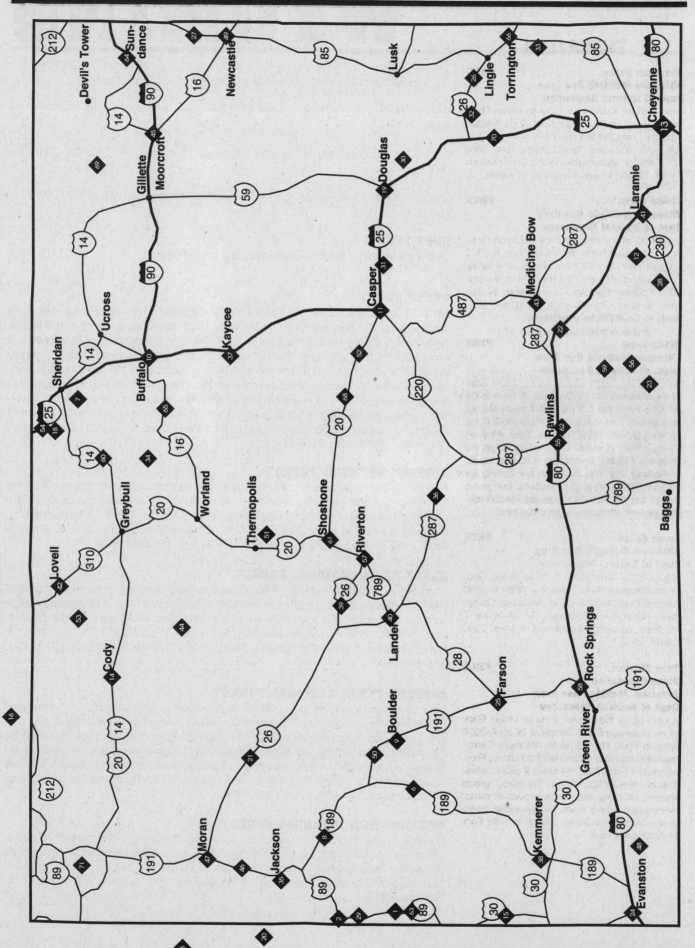

WYOMING

MISCELLANEOUS

Capital:
Cheyenne
Nickname:
Equality State
Motto:
Equal Rights
Flower:
Indian Paintbrush
Tree:
Cottonwood
Bird:
Meadowlark
Song:
"Wyoming"

Internet Address:
www.wyomingtourism.org

Toll-free number for travel information: 1-800-225-5996 (out of state).

Division of Tourism, I-25 at College Dr, Cheyenne, WY 82002: 307-777-7777 (in state).

Recreation Commission, Information Section, Cheyenne, WY 82002. 307-777-7695.

Game and Fish Commission, 5400 Bishop Blvd, Cheyenne, WY 82006. 307-777-4600.

REST AREAS

Overnight stops by self-contained vehicles are prohibited.

STATE PARKS

For 2007, overnight fees at state parks where camping is permitted are $6 per night for residents, $12 non-residents; no hookups, flush toilets or showers are available. An annual camping permit is available to Wyoming residents and non-residents; it allows camping in all parks; $30 for residents, $60 non-residents. The daily entry fee of $2 for residents and $4 for non-residents is included in the camping fee. Non-campers who use campground dump stations must pay the daily entry fees. No entry fees are charged at Hawk Springs Recreation Area, Conner Batlefield, Seminoe, Sinks Canyon and Medicine Lodge. Pets on leashes are permitted. For further information contact: Wyoming Division of Parks & Historic Sites, 2301 Central Ave., Cheyenne, WY 82002. 307-777-6323.

BIGHORN NATIONAL FOREST

A wide variety of dispersed camping opportunities are available. Thirty-six of the forest's developed campgrounds are now operated by concessionaire. Sites are managed from about Memorial Day weekend into October, but at 18 campgrounds, camping is free and water shut off in September until closed by snow. Columbus Bldg, 1969 S. Sheridan Ave., Sheridan, WY 82801. 307-672-0751.

BLACK HILLS NATIONAL FOREST

Camping is permitted outside of developed campgrounds with some exceptions. Free off-season camping (approximately 9/1-5/30) is permitted at developed campgrounds, but water and trash service are not provided. Bearlodge Ranger District, Black Hills National Forest, PO Box 680, Sundance, WY 82729; 307-283-1361. Or, Superintendent, Black Hills National Forest, 1019 N. Fifth St., Custer, SD 57730. 605-673-9200.

BRIDGER-TETON NATIONAL FOREST

Free off-season camping is permitted at developed campgrounds, but water and trash service are not provided; generally, the fee season is between Memorial Day and Labor Day. All campgrounds on the Jackson Ranger District are operated by a concessionaire. In the fall some campgrounds in the forest are left open at no charge, but water is not available due to freezing conditions. All campgrounds are closed during the winter. Forest Supervisor, Bridger-Teton National Forest, PO Box 1888, Jackson, WY 83001. 307-739-5500.

MEDICINE BOW NATIONAL FOREST

Located in the southeast quarter of Wyoming. Camping is permitted in developed campgrounds for up to 14 consecutive days. Dispersed camping outside campgrounds is allowed for up to 21 days. No overnight camping is permitted at day-use picnic grounds. Supervisor, 2468 Jackson St., Laramie, WY 82070-6535. 307/745-2300.

SHOSHONE NATIONAL FOREST

Since 1996, all campgrounds where fees are charged have been operated by concessionaires, and most overnight camping is $10. 808 Meadow Lane, Cody, WY 82414. 307/578-1200.

Wasatch National Forest, Evanston Ranger District, PO Box 1880 Evanston, WY 82731-1880.

Regional Forester, U.S. Forest Service, Rocky Mountain Region, 740 Simms St., Denver, CO 80401.

BIGHORN CANYON NATIONAL RECREATION AREA

The 71-mile-long Bighorn lake, created by Yellowtail Dam near Fort Smith, MT, provides electric power, water for irrigation, flood control and recreation. Daily entry fees are $5; annual pass, $30. Camping is available at the developed Horseshoe Bend Campground and at five less developed camping areas, including boat-in or hike-in sites. Backcountry camping also is available, but a free backcountry permit is required. A limited amount of shore camping, accessible by boat, is available at either end of the lake. Overnight parking for self-contained RVs is allowed in the upper parking lot at Ok-A-Beh and in the parking lot above the boat ramp at Barry's Landing. Summer activities include campfire campgrounds at Afterbay Campground in Montana and the Horseshoe Bend Campground amphitheater in Wyoming; topics include Indian culture, early settlers, geology, recreation and wildlife. Visitor center, 20 Highway, 14A East, Lovell, WY 82431; 307/548-2251.

Flaming Gorge National Recreation Area, Ashley National Forest PO Box 278, Manila, UT 84046; 801/784-3445.

YELLOWSTONE NATIONAL PARK

There are 1000 miles of hiking trails and 420 backcountry campsites. A $20 per vehicle park entrance fee is charged, valid for 7 days; or buy a $40 annual pass. Camping fees are $12-17. Superintendent, Yellowstone National Park, PO Box 168, Yellowstone National Park, WY 82190. 307/344-7381.

Bureau of Land Management, 2515 Warren Ave, PO Box 1828, Cheyenne, WY 82003; 307/775-6256.

Bureau of Land Management, Casper District, 1701 East E St., Casper, WY 82601.

Bureau of Land Management, Rawlins District, PO Box 670, 1300 3rd St, Rawlins, WY 82301.

Bureau of Land Management, Rock Springs District, P.O. Box 1869, Rock Springs, WY 82902-1170. Most of the Rock Springs District is open to unconfined camping, with requirements only on keeping vehicles on existing roads and trails, packing out all trash and limiting camping to 14 days. The Great Sand Dunes Off-Highway Vehicle Registration Area near Rock Springs has a parking and loading area with a vault-type toilet. It is not designated as a campground, but campers often camp near the facility; there is no drinking water.

Bureau of Land Management, Worland District, PO Box 119, Worland, WY 82401.

AFTON (1)

Lincoln County Park   **FREE**
9 mi N of Afton on US 89. Free. 5/1-10/31; 5-day limit. 10 sites. Tbls, toilets, cfga, no drkg wtr.

Swift Creek   **$5**
Bridger National Forest
1.5 mi E on county rd; qtr mi E on FR 10211. $5 during 5/15-10/15; free rest of yr when accessible, but no drkg wtr; 16-day limit except 10 days 7/1-8/31. 12 sites. Tbls, toilets, cfga, drkg wtr. Fishing, hiking, picnicking. Periodic Springs geyser nearby.

ALPINE (2)

Alpine   **$8**
Targhee National Forest
3 mi NW of Alpine on US 26. $8 base. MD-LD; 14-day limit. 17 sites (32-ft RV limit). Tbls, toilets, cfga, drkg wtr. Fishing, hiking, horseback riding. Palisades Reservoir. Snake River, Yellowstone & Grand Teton National Parks.

The Bridge   **$3**
Bridger National Forest
.8 mi SE of Alpine on US 89; 2.4 mi SE on Greys River Rd. $3 during 5/15-10/15; free rest of yr when accessible; 10-day limit. 5 sites (16-ft RV limit). Tbls, toilets, cfga, no drkg wtr. Swimming, boating, fishing.

Forest Park   **$5**
Bridger National Forest
.8 mi SE of Alpine on US 89; half mi SE on CR 1001; 35.3 mi SE on FR 10138. $5 during 6/1-10/30; free rest of yr, but no drkg wtr; 16-day limit except 10-day limit 7/1-8/31. 13 sites (22-ft RV limit). Tbls, toilets, cfga, drkg wtr. Fishing, picnicking. At Greys River. Elev 7000 ft; 8 acres.

Lynx Creek   **$3**
Bridger National Forest
.7 mi SE of Alpine on SR 89 (Greys River Rd); half mi SE on CR 1001; then 11.6 mi SE on FR 10138. Adjacent to Greys River. $3 during 6/1-10/30; free rest of yr when accessible; 16-day limit; 10 days 7/1-8/31. 14 sites. RV limit 16 ft. Pit toilets, no drkg wtr, cfga, tbls. Fishing in Greys River.

McCoy Creek   **$8**
Targhee National Forest
5 mi S of Alpine on US 89; 7 mi NW on FR 20058. Base $8. MD-LD; 14-day limit except 10-day limit 7/1-8/31. 19 sites (32-ft RV size limit). Tbls, flush toilets, cfga, drkg wtr. Boating(l), swimming, fishing, waterskiing. Elev 5500 ft; 4 acres.

Moose Flat   **$5**
Bridger National Forest
.7 mi SE of Alpine on SR 89, .5 mi SE on CR 1001, 22.5 mi SE on FR 10038. $5 during 6/1-10/30; free rest of year when accessible;

16-day limit. 10 sites; RV limit 22 ft. Pit toilets, drkg wtr, cfga, tbls; no wtr or trash service during free period. Fishing. Along Greys River. Elev 6400 ft; 11 acres.

Murphy Creek   **$5**
Bridger National Forest
.8 mi SE of Alpine on US 89; 11.2 mi SE on Greys River Rd. $5 during 6/1-10/30; free rest of yr when accessible, but no drkg wtr; 16-day limit except 10-day limit 7/1-8/31. 10 sites (30-ft RV limit). Tbls, toilets, cfga, drkg wtr. Fishing. Elev 6300 ft; 12 acres.

ASHTON, (IDAHO) (3)

Cave Falls   **$10**
Targhee National Forest
5 mi N of Ashton on SR 47; 7 mi E on CR 36; half mi S of Yellowstone National Park. IN WYOMING. $10. MD-10/15; 14-day limit. 23 sites (22-ft RV limit). Tbls, toilets, cfga, drkg wtr. Swimming, fishing. Elev 6200 ft; 16 acres.

BIG PINEY (6)

Middle Piney Lake   **FREE**
Bridger National Forest
20 mi W of Big Piney on SR 350; 4.3 mi W on FR 10046; W on FR 10024. Free. 7/1-9/30; 16-day limit. 5 sites. Tbls, toilets, cfga, no drkg wtr, no trash service. Fishing, hiking.

New Fork River Camp   **FREE**
Bureau of Land Management.
12 mi E of Big Piney on Hwy 351. Free. All year; 14-day limit. 5 sites. Tbls, no drkg wtr, toilets. Picnicking; fishing; boating. Names Hill, a "registry" for immigrants, is nearby.

Sacajawea   **$7**
Bridger National Forest
20 mi W of Big Piney on SR 350; 4.3 mi W on FR 10046; 1.2 mi W on FR 10024. $7 during 6/15-9/30; free rest of yr when accessible, but no drkg wtr 10-day limit. 26 sites (22-ft RV limit). Tbls, toilets, cfga, drkg wtr. Fishing, hiking trails. On Middle Piney Lake. Elev 8200 ft; 5 acres.

BIG HORN (7)

East Fork   **$10**
Bighorn National Forest
9.3 mi SW of Big Horn on CR 335; 8 mi SW on FR 26; half mi S on FR 293. RVs not recommended on FR 26 from Big Horn. $10 during 6/15-LD; 14-day limit. 12 sites (45-ft RV limit). Tbls, toilets, drkg wtr, cfga. Fishing, hiking. On East Fork of Big Goose Creek. Trails to Cloud Peak Wilderness. Elev 7600 ft; 6 acres.

Ranger Creek   **$10**
Bighorn National Forest
9.3 mi SW of Big Horn on CR 335; 10 mi SW on FR 26 (steep grades; RVs not recommended). $10 during 6/15-MD; 14-day limit. 11 sites (40-ft RV limit). Tbls, toilets,

cfga, drkg wtr. Fishing, hiking, picnicking. On Ranger Creek. Trails to Twin Lakes and Cloud Peak Wilderness. Elev 7800 ft; 5 acres.

BONDURANT (8)

Kozy   **$12**
Teton National Forest
8 mi NW of Bondurant on US 189. $12. MD-LD; 10-day limit. 8 sites (32-ft RV limit). Tbls, toilets, cfga, no drkg wtr. Fishing, hunting, picnicking. Elev 6500 ft.

BOULDER (9)

Boulder Lake   **FREE**
Bureau of Land Management
8.5 mi N of Boulder on BLM Rd 5106; on S shore of Boulder Lake. Free. 6/1-10/15; 14-day limit. 5 sites. Tbls, toilets, cfga, no drkg wtr. Fishing, boating, hunting.

Scab Creek Trailhead   **FREE**
Bureau of Land Management
7 mi E of Boulder on SR 353; N of Scab Creek Rd, then bear left (north) onto BLM 5423 for 7.5 mi. Free. 6/1-10/15; 14-day limit. 10 sites. Tbls, toilets, cfga, no drkg wtr. Fishing, hiking, horseback riding, hunting, climbing.

BUFFALO (10)

Bud Love   **FREE**
State Wildlife Management Area
6 mi N of Buffalo on Johnson Rd; 2 mi N on CR 131. Free. 5/1-11/15; 14-day limit. Primitive undesignated camping; no facilities, no drkg wtr. Fishing, hiking, hunting. The WMA is home to 500 elk, 200 deer & small herd of antelope.

Circle Park   **$11**
Bighorn National Forest
12.5 mi W of Buffalo on US 16; 2.5 mi W on FR 20. $11 during MD-9/20; 14-day limit. 10 sites (25-ft RV limit). Tbls, toilets, drkg wtr, cfga. Nature trails; trailhead to Cloud Peak Wilderness Area. Elev 7900 ft; 5 acres.

Crazy Woman   **$11**
Bighorn National Forest
26 mi W of Buffalo on US 16. $11 during MD-9/20; 14-day limit. 6 sites; 24-ft RV limit. Tbls, toilets, cfga, drkg wtr. Picnicking. Elev 7600 ft; 2 acres.

Doyle   **$10**
Bighorn National Forest
26 mi W of Buffalo on US 16; 5.5 mi SW on FR 32. $10 during 6/10-LD or as snow allows; 14-day limit. 19 sites (40-ft RV limit). Tbls, toilets, cfga, drkg wtr. Fishing, picnicking. Elev 8100 ft; 8 acres.

Hunter Corrals Horse Camp   **$10**
Bighorn National Forest
13 mi W of Buffalo on US 16; 3 mi NW on FR 19. $10; formerly free. 5/15-10/31; 14-day limit. Free during off-season but limited ser-

vices. 9 sites (30-ft RV limit) for horse camping only. Tbls, toilets, cfga, drkg wtr. Hiking, picnicking, horseback riding. Elev 7200 ft. Trailhead for Cloud Peak Wilderness.

Lost Cabin $11
Bighorn National Forest

26 mi SW of Buffalo on US 16. $11 during 6/10-LD; 14-day limit. 20 sites (45-ft RV limit). Six sites have 30-day limits. Tbls, toilets, cfga, drkg wtr. Fishing, picnicking. Along Muddy Creek. Elev 8200 ft; 5 acres.

Middle Fork $12
Bighorn National Forest

13.5 mi SW of Buffalo on US 16. $12 during 5/15-9/20; 14-day limit. 9 sites (60-ft RV limit). Tbls, toilets, cfga, drkg wtr. Fishing, picnicking. Elev 7400 ft; 3 acres.

South Fork $12
Bighorn National Forest

15 mi W of Buffalo on US 16; 1.6 mi E on FR 21. $12 (walk-in tent sites also $12) during 5/15-9/20; 14-day limit. 15 drive-in sites (35-ft RV limit); 5 walk-in sites. Tbls, toilets, cfga, drkg wtr. Fishing, picnicking; hiking trails nearby. Elev 7800 ft; 4 acres. Along South Fork of Clear Creek.

CASPER (11)

Alcova Lake $7
Natrona County Park
Bureau of Reclamation

23 mi W of Casper on Hwy 220 and CR 407. $7 base; $12 full hookups. 4/1-10/15; 14-day limit. 7 RV sites; 70 tent sites. Tbls, toilets, cfga, drkg wtr, dump, elec($), sewer($). Fremont Canyon. Fishing, swimming beach, boating(l). Marina, groceries. Elev 5500 ft; 3,370 acres.

Beartrap Meadow $7
Natrona County Park

7 mi S of Casper on Casper Mountain Rd., off SR 251. Poor road conditions. $7. 4/15-9/15; limited facilities in winter. 14-day limit. Undesignated tent camping, about 55 RV sites. Tbls, toilets, drkg wtr (no wtr 9/16-4/1). Ski trails, snowmobiling, tobogganing, horseback riding, biking. 160 acres.

Fishing tip: There's good angling for trout & walleye; brown and rainbow trout are stocked annually.

Casper Mountain $7
Natrona County Park

8 mi S of Casper on Casper Mountain Rd., off SR 251. Poor road conditions. $7. All year; 14-day limit; limited facilities in winter. Undesignated RV & tent sites. Tbls, toilets, drkg wtr (no wtr 9/16-4/1). Ski trails, snowmobiling, tobogganing, horseback riding, biking. 400 acres.

Gray Reef Reservoir $7
Natrona County Park
Bureau of Reclamation

26 mi W of Casper on SR 220. $7. 4/15-

10/15; 14-day limit. 12 sites (tents and very small RVs). Tbls, toilets, no drkg wtr. Fishing, boating(l). Elev 5500 ft; 43 acres.

Miracle Mile Area FREE
Kortes Reservoir
Bureau of Reclamation

54 mi SW of Casper on US 220, then on CR 407 & CRs 291 & 351; Miracle Mile stretches about 5.5 mi from Kortes Dam to Pathfinder National Wildlife Refuge. Free. All year; 14-day limit. 11 primitive camping areas. Tbls, toilets, drkg wtr, cfga, fishing pier. Hiking, fishing.

Fishing tip: Rainbow trout are stocked regularly, and fishing for them is excellent.

Lodgepole $5
Muddy Mountain
Environmental Education Area
Bureau of Land Management

9 mi S of Casper on Casper Mountain Rd; 6 mi to Muddy Mountain. $5 during 6/15-10/31; 14-day limit. 16 sites. Tbls, toilets, cfga, drkg wtr (at dam). Hunting, hiking trails. 200 acres.

Pathfinder Reservoir $7
Natrona County Park
Bureau of Reclamation

32 mi W of Casper on SR 220. $7. 4/1-10/15; 14-day limit. 65 sites. Tbls, toilets, cfga, drkg wtr. Fishing, boating(ld), dump, museum, groceries. Interpretive trail, visitor center at dam. Elev 5600 ft; 26,517 acres.

Fishing tip: There's excellent fishing in Pathfinder Reservoir for walleye and rainbow, brown & cutthroat trout, which are all stocked annually.

Ponderosa Park $7
Natrona County Park

10 mi S of Casper on SR 1301. $7. All year; 14-day limit. Undesignated tent sites only. Tbls, toilets, cfga, no drkg wtr. Hiking, snowmobiling.

Rim Campground $5
Muddy Mountain
Environmental Education Area
Bureau of Land Management

9 mi S of Casper on Casper Mountain Rd; 6 mi to Muddy Mountain. $5. 6/15-10/31; 14-day limit. 8 RV sites; tent spaces. Toilets, tbls, no drkg wtr except at Lodgepole Camp. Hunting, nature trails. Primarily a fall hunting camp.

Trapper's Route No. 1 FREE
Bureau of Land Management

About 27 mi SW of Casper on SR 220; just N of Grey Reef Reservoir. Free. All year, but limited access in winter; 14-day limit. Primitive undesignated sites. Toilets, tbls, cfga, no drkg wtr. Fishing, boating.

CENTENNIAL (12)

Aspen $10
Libby Creek Recreation Area
Medicine Bow National Forest

2 mi NW of Centennial on Hwy 130; qtr mi W on FR 351. $10. MD-9/30; 14-day limit. Dry camping off-season free. 8 sites (22-ft RV limit). Tbls, toilets, cfga, drkg wtr. Fishing, picnicking. Elev 8,600 ft.

Brooklyn Lake $10
Medicine Bow National Forest

9.5 mi NW of Centennial on FR 317. $10. 7/15-LD; 14-day limit. 19 sites (22-ft RV limit). Tbls, toilets, cfga, drkg wtr. Fishing, boating, hiking trails. Elev 10,500 ft; 7 acres. Trail to alpine lakes.

Nash Fork $10
Medicine Bow National Forest

8 mi NW of Centennial on SR 130; N on FR 317. $10. 7/1-LD; 14-day limit. 27 sites (22-ft RV limit). Tbls, toilets, cfga, drkg wtr. Fishing. Elev 10,200 ft; 16 acres.

North Fork $10
Medicine Bow National Forest

3.5 mi NW of Centennial on SR 130; 1.7 mi NW on FR 101. $10. 6/15-9/30; 14-day limit. 60 sites (30-ft RV limit). Tbls, toilets, cfga, drkg wtr. Fishing. Elev 8600 ft; 3 acres.

Pines $10
Libby Creek Recreation Area
Medicine Bow National Forest

2.3 mi NW of Centennial on Hwy 130; half mi NW on FR 351. $10. MD-9/30; 14-day limit. 6 sites (20-ft RV limit). Tbls, toilets, cfga, drkg wtr. Fishing. Elev 8600 ft.

Silver Lake $10
Medicine Bow National Forest

16 mi W on SR 130. $10. 7/1-9/15; 14-day limit. 17 sites (RVs under 32 ft). Tbls, toilets, cfga, drkg wtr. Elev 10,400 ft; 8 acres. Swimming, boating, fishing, trail to French Creek.

Spruce $10
Libby Creek Recreation Area
Medicine Bow National Forest

2.4 mi NW of Centennial on Hwy 130. $10. MD-9/30; 14-day limit. 8 sites (16-ft RV limit). Tbls, toilets, cfga, drkg wtr. Fishing. Elev 8600 ft.

Sugarloaf $10
Medicine Bow National Forest

13 mi NW of Centennial on SR 130; 1 mi N on FR 346. $10. 7/15-LD; 14-day limit. 16 sites (RVs under 23 ft). Tbls, toilets, cfga, drkg wtr. Boating, fishing, hiking trails to alpine lakes. Elev 10,700 ft; 4 acres.

Willow $10
Libby Creek Recreation Area
Medicine Bow National Forest

2 mi NW of Centennial on Hwy 130; half mi W on FR 351. $10. MD-9/30; 14-day limit. 16 sites (22-ft RV limit). Tbls, toilets, cfga, drkg wtr. Fishing. Elev 8600 ft.

✪ CHEYENNE (13)

Curt Gowdy State Park   **$12**
25 mi W of Cheyenne on Happy Jack Rd. to SR 210, then W to park. $12 ($6 for residents). Free after payment of $60 annual state park camping permit ($30 for residents). All year, but most wtr shut off after 10/1; 14-day limit. 150 sites (30 suitable for RVs); no RV length limit. Backpack & horse camping also available. Tbls, toilets, cfga, drkg wtr, dump, playgrounds. Boating(l), fishing, hiking, fishing pier, snowmobiling, beach (no swimming), birdwatching, ice fishing. archery range. Elev 7,200 ft; 1,635 acres. Crystal and Granite Reservoirs; waterskiing. Natural area. July bluegrass festival.

CODY (14)

Big Game   **$10**
Shoshone National Forest
28.6 mi W of Cody on US 14/16/20. $10. 5/15-9/30; 14-day limit. 17 sites (32-ft RV limit). Tbls, toilets, cfga, drkg wtr. Stream fishing. Elev 5900 ft; 10 acres.

North Fork Campground   **$12**
Buffalo Bill State Park
14 mi W of Cody on US 14/20/16 (North Fork Hwy). $12 ($6 for residents). Free after payment of $60 annual state park camping permit ($30 for residents). All year; 14-day limit; limited facilities 10/1-4/30. 56 pull-through RV sites & 6 tent sites, plus Trout Creek Group Camping Area). Tbls, toilets, cfga, drkg wtr, dump. Boating(l), fishing, swimming, hunting, picnicking, waterskiing, windsurfing, biking, hiking. Trout Creek Nature Trail is near the group camping area.

North Shore Bay Campground   **$12**
Buffalo Bill State Park
9 mi W of Cody on US 14/20/16 (North Fork Hwy). $12 ($6 for residents). Free after payment of $60 annual state park camping permit ($30 for residents). All year; 14-day limit; limited facilities 10/1-4/30. 35 RV sites (29 pull-through) & 3 tent sites. Tbls, toilets, cfga, drkg wtr, dump. Boating(l), fishing, swimming, hunting, picnicking, waterskiing, windsurfing, biking, hiking.

Clearwater   **$10**
Shoshone National Forest
31.8 mi W of Cody on US 14/16/20. $10. 5/15-9/30; 14-day limit. 20 sites (32-ft RV limit). Tbls, toilets, cfga, drkg wtr. Stream fishing, nearby trail along creek to North Absaroka Wilderness. Elev 6000 ft; 10 acres.

Elk Fork   **$10**
Shoshone National Forest
29.2 mi W of Cody on US 14/16/20. $10. 5/15-10/30; 14-day limit. 13 sites (22-ft RV limit). Tbls, toilets, cfga, drkg wtr. Stream fishing; trailhead; public corrals. Trail along Elk Creek into Washaki Wilderness. 4 acres.

Sunlight   **FREE**
State Wildlife Management Area
13 mi N of Cody on SR 120; 25 mi W on FR 101 (Chief Joseph Hwy). Free. 5/1-12/15; 14-day limit. Developed campground with undesignated sites. Toilets, cfga, no drkg wtr. Fishing, hiking, hunting, wildlife study. Area inhabited by grizzly bears; store all food.

   Fishing tip: Nearby stream are all stocked with cutthroat trout.

Three Mile   **$10**
Shoshone National Forest
48.6 mi W of Cody on US 14/16/20. $10. 5/15-10/30; 14-day limit. 33 sites (32-ft RV limit). Tbls, toilets, cfga, drkg wtr. Stream fishing, North Fork of Shoshone River. Hiking trails nearby. Elev 6700 ft; 9 acres.

Wapiti   **$10**
Shoshone National Forest
29 mi W of Cody on US 14/16/20. $10 (or $14 with elec). 5/15-10/30; 14-day limit. 42 sites (22-ft RV limit). Tbls, toilets, cfga, drkg wtr. Stream fishing, nearby hiking trails. Elev 6000 ft; 20 acres.

COKEVILLE (15)

Cokeville City Park   **FREE**
In town. Free. All year; 2-day limit. Tbls, toilets, cfga, drkg wtr.

Hams Fork   **$5**
Bridger National Forest
12 mi N of Cokeville on SR 232; 4 mi NE on county rd; 13 mi E on FR 10062. $5 during MD-10/31; free rest of yr when accessible, but no drkg wtr; 16-day limit except 10-day limit 7/1-8/31. 13 sites. Tbls, toilets, cfga, drkg wtr. Na-ture trails, fishing, snowmobiling, cross-country skiing. Elev 8000 ft; 7 acres.

Hobble Creek   **$5**
Bridger National Forest
12 mi N of Cokeville on SR 232; 8 mi N on FS rd; 10 mi N on FS rd. $5 during 7/1-10/31; free rest of yr when accessible, but no drkg wtr; 16-day limit except 10-day limit 7/1-8/31. 14 sites. Tbls, toilets, cfga, drkg wtr. Fishing, hiking.

COOKE CITY (MONTANA) (16)

Chief Joseph   **$8**
Gallatin National Forest
4.8 mi E of Cooke City on US 212. $8. 7/1-9/15; 15-day limit. 6 sites (22-ft RV limit). Tbls, toilets, cfga, drkg wtr. Picnicking, hiking. Nearby trailhead to Absaroka-Beartooth Wil-derness. Ranger programs. Elev 8000 ft.

Colter   **$8**
Gallatin National Forest
2.3 mi E of Cooke City on US 212 in Wyoming. $8. 7/1-9/15; 14-day limit. 23 sites (22-ft RV limit). Tbls, toilets, cfga, drkg wtr. Fishing, hiking trails along Lady of the Lake Creek. Elev 7900 ft; 15 acres.

Crazy Creek   **$10**
Shoshone National Forest
10.5 mi SE of Cooke City on US 212. Along Clarks Fork of Yellowstone River. $10. 6/1-10/20; 14-day limit. 16 sites (28-ft RV limit). Tbls, toilets, cfga, drkg wtr. Fishing, hiking, picnicking. Crazy Lakes trailhead to back-country lakes in Absaroka-Beartooth Wilderness. Scenic walk to Crazy Creek Falls. Elev 6900 ft.

Dead Indian   **$5**
Shoshone National Forest
40 mi SE of Cooke City, MT, on WY 296 (Chief Joseph Scenic Hwy). $5. All year; 14-day limit. 12 sites (RVs under 32 ft). Tbls, toilets, cfga, no drkg wtr, no trash service. Fishing, hunting, hiking. Adjacent to Dead Indian Trailhead. 42 mi from Yellowstone. Elev 6100 ft; 11 acres.

Fox Creek Campground   **$10**
Shoshone National Forest
7.5 mi SE of Cooke City on US 212. $10 with federal Senior Pass; others pay $20. 6/15-9/30; 14-day limit. 34 sites (32-ft RV limit). Tbls, elec hookups, toilets, cfga, drkg wtr. Fishing, hiking, boating, picnicking. At Fox Creek and Clarks Fork of Yellowstone River. Elev 7100 ft.

Hunter Peak Campground   **$10**
Shoshone National Forest
14.4 mi SE of Cooke City on US 212; 5 mi S on Hwy 296. $10. All year; 14-day limit. 9 sites (28-ft RV limit). Tbls, toilets, cfga, drkg wtr. Fishing, hiking, picnicking. Clarks Fork Trailhead nearby has horse facilities. Elev 6500 ft.

Lake Creek   **$5**
Shoshone National Forest
14.4 mi SE of Cooke City on US 212. $5. 5/1-9/30; 14-day limit. 6 sites (22-ft RV limit). Tbls, toilets, cfga, no drkg wtr. Fishing, hiking, picnicking. Elev 6900 ft.

Little Sunlight   **FREE**
Shoshone National Forest
In Sunlight Basin, 47 mi SE of Cooke City, MT, on WY 296 (Chief Joseph Scenic Hwy) & 13 mi on FR 101. Free. All year; 14-day limit. 4 sites (32-ft RV limit). Tbls, toilets, cfga, no drkg wtr. Horse corrals & hitchrails. Fishing, hiking, picnicking, horseback riding.

Soda Butte   **$9**
Gallatin National Forest
1.2 mi E of Cooke City on US 212. $8. 6/15-10/15; 15-day limit. 21 sites. Tbls, toilets, cfga, drkg wtr. Fishing, hiking.

DAYTON (18)

Dead Swede   **$11**
Bighorn National Forest
34 mi SW of Dayton on US 14; 4 mi SE on FR 26. $11 during 6/5-9/20 (some sites free later in fall, but no services); 14-day limit. 22 sites (40-ft RV limit). Tbls, toilets, cfga, drkg wtr.

Fishing; on the South Tongue River; hiking. Elev 8400 ft; 10 acres.

North Tongue $11
Bighorn National Forest
29 mi SW of Dayton on US 14; 1 mi N on FR 15. $11 during MD-9/20; $6 rest of yr as snow allows; 14-day limit. 12 sites (60-ft RV limit). Tbls, toilets, cfga, drkg wtr. Store, dump nearby. Some handicap sites. Fishing. Elev 7900 ft; 4 acres.

Owen Creek $11
Bighorn National Forest
34 mi SW of Dayton on US 14; qtr mi on FR 236. $11 during MD-9/20; 14-day limit. 8 sites (45-ft RV limit). Tbls, toilets, cfga, drkg wtr. Fishing. Elev 8400 ft; 3 acres.

Prune Creek $12
Bighorn National Forest
26 mi SW of Dayton on US 14. $12 during MD-9/20; 14-day limit. 21 sites (60-ft RV limit); some handicap sites. Tbls, toilets, cfga, drkg wtr. Store nearby. Fishing, hiking. On South Tongue River at Prune Creek. Elev 7700 ft; 8 acres.

Sibley Lake $12
Bighorn National Forest
25 mi SW of Dayton on US 14. $12 ($15 with elec) during MD-9/20; 14-day limit. 25 sites (60-ft RV limit). Tbls, toilets, cfga, drkg wtr. Fishing, boating(lr - no motors), hiking. Elev 7900 ft; 7 acres.

Tie Flume $11
Bighorn National Forest
34 mi SW of Dayton on US 14; 2 mi E on FR 26. $11 during 6/5-9/20; 14-day limit. 27 sites (60-ft RV limit). Tbls, toilets, cfga, drkg wtr. Fishing; hiking trails are nearby. Elev 8400 ft; 10 acres.

Tongue Canyon Camp FREE
Amsden Creek
State Wildlife Management Area
2.2 mi W of Dayton on CR 92; at the Y, turn left for 1 mi to the Tongue River Campground & follow dirt rd 1 mi. Free. 5/1-11/15; 14-day limit. Primitive sites; no facilities, no drkg wtr. Fishing, hiking, hunting, wildlife study.

Fishing tip: Catch small trout from Amsden Creek and larger ones in the nearby Tongue River.

DOUGLAS (19)

Ayres Natural Bridge FREE
Converse County Park
12 mi W of Douglas on I-25 to exit 151; 5 mi S on CR 13. Camp free, but donations suggested. 4/1-11/1; 7-day limit. 20 tent sites, 12 RV sites (32-ft RV limit). Tbls, toilets, cfga, drkg wtr. Picnicking; fishing, horseshoes, playground. Elev 5300 ft; Scenic mountain drives. Natural bridge. Reader says park open only 8-8 daily.

Campbell Creek $5
Medicine Bow National Forest
2 mi S of Douglas on SR 94 (Esterbrook Rd); right on Chalk Buttes Rd for 3 mi; left on SR 91 for 25 mi; continue S on unpaved Converse CR 24 for 14 mi. $5. 5/15-10/15. 8 sites; 22-ft RV limit. Tbls, Toilet, cfga, drkg wtr. Fishing, hiking.

Curtis Gulch $5
Medicine Bow National Forest
20 mi W & S of Douglas on SR 91; 14 mi S on CR 16; 1 mi NE on FR 658 (gravel rds 25 mi from Douglas); at LaBonte Canyon. $5. 5/15-10/15; 14-day limit. 6 sites; 22-ft RV limit. Tbls, toilets, cfga, drkg wtr. Fishing, hiking. Note: also numerous dispersed campsites along FR 658 between curtis Gulch & forest boundary along LaBonte Canyon.

Esterbrook $5
Medicine Bow National Forest
17 mi S of Douglas on SR 94 (Esterbrook Rd); 11 mi S on CR 5; 3 mi E on FR 633. $5. 5/15-10/15; 14-day limit. 12 sites; 22-ft RV limit. Tbls, toilets, cfga, drkg wtr. Hiking, fishing.

Friend Park $5
Medicine Bow National Forest
17 mi S of Douglas on SR 94 (Esterbrook Rd); 11 mi S on CR 5, then 15 mi SW on CR 5; 2 mi SE on fR 671. $5. 5/15-10/15; 14-day limit. 11 sites; 22-ft RV limit. Tbls, toilets, cfga, drkg wtr. Camp expanded in 1998. Fishing, hiking.

Riverside City Park FREE
Downtown Douglas on North Platte River; half mi E of I-25 from exit 140, cross river. Free. All year; 2-day limit. About 20 undesignated sites. Tbls, flush toilets, cfga, drkg wtr, showers, dump. Boating(l), fishing, hiking. Can be crowded in summer. 307/358-5544.

DRIGGS, (IDAHO) (20)

Teton Canyon $10
Targhee National Forest
6 mi E of Driggs on CR 009; 4.5 mi S on FR 009; in Wyoming. $10. 5/15-9/15; 14-day limit. 19 sites (22-ft RV limit). Tbls, toilets, cfga, drkg wtr. Beginning of Teton Crest Trail into Jedediah Smith Wilderness. Fishing, hiking. Elev 13,770 ft; 4 acres.

Pine Creek $8
Targhee National Forest
5.3 mi W of Victor on SR 31. $8. 6/1-9/30; 14-day limit. 11 sites (32-ft RV limit). Tbls, toilets, cfga, drkg wtr. No trash service; pack it out. Hiking, fishing. Elev 6600 ft; 3 acres.

Trail Creek $8
Targhee National Forest
5.5 mi E of Victor on SR 33; one-third mi S on SR 22. $8. 6/1-9/30; 14-day limit. 11 sites (32-ft RV limit). Tbls, toilets, cfga, drkg wtr. Fishing, hiking. Near Jedediah Smith Wilderness. Elev 6600 ft; 7 acres.

DUBOIS (21)

Brooks Lake $10
Shoshone National Forest
30 mi W on Hwy 287 from Dubois (gravel last 5 mi). $10. 6/15-9/30; 14-day limit. 14 sites (32-ft RV limit). Drkg wtr, toilets, cfga, tbls. Fishing, hiking, boating(l), picnicking. Elev 9200 ft; 9 acres.

Double Cabin $10
Shoshone National Forest
28 mi N of Dubois on FRs 508 and 285 (hazardous when wet). $10. 6/15-9/30; 14-day limit. 15 sites (32-ft RV limit). Tbls, toilets, cfga, drkg wtr. Fishing, hiking, picnicking. Elev 8053 ft; 8 acres. On edge of Washakie Wil-derness area.

Falls $10
Shoshone National Forest
25 mi NW of Dubois on US 26/287. $10. 6/1-10/30; 14-day limit. 44 sites (32-ft RV limit). Tbls, toilets, cfga, drkg wtr. Fishing, hiking, picnicking. Brooks Lake Creek Falls nearby. Elev 8000 ft; 18 acres.

Horse Creek $10
Shoshone National Forest
12 mi N of Dubois on FRs 508 & 285 (hazardous when wet). $10. 6/15-10/30; 14-day limit. 9 sites (32-ft RV limit). Tbls, toilets, cfga, drkg wtr. Fishing, hiking, picnicking. Trails to seclu-ded lakes. Elev 7500 ft.

Kirk Inberg/Kevin Roy FREE
State Wildlife Management Area
About 10 mi E of Dubois on US 26/287; 9 mi N on CR 277 & East Fork Rd to campground & headquarters. Free. 5/1-1/31; 14-day limit. Primitive undesignated sites. Tbls, toilets, cfga, no drkg wtr. Fishing, hiking, hunting, wildlife study, rockhounding. Permit required for fossil or artifact collecting. Once the traditional wintering site for the Sheepeater clan of Shoshone, and many artifacts remain.

Fishing tip: Try for trout & whitefish in the Wiggins Fork River.

Pinnacles $7.50
Shoshone National Forest
23 mi NW of Dubois on US 26/287; 15 mi N on FR 515. $7.50 with federal Senior Pass; others pay $15. 6/15-9/30; 14-day limit. 21 sites (32-ft RV limit). Tbls, toilets, cfga, drkg wtr. Fishing, hiking, boating, picnicking. Elev 9200 ft; 14 acres.

Spence/Moriarity FREE
State Wildlife Management Area
10.5 mi S of Dubois on US 26/287; 7 mi N on East Fork Rd. Free. 5/1-11/30; 14-day limit. Primitive sites. Toilets, cfga, no drkg wtr. Fishing, hiking, hunting, widlife study. Ruins of old stage station. 37,500 acres.

Whiskey Basin/ FREE
Little Red Creek
State Wildlife Management Area
4 mi E of Dubois on US 26/287. Free. Devel-

WYOMING

oped primitive campground. Toilets, cfga, no drkg wtr. Fishing, hiking, hunting, wildlife study. Former winter area of Sheepeater clan of Shoshone Indians, are has numerous petroglyphs & artifacts.

Fishing tip: Torrey Lake and 3 glacial lakes offer good fishing for brook & brown trout, whitefish.

ELK MOUNTAIN (22)

Bow River   **$7**
Medicine Bow National Forest
14 mi S of Elk Mountain on CR 101; 1.3 mi SE on FR 1013A; qtr mi W on FR 101. $7. MD-10/31; 14-day limit. 13 sites (32-ft RV limit). Tbls, toilets, cfga, well drkg wtr. Picnicking, fishing. Elev 8600 ft; 6 acres. Good wildlife viewing.

Wick/Beumee   **FREE**
State Wildlife Management Area
Along I-80, 6 mi SE of Elk Mountain. Free. 4/1-11/30; 14-day limit. Primitive undesignated camping. Toilets, cfga, no drkg wtr (wtr available at Wagonhound interchange rest area). Fishing, hiking, hunting, wildlife study.
Fishing tip: 4 streams drain the area, and all contain rainbow, brook & brown trout.

ENCAMPMENT (23)

Bottle Creek   **$10**
Medicine Bow National Forest
7 mi SW of Encampment on SR 70. $10. MD-10/31; 14-day limit. 16 sites (45-ft RV limit). Tbls, toilets, cfga, well drkg wtr. Picnicking, hiking, fishing. Elev 8700 ft; 4 acres.

Encampment River   **$7**
Canyon Trailhead
Bureau of Land Management
1 mi W of Encampment on SR 70; 1 mi S on CR 353; 1 mi on BLM rd. $7. 6/1-11/15 (weather permitting, free winter camping); 14-day limit. 8 sites; 25-ft RV limit. Tbls, toilets, cfga, no drkg wtr. Picnicking; fishing; swimming; hiking; horseback riding; rockhounding; kayaking. Trail access to BLM Encampment River Canyon Wilderness WSA & USFS Encampment Wilderness Area. Free primitive camping also allowed anywhere within canyon; best sites with first 9 mi of trail.

Haskins   **$7**
Medicine Bow National Forest
15.3 mi SW of Encampment on SR 70. $7. 6/15-10/31; 14-day limit. 10 sites (20-ft RV li-mit). Tbls, toilets, cfga, drkg wtr. Fishing. Elev 9000 ft; 5 acres.

Lakeview   **$10**
Medicine Bow National Forest
6 mi W of Encampment on SR 70; 22 mi SW on FR 550. $10. 6/10-10/31; 14-day limit. 50 sites (30-ft RV limit). Tbls, toilets, cfga, well drkg wtr. Hiking, picnicking, boating, fishing. On Hog Park Reservoir. Boat launch nearby. Elev 8400 ft; 33 acres.

Lost Creek   **$7**
Medicine Bow National Forest
17.3 mi SW of Encampment on SR 70. $7. 6/10-10/31; 14-day limit. 10 sites (22-ft RV limit). Tbls, toilets, cfga, well drkg wtr. Hiking, picnicking, fishing, rockhounding. Elev 8800 ft; 8 acres.

Six Mile Gap   **$10**
Medicine Bow National Forest
24.6 mi SE of Encampment on SR 230; 2 mi SE on FR 492. $10. 5/15-10/31; 14-day limit. 7 sites; 32-ft RV limit. Tbls, toilets, cfga, drkg wtr. Fishing, boating, hiking.

EVANSTON (24)

Bear River   **$10**
Wasatch National Forest
30.5 mi S of Evanston on SR 150. $10 plus special parking fee ($3 daily, $6 weekly or $25 annually). 6/15-9/15; 7-day limit. 4 sites. Tbls, toilets, cfga, drkg wtr. Fishing.

Beaver View   **$10**
Wasatch National Forest
38 mi S of Evanston on SR 150. $10 plus special parking fee ($3 daily, $6 weekly or $25 annually). 6/1-10/15, but no wtr after LD; 7-day limit. 18 sites (22-ft RV limit). Tbls, toilets, cfga, drkg wtr. Fishing, hiking trails. Elev 9000 ft.

Christmas Meadows   **$12**
Wasatch National Forest
40 mi S of Evanston on SR 150. $12 plus special parking fee ($3 daily, $6 weekly or $25 annually). 6/1-10/30, but no wtr after LD; 14-day limit. 11 sites (20-ft RV limit). Tbls, toilets, cfga, drkg wtr. Fishing, hiking, horseback riding. Elev 9000 ft. Site of High Uintas Wilderness trailhead; horse unloading facilities.

East Fork Bear River   **$10**
Wasatch National Forest
35 mi S of Evanston on SR 150. $10 plus special parking fee ($3 daily, $6 weekly or $25 annually). 5/1-10/1; 7-day limit. 7 sites. Tbls, toilets, cfga, no drkg wtr. Fishing.

Hayden Fork   **$10**
Wasatch National Forest
40 mi S of Evanston on SR 150. $10 plus special parking fee ($3 daily, $6 weekly or $25 annually). 6/1-10/1; 14-day limit. 9 sites. Tbls, toilets, cfga, drkg wtr. Fishing.

Little Lyman Lake   **$8**
Wasatch National Forest
34 mi S of Evanston on SR 150; 15 mi E on FR 058; half mi on FR 635. $8. 6/1-10/30, but no wtr after LD; 7-day limit. 10 sites (16-ft RV limit). Tbls, toilets, drkg wtr, cfga. Fishing, hiking, hunting. Elev 9300 ft.

Stillwater   **$12**
Wasatch National Forest
33 mi S of Evanston on SR 150. $12 plus

special parking fee ($3 daily, $6 weekly or $25 annually). 6/15-10/15, but no wtr after LD; 14-day limit. 21 sites (22-ft RV limit). Tbls, toilets, cfga, drkg wtr. Fishing. Elev 8700 ft; 7 acres.

Sulphur   **$12**
Wasatch National Forest
32.3 mi S of Evanston on SR 150. $12 plus special parking fee ($3 daily, $6 weekly or $25 annually). 6/15-10/15, but no wtr after LD; 14-day limit. 21 sites (22-ft RV limit). Tbls, toilets, cfga, drkg wtr. Fishing, hiking trails. Elev 9200 ft; 10 acres.

FARSON (25)

Big Sandy Recreation Area   **FREE**
Bureau of Reclamation
8 mi N on US 191; 2 mi E on co rd. 6/1-10/1; 14-day limit. 12 primitive sites. Tbls, toilets, cfga, no drkg wtr. Swimming, boating(l), fishing. Not well patrolled. Elev 6490 ft; 6190 acres.

FORT LARAMIE (26)

Chuckwagon RV Park (Private)   **$10**
1 block S on Hwy 160 from US 26. $10 base for tent & primitive sites; $16-18 full hookups. 4/15-10/15. 12 sites. Tbls, flush toilets, cfga, drkg wtr, showers($), handicap facilities, dump, elec($), sewer($), gift shop. 10% FCRV discount.

Ft. Laramie City Park   **FREE**
SW part of town. From Ft Laramie, 1 blk W on rd, 1 blk S of jct US 85/26 on Ft. Laramie Ave. Free. All year; 3-day limit. 25 sites. Tbls, toilets, cfga, drkg wtr, playground. Hunting; picnicking; fishing. Elev 4200 ft; 3 acres. Lake Guernsey. Old Ft. Laramie, Register Cliff. Sunrise Mine.

FOUR CORNERS (27)

Four Corners Campground   **$10**
At Four Corners, jct of US 85 & US 585 (N of Newcastle). $10 base tent sites. 10 tent sites; RV sites $25. Toilets, showers($), elec($), drkg wtr. Store, diner. Hunting, fishing, hiking, snowmobiling. Private campground.

FOXPARK (28)

Bobbie Thomson   **$10**
Medicine Bow National Forest
7 me NW of Foxpark on FR 512; 5 mi on FR 542, cross Douglas Creek bridge and bear right. $10. 6/1-10/15; 14-day limit. 18 sites (32-ft RV limit). Tbls, toilets, cfga, drkg wtr. Fishing. Rob Roy Reservoir nearby. Elev 8800 ft.

Lake Owen   **$10**
Medicine Bow National Forest
7 mi NE of Foxpark on FR 517; 3 mi S on FR 540. $10. 6/1-10/15; 14-day limit. 35 sites

(22-ft RV limit). Tbls, toilets, cfga, drkg wtr. Fishing, boating. Boat launch nearby. Elev 9000 ft.

Miller Lake $10
Medicine Bow National Forest
1 mi S of Foxpark on FR 512. $10. 6/1-10/15; 14-day limit. 7 sites (22-ft RV limit). Tbls, toilets, cfga, drkg wtr. Fishing, boating. Elev 9100 ft.

FREEDOM (29)

Pinebar FREE
Caribou National Forest
1 mi N of Freedom on CR 34; 9.5 mi W on SR 34. Free. 6/1-11/15; 14-day limit. 5 sites (16-ft RV limit). Tbls, toilets, cfga, drkg wtr, firewood. Horseback riding, picnicking, fishing.

GLENDO (30)

Glendo State Park Campground $12
3.5 mi E of Glendo on county rd; in state park. $12 ($6 for residents). Free after payment of $60 annual state park camping permit ($30 for residents). All year; limited facilities 10/1-4/1. 300 sites. Toilets, tbls, drkg wtr, cfga, dump. Hiking, canoeing, fishing, boating(l), playground. Elev 4700 ft; 9930 acres. Full-service marina nearby.
Red Hills Area: About 30 sites; close to lake; ground not level.
Reno Cove: About 30 sites; boat ramp; protected bay; ground not level, windy.
Custer Cove: About 40 sites; protected bay; some level sites.
Whiskey Gulch: About 100 sites; S side of large bay; many level sites.
Two Moon: About 200 sites; largest & best camping area; on bluff overlooking lake; most sites level.
Sandy Beach: Beach camping permitted, but no protection from wind; swimming; can be crowded in summer. Renovated in 2005; no RVs on beach, but tents okay.
Elk Horn: About 20 sites; close to lake; boat ramp seasonal.
Waters Point: Rock & gravel shoreline, protected bay for boats; ground not level, exposed to wind. About 15 sites.

GLENROCK (31)

ixby Public Fishing Area FREE
13 mi E of Glenrock on CR 27; at North Platte River. Free. All year; 14-day limit. Primitive undesignated sites at public access to North Platte River. Toilets, cfga, tbls, no drkg wtr. Fishing, boating(l).

Glenrock South FREE
City Recreational Complex
From Birch St in Glenrock, 2 mi S on Mormon Canyon Rd; right after going under I-25. Free. 5-day limit. Tbls, toilets, cfga, drkg wtr, dump. Ball fields, rodeo arena, fishing.

PP&L Public Fishing Area FREE
E of Glenrock on CR 27, then E on power plant rd, CR 27. Free. All year; 14-day limit. Primitive undesignated sites at public access to North Platte River. Toilets, cfga, tbls, no drkg wtr. Fishing, boating(l).

GUERNSEY (32)

Guernsey State Park $12
3 mi N of Guernsey, E on Hwy 26 from I-25 about 15 mi. $12 ($6 for residents). Free after payment of $60 annual state park camping permit ($30 for residents). All year; 14-day limit. Limited facilities 10/1-4/30. 142 sites at 7 campgrounds, including Fish Canyon on E side off Lakeshore Dr (good secluded tenting); Skyline on S end off Skyline Dr (best for large RVs). Tbls, toilets, cfga, drkg wtr, dump, beach. Fishing, boating (ld), hunting, picnicking, hiking, waterskiing, windsurfing. Visitor center; museum open 10-6 daily 5/1-10/1. Oregon Trail wagon wheel ruts; Register Cliff. On 2,375-acre Guernsey Reservoir. Elev 4300 ft; 6,227 acres.

HAWK SPRINGS (33)

Hawk Springs $12
State Recreation Area
Off Hwy 85, 3 mi E on dirt rd. $12 ($6 for Wyoming residents); free with $60 annual permit ($30 for residents). All year; 14-day limit; limited facilities 10/1-MD. 24 sites. Tbls, toilets, cfga, drkg wtr, beach, no dump. Boating(l), fishing, lake swimming, waterskiing, windsurfing. Elev 4400 ft; 50 acres. Blue heron rookery.

HYATTVILLE (34)

Medicine Lodge $12
State Archaeological Site
6 mi NE of Hyattville off Hwy 31; about 4.5 mi N on Cold Springs Rd; left at park sign on travel CR 268A. $12 ($6 for residents). Free after payment of $60 annual state park camping permit ($30 for residents). 5/15-11/1; 14-day limit. 25 sites. Tbls, toilets, cfga, drkg wtr, playground, no dump. Fishing, hunting, picnicking, hiking, birdwatching, nature trail, rockhounding, mountain biking, 4-wheeling. Interpretive center. One of America's major digs; prehistoric petroglyphs & pictographs on cliff walls.

Medicine Lodge FREE
State Wildlife Management Area
4 mi NE of Hyattville on SR 31; 1 mi N on CR 268A. Free. 7/1-11/30; 14-day limit. Primitive undesignated sites. Tbls, toilets, cfga, no drkg wtr. Interpretive programs, historic sites, exhibits. Fishing, hiking, hunting, wildlife study, nature trail to archeological features.

JACKSON (35)

Atherton Creek $12
Teton National Forest
2 mi N of Kelly on FR 30340; 5.2 mi E on FR 3040 (narrow rd with sharp curves). $12. MD-

9/30; 10-day limit. 20 sites (30-ft RV limit). Tbls, toilets, cfga, drkg wtr, fish cleaning station. Fishing, hunting, boating (l), swimming. Lower Slide Lake. Elev 7250 ft.

Crystal Creek $10
Teton National Forest
2 mi N of Kelly on FR 30340; 10.5 mi E on FR 30400 (5 mi of dirt rd). $10. MD-9/30; 10-day limit. 6 sites; 30-ft RV limit. Toilets, drkg wtr, cfga. Picnicking, fishing, hunting. On Gros Ventre River. Elev 7300 ft.

Curtis Canyon $12
Teton National Forest
1 mi E of Jackson on CR 25; 5 mi NE on FR 25; 3 mi E on FR 98 (6 mi of dirt rd; small RVs only). $12. MD-LD; 2-day limit. 11 sites (30-ft RV limit). Tbls, toilets, cfga, drkg wtr, firewood. Elev 6600 ft; 11 acres.

Red Hills $10
Teton National Forest
2 mi N of Kelly on FR 30350; 10.5 mi E on FR 30400. 4 mi of dirt rd. $10. MD-9/30; 10-day limit. 5 sites (30-ft RV limit). Toilets, cfga, drkg wtr. Swimming, fishing, hunting. On the Gros Ventre River. Elev 7300 ft.

JEFFREY CITY (36)

Cottonwood $6
Bureau of Land Management
6 mi E of Jeffrey City on US 287; 8 mi S on Green Mountain BLM Rd. $6. 6/1-10/31; 14-day limit. Free off-season. 18 sites. Tbls, toilets, cfga, drkg wtr. Hunting, fishing, hiking, mountain biking. Elev 7800 ft; 320 acres along Cottonwood Creek.

KAYCEE (37)

Ed O. Taylor FREE
State Wildlife Management Area
11 mi W of Kaycee on SR 190 & Barnum Rd, then S on any of the BLM rds into the WMA. Free. 4/15-11/15; 14-day limit. Primitive undesignated camping; no facilities, no drkg wtr. Fishing, hiking, hunting, widlife study.
Fishing tip: The primary reason for camping here is to catch cutthroat, brown, rainbow & brook trout from the creeks here and from the Middle Fork of Powder River.

Kaycee Town Park Donations
Just off I-25 and US 87; half block off Main St in Kaycee. Donations. All year; 4-day limit. 15 pull-through sites (RVs under 31 ft); 15 tent sites. Tbls, toilets, cfga. Store, food, ice, laundry nearby. Picnicking, hunting, fishing. Hole-in-the-Wall Outlaw Cave. Historical tours.

Outlaw Cave Campground FREE
Bureau of Land Management
1 mi W of Kaycee on Hwy 191; left on Hwy 190 for about 17 mi; left toward Bar C Ranch for 8.6 mi (past Hole-in-The-Wall overlook); 4WD necessary. Free. 5/1-11/1

(limited access in winter); 14-day limit. 4 tent sites. Tbls, toilets, cfga, no drkg wtr. Excellent overlook of Hole in the Wall.

KEMMERER (38)

Fontenelle Creek Recreation Area **$5**
Bureau of Land Management
32 mi NE of Kemmerer on SR 189. $5. 6/1-9/30; 14-day limit. 55 sites. Tbls, flush toilets, cfga, drkg wtr, dump ($2), fish cleaning station. Boating(l), playground, fishing.

Names Hill **FREE**
Bureau of Land Management
34 mi N of Kemmerer on Us 189. Free. All year; 14-day limit. Primitive undesignated sites. Tbls, cfga, no drkg wtr, no toilets. Thousands of westward immigrants passed near here and carved their names on the cliff faces; among them was trapper Jim Bridger.

Tailrace Campground **FREE**
Bureaus of Land Mgmnt/Reclamation
Rock Springs District
25 mi E of Kemmerer on Hwy 189, then 8.4 mi on SR 372; left onto County Line Rd; below Fontenelle Reservoir, cross dam; along the Green River. Primitive rds. Free. 5/1-11/30 (limited access in winter); 14-day limit. 3 sites. Tbls, 1 toilet, cfga, no drkg wtr. Canoeing, rafting (good river access), picnicking, birdwatching, fishing. Former gathering site of mountain men during their annual rendezvous.
Fishing tip: There's fine fishing here in the Green River for kokanee salmon and trout.

Weeping Rock Camp **FREE**
Bureaus of Land Mgmnt/Reclamation
Rock Springs District
25 mi E of Kemmerer on Hwy 189, then 8.4 mi on SR 372; left onto County Line Rd for 5 mi at the Fontenelle Reservoir dam. Primitive rds. Free. All year; 14-day limit. 4 sites. Tbls, 1 toilet, no drkg wtr. Canoeing, rafting (good river access), picnicking, birdwatching, fishing.

KINNEAR (39)

Morton Lake **FREE**
Bureau of Reclamation
1 mi N of Kinnear. Free. All year; 14-day limit. 12 primitive sites. Tbls, toilets, cfga, drkg wtr. Boating, fishing, swimming.

LANDER (40)

Atlantic City **$6**
Bureau of Land Management
30 mi S of Lander on SR 28; 1 mi on Atlantic City Rd. $6. 6/1-10/31; 14-day limit. Free off-season when free of snow, but no wtr. 18 sites. Tbls, toilets, drkg wtr, cfga. Hunting, fishing, historical sites, mountain biking, rock climbing. Elev 8100 ft; 40 acres.

Big Atlantic Gulch **$6**
Bureau of Land Management
30 mi S of Lander on SR 28; 1 mi on Atlantic City Rd. $6. 6/1-10/31; 14-day limit. Free off-season depending on snow, but no wtr. 10 sites. Tbls, toilets, drkg wtr, cfga. Hunting, fishing, historical area, mountain biking, rock climbing. Elev 8000 ft; 40 acres.

Fiddlers Lake **$10**
Shoshone National Forest
8.7 mi SW of Lander on SR 131; 14.7 mi SW on FR 300, Loop Rd. $10. 7/1-9/15; 14-day limit. Free off-season (no wtr). 20 sites (24-ft RV limit). Tbls, toilets, cfga, drkg wtr. Boating(l), fishing, hiking. Handicap facilities. Elev 9400 ft; 4 acres.

Louis Lake **$5**
Shoshone National Forest
8.7 mi SW of Lander on Hwy 701; 21.4 mi SW on FR 308. $5. 7/1-9/15; 14-day limit. 9 sites (16-ft RV limit). Tbls, toilets, cfga, drkg wtr. Boating(l), fishing, hiking. Elev 8550 ft.

Mexican Creek **FREE**
State Wildlife Management Area
8 mi W of Lander on Shoshone Lake Rd. Free. 9/1-12/31; 14-day limit. Primitive campground; no facilities, no drkg wtr. Horseback riding, hiking, hunting, wildlife study. Winter range for elk & deer; calving area for elk.

Ray Lake Campground (Private) **$8**
9 mi NW of Lander off Hwy 287; 39 Ray Lake Rd. $8 for tents; $15 for RVs. 5/1-10/1. 47 sites. Tbls, flush toilets, cfga, drkg wtr, elec ($), sewer($), sho-wers. Fishing.

Red Canyon **FREE**
State Wildlife Management Area
16 mi S of Lander on SR 28. Free. 5/1-11/30; 14-day limit. Primitive campground; no facilities, no drkg wtr. Hiking, hunting, wildlife study. Once site of a stagecoach stop; ruins of depot still visible. 1,783 acres.

Sinks Canyon **$10**
Shoshone National Forest
8 mi SE of Lander on US 287. $10. 5/1-10/31; 14-day limit. 9 sites (20-ft RV limit). Tbls, toilets, cfga, drkg wtr. Stream fishing, Middle Fork of Popo Agie River. Elev 6850 ft.

Sinks Canyon State Park **$12**
6 mi SW of Lander on SR 131. $12 ($6 for residents). Free after payment of $60 annual state park camping permit ($30 for residents). All year; 14-day limit; limited facilities 11/1-5/1. 30 sites; 40-ft RV limit. Tbls, toilets, cfga, drkg wtr, dump. Visitor center (MD-LD), nature program, fishing, trout display, hiking trails, fishing pier, birdwatching, rock climbing. River vanishes into a large cavern, then reappears in trout pool. Elev 6400 ft; 600 acres.

Sweetwater River **FREE**
Bureau of Land Management
Rock Springs Field Office
33 mi S of Lander (1 mi S of the South Pass rest area) on SR 28; 23 mi W on CR 453, then about 8 mi on BLM 4105 to two camping areas (Guard Station and Bridge). Free. All year; 14-day limit. Primitive undesignated sites. Toilets, cfga, tbls, no drkg wtr. Fishing, hiking.

Worthen Meadows **$8**
Shoshone National Forest
18 mi SW of Lander on SR 131. $8. 7/1-10/15; 14-day limit. 28 sites (24-ft RV limit). Tbls, toilets, cfga, drkg wtr. Boating(l), fishing, hiking. Trails to Popo Agie Wilderness. Elev 8500 ft.

LARAMIE (41)

Boswell Creek **$5**
Medicine Bow National Forest
38 mi SW of Laramie on SR 230; right on FR 526 for 3 mi. $5. 6/1-10/15; 14-day limit. 9 sites; 16-ft RV limit. Tbls, toilets, cfga, drkg wtr. Fishing, boating.

Pelton Creek **$10**
Medicine Bow National Forest
40 mi SW of Laramie on SR 230; 8 mi NW on FR 898. Along Douglas Creek. $10. 6/15-10/15; 14-day limit. 15 sites (16-ft RV limit). Tbls, toilets, cfga, drkg wtr. Fishing, hiking trails.

Rob Roy **$10**
Medicine Bow National Forest
22 mi W of Laramie on SR 130; 11 mi SW on Hwy 11; 9 mi W on FR 500. $10. 6/15-10/1; 14-day limit. 65 sites (35-ft RV limit). Tbls, toilets, cfga, drkg wtr. Fishing, boating(l), hiking. On Rob Roy Reservoir. Elev 9500 ft; 8 acres.

Sybille/Johnson Creek **FREE**
State Access Area
14 mi N of Laramie on US 30/287; 18 mi E on SR 34; near Johnson Reservoir. Free. All year; 14-day limit (visitor center open spring-fall). Developed campground; primitive sites. Toilets, cfga, no drkg wtr. Fishing, hiking, hunting, wildlife study, exhibits, interpretive programs. Facility manages endangered wildlife, including breeding the Wyoming toad.
Fishing tip: Good fishing for brook & rainbow trout at nearby Johnson Reservoir.

Vedauwoo **$10**
Medicine Bow National Forest
19 mi SE of Laramie on I-80; 1 mi E on FR 722. $10. 5/1-10/31; 14-day limit. 28 sites (32-ft RV limit). Tbls, toilets, cfga, drkg wtr. Rock climbing, hiking trails. Unusual rock formation. Elev 8200 ft; 5 acres.

Yellow Pine **$10**
Medicine Bow National Forest
12.3 mi SE of Laramie on I-80; 3 mi E on FR 722. $10. MD-9/30; 14-day limit. 19 sites (32-ft RV limit). Tbls, toilets, cfga, drkg wtr. Fishing, hiking. Elev 8400 ft; 2 acres.

LONETREE

Henry's Fork Trailhead   **FREE**
Wasatch National Forest
8 mi S of Lonetree on Cedar Basin Rd; 15 mi W on FR 58 to jct with FR 77 at Henry's Fork Creek. Free. 6/1-10/15; 14-day limit. 7 sites; 20-ft RV limit. Toilets, cfga, no drkg wtr. Hunting, horse trails, hiking trails, fishing. Elev 9600 ft.

LOVELL (42)

Bald Mountain   **$11**
Bighorn National Forest
33 mi E of Lovell on US 14A. $11 during 6/15-MD; 14-day limit. 15 sites (55-ft RV limit); some handicap sites. Tbls, toilets, cfga, drkg wtr. Fishing. Elev 9200 ft; 4 acres.

Barry's Landing   **$5**
Bighorn Canyon
National Recreation Area
2 mi E of Lovell on US 14A; 24 mi N on SR 37 into Montana. $5. Free, but entry fee charged. All year; 14-day limit. 12 open sites. Tbls, toilets, cfga, no drkg wtr. Boating(l), fishing, hiking.

Five Springs Falls   **$7**
Bureau of Land Management
Cody Field Office
22 mi E of Lovell on Hwy 14A; 2 mi N on steep, narrow access rd. $7. All year (but closed by snow); 14-day limit. 19 sites (25-ft RV limit on access rd). Tbls, toilets, cfga, drkg wtr. Hiking trails, nature program, hunting, bird watching.

Horseshoe Bend   **$5**
Bighorn Canyon
National Recreation Area
National Park Service
2 mi E of Lovell on US 14A to Jct 37; 14 mi N. $5 entry fee. All year; 14-day limit. 59 sites. Tbls, toilets, cfga, drkg wtr, dump. Fishing, boating(r), hiking, campfire talks. Pryor Mtn Wild Horse Range.

Lovell Camper Park   **FREE**
On Quebec Avenue in Lovell. Camp free, but donations encouraged. 5/1-9/30; 4-day limit. 15 sites. Flush toilets, showers, drkg wtr, cfga, tbls, dump. Store, laundry, ice, food nearby. Swimming, picnicking, fishing, golf, playground. Bighorn Canyon NRA nearby.

Medicine Creek   **FREE**
Bighorn Canyon
National Recreation Area
2 mi E of Lovell on US 14A; 14 mi N on SR 37 into Montana; 2 mi NW by boat or trail from Barry's Landing at dayboard 32. Free. Open late spring to fall; 14-day limit. 6 tent sites. Tbls, cfga, toilet, no drkg wtr. Fishing, hiking, boating, swimming.

Porcupine   **$11**
Bighorn National Forest
33 mi E of Lovell on US 14A; 1.6 mi N on FR 13. $11 during 6/15-LD; 14-day limit. 16 sites (60-ft RV limit); some handicap sites. Tbls, toilets, cfga, drkg wtr. Fishing. Elev 8900 ft; 5 acres.

Yellowtail   **FREE**
State Wildlife Management Area
6 mi E of Lovell on US 14A. Free. All year; 14-day limit. Primtve undesignated camping; no facilities, no drkg wtr. Fishing, hiking, hunting, boating, wildlife study.
Fishing tip: Good fishing here for walleye, trout, caftifh, crappie.

MEDICINE BOW (43)

Prior Flat   **$7**
Bureau of Land Management
22 mi N of Medicine Bow on SR 487; 9 mi NW on SR 77; 10 mi W on CR 102; left on Shirley Mtn Loop Rd about 3/4 mi. $7. 6/1-11/15; 14-day limit. 15 sites. Tbls, toilets, cfga, no drkg wtr. Hunting, mountain biking. Note: Dispersed camping is permitted throughout the adjacent Shirley Mountains.
Fishing: Try the good trout fishing in Sage Creek.

MEETEETSE (44)

Brown Mountain   **FREE**
Shoshone National Forest
5 mi SW of Meeteetse on Hwy 290; 15.8 mi SW on county rd; 3.2 mi W on FR 200. Camp free, but donations encouraged. 5/10-11/15; 14-day limit. 7 sites (16-ft RV limit). Tbls, toilets, cfga, drkg wtr. Fishing, hiking, picnicking. Elev 7600 ft.

Jack Creek   **FREE**
Shoshone National Forest
10 mi W of Meeteetse on Hwy 290; 20 mi W on FR 208. Camp free, but donations encouraged. All year; 14-day limit. 7 sites (RVs under 23 ft). Tbls, toilets, cfga, no drkg wtr. Fishing, picnicking. Access to Washakie Wilderness. Elev 7600 ft.

Oasis Motel & RV Park   **$8.99**
At 1702 State St. in Meeteetse. $8.64 base ($5.61 plus $3.38 per person) for self-contained RV or tent camping; $17.99 for 11 RV sites with hookups. All year. Tbls, toilets, cfga, drkg wtr, showers($).

Wood River   **FREE**
Shoshone National Forest
5 mi SW of Meeteetse on Hwy 290; 15.8 mi SW on county rd; 0.7 mi W on FR 200. Camp free, but donations encouraged. 6/1-11/15; 14-day limit. 5 sites (16-ft RV limit). Tbls, toilets, cfga, drkg wtr. Fishing, hiking, picnicking. Elev 7300 ft.

MOORCROFT (45)

Keyhole State Park   **$12**
12 mi E of Moorcroft on I-90; 6 mi N on paved co rd from Pine Ridge exit. $12 ($6 for residents). Free after payment of $60 annual state park camping permit ($30 for residents). All year; 14-day limit. 170 sites at 9 campgrounds overlooking lake (large RVs okay). Tbls, toilets, cfga, drkg wtr, dump, amphitheater, beach, playground. Fishing, boating(l), swimming, hunting, windsurfing, waterskiing. Limited facilities 10/1-5/1. Elev 4100 ft; 6256 acres.
Wind Creek Area: On W side of Pine Haven, accessed from I-90 at Moorcroft. Sites, tbls, restrooms.
Coulter Bay Area: Next to the town of Pine Haven. Sites, tbls, restrooms, shelters, boat ramp.
Pat's Point Area: Next to park headquarters & marina. Sites, tbls, restrooms, shelters, playground, boat ramp.
Pronghorn Area: Next to park headquarters & marina. Sites, tbls, restrooms, playgroujnd.
Arch Rock Area: Next to park headquarters & marina. Sites, tbls, restrooms.
Homestead Area: Past park headquarters. Sites, restroom, tbls.
Cottonwood Area: Past park headquarters. Sites, restrooms, tbls, playground, shelters.
Rocky Point Area: Near the dam. Sites, tbls, restroms.

MOOSE (46)

Backcountry Camping   **FREE**
Grand Teton National Park
At visitor center in Moose or from Jenny Lake Ranger Station, pick up free backcountry camping permits. Hike to backcountry areas. Camping free, but entry fee is charged. No facilities.

Colter Bay Campground   **$12**
Grand Teton National Park
25 mi N of Moose on US 89. $12. 5/15-9/15; 14-day limit. 350 sites. Tbls, tlush toilets, cfga, drkg wtr, dump, showers, store, coin laundry, visitor center. Swimming, boating(lr), fishing, rec program, horseback riding, biking(r). Entry fee.

Gros Ventre Campground   **$12**
Grand Teton National Park
S of Moose on US 89. $12. 5/1-10/15; 14-day limit. 360 sites. Tbls, flush toilets, cfga, drkg wtr, dump, no showers. Recreation program. Entry fee.

Jenny Lake Campground   **$12**
Grand Teton National Park
7 mi N of Moose on Teton Park Rd. $12. 5/30-9/30; 14-day limit. 49 sites. Tbls, flush toilets, cfga, drkg wtr, no showers. Boating(rl), fishing, horseback riding, rec program, hiking. Entry fee.

Signal Mountain Camp   **$12**
Grand Teton National Park

18 mi N of Moose on Teton Park Rd. $12. 5/30-10/1; 14-day limit. 86 sites. Tbls, flush toilets, cfga, drkg wtr, dump, shore, no showers. Recreation program, boating(lrd), fishing, hiking. Entry fee.

MORAN (47)

Angles   **$10**
Teton National Forest

Half mi NE of Cowboy Village Resort at Togwotee off the Old Togwotee Hwy Rd. $10 during 6/10-9/30; free rest of year; 14-day limit. 4 sites; 30-ft RV limit. Tbls, toilet, cfga, drkg wtr.

Black Rock Recreation Site   **$5**
Teton National Forest

About 11 mi E of Moran Junction on US 287 (about 25 mi S of S entrance to Yellowstone NP). For bicycle & walk-in campers only. $5 during 6/1-9/10; free rest of yr when accessible. 16-day limit. 9 tent sites. Tbls, toilets, cfga, no drkg wtr, bear-resistant food storage boxes. Picnicking, hiking.

Box Creek Campground   **$10**
Teton National Forest

About 4 mi E of Moran on US 287 (E entrance to Grand Teton NP); 8 mi NE on FR 30050. $10 during 6/10-9/30; free rest of yr when accessible; 14-day limit. 6 sites (30-ft RV limit). Tbls, toilets, cfga, no drkg wtr, corrals next to sites. Picnicking, fishing, hunting, horseback riding. Corrals. Within Grizzly Recovery Area; store food properly. Elev 8100 ft.

Hatchet   **$10**
Teton National Forest

8 mi E of Moran on US 26 (qtr mi W of Buffalo Ranger Station). $10 during 6/1-9/30; free rest of yr when accessible, but no wtr; 14-day limit. 9 sites (30-ft RV limit). Tbls, toilets, cfga, drkg wtr, food storage boxes. Hunting, picnicking. Within Grizzly Recovery Area. Elev 8000 ft.

Lizard Creek Campground   **$12**
Grand Teton National Park

17 mi N of Moran on US 89. $12. 6/15-9/14-day limit. 60 sites. Tbls, flush toilets, cfga, drkg wtr. Fishing, swimming, boating. On Jackson Lake.

Pacific Creek   **$5**
Teton National Forest

About 8 mi NE of Moran Junction on US 287 (access through Grand Teton NP), then N on Pacific Creek Rd (access rough). $5 during 6/15-9/30; free rest of yr when accessible, but no drkg wtr; 14-day limit. 8 sites; 30-ft RV limit. Tbls, toilets, cfga, drkg wtr, bear-resisent food storage boxes, corral, hitchrails. Picnicking, fishing, hunting, horseback riding. Elev 7000 ft. Camp hosts.

Sheffield Campground   **$5**
Teton National Forest

1 mi E off Hwy 89/287, 1 mi S of Flagg Ranch & across Sheffield Creek; high-clearance vehicles recommended. $5. 6/20-9/30; 14-day limit. Tbls, toilets, cfga, no drkg wtr. Fishing, hiking. Elev 8200 ft.

Turpin Meadow   **$10**
Teton National Forest

About 13 mi E of Moran Junction on US 287 (access through Grand Teton NP); N on FR 30050 (Buffalo Valley Rd). $10 during 6/1-10/1, free rest of year when accessible, but no wtr; 14-day limit. 18 sites; 30-ft RV limit. Tbls, toilets, cfga, drkg wtr, bear-resistent food storage boxes, corral, hitchrails at sites. Fishing, hunting. Stream. Elev 7300 ft. Primary access point for Teton Wilderness. Camp hosts.

MOUNTAIN VIEW (48)

Bridger Lake   **$12**
Wasatch National Forest

7 mi SW of Mountain View on SR 410; 16.5 mi S on CR 246 and FR 72; half mi S on FR 126. $12. 6/1-10/15, but no wtr after LD; 14-day limit. 30 sites. Tbls, toilets, cfga, drkg wtr. Fishing, hunting, hiking trails. Elev 9400 ft.

China Meadows   **$8**
Wasatch National Forest

7 mi SW of Mountain View on SR 410; 18.4 mi S on CR 246 & FR 72. $8. 6/1-10/15, but no wtr after LD; 14-day limit. 12 sites. Tbls, toilets, cfga, drkg wtr. Fishing, hiking. Elev 10,000 ft.

Deadhorse Trailhead   **$4**
Wasatch National Forest

7 mi SW of Mountain View on WY 2410; 19.4 mi S on FR 4072. $4 during 7/1-9/30; free rest of yr when access open; 14-day limit. 4 sites. Toilets, cfga, no drkg wtr. Hiking trails, hunting, horse trails. Trailhead into High Vintas Wilderness. Horse loading dock.

E. Fork of Black Forks Trlhd   **FREE**
Wasatch National Forest

S of Evanston on SR 410; SW on FR 073 past Meeks Cabin Lake to end of rd at Black Forks Trail. Free. Tbls, toilets, cfga, no drkg wtr. Hiking, fishing.

Hoop Lake   **$10**
Wasatch National Forest

23.5 mi SE of Mountain View on Hwy 414; .7 mi S on CR 264; 6.5 mi SE on FR 58. $10. 6/15-10/30, but no wtr after LD; 14-day limit. 44 sites. Tbls, toilets, cfga, drkg wtr. Fishing, boating, hiking. Elev 9000 ft.

Marsh Lake   **$12**
Wasatch National Forest

7 mi S of Mountain View on SR 410; 8.3 mi S on CR 246; 8.7 mi S on FR 72. $12. 6/1-

10/15, but no wtr after LD 33 sites. Tbls, toilets, cfga, drkg wtr. Hiking, hunting, boating (no motors), fishing, horse trails. Elev 9300 ft.

Meeks Cabin   **$10**
Wasatch National Forest

S of Mountain View on SR 410; W on FR 073. $10. 6/15-9/15; 14-day limit. 24 sites (20-ft RV limit). Tbls, toilets, cfga, drkg wtr. Swimming, fishing. Elev 8700 ft; 12 acres.

Stateline   **$12**
Wasatch National Forest

7 mi S of Mountain View on SR 410; 8.3 mi S on CR 246; 5.5 mi S on FR 72. $12. 6/1-10/15, but no wtr after LD; 14-day limit. 41 sites (32-ft RV limit). Tbls, toilets, cfga, drkg wtr. Boating, fishing, hiking trails. Elev 9200 ft.

NEWCASTLE (49)

Beaver Creek   **$8**
Black Hills National Forest

18 mi N of Newcastle on US 85; 6 mi E on FR 811; camp is just past forest boundary. $8 during MD-LD; free rest of year; 10-day limit. 8 sites; 45-ft RV limit. Tbls, toilets, cfga, drkg wtr. Fishing, picnicking. Elev 5600 ft.

Moon Campground   **FREE**
Black Hills National Forest

10 mi SE of Newcastle on US 16; 15 mi N on FR 117. Free, but donations accepted. 6/1-11/30; 10-day limit. 3 sites (RVs under 30 ft). Tbls, toilets, cfga, no drkg wtr.

Redbank Spring   **FREE**
Black Hills National Forest

14 mi NE of Newcastle. Free. All year; 10-day limit. 5 sites; 40-ft RV limit. Tbls, toilets, cfga, drkg wtr. Fishing.

PINEDALE (50)

Fremont Lake   **$12**
Bridger National Forest

1 mi NE of Pinedale on SR 187; 2.5 mi NE on CR 111; one mi E on Hwy 187. $12 during MD-LD; free rest of yr when accessible, but no drkg wtr; 16-day limit except 10-day limit 7/1-8/31. 54 sites. Tbls, toilets, cfga, drkg wtr, firewood. Boating(l), fishing, waterskiing. Elev 7600 ft; 77 acres.

Green River Lake   **$12**
Bridger National Forest

25 mi N of Pinedale on SR 352; 31 mi N on FR 91. $12 during 6/15-9/15; free rest of yr when accessible, but no drkg wtr; 16-day limit except 10-day limit 7/1-8/31. 39 sites (22-ft RV limit). Tbls, toilets, cfga, drkg wtr. Swimming, fishing, horseback riding. Elev 8000 ft; 19 acres.

Half Moon Lake   **$8**
Bridger National Forest

1 mi E of Pinedale on Hwy 187; 3 mi NE CR

111; 1 mi E on FR 134. $8 during 6/1-9/10; free rest of yr when accessible; 10-day limit. 18 sites (16-ft RV limit). Tbls, toilets, no drkg wtr. Fishing, swimming, boating (launch, docks nearby).

Half Moon   **FREE**
State Wildlife Management Area
9 mi S of Pinedale on Fayette-Pole Creek Rd. Free. 5/1-10/31; 14-day limit. Primitive undesignated camping. Toilets, cfga, no drkg wtr. Fishing, hiking, hunting, widlife study. Winter range for elk, mule deer, pronghorn antelope.
    Fishing tip: There's good angling for brook & brown trout in Pole Creek.

Narrows   **$12**
Bridger National Forest
9 mi N of Cora on SR 352; 4.5 mi E on FR 107; 2.5 mi E on forest rd. $12 during MD-9/15; free rest of yr, but no drkg wtr; 16-day limit except 10-day limit 7/1-8/31. 19 sites (30-ft RV limit). Tbls, toilets, cfga, drkg wtr, firewood. On New Fork Lake. Swimming, fishing, boating(l), waterskiing. Elev 7800 ft; 16 acres.

Soda Lake   **FREE**
State Wildlife Management Area
5 mi N of Pinedale on Willow Lake Rd. Free. 5/10-11/15; 14-day limit. Primitive campground; no facilities, no drkg wtr. Fishing, hiking, wildlife study.
    Fishing tip: Soda Lake is stocked with brook & brown trout.

Stokes Crossing   **FREE**
Bureau of Land Management
22 mi N of Pinedale on US 171. Free. All year; 14-day limit. 4 sites. Tbls, toilets, cfga, no drkg wtr. Fishing, hunting. Elev 7300 ft.

Trails End   **$5**
Bridger National Forest
1 mi E of Pinedale on Hwy 187; 3 mi NE on CR 111; 8 mi NE on FR 134. $5 during 6/25-9/10; free rest of yr when accessible, but no drkg wtr 16-day limit except 10-day limit 7/1-8/31. 8 sites (22-ft RV limit). Tbls, cfga, drkg wtr. Trail entrance to wilderness area.

Upper Green River   **FREE**
Recreation Area
Bureau of Land Management
24 mi N of Pinedale on Hwy 191 to Warren Bridge; 2 mi NE to site. Free. 6/1-10/31; 14-day limit. 12 sites (RVs under 33 ft). Tbls, toilets, cfga, no drkg wtr. Floating, fishing, picnicking.

Warren Bridge   **$6**
Bureau of Land Management
Pinedale Field Office
24 mi N of Pinedale on US 171. $6. 5/1-10/31; 14-day limit. 17 sites (30-ft RV limit). Tbls, toilets, cfga, drkg wtr, dump. Boating, fishing, hiking, nature program. 20 acres on Green River.

Whiskey Grove   **$5**
Bridger National Forest
36 mi N of Pinedale on SR 352 & FR 91 (20 mi N of Cora). $5 when wtr available; free when no wtr. 6/15-9/10; 10-day limit. 9 sites. Tbls, toilets, cfga, drkg wtr. Fishing (in Green River).

PIONEER (51)

Pioneer   **$10**
Wasatch National Forest
9 mi E of Pioneer on SR 242. $10 (formerly free). MD-11/1; 7-day limit. 18 sites; 20-ft RV limit. Tbls, toilets, cfga, drkg wtr. Hunting, fishing. Elev 5600 ft. 7 acres.

POWELL (53)

Homesteader Park   **FREE**
Park County
Hwy 14A, E city limits. Free. 4/15-10/31; 2-day limit. 25 RV sites, unlimited tent camping. Tbls, toilets, cfga, drkg wtr, dump. Sightseeing, picnicking.

RANCHESTER (54)

Connor Battlefield   **$12**
State Historic Site
2 blocks off Hwy 14 at Ranchester; in oxbow of Tongue River. $12 ($6 for residents). Free after payment of $60 annual state park camping permit ($30 for residents). 5/1-10/1; 14-day limit. 20 sites. Tbls, toilets, cfga, drkg wtr, playground, no dump. Fishing, picnicking, horseshoes, beach. Site of 1865 expedition against Arapaho village.

RAWLINS (55)

Chain Lakes   **FREE**
State Wildlife Management Area
32 mi NW of Rawlins on Riner Cutoff Rd; several dirt rds run east-west through the WMA; best place to camp is at N end near the lakes. Free. All year; 14-day limit. Primitive undesignated camping; no facilities, no drkg wtr. Fishing, hunting. Herd of wild horses waters here.

Interstate Bridge   **FREE**
Public Fishing Area
At the Ft. Steele exit off I-80, 15 mi E of Rawlings on both side of hwy. Free. All year; 14-day limit. Primitive undesignated sites at public access to North Platte River. Toilets, cfga, tbls, no drkg wtr. Boating(l), fishing.

Teton Reservoir   **FREE**
Bureau of Land Management
15 mi S of Rawlins on SR 71/CR 401. Free. All year; 14-day limit. 5 sites. Tbls, toilets, cfga, no drkg wtr. Fishing, picnicking, hunting, boating(l).
    Fishing tip: There's good trout fishing in this lake.

RIVERSIDE (56)

Bennett Peak   **$7**
Bureau of Land Management
4 mi E of Riverside on SR 230; 12 mi E on French Creek Rd; 7 mi S on Bennett Peak Rd. $7. Free off-season but no wtr. 6/1-1/15; 14-day limit. 11 sites. Tbls, toilets, drkg wtr, cfga. Fishing, floating, canoeing, hunting, boating (l), nature trails. On North Platte River.

Corral Creek   **FREE**
Bureau of Land Management
4 mi E of Riverside on SR 230; 12 mi E on French Creek Rd (CR 660); left for 7 mi on Bennett Peak Rd. Free. 6/1-11/15; 14-day limit. 6 sites. Tbls, toilets, cfga, no drkg wtr. Hiking trail, fishing, hunting. Popular big-game hunting site. Elev 7100 ft.
    Fishing tip: The nearby creeks provide good trout fishing all year.

RIVERTON (57)

Ocean Lake   **FREE**
State Wildlife Management Area
17 mi NW of Riverton on US 26; dispersed primitive camping around the lake. Free. All year; 14-day limit. Toilets, cfga, tbls, no drkg wtr. Fishing, hiking, hunting, boating(l). Developed day-use facilities managed by Bureau of Reclamation. Nesting habitat for sandhill & whooping cranes, other waterfowl. Several thousand pheasants released each year for hunters.
    Fishing tip: There's excellent fishing here for bass, trou; perch, walleye.

ROCK SPRINGS (58)

Three Patches   **FREE**
Bureau of Land Management
Rock Springs Field Office
S of Rock Springs on SR 130, then 10 mi S on Aspen Mountain Rd; near top of Aspen Mountain. Free. May-Oct; 14-day limit. Primitive undesignated sites, popular for picnicking. Tbls, toilets, cfga, no drkg wtr. Hiking.

SARATOGA (59)

Foote Public Fishing Area   **FREE**
5 mi N of Saratoga off Hwy 130/230. Free. All year; 14-day limit. Primitive undesignated sites at public access to North Platte River. Toilets, tbls, cfga, no drkg wtr. Fishing, boating(l).

Frazier   **FREE**
Public Fishing Area
7 mi N of Saratoga on SR 130; 4 mi W on Pick Bridge Rd. Free. All year; 14-day limit. Primitive undesignated sites at public access to North Platte River. Toilets, cfga, tbls, no drkg wtr. Boating(l), fishing.

French Creek   **$7**
Medicine Bow National Forest
24 mi E of Saratoga on SR 130; 15 mi S on FR 206 (South Brush Creek Rd). $7. 5/15-10/31; 14-day limit. 11 sites (32-ft RV limit). Tbls, toilets, cfga, drkg wtr. Fishing, hiking.

Jack Creek   **$7**
Medicine Bow National Forest
19 mi W of Saratoga on CR 500; 8 mi S on FR 452. $7. MD-10/31; 14-day limit. 16 sites (22-ft RV limit). Tbls, toilets, cfga, well drkg wtr. Picnicking, fishing, hiking. Elev 8500 ft; 5 acres.

Lincoln Park   **$10**
Medicine Bow National Forest
20.2 mi SE of Saratoga on SR 130; 2.6 mi NE on FR 101. $10. 5/15-10/1; 14-day limit. 12 sites (32-ft RV limit). Tbls, toilets, cfga, drkg wtr. Picnicking, fishing. Elev 7800 ft.

Pennock Mountain   **FREE**
State Wildlife Management Area
5 mi NE of Saratoga on CR 504; at Lake & Goetz Creeks. Free. 5/1-11/30; 14-day limit. Primitive undesignated camping; no facilities, no drkg wtr. Fishing, hiking, hunting, wildlife study. 9,800 acres.

Pick Bridge   **FREE**
Public Fishing Area
6.5 mi N of Saratoga on Hwy 130/230; W on Pick Bridge Rd for 3 mi to river. Free. All year; 14-day limit. Primitive undesignated sites at public access to North Platte River. Toilets, cfga, tbls, no drkg wtr. Fishing, boating(l).

Ryan Park   **$10**
Medicine Bow National Forest
23.3 mi SE of Saratoga on SR 130. $10. MD-10/31; 14-day limit. 49 sites (32-ft RV limit). Tbls, toilets, cfga, well drkg wtr. Picnicking, fishing, hiking. Elev 8900 ft; 18 acres. Reservations available.

Saratoga Lake Campground
$7.50
1 mi N of Saratoga on Hwy 230; 1 mi E on Saratoga Lake Rd. $7.50 primitive camping; $10 with elec. May-Sept. 65 sites. Tbls, toilets, cfga, drkg wtr, dump, elec($). Swimming, boating(ld), fishing, horseshoes.

South Brush Creek   **$10**
Medicine Bow National Forest
20.2 mi SE of Saratoga on SR 130; qtr mi NE on FR 101; 1 mi E on FR 200. $10. MD-10/31; 14-day limit. 20 sites (32-ft RV limit). Tbls, toilets, cfga, well drkg wtr. Picnicking, fishing. Elev 7900 ft; 7 acres.

Treasure Island   **FREE**
Public Fishing Area
9 mi S of Saratoga on Hwy 230; E on dirt rd, following signs. Free. All year; 14-day limit. Primitive undesignated sites at public access to North Platte River. Toilets, tbls, cfga, no drkg wtr. Fishing, boating(l).

SHELL (60)

Cabin Creek   **$10**
Bighorn National Forest
15.8 mi NE of Shell on US 14; half mi E on FR 17. $10 during 5/15-9/20; 14-day limit. Also $10 daily or $200 per month camping by monthly permit, by reservation, only on 26 sites). 4 overnight RV sites (RVs under 30 ft). Toilets, drkg wtr. Elev 7500 ft; 3 acres.

Medicine Lodge Lake   **$10**
Bighorn National Forest
15.7 mi NE of Shell on US 14; 25 mi SE on FR 17. $10 during 6/20-LD; 14-day limit. 8 sites (45-ft RV limit). Tbls, toilets, cfga, drkg wtr. Boating, fishing, hiking trails. Elev 9300 ft; 5 acres.

Paintrock Lakes Complex   **$10**
Bighorn National Forest
15.7 mi NE of Shell on US 14; 25.7 mi SE on FR 17. $10 during 6/20-LD; 14-day limit. 8 sites; (4 at Upper Paintrock, 4 at Lower Paintrock); 40-ft RV limit. 2 campgrounds about half mi apart. Tbls, toilets, cfga, drkg wtr. Boating, fishing, hiking.

Ranger Creek Recreation Area   **$10**
Bighorn National Forest
15.7 mi NE of Shell on US 14; 2 mi S on FR 17. $10 during 5/15-9/20; 14-day limit. 10 sites (35-ft RV limit). Tbls, toilets, cfga, drkg wtr. Fishing, hiking. Horse rentals, ranger station nearby. Elev 7600 ft; 2 acres.

Shell Creek   **$11**
Bighorn National Forest
15.7 mi NE of Shell on US 14; 1.2 mi S on FR 17. $10 during 5/30-10/31; 14-day limit. 15 sites (55-ft RV limit). Tbls, toilets, cfga, drkg wtr. Fishing, hiking trails; riding stable nearby. Elev 7500 ft; 7 acres.

SHOSHONI (61)

Boysen State Park   **$12**
12 mi NW of Shoshoni on US 20. Access also from Hwy 26 S of lake. $12 ($6 for residents). Free after payment of $60 annual state park camping permit ($30 for residents). All year; 14-day limit; limited facilities 10/1-3/31. 202 sites at 11 campgrounds (9 around lake). Tbls, toilets, cfga, drkg wtr, dump, group shelters, beach, playgrounds. Swimming, boating(ldr), fishing, hunting, waterskiing, windsurfing. Wind River Canyon. Elev 4820 ft; 19,560 acres.

Lake Cameahwait   **FREE**
State Game & Fish Dept.
15 mi W of Shoshoni off US 26. Free. All year; 14-day limit. Primitive undesignated sites. Tbls, toilets, cfga, no drkg wtr. Fishing, hiking, boating(l), hunting, wildlife study. 365 of 1,057 acres set aside for recreation.

Fishing tip: There's good fishing here for trout, bass, perch, bluegill, sunfish & crappie.

Sand Mesa   **FREE**
State Wildlife Management Area
25 mi W of Shoshoni on US 26, then N on Bass Lake Rd. Free. All year; 14-day limit. Primitive undesignated sites. Toilets, cfga, no drkg wtr. Hiking, fishing, hunting, wildlife study, boating(l).

SINCLAIR (62)

Seminoe Boat Club Area (Private)   **$12**
6 mi E of Rawlins on I-80; exit at Sinclair; 25 mi N on Seminoe Dam Rd; 2.5 mi E on Club Drive. $12 for tent & primitive sites; $18 full hookups. 4/1-10/31. 46 sites. Tbls, flush toilets, cfga, drkg wtr, elec($), sewer($), dump, store, showers($). Boating, fishing, swimming at Seminoe Reservoir. Fees not verified for 2005.

Seminoe State Park   **$12**
30 mi N of Sinclair on Seminoe Rd. $12 ($6 for residents). Free after payment of $60 annual state park camping permit ($30 for residents). All year; 14-day limit. 94 sites (35-ft RV limit). Tbls, toilets, drkg wtr, cfga, dump. Limited facilities 9/15-5/15. Swimming, boating(l), fishing. Seminoe Dam, sand dunes, North Platte River. Travel difficult Dec 1-Apr 15; snow; 4WD may be needed. Elev 6350 ft; 3821 acres.

The Dugway   **FREE**
Bureau of Land Management
8 mi N of Sinclair on CR 351 (Seminoe Rd) to North Platte River. Free. All year, depending on weather and accessibility; 14-day limit. 5 sites. Tbls, toilets, cfga, no drkg wtr. Hunting, fishing, canoeing, boating. Take-out for canoers & kayakers.

SMOOT (63)

Allred Flat   **$5**
Bridger National Forest
15.5 mi S of Smoot on US 89; qtr mi N on FR 10131. $5 during MD-10/31; free rest of yr when accessible, but no drkg wtr; 16-day limit except 10-day limit 7/1-8/31. 32 sites (22-ft RV limit). Tbls, toilets, cfga, drkg wtr. Hiking, fishing, picnicking. Elev 7000 ft; 8 acres.

Cottonwood Lake   **$5**
Bridger National Forest
1 mi S of Smoot on US 89; 1.1 mi E on CR 153; 6.7 mi E on FR 10208. N end of Cottonwood Lake. $5 during 5/15-10/15; free rest of year when accessible; 16-day limit. 10-day limit July & Aug. 17 sites (RVs under 23 ft). Tbls, toilets, cfga, drkg wtr. Boating, fishing, picnicking, canoeing.

SUNDANCE (64)

Cook Lake   **$11**
Black Hills National Forest
2.1 mi W of Sundance on US 14; 14 mi N on FR 838; 5 mi E on FR 843; 1 mi NW on

FR 842. $11 & $15. Fees charged 5/23-9/9; free rest of year. 10-day limit. 34 sites (RVs under 45 ft). Tbls, toilets, cfga, drkg wtr, trash pickup. Accommodations for handicapped. No wtr or trash service during free period. Hiking, biking, fishing, canoeing, swimming. Scenic spot. Lake approx 30 acres; has trout.

Reuter   **$10**
Black Hills National Forest
2.1 mi W of Sundance on US 14; 2.5 mi N on paved FR 838. $10. Fee charged 5/23-9/9; free rest of year. 10-day limit. 24 sites (RVs under 31 ft). Tbls, toilets, cfga, drkg wtr. No wtr or trash service during free period. Hiking, picnicking.

TEN SLEEP (65)

Boulder Park   **$11**
Bighorn National Forest
20 mi NE of Ten Sleep on US 16; half mi W on FR 27; 1.5 mi S on forest rd. $11 daily or $220 monthly during MD-9/20; 30-day limit. Concession-operated; reservations available. 39 sites (40-ft RV limit). Tbls, toilets, cfga, drkg wtr. Store. Fishing, hiking. On Tensleep Creek. Elev 8000 ft; 10 acres.

Bull Creek   **$9**
Bighorn National Forest
25 mi NE of Ten Sleep on US 16; half mi N on FR 433. $9 during 6/10-LD; 14-day limit. 10 sites (16-ft RV limit). Tbls, toilets, cfga, no drkg wtr. Groceries. Boating(l), fishing. Elev 8400 ft; 4 acres. Closed early in 2007 for hazardous tree removal.

Castle Garden Scenic Area
FREE
Bureau of Land Management
1 mi W of Ten Sleep on Hwy 16/20 to Castle Garden Turnoff; left on unpaved Two Mile Hill Rd for 6 mi. Free. 6/1-10/31; 14-day limit. 2 sites (RV under 18 ft). Tbls, toilets, cfga, no drkg wtr. Hunting, picnicking.

Deer Park   **$10**
Bighorn National Forest
20 mi NE of Ten Sleep on US 16; 6 mi N on FR 27. $10 during 6/10-LD; 14-day limit. 7 sites (35-ft RV limit). Tbls, toilets, cfga, drkg wtr. Hiking, fishing. Trails to East Tensleep Lake and Cloud Peak Wilderness. Elev 8400 ft; 3 acres.

Island Park   **$10**
Bighorn National Forest
20 mi NE of Ten Sleep on US 16; 4 mi N on FR 27. $10 during 6/15-LD; 14-day limit. 10 sites (32-ft RV limit). Tbls, toilets, cfga, drkg wtr. Fishing, hiking. Along Tensleep Creek. Elev 8400 ft; 4 acres.

Lakeview Recreation Area   **$11**
Bighorn National Forest
24 mi NE of Ten Sleep on US 16. $11 during 6/10-LD; 14-day limit. 24 sites (22-ft RV limit). Tbls, toilets, cfga, drkg wtr. Groceries. Boating(lr), fishing, hiking. On NE shore of Meadowlark Lake. Elev 8300 ft; 5 acres.

Leigh Creek   **$11**
Bighorn National Forest
8 mi NE of Ten Sleep on US 16; 1 mi N on FR 18. $11 during 5/15-9/20; 14-day limit. 11 sites (40-ft RV limit). Tbls, toilets, cfga, drkg wtr. Fishing in Leigh and Tensleep Creeks for brook trout. Elev 5400 ft; 5 acres.

Middle Fork   **FREE**
of Powder River
Bureau of Land Management
S of Ten Sleep on SR 434 to Big Trails, then E on BLM Dry Farm Rd. to Hazelton Rd., then S to the camp. Free. 6/1-10/31; 14-day limit. 5 sites. Toilets, cfga, no drkg wtr (proposed for future), no trash service. Hunting. S of here on Arminto Rd is Hole in the Wall, where Butch Cassady & gang hid out.

Fishing tip: Trout angling is quite good here.

Sitting Bull   **$12**
Bighorn National Forest
23 mi NE of Ten Sleep on US 16; 1 mi N on FR 432. $12 during 6/5-9/20; 14-day limit. 42 sites (45-ft RV limit). Tbls, toilets, cfga, drkg wtr. Boating, fishing, hiking & nature trails. Elev 8600 ft; 21 acres.

Tensleep Creek   **$11**
Bighorn National Forest
8 mi NE of Ten Sleep on US 16; 2 mi E on FR 18. $11 during 5/15-1LD; 14-day limit. 5 sites; 35-ft RV limit. Tbls, toilets, cfga, drkg wtr. Fishing. Elev 5400 ft; 2 acres.

West Tensleep Lake   **$11**
Bighorn National Forest
20 mi NE of Ten Sleep on US 16; 7.5 mi N on FR 27. $11 during 6/10-9/20; 14-day limit. 10 sites (35-ft RV limit). Tbls, toilets, cfga, drkg wtr. Fishing, hiking. Trail to Cloud Peak Wilderness. Elev 9100 ft; 4 acres.

TORRINGTON (66)

Pioneer Municipal Park   **FREE**
At W 15th Ave & West E St, Torrington. Camp free, but donations requested for elec. 5/1-9/30; 10-day limit. 30-35 sites. Tbls, flush toilets, cfga, drkg wtr. Picnic area.

Springer/Bump Sullivan   **FREE**
State Wildlife Management Area
15 mi S of Torrington on SR 134 & CR 133. Free. All year; 14-day limit. Primitive campground. Toilets, cfga, no drkg wtr. Boating(l), fishing (not recommended), hiking, hunting, wildlife study.

Table Mountain   **FREE**
State Wildlife Management Area
Bureau of Land Management
About 16 mi S of Torrington on SR 92, then on either SR 158 or CR 166. Free. All year;

14-day limit. Primitive undesignated camping. Toilets, cfga, no drkg wtr. Fishing, hiking, hunting, wildlife study. Waterfowl nesting area.

WALTMAN (68)

Buffalo Creek   **FREE**
Bureau of Land Management
From Waltman (W of Casper on US 20/26), 12 Mi N on Buffalo Creek Rd to Arminto, then NW 8.5 mi on Big Horn Mountain Rd. Free. All year; 14-day limit. Undesignated primitive sites. Toilets, no drkg wtr. Hunting, fishing.

Grave Springs   **FREE**
Bureau of Land Management
From Waltman (W of Casper on US 20/26), 12 mi N on Buffalo Creek Rd to Arminto, then NW 11.5 mi on Big Horn Mountain Rd. Free. All year, but limited access in winter; 14-day limit. Undesignated primitive sites. Toilets, no drkg wtr. Hunting, fishing.

WESTON (69)

Weston Hills   **FREE**
Recreation Area
Bureau of Land Management
6 mi S of Weston on SR 59; just W of Thunder Basin National Grassland segment. Free. All year; 14-day limit. Primitive undesignated sites; no facilities, no drkg wtr. Hiking, horseback riding, hunting, OHV activity. 2-mi ATV trail open 10/16-9/14 but closed during hunting season. Dispersed camping permitted throughout the area and the grassland.

WHEATLAND (70)

Festo Lake   **FREE**
Platte County Campground
Near Wheatland; follow signs. Free. Primitive undesignated camping; no facilities. Fishing, boating.

Grayrocks Reservoir   **FREE**
State Wildlife Management Area
9 mi NE of Wheatland on Grayrocks Power Plant Rd. Free. All year; 14-day limit. Toilets, tbls, cfga, no drkg wtr. Fishing, hiking, hunting, wildlife study, boating(l).

Fishing tip: This lake contains big walleye as well as other species, but you'll have to compete for them with flocks of white pelicans.

Rock Lake   **FREE**
Public Campground
Next to Wheatland Reservoir #1. Free. All year; 5-day limit. Primitive undesignated sites. Fishing, boating.

Wheatland Reservoir #1   **FREE**
Near Wheatland. Free. All year; 5-day limit. Primitive undesignated sites. Fishing, boating.

Wheatland Campground — FREE
Lewis City Park

In downtown Wheatland. Donations accepted, but camp free. All year; 3-day limit. 28 RV sites; 5 tent sites. Tbls, cfga, toilets, drkg wtr, hookups, showers($).

YELLOWSTONE NATIONAL PARK (71)

Indian Creek — $12
7.5 mi S of Mammoth Hot Springs Junction on the Mammoth-Norris Rd. $12. 14-day limit 6/15-LD, 30-day limit otherwise. 75 sites. Tbls, toilets, cfga, drkg wtr. Fishing. Elev 7300 ft.

Lewis Lake — $12
10 mi S of W Thumb Junction, on Lewis Lake. $12. 14-day limit 6/15-LD, 30-day limit otherwise. 85 sites. Tbls, toilets, cfga, drkg wtr. Fishing. Elev 7800 ft.

Pebble Creek — $12
7 mi S of Northeast Entrance of Yellowstone NP. $12. 14-day limit 6/15-LD, 30-day limit otherwise. 32 sites. Tbls, toilets, cfga, drkg wtr. Fishing. Elev 6900 ft.

Slough Creek — $12
10 mi NE of Tower Fall Junction of Yellowstone NP. $12. 14-day limit 6/15-LD, 30-day limit otherwise. 29 sites. Tbls, toilets, cfga, drkg wtr. Fishing. Elev 6250 ft.

Tower Fall — $12
3 mi SE of Tower Junction, Yellowstone NP. $12. 14-day limit 6/15-LD, 30-day limit otherwise. 32 sites. Tbls, toilets, cfga, drkg wtr. Fishing, horseback riding. Store. Elev 6600 ft.

UNITED STATES MAP

NOTES